CLEY-NEXT-THE-SEA
547

Cromer
676

NORTH

SEA

Holt
1004

1811

Briston
750

North
Walsham
1959

am

Cawston
840

Aylsham
1667

1794

1797

R.
ANT

R.
THURNE

The

VENSUM

Horsham
St Faith with
Newton
883

R.
BURE

Broads

GREAT
YARMOUTH
14,845

NORWICH
36,832

1770

1770

all

R.
YARE

1770

1769

R.BURE

1770

The

R.
YARE

Broads

1695

Wymondham
1563

Loddon
799

R.
CHET

1785

Buckenham
845

1772

Carleton
Rode 767

Hempnall
879

R.
WAVENEY

1796

New
Buckenham
664

Banham
1015

Pulham St Mary
Magdalen
767

Pulham St Mary
the Virgin
801

Kenninghall
1052

1769

Diss
2246

Harleston
with Redenhall
1459

N

SUFFOLK

M B20
20

front endpaper Norfolk's communications network. The county had four seaports with customs houses: King's Lynn, Wells, Blakeney and Cley (with the Customs at Cley), and Gt Yarmouth. These harbours were augmented by staithes along silting creeks where small ships could berth, and by the open shore, where colliers would beach to unload their coal. The county's towns were mostly small in population terms, even where they lay on turnpike roads. A few villages had workhouses, or houses of industry, housing the poor of a number of nearby parishes. Mary Hardy had lived at Coltishall on the Broads, on a network of navigable rivers linked to the sea for freight transport. However Letheringsett, west of Holt, lay in a very large area remote from fast roads and navigable waterways

THE AUTHOR

Margaret Bird is the editor of the complete text of the diary of Mary Hardy, published in 2013.

An honorary research fellow in the History department of Royal Holloway, University of London since 2006, she was elected a fellow of the Royal Historical Society in 2016. She was born in central London in 1946, read Modern History at St Anne's College, Oxford and gained her master's degree in Modern History at Royal Holloway. For both degrees she specialised in aspects of English history in the eighteenth century.

She has lived in Kingston upon Thames in Surrey since 1970 and was a partner with her husband Tony in the economic consultancy they founded and ran for 22 years.

She has a deep love of the landscape and waterways of the Norfolk Broads in eastern England. All her life she has spent as much time as possible on the family boat, at first with her parents, later with her husband and three sons and, in recent years, the new boating generation.

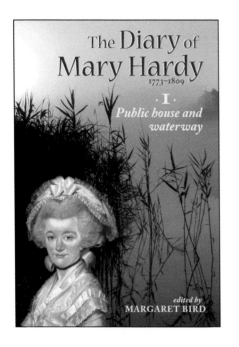

The Diary of
Mary Hardy
1773–1809

· 1 ·
*Public house and
waterway*

edited by
MARGARET BIRD

The Diary of
Mary Hardy
1773–1809

· 2 ·
*Beer supply, water power
and a death*

edited by
MARGARET BIRD

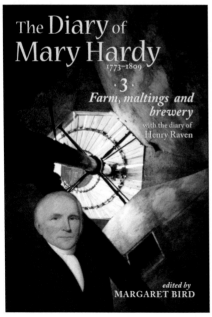

The Diary of
Mary Hardy
1773–1809

· 3 ·
*Farm, maltings and
brewery*
with the diary of
Henry Raven

edited by
MARGARET BIRD

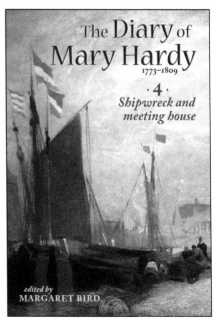

The Diary of
Mary Hardy
1773–1809

· 4 ·
*Shipwreck and
meeting house*

edited by
MARGARET BIRD

Praise for *The Diary of Mary Hardy 1773–1809* edited by Margaret Bird and published 2013

THIS DAILY RECORD, meticulously kept over thirty-six years, of working life and entrepreneurship in late eighteenth- and early nineteenth-century England offers one of the most consistent, enduring and revealing primary sources of its period . . .

Having devoted twenty-five years to the task, Margaret Bird has completed a most impressively professional edition, with meticulous annotations arranged in side-notes . . . The index to each volume is impeccably comprehensive and lucidly arranged . . .

This is a source which illuminates much of the social as well as the topographical landscape of its time, revealing the possibilities of upward social mobility . . .

On account of the handsome appearance and painstaking thoroughness of the editing, the cost of the four diary volumes plus the *Remaining Diary* can be considered a real bargain at present-day book prices.　　　PROF. G.M. DITCHFIELD [1]

A WONDERFUL VIEW of an upwardly mobile 'middling' family immersed in making their way . . . Their social and domestic life was not a retired one . . .

All half a million words of them [the diaries] are edited . . . by Margaret Bird. It is a most remarkable venture, the outcome of a quarter of a century's intense and enthusiastic labour. They are a notable addition to the long roll-call of English diaries, one of the great joys of our historical record.　PROF. RICHARD G. WILSON [2]

THIS PROJECT really is in a class of its own. In fact, I would go so far as to describe it as possibly the greatest single piece of scholarship on a Norfolk topic since the Rev. Francis Blomefield embarked on his monumental survey of the county in the 18th century.　　　　　　　　　EASTERN DAILY PRESS [3]

EVERYTHING ABOUT THE PRESENTATION of this incredibly rich material has been considered with the reader in mind . . . Published together in five volumes, it [is] . . . a work of an outstanding scale.　　　FORMER SURREY COUNTY ARCHIVIST [4]

THESE ARE A SET OF REFERENCE BOOKS that can be used by scholars and researchers across many disciplines and at all levels . . . Everything in the books describes in great detail the social, economic and financial environment common in the 18th century.　　　　　　　　　　BREWERY HISTORY [5]

[1] *G.M. Ditchfield* Emeritus Professor of Eighteenth-Century History at the University of Kent, in a book review in *The English Historical Review*, vol. 130, no. 542 (Feb. 2015), pp. 219–21. *The Remaining Diary of Mary Hardy* contains the entries omitted from the four-volume set

[2] *Richard G. Wilson* Emeritus Professor and former Director of the Centre of East Anglian Studies at the University of East Anglia, in a Diary book review in the *Parson Woodforde Society Quarterly Journal*, vol. 46, no. 4 (winter 2013), pp. 21–6

[3] *Eastern Daily Press* Trevor Heaton, Books Editor, in a review in the regional daily newspaper (Weekend supplement, 8 June 2013, p. 21)

[4] *former Surrey County Archivist* Maggie Vaughan-Lewis, in a book review in the *Journal of the Aylsham Local History Society*, vol. 9, no. 8 (Aug. 2013), pp. 294–6

[5] *Brewery History* Ken Smith, former editor of *Brewery History*, the journal of the Brewery History Society, in a book review, no. 154 (autumn 2013), pp. 89–90

Mary Hardy
and her World
1773–1809

title page 'Charge Your Bayonet': a Norfolk Militiaman takes a determined stand in a manual devised by William Windham of Felbrigg Hall and Lord Townshend of Raynham Hall during the Seven Years War.

The Regulars, the Militia and the Volunteers were all engaged in the nation's defence during the repeated threats of invasion by the French
[*W. Windham, A Plan of Discipline…for the use of the Militia of the county of Norfolk (1759): Norfolk Heritage Centre, Norwich*]

half-title An early-19th-century pewter tankard holding two pints, in use at Coltishall's Anchor Hotel until the 1960s.

Mary Hardy wrote the early years of her diary at Coltishall
[*photograph Margaret Bird 2013*]

Mary Hardy
and her World
1773–1809

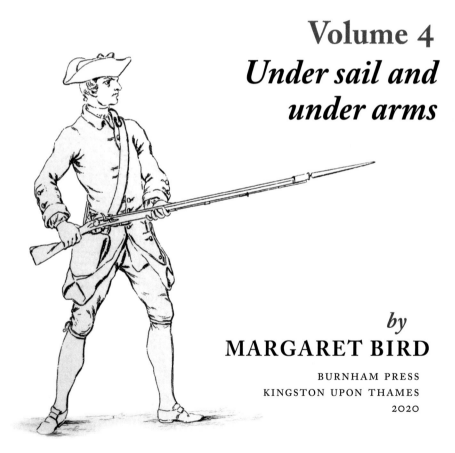

Volume 4
*Under sail and
under arms*

by
MARGARET BIRD

BURNHAM PRESS
KINGSTON UPON THAMES
2020

BURNHAM PRESS

2020

❋ KINGSTON UPON THAMES ❋

www.burnham-press.co.uk

Published by
Burnham Press, Burnham Lodge,
193 Richmond Road, KINGSTON UPON THAMES,
Surrey, KT2 5DD, United Kingdom

First published 2020

Design and typesetting in Adobe InDesign
by Margaret Bird
Main text set in Plantin MT Pro 9½ on 11½
Sidenotes in Plantin Light 8¾ on 9¼
Captions in Adobe Caslon Pro semibold 9¼ on 10
Display text Nueva Standard bold and
Adobe Caslon Pro semibold
Printers' floral ornaments by the Norwich Press 1796

gomerprinting.co.uk

MIX
Paper from responsible sources
FSC® C114687
www.fsc.org

Printed and bound in the UK by Gomer Press Ltd,
Llandysul, Ceredigion SA44 4JL, United Kingdom
on 100 gsm Claro silk-coated, archive-quality paper,
woodfree and FSC accredited

ISBN for VOLUME 4 as an individual volume:
ISBN 978–1–9162067–4–8

more on Mary Hardy:
**www.burnham-press.co.uk/
mary-hardys-world**
and
**www.burnham-press.co.uk/
mary-hardys-diary**

A CIP record for this title is available from the British Library

VOLUME 4 is one of four individual volumes in the set
Mary Hardy and her World 1773–1809, published 2020

ISBN for the complete set of four World volumes:
ISBN 978–1–9162067–5–5

Contents

Volume 4

TO THE MEMORY OF

THE HONOURABLE BERYL COZENS-HARDY
(1911–2011)

OF LETHERINGSETT, NORFOLK

BOTH GREAT-GREAT-GREAT-GRANDDAUGHTER AND

GREAT-GREAT-GREAT-GREAT-GRANDDAUGHTER OF

MARY HARDY

THESE FOUR VOLUMES ARE DEDICATED

A descendant's preface

by Beryl Cozens-Hardy

The Hardy, Cozens-Hardy and Phelps families have in turn been custodians of Mary Hardy's manuscript diary since it was written. In November 2009 Beryl Cozens-Hardy received a letter from Margaret Bird inviting her to write some opening words for this book.

Two days later, and one week short of her 98th birthday, Beryl replied in her own hand with these thoughts from her room at Letheringsett Hall—the room built as his study by Mary Hardy's son William and in which Beryl died on 25 September 2011.

She begins with words from Margaret's letter.

from The Hon. Beryl Cozens-Hardy, OBE

LETHERINGSETT HALL · HOLT · NORFOLK · NR25 7AR

23 November 2009

'I AM NOW CLOSE TO COMPLETION.' Magic words from Margaret Bird which will create joy among all those who have been waiting for this tremendous work.

Her writing is so clear and skilled, so well illustrated, so comprehensive, and so interesting, that I feel sure it will be much read and studied by generations of people wishing to learn more about life in Mary Hardy's time. The whole exercise is very serious and yet this mine of information remains 'a good read'.

Our thanks go to Margaret, and to all her family for giving her the support she needed. They have all played a valuable part. Her husband Tony has encouraged and helped Margaret again and again, as have their three sons Roger, Christopher and Michael, now all married, who grew up in the book's shadow.

I saw how much they all contributed to her great work, and I want to thank them and congratulate them too for helping her to produce these volumes.

above Beryl Cozens-Hardy in 1961 as Chief Commissioner for England, Girl Guides Association
[*Press Photographic Services*]

facing page In the Amalienborg Palace, Copenhagen, 1984: Beryl Cozens-Hardy is honoured for her service in leading the Girl Guide movement worldwide
[*photographer not known*]

Foreword
by Penelope J. Corfield

Penelope J. Corfield is Emeritus Professor at Royal Holloway, University of London, and Visiting Professor at Newcastle University, UK.
  She is also a member of the *Academia Europaea*/European Academy; and President of the International Society for Eighteenth-Century Studies   [*Anthony Bird 2013*]

BATTERSEA, 8 August 2018

THE MAGNIFICENT ENTERPRISE that appears here in the form of *Mary Hardy and her World* is the stuff of a historian's (happy) dream. For some time now, there has been an awakening interest in discovering personal documentation relating to women in history. They are, generally speaking, less famous and publicly important than men. Their lives are less well recorded. And, as a consequence, their fortunes have, until recently, been less well studied. So that makes every new discovery a matter of some moment. Hence this full analysis of the voluminous diaries of Mary Hardy (1733–1809) is positively epic.

  One fascinating sign of historians' eagerness to find women's personal records appears in the story of a fake (or at least a semi-fake). Anne Hughes's *Diary of a Farmer's Wife, 1796–7*, published in different editions in 1964, 1980 and 2009, has been serially discovered, published, and debunked, before being re-discovered, re-published and re-debunked. This source originated in a genuine document, now lost. It then came into the hands of a local historian in the 1930s, who, seeking to add interest, inserted extraneous nineteenth-century materials relating to cookery and folk customs.

The outcome was a hybrid. One sign of its doctored contents was a certain archness of style: 'Men be just like childer and as much trubble in many wayes . . .'. As a result, this diary does not pass muster as a *bona fide* source document. A similar archness was apparent in a known fake. Cleone Knox's *Diary of a Young Lady of Fashion in the Year 1764–5* (1925) was written as a spoof and its real author was taken aback to find it taken seriously. At one point, the fictitious heroine muses: 'Men are such Silly Fools'. Diary-hunters be warned. Any newly-discovered diary which generalises about male–female relations in such knowing terms (trying to raise a smile), should be regarded with instant suspicion.

No such generic meditations worried Mary Hardy during her busy life in eighteenth-century Norfolk—or, if they did, such views did not appear in her long-unpublished diaries. Her recorded concerns were immediate, quotidian, and practical. That indeed is one prime characteristic of diaries. Of course, these highly personal records vary considerably. There are no rules. Nonetheless, diaries share some common features. Overwhelmingly, they tend to concentrate upon everyday affairs, often written in terse prose. And it's not uncommon to mention the weather. (So it's interesting but not surprising to learn that Mary Hardy's very first diary entry, on 28 November 1773, was: 'Fair weather').

Within a fairly common format, however, there is plenty of scope for personal variation. Different diarists use this private medium to record a range of different preoccupations. For instance, there are religious diaries, food diaries, work diaries, travel diaries, military diaries, political diaries, prison diaries, and so forth. For many diarists, writing daily (or sometimes more intermittently) allows them to gather their thoughts and then to free their minds by logging the key points. The resultant document functions as a personal *aide-memoire*.

An example can be seen in the prison jottings, scribbled in Newgate in the years 1794-6 by a young radical named Thomas Lloyd. He tried to keep some sense of control by secretly diarising his grim experiences. No doubt, too, his developing facility of speed-writing helped him in his later career, when he emigrated to the USA and pioneered the American version of shorthand.

Reference to secrecy highlights one important point about diaries. It's important always to assess for whom they were written. The greater the privacy a diarist can maintain, the greater the frankness of the entries. So diaries that are written deliberately as semi-public resources, to be read or shown to others, are habitually the most carefully composed and the least spontaneous. A majority of diaries, meanwhile, are written as private records. But if the resultant document is not well hidden, there is always the risk that it might be read casually by others. So most private diaries are candid but usually with some reservations. By contrast, those records which are kept in complete secrecy—and, especially, those written in secret codes—are usually the most explicit.

Sex provides one test. Personal sexual encounters (as opposed to gossip about other people's escapades) are not often described frankly in diaries. However, the more secretive the format, the more likely are such matters to be included. Samuel Pepys is the paradigm case. He wrote in his own variant of a standard seventeenth-century shorthand code. Yet what would Pepys have thought in the 1660s had he known that his cipher would be cracked and that, with the publication of his diaries from 1825 onwards, every interested reader to this day could read full details of his sex life, which were concealed from even his closest family? Possibly he might have been pleased. After all, he had saved copies of his diaries and (separately) a code to the cipher. Either way, Pepys's fate sends a clear message. Diarists seeking complete retrospective privacy should ultimately destroy their handiwork. Otherwise, all surviving personal documents—coded or otherwise—are considered by historians as fair game.

Generally, however, the greatest safeguard against casual diary readings by nosy friends and neighbours is the sheer ordinariness of most diary entries. They are often repetitive, sometimes boring. Sometimes cryptic. There is no overarching narrative line, other than the passing of the days. Not much humour except at times inadvertently. And, above all, the sheer abundance of many terse entries on many diverse topics can be hard for an uninitiated reader to process mentally. Diaries are thus, on the one hand, highly accessible historical documents but, on the other hand, they are very opaque—hiding bigger pictures among a forest of mundane details.

These preliminary observations serve to highlight the utter magnificence of Margaret Bird's interpretation of Mary Hardy's diaries. The basic entries in themselves constitute invaluable historical evidence. As already noted, there is a dearth of personal documentation relating to non-elite eighteenth-century women. But between 1773 and 1809 Mary Hardy penned half a million words on an exceptionally wide range of topics. Indefatigably, she recorded details of her daily housework and family dynamics, her practices of childcare, her business as the working wife of a Norfolk farmer and brewer, her relationships with workers and servants, her active social life, her questing religious life, her observations on significant local and national events, and so forth, not excluding the weather . . .

In short, a veritable cornucopia. This resource stands comparison with already treasured big diaries from the eighteenth century, such as those of (in Britain) Parson James Woodforde (1740–1803), another Norfolk resident, or (in North America) the Philadelphian Quaker Elizabeth Drinker (1735–1807).

Yet voluminous diaries cry out for expert guides. That is where Mary Hardy has had the posthumous good fortune of finding her ideal editor and interpreter. It takes a lot of energy, pertinacity, and powers of self-organisation to maintain a daily diary over many years. Margaret Bird has proved equally pertinacious in studying these materials in depth. Not only has she already presented the diaries immaculately in a stylish layout, but here she elucidates the material in a series of sustained essays. These convey Margaret Bird's big-picture analysis of the world of Mary Hardy, accompanied by well-chosen illustrations, tables, graphs, maps, family trees and extensive side-notes. There is much to savour, to learn, to debate.

Mary Hardy and her World constitutes a publication *de luxe*. It is worthy both of the diarist herself and of Margaret Bird, her editor and historian. Now, readers, please read on . . .

Introduction —
the diaries' significance

by Margaret Bird

The author with the five huge ledgers containing Mary Hardy's diary, written daily over nearly 36 years 1773–1809. This manuscript, with that of the nephew and brewery apprentice Henry Raven, remains in the descendants' possession in north Norfolk   [*Christopher Bird 2012*]

KINGSTON UPON THAMES, 22 December 2019

¹ *diaries* They remain in private hands. Their full text was published in Apr. 2013. As told on p. 1 of each World volume a full set of photocopies, on A3 paper, was lodged in the Norfolk Record Office, Norwich, securing free public access to the MSS

² *valuable material* See the extracts from the reviews of *The Diary of Mary Hardy 1773–1809* at the start of each World volume

³ *unique* This verdict by Richard G. Wilson, former head of the Centre of East Anglian Studies, is in his book review of 2013 and is quoted in vol. 1, p. 142. It is cited on the reviews page for the Diary at the start of each World volume

DEVOTING ALMOST A THIRD OF A CENTURY to just one uninterrupted quest requires some justification. So here it is.

It has taken 32 years of continuous research and writing to publish the diaries of Mary Hardy and her young nephew Henry Raven in full for the first time and to prepare these four companion volumes of commentary and analysis.

This introduction to the two diaries is common to all the commentary volumes, *Mary Hardy and her World*.

Mary Hardy wrote her 500,000-word diary every day during 1773–1809 in what by the end were five thick ledgers. Henry too wrote daily for four of those years, contributing a further 73,000 words in his own ledger.¹ It is exceedingly unusual to find a woman of little formal education creating such a sustained piece of what is now seen as valuable primary source material.² The teenage brewery apprentice's record is thought to be unique for the eighteenth century.³

Publishing their work has generated its own statistics. The Diary volumes contain just under 2350 pages, of which more than 460 are pages of index; there are 1300 black-and-white illustrations. The World volumes, this study, contain 3240 pages with 1450 black-and-white illustrations and 360 pages of index, plus 96 pages of 190 colour plates. They also have 188 tables, graphs, maps and family trees. Both works contain numerous appendices. The project to bring them before the public has taken almost as many years as it took Mary Hardy to compile her journal: 32, to her 35½.

The opening chapters in volume 1 of this study examine the diaries as sources and chronicle the lives of their writers. In order to keep the bulk of this inordinately long work within manageable bounds the other three volumes launch into their subject matter without covering that ground again other than in the summaries, on page 1, of the careers of Mary Hardy (1733–1809), her farmer and brewer husband William, their children Raven, William and Mary Ann, and her fellow diarist Henry Raven (1777–1825). He was the son of her brother Robert, who died in 1783 when Henry was six years old. Henry lived in the Hardys' household in north Norfolk for eight years from the age of fourteen and was formally bound as their apprentice for five of those years.

below On the left: the spines of the set of four Diary volumes; Henry Raven's text is intercut with his aunt's entries in the third volume.

The spines on the right are this study: the four companion volumes of commentary and analysis, *Mary Hardy and her World 1773–1809.*

Each of the eight is fully annotated, illustrated and indexed.

They are available as sets of four or singly: www.burnham-press. co.uk

THE DIARY OF MARY HARDY	THE DIARY OF MARY HARDY	THE DIARY OF MARY HARDY	THE DIARY OF MARY HARDY	MARY HARDY AND HER WORLD	MARY HARDY AND HER WORLD	MARY HARDY AND HER WORLD	MARY HARDY AND HER WORLD
❋	❋ ❋	❋ ❋ ❋	❋ ❋ ❋ ❋	❋	❋ ❋	❋ ❋ ❋	❋ ❋ ❋ ❋
1773–1781	1781–1793	1793–1797	1797–1809	1773–1809	1773–1809	1773–1809	1773–1809
MARGARET BIRD	MARGARET BIRD	MARGARET BIRD	MARGARET BIRD	MARGARET BIRD	MARGARET BIRD	MARGARET BIRD	MARGARET BIRD
William Hardy	Mary Hardy	Mary Hardy	William Hardy	William Hardy 1732– 1811	Mary Hardy 1733– 1809	William Hardy jnr 1770– 1842	Mary Ann Hardy 1773– 1864

THE SPINE PORTRAITS

above A sample page from Mary Hardy's MS diary: her entries for 23–29 Oct. 1797, when she was nearly 64. The long, narrow layout was imposed on her by the use of a counting-house ledger.

The first two of the seven days are transcribed in a separate publication *The Remaining Diary of Mary Hardy* (Burnham Press, 2013). This contains all the entries not included in the four-volume Diary set. Such extracts are cited as 'Diary MS' in the editorial sidenotes in the Diary and World volumes [*Cozens-Hardy Collection*]

The Coltishall diary 1773–81 appeared in full in the first Diary volume. Henry Raven's Letheringsett diary 1793–97 is in full in the third volume. But to spare the reader unnecessary repetition Mary Hardy's Letheringsett diary 1781–1809 was abridged. The 44 per cent of her diary text not included in the set of four Diary volumes was published by Burnham Press in 2013—without annotation or an index—in a separate work, a paperback: M. Bird, ed., *The Remaining Diary of Mary Hardy 1773–1809*.

For brevity the Diary volumes are cited in the editorial notes '*Diary 1*', '*Diary 2*' etc. *The Remaining Diary* is cited as 'Diary MS'.

Other volumes within this study, *Mary Hardy and her World*, are cited merely as 'vol. 1', 'vol. 2' etc, again for brevity.

Each of the four World volumes draws heavily on material from the full text of the two diaries. While containing frequent cross-references to other volumes each stands on its own and is constructed around related themes:

1 · A working family
Family life, marriage, children and schooling
Creating and running a home
Managing maidservants
Gardens and pleasure grounds

2 · Barley, beer and the working year
The workforce, farming, enclosure and the weather
Malting, brewing and milling
Running and supplying the public houses
The excise service, debt and business finance

3 · Spiritual and social forces
Church of England clergy and Nonconformist preachers
Sunday schools
The reactions of the flock
Local society, civil unrest, crime and the poor
Market towns, trades and professions

4 · Under sail and under arms
Transport by road, inland waterway and sea
Tourism, the theatre, fairs and other leisure pursuits
Politics and home defence

It will immediately become obvious that the two diarists cover an extraordinary range, broken down in this study into 39 distinct topics. These 39 chapters, listed at the end of each of the World and Diary volumes, paint an unusually wide canvas of eighteenth-century life, work and outlook.

The topics are remarkable not only for their range but for their depth, for Mary Hardy and Henry Raven had an eye for detail and were meticulous in keeping the record. They came from modest shopkeeping and farming backgrounds in central Norfolk, as described in volume 1, chapter 2 and seen in the outline family tree facing page 1 of each World volume. Yet they were keen to record life beyond the physical limits of the villages in which they wrote, this feature being particularly true of the aunt's entries.

The nature of their work fostered an outward-looking approach. As well as farming, the Hardy family were engaged in malting, brewing and the supply of up to 25 tied houses at any one time, with the addition of many further outlets not secured by tie.[1] Mobility is one of the hallmarks of the diaries partly as a consequence of the daily need to deliver beer across a radius of up to 25 miles from the brewery and also to sort out problems as they arose. As shown in two of the volumes, a drayman might cover 555 miles in five weeks with the beer cart or beer wagon—on top of his many other duties in this family-run enterprise.[2]

So precise is the source material that we can calculate the hours worked a year: 3760 in the mid-1770s; 3617 in the mid-1790s. These figures are way beyond anything performed today. In the United Kingdom the average working year for those in full-time employment in recent years was 1677 hours.[3] Such calculations are made possible only through the time-awareness displayed by both diarists and by the Hardy family generally. Not a moment could be wasted. As a result the pages devoted to their leisure hours are few. Their lives were governed by the clock, as were the lives of the male workforce and the maidservants. In many ways the diaries serve as workaday logs; they are certainly not literary journals.[4] In this lies their strength. By keeping her entries terse, as pictured opposite, noting the day's events did not take too much time. Hence Mary Hardy's ability to keep to her task for nearly 36 years until released by death.

[1] *tied houses* A later term, but the concept was familiar at the time. It refers to retail outlets (the public houses), owned or hired by the brewer or where the innkeeper is bound by debt to the brewer (see vol. 2, chaps 8, 9, 10 and 11)

[2] *workforce* The demands made of the versatile yearly-hired men who turned their hand to work on the farm, in the maltings and brewery and as draymen are analysed principally in vols 2 and 4

[3] *working hours* This subject is analysed in vol. 2, chap. 1. Comparisons are made with modern working conditions using OECD data. Mary Hardy is the source for the 1770s and Henry Raven for the 1790s

[4] *logs* To be true to the original MSS, the Diary volumes transcribe the words as the diarists wrote them, faithfully reflecting original spelling, use of super-scripts (as in W^m for William) and capital letters at the start of words.

For greater ease of reading I have modernised spelling and orthography in these World volumes

[1] *by water* In 1776 William and Mary Hardy commissioned the building of a wherry, a small sailing vessel, to carry their produce along the inland waterways of the Norfolk Broads and to bring Tyneside coal upriver from Gt Yarmouth. They named her *William and Mary*.

Their son William owned a seagoing sloop *Nelly* for similar purposes, but she could venture round the coast and to Norway. *Nelly* sailed from Blakeney on the north Norfolk coast until she was wrecked there in 1804.

Owning their own vessels sprang from the twin urges to integrate all aspects of the business and exert control

[2] *hailstones* They measured 17·8 cm. See vol. 1, chap. 2 and vol. 2, chap. 4 relating the strange phenomena to the volcanic fissure eruptions in Iceland

Distinct the topics may be, but common threads emerge. Any notion of Georgian country life as remote, static and changeless is exploded. We learn how much movement there was not only by road but by water.[1] Itinerancy was a way of life, engaged in by very many sections of the population: by bishops, curates and preachers, by excise officers (the severe service William Hardy endured for twelve years in his younger days), and by professional men, tradesmen and theatre troupes. Services were brought to the client in a world largely without offices. The roads were packed with men—and to a lesser extent women—on the move.

Other general themes include the effects of harsh weather patterns: in July 1783 Mary Hardy noted hailstones near seven inches in size.[2] Poor harvests, food shortages and riots became a feature of the period. The overarching theme is that of control: control of the workforce and servants; of the poor in workhouses or through suppressing the fairs and sports they prized; of the children of the poor in Sunday schools; and self-control to the point of self-abasement, as urged by Wesleyan Methodists and Anglican Evangelicals.

Justices pursued control through the licensing of a wide variety of institutions from public houses to madhouses, as these were then known. Even the landscape was controlled and tamed through enclosure, road diversions and the creation of parks. William Hardy's adoption of a business model known today as vertical integration, whereby the one enterprise undertakes all the elements required to make a product (in his case beer), was both a rational response to the pressures of the time and a symptom of the desire to control.

What prompted me to embark on this demanding mission? It began more than a year before the Berlin Wall fell; Mikhail Gorbachev and Margaret Thatcher were still in power. The internet, worldwide web and e-mails did not exist. Google was not founded until more than ten years after I first shoul-

left Starting young: the author aged eight months on the Norfolk Broads. My father Cecil, mother Enid and I lived on this small boat from April to October every year until the demands of school in London reduced our annual boating time to three months   [*Cecil Perham 1947*]

dered my burden. Readers will conclude I am just slow, but at the start I had no idea of the enormity of what lay ahead. As recounted in the Preface by Michael J. Sparkes to the first of the Diary volumes, I was inspired by his article of 1988 giving extracts from Mary Hardy's diary about the Hardys' wherry and their son's doomed sloop.[1] I was already familiar with the extracts by Basil Cozens-Hardy from his ancestor's diary, published in 1968.[2] I felt an immediate bond with this diarist. She lived at Coltishall, a village I knew well as the home berth of my parents' boat.[3] She moved to Letheringsett, near the sea, a place I had come to know through friends from 1967. I could visualise the setting for her life and work. The Sinclairs were close friends and Letheringsett neighbours of the Hon. Beryl Cozens-Hardy, doubly descended from Mary Hardy and the manuscript's custodian for more than fifty years. They effected an introduction in November 1988, and to Beryl's memory I dedicate these volumes in tribute to her lively support.

Her first cousin once removed, Basil Cozens-Hardy, had confined himself to very brief extracts and did not transcribe any of Henry Raven's text. As a result I did not realise what a mass of material awaited me in my quest to learn more.

The long list of Acknowledgments overleaf attests to the debt I owe to so many. I am particularly grateful to members of the extended Cozens-Hardy family for welcoming me into their lives and freely granting access to the precious family archives. The debt I owe Beryl's nephew John Phelps and his wife Linda, and Basil's son Jeremy Cozens-Hardy and grandaughter Caroline Holland, principal custodians of the Cozens-Hardy Collection, is incalculable.

I also wish especially to thank my tutors at Royal Holloway, Penelope J. Corfield and Nicola Phillips, for inspirational teaching. My history skills, honed at Oxford in the 1960s under the gifted Marjorie Reeves, Betty Hughes, Howard Colvin, T.M. Parker and others, had grown rusty after forty years. Professor Corfield and Professor Richard G. Wilson of Norwich read my work as it progressed. It has been very greatly improved by their comments. Above all I thank my husband Tony, our mothers Enid and Madge and our sons Roger, Christopher and Michael. Unfailingly enthusiastic participants, they enriched the project—and made it fun.

[1] *preface* 'A skipper's preface', in *Diary 1*, pp. vii–ix; Mike Sparkes has long been a volunteer skipper on the preserved trading wherry *Albion*. See his article 'The *William and Mary* and the *Nelly*', *Journal of the Norfolk Wherry Trust* (spring 1988), pp. 38–42

[2] *extracts* B. Cozens-Hardy, ed., *Mary Hardy's Diary* (Norfolk Record Soc., vol. 37 (1968)). See also his earlier work *The History of Letheringsett in the County of Norfolk with extracts from the diary of Mary Hardy (1773 to 1809)* (Jarrold & Sons, Norwich, 1957)

[3] *home berth* My father Cecil Perham (1882–1964) started boating on the Broads in 1925.

He married late, and was retired when I arrived in 1946. Half the year we lived in Bayswater, in London, and the rest on our beloved 24-foot (7.3-metre) motor cruiser.

Clifford Allen's boatyard at Coltishall became our new base in 1948. My husband Tony and I, with our baby son Roger, moved from that yard in 1973 just before it closed.

Since then we and our family have kept the boat, and her two successors, at Horning on the Bure and then at Brundall on the Yare

Acknowledgments

I AM VERY GRATEFUL to the individuals, societies and institutions who have helped me in my task since 1988. The hundreds named here gave generously of their time; many allowed me to copy documents in their care.

A bullet additionally denotes permission to reproduce illustrations, for which I am also most grateful. Every effort has been made to identify and attribute copyright; I should like to be told of any unwitting omission or infringement.

There are also those whose names I never discovered: owners of former public houses; serving publicans; brewers, farmers, stockmen and gardeners; and many encountered in churches, chapels and on the water.

They passed on their knowledge of their patch, and were patient with a total stranger pursuing them with improbable questions or enquiring about their property deeds.

I owe a great debt to the clergy and parish officers, ministers and congregations whose archives I studied in libraries and record offices; and subsequently to the staff caring for these records whose expertise speeded me on my way.

I pay a special tribute to the descendants of Mary Hardy. As members of the extended Cozens-Hardy family and as custodians of the diaries and other family archives they have been stalwart throughout in granting me access and giving me encouragement.

Michael Sparkes of the Norfolk Wherry Trust and David Mayes of Letheringsett were there for me at the beginning and have steadfastly been by my side throughout my thirty years of research.

Unless otherwise shown here, the individuals listed separately from the institutions and societies are, or were, Norfolk based.

A great many died before my work was done. Happy to help me, they suspected they were unlikely to see the fruits. They especially are not forgotten. M_B

Bob Adams of Rowley Regis, W. Midlands
Adnams Brewery, Southwold: Robert Porter
Ann Allen, Clifford E. Allen and Paul Allen of Coltishall
Aylsham Local History Society: Valerie Belton, Tom Bishop, Dr Julian Eve, Elizabeth Gale, Derek Lyons, Tom Mollard, Diana Polhill, Dr Roger Polhill
• **Aylsham Town Council**: Lloyd Mills, Ron Peabody, Mrs M. Reynolds
Esmé Bagnall Oakeley and Jeremy Bagnall Oakeley of Brinton
Anthony J.M. Baker of W. Runton
Jim Baldwin of Fakenham
Billy Barstard of Blakeney
Michael Barter of Colkirk
Józef Beck of Herne Bay, Kent
June Betts and Russell Betts of Reepham

Blakeney Area Historical Society: Richard Daley, Mary Ferroussat, Jonathan Hooton, Eric Hotblack, Richard Kelham, John Peake, Pam Peake, John Wright
• **The Bodleian Libraries**, University of Oxford
Richard Bond of Coltishall
• Roger Bradbury of Coltishall
• Harvey Brettle and Lindsay Brettle of Letheringsett
Brewery History Society: Ray Anderson, Geoffrey Ballard, Colin Bridgland, Chris Marchbanks, Amber Patrick, Lynn Pearson, • Ian P. Peaty, Jeff Sechiari, Ken Smith
Briston Methodist Church: Roger Williamson
• **British Library**
Broads Authority, Norwich: Mary Muir
Broads Society: Major Roy Kemp

- Mrs B. Brockdorff of Ingworth
  Sharon Brooks and Steve Brooks of Holt
- Cambridge University Library:
  Arthur Owen
  Gordon Camm and Valerie Camm
  of Upton
- Bettina Carter of Bale
- Charlotte Carter and Robert Carter
  of Letheringsett
- The Cheshunt Foundation at
  Westminster College, Cambridge:
  Margaret Thompson, Revd Dr Janet
  Tollington, Helen Weller
  Alice Childs of Coltishall
  Stephen Clarke of Oxford
  William Clowes Printing Museum,
  Beccles, Suff.: Bert Walding, Ernie Ward
  Shaun Colby of the Star, Lessingham
  Coltishall Parish Church: Revd Roger
  Hawkins, Revd Heinz Toller
  Joanna Cooper of London
- Country Life Picture Library
- Courtauld Institute of Art: Photographic
  survey, London
  Bill Cowles of Strumpshaw
- Cozens-Hardy Collection: Ann Solberg
  Clark, ◆ the Hon. Beryl Cozens-Hardy,
  ◆ Jeremy Cozens-Hardy, ◆ John Cozens-
  Hardy, ◆ Raven Cozens-Hardy, Duncan
  Gordon, Isabel Pilkington Henniger,
  ◆ Caroline Holland, David Horne, Laura
  Loane, Richard J. Lyne, the Hon. Mrs
  Douglas Phelps, ◆ John Phelps, Linda
  Phelps, Mary Pickard, Peter Rosser,
  Sue Rosser
  Cozens-Hardy & Jewson, Norwich:
  Matthew Martin, David Taylor
- Albert Daniels and Phyllis Daniels,
  John Daniels and Vivienne Daniels
  of Whissonsett
- Hubert Dawson of Dereham
  Kim Dowe of Potter Heigham
  Shirley Drew of Whissonsett
  Rhoda Drummond of Ingworth
- Dundee City Council, Central Library
- Eastern Counties Newspapers/Archant,
  Library: Rosemary Dixon, Alison
  Maloney, Frances Pearce
  Elgoods Brewery, Wisbech, Cambs

Mundy Ellis of S. Walsham
Ann English of Whissonsett
Simon Evans of Banstead, Surrey
- Viki Fairhurst of Worstead
- The Fitzwilliam Museum, Cambridge
  John F. Fone of Norwich
- French & Jupps Ltd, Stanstead Abbotts,
  Herts: Doug Horton, David Jupp
  Friends of Norfolk and Norwich Heritage:
  Tony Eggleston
- Revd Barry Furness of Honing
- Gainsborough Construction Ltd, Bishop's
  Stortford, Herts: Ian Irvine-Fynn
- George Gale & Sons Ltd, Horndean, Hants
  Dr Denis Gibbs of London
  Heather Gooch of Horningtoft
  Dr Gerry Gregory of Twickenham, Middx
  Gomer Press Ltd, Llandysul, Ceredigion:
  Carys Hughes, Sulwyn Lloyd, Dai Noble
- Gresham's School Archive, Holt:
  Elizabeth Larby, Sue Smart
- Hargham Archive: Sir Thomas Beevor, Bt;
  Anne Carter, honorary archivist
  Peggy Harris and Peter Harris of Tuttington
  Dr Alan Harrison of Loughton, Essex
- Jean Hart of Whissonsett
  Holkham Hall Archives: Christine Hiskey
  Holt Society: Steve Benson, Dr Tony Leech
- Horstead Parish Church: Revd Neville
  Khambatta and Mrs Khambatta
- Houghton Hall Archives:
  the 7th Marquess of Cholmondeley;
  Susan Cleaver, administrator;
  David Yaxley, honorary archivist
- Kristian Howlett and Susan Howlett
  of Coltishall
- Hull Central Library, Kingston upon Hull
  Itteringham History: Maggie Vaughan-
  Lewis, William Vaughan-Lewis
  The Ven. William M. Jacob of London
  Alison Kelly of London
  Jackie Kendall of Cradley Heath
  Peter Kent of Norwich
- King's College, Cambridge: the Provost
  and Scholars; also Dr Michael Halls,
  Mr K.A. Hook, Dr Rosalind Moad,
  John Phillips
  Lancashire Record Office, Preston:
  Simon Jelf

ACKNOWLEDGMENTS

- **Larks Press**, Guist Bottom: Susan Yaxley
Letheringsett Parish Church:
  Dr Wallace White
John Leveridge of Letheringsett
Rosemary Lewis of Holt
Linnean Society: Lynn Crothall,
  Gina Douglas
Alex Lister of Canterbury, Kent
Joy Lodey of Etling Green, Dereham
- Robert Malster of Holbrook, Suffolk
- David Mayes and Stella Mayes
  of Letheringsett
Derek Moody of Dorchester, Dorset
- **Museum of English Rural Life**, Berks
- **The National Archives**
- **National Maritime Museum**, Greenwich,
  London
Norfolk County Council: Michael Knights,
  Historic Buildings Officer
- **Norfolk Heritage Centre** at the Norfolk &
  Norwich Millennium Library, Norwich:
  Clare Agate, Dr Clive Wilkins-Jones,
  Rachel Willis, and all the staff; also
  Norfolk County Council Library &
  Information Service's branch libraries
  at Great Yarmouth and Holt
Norfolk Industrial Archaeology Society:
  David Durst, Barré Funnell,
  Derek Manning, Mary Manning,
  James Oxley-Brennan, Philip Tolley
Norfolk Museums & Archaeology Service:
  Bridewell: David Jones, John Renton
- Museum of Norfolk Rural Life and
  Union Farm, Gressenhall: Frances
  Collinson, Catherine Littlejohns
- Norwich Castle Museum & Art Gallery:
  Paris Agar, Norma Watt
- Strangers' Hall: Helen Rowles
- **Norfolk Record Office**, Norwich: Dr John
  Alban, Jean Kennedy, Susan Maddock,
  Ian Palfrey, Gary Tuson, Jenny Watts,
  Freda Wilkins-Jones, and all the staff
Norfolk Record Society: John M. Barney
- **Norfolk Wherry Trust:** ◆ David Bray,
  Mike Fuller, Henry Gowman, John
  Perryman, ◆ Michael J. Sparkes
Ray Norman of the White Horse, Upton
North Yorkshire Record Office,
  Northallerton
Norwich Cathedral Library:
  Gudrun Warren

Desmond O'Brien of Panxworth
Open University: Dr Anne Stott
- Richard Palmer and Wilma Palmer
  of Whissonsett
- **Herbert Parker Ltd**, Bramerton
Parson Woodforde Society: Clifford Bird,
  Martin Brayne, Dr David E. Case, Revd
  Peter Jameson, Phyllis Stanley
Paston Sixth Form College,
  North Walsham: Irene Golden
John Pegg and Lesley A. Pegg
  of Whissonsett
Pat Perrin of Ontario, Canada
- George A. F. Plunkett of Thorpe St Andrew,
  Norwich
David Pooley of Panxworth
Gladys Preston and Robin Preston
  of Letheringsett
Mr L. Price of Cromer
Helen Rees of Mount Gambier,
  South Australia
- Gill Riley and Margaret Riley of Coltishall
- **Rowley Regis Parish Church**,
  W. Midlands: Revd Ian Shelton and
  Matthew Shelton
Royal Artillery Historical Trust: Colonel
  M.B. Cooper, Brigadier K.A. Timbers
Andrée Shepherd and Ian Shepherd
  of Little Thornage
Marion Sinclair and Professor Peter
  Sinclair of Letheringsett
Olga Sinclair of Potter Heigham
- David Smith and Jayne Smith of Coltishall
- Laura Smith of Letheringsett
Shirley Heriz Smith of Diss
James Smithies of London
Sir John Soane's Museum, London:
  Helen Dorey, Susan Palmer
Ivan Spinks of Coltishall
Mr S.H. Steel of Grantham, Lincs
- William H. Stibbons and Mabel H. Morse
  of Coltishall
Suffolk Record Office, Ipswich
- Alan Taylor and Brenda C. Taylor
  of Horsham St Faith
John Thorne of Dagenham, Essex
- Michael Thurlow of Letheringsett
  Watermill
- The 8th Marquess Townshend,
  Raynham Hall
Elaine Ulph of Old Costessey, Norwich

University of Bradford: Dr Paul Jennings
University of East Anglia: Professor
  A. Hassell Smith, Professor Tom Williamson, Professor Richard G. Wilson
University of Kent: Professor Grayson
  Ditchfield
University of London (Royal Holloway):
  Professor Sarah Ansari, Professor
  Penelope J. Corfield, Dr Nicola Phillips
University of Manchester: Dr James
  Sumner
University of Oxford (Department for
  Continuing Education): Joyce Martin;
  (St Anne's College): Dr Marjorie Reeves
Sarah Warbrick of Long Ditton, Surrey
Douglas Warren of Dudley, W. Midlands
David Websdale and Evelyn Websdale
  of E. Bilney
Juliet Webster of Norwich
Wells Local History Society:
  Revd Canon Roger Arguile
Paul Welters of Norwich

Wesley Historical Society: Revd Elizabeth
  Bellamy, Norma C. Virgoe
West Sussex Record Office, Chichester
✦ West Yorkshire Archive Service,
  Wakefield
Betty M. Wharton of Langham
✦ Whissonsett Parish Church:
  The Rector and PCC; Janet Stangroom
Whitbread plc, London: Nick Redman
✦ Wigan History Shop and Wigan Archives,
  Lancs: Brian Blakeman, Mr A. Gillies,
  David Tetlow
✦ Felicity Wiley and Reginald Wiley
  of Little Plumstead
Squadron Leader Geoffrey Williams
  of Coltishall
Audrey Wilson of Thorpe, Norwich
Wolterton Hall Archives:
  the Lady Walpole
✦ Woodforde's Norfolk Ales: Ray Ashworth,
  Neil Bain
John Yaxley of Barton Turf

Currency symbols and conversion

£   s   d   =   pounds · shillings · pence

pre-decimal		decimal		
one pound	= 20s	= 100p	= £1.00
one shilling	= 12d	= 5p	= £0.05
half a crown	= 2s 6d	= 12½p	= £0.125
one crown	= 5s 0d	= 25p	= £0.25
one guinea	= £1 1s	= 105p	= £1.05

Sources: the original manuscripts

The diary of Mary Hardy
Ledger 1 · 28 Nov. 1773–6 Jan. 1778
Ledger 2 · 7 Jan. 1778–22 Sept. 1782
Ledger 3 · 23 Sept. 1782–20 July 1790
Ledger 4 · 21 July 1790–7 May 1800
Ledger 5 · 8 May 1800–21 Mar. 1809

The diary of Henry Raven
10 Oct. 1793–25 Oct. 1797

Citations and conventions

Alum. Cantab.	*Alumni Cantabrigienses*
Alum. Oxon.	*Alumni Oxonienses*
CHESHUNT	The Cheshunt Foundation at Westminster College, Cambridge
Diary	Volume in the 4-volume Diary set, eg *Diary 2*
Diary MS	*The Remaining Diary of Mary Hardy*
King's Coll.	King's College, Cambridge
Norw. Merc.	*Norwich Mercury*
NRO	Norfolk Record Office
TNA: PRO	The National Archives: Public Record Office

Dates Those before the calendar alteration of 1752 are adjusted to the New Style by altering the year date but not the day. William Hardy was born 26 January 1731. This is given as 26 January 1732; not 26 January 1731/2, nor 6 February 1732

FIGURE 4.A
The Hardys and the Ravens

The diarists Mary Hardy (writing 1773–1809) and Henry Raven (writing 1793–97) are shown in capitals in italic type. Mary Hardy's husband and three children all made entries in her diary and are also shown in italic

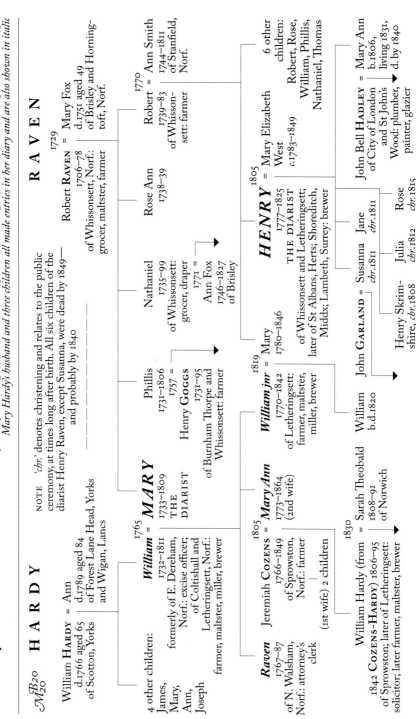

NOTE '*cbr:*' denotes christening and relates to the public ceremony, at times long after birth. All six children of the diarist Henry Raven, except Susanna, were dead by 1849— and probably by 1840

Getting acquainted

Introducing Mary Hardy and Henry Raven

THIS BRIEF SUMMARY OF THE LIVES of the two diarists and of Mary Hardy's immediate family is common to all four volumes.

The diaries

The original manuscripts remain in the care of Mary Hardy's descendants in north Norfolk. Her diary, written daily 1773–1809, is 500,000 words long; her nephew Henry Raven's, written daily 1793–97, is 73,000 words.[1] The complete transcription of both manuscripts, with editorial notes, was published in April 2013.[2]

Mary Hardy (1733–1809)

The diarist was born Mary Raven on 12 November 1733 in the central Norfolk village of Whissonsett. She died 23 March 1809 at her north Norfolk home, Letheringsett Hall, near Holt.

William Hardy (1732–1811)

She married a serving excise officer, William Hardy, in her home parish 22 December 1765. They settled at East Dereham, where he was stationed. He left the service in 1769 and in 1772 moved with his family to the village of Coltishall, near Norwich, where he became manager of Wells's maltings and brewery and occupier of the attached 60-acre farm. In April 1781 they moved to Letheringsett, where he prospered as owner of a 56-acre farm and 40-coomb maltings and brewery across the road from their home. He died 18 August 1811 at their daughter's home at Sprowston, Norwich.

The Hardy children

RAVEN was born at East Dereham 9 November 1767 and died of tuberculosis at Letheringsett Hall on 12 February 1787 while articled to an attorney in the market town of North Walsham. WILLIAM was born 1 April 1770 at Litcham, Norfolk; he married his cousin Mary Raven 17 November 1819, and died 22 June 1842 at his home Letheringsett Hall. He followed his father as farmer, maltster and brewer and greatly expanded the business. MARY ANN was born 3 November 1773 at Coltishall; she married the widowed farmer Jeremiah COZENS 12 November 1805 and they had one son, William. She died 28 October 1864 in Norwich.

Henry Raven (1777–1825)

He was born 31 August 1777 at Whissonsett Hall, his father's farm. His father died in 1783, and Henry came to live with his aunt, the diarist, at her Letheringsett home in 1792. After his apprenticeship there 1794–99 he moved in 1800 to breweries in St Albans, Herts and in London. He was buried on 27 March 1825 in Lambeth.[3]

[1] *the manuscripts* Paper photocopies were lodged in the Norfolk Record Office (NRO) in Norwich in 2013 and are accessible to the public. Their general catalogue reference is FX 376.

The photocopies of Mary Hardy's, in five large boxes, have the references FX 376/1–376/5. Henry Raven's photocopies are in a sixth box, FX 376/6

[2] *the Diary publications* M. Bird, ed., *The Diary of Mary Hardy 1773–1809* (4 vols, Burnham Press, Kingston upon Thames, 2013); 2348 pages. Henry Raven's is intercut with hers in the third volume, *Diary 3*.

The diary entries not included in the four-volume edition were published separately: M. Bird, ed., *The Remaining Diary of Mary Hardy 1773–1809* (Burnham Press, Kingston upon Thames, 2013); 168 pages

[3] *Henry Raven* He qualified as a brewer under the Hardys. He married Mary Elizabeth West in 1805 and they had six children.

She and some at least of their surviving family were in poverty and want by the 1840s

1 · Figures and tables

*Biedermann's
compass rose, p. 72*

I · Wide horizons

top The Norwich Mail in a thunderstorm on Thetford Heath in 1827. This dramatic image was chosen by the UK Post Office in 1984 for one of the postage stamps celebrating the 200th anniversary of the introduction of the mail-coach service, between Bath and London; the Norwich–London Mail was inaugurated a few months later. Passengers bowled along at 8–9 mph [*drawing by J. Pollard*]

above The Bull and Mouth Inn, St Martin's-le-Grand, London *c*.1831. Early one October morning in 1787 William and Mary Hardy boarded the Liverpool stage coach at this busy centre and travelled through the night with minimal stops, arriving 36 hours later 130 miles away near Newcastle-under-Lyme, Staffordshire: a speed of 3·6 mph, with stops [*drawing by T.H. Shepherd; engraving by W. Watkins*]

I

The roads

More than ordinary exertion

A showery day. William Lamb at Hevingham, Buxton, Neatishead and Tunstead . . .   MARY HARDY, 1781

A rainy forenoon, close afternoon . . . Will Lamb went with the wagon to Swanton, Smallburgh and Horning . . .   RAVEN HARDY, 1781 [1]

The said wagons and carts should be bound to travel at the rate of five miles in every two hours: twenty-five miles when loaded, and thirty miles when empty, in every twenty-four hours; and in either case as much further as possible, if the urgency of the service should require more than ordinary exertion.

PLAN FOR THE DEFENCE OF THE EASTERN DISTRICT, 1797 [2]

AT FIRST SIGHT THESE WOULD APPEAR prosaic topics: the use of roads for travel, and the types of vehicle to be found on them. It is in reality one of the most absorbing. Waterways and the sea were used for a great deal of freight transport. But the roads took by far the greatest proportion of passenger traffic, and road improvements resulted in a transformation of the lives of the better off in our period. The term revolution can be overworked, but it applies to road travel. The institution of mail coaches from 1784 meant that well-to-do travellers sped through England at between twice and three times the speed of the stage coaches.

Other improvements stand out in Mary Hardy's diary. For men these included a diminished reliance on riding on horseback and an increasing preference for horse-drawn vehicles such as the chaise and the whiskey—a light gig. As a result travelling became a safer occupation, for a fall from a horse would often result in serious injury or death.

For women the difference was even more marked. In Mary Hardy's circle the new freedom granted by the spread of light vehicles and improved roads resulted in increased

[1] *Lamb Diary 2*: 9 Apr. 1781, by Mary Hardy; 12 Apr. 1781, by 13-year-old Raven Hardy.

On his beer deliveries to public houses in the space of four days the Hardys' drayman covered 110½ miles: 62 with the loaded beer wagon and 48½ miles returning light on 10 and 13 Apr., as charted in fig. 4.1B (p. 11). He spent a fifth day, 11 Apr., at Letheringsett. He exactly matched the 110 miles proposed by the military expert for civilian haulage of loaded and unloaded wagons over four days

[2] *defence* TNA: PRO WO 30/100, p. 5: 'Proposed plan for the supply of an extra number of wagons and carts for the service of the Army in the Eastern [Military] District during the war', by Henry Motz, Esq., Commissary General, Chelmsford, Essex, 11 July 1797.

The role of civilians in the wars against France is analysed in chap. 9

[1] *Mail ticket Norw. Merc.*, 12 Mar. 1785 (pictured p. 42). The postchaise was nearly double the price, costing the Hardys £8 4s 6d for three seats one way in 1800

[2] *wages* For the workforce see vol. 2, chap. 1. Non-beneficed clergy needed multiple curacies to make ends meet (vol. 3, chap. 1)

[3] *distribution* See vol. 2, chaps 1, 9 and 10.
A cart has two wheels; a wagon has four. Where possible, the Hardys and their workforce used the more manoeuvrable cart in preference to the heavy wagon with its long wheelbase. Their vehicles are listed on p. 34

[4] *draymen* The chapters in vol. 2 on the workforce and public houses describe the workload of the draymen.
The wide area they covered is charted in fig. 2. app. in vol. 2.
All four volumes of *The Diary of Mary Hardy*, but particularly the early entries by Mary Hardy and later Henry Raven (*Diary 1* and *Diary 3*), log the dates of public house supply. The editorial indexes to the towns and villages, compiled by date of entry, enable patterns to be plotted

mobility and new opportunities to travel short distances in the company of their young children and without spattering their clothes with mud. Horse-riding other than occasionally as pillions behind male relatives was only very rarely attempted by the women of Mary Hardy's diary, as also by women of all classes other than nobility and upper gentry.

On the majority of their road journeys the passengers were exposed to the elements. They were not under cover unless protected by the postchaise and, for other long-distance journeys, the much slower carrier's cart, mail cart and stage coach—if paying extra as inside passengers. There is no mention in the diaries of the Hardy family seizing the new opportunities provided by the mail coach. Like most of the population they may have considered the cost prohibitive. At £1 11s 6d for a one-way ticket on the Norwich Mail, a family of three would have paid just under £9 10s for a trip to and from London, quite apart from the cost of getting to Norwich.[1] When he left the Excise in 1769 William Hardy's annual salary was £50, out of which he paid for a horse. In the 1790s his miller's annual wage was £31 10s; a curate might receive only £15 a year from his non-resident incumbent.[2] For the vast majority of the population the costly mail service, and indeed almost all forms of relatively fast and comfortable transport, were out of reach. Going on foot, on horseback, in an open cart or, on the water, taking passage in a trading vessel were the best options on offer.

Nevertheless it has been a central theme of the earlier volumes that life in the countryside as seen through the eyes of Mary Hardy and her diarist nephew Henry Raven was far from isolated and static. Thanks to a generally buoyant local economy it was characterised by the constant movement of people and goods. Carts and, to a lesser extent, wagons predominated on the roads and byways. Distribution, already covered in volume 2, is examined afresh at the start of this chapter.[3] The brewer's draymen routinely drove more than a hundred miles a week supplying the public houses—on top of their other errands such as fetching coal. The valiant William Lamb lumbered 555½ miles in five weeks with the beer wagon in 1781, as the next section will record.[4]

The passenger transport revolution, while much discussed, is not the full story. Quietly and routinely huge distances were being covered when carrying freight within local areas, linking villages with market towns and supplying the retail networks of rural manufacturers.[1] The possibilities opened up by the mail service dazzled the opinion formers. But very few wrote of the daily grind endured by those ceaselessly jolting along at slower than walking speed. Loaded wagons could be drawn at only 2–3 miles an hour. When employed about the farm these speeds were of little consequence; but brewers were reliant on the dedication of their draymen, who might have to drive a wagon over 30 miles a day.

A preoccupation with the social revolution accomplished by the railways can obscure other real changes made in the sixty years before the steam train's arrival. Coaching and turnpike roads reached a sophistication which transformed the lives of the better off, only for that achievement to be thrown over within a few years of the railways. The coaching trade never recovered. The mail coach, introduced with such pride and optimism in 1784 and offering fast, reliable long-distance travel for passengers on main routes, had only a brief flowering. The last London-based mail ceased to run in 1846, just 62 years after the inauguration of the service.

Carrying bulk goods

The most startling of the revelations about road transport to be found in the diaries of Mary Hardy and Henry Raven is their careful log of the distances regularly completed by the draymen. There was no change of drayhorse on the beer deliveries, and 35 miles is generally accepted as the daily maximum—as was the case with freight transport to the local market town.[2] The Norfolkmen's mileages were truly astonishing. A 35-mile round trip with the beer wagon in one day, as in the deliveries to Burnham Market from Letheringsett, or a 50-mile round trip to Stalham in two days, formed part of the service offered to the more outlying public houses. William Lamb managed 37 miles in one day on 9 April 1781, with a fully loaded beer wagon (figure 4.1B).

In the extremely testing period 1781–82, when William Hardy had to supply the public houses of his old Coltishall enterprise from his new Letheringsett base, the greatest part of the burden fell to his head drayman. William Lamb served not only the public houses of his master's Leth-

above The Crown at Smallburgh, near Stalham, one of the outlets quoted at the chapter head which Lamb supplied from Letheringsett, 22 miles away [*MB · 2007*]

[1] *revolution* The term is used in the title of a well-illustrated study of the infrastructure: P. J. G. Ransom, *The Archaeology of the Transport Revolution 1750–1850* (The Windmill Press, Kingswood, 1984)

[2] *towns* R. Perren, 'Markets and marketing', *The Agrarian History of England and Wales: Volume VI 1750–1850*, ed. G. E. Mingay (Cambridge Univ. Press, 1989), pp. 218–19

¹ *source* Extract from the 'Proposed plan for the supply of an extra number of wagons and carts for the service of the Army in the Eastern [Military] District during the war', by H. Motz, Esq., Commissary General, Chelmsford, Essex, 11 July 1797.
His figures, for haulage by civilian wagons and carts, were given in hundredweight; they are here converted to tons (defined in the Glossary)

TABLE 4.1.1

Road-haulage capabilities in East Anglia 1797, as seen by the military (*tons*)

source TNA: PRO WO 30/100, p. 5, 11 July 1797 ¹

team	heavy items (*tons*) eg flour, grain, fuel	bulky items (*tons*) eg bread, biscuit
wagon		
4 or more horses	3	1
3 horses	2	0·75
cart		
3 or more horses	1·5	0·5
2 horses	1	0·5

² *military estimate* TNA: PRO WO 30/100, p. 6, 11 July 1797. Weybills (dockets for freight) and conductors, in addition to easing bulk carriage, helped to prevent embezzling.
It was also essential to keep the roads clear. Later in 1797 Henry Motz proposed to HRH Field Marshal the Duke of York (the British Commander-in-Chief) that to prevent 'fatal impediments' blocking the operations of the Army the unmarried civilian inhabitants forced to leave their homes under the threat of invasion should form 'a voluntary Corps of Pioneers' (TNA: PRO WO 30/100, p. 31, the Commissary General writing from Westminster Bridge, London, 27 Dec. 1797)

eringsett brewery in north Norfolk but also those of the Coltishall brewery of John Wells, on the Broads, which the diarist's husband still managed for up to eighteen months following the family's removal to Letheringsett on 5 April 1781. The tireless Lamb notched up distances which even that high priest of eighteenth-century road travel, John Wesley, would have marvelled at. Loading his wagon the night before, Lamb would have perhaps a fourteen-hour day on the road if travelling 35 miles, and eight hours if travelling 20 miles—not allowing for the time spent unloading the 36-gallon barrels at each house and collecting the empty barrels. At these stops he could rest his horses and himself.

In one five-week period in 1781, as figures 4.1A and 4.1B show (overleaf), Lamb completed 555½ miles on the roads of north-east Norfolk—and not on horseback, where he could trot at five or six miles an hour, but with a heavy wagon negotiating the main roads, lanes and byways of the county at less than three miles an hour.

Table 4.1.1 sets out the military estimate of the load that civilian carts and wagons could haul in East Anglia. The Commissary General of the Eastern District, while describing in impressive detail the system to be adopted during an invasion threat, with weybills and conductors for the goods and a pioneer corps to keep the roads open, did not make calculations for the bulk transport of liquids such as beer.²

above A sample of the source for the drayman's mileages (figures 4.1A, 4.1B): Mary
Hardy's diary for 14–20 Apr. 1781, written
at Letheringsett. 'WL' [William Lamb]
journeyed 29½ miles with the loaded beer
wagon on 16 Apr. to N. Walsham, Lessingham and Stalham. We do not hear how many
barrels were carried [*Cozens-Hardy Collection*]

FIGURE 4.1A

74½ miles with the beer wagon in three days: the daily mileage covered by the Hardys' drayman William Lamb on his deliveries from the Letheringsett brewery, 19–21 Apr. 1781

source Diary of Mary Hardy. The location of all the outlets is charted on the endpaper maps in vol. 2, and in fig. 2.app. in that volume

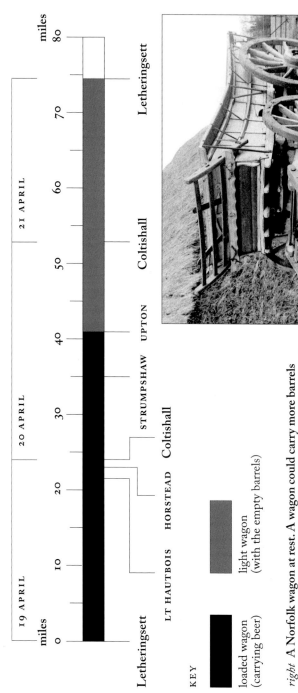

19 APRIL	20 APRIL	21 APRIL
miles 0 10 20 30	40 50 60	70 80 miles

Letheringsett

LT HAUTBOIS   HORSTEAD   Coltishall

STRUMPSHAW   UPTON   Coltishall

Letheringsett

KEY

loaded wagon (carrying beer)

light wagon (with the empty barrels)

right A Norfolk wagon at rest. A wagon could carry more barrels than a two-wheeled beer cart, and on his three-day pilgrimage Lamb supplied four public houses (shown above in small caps). He stayed both nights at Coltishall. On this route Upton, towards Gt Yarmouth, lay 41 miles from the brewery base near Cley on the north coast
[*photograph Miss F. Foster, nd: Norfolk Heritage Centre, Norwich*]

FIGURE 4.1B

555½ miles with the beer wagon in five weeks: the daily mileage covered by the Hardys' drayman William Lamb on his deliveries, 9 Apr.–12 May 1781

source Diary of Mary Hardy

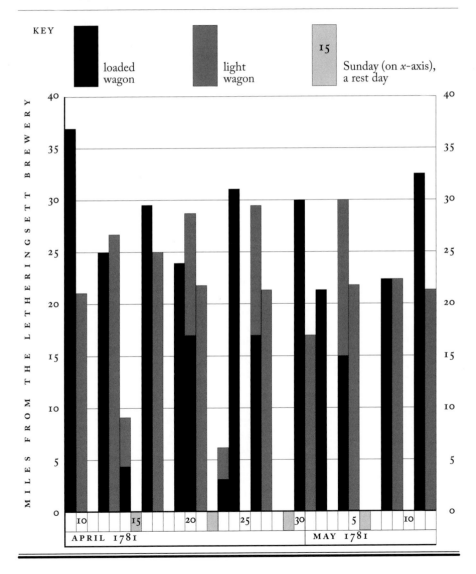

KEY

loaded wagon

light wagon

15 Sunday (on *x*-axis), a rest day

[1] *horse power* J. Vince, *Discovering Carts and Wagons* (3rd edn Shire Publications Ltd, Princes Risborough, 1987), p. 8.
There are 2240 lb, or 20 hundredweights (cwt), to the ton; a ton equates to 1016 kg, or 1·016 metric tonnes (see the Glossary). A key consideration for a dray would be braking power, and not only tractive power

[2] *land carriage* N. Kent, *General View of the Agriculture of the County of Norfolk* (London, 1796), p. 20.
The quotation was from a letter to Sir John Sinclair, Chairman of the Board of Agriculture, presumably by the MP for Bedford, William MacDowall Colhoun (d. 1821), who lived at Wretham, six miles north of Thetford.
Colhoun regretted the failure in 1790 of the Bill to link King's Lynn to London by inland waterway along the Lt Ouse (on which Thetford lies), Stort and Lea navigations so that Norfolk's farm produce could be conveyed safely and more cheaply than by land, avoiding storms and enemy attack at sea (N. Kent, *General View of the Agriculture of the County of Norfolk*, p. 19)

[3] *millstones Diary 2*: 20 Aug. 1784

Probably the military assumed that this most difficult of commodities to convey would be available locally. The long-established practices of billeting troops in public houses and of entering into local contracts for supplies to military canteens would have meant that the soldierly mind did not see the provision of beer as a problem. For the local brewer, by contrast, any interruption in the availability of coal and cinders (coke) for his brewery and maltings and of hops for the brew, to say nothing of the many hazards to the barley harvest in a war zone, would have compromised production.

Present-day transport historians have calculated the power required to pull freight by road. Carts, although less capable of hauling large loads, were less costly than wagons:

A cart can be worked by a single horse, and in terms of horse power carts were more easily drawn than wagons. On a good road surface a horse with a cart had to exert a pull of 51·4 lbs to move a ton. This compared with the 68·1 lbs of effort per ton required to pull a wagon. On arable land the difference was even more striking. The cart horse had to exert a pull of 201 lbs per ton, and a two-horse wagon needed 295·2 lbs of energy for the same load. In other words a cart needed about 28 per cent less pulling than a wagon.[1]

Transport ratios will be further considered in chapter 5, but it was glaringly obvious to economists and agriculturalists at the time how expensive land carriage was. In his report of 1796 to the Board of Agriculture, Nathaniel Kent quoted the observation of Mr Colhoun that the cost of land carriage from Thetford to London or back was four pounds (sterling) a ton. If the proposed linkage of Thetford by water to the capital had gone ahead the calculation would have fallen to under one pound a ton, 'a saving of near eighty per cent. The like saving would have been made on all the articles of trade, extending to the city of Norwich.'[2]

As well as the heavy barrels of beer routinely delivered to the public houses, and the special collections of such items as a pair of French burr millstones 25 miles distant in Stalham,[3] the Hardys had to organise wagon teams to convey items they could not handle themselves. As related in chapter 5, special arrangements were put in place in 1791–92 over hiring teams to carry export orders of beer overland to the ports, from where the consignments were taken by sea to Liverpool, Newcastle and Norway. A local farmer, John Minns of Edgefield, lent the Hardys his timber drug—a four-wheeled vehicle specially adapted for carrying logs—when they needed to take delivery of a storage cask from a Norwich brewery. This was probably the 208-barrel cask offered for sale in the press. Lamb, predictably, was despatched the 22 miles to the city to pick up a second, smaller cask from Isaac Jackson's brewery.[1]

The great difficulty of moving domestic goods and furniture on the roads may well explain why so many in the diarist's circle put their goods on the market when moving house. Attending house sales in the neighbourhood was the Hardys' principal means of purchasing large items such as mahogany furniture. Sometimes this stratagem could not be resorted to, as when twelve-year-old Mary Ann's brand-new organ was delivered to Letheringsett from Norwich.[2]

Carriage of heavy items by road was not necessarily performed by wheeled traffic. On a memorable occasion in 1793 James Woodforde took delivery at his Weston parsonage of a mahogany sideboard and a mahogany drinks cabinet which two men had carried on their backs the twelve miles from Norwich. The kindly parson did not forget the men in his delight at taking possession of these handsome pieces:

[1793] APRIL 4, WEDNESDAY . . . About 2 o'clock this afternoon two men of Sudbury's [the upholsterer] at Norwich came with my sideboard and a large new mahogany cellaret bought of Sudbury, brought on the men's shoulders all the way, and very safe. The men's names were Abraham Seily and Isaac Warren. I gave them whatever they could eat and drink, and when they went away gave them 1s 0d to spend either on the road or at home and sent word by them to Sudbury to pay them handsomely for their day's work.[3]

Itinerancy a way of life

The diaries of Mary Hardy and Henry Raven reveal that their areas of the Norfolk countryside were a heaving mass of people and animals. Weekly markets and annual fairs were treated as reunions, a chance to meet family and friends as well as transact a large amount of business. As seen in the previous volume, both itinerant and local Wesleyan preachers were moving from class to class and meeting to meeting on their carefully planned circuits. Similarly

[1] casks Diary 2: 2–3 Oct., 8 Oct. 1788. See vol. 2, chap. 7 on the equipment in the Hardys' brewery, including the huge casks in the tun room in which the strong beer matured

[2] organ Diary 2: 15 Oct. 1785; it was destined for the parlour

[3] sideboard and cellaret J. Woodforde, The Diary of a Country Parson, ed. J. Beresford, vol. 4 (Oxford Univ. Press, 1929), p. 20

above A tumbril in a marlpit. This was a very sturdy type of cart, used on rough ground and for carrying heavy loads, as here at Whitlingham, near Norwich [painting by J. Stark; engraving by W. Radclyffe 1828, detail]

[1] *attending services* The topography of the areas around Coltishall and Letheringsett is examined in detail in vol. 3, chaps 1 and 4: see esp. figs 3.1A, 3.1B, 3.4A and 3.4B

[2] *novelty* R. Southey, *The Life of Wesley and Rise and Progress of Methodism* (new edn London, 1864; 1st pub. 1820), vol. 1, pp. 247–8

[3] *tax-collecting rotations* Such rounds were advertised in advance, so that taxpayers could plan their journeys accordingly: eg Roger Kerrison's schedule of visits around Norfolk to collect the land tax (*Norw. Merc.* 7 Apr. 1781). For the Excise see vol. 2, chap. 11

[4] *customs* In the small outport of Blakeney and Cley, of the total complement of 13 customs officers including the Collector, three served as riding officers on patrol from Mundesley to Pit's Point (the borders of the jurisdiction to Gt Yarmouth and to Wells) (TNA: PRO CUST 96/165, 20 July 1798). The customs service is described in chap. 5

[5] *pedlars and drovers* Pedlars are covered in vol. 3, chap. 7. The infrastructure supporting drovers is very well illustrated in W. Smith,

Anglicans, both the clergy and their flock, were on the move on Sundays. In addition, weekday evening services increasingly attracted numbers of Nonconformists and Anglicans.

Only a sound infrastructure, in the form of an intricate network of good roads and numerous public houses for refreshing travellers and their horses, could have supported this level of intensity of movement. Mary Hardy and her energetic sermon-tasting circle were prepared to travel up to nineteen miles on a Sunday to attend a variety of church services and Nonconformist meetings across a swathe of parishes. From the villages where she wrote her diary the spiritually adventurous Mary Hardy had easy access to a lavish provision for worshippers. At Coltishall seventeen other parishes lay within three miles of her house. At Letheringsett 25 other parishes lay within 4½ miles. These distances, respectively, were less than an hour's walk and probably less than an hour's cart ride from her home.[1]

Robert Southey attributed the early successes of the Methodists to the novelty of itinerancy.[2] It was not a novel concept in Norfolk, as a leaderless curate serving three parishes on a Sunday knew all too well. While Saxon preachers and mediaeval friars would long have been forgotten as itinerants (as Southey pointed out), in Mary Hardy's period the circuit formed part of the normal daily experience of a wide range of religious and other service providers.

Just as a brewery drayman had his rounds and served the public houses in rotation as faithfully as a Wesleyan preacher his meetings, so too lawyers, surgeons, tailors, wigmakers, millers and the brewers themselves had 'rounds' when they called on clients and pocketed the fees due to them. The Collectors of Excise and Receivers General of the Land Tax journeyed on their regular rotations around the market towns to receive the monies that financed the wars,[3] while hard-pressed excise officers adhered to 'rides' and 'footwalks' to monitor the commodities they gauged. Customs officers, in addition to many other duties, patrolled the coast roads as riding officers,[4] while drovers and pedlars kept to their well-trodden, carefully planned cross-country routes.[5]

Wholesale grocers had their pre-set pattern of 'waiting upon' the scattered village retailers they supplied, as recorded by the prominent Norwich firm founded by John

Cozens, the future brother-in-law of Mary Ann Hardy.[1] The Hardys themselves often entertained 'riders', the travelling sales representatives of London factors and merchants supplying the brewing industry. Mr Potts, a rider for the London liquor merchant Mr Hudson, called annually in November at Coltishall, and in the Letheringsett years the riders of hop suppliers came visiting regularly.[2]

To suit the magistrates, grand jurors, parish officers and all the parties contesting lawsuits, the county sessions were adjourned in rotation every quarter from Norwich to the sessions towns of Holt, Walsingham, King's Lynn and Swaffham. Nevertheless all those involved still had lengthy journeys of up to twenty miles to reach the seat of justice. Assize judges, bishops and archdeacons too had their pre-ordained circuits as they toured their courts and conducted long-drawn-out visitations of their dioceses and deaneries.

Away from these ecclesiastical, official, fiscal, commercial and judicial worlds, troupes of entertainers and individual specialist teachers kept to their circuits in the countryside; as a result they were on the road for much of their working lives. Travelling players would jolt with their costumes, musical instruments, props and scenery from town to town, uprooting themselves every few weeks. Dancing masters toured the market towns on their weekly rotations. François Veron, teaching schoolchildren and individual private pupils across north-west Norfolk—as did John Browne for Norwich and the north-east—hardly touched base during the summer. Monsieur Veron set out his breathless schedule at the start of the dancing season in March 1785: Mondays at Narford, Tuesdays at Bagthorpe and Thursford, Wednesdays at Wells and Walsingham, Thursdays at Fakenham (where he would have taught Mary Ann Hardy), Fridays at King's Lynn, and Saturdays at Swaffham. His was a weekly circuit of 80–85 miles.[3]

It is little wonder that an eighteen-year-old Frenchman marvelled at the bustle of the East Anglian roads he travelled in 1784. The 'post' is a staging post such as an inn:

You cannot imagine the quantity of travellers who are always on the road in England. You cannot go from one post to another without meeting two or three postchaises, to say nothing of the regular diligences.[4]

The Drovers' Roads of the Middle Marches: Their history and how to find them today (Logaston Press, Woonton Almesley, 2013)

[1] *grocers* W.O. Copeman, *Copemans of Norwich 1789–1946* (Jarrold and Sons, Norwich 1946), pp. 15–17 and illustration facing p. 18. See vol. 3, chap. 7 on shops and shopping

[2] *riders* Mr Potts kept to a regular schedule for Coltishall, taking orders in the same week every year (*Diary 1*: 16 Nov. 1774, 13 Nov. 1775, 13 Nov. 1776, 16 Nov. 1777). For hop suppliers see vol. 2, chap. 5

[3] *Veron Norw. Merc.* 19 Mar. 1785. See also vol. 1, chap. 6 on dancing tuition, and chap. 6 in this volume on travelling players and the playhouse

[4] *Frenchman* F. de La Rochefoucauld, *A Frenchman's Year in Suffolk, 1784*, ed. N. Scarfe (The Boydell Press and Suffolk Records Soc., vol. 30 (1988)), p. 96. The young aristocrat noted Bury St Edmunds as having 125 horses to serve the postchaises and coaches (p. 96). This hardly seems sufficient. The King's

Head at Holt alone had stabling for 100 (*Norw. Merc.* 7 Jan. 1797)

---

[1] *best of roads* J. Woodforde, *The Diary of a Country Parson*, ed. J. Beresford, vol. 1 (Oxford Univ. Press, 1924), p. 151, 13 Apr. 1775. His enthusiasm was boundless. Norwich proved next day to be 'the finest city in England by far' (p. 151). St Stephen's Gate, which customarily was barred at 10 pm, was demolished with four others in 1792 (*Norw. Merc.* 29 Sept. 1792). Magdalen Gate was the last to go, in 1808, in a prolonged programme of urban modernisation following London's lead in the 1760s. Gates were seen as a relic of the past as well as an obstruction to traffic

---

facing page **Norwich: St Giles's Gate (left), viewed from without the walls; and (right) St Stephen's Gate, from within.** This last was the one which Woodforde found barred at night— a tradition soon to be jettisoned. Also narrow gates could not cope with the increasing levels of wheeled traffic [*drawings by J. Kirkpatrick 1720; engravings by H. Ninham 1864*]

The circuit was historically a response to slow road communication and unreliable mails—disadvantages which were gradually being surmounted in the diarist's period. Later, over the nineteenth and twentieth centuries, as communications improved, so the travelling service provider could increasingly be dispensed with. It was similarly no longer necessary to give notice of meetings and forthcoming visitations through the medium of local newspapers. Customers, taxpayers and recipients of services would instead receive a personal letter. Until then the weekly newspaper played a vital role as a public information service, without which itinerancy would have faltered.

In the Hardys' world it was still more practical to bring the service provider to the client, the tax collector to the taxpayer, the judge to the defendant, the bishop to the confirmation candidate and the dancing master to the pupil. There was a residual requirement for short-distance road transport to meet the needs of all these circuits. Changes in the nature of short-distance journeys, as well as the more dramatic improvements in long-distance travel, are discernible in the 36-year chronicle of Mary Hardy.

The state of the roads

What was the state of the roads carrying this busy traffic; and—a question at times overlooked in an area bi-sected by water—what was the condition of the bridges? The Broads network had about 115 miles of lock-free navigable waterway: a blessing for freight transport. But such areas are not necessarily blessed with numerous bridges. Masters of vessels with tall masts and running at perhaps 7 knots (with a favourable wind and tide) look unkindly on fixed crossings.

While independent observers, especially those from outside the county, would seem a reliable source, no consistent answer energes. In 1775 the Revd James Woodforde, buoyed up with pride and enthusiasm after securing the lucrative living of Weston Longville, arrived at 11 pm as a stranger to Norwich to find the city gate on the approach road from the capital locked for the night. But he was in no doubt about the roads, if not the gates. He pronounced this oft-repeated panegyric: 'From London to Norwich 109 miles, and the best of roads I ever travelled'.[1]

The statistically-minded agriculturalist Nathaniel Kent, writing twenty years later, was also favourably struck by the state of the Norfolk roads, and offered factual evidence in support:

> The roads in this county afford the farmer a very great advantage over many other parts of England, being free from sloughs [mires], in all parts (except the marshes), and though the soil is sandy, it resists the pressure of the wheels at a small distance from the surface, and the ruts are kept shallow at a very little expence . . . In short, the roads, though often called bad by Norfolk men, are so good, comparatively with those in other counties, that where the common statute duty is fairly done, a traveller may cross the country in any direction, in a post-chaise, without danger; and where the duty is not done, may trot his horse from one parish to another, at the rate of six miles an hour.[1]

Arthur Young, well used to travelling about the kingdom in his role as Secretary to the Board of Agriculture, considered that Norfolk had made great strides since his first tour of 1770. Following his 1802 visit he could say that the county

[1] *roads* N. Kent, *General View of the Agriculture of the County of Norfolk*, pp. 16–17.

The 'statute duty', as described later in this section, was the parochial obligation under the Highways Act of 1555 to keep the roads in good repair.

One of the elected parish officers, serving alongside the churchwardens, overseer of the poor and parish constable, was the surveyor of the highways: a man chosen by the ratepayers to collect the rates for the parish roads and supervise road repairs

[1] *exertions* A. Young, *General View of the Agriculture of the County of Norfolk* (London, 1804), p. 489. His earlier tour had been published in two volumes as *The Farmer's Tour through the East of England* (London, 1771)

[2] M.J. Armstrong *The History and Antiquities of the County of Norfolk* (Norwich, 1781), quoted by C.W. Haines, 'Norfolk milestones, Part 2', *Journal of the Norfolk Industrial Archaeology Society*, vol. 4, no. 2 (1987), p. 49. Carol Haines' sevenpart article, published in the NIAS journal 1986–97, is a massive contribution to the subject

[3] *intricate network* A point reinforced by a redrawing of Faden's map of 1797, highlighting just the roads, by Andrew Macnair and Tom Williamson in *William Faden and Norfolk's 18th-century Landscape* (Windgather Press, Oxbow Books, Oxford, 2010), p. 166

[4] *article* It was published in the *Eastern Daily Press* 2 Mar. 1895, and reprinted in Sydney Cozens-Hardy's memoir of his father, *Memorials of William Hardy Cozens-Hardy of Letheringsett, Norfolk* (Norwich, 1936), pp. 34–40

had made 'considerable exertions' in the previous twenty years, the consequent improvements being brought about in part by the creation of turnpikes on the main routes: 'the roads, in general, must be considered as equal to those of the most improved counties.'[1]

The turnpike roads will form a recurring topic in this chapter. Each run by a non-profit-making trust and requiring an individual Act of Parliament as they ran counter to the communal right of free passage on the highway, they were allowed to charge tolls to pay for their building and maintenance. Some observers shared Young's view that they brought marked improvements in getting about by road. Others differed: non-turnpike routes could be equally as good. This was the opinion of Mostyn John Armstrong, author of a ten-volume Blomefield-like survey of Norfolk in 1781: 'Besides the turnpike roads, there are some great leading roads which have milestones, and in other respects [are] no less commodious for travelling.'[2]

The turnpikes should not dominate discussion of the road system. It was visitors and well-to-do tourists, prepared to pay the tolls and able to afford mail coaches and postchaises, who tended to comment on them. In reality there were few turnpike roads in Norfolk, and none at all in most of the north and north-west of the county in Mary Hardy's time, as the front endpaper map shows. Secondly, what was important for most road users, including those on circuit, was not the quality of a handful of principal roads, but the availability of an intricate network of acceptable roads, making cross-country journeys as direct and endurable as possible. In this the county scored highly, especially in those parts in which Mary Hardy lived: the central area around Whissonsett, East Dereham and Litcham; the whole Broads area; and north and north-east Norfolk.[3]

An entirely contrary picture to the favourable one painted by the agriculturalists and Armstrong is presented in the recollections of Mary Hardy's grandson, written and published a few weeks before his death in 1895 aged 88. In an article for the *Eastern Daily Press* entitled 'Old Norfolk Highways' he was scathing about the condition of most of the local roads during his childhood.[4] Even allowing for the passage of eighty years, William Hardy Cozens-Hardy's indictment is packed with factual information and is by no means a vague, imprecise series of anecdotes. He carefully gives detailed reasons for the weak performance of the statute labour teams overseen by the surveyors of the highways, the annually elected (and unpaid) parish officers who supervised road mending as laid down by the Highways Act of 1555. Under this system, in force until 1835, landholders were required at slack times in the farming year to provide men, horses and tools for four days' work a year, with no expenses reclaimable. It did not work well. These are the recollections of an observant man born in 1806:

> When I was a boy road-hammers were unknown, and none of the large stones were broken; they were simply carted out of the gravel-pits and 'tumbled on to the roads' without any regard to size, leaving the heavy carts and waggons to break them to pieces . . .
>
> The formation of roads was very defective in most parts of the country. They were made high in the middle, by which means carriages were compelled to go on a dangerous slope unless kept in the very centre of the highway. In the winter time, after severe and protracted frosts, these sloping roads became so bad that it was scarcely possible to travel more than five or six miles an hour.[1]

He went on to praise the great improvements introduced from about 1818 by the Scottish civil engineer John Loudon McAdam (1756–1836) and emulated by William Hardy junior, the writer's uncle, whereby the road surface was to rise no more than three inches (7·6 cm) across a width of 30 feet (9·1 metres). No piece of stone was to exceed one inch.[2]

Yet even this clear testimony can be called into question. William H. Cozens-Hardy had a vehement way of expressing himself which could lead to exaggeration. Road hammers were by no means unknown in his area, unless he meant mechanical ones, and sieves were used for gravel to grade large and small stones. When this witness was a boy of nine the surveyor of the highways for Thornage, the neighbouring village to Letheringsett, claimed as his expenses: '1 road hammer, 1 iron rake, 1 double pick, 1 hoe with pick and 1 gravel screen' [a coarse sieve].[3]

Further problems were caused to road users by the hills of the Cromer ridge. North Norfolk, while hardly alpine— as one eighteenth-century diarist claimed—is decidedly undulating.[4] The hill near the former racecourse on Holt

[1] *defective* S. Cozens-Hardy, *Memorials of William Hardy Cozens-Hardy*, p. 35

[2] *praise* S. Cozens-Hardy, *Memorials of William Hardy Cozens-Hardy*, pp. 34,36.
Mary Ann's son had much to say on the problems of ruts, whereby gig horses, unable to follow the tracks gouged by wider-axled coaches, would constantly move from one rut to another; also on bridges, falgates (foldgates) and road diversions

[3] *tools* NRO: MC 1858/17, 860 x 5, Holt hundred: Thornage surveyor's [account] book 1776–1816, note on the flyleaf dated Jan. 1816

[4] *alpine* 'We drove for about a quarter of a mile on the brink of a precipice not much inferior to some described by those who have crossed the Alps' (Letitia Beauchamp Proctor's account of her 1764 journey from Holt to Holkham, quoted by R.W. Ketton-Cremer, 'The Tour of Norfolk', *Norfolk Assembly* (Faber and Faber Ltd, London, 1957), p. 190).
Lady Beauchamp Proctor was probably describing the high ground above the Glaven at Bayfield close to Letheringsett

below The mid-18th-century roadside milestone in the woods near the inn at Blickling [*MB·1996*]

above The Buckinghamshire Arms at Blickling, remodelled in the mid-18th century when it became an inn. In the Hardys' time the road ran right beside the main gates of Blickling Hall just out of view to the right, the dip in the ground under the trees tracing the course of the old route which then passed in front of the inn.

With its large barn-like stable to the rear it was a busy staging post for those on the move   [*MB·2002*]

Heath (later Holt Country Park) on the Holt–Norwich road approaching Edgefield, was so pronounced that the Wells–Holt–Norwich stage coach had to avoid this treacherous route and take a detour via Hempstead, Itteringham, Blickling and Aylsham.[1] The very sharp drop to the Glaven valley from the top of that hill is depicted in the sepia wash of 1815 by twelve-year-old Mary Anne Turner, daughter of Dawson and Mary Turner, illustrated as *plate 15* in volume 2.

Given these contradictory sources we have to seek other means of judging the state of the roads. How easy was it for people to get about by carriage, cart and on foot? The starting point can be found in the quarter sessions records, as the justices of the peace were responsible for enforcing the Highways Acts. As with other matters, any elected parish officer failing to carry out his appointed task was answer-

[1] *detour* B. Cozens-Hardy, 'The Holt road', *Norfolk Archaeology*, vol. 31 (1957), p. 176

able to the magistrates. The minutes and orders of Norfolk Quarter Sessions held in Norwich and by adjournment elsewhere do admittedly record hearings of cases of 'Bad Roads', as the marginal annotations refer to the item, but not so often as to indicate a general, recurrent, poor state of repair.

Interestingly, and running counter to Arthur Young's 1802 impression, the number of cases involving roads— as opposed to bridges—increased markedly in the 1790s. This suggests that the authorities were less prepared to put up with poor roads as the transport system became more sophisticated and as turnpike trusts proliferated: the Norwich–Aylsham road was turnpiked in 1794–95 and the Norwich–North Walsham in 1797. The Norwich–Great Yarmouth turnpike had been one of the earliest to be built in Norfolk, in 1768–69, while the Norwich–Fakenham was one of the last, not being opened until 1823.[1]

Parish officers in the Fens and Fleggs were indicted at Norwich Sessions in 1795, and a few months later there were allegations of bad roads at Gunthorpe and Bale; these two parishes lay close to Letheringsett and had Hardy public houses. The nearby parish of Fulmodestone proved an intractable case, the charge that the inhabitants kept bad roads having to be respited and coming before the magistrates on four different occasions.[2] In 1804 the inhabitants of Edgefield and Saxthorpe, again close to Letheringsett, were indicted for the nuisance caused by their bad roads.[3]

Magisterial oversight seems to have been effective. Orders to see to road repairs would appear generally to have been enforced, as cases against individual parishes rarely recur. One of the local JPs serving the quarter sessions at Holt and Walsingham was the Revd Charles Collyer, who held the consolidated living of Gunthorpe and Bale; another was the Revd Peter Sandiford, Rector of Fulmodestone. The increased energy devoted to road cases may be attributable at least in part to the impatience of the new generation of clerical JPs over these impediments to free movement around their parishes: the 1790s saw an appreciable rise in the number of clerical appointments to the bench.[4]

One of the beneficial consequences of turnpiking was the greater use of milestones and direction posts to guide

[1] *turnpikes* See A. Cossons, 'The turnpike roads of Norfolk', *Norfolk Archaeology*, vol. 30 (1952), pp. 189–212; also V. Belton, *The Norwich to Cromer Turnpike* (Ingworth, 1998).
The Hardys had long left Coltishall before its main highway to Norwich was turnpiked in 1797 as part of the N. Walsham Act. Mary Ann's marital home at Sprowston from 1805 was to stand facing this road.
The Aylsham turnpike was the nearest to the Hardys at Letheringsett. The extension to Cromer was not completed until 1811, as shown on the front endpaper map

[2] *bad roads* NRO: C/S 1/15, Norfolk Quarter Sessions, minute book 1791–1800: Norwich, 7 Oct. 1795; Walsingham, 14 Apr. 1796; Holt, 17 Oct. 1799; Walsingham, 1 May 1800, 24 July 1800; Holt, 16 Oct. 1800

[3] *bad roads* NRO: C/S 1/16, Norfolk Quarter Sessions, minute book 1801–04: Holt, 20 Jan. 1804

[4] *clerical justices* The whole system of quarter and petty sessions and parish government is analysed in vol. 3, chap. 6, entitled 'Upholding the Peace'

right and *below* The Holt obelisk, at the top of Letheringsett Hill at its opening onto the town centre. The ornamental 17th- or 18th-century milestone crams a huge amount of information onto its four faces, including distances to most of the county's market towns and ports. Mileages to north Norfolk's great country houses, including Blickling, Holkham and Houghton, occupy one face. It is alleged to have been one of a pair of gate-piers at Melton Constable Hall, 5½ miles away—although the distances marked are inaccurate from that point.

Since the mileages are exact if Holt is taken as the departure point they may have been incised post-removal [*MB·2011*]

facing page An orginal tollhouse on the 1797 Norwich–N. Walsham turnpike. Still facing the main road just south of N. Walsham, its small window in the gable end enabled the keeper to watch for approaching vehicles [*MB·2011*]

To	Miles
Harleston	41
Hingham	27
Loddon	33
Lynn Regis	34
NORWICH	21
Reepham	12
Swaffham	28

[1] *compulsory* W.G. Hoskins, *The Making of the English Landscape* (Penguin Books Ltd, Harmondsworth, 1970), p. 246

[2] *milestones* C.W. Haines, 'Norfolk milestones, Part 7', *Journal of the Norfolk Industrial Archaeology Society*, vol. 6, no. 2 (1997), p. 45

[3] *Faden's map* NRO: c/s 1/15: Norwich, 18 Apr. 1798. Mapmaking grew out of military surveying, the Ordnance Survey being one principal link

the traveller; indeed these became compulsory on all turnpike roads under an Act of 1773.[1] Carol Haines has tracked down approximately 340 surviving milestones in Norfolk,[2] many of them predating the Act and springing from independent enterprise. They serve as a useful record of road mileages before modern straightening and bypassing.

Interest in the county's roads would have been fired by Norfolk's first large-scale map. William Faden published his meticulous and informative county map in 1797. The magistrates at the Shirehouse in Norwich Castle certainly appreciated his efforts, and moved swiftly to place their order: 'Ordered that Mr Faden of St Martin's Lane, London, be wrote to for a map of this county to be hung up in the Grand Jury chamber'.[3]

After the orders and minutes taken at quarter sessions another source of non-impressionistic evidence is the daily journal written over a long period, enabling the reader to build up a picture of the writer's ease of movement. There is a wealth of material in the diaries of James and Anna Maria Woodforde and of Mary Hardy about the state of the roads and the effects of the weather on mobility. Despite his initial optimism the Revd Mr Woodforde, and more especially his niece Anna Maria (Nancy), frequently give the impression of being prisoners in their rectory. Yet it lay under half a mile from the centre of the village, approximately 1½ miles from the main Norwich–Fakenham road, and 2½ miles from the Norwich–Dereham turnpike of 1770. Their journals constantly lament their inability to get about, and the necessity of cancelling or postponing social engagements at no notice owing to the miry roads of the neighbourhood.

Whether their testimony is representative of others' lives is questionable. Nancy Woodforde was born in 1757; she was only 34–35 and in reasonably good health when she wrote her surviving diary. She so often resolved not to attend service at her uncle's church on account of the weather and dirty lanes that the reader is left wondering whether the lanes were really that bad—especially as others seemed able to get about—or if her heart quailed at the thought of the unheated church.[1] Nancy, like her uncle, had a very warm and close relationship with the Custances up at the big house only 1¼ miles from the rectory. However time and again she would set off for Weston House and then turn back on the short walk, usually owing to rain.[2]

[1] *church* 'Could not go to church on account of the dirty road' (D.H. Woodforde, ed., 'Nancy Woodforde: A diary for the year 1792', *Woodforde Papers and Diaries* (Parson Woodforde Soc. and Morrow & Co., Bungay, 1990), p. 85, 30 Dec. 1792). It was the wind which had prevented churchgoing on 25 Mar. Nancy managed a good walk in the parsonage garden nonetheless (p. 51)

[2] *weather* D.H. Woodforde, ed., 'Nancy Woodforde: A diary for the year 1792', p. 52. The rain prevented even her uncle from walking to Weston House on 23 Mar. (pp. 50–1).

The wind stopped Nancy from walking to

Weston Church 15 Apr. (p. 54), yet the previous day, as her uncle noted, the boy and his mother had walked to Norwich and back—a 24-mile round trip (J. Woodforde, *The Diary of a Country Parson*, ed. J. Beresford, vol. 3 (Oxford Univ. Press, 1927), p. 344)

[1] *Woodfordes* D.H. Woodforde, ed., 'Nancy Woodforde: A diary', pp. 48–9; J. Woodforde, *The Diary of a Country Parson*, ed. J. Beresford, vol. 3, p. 338

[2] *Hardys Diary 2*: 4–5, 7–9 Mar. 1792; Diary MS: 3, 6, 10 Mar. 1792

Nancy Woodforde's diary has come down to us in full only for the year 1792, so it makes a useful exercise to compare the movements of Nancy, her 51-year-old uncle and the brewer's family at Letheringsett, by studying the three daily records compiled that year and separated by only 17–18 miles. Reactions to adverse weather differed at Weston Rectory from those at the brewer's house, and it would be unwise to rely on just one source to draw conclusions on the state of the roads and rural isolation in general.

Poor Nancy, marooned with her bachelor uncle, recorded on 10 March 1792 during a cold spell: 'Frosty weather with snow. Not a soul has called on us this week. No letters from our friends. We spend our time in reading.' Yet that same day James Woodforde logged some business letters being sent to Norwich 'by some of Cary's people who are to bring back my newspapers', so letters were expected to get through.[1]

By contrast, over at the Hardys' that same week there was the customary pattern of work, movement and socialising. On 5 March 1792 the brewery clerk journeyed 18 miles to to East Dereham; five of the Hardys' friends, including one female, came over from Holt to tea and supper. On 3 and 6 March 58-year-old Mary Hardy and her daughter Mary Ann walked to Holt, one mile away, for tea with friends. On 7 March William Hardy senior and junior bought trees nearby at Edgefield, and then saw to the letting of the Horseshoes eight miles away at Corpusty; four female friends from Holt came to tea; and the drayman Robert Bye completed a 21-mile round trip delivering beer to Wells. On 8 March the male Hardys were supervising tree-planting in the snow in the Furze Closes a mile away, and the following day the seamstress arrived at their house. The Rector of Letheringsett journeyed to Cambridge that week.[2]

Although the challenges posed were the same there is no similarity over the way they were met. The Rector of Weston and his niece were susceptible to cold and wet and managed to trigger a melancholic strain in one another. The resort to hibernation was a response which farming, professional, mercantile and manufacturing families—to say nothing of the labourers—could not adopt. A very comfortable rectorial living provided a more secure source of income than most. The indomitability of Mary Hardy and her family

runs through volume I, and it is unnecessary to labour the point here. It is evident the Hardys and their circle rose above the sometimes unsatisfactory condition of the roads with a will not shared by the timorous Woodfordes. As the rector grew older his lifestyle became far more restricted and the little group at Weston endured endlessly 'dull' days, as Nancy characterised them.[1] As will become apparent in this chapter the family at Letheringsett, by contrast, became much more mobile and took advantage of new opportunities afforded by faster roads and lighter vehicles.

As a final indication of the state of the roads, let us look at the diary entries made daily by Mary Hardy for just under 35½ years—roughly, allowing for two gaps for incapacitating illness, 12,850 days. In that period on how many days did she describe the roads as impassable, including those occasions when she and her circle were prevented from moving about on their daily rounds usually owing to floods, snowdrifts or a thaw? The answer is 32 days (*plate 1*). Even though, as we saw in volume 2, the age witnessed some truly appalling winters in which people lost their lives in the snow, for only 0·25 per cent of the time were the roads impassable. Hence the survival of itinerancy as a way of doing business, ministering to the spiritual and judicial needs of the populace and bringing entertainment to townsfolk and villagers.

above Lenwade Bridge on the Wensum, close to the Woodfordes' parsonage at Weston.
The cart driver sits hunched against the cold, emphasising the exposed nature of most road travel [*drawing by F. Stone & Son 1831; lithograph by D. Hodgson*]

facing page A cross-boarded cart, giving extra strength to the construction. Muck carts had long-boarded floors, for ease of use.
The Hardys relied on a number of sturdy carts for getting about [*MB·1989*]

[1] *dull days* Worsening on the Custances' move to Bath in Oct. 1792

The 86 county bridges of Norfolk 1831

source F. Stone & Son, *Picturesque Views of the Norfolk Bridges,* pts 1–4 (Norwich, 1830, 1831) [1]

Acle
Alderford
Attlebridge
Aylsham Burgh
Aylsham 1
Aylsham 2
Banningham
Barford
Barney
Barnham Broom 1
Barnham Broom 2
Bawburgh
Blickling
Bodney 1
Bodney 2
Bodney 3
Brandon Creek
Brettenham
Bridgham
Carlton Forehoe
Chapel Mill
Coltishall
Cringleford
Crostwick
Ditchingham and
  Bungay
Ditchingham 1
Ditchingham 2

Ditchingham 3
Ditchingham 4
Earlham
Earsham and
  Bungay
Earsham 1
Earsham 2
Earsham 3
Earsham 4
Erpingham
Eshingham
Filby
Gillingham and
  Beccles
Great Snarehill
Harpham [Hargham]
Hartford 1 [Harford]
Hartford 2 [Harford]
Hilgay
Honingham 1
Honingham 2
Igburgh [Ickburgh]
Ingworth
Itteringham
Lakenham
Larlingford 1
Larlingford 2
Lenwade

Little Ryburgh
Mayton
Mendham
Modney
Mundford
Narborough Mill
Newton Flotman
Nordelph
Potter Heigham
Reepham
Scole
Sedge Fen
Setchey
Shotford
Shropham and
  Snetterton
Skeyton

Sluice Drain
Southery Ferry
Spixworth
Starston
Stoke Ferry
St Olaves
Swanton Morley
Trowse 1
Trowse 2
Trowse 3
Tuttington
Wayford
Wiveton
Witton Run
  [east of Norwich]
Wortwell
Wroxham
Wymondham

[1] *Francis Stone* The County Surveyor of Norfolk. Maintenance was financed from the county budget (raised by means of the county rate), under the supervision of the JPs and Clerk of the Peace. Other bridges were paid for by parish ratepayers or by private subscription. The names given here are Stone's. Aylsham Burgh is Burgh-next-Aylsham; Aylsham 1 is Anchor Bridge in Millgate, Aylsham. Chapel Mill is in Gressenhall, on the Whitewater

Bridges

[2] *turnpike* The front endpaper map gives the dates of the turnpikes. The Norwich–N. Walsham turnpike through Horstead and Coltishall did not open until 1797, long after the Hardys' departure for Letheringsett

There were, and are, only three bridges along the 32 miles of the River Bure from the Hardys' village of Coltishall to the approach to the seaport of Great Yarmouth. They linked Horstead to Coltishall, Wroxham to Hoveton, and Acle to Clippesby; this last carried the Norwich–Great Yarmouth turnpike of 1769.[2] There were no locks until Coltishall's was opened in 1775. And there were no fords, unlike the position at Letheringsett and other villages on the unnavigable, comparatively shallow upper Glaven. There were however two

above A heart-stopping prospect for helms-
men. Potter Heigham Bridge straddles the
tidal River Thurne on the Norfolk Broads
and is seen here from downstream. It has
an air draught averaging under seven feet
in normal conditions. At average high water
the clearance drops to little more than 78
inches (just over 2 metres). The swans

silhouetted under the main arch help to give
a sense of the constricted width and height.
  This 14th-century road bridge, with later
remodelling, was one of 86 paid for out of
the county rate in Mary Hardy's time. Most
were rebuilt during the 20th century following flood damage and the arrival of high-
tonnage road vehicles   [*MB · 2008*]

ferries along the 32 miles, at Horning and Stokesby. Coltishall Bridge was important in enabling the diarist, her family
and the workforce to have direct access to the villages south
of Coltishall, as well as to Norwich and Aylsham.[1]
  The quarter sessions orders reveal the tremendous drain
on funds brought about by Norfolk's waterways. Under an
Act of 1530 certain bridges were not entrusted to the parish,
as footbridges might be, but were classed as county bridges.
A county levy was raised quarterly to pay for repairs and rebuilding. These bridges, generally sited outside towns, were
ones not already falling under the care of another authority
or person; many were important bridges carrying the king's
highway. The city of Norwich and boroughs of King's Lynn
and Great Yarmouth had no county bridges, and had to find
means other than the county rate of paying for them.

[1] *Coltishall Bridge*
Pictured in vol. 1, p. 24.
  As well as Wroxham
Bridge, nearly three
miles away by road,
there were crossings
within reach upstream,
the nearest being
Mayton Bridge on the
northern border of
Horstead. However
without Coltishall
Bridge William Hardy
could not have farmed
at Horstead, nor easily
have supplied many of
his public houses

[1] *Stone* At his death in 1835 Stone had been the county surveyor for 30 years. He dedicated his *Picturesque Views of all the Bridges belonging to the County of Norfolk* to the Lord Lieutenant and justices

above The wooden bridge at Southery Ferry on the Gt Ouse, showing lithographic reversal: the dinghy's name can be read in a mirror as *F^s Stone*. The boat has no oars, probably as a precaution against theft. The solitary figure carries them on his shoulder [*drawing by F. Stone & Son 1831; lithograph by D. Hodgson, detail*]

right The Ferry House at Surlingham, near Norwich, with a date stone of 1725, faces one of many now-disused crossings on the Yare. Most ferries had public houses on the bank, supplying the needs of travellers   [*MB·2011*]

There were 86 bridges maintained by the county at the time the architect and county surveyor Francis Stone drew them, the four-volume set of lithographs by David Hodgson being published in 1830–31.[1] They were built of stone or of brick with stone dressings; a very few, such as Southery Ferry south of Downham Market, were of wood. Although intended as architectural drawings to display the state of the bridges to the justices Stone's work was enlivened with human touches giving scale. His scenes are busy with various types of road and river traffic, and he shows workmen (wearing all manner of clothing and assorted headgear), gleaners, anglers, loafers and public houses.

As with the roads, so with the bridges: the magistrates seem to have taken their duties seriously. By 1831 the bridges depicted by Stone were evidently in good repair. But the outgoings to keep them up to standard were large. A useful crossing used by the Hardys' Coltishall draymen was Ingworth (later to carry the Cromer turnpike), which in 1773–74 required an outlay of £170 at a time when the total quarterly levy across the county, in support of the county

above Wiveton Bridge over the Glaven, one of the routes from Holt and Letheringsett to Blakeney and Cley; the tidal river on its approach to Cley is shown as a trickle at low water. Local JPs were called on to supervise repair work funded by the county rate [*drawing by F. Stone & Son 1831; lithograph by D. Hodgson*]

gaol, bridewells, shirehouses and, in time of war, the families of Militia substitutes, was £1200. This total varied according to the demands made upon it. In some quarters the figure was only £900, £600 or even £300. In 1778 Coltishall Bridge was granted a sum not exceeding £90, probably to cope with alterations required by the Aylsham navigation; further repairs were needed two years later.[1]

The nearest county bridge to the Hardys at Letheringsett was Wiveton, a fifteenth-century stone bridge. In 1794 repairs were ordered not exceeding £100 'for the repairing and raising the parapet walls of Wiverton Bridge';[2] Burgh-next-Aylsham, Potter Heigham and Wroxham Bridges were also undergoing repairs at this time. The Norwich papers would warn their readers about such works,[3] which when prolonged must have been highly inconvenient for road users.[4]

Although bridges attract the attention of architectural and transport historians and urban geographers, their social

[1] *bridges* NRO: C/Sce 1/8, Norfolk Quarter Sessions, order book 1773–84: Norwich, 14 July 1773, 12 Jan. 1774; 15 July 1778, 12 July 1780

[2] *Wiveton* NRO: C/S 1/15, Norfolk Quarter Sessions: Norwich, 15 Jan. 1794

[3] *newspapers* eg *Norw. Merc.* 5 Sept. 1778, warning readers about Coltishall Bridge: '. . . No carriages can pass over the said bridge after Wednesday next until further notice'

[4] *prolonged* For a full account of the costly repairs at Wroxham Bridge in 1576, see P. Millican, 'The rebuilding of Wroxham Bridge in 1576', *Norfolk Archaeology*, vol. 26 (1938),

pp. 281–95. During the months the bridge was out of use a ferry service was in operation (p. 282)

¹ *Norwich* S. Cocke and L. Hall, *Norwich Bridges Past & Present* (Norwich Soc., Norwich, 1994), p. 3. The authors add that the River Yare running nearby south of the city also had four bridges

² *William Hardy Diary* 2: 4 Sept., 6 Oct. 1790. As the parish ratebooks have not survived it is not known whether he was acting as churchwarden or surveyor of the highways; he could have been both

³ *Horning Diary 1*: 2 July 1774. It was cheap to cross by ferry if on horseback, at only 1½d a horse. A wagon and team cost 20 times as much at 2s 6d, a cart and two horses 1s, and a chaise, whiskey or cart each with one horse 6d (*Norw. Merc.* 2 Nov. 1805)

and economic significance may sometimes be overlooked. The striking feature about Norfolk's bridges is their number. A wealth of bridges points to economic wellbeing, for ease of movement along a network of roads and river-crossings is a prerequisite for successful commerce. Many of the county bridges, or their predecessors, were in existence before the Act of 1530 transferring responsibility for their maintenance out of private hands. Their abundance can reflect mediaeval glory as much as eighteenth-century vitality, as Norwich demonstrates. As early as 1300 'there were five bridges over the Wensum in Norwich, more than any other city in England, including London'.¹ The JPs ensured that the county legacy was maintained for the future.

There were alternative river crossings to bridges. Along the shallower streams a popular and cheap choice was the ford combined with a wooden footbridge, as can still be found today. Wheeled traffic and those on horseback would cross by the ford; pedestrians by the bridge. William Hardy, presumably in his role as parish officer, was responsible for rebuilding the footbridge by his Letheringsett maltings and brewery carrying pedestrians on the King's Lynn–Cromer road.² Fords spelled danger. Following prolonged heavy rain normally well-behaved rivers could be transformed into surging torrents, knocking horses off their feet and smashing down footbridges, with fatal results. A deadly accident at the Letheringsett ford is described on page 47.

Ferries were funded by tolls. During her Coltishall years Mary Hardy appears to have taken Horning Ferry as a means of cutting down the length of a journey.³ Mounted on the small horse or 'hobby' belonging to the surgeon's wife Elizabeth Bendy, the diarist rode beside her husband on a very long day trip to one of their outlying public houses, stopping for dinner at Horning and having tea at the Shoulder of Mutton at Strumpshaw. They did not get back to Coltishall until 11 pm, so for the last part of the journey the diarist, who was no horsewoman, was riding in the dark.

Riding on horseback held little appeal for the overwhelming majority of women. In the years after her Strumpshaw adventure on that fine midsummer day in 1774 Mary Hardy had very little need to ride. New ways of getting about were shortly to come within her reach.

From horseback to whiskey

Mary Hardy's record of her 22-mile round trip to Strumpshaw is notable for being the first of only five occasions in 36 years when she rode on horseback. On the two occasions out of the five when she sat alone, as on that day, she borrowed a slow, small and safe hobby, not a riding horse. The following month she rode an innkeeper's hobby to and from Norwich,[1] and shortly afterwards she rode pillion behind a comparative stranger returning from St Faith's Fair, five miles from her home. The new boy at the brewery had lost his way in the maze of lanes between Coltishall and Horsham St Faith—those very lanes which made effective distribution possible for manufacturers:

[1774] OCTOBER 17, MONDAY ... Childer [children] and I walked to St Faith's Fair, Mr Hardy, Mr Farewell and Mr Smith followed us. Childer came home in Mr Oakes's cart, I came behind his cousin. The boy should have met Mr Hardy with the cart but missed his road and they were obliged to come home a-foot.[2]

The diarist appears to have ridden pillion behind her husband the seven miles to Norwich when setting off and returning from their London trip of 1777.[3] She never mounted a horse again between that visit and her death in 1809.

This great reluctance to ride on horseback was shared by most of her female acquaintance. Her daughter Mary Ann, born in 1773, rode pillion or on a hobby on only very rare occasions.[4] Few others feature in the diary. Mary Hardy's first cousin Hannah Raven rode pillion behind her husband Robert, who farmed nearby, only to come to grief on the way home: 'Mr and Mrs Raven of Tunstead drank tea and supped here; heard since they got a fall from their horse in going home but received very little hurt.'[5] The diarist's maidservant was rather bolder. In the summer of 1781, soon after the move to Letheringsett, at first light Mary Moys 'set off for Smallburgh morning 5 upon our old black mare', probably bound for Ingham Fair—26 miles distant.[6] Such horsemanship by a woman was not recorded again.

The majority of references to women on horseback can be found in the early diary years. It was the same with the men. At Coltishall William Hardy had routinely ridden his reliable mare on his frequent rounds and his weekly 14-mile round

1 *Norwich Diary 1*: 4 Aug. 1774. It cannot have been an easy 14-mile round trip to the city. Setting out before breakfast, William Hardy carried six-year-old Raven, presumably on his horse, and the Coltishall curate walked beside them.
They returned in the rain at 2.30 am—a fairly normal part of child-rearing in the Hardy household (vol. 1, chaps 5 and 6)

2 *fair Diary 1*

3 *Norwich Diary 1*: 21 Sept., 29 Sept. 1777

4 *Mary Ann* eg *Diary 2*: 4 Oct. 1784, 11 July 1788, 20 July 1792; *Diary 4*: 28 May 1801, 7 Dec. 1807.
She had a side saddle among her possessions, as noted in the inventory made in 1797 by her father (*Diary 2*: app. D2.C, p. 421)

5 *the Ravens Diary 1*: 10 Feb. 1780

6 *maidservant Diary 2*: 10 June 1781

facing page Horning Ferry was used by the Hardys to reach one of their outlets at Strumpshaw in the Yare valley.
The ferry formed a vital part of the infrastructure of the Broads [*Faden's Map of Norfolk 1797: Larks Press 1989*]

¹ *William Hardy Diary* 3: 11 June 1795; *Diary 4*: 24 Jan. 1798

² *fast* A speed of 10¾ mph over a distance of 50 miles was attained in a wager won by a neighbour (*Diary 2*: 7 May 1787)

³ *Yarmouth cart Diary 2*: 21 July, 5 Oct. 1783. The design was derived from the troll cart, for carrying goods. 12 feet long, including the shafts, and 3½ feet wide (3·7 metres by 1·1), these carts were able to cope with the port's narrow Rows leading away from the quays, as the wheels were tucked under the load-carrying frame.

A variant was produced in the 18th century to enable tourists to ride about the town and across the Denes to the sea. Such excursions are described in a tourist guide: 'For a company to have been at Yar-

trips to North Walsham market. Once at Letheringsett he liked to use the little cart regularly, while yet not altogether neglecting riding. Once past sixty he rarely mounted a horse, apart from the day he followed the Army in procession to Weybourne Camp. Subsequently he had the occasional ride to Holt Heath Farm, about 1½ miles away.¹

William Hardy's twelve years as a young exciseman would have hardened him to the rigours of the saddle. He is likely to have been an accomplished rider, for the diarist never records a fall by her husband. Their sons, and particularly their younger son, showed little liking for riding, in spite of the fast speeds which could be achieved in the saddle.² In the Letheringsett years 1781–1809 the male members of the family, like their womenfolk, generally did not ride if they could use a vehicle. Greater comfort was within their reach.

William the younger took up driving as a child. He was far more at home with a vehicle, whether the little cart, which was the workaday means of getting about even over long distances, or one of their later light, two-wheeled purpose-built passenger vehicles such as the Yarmouth cart, the gig and the whiskey. When he was only thirteen he drove his mother and sister to the funeral of his uncle Robert Raven at Whissonsett, using the Yarmouth cart which they had started to build in July 1783. The trio endured a three-hour journey of fifteen miles in showers and a high wind.³

This light cart was not however a success. Like the chaise, bought just before they left Coltishall, it was not used regularly after the initial burst of enthusiasm and pride of ownership. Problems associated with the taxation of pleasure

facing page 'A trifle from Yarmouth'. A Yarmouth cart, such as the Hardys commissioned in 1783: one of the souvenirs decorated by William Absolon (1751–1815). A smartly dressed couple bowl along, whip streaming in the wind, in this example from the town's former Maritime Museum   [MB·1989]

right A silver-plated livery button with the Cozens-Hardy crest: one of a set on the greatcoat worn by Robert Moore, coachman to Mary Hardy's grandson William Hardy Cozens-Hardy (1806–95).

Moore's 19th-century livery (jacket in French navy blue, cream nankeen breeches and tall boots) is still held by the Cozens-Hardy family (overleaf)   [*Cozens-Hardy Collection*]

vehicles, as described in volume 2,[1] determined the Hardys' choice of transport. The general-purpose 'little cart' became the most widely used of the vehicles in the Letheringsett years apart from the beer carts and farm carts.

As he grew older William did not ride on horseback nearly as often as his father in his younger and middle years. If a cart were unavailable William often chose to go on foot. Aged 21, he walked long distances to Corpusty and back on three occasions when repairs were being undertaken at the public house; these were round trips of sixteen miles, and one of the days was wet.[2] Many of his male relatives, and others in the diary, walked comparable distances. His first cousin Nathaniel Raven junior, from the Whissonsett shop, and his mother's first cousin Thomas Fox, a former shopkeeper at nearby Brisley, walked the fifteen or sixteen miles to Letheringsett in 1798.[3]

As with his cousins Nathaniel Raven junior, Robert Raven junior and Henry Goggs, it frequently fell to William from an early age to collect and deliver female members of the family attending their various engagements: all four young men routinely drove their family between Whissonsett and Letheringsett and beyond. Women in the early part of the diary never held the reins, so it usually fell to the farm boy or to William to take Mary Ann Hardy to and from her Fakenham boarding school 1783–86 (*Diary 2*).

The first woman recorded by Mary Hardy in charge of a horse-driven vehicle was her seventeen-year-old niece Rose Raven in 1791—and then only because Rose had no choice in the company of the commanding brewer from Letheringsett. Life in the Hardy household was never dull. When Rose's brother Robert came from Whissonsett to collect her he found she was 22 miles away. Rose had, without notice, found herself accompanying her uncle to Norwich in the little cart to try to find a Holt innkeeper, William Shilling, who had recently absconded leaving a trail of debts. William Hardy set off with Rose 'to see if he could happen of Shilling'. He succeeded, getting home in the dark at 10 pm:

[1791] JULY 30, SATURDAY Mr Hardy came home from Norwich evening 10, sued Shilling, rid home on his [Shilling's] fine mare valued at £45 and got £30 in cash and the old horse . . . R. [Rose] Raven came home in little cart.[4]

mouth, and not to have rode in one of these carts . . . is to lose perhaps one of the greatest pleasures this town is able to afford . . . The Yarmouth cart-coach is the most convenient, useful and whimsical carriage used in the kingdom' (R. Beatniffe, *The Norfolk Tour, or Traveller's Pocket Companion* (5th edn Norwich, 1795), p. 17).

Plate 3 shows a creamware jug depicting a Yarmouth cart

[1] *taxation* The changes in levels of duty on riding horses and leisure vehicles meant that taxpayers changed their habits to try to reduce their payments (vol. 2, chap. 11)

[2] *Corpusty* Diary MS: 13 Apr., 14 Apr., 20 Apr. 1791

[3] *walking* Diary 4: 26 Feb. 1798

[4] *Rose Raven* Diary 2: 29, 30 July 1791

Vehicles used by the Hardys for personal transport 1773–1809

source   Diaries of Mary Hardy 1773–1809 and Henry Raven 1793–97

KEY   H   horse/horses   P   persons   W   wheels

vehicle	characteristics	use [1]
PRIVATELY HIRED		
carriages		
chaise	2 W, 1–2 H, 2–4 P + driver; light; open; fast	often borrowed from friends and hired 1773–96
postchaise	4 W, 2 or 4 H, 3 P + driver; enclosed; fast	lifts taken in others' and often hired 1775–1808
sociable	4 W, 2 H, 4 P + driver; semi-open barouche	used once for a local pleasure trip 1804
whiskey (self-driven)	2 w fixed to shafts, 1–2 H, 2 P; light; fast	occasionally borrowed and lifts taken in others' 1778–1808
PRIVATELY OWNED		
2–wheel, 1–horse open carts		
donkey cart (self-driven)	1 donkey ('dickey'), 2–3 P; slow	frequently by women and children in Mary Ann's 1808
little cart (self-driven)	1–2 P; strong and long-lasting; slow	frequently-used general-purpose passenger transport 1773–1808
Yarmouth cart (self-driven)	1–2 P; modelled on troll cart; fast	built to order 1783; used locally; sold c.1789
carriages		
chaise	2 W, 1–2 H, 2–4 P + driver; light; open; fast	bought 1781, replaced 1787; replaced 1794 (1 H); ? sold c.1805
gig (self-driven)	2 W, 1–2 H, 3 P; light; open; fast	bought by William ?1797, ? soon sold; replaced 1805; often used
postchaise	4 W, 2 or 4 H, 3 P + driver; enclosed; fast	bought 1788, sold c.1791
whiskey (self-driven)	2 w fixed to shafts, 1–2 H, 1–2 P; light; fast	often used 1799–1805, sold; another bought by J. Cozens 1805
PUBLICLY HIRED		
hackney carriage	2 W, 1 H, 2–3 P; enclosed; for urban use	used during London visit 1777
mail cart	2 W, 2 P + driver; semi-open	scheduled services used in Norfolk 1786–89
stage coach	4 W, usually 4 H, many passengers (inside and out) + driver; enclosed; fairly fast	scheduled services often used long-distance 1773–1806; Wells–Norwich coach (financed by private subscribers) used 1785–86

[1] *use* Not shown here is the use of the Hardys' working vehicles for transport, such as their malt cart and turnip cart (never the muck cart). Their maids would also take lifts on the beer cart and wagon

The range of vehicles used by the Hardys for personal transport is shown opposite. Some, such as their chaises and postchaise, required a coachman to sit as driver on the box. Since this meant taking one of the workforce away from his duties or else postponing use of the carriage until after the end of his working day—the solution generally adopted—the coachman-controlled vehicle was somewhat impractical.

It would have struck the townsfolk of Holt and the surrounding area that the Hardys' public profile had changed. They took to using their new chaise even the one mile to or from the town, complete with coachman. (The outspoken opinions of William Cobbett on jumped-up farmers are quoted in volume 2, chapter 10, in 'Old Hospitality'.) In the years 1788–91 the role of drayman-cum-coachman fell to William Lamb. There are frequent references in those four years to the loyal farm servant and drayman, after an arduous day's work delivering beer and carrying out other duties, being required to stay up very late as coachman. For this he shed his working clothes and donned his new blue jacket:

[1789] NOVEMBER 30, MONDAY I and William and Mary Ann went to the assembly at Holt evening 8, came home morning 2, Lamb had a new blue jacket . . .

DECEMBER 19, SATURDAY Mr Hardy, I, Mary Ann and Miss Billing walked up to Holt, drank tea at Mr Davy's, William followed us. Lamb went to Wells and met us with the carriage coming down from Holt . . .

[1790] JANUARY 9, SATURDAY . . . Lamb went to Sheringham and came for us to Holt evening 8 . . .

JANUARY 14, THURSDAY . . . William brewed. Mr Hardy, I & Mary Ann walked up to Holt, drank tea and supped at Mr Bartell's, Lamb came for us with the carriage. William rid [rode] up after tea. Lamb went to Sheringham . . .

JANUARY 26, TUESDAY . . . Lamb went to Hildonveston [Hindolveston] forenoon, drove us to Mr Forster's [at Bayfield] afternoon, we drank tea and supped there . . .

top and *above* The Cozens-Hardy livery from the mid-19th century; the buttons bear the family crest.
The coachman for whom it was made, Robert Moore, was very slim. The heavy navy jacket, unyielding collar, stiff breeches and top boots were far too tight for Michael Bird, here aged 12¼ and 5 feet 2 inches tall (1·57 metres) [*MB · 1994*]

This state of dependence on a coachman did not last, and from 1791 to 1809 the Hardys experimented with different vehicles, variously hired, borrowed and owned, which gave them a measure of control over their movements. The term 'self-driven' in the lists opposite means that the vehicle did not require a coachman; William Hardy senior or his son

1 *boys* See vol. 1, chap. 8 on the farm boys; also vol. 2, chap. 5 on the brewery clerks. Girling started as a boy at 16, but rose to the position of William Hardy jnr's confidential clerk

2 *saddle* Instances of riding on horseback are indexed in all four Diary volumes under 'horses, riding horses'

3 *carrier* eg *Diary 2*: 30 Jan. 1787, when William Wade the carrier took Mrs Molly Prior to Norwich; she had worked for Mary Hardy at Coltishall as a maidservant in emergencies (vol. 1, chap. 8); also Diary MS, 31 July 1787, when Wade took Mrs Sheppard to Norwich.

The new cook, Martha Dawes, came by Wade when starting work at the Hardys (*Diary 4*: 17 Oct. 1805)

4 *mail cart Diary 2*: 14 May, 16 May 1789. William Hardy snr and jnr had earlier taken the mail cart from Norwich (via Aylsham) to Holt (*Diary 2*: 8 Oct. 1786). The Yarmouth mail cart went fast, at about 6½ mph.

Mail carts linked their timings to the mail coaches, providing a service to towns beyond Norwich. Both the mail cart and the carrier's cart offered some protection from the weather

usually took the reins. However if women were using the vehicle they almost without exception turned to a male relative or friend or to one of the workforce or the farm boy to drive them. As described earlier, Mary Hardy became very dependent on the boys, especially William Girling, to drive her to and from her Nonconformist meetings at Cley, Briston and beyond in her later years.[1]

By that time it was almost universal for men and women in the Hardys' circle—and with money—to get about on wheels. The age of riding had largely passed, arguing that the roads had improved and that new types of light vehicles had become popular. Men were prepared to mount into the saddle if there were special circumstances such as riding to catch a coach some miles away, or a shortage of vehicles for a large party. Generally they preferred to drive.[2]

New opportunities

Mary Hardy's diary depicts a social revolution. Women and children gained greater independence, being able to travel unaccompanied in a range of vehicles for public hire. As well as the carrier's cart, used by some of the Hardys' poorer visitors—but not the Hardys themselves[3]—there was the mail cart, used by Mary Hardy and her daughter to get to and from Great Yarmouth while at Norwich.[4]

WELLS and HOLT COACH.

THE Proprietors of the above COACH beg Leave to inform their Friends and the Public in general, that the great Inconvenience attending Passengers riding so far over the Stones, has induced them to remove it from the ANGEL, in the Market-Place, to the MAID's-HEAD, in St. Simon's, Norwich; and that the same will only go and come twice a Week in future, viz. from WELLS every Monday and Friday, and return from NORWICH every Wednesday and Saturday, at Nine o'Clock.——The Fares as usual.

N. B. For the Convenience of the Public, Places and Parcels will be ta'ken in he Mail-Coach Office, King's-Head, and at the Maid's-Head, St. Simon's.

above The Wells–Norwich twice-weekly coach service, funded by private subscription, was first proposed at the end of 1784. Mary Hardy herself was an early subscriber and user of the service [*Norwich Mercury, 14 Jan. 1786: Cozens-Hardy Collection*]

An exciting development followed in the wake of the new assessed taxes which Pitt's administration imposed from 1 October 1784, when the Hardys seem to have discontinued using their first chaise owing to the duties. This was the Holt stage coach or postcoach, financed by private subscribers:

Such gentlemen as wish to support a diligence to run from Holt to Norwich are requested to meet at the Feathers, in Holt, on Friday 5 November . . . John Mann in the chair.

Another meeting 'for the proprietors of the Wells, Holt, Aylsham and Norwich postcoach' was held in Wells a few months later.[1] It was for gentlewomen too, as well as gentlemen, since Mary Hardy took out a subscription.[2]

above A carrier's cart at Lakenham, south of Norwich. Carriers kept to strict schedules.

Primarily for taking goods locally, they had room for one or two passengers and were used by the Hardys' poorer visitors [*drawing by F. Stone & Son 1831; lithograph by D. Hodgson, detail*]

THE Public are hereby respectfully informed that for the speedy conveyance of Passengers and small Parcels a POST CHAISE will set out on Wednesday the 20th of April instant, at Eight o'clock in the morning, from the Feathers, in Holt, and will arrive at the King's-Head, in the Market-place, Norwich, at One, by way of Aylsham ; to carry Three Inside Passengers at Seven Shillings each ; and will leave the King's-Head on its return for Holt on Thursday the 21st instant, at One in the afternoon, and continue that course weekly.— ☞ The greatest care will be taken of small parcels, and all favors gratefully acknowledged by their humble Servant,

Holt, April 14, 1781.   E. SHEPPARD.

April 14, 1791.

LYNN and NORWICH POST COACH will set out from the Duke's-Head, Lynn, next Monday, Wednesday and Friday ; and from the White Swan, St. Peter's, Norwich, next Tuesday, Thursday and Saturday, at 7 o'clock in the Morning, dine at Norwich and Lynn, will then be in time for the Yarmouth Machine & the London Mails, performed by the public's most humble servant,

G. GIRLING, Dereham.
G. CROWN, Swaffham.
D. DIMOND, Lynn.

To continue till notice be given to the contrary.
N. B. The Proprietors cannot be accountable for any writings, money, plate, &c. above 5l. unless entered and paid for as such.
(6-3

above A proliferation of regular services by 1791, though slow and costly: five hours to Norwich (21 miles) by postchaise; 7s for an inside fare. Elizabeth Sheppard ran the Feathers at Holt [*Norwich Mercury, 16 Apr. 1791* [*not 1781*]: *Norfolk Heritage Centre*]

[1] *postcoach Norw. Merc.* 30 Oct. 1784, 19 Feb. 1785. The paper published the details on 12 Mar. 1785: 'It carries six inside passengers, each to pay from Wells to Norwich 8s, from Holt 5s. Passengers taken up on any other part of the road, threepence a mile. Outside passengers half price. Each to be allowed 14 lb [6·4 kg] luggage; all above that weight one penny per pound'

[2] *subscription Diary 2:* 17 Dec. 1784

¹ *coach* The service
needed a good number
of suitable horses 'of
the light cart kind, or
able road horses, from
five to eight years old,
about fifteen hands
high'; the subscribers
were short of nine such
horses at the start
(*Norw. Merc.* 4 Dec.
1784). The horses did
not have to match in
colour: this was not a
fashionable equipage.
The service began a
few months later (*Norw.
Merc.* 12 Mar. 1785)

² *profits Diary 2*: 13
May, 14 May 1785,
13 June 1785

The coach service, originally running three times a week
each way but very soon reduced to twice weekly each way,
started from the Royal Standard of England on Wells Quay
with half-hour stops at Holt and Aylsham respectively and
then on to Norwich.¹ Presumably many of those travelling
to the city from north Norfolk had put aside their carriages
under the burden of William Pitt's taxation. Instead they
found it cheaper to use a regular service or to hire a chaise
or postchaise when required, as the Hardys sometimes did.

The coach offered women in the hinterland new opportunities. They now became subscribers, although may not
have attended the meetings to arrange the details. It was
William Hardy who went to the meeting in December 1784
at the Feathers, Holt at which he paid his wife's subscription; and he, not the diarist, attended subsequent meetings.
Mary Hardy would at times note down the number of inside
and outside passengers, as though calculating profits,² and
she and Sarah Bartell, the wife of the Holt surgeon, used the

right Aylsham market place: the Black Boys.
This inn served as a staging post for the
Wells–Norwich coach which began running
in Mar. 1785. Its introduction coincided
both with new taxation of private carriages
(and of riding horses and carriage horses)
and the institution of the London Mail.
Some of the named subscribers to the
service were leading proponents of the
Sunday school movement. As the schools
spread quickly round north Norfolk from
the spring and summer of 1786 the coach
owners announced that the profits would go
towards the schools. Mary Hardy was very
active in the movement   [*MB·2000*]

facing page Lenwade, the Bridge Inn, on
the Fakenham road nearly 10 miles from
Norwich. It was a staging post for stage
coaches and postchaises, and the halfway
point for Mary Hardy between her childhood home at Whissonsett and the
Coltishall brewery. The main road used to
run in front of the inn, the crossing then
lying a short way downstream   [*MB·1999*]

[1] *alone* eg Diary MS: 9 Apr. 1785

[2] *young women* Diary 2: 27 Jan. 1786, 27 Dec. 1785. This was by no means an all-female coach. Mary Hardy records male passengers including her husband and their sons Raven and William, and the Rector of Holt and his son (*Diary 2* and Diary MS, entries from May 1785 to Oct. 1786)

[3] *Sunday schools Norw. Merc.* 22 Apr. 1786. For Mary Hardy's role in Letheringsett Sunday School, and that of others locally, see vol. 3, chap. 2

[4] *inns* J. Chartres, 'The eighteenth-century English inn: a transient "Golden Age"?', in *The World of the Tavern: Public houses in early modern Europe*, ed. B. Kümin and B.A. Tlusty, (Ashgate, Aldershot, 2002), pp. 218–19

[5] *posting inns* Stable size can be an indicator in this trade: very many houses on major routes were not in the business of serving postchaises and postcoaches as their stabling was minimal. The tied houses of the Coltishall Brewery lying within eight miles of Norwich usually had few stalls for horses as 10–12 miles was the staging distance: see the details of the 53 tied

Holt stage coach for a visit on their own to Norwich 27–30 April 1785. The two travelled alone on other occasions.[1]

The coach, carrying mail and instituted in the same month that the London–Norwich Mail began running, was appreciated by single young women and girls. They evidently felt happy to travel in mixed company. Mary Hardy and young William put twelve-year-old Mary Ann on the coach for Norwich a month after Mary Ann's friend, the Holt shopkeeper's young daughter Ann Davy, had been a passenger.[2] Mary Hardy, Mrs Bartell and the Cley merchant John Mann (one of the principal progenitors of the coach service) were all active in their local Sunday schools, and from early 1786 the profits of the coach were to support the schools.[3]

The diarist does not say why the service, valued by her family and close friends, came to a halt. She merely notes that when the coach was put up for auction at the Feathers on 25 April 1788 it sold for seven guineas, which seems extraordinarily little. She had recorded the sale of the horses and harness at Holt as early as 29 November 1786 (*Diary 2*). The service was reintroduced 8 December 1794 (*Diary 3*).

Posting inns feature increasingly in the diary as the years pass; they were crucial to the success of the postcoach and postchaise from the mid-century onwards.[4] Like the King's Head and Feathers at Holt, and the Black Boys at Aylsham, the Bridge Inn at Lenwade was a well-known posting inn; all four would appear to have been popular with travellers.[5]

houses put up for sale in 1841 (NRO: MS 7351, 7 D4, Coltishall Brewery estate: sale particulars 14–17 Sept. 1841)

---

1 *postchaises for hire* eg *Norw. Merc.* 16 Apr. 1791 (pictured on p. 37 in this chapter), 16 Nov. 1793 (also Holt Feathers); 10 Oct. 1795 (Wells Fleece); 22 Sept. 1804 (Holt King's Head). Such notices would emphasise the capabilities of the 'able horses and careful drivers'

---

below right A dickey or donkey cart, used on a delivery round in Diss *c.*1890.

William Hardy jnr, aged 14, acquired a donkey in 1784 just when new taxes were levied on horses; this was presumably to pull his cart. A donkey cart gave his sister new independence after her marriage. Driving herself and the children in and about Norwich she no longer relied on her menfolk.

Even donkey carts could be dangerous. Mary Ann's 74-year-old mother, the diarist, was injured in an accident in Mary Ann's in 1808 [*Norfolk Rural Life Museum*]

From the 1790s onwards the Hardys did not rely so much on regular services such as the Holt coach (which was not mentioned again after 1794) or scheduled postchaises. They either hired postchaises for their own use or used their own light one-horse two-wheelers, the gig and the whiskey. Both types of transport needed places to 'bate', where passengers could refresh themselves and their own horses or change their hired horses. From about 1791 the *Norwich Mercury* increasingly published advertisements for postchaises available for hire from the larger public houses.1

The route taken by the Holt coach in the 1780s (before the opening of the Norwich–Aylsham turnpike), of going north from Norwich and then at Aylsham heading northwest to Holt, would have threatened the Woodrow Inn at Cawston. This prominent staging post on the Holt road was often used by the Hardys in their private vehicles. The direct Holt road was never turnpiked, and the Aylsham route was increasingly favoured after 1794. When driving in their own vehicles on the Aylsham turnpike the Hardys and their circle seem generally not to have bated at the Black Boys at Aylsham but at the Buckinghamshire Arms nearby at Blickling. Such stopping places make more appearances in the diary as getting about became easier and more frequent.

The Hardys were a most united family. The marriage of the diarist's only daughter Mary Ann in 1805 to a Sprowston farmer over twenty miles away near Norwich was not

above The tollhouse at Marsham, south of Aylsham on the old turnpike taken by the Hardys on their visits to Sprowston and Norwich. It is not the original house of 1794, which stood nearby.

The modern road, the A140, lies a few paces to the west of this old highway—now a shady lane [*MB · 2003*]

the severe blow it could have been twenty or thirty years earlier, and communication between the two families became frequent and intense along the Aylsham turnpike.[1]

However this growing reliance on their own vehicles meant that women could not get about independently: they needed a male relative, farm servant or boy to drive them, as already explained. In the Hardys' extended family there was no shortage of such accommodating drivers, and the greater freedom of movement heralded by developments in scheduled services in the 1780s was not compromised over the next two decades as some of these services atrophied. While it is clear the diarist and her daughter did not lose out, other less fortunately placed women—like Anna Maria Woodforde—may well have done so. Also the light vehicles of the later years were very exposed; with only one horse they went slowly. Long journeys in the snow, hail and rain had to be endured. A hired postchaise, or the Holt postcoach, both enclosed, would surely have seemed a fond memory.[2]

One last option should not be forgotten. It was used particularly by women and children. This was the donkey cart, or, in Norfolk parlance, the dickey cart. Donkeys were not subject to taxation, and their pulling power was small. Being docile they could easily be managed, the *Norwich Mercury* reporting on 16 August 1806 that the donkey cart was fast becoming popular: 'another instance of the fashionable estimation in which asses are coming to be held in all parts

[1] *Aylsham turnpike* A well-illustrated survey describes the Norfolk turnpikes and their tollhouses: P. Taylor, *The Tollhouses of Norfolk* (Polystar Press, Ipswich, 2009).

Valerie Belton narrates in entertaining detail how travellers tried to evade paying by entering fields a short way before the tollgate and rejoining the road once the danger was passed (V. Belton, *The Norwich to Cromer Turnpike*, pp. 24–6)

[2] *open vehicles* There are many examples in these later years 1792–1809, as when William and his sister Mary Ann set off on the three-hour journey to Whissonsett in a frost, high north wind and 'frequent storms of hail and snow' (Diary MS: 31 Dec. 1801)

right Mar. 1785: two mail-coach services are instituted, running daily both ways between London and Norwich. A revolution was effected in journey times: stage coaches went at 3–4 mph; the mails at 8–9 mph. One stop, of half an hour, was permitted on the new services: at Thetford on the western route and at Ipswich on the eastern route (today's A11 and A12/A140). The service ran between Fetter Lane, near Fleet Street in the City of London, and the King's Head in Norwich market place.

The reader's eye is drawn to the historic announcement by the new printer's ornament of the Royal Arms, such ornaments being the only form of illustration in the newspapers of the time.

While the Hardys seem not to have taken seats in the mail coaches they benefited greatly from the improved postal service [*Norwich Mercury, 12 Mar. 1785: Norfolk Heritage Centre, Norwich*]

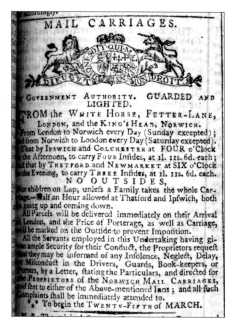

¹ *asses Norw. Merc.* 16 Aug. 1806.
Given the inflamed political atmosphere in Norfolk at this time, as the hotly contested general election of Nov. 1806 approached, this may be an ironic reference not so much to donkey carts as to party opponents and the much-derided Ministry of All the Talents, which was in power 1806–07 after Pitt's death

² *donkey cart Diary 4*: 16–18 June, 21 June, 16, Aug., 17 Aug., 20 Aug., 21 Aug., 28 Aug. 1808

of the country'.[1] One of the consolations of Mary Hardy's last summer was her daughter's donkey cart, treated by Mary Ann as a runabout for getting into and around Norwich from her Sprowston home. Sometimes it was brought over to Letheringsett, and mother, daughter and toddler grandson would go riding in the cart on their own, with no male driver. They drove round the farm and in the Thornage lanes in June 1808 and, after two of the maidservants had driven it back to Sprowston, mother and daughter used it to get to Nonconformist meetings and family visits that August. Mary Ann also took her mother and children into the harvest field in the cart, which seems to have been a most versatile vehicle. Male relatives, if accompanying them, would go on horseback or in the gig into Norwich.[2]

The story that emerges over the 36 years of the diary is not only of a better infrastructure in the form of better roads, faster coaches and inns adapted to the needs of a larger body of travellers, but of a much wider range of options. In the last two decades at Letheringsett the manuscript is peppered almost daily with references to getting out and about in the cart, chaise, postchaise, gig or whiskey: a startling contrast with life in the 1770s when, apart from booking hired vehicles or seeing his wife and children accepting occasional lifts from others, William Hardy was a solitary horseman.[1] Life for the Hardys had become less confined, speedier, more comfortable and more companionable.

As seen earlier, mail coaches were costly. For most long-distance journeys the Hardys stayed loyal to the stage coach with its cheaper fares and greater number of stops. If speed and convenience were at a premium a two-wheeler was brought into service: William Hardy drove a borrowed whiskey for a trip to collect his mother from Yorkshire in 1778.[2] However the Hardys relied on the mail-coach service in one obvious way: they appreciated the enhanced speed of the post. Exchanging letters underpinned family bonds, as seen in volume I.[3] Mary Hardy turned to an ad hoc system in the 1770s for keeping in touch with her Whissonsett family 22 miles away cross country, for callers and strangers often brought her letters. Long-distance mails were slow. When her husband set off on 18 May 1778 for Yorkshire in the two-wheeler she did not hear from him until a week later.[4] A worrier, the diarist would have found this waiting painful.

The mail coaches brought huge changes in their wake. The human dimension is highlighted by Susan Whyman, who sees the change as dramatic. In 1775 there were 444 English post towns, but in 1800 there were over 783; and 'by 1800, high-speed coaches crammed with letters and newspapers sped to every corner of the land.'[5] One of these post towns was Holt. Elizabeth Sheppard, innkeeper of the Feathers, excise officekeeper and postmistress, provided the staging post for the Norwich coach and mail cart. Mary Hardy and her family would go up to check for letters, and the speed with which she heard from her husband and son on their business trips after 1785 was impressive. On 8 January 1788, in a cold north wind, William Hardy set off for Lancashire on his son's mare at the start of a complex journey with many stages. On the second day he was to go from Whissonsett to King's Lynn and there take a postchaise to Wisbech before heading north. He arrived three days later, and on 15 January his wife heard by letter of his safe arrival (*Diary 2*).

[1] *lifts* Mary Hardy, her children and the maids would accept lifts from various acquaintances, such as the Coltishall shoemaker William Hill. He took them by cart into Norwich to watch a public hanging (*Diary 1*: 12 Apr. 1775). The diarist's relations were rather better off, her father Robert Raven and brother Nathaniel Raven each having a chaise. The Hardys did not acquire a chaise until just before their removal to Letheringsett (*Diary 1*: 20 Mar. 1781)

[2] *whiskey Diary 1*: 18 May 1778; he took his own horse and brought his mother to Coltishall three weeks later for a year-long visit. Ann Hardy, then in her mid-seventies, went home by sea

[3] *family bonds* See vol. 1, chap. 4 on letters and Mary Hardy's anxiety to receive news

[4] *Yorkshire letter Diary 1*: 25 May 1778

[5] *change* S.E. Whyman, *The Pen and the People: English letter writers 1660–1800* (Oxford Univ. Press, 2009), pp. 56, 4. This elegant study charts the speed and efficiency of the postal service and the family relationships strengthened by it

[1] *William Diary 2.* In the later years there are many such examples of fast turnarounds between saying goodbye and receiving a letter, often from London. William left for London on 31 May 1799, and his mother received a letter from him there on 2 June— a Sunday (*Diary 4*)

[2] *capital* On 23 Oct. 1804 William and Mary Ann set off for London taking the Fakenham coach to the malting town of Ware, Herts (*plate 2*) and then on to London. They arrived late on 25 Oct., and *on 26 Oct.* their mother received a letter from them with news of their safe arrival (*Diary 4*)

[3] *danger* Vol. 2, chap. 1; also table 2.1.6

[4] *falls* Drink was established as a contributory factor in some of these deaths, as with the Hardys' innkeeper from Edgefield and Valentine Lound riding late from a sheep show. A Blakeney merchant died returning in the small hours from Holt market (*Diary 2*: 10 Mar. 1784, 29 Aug. 1792; *Diary 3*: 24 May 1794)

[5] *falls* Both William III, in 1702, and Sir Robert Peel, in 1850, died from complications following a fall from a horse

She had an even shorter wait five years later. Her son William set sail from nearby Blakeney for Newcastle upon Tyne on 1 June 1793 at 10 am. Only four days later, on 5 June, his anxious mother learned from his letter of his safe arrival on 2 June. She had bid farewell to him at home on the Saturday and received news the following Wednesday of his arrival 200 miles up the coast on the Sunday.[1] William had however been held up since 27 May at home waiting for a favourable wind, and the disadvantages of sea passages over road travel will be described later.[1]

The mail service not only oiled the wheels of commerce but brought essential news and reassurance to apprehensive loved ones. The interval between the goodbyes and the news that all was well became astonishingly short. Evening collections and Sunday mail services produced postal statistics not seen today. In 1804 Mary Hardy's son and daughter arrived in London by scheduled coach service late in the evening ('night') of 25 October. *The next day* their mother at Letheringsett received a letter from them in the capital.[2]

Accidents

Life also become safer. It has already been shown that the greatest danger posed to the Hardys' workforce came from the horse.[3] It is clear from the catalogue of road accidents recorded by Mary Hardy that a fall from a horse was far more likely to prove fatal than being thrown from an open vehicle. Injuries sustained when riding were also more likely to be grave than when being driven, unless the driver or drayman fell under the wheels. She does not record any mishaps involving the enclosed stage coach and postchaise. The evidence has to be handled carefully as inquests, if called at all, could be brief affairs. Given the state of medical knowledge at the time it is not clear from the report if the fall had been occasioned by a stroke, heart attack or seizure. In other words the rider could have been unconscious or dead before he hit the ground.[4]

The danger of riding is likely to have been in the forefront of everyone's mind. A monarch had been killed that century by a fall, as a former prime minister was to be in the next.[5] In the Coltishall years 1773–81, the period when travel was still often on horseback, the diarist records three deaths in

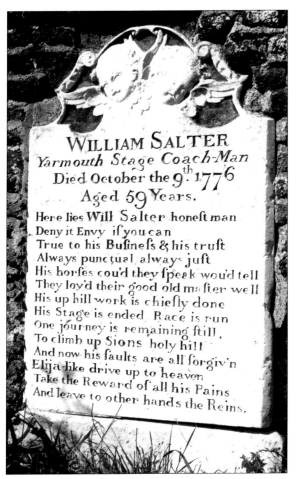

WILLIAM SALTER
Yarmouth Stage Coach-Man
Died October the 9th 1776
Aged 59 Years.

Here lies Will Salter honeſt man
Deny it Envy if you can
True to his Buſineſs & his truſt
Always punctual always juſt
His horſes cou'd they ſpeak wou'd tell
They lov'd their good old maſter well
His up hill work is chiefly done
His Stage is ended Race is run
One journey is remaining ſtill,
To climb up Sions holy hill
And now his faults are all forgiv'n
Elija like drive up to heaven
Take the Reward of all his Pains
And leave to other hands the Reins.

left 'True to his Business and his trust / Always punctual always just / His horses could they speak would tell / They loved their good old master well': the mural tablet to the Yarmouth stage-coach driver William Salter on the outer wall of Haddiscoe churchyard. It overlooks the spot where he was killed in a crash in 1776 on what was then the highway to Gt Yarmouth from the south-west. Coaches were however generally a safe means of transport.

The Rector of Haddiscoe, composer of the epitaph, imagines Salter as driving 'Elija-like' up to heaven [MB · 1996]

---

[1] *falls Diary 1*: 5 Oct. 1776, 31 Aug. 1777, 24 Apr. 1779; 20 Apr. 1775

[2] *accidents Diary 1*: 7 June 1774 (when the Ravens' own chaise was broken 'all to pieces' and Mary Hardy's sister and little nephew were injured), 9 Aug. 1776, 21 Apr. 1778. It was feared six-year-old William jnr had broken his thigh (9 Aug. 1776). Mary Hardy's cousins Robert and Hannah Raven, who, as seen earlier, were to fall from their horse in 1780, were also injured in their chaise (21 Apr. 1778)

falls from a horse; she also records that the excise supervisor, holding a senior post, broke his thigh falling from his horse.[1]

Driving in open vehicles too brought its dangers. Mary Hardy and her extended family were involved in accidents in two chaises and a cart at Coltishall, but all escaped with minor injuries.[2] The early Letheringsett years 1781–93 saw deaths and serious injuries in road accidents. Three children were run over and killed by carts, the drayman Robert Lound broke his thigh under the wagon, the Revd John Burrell dislocated his shoulder, and the innkeeper Richard

right A mid-20th-century view of the bridge over the Glaven built in 1818 by private subscription under William Hardy jnr's direction to replace a footbridge. It was designed by the local architect William Mindham, who also designed the first Foundry Bridge in Norwich across the River Wensum, right by the later railway station.

Carrying all the traffic on this very busy main road, Letheringsett Bridge is sited at the point of the old ford by the Hardys' maltings where the Binham dray mare drowned in 1796
[*photograph Basil Cozens-Hardy 1952: Cozens-Hardy Collection*]

facing page, top 'W. Mindham', the signature below the architect's drawing of one of the bridge piers. The fixed crossing at Letheringsett made the main road much safer
[*Cozens-Hardy Collection, detail*]

---

[1] *accidents Diary 2*: 4 Aug. 1786, 29 Aug. 1792; 1 Sept. 1781, 4 Nov. 1785; 28 Nov. 1782, 13 July 1785, 23 Aug. 1788, 13 Sept. 1787

[2] *draymen* Vol. 2, chap. 1, table 2.1.6; *Diary 3*: 15–17 Oct. 1793 (entries by William Hardy jnr), 28 Nov. 1794, 23 Dec. 1794, 9 Dec. 1796

[3] *injuries Diary 3*: 3 July 1794, 21–22 May 1795, 17 Jan. 1797

[4] *horse fell down Diary 3*: 3 July 1794

Mayes broke his leg falling from a cart. The diarist herself was injured when the Hardys' little cart overturned.[1]

The other Letheringsett diarist, her brewery apprentice nephew Henry Raven, does not record any falls from horses, fatal or otherwise, in the years 1793–97. However the injuries he recorded to the draymen Robert Bye and Thomas Baldwin, some serious, feature in volume 2.[2] As well as the draymen's accidents Mary Hardy records injuries to herself and her husband in the chaise, and a fatality when a cart overturned and killed the Norwich driver. A local curate, the Revd William Wilcocks, was injured overturning his cart in the Hardys' field, 'being very much in liquor'.[3]

The roads were also a place of danger for the horse, a badly maintained road being responsible for some of the accidents befalling Mary Hardy. An inexperienced horse would find a rutted road difficult, and the diarist and her husband were injured at Swanton Novers when 'the horse fell down with us, bruised my head and hurt Mr Hardy's side, broke one of the shafts of the chaise.'[4] There are consequently many references in both diaries to training young colts for the chaise and gig.

Only one fatal accident to a horse is recorded, but it took place right beside the Hardys' house and malthouse at the ford on the Holt–Fakenham road. There had been heavy rain on 3 June 1796, so the Glaven was swollen the following day when the dray cart belonging to the widow of the Binham brewer John Booty approached the crossing. Both Mary Hardy and Henry Raven were on the spot:

[1796] JUNE 4, SATURDAY
[*by Mary Hardy*] A wet morning, the water higher in the river than ever was remembered. Mrs Booty's brew cart attempting to pass through was drawn under the bridge and one of the horses drowned. A man who was riding on the cart was thrown into the river (for the cart was overturned), was providentially saved . . .

[*by Henry Raven*] A very wet day. No work done except helping to get Mrs Booty's horses out of the river which were taken under the bridge with the stream, one mare was lost . . .[1]

[1] *mare lost Diary 3*

above A French phaeton of 1903 at Letheringsett, with horse and driver picking their way carefully over the stones of the Glaven to Lt Thornage.

This ford lies upstream of the main crossing (seen opposite) on the King's Lynn–Cromer road through the village. The drayhorse of the Binham brewer Mrs Booty was drowned in 1796 by being swept under the footbridge at the former ford. Here the footbridge (foreground) has been placed at the safer end, *upstream* of the ford [*MB · 2003*]

¹ *rector's son* Robert Thomlinson jnr (*Diary* 4: 22 Feb. 1809). His death 'was occasioned by a fall from a restive horse' (*Norw. Merc.* 25 Feb. 1809)

² *donkey cart* 'A very fine day. Mr Hardy and Mr Cozens in gig, I and Mrs Cozens [her daughter Mary Ann] in dickey cart went to Norwich to Wilks's meeting forenoon.
Going home the dickey was frightened and ran into a hedge and threw us both out, I was hurt a good deal and Mrs Cozens a little, I could not go to meeting afternoon' (*Diary 4*: 28 Aug. 1808. The Trevecca-trained Mark Wilks was by then a Calvinistic Baptist minister: see chap. 8).
The other accident was to the milliner Miss Scott, who 'overturned a gig at Holt and hurt herself very much' (*Diary 4*: 31 Aug. 1806)

³ *shipwrecks* The sea, shipping, cargoes and customs service are covered in chap. 5.
William Hardy jnr's sloop *Nelly* was lost with all hands in a storm off Blakeney, her home port, in Feb. 1804

⁴ *winds* The Norfolk ports lay up creeks and estuaries, and square-rigged ships could not battle against a head wind to get out to sea

In the last part of the diary, 1797–1809, the number of accidents decreased even though there would have been more traffic in the form of pleasure vehicles such as gigs. There was only one fatality on the road, when the Rector of Cley's 23-year-old son fell from his horse.¹ The two accidents in falls from vehicles were minor, one involving Mary Ann's donkey cart and the other the Holt milliner's gig. In both cases the women were driving.²

In a period characterised as dangerous for women owing to the risks associated with childbirth, it was also hazardous for men, whose daily demands and frequent business trips took them away from home and exposed them to death or injury as riders and drivers. As the years passed, and as the roads improved and the use of vehicles rather than riding took hold, the number of dangerous accidents diminished.

The Hardys' preferred long-distance vehicle, despite its expense, was the postchaise, as we shall see later in this chapter. This had an excellent safety record. It is also clear that Mary Hardy in particular did not relish the prospect of going by sea. Whereas her husband and both sons were prepared occasionally to brave sea passages, neither the diarist nor her daughter shared their courage—or perhaps, in their eyes, their foolhardiness. Indeed, Mary Ann is never recorded as venturing out to sea.

'Sick and weary': road and sea comparisons

There was always the alternative of a sea passage for long-distance travel. Many in the diarist's extended family seem to have resolved to risk their lives as little as possible on the sea; however some of their business acquaintances were more prepared to do so. Fear of the deep, combined with impatience at the uncertainties and delays associated with shipping, would appear to have lain behind the family's resolve, the Norwich newspapers all too often carrying reports of vessels lost on the east coast.³

After two bad experiences in 1775 Mary Hardy seems to have determined never go to sea again. Thereafter all her long-distance travel was by road. While expensive it was much safer, far less chancy, and often quicker in the end: adverse winds persistently prevented ships on the east and north coasts of Norfolk from leaving port.⁴ Friends and

above Yarmouth Quay, near the town hall and customs house: the sight which became all too familiar to the Hardys at the start of their voyage to Hull in Sept. 1775.

Large ships and most warships had to anchor 'in the roads' out at sea, but the smaller trading vessels could moor right against the quayside, as seen here, and load and unload with comparative ease.

William and Mary Hardy and their very young sons had to wait three days before the trader in which they had booked their passage was ready and the wind favourable. All except the five-year-old succumbed to seasickness until they reached Hull six days after leaving their Coltishall home.

Road travel held much greater appeal for the Hardy family, despite the expense [*painting by J. Stark; engraving by G. Cooke 1831, detail*]

acquaintances sailing from the north Norfolk ports would often be held up for days waiting for a favourable wind.[1] Her diary demonstrates the competitive advantage enjoyed by the roads. Unless the maritime passenger wished to do business in a port such as London, Hull or Newcastle, further delays would be caused by having to reach the eventual destination overland, and the diary tracks the road journeys which added to the time spent at sea.

[1] *held up* The twin harbours of Blakeney and Cley, four miles from Letheringsett, handled little passenger traffic in this period. Norfolk residents had the choice of King's Lynn, Wells or Gt Yarmouth if

travelling by sea. Just getting to a port could take one day out of the journey time.

When sailing for Hull in June 1783 Raven and William were held up for three days at Wells, 10 miles away from their home, waiting for a fair wind.

Their father waited at Wells for three days or more in May 1791, when waiting for the wind to change for Newcastle. The captain's patience with his passenger must have been sorely tried, as with the wind remaining unfavourable William Hardy had at first waited at home. The delay caused by summoning him from Letheringsett very early on 8 May lost the ship her sudden fair wind.

After that the brewer spent the remaining days of waiting at Wells —firmly under the captain's eye (*Diary 2*)

---

[1] *Gt Yarmouth Diary 1*: 18–22 Sept. 1775

[2] *Humber Diary 1*: 23–24 Sept. 1775.
They had set sail once the wind had changed from the south-west. They entered the River Humber at noon and reached Hull three hours later

[3] *sick and weary Diary 1*

The Yorkshire trip of September 1775 was certainly character forming. William and Mary Hardy took their sons, then aged seven and five, with them for a visit to the Yorkshire family. Living on the Broads only 23 miles by road from Great Yarmouth they chose to sail. Their experience was not a happy one. Almost all passenger voyages in this period were booked on trading vessels, and the needs of the cargo over unloading and loading took priority. The Hardys were held up for nearly four days at the port waiting for the ship to be got ready for the voyage to Hull and for the wind to change.[1] Had they gone by road they would have been in Knaresborough by then.

For the first and second days they paced restlessly about the port, 'looked at the Dutchmen and the sea', and took a close interest in the direction of the wind. They eventually sailed with the wind in the south-east. All fell seasick except young William. It was mercifully a fast passage: they crossed the Yarmouth Bar at 5 pm and entered the Humber the following day at noon. Their confidence in waterborne transport would have been further shaken on hearing the day after their arrival that five boys had been drowned that afternoon crossing the Humber.[2] The Hardys had set out from Coltishall on the Monday morning and had reached Hull on Saturday afternoon.

The return passage was equally unpleasant. They were lucky to chance upon a ship at Hull about to sail to King's Lynn, and they secured their berths. But the initial fair wind failed them and *Providence* met a head wind:

[1775] OCTOBER 7, SATURDAY At morning 2 [2 am] the wind rose very high and at morning 6 we anchored being unable to proceed any further, at this time we fell very sick, and at morning 9 they took up their anchors and purposed to return to the Humber and anchor in smoother water, we had not run above an hour when the wind suddenly changed again fair for Lynn where we arrived in about five hours very sick and weary . . .[3]

The final sea voyages taken by the Hardys and recorded in the diary were by William Hardy from Wells in 1791 and by his son from Blakeney in 1793, both bound for Newcastle where they were arranging sales of their produce. William Hardy junior was delayed even longer than his father had been: he and his friend the Holt miller John Wade were held up for six days waiting for a favourable wind before they had even left the Norfolk port.[1] For busy manufacturers with mills, maltings and breweries to run such delays were intolerable. Roads offered the reliability, freedom, independence and control prized by the commercial world, while for the leisured seeking a holiday the roads provided a faster and safer means of transport than the sea.

Tourism

This portrait of the roads and road transport ends with a look at the concept of the holiday taken away from home. We have seen already in volumes 2 and 3 that the great bulk of the population—the labouring sort, or industrious poor—did not have dedicated holidays. The most they could hope for was to be granted a day off to attend their local fair, home fair, boxing match or other attraction. The loss of customary ways and the severer tone of the 1790s brought far fewer leisure opportunities for the working man and his family: bishops and justices were opposed to holidays whereby the habit of work risked being broken.[2]

The employers known to Mary Hardy were likewise not much given to holidays for pleasure. Most masters and farmers could not afford to take more than a day or two off when they had a maltings, brewery, mill, shop or landholding to run; innkeepers and most tradesmen were not generally free to leave their business in other hands. Even overworked senior excise and customs officers had to plead to be granted a brief respite which they could spend visiting their families.[3] As a consequence, wives often took holidays with their children separately from their husbands unless such breaks could be combined with business, and unless there were a responsible person who could be left at home.[4]

Women similarly were often constrained. Most in Mary Hardy's circle, such as the wives of shopkeepers and innkeepers, shared the workload and faced the same difficulties as their husbands. Others were single women or widows with businesses to run as innkeepers, schoolmistresses, milliners and seamstresses; one unmarried friend, Miss Billing, was a considerable arable farmer. Many of these women, including the diarist, had domestic responsibilities towards

[1] *Blakeney Diary 2*: 27 May–1 June 1793

[2] *holidays* For the deep roots of the conviction that 'the working classes must be made to work', see the latter part of Keith Thomas's article, 'Work and leisure in pre-industrial society', *Past & Present*, no. 29 (1964), pp. 60–2. The long working year of the Hardys' workforce, who had very few days off, is examined in detail in vol. 2, chap. 1. Their highly valued fairs, with other recreations such as boxing, are covered in chap. 7 in this volume

[3] *officers* For the Excise see vol. 2, chap. 11. For the Customs see chap. 5 in this volume

[4] *left at home* In 1775 William and Mary Hardy took Raven and William for three weeks to see the brewer's Yorkshire family. The diarist's father, aged 68, came to look after the Coltishall business. When Mary Hardy and her husband went to London at hop-buying time in 1777, his 25-year-old brother Joseph came from Yorkshire to take charge at Coltishall—doubtless aided by Raven and William, aged nine and seven and already well versed in their parents' affairs

Mary Hardy's 13 holidays 1773–1809

source Diary of Mary Hardy *notes* Norfolk family visits (to Whissonsett or Sprowston) are excluded. Unless stated, all vehicles are hired

year	duration	companions	destinations	transport	purpose
1775	18 Sept.–10 Oct.	husband; sons	Yorkshire	ships; postchaises; stage coach	visits to family; tourism
1777	21–29 Sept.	husband	London	stage coach; horseback	business; tourism
1779	2–8 Oct.	friends Mary Neve and Miss Flamwell	Suffolk	postchaise	tourism; visits to friends
1783	22–26 Mar.	son Raven; friend Sarah Bartell	Norwich	postchaise	tourism; visits to friends
1783	15–19 July	husband	Gt Yarmouth	? own chaise	business; tourism
1783	9–11 Nov.	husband	Gt Yarmouth	chaise	business; tourism
1785	27–30 Apr.	son Raven	Norwich	Holt stage coach	visits to family and friends
1787	28 Sept.–14 Oct.	husband	London; Lancashire	stage coaches; postchaises	business; visit to family; some tourism
1789	10–24 May	daughter; friend Sarah Bartell	Norwich; Gt Yarmouth	postchaise; mail cart; own carriage	tourism; visits to friends; tours of Sunday schools
1792	22–26 May	husband	Norwich; Gt Yarmouth	own little cart	business; visits to friends

WILLIAM HARDY'S RETIREMENT, OCTOBER 1797

year	duration	companions	destinations	transport	purpose
1800	8 May–19 June	husband; daughter	Cambridge; London	postchaises	tourism; some business
1803	9 May–? 11 June	husband; daughter	Leziate; Yorkshire	postchaises	visit to family; tourism
1804	17–21 Sept.	husband	Coltishall; Norwich	own gig	visits to friends

very young children or ailing and elderly relatives whereby taking a long trip from home was impracticable. Maidservants could not be expected to shoulder these extra duties, and female relatives would be called upon to step in. Mary Hardy herself had to turn to her young niece Mary Raven from Whissonsett Hall to keep house during her long holidays in London and Hull after her husband's retirement.[1]

The list opposite of Mary Hardy's thirteen holidays in 36 years (not including visits to her family at Whissonsett and Sprowston) shows that she took four without her husband, all before his retirement in October 1797. Six of the thirteen were a combination of business and pleasure. Those within Norfolk were not only for work as well as a break but were very short, lasting only three or four days including the long travel time. Apart from the Yorkshire visit of 1775 and until after his retirement Mary Hardy had only one other long holiday in the company of her husband—to see his mother and brother Joseph in Wigan in 1787. In the intervening years they generally undertook only short visits together. Longer trips had to be arranged separately.

Not including the leisured classes, who did not have to work, and the labouring classes, who were made to do nothing but work, it was almost universal for holiday-makers to embrace more than mere tourism and sightseeing. Maintaining face-to-face contact with far-flung family members had a high priority, and ideally business could be conducted at the destination or along the way. William Hardy would make a point of calling at his tied houses when travelling to and from Great Yarmouth and Norwich.

Just as women would visit the playhouse without their menfolk,[2] so they undertook excursions in one another's company. The diarist accompanied her friends Mary Neve and Mrs Neve's sister on their visit to the Flamwells in Suffolk in 1779, and she and Sarah Bartell, wife of the Holt surgeon Edmund Bartell, visited Norwich for the theatre and to tour the Sunday schools in 1789. Not being drivers or capable horsewomen, the women in the diarist's circle were reliant on sometimes slow means of transport. The trip to Great Yarmouth with Mary Ann in 1789 could have proved trying. The Norwich mail cart to the town, while faster than many other carts, still took 3½ hours.[3]

[1] *keeping house* During the holidays of 1800 and 1803 (*Diary 4*). The housekeeper's role, normally taken by the wife, was an onerous one (vol. 1, chap. 7).
Mary Ann could have taken it on behalf of her mother had she not accompanied her parents on both trips

[2] *playhouse* See chap. 6 in this volume. Again someone had to be left at home to run the business

[3] *Gt Yarmouth* The port lay 23 miles from Norwich, reached along the turnpike via Acle, Filby and Caister (*Diary 2*: 14, 16 May 1789). The direct, southern 19-mile marsh road was not built until 1831

above Acle: the route taken by Mary Hardy and her 15-year-old daughter to Yarmouth [*drawing by F. Stone & Son 1830; lithograph by D. Hodgson, detail*] *right* The Buck's Head at Thwaite, Suffolk: a modest inn for travellers on the Ipswich road from Norwich. Here in 1779 Mary Hardy and her friends Mary Neve and Miss Flamwell stopped for a meal on their outward journey to Nacton, on the River Orwell in Suffolk, and here the diarist stayed overnight on the return journey in the company of Mr and Mrs Neve.

She was travelling in the comfort of a post-chaise hired from the Coltishall plumber and auctioneer Robert Ansell. The three women were happy to undertake expeditions unaccompanied by male relatives and to stay in roadside hostelries such as this and the Ram at Tivetshall St Mary [*MB · 2003*]

[1] *postchaise from London* Mary Hardy gives a very detailed break-down of times, costs and staging posts (*Diary 4*: 17 June 1800).

Their route from the City was Epping, Hockerill, Gt Chester-ford, Newmarket, Barton Mills, Brandon, Swaffham, Whissonsett. Unusually, Mary Hardy makes no mention of food or drink; perhaps they just pressed on

Lack of leisure time was not the only constraint. Mary Hardy's often detailed logs of her journeys illustrate the very high costs of travel. The vehicle preferred above all others for comfort and convenience was the postchaise. Unlike the chaise, gig, whiskey or cart it was covered; unlike the stage coach, mail coach or carrier's cart it would run almost door-to-door and to the traveller's schedules. It was fast and flexible, but also very expensive. The published tables setting out the fixed rates for hiring postchaises—and given in French even in the wartime edition of 1794 seen opposite—present only part of the picture. The rates do not include the incidental costs of road travel, as Mary Hardy shows.

The additional expenses, some of them discretionary, included payments to the driver. These seem to have varied according to individual performance, the same mileage commanding different payments. Other outgoings included tolls on turnpikes and at bridges, also the high cost of meals on the road, with accompanying beer and brandy. The final figure for one day's journey—not including food, if any—when William and Mary Hardy and Mary Ann went by postchaise non-stop from London to Whissonsett in 1800 was £8 4s 6d. They left London one midsummer day at 6.30 am and arrived at the diarist's family at Whissonsett at 9.30 pm: 108 miles in 15 hours.[1] The London to Norwich stage—cheaper, but less private—would have taken only 2½ hours longer, but stopped well short of their destination.

The great rarity of these trips meant that the minutiae of the journey held a fascination for Mary Hardy. She noted the stages, changes, vehicles, tolls, delays and refreshments in exacting detail. Just two days from her account of the

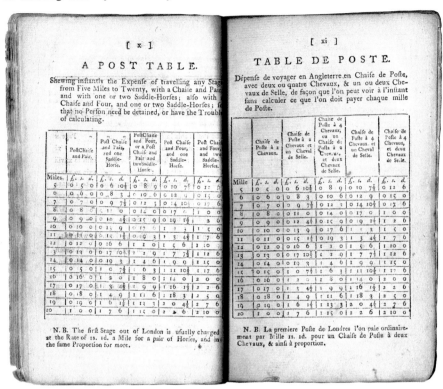

above Tables for calculating the cost per mile, in English and French, of hiring a postchaise with six different configurations of horses. These range from a chaise and pair to a chaise and four with additionally two saddle-horses. The cost of travelling 20 miles by postchaise rose from £1 0s with just one pair to £2 10s with six horses.

The page in English in this copy of the popular road atlas by Daniel Paterson has been so well thumbed the print has faded through chafing. Such road atlases were essential for long-distance travel, showing the cross-country routes ('cross roads') and interconnections with coaches. Postchaises were popular as being rapid and private; they were however one of the most expensive ways of travelling. William and Mary Hardy and Mary Ann took a postchaise from London to Whissonsett in June 1800, taking only 15 hours to cover 108 miles and having the carriage all to themselves—but the cost was £8 4s 6d
[*D. Paterson, A Description of all the Direct and Principal Cross Roads in England and Wales* (*10th edn London, 1794*), pp. x–xi]

[Margin notes:]

¹ *whiskey* A second, hired, whiskey was required, to enable William Hardy jnr and the boy William Girling to bring the first back from Fakenham: travellers depended on family and servants for support services

² *Germans Bridge* Over the Gt Ouse at Wiggenhall St Germain (St Germans), the main western route from King's Lynn

³ *Spalding ditto* The Spalding turnpike, the toll paid being sixpence

⁴ *close* Cloudy

⁵ *10 minutes before 4 o'clock* This is a highly unusual level of precision over clock time.

Normally the time-obsessed diarist refers only to the hours, half hours and sometimes the quarters, suggesting she may have been used to clocks at home with just an hour hand.

Here perhaps she met something which really intrigued her: a *two*-handed clock, for regulating scheduled services on the road but also giving her much more scope for dividing the day

⁶ *Brigg navigation* West of the River Ancholme, it was created in 1635 by Sir John Monson, who drained the valley and created the new cut alongside the old river

[Main text:]

four-day journey from Letheringsett to Hull in May 1803 give a flavour of her manner of recording.

The Hardys and their daughter started off in a whiskey, soon changing to a postchaise at Fakenham.¹ This excerpt, in the diarist's own style of writing and from *Diary 4*, begins at Holt House, Leziate, near King's Lynn, where the trio spent the first two nights with their farming friends, the Forsters. Over the next two days they travelled through Lincolnshire and, after a night at Sleaford, reached Brigg:

[1803] MAY 11, WEDNESDAY Breakfstd at Mʳ Forsters, had a Post Chaise from Lynn, sett of at 9 oClock, changd Horses at Linn [Lynn] & got to Wisbeach ½ after 12. Chaise from Holt House to Wisbeach 21 Miles £1 6s 3d, Servᵗ [servant] 2/6d, Lynn Turnpike 8d, Germans bridge 1/8d,² Walpole Turnpike 8d, Wisbeach Turnpike 8d, took a Post Chaise from Wisbeach to Long Sutton 10 Miles 12/6d, Turnpike out of Wisbech 1/-, Tid Goat [Tydd Gote] Turnpike 9d, Driver 2/- [2s], Chaise from thence to Long Sutton 10 Miles 12s 6d, Driver 2/-, Brandy & Water 6d, Fleet Turnpike 9d. From thence we took a post Chaise to Spalding 13 Miles 16s 3d, Driver 2/-, Turnpike 6d, Spalding Do 6 [Spalding ditto 6d].³ From Spalding to Donington 10 Miles, Chaise 12s, Driver 2/4d, Tea 3s, we were oblidgd to stop there for a Chaise near 2 hours, set of from thence Eveng 8 for Sleaford 16 Miles £1, Turnpikes 1/8d, Driver 2/4d, Supper 6/-, Brandy & Water 1s, Beer 1s, Servᵗ 2s.

MAY 12, THURSDAY A Windy Close day.⁴ Set of for Lincoln Morng 10, 18 Miles £1 2s 6d, Driver 2s 6d, Turnpikes 1s 6d, got to Lincoln abt Noon, look'd at the Minster which is a very hansome Building, so large, so lofty, yet so light, the Town stands on the side of a Prodigious high hill, the Streets are narrow. We dind there & set of for Spittel [Spital] 10 minuets [minutes] before 4 o Clock,⁵ arivd there after 5, Chaise hire 12 Miles 15/- [15s], Driver 1s 6d, turnpk 6d, took a Chaise to Brig 12 Miles 15[s], Driver 1s 6d. Brig is a trading place, there is A Navigation & 2 Bridges into the Town.⁶ The Church is a Mile & ¼ from the Town, there is a Chaple of Ease in the town, almost all the Town belong to one Man. Slept at the Angel Inn, Supper 6/-, Ale 9s [? 9d], Brandy &c 1[s], Breakfast 3/6d.

For those in Mary Hardy's circle long-distance travel was too expensive and time-consuming to be devoted purely to what could be regarded as self-indulgent pleasure. There are few nods to sightseeing in this detailed Lincolnshire extract: in a passing reference Lincoln Cathedral is noted as handsome, large, lofty and light. By contrast, tourism for

left The golden age of coaching: the Norwich stage coach about 1790, by an unknown artist

below The Norwich Mail of 1832 passes the Eagle, Snaresbrook, on the northern outskirts of Epping Forest, Essex. Tickets were cheaper for the outside seats, but the hardy passengers were exposed to the worst of the weather [*from a print after J. Pollard*]

the wealthy and the nobility, represented at its apogee by the Grand Tour, had the sole purpose of the acquisition of knowledge and culture.[1] But for the professional, trading, mercantile, manufacturing and farming families, with whom Mary Hardy's record is primarily concerned, travel

[1] *tourism* For an analysis of 'specialized leisure', as exemplified by the spa towns, see P. J. Corfield, *The*

[1] *John Taylor* His son
Joseph (1785–1864), who
wrote the admiring
account of William
Hardy jnr's Letheringsett
property (see the inset in
vol. 1, chap. 9), accompanied his father and his
brother William on these
regular annual business
trips to the 'congress'.
  On their father's
death in 1827 Joseph and
William carried on his
business as 'maltsters,
malt-factors and malt-
masters' (P. Mathias, *The
Brewing Industry in Eng-
land*, p. 463)
[2] *Mr Hardy* William jnr;
he would also have
known this business
circle at Ware (*plate 2*)
[3] *Searle and Clough* Also
in the malt trade in Hert-
fordshire. Crisp Brown
was a Norwich maltster

Cromer's 'informal congress' of brewers and bankers c.1824

source P. Mathias, *The Brewing Industry in England 1700–1830* (Cambridge Univ. Press, 1959), pp. 462–3 (drawing on the MS diary of John Taylor, of Stortford, Essex, malt-factor) [1]

ROUND THE DINNER TABLE and at breakfast in the country houses, in the market, at the evening promenade along the sands and on the jetty, at the parish church and the meeting-house (both of which John Taylor attended impartially) he mingled with the families who were to be his main customers in the ensuing year, once the barley had been gathered and malted which was ripening in the fields around Cromer while they chatted, entertained and worshipped.

Mr Green, 'the brewer at Reid's House [in London] and his sons', Mr Prior, 'brewing at Islington', Mr Hardy, brewing at Holt, were there [2] . . . At different times he met Crisp Brown, Samuel Searle, Fison (of Thetford and Norwich), and W. Clough—all in his own trade.[3] And most of the brief entries mentioning the people he met include also their comments on the barley. Evidently, Cromer at holiday in July and August became an informal congress of brewers, bankers, landowners and malt merchants, many of them linked by ties of kinship, and all by a common concern with the barley harvest.

*Impact of English Towns
1700–1800* (Oxford
Univ. Press, 1982), p. 52.
  For a study of tour-
ism and the growing
enthusiasm for visits
to stately homes, see A.
Tinniswood, *A History
of Country House Visit-
ing: Five centuries of
tourism and taste*
(Basil Blackwell and the
National Trust, Oxford
and London, 1989),
esp. pp. 88–108

had to have more than one purpose if the massive investment of time and money were to be justified. As the list of Mary Hardy's holidays shows, and as Peter Mathias's view of Cromer in high summer also indicates (above), long-distance travel for the middling sort was undertaken for the dual purpose of business and visits to family and friends. Pure tourism and outdoor recreation performed very much a subsidiary function.

Departing from the way eighteenth-century leisure is at times portrayed, the vocabulary used by Mary Hardy does not include the nouns 'politeness', 'gentility' and 'taste', nor their related adjectives. She had a thirst for information and responded to the stimulus of new places, but was not given to expressing herself in the language of social aspiration. That she could be introduced to the 'neat', the 'elegant', the 'curious', the 'remarkable' and the 'odd' were sufficient for

above A deceptive portrait of Cromer, seen from the north-west. By the local surgeon Edmund Bartell jnr, it forms the frontispiece to the second edition of his study *Cromer considered as a Watering Place* (London, 1806). The coastal town, whose population was still under 700 in 1801, clusters on the edge of the cliffs and near the foot of the massive church. During the previous ten years it had become fashionable as a bathing resort and place of recreation.

Bartell's depiction in his tranquil images and flowery prose fails to reflect the whole scene. He concentrates almost exclusively on aspects of the area which would appeal to an artist's sensibilities and the seeker after the Picturesque.

The economic historian Peter Mathias pithily describes the more hard-headed reality. Early-19th-century Cromer in high summer became 'an informal congress of brewers and bankers, landowners and malt merchants', all drawn there by their 'common concern with the barley harvest'. Bartell's good friend William Hardy jnr was of their number [*Author's collection*]

---

her. Gibbets, chains, skeletons and murderous implements such as an adze, an axe and an iron rod are to the fore with this diarist in place of the polite and the genteel.[1]

The early-nineteenth-century artists of the Norwich School, with some down-to-earth exceptions, created for posterity a tranquil, timeless image of the Broadland landscape, and

[1] *gibbets and chains etc* Terms and objects all noted on her first recorded holiday in Yorkshire (*Diary 1*: 23 Sept.–7 Oct. 1775). Her writing may reflect the

preoccupations of two of her companions: her sons aged seven and five

[1] *watering places* 'The pleasant town of Cromer increases in celebrity as a bathing place', seeing 'a great deal of genteel company, amongst whom are some of the first persons in this country' (*Norw. Merc.* 3 Sept. 1791). Not only Cromer was becoming fashionable. Lower Sheringham had perhaps too much the feel of a fishing station, but Mundesley was starting to attract tourists. The Hill House at Happisburgh offered bathing machines (*Norw. Merc.* 15 June 1799), and some of the diarist's relatives took up sea-bathing (vol. 1, chap. 2)

[2] *Cromer* Edmund Bartell jnr, *Cromer considered as a Watering Place* (enlarged 2nd edn London, 1806), pp. 17–31. Fellow members of the Norwich Society were tempted over to Cromer to commit to canvas the scenes Bartell depicted in prose (D. Blayney Brown, A. Hemingway and A. Lyles, *Romantic Landscape: The Norwich School of Painters* (Tate Gallery Publishing, London, 2000), pp. 132, 133)

painted sailing vessels drifting gently past idly grazing cattle. Their images are at odds with the semi-industrial nature of the Broads, with busy staithes and warehouses, timber yards, coal wharves and cinder ovens, as the next three chapters will show. So too the promoters of genteel watering places along the Norfolk coast deftly painted a canvas which masked the true business and commercial realities.[1]

William Hardy junior's friend Edmund Bartell junior was an amateur member of the Norwich Society of Artists as well as a surgeon. In his guide to his adopted town Bartell almost wholly obliterates in text and illustration any trace of commercial activity in Cromer and the surrounding area. His references to fishermen are in the context not of their economic function, but of the picturesque nature of their calling and of the dramatic seascapes visible from the cliffs when on stormy nights they fight for their lives in the surf.[2]

When considering watering places, outdoor pursuits and tourism we need to be on our guard against the image-creation at work in the contemporary sources, including even the commercially minded newspapers. They sought to emphasise the polite and the Picturesque, the select and the solitary. But the dusty, sober-suited travellers invading these places of genteel retreat might in fact have been focused on purchasing raw materials, securing manufacturing contracts and sealing trade agreements within the compass of an agreeable resort in which they could pass a pleasant few days. Tourism placed too many demands on time and financial budgets to be confined to idle, self-indulgent recreation.

We have seen the Hardys rising in social consequence by acquiring a coach of their own after years of going without at Coltishall, and then purchasing all manner of vehicles over subsequent years. The familiar theme of gentrification took many forms. We have seen it in volume 1, with the desire for privacy and exclusion. Those with anything approaching a country seat, including William Hardy junior at Letheringsett, formed parks around their houses, with the consequent removal from sight of anything redolent of industrial or working life. The push for enclosure, charted in volume 2, ran parallel with this preference for a controlled landscape denuded of straggling and unproductive heaths and, perhaps, straggling and unproductive cottagers.

As the desire for personal, business, spiritual and social control took a grip, as explored in all four volumes, so the landscape was plotted and committed to paper. Mapmaking had military origins, and the road atlas on which the Hardys relied was compiled by the Assistant to the Quartermaster General of His Majesty's Forces.[1] Armed with their atlases, travellers extended their horizons and watched out for the landmarks along the way. By the 1840s, when turnpike trusts were on the verge of being put out of business by steam, the land had been bisected by 20,000 miles of turnpike road overseen by more than a thousand turnpike trusts.[2]

It is a popular notion that before the railway, and perhaps even the motor car, people in rural areas rarely strayed far from their villages. This chapter, like that on the workforce in volume 2, shows that people were constantly on the move, across many classes and callings. Lamb's 555 miles in five weeks dispel any notions of a static world. This was one with wide horizons, where even some with little money to spare were able to get about by hitching lifts, working their way or taking the humble carrier's cart. And barring accidents they seem to have travelled safely. Not once in 36 years does Mary Hardy refer to her family or workforce being robbed while out and about. Highwaymen do not feature at all other than in the sobering mementoes in York Castle of Dick Turpin and William (John) Nevison as they awaited execution.[3]

Control lay at the heart of the Hardys' marked preference for road travel. Even scheduled coach services had their limitations, the cross-country routes being poorly served. The deeply held need for command over their lives recurs time and again with the Hardys. They opted for self-drive vehicles rather than coachman-driven carriages. Wind, tide, imperious captains and the needs of the cargo reduced sea-going passengers to a state of bewildered impotence. Mrs Ann Hardy, who seems to have enjoyed taking lifts in keels and wherries (types of trading vessel plying the Norfolk rivers), had a particularly bad time of it trying to get back to Knaresborough in 1779.[4]

The next four chapters take us onto the waters of the Broads and out to sea: not for passenger transport, but freight. Water came into its own over the carriage of bulk goods, and the Hardys owned two vessels for that purpose.

[1] *atlas* Paterson's. He had consulted mapping experts such as William Mudge (R. Hewitt, *Map of a Nation: A biography of the Ordnance Survey* (Granta Publications, London, 2010), p. 147). Atlases advertised in the Norwich papers included those by W. Owen and Paterson, both running to multiple editions (eg *Norw. Merc.* 20 Sept. 1788, 16 June 1792). Surveying is examined in vol. 2, chap. 3

[2] *turnpikes* P. Taylor, *The Tollhouses of Norfolk*, p. 11. The trusts were finally wound up in the 1870s

[3] *highwaymen* 'Turpin's irons he wore in prison, near a yard long and very heavy; Nevison's irons, very near as long as Turpin's . . .' (*Diary 1*: 26 Sept. 1775). Incidents of violence against the person and of criminality generally are few in Mary Hardy's record (vol. 3, chap. 6)

[4] *Ann Hardy Diary 1*: 30 May 1779 and note. Mary Hardy's mother-in-law reached home on 11 June, having waited a week at Gt Yarmouth for a berth. Boating for pleasure as a leisure activity rather than as a means of transport is covered in chap. 7 in this volume

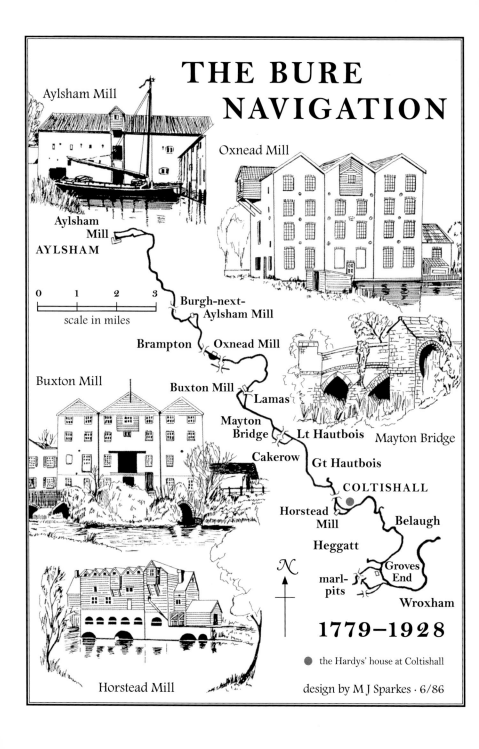

THE BURE NAVIGATION

Aylsham Mill

Oxnead Mill

Aylsham Mill
AYLSHAM

0   1   2   3
scale in miles

Burgh-next-
Aylsham Mill

Brampton   Oxnead Mill

Buxton Mill

Buxton Mill   Lamas

Mayton
Bridge   Lt Hautbois   Mayton Bridge

Cakerow   Gt Hautbois

COLTISHALL

Horstead
Mill   Belaugh

Heggatt

marl-
pits   Groves
End

Wroxham

𝒩

1779–1928

● the Hardys' house at Coltishall

design by M J Sparkes · 6/86

Horstead Mill

2

The new navigation

Injurious to this property

Mr Hardy went morning 10 to Aylsham with Mr Ansell in the *Grampus* with four other boats, one of them was overset near Lamas, got to Aylsham evening 5.　　　　　　　MARY HARDY, 1779 [1]

The situation [of the manor house at Coltishall] is on a river which is navigable from Aylsham to Yarmouth—no river dues are paid. This was originally the head of the navigation; the new cut must have been injurious to this property.

　　　REPORT TO KING'S COLLEGE, CAMBRIDGE, 1805 [2]

M ARY HARDY LIVED AT A SIGNIFICANT TIME for the inland waterways of her area, the Norfolk Broads. It proved an uncertain one for her home village of Coltishall. Its economy, buoyant until then, was damaged when water-borne trade was extended up the River Bure. For centuries a thriving inland port, benefiting from its position as head of navigation, Coltishall was no longer the most inland of an extensive network of towns and villages on the northern Broads. Its coal wharves and timber yards serving the hinterland lost ground, as did its principal industry, malting.

The diarist, married to a maltster and brewer, lived at the point where the navigation started on its winding course. An eye-witness to its construction, she is at times our only written source. The Act of Parliament authorising the navigation was passed in 1773, the year she began her Coltishall diary.

facing page The Bure navigation, also known as the Aylsham navigation, was created 1774–79 by deepening and improving the existing, non-navigable Bure along the 9¼ miles upriver from just below Coltishall Lock (near Horstead Mill) to the market town of Aylsham. The watermills were long established. Bypass channels and locks had to be dug to allow wherries with their cargoes to negotiate the waterway　　　[*map © M.J. Sparkes 1986*]

[1] *overset* Capsized (*Diary 1*: 20 Oct. 1779), recounting the opening day of the navigation from Coltishall right through to Aylsham. It took the little flotilla seven hours to cover 9¼ miles. *Grampus* (a dolphin) was the name of the wherry owned by the Coltishall plumber and auctioneer

[2] *injurious* Report on the estate for King's College, Cambridge, manorial lords of Horstead and Coltishall, by John Josselyn jnr, 15 Jan. 1805 (King's Coll.: KCAR/6/2/38, COL/505). The Hardys lived just upstream of Coltishall Manor House.

A navigation is a river improved to make it passable by boat; a canal or cut is purpose-built. Tolls were not paid on the tidal river below Coltishall Lock.

A wherry is a trading vessel with a single sail, rigged fore and aft. The boats of the Norfolk and Suffolk Broads are covered in this chapter and in chaps 3, 4 and 7

[1] *farming, enclosure* See vol. 2, chaps 2–4

[2] *maltings, breweries* Vol. 2, chaps 5–8. Cinders (coal treated in a coking oven) did not taint the grain during malting

[3] *supply* See vol. 2, chap. 10

[4] *Desmond Best* His unpublished 1976 Keswick Hall thesis, 'The Aylsham Navigation', has meticulous annotations; the original, full version is held in the Norfolk Heritage Centre, Norwich.
Extracts, without Best's essential footnotes and appendices, appeared as 'The Aylsham Navigation' in the *Journal of the Norfolk Industrial Archaeology Society* (vol. 7, no. 1, (2001), pp. 53–73) and, with fresh illustrations, in *The Wherry*, the journal of the Norfolk Wherry Trust (2003), pp. 10–25, 32

[5] *commemorative study* S. Spooner, ed., *Sail and Storm: The Aylsham navigation* (Aylsham Local History Society, 2012). Led by Sarah Spooner of UEA, this was a collaborative venture drawing on the research and fieldwork of Aylsham Local History Society members and on the archives held by Aylsham Town Council.
Desmond Best died in 1991. The book

The creation of canals (new-dug, manmade waterways) and improved rivers (called navigations) was spurred on by the general spirit of 'improvement' at this time. Volume 2 in this study has described some of the new, more productive farming methods and new breeds of livestock; enclosure too was driven by the need to feed the nation through expanding and improving the amount put to arable from the 'wastes', as the old heaths and warrens were called.[1] The previous chapter in this volume has touched on the turnpike trusts as striving to improve the roads, making them faster and better able to support the new types of vehicles—whether long-distance coaches or light two-wheelers for everyday use. Mail coaches were 'improved' versions of the stage coach.

So too navigations reflected the desire to speed up transport and distribution. When the agricultural reporters prepared their county volumes they used templates dictated by the Board of Agriculture. These templates included a section on navigations, seen as central to farming and the local economy. There was little benefit to be gained from enhancing crop yields if the abundance supplied by the good earth and enlightened farmers could not be carried efficiently, rapidly and as cheaply as possible across the kingdom.

Production at the maltings and breweries whose story has dominated much of volume 2 would have ground to a halt without the cinders (coked coal) and coal which fuelled them.[2] Where at all possible coal was brought round from the North-East by water: by sea, and then inland by waterway, whether a natural river or an improved one. The last chapter and that in volume 2 on supplying the beer have shone a spotlight on distribution by road.[3] This chapter and the next three go to the heart of waterborne distribution, covering the staithes or wharves, inland ports, seaports and the vessels used for freight transport by river and sea.

There have been earlier studies of the Aylsham navigation, the scheme built on Mary Hardy's front doorstep. Desmond Best produced a much-respected thesis in 1976 which was never published.[4] However it inspired the highly readable and well-illustrated study of the navigation, *Sail and Storm*, published in 2012 by the Aylsham Local History Society to commemorate the ending of the navigation following the destructive floods a century earlier.[5]

This chapter will largely avoid overlapping with these two major studies; it can instead be seen as complementary to them. While outlining the planning, construction and early economics of the navigation it will focus on issues highlighted by Mary Hardy's diary. It will also portray the new waterway not from the perspective of the 'victor' or prime beneficiary, the market town of Aylsham, but from that of the loser. Coltishall lost out. Horstead, across the Bure, suffered rather less: most of the village centre lay upriver of the new lock. Its watermill and manor house downstream, at the old head of navigation, became Horstead's prime losers.

Loss was the fate of almost all former heads of navigation. When thrusting new commercial centres sprang up further upstream it was inevitable that local trade patterns would shift. The words of John Josselyn junior, the surveyor and valuer reporting to King's College in 1805 (at the chapter head), will reflect the views of the corn and coal merchant who was the college's copyholder at the manor house, William Palgrave. It was a considered judgment, delivered after the navigation had been in full operation for a quarter of a century. The extension to Aylsham had injured his business. It had consequently devalued the college estate.[1]

Finally this chapter will set the navigation in context, and compare it with some contemporary projects. Although those financing the Aylsham scheme had to withstand some early shocks, and although the original estimate of 1772 had more than doubled by the time the waterway opened to Aylsham seven years later, it can be seen as a model of prudent execution in comparison with most others.

Calculations over the waterway's approximate cost vary between £6551 and £8886.[2] At 9¼ miles long it thus cost between £708 and £960 a mile to improve. Whichever of the two figures is adopted, the table on page 111 in this chapter places Aylsham at the modest end of the scale. Another Broads navigation, the New Cut, giving Norwich direct access to the North Sea via Lowestoft and completed in 1833, cost £21,429 a mile. The construction of Mutford Lock west of Lowestoft and the need to deepen existing rivers and dig a new linking waterway from scratch—all to suit seagoing traders—will explain much of the outlay.[3] The far less ambitious Aylsham scheme could be seen as a snip.

was dedicated to his memory, and his widow Lucie was present at the launch of *Sail and Storm* to great acclaim at Aylsham in Sept. 2012

---

[1] *Aylsham* The new waterway had various names. Mary Hardy refers to it as 'the new river' on the day work began (*Diary 1*: 29 June 1774). John Josselyn jnr, writing to King's 1805, calls it 'the new cut', though the great majority was not newly cut.

Historically and today it is known as both the Aylsham navigation and the Bure navigation, both names being correct

[2] *costs* The lower figure was already an increase from the surveyor's original tender of 1772, for £4006, as described later. Costs rose steadily. The figure of £6551 appears in table 4.2.1 and is derived from the cited source; it is retained there to preserve comparability with all the other cost figures in the table.

However Aylsham's final tally shortly before opening actually came to £8886 4s 5¼d (S. Spooner, ed., *Sail and Storm*, p. 32)

[3] *comparisons* See table 4.2.1. Aylsham, unlike a few others listed, did not cater for seagoing ships

1 *Repton* S. Yaxley, ed., *Sherringhamia: The journal of Abbot Upcher 1813–16* (Larks Press, Guist Bottom, 1986), p. 2

2 *Green* In 1779 he entered into partnership with the existing engineer John Smith, as described later

3 *by water* S. Yaxley, ed., *Sherringhamia*, pp. 18–19, entry for 13 Apr. 1815. Abbot was the diarist's forename

4 *valuer* He is not named. The pressure was on him to talk up the proposal. Mayton is rather more than six miles by road from Norwich, and the local fair, near Mayton Hall at Cakerow, to which he attaches significance was not up to much by Mary Hardy's time: she refers to it as Scarecrow Fair (*Diary 1*: 7 Apr. 1777). The Hardys attended it regularly, but it was far from a major event other than for entertainment, socialising and drinking: see chap. 7 on fairs, in this volume.

For the story of the later Pastons and their financial woes, in their own words, see J. Agnew, ed., *The Whirlpool of Misadventures: Letters of Robert Paston, First Earl of Yarmouth, 1663–1679* (Norfolk Record Soc., vol. 76 (2012))

Inland ports and heads of navigation

Sheringham Park is a popular attraction for locals and tourists on the north Norfolk coast west of Cromer, its varied plantations and grounds looked after by the National Trust. Humphry Repton, who designed the new villa named Sheringham Bower and advised on the grounds in 1812, regarded this project as his 'favourite and darling child in Norfolk'.[1] Snuggling into protectively sloping ground to the north-east the house looks out across a gentle, sheltered valley.

Its white facing bricks are not local. They came from a builder in Wroxham, on the River Bure downstream from Coltishall. That builder, John Green, had been a contractor and one of the engineers constructing the Aylsham navigation.[2] Sheringham's delighted owner, Abbot Upcher, wrote in his diary in 1815: 'Our white bricks for frontage we had from Mr Green's of Wroxham, he delivering them at Aylsham by water from whence our wagons brought them.'[3] Had the navigation not been built these bricks could well have come via Coltishall, bringing business and fees not only to the staithe owner or wharfinger concerned, but to nearby public houses where the drivers and wagon horses would have slaked their thirst. Staithes and public houses go hand in hand.

Town and village inland ports were entrepots in miniature. They provided landing places, called staithes, where goods destined for distant ports were loaded. Incoming goods too came from far and wide. The observation (opposite) by a valuer a century before the Aylsham scheme was completed spells out the potential advantages for just one manor house new-linked to the North Sea. Mayton Hall was at that time stranded high and dry when it came to commerce, the navigable river stopping at Coltishall and Horstead. Were the Bure improved a few miles upriver vessels 'of great burden', carrying appreciable tonnage by way of cargo, could bring up coal and other commodities brought round by sea either coastwise within Britain or from overseas, and carry down to Great Yarmouth all the local produce, notably corn and timber. Benefits would accrue to the local area. These advantages, in this 'noble, sweet country', were Coltishall's at the time the valuer wrote this. They became Mayton's in 1775, on the opening of the new waterway's first stage.[4]

'A huge advantage': the navigation is anticipated *c.*1673

source   NRO: MS 3332, 4 B3 (Clayton MSS 123), A particular of
the manor of Meyton in the county of Norfolk, parcel of the estate
of the Right Honourable the Lord Viscount Yarmouth [1]

THE MANOR HOUSE [MAYTON HALL] WITH BARNS, stables, and
other outhouses convenient, a garden, and orchard, and above twelve
score acres of land, being meadow, arable, and pasture ground lying
in many several inclosures, joining to one another, without one rood
of land of any other person lying within it, leased out at the yearly
rent of seventy pounds but capable of improvement—*£*70 0*s* 0*d*.
. . . The grounds are reasonably stored with wood and timber.
The manor house stands upon the river that runs to Yarmouth
which is navigable within a mile of the said house, bearing vessels
of great burden which bring up coal and diverse other commodities from the said town, and carry down to it corn, timber, billet
[wood for fuel], and what else the country affords [provides], at
very cheap rates, to the great benefit of the country, especially of
such places as are near it [the navigable river].

It is thought that in time the river may be made navigable to the
said manor house, which will be a huge advantage to that estate. It
stands within six miles of the city of Norwich, within four miles of
North Walsham, and within three miles of Aylsham, good market
towns; and in a noble sweet country. There is yearly a fair holden
and kept near the said house belonging to the manor, to the advantage thereof, and to the benefit of the neighbour towns thereabouts.

[Endorsement, nd:]
Mr William Paston thinks to borrow £1000 on the manor of Meyton in Norfolk. [2]

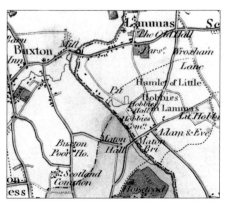

[1] *source* The MS is undated, but presumably dates from 1673–79, the only period when the owner of the manor of Mayton near Horstead bore the title Viscount Yarmouth.

Sir Robert Paston, Bt (1631–83), FRS 1663, MP for Castle Rising 1661–73, Lord Lieutenant of Norfolk 1676–83, was created Viscount Yarmouth and Baron Paston in 1673, the year after his eldest son William (1654–1732) had married King Charles II's eldest illegitimate daughter, the widowed Charlotte Jemima Howard.

Viscount Yarmouth was created 1st Earl of Yarmouth in July 1679, being succeeded in 1683 by his son William, with whose death the title became extinct; the Earl's heir took the courtesy title of Lord Paston. Unless the valuer mistook the peer's title, the MS cannot be as late as 1685, the date ascribed to it by Percy Millican (*A History of Horstead and Stanninghall, Norfolk* (Norwich, 1937), p. 6)

[2] *Mr Paston* Viscount Yarmouth's heir, with no courtesy title until 1679

left Mayton Hall and bridge, from Bryant's 1826 map of Norfolk. The Pastons, hugely indebted, had hoped to raise money in the 1670s by talking up a project for a navigation just after the Act for Bungay's in Suffolk had been passed [*Cozens-Hardy Collection*]

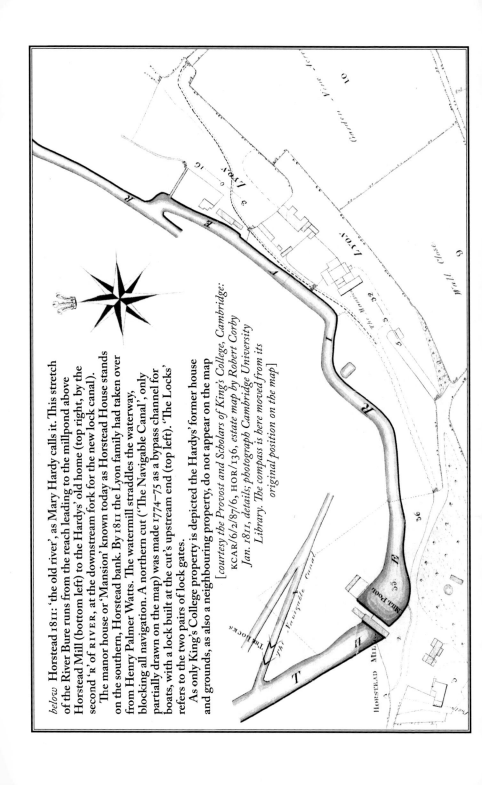

below Horstead 1811: 'the old river', as Mary Hardy calls it. This stretch of the River Bure runs from the reach leading to the millpond above Horstead Mill (bottom left) to the Hardys' old home (top right, by the second 'R' of RIVER, at the downstream fork for the new lock canal).

The manor house or 'Mansion' known today as Horstead House stands on the southern, Horstead bank. By 1811 the Lyon family had taken over from Henry Palmer Watts. The watermill straddles the waterway, blocking all navigation. A northern cut ('The Navigable Canal', only partially drawn on the map) was made 1774–75 as a bypass channel for boats, with a lock built at the cut's upstream end (top left). 'The Locks' refers to the two pairs of lock gates.

As only King's College property is depicted the Hardys' former house and grounds, as also a neighbouring property, do not appear on the map

[courtesy the Provost and Scholars of King's College, Cambridge: KCAR/6/2/87/6, HOR/136, estate map by Robert Corby Jan. 1811, details; photograph Cambridge University Library. The compass is here moved from its original position on the map]

Once sown, the idea of a navigation took root. On 3 January 1723 it was proposed that a company be formed to seek parliamentary authority for such a scheme.[1] Pressure for this extension of the waterway then came, as it did much later in 1772–73, from the leading inhabitants, estate owners and merchants of Aylsham and the immediate area. Achieving the status of head of navigation was the prize.

Why was this important? Admittedly, all inland ports shared in the buoyancy afforded by access to a prime distribution network. As the front endpaper map shows, the Broads formed a system of approximately 130 miles of navigable waterway linking villages to market towns, to the provincial capital of Norwich and to the North Sea (lock-free) at Great Yarmouth. In addition there were the large sheets of water of the broads themselves, formed centuries earlier when mediaeval peat-diggings were flooded as sea levels rose. The former open-cast quarries, no longer able to provide peat turves for heating and cooking, were put to good use by becoming connected to nearby settlements and rivers along specially dug dykes or cuts. The parishioners thus gained access to the water even if their village centre lay distant a mile or more. These dykes, once numerous, are now often overgrown and choked with vegetation unless kept open for holiday and leisure traffic.

The furthest upriver settlements did however gain particular advantages by penetrating deepest into the hinterland. With some exceptions, bulk cargoes were taken by water if at all possible, as chapter 5 will demonstrate in relation to the sea. Abbot Upcher could have sent his wagons straight to Wroxham to pick up his bricks, but he chose to get the bricks as close as possible to Sheringham by water—to the inland port of Aylsham. Only then were they taken by road. So busy was the trade and onward despatch at heads of navigation that canal basins had to be built, as at Aylsham from 1779; or a long series of staithes maintained along the bank, as at Coltishall until its trade was hit from then onwards.

Horstead was similarly hit. The map commissioned by King's College in 1811 (opposite) depicts the 'old river' running from the millpool past the college's manor house. The lane east to Heggatt, a hamlet of Horstead, skirts the millpool, the meeting point of road and water marking

[1] *company* Aylsham Town Council, Box 34; a survey was made, and sites for public staithes chosen. I am very grateful to the town clerk Mrs M. Reynolds and hon. archivist Ron Peabody for granting me access in 1990 and 1995

above The long, straight cut to Upton across Upton Marsh, dug from the Bure upriver of Wey (Acle) Bridge to link the small village with the great artery that was the tidal waterway.

A staithe house, warehouses and all the support structures of an inland port grew up at the head of Upton Dyke. The Hardys' public house (the White Horse or the Cock) also played its part in the infrastructure [*Faden's Map of Norfolk 1797: Larks Press 1989*]

¹ *Biedermann* Son of Otto and Maria Biedermann: born 1743 or 1744 at Blankenburg [? Blankenburg am Harz, in Saxony-Anhalt] and buried at Tetbury, Gloucs, 15 Mar. 1816, a surveyor specialising in navigations and enclosures. His career is summarised by Peter Eden, 'Land surveyors in Norfolk 1550–1850, pt 2', *Norfolk Archaeology*, vol. 36, pt 2 (1975), p. 130. Biedermann worked 1777–78 for the Holkham estate in Norfolk and lived at Woodbastwick for a time before moving to a farm in Wiltshire and later settling at Tetbury. He was naturalised in 1804

² *upriver* William Palgrave snr (d. 1780), the uncle of the later copyholder at Coltishall, built a maltings just upstream of Coltishall Bridge in 1776, as seen in the Horstead church ratebook (pictured in vol. 2, chap. 5, under 'Village entrepreneurs')

³ *houses* The Norfolk Mead Hotel was known in the 16th century as Cockerells; the manor house was known up to the 18th century as Postills (Postles). These and other properties referred to by Mary Hardy are located on the map of Coltishall in 1780 (rear endpaper in vol. 1 of this study)

the mill staithe. This had been the head of navigation for Horstead, the most upstream point on the Bure. Yet by 1811 the features we might expect to see in a canal basin at a head of navigation had evaporated. The pool had been the basin, despite the danger and inconvenience of loading and unloading in a cauldron of foaming, churning water. The buildings seen on the south bank by the staithe, including the large house, primarily served the miller's needs; the long building on the north bank may be a granary. Apart from the support structures associated with cornmilling this area lacks all sense of a thriving, commercial hub. It had ceased to be one thirty years earlier.

The Hardys lived on the north bank, by the downstream fork shown on Corby's map. They had arrived at Coltishall in 1772, the year that Henry Augustus Biedermann drew up his plan for the navigation, as described in the next section.¹ Coltishall faced different problems from its neighbour across the stream. Horstead's parish boundary stretched far north and west, so the village had the option of establishing new commercial premises and staithes upriver of the lock and on the navigation itself—an opportunity it seized as early as 1776.² This rearguard action notwithstanding, its role as joint head of navigation had been forfeited.

Coltishall found itself geographically more constrained. The parish boundary ended at Coltishall Bridge, a short way upstream from the lock; Great Hautbois straggled along the new navigation on the other bank from Horstead. One of Coltishall's two large riverside commons, known then as West Common and belonging to King's College, occupied an uninhabited area, with no access road, north of and upstream from Horstead Watermill (also a King's College property). Cutting the canal across this common required the consent of the college, and we shall see that some guile was needed on the part of the manorial steward Henry Smith to obtain their permission—retrospectively.

With this topography, landing places at Coltishall could begin only *downstream* of the common. A string of three private staithes could be accessed from the main road along a narrow lane or 'loke' and a private drive: at what is now the Norfolk Mead Hotel (formerly The Mead); at the Hardys' at what is now Holly Lodge; and at the manor house.³

left Coltishall, the Norfolk Mead Hotel: the property at the fork of the old river and new canal. The Hardys lived immediately downstream, and were reached along the lane shared with this house south of the church. It was remodelled in 1740 by Joseph Smith (d.1761). His brother Henry (d.1788), the manorial steward for Horstead and Coltishall, was careful not to keep King's College fully informed over the navigation. Their brother John was Vice-Chancellor of Cambridge University and head of Caius College; Joseph Smith jnr was an undergraduate there and later Senior Fellow, his widowed mother Margaret keeping house for him in Cambridge. In 1786 he became private secretary to the Prime Minister, William Pitt. They were a distinguished family with an interesting history. Their forebear Henry Smith was a regicide, his firm signature authorising Charles I's execution on the 1649 warrant (volume 3, chapter 8)   [*MB · 2018*]

The really significant staithe for Coltishall lay behind the King's Head, on the main road a short way east of the manor house. This coaling staithe is frequently referred to by Mary Hardy even though the Hardys relied heavily on their own staithe in front of their house, maltings and brewery. The innkeeper of the King's Head, Joseph Browne, was also the wharfinger, and a great deal of business was conducted at the King's Head Staithe (chapter 3). This, with the three private staithes just upstream and John Browne's at the brewery downstream, effectively formed the head of navigation for mercantile purposes on the Coltishall bank until that vital role was lost when the Aylsham waterway opened.

A succession of local businesses failed shortly afterwards. The death of Joseph Browne in 1780 at the age of 49, less than six months after the full opening to Aylsham and with his affairs 'desperate', in Mary Hardy's words, has already been described. The powerful brewer Chapman Ives, one of East Anglia's leading manufacturers, also fell on hard times. He was twice bankrupted before dying aged 46. Economic activity slowed at Coltishall.[1]

[1] *Browne and Ives* See vol. 2, chap. 8. Both men were from malting and brewing dynasties in the village. The consequences of the navigation generally for Coltishall are described later in this chapter.

Although the Hardys' property, owned by John Wells, and Mrs Smith's, which she let to the Glover family in the 1770s, had staithes they did not handle the same level of business as the two downriver.

Horstead had farm staithes and marlpit staithes downstream of its manor house: see the map at the chapter frontispiece (p. 62)

[1] *surveys* P. Holman, 'The Bure Navigation 1779–1912', in *A Backwards Glance: Events in Aylsham's Past*, ed. G. Gale *et al.* (Aylsham Local History Soc., 1995), unpag., complete with useful OS grid references. The society made a field survey and held an exhibition of photographs and their other findings in 1994.
The Norfolk Industrial Archaeology Society (NIAS) undertook a field survey in 1979, some gallantly taking

Planning the Aylsham navigation

The 'improvement' of the River Bure has fascinated local writers long since the waterway authorised by Parliament ceased to have much economic function. Its lock gates were smashed in floods following prolonged heavy rain in late August 1912, and the navigation was officially closed in 1928. Horstead and Coltishall once more resumed their old role as joint heads of the navigable river to Great Yarmouth.

Archival research fails to do full justice to the navigation, and all those publishing on the subject in recent decades have experienced the need to get out and explore. As well as the fieldwork in preparation for the 2012 centenary, two very well documented surveys were made, in 1994 and before then in 1979, by members of local societies prepared to get more than just their feet wet.[1] They were stepping in the footprints of H.A. Biedermann in 1772.

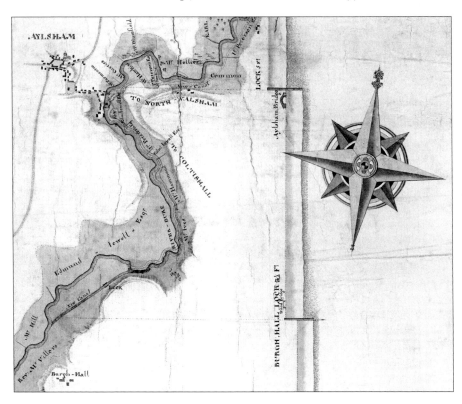

right Buxton Mill from downstream, along the channel from the millpool; the cut to the former lock lies out of sight to the right.

One of the wherries in the flotilla sailing from Coltishall on 20 Oct. 1779, the day the navigation was opened fully to Aylsham, capsized just upstream of this point

below Burgh Mill from upstream, with its large millpond; the remains of the lock in its own cut lie a short way downriver. The Mermaid Stream joins the waterway near this point, long proving troublesome and causing the navigation to overtop its banks [*MB · 2002, 2004*]

facing page Part of H.A. Biedermann's plan of 1772 for the projected Aylsham navigation. Still held at Aylsham it is a very skilled piece of work, nearly 5 feet long (1·5 metres), by the German surveyor still in his twenties.

Combining a mass of information with elegance and restrained colouring, it is shown in full at *plates 10, 11*. Its graphic design has some of the qualities of the most stylish draughtsmen of their day, William Playfair and Charles Joseph Minard.

It plots the bridges and drops at the locks in a vertical axis alongside their position on the course of the waterway. A proposed lock canal, never built, is shown here at Burgh Hall. A busy waterside settlement very soon developed along Millgate and Dunkirk, north-east of Aylsham town centre [*Aylsham Town Council, detail*]

Biedermann's plan, created after his initial survey, is a work of beauty and ingenuity and is seen in full in the colour section. A plan of the proposed navigation or canal formed a necessary accompaniment when presenting a Bill before Parliament, and this skilful young surveyor from the Harz Mountains packed a huge amount of information into his. It was at first envisaged that the navigation would extend

to canoes which sank at Aylsham. I am grateful to NIAS's records officer Derek Manning and to John Renton of Norwich's Bridewell Museum for letting me examine the papers

right The mural tablet in the chancel of
Aylsham Church to the local attorney John
Adey (1736–1809), drafter of the 1773 Bill and
Clerk to the Commissioners of the Aylsham
navigation. His wife Dorothy (d.1822) was
the daughter of the Collector of Norwich,
one of the two top excise officers in Norfolk,
and sister to Humphry Repton   [*MB · 2006*]

facing page, bottom John Adey regularly
alerted subscribers to meetings and other
developments—including pleas for further
injections of cash. The Commissioners met
monthly at the Black Boys in the town
[*Norwich Mercury, 21 July 1781: Norfolk
Heritage Centre, Norwich*]

SACRED TO THE MEMORY OF
JOHN ADEY, ESQ.ᴿᴱ
FORMERLY OF LICHFIELD AND LATE OF THIS PLACE;
WHO DIED ON THE 4ᵀᴴ OF MAY 1809, AGED 73 YEARS.

AND OF DOROTHY ADEY, HIS WIDOW,
WHO WAS THE DAUGHTER OF JOHN REPTON, ESQ.ᴿᴱ OF NORWICH,
AND WHO DIED ON THE 21ᵀ OF APRIL 1822, AGED 75.

THE UNION OF THIS AFFECTIONATE PAIR
WAS BLESS'D
WITH AN UNINTERRUPTED HAPPINESS
OF THIRTY NINE YEARS.

---

[1] *locks* The plan and its
subsequent alterations,
drafting of the Bill and
the original backers are
covered with a wealth
of illustrations in S.
Spooner, ed., *Sail and
Storm*, pp. 11–36

[2] *optimism* The open-
ing of the navigable
Waveney to Bungay in
the 1670s could have
inspired them (see table
4.2.1 on p. 111).

It had also early been
proposed to link the
Waveney and Lt Ouse
in 1656; a later hope of
1818 was to link Diss to
Bungay. As always,
obtaining a 'large and
cheap supply of coal'
other than by costly
land carriage proved
the spur; local marl and
timber could also be
moved more cheaply
(C. Barringer, *Exploring
the Norfolk Market Town*
(Poppyland Publishing,
Cromer, 2011), p. 43)

beyond Aylsham to Ingworth Bridge, a county bridge later
carrying the Cromer turnpike, but this idea was dropped
early. Biedermann calculated a drop of 35 feet (10·7 metres)
from Ingworth to Coltishall. In the end only five locks were
built: at Aylsham below the town, Burgh (near the watermill), Oxnead, Buxton and Coltishall/Horstead. Another
two, proposed at Burgh Hall and between Aylsham and
Ingworth, were never built, largely on grounds of economy.[1]

Biedermann lived in an age of optimism and vision, when
great projects captured the imagination of those with the
power and the purses (sometimes) to carry them through.[2]
As soon as Aylsham started to dust off its old survey and
proposals from much earlier in the century the market town
of North Walsham, seven miles away, caught the mood of its
neighbour and competitor. When not a spadeful of soil had
been dug for the Aylsham scheme Sir Harbord Harbord, Bt,
of Gunton Hall, MP for Norwich and later 1st Lord Suffield,
chaired a meeting at North Walsham on 30 November 1773
in support of a navigation of their own (opposite). The plan
and estimate were already complete, and a subscription
book had been opened. The town had to wait until 1826.

Aylsham was fortunate to have the Staffordshire-born
attorney John Adey as Clerk to the Commissioners. Hardworking and astute, and despite all the other calls on his
time, he oversaw the progress of the Bill, liaised with London and supervised much of the day-to-day business.

WICH MER

CHASE, in the C

FRIDAY, *December* 24, 1773.

A foreign paper mentions that, among the papers of the Ex-jesuits at Rome, it was found that that Society have kept a correspondence with the King of Prussia for many years past, and, foreseeing their present fate, had remitted their money and best effects to Berlin, on the royal promise of protection.

There has lately been discovered in the neighbourhood of Neusolh, in Hungary, a rich silver mine, the veins of which are not more than ten fathom deep. Miners are set to work, and great things are promised from it. In another Canton a gold mine has been discovered, and the Jews who are seated near it have received orders to retire ten leagues from the spot.

Letters from Vienna advise, that the Empress Queen having expressed an earnest desire to know whether the practice of burying the dead in churches was really hurtful, Mr. J. Habermann had just published a dissertation, entitled *De Salubri Sepultura*, wherein he proves that "this custom being indecent, barbarous, and often dangerous, ought to be abolished."

Yesterday was held a Court of Lord-Mayor, Aldermen, and Common-council at Guildhall, in order to elect a Common Cryer for this City,

Lady K——N to her Daughter Mrs. G——T, with a Present of a Watch.

ACCEPT this watch, a toy at best,
Yet trifles wisdom may suggest.
Mark how each moment as 'tis past,
Brings you still nearer to your last.
Prompted by this well-going toy,
May you your moments so employ,
As that when time shall be no more,
You safe may reach the Heav'nly shore.

NORTHWALSHAM NAVIGATION.

AT a Meeting held on Tuesday the 30th of November last, at the Bear in Northwalsham, of Gentlemen and Others interested in the intended Navigation from Dilham to Northwalsham, a Plan of the said Navigation, with an Estimate of the Expence attending the same, was produced, laid before, and approved by them; which Plan and Estimate, with a Book for entering Subscriptions are left in the Hands of John Howse, of Northwalsham, for the Inspection of all Persons interested in, or inclined to promote the Execution of the Plan, who are requested to call on him previous to the next Meeting, which will be held on Tuesday the 28th of December inst. at Eleven o'Clock in the Forenoon, at the Bear abovementioned.

Sir HARBORD HARBORD, Bart. in the Chair

AYLSHAM, July 18, 1781.
AYLSHAM NAVIGATION.

NOTICE is hereby given, that the General Annual Meeting of the Commissioners (as by Act of Parliament directed) will be held at the Black Boys in Aylsham, on Wednesday, the first of August next, at Ten o'Clock in the Forenoon, to audit and settle the Treasurer's Account: And that the said Commissioners of the said Navigation will meet at the Black Boys in Aylsham upon the first Tuesday in every Month after August next, at Ten o'Clock in the Forenoon, until the General Annual Meeting to be held in August, 1782.

JOHN ADEY, Clerk to the Navigation.

above Eye-catchingly under the masthead, a notice on Christmas Eve 1773 invites examination of the proposals for a North Walsham navigation. The plan, estimate and subscribers' book were held by the attorney John Howse.

The Act was not passed until nearly 40 years later; the waterway did not open until 1826. The Aylsham navigation had itself been a century in gestation [*Norwich Mercury, 24 Dec. 1773: Norfolk Heritage Centre, Norwich*]

'A great advantage': the legislation authorising the Aylsham navigation 1773

source Extracts from the Act of Parliament 13 Geo. III cap. 37 [1]

AN ACT FOR MAKING AND EXTENDING the Navigation of the River Bure (commonly called the North River) by and from Coltishall to Aylsham Bridge, in the County of Norfolk

PREAMBLE

Whereas the River Bure ... is navigable for boats and other vessels from the town of Great Yarmouth to the town of Coltishall: and whereas the said river is capable of being made navigable up to a bridge near the town of Aylsham called Aylsham Bridge: and whereas the extending the navigation of the said river by and from the said town of Coltishall to Aylsham Bridge aforesaid will be a great advantage to the said county of Norfolk, and the public in general ...

PERSONS TO PAY TOLL ON THE CANAL

[1] *the Act* These brief extracts from the Act of 1773 authorising the navigation are helpful in establishing the nature of the waterborne trade above Coltishall, as envisaged by champions of the navigation, in the year in which the diary opened. The provisions relate only to the navigation and not to the 32 miles of the tidal River Bure from Coltishall Lock to Gt Yarmouth.

The Act shows that the original scheme to create an 11-mile waterway to Ingworth, above Aylsham, had been abandoned. The upper limit is Aylsham Bridge, near the watermill

[2] *terras* Earths (a legal term). Marl and clay would normally have been included in the term, but the legislators specifically exempted them from toll

And, for defraying the necessary expenses of putting this Act in execution, be it further enacted that at such place or places upon or adjoining to the said river, navigable cuts, canals, trenches, or passages, as the said Commissioners, or any seven or more of them, shall ... appoint, there shall be paid to the Collector or Collectors to be nominated as hereinafter is directed, by all and every person and persons who shall carry or convey any goods, wares, merchandises, or commodities whatsoever (except as hereinafter excepted) up or down the said river, or any of the said navigable cuts, canals, trenches, or passages, such sum and sums of money as and for a toll as the said Commissioners ... shall think proper to appoint, not exceeding the sums following; that is to say,

THE TOLLS

For every ton weight of coals, cinders, bricks, pavements, tiles, lime, and terras,[2] the sum of one shilling; and for every ton weight of corn, grain, meal, flour, timber, goods, wares, merchandises, or commodities whatsoever, not before enumerated, the sum of one shilling and sixpence; and so in proportion for any greater or lesser weight than a ton ...

MANURE ETC EXEMPTED FROM TOLLS

Provided always, and be it further enacted, that no toll shall be demanded or taken at any lock or locks to be erected by virtue of this Act for any boat, barge, or any other vessel, which shall be loaded with any straw, muck, marl, clay, or any other materials to be used in the improving or manuring of lands only, nor for any such boat, barge, or other vessel, laden with materials for the repair of any mill or mills upon the said river; anything in this Act contained to the contrary notwithstanding ...

'A great advantage': the legislation authorising the navigation 1773 *(cont.)*

OWNERS OF VESSELS TO GIVE ACCOUNT OF LADING

And for the more easy collecting the said tolls herein before granted, be it further enacted that every person having the charge of any boat, barge, or vessel passing on the said river, navigable cuts, canals, trenches, or passages, shall give a true report ... of the quantity, quality, and weight of the goods, wares, merchandises, and commodities, which shall be in or belonging to such boats, barge, or vessel ...

OWNERS TO PLACE THEIR NAMES AND ABODES ON THEIR BOATS

And be it further enacted that the owner or owners of any boat, barge, or vessel, passing upon the said river, navigable cuts, canals, trenches, or passages, shall cause his, her, or their name or names, place and places of abode, at full length, to be placed and set in large capital letters, four inches long, and broad in proportion, on the upper part of the boat, on both sides of every such boat, barge, or vessel, and painted white, so that the same shall, from time to time, and at all times, be plain and legible; and shall also permit and suffer every such boat, barge, or vessel, to be measured, whenever it shall be required by the said Commissioners, or any seven or more of them, or such person or persons as shall be appointed by them ...

OWNERS AND OCCUPIERS OF LANDS ADJOINING MAY USE PLEASURE BOATS

Provided also, and be it further enacted, that it shall and may be lawful for the owners and occupiers of any lands or tenements adjoining to the said river, cuts, canals, trenches, or passages ... to use any pleasure boat or boats upon the same ... without paying any of the tolls aforesaid, so as such pleasure boat shall not be used in carrying any goods, wares, or merchandises charged or chargeable with any of the tolls by this Act granted and made payable ...

LORDS OF MANORS MAY ERECT WAREHOUSES ETC

Provided also, and be it further enacted, that nothing in this Act contained shall be construed to obstruct or hinder the lord or lords of the manor or manors, or the owner or owners of the lands or grounds lying upon or near the banks of the said river, or any of the lands or grounds through which the said river, cuts, canals, trenches, or passages shall be made, from making or erecting any warehouses, weigh-beams, cranes, quays, landing places, or wharfs upon the banks of the said river ... in or upon their own lands, wastes, or grounds, or erecting any bridge or bridges over the said river ... or sinking or laying any pipe, arch, or conduit under the said river ... so that the erecting or using such warehouses, cranes or wharfs, bridge or bridges, pipe, arch or conduit do not obstruct or prejudice the said navigation ...

facing page '... large capital letters, four inches inches long, and broad in proportion ...'

Owners of wherries in the 21st century do not have to comply with the Act, but ornate artwork often appears on the boards in the bows—as seen here with *Maud* [*Roger Bird 2000*]

below '... making or erecting any warehouses, weigh-beams, cranes, quays ... upon the banks of the said river ...'

A small warehouse on the riverbank at Coltishall Manor House, a short way downstream of the start of the navigation. Secure warehouses were vital for trade [*MB · 1989*]

1 *Henry Smith* (1710–88), an attorney, like his father Henry. For details see the note to *Diary 1*: 7 Dec. 1773

2 *Watts* Henry Palmer Watts snr (d.1780), copyholder of King's College, Cambridge at Hallbergh (now Horstead House) and their tenant at the mill

3 *letter* King's Coll.: KCAR/6/2/38/9, COL/517. The original sketch by Henry Smith has survived, but while clearing the muniments room at King's in 1911 Mr F. L. Clarke typed copies of many documents before destroying the originals, his typed version being transcribed here.

I am most grateful to the Provost and Scholars of King's for their permission to consult the college records, and to Dr Michael Halls and Dr Rosalind Moad of King's and Mr A.E.B. Owen of the Cambridge University Library for enabling me to work in the archives since 1990

4 *Master of Caius* John Smith (bapt. Coltishall 14 Oct. 1711, d. 17 June 1795, bur. Caius Chapel, Cambridge); educ. Norwich School and Eton, adm. Caius College, Cambridge 1732, BA 1735–6, MA 1739, DD 1764, Fellow 1739–44, Master 1764–95, Vice-Chancellor of Cam-

Keeping Cambridge informed—or in the dark

King's College, Cambridge had been lords of the manors of Coltishall and Horstead since the mid-fifteenth century, the college archives yielding a wealth of information on both parishes. They have rather less on the navigation, for a reason. Their manor court steward, Henry Smith, was keeping them in the dark.[1] A prominent lawyer, who makes many appearances in Mary Hardy's diary, he lived next to the White Horse at Great Hautbois upstream of Coltishall Bridge—and would benefit from coals brought to his door.

It might have been expected that Lawyer Smith would be keeping the manorial lords informed of what was afoot. Biedermann's plan shows that the new canal and Coltishall Lock were to be carved out of the edge of the common owned by the college. But, given the location of his home, Henry Smith was in danger of suffering from a conflict of interest. He penned a remarkable letter to the college bursar in which he dismissed the proposed works as trivial and of little significance. At the end of 1773 Mr Paddon learned, seemingly for the first time, about the route of the new cut:

Sir, The Commissioners [of the navigation], acting under an Act for extending a navigation from Coltishall to Aylsham, desired me to acquaint your Society [King's] that in order to pass by Horstead Mill belonging to your Society and in the possession of Mr Watts,[2] it is necessary to fix a sluice just above the Mill on Coltishall Common, and to take off the said common 37 rods or perches, and so go on down a water ditch (to be enlarged by them) dividing the meadow belonging to the mill, as by the sketch on the other side: the gentlemen did not think proper to do anything without previously informing your Society with it, and Mr Watts is likewise acquainted with it; the affair is of such little consequence, that the Commissioners do not in the least doubt of their [the Provost and Fellows'] free consent, and the small piece of land will be laid to the Mill Meadow; you will be kind enough to inform the Provost and your Society with it, as soon as may be, and if consistent [?consentient], should be glad of an answer against the Commissioners' next meeting, which I think will be on Tuesday s'e'nnight, which will be esteemed a favour,

By your very humble servant

HENRY SMITH

Coltishall, 27th December 1773 [3]

NB If any further explanation necessary, be so obliging to call on the Master of Caius College who is well acquainted with the situation.[4]

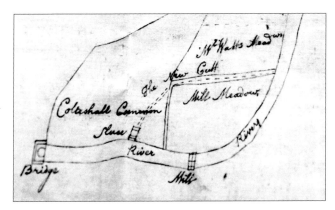

above Coltishall: the lawyer Henry Smith's sketch map, on the back of his letter of 27 Dec. 1773 to King's College. He explains, extremely tardily, what was being proposed across their land.

Oriented (loosely) east, it shows the drain across Upper or West Common which probably relieved pressure on Horstead Watermill when river levels upstream were high. This drain had to be enlarged to create the new lock canal, 'The New Cutt'.

Its upper section had to be re-sited a short way upstream, as denoted by the double dotted lines, so that vessels stayed clear of the powerful pull from the mill leat.

Unaccountably, and perhaps intending to deceive, the college's manor court steward describes the proposed lock as a sluice. He deliberately plays down the significance of the proposal: 'the affair is of such little consequence . . .'
[*courtesy the Provost and Scholars of King's College, Cambridge:* KCAR/6/2/38/9, COL/517, *detail*]

bridge 1766–67. Priest Norwich 1739, Curate of Coltishall; Lowndean Professor of Astronomy 1771–95, Chancellor of Lincoln (*Alum. Cantab.*).

The brothers had been brought up on the spot. The Smith family lived at Point House, Gt Hautbois (vol. 3, *plate 30*—the fine 18th-century house on the main road just north of Coltishall Bridge), and Cockerells—the 16th-century house, later the Norfolk Mead Hotel (p. 71 in this chapter)

above King's College, Cambridge: the view to the 15th-century chapel from the muniments room where the Horstead and Coltishall manorial archives are housed   [*MB · 2012*]

There is guile, even effrontery, behind the lawyer's words. The college owned the watermill at Horstead, the manor houses at Horstead and Coltishall very close to the existing head of navigation (all three properties being threatened economically), and also the common at Coltishall which was to be cut into by the canal. It was not proposed to 'fix a sluice', but to dig a deep lock for trading vessels. The new cut, while in strict truth being built along the course of a meadow drain, was very considerably to widen this 'ditch'.

The college, out of term, was required to take a decision on the matter in less than a week—allowing for delivery of two letters. Further, the college head, the Provost of King's, was invited to be thankful that he had been consulted at all.

¹ *staked out* Aylsham
Town Council, Box 36:
Commissioners' minute
book 1772–1811, meet-
ing of 10 Aug. 1774

² *robbery* *Norw. Merc.*
11 Feb. 1775 [my italics].
This notice appeared at
the time Mary Hardy
was noting visits to see
progress at the lock on
29 Nov. 1774 and 26
Feb. 1775 (*Diary 1*).

Joseph Smith has a
fine ledger stone in the
sanctuary of Coltishall
Church. The ledger
stone of his brother
Henry, the lawyer and
court steward, lies
between the south door
and the font where
both were baptised

To cap it all the Bursar of King's was summarily despatched
up the road to consult the Master of Caius, who happened
to be Henry Smith's brother John.

The Cambridge college was not alone in this treatment.
Henry Smith's sister-in-law was Margaret, widow of his
youngest brother Joseph Smith. Her consent had still not
been obtained by August 1774, even though Biedermann
had by then staked out the route across her land: digging
the lock was to begin in November 1774.¹ Mrs Smith lived
in Cambridge, renting her property to the Hardys' neighbours Edward and Sarah Glover, featured in the diary. The
Glovers were soon to have their own problems as a consequence of the digging of the canal across the land they
occupied. Their new river frontage brought its irritations:

> Whereas the fowl house of Mr Edward Glover, of Coltishall, was,
> in the night of Thursday the 26th of January last, broke open and
> robb'd of eleven fowls: This is to give notice, that a man trap will
> be set every night either about the dwelling-house, outhouses or
> yards, *and to forewarn all persons that come by water*, in crossing the
> meadows or yards, as they will be liable to be caught.²

The building had begun.

---

right **Gt Hautbois to Coltishall
and Horstead: the most downstream section of Biedermann's
plan of 1772.** A drop of 5 feet (1·5
metres) is shown for the lock; the
canal is to cut across the common.
Riparian owners include Henry
Smith, with his very long frontage
north from the bridge. John Wells,
from whom the Hardys rented
their house, maltings, brewery and
land, owned fields [Sergeant Close
and Sergeant Piece] along the navigation. John Ives (d.1766) is named
below the bridge [for Mill Close
and Mill Piece], but the owner
was his widow Rose (d.1780), for
whom Henry Smith acted. William
Hardy farmed all four fields
[*Aylsham Town Council, detail*]

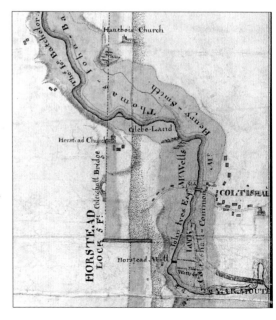

above A wherry raises her mast on leaving Coltishall Lock; vessels were not permitted to navigate locks under sail and had even to lower their masts. The footbridge just visible by the downstream gates enforced this rule as well as enabling pedestrians to reach the watermill from the common. The lock cottage was built in the mid-19th century. This view, dating from probably the late 19th century or early 20th, is taken looking downstream; the fork to Horstead Mill, along the old river, is glimpsed to the right.

At the next lock, Buxton, the wherry cut bypassing the mill was sited dangerously close to the millpond. The resulting currents may have caused the capsizing of the wherry on the opening day in 1779, as related by Mary Hardy   [*Norfolk Rural Life Museum*]

Building the navigation

Progress on constructing the navigation can be monitored through the commissioners' records held at Aylsham Town Hall, the notices they placed in the local newspapers, and the pages of Mary Hardy's diary. Local disquiet over the project can be found in the manorial archives at King's.

Important meetings were held after the Act had passed in 1773.[1] The landowners whose lands were to be cut through were invited to Aylsham to negotiate the sale of their property. At the same time contractors were being engaged:

AYLSHAM NAVIGATION. The next meeting of the Commissioners[2] will be held on Tuesday next the 21st of December, at ten in the forenoon, at the Black Boys in Aylsham, when the proprietors of

[1] *Act* It received the Royal Assent on 7 Apr. 1773

[2] *Commissioners* In Aug. 1773 the 15 men included Lord Walpole (of Wolterton), Robert Marsham snr and jnr (of Stratton Strawless), William Wiggett Bulwer (of Heydon), Peter Elwin jnr (of Booton) and Revd Richard Baker (Rector of

Cawston). Thomas Durrant (d.1790 aged 56), JP, Bt 1784, of Scottow Hall, became as active and conscientious a treasurer to the navigation as he was as secretary to the governors of N. Walsham's Free Grammar School (vol. 1, chap. 6). The scheme's backers were too exalted to be part of the Hardys' circle, but the brewer would have encountered many, as JPs, at licensing sessions

---

1 *staked out Norfolk Chronicle,* 11 Dec. 1773

2 *tendering* R. Malster, *Wherries and Waterways* (Terence Dalton, Lavenham, 1971), p. 27. By 16 June 1774 the figure was £4200, not including the building of a new bridge at Mayton, a new road at Buxton Mill and a quay at Aylsham (Aylsham Town Council: Box 36, minute book)

---

right Honing's deep lock on the old N. Walsham and Dilham Canal, seen from downstream; sluices now control the flow. The Aylsham navigation's locks gave a great deal of trouble, with skippers of keels and wherries passing through at night and breaking the gates [*Christopher Bird 1989*]

the lands now staked out, and intended to be cut through, are requested to attend and agree with the Commissioners for the sale thereof.

And all persons willing to contract for digging the canals, or any part of them, or for depthening [deepening] the river, are desired before the said meeting to send their proposals in writing to Mr John Adey of Aylsham, Clerk to the said Navigation. Lord WAL-POLE in the Chair. 1

Work began in the expectation of a total expenditure of £4006 5s 4½d, Biedermann's estimate being described by Robert Malster as 'a nice if inaccurate piece of tendering'. 2 No reports of progress were made in the local papers apart from occasional brief statements in notices by the Clerk to the Commissioners when summoning a meeting, but the treasurer's payments and Mary Hardy's occasional references provide insight into the way the work was going in the early period of the navigation.

The Commissioners' minute book opens on 15 December 1772. The account book of the navigation's treasurer opens on 23 November 1773, five days before Mary Hardy began her diary in the house immediately downstream of the lock cut. Over the coming months Thomas Durrant neatly listed

all the subscribers with the date and amount of their donations; many were riparian owners upstream of Coltishall.[1]
Biedermann, the engineer as well as surveyor, appears to
have been in charge of paying the workmen on the navigation, the sums issued to the surveyor weekly in December
1774 being one of £50 and three of £30. A separate contractor, James Frost of Norwich, was engaged for Coltishall
Lock itself, undertaking the work on 25 June 1774 for the
sum of £560.[2] Frost was paid £130 at the end of 1774 and
an additional sum of £84 on 20 February 1775; he was paid
in full on 30 December 1774.[3]

These accounts record payments to local men, some of
them familiar from Mary Hardy's diary. Thomas Fuller
provided the lime in the opening years, while the Horstead
farmer John Pike sold marl and clay (presumably for lining
or puddling the river bed along the new cuts and for the
lock). Another Horstead farmer Stephen Hammond helped
with masonry work.

The diarist and her friends found the work on Coltishall
Lock a source of some interest. The Hardys went to check
on progress in November 1774 in the company of their close
friends, the master of Coltishall Free School John Smith and
his wife and daughter. The labourers digging the lock had
evidently repaired to the nearest public house, the White
Horse, Great Hautbois, where Thomas Neve was innkeeper;
he had not yet ventured into the timber trade which was to
plunge him into financial ruin. Neve's brewer was Rose Ives
of Coltishall, who provided the men with a barrel of beer.
The Hardys brought them bottles of gin:

[1774] NOVEMBER 29, TUESDAY . . . Mr and Mrs and Miss Smith
went with us to the new river to see the lock, carried the men two
bottles of gin. Mrs Ives gave the men a barrel of beer at T. Neve's
and he forced them to drink it abroad . . .[4]

Evidently the innkeeper did not want to have the muddy
boots of the workmen in his parlour. During the construction stage the public houses nearest the navigation would
have become miniature offices of works. Biedermann would
have struck up a close working relationship with the innkeepers, and it was at the White Horse in 1778 that Mary
Hardy met Biedermann and his English wife Mary.[5]

[1] *subscribers* Aylsham
Town Council: Box 34,
Account book. These
aspects of the project
are comprehensively
covered in Desmond
Best's thesis 'The
Aylsham Navigation'
and in Sarah Spooner's
Sail and Storm

[2] *Frost* Aylsham Town
Council: Box 36. Frost,
a builder and joiner,
was also a valuer who
handled the sale of the
stock of the timber
merchants George
Boorne and Thomas
Neve, formerly con-
tractors to the naviga-
tion, at Coltishall in
1781 (*Diary 1*: 1 Feb.,
7 Feb., 11 Feb. 1781)

[3] *Coltishall Lock* Aylsham Town Council:
Box 34

[4] *gin Diary 1*. 'Abroad'
means outside; in the
open.
   The Free School
Smiths were not related
to Henry or Margaret
Smith. The Hardy boys
attended the school at
the church crossroads.
   Rose Ives owned one
of Coltishall's three
breweries during her
son Chapman's minor-
ity (vol. 2, chap. 8)

[5] *Biedermann Diary 1*:
20 Aug. 1778. The
name gave her some
difficulty, and she
renders it 'Biddemon'.
   He would have been
there for old time's
sake, his work on the
project having ended

[1] *barrows* Aylsham Town Council: Box 36, minutes, 25 June 1774

[2] *labourer's pay* See vol. 2, chap. 1

[3] *Royal Military Canal* B. Lavery, *We shall fight on the Beaches: Defying Napoleon and Hitler, 1805 and 1940* (Conway, London, 2009), p. 176. The soldiers building the canal had 2s a day plus their normal wages and their rations. The canal, 60 feet wide (18·25 metres), ran 28 miles just inland from the south coast: see P.A.L.Vine, *The Royal Military Canal: An historical account of the waterway and military road from Shorncliffe in Kent to Cliff End in Sussex* (Amberley Publishing, Stroud, 2010)

[4] *work* A. Burton, *The Canal Builders* (2nd edn David & Charles, Newton Abbot, 1981), p. 192. He gives general rates of pay as about 12d a day in 1770, rising by 1793 to 2s 6d a day (p. 200). (The farm labourer saw no comparable rise.) In one day a navigator could dig a trench 3 feet wide, 3 feet deep and 36 feet long (nearly 1 metre by 1 metre by 11 metres) (p. 158). The book sets out the national picture, with a building chronology and the various problems which could arise

Mary Hardy's entry that November day in 1774 is of significance as being one of very few references—indeed perhaps the sole reference—to the men who actually built the navigation. The Aylsham archives reveal something of the contractors and sub-contractors, but the labourers were not paid directly by the treasurer or dealt with by the clerk and thus do not flit across the pages at all. Only a brief direction by the Commissioners to Mr Biedermann to collect a set of barrows at the start of digging in June 1774 testifies to the manual labour by which the navigation was built.[1]

The Norwich newspapers had nothing to say about the navigators or, as they were later known, the 'navvies' who carried out the gruelling manual work. This absence of comment does at least suggest there were no major incidents or brawls with local men. The 1770s were long before migrant labour was employed to build the later canals and the railways. The men given beer and gin by the Coltishall brewers are likely to have been local men themselves, known and trusted by the contractors and paid the statutory day labourer's rates for winter and summer hours, as laid down in the justices' manual: variously 12d (1s) to 16d a day.[2]

If so, the pay of the men building the navigation was a very far cry indeed from that of the builders of the costly project known as the Royal Military Canal, carved out at great speed across Kent and Sussex to protect England from Napoleon. It was an unusual enterprise, being one of only two waterways built in Great Britain by the Government. Perhaps as they were under the control of the military rather than the magistrates at a time of national crisis, the civilian labourers received about five times the statutory rate: 5s 6d a day, not 1s 3d, totalling an astonishing £1 13s a week as opposed to the more usual 7s or 7s 6d for a six-day week.[3] The exhausting tasks of the canal builder are listed by Anthony Burton: digging out the new cuts, dredging and deepening the existing waterways, working the barrow runs, filling and emptying the lighters carrying the spoil, and puddling—lining the bed and sides with clay to provide a non-porous membrane.[4]

The Smiths and Hardys visited Coltishall Lock again on 26 February 1775, shortly before Mary Hardy recorded the

left Geldeston Lock, also known as Shipmeadow Lock; a wherry with lowered mast passes through. This was the most downstream of the locks on the Waveney navigation to Bungay authorised in 1670 [*painting by J. Stark; engraving by W. Forrest 1831, detail*]

below The disused Geldeston Lock today, its old brick walls smothered in vegetation   [*MB · 2014*]

opening of the lock to river traffic (to just below Buxton) on Thursday 16 March 1775. With her husband and two of their ploughmen Zeb Rouse and Robert Manning at work in a field on the Horstead riverbank above Coltishall Bridge, she made the sole record to have survived giving the date and the name of the first vessel to negotiate the lock: 'Mr Ansell's *Grampus* went through the new lock today, being the first that ever went through that lock.'[1] The wherry *Grampus*, belonging to the Coltishall plumber, glazier, auctioneer and valuer Robert Ansell, was also the first to enter the completed navigation four years later, as quoted at the beginning of this chapter.

The Commissioners and the engineer had to be flexible over making last-minute alterations. Months after the route had been agreed, and a little over three weeks before Coltishall Lock opened, Henry Palmer Watts of Horstead took out a legal agreement with the Commissioners and the treasurer under which, for a fee of £50, Mr Watts regularised the existence of a navigable cut made at his request linking the millpool directly to the lock canal; it was formed out of lands belonging to King's College, Mr Watts and Mrs Margaret Smith. Mr Watts thereby secured right of passage for his boats, free from toll or charge as it was tidal, in the area of his staithe and mill along the 'old river' and along the lockstream. The link channel may also have allowed his wherries to take a short cut from the mill to the lock.[2]

[1] *Grampus Diary 1*: 16 Mar. 1775

[2] *Watts* NRO: BRA 926/XIII/28, 110x1, Tripartite indenture of 21 Feb. 1775, with one-year lease of meadow land owned by Henry Palmer Watts and Mrs Margaret Smith, 20 Feb. 1775. His link cut still exists.

The indenture refers to 'a small island' bounded by the dual streams to the mill and lock. This island, now thickly planted, was formed out of Mill Meadow and Watts's meadow on the north bank of the old river

right Horstead: the old river, now the mill-stream, winding east from the millpool. This section of the old Bure lies just upstream of the 'mansion', Horstead House, shown on Corby's estate map of 1811. Henry Palmer Watts' Mill Meadow, leased from King's and from 1774 part of an island, is seen on the far side of the fast-flowing stream   [*MB · 2011*]

¹ *remains* Aylsham Town Council: Box 34

² *lock design* Aylsham Town Council: Box 36, minutes, 16 June 1774.

Coltishall lies on the north-east bank of the Bure and Horstead on the south-west. The lock east of the water-mill is generally known as Coltishall Lock and the mill as Horstead Mill; the bridge has been called over the years by either name

³ *Biedermann* The surveyor and engineer was not forgotten following his departure for the West Country, the *Norwich Mercury* reporting 31 May 1800 that the daughter of Henry Augustus Biedermann, of Tetbury, Gloucs, and formerly of Woodbastwick, Norfolk, had just been married at Tetbury

Weekly payments, usually of £50, continued to Biedermann throughout most of 1775. On 2 August 1775 the treasurer made this alarming calculation:

Total received on account of Navigation	£4376	5s	0d
Expended on the other side	£4131	7s	4½d
Remains in the Treasurer's hands	£ 244	17s	7½d ¹

Expenditure had exceeded Biedermann's original estimate. Yet only one of the seven locks he marked on his plan had been completed. With no expertise locally, the last navigation in this part of the world having been built in the 1670s, the lock design was modelled on an unnamed one visited in Suffolk.²

The last payment by the Commissioners was made to Biedermann on 3 November 1775, after which he no longer appears in the Aylsham records. He moved on, evidently keeping in touch with his old friends Thomas and Mary Neve at the White Horse. Mary Hardy does not refer to him again after their encounter in the summer of 1778.³

Mounting problems

Toll income started to trickle in to the Commissioners' accounts from 22 August 1775. William Pepper of Buxton Watermill, one of the Commissioners, served as collector at first; John Colls, the miller at Horstead, took over as collector from 1778. But the sums were small. Even by 1778 the navigation was not proving a success, perhaps as it was finished only to below Buxton and because it was not at this stage deep enough to take other than small, shallow-draughted wherries. The sum of only £14 was collected in tolls for the period 20 August–26 September 1778, and £19 15s for the following period to 31 October.[1]

There were still massive outgoings, with new cuts being required near Burgh-next-Aylsham.[2] Also the materials for the locks underwent a change of plan, with expensive bricks being substituted for oak timber to line the walls. On his 1772 plan Biedermann had specified that the locks be lined with wood, showing only one as brick-lined (near Burgh Mill, and sited near a brickworks). However it seems that only Coltishall Lock was built of timber. All the others were

[1] *tolls* Aylsham Town Council: Box 34

[2] *new cuts* Summarised by P. Holman, 'The Bure Navigation 1779–1912', unpag.; also by S. Spooner, *Sail and Storm*, pp. 63–6

---

below left An early appearance of the name Bure for the river then known as the North River. The surveyor Samuel Bellard, who prepared a set of maps of Scottow and the surrounding area for Thomas Durrant's father Davy Durrant in 1742, here renders the name 'Buer'.

The river is pronounced locally 'Burr', rather than to rhyme with 'pure', perhaps as it rises in Burgh Parva near Melton Constable.

Mayton Bridge is here shown with a wide stream running under its twin arches; it was to be bypassed by the navigation.

Bellard (d.1763) became master of Coltishall Free School. He was probably the father-in-law of the contractor George Boorne, whose wife was Frances, née Bellard [NRO: MC 662/15/1, *Map by Samuel Bellard c.1742, with later pencilled annotations, detail*]

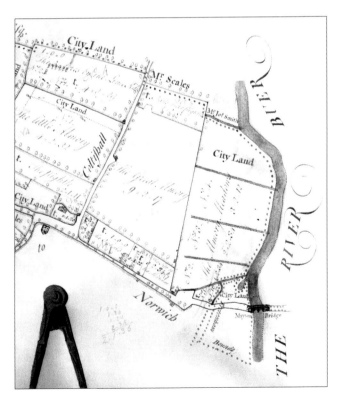

right The county bridge at Mayton had to be by-passed as vessels could not squeeze under it, such re-routing being very costly. The stream seen on the previous page was diminished to a trickle, as shown here [*drawing by F. Stone; lithograph by D. Hodgson 1831*]

¹ *Coltishall Lock* On 30 Nov. 1774, the day after the men were given their beer and gin, the Commissioners asked John Neve and his son John Neve jnr, both Coltishall carpenters, to 'inspect and give their opinion of the plank timber in the inside of the said lock whether the same is good sound heart of oak and free from sap' (Aylsham Town Council: Box 36, minutes). They must have been worried about it, as by 1778 they had determined to build brick-walled locks

² *Boorne* Aylsham Town Council: Box 36

³ *bricks Norw. Merc.* 7 Feb. 1778; later in the notice he emphasises the need for 'well-burnt bricks'. The Hardys used clinkers to line their malting cistern or the floor around it, as Henry Raven recorded (*Diary 3:* 11 Sept. 1797 and note)

brick-lined.¹ On 15 May 1774 the Commissioners entered into an agreement with George Boorne, who had newly given up shopkeeping to become a Coltishall timber merchant, that he should 'deliver at Buxton Mill . . . sufficient quantity of sound oak body-timber for completing a lock and bridge'.² Boorne, the Hardys' close friend, was to supply the wood for their own wherry in 1776 (chapter 4).

By early 1778 there had been a change of plan. Buxton Lock was to be built of brick, as made clear by the clerk John Adey in a press notice. The hard-burnt bricks on which he placed great emphasis were 'clinkers' or 'iron cinders', as used in brewhouses and wash houses and fired to a very high temperature to render them impervious to water:

AYLSHAM NAVIGATION. Any person having hard-burnt BRICKS, either red or white, are desired to send in their proposals before the 20th day of this instant February, to Mr JOHN ADEY, of Aylsham, for delivering of a sufficient quantity at Buxton Mills to build a lock there . . .³

The minutes convey a sense not of smooth, purposeful momentum but of faltering progress and, at times, high anxiety. The Commissioners had been in doubt as early as 23 August 1775, three weeks after Thomas Durrant's alarming calculations, whether to proceed with the navigation at all. John Colls of Horstead Mill was ordered to place a lock on Coltishall Lock to prevent its use by boats; and Biedermann was ordered to present a revised estimate. Meanwhile there were insufficient funds to pay the contractors, the Commissioners resolving on 20 September 1775 that George Boorne be paid only £100 'in part of £333 4s 11d' due to him for oak timber. (Four years later he was in deep financial trouble, William Hardy having to underwrite the partnership of Boorne and Thomas Neve, the former innkeeper, for £1000.) Not until 6 April 1778 did Boorne at last receive full payment, with 5 per cent interest from 1775.[1]

The Commissioners were slow with their payments in the early years as they had little toll income on which to draw. In this they were not alone, the finances of navigations pursuing a perilous course. It was generally financial problems, and not engineering ones, which delayed the construction of canals and navigations.[2] Even so, the Aylsham scheme with, in its revised form, five locks in the short space (for a flat region) of nine miles proved burdensome: 'The major obstacle facing the canal engineer was the change in the level of the ground.'[3]

Further trouble developed at Coltishall Lock (also known as Horstead Lock). Thomas Durrant desired the Commissioners to attend a meeting at the Black Boys at Aylsham on 6 July 1778 'to consider of the best method of making Horstead Lock passable'.[4] The previous year the gates had been broken and damaged by keelmen passing through at night, and on 15 December 1777 the Commissioners passed a bye-law forbidding vessels to pass through the lock between 8 pm and 6 am until 25 March 1778 and then between 10 pm and 4 am from 25 March until 29 September 1778, John Colls being responsible for locking the gates.[5]

The clerk John Adey announced some months later that Horstead Lock 'is now in good condition and the amount of the tolls, clear of all charges of collecting, from the 24th November 1777, the time of its opening, to the 31st October last (although it has been full two months in the summer impassable) is £106 4s 5½d'.[6]

With Biedermann's departure overall supervision of the work was probably lacking. On 14 October 1777 a new name appears in the minute book: that of John Smith, engineer, who had prepared a revised plan and, with £3600 already spent, declared that a further £2951 would be needed.[7] He was described, in a notice calling a meeting, as engineer to

[1] *Boorne* Aylsham Town Council: Box 36; *Diary 1*: 18 Feb. 1779 and numerous entries 16 Feb. 1779–7 Mar. 1781. His business was stopped 31 Jan. 1781

[2] *delays* A. Burton, *The Canal Builders*, p. 68.
As happened with the Aylsham scheme, the Act authorising the project set an upper limit of expenditure which became unrealistic as problems mounted (p. 68)

[3] *locks* A. Burton, *The Canal Builders*, p. 75

[4] *lock* Norw. Merc. 27 June 1778

[5] *locking gates* Aylsham Town Council: Box 36. Commissioners were empowered under the 1773 Act to make by-laws regulating the 'keelmen, watermen, and boatmen', ie the skippers and mates of wherries and, if they could fit into the locks, keels

[6] *toll income* Norw. Merc. 7 Nov. 1778. The date of 24 Nov. 1777 must refer not to the opening of the lock (recorded by Mary Hardy 2½ years earlier), but to the completion of the waterway as far as just below Buxton

[7] *Smith* Aylsham Town Council: Box 36. The figure of £3600 does not accord with Thomas Durrant's

balance sheet of 2 Aug. 1775 quoted earlier, stating that £4131 had been expended

---

[1] *estimate Norw. Merc.* 31 Jan. 1778; Aylsham Town Council: Box 36. There is nothing in the records to suggest that the canal engineer was related to any of the Coltishall families named Smith

[2] *Smith* J. Boyes and R. Russell, *The Canals of Eastern England* (David and Charles, Newton Abbot, 1977), pp. 198–201.
For the Leicester navigation on the Soar, see J. Priestley, *Historical Account of the Navigable Rivers, Canals, and Railways, throughout Great Britain* (David & Charles Reprints, Newton Abbot, 1969; 1st pub. 1831), pp. 578–80. As a 7-mile navigation with an additional 1½ miles of canal it was comparable to Aylsham. It proved lucrative once problems 1766–76 were solved as it fed into the Trent and linked into the Grand Union Canal

[3] *Northampton to Peterborough* See J. Priestley, *Historical Account of the Navigable Rivers*, pp. 463–5; 20 large locks were proposed

[4] *payments* Aylsham Town Council: Box 34

[5] *Mr Smith Diary* 1

the Loughborough navigation in Leicestershire, and it was announced that his 'estimate and model' had been accepted for completing the scheme from Buxton Lock (as yet unfinished) to Aylsham.[1] On 9 March 1778 he was formally appointed, the date of his articles of agreement being noted on the original plan of 1772 (*plate 11*).

The navigation which he had just been working on was the canalisation of the River Soar from Loughborough to Leicester, in the heart of the canal network. John Smith may have worked alongside the consulting engineer to that navigation and one of the foremost canal engineers of his time, William Jessop (1745–1814). Smith, from Attercliffe near Sheffield in Yorkshire, was the son of a canal engineer of the same name. John Smith junior had earlier been both engineer and contractor for the Nene navigation between Northampton and Peterborough, his skill in its construction being much praised in the years 1758–61.[2] This latter navigation was a massive undertaking requiring four Acts of Parliament and a whole series of new cuts.[3] The younger Smith had already been through the furnace before he came to deal with Aylsham's problems.

A payment of £160 was made to the new engineer on 4 August 1778 'in full for Horstead Lock', with a further £400 the following day, 'according to his contract'.[4] As with Biedermann, numerous regular payments were made to Smith in 1778, of £100 and £150, suggesting that he was once more paying the workmen who were digging the new cuts along the upper reaches of the navigation.

Mary Hardy had met John Smith months before his name appeared either in the press or in the minutes, and his visit to the Hardys with his family helps to identify the location of their house: their grounds and staithe commanded a view of the fork to the lock. The diarist noted on 11 July 1777 that 'A Mr Smith came to look at the lock and river; his wife and daughter came into our garden.'[5] This would have been when John Smith was familiarising himself with the area. Had the Hardys lived further downstream it was unlikely he would have called, for he could have examined the Bure easily from the open spaces near the King's Head. The reaches by the Manor House and upstream, however, were edged on the Coltishall bank by private staithes only.

Problems continued to mount. John Colls of Horstead Watermill, the toll collector on whose goodwill the Commissioners depended, declared in November 1778 that he had insufficient water to power his mill. High-water and low-water marks had to be erected on the upper gate posts at Coltishall Lock by agreement.[1] It was also arranged from 7 December 1779 that the sum of £30 a year had to be spent on dredging, as when the millers opened their gates in times of heavy rainfall this washed accumulated gravel, silt and rubbish into the stream.[2] The Upper Bure is fed by numerous headstreams called becks, and these too would have carried additional silt into the navigable waterway.

Worse was to follow, as the minutes for 14 September 1779 record:

. . . Mr John Smith, Engineer, having on or about the first day of this instant September deserted the work of the the said Navigation and left the county of Norfolk, *Ordered* that Mr John Adey cause advertizements to be immediately inserted in the York and one of the London newspapers for the said Mr John Smith to return and finish the said work . . . agreeable to his contract with the Commissioners . . . dated 9 March 1778.[3]

The absconding engineer, who was evidently suspected of returning to his home county, did return. John Green, the Wroxham builder who had called at the Hardys on the day John Smith inspected the river from their grounds,[4] now joined the project and saw it through to completion. Green agreed to enter into partnership with Smith, as minuted by the Commissioners on 31 March 1779.[5] The future of the great scheme to bring increased prosperity to the hinterland north and west of the former head of navigation was assured. The flotilla of trading vessels, with William Hardy on board, sailed—or quanted—into Aylsham less than seven months after the signing of the partnership.

Navigating the waterway

If we wander now along the banks of the waterway on a fine day we are presented with an attractive pastoral panorama. Cattle graze in lush meadows, showy wild flowers sway in the breeze on the river's edge, and clear streams nudge the old bridge piers (*plates 7, 8, 9*). But it is extremely doubt-

[1] *Colls* Aylsham Town Council: Box 36, 3 Nov. 1778. It was determined 'that the high-water mark be cut 13 inches lower than the upper side of the top bar of the upper gate and the low-water mark 6 inches lower as agreed' (33 cm and 15.25 cm).

These marks would have been similar to the one erected at Letheringsett Watermill in 1765 (illustrated in *Diary 2*, p. 172)

[2] *silt* Aylsham Town Council: Box 36. It was a common problem for feeder streams to introduce soil and debris into navigations (A. Burton, *The Canal Builders*, p. 80)

[3] *Smith* Aylsham Town Council: Box 36

[4] *Green Diary 1*: 11 July 1777. Years later he supplied the white bricks for Sheringham (p. 66). He was probably the John Green who in the 1770s designed Rollesby House of Industry, still standing in the Fleggs near Gt Yarmouth (A. Digby, *Pauper Palaces* (Routledge & Keegan Paul, London, 1978), p. 37).

The brick-kiln at Wroxham is marked on Faden's county map 1797 on the west bank of Wroxham Broad

[5] *partnership* Aylsham Town Council: Box 36

right The wherry *Albion*, built in 1898 and, like the keel *Trial* seen opposite, carrying 40 tons. She is decked overall on Coltishall Lower Common 26 Aug. 2012 after her voyage (from downstream) to commemorate the exact centenary of the ending of the Aylsham navigation [*MB · 2012*]

facing page The Gt Yarmouth register of keels and wherries on the Broads. In all, 156 vessels were registered 1795–98, by Act of Parliament.

The 40-ton keel *Trial*, home berth Panxworth (near S. Walsham), plies Aylsham to Gt Yarmouth with a skipper and a boy. The 58-ton keel *Royal Oak*, home berth Bungay, plies Bungay to Gt Yarmouth with a skipper and a mate. These sailed on the Aylsham and Waveney navigations.

Tonnage refers not to their displacement but to the capacity of the hold; it is 'tons burden' (chapter 4) [NRO: YC 38/3, *10 Aug. and 31 Aug. 1795*]

---

[1] *press gang Diary 1*: 8 Apr., 12 July 1777. The American war soon escalated into war with the French

ful whether the watermen who worked the navigation found it idyllic. It presented them with a set of hurdles they did not have to encounter on the tidal rivers of the Broads. The Hardys' 'wherry captains' make their appearance in chapter 4, where the Broadland vessels are also described. Here we try to answer the question of what was it like to take a boat up the nine miles of the navigation.

The skippers and, if they had them, their mates have not left us a written record in Mary Hardy's time at Coltishall. But we can visualise some of their difficulties. Firstly we can put names to them and their boats at the end of the century. As operators of commercial vessels on inland waterways they appear in person in the years 1795–98 to be recorded, with details of their craft, by the town clerk of Great Yarmouth.

These registers were being maintained around the country as it was a time of war. If watermen on the inland waterways were to avoid being pressed into the Royal Navy they needed proper protection from the press gang, and it was by means of the register that exemptions were certificated. As a result the names of the skipper and his mate or boy, not the vessel's owner, appear in the record (illustrated opposite). The press gang posed a real threat to those making a living on Norfolk's waterways, Mary Hardy twice referring to their operations as far upstream as Coltishall and Horstead, 32 miles from the sea, after the outbreak of the American war.[1]

As chapter 4 explains, the system was in place following the Quota Act of 1795: the French Revolutionary War 1793–1801 is the reason for the Yarmouth register's compilation. The Quota Acts were designed by William Pitt's government to supplement recruitment into the Royal Navy. But once the skipper or mate of a Norfolk keel or wherry had his name on the Yarmouth register he was granted a card of protection, which he needed to carry at all times to show he was exempt from pressing and from forming part of the county's quota of seamen.[1]

Unfortunately for these men their protection was dropped in new legislation in the more desperate times of 1798, and the register abruptly ends. Apart from those three years any skipper and crew approaching Yarmouth in wartime had more than weather, wind and tide to contend with, or the cargo's obstruction of their view. They feared impressment.

[1] *register* For vessels over 13 tons only, as set out further in chap. 4; the backdrop of fears of invasion and the civilian response is described in chap. 9.

The register yields very useful information: the names and standing of the crew ('waterman' here meaning a mate), the residence of the skipper (the 'master'), the vessel's type, name, capacity in tons, home berth and, crucially, the waters she customarily sailed (NRO: YC 38/3)

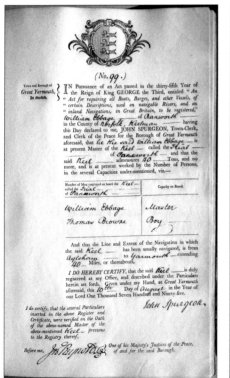

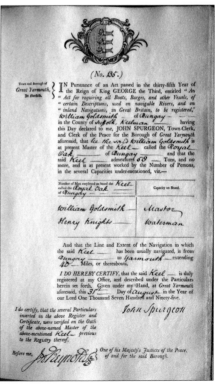

¹ *Dee-Dar* Pictured in chap. 4 and *plates 22, 23, 29*

² *Venture* No. 100 in the register: berthed at Panxworth, skipper William Noughton of Panxworth (sailing single-handed, this being a small vessel); entry dated 10 Aug. 1795 (NRO: YC 38/3)

³ *register* NRO: YC 38/3, nos 139, 145 and 147, dated 8 Sept., 10 Oct. and 23 Oct. 1795. Two of these wherries were berthed at Aylsham; *Oxnead* was berthed at Oxnead. All traded to Gt Yarmouth. Wherry

This invaluable register appears to be our only evidence that the Norfolk keel, with its centrally stepped mast and square sail, could get up the Aylsham navigation. Keels have frequently been portrayed as wide, ungainly, bluff-bowed, unmanageable tubs. Some were evidently slender, otherwise they could not have negotiated the locks. *Dee-Dar*, the only one to have survived into recent times until her demise in 2012, demonstrates that the keel could be slim in build and, probably, responsive in handling.[1] Two keels appear in the register as serving Aylsham: the 40-ton *Trial*, number 99 in the register (illustrated), and the 20-ton *Venture*.[2]

Wherries too were registered as plying the Aylsham navigation. Clement Cook of Horning had the 36-ton wherry *Olive Branch*, which he worked Aylsham–Yarmouth with the boy Charles Cook. John Maidstone of Aylsham had the 18-ton wherry *Brothers*, with James Moore as boy. William Spinks of Aylsham skippered *Oxnead*, with John Moore as boy.[3]

right Plantation Bridge, near Oxnead Hall. This accommodation bridge, which is not depicted on Biedermann's original plan, was built to provide ease of movement around the farm. The piers are set close, leaving only a narrow gap for keelmen and wherrymen to squeeze through.

Oxnead Hall, built in the 1580s and with 79 rooms a century later, was 'the sweetest place in the world' for Sir Robert Paston, 1st Earl of Yarmouth. It has a haunting quality even today. Charles II, Queen Catherine and their retinues were entertained in style by the river here in 1671 just when the Paston fortunes were crashing down and debts crowding in; the bills for the King and Queen's reception were still unpaid years later.

Much of this bridge was washed away in the flood of 26 Aug. 1912. The former warm red-brick humpbacked crossing now has a dejected air with its concrete deck and wooden rails, softened by the meadowsweet and Norfolk reed reflected in the fast-flowing Bure   [*MB · 2011*]

left The bridge at Burgh-next-Aylsham, from downstream. The brick piers are original, as are those at Oxnead Bridge, Mayton (New) Bridge and Plantation Bridge (opposite).

The upper part of the structure was rebuilt after the 1912 floods [*MB · 2012*]

sizes varied a great deal on the navigation; all were rigged fore and aft. Matthew Bidney, of Burgh-next-Aylsham ('Aylsham Burgh'), had a 16-ton wherry, *Endeavour*, which he worked alone to Gt Yarmouth. William Sago of Aylsham also had a 16-ton wherry, *Mayflower*, which he sailed alone (NRO: YC 38/3, nos 132 and 118, 28 Aug. and 17 Aug. 1795)

[1] *Mary Gant* The toll collectors from 1775 are listed in S. Spooner, ed., *Sail and Storm*, p. 107

[2] *Act* '. . . and every such owner or owners shall also cause figures to be placed on the head and stern of every such boat, barge, or vessel . . . to denote the draught of water, and how deep such boat, barge, or vessel is laden . . .' (from the Act)

The skippers would not have appreciated the increased level of bureacracy, compared with the freedom of the tidal stretches, nor the physical obstacles in their course in the way of locks and low bridges. The rest of the Broads, apart from the short stretch between Geldeston and Bungay, was free from locks at this time, and bridges were few. Raising and lowering the mast and sail were time-consuming, laborious operations to be avoided if at all possible—especially when single-handed, as many skippers were. To have to do this time and again through the locks and bridges would have tried the men's' patience. Further, the Commissioners had suppressed their old freedom to sail at night.

Under the navigation's regulations the skippers had to pay tolls to John Colls to enter the waterway; on his death in 1806 Mary Gant took over as collector at Great or Little Hautbois.[1] Paying would have caused a delay while the busy miller was winkled out or his deputy found. Secondly the Act of 1773 required additional signwriting on the vessels which was not needed on the tidal reaches. The provisions specified that not only the vessel's name but her draught and an early type of Plimsoll line had to be displayed.[2]

The strong current on a fall of over 30 feet (9 metres) would further have slowed the boats' upstream passage. It is likely the men had to pole their way along the majority of

¹ *quants* 24 feet long (7·3 metres) for a 40-tonner; progress is by muscle power. As a child I rowed our hefty wooden dinghy up to Coltishall Lock and Horstead Mill most days when we were moored at the downstream end of Coltishall. It is a hard pull against the current when rowing; a 30- or 40-tonner would have to be inched along

² *locks* A. Burton, *The Canal Builders*, pp. 79–80; this equates to 254,581 litres.

By contrast, a notice in 1814 for Oxnead Mill, then a papermill, claimed: 'It has a good fall, and a very plentiful supply of water' (*Norfolk Chronicle*, 4 June 1814). Perhaps the problems were solved

the reaches, pushing against their heavy wooden quants.¹ Unlike canal barges the Broads boats did not turn to horses for a tow, and the concept of a towpath was non-existent. Instead, beyond the reeds, there was usually a raised bank called the rond or rhond, formed of layers of dredged mud.

This silt presented an additional hazard. The Aylsham navigation suffered from constant silting, as noted earlier and as the millers were quick to point out to the Commissioners. As if that were not enough we have already seen that John Colls was short of water for his mill. The boats would be facing the same difficulty and be in danger of grounding on shoals. The average lock on the Grand Junction Canal held 56,000 gallons of water, and canal engineers had to cast about for ways of keeping a sufficient flow.²

The consequences for Coltishall and Horstead

When the 32-page Act authorising the navigation passed through Parliament on 7 April 1773 it launched a bold enterprise intended, in its opening words, to be 'a great advantage to the said county of Norfolk, and the public in general'. It proved not to the advantage of the merchants at the head of the tidal Bure; nor to some riparian owners on the navigation. A good deal of trade and manufacturing moved up-

facing page **Aylsham: the county bridge in Millgate near the new canal basin.** The town gained an economic boost from its new link to the North Sea, this area fast developing to serve the needs of trade. The private house with the large chimney became the Anchor Inn in 1781, meeting other needs [*drawing by F. Stone; lithograph by D. Hodgson 1831*]

left The old Anchor Inn, no longer licensed [*MB · 2012*]

stream. It is a striking tribute to the social cohesion of the area that rioting did not break out and that the locks were not vandalised (other than by impatient watermen battling to get through at night). In the detailed minutes recording progress in the navigation's early years and in the two local newspapers of the time there is no mention of violent protests. Any attacks tended to be verbal, the most vigorous and outspoken campaigners being those reporting to King's College. Yet the college, despite the diminished status of its manors of Horstead and Coltishall, chose not to oppose the scheme, and the formative first decade witnessed a remarkably harmonious transition to Aylsham hegemony.

It is tempting to view the Aylsham navigation as an unquestionable success. It was used by keels and wherries from 1775 to 1912 and managed to survive the coming of the railways to Aylsham in 1880 and 1883. Its chronicler Desmond Best and the historian Robert Malster pay tribute to its role in promoting the prosperity of the market town of Aylsham:

For more than a century the navigation played an important part in the mercantile life of the town, a brisk trade being carried on in corn, coal, timber and other cargoes. At one time as many as 26 wherries were trading to Aylsham, a number being owned in the town.[1]

[1] *Aylsham* R. Malster, *Wherries and Waterways*, p. 27.

Desmond Best in his thesis 'The Aylsham Navigation' concludes that in 1779 'Aylsham and its environs now had a cheap and reliable transport route which was to serve it well for 133 years.'

Sarah Spooner highlights the 'much-needed economic boost' given to formerly landlocked towns and villages. The navigation 'allowed Aylsham and the villages along its course to participate more fully in the developing economy of the late Georgian period' (S. Spooner, ed., *Sail and Storm*, p. 6)

[1] *Manchester* A. Burton, *The Canal Builders*, pp. 3, 12

[2] *Aylsham expansion* Chronicled in detail by T. Mollard and G. Gale, eds, *Millgate, Aylsham* (2nd edn Aylsham Local History Soc., 2006; 1st pub. 1993) and by S. Spooner, ed., *Sail and Storm*, pp. 75–90, 106–25

[3] *Buxton Mill Norfolk Chronicle*, 7 Dec. 1782. Oxnead Lock was finished by Feb. 1779 (*Norw. Merc.* 27 Feb. 1779), navigation construction recovering after having stalled just below Buxton

[4] *Bawtry* J. Chartres, 'Rivers, Canals and the Port Activities of the Eighteenth-century English Town', given at the annual conference of the British Society for Eighteenth-Century Studies, St Hugh's College, Oxford, 6 Jan. 2009. See also J. Priestley, *Historical Account of the Navigable Rivers*, pp. 148–51, 345–6.
In response to its predicament Bawtry turned itself into a coaching town—a strategy which could not withstand the coming of the railway age

[5] *Batchelor* Aylsham Town Council: Box 36.
His fears over loss of privacy were justified, as set out on pp. 100–1 and 107

The statistics on the benefits gained by building canals and navigations are arresting. When the Duke of Bridgewater's canal reached Manchester in 1761 the price of coal in that fast-expanding city halved.[1] Coal was vital to industry as well as bringing domestic comfort to those who could afford it; the maltings and breweries of the Broads relied on cinders and coal to fuel them. Aylsham had no commercial breweries at this time as it had no good brewing water or 'liquor', but its cornmilling and malting capacity expanded greatly from the 1770s.[2] Similarly, three years after the opening of the new waterway through Buxton, the village's watermill announced massive expansion. It was now 'capable of performing more work than any in this part of the kingdom'. Also it was 'excellently well situated for a foreign trade' from its 'communication by water with the port of Great Yarmouth'.[3] Horstead Mill a few miles downstream would have seen trade hit by this new competition.

This section and the next will focus on the losers from the Aylsham navigation: those who lost out when trade patterns shifted in favour of others. It was a shift repeated across the country, as when Bawtry faltered at the same time as Coltishall through the opening of the Chesterfield Canal in 1777. Bawtry, south of Doncaster, had until then been the head of navigation on the River Idle—an inland port supplying Hull. The town was bypassed with the opening of the 46-mile Chesterfield Canal with its link to the Trent.[4] The most obvious illustration of shift caused by a new waterway is the opening of the Manchester Ship Canal to oceangoing ships in 1894, in the teeth of vehement opposition from Liverpool.

This part of the story will give voice to the individuals who heartily opposed the Aylsham navigation. Thomas John Batchelor of Horstead Hall, a short way upstream of Coltishall Bridge, had been against the scheme right from the start, as he made plain to the Commissioners. At their meeting of 15 December 1772 they noted: 'Thomas John Batcheler Esq. of Horstead objects to the whole Navigation.'[5]

The plight of the villages supplanted by upstarts upstream was commented upon at the time: by the vocal rector, by the King's College copyholders at the manor houses and, tellingly, by the level-headed and impartial Excise. Chilling indicators of the depressive effect on trade of removing the status of head of navigation came in decisions by the Excise Commissioners in London. They resolved firstly to reduce the two divisions in Coltishall in 1789 and then, nearly twenty years later, to downgrade it from its very high status of excise district which it enjoyed continuously 1758–1808 as a producer of dutiable commodities.

It was John Adey's future father-in-law John Repton who as Collector of Norwich made Coltishall an excise district in 1758.[1] It then had two divisions.[2] However in 1789 it was demoted to a division and a ride, for malt and beer respectively. Coltishall was still one of four districts in the Excise Collection, the others being the leading manufacturing areas of Norwich, Yarmouth and Bungay.[3] Such alterations in excise monitoring reflected rises and falls in production. In 1779, when the waterway was about to open, Coltishall had eleven maltings. By 1792 this figure had dropped to seven.[4]

Further humiliation followed in 1808, nearly thirty years after the full opening of the navigation. The Excise Commissioners downgraded Coltishall to just two rides and removed its district status, for the reasons that 'Several trades have discontinued working in Coltishall Division and … there being no malt made for exportation therein . . .'[5] The Excise could be better served by moving the district supervision and its senior officer, the supervisor, elsewhere. Also the three wholesale breweries of the 1770s had dropped to one, owned and run by William Hardy's successor at Wells's brewery Siday Hawes, although this was not wholly as a result of competition brought about by the navigation.[6]

Horstead Mill injured and its trade prejudiced

An articulate and outspoken cleric was watching all these developments with mounting concern. King's College was kept fully informed by the Revd Dr Charles Grape, Rector of Horstead and Coltishall and resident at Horstead Rectory from 1786 until his death in 1815. Dr Grape—a Kingsman, as were all the Horstead and Coltishall incumbents at that time—was devoted to the interests of his college and much given to the use of exclamation marks. In 1791 he complained indignantly that the college meadows near the watermill were subject to flooding;[7] the occupier Siday

[1] *district* TNA: PRO CUST 47/222, p. 59, 21 June 1758. The structure of the excise service is described and illustrated in vol. 2, chap. 11 (see esp. fig. 2.11A) and in vol. 2, app. 2.A

[2] *two divisions* TNA: PRO CUST 47/219, pp. 119–20, 4 Oct. 1757

[3] *division and ride* TNA: PRO CUST 47/363, pp. 69–71, 13 Jan. 1789; CUST 47/365, pp. 44 onwards, 3 Apr. 1789

[4] *maltings* NRO: PD 598/37, Coltishall churchwardens' account book 1776–1830; see also vol. 2, chap. 5, the section 'Village entrepreneurs'

[5] *no malt exported* TNA: PRO CUST 47/457, pp. 88–9, 24 Mar. 1808. 'Exportation' relates to goods passing through a seaport such as Gt Yarmouth. The term embraces all produce shipped coastwise around Britain as well as overseas

[6] *breweries* Described in vol. 2, chap. 8

[7] *flooding* King's Coll.: KCAR/6/2/087/14, HOR/18, Letter 27 June 1791 sent in high dudgeon by Dr Grape to the Provost, revealing that the rector was at loggerheads with Henry Palmer Watts of Horstead House, with Lord Suffield (the former MP Sir Harbord Harbord), and with Sir Thomas

Durrant (by now a baronet): 'Competitors with whom no Rector of Horstead, or Colteshall, will be desirous of engaging, though he may fight under the banner of King Henry the VIth . . . God grant that I may have no further trouble!'

---

[1] *map* NRO: PD 597/78, dated 29 Apr. 1788; Dr Grape marks the marl-pits in the south of the parish near the Bure and draws a much-begabled watermill. He uses the manorial spelling, Colteshall. His comments are transcribed in P. Millican, *A History of Horstead and Stanninghall*, p. 9.

Mr Batchelor's fish ponds and swannery were on his land on the Gt Hautbois bank, as marked on Biedermann's plan. The rector alleges that wherrymen were helping themselves and living off the land.

Mr Batchelor had feared incursions into his property by those using the new waterway. Loss of privacy was frequently complained of by riparian owners who were unconnected with trade and now had to share the delights of their pleasure grounds with every passing waterman (A. Burton, *The Canal Builders*, p. 42)

Hawes, who farmed them, had not cleared the drainage ditches. The ditches would have been affected by changes in water level associated with the navigation, and it seems at this point that the riverside fields formerly tilled for arable crops, as recorded by Mary Hardy 1773–81, became water-logged pasture.

Dr Grape was no champion of the navigation, which he depicts on his parish map of 1788. The scheme had been 'to the prejudice of the trade of Horstead Mill . . . and to the great damage of T.J. Batcheler, Esq.'s meadows and royalty from Colteshall to Meyton Bridge, the land being frequently flooded and the fish and swans disturbed or stolen'.[1]

In fact the situation was more complex than the rector stated in his exclamatory way. By 1790 it was clear that the changes to the waterway, including raising the water level to ensure enough flow passed to the locks and mills, had damaged the meadows on the Horstead side; these bordered the navigation from the watermill to close to Horstead Church upstream. They were the former arable fields known to Mary Hardy as Mill Piece and Mill Close and, above the bridge, Sergeant Piece and Sergeant Close. Henry Palmer Watts, occupier of Mill Piece and Mill Close in 1790, came to a legal agreement at the request of Dr Grape at the Rectory and of John and Ann Darby, owners of Sergeant Piece and Sergeant Close. Mrs Darby was the former Ann Wells, the brewery heiress; Siday Hawes farmed her land (volume 2).

The terms of the agreement explained what had gone wrong. When the river was made navigable it was embanked, but there was seepage from the waterway onto the fields which lay below river level. These embankments (probably formed from dredged spoil when the river was deepened) then blocked the drainage dykes formerly emptying into the river. The raised level of the navigation, whereby those working the vessels looked down onto the meadows, can be seen at Brampton at *plate 7*.

Unhelpful actions on the part of Mr Batchelor just upstream of these Horstead fields exacerbated the problems:

. . . Know ye that whereas the waters issuing out of certain meadows belonging to John Darby and Anne his wife in the occupation of Siday Hawes lying in Horstead . . . of late have and of right ought to flow into the common river, but the usual outlets into the said common river being blocked up, the said waters have been directed and led up to and through an arch (built across Coltishall Causeway) into the lands late of Chapman Ives Esquire and now of Henry Palmer Watts Esquire and not only the water issuing from out of the herein-above-described meadows, but the owners and occupiers of certain other meadows lying above the same by connivance taking advantage of the passage for the said water cut drains . . . whereby large flows of water were let down upon the lands and meadows . . . to the great injury of the same and to the lessening the power of the water in the said common river to the great injury of a certain watermill called Horstead Mill belonging to King's College in Cambridge and now in the occupation of John Colls as lessee to the said Henry Palmer Watts . . . [1]

The agreement refers to the tension between Siday Hawes and John Colls: the first anxious to drain his fields, in their new and unwelcome state of bogginess, by other means now that the drainage dykes could no longer enter the raised stream; and the other insistent on having all water directed into the river to preserve the flow to his mill.[2]

This was a common problem where there were watermills, and not all the blame can be laid to the navigation; it merely worsened an existing situation. The agriculturalist Arthur Young, applauded by William Marshall in a most uncharacteristic display of unity, matched Dr Grape in outspokenness in his assault on the damage done to field drains by

[1] *great injury* NRO: BRA 926/XII 56/4, 110x4, Agreement over a watercourse in Horstead permitted by Henry Palmer Watts to John and Anne Darby and Charles Grape, 9 Jan. 1790. Dr Grape was required to ensure that the banks of Rectory Meadow were firm 'so as to prevent the water of the common river escaping and issuing through the same'.

Also at issue was the culvert or 'arch' under the causeway carrying the main road to Coltishall Bridge from the Recruiting Sergeant (illustrated below)

[2] *drainage* For the damaging consequences of embanking, draining and culverting the meadows beside the navigation at Burgh-next-Aylsham, see P. Holman, 'The Bure navigation': 'Because of these changes there were problems . . . with draining the low-lying fields—a maze of ditches, some passing under others by culverts, resulted' (unpag.)

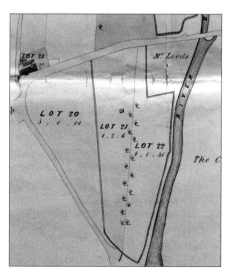

left Mill Close and Mill Piece at Horstead, beside the navigation downstream of Coltishall Bridge (top right) and the subject of a heated dispute over flooding. The causeway runs from the Recruiting Sergeant (top left). The mill and lock lie just downstream [NRO: MS 7351, 7 D4, *Plan by W. S. Millard & Son for the Coltishall Brewery sale 1841, detail*]

¹ *watermills* 'Bravo!
Bravo!' adds Marshall
to this extract from
Young's 1804 Norfolk
report (W. Marshall,
*The Review and Abstract
of the County Reports to
the Board of Agriculture*,
vol. 3 (York, 1818; 1st
pub. 1811), p. 363).
The original
comments are in A.
Young, *General Report
on the Agriculture of the
County of Norfolk*, p.
391, where he refers
to Sculthorpe Mill

² *Horstead manor house
and mill* King's Coll.:
KCAR/5/1/26 76, p. 86,
dated 2 June 1802

millers. Watermills sabotaged attempts at improved farming methods: 'Of the nuisances that a country can be plagued with, certainly watermills class very high in the black catalogue'; what should have been a rich meadow in central Norfolk was 'poisoned with water, and producing rushes, flags, sedge, and all sorts of aquatic rubbish'.¹

In 1802 the college's surveyor and valuer wrote in more measured terms than Dr Grape, alerting King's to the loss of college income occasioned by the Aylsham navigation. The Horstead manor house and adjoining watermill had evidently been a trading post of some size. John Josselyn junior, of Belstead Hall, near Ipswich, submitted his report in 1802 entitled, 'An estimate of the annual value of estates belonging to the Provost and Fellows of King's College in Cambridge, situate at Horstead'. The manor estate of 268 acres had an annual value of £208 15s; the college-owned watermill (Horstead Mill)—with its coal wharf and lime-kiln—had an annual value of £150; and two additional items brought the total annual value to £363 3s.²

above The manor house now called Horstead House, from the mill-stream   [*MB · 1989*]

right From Josselyn's report to King's of 1802 [*courtesy the Provost and Scholars of King's College, Cambridge:* KCAR/5/1/26 76, p. 86, *detail*]

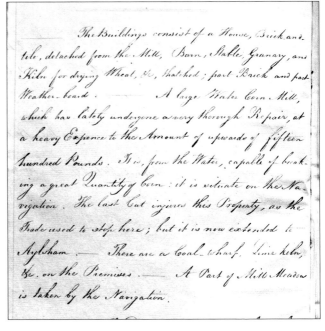

The brick-and-tile manor house had a barn, stable, granary and kiln for drying wheat on the home premises. Mr Josselyn had also surveyed the neighbouring mill, which had been injured by the navigation:

A large water cornmill, which has lately undergone a very thorough repair, at a heavy expense to the amount of upwards of fifteen hundred pounds.[1] It is, from the water, capable of breaking a great quantity of corn: it is situate on the Navigation. The last Cut injures this property, as the trade used to stop here; but it is now extended to Aylsham. There are a coal wharf, lime-kiln, etc on the premises. A part of Mill Meadow is taken by the navigation . . .[2]

It was of course in the interests of Henry Palmer Watts, the occupier of the estate, to impress upon King's the difficulties of his position in the hope that this would influence the level of rent he was to be charged on the renewal of his lease. Mr Josselyn, caught in the middle, made an observation in his accompanying letter with some diffidence:

On the Horstead estate, Mr Watts has expended much money; it might therefore probably be thought hard if the College on this renewal were to take the advantage of it, the old mills having been a very moderate building. I beg your pardon for mentioning this.[3]

At first sight there are contradictions here. If the mill had suffered so severely, it would seem odd that Mr Watts should have expended so much of his own and John Colls's money on rebuilding it. However Mr Josselyn clarifies the ambivalent positions of the manor copyholders in his report of 1805 on the Coltishall estate. He points out that William Palgrave had other landholdings and trade interests, in his own right, and was thus able to view with relative equanimity the loss of income on the premises he held from King's.[4]

Mr Josslyn probably surveyed the college's estate at Coltishall early in 1805, making his report to William Johnson in mid-January 1805 (overleaf) and enclosing it with a letter dated 24 January written from his home at Belstead. The manor estate at Coltishall totalled 30 acres, which with the manor house and attached buildings he valued at £52 10s a year. The coal yard, cinder ovens, malthouse, wharf and granary on the manor house premises he valued at £50, bringing the total to £102 10s: 'NB I think to keep these premises in fair repair it will annually cost twenty pounds'.

[1] *thorough repair* The mill had been been remodelled and enlarged between 1789 and 1797: see vol. 2, chap. 7. It had a very high capacity by 1797, being capable of milling 300 quarters of wheat a week, or 15,600 p.a. (*Norw. Merc.* 8 Apr., 6 May 1797; also table 2.7.3 in vol. 2, chap 7). This was a time when millers were doing well during the recurrent wheat shortages, thus probably offsetting for Horstead Mill some of the losses caused by the navigation

[2] *report* King's Coll.: KCAR/5/1/26 76. A valuer had reported to King's in Oct. 1725 that 'the mills' (presumably the corn watermill and not also the college's fulling mill at Horstead) were let at £25 p.a., and that Mr Warren, of the manor house, had lately rebuilt them (King's Coll.: KCAR/6/2/087/4, HOR/24, Report on the Horstead estate)

[3] *letter* King's College: KCAR/5/1/26 76, also dated 2 June 1802

[4] *Palgrave* King's Coll.: KCAR/6/2/38, COL/505, Report by John Josselyn jnr to King's, 15 Jan. 1805 (extracts overleaf). Coltishall Manor House, its staithe and the Palgraves are described in the next chapter

above **Coltishall Manor House, late 19th century**
[*courtesy the Provost and Scholars of King's College, Cambridge, detail*]

¹ *the Waste* This may refer to Siday Hawes's expansion stretching across Upper Common from the road by his brewery at the Old House; this included a new malt-house (vol. 2, chap. 8)

The new cut has injured the Coltishall manorial estate by 1805

source King's College, Cambridge: KCAR/6/2/38, COL/505, Report by surveyor and valuer John Josselyn jnr, of Belstead Hall, Suff., to King's College, lords of the manor of Coltishall, 15 Jan. 1805

THESE PREMISES CONSIST OF A GOOD SUBSTANTIAL bricked dwelling house with convenient offices—stables, brick barn, hay-house, cart sheds, bullock sheds, coal yard, wharf, granary, malt-house (near fifty coombs steep) and other buildings. The situation is on a river which is navigable from Aylsham to Yarmouth—no river dues are paid. This was originally the head of the navigation, the new cut must have been injurious to this property . . .

The buildings on this property are very numerous, much more than can possibly be wanted for the land and trade, but the tenant having other land of his own adjoining is the reason. The trade etc etc being established ought in a certain degree to be calculated upon but not upon too large a scale as there are other wharfs near and liable to be opened and one now erecting on the Waste ¹ which if suffered will be injurious to this estate . . . I should strongly recommend not to make any grants.

Mr Palgrave has no doubt expended very large sums of money on this estate and materially improved it. I believe after labouring for forty-five years he has not done anything great for himself and family—his having freehold adjoining this I rather wonder he should expend so much on the college estates.

facing page **Horstead Mill, seen from downstream on the old river. It burned down in Jan. 1963. The loss of this late-18th-century mill in its once beautiful setting is still mourned** [*Cecil Perham 1948*]

² *Horstead* Depicted by Percy Millican in his classic study: *A History of Horstead and Stanninghall, Norfolk*

Josselyn's observations echo those he had made over Horstead House. The manorial property was equipped to serve as a busy trading post, but its pre-eminence had been materially prejudiced by the extension of the navigable river to Aylsham; 'the new cut' must have injured it. In his covering letter he again strongly urges King's to 'prevent any grant being made of the waste of your manor adjoining the river', with consequent further losses of income. Coltishall's large commons near the mill and the King's Head bordered the river and were evidently viewed hungrily by enterprising merchants and manufacturers wishing to establish themselves on the bankside open spaces.

Horstead probably lost out to lesser extent than Coltishall as it was less mercantile.² It was principally a farming community, served by only one public house; its leading inhabitants, with the exception of Watts and Colls, were not immersed in trade. Coltishall presented a total contrast, as has been described under 'Village entrepreneurs' (volume 2, chapter 5). The village's bustling staithes are portrayed in the next chapter.

There was one route available to canny traders seeking to adapt to the new situation: the extension of their business upriver. Both William Palgrave and his uncle of the same name adopted this course. (They died in 1822 and 1780 respectively, both had strong Great Yarmouth connections, and both were corn and coal merchants and manufacturers and traders at Coltishall Manor House.) We have already seen the elder Palgrave establishing himself at a new malthouse at Horstead in 1776, as recorded in the Horstead ratebook; this was almost certainly the one on the navigation just above Coltishall Bridge, later rebuilt.[1]

By 1779 both Palgraves were occupiers of 'two very good malthouses' at Buxton which were 'well situated for trade, the river being navigable from thence to Yarmouth'—a refrain which would have been increasingly galling for Horstead and Coltishall traders.[2] It is not certain these maltings were in Buxton. The village on the opposite bank, Lamas, was often classed as Buxton and the settlements treated as one, 'Buxton Lamas', despite being parted by the river. The pair may have been the early malthouses still standing in the village street at Lamas. This village, like Coltishall, had staithes running along the bank; even the church stands by the river. Buxton, like Horstead, tended to shun the river other than at the mill. Either way, the Palgraves were in place to seize opportunities when the navigation opened.

However none of the Coltishall and Horstead commercial boats took advantage of the navigation. The register of keels and wherries enables us to identify all the vessels with home berths in the two villages, and none worked upstream: all plied only downstream to Great Yarmouth (table 4.4.2). The Coltishall-berthed 43-ton wherry *William and Betsey* will have been the Palgraves', the younger William Palgrave having married Elizabeth Thirkettle in 1771; his uncle never married. Their skipper Edward Smith and mate John Smith traded only downstream.[3]

[1] *Horstead* NRO: NRS 18386, 33 B7 (illustrated in vol. 2, chap. 5)

[2] *Buxton Norw. Merc.* 8 May 1779. The malthouses may not have been built as a response to the navigation. 'Two convenient malthouses', with 30-coomb and 40-coomb steeps, had been advertised at Buxton (or Lamas) as early as 1756 (*Norw. Merc.* 18 Sept. 1756).

When Irmingland Hall, by Aylsham, was being partially demolished in 1787 the auction of the heavy building materials such as bricks, tiles, lead and iron was held at the Black Boys at Aylsham. The town's proud boast was that it stood 'on the navigable river to Yarmouth' (*Norw. Merc.* 17 Nov. 1787)

[3] *William and Betsey* NRO: YC 38/3, no. 27,

17 July 1795. The next
village downstream was
Belaugh, and the
wherry there traded
only downstream too.
The skipper William
Martin sailed his 30-
ton *Friendship* single-
handed (no. 47, 20 July
1795)

---

[^1] *towns* J. Priestley,
*Historical Account of the
Navigable Rivers*, p. 109;
he was a canal manager

above Halesworth,
Suffolk. The old Blyth
navigation is now
choked with lilies on
the approach to the
canal basin. Perversely,
opposition in 1753 was
led not by Southwold,
threatened by the open-
ing, but by traders in
Halesworth in cattle,
leather and dairy
products   [*MB · 2012*]

The picture is mixed. While there were some clear win-
ners and losers through the opening of the navigation and
the extension of trade some at least of the losers tried to
remedy the threats to their business interests to which the
proponents of the Act had exposed them. But the frequency
with which alarming phrases are heard from those who were
not Aylsham based points to the damage done by the new
enterprise. The local squire Mr Batchelor, the rector and
the Suffolk-based valuer spelled out in uncompromising
terms that many had suffered. We have seen that in the clear,
forceful speech of the time they used phrases such as 'great
injury' (often repeated), 'great damage', 'to the prejudice of
the trade of Horstead Mill', 'prejudice to the estate', 'injurious to this property' and, in the verdict expressed to London by the Excise, 'Several trades have discontinued working in Coltishall Division.' So why did these perceived hurts
not spill over into violent protest by those who lost livelihoods—working floor maltsters, journeymen millers, corn
and coal merchants' carters and wagoners, and apprentices?

The absence of rioting

A telling observation was made in 1831 about the impact
of the Aylsham navigation. It was at its zenith, following
its deepening after the initial building; the railway did not
come to Norfolk until 1844. Joseph Priestley, in his study
of navigable waterways nationally, pointed to the benefits
derived by market towns at the head of navigation and in
the neighbouring area who could participate more directly
in the notable gains to be had. By implication, settlements
along lower parts of the Bure had been less fortunate:

As the navigable part of the North River and River Bure, from the
head of navigation at Aylsham to the sea at Yarmouth, is by its
course forty-two miles, and as it passes through one of the finest agricultural districts of which this kingdom can boast, the advantages
arising from the facilities it affords for the export of the natural
productions of its vicinity are incalculable. The towns of Aylsham,
Cawsham [Cawston], Reepham, and the immediate neighbourhood
participate, perhaps, more directly in the advantage thus derived ... [^1]

The 1770s could have been years of turmoil for Coltishall
and the surrounding area. Some towns when threatened by
the extension of a navigable river had resorted to violence:

left The Lamas bank near the former Anchor of Hope, seen across the navigation from Buxton; the outlet was well placed to serve watermen waiting at the lock. It was not licensed in the late 18th century, as the alehouse register shows. It soon sprang up to serve the navigation [*MB·2008*]

left Gt Hautbois: a cut from the navigation facing Horstead Church and Rectory, close to the site of Thomas John Batchelor's former swannery and fish ponds.

The rector indignantly reported in 1788 that the swans and fish had been disturbed and stolen by those using the navigation [*MB·2007*]

Improvements were carried out to most navigable rivers during the eighteenth century, sometimes involving extensive engineering work. The Kennet Navigation, undertaken betwen 1718 and 1721, was quite a major piece of work as eighteen locks were required along the eighteen miles of river from Newbury to Reading. The Navigation was a boon to Newbury, but its construction had aroused violent opposition from Reading, since goods formerly had to be transhipped there. The mayor of Reading even took gangs of his townsmen out to destroy the locks as they were being built.[1]

Coltishall had no mayor. Even so, nowhere do we read in Mary Hardy's diary that her husband, a leading parishioner, churchwarden, holder of other parish offices and one of the principal manufacturers locally, led gangs of fellow tradesmen to destroy Coltishall Lock. Instead he gave the workmen building it bottles of gin.

Robert Malster chronicles the vigorous opposition to the North Walsham and Dilham Canal eventually built in 1825–26.[2] Under the scheme the River Ant was to be made navigable beyond Wayford Bridge to its source at Antingham, passing through North Walsham. The market town had itself suffered from the Bure navigation which promoted the

[1] *Reading* J. Brown, *The English Market Town: A social and economic history 1750–1914* (The Crowood Press, Marlborough, 1986), pp. 97–8. 'Townsmen' may here have the precise contemporary meaning of the leading ratepayers, rather than the more general sense of fellow citizens or fellow parishioners, drawn from across all social classes

[2] *N. Walsham* R. Malster, *The Norfolk and Suffolk Broads* (Phillimore, Chichester, 2003), pp. 95–7. It was a canalisation of the Upper Ant on the northern Broads: see table 4.2.1 on p. 111

[1] *N.Walsham* The arguments are summarised by Theole Douglas-Sherwood in her unpublished M.Litt. thesis: 'Whereas the north end of the main Bure channel had been extended to reach Aylsham . . ., the market town of North Walsham had suffered in competition through having to use the far more expensive mode of transport provided by cart' ('The Norfolk keel' (St Andrews, 1987), p. 44). A copy is held in the Norfolk Heritage Centre, Norwich.
Theole Douglas-Sherwood, a marine archaeologist, organised the lifting of the Norfolk keel *Dee-Dar* from a watery grave at Whitlingham, near Norwich (chap. 4)

[2] *Dilham* M. Allthorpe-Guyton, *John Thirtle 1771–1839: Drawings in Norwich Castle Museum* (Norfolk Museums Service, Norwich, 1977), pp. 66–7, cat. nos 115–118

[3] *opposition* R. Malster, *The Norfolk and Suffolk Broads*, p. 96

[4] *guidebooks* 'Coltishall is a typical English village, and picturesque withal' (G.C. Davies, *Norfolk Broads and Rivers* (London, 1883), p. 65); 'Coltishall . . . is in many respects a delightful place: undoubtedly

town's competitor Aylsham, the Act of 1812 authorising the new scheme declaring that the navigation was to facilitate and render less expensive 'the conveyance of all kinds of commodities'.[1]

The previous head of navigation had been the village of Dilham, with its busy staithe and warehouses twice depicted by the Norwich artist John Thirtle.[2] The people of Dilham and neighbouring Worstead at first opposed the Bill. After the passing of the Act they may, Robert Malster considers, have been responsible for the long delay before money was raised and digging could begin:

There were sufficient people in the adjoining parishes of Dilham and Worstead whose livelihoods seem to have depended on the trade through this staithe for there to be spirited opposition to the canal proposal.[3]

Yet there is no trace of public protest against the Aylsham scheme in the contemporary sources consulted. The Norwich newspapers are likely to have given accounts of unrest and riots had they occurred, as they did in full during the wheat-famine riots (narrated in volume 3, chapter 6). Mary Hardy too is silent upon the subject. Her lack of comment suggests that the economic casualties referred to indirectly by the Excise in 1808 accepted their fate stoically. Like the Beccles traders a century earlier they had to adapt, or else fail in business. She records no recourse to law, as might be expected from property-holders on suffering a commercial injury—and such as she describes in 1786–87 over Letheringsett Watermill (volume 2, chapter 7). The transformation of Coltishall from a diversified manufacturing and trading hub took just over a century. It became principally a malting town by the mid- and late nineteenth century; and then—as characterised by guidebook compilers—a picturesque backwater.[4]

The reason for the silence is that the rioting classes, variously seen as the labouring poor, the industrious poor and the mob, were not directly hit unless they lost their jobs at the maltings, breweries, mill and staithes. Such workers were few, none of the workforces constituting more than a handful of men (volume 2, chapter 1). It was their employers who suffered directly, and at Horstead and Coltishall they chose to remain silent—at least in public. Rioters poured out onto the street and into the market square when they were starving or, in later decades, when mechanisation threatened their future. However it is possible that before November 1780, when William Hardy bid successfully to buy his own concern at Letheringsett, he had determined that Coltishall would not become his family's permanent home. Tellingly, the talks over the Wells brewery merger with John Browne's business at Coltishall came to nothing in July 1780, less than a year after Aylsham's full opening; again perhaps he saw the writing on the wall. George Boorne and Thomas Neve, struggling with illiquidity brought on in part at least through their role as timber contractors to the navigation, had little room for manoeuvre. They went under early in 1781.[1]

The principal and overriding driver of canals and navigations was the demand for coal. Coal predominated in all pro-canal writing: 'The lower cost of coal, the increased supply of coal—the same point is banged home again and again by the pamphleteers and letter writers.'[2] Cheap coal was a public good in which all could share. Hence perhaps the absence of voices raised in protest?

Canal mania

A sustained effort was made in the eighteenth century to transport goods by water rather than by road. Canal mania did not hit the southern and eastern counties of England as feverishly as it did the North and Midlands. Agricultural produce, timber, building materials and fuel coal formed the principal freight in the south, rather than the bulk iron and mined coal of the counties of the industrial heartlands.

Nonetheless there was a prolonged bout of navigation fever in eastern England, Aylsham being one of many schemes. As table 4.2.1 shows (overleaf), it was the second of four Broadland projects. It was completed in good time and with a comparatively modest outlay, being fortunate in having an active group of commissioners who took their duties seriously and gave the undertaking leadership and direction. The Blyth scheme, completed in eight years, most closely matched Aylsham's and was very reasonable in price at about £425 a mile; Aylsham, at between £708 and £960, as explained on page 65, cost rather more to build.[3] (All figures are quoted in the money of the day, and are not

it is the most picturesque waterside village in Broadland' (W.A. Dutt, *The Norfolk Broads* (Methuen, London, 1903), p. 146). Its inns were 'quaint', its malthouses 'old', its reaches wooded (hardly helpful to wherries under sail), its watermill 'old', and its lock worn by weather and water (Dutt, p. 146).

Tourism, not trade, predominates

---

[1] *businesses* Charted elsewhere: see esp. vol. 2, chaps 8 and 11; also vol. 1, chap. 2 on the Hardys' search for a brewery of their own. Day-by-day accounts are given in *Diary 1*.

The Hardys' waterborne trade was still all downriver even after the opening of the navigation (chap. 4)

[2] *coal* A. Burton, *The Canal Builders*, p. 45

[3] *Blyth* The nine-mile Suffolk navigation from Southwold to Halesworth was a fairly early scheme in the region. Of its five locks two were built of brick, three of wood faggots. Keels and wherries used the waterway (M. Fordham, *Halesworth Quay and the Blyth Navigation* (Halesworth and District Museum, 2012), p. 6).

Unlike Aylsham, the push for the project

came not from the new head of navigation. Of the £3587 raised in subscriptions at the start only £225 came from Halesworth (p. 5)

---

¹ *N. Walsham* After its linking to the Broads it found itself in a less happy position than that of Aylsham. The vessels on its canal were perforce very small, and the waterway chronically short of water. Collecting coal by cart using the gaps in the cliffs at Mundesley and Bacton still had its attractions, the colliers beaching themselves on the sand to be unloaded at low tide

---

right Bishop Bridge: the oldest surviving crossing on the River Wensum in Norwich, and now the head of navigation for hire craft. Aylsham lies a mere 12 miles from Norwich by road, but just under 70 by water to New Mills, a short way upstream from here. But it still made economic sense to convey goods by water rather than by land.

New Mills was the ultimate head of navigation in the 18th century, and remains so today   [*MB · 2016*]

adjusted for inflation which struck hard during and after the French wars.) The table does not distinguish between schemes intended for inland shipping only and ones accommodating larger, deep-draught seagoing vessels as well.

The Aylsham navigation seems insignificant in comparison with some later enterprises It also appears something of a bargain in comparison with its closest neighbour, the North Walsham and Dilham Canal, built fifty years after Aylsham, at £3349 a mile.¹

The cost calculations in the table opposite can be treated as only approximate; different sources produce conflicting results. The figures quoted by the single source, a published work of 1977, are retained in the table for comparability. The six navigations listed at the foot of the table lack costings but are otherwise striking. The Nene navigation, a very important link waterway and one in which the Aylsham engineer John Smith was briefly engaged, had 44 locks (now in the 21st century reduced to 38). In the table the entry first quotes the waterway name, followed in brackets by the town by which the scheme is commonly known: hence Bure (Aylsham); Waveney (Bungay). Some have only one name.

The table thus puts Aylsham in context as very modest compared with the grander projects. Overleaf the plan of 1777 for the Basingstoke Canal in Hampshire and Surrey shows a much more complex affair: 44 miles long, not nine; 29 locks, not five; and—a huge undertaking which all the eastern region navigations were luckily spared—a tunnel.

TABLE 4.2.1

Canal mania: from prudence to runaway costs for the 16 principal navigations and canals in eastern England 1670–1833

source Extracted from data in J. Boyes and R. Russell, *The Canals of Eastern England* (David & Charles, Newton Abbot, 1977), app. 1, pp. 336–60

notes Bold type denotes navigations on the Broads. The table is arranged in ascending order of *approximate* costs per mile. A dash denotes lack of firm information on costs, those six navigations being in order of date of opening. The source makes no adjustment for inflation

waterway (*name*)	*Act*	*fully opened*	*miles*	*locks*	*cost at opening* (£), *approx.*	*cost per mile* (£), *approx.*
Nar	1751	1759	15	?4	2600	173
Stour	1705	c.1709	25	15	6500	260
Blyth (Halesworth)	1757	1761	9	4 [5]	3822	425
Bure (Aylsham)	**1773**	**1779**	**9·25**	**5**	**6551**	**708**
Gipping (Ipswich and Stowmarket)	1790	1793	17	15	35,300	2076
(Wisbech Canal) [1]	1794	1796	5·25	2	16,500	3143
Ant (North Walsham and Dilham)	**1812**	**1826**	**8·75**	**6**	**29,300**	**3349**
Chelmer and Blackwater	1793	1797	14	13	50,000	3571
Bain (Horncastle) [2]	1792	1802	12	11	45,000	3750
New Cut (Norwich and Lowestoft)	**1827**	**1833**	**7** [3]	**1**	**150,000**	**21,429**
Waveney (Bungay)	**1670**	**1670s**	**23** [4]	**4**	——	——
Little Ouse	1670	c.1677	22·5	8	——	——
Cam	1702	[?]	14·5	4	——	——
Lark	1700	c.1720	24	25	——	——
Nene	1724	1761	91·5	44	——	——
Old Nene	1753	[?]	26	1	——	——

[1] *Wisbech Canal* This was a fresh cut, and not along the course of an existing waterway

[2] *Horncastle* A canalisation of the Bain between Horncastle and Witham, Lincs

[3] *New Cut* The figure of seven miles includes not only the new canal linking two rivers but also dredging and widening elsewhere, as in Oulton Dyke leading to the Waveney. The costs figure includes building Mutford Lock

[4] *Waveney* The Bungay navigation was effectively nine miles long, from Beccles to Bungay. The figure of 23 miles includes further improvements along the 20 miles of the navigable Waveney downstream of Beccles to the confluence with the Yare below Burgh Castle; also dredging and a new cut upstream to link the village of Geldeston with the river and create a large staithe (chap. 3). It was built with four locks, later reduced to three

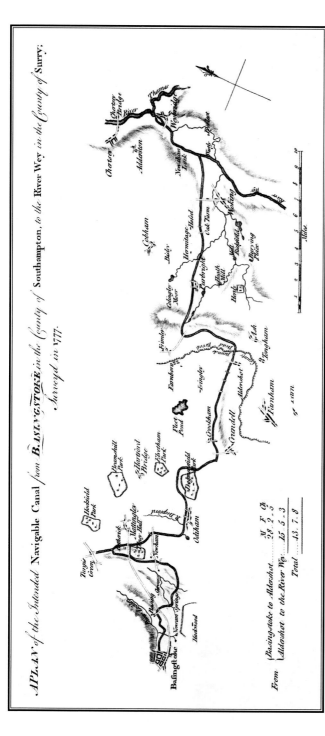

A PLAN of the Intended Navigable Canal from BASINGSTOKE in the County of Southampton, to the River Wey in the County of Surry: Surveyed in 1777.

From { Basingstoke to Aldershot 28. 2. 3
Aldershot to the River Wey 15. 5. 3
Total 43. 7. 8

above A contemporary, much larger project in Hampshire and Surrey: the plan of 1777 showing the route of the intended 44-mile canal from Basingstoke through Odiham, Aldershot and Pirbright to the Wey and thus the Thames near Weybridge.

This canal, authorised by an Act of 1778 and with 29 locks and a long tunnel, was built shortly after the Aylsham navigation

in the expectation that Basingstoke's economy would be boosted by its transformation into an inland port.

But, as with another such scheme north of Swindon at Cricklade, 'the Basingstoke Canal never paid its way, and in 1800 carried only about 18,000 tons of goods, well below the 30,000 tons a year forecast when the canal was promoted. No revival

of old textile industries resulted at either Basingstoke or Cricklade' (J. Brown, *The English Market Town* (1986)).

Many schemes proved to be crippling financially. One on the Broads, the Norwich and Lowestoft scheme of 1827–33 designed to make Norwich a deepwater port, cost well over 20 times as much as the Aylsham navigation   [*Author's collection*]

above The shape of things to come. Canal mania had peaked in the 1790s; the railway was to kill the viability of most navigations. Aylsham's demise was postponed as its two railways came late to that part of north Norfolk, in the 1880s, and trade on the waterway held on until the 1912 floods. Here Reedham Swing Bridge over the River Yare carries the Lowestoft line, built in 1845–47; a further swing bridge takes the line across the Waveney at Somerleyton. Its coming wrecked the hopes of promoters of the New Cut, which runs beside the railway. That hugely expensive Norwich–Lowestoft project had been completed only 14 years earlier   [*MB · 2018*]

The table does not reveal the isolated nature of the eastern region's new schemes. Many of these did not link to the interconnected canals thrusting across the central core of the country. Birmingham, Manchester and Leeds remained out of reach from the Broads; London could be gained only by sea from eastern Norfolk. (The canals emptying into the Wash form an exception.) It was a grave disadvantage for the Broadland economy that not one of its waterways could link into the massive central network then fast being built.[1]

Despite this, the navigations brought marked benefits. They also had their detractors. One objector ascribed the marked worsening of the climate to the prevalence of canals and aqueducts. All that damp was influencing the weather.[2]

[1] *network* The importance of the waters flowing into the Wash is highlighted by T. S. Willan (as it had been by Daniel Defoe) in 'River navigation and trade from the Witham to the Yare, 1600–1750', *Norfolk Archaeology*, vol. 26 (1938), pp. 296–309

[2] *climate* A. Burton, *The Canal Builders*, p. 45.
Climate is covered in vol. 2, chap. 4, where

the effect of the Laki fissure eruptions of 1783–84 is analysed

[1] *mania* A. Burton, *The Canal Builders*, p. 52; 19 of the Bills received the Royal Assent during the year. The simpler days of the Aylsham groundwork were over, 200 witnesses being brought up to London for the Birmingham Canal Bill of 1791 (A. Burton, p. 52)

[2] *New Cut* House of Commons Parliamentary Papers 1826 (369), vol. IV, Norwich and Lowestoft Navigation Bill, Minutes of evidence to the committee, pp. 85–95, 181–86. Crisp Brown, Daniel Harmer, John Cozens and James Boardman, all of Norwich, in a precise and assured manner, told of wherry passages, damage to cargoes, pilfering from vessels, the use of warehouses and other day-to-day aspects of the waterways.

The grocer John Cozens, Mary Ann Hardy's brother-in-law, considered the Yare one of the best and cheapest waterways in the kingdom (Minutes, p. 184)

Canal mania took hold in the early 1790s. In 1793, just as war was about to break out, 36 Bills were under consideration.[1] Parliamentary preparatory work prior to authorising a canals or navigation had become more sophisticated than at the time of the Aylsham Bill, and we can hear the verbatim testimony of promoters and opponents of these projects as they appeared before a committee of MPs. The minutes of the evidence taken by the 1826 committee for the Norwich and Lowestoft navigation, commonly known as the New Cut, are invaluable and will be examined in chapter 4.[2]

The Aylsham navigation, its trade already under threat from the railways which arrived in the town in 1880 and 1883, was brought to an end not by manmade developments but by a dramatic natural disaster. Prolonged heavy rain caused its demise. The floods of 26 and 27 August 1912 tore at the banks, smashed the lock gates and swept away most of the bridges; houses were demolished and wherries cast adrift across the meadows. The navigation could not recover and was not worked again. After much deliberation it was formally wound up in September 1928.

Part of the appeal of the old navigation lies in the poignancy of a busy trade long since ended, but it also lies in its seclusion. Like most of the Broads network it needs to to be experienced, ideally, from a boat. These waters with their mysterious beauty cannot work their power by means of snatched glimpses through car windows on bridges or across rush-edged meadows.

What remains these days of H.A. Biedermann's vision? Unrestrained by locks, water surges clear and sparkling down his navigation from the reaches of the Upper Bure through sluices and along millstreams. Bright green fronds of waterweed swirl below the surface in the force of the stream; encroaching vegetation narrows a once open waterway. The public houses which thrived on trade from passing

right The scale on H.A. Biedermann's plan [*Aylsham Town Council, detail*]

watermen are now mostly closed: houses such as the White Horse by Coltishall Bridge, the Anchor of Hope at Lamas, and the Maid's Head and Cross Keys at Brampton. Traces of some of the rest of the infrastructure of the waterway can still be found. Only one watermill has disappeared, at Horstead; only one lock has been built over, at Buxton.

Public access onto the bankside paths is easy along the stretches from Coltishall to Burgh-next Aylsham. The Bure Navigation Conservation Trust, founded in 2012, aims to encourage access and understanding of the navigation's history; it also works for the conservation of the waterway. Much of the nine-mile route can still be explored on foot or in a canoe or rowing dinghy, from where you can pick out silent monuments in the form of low walls of red and pink brick behind the climbing ivy, their mortar brittle and crumbling, vestiges of the warehouses, maltings and kilns once lining the banks.

And in the town hall in the centre of Aylsham proudly hangs the plan of 1772, almost as tall as those viewing it. Skilfully delineating the route in blended russet, beige and brown it gave direction and form to this great enterprise.

above The Aylsham navigation inspires great interest. Crowds flocked all day to the centenary event on Coltishall Lower Common on 26 Aug. 2012, some of them coming from overseas. The stalls of societies connected with the navigation were kept busy from well before the scheduled opening time.

The site of Ives's upstream brewery is out of the picture to the left. Rose Ives, who gave the lock-builders a barrel of beer in 1774, lived at Coltishall Hall, behind the trees on the left [*MB · 2012*]

NORWICH: two views by James Stark of staithes on King Street, a manufacturing quarter with rows of warehouses, malthouses, breweries and granaries lining the River Wensum

top Looking upstream towards the Castle on the skyline; two wherries and a keel are moored opposite the Devil's Tower. The left bank is staithed, the timbers supporting the bank enabling boats to moor securely.

The right bank is not staithed, its rushy edge offering no firm landing place; one man has to wade deep [*engraving by G. Cooke 1831*]

right Looking downstream beside Harrison's Wharf. Two transom-sterned wherries are alongside a small maltings with a pantiled roof and characteristic vent or cowl. A tumbril is at rest beside an array of goods on the bank. The sawn planks are to be carted: they have no risers allowing air to pass during weathering [*engraving by J. H. Kernot 1829, detail*]

3
Riverside staithes

A small town of warehouses, malthouses etc

This situation [Geldeston Staithe], for trade, is admirably fine, being so entire within itself that no opposers can ever hurt it, lying between the towns of Beccles and Bungay, and having a fine navigable canal cut from the River Waveney half a mile up to it, upon which stands a small town of warehouses, malthouses, granaries, etc, all adjoining to the canal and locked up every night . . .

NORWICH MERCURY, 1776 [1]

William Frary in malthouse. Zeb Rouse and Robert Manning fetched bricks from the staithe forenoon . . .

William Frary in malthouse. Zeb Rouse and John Thompson fetching Welsh coals from the staithe.   MARY HARDY, 1775, 1778 [2]

VISITORS TO THE BROADS in Norfolk and Suffolk who choose to keep their feet on firm ground will marvel at the amount of time and consideration devoted by sailors to finding a good mooring place. The Broads can be seen by road from only a relatively few places. It is hard to appreciate from a pub garden, boatyard dyke or village green how inhospitable the great majority of the banks can be. Marsh-softened edges and reedy fringes look picturesque, but they are treacherous for anyone attempting to land there.

Those on the water find getting about not too burdensome, aside from various often-chronicled hazards. These range from high winds, low bridges, overhanging branches, submerged stakes and undredged riverbeds creating risk of grounding to strong tides on the approaches to Great Yarmouth. It is when a mooring is sought that anxiety levels rise. A poorly chosen one will result in damage to the boat—and in public humiliation in front of the crowd which instantly emerges from nowhere to observe the action.

[1] *small town Norw. Merc.*, 13 Jan. 1776. The advertisement is transcribed more fully on pp. 140–1.

The River Waveney forms the eastern end of the dividing line between Norfolk and Suffolk. The small village of Geldeston stands on the northern, Norfolk bank; the market towns of Beccles and Bungay are on the southern bank.

Those drafting the notice did not foresee the 'opposers' who were to arrive in the 19th century promoting Bungay and Beccles by deepening the Waveney as part of the Norwich and Lowestoft Navigation in 1831.

In 1863 a further danger was posed by the opening of the Waveney Valley Railway

[2] *bricks, Welsh coals Diary 1*: 10 May 1775, 28 Nov. 1778, at Coltishall. This is the only reference by Mary Hardy to Welsh coal in 36 years

above The approach to Rockland Broad and village from the River Yare along the upstream dyke. This large broad has two manmade cuts linking the flooded open-cast peat quarry to the Norwich–Gt Yarmouth waterway. The reed banks offer no landing place for boats, and similarly no footing for anyone attempting to come overland

facing page Looking back to the same point from the expanse of the broad. The posts and buoys mark the dredged channel.
    Another dyke off this channel, behind the photographer, leads to Rockland Staithe and its public house, the New Inn. As with much of the Broads the only way to experience these waters is by boat   [*MB · 2011*]

---

[1] *staithe* From Old English *staeth*, a landing place for merchandise; akin to hythe (Anglo-Saxon in origin), a wharf. 'Staithe' can be found in places with early Danish settlement, including Hull, York and Tyneside: the word has its origins in Old Norse (R. Malster, *The Mardler's Companion: A dictionary of East Anglian dialect* (The Malthouse Press, Holbrook, 1999), p. 73)

If this holds true today for those with engines the hazards were far greater for watermen under sail in Mary Hardy's time. A firm bank perhaps with piling and mooring posts, a safe landing with no harm to vessel or cargo, and a warm well-lit alehouse will have been at the forefront of a shivering waterman's mind as, often wet through, his long day ended and he faced the prospect of turning in to his cramped bunk with only bread and cheese and cold tea for supper.

An inland waterway requires numerous landing places if it is to be put to full use. One of the fascinations of the Broadland rivers is the frequency with which the old wharves and quays line the banks, many still used today by pleasure craft on the Broads. These staithes, as they are called, were once busy with keels and wherries loading and unloading their goods,[1] and Mary Hardy records the variety of cargoes

carried on the rivers in the years she was writing her diary at Coltishall from 1773 to 1781. As this chapter will show, the individual and sometimes elaborate layouts of staithes in towns and villages enabled them to perform a multiplicity of roles vital to the economy: manufacturing, supply, warehousing, coking of coal and victualling of watermen.

The staithe was absolutely central to efficient distribution, serving as the interface between land- and water-based transport. These commercial premises, often privately owned, furnished boats with essential support structures. The most important of these, apart from the ubiquitous watering hole, was the presence of a road or lane firm enough to permit horse-drawn traffic. The majority of staithes spelled bustle, commerce and human interaction, as seen at the chapter frontispiece. The contrast with marshy, reedy banks along unstaithed rivers and broads could not be stronger.

The characteristics of a staithe

A staithe offered a safe haven for a boatman and a means of livelihood for the staithe owner or manager, the wharfinger. It could be in a remote spot away from any local settlement, as at the head of a purpose-built dyke to carry away barley, malt, wheat and manure and bring in coal and timber.

above **Norfolk reed** (*Phragmites australis*), constantly swept by the wind. Its summertime purple-brown flowers and its golden seed cases and stems in winter are very distinctive [*MB · 2010*]

above Stokesby Staithe on the Bure, nine miles
from Gt Yarmouth. It has the typical components
of a staithe: cottages for workmen and wherrymen; a small lockable warehouse (right) for goods
going to or from the vessels; and a riverside public
house, the Ferry. The staithe owner's house stands
out of sight beside the cottages.

The Coltishall brewers John and Rose Ives and
their son Chapman owned a maltings near the
staithe, the cottages for their workforce having a
date stone 1757 (illustrated in volume 2, chapter 1).

The Ferry House at Stokesby was supplied with
Coltishall beer from Wells's brewery in the mid-
18th century (volume 2, table 2.8.4)   [*MB·1992*]

right The Stokesby warehouse, seen from downstream, appears on the tithe map of 1840. The
inlet was to accommodate the ferry   [*MB·1989*]

---

[1] *goods* The warehouse
at S. Walsham's staithe
in Fleet Lane bears the
date 1786 (e-mail from
Mundy Ellis of Fleet
Lane, 23 Dec. 2015)

It could alternatively lie in the heart of a town, a hamlet growing up nearby; the staithes at Aylsham and Loddon
were near the watermills. Stokesby benefited from its close-
ness to Great Yarmouth, where goods could be transhipped.[1]

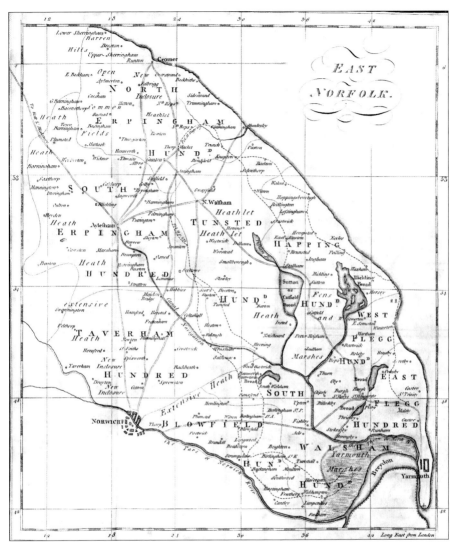

above East Norfolk and its rivers in 1787. The number of simplifications creates the effect of a diagram rather than a map. The Yare (in the south) and Bure (centre) are depicted as considerably straighter than their actual winding course; the Aylsham navigation is shown as extending to Wroxham. Many large broads including Hoveton, Wroxham and S. Walsham are omitted.

Undue deference to local pronunciation, as in 'Burrow' for Burgh-next-Aylsham, renders some places almost unrecognisable; 'Hoston' for Hoveton (sited too far west) is a misreading of Hofton. The 'extensive heath' north-east of Norwich is Mousehold.

Broadland as yet had no accurate mapping [*W. Marshall, The Rural Economy of Norfolk (London, 1787), vol. 1, frontispiece*]

above Barrowing coal by hand from the wherry *Meteor c.*1901 at Surlingham Ferry on the Yare; loose coal has to be shovelled out of the hold. The gaff is raised clear of operations and the hatches lie stacked by the mast [*courtesy Norfolk Wherry Trust*]

below left The Staithe House at Upton on the Bure, up a long narrow dyke [*MB·1992*]

Those drafting the legislation for the Aylsham navigation, while not employing the local term for a wharf, were careful to confirm the rights of manorial owners and riverside residents to build and manage staithes. The Act of 1773 permitted the creation of cuts and the erection of 'warehouses, weigh-beams, cranes, quays, landing places, or wharfs upon the banks', so long as such works did not 'obstruct or prejudice the said navigation' (quoted more fully on page 77).

Some were public and parish staithes, often on the banks of common land. Others were private, generally to be used only by the owners and occupiers of the property on the riverside at that spot, such as a watermill, tannery, brickworks, brewery, malthouse, lime-kiln, manor house or farm. Staithes have a long history, Tom Williamson pointing out that reference to them in the award and allotments following parliamentary enclosure was essentially to confirm pre-existing, time-honoured rights:

Before the late nineteenth century . . . the waterways played a more fundamental role in the wider economy of the region. They were arteries of trade, and the ease of transport which they afforded ensured that industry was a far more prominent feature of the landscape than it is today . . .

Both public and private staithes had existed in some numbers since medieval times. The suggestion sometimes made, that most originated with the Enclosure Acts of the early nineteenth century, is erroneous: the pre-enclosure landscape was littered with them.[1]

Before describing the operations of some eighteenth-century staithes and the vital services they performed on the Broads we need to arrive at some definitions. As Tom Williamson makes clear, this can be contentious. The question of how—and whether—to distinguish between a public staithe and a parish staithe is complex and at times bewildering; there can for instance be some overlap between the two types and they are not always distinguished in the sources.

Roy Kemp of the Broads Society, the author of a survey and register of 56 Broadland staithes which he had researched over twenty years, worked with the Broads Authority in 1984–85 before publishing the results of his labours in the form of a provisional, incomplete register.[2] When the Rivers Officer for the Great Yarmouth Port and Haven Commissioners—the body based at Great Yarmouth then responsible for river maintenance, navigational issues and toll-collecting—learned of Roy Kemp's endeavours, he wrote to Basil de Iongh on the survey's editorial team:

It is certainly a useful project, but I can think of less frustrating ways of passing my time . . . The whole subject is so complicated that my knowledge tends to be as vague as that of everybody else.[3]

Roy Kemp offers these definitions, distinguishing between rights confirmed by Parliament and rights based on customary use from time immemorial:

A PARISH STAITHE is one allotted in an Inclosure Award. For the most part these were specifically nominated as public staithes by the Commissioners for Inclosure, and the Act of Inclosure gives them statutory protection. In a few cases they formed part of the 'Poors Allotment' and became subject to the law relating to charities.

A PUBLIC STAITHE is one which is in general use by the public, and their status stems from various sources. In some cases a cus-

[1] *landscape* T. Williamson, *The Norfolk Broads: A landscape history* (Manchester Univ. Press, 1997), pp. 137, 138–9

[2] *register* Roy A.F. Kemp, *Staithes: A survey and register* (The Broads Authority, Norwich, 1986). Almost all these 56 staithes had rights of public access. The inclusion of private staithes would have more than quadrupled or quintupled the total.

The Broads Authority, a statutory body responsible for conservation, tourism and navigation on the Norfolk and Suffolk Broads, holds a series of files on staithes.

I am most grateful to the survey's author Major Kemp and to Mary Muir of the Broads Authority for granting me access to the working papers (MD14) in Norwich in Oct. 1990.

The Broads Society is a non-statutory body founded in 1956 by a group of Broads-lovers devoted to helping to secure a sustainable future for the Broads as a unique landscape in which leisure, tourism and local economy can thrive in harmony with the natural environment

[3] *complicated* Letter from Mr J.A.D. Hart, 3 Apr. 1984 (Broads Authority: MD14)

[1] *definitions* R.A.F. Kemp, *Staithes*, p. 1. For a discussion of the legal status of staithes and historic rights of public access to them, see also M. George, *The Land Use, Ecology and Conservation of Broadland* (Packard Publishing, Chichester, 1992), pp. 353–5

[2] *in perpetuity* Roy Kemp, discussion paper prepared for the Broads Authority, 22 Oct. 1984 (MD14).
The Authority had earlier commissioned a report from a team of Cambridge consultants on improving the design of staithes with public access, bearing in mind the different and at times conflicting interests of local residents, the boating fraternity, visitors by car, and conservation needs. The very popular Ranworth Staithe on Malthouse Broad was chosen for a case study 1982–83.

Many parishes on the Broads did not undergo parliamentary enclosure yet have parish staithes. It is evident that, as argued by Tom Williamson, the right predated the Acts of Enclosure of the 18th and 19th centuries. For enclosure and rights of access see vol. 2, chap. 3 and vol. 1, chap. 10 in this study

tomary use over a long period has been established; some are provided by an Authority—usually the Navigation Authority—others by gift or permission of a landowner. Where a public staithe is in private ownership problems relating to public use may arise . . .

A PRIVATE STAITHE is one where there are no public rights although in some cases the landowner permits a degree of public use.[1]

The function of staithes was not only the economic one of aiding the conveyance of goods, and they offered more than a valuable support mechanism in the distribution network. Roy Kemp acknowledged at the pre-publication discussion stage that access to parts of the riverside by the local inhabitants for recreational purposes was a time-honoured right. He also at this early stage put forward a broader definition of a parish staithe than appeared in the published survey, stating that the establishment of parish staithe status predated parliamentary enclosure and was not confined to awards and allotments as part of that process:

There is no doubt that prior to the Acts of Inclosure parish staithes were a part of the common wastes of the village. Following the inclosures the staithes remained unfenced and were dedicated to public use; thus the customary public rights remained unaffected and the villagers were able to resort to the staithes for purposes of recreation and enjoyment 'As in times past'.

Inclosures were the product of measures taken by Parliament in the interests of good husbandry. Recognising the continuing importance of parish staithes in the pattern of the rural economy Parliament gave them statutory protection.

The staithes were allotted to a public body representative of public interests (in many cases the Commissioners of Drainage) and dedicated to public use. The Acts make it quite clear that the public rights exist in perpetuity.[2]

Parish staithes can give rise to disputes. Many villages on the Broads now treat them not as interfaces between land and water for commerce and recreation, but as year-round berths for their parishioners' boats. Often a stretch of the public staithe is set aside for this purpose as well. The parish staithe becomes in effect a miniature marina, thereby losing one of the principal elements by which a staithe was defined historically: as a landing place. Instead of bustle, movement and endless coming and going the parish staithe of today can present a scene of stillness and inactivity.

There is no hint in Mary Hardy's diary of any disagreements or disputes over the use of staithes; active supervision by staithe owners and occupiers ensured smooth running. Almost all the staithes to which the diarist refers were private, and clear of controversy. Joseph Browne, innkeeper of Coltishall's leading establishment the King's Head, was also wharfinger of the equally prominent King's Head Staithe.

Neither Coltishall nor Horstead underwent parliamentary enclosure, and no statutory definition of a staithe in the two parishes appears to have been made at this time. Staithes do however feature in conveyances and other legal agreements, being valued as significant assets attached to a riverside property. When John Simpson, father-in-law and executor of the Coltishall brewer Robert Wells, was making over the business to Robert's cousin William Wells in 1744 he listed all the leases of the public houses belonging to the brewery. One lease specifically mentioned two staithes in Hoveton St John, across the River Bure from Wroxham, in the occupation of the subtenants Henry Brown and John Wright respectively and belonging to Robert Smith of Hoveton St Peter. Dated 7 August 1739, the 21-year lease related to the King's Head at Hoveton with its staithe and garden, and to a second unidentified house with its yards, gardens, staithes and privileges.[1]

A search for staithes in the parish taxation records, the ratebooks, yields nothing. It might be thought that an ingenious parish officer looking to raise new sources of revenue for the parish church or the poor, or those attending the annual meeting to set the rates, would have found a way of including an asset like a commercial staithe in the schedule of properties with a rateable value. But the Coltishall and Horstead ratebooks for the mid- and late eighteenth centuries, while carefully recording rating payments by the occupiers of malthouses, brewhouses, granaries, mills and farms, contain no references to staithes.[2]

The central part of this chapter will examine some individual staithes and their workings, starting with the public staithe immediately downstream of Joseph Browne's at Coltishall. Two private staithes, both with interesting features, will follow: the Manor House Staithe just upstream of Browne, and a model staithe at Geldeston on the Waveney.

[1] *Hoveton* NRO: BRA 1164/16/18, 760 x 7, Indenture of 23 June 1744 endorsed, 'Mr Simpson, executor of Mr Wells, his assignment of several leases as also of the possession of several estates unto Mr William Wells'.

For Wells's brewery at Coltishall, managed by William Hardy 1772–82, see vol. 2 chap. 8

[2] *ratebooks* See table 2.5.3 in vol. 2, chap. 5.

In 1777 Joseph Browne paid rates on his dwelling (the King's Head), on a maltings he occupied and a granary he owned (this last probably standing on the King's Head Staithe), but not on the staithe as such (NRO: PD 598/ 37, Coltishall churchwardens' account book)

above The King's Head, Coltishall   [*MB · 2010*]

below right Coltishall: looking to Lower Common from the approximate boundary of the King's Head Staithe and public staithe [*Christopher Bird 2004*]

[1] *terrier* NRO: DN/TER 48/3, Coltishall glebe terrier, 20 June 1770.
The full text is transcribed in *Diary 1*, app. D1.B, the staithe reference being on p. 429 of the appendix

[2] *wherry Diary 1*: 11 Apr. 1776. This was the Hardys' wherry *William and Mary* (chap. 4)

[3] *King's* The college had owned Coltishall's three commons since the mid-15th century, King Henry VI giving part of what had been his personal estate as Duke of Lancaster to endow his new Cambridge college founded in 1441. For an overview of mediaeval Coltishall and its manor of Hackford see vol. 3, chap. 5 in this study.
    In 1992, after 550 years of ownership and management by King's, the commons were sold by the college to a new management trust, formed 'to ensure future sound management and preservation of the commons' and with local parish council representation on the new body; the purchase money (£37,000 plus legal fees) was raised by grants and donations (Sally Barber, 'The Coltishall Commons Management Trust', in *The Marlpit: The community paper for the villages of Horstead, Coltishall and Great Hautbois* (Horstead, Sept. 1991), p. 16).
    I am very grateful to Mr W. H. Stibbons of Coltishall for posting me *The Marlpit* every month for many years. It has in recent times been available to all online: <www.themarlpit.co.uk>, accessed 25 May 2019

A public staithe at Coltishall

In the 1770 Coltishall terrier there is mention of a staithe, in terms suggesting a public staithe, which lay at one end of 'the common way leading from Coltishall Staithe to Sco Ruston'.[1] This is likely to have been the public staithe at the south-western corner of Coltishall Lower Common near the King's Head (also used in later years as moorings for the Rising Sun public house); it lies close to the start of the present White Lion Road, which forks at Coltishall Old Hall to Sco Ruston and Tunstead. It was a very busy stretch of the river. Wright's boatyard lay immediately upstream of the King's Head, Mary Hardy on five occasions coupling wherry building by Wright 1776–77 with the name of Joseph Browne: as, for example, 'Mr Hardy at Joseph Browne's forenoon, began to build a wherry'.[2]

    The staithe named in the terrier is probably one of the public staithes referred to in documents at King's College, Cambridge, the owners of all the commons at Coltishall.[3] As

we have seen, public staithes were associated with common land. Over a long period the college received reports from local people anxious about encroachments on and misuse of the staithes. As early as 1725 the lawyer Henry Smith of Great Hautbois, who like his son Henry served as manor court steward to King's, forwarded to John Burford, Bursar of King's, the complaint that several persons who were neither owners nor occupiers of lands in Coltishall were using the staithes without payment of any recompense and without contributing towards the charge of such staithes. He requested the college's help over remedying the grievance.[1]

Encroachments continued into the following century. Mr Clarke, apparently the college's early-twentieth-century archivist, noted that the years 1817–49 saw further erosion of the public rights over the staithe near the King's Head, these being years when that end of Lower Common became more commercial and industrial. On 10 June 1828 the college gave notice to Thomas Watson to remove the buildings he had erected on 'the waste' (the common). On 29 May 1849 George Ives, shown in White's directory of 1845 as a butcher and coal merchant as well as innkeeper of the White Lion nearby, applied for permission to enclose a portion of

above **Coltishall:** the view from Lower Common with (in the foreground) the area of the public staithe and, where the Rising Sun now stands, the King's Head Staithe. The old granary with its tarred gable end fronting the water's edge may be a successor to Joseph Browne's granary [*Christopher Bird 2004*]

[1] *Smith* King's Coll.: KCAR/6/2/38/9, COL/517, notes by F. L. Clarke, dated May 1911, on the contents of a letter from Henry Smith dated 21 July 1725; the original was destroyed in 1911

[1] *perch* In square measure 40 perches equate to one-quarter of an acre. 4 perches is thus 2·5% of one acre

[2] *encroachments* King's Coll.: KCAR/6/2/38/9, COL/517; W. White's *Norfolk directory* (Sheffield, 1845), p. 464; F. White's *Norfolk directory* (Sheffield, 1854), p. 422

[3] *revival* R. Bond, *Coltishall: Heyday of a Norfolk Village* (Poppyland Publishing, N. Walsham, 1986), pp. 1–2. He identifies the village's heyday as ending about 1914.

Yet as early as 1841 the last of the wholesale breweries had closed (vol. 2, chap. 8)

[4] *public staithe* I recall that around 1968–74 Clifford Allen, the Coltishall boatbuilder, unveiled a large board confirming this staithe's existence downstream of the Rising Sun. The board did not last long

the waste abutting on the river 'at a place called the Staithe near the King's Head Inn and to erect a building thereon' for the purpose of landing coals from barges navigating the River Bure.

At first, in 1850, Congregation (the college body) voted that he could be allowed to enclose 4 perches, although this decision was rescinded in 1852.[1] In 1851 and 1852 Samuel Buck and Thomas Wright the Elder were also pressing to take over small pieces of waste at the staithe near the King's Head, and this may have been the moment when the future public house, to be licensed later as the Rising Sun, appeared on the scene. Samuel Buck is named as running a beerhouse at Coltishall in White's directory of 1854, but no beerhouse is listed in the village in 1845.[2]

The second quarter of the nineteenth century marked the start of Coltishall's partial revival after the depression brought about in part by the Aylsham navigation, Richard Bond singling out the abundance of craftsmen, numerous malthouses, busy wherry traffic and the boatbuilding yard as contributing to Coltishall's Victorian emergence as a 'boom town'.[3] It is possible that King's College tried to help the process along by agreeing to measures which would promote trade and industry even at the expense of former customary rights, although no such resolve appears to have been expressed in the surviving college records.

The history of Coltishall's Lower Common staithe shows how rights and public access could be whittled away over time.[4] King's College may have been enticed by the prospect of quit-rents (annual payments to the manorial lord)

---

facing page The tithe map of Coltishall, surveyed 1841 and oriented north. It shows the King's Head Staithe in the centre [323], on a gentle bend in the river.

A narrow stream, culverted under the main west–east Coltishall–Wroxham road, runs from Tunstead to enter the Bure just east of the King's Head Staithe. The public staithe, then under threat from commercial expansion by local entrepreneurs, lay in this area, on cither side of the stream.

The King's Head itself stands on the main

road opposite a long narrow malthouse. Another very long, narrow malthouse, west of [323], occupies the site of Wright's yard where the Hardys' wherry was built in 1776.

A large private staithe [11] is seen at the manor house upstream, near the foot of this portion of the very large map. An L-shaped wherry cut has been dug at the downstream end of the staithe. The Manor House Staithe is depicted on Corby's map of the King's College estates in 1811 on page 136 in this chapter   [TNA: PRO IR 30/23/146, *detail*]

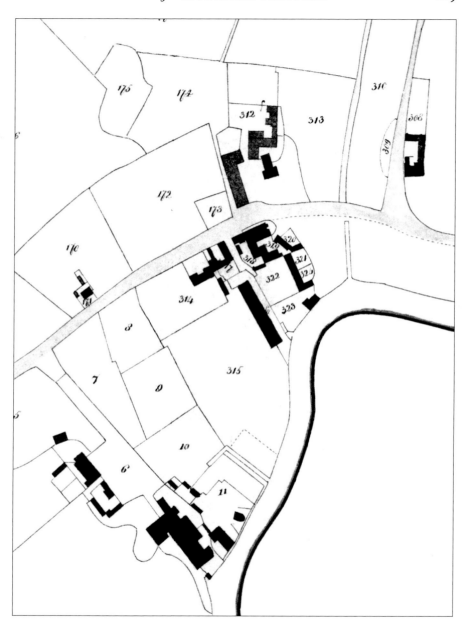

[2] *acreage* King's Coll.: KCAR/6/2/38/9, COL/517, Coltishall Commons, May 1911.
The principal part of Lower Common between the grounds of the Hall and the Bure then totalled 2 acres 3 roods 3 perches: approx. 2¾ acres.
It had been much larger. In 1782 a grant of 3 acres 1 rood 16 perches (only a portion of the then extent of common land) had been made by King's College Congregation to the brewer Chapman Ives of Coltishall Hall, with the consent of Coltishall residents with rights of commonage (including William Hardy), so that he could empark his house: see vol. 1, chap. 10.
Lower Common is known in the college records by its old names of Newgate Common and Parsonage Common. The other large riverside common, Upper Common, had the historic name West Common

[3] *warehouses* John Yaxley describes the distinctive former 'Coal House' on Barton Turf's public staithe (J. Yaxley, *A Jam round Barton Turf* (Barton Turf, 2006),

when granting permissions to enclose and build on hitherto common land, since on 13 December 1850 Congregation specified that George Ives and Samuel Buck should pay quit-rents.[1]

Nineteenth-century photographs show housing on part of the staithe, and Buck's bakery and the Salvation Army Hall were also on the site between the two public houses until the 1950s. By May 1911 King's College calculated that the part of Lower Common near the Rising Sun adjoining the River Bure (presumably the public staithe) totalled just 1 rood 19 perches—well under half an acre.[2] Stalham Staithe, pictured opposite, shows the type of small-scale building taking place in the nineteenth century on the public staithe at Coltishall: the 'small town of warehouses' referred to at the chapter head.[3]

We shall return to the King's Head Staithe, an important coaling staithe often referred to by Mary Hardy, in the section on staithes used by the Hardys. Given the significance of the rights of access vested in them, it is disappointing that public staithes have relatively little documentation: an absence of firm evidence beset Roy Kemp in his researches.

Public access in the form of non-permanent (often 24-hour) moorings is vital to tourism on the Broads: the boats need a firm, safe bank; the local shops and public houses need their custom. The riverbank at Coltishall Lower Common, apart from the small island once used for pleasure boating by the owners of Coltishall Hall, has long been treated as short-term mooring by boat-users. The common serves in effect as a popular public staithe (*plate 56*).

Coltishall, like most other villages on the Broads, also had another type of staithe affording public access. These were the narrow scores associated with built-up areas. Now under threat, they too have a largely undocumented history.

Scores: staithes in miniature

The port of Lowestoft has narrow scores, often steeply sloping, linking the High Street to the beach. The score is a particular type of public footpath or bridleway associated with access to water; some could take small wheeled vehicles. The rows of Great Yarmouth, running from the town centre

left Stalham Staithe, on the River Ant. This flint-and-brick warehouse may pre-date its date stone of 1837. The large opening will have been made when it became a garage, but its old doors were almost certainly lockable when the building stored goods brought by water such as coal and bricks   [*MB · 1998*]

right Stalham Staithe: a former warehouse converted for use as the Museum of the Broads. Bundles of thatching reed harvested from the marshes rest beside a beached reed lighter. Many towns and villages—such as Stalham, Sutton, Barton Turf, Stokesby and Beccles—retain structures associated with staithes   [*MB · 2001*]

to the quays along the River Yare, serve the same function as scores. Slim carts known as troll carts had been developed well before the eighteenth century to cope with these narrow rows (note on page 32). Cart gaps in the cliffs similarly linked villages to the beaches along the coast.

Scores were a feature of Broadland towns and villages.[1] Some, as depicted on the map of Coltishall Manor House Staithe in 1811, seen on page 136, were not for public use. Another score downstream, in Anchor Street, gave access from the lane to the river, but was blocked off and incorporated into a neighbouring riverside garden in the late 1960s. Like footpaths, they are vulnerable to seizure by private owners. The scores of Beccles are likewise under threat.

p. 36; it was used to store perishable goods as well as coal

---

[1] *scores* Almost certainly they once were more numerous than today. One, a valuable village asset, runs from Horning Lower Street to the river below the New Inn, and is so narrow as to be missed by most passers-by

Beccles staithes and scores: the Suffolk market town of Beccles, on the River Waveney, has a wealth of features from its days when it depended on the river for its trade.

It also has the best preserved series of scores on the Broads. On Puddingmoor and Northgate, they serve as miniature public staithes for residents and visitors—if mooring continues to be permitted

top A former maltings, now converted to housing, its cowl above the old kiln attesting to its past life.

These garden moorings served as the maltings' private staithe, with wherries delivering barley, coal and cinders and taking the malt to Yarmouth and Norwich

left Church Score, newly staithed in timber, seen from the road and (below) from the river

right The Score, seen from the road at the top of a steep flight of steps and (below) from the river. [*MB · 2014*]

above Another former maltings at Beccles. It stands close to The Score, the widest of the scores along Northgate. As on the coast at Blakeney, and elsewhere on the Broads including Coltishall, most working buildings such as malt-houses, granaries and tanneries were built gable end to the water

STAITHE
SMITH & EASTAUGH
CORN & COAL MERCHANTS.
Dealers in Malt & Hops of the best quality.
BEANS. PEAS. OATS. POLLARD. CINDERS
WHOLESALE & RETAIL
Wherries constantly attend the Traders & Steam Vessels for conveying goods to and from the wharf.

above right The gable end of the maltster's house in Northgate, Beccles, seen set back from the river at the top of the opposite page. The sign's reference to steam vessels shows that it dates from well after Mary Hardy's time, but it clearly demonstrates the varied nature of the trade at this spot.

Merchants frequently dealt in both corn and coal, as did the Palgraves at Coltishall. They sold wholesale and retail, as did the Hardys at Coltishall and Letheringsett.

As dealers in hops, brought by sea from Kent, these merchants supplied brewers: Beccles was a brewing as well as a malting town. Pollard is coarse-ground flour; the cinders (coke) for malting would probably have been coked on this staithe from the Tyneside coal brought here from Gt Yarmouth and, after 1833, from Lowestoft.

This waterborne trade ended with the coming of the railways, one of the lines crossing the river right by this staithe   [MB · 2014]

[1] *laundry* J. Crome, *Back of the New Mills* (c.1814–17)

[2] *row* eg J. Thirtle, *A View of Thorpe, with Steam Barge working up—Evening* (1815); J. Crome, *Norwich River: Afternoon* (c.1819)

[3] *wading* J. Crome, *New Mills: Men wading* (?1812)

[4] *wherry cut* Now almost hidden from the river by trees, it has been narrowed over the past century by encroaching vegetation. Mr W. H. Stibbons (1908–97), of The Limes and part-owner of the wherry cut, told me on 10 Aug. 1990 that many of the meadow dykes run into the cut, necessitating constant dredging and cleaning of the cut to keep the fields drained.

He added on 28 June 1991 that when he was a small boy 'you could get three boats side by side in the wherry cut'. Thus even into the 20th century the staithe retained something of its former capabilities

As well as being used for quick loading and unloading of small goods, scores had a multiplicity of other functions. A painting by John Crome, a leading member of the Norwich Society of Artists with a strong affinity with workaday subjects, shows what appears to be a score in Norwich being used by a woman washing laundry. Such a facility would have been greatly valued in built-up areas with few wells.[1]

Scores had leisure functions. Those with boats could moor up briefly to collect friends and take them for a row or sail, as also seen in Norwich School paintings.[2] Townsfolk would wade into the water, where it shelved, to cool off on a summer's day.[3] Residents of cottages with no river frontage liked to take the evening air by the water's edge, as did those in Anchor Street at Coltishall until the score was blocked. Watching the mist settle on the Horstead pastures across the Bure enabled them to forecast the next day's weather.

Until very recently those coming up from a mooring at Gillingham, downstream of Beccles, or from Geldeston upstream, could moor their dinghies at the Beccles scores while shopping in the town or having a pub meal. The scores are not treated as long-term berths, which would destroy their availability for others. As the governing body of King's came to realise over Coltishall's public staithe in the nineteenth century, there is a hunger for riverside access. Unless measures are in force to preserve scores and public staithes they will be encroached upon and then taken over entirely.

Two private staithes

Private staithes looked different, being more complex. As we shall see, instead of small warehouses such as Stalham's some had massive, well-designed buildings with special features such as spouts for shooting malt into the holds of wherries and keels, or a raised ground floor to allow vessels to squeeze under the building to unload. Two private staithes are well documented, at Coltishall and Geldeston.

One of Coltishall's largest private staithes was owned by King's and run by the college's tenants, the Palgraves. The 1811 estate map by Robert Corby of Kirstead, Norfolk (overleaf) shows that the area right beside the manor house was an industrial site, bordered by an L-shaped wherry cut leading from the Bure to the cinder yard and wood yard.[4]

A long straight drive runs from the main road past the barn, the wide turning circle for the wagons in the road clearly marked. The corners of the start of the drive have deliberately been sheared away at the main gate, and a less pronounced easing has been created on the opposite side of the road by the field gate into five-acre Pasture Close. This drive provided the only road access to the house and staithe in the early nineteenth century, with the result that the Palgraves not only lived in the bustle of mercantile activity but shared the drive with the carts and wagons. Later in the nineteenth century a second, curving drive was created from the west and across the seven-acre lawn, affording a more private and picturesque approach to the main front.[1]

The icehouse and large seventeenth-century barn stand a little distant from the house. But the remains of the malthouse and other staithe buildings near the river, some incorporated into garden walls and other features, lie exceptionally close to the main house, the nearest being only 20 feet (6 metres) from the south wall of the house. In the Palgraves' time, as the 1811 map shows, the large malthouse was actually joined to the house.[2]

A remarkable feature of the estate map of 1811 is the number of field gates it depicts at the manorial property. While some were presumably to keep stock penned, others would have been to prevent thieves driving away goods by the cartload. Nine gates are shown, the hay, barley, wheat, malt, timber, coal, cinders and other commodities stored on the premises being extremely valuable.

Shortly before the death of William Palgrave in November 1822 this 'concern of magnitude' was put on the market, together with all the lands and houses he owned in his own right (overleaf). As with the advertisement for Geldeston Staithe in 1776, transcribed in this section, the particulars of 1822 make no mention of the impact on trade and profits caused by the upstream navigation, although the college as owners were well aware of the difficulties (chapter 2).

In Mary Hardy's time at Coltishall there were many other private staithes, serving the village's many maltings, three common (wholesale) breweries and the merchants. References and descriptions occasionally follow the bankruptcy or death of the owners and occupiers. When John Fiddy

[1] *west drive* Shown on the 25-inch OS map, 1906.
The north entrance also remains in use today, much narrowed now that it no longer leads to an industrial site. The old rounded corners required by the long wheel base of horse-drawn vehicles once bound for the staithe can still be discerned in the banks of ivy and under the trees

[2] *house* I should like to thank Squadron Leader and Mrs Geoffrey Williams of the Manor House and Richard Bond, also of Coltishall, for devoting hours to showing my family and me round the house and grounds on 22 Aug. 1989

right The Manor House
Staithe at Coltishall in
1811, a short way down-
stream from the watermill
and manor house at
Horstead. Both houses
stand on the River Bure:
the 're' of 'bure' is seen
at the foot of the map.

The map is shown here
oriented north-west,
being rotated from its
original orientation so
that the labelling is level.

William Palgrave
(1745–1822), the corn and
coal merchant based here,
privately owned much of
the surrounding property.

The features of an active
working staithe are clearly
mapped. The wharfinger
Mr Palgrave lives in the
manor house fronting the
curving drive south-east
of the yard [45]. A large
riverside malthouse adjoins
the house, reached by a
field gate and from the
long manor house 'score'.

Close by are the cinder
yard, with its coking ovens
[50], and the wood yard
[49]. A long wherry dyke
from the river edges two
sides of the cinder yard.

Barns, stables and other
outbuildings lie between
the house and the hedged
main road
[*courtesy the Provost and
Scholars of King's College,
Cambridge:* KCAR/6/2/87/6,
HOR/136, *estate map by
Robert Corby, Jan. 1811,
detail; photograph Cam-
bridge University Library*]

The 'large and commodious staithe' at Coltishall Manor House in 1822

source King's College, Cambridge, KCAR/6/2/38/8, COL/407: Conditions of sale of the capital freehold and leasehold estates . . . belonging to Mr Palgrave . . . to be sold by auction . . . at Gurney's Hotel, Chapelfield, Norwich, on Saturday 7 September 1822 . . . in twenty-two lots [1]

THE ESTATES ARE SITUATE AT COLTISHALL, in the county of Norfolk, and partly adjoin the River Bure, which is navigable to Yarmouth, and consist of excellent dwelling houses, with gardens, offices, and outbuildings adapted for the residence of genteel families; cottages well worth the attention of persons desirous to secure votes; [2] spacious malthouses, granaries, and mercantile buildings, upwards of 95 acres of arable and pasture land, of the best quality, in high cultivation, adjoining the river, where an extensive business in the corn and coal trade has been carried on for more than seventy years.[3]

Coltishall is a populous village, and the poor's rates are moderate. It is situated in a good corn country, distant only seven miles from Norwich and the market towns of North Walsham and Aylsham, twenty from Yarmouth, and with a daily post and a stage coach passing through each day . . .

LOT 20. A most valuable LEASEHOLD ESTATE, in the occupation of Mr Palgrave; consisting of a capital messuage and the undermentioned lands, containing about 31 acres,[4] and numerous mercantile and agricultural buildings and yards of the first description, eligibly situated on the banks of a river, with a large and commodious staithe . . .

The MESSUAGE possesses every accommodation for a respectable family, and commands a delightful view over a considerable tract of rich and well-timbered pastures, and has near it a large garden, well stocked with the best fruit trees and thriving plantations.[5]

The MERCANTILE BUILDINGS consist of a counting house, malt-house with a 60-coomb steep, malt-mill, granaries, [private] brewery, wine vault, cinder ovens, coal yard, hay house, chaise house, cart lodge, and granary over it, bullock shed, cow houses, piggeries, four stables, and other buildings necessary for a concern of magnitude . . .

This Lot is held of King's College, in Cambridge, under a lease for 20 years (usually renewable every seventh year for 21 years) whereof 17 years will be unexpired at Michaelmas next, at the yearly rent of £1 7s 4d in money, and one quarter of wheat and one quarter and four bushels of malt, or of money in lieu thereof, after the rate the best wheat and malt shall be sold for in Cambridge Market on [   ].

LAND TAX £2 17s. The lessee is allowed the sum of £3 6s 8d yearly, for collecting the quit-rents due in the manors of Coltishall and Lessingham, of which the lessors are the lords . . .

[1] *source* Transcribed courtesy King's College

[2] *votes* A telling pointer to the way a landlord, if he chose, could command his tenants' votes in the days before secret ballots

[3] *business* William Palgrave (1745–1822) was the only survivor of the 11 children of Capt. Thomas Palgrave (1715–75) and his wife Mary Manning.

Capt. Palgrave and his brother William (1718–80) had been in partnership at Gt Yarmouth and Coltishall. For details of their careers see C.J. Palmer and S. Tucker, eds, *Palgrave Family Memorials* (Norwich, 1878), pp. 45–66.

The younger William Palgrave served as Mayor of Gt Yarmouth in 1782 and 1805. His wife Elizabeth, herself the sole survivor of 11 children, died aged 58 during his second term

[4] *lands* Omitted in this transcription. The college lands totalled 31 acres, the remaining 64 acres belonging personally to William Palgrave

[5] *fruit trees* The orchard was sold in about 1928, the large house named Orchard Hill being built in this part of the Manor House gardens

[1] *wharf* Norw. Merc. 9 Oct. 1802.
    The local term may not have been used as Ives was casting his net wide, as far as London, in the hope of finding a buyer. The term 'staithe' may not have made much sense to metropolitan manufacturers and entrepreneurs

[2] *chaldron* A measure of volume equating to about 1·2 or 1·3 tons: see chap. 4 and the Glossary.
    Robert Ansell's sale advertisement for the Hardys' wherry gave her carrying capacity as 12 chaldrons of coal (*Norfolk Chronicle*, 21 July 1781)

[3] *Ansell's wherry Diary* 1: 20 Dec. 1775

[4] *steep* The cistern is which barley is wetted at the start of malting: see vol. 2, chap. 6.
    Malting capacity was judged by steep size

junior, the young dancing friend of Raven Hardy and William Hardy junior, was bankrupted in 1801, the notice in the *Norwich Mercury* of 16 May 1801 referred both to his freehold house at Coltishall, with an orchard, granaries and large maltings, and to the staithe at Wroxham or Hoveton which he rented from the Vicar of Wroxham, the Revd Daniel Collyer. This staithe's maltings, coal yard and cinder oven, held on a long lease, had sixty years yet unexpired.

Chapman Ives's immense steam brewery at Coltishall, capable of brewing 26,000 barrels a year, stood in what later became known as Anchor Street (then Lowgate). It had its own 'wharf' just downstream of Lower Common; the site is illustrated as the frontispiece to chapter 8 in volume 2.[1]

The clearest way to picture a private staithe of the 1770s, the period of the Hardys' time at Coltishall, is to quote the sale particulars from the *Norwich Mercury* of 13 January 1776 (overleaf) describing a thoroughly up-to-date staithe. It was owned by the merchant Samuel Robinson at Geldeston, on the Norfolk bank of the Waveney at the furthest extremity of the Broads from Coltishall. Even allowing for the hyperbole of the times Geldeston Staithe had all the elements of a well-designed integrated enterprise.

Served by a long manmade cut, it was on the tidal river to Great Yarmouth and thus free from the tolls and dues to which navigations such as the Aylsham and Bungay schemes were subject. Its 'small town' on the cut, of warehouses, malthouses and granaries, could be securely locked at night to prevent pilfering. Its coal wharf was large, being capable of handling 2000 chaldrons of coal—nearly 170 wherry loads if shipped by the Hardys' 12-chaldron wherry *William and Mary*.[2] The granary of 1773 could store 1000 quarters of grain. Couched in terms familiar to Mary Hardy this was the equivalent of 2000 coombs or 100 lasts of corn (more than 203 metric tonnes)—a little more than ten wherry loads for a large Coltishall boat, Robert Ansell's wherry being capable of shipping at least 8½ lasts of malt (more than 17·25 metric tonnes).[3]

The 1775 malthouse at Geldeston Staithe had a 40-coomb steep, the same size as the one at Letheringsett bought by William Hardy in 1780.[4] Like his maltings at Coltishall and Letheringsett it had two malting floors and a granary in the

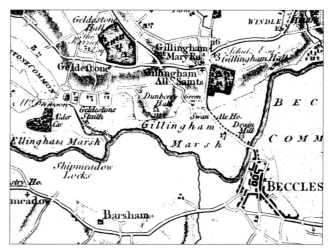

left Norfolk's first accurate, large-scale map, of 1797. The cut to Geldeston Staithe is marked 'Navigation'; Shipmeadow Lock, also known as Geldeston Lock, lies on the main river.

Benjamin Dowson, the new owner of the staithe, is named at Staithe House [*Faden's Map of Norfolk 1797: Larks Press 1989*]

facing page The half-mile-long dyke as it nears Geldeston Staithe. The unmade-up bank, with no piling and a minimal number of mooring posts, is typical of some rural staithes   [*MB · 2014*]

roof area, the store over the Geldeston malthouse being capable of holding an additional 1000 coombs of barley.

The malt granary described in the sale advertisement as accommodating another 2000 coombs of malt was of an unusual design. It straddled an inlet off the dyke so that wherries and keels could nudge under the store, the malt being poured down chutes into the hold and thus saving days of laborious loading. Shallow-draughted vessels like those on the Broads could squeeze under a granary, malthouse or warehouse for loading and unloading. A timber-clad granary of 1808 similarly built across a dyke survives at Stalham's substantial staithe on the River Ant; the windows date from its conversion to a home (*plate 12*).[1]

Samuel Robinson owned three wherries. Perhaps keels found Geldeston Dyke too narrow or shallow, although, as seen in chapter 2, the 58-ton keel *Royal Oak* could get up the Bungay navigation. He was also part-owner of two sea-going ships plying from Great Yarmouth, presumably giving him control of his malt shipments to London and elsewhere. William Hardy junior similarly expanded into shipowning in 1800, as chapter 5 relates, such diversification forming part of the complexity which characterised so many enterprises including the Hardys'.[2] Robinson also had stables, and a cinder oven for making the fuel for the maltings. None of these features survives today at this quiet, tree-lined spot.

[1] *granary access* Such loading bays were not new. Caister Castle, north of Gt Yarmouth, has a 15th-century watergate under which barges could dock. It is linked via the Pickerell Fleet to the River Bure.

An 18th- or early 19th-century arched loading bay under a brick warehouse survives at the back of Grove Farm House, west of Gay's Staithe, Neatishead, served by a cut from Limekiln Dyke, off Barton Broad

[2] *diversification* Analysed in vol. 2, chap. 5

Geldeston, on the River Waveney in Norfolk: a model private staithe 1776

source Norwich Mercury, 13 Jan. 1776

---

[1] *canal* The dyke (illustrated on the previous
page) linking the river to
the village of Geldeston
was dug following the
formation of the Bungay
navigation under the Act
of 1670 (22 Chas II, cap.
16: see p. 111, table 4.2.1).
The cut lies a short
way below the most
downstream of the
navigation's locks

[2] *teams* Of horses

[3] *Wherry* In the late 18th
century this was the only
public house at Geldes-
ton Staithe (NRO: c/Sch
1/16, Alehouse register
1789–99).
In about 1850 a second
public house, the Garden
House, was built in Big
Row even closer to the
staithe

GELDESTON STAITHE, ETC   To be sold by private contract:
All that well-known staithe and wharf with the sole and exclusive
right of navigation belonging thereto, extending to and from the
port of Great Yarmouth, at which is now carried on a very considerable and well-established mercantile trade in coals, corn, deal, etc
etc etc with great advantage and in great repute, being so situated
that the trade is entirely free from all encumbrances of tonnage,
lockage, etc to which most other inland navigations are subject;
being a singular and very considerable advantage to the trade of
this navigation.

This situation, for trade, is admirably fine, being so entire within
itself that no opposers can ever hurt it, lying between the towns of
Beccles and Bungay, and having a fine navigable canal cut from the
River Waveney half a mile up to it,[1] upon which stands a small town
of warehouses, malthouses, granaries, etc, all adjoining to the canal
and locked up every night; with an exceedingly fine coal wharf
capable of containing two thousand chaldron of coals, which are
landed with little or no expense, with a very quick sale for the same.

Likewise close to the waterside is an exceeding well-built fine
granary, capable of containing one thousand quarters of corn, built
in 1773, adjoining to which is an exceedingly good compting house,
from which is commanded the canal, the wharf, and all the buildings etc upon it.

Also an exceeding good brick and tiled malting office built last
summer, forty coomb steep, with two exceeding good working
floors, one plaster of Paris, the other brick, and a fine granary over
the same, capable of containing five hundred quarters of corn, with
storerooms and drying chambers for laying dry malt so conven-
iently adjoining and built over the canal that vessels may lay under
the chambers to receive their loading without any expense, and the
same is capable of containing one thousand quarters of malt.

Adjoining is a strong-built brick cinder oven, with large yards
boarded in for laying a large quantity of coals and cinders. Also
new-built stables for the convenience of teams coming to the
staithe;[2] and also adjoining is a large spacious quay and yard; and
near thereto stands an exceeding good and convenient messuage
with very pleasant gardens, orchard, with great variety of fruit trees,
fish pond etc, pleasantly situated against the road leading from
Bungay to Beccles, with a barn, stables and convenient outhouses;
and a public house, known by the sign of the Wherry, let to John
Brown at the yearly rent of five pounds:[3] also about nine acres of
pasture or meadow land adjoining to the navigation, with six tene-

right The Wherry Inn at Geldeston, opposite the fine staithe house with its crinkle-crankle wall [*MB · 2014*]

ments, four of which are new built, brick and tiled, with large yards and gardens to each, very convenient for watermen etc employed in the said navigation.

The whole is freehold, and upwards of two thousand pounds have been laid out upon the premises within five years, which has rendered it one of the most compact situations for a merchant that is in the counties of Norfolk or Suffolk, and which opens itself into a fine extensive country for trade, which is large and well established, and carried on with great advantage, and is in great esteem.

The reason for all the premises being to be disposed of, arises from the present proprietor's intention of going to reside in London in a capital mercantile business.[1]

Likewise are to be sold three wherries or lighters with their masts, sails, ropes, rigging and furniture now in employ, and belonging to the said navigation, in conveying merchandise to and from Yarmouth.

Also a sixteenth part of the ship called the *Shrimp*, of Yarmouth, burthen 100 tons, John Moore, Master; and an eighth part of the ship called the *Good Intent*, of Yarmouth, burthen 120 tons, Simon Smith, Master; and two pleasure boats, with sails and rigging.

Also an estate in Geldeston aforesaid, called and known by the name of the Old Staithe, with a messuage, outhouse, and about two acres of land let to Elias Clear, tenant at will, at the yearly rent of seven pounds ... [There follow details of the Old Staithe property and 4 acres of arable, the river marshes, and 5½ acres of arable and meadow land, the whole to be entered upon at Michaelmas or earlier.]

For further particulars enquire of the proprietor, Mr Samuel Robinson, merchant, on the premises; or of John Kerrich, Esq. at Harleston;[2] John Gay, Esq. at Norwich; Mr Christopher Eaton, merchant, at Yarmouth; or Mr Joseph Shrimpton and Co., merchants, in Mark Lane [Corn Exchange], London.

[1] *proprietor* Samuel Robinson did not retire from the Geldeston business until 1785. He had by then built two new malthouses, each with 35-coomb steeps (*Norwich Mercury,* 20 Aug. 1785).

He may be the same Samuel Robinson of Houndsditch, London, or a relative, who had engaged to build the Aylsham navigation in 1774 in partnership with James Frost.

However he failed to attend meetings. Biedermann quickly succeeded him as engineer (Aylsham Town Council: Box 36, minutes of 16 June and 25 June 1774)

[2] *Kerrich* Brewers at Harleston, Suff. (vol. 2, table 2.8.2). Faden's map shows Thomas Kerrich at Geldeston Hall

above Geldeston Staithe: the four riverside cottages described in the 1776 particulars as 'new built, brick and tiled, with large yards and gardens to each, very convenient for watermen etc'. These are the only standing remains of Robinson's complex by the water.

The railway which cruelly drew attention to itself by running beside and almost across the staithe would have severely damaged the waterborne trade. By the middle years of the 20th century the small town of warehouses had given way to a boatyard   [*MB · 2014*]

1 *public house* The Locks Inn at Geldeston Lock, a long walk from the staithe, lies in Ellingham parish

2 *spouts* Norw. Merc. 15 Oct. 1785 (opposite).
An almost identical notice for the same three malthouses was published in the *Norwich Mercury* of 14 Oct. 1786; again all three had the labour-saving spouts

The staithe owner's red-brick house (now the Old House) had its own range of outbuildings, and still stands against the main road, its gardens bounded by a very fine crinkle-crankle wall. A common accessory for a staithe was advertised in the sale notice of 1776: the public house, then the only one in the parish, aptly named the Wherry and evidently belonging to the staithe owner.[1]

This was a sophisticated staithe for a small village. Speed, efficiency and economy over labour costs were more usually highlighted in relation to the large malthouses of a city: some maltings on the River Wensum in Norwich had spouts overhanging the river so that malt could be poured from the upper storerooms into boats lying alongside.[2]

While manufacturers would have appreciated the much-improved turn-round times provided by internal loading bays and spouts, one of the notices makes it plain that the reduced labour cost, the 'saving for porterage', was a consideration worth emphasising. A 60-coomb malthouse in Green Man Yard, Conisford (along King Street, and perhaps similar to one seen at the chapter frontispiece) had 'one storeroom very advantageously situated for conveying malt on board the keel by spouts, which is a considerable saving for porterage'.[1]

The grain would presumably be bagged as it poured into the hold, to enable it to be transhipped more easily at Great Yarmouth and to keep it clean; the boat's previous load was likely to have been coal or cinders. Any vessel carrying grain would also need to be hatched to protect the malt from the weather, as described in the next chapter.

According to the Geldeston notice more than £2000 had been spent on the staithe and its buildings between 1771 and 1776. While the business was in many respects vertically integrated some important elements were missing. Samuel Robinson had to buy in his barley, very little arable land being advertised. He malted it and could carry it in his own vessels; his men, six of whom he could house, could quench their thirst in his own public house. At the end of his working day he could go sailing on the Waveney in one of his own pleasure boats. But there was no brewery. His successors, the Dowsons, filled these vital farming and brewing gaps.[2]

[1] *saving Norw. Merc.* 21 Aug. 1779. A riverside malthouse in Bishopgate in Norwich with a 60-coomb steep also had 'spouts to convey the malt immediately out of the malt rooms into keels' (*Norw. Merc.* 21 Sept. 1776).

All these maltings had a much larger capacity than village enterprises like those of William Hardy and Samuel Robinson

[2] *Dowsons* They prospered and stayed for generations, founding the Geldeston Brewery in the early 19th century. They used their wealth to found the British School in 1825 (White's *Norfolk Directory*, 1845, p. 808).

As a mural tablet above the door records, Elizabeth and Susanna Dowson gave the village hall built near the staithe in 1928 to the parish 'to commemorate the connection of the Dowson family with the village since 1788'

MALT HOUSES to be LET, and entered upon immediately,

I. A Large MALT HOUSE, in St. Michael Coslany, near the Bridge; consisting of two Steeps, of sixty Coombs each, two Kilns, &c. besides a large Granary.

II. A MALT HOUSE situated at the lower End of Fyebridge Quay; consisting of two Steeps, forty-two Coombs each, one large Kiln, &c. besides a large Granary.

III. A MALT HOUSE in the Rainbow Yard, Kingstreet; consisting of three Steeps, thirty Coombs each, and two Kilns, &c. besides a very large Granary.

The above Premises are very Convenient for the delivery of Corn by the Farmers, and also for sending it to Yarmouth; being all situated next the River, and have Spouts for loading the Corn directly into the Craft.

Inquire of the Printer of this Paper.

left Norwich malthouses at some up-to-date staithes. All three have 'spouts for loading the corn directly into the craft' moored below [*Norwich Mercury*, 15 Oct. 1785: *Norfolk Heritage Centre, Norwich*]

¹ *Ranworth Norw. Merc.* 6 Nov. 1790. Mr Steward, a Gt Yarmouth attorney, had the sale particulars. The Geldeston complex could also store 100 lasts.

Anyone climbing Ranworth Church tower today gets a good view of part of the walls and other remains

² *Norwich* J. Stark and J.W. Robberds jnr, *Scenery of the Rivers Yare and Waveney, Norfolk*, pt 2 (London, 1830), unpag.

above **A busy staithe at Beccles. It is not clear if the dilapidation often portrayed by Stark and other Norwich School artists is an accurate depiction or a device to dress up the staithes in Picturesque garb** [*painting by J. Stark; engraving by W.F. Cooke 1833, detail*]

These two private staithes, at Coltishall Manor House and Geldeston, had complex layouts; many would not have had malthouses, cinder ovens and timber yards. Almost all staithes however, public and private, would have needed a secure place or warehouse in which to store that most vital commodity, coal.

An advertisement for a private staithe at Ranworth is probably more typical. It was a maltings staithe on Malthouse Broad, lying on the slope below the church. Interestingly, being linked by water to Norwich as well as Great Yarmouth (as indeed all places are on the Broads) was considered a selling point. A freehold estate was for sale, with some huge granaries. It had two 'substantial malthouses, in excellent repair, that will wet upwards of 60 coombs of barley, with storerooms that will contain between 90 and 100 lasts of corn', together with a house, stables, land, and the liberty of fishing in the broad at Ranworth 'next the navigable river to Yarmouth and Norwich—to which belongs a good staithe'.¹

The somewhat ramshackle buildings and staithes seen in Norwich at the chapter frontispiece were nearly demolished as not having enough capacity—and sufficient elegance— for the great endeavour envisaged by the Norwich and Lowestoft Navigation Act (table 4.2.1). In his accompanying text to Stark's depiction of the existing staithes at Harrison's Wharf James Robberds junior described the large deep-water basin along King Street designed to bring the city up to date: 'As it is intended to make the head of the ship navigation near this point, it will undoubtedly soon assume a very altered aspect.' He imagined the 'lofty warehouses, capacious docks and handsome quays, with all the more splendid accompaniments of foreign commerce' where lines of malthouses, breweries and granaries at present stood.²

The scheme was only partially realised in 1833, and Norwich never got extensive deepwater docks. The 'humbler fabrics', in Robberds' eyes, remained with their jumble of pantiled roofs and cluttered yards—a feature of even the more substantial staithes. Norwich was fated not to develop into one of the great mercantile centres of Europe in the centuries to come.

Staithes used by the Hardys

Staithes were such workaday affairs that they received little in the way of specific notice. They were just landing places for goods. By contrast the mills, maltings, breweries and granaries on their banks did attract attention and, if we are lucky, make their appearance in the archives. The working staithes' humble, everyday character, highlighted by Robberds in his lofty prose, causes problems for those researching their history. For the same reason Mary Hardy never names the river which ran past her house. It was merely 'the river'. Goods came and went 'by water'.[1] Like the staithe beyond her front garden it was just there. We never learn whether she called it the Bure or the North River—both names in use at the time. Nevertheless her Coltishall diary does tell us about the seven staithes, listed below, on which the Hardys' business depended.

[1] *the river* Mary Hardy was not writing for posterity, and makes no concessions to any future reader unfamiliar with her world.

Even in her opening entry in the 36-year-long record she fails to name the river flowing past her home: 'Mr Hardy and Raven went to Yarmouth by water' (*Diary 1*: 28 Nov. 1773).

Nowhere does she use the port's full name of *Great* Yarmouth, but that practice was near universal at the time

TABLE 4.3.1

Staithes used by the Hardys and by their wherry *William and Mary* 1773–81

source Diary of Mary Hardy

town/village, river	staithe, wharfinger	recorded vessels
1. **Coltishall** Bure	Wells's private staithe, William Hardy, brewer (home berth)	*William and Mary*; Colls's wherry; Symonds' keel; unidentified keels and wherries
2. **Coltishall** Bure	King's Head, Joseph Browne, innkeeper	unidentified keels and wherries
3. **Coltishall** Bure	Manor House, William Palgrave (d.1780), merchant	*William and Mary*
4. **Coltishall** Bure	Upper Common, ?William Hardy, ?parish	*William and Mary*
5. **Gt Yarmouth** Bure	Symonds' Wharf, Jonathan Symonds, grocer	Symonds' keel; *William and Mary*
6. **Horstead** Bure	Horstead Watermill, John Colls, miller	Colls's wherry
7. **Strumpshaw** Yare	?Strumpshaw Staithe, ?public staithe	unidentified keel; Symonds' keel

above and *facing page* From the Coltishall tithe map of 1841: the great curve of the River Bure flowing west to east along the parish's southern boundary with Horstead.

The Hardys' private staithe is the triangle of land [16] at the downstream end; their maltings and brewery are the long buildings set well back [18]. Their house, tiny in comparison, lies behind the industrial complex at the foot of the southern slope from the church on the main road [19].

The Aylsham navigation begins at the fork by their staithe. Upper Common occupies the huge expanse between the watermill (bottom left), the bridge (far left), and east to the Hawes maltings [41] and brewery on both sides of the road (centre).

The short-lived staithe William Hardy created on Upper Common was just below the lock, east of the upstream fork. Drains criss-cross the common and meadows [TNA: PRO IR 30/23/146, *details*]

The home berth of the Hardys' wherry *William and Mary* was to be found at the private staithe belonging to their house, now called Holly Lodge. It presumably formed part of the property rented from their landlord John Wells, owner of their house, maltings and brewery.[1] As well as recording sailings from other wharves at Coltishall and at Great Yarmouth and Strumpshaw (listed in the next chapter's tables and wherry log) Mary Hardy chronicles the day-to-day work of loading and unloading at their staithe.

The cut for keels and wherries calling there has a distinctive triangular shape, creating the small island which survives today. As seen clearly on the tithe map, illustrated, a grid of narrow meadow dykes drains into the cut from the land belonging to the property immediately upstream (now the Norfolk Mead Hotel), and from the Hardys' meadow adjoining the manor house, immediately downstream.[2]

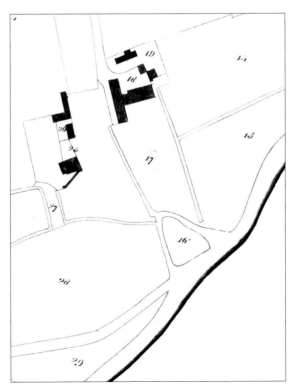

[1] *Holly Lodge* I am very grateful to Ivan Spinks (b. 1934) for showing my family and me round the island staithe and the area of the Hardys' former malt-house and brewhouse on two occasions in Aug. 1990 while he was watching over a Muscovy duck hatching 16 eggs on the island.

He told us that in 1960 he and Michael Durrant, owner of the staithe, had discovered that the small basin at the head of the triangle, the most inland point, had a firm shingle bottom beneath the mud and that a spring of clear water ran over a York-stone rockery into the cut (see also vol. 1, chap. 7 on the Hardys' house)

[2] *dykes* A roughly drawn sketch map held at King's, undated but perhaps early or mid-19th century, clearly shows the triangular cut, the set of meadow drains into it, and the fork to the millstream and the navigation or lockstream (King's Coll.: KCAR/6/2/087/6, HOR/90).

It is not clear from either this map or the tithe map whether a small wherry like *William and Mary* could push inland along the dyke right to the coal store (probably the small square building at the head of the eastern dyke seen in the close-up, left) and to the maltings and brewery, but it would have made sound sense. Barrowing heavy goods across uneven turf would have been exhausting

[1] *Taylor* The presence of the staithe is implied in the sale particulars: 'LOT 8 . . . This Lot is very desirable for a merchant; the dwelling-house and malthouse stand nearly in the centre of the land, which lies together, and is bounded by the River Bure for a considerable extent to the southwest' (King's Coll.: KCAR/6/2/38/8, COL/407, Sale of estates belonging to Mr Palgrave, 7 Sept. 1822)

[2] *refrains Diary 1*: 28 June 1775, 21 Dec. 1775, 13 Feb. 1776, 11 Mar. 1776, 22 Mar. 1776, 5 Jan. 1780

[3] *Peirson* TNA: PRO CUST 47/299, p. 101, 13 June 1775. There is nothing to suggest the letting of the staithe triggered the officer's removal. He had just challenged the local schoolmaster to a duel with sword and pistol for 'hurting his childer [children] at school', an intemperate response which would have displeased his Excise masters (see vol. 1, chap. 6; also *Diary 1*: 10 June, 12 June 1775). The order for his posting came the day after the challenge

[4] *oats, coal Diary 1*: 5 Dec. 1774, 28 Oct. 1776. Half a last is 10 coombs (approx. 1016 kg, or just over one metric tonne)

The triangular cut is also shown, less precisely than on the later tithe map, on the plan accompanying the sale particulars of William Palgrave's property in 1822. By this time his son-in-law, the surgeon Walford Taylor, was living at the Hardys' house, with Palgrave himself part-occupier of the adjoining six-acre riverside meadow.[1]

The maps and the sale particulars convey nothing of the bustle and backbreaking labour forming the daily backdrop to the life of the staithe. Despite its laconic style, the significance of Mary Hardy's record of her Coltishall years is its glimpse into that largely undocumented mercantile world of the staithe: a world of movement, of loading and unloading, collecting and delivering, manufacturing and trading. Echoes of this lost world resound in the diary refrains: 'Zeb Rouse fetched 13 chaldrons of coals from the keel'; 'Mr Hardy at the staithe all the forenoon'; 'Zeb Rouse and Isaac Pooley and labourer fetching cinders home from the staithe'; 'Zeb Rouse fetching home bricks'; 'Zeb Rouse and Isaac Pooley fetching cinders from the staithe'; 'Zeb Rouse carrying tree nails down to the staithe for Boorne and Neve'.[2] The words repay study. In the first, during one long midsummer day, one man, the steadfast farm servant Zebulon Rouse, shifted about 16 tons of coal single-handed.

Apart from the references to goods passing through the staithe Mary Hardy makes a somewhat surprising reference on 3 October 1774 to her husband's letting of the staithe to the local excise officer, Thomas Peirson: 'Let the staithe to T. Pearson, he to be allowed 3*s* in the pound of all the staithe money'. It was highly irregular for an exciseman to come to a private commercial arrangement with one of the manufacturers under his survey, and the agreement may not have lasted long. Thomas Peirson was posted to a Norwich excise division in June 1775.[3]

One nearby staithe which the Hardys also used was the busy one at the King's Head, already described in this chapter. The innkeeper's name is synonymous at times with his staithe, as in 'Zeb Rouse fetched half a last of oats from Joseph Browne's'. When Zeb was holding things together during an innkeeping interregnum at the Recruiting Sergeant, the Hardys' Horstead tied house, his master and mistress arranged to send coal to him 'from Joseph Browne's'.[4]

William Hardy seems to have been instrumental in creating a new staithe from scratch at Coltishall Lock, although his wife's entries are unhelpfully brief. He is recorded using it in 1777–78. On 27 March 1777 Henry Edwards, one of the Hardys' men, supervised by his master, 'began making a road cross the Common to the Lock, Mr Hardy with him all day'. Mary Hardy also records work on the road in April and August that year and road repairs there early in 1778.[1] As the tithe map shows, the lock lay some distance south of the main Norwich road and the bridge, but the bank there is firm and only one meadow drain would have had to be bridged—probably with timber—to support a cart.

On 6 April 1777, a Sunday, the Hardys walked to their wherry *William and Mary* moored at the lock, suggesting the existence of a staithe just downstream of the lock: 'All walked to our wherry at the Lock and then went to Horstead Church.' The mooring at the lock had the attributes of a working staithe, even though this was on Upper Common which belonged to King's College, no mention being made either in the diary or in the manor court books and surviving letters at King's of negotiations and terms for a further development on common land. Mary Hardy records coal and cinders being collected from the lock,[2] and nog (strong beer) for London being delivered by the Hardys' men to *William and Mary* which was apparently moored at the lock rather than their home staithe:

John Thompson and William Frary raking Sergeant Piece and got them [the rakings] up, then fetched coals from the Lock and carried six barrels of nog to the wherry for London.[3]

It is hard to know what explanation to offer for these entries. Given the arduous nature of collecting coal and cinders by road it would have made sense to bring the wherry to the Hardys' staithe rather than send a cart a quarter of a mile towards the bridge and then take the new road for a few hundred yards over the common to the staithe on the lock-stream. This improvised staithe on Upper Common is not referred to after December 1778, and Coltishall residents born in the early years of the twentieth century and consulted on the matter had no recollection of any road over the common, nor of a staithe on the lock canal.[4]

above **A malt-kiln cowl: often the first sight a skipper had from afar of the staithe for which he was heading. This converted maltings is on the main quay at Beccles** [*MB · 2011*]

[1] *road Diary 1*: 4 Apr. 1777, 13 Aug. 1777, 20 Jan. 1778, 27 Jan. 1778

[2] *coal, cinders Diary 1*: 6 Sept. 1777, 21 Jan. 1778, 16 Dec. 1778

[3] *nog Diary 1*: 6 Sept. 1777. The verb 'carried' suggests the distance was greater than just the short way down to the home staithe

[4] *new road* Once the college was alerted to their existence the short-lived road and staithe could have been closed by King's using informal channels, perhaps by a word to Henry Smith who lived close by at Gt Hautbois

[1] *Colls, Palgrave Diary 1:* 2 Dec. 1775, 29 Feb. 1776; 1 Feb. 1777

[2] *Symonds Norw. Merc.,* 25 Apr. 1801; the main road led north to Caister-on-Sea and Martham. He did not have long to enjoy his retirement, dying at Ormesby St Margaret on 9 Aug. 1803 aged 65 (*Norw. Merc.,* 13 Aug. 1803). The Hardys often visited the Symonds family and had them to stay.

For a study of the family, prominent in Gt Yarmouth for generations, see A.W. Ecclestone, *The Old White Lion, Great Yarmouth, and the Symonds Family* (E. Lacon & Co. Ltd, Gt Yarmouth, nd [*c.*1946])

There are occasional references to two other staithes at Coltishall. The Hardys twice turned for help to John Colls at Horstead Watermill over taking their malt to Great Yarmouth, and they in turn helped out William Palgrave at the manor house by carrying his barley in their wherry also to Great Yarmouth.[1] Links to the port 32 miles downstream from Coltishall were strong. The key person there on whom the Hardys relied was Jonathan Symonds, the owner of a large staithe on the last stretches of the Bure.

Symonds, the Great Yarmouth grocer, merchant, salt-refiner, wharfinger and member of the town's Common Council, is shown in the diary to have supplied the Hardys with coal and cinders on a regular basis, as the next chapter will describe. His staithe, Symonds' Wharf, with its extremely long 500 feet (152 metres) of frontage to the Bure was advertised in 1801 at the time he retired from trade to live at the Old Hall, Ormesby St Margaret. His house in the seaport was for sale, together with two lime-kilns, chalk-houses, warehouses, a coal yard, wreck yards and wharves, all situated 'on the banks of a navigable river and communicate with the main road leading to the hundreds of East and West Flegg'.[2]

right The ledger stone in Gt Yarmouth Parish Church (now the Minster) to Jonathan Symonds, owner of a huge staithe, and his wife Phillis (d.1803 and 1826).

Mary Hardy, being from the same background, was particularly drawn to shop-keepers. The Hardy and Symonds families became close. They kept in touch even after the move to Letheringsett in 1781, Phillis, the Symonds' only child, making a number of visits. She married Edmund Preston, from another influential family at Gt Yarmouth, but died aged 26 in 1805.

The Symonds and Preston ledger stones in the west end of the north aisle are rare survivals in a magnificent church whose tower, roof and interior were almost totally obliterated by wartime bombing in 1942. Only some walls were left standing   [*MB · 2011*]

above Gt Yarmouth in the 1860s. The mid-14th-century tower stands close to the site of Symonds' Wharf on the last reaches of the Bure before its confluence with the Yare. The parish church of St Nicholas (left), a prominent seamark, can also be seen for miles across the marshes on the approaches by river.

The Hardys berthed their wherry *William and Mary* here 1776–81 when their close friend Jonathan Symonds, a Gt Yarmouth grocer, was the wharfinger. The large vessels on the right are two wherries (gaff-rigged) and a keel (with the square sail), all hatched.

The bank is staithed in the traditional manner with horizontal planking held in place by vertical piling driven deep. The large pantiled warehouse has seen better days [*painting by W.H. Hunt: Norfolk Museums & Archaeology Service (Great Yarmouth Museums)*]

The Hardys used Jonathan Symonds' keel not only for coal and cinders brought south from Tyneside by sea and transhipped from the colliers, but for goods taken along the Yare from the village of Strumpshaw. This, the last of the staithes forming part of the infrastructure of their small empire, lay more than 50 miles from their base, requiring a round trip of 101 miles. Boats plying between Strumpshaw and Coltishall sailed east along the Yare and crossed the treacherous tidal sheet of open water and mudflats of Breydon before entering the River Bure.[1]

[1] *keel* Table 4.4.4 logs the movements of Jonathan Symonds' keel bringing bricks and floor tiles (pamments) from Strumpshaw and coal and cinders from Gt Yarmouth, and returning to Yarmouth with malt from the Hardys

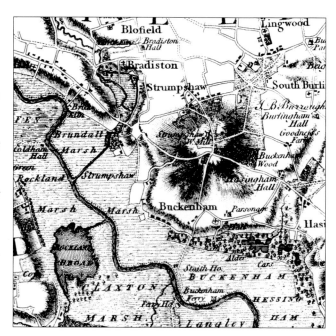

¹ *Staithe House* Shown on the OS one-inch map of 1838 (1st edn)

² *Low Road* This skirts the old access points to the dykes leading to the large broad and thence to the main river—a clear example of a service road supporting the interface between land and water.

I am most grateful to Mr and Mrs Cowles for welcoming my son Roger and me to their house (unannounced) on 31 July 1990 and to Mr Cowles for drawing a map of the old layout of the staithes based on accounts he had heard when young. It shows the route taken by wherries in the 19th century along the dyke from the main river which then forked, leading to two separate broads.

Wherries calling at Low Road's staithes would fork right and cross the broad later mudpumped by the RSPB. The northern wherry cut led to the public staithe (near the RSPB car park), bringing coal and other materials to the village.

Unlike the later hall, Strumpshaw Old Hall lies very close to Low Road, where it had its own private staithe

Symonds' keel transported bricks on a regular basis from Strumpshaw, where one of the tenants of a Hardy tied house, John Clarke of the Shoulder of Mutton, was also a brickburner. The laying of the Norwich–Great Yarmouth railway line in 1843–44 through the area of the public and private staithes at Strumpshaw and, from 1975, the creation of parking and visitor arrangements in Low Road for the Strumpshaw Fen nature reserve of the Royal Society for the Protection of Birds (RSPB) have made it difficult to reconstruct the old staithes' layout today (*plate 6*).

A local resident of Low Road, Bill Cowles (born 1905), recalled that the public and private staithes were located on either side of Staithe House, which by 1990 had become the RSPB warden's house.¹ These had not been working staithes in his lifetime, as the dykes leading to Strumpshaw Broad and thence to the River Yare had been too clogged up to be used by wherries. Mrs Cowles could however recall the days when marshmen would cut reed from the broad and carry it on shallow-bottomed boats 'to the village staithe, from where it was taken away along Low Road'.²

facing page The long dyke joining Strumpshaw to the River Yare beside Brundall Marsh was navigated by the keels and wherries recorded by the diarist on their round trips to Coltishall. It lies upstream of the dyke to Rockland Broad, on the opposite bank.

Low Road runs to the staithes at the foot of the western slopes of Strumpshaw Hill. The broad is not shown; instead that large expanse is depicted as marsh. Another staithe, with its Staithe House, is shown downstream, opposite the public house at Buckenham Ferry   [*Faden's Map of Norfolk 1797: Larks Press 1989*]

Mary Hardy does not tell us where in Strumpshaw the keels and wherries would call to collect the bricks. Typical entries read: 'Symonds's keel came up from Strumpshaw laden with bricks;' or 'Our wherry came up from Strumpshaw loaden with bricks etc.'[1] One keel-load could contain as many as 7000 bricks, plus pamments.[2] The only riverside brickworks in the area marked on William Faden's map of 1797, the brick-kiln on the Yare itself, lay upstream of the dyke leading to Strumpshaw Broad and staithe. This kiln was reached by a road to the river south-west of Braydeston Church. However the kiln, if Faden is accurate, was not in Strumpshaw but in the parish of Braydeston ('Bradiston' on the map), in the area south of Brundall station occupied from the early twentieth century by boatyards.[3] Almost certainly this was not the kiln to which Mary Hardy refers. The staithe used by boats bound for Coltishall was to be found in Strumpshaw parish, serving Clarke's brickworks.

The question arises as to why the Hardys persisted for three years 1774–77 in bringing bricks on a 101-mile round trip by water. Coltishall lay in good brickmaking country, and rather more local suppliers could be found. It may be that William Hardy was trying to keep his innkeeper afloat financially; or that there was some contract with the Wells family over Strumpshaw bricks.[4] Possibly a return cargo, unrecorded by the diarist, made the round trip economic.

A likely explanation is that the economics of water transport, as against land, made Strumpshaw an attractive proposition in the eyes of the Coltishall farmer and brewer. In a similar operation, presumably before the Horstead marlpits were developed, it made sense to take marl, used as a fertiliser, 47 miles by water from the pits outside Norwich round to Woodbastwick rather than seven miles by road.[5]

[1] *bricks Diary 1*: 17 Nov. 1775, 28 July 1777

[2] *keel-load Diary 1*: 14 Nov. 1774

[3] *brick-kiln* G. J. Levine in *A Concise History of Brundall and Braydeston* (Brundall, 1977) refers to the public staithe which existed until the two parishes were amalgamated in 1883; it lay in one of the dykes later used by Broom's (pp. 19–20). But he makes no mention of a brickworks in this area

[4] *Wells* William and Mary Hardy met John Wells, owner of their Coltishall brewery, at Strumpshaw in 1774 (*Diary 1*: 2 July 1774). Another member of the Wells family, Jonas, was based at Strumpshaw (*Diary 1*: 1 Sept., 11 Sept. 1774, 2 Feb. 1776).

John Clarke did not manage to keep afloat. His affairs took up a great deal of William Hardy's time, including settling the Strumpshaw brick-kiln.

The innkeeper-cum-brickburner spent a year in the debtors' gaol in Norwich Castle (*Diary 1*: many entries 1774–79)

[5] *marl* W. Marshall, *The Rural Economy of Norfolk* (2 vols London, 1787), vol. 2, p. 99.

The villages were on the Yare and Bure respectively

right The staithe at Coltishall Manor House, its hydrangeas shimmering pink in the August sun.

The flint-and-brick walls formed part of the private staithe seen earlier on Corby's 1811 map   [*MB·1999*]

below Terracotta malt-kiln tiles, uprooted in 1928 during demolition of the riverside malt-ings beside the King's Head, Coltishall. The maltings took over the site of Wright's boat-yard when the yard moved downriver in 1800.

The tiles were relaid close by to pave the piggery yard of The Limes. Fragments of such tiles used to be dredged up in the silt and dropped on the Horstead bank as late as the 1960s [*MB·1988*]

That type of calculation preserved the staithes as essential components of the local economy until the railways under-cut them during the extension of the rail network across the hinterland, away from the main routes, in the 1880s.

Until then the river, not the road, ruled supreme in the mercantile world as the principal highway for carrying bulk goods. At inland ports the merchant houses turned their main fronts to their staithes and to the warehouses and manufacturing buildings straggling across them; from these they derived much of their wealth. Even now, long after the withering of the river trade, a great deal of visual evidence can be recorded if the determined explorer takes to the water.

The Hardys' house, the manor houses of Coltishall and Horstead and the two brewery houses associated with Ives's at Coltishall all face the Bure. The rear elevations of the first three are turned towards the road from which they are largely invisible. Their principal gardens once graced the back or sides of the houses, and did not extend down to the water where the vital activity of the staithe held sway. At Coltishall only properties cut off from the river turn their faces towards the road—houses such as the Hall, Old Hall, The Limes (lying between the Manor House and King's Head and with no river frontage until the land purchases of the twentieth century), and the Old House, the former Hawes brewery inland from Upper Common.

left A complete con-
trast with the setting of
a working staithe. As
seen at Rockland at the
start of the chapter, the
edges of Hoveton
Little Broad, upstream
of Horning, are formed
of reed beds which offer
no landing place.

Faden's map of 1797
marks this area as
Horning Fen, and
shows no road here
to the broad's edge.

This appears to be
the thatched cottage
chosen by John Thirtle
for his watercolour
Hoveton Little Broad,
*c.*1815–20. The house's
charm lies in its air of
quiet retreat in an
isolated situation.

These may have been
the very characteristics
which appealed to the
artist's aesthetic sense.
They, and the reeds,
have nothing in
common with a manu-
facturer's wharf or a
village coaling staithe
[*MB·*2000]

The standing remains of staithes from Mary Hardy's time
are few: perhaps only some salvaged malt-kiln tiles trans-
planted into a yard or terrace, or a length of ancient brick
wall put to an ornamental use by supporting a colourful
climbing plant. Lawns and flower beds now often hide
the old foundations of the warehouses. Reeds colonise the
crumbling banks.

In the days when dredged silt from the river bed could
still be deposited upon the bank the drying mud would
reveal fragments from the past: lumps of coal and coke,
a broken brick, or a jagged piece of resilient kiln tile with
its daisy-patterned perforations. Graceful weeping willows
and rambling roses now soften the staithe edge; branches of
dense foliage arch over the yards and wherry cuts where coal
wharves and timber stacks once lined the banks. The scent
of roses and meadowsweet now drifts across the staithes
where the heady smells of malting, brewing and coking coal
would have signalled to the wherry skipper on a night passage that he was drawing near his berth.

Those watermen and their boats are featured in the next
chapter.

above The view from the helm of a Norfolk wherry. Here *Albion*, built at Oulton Broad in 1898, passes St Benet's Level Mill, a drainage mill seen by *William and Mary* on her regular passages to and from Gt Yarmouth.

The tea party at her launch would have gathered in the empty hold, the only place with room for them all   [*MB · 2001*]

= 4
Keels and wherries

Launched the new wherry this afternoon

Launched the new wherry this afternoon, named her the William and Mary; Mr and Mrs Danser and Miss Gooch dined here and drank tea on board the wherry. Mr and Mrs Smith, Mr Fiddy and daughter, Mr Ansell and Mr Easto drank tea with us, the gentlemen stayed till past 12 o'clock [midnight] and were very drunk.

MARY HARDY, 1776 [1]

The present wherries are much smarter craft than those of a couple of generations back. At that time there was another class of vessels called 'keels', which were fitted with huge square lug-sails, and were chiefly used for carrying timber. These are now unknown.

The last we saw was some ten years back on the Bure. We had moored opposite St Benedict's Abbey one chilly gloomy evening, when a keel came up the river before the strong easterly breeze. The immense square sail, as she passed us and drove on, shut out the narrow feeble sunset, and seemed to deepen the gloom around us. She was a very old-looking craft, and so far as we know, she has never reappeared from the faint western glow in which she then disappeared. GEORGE CHRISTOPHER DAVIES, 1883 [2]

'A VERY SHADOWY PERIOD'. These words of Robert Malster are by an authoritative writer reflecting on current knowledge of the waterborne trade on the Broads in the eighteenth century. A specialist in maritime history, and having devoted a lifetime to the study of Norfolk and Suffolk, he concludes in one of his many portraits of the Broads that 'Information on 18th-century trade on the waterways is hard to come by.' [3]

Mary Hardy's light penetrates some of the shadows.[4] But the lantern is swung so delicately, her presentation being low-key and unobtrusive in the extreme, that the reader of her Coltishall diary is hardly aware of the uniqueness of the keel and wherry material lying heaped among her jumble

[1] *very drunk Diary 1:* entry for 22 Aug. 1776

[2] *old-looking craft* G.C. Davies, *Norfolk Broads and Rivers*, pp. 29–30

[3] *shadowy* R. Malster, *The Norfolk and Suffolk Broads*, p. 115

[4] *Mary Hardy* Michael Sparkes, volunteer wherry skipper and honorary archivist of the Norfolk Wherry Trust, saw ahead of me into the shadows.

The publication of his article 'The *William and Mary* and the *Nelly*' in the *Journal of the Norfolk Wherry Trust* (spring 1988, pp. 38–42) under David Bray's editorship spurred me into my resolution of 1988 to transcribe the MS diary of Mary Hardy and write a commentary on it.

I am grateful to them both—now that the penal servitude is over

top **Good fortune to the wherry: a red and blue 'bunch of pears' on** *Albion*'**s mast** [*MB·2014*]

[footnote 1] *wherry log* Summarised in the section on the working days of the Hardys' small wherry (pp. 220–3)

[footnote 2] *register* NRO: Y/C 38/3. In addition to sections devoted to the register, two of this chapter's tables (4.4.2 and 4.4.3) derive from that source.

   The map opposite is constructed from the register. The 47 parishes providing home berths, omitting the 'away' berth at Hardley, are listed in this chapter, with the tonnages of the vessels using them (p. 194)

of entries on the weather, the workforce, the public houses, scriptural texts and the children's illnesses. What in fact emerges from the shadows is a revelation, and includes the only approximation to a wherry log known to survive from the eighteenth century. The diarist catalogues some of the dates and destinations of the passages made by the small wherry *William and Mary* built for William and Mary Hardy at Coltishall in 1776, identifies the freight carried on many of the voyages, and gives much otherwise unrecorded detail including firm evidence that it was the Hardys' workforce who did the loading and unloading.[1]

   This chapter will describe the state of the waterways of the Norfolk Broads in the diarist's time before defining the characteristics of the two principal cargo-carrying sailing vessels, the keel and the wherry. Then follows an analysis of the wealth of intelligence provided by an invaluable source already touched on in chapter 2: the register of Broadland keels and wherries maintained 1795–98.[2]

right Turf Fen Mill. George Christopher Davies in his 1883 portrait of the Broads refers to 'scores of windmills all twirling merrily round'. These were drainage mills, like this one on the River Ant, to pump water from field and pasture into the rivers.

   In the 19th century the rivers and broads were not heavily wooded, and keel and wherry passages could be fast to Gt Yarmouth if the wind and tide were right. Now only the middle and lower reaches resemble the rivers of Mary Hardy's time, with reed banks stretching into the horizon [*MB · 2001*]

facing page The 47 places in which all 156 keels and wherries of 13 tons burden and above had their home berths, as revealed by the Gt Yarmouth register of vessels 1795–98 now held in the Norfolk Record Office. The entries are described in full later.

   One further village, Hardley, on the Yare, was recorded as a destination for a wherry berthed at Geldeston, far up the Waveney [*map © Margaret Bird 2020*]

KEY

⌐ navigable river

⌐ river ? unnavigable

⹀ new cuts 1833 for Norwich & Lowestoft navigation

‖ lower end of canalised river (Aylsham and Bungay navigations)

● named city/parish with berths

NOTE
The broads (lakes) are not shown

miles 0 — 7

km 0 — 11

BROADLAND
The six navigable rivers 1795–98
48 PLACES NAMED IN THE GT YARMOUTH REGISTER (NRO: Y/C 38/3)
AS HOME BERTHS AND/OR DESTINATIONS FOR KEELS AND WHERRIES

¹ *Gt Yarmouth* Another
seaport shown on the
map is Lowestoft. One
vessel, a 20-ton wherry,
gave her berth in 1795
as Lowestoft (NRO: Y/C
38/3, no. 60).
    She gave her route as
Lowestoft–Yarmouth.
This would have been
not by sea but across
Oulton Broad, down
the narrow and winding
Oulton Dyke (as it was
then), along the River
Waveney and over
Breydon, otherwise she
would not be listed in
the register of craft on
the inland waterways
of the Broads. Faden's
map of 1797 shows that
there was no eastern
exit to the sea from the
Broads via Lake Loth-
ing, an expanse of water
east of Oulton Broad.
    The wherry might
have been based within
Lowestoft parish at the
very western end of
Lake Lothing and have
passed under Mutford
Bridge, where Mutford
Lock was built in 1833,
to enter Oulton Broad.
    Lowestoft harbour
was not built until 1833
as part of the Norwich
& Lowestoft navigation
scheme (see chap. 2
under 'Canal mania').
At the same time the
New Cut was dug to
link the Rivers Waveney
and Yare as a short cut
to Norwich from the
sea and as a way of
bypassing Gt Yarmouth,
as shown on the map

The second half of the chapter centres on the material yielded by Mary Hardy. Passengers as well as goods travelled under sail. The diary is the only evidence we have for the existence and location of Wright's boatyard at Coltishall, forerunner of the locally famous wherry-building yard of the Allens just downstream. Mary Hardy relates that their small wherry was built in the surprisingly short time of five months from ordering the timber to launch date. The wherry carried 12 chaldrons: perhaps 14½–16 tons of coal. Chaldrons and tonnages, referring to carrying capacity, are defined in the next section on page 165 and in the Glossary.

It is hard to draw general conclusions about the Broads craft. They varied between 8 tons and 97 tons burden (their carrying capacity) and kept to different patterns for their voyages. One feature united them. Various sources show that each, from the smallest wherry to the largest keel, travelled to, from or via Great Yarmouth on their regular routes— even the Geldeston-berthed wherry (in the register) plying to Hardley. The seaport was an extremely busy import and export centre, and the function of these vessels was a simple one: to bring goods, notably coal, upstream from Yarmouth and carry other goods, notably farm produce and manufactures, down to the sea for onward carriage.¹

As keels and wherries were generally not seagoing all the cargoes had to be transhipped at the quays of Great Yarmouth or lightered there and then transhipped at sea, 'in the roads'. Some river-based craft did venture out to the great ships at anchor to load and unload, but the sea conditions had to be calm to enable them to do so.

It is also a human story. We learn something of the watermen themselves: the skippers, mates (male and female), their work patterns and the accidents that befell them. The teams of volunteers on the two preserved trading wherries still sailing today, *Albion* and *Maud*, know the dangers the vessels can pose. They treat them with great respect.

Tonnages and the state of the rivers for trade

How fit were the waterways for this traffic? As we have seen in the last three chapters, an infrastructure capable of supporting road- and river-based trade was vital to the success of the nation's economy, especially one so wracked by war as

left Danger while under way. Decks can be slippery even in dry weather. Newspapers would occasionally report the deaths of keelmen and wherrymen while under sail. Most could not swim, and falling in was often a death sentence in the cold water and strong tides.

This cruiser left Stokesby at 5.30 am on a fine July day to catch the tide through Gt Yarmouth, nine miles down the Bure. The rails and decks are dripping with a heavy dew despite the early morning sun. Two drainage mills can just be seen through the pale grey mist   [*Christopher Bird 2011*]

below Stokesby retains in its buildings the infrastructure of an 18th-century inland port, as illustrated in chapter 3 (page 120).

The inn board of the Ferry Inn depicts the ferry which used to operate here for those wishing to reach Acle. The western road over Muck Fleet to Acle Bridge and the town was not built until the 19th century: it does not appear on the maps by Faden in 1797 and Bryant in 1826 [*MB · 2011*]

Britain's. The Broadland map locates the 48 places named in the register, but in reality there were far more staithes serving the network. The register records either the parish name or, in the case of Norwich with its numerous parishes edging the Wensum, the city name. Within the parish, as seen in chapter 3 with Coltishall, there could be a series of private, parish and public staithes. Wroxham, Horning, Ludham and many others had a string of such staithes.

Only the smallest places, such as Tunstall and Flixton, with village centres often far from the manmade dykes leading to their marsh tracks, had just one staithe. Even a tiny outpost needed a constantly dredged cut, well-maintained banks and one or more lockable warehouses; a public house would be an added bonus. The bridge staithe at St Olaves, between Herringfleet and the Waveney's confluence with the Yare, shows these features in the illustration overleaf.

above St Olaves Bridge on the Waveney, linking Norfolk and Suffolk, seen from downstream; the Bell Inn is on the left. The skipper or mate rests his weary back against the wherry's tiller. The gaff, from which the sail hangs, is lowered right down and the sail droops over the hatches like a tarpaulin.

The transom (squared-off) stern and back of the cabin are painted white, probably as a safety measure to give warning at night.

An immaculately thatched warehouse stands at the staithe, buttressed on the river side apparently owing to subsidence. The bank edge is reinforced with horizontal boarding to give it protection from vessels coming alongside at a point where the narrowing of the river and the very strong tide would be hazardous [*drawing by Francis Stone & Son; lithograph by D. Hodgson 1830*]

---

[1] *navigable rivers* The Chet may not have been navigable, neither Loddon nor Chedgrave at the head of that short tributary of the Yare featuring in the register.

None of the Trinity Broads is mentioned either (Ormesby, Rollesby and Filby, north-east of Stokesby), suggesting that Muck Fleet could not by then be used by trading craft

The Broadland map names the six rivers definitely navigable for keels and wherries in the last decade of the eighteenth century: the Bure, Ant and Thurne; the Yare and Wensum; and the Waveney.[1] The Hardys lived 32 miles up the Bure from Great Yarmouth, just below the point where the Aylsham navigation then continued into the hinterland of north-east Norfolk. Two tributaries flowed into the Bure from the north, the Ant and the Thurne, close to the midway point between Coltishall and Yarmouth, but these may not have been sufficiently deep and wide to enable large and even middle-sized vessels to use them. In the register the largest on the Ant was a 30-ton wherry based at the head of navigation at Dilham; while the largest on the Thurne was also of 30 tons: a wherry based at Repps. A 28-ton wherry could reach West Somerton, the head of navigation on one of the branches of the Thurne.[1]

By contrast, the largest vessel berthed on the upstream reaches of the Bure was the 43-ton wherry *William and Betsey*, which features later in this chapter; she was a little larger than the present-day *Albion* and about the same size as *Maud*, also seen on the rivers today. Very much larger craft could get up to Coltishall however, the skipper of a vast Yarmouth-based keel of 85 tons declaring that he routinely plied between Norwich and Coltishall.[2]

These vessels and their routes will be analysed later, in the section on the register. The figures for carrying capacity are quoted here to demonstrate that the northern rivers could cope with vessels of a very useful size from the point of view of distribution by water, showing that the rivers were well maintained. It is impossible to visualise these days an 85-tonner, with a great draught of water when loaded (the depth figure depending on her beam) struggling all the way up to Coltishall. How she coped with the low bridges at Acle and Wroxham, of a type similar to St Olaves Bridge seen opposite, is also a puzzle; perhaps her load-bearing capability lay in her beam. *Albion*, at 40 tons, has trouble getting up to Coltishall.[3] In 1795 a 42-ton wherry was based at Aylsham—a far cry from the tonnages well below half that size for which the navigation had been designed in 1773, as we shall see.[4]

The Yare probably had the busiest traffic; it certainly had the largest vessels. Just before it reaches Norwich the river swings to the south, leaving to its tributary the Wensum the honour of taking craft into the heart of the city.[5] The length of the two combined waterways from the quays at Great Yarmouth to the head of navigation at New Mills in Norwich is just under 29 miles. Here again the river was evidently well maintained in the 1790s. The register does not disclose the individual city staithes at which the keels and wherries called or had home berths, but it is likely that the largest stopped short of the Cathedral watergate, upriver from the King Street moorings. Monster keels of 95 and 97 tons could reach Norwich (numbers 2 and 131 in the record); the largest wherry was 50 tons (number 9).

[1] *Ant and Thurne* The Dilham wherry was no. 88 in the register (NRO: Y/C 38/3); the Repps wherry no. 28; and the Somerton wherry no. 34

[2] *Bure* The Coltishall wherry was no. 27 in the register (illustrated later in this chapter); the 85-ton keel no. 72

[3] *Albion* Skipper Henry Gowman gave me a colourful description of his adventures getting *Albion* under Wroxham Bridge on 25 and 27 Aug. 2012 after the high rainfall immediately preceding Coltishall's centenary commemoration of the floods of 26 Aug. 1912 (his e-mails to me of 9, 10 and 11 Mar. 2013)

[4] *Aylsham* No. 97 in the register

[5] *Wensum* The longest of the county's rivers, it takes a perversely winding course down from central Norfolk. One of its headstreams, sometimes characterised as the source, rises in Horningtoft close to the house left to Mary Hardy by her mother Mary and passed on in turn by the diarist to her son William.

As copyhold, and subject to manorial law, the property could be devised by married women (see vol. 1, chap. 4)

[1] *Waveney* The Oulton wherry is no. 37 in the register; the largest Bungay wherry no. 135. Geldeston Dyke, a man-made cut (chap. 3), was kept dredged, the largest of the six wherries berthed at its head being 35 tons (no. 75).

The great engineer William Cubitt was brought in at an early stage to advise the pro-moters of the Norwich & Lowestoft navigation. He provided detailed statistics about the Waveney from Oulton Broad upstream to Beccles in Dec. 1827, with the idea of making Beccles a deepwater port as part of the Lowestoft scheme.

He proposed a new shortened route for the Waveney, with map, to make passages faster, as well as widening and deepening on the upper reaches. His proposals were implemented only in part (R. Malster, *The Norfolk and Suffolk Broads*, pp. 102–6); yet his presentation of the depth of water and the tonnages which could be attained on improve-ment are illuminating for a later period than Mary Hardy's (W. Cubitt, *A Report and Estimate on the River Waveney between Beccles Bridge and Oulton Dyke towards making Beccles a Port* (London, 1829), see esp. pp. 6–11)

above The sight greeting the crews of keels and wherries as they drew into Gt Yarmouth. Here a wherry with four people on board (right) approaches Hall Quay, her mast lowered as she had just passed under the Haven Bridge; her momentum carries her along despite what appears to be a flood tide.

Two other wherries lie alongside the seagoing ships at the quay (left). Loading and unloading were time-consuming operations, with the pressure on to catch the tide and any favourable wind [*painting by J. Stark; engraving by G. Cooke 1831, detail*]

The sixth river, and the most southerly, is the Waveney. Unlike the two other long rivers on the Broads it has no navigable tributary. It pursues a solitary course for 22 miles from the south end of Breydon to Geldeston Lock, apart from a branch from the south-east and Oulton Broad which was straightened and deepened 1827–33 for the Norwich and Lowestoft navigation. Oulton Dyke in Mary Hardy's time, before improvement, was nevertheless a useful water-way, the two wherries whose home berths took them along it in 1795 being of 34 and 20 tons. The tidal part of the Waveney and even the navigation to Bungay were as well maintained as the other rivers, having vessels of up to 58 tons using the navigation—considerably larger in size than the 42 tons for Aylsham.[1]

This early part of the story of keels and wherries has relied on tonnages to make the point that large inland vessels could use all of the principal Broadland rivers and carry large tonnages. The moment has come to grapple with a controversial subject. Measurements by weight and by volume are a bramble thicket as thorny as crop yields proved to be in volume 2. Tonnage in this study refers neither to the dead weight nor the displacement of the vessel but to the carrying capacity of the hold: tonnage burden, or 'burthen'. An imperial ton (Winchester measure) was 20 hundredweight (2240 lb or 1·016 metric tonnes), but a ship's ton was 2000 lb (40 cubic feet, or 0·9 of a tonne).[1]

It is not certain which type of tonnage is quoted in the register and the press advertisements of the time; nor is it clear which chaldron (a measure of coal by volume) the Broadland boats used. The London chaldron, at 26½ hundredweight, was half that of the Newcastle measure at 53 hundredweight. The Great Yarmouth chaldron used in the mid-eighteenth century was 24½ hundredweight; there is no evidence however that this was used for the 1795 Yarmouth register and in the Norwich newspapers.[2] (Henry Raven's diary, by the way, implies that the north Norfolk ports used the London chaldron.)[3]

We have two firm but contradictory statistics relating to the Hardys' wherry which muddy the waters when we try to judge the measures used on the Broads. One is quoted by the Coltishall auctioneer, valuer, plumber and wherry owner Robert Ansell when advertising the vessel for sale following the Hardys' move to Letheringsett in 1781. He tells us that *William and Mary* carried 12 chaldrons of coals.[4] This could work out at perhaps 14½ imperial tons (Yarmouth measure) or 16 imperial tons (London measure).

However in 1777 Mary Hardy refers to an extremely large load carried onto this same wherry at Coltishall: 10 lasts of malt.[5] This consignment, equating to 100 quarters in volume and 20·3 metric tonnes in weight, indicates that the wherry could carry as much as 20 imperial tons approximately. (We cannot be certain which measures to adopt, and whether to use imperial tons or ship's tons.)

So, how could a 12-chaldron coaling vessel carry 20 tons of malt? The answer may lie in the manner of loading. If a

[1] *ship's ton* I am very grateful to Robert Malster for his guidance on this and other points relating to tonnage and chaldrons in his letter to me of 7 August 2000.
The standard abbreviation for hundredweight is 'cwt'. The measure was also called 'hundred' in the 18th century, that term being the one adopted by Mary Hardy

[2] *chaldrons* Roy Clark in *Black-Sailed Traders* gives the Gt Yarmouth measure (p. 100).
The coal trade is discussed in the next chapter, where the gravity-propelled and horse-drawn truck used to bring coal down from the pits to the colliers at the Tyneside staithes is illustrated.
That type of truck, known as a chaldron, carried 53 cwt—the Newcastle measure

[3] *Henry Raven Diary 3*: 1 Aug. 1797 and note. For more details see chap. 5 on coal

[4] *12 chaldrons Norfolk Chronicle* and *Norw. Merc.*, 21 July 1781 (illustrated on p. 214, above the particulars of the wherry)

[5] *malt Diary 1*: 19 Feb. 1777. Mary Hardy states that the load could actually have been more: '10 last or upwards'

below right The hatches of the wherry *Albion* are piled on the bank after repainting in the traditional bright scarlet   [*MB·1999*]

facing page Hatch no. 5 on *Albion*. Wherry hatches are incised with Roman numerals (all straight lines) to distinguish them, as each hatch is shaped to the curves of the vessel to ensure a snug fit [*MB·1998*]

---

[1] *paintings* Joseph Stannard's engraving of a hay wherry is reproduced in R. Malster, *The Norfolk and Suffolk Broads*, p. 112.

Marsh litter is the vegetation mowed by hand on the banks and taken by water in flat-bottomed boats for animal bedding. The work is depicted in C.S. Middleton, ed., *The Broadland Photographers* (Wensum Books, Norwich, 1978), unpag.

[2] *Harmer* House of Commons Parliamentary Papers 1826 (369), vol. IV, Norwich and Lowestoft Navigation Bill, Minutes of evidence to the committee, p. 181, 26 Apr. 1826.

On the Bure the grain would have had to be so loaded as to enable the mast to be lowered for bridges

low-density load is carried it can be built upwards; marsh hay and marsh litter are seen heaped high in nineteenth-century paintings and photographs of Broads vessels, the mate standing on top of the cargo to direct the helmsman over whom he towers.[1] Coal however could not be piled at all high, for the weight would make the boat unstable.

Malt by volume is lighter than coal, and indeed we hear from a Norwich maltster how it could be safely loaded to make maximum use of the hold. If the Hardys' men adopted the system described by Daniel Harmer in his evidence to the House of Commons committee in 1826 they could well have loaded the malt well above the normal level, to rest much higher than the uprights supporting the hatches:

We have tarpauling provided, that we can carry a quantity above deck to enable the craft to load herself; we carry one third of our light property above the hatches.[2]

The key to this answer before the committee may lie in the adjective 'light'. A light commodity—light, that is, as low density—could be built up in this way and then protected with a waterproof covering, although securing the tarpaulin in a high wind would not have been easy and the malt would surely have been at some risk from the weather. The wooden hatches designed to protect the perishable grain may have had to be dispensed with on some occasions.

In addition to well-maintained rivers, and a good depth of water, sailing vessels of course require wind. It is very clear from the photographs of G.C. Davies, P.H. Emerson and J. Payne Jennings in the last quarter of the nineteenth century that the waterways were kept more open than they are today, at least along many of the upper reaches of the navigable rivers. The testimony of those who knew the Broads then and in the early twentieth century bears this out.

Charles Carrodus, reminiscing in 1949 about the rivers he had known for much of his long life, stated that Horning Church tower (seen on page 207) was becoming blanked from view. In earlier times he had seen this great landmark for miles across the open landscape of the Bure:

Nor have I said anything of the beautiful church set on what may be called a hill in this neighbourhood and in my time in view of voyagers on the river nearly all the way from Acle Bridge in one direction, and from beyond Hoveton Great Broad [near Wroxham] in the other.[1]

It is the same tale of regret and loss at Barton Turf. Trees have grown up around the broad largely since the Second World War. These trees and other dense vegetation now cast a deep pall over many of the banks and dykes and prevent wild flowers and the other formerly vigorous wildlife from flourishing. They also blanket the wind from sailing vessels. John Yaxley (1928–2019), heir to generations of Barton wherrymen from the time of the 1795 register and perhaps earlier, reflected on the changes he had himself witnessed over the twentieth century from his house beside the staithe:

From here it is now [in 2006] impossible to see even one of the seven churches that were visible from this area in years gone by. Quite recently Sutton Windmill, nearly due east, could be seen, and a little to the south, till the line was shut [in 1959], the lights of Catfield railway station, but now all is obscured by the neglect of the overgrown marshes.[2]

As the trees grew, so the speeds attainable by the wherries declined. Passages used to be very fast if the conditions were right. Skipper Rump, of the wherry *Hilda*, recalled for Robert Malster the increasing difficulties he had faced in the first half of the twentieth century. Accustomed to sailing from Great Yarmouth to Coltishall (32 miles) in five hours, he found that by 1930 he was lucky to make it over the lesser distance to Wroxham in six and a half hours. In his Norfolk voice he explained, 'We don't get the winds we use to.'[3] In those same years a wherry could leave Barton Turf Staithe in the morning and reach Great Yarmouth by 4 pm, a distance of 22½ miles, nearly five of them along the particularly narrow, winding River Ant.[4]

[1] *Horning Church* C. Carrodus, ed., *Life in a Norfolk Village: The Horning story* (Soman-Wherry Press, Norwich, 1949), p. 49. He was a friend of my parents, who liked to moor at Horning, and I knew him in my early childhood as someone with a fund of knowledge of the past. Like him I have watched the Broads churches being swallowed up by trees.

Riverside trees also make night sailing more difficult by obscuring the line of the bank and reducing reflections

[2] *Barton* J. Yaxley, *A Jam around Barton Turf*, p. 23. A postcard of the view from Barton Turf Staithe in the 1930s (his p. 26) depicts the wide vistas of a past age

[3] *C. Rump* R. Malster, *Wherries and Waterways*, p. 45

[4] *Ant* A. Wilson, *Wherries and Windmills* (Barton Turf, 1982), p. 16

TABLE 4.4.1

'The fastest sailor on the stream': 15 keels and wherries advertised for sale in the *Norwich Mercury* 1779–1808

source The weekly *Norwich Mercury*

notes 'Capacity' is carrying capacity; a chaldron is approx. 1·2–1·3 tons; a dash denotes lack of data. None of these vessels is identifiable in the Gt Yarmouth register 1795–98 of vessels above 13 tons (NRO: Y/C 38/3)

date of notice	sale berth	type	capacity	built	name of vessel	draught	owners (or skippers)
1779, 13 Mar.	Gt Yarmouth	wherry	20 chaldns	'new'	—	—	Peter Kirkman's widow
1779, 20 Mar.	Norwich	keel	50 tons	—	*Dolphin*	—	(Isaac Dye, skipper)
1779, 23 Oct.	Coltishall	keel	50 tons	—	*John and Joseph* [1]	—	John Fiddy & Jos. Browne
1780, 22 Apr.	Gt Yarmouth, the Bear	keel	36 chaldns	—	*Success*	'small'	John Clarke
1780, 16 Sept.	Gt Yarmouth, haven	keel	40 tons	—	*John and Elizabeth*	—	(John Clarke, skipper)
1781, 17 Mar.	Aylsham, Anchor Inn	wherry	12 tons	1780	*Buckenham*	2 ft 6 ins	(Edward Roofe, skipper)
1781, 21 July	Horning, White Swan	wherry	12 chaldns	1776	*William and Mary*	2 ft 10 ins	[William & Mary Hardy]
1786, 8 July	Norwich, King Street	keel	30 tons	—	*William and Mary*	—	—
1787, 16 June	Potter Heigham [2]	wherry	13 tons	—	—	—	—
1794, 22 Feb.	Gt Yarmouth	wherry	10 tons	—	*Mayflower* [3]	—	—
1796, 28 May	Norwich, King Street	keel	50 tons	—	*British Queen* [4]	—	—
1804, 1 Sept.	Norwich, King Street	wherry	27 tons	1801	*Recovery*	—	—
1805, 2 Mar.	Norwich, Carrow	wherry	18 chaldns	1805	*Mayflower* [5]	—	—
1808, 23 July	Dilham, Barnes's staithe [6]	wherry	13 tons [7]	1805	—	'easy'	—
1808, 23 July	Dilham, Barnes's staithe	wherry	18 tons [7]	1808	—	'very easy'	—

ADDITIONAL DETAILS IN THE NOTICE

[1] *keel* Hatched; lately thoroughly repaired
[2] *Potter Heigham* On the River Thurne
[3] *wherry* Hatched; of Martham, on the Thurne
[4] *keel* '... reckoned the fastest sailor on the stream [the River Yare]'
[5] *wherry* Fitted with a new sail; of Beccles
[6] *Dilham* Head of navigation on the River Ant
[7] *two wherries* Clinker-built; 'well adapted for the Aylsham or Beccles navigation'

Keels and wherries did not sail light or in ballast on a return trip, the river trade being handled as economically as possible. A laden vessel also gets up momentum—so much so that one with only a cargo of a dozen people on board, like *Albion*, requires up to a quarter of a mile, with the sail lowered, to come to a gentle halt. Her former volunteer skipper David Bray confirms that an unladen *Albion* can make 8–9 knots landspeed with a following tide and a fair wind.[1]

In some ways the canvases of the artists of the Norwich School have misled us. Almost all their depictions of keels and wherries under way show vessels drifting in light airs, and not the great bow wave as the vessels powered their way through the water. Owners of commercial vessels were hard-headed men, as their detailed testimony to the House of Common committee confirms. They were acutely aware of prices, costs and speeds. Similarly those advertising boats for sale were at pains to draw attention to the particular merits of individual vessels, as seen in the table opposite. *British Queen*, the keel named for Boudicca and berthed at a King Street staithe, is described as 'the fastest sailor on the stream', meaning that she was the fleetest of all the keels and wherries on the Yare and perhaps even on the Broads. These attributes mattered. Time was money, even then; and skippers and crew perforce led pressurised lives.

The 50-ton *British Queen* may well show Roy Clark's easy dismissal of keels in general as ungainly sluggards to be unjust.[3] Advertisers are admittedly not on oath. However this description of a keel would have invited ridicule if wide of the mark, and even the most cursory enquiry would have discovered whether there were any foundation to the claim.

Sometimes the press notices would state whether the boat were clinker-built, with overlapping strakes along the hull, or carvel-built, where the seams of the horizontal planks lie flush; clinker construction is usually thought to offer greater strength and springiness. Another selling point would be that the vessel was hatched. The 50-ton hatched keel *John and Joseph*, seen opposite for sale in 1779, belonged jointly to two friends of the Hardys who feature in the Coltishall diary: the farmer and merchant John Fiddy, present at the launch of their own wherry, and the coal merchant and innkeeper Joseph Browne, whom we met in chapter 3.[4]

[1] *Albion* D. Bray, 'Albion: Notes for skippers and mates' (privately circulated, Lowestoft, *c.*1990), p. 20. A 28-page distillation of Skipper Bray's 25 years' experience of *Albion*, it was compiled from his illustrated lectures in the *Journal of the Norfolk Wherry Trust* during the 1980s for trainee skippers and mates.

My son Roger recalls being overtaken in the family motor cruiser by *Albion* on the Bure below Thurne Mouth in 2006: 'I was doing 6 mph landspeed with the ebb and watched a silent *Albion* gliding past in parallel, with the wind behind her and little wash—going at 8 mph'

[2] *British Queen* She does not appear under that name in the register compiled only a year later; indeed none of the vessels in table 4.4.1 can be traced in the register. It would seem that names were changed readily by a new owner, with no superstition that bad luck might ensue

[3] *keels* R. Clark, *Black-Sailed Traders*, p. 48

[4] *John Fiddy* Mary, his daughter, and playmate of the Hardy children, was at the launch.

Mary Hardy paid his wife Mary for the broken glass the day after the event (*Diary 1*). The

Coltishall wherry *John and Mary* belonging to John Fiddy jnr features in table 4.4.2.
Financial troubles precipitated the sales of the keel and wherry

---

[1] *Harmer* House of Commons Parliamentary Papers 1826 (369), vol. IV, Norwich and Lowestoft Navigation Bill, Minutes of evidence to the committee, p. 181, 26 Apr. 1826

[2] *Cozens* House of Commons Parliamentary Papers 1826 (369), vol. IV, Minutes of evidence to the committee, p. 184, 26 Apr. 1826. Crisp Brown's evidence earlier that day is on pp. 85–95; he was also a corn and coal merchant

[3] *Boardman* House of Commons Parliamentary Papers 1826 (369), vol. IV, Minutes of evidence to the committee, p. 185, 26 Apr. 1826. He, like Cozens, gave the distance by river from Norwich to Gt Yarmouth as 32 miles. They might have meant to Yarmouth Bar, where the Yare empties into the sea, as they were considering the transhipment of goods

[4] *Jennings* C.S. Middleton, ed., *The Broadland Photographers*, Introduction, unpag.

Lastly in this survey of the fitness of the waterways for trade we need to look at some hazards highlighted by the Norwich manufacturers and traders in their evidence to Parliament. It was Daniel Harmer's view that the Yare and Waveney were not wide enough in some parts to permit two square-rigged vessels (keels) to pass one another in safety. The bends in the river, forming sharp points as at Whitlingham, below Norwich, meant that one of the two skippers had to run into the shore to let the other pass.[1]

John Cozens, by contrast, spoke up for the Yare in 1826. Unlike Harmer and another critic of the existing waterways, the Norwich maltster Crisp Brown, he did not think a new navigation necessary. Cozens, the Norwich wholesale grocer whose brother Jeremiah had married Mary Hardy's daughter in 1805 (volumes 1 and 3), was not himself a keel or wherry owner, but he relied heavily on the vessels for his livelihood. In his opinion 'the expedition and condition of those craft' could not be exceeded, and the tidal Yare was 'one of the cheapest and best navigations in the kingdom'.[2] James Boardman, a wharfinger at Norwich and ship agent for seagoing ships from Hull and Selby, agreed with John Cozens that the unimproved Yare was the cheapest and most expeditious navigation 'in the whole kingdom'.[3] As so often happens the evidence is contradictory, but since Brown and Harmer were owners of river craft, whereas Cozens and Boardman were not, perhaps greater reliance should be placed on their strictures. The two maltsters and traders would have heard of the crew's difficulties at first hand, as they were often at the staithes as part of their work.

The work of the Norwich artists at the time of this House of Commons investigation into the ability of the Broads network to support waterborne trade strikes a vivid contrast with the pragmatic, practical turn of mind of these businessmen. Similarly the trio of Broadland photographers and writers sixty years later chose not to portray the economic pressures of their time. By the 1880s the railways had started to undermine the viability of the wherry trade; indeed Jennings was commissioned by the Great Eastern Railway to capture this watery world for the tourists being brought in by the trainload.[4] When we read the beguiling prose of these wordsmiths and admire the beauty of their images we

left The Yare, the widest of the rivers and the one carrying the most freight in 1795–98 (table 4.4.3 on numbers and tonnages). This long reach is at Strumpshaw, the village where the craft used by the Hardys would call. Here four large yachts can sail abreast.

But some of the Norwich traders who gave evidence to the Commons committee in 1826 pointed out the difficulties for the watermen working these waters. Even the Yare had some reaches where keels could not pass, and one vessel would have deliberately to be driven into the bank to enable the other to sail by   [*Christopher Bird 2012*]

[1] *wordsmiths* Davies writes of wherries 'gliding' along. In his many studies we usually get little insight into the precarious economy of the area he captured so skilfully on film: 'The marshes often present a curious sight. If the spectator is on the same level, scarcely any water may be visible, and the expanse of marsh may seem continuous; yet here and there and everywhere are the sails of yachts and wherries gliding through it, their hulls invisible' (G.C. Davies, *Norfolk Broads and Rivers*, p. 7). *Plate 28* illustrates his point

[2] *keel* The Norfolk keel was 'quite different in hull form from the keels of the Yorkshire and Lincolnshire waterways and from those of the Tyne. It need not surprise us that craft so different in design should have the same name, for the word is descended from the Anglo-Saxon *ceol* and the Old Norse *kjoll*, both of which are synonyms for "boat"' (R. Malster, *The Norfolk and Suffolk Broads*, p. 111)

need to bear in mind that they are carefully constructing a depiction of Broadland removed from the harsh realities.[1] It is those realities which Mary Hardy records for us and which the later parts of this chapter will describe.

The Norfolk keel

So far the keels and wherries of the Broads have entered the story without any detailed analysis of their characteristics; this section and the next will analyse their looks and capabilities. A keel in the sense used in this study is not the lowest part of a ship, nor is it one of the sailing vessels of the Humber and the Tyne, although the derivation is the same, from the Anglo-Saxon and Scandinavian words for a boat.[2] The Norfolk keel was a square-rigged sailing barge which differed in its development from other mediaeval vessels; the gaff-rigged Norfolk wherry which supplanted the keel in

facing page A small keel below Carrow Bridge on the approach to Norwich, showing the number of stays for the mast; a wherry has only one stay, the fore-stay (to the bow).

The sail is nowhere to be seen as it would get in the way of this six-man operation to manhandle the timber in or out of the moored boat.

On the right a small wherry is being quanted (poled) forward, her mast lowered for the bridge. A white-sailed yacht, in danger of crashing her mast into the bridge, is right in her path.

Upstream of the bridge can be seen a line of malt-kiln cowls [*painting by J. Stark; engraving by W. Miller 1833, detail*]

[1] *square rig and gaff rig* Large RN and merchant ships in the 18th century had square-rigged main-masts, with sails billowing in a tail wind; a head wind presented problems.

A gaff rig is a particular type of fore-and-aft rig. In a tail wind the sail swings well out to the side of the vessel; with the wind on the beam the rig enables the vessel

the nineteenth century was not a refinement of the older keel, but probably derived from slender row barges carrying passengers on the Broads and the Thames at the rowing boats' height in the sixteenth to eighteenth centuries.[1] Replicas of such barges can be seen on the Thames today, such as the strikingly beautiful royal barge *Gloriana*, lead vessel in the Thames Diamond Jubilee pageant of 2012.

The valedictory note struck by G. Christopher Davies after his last (and only) sighting of a Norfolk keel in about 1873, quoted at the beginning of this chapter, is tinged with awe, as though he had just seen the last of the great auks or a reincarnated dodo. Davies and his party gaze at the strange, unfamiliar shape scudding up the Bure past St Benet's Abbey into the sunset, and it is all too easy to catch Davies's spirit and sense an air of mystery in the evening chill.

The Norwich artists from earlier that century chase away all mystery and show us how the keel was handled, as seen here in the colour plates and in the engravings of James Stark's paintings. *The River at Thorpe* by Joseph Stannard (*plate 21* and on the jacket cover) depicts a broad-beamed keel moored at an unmade-up bank. The two-man crew in their close-fitting hats have two visitors on board, with a dog, who join their hosts in balancing on top of the cargo of Norfolk reed. This vessel can carry a good load and yet have a minimal draught, so she can probably get up shallow dykes when collecting the harvested reed.

The tanned sail is loosely furled while the boat is moored; the white sail belongs to the pleasure yacht fast approaching at the bow. The winch at the stern for raising and lowering the sail is clearly shown, as also the wooden block on one of the stays for the mast. The living quarters at the bow are obscured by the bundles of reed. A ring, which could have been used to secure the stern mooring rope, is set into a post on the bank, showing this was not some random mooring place but probably a well-used staithe. The boat appears to be moored only by her bow, the tide holding the stern in.

John Thirtle's *View of the River near Cow's Tower, Norwich* (*plate 18*) shows a keel under way, propelled by hand. The boat inches her way down the River Wensum. The two-berth cabin or 'cuddy' is shown at the bow. The centrally-placed mast, lowered for the approach to Bishop Bridge, has been

unstepped from its customary position in the 'tabernacle' or pair of massive timber supports (which allow it to pivot up and down by means of a counterweight) as it is swinging over the port side in a way that would not happen with a wherry mast. The skipper stands at the helm, his right arm holding the ropes (sheets) clear of the action. The mate, on the quant pole at the bow, is thrusting with the full force of his body to keep the keel off the shallow bank on the bend later known as Petch's Corner.

John Perryman, then Chairman of the Norfolk Wherry Trust, gave an authoritative appraisal of a keel's sailing capabilities; extracts from his 1989 study are given on the following pages. He had examined the one surviving Norfolk keel, named *Dee-Dar*, which after a twilight existence serving as a dredger for the firm of James Hobrough at Thorpe St Andrew, downriver of Norwich, had been deliberately sunk nearby at Whitlingham in 1890. There she lay preserved in the mud and only briefly disturbed.[1]

still to catch the wind, while in a head wind she has to tack.

For a chronology of cargo-carrying Norfolk keels and wherries and the passenger-carrying row barge see R. Malster, *Wherries and Waterways*, pp. 57–9

---

[1] *Dee-Dar* Robert Malster has pointed out (*The Norfolk and Suffolk Broads*, p. 117, with a photograph of *Dee-Dar*) that the unlikely name could result from the Norfolk tongue's grappling with *Deodar*, the name of the Himalayan cedar suiting a boat well adapted to carrying timber.

The process of finding, lifting and investigating the Whitlingham keel, as *Dee-Dar* is also called, in 1984–85 is described in Theole Douglas-Sherwood's 253-page thesis 'The Norfolk keel'. She also covers the history of keels in general (eg pp. 22–6, 97–100).

Dee-Dar was later kept in a barn at Hales Hall, near Loddon, and at a staithe in Norwich before being moved in 1998 to a Norwich industrial estate.

Reports on this keel, with colour photographs, were published in *The Times*, 2 Mar. 1993, and *Eastern Daily Press*, 5 Aug. 2000

An appraisal of the Norfolk keel's sailing qualities 1989

source   Extract from an article by 'Boy John' [John Perryman], 'The Norfolk keel', *Journal of the Norfolk Wherry Trust* (spring 1989), pp. 6–9 [1]

EXAMINATION OF THE RECENTLY RAISED Norfolk keel, now being conserved at Norwich, revealed some very interesting areas of conjecture. Being a wherry buff, I had never given much thought to the ubiquitous keel. Somehow, I had considered them to be bluff-bowed, unhandy, downwind barges.[2] But now I am not so sure.

The keel raised from Whitlingham is a shallow-draught hull of fine form not unlike the average wherry. Although the bow of the relic is missing, photographs of the boat when used by Hobrough,[3] as part of a dredging complex, show what seems to be the original bow including the forward cabin so distinctive of the keel. The bottom planking is clencher form notched into the frames in wherry fashion, but the topsides are carvel-planked exactly as *Albion*.[4] The shape of the frames and reference to many of the Norwich School of paintings show this to be a common feature. The 'Norfolk' keel also has a small transom, again not unlike some early wherries.

A study of the Norwich School paintings, allowing for artists' licence, suggests that there were two classes of keel. Some have a full (large) transom suggesting a deep-bodied vessel, and others, like the Whitlingham boat, have a fine transom suggesting a more shallow form.[5] Indeed the Whitlingham boat has a hold-depth of about half that of *Albion*, given that the overall length and beam are the same.[6] As *Albion* is conceded to be a 40-ton wherry it is reasonable to assume that the keel relic is about 15–20 ton capacity, and the somewhat light scantlings, compared with a typical wherry, suggest a north-river boat used for light cargo—marsh hay, reeds and the like.[7]

Doubtless, there were keels and keels . . . The rig, however, was common to all. The sail was a square sail with reef points across the foot. The yard was hoisted by a winch mounted on the aft deck and controlled by braces led aft. The mast was placed about amidships in a tabernacle and hoisted by a forestay and tackle which again led to a winch.[8] Shrouds were arranged to give support. The Whitlingham boat is fitted with lacing-type shroud-plates both forward and aft of the mast. Clearly, raising and lowering the mast was not as easy as on *Albion*, and just why shrouds on the fore side of the mast were required is not clear, unless these forward shrouds were adjusted to keep the mast steady when lowered. The paintings show that as the tabernacle was relatively small, the mast did not lower to a horizontal position . . .

[1] *source* Reproduced courtesy the author and David Bray, then editor of the journal. I am very grateful to them both for allowing these long extracts to be quoted and to David Bray for permission to reproduce his line drawing of a keel which accompanied the article.

The Whitlingham keel to which the author refers is *Dee-Dar*, raised from a watery grave on the Yare at Whitlingham

[2] *bluff-bowed* With blunt, rounded bows, unlike the wherry's pointed bow

[3] *Hobrough* The firm specialising in dredging and river management founded by James Hobrough. Their docks lay on the Thorpe bank opposite Whitlingham, and they used retired keels and wherries as lighters for carrying the dredged spoil and silt

[4] *carvel-planked* The seams flush and smooth; the opposite of the much more prevalent clinker-built hulls where the timber strakes overlap

[5] *transom* The squared-off stern of a vessel; the opposite of the pointed stern of later wherries

[6] *Albion* 58 feet long, 15 wide (17·7 metres by 4·6)

[7] *scantlings* Cross-timbers; ribs

[8] *tabernacle* The strong elbow-shaped timbers housing the mast,

above **The stern of the Whitlingham keel, supported in her steel cradle 26 Apr. 2012. A few months later she was a small pile of ashes** [*Christopher Bird 2012*]

Historians write off the keel as being only able to sail with a following wind and as having no windward performance at all. Having now studied the form of the Whitlingham keel and having sailed in square-rigged ships I believe that the keel did have quite a reasonable windward performance. Admittedly it could not tack wherry fashion, but a laden keel could claw to windward on a long stretch. A Humber keel, a bluff-bowed blunt-ended vessel, goes to windward very well and is about as efficient as a loose-footed lugsail.[1] The Humber keel is fitted with lee-boards after the fashion of the Thames barge, and it is possible that some Norfolk keels were so arranged with Dutch influence. However, a fine-ended boat gains lateral area from the vertical sections at the stem and stern.

Using the Humber-keel rig as a guide it is possible to see some of the tricks o' the trade. With a following wind the sail would be set athwart-ships with sheets and braces equal-spaced. As the wind comes further ahead one edge of the sail becomes the luff and the other edge becomes the leach.[2] At some point the 'luff' will not stand to the wind and will collapse. The weather-side sheet is taken forward to an eye on the deck-edge somewhere forward of the mast, the lee brace is pulled tight to put a strain on the 'luff', and a quant is inserted into a reef cringle in the 'luff' and lodged at the deck on the weather side. Presto! The square sail is now braced and set with the stiff luff like a dipping lugsail. Tacking with this arrangement could be achieved in light airs and with a following tide, but in anything like a breeze the sail would be caught back. James Stark, renowned for his attention to detail in his engravings,

through which it pivoted (illustrated overleaf)

[1] *lugsail* A four-sided sail hoisted on a yard; with no boom along its bottom edge it is loose-footed. Wherries, like keels, also have no boom

[2] *luff* The leading edge; in David Bray's sketch (overleaf) the luff is to starboard, the 'leach' to port.

He also shows the quant wedged into a cringle (an eye-hole) on

right **A narrow-beamed unhatched Norfolk keel, lightly stacked with reed, sails to windward. The mate, perhaps the skipper's wife, stands on the steps to the living quarters or 'cuddy' towards the bows; the cuddy in a wherry is at the stern.**

As described in the article, the quant is wedged against the luff edge of the sail to make the vessel perform in the manner of a gaff-rigged wherry.

The drawing is by David Bray, then editor of the *Journal of the Norfolk Wherry Trust* [*David Bray 1989*]

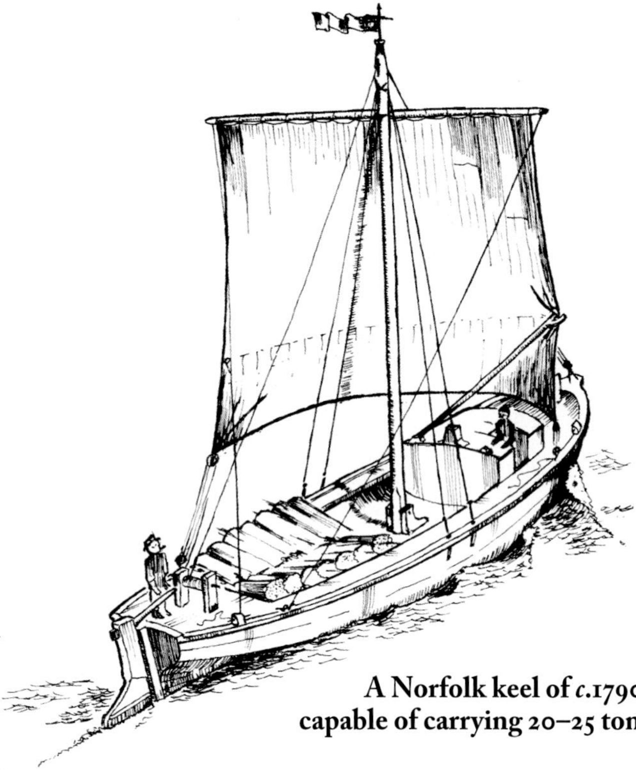

A Norfolk keel of *c*.1790, capable of carrying 20–25 tons

the luff-edge and the lee-edge pulled taut, so that the keel sails almost as if rigged fore and aft

shows a timber-laden keel close-hauled at Norwich, with the rig trimmed as described . . .[1]

Finally, it is worth noting that there are many features common to both keels and wherries. This is to be expected of course, because although the wherry-hull form was a development of the rowing wherry with a sprit-sail rig, many parts were common where there was no need for change. A superb series of contemporary sketches of the working parts of a keel shows similarities with the wherry in respect of the stayfall block, the halyard winch (no patten bar), the swipe (pump), the timber heads, the quant and the co'burgh.[2]

Whilst archeologists write off the keel as being an inefficient lumbering barge with Saxon origins, it is my view that this is far from true. A deep-laden keel stacked high with reeds in a strong breeze would be quite a handful with two mainsheets and two braces to handle.

Would that we could rebuild the Whitlingham keel and find out if my theory is true . . .

[1] *Stark* The keel passing Harrison's Wharf (illustrated opposite)

[2] *coburg* The wooden support for the stove-pipe chimney poking through the top of the little cabin (illustrated, above, on the cuddy in the bow; the chimney is unshipped under way)

left A timber-laden keel passing Harrison's Wharf, King Street, Norwich—the painting referred to in John Perryman's article.

The close-hauled keel is clinker-built, with a narrow transom. The skipper is standing on top of his cargo, to see ahead. He seems to have two mates, unless one is about to board the rowing dinghy coming alongside [*painting by J. Stark; engraving by J.H. Kernot 1829, detail*]

The first time the Whitlingham keel was lifted was in 1912, when measurements were taken preparatory to the construction of the models of *Dee-Dar* lodged in the Bridewell Museum in Norwich and Science Museum, London. The keel, of oak, was 55 feet 9 inches long, with a beam of only 13 feet 8 inches (17 by 4 metres). Her name was not known then. It was the 83-year-old naturalist Arthur H. Patterson ('John Knowlittle') who identified her in the mud eighteen years later as *Dee-Dar*, formerly skippered by 'Dilly' Smith.[1]

The marine archaeologist Theole Douglas-Sherwood organised the raising of *Dee-Dar* by volunteer Royal Navy and Royal Air Force divers in 1985, with the intention that the sole example of this type of vessel be conserved and put on public display—Norfolk's *Mary Rose*, as the project was characterised. In his article John Perryman ('Boy John') sought to demonstrate why the keel had persisted for centuries on the Broads. He judged that the centrally-placed mast and single square sail offered considerably better performance and flexibility than had hitherto been thought.

The physical presence of the resurrected keel on dry land led to greater understanding of these vessels. Until then our knowledge had derived largely from the artists and from

[1] *Dee-Dar* T. Douglas-Sherwood, 'The Norfolk keel', pp. 175, 216. Robert Malster gives the skipper as 'Tiger' Smith (*The Norfolk and Suffolk Broads*, p. 116)

above Dee-Dar's black-smith's work in the form of metal eyes, bolts and plates stayed well preserved, as seen here at Whitlingham Barns 26 Apr. 2012 [*MB · 2012*]

[1] *transom* This was just under 5 feet at its widest point, 2 feet 4½ inches at its highest point, and the timber 4 inches thick (150·5 cm by 73 by 10) (T. Douglas-Sherwood, 'The Norfolk keel', p. 184)

[2] *hold* Just under 35 feet long by 10 feet 4 inches wide amidships and 8 feet 10¼ inches wide at the stern (10·6 metres by 3·15 by 2·7) (T. Douglas-Sherwood, 'The Norfolk keel', pp. 215, 193)

[3] *hull and plankways* T. Douglas-Sherwood, 'The Norfolk keel', pp. 189, 204

[4] *period* As well as the huge vessels of the 1790s there were keels of *Dee-Dar*'s size in the 1795 register (though none named *Deodar* or *Dee-Dar*): eg no. 39, a Gt Yarmouth keel of 30 tons plying Yarmouth–Norwich; and no. 100, a Panxworth keel of 20 tons plying Aylsham–Gt Yarmouth (NRO: Y/C 38/3)

[5] *tonnage* T. Douglas-Sherwood, 'The Norfolk keel', pp. 23–4

[6] *Blyth navigation* T. Douglas-Sherwood, 'The Norfolk keel', pp. 24–5. The first vessel to reach Halesworth was a keel carrying coal (M. Fordham, *Halesworth Quay and the Blyth Navigation*, p. 6)

press advertisements such as those in table 4.4.1. Like many eighteenth- and early-nineteenth century river craft *Dee-Dar* did not have a pointed stern but a transom stern (*plate 22*). This remained her best-preserved feature until she was destroyed by fire at Whitlingham Barns in 2012.[1]

Calculating tonnage remained as problematic as ever. Theole Douglas-Sherwood considered that the size of *Dee-Dar*'s shallow hold would indicate a vessel capable of carrying about 30 tons.[2] John Perryman, who had also been an active participant in the keel project, thought 15–20 tons the more likely maximum, as seen in his article. (However his figures give a somewhat meagre capacity for a 55-foot vessel, a great deal of sailing effort being required but not much in the way of freight shifted.) The upper three strakes of the keel's hull were of carvel construction and the lower ones clinker. The noticeably wide plankways (the catwalks, or sidedecks) were tarred,[3] as could still be seen in 2012.

Theole Douglas-Sherwood estimated from the keel's looks and timbers that *Dee-Dar* dated from the period 1790–1820.[4] In her researches into newspaper notices and the Norwich and Great Yarmouth records she concluded that keels had increased markedly in size thanks to the greater effort being put into deepening and dredging the rivers. She found evidence that in the seventeenth century 20 tons was the maximum for a Broads vessel; by 1727 this figure had risen to 40 to 50 tons, and in 1766 to 50 or 60 tons for the Wensum.[5] As we have seen earlier in this chapter, even these tonnage figures had been exceeded by the time of the 1795 register of keels and wherries.

Like wherries, keels could sail out to sea if the conditions were right. They were used as lighters during transhipping, and even sailed south from Great Yarmouth to Southwold in Suffolk: the first vessel to use the Blyth navigation up to Halesworth in 1761 was a Norfolk keel.[6]

We shall return to the keel later in this chapter with a section on the keels known to Mary Hardy in her time at Coltishall. First the characteristics and capabilities of the wherry need to be considered, and the wealth of data from the somewhat neglected 1795 register analysed. This was not perhaps such a 'shadowy period' after all.

above The Yare: waters well known to *Dee-Dar* and to the keels and wherries bringing bricks to the Hardys at Coltishall. Downstream of Strumpshaw the banks are no longer shrouded by trees, and the view over the grazing marshes to Langley remains unobstructed. In 1795 two wherries, of 29 and 30 tons, had Langley as their home berth, so the dyke to the village staithe was then navigable by sizeable craft   [MB · 2010]

The Norfolk wherry

The wherry is held in great affection today, by the people of Norfolk and by visitors to the Broads. The only two surviving trading wherries, *Albion* and *Maud*, were rescued from oblivion: the first by a trust specially formed for the purpose in 1949; and the second by a husband-and-wife team from Essex, Vincent and Linda Pargeter, who, as was to happen shortly afterwards with *Dee-Dar*, raised *Maud* from a muddy grave in 1981. *Albion* had been built at Oulton Broad on the Waveney by William Brighton in 1898, and *Maud* at Reedham on the Yare by Hall's yard in 1899. Both wherries led active working lives. These dramatic vessels with their tarred hulls, tall masts, huge black sails, long red streamers or pennants and colourful hatches turn heads wherever they go.[1]

They are called trading wherries as both have retained their hatched holds from their cargo-carrying days; neither takes commercial cargoes these days other than animate

[1] *Albion and Maud* As well as the studies already cited in this chapter see the works covering these vessels in detail: D. Bray, *The Story of the Norfolk Wherries* (Jarrold Colour Publications, Norwich, [1978]); M. Kirby, *Albion: The story of the Norfolk trading wherry* (Norfolk Wherry Trust and Jarrold Publishing, Norwich, 1998); and V. and L. Pargeter, *Maud: A Norfolk wherry* (Ingatestone, 1990)

above The trading wherry *Albion*, preserved in full working order by the Norfolk Wherry Trust since 1949. Here she lies peacefully on the Yare at Cantley, upstream of the sugar beet factory, on 10 Aug. 2014 after a long members' voyage earlier that day from Oulton Broad, on the Waveney—endured in the storm-force winds and driving rain of the tail end of Hurricane Bertha.

The 42-foot mast (12·8 metres) is in the horizontal position, the lead counterweight clearly seen at the bow where it pivots in the tabernacle or timber housing. The hatches are hidden by the awning stretched over the hold and the cabin to keep her watertight.

The white nosings, introduced during the 19th century to enable vessels to show up in poor light and at night, are new painted and reveal the clean carvel lines of the hull. Unlike the wherry shown opposite, *Albion* is unusual in not being clinker-built (with overlapping planking)   [*MB·2014*]

---

[1] *Hathor* Built by Hall's of Reedham for descendants of Mary Hardy. *Hathor*'s story is told by her skipper Peter Bower, who founded Wherry Yacht Charter: *Hathor: The story of a Norfolk pleasure wherry* (Broads Authority, Norwich, 1989)

ones in the form of enthusiasts and members of the public who try their hand at wherrying under the watchful eye of trained volunteer skippers and mates.

Three pleasure wherries also sail the Broads: *Solace* (built in 1903), *Hathor* (1905) and *Ardea* (1927); *Hathor* is seen at anchor in *plate 52*. They have the same rig and handling qualities as the traders, but in place of the hold they have purpose-built cabins with bunks.[1] Completing the set of eight preserved wherries at the time of writing (June 2019) are the wherry yachts *Olive* (1909), *Norada* (1912) and *White Moth* (1915), of a slightly different design and with white-painted hulls and white sails; they too were intended for comfort rather than cargo. Pleasure boating will feature in chapter 7; this chapter relates only to trading wherries.

David Bray's diagram (below) depicts the design of the trading wherry in its final flowering. Vessels of this late period (the late nineteenth century and early twentieth) do not however resemble the earlier wherries in all particulars.[1]

[1] *final flowering* The smaller wherries in this late period were sometimes fitted with slipping keels, as seen below, which were unbolted and removed (with difficulty) to enable them to navigate in shallow waters

The design of the Norfolk wherry in its final form
[*reproduced courtesy David Bray*]

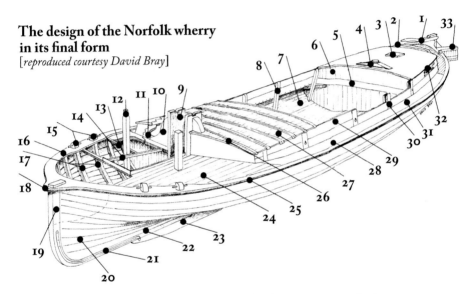

above The construction of the Norfolk wherry *c.*1900, as depicted by one of *Albion*'s former volunteer skippers:		
1 tiller	9 tabernacle for the mast	22 keel
2 mainsheet	10 tabernacle knee	23 slipping keel
3 cabin skylight hatch	11 main beam	24 foredeck
4 coburg	12 winch stanchions	25 bin iron
5 after beam	13 deck beams	26 dead hatch
6 cabin bulkhead	14 carlin beams	27 portable hatches
7 hold ceiling	15 timber heads	28 standing rightup
8 rightup stanchion	16 planksheer	29 shifting rightup
	17 timbers	30 rightup iron
	18 harpen iron	31 plankway
	19 stem	32 cabin window
	20 clinker planking/strakes	33 rudder
	21 slipping keel iron	[*David Bray 1978*]

[1] *wherry sail* D. Bray, 'Albion: Notes for skippers and mates', p. 7.
Davies described the way the wherry could 'shoot' a bridge: that is, approach at speed, lower the mast and sail in one movement, rely on the vessel's momentum to take her through, and then raise the mast and sail all 'without a pause' and without coming in to the bank.
The operation required great skill and even more nerve on a vessel that might be going at 7–8 mph (G.C. Davies, *Norfolk Broads and Rivers*, pp. 27–8)

[2] *mast* G.C. Davies, *Norfolk Broads and Rivers*, p. 27.
Lead is easier to cast than iron as its melting point is lower. For its volume, lead is heavier than iron and thus the preferred material for a mast. Lead is also more malleable than iron in case it should need reworking later

The key feature of the Norfolk wherry, through the centuries following its adaptation from the row barge, is its rig in the form of the mast and sail. Unlike the keel the mast has only one stay, the forestay, and no side stays; with the counterpoise this made it possible for one man on a fairly small wherry to raise and lower both mast and sail while under way. David Bray adds, 'A wherry sail is unique in that it is hoisted by means of a single halyard. All other gaff sails have separate peak and throat halyards.' In his vivid prose G.C. Davies expressed awe at both the design and the helmsmanship displayed,[1] identifying the counterweight at the foot of the mast as fundamental to the success of the wherry. Speaking of these masts, he observed:

They are made of spruce fir, and are very massive, yet we have seen a little girl amuse herself by rocking a mast up and down, so carefully was it balanced. A weight of two tons being played with by a little girl was a curious illustration of the triumph of man's mechanical mind over matter.[2]

As well as their distinctive design, the measurements and tonnages of keels and wherries are central to the story, as has become clear. The two trading wherries are broader in the beam than *Dee-Dar*, a particularly slender keel. *Maud* is the larger at 60 feet long by 16 feet 6 inches beam (18·3 metres by 5); *Albion* is 58 feet by 15 feet (17·7 metres by 4·6). *Maud*'s hold is 33 feet long (10 metres), and is lined

right The clinker construction of *Maud*'s hull. The mast, 46 feet long (14 metres), is lowered, showing the white-painted counterpoise which rests near the bottom of the boat when the mast is raised. The quants are stowed at the bow [*MB · 2000*]

above Wayford Bridge on the River Ant: the branch leading north-west to Dilham, seen from downstream. No keels were registered as using the Ant or the Thurne 1795–98. The register shows that four wherries, of up to 30 tons, and one 'boat' of unknown rig were based at Dilham and thus had to get through this narrow arch.

The timber boarding protected the bridge from vessels in case of grazing, and perhaps offered a handhold for the crews as they eased their way along.

The soft-edged banks provided an easy landing for the wherry, one of the most difficult manoeuvres being to bring the vessel to a gentle halt. In the dark, unstaithed banks can be dangerous. It is easy to fall in under the boat if part of the bank gives way [*drawing by Francis Stone & Son; lithograph by D. Hodgson 1830*]

with pine boarding. Those working under the hatches have to bend double during a trip on *Albion*. When emptying the contents of one of the vast teapots overboard by climbing the companionway to the deck they find themselves lurching unsteadily across the pronounced slopes forming the floor of the hold, hitting their head in the process. Those unused to a wherry's motion can be identified by their bruises.

Albion has a draught of 3 feet 6 inches when light, and 5 feet 6 inches (1·1 and 1·7 metres) when laden to her full 40-ton capacity; *Maud* can carry a few extra tons.[1] Each has sixteen cambered hatches, one of the middle ones remaining fixed. Summarising the design of these gaff-rigged vessels David Bray considers them 'perhaps the most graceful of

[1] *draught* Table 4.4.1 gives the draught on some early wherries.

The heavy counterpoise could cause problems for wherries—but not for keels, where the mast was stepped centrally. The lead at one end and the heavy rudder at the other would break a wherry's back, causing her to become 'hogged' if not kept fully laden. I am grateful to Mike Fuller, of the Norfolk Wherry Trust and author of 'How a Wherry was Built in about 1825' (privately circulated, Ludham, 2002), for his guidance on hogging and how to prevent it (our phone conversation of 15 June 2002)

---

[1] *graceful* D. Bray, *The Story of the Norfolk Wherries*, unpag. Commenting on the unstayed mast he adds, 'All the sailing stresses were taken by the massive tabernacle or mast case'

[2] *red-brown* G.C. Davies, *Norfolk Broads and Rivers*, p. 6

[3] *sail* R. Clark, *Black-Sailed Traders*, pp. 55–7: 'It is just simply black . . . Only someone suffering from colour blindness could make any mistake about it' (p. 55)

[4] *black* G.C. Davies, *Norfolk Broads and Rivers*, p. 177: 'Very graceful are the forms of those black high-peaked sails, and very busy is the sight when the change of tide lets loose the waiting craft'

[5] *Michael Sparkes* His letter to me of 22 Nov. 1995. The dyke is the stream from Tunstead at the point where it enters the Bure at Lower Common

inland cargo-carrying craft ever built'.[1] The colour plates of *Albion* in this volume illustrate his point (*plates 25–28*).

Colour brings us to the contentious topic of the colour of the sail. As Stannard's *River at Thorpe* indicates (*plate 21*), together with many other Norwich School paintings, the sails were tanned a rich russet in the early nineteenth century and probably earlier; Mary Hardy does not help since she does not comment on the subject. Davies too says that they were russet: 'the red-brown canvas of the wherries'.[2]

However that type of remark irritated Roy Clark, who chose to give the title *Black-Sailed Traders* to his highly readable tale of the wherries. He held that wherry sails were *always* tarred, not tanned. He had his supporters, bringing up big guns like Jacob Cox of the boatbuilding dynasty at Barton Turf. Cox, his memories going back to the 1890s, affirmed that sails were black, he and Roy Clark inveighing against 'those fancy colours you read about in books' and 'such fairy-tale descriptions'.[3]

It does not further the quest for truth to find Davies contradicting himself and stating elsewhere in his book that wherry sails were black.[4] The most likely explanation is that he was witnessing a change in practice from perhaps the mid-century onwards, and that by old Jacob's time the change to tarring was complete.

Wherries of 40 tons and more are long. *Albion* and *Maud* can be troublesome in confined spaces such as dykes. Even on the main river they give their crews headaches. *Albion*'s skipper Michael Sparkes recounted some testing moments one autumn at Coltishall, by the old King's Head Staithe:

> . . . We moored next to the Rising Sun on the Saturday evening. We lit the stove [in the little cabin] before turning in for the night; we were lucky as the wind blew the smoke down river towards the green and not into the pub.
>
> Turning the wherry round was difficult because of the narrow river. We turned Albion near the dyke just before the Rising Sun; because of the water coming down from the mill [at Horstead] a mudweight was used to control the turn.[5]

left Maud with her majestic black sail passes a moored boat at Irstead Staithe on the Ant. She was deliberately sunk on Ranworth Broad in the 1960s to shore up the bank, only to be restored lovingly to her old glory by her owners Vincent and Linda Pargeter

below Albion's forestay, with the rope stowed in readiness just as seen in Stone's *Wayford Bridge* 1830 [*MB · 2008, 2012*]

Most wherry experts consider that gaff-rigged vessels are easier to handle than square-riggers like the keel: the craft co-operate more willingly in adverse winds. It therefore follows that a wherry will perform better on a winding river, where every bend brings a new challenge. Since the Bure has 103 reaches on the 32 miles to Coltishall, as against the 54 reaches on the Yare and Wensum on the 28½ miles to Norwich,[1] it might be expected that the wherry would predominate on the sinuous Bure. That is exactly what the Great Yarmouth register tells us 1795–98: a far greater keel tonnage is found on the Yare and Wensum than on the Bure, but a massively greater wherry tonnage on the Bure.[2] Now is the time to turn to that remarkable source.

[1] *reaches* R. Malster, *Wherries and Waterways*, pp. 157–8, 160. A reach is the stretch of water you can see between two bends. He lists the names of the reaches, as used by the watermen, on all the rivers

[2] *register* Numbers of vessels and comparative tonnages are given in table 4.4.3

The Great Yarmouth register 1795–98

[1] *chap. 2* Two pages from the register (for the Panxworth keel *Trial* and the Bungay keel *Royal Oak*) are reproduced on p. 93

The background to the register has already been outlined in chapter 2.[1] The register, consisting of 156 printed forms, filled in by hand, with a large number of forms which were never used, are bound into one large volume. It was maintained by the 'Town and Borough of Great Yarmouth in

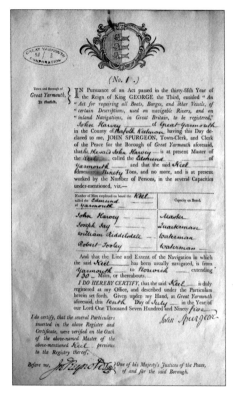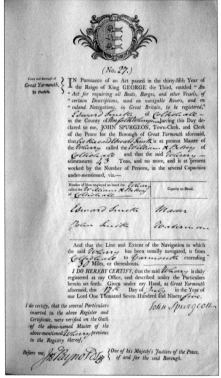

above The Gt Yarmouth register of keels and wherries on the Broads.

The first of the 156 vessels in the ledger is the extremely large keel *Edmund* (left), of 90 tons, home berth Gt Yarmouth. The skipper John Harvey of Yarmouth routinely sailed on the River Yare to Norwich and needed three men to help him.

The 43-ton wherry (no. 27) *William and*

Betsey, home berth Coltishall, plied between Coltishall and Gt Yarmouth with a skipper Edward Smith and a mate John Smith—possibly a younger brother or son being trained to wherrying. Almost certainly this was the wherry belonging to the corn and coal merchant William Palgrave and his wife Elizabeth, of Coltishall Manor House [NRO: YC 38/3, *10 July and 17 July 1795*]

Norfolk', as the printed preamble dated 7 July 1795 makes clear at the start of the register. It explains the provisions of the Act leading to its compilation:

WHEREAS by an Act made and passed in the last Session of Parliament intitled,—'An Act for requiring all Boats, Barges, and other Vessels, of certain Descriptions, used on navigable Rivers, and on inland Navigations, in Great Britain,' to be registered . . .[1]

The Act covered 'every lighter, barge, boat, wherry, or other vessel, exceeding the Burthen of thirteen Tons' worked from and after 15 June 1795. The Act would continue in force until 5 April 1798, which explains why all further entries cease from that date.

Persons working the vessels had to appear before the Clerk of the Peace or the Town Clerk of the issuing authority throughout the kingdom to obtain their certificates.[2] The Great Yarmouth certificate required only the 'men employed on board' to be named, as seen in the printed box opposite, although the Act referred not to 'men' but to the 'person or persons' employed on board.[3] Great Yarmouth chose to exclude women, none being noted among the hundreds of names in the register, as will be discussed later.

Failure to comply would result in forfeiture of the vessel and the fining of 'the master' (the skipper) ten pounds *a day* for every day the boat was worked without a certificate—a huge penalty.[4] We can assume that all or very nearly all the vessels over 13 tons are listed, assuming the borough officers took their enforcement role seriously. Some leeway would have been given at the start of the scheme, as the skippers had to be told and as Great Yarmouth would have found it difficult to handle 156 boats moored all at once at the quays in addition to the seagoing vessels. In the event the initial burst of licensing lasted many weeks into September 1795.

With one or two exceptions the boat owner's name is not given: it was the skippers and crew who were required to be named. On the forms their roles are entered in manuscript under the heading 'capacity on board'. The term 'master' means skipper; 'waterman' is his assistant or mate. ('Watermen' is also the generic term applied to all who worked craft on the inland waterways.) Very unusually the largest vessels also had a 'quarterman', as illustrated for the 90-ton keel

[1] *preamble* NRO: Y/C 38/3, unpag. The key figure by which any vessel can be identified and located is the number in the register, entered clearly by hand in chronological order of registration at the head of each form (as seen opposite for the vessels numbered 1 and 27 in the ledger).

Theole Douglas-Sherwood explains that the Act of 1795 (distinct from the Quota Act of the same year) was one of a series of Navigation Acts passed to give the Government essential data on manpower and shipping (T. Douglas-Sherwood 'The Norfolk keel', p. 27)

[2] *authority* Gt Yarmouth was the port and borough with responsibility under the Act for all Broads-based vessels.

Each certificate is signed and counter-signed, as seen opposite

[3] *person or persons* Terms taken from the Act and quoted in the preamble to the Yarmouth register (NRO: Y/C 38/3)

[4] *penalty* William Hardy was then paying his farm servants at Letheringsett £21 and his miller £31 *a year* (vol. 2, chap. 1). We do not learn how his wherry skipper was paid in the 1770s, but it was almost certainly by the job or out-and-return voyage

[1] *helm* With a 40-ton wherry like *Albion* the same person can be at the tiller and also hold the mainsheet (the rope controlling the sail).

Usually in anything other than a light wind the helmsman controls the tiller with his or her body, but a large keel may have needed one person at the helm, another at the sheets and a third atop the cargo. The two watermen on *Edmund* would have quanted when necessary, and helped to adjust the sail

[2] *boy* One such was 'Stephen Darby junior', 'boy', who sailed the 24-ton wherry *Perseverance*, berthed at Wainford with Stephen Darby as skipper; they worked her between Wainford on the Bungay naviga-tion and Gt Yarmouth (NRO: Y/C 38/3, no. 58, 22 July 1795)

[3] *Navy* J. Ehrman, *The Younger Pitt: The con-suming struggle* (Con-stable, London, 1996), p. 126

[4] *pressing Diary 1*: 2 Nov. 1776. The Royal Naval Museum, Ports-mouth gives details: <http://www.royalnaval-museum.org/info_ sheet_impressment. htm>, accessed 4 June 2019

[5] *strike* T. Douglas-Sherwood 'The Nor-folk keel', p. 43

Edmund (number 1). This post may have resembled that of a naval quartermaster, the person at the helm, but it may here just mean a senior hand, a cut above waterman.[1] The last category under 'capacity' on the form was that of boy: a young person being trained to boatwork who, as we see from the surnames, was often related to the skipper.[2]

As described in chapter 2, these skilled and responsible men were an obvious target for the press gang, the teams forming the Royal Navy's Impress Service. John Ehrman descibes the vulnerability of the men of the inland water-ways in the face of the Navy's insatiable hunger for seamen: 'One obvious if unpopular source lay to hand: the men pro-tected, in an uneasy balance with naval needs, in the sea and river trades. In May 1798 Government decided to suspend all such exemptions for five months, except in the coastal coal trade for one month.'[3]

A 'hot press', or 'press from all protections', of the type recorded by Mary Hardy in November 1776, meant that all certificates of protection were suspended, so great was the Royal Navy's need for men. Summarising in her diary an item from the newspaper, she noted:

Pressing for seamen very hot on the Thames, Portsmouth and other places, above 1000 men pressed at the above places and many lost their lives endeavouring to escape from them. A war with France talked of.[4]

Feelings ran high among the men of the inland waterways over their predicament. Theole Douglas-Sherwood refers to the 1803 strike of the Tyne keelmen who, at a time of severe national emergency after the renewal of war with France, 'brought all coal carriage to a halt as a protest when several were captured by the Tyne Regulating Officer'—the head of the Impress Service in that area.[5]

Before deriving conclusions about the tally of 156 vessels in the register some problems need to be highlighted. The first relates to the three catageories of river craft which it records. The 36 keels and 117 wherries listed are clearly dis-tinct, having, as we have seen, very different deck layouts and rigs. But what are we to make of the three 'boats'? No guidance is given as to these vessels, which were all based on the Ant and Thurne: a 16-ton boat berthed at Dilham but sailing between Barton Turf and Great Yarmouth; a 16-ton boat just downstream at Stalham; and a 14-ton boat at Martham.[1] Occasionally the Norwich artists depict boats with rigs which wander far from those of the keel and wherry. John Thirtle in his painting of a boatyard opposite Cow Tower in Norwich shows a strange, small craft with two masts and two square sails (*plate 17*). In an engraving of Joseph Stannard's *Boats on Breydon* (1825) a hay wherry has been fitted with a square sail, forward of the single mast, in addition to the normal wherry sail. A small boat to starboard of the wherry is rigged with a spritsail and jib.[2] It is possible that any or all of these three vessels might fall into the catch-all category 'boat'.

The next problem is the duplication of names for vessels, some names appearing time and again in the register.[3] The citation of the unique registration number prevents misidentification, despite the many examples in the register of *Success, Endeavour, Royal Oak*, and even two vessels *William and Mary*—the Hardys' choice of name in 1776.[4] The name *Mayflower* proved the most popular on the Broads in the 1790s, despite its associations with the Pilgrim Fathers and thus with the colonists who had risen in revolt twenty years earlier and precipitated the struggle in which France, Spain and the Dutch had joined forces with the Americans against the British. Possibly fellow-feeling for those seeking freedom of worship triumphed over patriotic inclinations. Table 4.4.2 (overleaf) shows two wherries named *Barley Corn* with Coltishall as their home berth. Their size and the colour of their paintwork would have distinguished them.

The register quotes the mileages along rivers navigated by each vessel. These are rough figures. Geldeston and Beccles (nearly four miles apart on the Waveney) are both given as 30 miles from Great Yarmouth in two entries. Sometimes the distance between Coltishall and Yarmouth is given as 30 miles, yet the distance between Horstead (just over the river from Coltishall) and Yarmouth is entered as 35 miles. Given this inexactitude we cannot calculate whether skippers took short cuts to speed up their journey times. Robert Malster recounts that some were able to sail between Horning and Wroxham not along the very winding River Bure but across

[1] *boats* Nos 40, 43 and 29 in the register. The map near the start of this chapter (p. 159) locates the places named in the register

[2] *Stannard* Illustrated in R. Malster, *The Norfolk and Suffolk Broads*, p. 112. A long boathook keeps the wherry's mainsail far out to port (rather as the quant does in David Bray's illustration of the keel seen on p. 176). One of the crew as a result feels free to have his hands in his pockets, and the other two (one female) seem to be chatting with the group on the boat alongside—a lackadaisical trio on the treacherous waterway

[3] *names* Mrs Douglas-Sherwood refers to 'a striking lack of imagination in the naming of vessels' ('The Norfolk keel', p. 40)

[4] *William and Mary* eg the 40-ton keel *William and Mary*, of Gt Yarmouth, skipper John Ward of Gt Yarmouth, sailing between Yarmouth and Norwich (NRO: Y/C 38/3, no. 13, 16 July 1795); and the 75-ton keel *William and Mary*, of Norwich, skipper Richard Thorning of Norwich, mate John Blackmore, sailing between Norwich and Yarmouth (no. 48, 20 July 1795)

TABLE 4.4.2

From the register: the 14 keels and wherries above 13 tons based at Coltishall, Horstead and Belaugh 1795–98

source NRO: Y/C 38/3 [1]   *notes* All the skippers give their regular destination as Gt Yarmouth. Mean tonnage = 31·8 tons

1795	reg. no.	home berth	type	tons	name of vessel	skipper [2]	mate [2]
17 July	27	Coltishall	wherry	43	*William and Betsey* [3]	Edward Smith of Coltishall	John Smith
18 July	31	Horstead	wherry	21	*Crostwick* [4]	Edmund Reynolds of Horstead	*none named*
18 July	32	Horstead	wherry	28	*Union*	John Reynolds of Gt Yarmouth	*none named*
20 July	46	Coltishall	wherry	35	*Friends' Adventure*	William Horn of Gt Yarmouth	William Horn jnr
20 July	47	Belaugh	wherry	30	*Friendship*	William Martin of Belaugh	*none named*
20 July	50	Coltishall	wherry	20	*Barley Corn*	Samuel Parson of Gt Yarmouth	*none named*
20 July	51	Coltishall	wherry	20	*Harvest Home*	John Fox of Coltishall	*none named*
23 July	67	Coltishall	wherry	42	*Wheat Sheaf*	Gould Scott of Gt Yarmouth	*none named*
28 July	78	Coltishall	wherry	37	*Industry*	James Wilkins of Coltishall	*none named*
1 Aug.	84	Coltishall	wherry	36	*Barley Corn*	Gazeley Kettle of Coltishall	*none named*
3 Aug.	85	Coltishall	wherry	42	*Coltishall*	Samuel Thaxter of Coltishall	*none named*
3 Aug.	86	Coltishall	wherry	38	*John and Mary* [5]	Joseph Chamberlain of Coltishall	*none named*
18 Aug.	120	Coltishall	keel	28	*Two Friends*	Elisha Royal of Coltishall	Henry Press (boy)
27 Aug.	129	Horstead	wherry	25	*Fancy*	Robert Blyth of Horstead	*none named*

[1] *register* Introduced for vessels above 13 tons for a three-year term by Act of Parliament, to expire on 5 Apr. 1798. Gt Yarmouth's runs from 10 July 1795. No signatures by skippers and mates were required; no owners are listed

[2] *skipper, mate* The terms keelman/wherryman and waterman are used to denote skipper and mate. Where no mate is listed the vessel may have been single-handed. If the skipper's wife served as mate her name was not recorded, as only the men employed on board were noted

[3] *William and Betsey* ? Owned by William and Elizabeth Palgrave of Coltishall Manor House

[4] *Crostwick* ? Owned by a Watts of Horstead (Manor) House; the family had Crostwick connections

[5] *John and Mary* Probably owned by the farmer and maltster John Fiddy jnr and his wife Ann and named for his parents; John jnr owned two trading wherries and a pleasure boat at his bankruptcy in 1801 (*Norw. Merc.* 16 May 1801)

the great open sheet of water forming Hoveton Great Broad.[1] They could well have accessed Hoveton Little Broad and Wroxham Broad as well, to complete a fast run.

Table 4.4.2 does not record all the vessels which called regularly at Coltishall. Three additional keels gave Coltishall as their destination. Samuel Betts, of Great Yarmouth, keelman, skippered an 80-ton Yarmouth-based keel *July Flower*, which he sailed between Yarmouth and Coltishall with William Drake as waterman. The 85-ton keel which came up to Coltishall from Norwich has already been mentioned in connection with the state of the rivers. Another Yarmouth-based keel, this time of 45 tons, also sailed between Norwich and Coltishall.[2] Lastly the register reveals a skipper resident at Coltishall who does not show up in the table since his vessel's berth lay elsewhere. George Tuck was master of the 42-ton wherry *Defiance*, berthed at Aylsham, which he sailed beween Aylsham and Yarmouth.[3] It is evident from these and other examples that many crews (probably the great majority) lived on board their vessels for long periods.[4]

Each entry in the register gave the vessel's principal route, as required by the 1795 Act. Very frequently that route was along only one river.[5] A problem with trying to derive firm conclusions about the waterways is highlighted by Mary Hardy's diary. As table 4.4.4 will show in the section on keel movements, the keels bringing goods for the Hardys at Coltishall did not take a route associated with just one river, although historians and other analysts have tended to interpret the data from the register in terms of the trade on individual rivers—as set out in table 4.4.3. During 1774–76 the Hardys regularly had bricks and pamments (terracotta floor tiles) brought to them from Strumpshaw on the River Yare, with the same keel stopping at Great Yarmouth for a further load—of coal and cinders (coke)—before sailing up the Bure; the keel would return with malt for Yarmouth and beyond. The scribe entering the principal route of the brick keel in the register might decide to record it as Strumpshaw–Yarmouth or Yarmouth–Coltishall, and not Strumpshaw–Coltishall. Only two vessels, the Yarmouth keels of 85 and 45 tons plying Norwich–Coltishall, are shown as having their principal routes along *two* major waterways. There may consequently be some examples of data-distortion.

[1] *short cut* R. Malster, *Wherries and Waterways*, p. 24. Many broads had both downstream and upstream access dykes from the river, making them water highways

[2] *Coltishall destination* NRO: Y/C 38/3, nos 138, 72 and 148

[3] *Coltishall skipper* No. 97, 8 Aug. 1795

[4] *living on board* Clement Cook, resident at Horning, had a 36-ton wherry *Olive Branch*, berthed at Aylsham, which he worked between Aylsham and Yarmouth with Charles Cook on board as boy (no. 139, 8 Sept. 1795).

Similarly, as we have seen, a Geldeston-berthed wherry sailed between Hardley on the Yare and Gt Yarmouth; and the small Dilham-based 'boat' sailed between Barton Turf and Gt Yarmouth (nos 62 and 40)

[5] *route* Expressed not by naming the river or rivers, but by naming the places at the furthest extent of the voyages customarily made by the vessel.

Sometimes two rivers were navigated, in the form of a tributary and then the main river: eg the Wensum and Yare (Norwich–Yarmouth), the Ant and Bure (for Dilham–Yarmouth), the Thurne and Bure (Repps–Yarmouth)

---

[1] *Ives and Wells* Covered in detail in vol. 2, chaps 5–8. Ives's may have been the largest brewery on the Broads (including Norwich) in the early 1790s.

William Hardy had been manager of Wells's maltings and brewery at Coltishall

[2] *Dilham Norw. Merc.*, 23 July 1808

[3] *Potter Heigham Norw. Merc.* 16 June 1787

[4] *data compilation* 'The passion for data collection' is discussed in vol. 2, chap. 2, but it is a theme running through this study.

Religious adherence and churchgoing practices are covered in vol. 3, chaps 1–4

The register does not record cargoes, so we cannot come to definite conclusions as to why those two keels had the Yare *and* the Bure as their main route. We can however speculate. The steam-powered brewery of Chapman Ives beside the river at Coltishall may be the reason. His voracious coppers, capable of brewing a massive 20,000 barrels of beer and more a year, would have needed more grain than the maltings of the Coltishall area could have produced. The rival, but smaller, Wells's brewery (later Hawes's) in the village was also taking regular quantities of malt.[1] The rows of maltings along the Wensum wharves in Norwich may provide the answer over the two keels.

As a final reflection on the difficulties of using the register, the omission of vessels below 13 tons under the Act will almost certainly mean that we are missing a sizeable number of working vessels on the Broads at that time; and the pleasure craft do not appear at all. The press advertisements can fill the gap only up to a point. A small 8-ton wherry was for sale at Robert Barnes's staithe at Dilham in 1808, the notice implying that only extremely small vessels would be able to cope with the restricted access to parts of the Upper Ant: 'Built in 1807, burthen 8 tons (or thereabouts), and is well adapted for the Dilham, Stalham, or Sutton dykes'. Like the other two for sale at Dilham at that time (table 4.4.1) this diminutive craft was clinker-built.[2] Small wherries were nevertheless held to be profitable, in waters suited to them. It was said of the Potter Heigham wherry of 13 tons, for sale in 1787 (table 4.4.1): 'There has been a constant and profitable employ for the wherry.'[3]

Firm data from the Great Yarmouth register

Despite these difficulties the register yields vital information about vessels, crews, staithes, tonnages and routes. It was an age of data compilation in farming, manufacturing, taxation and even (through the episcopal visitation returns) in religion.[4] As the Government had anticipated, keeping such detailed records as Great Yarmouth's shone a light on waterborne distribution during the national emergency which persisted almost without a break from 1793 until the final resolution on the field of Waterloo. Tabulating the data, as in table 4.4.3, produces results which leap off the page.

One of the most striking features on first examining the register is the small number of crew members for the larger vessels. It seems impossible to believe that James Wakefield, of Great Yarmouth, handled the keel *Flora*, of 70 tons, on his own along the Yare to Norwich. Yet his name is the only one on the form.[1] Almost as incredible is that John Thomas, also of Yarmouth, sailed the 43-ton wherry *Robert and Frances* single-handed, on the same route;[2] or that John Kirk, of Horning, sailed the 40-ton wherry *Providence* alone between Horning and Yarmouth.[3]

Either they were extraordinarily skilled boat-handlers or, as is likely, the skippers were helped by their womenfolk whose presence was not recorded. As we have seen, the Norwich artists often depicted women on board keels and wherries. In this chapter we shall meet two known to Mary Hardy: Mrs Starkey, whose husband had a keel which called at Coltishall, and Mary Ann Pooley, wife of a wherryman, Thomas; he was later killed in an accident on his craft.

In one instance the mate is entered in the register as the *father* of the skipper: a nice reversal of the practice of ship's boys accompanying their fathers or older brothers.[4]

[1] *Flora* NRO: Y/C 38/3, no. 63, 23 July 1795

[2] *Robert and Frances* No. 49, 20 July 1795

[3] *Providence* No. 61, 23 July 1795.
Other examples include an 85-ton keel with only two people, and an 80-ton keel with only a skipper and boy; both sailed on the Yare

[4] *father* On the 80-ton keel *Polly*, on the Yare, the master is given as 'Permeter Ansell the Younger', of Yarmouth, keelman. His 'waterman' is 'Permeter Ansell senior' (no. 101 in the register, 11 Aug. 1795). Given the size of the keel it is likely a Mrs Ansell was on board too

The 47 parishes of Norfolk and Suffolk in which 156 keels and wherries had their home berths 1795–98, with numbers of vessels and range of tonnages

source   Register of 36 keels [K], 117 wherries [W] and 3 'boats' [B] (of unspecified rig) at Gt Yarmouth 1795–98 (NRO: Y/C 38/3). All the vessels sailed to or from, or via, Yarmouth
notes   Tonnage relates to carrying capacity: tonnage burden or 'burthen'.
Rivers, towns and villages are located on the Broadland map on p. 159

home berth	numbers	tons	home berth	numbers	tons
Acle	2W	16–20	Norton	1W	34
Aylsham	5W	16–42	NORWICH ²	9K·15W	17–80
Barton Turf	2W	14–19	Oulton	1W	34
Beccles	4W	22–29	Oxnead	1W	18
Belaugh	1W	30	Panxworth	2K	20–40
Bungay	1K·7W	18–58	Potter Heigham	2W	24–24
Burgh-next-Aylsham	2W	16–18	Ranworth	1W	20
Burgh St Peter	1W	20	Reedham	1K· 1W	15–59
Cantley	1W	17	Repps	1W	30
Carrow	1K	60	Salhouse	3W	26–40
Catfield	1W	20	[West] Somerton	1W	28
Coltishall	1K·9W	20–43	South Walsham	3W	16–29
Dilham	4W·1B	15–30	Stalham	1W, 1B	14–16
Flixton	1W	20	Stokesby	1W	20
Geldeston	6W	18–35	Sutton	5W	16–20
GREAT YARMOUTH	21K·8W	15–97	Tunstall	1W	14
Herringfleet	1W	18	Upton	1W	30
Hickling	2W	20–24	Wainford	2W	20–24
Horning	4W	17–40	Whitlingham	1W	22
Horstead	3W	21–28	Woodbastwick	1W	23
Hoveton ¹	1W	20	Wroxham	3W	22–25
Irstead	2W	14–16			
Langley	2W	29–30	¹ *Hoveton* Given as 'Overton' in the register
LOWESTOFT	1W	20	² *Norwich* The city's many parishes are not
Ludham	1W	18	distinguished in the register. Carrow was
Martham	1B	13	recorded as separate from the city staithes

³ *staithes* Where there was a riverside cornmill, maltings, brewery, brickworks, lime-kiln or other such concern there was a staithe. Robert

It has long been known that small staithes were dotted about the Broads in the eighteenth century; finding firm evidence of their presence has been trickier (chapter 3).³ The register provides just such evidence, as charted in the list above and on the Broadland map on page 159.

The list of 47 parishes, plus Hardley (given as a destination for a Geldeston-based wherry, as explained earlier), is fascinating for the light it throws on lesser-known staithes. While many of the moorings opposite are very popular today with holidaymakers on the Broads—as at Hoveton, Wroxham, Horning, Ranworth, Ludham, Potter Heigham and Hickling on the northern rivers, and Reedham, Oulton and Beccles on the southern rivers—it is the forgotten places which stand out. These were often reached by dykes long overgrown, silted and now inaccessible.

No one on the rivers these days would be able to get up Flixton Dyke on the Waveney, Tunstall Dyke on the Bure or Panxworth Dyke off South Walsham Inner Broad. Yet here they are shown, able to cope with vessels of 20, 14 and 40 tons respectively. Tunstall makes an interesting study. Its long dyke, unimpeded in the 1790s across the low ground in the parish, was compromised by the building of Acle New Road, the 'Acle Straight', in 1830 and the railway in 1882:

> To get up to the staithe wherries had to negotiate two awkward bridges, a hump-backed bridge carrying the Acle New Road and a girder bridge carrying the Acle–Yarmouth railway line. It was too narrow for a wherry to tack, and when the wind was contrary the wherry had to be bow-hauled by helpers from Tunstall.[1]

In this instance the coming of the railway hampered the wherry trade even more directly than was the norm.

Maltster, in *Wherries and Waterways*, refers to many such staithes, in often out-of-the-way places: see esp. pp. 71–90. Roy Clark has a fund of anecdotes about the staithes and cargoes in his work *Black-Sailed Traders*: see esp. pp. 88–109.

However their examples date from the 19th and 20th centuries

---

[1] *Tunstall* R. Maltster, *Wherries and Waterways*, p. 25. The dyke fell into disuse about 1897, the last wherry along it being owned and sailed by the coal merchant Joseph Powley (perhaps descended from the 1795 skipper). 'If the water was too high the wherry could not get under the bridges; if it was too low there was not sufficient depth to float the craft' (p. 25)

left Tunstall: the village, on high ground, and dyke (labelled 'Navigation') on Faden's map of 1797. Stokesby lies upstream and on the other bank. The Gt Yarmouth register records that William Powley, of Tunstall, had a 14-ton wherry *Maid*, of Tunstall, which he worked Tunstall–Yarmouth (NRO: Y/C 38/3, no. 71, 25 July 1795). The staithe house at the head of the dyke is also marked.

A vessel of *Maid*'s size could be sailed single-handed. The Bure, while heavily tidal in its lower reaches, was clear of bridges and other impediments to navigation [*Faden's Map of Norfolk 1797: Larks Press 1989*]

[1] *Panxworth* NRO: Y/C 38/3, nos 99 and 100, 10 Aug. 1795. The larger keel, skippered by a Ranworth man, William Ebbage, had a boy, Thomas Browne (the register entry being pictured on p. 93 in chap. 2 under 'Navigating the waterway').

The staithe as a working area had passed from memory by the time Roy Clark and Robert Malster were researching the waterways and conducting interviews with retired wherrymen. It receives no mention in Clark's *Black-Sailed Traders*, and only an oblique reference in Malster's *Wherries and Waterways* (p. 77)

[2] *two keels* R. Malster, *The Norfolk and Suffolk Broads*, p. 115.

These were not 'the only two keels' from the Bure. Coltishall was the home berth of *Two Friends* (table 4.4.2), and the berths of some of the Gt Yarmouth keels would have been on the last reaches of the Bure, as we know from Mary Hardy's references to Jonathan Symonds' keel or keels (table 4.4.4)

[3] *boundaries* The parish boundaries are marked on Bryant's map of Norfolk of 1826, but not on Faden's map of 1797

Flixton Dyke, on the Waveney between Somerleyton and Oulton Dyke, has similarly not been used for well over a century. That Panxworth had its own staithe is likewise no longer recalled, yet in 1795 two keels registered their home berths there: the 40-ton *Trial* (as illustrated in chapter 2), and the 20-ton *Venture*. This smaller keel was skippered by William Noughton of Panxworth. Both masters gave their principal route as Aylsham–Yarmouth.[1]

These vessels perplexed Robert Malster, causing him to question whether the register were really a reliable source:

> How does it come about that the only two keels from the North River [the Bure], the 40-ton *Trial* and the 20-ton *Venture*, belong to Panxworth, a parish which does not lie on any waterway?[2]

The answer lies in parish boundaries. The register followed the practice of the licensing authorities for public houses, and much other eighteenth-century regulation, by recording entries under the appropriate parish. A salient of Panxworth parish juts out along a stream which runs into the north-western corner of what is now South Walsham Inner Broad; in 1797 that end of the broad extended further across towards Panxworth than it does today.[3] Faden's map shows that a staithe could have been sited at the point north-east of Panxworth Carr ('Cars'), where a road bridge carries the lane running between the Ship at South Walsham and the Maltsters at Ranworth.

And so the register tells us of these neglected waterways which once brought coal to the villages and took away their produce: Panxworth had a small maltings on the main road near the Red Lion, that house also being marked on Faden's map. The register pierces the mists which were to lift finally only in the age of the camera and the oral-history interview.

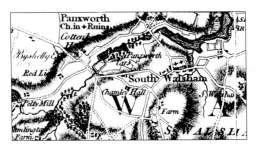

left The 18th-century staithe house at Stokesby stands right on the riverbank behind the old brick warehouse and beside the Ferry Inn. Staithe houses can be found in many Broadland villages, as at nearby Upton at the head of the long manmade dyke from the Bure to Upton village　　[*MB · 2011*]

facing page The likely location of Panxworth Staithe at the time that the Gt Yarmouth register of keels and wherries was compiled. S. Walsham Broad, reached along a winding dyke from the River Bure (off the top of the map), snakes across the north-east corner. S. Walsham's two churches in the one churchyard are marked south of the broad: ✝ ✝ The lane to Ranworth heads north-west from the churches and crosses a tree-lined inlet from the broad which carries on under the bridge to 'Panxworth Cars' [Carr, meaning marshy woodland]. The staithe probably lay just east of that bridge [*Faden's Map of Norfolk 1797: Larks Press 1989*]

Checking the list of staithes against Faden's county map illustrates the register's uses in conjunction with other documentary sources; newspaper advertisements also provide a cross-check. Wills and inventories help with the interpretation of the evidence, and can suggest clues as to ownership.[1] The farmer at Oxnead Hall on the Aylsham navigation, John Repton, brother of the landscape gardener Humphry, had 'a capital wherry' berthed at Oxnead which was sold for £50 in 1828, John Spinks having taken Repton's farming equipment, livestock and other possessions on lease on Repton's death in 1809.[2] The register sheds light on the Spinks family and the wherry. In 1795 William Spinks, of Aylsham, was skipper of the 18-ton wherry named *Oxnead* which appears under Oxnead, the home berth, in the list of 47 parishes seen earlier.[3] We do not learn from a comparison of the sources whether Repton's capital wherry was the one of 1795 or a replacement, but he is likely to have been the owner of the wherry *Oxnead* in the register. Also the Spinks connection with Oxnead Hall can be traced back to 1795.

The use of the problematic term 'boat', discussed in the previous section, surfaces in the Barton Turf will of a member of the wherrying family of Amies or Amis. Just as the

[1] *ownership* The sole owner whom I found named in the register was Anthony Cheeper, of Gt Yarmouth. He may have been singled out as he owned the largest vessel, the 97-ton keel *Success*, master John Rant, waterman Benjamin Harmer, working Yarmouth–Norwich (NRO: Y/C, 38/3, no. 131, 28 Aug. 1795)

[2] *Repton* W. and M. Vaughan-Lewis, *Aylsham: A Nest of Norfolk lawyers* (Itteringham History, 2014), p. 177

[3] *wherry Oxnead* No. 147, 23 Oct. 1795. Although this was only a small wherry Spinks had a boy on board, John Moore

¹ *Amies* James Amies (bapt. Barton Turf 12 June 1749), of Barton Turf, 'boatman' (NRO: ANF 1805, f. 50, no. 34, Will dated 6 Jan. 1805, proved 1 Apr. 1805).
    He left his 'boat' with tackle, apparel and furniture to his son, James Amies; his son-in-law, also a beneficiary, was William Yaxley. The son, James Amies/Amis (1774–1846), was by contrast a wherryman and left his 'wherry' to his son James Amis (b. 1807). Details of the wills are given on the Norfolk Wills website: <www.norfolkwills. co.uk/1805-001.pdf> and <www.norfolkwills. co.uk/1846-001.pdf>, accessed 4 Nov. 2014

² *figures* Robert Maltster, *The Norfolk and Suffolk Broads*, p. 115.
    Tom Williamson echoes Robert Malster's findings but also states, surely inexplicably, that the keel was smaller than the wherry (*The Norfolk Broads*, p. 137). He adds, without citing the evidence, that the wherry was 'the principal craft to ply the rivers' as early as the early 17th century (p. 137).
    Both Roy Clark and Theole Douglas-Sherwood make determined assaults on the register. They give interesting analyses and make the key point on tonnages,

skipper of a keel or wherry, on appearing before the Great Yarmouth authorities to register his vessel, is described on the form as a keelman or wherryman, so the skippers of the three boats are each called 'boatman'. That too is how James Amies describes himself in his will of 1805. He could not categorise his craft as a keel or a wherry, although his son later had a wherry.¹

And so we come to the tablulated data from the register, seen opposite in table 4.4.3. A superficial glance at the numbers, showing 36 keels, 117 wherries and three 'boats', would seem to indicate that by 1798 the day of the keel was well past. We would be wrong. A head count (or mast count) is deceptive; indeed, it is thoroughly misleading. Capacity, not numbers, should form the basis of comparison. When assessing the fighting force of two opposing states, no naval analyst would rely on the weight of numbers alone, but would enquire into capability. If the countries had fifty ships each they might at first glance seem evenly balanced—until investigation revealed that the first had forty patrol boats and ten frigates and destroyers, while the second had ten patrol boats and forty frigates and destroyers.

In the case of the register it is the tonnages which matter. Yes, there are only 36 keels. But in tonnage terms they represent 2271 tons. The 117 wherries together muster not a great deal more: 3068 tons. (The three boats, being small vessels, total only 46 tons.) The day of the keel was far from over.

And on the Yare, the principal thoroughfare of the Broads for freight at that time, the keels were the workhorses, carrying well over twice the tonnage of the wherries on that river: 1915 tons to 845 tons. As the table shows, the Yare carried a great deal more freight than the other rivers, including the Bure. The figures at the foot of the columns show us what was happening: the average keel could carry 63 tons; the average wherry only 26 tons. Keels, many of them broader in the beam than any gaff-rigged craft could be, were particularly well adapted to conveying loads like coal and timber.

Unless the figures are set out fully the position may be misconstrued. Robert Malster and Tom Williamson confine themselves to the comparative number of vessels, without heeding the *tonnages*; others have since echoed their words.²

TABLE 4.4.3

Numbers and gross and mean tonnage burden of keels and wherries above 13 tons on the Broads 1795–98

source Register of 36 keels, 117 wherries and 3 'boats' (of unspecified rig) at Gt Yarmouth 1795–98 (NRO: Y/C 38/3). All 156 vessels were declared as sailing to or from, or via, Yarmouth

waterway	*keels*	*wherries*	*'boats'*
numbers			
River Ant [1]	0	14	2
River Bure (and Aylsham navigation)	4	43	0
River Thurne [1]	0	7	1
River Yare (and River Wensum) [2]	29	29	0
River Waveney (and Bungay navigation)	1	24	0
Rivers Bure and Yare	2	0	0
TOTAL NUMBERS	36	117	3
gross tonnage			
River Ant [1]	0	253	32
River Bure (and Aylsham navigation)	168	1160	0
River Thurne [1]	0	168	14
River Yare (and River Wensum) [2]	1915	845	0
River Waveney (and Bungay navigation)	58	642	0
Rivers Bure and Yare	130	0	0
GROSS OVERALL TONNAGE	2271	3068	46
MEAN OVERALL TONNAGE	63	26	15

[1] *Ant and Thurne* Vessels sailing on these rivers, both tributaries of the Bure, perforce also sailed on the Bure to reach Gt Yarmouth. In this table Catfield is treated as on the Ant, Ludham on the Thurne. They have staithes on both rivers, but the register does not specify the location of the staithe

[2] *Wensum* A tributary of the Yare, running through Norwich. The Chet, with its twin inland ports of Loddon and Chedgrave, is also a tributary of the Yare, but it does not appear in the register. It may not have been navigable then

right The arms of the Borough of Great Yarmouth appear at the head of each printed form in the register [NRO: Y/C 38/3]

while compiling slightly different totals and averages from my own (R. Clark, *Black-Sailed Traders*, pp. 48–50, and his appendix pp. 201–37 which has been mined over the years by many researchers; also T. Douglas-Sherwood, 'The Norfolk keel', pp. 28–36, including graphs and tables).

Both she and Robert Malster point out that there may be a duplicate vessel in the register. The Yarmouth keel *Flora*, of 57 tons, may appear twice, probably as a new skipper was appointed and had to re-register *Flora* in 1797 (nos 151 and 154).

However since there is no note in the ledger declaring this to be the case I have discounted it and entered the keel into the calculations as two separate vessels.

It is entirely possible, given the fondness for certain names, that there *were* two keels of the same size and bearing the same name

---

[1] *Bure and Yare* The two keels, totalling 130 tons, which used both rivers are not included in these totals (nos 72 and 148 in the register)

[2] *Aylsham and Bungay* The registration numbers of the craft plying the Aylsham

The table yields further nuggets. Whereas in number terms the keel was level-pegging with the wherry on the Yare, at 29 vessels each, the wherry was the far more popular vessel on the Bure: only four keels to 43 wherries. On the Waveney the keel was even more heavily outnumbered: one keel to 24 wherries. In comparison with the Yare and the Bure, the Waveney was a less useful waterway. It carried only 700 tons (as measured by the capacity of the vessels recording it as their principal route), against the 2760 tons and 1328 tons of the other two. If the Ant and Thurne are included in the Bure's totals, since they are tributaries, the Bure's figure rises to 1795 tons.[1] The Ant and Thurne almost certainly carried a larger tonnage than is shown. The requirement under the Act to register vessels of only 13 tons and above will have prevented their true tonnage from being reflected.

The Waveney's day was yet to come (if in a brief flowering), with William Cubitt's proposals of 1827 for making Beccles a deepwater port and then in 1833 the opening of the Norwich and Lowestoft navigation and creation of Lowestoft harbour, as touched on in the note on page 164.

The two navigations—on the Bure from Coltishall Lock to Aylsham, and on the Waveney from Geldeston Lock to Bungay—share a fairly similar profile in the register. The first had two keels on its waters (the pair berthed at Panxworth) and nine wherries; the second had one 58-ton keel (*Royal Oak*, the largest vessel on the Waveney), and nine wherries. Bungay had the larger craft, the biggest on the Aylsham navigation being the 42-ton wherry *Defiance*, skippered by the Coltishall resident, George Tuck.[2]

Keels at Coltishall 1773–81

The fourteen vessels with home berths at Coltishall and the neighbouring parishes of Horstead and Belaugh in 1795–98 have already been listed (table 4.4.2). The one keel, of 28 tons, was outgunned by the thirteen wherries with a total capacity of 417 tons. Now we can observe their predecessors in operation through the eyes of Mary Hardy at Coltishall.

Tables 4.4.4 and 4.4.6 list the number of keel and wherry freight movements at Coltishall recorded in the diary 1773–81. (Tables 4.4.5 and 4.4.7 relate to the carriage of passengers by keel and wherry.) Revealingly, and suggesting the predominance of the keel still in this period, there are 23 keel movements, as opposed to three for wherries—with the significant omission of the Hardys' own wherry, the log for which is featured separately. However the last keel movement came in August 1776, the month that the Hardys launched their wherry, and the diarist does not thereafter refer to keels in connection with freight. This does not mean the keels had disappeared; it was just that the Hardys no longer had need of them.

Keels would still have been coming and going at Coltishall. We have already seen the 50-ton hatched keel belonging to John Fiddy and Joseph Browne for sale at Coltishall in 1779 (table 4.4.1). Many of the references to cargo and passenger travel in the diary are vague, with terms such as 'by water' or 'by boat'; some of these imprecise movements were probably made by keels. Mary Hardy's opening entry, for instance, on 28 November 1773, records that 'Mr Hardy and Raven went to Yarmouth by water.'[1] Such references have been omitted from the tables.

Coltishall was a keel-building village in the years she lived there, the diarist noting that on 29 December 1774, a 'very fine dry day', her husband and the village schoolmaster John Smith 'walked to see the keel building'. She does not state where the yard lay, but it was probably the Wrights' yard, where the Hardys' own wherry *William and Mary* was to be built two years later.[2]

In the years before the Hardys had their own vessel they used others', notably a keel belonging to Jonathan Symonds of Great Yarmouth; his Bureside wharf by the North-West Tower has already been described in chapter 3. As table 4.4.4 shows (overleaf), a typical passage was for the keel to collect bricks from Strumpshaw on the River Yare and add to her cargo at Great Yarmouth by stopping to collect coal and cinders before starting on the long passage from Symonds' Wharf to Coltishall. On two occasions a load is quoted as 12 chaldrons,[3] so the men would have had to load 144 sacks of coal onto the keel, unless it was loose coal.[4]

The keel making the passage to Coltishall on 14 November 1774 was a big one, Mary Hardy noting that as well as 12 chaldrons of cinders (about 14½–16 tons) 7000 Strumpshaw bricks were on board and a number of pamments,

navigation are 96, 97 (*Defiance*), 99 (keel), 100 (keel), 117, 118, 125 (berthed on the Ant at Irstead), 132, 139, 145, 147.

Those for the Bungay navigation are 58, 59, 123, 124, 126, 128, 135 (keel), 136, 137, 141 (NRO: Y/C 38/3).

The entry for the Bungay keel, *Royal Oak*, is pictured on p. 93 in chap. 2

---

[1] *opening entry Diary 1.* Raven their elder son, was then aged six; his mother had been born Mary Raven

[2] *keel building Diary 1.* The Wrights and their yard are covered in a later section

[3] *12 chaldrons Diary 1*: 14 Nov., 16 Nov. 1774 (up to about 16 tons)

[4] *sacks* Nationally, at that time, one chaldron of coal represented 36 heaped bushels (also a measure of volume) or 12 sacks, so there were 3 heaped bushels to the sack.

Each sack measured 50 inches by 26 (127 cm by 66).

The Gt Yarmouth coal measure was 137 lb to the sack (62·1 kg), but we do not learn which measure Mary Hardy was quoting

TABLE 4.4.4

Keel movements at Coltishall noted by Mary Hardy 1774–76: goods

source Diary of Mary Hardy   *note* A chaldron is approx. 1·2–1·3 tons

date	owner of keel	cargo	passage
1774			
29 Aug.	?	bricks, tiles	from Strumpshaw
14 Nov.	? Jonathan Symonds	7000 bricks, pamments, 12 chaldrons cinders	from Strumpshaw, from Gt Yarmouth
16 Nov.	Jonathan Symonds	12 chaldrons cinders	from Gt Yarmouth
1775			
22 Jan.	Jonathan Symonds	bricks, pamments	? from Strumpshaw
17 Feb.	Jonathan Symonds	bricks	from Strumpshaw
19 Mar.	Jonathan Symonds	bricks, pamments, coal, cinders, salt	? from Strumpshaw ? from Gt Yarmouth
23 Mar.	Jonathan Symonds	malt	? for Gt Yarmouth
24 May	Jonathan Symonds	bricks, pamments	? from Strumpshaw
28 June	?	13 chaldrons coal	? from Gt Yarmouth
14 Aug.	Jonathan Symonds	bricks, cinders	? from Strumpshaw ? from Gt Yarmouth
8 Sept.	Jonathan Symonds	coal, cinders	from Gt Yarmouth
16 Oct.	Jonathan Symonds	?	from Gt Yarmouth
3 Nov.	?	wheat	for Gt Yarmouth, for transhipping to Yorkshire
1 Dec.	Robert Ansell	sea sand	? from Gt Yarmouth
26 Dec.	Jonathan Symonds	bricks	? from Strumpshaw
27 Dec.	Jonathan Symonds	malt	for Gt Yarmouth, for transhipping to London
1776			
14 Feb.	?	malt	? for Gt Yarmouth
26 Feb.	Jonathan Symonds	cinders	? from Gt Yarmouth
28 Feb.	Jonathan Symonds	malt	? for Gt Yarmouth, for transhipping
7 Mar.	John Colls	bricks	from Strumpshaw
18 Mar.	Jonathan Symonds	malt	? for Gt Yarmouth
22 May	?	malt	? for Gt Yarmouth
3 July	?	malt	for Gt Yarmouth, for transhipping to London
1 Aug.	?	malt, wheat	malt for Gt Yarmouth, for transhipping to London; wheat for Gt Yarmouth

which she calls 'pavements'.[1] Mary Hardy shows that loading and unloading of keels and wherries was performed by their farm and brewery workforce—not by the skipper and mate, as was the practice in the nineteenth and twentieth centuries once times were hard and the wherries were trying to compete with the railways.[2] A history of the brickyard at Somerleyton (a village which does not appear in the Great Yarmouth register), served by its own wherry cut from the River Waveney, shows that in the mid-nineteenth century a wherry could hold between 12,000 and 14,000 bricks:

The title deed [of 2 March 1849] refers to the canal, running from the River Waveney, now used by Ripplecraft Ltd, and known as the Cut, but which used to be called Wherry Dyke.[3] Here the bricks were loaded onto the black-sailed wherries long before the coming of the railways; and even after the line between Somerleyton and Lowestoft was opened in 1847, to connect with the line to Norwich at Reedham, wherries continued to be used for the brick-carrying trade, right into the present century [the 20th century].

The wherrymen did their own unloading and were paid 6d per thousand bricks. The average load was 12–14,000 bricks and the carriage rate 2s 6d per thousand.[4]

[1] *bricks* William Marshall gives the dimensions of stock bricks in north-east Norfolk in 1782 as 9 inches by 4¼ by 2⅛ (22·9 cm by 10·8 by 5·4) (W. Marshall, *The Rural Economy of Norfolk*, vol. 1, p. 388)

[2] *workforce* The diarist records that unloading Symonds' keel just of bricks and pamments took five man-days at Coltishall, in rain, sharp frost and high winds (*Diary 1*: 23–25 Jan. 1775; see also 21–22 Mar. 1775)

[3] *Wherry Dyke* Not on the 1783 county map (J. Hodskinson, *Hodskinson's Map of Suffolk in 1783* (Larks Press, Guist Bottom, 2003)

[4] *bricks* A. and A. Butler, *Somerleyton Brickfields* (Somerleyton, 1980), p. 5. Somerleyton bricks were used for Liverpool Street Station, London (1875), York Station (1877), and a Belgian royal palace (p. 7).

The wherry cut and brickfields remain, near the station also built with the local material

left Pamments: terracotta floor tiles fired in the upper part of a brick-kiln and called 'pavements' by Mary Hardy.
These examples are in Cantley Church, near the brickfields of Strumpshaw which provided the Hardys with their cargoes of tiles. John Clarke, the innkeeper of their Strumpshaw tied house, the Shoulder of Mutton, was also a brickburner [*MB · 2010*]

[1] *wheat* 'Mr Hardy at Thomas Nash's fore-noon putting up some wheat for Mr Hawk-ridge of Yorkshire, put it aboard a keel for Yarmouth afternoon' (*Diary 1*: 3 Nov. 1775).
Thomas Nash was a Gt Hautbois farmer. The keel, if small, could have loaded at his farm near new Mayton Bridge: the navigation was open to Mayton by then

[2] *malt* eg 'A sharp frost, a fine day ... Zeb Rouse and Isaac Pooley and Thompson unloading Mr Symonds' keel of bricks and loading of it again with malt for London' (*Diary 1*: 27 Dec. 1775); also 'Ex-cessive hot day. Men loading a keel with malt for London, sent 2 last of wheat to Yarmouth ... Mr Hardy with the men forenoon and afternoon' (1 Aug. 1776).
'2 last' is 20 quarters, or 40 coombs of grain: approx. 4 metric tonnes

[3] *Sunday bar* R. Malster, *The Norfolk and Suffolk Broads*, p.113

[4] *Symonds' keel laden* William Hardy was at the keel at 8 am the next day.
After the unloading, on 22 Mar. they loaded her with malt, with William Hardy present, the loading finishing on

As table 4.4.4 shows, Mary Hardy started to record the cargo being taken to Great Yarmouth from March 1775. Wheat was carried on 3 November 1775, for transhipping to Yorkshire,[1] and malt was sometimes carried in 1776 for tran-shipment to London.[2] Mary Hardy makes no reference to any of the river craft going out to sea, but she would be un-likely to include such downstream snippets of information.

In addition to the general Sabbatarian laws, enforced by the magistrates, watermen were subject to a specific bar on Sunday working.[3] This they evidently flouted. Jonathan Symonds, although prominent as a common councilman in the borough of Great Yarmouth and of a distinguished mercantile family, did not debar his skipper from sailing on Sundays, Symonds' keel arriving at Coltishall on Sunday 22 January 1775. Two months later the keel again came up on the Sabbath:

[1775] MARCH 19, SUNDAY A wet day. Mr Symonds' keel of Yar-mouth [came up] laden with bricks and pavements and coals and cinders and salt. All went to Horstead Church afternoon ... [4]

As seen later, the Hardys' own wherry skipper would also sail on Sundays.

Boats did not display lights in this period. Mary Hardy records some night-sailings, even in winter:

left Shimmering moonlight at Reedham, with the Yare lit up at midnight.
Keels and wherries regularly sailed at night from Coltishall. While they did not display lights many would have had the white-painted transom stern seen earlier on the St Olaves wherry (page 162). The white quadrants at the bow were not introduced until the mid-19th century.
Even with little or no moon at night there is usually just enough light on the water to navigate by—as long as there are no trees   [*MB · 2010*]

[1776] FEBRUARY 28, WEDNESDAY A cold dry day . . . Zeb Rouse and Isaac Pooley and labourer loading the keel with malt, old Stephen Cox dined here and set sail at sunset. Mr Hardy with the men all day . . . [1]

As the next day was stormy the skipper might have wanted to get away quickly. It was not full moon until 5 March, as Mary Hardy noted, so Stephen Cox could not gain the benefit of maximum moonlight. Despite the evident dangers, many sources confirm that the crews of the past did not rely on navigation lights. As late as the 1960s and early 1970s Clifford Allen (1908–77), of the family of Coltishall boat-builders, was emphatic on the point: 'The wherrymen never used lights. There is always enough light to see the bank, as the water reflects every bit of natural light.'[2] However in recent decades the growth of trees on the banks and spread of low-hanging branches onto the stream have made night-sailing difficult. The dark vegetation reduces the glimmers and plays tricks with reflected light, causing hazards the wherrymen were spared in days when the banks were open.

As well as the maltings at Wells's brewery at Coltishall, south of the church, William Hardy ran a maltings at Wroxham or Hoveton (volume 2, chapter 6). Two entries relating to keel movements at this downstream malthouse are not shown in table 4.4.4:

[1776] MARCH 20, WEDNESDAY   A fine day . . . Zeb Rouse and Isaac Pooley at Wroxham carting malt aboard a keel . . . Mr Hardy at home forenoon, went to Wroxham malthouse afternoon . . .
[1776] APRIL 19, FRIDAY   A very fine warm day . . . Zeb Rouse and Isaac Pooley at Wroxham loading a keel with malt. Mr Hardy with the wherry-builders . . .

The wherry-builders were a new presence in the Hardys' lives. By this stage the Hardys had decided no longer to rely on others' keels, and were having their own wherry built.

What comes across clearly in the mass of entries by Mary Hartdy on loading and unloading is the pressure that her husband and the men were under to fulfil a sustained series of malt contracts. Not until 1777 did they ship strong beer to London in the form of nog, the local brew. The experiment may not have been a success. Malt and beer can be spoiled in handling and by exposure to damp air and extremes of temperature.[3]

the morning of 23 Mar. On 24 Mar. William Hardy set off by road to Gt Yarmouth, where he presumably saw to the transhipment and signed the export papers (for London) at the Customs House. On 25 Mar. Mary Hardy recorded, 'Mr Hardy came from Yarmouth evening 9, sold his malt for 16s [a coomb]' (*Diary 1*)

[1] *Cox* The keel's skipper (*Diary 1*). Three of the Hardys' men had spent two days unloading and loading the vessel.
   Stephen Cox is not listed in the *Calendar of the Freemen of Yarmouth 1429–1800* (Norfolk and Norwich Archaeological Soc., 1910), although keelmen were regularly admitted

[2] *Clifford Allen* Conversations with my husband and me at the Coltishall boatyard where we kept our boat until the yard closed in late 1973

[3] *contracts* The nog shipment came on 6 Sept. 1777. The many other arrangements and shipments, with meetings till 2 am with malt-factors, are indexed under 'keels', 'malt' and 'wherries' in *Diary 1*: see, eg, 1 Dec., 20 Dec. 1775, 2 July 1776

TABLE 4.4.5

Keel movements at Coltishall noted by Mary Hardy 1774–79: passengers

source Diary of Mary Hardy

date	skipper of keel	passengers	passage
1774, 7 July	John Clarke	Mary Hardy, her husband and children and the curate Revd Phillips Farewell	to Horning
1778, 26 Sept.	Mr Starkey	Ann Hardy (diarist's mother-in-law)	from Gt Yarmouth
1779, 2 July	Mr Starkey	Mary Hardy and Mary Neve	to Belaugh

[1] *Starkey* Joseph Jay was his mate in 1795. They customarily sailed Yarmouth–Norwich; the keel was berthed at Yarmouth (NRO: Y/C 38/3, no. 24, 17 July 1795)

[2] *to tea* Diary 1: 29 Apr. 1779

[3] *treat* Diary 1: 2 July 1779. The evening trip to Belaugh is described in chap. 7, p. 412

[4] *Clarke Success* was a 36-chaldron vessel (up to 48 tons), with 'a small draught of water, and in very good repair'. *John and Elizabeth* was of 40 tons (table 4.4.1). Both were for sale at Gt Yarmouth in 1780 (*Norw. Merc.* 22 Apr. 1780 and 16 Sept. 1780, *Success* being still unsold in the November: *Norw. Merc.* 18 Nov. 1780).

Mary Hardy writes in 1774 that their party visited Mrs Barwick at Horning. This was the

Watermen did not like their boats to sail light. A load gave a boat stability, and it made no sense economically to be without freight, unless perhaps there were passengers and their luggage to take, as when Mary Hardy's mother-in-law sailed up from Great Yarmouth by 'Starkey's keel' in 1778 (table 4.4.5). Even so, it is likely there was commercial cargo on board as well. It is possible this was John Starkey, who appears in 1795 as skipper of the 70-ton keel *Royal Oak*.[1]

Mrs Starkey accompanied her husband on the voyages. The diarist struck up a friendship with the Starkeys, having them to tea at her house in 1779; Mrs Starkey stayed on for supper.[2] It was with them that Mary Hardy chose to have a very rare treat indeed: a pleasure-boating trip on the keel just with the keelman, his wife and the diarist's close friend Mary Neve, wife of the Coltishall timber merchant and former innkeeper. They had a golden July evening.[3]

When the Hardys sailed with the curate down to Horning in July 1774, as shown in the table, they were passengers on board John Clarke's keel. This was not the brickburner and innkeeper at Strumpshaw but the 'occupier' of a keel named *Success* and 'master' of the keel *John and Elizabeth*.[4]

The tables are sketchy. Mary Hardy was presumably making no effort to maintain a keel log, and was merely setting down what she happened to learn from her husband, her children and the workforce. The record was made in order to note the work of the men and not to keep a tally of comings and goings on the river. There will be a large number of

above Horning Church Staithe. On a 'fine, dry day' in 1774 Mary and William Hardy, their children and the eccentric curate, the Revd Phillips Farewell, sailed 12 miles down the Bure to call on Mrs Barwick, wife of the Vicar of Horning who had been Mr Farewell's predecessor as Curate of Horstead and Coltishall.

Mary Hardy called the skipper of this keel 'Mr' Clarke. She could be respectful of skippers. When the Hardys had a wherry of their own she referred to 'our wherry captain' [*MB·1990*]

vicar Anthony Barwick's wife Agnes.

Horning had no habitable vicarage at this time, as an earlier vicar Revd George Kenwrick had noted in the Horning parish register (NRO: PD 692/2, endnotes); we do not learn where the Barwicks lived.

In 1820–21 Revd Charles Carver built the vicarage (seen here to the right of the church), at his own expense, for £1200: see *Diary 1*: 7 July 1774 and note.

At the end of their boating trip and social call the Hardys and their young children had a long walk home, arriving back at 10 pm

passages by keels and wherries not shown in the tables, as noting voyages 'by water', without distinguishing the vessel, was common in the diary. Yet we learn of the interaction between the river-based and land-based working people of the time. Far from leading isolated lives, the watermen and their families were connected through work and friendship with those along the riverbank.

Wherries at Coltishall 1773–81

This part of the story will not cover the Hardys' own small wherry, which is told towards the end of the chapter. The term 'wherryman', which recurs throughout the register of 1795, seems then to have been a new one—a pointer perhaps to the longer antecedents of the keel. A 'keelman' makes an appearance earlier in the diary than 'wherryman', young

above Early-morning fishing at Horning. Herons abound on the Broads
[*Christopher Bird 2012*]

¹ *keelman* Nine-year-old Raven, on the drowning of John Oliver in the Bure. He had originally added the gloss 'the keelman' before drawing a line through it (*Diary 1*: 13 Feb. 1777). Mary Hardy soon afterwards noted buying a swan 'off a keelman' (8 Mar. 1777)

² *Norwich* Only two keelmen appear in the register of Norwich Freemen for the first half of the 18th century, in 1714 and 1728; there are no wherrymen.
There are however 22 'watermen' (P. Millican, *The Freemen of Norwich 1714–1752*, vol. 23 (Norfolk Record Soc., vol. 23 (1952)), pp. 40, 55)

³ *Gt Yarmouth Calendar of the Freemen of Yarmouth*, pp. 227, 239

⁴ *last* One last is about 2032 kg, the level of moisture in the grain affecting the weight

Raven Hardy noting the term even before his mother does.[1] Keelman was of long duration, as we know from the admissions of Freemen in Norwich.[2] It was not until 1783 that a wherryman, described as such, was granted the Freedom of Great Yarmouth. He was Jonathan Symonds' apprentice, Matthew Underwood. A second wherryman was not admitted until 1790: Charles Ingram, admitted by birth as the son of his Freeman father.[3]

Table 4.4.6 shows the three references by Mary Hardy to the taking of their produce by others' wherries in the years before they had their own. As shown in chapter 2, John Colls was the miller at Horstead Watermill and Robert Ansell the Coltishall plumber and auctioneer. These cargoes may not represent a full load for the wherries, apart perhaps from the malt taken by Mr Ansell's wherry: 8½ lasts equal just under 17 ship's tons.[4] The Hardys may have added their own goods to the consignment about to set off downstream. If so this indicates their malt was bagged, and not loose.

The hardships of the men and women on the waterways were immense, for they worked in all weathers unless the river were frozen solid. Early-nineteenth-century painters generally show us summer days and light breezes, for no member of the Norwich Society of Artists would be likely to set up his stool, board and palette in a howling gale or hailstorm. (Similarly the holiday brochures of today invariably show us blue skies and bikini-clad sunbathers on the topdecks.) It is important to look for sources which do open our eyes to the hardships of those who had to work for their

---

TABLE 4.4.6

Wherry movements at Coltishall noted by Mary Hardy 1775–76: goods

source Diary of Mary Hardy   *note* The Hardys' wherry is excluded: see log on pp. 220–3

date	owner of wherry	cargo	passage
1775, 2 Dec.	John Colls	malt	for Gt Yarmouth
1775, 20 Dec.	Robert Ansell	8½ lasts malt	for Gt Yarmouth, for transhipping to London
1776, 29 Feb.	John Colls	4 lasts malt	for Gt Yarmouth

left A small wherry being loaded with hay or with marsh litter for animal bedding. Care is being taken not to load the top of the cabin at the stern and thus smother the flue for the stove inside.

The wherry has a two-man crew. The two bringing another heap of mowings on a hurdle will be land based: the figure second from the left (on the boat) has a head-hugging hat which will not blow off, whereas the man on the right (on land) has a brimmed hat unsuited to boating.

Keels and wherries have loose-footed sails, with no boom at the bottom of the canvas. Even so, it looks as though this load will foul it unless the crew adjust the set of the sail [*painting and ? engraving by J. Stark c.1833, detail*]

living on the water, and in this the interviews given to Roy Clark and Robert Malster are invaluable. In icy conditions skippers would struggle to unbolt the slipping keel when about to enter shallower waters, as related by Desmond Best in his 1976 thesis. He interviewed the wherryman Jack Powley many times, and heard 'Wherry-skipper Powley's tales of the North River [the Bure] and the dislike wherrymen had of sailing up to Aylsham'.[1]

[1] *Powley* D. Best, 'The Aylsham Navigation', Preface, p. 1. The slipping keel was a late addition (R. Clark, *Black-Sailed Traders*, pp. 69–70, and V. and L. Pargeter, *Maud*, p. 1)

TABLE 4.4.7
Wherry movements at Coltishall noted by Mary Hardy 1775–79: passengers
source Diary of Mary Hardy

date	wherry	owner/skipper	passengers	passage
1775, 16 Mar.	*Grampus*	Robert Ansell	those celebrating opening of lock	through Coltishall Lock
1778, 20 Aug.	?	Thomas Pooley	Ann Hardy	to Gt Yarmouth
1779, 20 Oct.	*Grampus*	Robert Ansell	William Hardy and those celebrating navigation opening	to Aylsham; one of the wherries in the flotilla capsizes at Lamas

[1] *Pooleys Diary 1*: 30 Dec. 1776; also 26 July 1780, when 'Pooley removed into the laundry'. The second entry may indicate that the wherry was then his only home; his wife may have been more comfortably installed elsewhere on shore

Two of the three wherry movements in table 4.4.7 relate to events connected with the Aylsham navigation, as recounted in chapter 2. The third entry, for 'Pooley's wherry', refers to the trip taken by the Yorkshire-based Ann Hardy to Great Yarmouth during her year-long stay with her son William and his family. Mary Hardy knew the wherryman's wife Mary Ann, who had helped her and the maids with the heavy washing in 1776; and for some reason which is not clear Thomas Pooley moved into the Hardys' wash house in 1780.[1]

right Albion: the handle for the winch is always stowed out of the barrel when not in use. Thomas Pooley, the wherry skipper, was killed in 1788 aged 50 when 'the crank of the winch flew off the barrel [and] struck him on the head' while he was lowering the sail (*Norwich Mercury*, 12 July 1788, reporting the inquest of 8 July)   [*MB · 2014*]

facing page, below Trainee mate Steve Bensley lowers *Albion*'s sail, carefully keeping control of the handle with both hands throughout   [*MB · 2014*]

facing page, top Coldham Hall. Mary Hardy noted that 'a waterman belonging to Norwich was by the violence of the wind hauled overboard and lost' here on the Yare in a winter storm in 1774. That same night a wherry sank while crossing Breydon and two people were drowned   [*MB · 2011*]

Accidents on the waterways

Mary Hardy repeatedly gives accounts of seagoing ships driven ashore and lives lost, some of the shipwrecks being described in the next chapter. Occasionally we read in her diary of drownings on the Broads, as when William Bell was 'hauled overboard' when passing Coldham Hall, a public house on the Yare. That same evening two people were lost on Breydon Water when a wherry bound for Bungay sank in 'a violent storm of wind at north-east'.[1]

Keeping a grip on a deck slippery with ice and frost, rain and snow cannot have been easy; there were no deck shoes with rubber soles then. One solution was to rub sawdust or grit into the molten pitch smeared on the plankways. The pitch kept the vessel watertight, while the sawdust provided a roughened surface for a foothold. This gritting and tarring was still evident on a visit to the keel *Dee-Dar*, despite her near-century of immersion and years of neglect on land.[2]

Breydon had to be crossed by all the vessels recorded by Mary Hardy sailing south from the Bure to the Yare. More than three miles long by nearly a mile wide, its conditions at times can be as bad as those at sea. Even the crews of the Royal National Lifeboat Institution find Breydon challeng-

[1] *drowned Diary 1*: 3 Dec. 1774, reporting the news items from the *Norwich Mercury*

[2] *Dee-Dar* At Whitlingham, 26 Apr. 2012. The edge of the deck, the planksheer, was often painted white to mark the drop to the water

above The pleasure wherry *Hathor*, seen at anchor on Surlingham Broad (also at *plate 52*), has a family connection with the diarist. She was built in 1905 for Ethel and Helen Colman; their mother Caroline was Mary Hardy's great-granddaughter.

Hathor's two small boats play a vital safety role: if anyone falls overboard a dinghy can instantly be rowed to them. Turning the wherry would take a long time, and by then she would have moved far on. Dinghies under tow can slow a vessel, and the Norwich artists show keels and wherries sailing without them   [*Christopher Bird 1995*]

[1] *lifeboat* See the vivid account of the rescue, by the crew of the RNLI inshore lifeboat, of all on a sinking cruiser on Breydon, 1 Dec. 2010 (V. French, 'Ice, wind and snow', *The Lifeboat*, issue 596 (summer 2011), pp. 23, 25). The waves were more than 8 feet high (2·5 metres)

[2] *winch* D. Bray, 'Albion: Notes for skippers and mates', pp. 9, 8

ing in bad weather, when spray can freeze on the decks and make them skating rinks.[1]

There are countless ways to lose a member of the crew on the Broads. They have to be alert and if at all possible keep one hand for the boat and one hand for themselves. Skipper David Bray devised a set of standing orders for the crews on *Albion*, as in connection with the winch which had killed Skipper Pooley: 'Always unship the winch handles at all times when not in use.' Raising and lowering the sail now takes a team of up to four people, for maximum safety—a far cry from the conditions experienced by the watermen of the past—'otherwise it is possible for the sail to come down at the run, with flying crank handles'.[2]

In 1826 the Norwich grocer John Cozens told the House of Commons committee of an accident on the Yare. He had lost £100 by the sinking of a wherry through a light craft running down the laden one—caused, he observed, by the carelessness of the pilot on board the unladen vessel. It was not his wherry, so he did not have to bear that cost, but he was not insured for the loss of the goods on board.[1]

Building the Hardys' wherry at Wright's yard

On 12 March 1776, a dry but cold and cloudy day, Mary Hardy gives us the news that they were to have a wherry of their own. The arrangements with the timber merchant George Boorne and with the boatbuilder at the boatyard behind the King's Head were put in train before breakfast:

[1776] MARCH 12, TUESDAY . . . Mr Hardy at Boorne's morning before breakfast, agreed with him for timber to build a wherry with, and at Joseph Browne's with the man that is to build her, came home morning 10 and breakfasted, then went to Norwich . . .[2]

Although from a central Norfolk background unconnected with boating the diarist had instantly adopted the tradition that a boat is referred to respectfully as 'her' and not 'it'. Again, during the wherry's fitting out, we are told: 'She lies to be hatched.'[3] Only after the launch and fitting out comes any mention of paying for the wherry; and only then do we learn that the builder, 'the man', was named Wright.[4]

From the start of building on 11 April to the launch on 22 August is a remarkably short time: old Jacob Cox reckoned on building one wherry a year at Barton Turf.[5] It is a particular achievement as the Hardys came in a constant stream to watch progress. 'The man' was very forbearing, for William Hardy may have spent as much as thirteen hours with him one day. A week after the start of operations two builders are mentioned, the minimum needed for wherry-building.[6] When the Hardys, their children and friends arrived en masse to inspect progress they had the delicacy to choose a Sunday—presumably the boatbuilders' day off.[7]

For the tonnage and draught of the wherry we are wholly reliant on the notice the Coltishall keel and wherry owner Robert Ansell placed in the two Norwich newspapers, the Norfolk Chronicle and the Norwich Mercury, on 21 and 28

[1] Cozens House of Commons Parliamentary Papers 1826 (369), vol. IV, Minutes of evidence to the committee, p. 183, 26 Apr. 1826. It was common not to insure cargoes, and often not even the vessel

[2] wherry Diary 1. For Boorne and Browne see chaps 2 and 3. Boorne provided oak timber for the navigation. Like almost all wherries the Hardys' would have been of oak

[3] she lies Diary 1: 8 Jan. 1777

[4] paying Diary 1: 4 Feb. 1777

[5] Cox R. Clark, Black-Sailed Traders, pp. 54–5; see also his pp. 52–71 on building a wherry

[6] two builders John Wright was probably the principal trader then. The young Stephen Wright, possibly his son, was newly established at the yard, as described in this section; within a very few years Stephen was in sole charge

[7] wherry-watching Diary 1: 28 Apr. 1776; also 12 Apr., 15 Apr., 18 Apr., 19 Apr. William Hardy was also keeping an eye on progress 25 Apr., 2 May, 23 July and 21 Aug., and probably on many other occasions when he was recorded by his wife at Browne's

I *tonnage* Revd Dr Grape stated the new waterway took 'boats of 13 tons burden' at its opening in Oct. 1779 (P. Millican, *A History of Horstead and Stanninghall*, p. 9). It had been much enlarged by 1795

July 1781, when the Hardys put her up for sale at Horning after their move to north Norfolk. At roughly 15–16 tons she was too big to get up the Aylsham navigation in its early years of operation.[1]

right Two vital pieces of information: the tonnage and draught of the Hardys' wherry. The White Swan was then one of their tied houses [*Norfolk Chronicle, 21 July 1781: Norfolk Heritage Centre, Norwich*]

To be SOLD by AUCTION, By ROBERT ANSELL, On Tuesday the 31st of July, Instant, between the Hours of Four and Five in the Afternoon, at the White Swan in Horning, Norfolk,

ALL that WHERRY known by the Name of the WILLIAM and MARY, Burthen twelve Chaldron of Coals; she is allowed to be as compleat a Vessel as ever was built, but four Years old, draws two Feet ten Inches Water.

☞ Further Particulars may be had of the Auctioneer, at Coltishall.

Particulars of the Hardys' wherry *William and Mary* of Coltishall 1776–81

sources   Diary of Mary Hardy; sale notice, *Norfolk Chronicle*, 21 July 1781

type	Norfolk hatched wherry with gaff rig
draught	2 feet 10 inches (0·86 metres)
tonnage burthen	12 chaldrons of coal:
	approx. 16 tons (London measure) or 14½ tons (Gt Yarmouth measure)
builders	Wright's boatyard, Coltishall (just upstream of the King's Head); timber supplied by George Boorne of Coltishall; boatbuilder named Wright paid by William Hardy 4 Feb. 1777
launched	Wright's boatyard, 22 Aug. 1776; celebrations last beyond midnight
fitting out	Initial work completed 3 Sept. 1776; sailing and trading by 14 Oct. 1776; hatches fitted 15–31 Jan. 1777; new sail cloth boiled 8 Mar. 1779
first owners	William and Mary Hardy of Coltishall
skippers	1] L. Neve 1776–80 2] —— Wells 1780
home berth	Coltishall: Wells's brewery [private staithe, now by Holly Lodge]
other berths	1] Coltishall Upper Common, near the lock
	2] Gt Yarmouth: Symonds' Wharf [private staithe on the Bure]
auctioned	The White Swan, Horning, 31 July 1781; by Robert Ansell of Coltishall
registration	Not listed in the Gt Yarmouth register 1795–98 under her original name

above Building a wherry at Carrow, just downstream from one of Norwich's manufacturing quarters lining the staithes of the River Wensum along King Street.

The figure on the right is heating the tar. The rudder is propped up in the foreground, to the right of the figure standing by the hull. The lines of the vessel are emerging. The engraving suggests she is carvel-built, with flush seams; on clinker-built boats overlapping strakes form the hull.

She is transom sterned (squared off, rather than having a pointed end for the rudder). The cabin or 'cuddy' looks close to completion. The iron 'horse', the arching structure along the top of the cabin, is silhouetted against the bank. When rigged, the large timber block for the mainsheet will slam along this arch with tremendous force and noise, shattering the hand of anyone gripping the horse in an effort to keep upright as the wherry heels in the wind.

The wide catwalk or plankway has a pronounced 'sheer' or curve. The tabernacle, through which the mast will pivot, takes shape in the bow.

John Wright, of the Horning, Belaugh and Coltishall family of boatbuilders, moved to this yard in 1784; he may be the John Wright who built the Hardys' wherry in 1776 [*drawing by J. Stark; engraving by W.J. Cooke 1830*]

James Stark depicts a yard with a wherry on the stocks at Carrow (above) which probably resembles the Wrights' yard at Coltishall two generations earlier. John Thirtle similarly shows a wherry being built out in the open (*plate 17*).[1]

[1] *in the open* The sheds in both pictures are for storing equipment and tools, not boats

above Coltishall: Allen's boatyard in May 1881, downstream of the Anchor bend. The wherry yacht *Kiama*, her white sail furled, is moored on the main river; her overhanging counter stern partially blocks the mouth of the boatyard dyke. A trading wherry with a white-painted nosing lies at her bow.

A mast supported clear of the ground on the Horstead bank (foreground) is evidently receiving treatment.

Allen's yard retained this appearance of a craftsman's working area until its closure in the winter of 1973–74. Its stacks of oak planks on risers (seasoned for 10 years), with the smell and clutter of dry sheds, wet shed, engine shop, carpenter's shop, greased slipways and dim storehouses, were a far cry from Coltishall's manicured banks of today [*Horace Bolingbroke Collection: courtesy Robert Malster*]

[1] *yard* Clifford E. Allen and his son Paul, also a boatbuilder at the yard, kept the ledgers dating from the 19th century.

John Allen appears to have bought the business in 1864 (V. G. Cole, 'Birthplace of the wherries', *The Norfolk Magazine*, vol. 6, no. 6 (Nov.–Dec. 1953), p. 46). Census data, the trade directories and the 1841 tithe award (NRO: DN/ TA 438) also shed light

Mary Hardy is the sole source for the existence of Wright's boatbuilding yard at Coltishall as early as 1776, and for its establishment near Joseph Browne's public house, the King's Head. The boatyard, on that site and then from about 1800–01 downstream in Anchor Street, had a continuous history through the names successively of Wright, Press, Collins, Wright, Allen, Allen and Blackburn, and lastly Allen until the winter of 1973–74 when Clifford Allen sold the yard, land and dyke for redevelopment as housing.[1]

At the time that *William and Mary* was being completed, in 1777, the church ratebook establishes John Wright as a tenant of Mr [William] Bell; the rateable value of the property was £1 10s. Bell, a former churchwarden, lived just up the main road from the King's Head at the substantial house later known as The Limes. Wright's property had the same rateable value as Joseph Browne's granary, which probably also stood by the river just behind the King's Head.

Some time soon afterwards Stephen Wright took over. By March 1785 Stephen Wright was the tenant of Mr [Chapman] Ives, but at the same place and with the same rateable value: William Bell had sold his 'estate', as Mary Hardy calls it.[1] The churchwardens seem to have been uncertain how to log the tenants of the bankrupt farmer, maltster and brewer Chapman Ives, for in the late 1790s the owner of the boatyard's premises is not named. It is never described in the eighteenth-century ratebook as a boatyard, nor are the occupations of John and Stephen Wright given. All we know is that they in turn held the premises on lease from first Bell and then Ives.

The roadside end of their site was known from the nineteenth century, and possibly earlier, as Wright's Yard. It is not known which member of the Wright family gave his name to this loke running beside The Limes down to the maltings built in the early nineteenth century.[2] The maltings, demolished in 1928, came into being almost certainly as the boatyard had moved from that site to Lowgate, later named Anchor Street. There it occupied the area at the mouth of the dyke dug to serve an earlier maltings (seen below), which may have been built by Chapman Ives.[3]

[1] *ratebook* NRO: PD 598/37, 24 Mar. 1777, 24 Mar. 1778, 24 Mar. 1785; the book opens at the year 1776–77.
The brewer Chapman Ives and then the merchant William Palgrave appear to have owned Bell's former estate (vol. 2, chaps 5 and 8; also *Diary 1*: 7 Feb. 1774, 2–3 Jan. 1776).
To put the very modest rateable value of £1 10s in context, see vol. 2, table 2.5.3

[2] *Wright's Yard* The name by which William Stibbons knew the area beside his house, The Limes (our many conversations 1988–95)

[3] *Anchor Street* Mr Allen told me in the 1960s that an old shed, long demolished, had borne the date 1801.
When the malthouse closed in 1932 the boatyard took it over for storage and an office

left Clifford Edgar Allen at work on *Gwenda*, the sole yacht in his post-war hire fleet at Coltishall. He pauses in characteristic pose, a pencil behind his ear and a long-stemmed pipe in his mouth. Behind him, towards the head of the boatyard dyke, stands the former maltings dating probably from the late 18th century. When in about 1800–01 Wright's yard moved down to this spot boatbuilding and malting had to rub along together in the narrow dyke.

Mr Allen died on 20 Mar. 1977 aged 68, just over three years after his yard had closed. It had a continuous history at Coltishall of at least 200 years. *Ella* (24 tons), the last wherry to be built on the Broads, was launched here in 1912   [*Cecil Perham 1953*]

[1] *ratebook* NRO: PD 598/37

[2] *Wright* I am very grateful to Michael J. Sparkes for his help 2000–14 in piecing together the various threads forming the wherry-building Wrights of the late 18th and early 19th centuries. Mike is descended from Francis Wright of Horning and Belaugh who married Margaret Garrod, formerly of Ranworth, at Horning in 1783 (NRO: PD 692/4)

[3] *Lydia Rouse* Her surname is given in the Horning register as Rounce; at Coltishall it is Rouse. Stephen jnr was baptised at Horning in 1775 and Thomas in 1776. Lydia was their first child baptised at Coltishall, in 1780, followed by Thomas (1783), Meshach and Sarah (NRO: PD 692/4, 692/2, Horning marriages and baptisms; PD 598/2, 598/14, Coltishall baptisms and burials)

[4] *Thomas Wright* White's directories 1836, p. 528, and 1845, p. 464. If he was the T. Wright of Coltishall subscribing to W. Stone's *The Garden of Norfolk* (Norwich, c.1823), a tribute to William Hardy jnr and Letheringsett, he was probably a Methodist (vol. 1, chap. 9)

[5] *John Wright Norfolk Chronicle*, 6 Mar. 1784;

By Easter 1802 there had been a change at Wright's. For the first time Stephen Wright's rateable value is given as £2. Unfortunately the ratepayer listings lack some of their earlier precision, but the period 1800–01 probably marks the yard's move downstream. Further changes followed. At Easter 1808 the entry reads, 'Stephen Wright (now Press) £2 0s 0d': the yard had changed hands 1807–08. In 1809 Thomas Press is named in place of Stephen Wright.[1]

Who were the Wrights who built the wherry in 1776? The name crops up in the parish registers of villages along the Bure in the eighteenth century: at Coltishall, Horstead, Belaugh, Horning, Ranworth and Upton.[2] This extended family can be traced through their marriages and the baptism and burial of their children as they moved along and across the river to start up afresh in trade, but at this time the parent branch seems to have been established at Horning. It retained a base there, which may explain the choice of Horning for the auction of the Hardys' wherry in 1781.

Stephen Wright married Lydia Rouse by banns at Horning in May 1774. Both were single and made marks. Their first two children were christened there in 1775 and 1776, but the parents could have brought them down by water for the ceremony in their old parish. Subsequent children were baptised at Coltishall, where Stephen Wright and his widow Lydia were buried in 1822 aged 68 and in 1832 aged 76.[3] The Wrights re-established themselves at the Anchor Street yard after the Press family: Thomas Wright, possibly their second son of that name, is shown in the 1836 and 1845 Norfolk directories as a Coltishall boatbuilder; another Thomas Wright was a corn, coal and timber merchant.[4]

John Wright, the boatbuilder known to the Hardys in 1776–77, could have moved from Coltishall back to Horning and then to Carrow. In 1784 'John Wright, of Carrow Abbey, near Norwich, boatbuilder', announced that he had moved there from Horning. He took on an apprentice at Carrow in 1794.[5]

Little is clear about the Wrights in this period. The near-universality of the name in a great number of Broadland villages and the popularity of certain forenames such as John and Thomas make firm identifications elusive. (To add to the difficulties another John Wright, a tailor and probably unrelated, was active at Coltishall at the same time. He appears in the diary and the parish registers, and died in 1836 aged 86.) Were it not for the evidence of the diary, backed up by the Coltishall churchwardens' ratebook, we would know nothing of the early years of Wright's boatyard.

The working days of *William and Mary*

After months of wherry-watching came the launch on the afternoon of Thursday 22 August 1776, 'a very fine day'. The celebrations, as described by Mary Hardy at the chapter head, began decorously enough with a select dinner at home followed by tea on board the wherry. But things then got out of hand with some of the party: 'The gentlemen stayed till past 12 o'clock and were very drunk.'[1] William Hardy was laid up the next day 'very ill' (his wife's euphemism for a hangover), and it was she who had to pay Mrs Fiddy for the broken glass first thing the next morning.[2]

Mary Hardy does not record the maiden voyage from Coltishall, but *William and Mary* was working her way by mid-October: 'Our wherry came up from Yarmouth laden with 17 bags of hops and 1 puncheon of rum and 5 or 6 loads of sand.'[3] It was a dry day, mercifully: the wooden hatches for covering the hold were not yet fitted. The log compiled by Mary Hardy 1776–81 now tells its own story.

TNA: PRO IR 1/67, no. 9, 30 Aug. 1794. Mike Sparkes has worked on the history of the Carrow yard (M. Sparkes, 'A passage in time, industry and sport on the Norwich River', *Harnser: The magazine of the Broads Society* (Apr. 2014), pp. 22–8).

Lydia Wright was Zeb Rouse's sister (e-mails from June Betts of Reepham, 7, 14, 15 Aug. 2019)

---

[1] *launch Diary 1.* The male guests were the Norwich hop merchant and household broker Thomas Danser, the Coltishall schoolmaster John Smith, farmer and merchant John Fiddy, plumber and auctioneer Robert Ansell and butcher Nathaniel Easto

[2] *glass Diary 1:* 23 Aug. 1776; presumably Mary Fiddy had lent the Hardys some of her glassware. The term 'morning', rather than 'forenoon', indicates that it was early

[3] *laden Diary 1:* 14 Oct. 1776. The load of hops was large. Each bag weighed 2½ cwt (127 kg) and measured 7½ feet long by 8 in circumference (2·3 and 2·4 metres): a total of 2159 kg, or well over two metric tonnes

---

left Albion on the Yare, with lowered mast; the masthead decoration of the 'bunch of pears', a traditional protective talisman, is painted in bright scarlet and royal blue.

An informal and incomplete log of the Hardys' wherry starts overleaf, showing the dates of sailing, destinations, cargoes and loading and unloading times   [*MB · 2014*]

Incomplete, informal log of the Hardys' wherry *William and Mary* 1776–81

source   Diary of Mary Hardy; her entries form only a partial log of sailing and loading

date	passage [1]	cargo	further information
1776	**Building**		
12 Mar.			COLTISHALL: William Hardy places order with timber merchant Boorne and boatbuilder Wright
11 Apr.			WRIGHT'S YARD: building begins
22 Aug.			WRIGHT'S YARD: wherry launched
	Early voyages		
14 Oct.	Yarmouth–Coltishall	hops, rum, sand	
30 Oct.	Yarmouth–Coltishall	bricks	
2 Nov.			COLTISHALL: 2 men unload bricks
7 Nov.	Yarmouth–Coltishall	coal	
9 Nov.	Coltishall–Yarmouth		
23 Dec.	Yarmouth–Coltishall	bricks	
24 Dec.		malt	COLTISHALL: 3 men and boy load malt
31 Dec.	Yarmouth–Belaugh	cinders	BELAUGH: wherry stuck fast in ice
1777	**Fitting out; regular passages to and from Gt Yarmouth**		
1 Jan.	Belaugh–Coltishall	cinders	2 extra men help wherry through ice
2 Jan.			COLTISHALL: 1 man unloading cinders
8 Jan.			COLTISHALL: river still frozen; skipper paid by Hardys; awaiting hatch-fitting
13–16 Jan.			HORSTEAD: skipper lodges at Recruiting Sergeant during fitting out
31 Jan.	Coltishall–Yarmouth	barley	cargo owned by William Palgrave
7 Feb.	Yarmouth–Coltishall	cinders	
18 Feb.	Yarmouth–Coltishall	casks, iron, wheat	
19 Feb.		malt	COLTISHALL: 2 men load more than 10 lasts of malt
20 Feb.	Coltishall–Yarmouth	malt	COLTISHALL: sets sail at 4 am with William Hardy and son Raven aboard
24 Feb.			YARMOUTH: river high; sailing delayed
26 Feb.	Yarmouth–Coltishall		
27 Feb.	Coltishall–Yarmouth	wheat	COLTISHALL: sets sail during night
5 Mar.	Yarmouth–Coltishall	wheat, flour barrels	
7 Mar.	Coltishall–Yarmouth	flour	
12 Mar.	Yarmouth–Coltishall	muck [manure]	COLTISHALL: muck unloaded and flour loaded with 1 extra man helping
18 Mar.	Coltishall–Yarmouth	flour	COLTISHALL: sets sail at 5 pm

date	passage [1]	cargo	further information
1777		**Regular passages to and from Gt Yarmouth** (*cont.*)	
23 Mar.	Yarmouth–Coltishall		
30 Mar.	Yarmouth–Coltishall	wheat	COLTISHALL: arrives on Easter Day
1 Apr.	Coltishall–Yarmouth	flour	
7 Apr.	Coltishall–Yarmouth	wheat	COLTISHALL: sets sail at 6 pm
11 Apr.	Yarmouth–Coltishall	wheat	
29 Apr.	Yarmouth–Coltishall	wheat	
5 May [2]	Yarmouth–Coltishall	4 chaldns coal, 3 lasts wheat	

New focus on loading and unloading at Coltishall

8–9 May		malt	COLTISHALL: loading takes 2 days
24 June		malt	COLTISHALL: 3 men loading malt
19 July		malt	COLTISHALL: 4 men loading malt
28 July	Strumpshaw–Coltishall	'bricks etc'	
30 July			COLTISHALL: men unloading bricks
11 Aug.	Coltishall–Yarmouth	malt	
25 Aug.			COLTISHALL: William Hardy's brother Joseph helps unload unidentified cargo
27 Aug.	Coltishall–Yarmouth	[ ]	Joseph Hardy sails as passenger
6 Sept.	Coltishall–Yarmouth	beer	6 barrels of nog carried for London
24–5 Nov.		cinders	COLTISHALL: men unloading cinders
19 Dec.			COLTISHALL: 1 man unloading wherry
20 Dec.		barley	COLTISHALL: 2 men loading barley
1778			
1–2 Jan.		malt	COLTISHALL: 6 man-days loading malt for London
28 Jan.		'bricks etc'	COLTISHALL: 2 men unloading bricks
9 Feb.		malt	COLTISHALL: 2 men loading malt
14 Aug.	Yarmouth–Coltishall		Mrs Ann Dixon and 2 children sail as passengers; cargo not identified
8 Sept.		coal	COLTISHALL: men unloading coal
9–10 Sept.		malt	COLTISHALL: malt loaded for London
22–4 Sept.		coal	COLTISHALL: men unloading coal
24–5 Sept.		malt	COLTISHALL: malt loaded

[*continued overleaf*]

---

[1] *passage* This, with the date, refers to the day of arrival at or departure from Coltishall. The 32-mile voyage to Gt Yarmouth could take a few hours or more than one day

[2] *5 May 1777* After this entry the diarist tends to refer less frequently to sailings and more often just to loading and unloading of goods at Coltishall

Incomplete, informal log of the wherry *William and Mary* 1776–81 (*cont.*)

date	passage [1]	cargo	further information
1778		**Focus on loading and unloading at Coltishall** (*cont.*)	
7 Oct.		bricks	COLTISHALL: 2 men unloading bricks
17 Oct.		cinders	COLTISHALL: 2 men unloading cinders
28 Oct.	Yarmouth–Coltishall	hops, bricks	also brings Yorkshire kitchen oven
29 Oct.			COLTISHALL: 2 men unload hops, bricks
12 Nov.		hops, sand	COLTISHALL: 2 men unload hops, sand
13 Nov.		malt	COLTISHALL: 2 men load malt for London
1779		**Loading malt at Coltishall for transhipping for London**	
7–8 July		malt	COLTISHALL: men loading malt
19–20 July		[ ]	COLTISHALL: men unloading
2 Aug.		malt	COLTISHALL: malt loaded for London
15 Nov.	Yarmouth–Coltishall	muck	
18–19 Nov.		malt	COLTISHALL: 5 man-days loading malt for London
28–9 Dec.		malt	COLTISHALL: 5 man-days loading malt
1780		**Malt for London—and two skippers leave in turn**	
8–10 Feb.	Coltishall–Yarmouth	malt	COLTISHALL: 1½ man-days loading malt
6 Mar.		malt	COLTISHALL: 2 men loading malt
3 Apr.		coal	COLTISHALL: 2 men unloading coal
5 Apr.		malt	COLTISHALL: 2 men loading malt
29 June		coal	COLTISHALL: coal unloaded
6 Aug.			Skipper L. Neve abandons wherry
19 Sept.		malt	COLTISHALL: new skipper loads malt; [2] illness obliges him to go to Norwich
19–21 Sept.		malt	COLTISHALL: 5 man-days, in addition to skipper's, loading malt
5 Oct.		barley	COLTISHALL: men loading barley
1–2 Dec.		malt	COLTISHALL: 4 man-days loading malt; William Hardy pays off Skipper Wells
23 Dec.		[ ]	COLTISHALL: 2 men loading
1781		**Cargoes often not recorded**	
26 Jan.		[ ]	COLTISHALL: 2 men begin loading in snow near nightfall
27 Jan.		[ ]	COLTISHALL: 4 men loading wherry
5–7 Feb.		malt	COLTISHALL: 6 man-days loading malt
2–3 Mar.		[ ]	COLTISHALL: 4 man-days loading
14 Mar.		malt	COLTISHALL: 3 men loading malt
26 Mar.		[ ]	COLTISHALL: 2 men loading

above and *left* **Portraits by Huquier in 1785 of William and Mary Hardy and their 11-year-old daughter Mary Ann.**

The new wherry was named *William and Mary* at the launching near the King's Head at Coltishall on 22 Aug. 1776; many vessels were named after husbands and wives
[*Cozens-Hardy Collection*]

[1] *passage* This, with the date, refers to the day of arrival at or departure from Coltishall. The 32-mile voyage to Gt Yarmouth could take a few hours or more than one day

[2] *new skipper* The only occasion on which Mary Hardy records their skipper loading or unloading. The time-consuming work almost always fell to the Hardys' men

above The tedium of unloading by barrow balanced on a narrow plank. This wherry is moored in Horning village centre at the same staithe where the Hardys' wherry *William and Mary* was sold in 1781.

The Swan, formerly a Hardy tied house, stands in the foreground; sawn tree trunks prevent damage to the frontage from carts and wagons. Two maltings loom higher than the Swan on what is now a small green.

The wherry's hatches are stacked out of the way during operations. The next cargo may be malt bound for Gt Yarmouth, the grain needing the protection of the hatches [*photograph by J. Payne Jennings c.1890: Norfolk Heritage Centre, Norwich*]

---

[1] *stopovers* For detailed comments on sailings, cargoes and unloading times see the editorial notes to *Diary 1*

[2] *trouble* 'Our wherry laid fast at Belaugh coming up from Yarmouth' (*Diary 1*: 31 Dec. 1776)

The new wherry was kept very busy in her early weeks, sailing up from Great Yarmouth on 14 and 30 October and 7 November 1776. It is not always clear from the diarist's jottings whether *William and Mary* had come round from Strumpshaw on the return trip, with Yarmouth serving just as an extra stopover: the cargo of bricks on 30 October may well indicate that Strumpshaw had been a port of call.[1]

Then trouble struck. On a day of 'sharp frost and deep snow' the wherry—'our wherry', as the diarist often calls her—was stuck in the ice downstream at Belaugh.[2] The next day two of the Hardys' farm servants were taken off other duties and beer deliveries to help the wherry up to Coltishall; they probably had to break the ice with the quant poles. A week later, with the river still frozen during 'the sharpest frost that have been this winter' the Hardys' skipper decided to make the best of it: 'Our wherry man here and reckoned, she lies to be hatched, the river froze up.'[1] The timbers had perhaps been left to settle for five months before the hatches were fitted. During this work 'our wherry captain' took himself off to the Hardys' tied house nearby, the Recruiting Sergeant at Horstead, where he lodged for three nights and very probably ordered beer on the house.[2]

On 31 January 1777 the fitting out was complete: 'Our wherry finished'. The log continues as compiled by Mary Hardy, the entries tumbled among all her other references to the work of the farm, maltings and brewery and family and other matters. It is a unique record for this period: the only keel or wherry log surviving from the eighteenth and early nineteenth centuries. The huge load placed, literally, on the shoulders of the Hardys' workforce emerges with clarity. The variety of the cargoes would also have caused problems. On 12 March 1777 manure had to be unloaded from the hold and flour loaded all in the one day. Cleaning the boards of the open hold on a day of sharp frost would have been tough for Zeb Rouse, who was plucked from the heat of the Hardys' brewhouse to carry out that task.[3]

The log shows William Hardy and others taking passages on the wherry. On 20 February 1777 he and his nine-year-old son Raven set off at 4 am for Yarmouth, with three hours of darkness and the bitter cold ahead of them: it was a day of 'excessive sharp wind frost'.

We learn very little about the skippers. One, perhaps the wherry's original skipper and named L. Neve, left his post without any warning in 1780: 'Mr Hardy not at church, went after the wherry, L. Neve left her.'[4] A new regime was attempted with the new skipper, named Wells, who was detailed to help with loading malt. He instantly fell ill and declared himself unable to continue, taking himself off to Norwich to make the point. He was paid off less than three months later.[5] As far as we can judge, the wherry had three skippers in under five years. No mate is mentioned.

[1] hatched Diary 1: 8 Jan. 1777. William Hardy had spent a great deal of time at the wherry in the days following the launch, presumably overseeing arrangements such as stepping the mast and rigging the sail.

The hatches were painted (or repainted) on 11 July 1777 by John Ellingham of Coltishall

[2] wherry captain Diary 1: 16 Jan. 1777. Watermen suffered during severe winters. In 1799 a local farmer, T. Layton, Esq., gave the poor of Salhouse a 64-stone ox 'to their very great relief at this inclement season'—the 24th ox presented by him. He also gave hot dinners twice a week to the boatmen (Norw. Merc. 28 Dec. 1799).

Boats had to moor up in the worst of the weather—with no pay for their crews

[3] Zeb Rouse One of the farm servants (Diary 1). I have not traced any connection between him and Stephen Wright's wife Lydia, née Rouse.

For very strenuous loading days see Diary 1: 19 Feb., 19 July 1777 and 7 Feb. 1781

[4] L. [? Leonard] Neve Diary 1: 6 Aug. 1780

[5] Wells Diary 1: 19–21 Sept., 1–2 Dec. 1780

[1] *Horning and Acle Diary 2*: 31 July, 1 Aug. 1781. The new owner is not mentioned, nor does the wherry appear under her original name and tonnage in the 1795 register

[2] *Brown* House of Commons Parliamentary Papers 1826 (369), vol. IV, Minutes of evidence to the committee, pp. 92, 94, 26 Apr. 1826. He supplied the London brewers Barclays and Whitbread (p. 93). Dying in 1830, Crisp Brown did not see his vision realised

[3] *malt* House of Commons Parliamentary Papers 1826 (369), vol. IV, Minutes of evidence to the committee, pp. 85, 86, 88–9, 26 Apr. 1826. The sea passage to London took 24 hours (p. 86). Brown's evidence reveals his preoccupation with 'plunder', and the way fraud and theft during carriage could undermine his business: the hatches of his wherries were always kept locked down (p. 89)

[4] *Harmer* House of Commons Parliamentary Papers 1826 (369), vol. IV, Minutes of evidence to the committee, p. 181, 26 Apr. 1826. He testified that wash from the steam packets could (and did) capsize other boats and damage the banks

Ascendancy and decline

We hear no more of the Hardys' wherry after their move to Letheringsett in April 1781. William Hardy still had to come back to Coltishall regularly, as did his men, for he continued to manage the maltings and brewery and supply the outlets until Siday Hawes replaced him fifteen or eighteen months later. Mary Hardy records that her husband and eleven-year-old William left early for Horning on 31 July 1781, but she does not say why. It was the date of the boat's sale. The next day the pair were at Acle and Great Yarmouth, suggesting that the wherry may have found a new berth at Acle.[1]

The river trade increased markedly in the coming years, the early nineteenth century proving the golden years for wherrying. The maltster Crisp Brown, the man who in 1827 was to dig the first spadeful of earth at Mutford Bridge for the Norwich and Lowestoft scheme, told the House of Commons committee that in 1801 or 1802 about 77,000 chaldrons of coal came through Great Yarmouth. By 1825 this figure had reached 153,000 chaldrons, of which one-half went on to Norwich. He described the loading of the coal onto wherries at Yarmouth and the great host of sails crossing Breydon Water: 'The wherries accumulate together waiting for the tide going over Breydon . . .'[2]

While Norwich had many riverside maltings Crisp Brown explained to the committee that there existed 'malthouses all over the city to receive the barley from the growers'; the malted grain then had to be carted to the staithes. He alone sent 900–1000 quarters of malt by wherry from Norwich to Great Yarmouth every eight or nine days. Tellingly, he does not mention keels as serving his great concern.[3]

Daniel Harmer, another Norwich promoter of the Lowestoft scheme, testified to the thriving waterways and reliance on wherries; he too does not mention keels. In an average week 1000 sacks of flour were carried to Yarmouth. He confirmed that trade on the Broads was free from toll (a refrain by users of the tidal rivers, putting the Aylsham navigation at a disadvantage by comparison.) However he sounded a warning note for the days of sail: two steam vessels were also employed out of Norwich, capable of a steady 8 mph.[4]

Steam was not the only threat facing the wherries. Brown, Harmer and the other supporters of the project to make

above Mutford Bridge, from Oulton Broad: a busy approach to Lowestoft by road from the south. Lake Lothing lies beyond. This was the joyous morning (for the people of Norwich and Lowestoft) of 4 Sept. 1827, when work began on the scheme to create a southern link to the sea from the Broads.

By 1830 a 90-foot lock and a swing bridge had replaced this crossing; the quarter-mile-wide bank separating Lake Lothing from the sea was cut through in 1831. Yarmouth with its controls and port tolls was bypassed [*painting by J. Stark; engraving by W.J. Cooke 1827*]

'Norwich a Port' through the projected new opening to the North Sea were thus inviting seagoing vessels onto the Broads, with no need for lightering or transhipment. Even though the hoped-for capacious deepwater harbour was never built at the downstream end of Norwich, small sea-going vessels of 70–80 tons burden did in fact moor in the city from 1834, endangering the livelihood of wherrymen on the southern Broads and striking even at those waters which such ships could not penetrate. Coal, grain and all the other cargoes of the river craft could henceforth be carried more cheaply; however only wherries and keels could get under the city bridges to the upstream staithes. The coming of the railways from 1844 dealt a third blow to the wherry trade.[1]

[1] *Norwich a Port* J.W. Robberds jnr's anticipation of the scene is quoted in chap. 3 at the end of the section on two private staithes (p. 144).
For an illustrated survey of what was achieved see R. Malster, *The Norfolk and Suffolk Broads*, pp. 98–109

right The trading wherry *Victory*, converted into a pleasure wherry in about 1912 and abandoned after the Second World War in a dyke beside Barton Turf Staithe. Here she slowly rots in the silt, her hull pierced by the vegetation. The curving 'knees' of the mighty mast-bearing tabernacle, generally some of the last of a wherry's timbers to survive, rear up among the yellow flags and kingcups, water mint and young nettles.

This photograph was taken in 1990. Now, nearly thirty years later, nothing can be seen of *Victory* in her final resting place   [*MB · 1990*]

¹ *last years* T. Douglas-Sherwood, 'The Norfolk keel', pp. 97–100.

She considers that steam was introduced from 1819 principally for passenger-carrying (p. 97)

² *public meeting* Chaired by Lady Mayhew, née Colman. A distinguished yachtswoman, Beryl Mayhew lived to see not only her own centenary in 1997 but that of *Albion* at the celebrations on Wroxham Broad 4–5 Apr. 1998 (*Eastern Daily Press*, 6 Apr. 1998).

Martin Kirby tells the story of the founding of the Trust and *Albion*'s resurrection (*Albion*, pp. 28–32).

Wherry wrecks can still be seen, submerged to prevent bank erosion. Surlingham Broad and Rockland Broad have extensive wherry graveyards; ribs and tabernacles break the surface at low water

Theole Douglas-Sherwood charts the decline of the keels. They were finally ousted by the wherries between 1830 and 1850 and spent their last years not as cargo vessels but as ballast boats, dredgers and lighters. A few, such as the one spotted at St Benet's Abbey in 1873 by George Christopher Davies, clung on as timber carriers. The wherries survived for longer, she believes, thanks to their rig: they needed fewer crew to work them and could keep wage costs down. They could also reach parts of the Broads which neither seagoing vessels nor railways could manage: hence the presence of working wherries on the waterways until road transport in the form of petrol-fuelled lorries took over. (Further delaying the wherries' end the railway system was extended around northern Broadland rather later than in the south.)

By the end of the war in 1945 the future of the wherry looked bleak indeed. Then a small group of Norfolk boating enthusiasts, including Roy Clark, James Forsythe and two of Mary Hardy's descendants Humphrey Boardman and Beryl Mayhew, got together to see if just one wherry could be saved. The public meeting of 23 February 1949 in Norwich led swiftly to the formation of the Norfolk Wherry Trust. *Albion*, by then renamed *Plane* and in a sorry state as a mastless lighter serving Colmans of Norwich, was the lucky one chosen to live. By 13 October 1949 the restored wherry could sail unaided from Yarmouth to Norwich.²

The last word should go to the much-respected if fearsome Nat Bircham, a great wherry skipper of the twentieth century; he died in 1981. His voice is heard, an outspoken comment never far from his lips, in his interview with David Cleveland.[1] He could be lyrical about his lifelong love of sailing, reminiscing over the last wherries to be built on the Broads at Coltishall and the excitement and mystery of night passages in 1919–20. Such experiences had also been familiar to William Hardy and Raven and formed a regular feature of working life for the keelmen and wherrymen known to the Hardys.

This is part of Nat Bircham's lament on the passing of a centuries-long sailing tradition:

My memories carry me back to the end of World War I, when I joined my father on the *Emily*, starting out from Rockland Staithe where she had laid idle owing to the closing of Brickyard to water traffic. This wherry, a sister ship to *Ella*,[2] was built at the well-known yard at Coltishall, designed to go through locks to Aylsham, but alas the flood [of 1912] ended her days on the upper reaches.

Many times we left Great Yarmouth, Wroxham bound, in the company of such wherries as the *Cornucopia, Dispatch, Stalham Trader, Bertha, Ella, Ethnie, Hope, Violet, Gleaner, Rambler*, the *Lord Roberts, I'll Try, Dauntless* and many others that were plying trade on northern waters.[3] Sailing at night was perhaps the most exciting, especially with a strong and favourable breeze, with sail doused, one of the crew forward using the winch all the time replacing use of main sheet.[4] No one could describe the feeling who never took part. In practically every reach was a windmill with sails creaking and mechanism groaning under the strain; water cascading from the paddles causing a trail of foam along the river; a dim light flickering in the little windows telling us the miller was near at hand in case of emergency.[5] 'There you go', was heard from the doorway, 'Dirty old night', or some other remark.

Sometimes a flock of geese could be heard flying high (a sign of bad weather) with destination only themselves knew. As the sail brushed the reeds, water hens [moorhens] and coots fluttered down from their precarious perches. Approaching moored wherries, the cabin door would open and a voice call out, 'There you go, Jimmy (or Jack), blow hard, where you bound, good night'. They always knew which wherry passed by the shape of sail, or masthead if it could be seen . . .

Alas, today there is but one trader left, and even this is no longer skippered by a wherryman.[6] The thrill of seeing one sail single-handed, or watch such a craft tack unaided up a narrow river is gone for ever.[7]

[1] *interview* eg *A Look Back at the Broads* (E. Anglian Film Archive, 1998), with stills and film 1834–1987. Nat Bircham describes the harsh life afloat in 1928, when he worked an 18-hour day seven days a week, for 4½d an hour, piecework. He did all the loading and unloading, being paid 2d a ton for loading sugar beet

[2] *Ella* A small vessel (24 tons), the last wherry built on the Broads—by Allen's, in 1912; she lies scuttled at the bottom of the upstream dyke leading to Decoy Broad, Woodbastwick. Nat Bircham was her last owner and last skipper (R. Clark, *Black-Sailed Traders*, p. 212); he also skippered *Albion* for the Norfolk Wherry Trust in the 1950s

[3] *northern waters* The Bure, Ant and Thurne

[4] *doused* Partially lowered, as when expecting bad weather: see R. Clark, *Black-Sailed Traders*, p. 69

[5] *miller* The marshman at a drainage windmill

[6] *one trader Maud* has since joined *Albion* as the second under sail

[7] *memories* N. Bircham, 'My Opinion', *Bulletin of the Broads Society* (Sept. 1970), p. 12

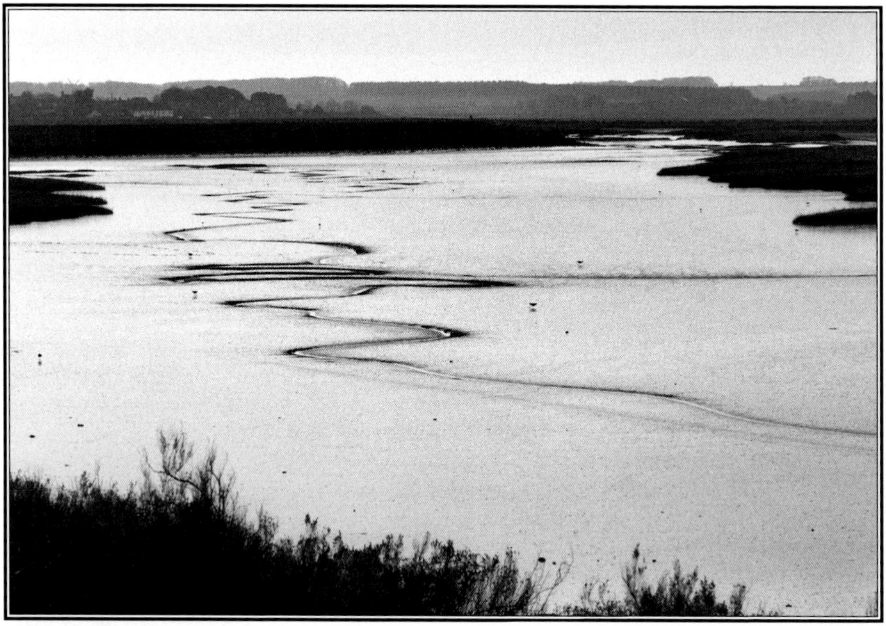

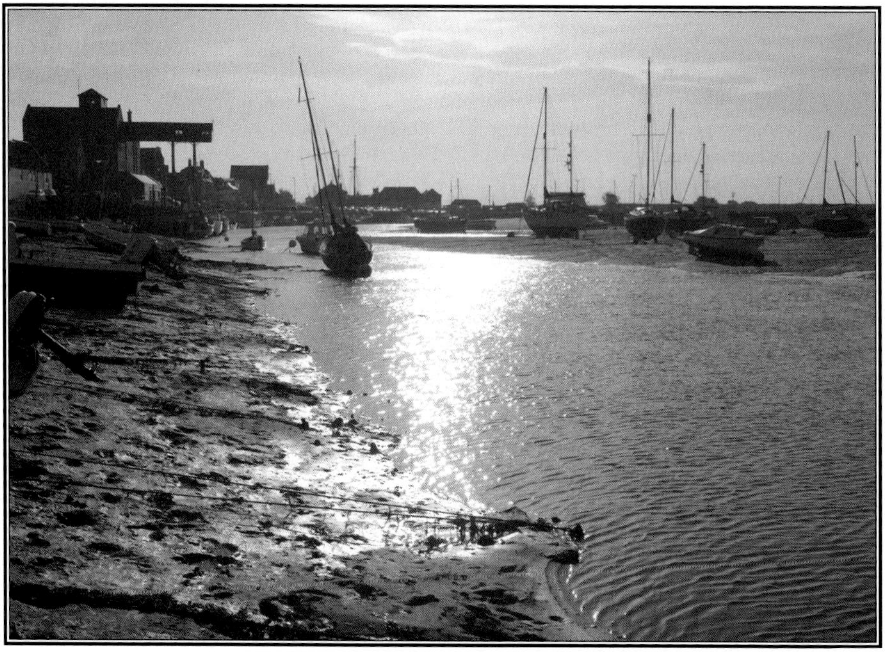

5
The sea

Captured upon the high seas by a Dutch privateer

Robert Mathew of Dundee in the county of Forfar, mariner, late master and part-owner of the sloop or vessel called the *Nelly*, of Dundee . . . maketh oath . . . that . . . on the 28th day of December 1797 the said sloop . . . was captured upon the high seas by a Dutch privateer and carried into Amsterdam; . . . about the month of April 1799 the said sloop . . . was retaken by His Majesty's sloop-of-war *L'Éspiègle* . . . and sent into the port of Yarmouth, and . . . the same hath been sold . . . to William Hardy the younger, . . . beer brewer.

ROBERT MATHEW, DUNDEE, 1800 [1]

Wind very high all day and stormy . . . Heard at evening that William's ship the *Nelly* was wrecked near Blakeney Pit and the whole crew consisting of the captain John Coe, 3 men and one boy perished. (She was coming from Newcastle loaden with coals and oilcake) no part of which was insured.   MARY HARDY, 1804 [2]

T HE STORY OF THE SMALL SCOTTISH SLOOP NELLY is the most dramatic of all those told by Mary Hardy in 36 years. Only the death of her elder son Raven, following a six-month-long decline, matches *Nelly*'s tale in poignancy. The 60-ton sloop and her crew met their sudden and brutal end on 12 February 1804, the seventeenth anniversary of Raven's death.[3]

The diarist's characteristically restrained language belies the emotion felt by the family. Following Mary Hardy's account of the wreck and partial salvage *Nelly* is never again mentioned. William Hardy junior, his venture into shipown-

[1] *Dundee* Part of the statement of the former master of *Nelly*, dated 25 Apr. 1800 (TNA: PRO CUST 97/31, Customs outport book, Gt Yarmouth), at the time William Hardy jnr purchased the ship at Gt Yarmouth for £590.

Robert Mathew's affidavit is reproduced in full on p. 278. In it he describes *Nelly*'s capture by the Dutch, and her recapture at sea by the Royal Navy as a prize 16 months later

[2] *Nelly Diary 4*: 12 Feb. 1804, recounting the loss of William's sloop within sight of home. The parentheses are the diarist's

[3] *Raven* His illness and death at the age of 19 are narrated in vol. 1, chap. 5

---

facing page Two north Norfolk havens. Like so many, Burnham Overy (top) and Wells face the constant problem of silting.

William Hardy jnr bought a Dundee-built ship, *Nelly*, in 1800 after the Royal Navy had recaptured the sloop from the Dutch. *Nelly* was wrecked off Blakeney in 1804, with the loss of all on board. The only body recovered was that of 28-year-old Richard Randall of Cley. He was found at Burnham Overy and buried at Wells [*Christopher Bird 2013, 2014*]

above The view looking north-west from Blakeney Church tower, showing how close *Nelly* was to home when she foundered. Just in from the horizon a white line of surf breaks over the seaward side of the long sandy spit leading west to Blakeney Point.

Blakeney Pit, protected by the spit, is the deep anchorage beyond the saltflats close inland; the tiny white specks (left) are the masses of small craft at anchor in the Pit.

The creek leading to the quay and *Nelly*'s old berth winds to the left of the stone pinnacle and past the bevy of sailing boats drawn up on the hard   [*MB · 2008*]

---

[1] *accounts* Transcribed in *Diary 4*, app. D4.B

[2] *lifeboat Norw. Merc.* 3 Nov. 1804; many others gave much more, the boat's likely cost being £300. Later William also gave a guinea to a fund for the families of seven Sheringham fishermen lost at sea (*Norw. Merc.* 5 Dec. 1807)

[3] *Act* 'For Improving the Harbour of Blak-

ing brought abruptly to a halt, never bought another ship. There is likewise no mention of writing off *Nelly* as an asset in his 1804 accounts.[1] In a humanitarian response he subscribed a modest one guinea to the Cromer lifeboat fund later that year, the first occasion on which either he or his parents were listed in the press as charitable donors.[2] At a practical level he was named as a subscriber to the Blakeney Harbour improvement scheme enacted by Parliament in 1817, by which the approaches to the haven were to be made safer for shipping.[3] Beyond the tale of one ship, the sea forms a constant backdrop to the diary and we learn much that the official records do not disclose.

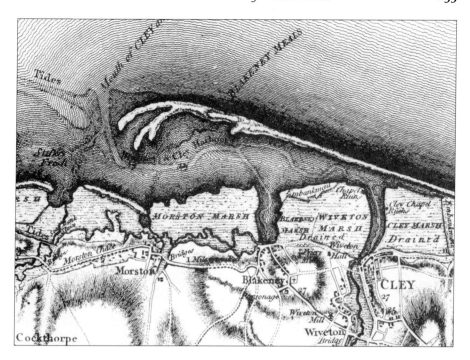

above The coast, as surveyed 1790–94; maps, charts and harbour plans needed constant updating to reflect changes in the shifting marshes. The Pit is labelled 'Blakeney & Cley Harbour', although the wharves of both havens were reached along shallow creeks.

Blakeney Church, on high ground a mile north-west of Wiveton Bridge, is represented by a cross: **✚** The bridge crossed one of the lower reaches of the Glaven above the head of the estuary; Letheringsett, off the map, straddled the river four miles south of Blakeney and Cley [*Faden's Map of Norfolk 1797: Larks Press 1989*]

eney, within the Port of Blakeney and Clay'; it received the Royal Assent 10 July 1817.

William Hardy Esq. was named as one of eight proprietors of the new Blakeney Harbour Co. (p. 2 of the Act)

This chapter tells a very small part of the story of Britain's Merchant Navy, a topic often neglected when the Royal Navy is seen as the nation's saviour at this time. Yet without the merchant fleet the economy would have collapsed in weeks, or even days. Coal and cinders (coke), grain, timber and all manner of foodstuffs were taken by sea. In 1803 Britain had more than 18,000 registered ships, totalling more than two million tons. When fully manned they gave employment to 105,000 merchant seamen.[1] For comparison, the Royal Navy had about 100,000 men. Napoleon's Grande Armée, 'the

[1] *tonnage* B. Lavery, *We shall fight on the Beaches*, p. 36. Goods carried round the British coast were taken 'coastwise'. Those going abroad were exports, although the term 'export' was at times also applied to coastwise cargoes. Peter Mathias carefully differentiates between the

two categories: 'For example, 54,800 quarters of barley left [Gt] Yarmouth coastwise in the year ending Christmas 1742 and 8800 quarters of malt (whereas her barley exports were 9900 quarters in the same year and malt exports 105,900 quarters)' (P. Mathias, *The Brewing Industry in England 1700–1830*, p. 433)

---

[1] *Grande Armée* B. Lavery, *We shall fight on the Beaches*, p. 386

[2] *doubled* S.P. Ville, *English Shipowning during the Industrial Revolution: Michael Henley and Son, London Shipowners, 1770–1830* (Manchester Univ. Press, 1987), p. 11

[3] *growth* A.D. Harvey, *Collision of Empires: Britain in three World Wars 1793–1945* (Phoenix, London, 1994), pp. 62, 57–61

---

most formidable land force in the world', camped above Boulogne in the summer of 1804, had 130,000 men.[1]

By the time the French wars drew to a close in 1815 the British Merchant Navy had expanded even further:

The size of the mercantile marine doubled between 1786 and the end of the French wars to reach a peak of 2·6 million tons which was not surpassed for another twenty-five years.[2]

Arnold Harvey tabulates the growth 1789–1815 of the merchant fleets of England and of Britain, Ireland and the Colonies, and gives a wealth of statistics on overseas trade comparisons between Britain and her commercial rivals. In 1789 Britain and France were evenly matched when it came to the volume of foreign trade. A decade later France's level had sunk to just half of Britain's. By 1804 the trade of the Genoese, Venetians and Dutch had suffered an even worse decline.[3]

The Mill, Cley-next-the-Sea.

right The Glaven estuary in the early 20th century looking downstream on the northern, seaward side of Cley; the mill was built shortly before 1819. In the Hardys' time the Customs House faced the wharf on the far right, and a line of malthouses and cinder ovens stood just upstream.

By then only the smallest seagoing ships could reach these quays, and lighters generally had to be used to bring goods from the Pit. *Nelly* paid only one recorded visit here, in Mar. 1801   [*from a postcard dated 1909*]

above Blakeney Pit from the dunes of the Point, looking south-east to the tower of Blakeney Church among the distant trees (left). The sandy dunes with their tussocks of marram grass are labelled 'Meals' on Faden's map. It is close to high water, and the Pit is crowded with boats at anchor and under sail   [*MB·1995*]

The effects of prolonged war took their toll on many of the belligerents, as Harvey charts into the time of the Anglo-American War of 1812. The volume of United States trade 'virtually collapsed' between 1811 and 1814; yet the British share was maintained and even expanded. Assessing the period 1791–1814 in general, Harvey concludes:

The growth of the British merchant fleet was nothing less than phenomenal, especially given that it was already the largest in the world when the wars began [in 1793], and had moreover to sustain the burden and disruption of its merchant seamen being system-atically pressed into naval service.[1]

He gives a chilling quote from an observer at La Rochelle in 1809: 'The silence of death reigns there; one goes through the streets without meeting a living soul; there is as much grass here as in a field . . .'[2] Driving the point home, Harvey highlights the dual function of the Royal Navy as being not only to protect their home islands from foreign invasion but also the clearing of the seas for the British merchant fleet:

The key feature of Britain's part in the French wars was less the defeat of the enemy battle fleets than the driving of the French and later Danish and finally American commerce from the oceans, while keeping them open for the expansion of British trade.[3]

[1] *growth* A.D. Harvey, *Collision of Empires*, p. 61. He offers a series of tables to illustrate his points (pp. 58–61).
  For Norfolk's civilian response to war see chap. 9 in this volume

[2] *La Rochelle* A.D. Harvey, *Collision of Empires*, p. 122. La Rochelle's population had been reduced by half since the outbreak of war in 1793. Gt Yarmouth, by contrast, greatly expanded, as we see later in this chapter and in vol. 1, chap. 1, table 1.1.3.
  The La Rochelle observer maintained that the same silence could be found in once-flourishing ports like Le Havre, Ostend, Dunkirk and elsewhere. Harvey offers Amster-dam, Hamburg and Copenhagen as well (A.D. Harvey, p. 122)

[3] *La Rochelle* A.D. Harvey, *Collision of Empires*, p. 122

above A protective presence at Gt Yarmouth: St Nicholas, patron saint of children, fishermen and sailors. The statue was saved from the flames of the 1942 incendiary bombing and restored to the south porch [*MB·2011*]

Much of this chapter will point to the buoyancy of the fortunes of comparatively small Norfolk ports at a time when many great continental trading posts were in severe decline. Despite numerous difficulties, caused variously by nature and human conflict, as will be described, in some ways these minor outposts had a 'good' war. Great Yarmouth perhaps benefited the most, as host to the Royal Navy fleet anchored in the Roads. Yarmouth, where William bought his *Nelly* during the French Revolutionary War—only to lose her in the next—will be featured in the later sections 'Strains placed on the Customs' and 'The Excise at sea'.

It is doubtful whether those striving to make a living from the sea during the wars saw it as a good time. As we shall see, there were few natural harbours along the inhospitable Norfolk coast. Only King's Lynn and Great Yarmouth, close to the mouth of the Great Ouse and the combined waters of the Bure, Waveney and Yare, had fairly deepwater wharves and quays. The handful of other havens lay up shallow creeks. Many landing places were no more than an exposed open beach onto which ships were driven at high tide, counting themselves lucky to escape stranding on the sands offshore. They were loaded and unloaded on the beach when the sea had receded. Importantly, no Norfolk port had a wet dock above the size of a wet shed or boathouse.

Merchants, shipowners and seamen endured financial uncertainty and the consequences of frequent shipwreck

facing page A weather eye over Gt Yarmouth: the weathercock of 1738, four feet wide (1·2 metres), which swivelled atop the tall spire of the parish church in Mary Hardy's time.
Rescued from the near-total destruction of 1942 it now perches, immobile, high inside the north aisle   [*MB·2011*]

left The figurehead of HMS *Unicorn*, a 46-gun frigate launched at Chatham in 1824 and here moored in the wet dock at Dundee just downstream from where *Nelly* was built and berthed in 1792. Frigates and sloops of war strove to sweep the seas of marauding ships such as the Dutch privateer which seized *Nelly*   [*MB·2007*]

and drowning. Insurance, of either craft or cargo, proved a near-impossibility in wartime. Further, the wars brought the press gang, the enemy privateer, delays in waiting for convoys while cargoes rotted, and the grim knowledge that the North Sea Fleet could not protect the whole seaway from Scotland to the Channel. Once at sea, getting news became another major hurdle. In May 1803 many ships were captured, on both sides, whose crews did not realise that hostilities had broken out once more. These seafaring hazards will emerge in this portrait of the Merchant Navy and in the story of just one ship, *Nelly*.

Despite these many tribulations the ships of the mercantile marine pressed on and kept the industries and people of the British Isles supplied. Not once in 36 years at Coltishall and Letheringsett does Mary Hardy record the family being short of the coal and cinders so vital to their manufacturing. Sufficient numbers of colliers must have got through, even if disaster at sea occasionally struck the Hardys and other manufacturers when crews and cargoes were lost.

In some ways Norfolk seafaring was still a considerable affair. Its seaboard formed half the county boundary, and it had a centuries-old proud tradition of trading overseas. But the glory days lay in the past. Great Yarmouth had commanded a far more prominent place in the nation's affairs in the fourteenth century than it enjoyed in the eighteenth. At the Battle of Sluys in 1340 the town had provided more ships than all the Cinque Ports combined, Edward III granting new arms by which the town's three silver herrings were halved with the royal arms of three golden lions.[1] King's Lynn (*plates 30–35*) had then been a Hanseatic port, with strong international connections, being knitted into the trade and economy of northern Europe and Russia.[2]

Establishing firm, comparable statistics can be tricky, as there are suspicions of over-estimates,[3] but David Macpherson's contempory compilations show the way the small north Norfolk ports had been massively overtaken. In 1800 the five chief British ports, assessed by total tonnages of ships registered at each location, were: London 568,262 tons, Liverpool 140,633, Newcastle upon Tyne 140,055, Sunderland 75,319 and Hull 68,533.[4] Against these can be set Wells-next-the Sea at 3078 tons (with 52 ships and 237 seamen)

[1] *arms* The distinctive mermaid-like creatures, with lion's heads and fishy tails, are retained on the town's arms today (A.A.C. Hedges, *Yarmouth is an Antient Town*, p. 16)

[2] *Lynn* P. Richards, *King's Lynn* (Phillimore, Chichester, 1990); see esp. pp. 22–5, 59–64

[3] *statistics* J.M. Bellamy, *The Trade and Shipping of Nineteenth-Century Hull* (E. Yorkshire Local History Soc., 1971), p. 13. Joyce Bellamy points out that many of Hull's 611 vessels were employed in the transhipment of goods; in 1801 there were 3770 seamen employed on Hull's ships (p. 11). (Gt Yarmouth too was heavily into transhipment)

[4] *tonnages* D. Macpherson, *Annals of Commerce, Manufactures, Fisheries and Navigation* (London, 1805), vol. 4, p. 535. Gt Yarmouth was eighth (at 32,957 tons and with 375 ships)—one place ahead of Bristol; Lynn was 16th (12,639 tons and 119 ships) (vol. 4, p. 535)

1 *Norfolk* D. Macpherson, *Annals of Commerce, Manufactures, Fisheries and Navigation*, vol. 4, p. 535. Comparable to Wells, Blakeney and Cley in tonnage were Southwold and Woodbridge in Suffolk; Pembroke, Aberystwyth, Llanelli and Milford in Wales; Deal, Chichester, Arundel and Cowes along the Channel coast; and St Ives and Bridgewater in the South-West (p. 535).

Paul Richards offers statistics across a wider range of years. King's Lynn had 85 ships in 1776 and 116 in 1831, and 16,800 tons in 1788 (*King's Lynn*, p. 32)

2 *Yarmouth* D. Defoe, *A Tour through the Whole Island of Great Britain* (2 vols J.M. Dent & Sons, London, 1962; 1st pub. 1724–6), vol. 1, pp. 69, 65

3 *quay* F. de la Rochefoucauld, *A Frenchman's Year in Suffolk, 1784*, p. 212. His tutor Maximilien de Lazowski states that the quay was 103 yards wide (94·2 metres), similar to Defoe's 1723 figure of 100 yards (D. Defoe, *A Tour through the Whole Island of Great Britain*, vol. 1, p. 65)

4 *empire* J. Storer, in the caption to 'The South Gate' in *The Antiquarian and Topographical Cabinet* (London, 1807)

facing page Gt Yarmouth: the South Gate's intricate flint and brick chequerwork. Atop the quayside tower is the commercial telegraph which had earlier served the Admiralty. The gate led from South Quay onto the Denes and to the fort. Naval prizes were held at the dockyard beside it on the River Yare (left). The accompanying text in the 1807 publication reads: 'On the top of the western tower is a telegraph, the head of a line of communication between Yarmouth and Norwich, erected and maintained at the expense of the merchants and traders of these places, for conveying speedy information respecting their affairs … Yarmouth Quay is the largest in the British Empire, being near three quarters of a mile in length, and from 150 to 200 feet in breadth' [*drawing by W. Brand; engraving by J. Storer for The Antiquarian and Topographical Cabinet (1807)*]

and the port of Blakeney and Cley at 1876 tons (with just 24 ships, in the two havens together, and 115 men).[1] *Nelly* was thus one of 24, some of those being unable to reach the quays and having to remain in the Pit while being lightered.

It is not enough however to judge a port by the total tonnage of the vessels registered there. Norfolk's ports were visited on a daily basis by ships berthed at four of the five principal ports just listed: London, Newcastle, Sunderland and Hull. Liverpool, the only one on the western rather than the eastern seaboard, was a more distant trading partner.

Norfolk had some claims to distinction and still attracted superlatives, even if some were not altogether welcome. Daniel Defoe in 1723 considered the coast around Great Yarmouth as 'particularly famous for being one of the most dangerous and most fatal to the sailors in all England, I may say in all Britain', especially with a wind from a north-east to south-east quarter driving the ships onto the beach and treacherous sands. At the same time he called Great Yarmouth's quayside 'the finest key in England, if not in Europe, not inferior even to that of Marseilles itself'.[2] In 1784 the tutor–companion of the young French aristocrat La Rochefoucauld was impressed, calling the quay superb.[3] Twenty years later the quay was held to be the longest in the British Empire.[4]

Penetrating the hinterland

Chapters 2–4 featured the supplying of inland ports on the waterways of the Broads. Great Yarmouth and King's Lynn

[1] *Lynn* D. Defoe, *A Tour through the Whole Island of Great Britain,* vol. 1, p. 73. He added that the Humber (and thus Hull) represented a second exception

[2] *Glaven* For an authoritative topographical study built on 80 years of living beside the river see B. Cozens-Hardy, 'The Glaven valley', *Norfolk Archaeology,* vol. 33 (1965), pp. 491–513. He shows that in the early 19th century, and possibly before, the river was still tidal above Glandford, the tides sometimes passing through the waterwheel into the mill dam upstream (p. 506). This would have had implications for brewers and millers at Letheringsett (vol. 2, chap. 7)

and, further up the coast, Hull each stood at the entry point to a system of rivers, navigations and canals going deep into the hinterland; Hull, with its access to the Humber, Ouse and Trent, could serve the towns of the West Midlands and the North. Defoe immediately appreciated the significance of King's Lynn's situation. While it had 'more gentry' and consequently 'more gayety' than Great Yarmouth—and even Norwich—it too was rooted in commerce and shipping. Lynn enjoyed access by inland waterway to six counties and to parts of three others:

It is a beautiful well built and well situated town, at the mouth of the River [Great] Ouse, and has this particular attending it, which gives it a vast advantage in trade; namely, that there is the greatest extent of inland navigation here, of any port in England, London excepted.[1]

The Glaven harbours of Blakeney and Cley were not so fortunate. They lay on what was by the late eighteenth century the shallow, silted estuary of a short (twelve-mile) river which, while it provided economic muscle in powering a large number of corn watermills and a brewery, was unnavigable from just upstream of the estuary. Like other north Norfolk rivers such as the Stiffkey and Burn, but unlike the rivers of the Norfolk Broads and the Fens, there were no inland ports on its banks.[2] Any vessel managing to squeeze

above The Glaven at Letheringsett: providing power and ornament, but without any wharves   [*MB·1998*]

[1] *advertisements Norw. Merc.* 29 July (and 5 Aug., 12 Aug.) 1780, illustrated at the start of vol. 2, chap. 5

[2] *cart Diary 3*: 1 Aug. 1797. The point is amplified later under the coal trade (pp. 268–70). See also table 4.4.1 on p. 168 in chap. 4 for the capacity of 15 keels and wherries, expressed in terms of tons and chaldrons

[3] *Diocletian* R. Duncan-Jones, *The Economy of the Roman Empire* (2nd edn Cambridge Univ. Press, 1982), app. 17, p. 368. The difference in road transport from the English figure was partly caused by the primitive Roman method of harnessing (p. 368).

Emperor Diocletian's price edict was passed in AD 301 and promulgated only in the Eastern Empire, at a time of dislocation; but the author adds that 'the amount by which transporting wheat by sea from a producing area increased its cost . . . would normally have been greater than the Edict's figures show' (p. 368)

[4] *canals* D.C. Earl, *On the Absence of the Railway Engine* (University of Hull, 1980), p. 6. The canal horse pulled its load slowly, at a maximum of 4 mph

under Wiveton Bridge would have been forced to stop at the mill straddling the waterway at Glandford.

The diaries of Mary Hardy and Henry Raven are of value in pointing up the differences between commercial life at an inland port and in a hinterland village. At Coltishall there was comparatively easy access to coal, thanks to the keels and wherries. At Letheringsett, although the advertisement of 1780 for the maltings and brewery drew attention to the proximity of the 'sea-ports' (as opposed to inland ports) of Blakeney and Cley,[1] the Hardys' cart had to lumber four miles across rolling terrain to pick up only a relatively small amount of coal (1½ chaldrons) at a time.[2]

The previous four chapters, devoted to transport by road and waterway, have highlighted the advantages attaching to waterborne freight. The costs of bulk carriage before the coming of the railways have been analysed by ancient, mediaeval and modern historians alike, the figures producing emphatic evidence in favour of the sea. Cost ratios across the Roman Empire at the time of the Emperor Diocletian (in the early fourth century AD) when compared to those of eighteenth-century England before the coming of macadam roads, canals and the expansion of navigations, show some remarkable similarities:

Taking the Diocletianic figures for sea transport and road transport by wagon, the cost ratios for the three types are sea 1, inland waterway 4·9, and road 34–42 . . . Some approximate ratios for England in the first half of the eighteenth century are as follows: sea (transatlantic shipment) 1, river 4·7, and road 22·6. It is interesting that these ratios show some mutual resemblance.[3]

Donald C. Earl recounts the demonstration by the canal engineers John Smeaton and Thomas Telford that a single horse pulling a stage wagon on a soft road could haul five-eighths of a ton and on a macadam road two tons, but that beside a river one horse could pull 30 tons and on a canal no less than 50.[4] Like Defoe contemplating the vigour of Lynn, Earl draws attention to the importance for Roman bulk transport of Arles, Marseilles, Ephesus and Alexandria at the mouth of extensive river systems: 'It has been calculated that it was cheaper to transport wheat from one end of the [Roman] empire to the other by sea than to cart it 75 miles overland.' The only sensible option in the pre-railway age was to carry bulk goods by water where at all possible.[1] The central parts of this chapter examine this assertion in relation to the havens nearest to the Hardys at Letheringsett.

The port of Blakeney and Cley

The types of vessel which traded along the east coast are listed on this page. Before the first canal was opened bisecting Scotland (the Forth and Clyde, in 1790) it could on occasion take longer to sail round the north of Scotland from the east coast to the west coast of Britain than from Newcastle upon Tyne to Bombay.[2] Unfavourable winds, storms and consequent damage to the ship would conspire against the sturdy merchant vessel, such as a schooner or brig, and cause delays.

The comparison is far from preposterous. Chapter 1 described the delays the Hardys endured on their voyages to and from Hull in 1775. The diarist never travelled again by sea. The Forth and Clyde Canal, linking Grangemouth to Bowling, did not provide much of a solution at first: it could take only small seagoing vessels with a draught of seven feet (2·1 metres). William Hardy junior's 60-ton sloop could negotiate locks used by 80-tonners. But, as noted later, her draught when fully laden was *nine* feet (2·7 metres). *Nelly* took more than two months to complete her voyage from Blakeney to Liverpool (overleaf) via 'the Scotch Canal'.[3]

[1] *overland* D.C. Earl, *On the Absence of the Railway Engine*, p. 8. The whole force of his argument concerns the extraordinary transformation wrought by the steam railway

[2] *to Bombay* Anthony Burton cites the contrast over passage times. Sir Edward Parry, championing the cutting of the Caledonian Canal, had quoted in evidence to Parliament this case of the two ships leaving Newcastle on the same day (A. Burton, *The Canal Builders*, p. 11). The Act authorising the project was passed in 1803

[3] *Nelly Diary 4*: 9 Aug., 11 Oct., 16 Oct. 1800. An 80-ton vessel was the first to use the canal in 1790. The next section explains that *Nelly* presumably sailed light-laden

---

Types of merchant ship on the east coast of England 1770–1810

source   Norwich Mercury: vessels commonly reported as trading along the Norfolk coast

sloop	one mast; fore-and-aft rig; one sail ahead of mast (Royal Navy sloops differed)
cutter	one mast; fore-and-aft rig; two or more sails ahead of mast
schooner	two or more masts; fore-and-aft rig on all masts; jibs *or* (for topsail schooner) with square topsails on foremast only; jibs
brig	two masts; square sails on both masts; three jibs
brigantine	two masts; square sails on foremast; fore-and-aft rig on mainmast; three jibs
bark/barque	three or four masts; all with square sails except for fore-and-aft rig on mizzen (aft mast); jibs
barquentine	three or four masts; square sails on foremast only; fore-and-aft rig on others; jibs

above An unsigned view of Liverpool, seen from across the River Mersey in 1775. It was the first port in the world with a commercial wet dock, with lock, quays and warehouses.

By 1778 Hull had the largest British wet dock. London followed from 1800 onwards.

The Hardys first shipped barley, malt, wheat, flour and porter to Liverpool from Blakeney in Jan. 1788. William Hardy travelled overland to Lancashire to arrange the sale of the valuable cargo. It arrived damaged after a bad passage, but was insured.

Nelly's voyage to this Atlantic port in 1800 was unusually long, taking over two months via the Forth and Clyde Canal of 1790. The fast-industrialising population of the North-West relied on supplies from the E. Anglian grain basket [*Author's collection*]

Jonathan Hooton, author of a major work on the Glaven ports of Blakeney, Cley and Wiveton, has researched the shipping there in the decades before and after the 1817 Blakeney Harbour Improvement Act. Whereas photographs of Blakeney Quay from the late nineteenth century onwards show billy boys (wide-beamed, single-masted craft) and brigs moored near the granaries and coal houses this was not possible in Mary Hardy's time at Letheringsett. Generally only sloops and schooners were small enough to make it up the creek. Little information has survived on the ships' draught of water pre-1820.[1] In the decades before the Act brigs, brigantines and barques had to anchor offshore or in the Pit and be lightered. Unlike the ports of King's Lynn, Wells and Great Yarmouth, there were no shipbuilding or ship repair yards at Blakeney and Cley to bring in business.

As the customs service classed the harbours of Blakeney and Cley as one port it did not distinguish between the two havens. It is thus impossible to assess which was the busier from the official data on goods shipped inward and outward.[2] The population returns of 1801 and 1811 were necessarily misleading, as on any one night large numbers of seafaring men could be away from home. Blakeney returned totals of 618 and 583 for 1801 and 1811; Cley 547 and 595. These figures would seem to suggest that Cley was prospering at the expense of Blakeney, were it not for the observations of the former Cambridge wrangler and statistically-minded Rector of Cley, the Revd Robert Thomlinson. He had compiled his own series of data showing marked fluctuations in the last quarter of the eighteenth century. On 26 May 1777 Cley had 587 inhabitants, but on 6 April 1789 there were only 422, causing him to observe for 1789: 'NB About this time the trade of the town declined very much. Many of the principals being dead, people went to Blakeney etc.'[3]

Less than two years later, on 1 January 1791, the rector could declare, 'I believe we are now as full of inhabitants as in the year 1777, trade being very brisk and two merchants in the town'. And by 17 December 1800 matters were even better: 'The trade of the town has increased very much these last two years. Mr Coleby, a Quaker, bags and ships a considerable quantity of corn, which finds great employment for the poor.'[4]

[1] *sloops and schooners* J. Hooton, 'The Glaven in decline in the 19th century', a talk given to the Norfolk Industrial Archaeology Society in Norwich, 3 Apr. 2014. He is the author of *The Glaven Ports: A maritime history of Blakeney, Cley and Wiveton in north Norfolk* (Blakeney History Group, Blakeney, 1996), the most detailed study of these ports yet produced and ranging from their origins to the mid-20th century

[2] *official data* The port books were withdrawn in 1780, the year before the Hardys' arrival. In 1786 Blakeney and Cley became classified by Customs as a headport, not an outport under Gt Yarmouth; it remained so until 1853, when the Customs House at Cley was closed and its business transferred to Wells. Official figures on the coasting trade in this region range from the patchy to the absent (P. Mathias, *The Brewing Industry in England 1700–1830*, pp. 429–30, 433–5)

[3] *Thomlinson* NRO: PD 270/5, Cley parish register 1779–1814, flyleaf

[4] *Quaker* Charles Coleby (d. 1802), a Cley merchant; like most of the merchants and ship-owners of Blakeney and

right Blakeney harbour, looking north from the High Street. Following the Blakeney Harbour Improvement Act of 1817 this creek was considerably straightened by means of a new cut.
   In *Nelly's* time it had taken an even more winding course [*MB·2004*]

Cley he had dealings with the Hardys.
   One of the two merchants referred to in 1791 would have been John Mann, whose actual finances failed to match his outward show of wealth (*Diary 3*: 17 Aug., 23 Aug. 1794)

¹ *gale Norw. Merc.* 10 Oct. 1807, reporting the storm of 30 Sept. 1807 [my italics]. The average rise and fall at Cley of 2·4–3·7 metres suggests that there was still a good tidal scour.
   Mary Hardy noted that in the very high tide of 30 Sept. three ships had been driven on shore between Blakeney and Salthouse (*Diary 4*). Revd Robert Thomlinson had also recorded 'rages', as these tidal floods were called, in the parish register on 2 Jan. 1767, 1 Jan. 1779 and 2 Feb. 1791 (NRO: PD 270/5)

This useful series ended with the rector's death in 1801. The upward trend he noted shows that Cley was still able to attract a fair amount of trade, suggesting that there was water enough for lighters at the quayside by the customs house, malthouses and coal wharves. But Blakeney was silting up, as the press report of a storm in 1807 makes clear:

The north-east coast of Norfolk felt the effects of the gale which blew so violently from the North on Wednesday se'nnight. The levelness of the coast, the height of the tide, and the fury of the wind, made the sea rush in upon the land with such force and velocity as had hardly ever been experienced. Blakeney harbour, *which is dry at low water,* was filled by the sea in the space of a few minutes; the tide rose above the banks, and the boats and vessels which were in the harbour soon floated unto the quay, and stove against the buildings.
   Cley, which is about a mile from Blakeney, afforded as extraordinary a spectacle. *The tide usually rises at this place from 8 to 12 feet,* and this time it rose not less than 18; the streets were completely inundated, and nothing but closed doors and stopped crevices prevented several feet of water penetrating into the ground floors of the houses.
   The road from Blakeney to Cley lies over a part of the land which is always covered by a few inches of the water which comes up to Cley.¹

Mary Hardy frequently records problems associated with storm and tidal surges, coastal flooding and erosion. When the family first moved to Letheringsett the sea proved to be something of a novelty as a neighbour. William and Mary Hardy had been reared deep inland in Yorkshire and Norfolk, and their married life had until then taken them to homes far from the sea at East Dereham, Litcham and Coltishall. But now they lived a little over an hour's walk from the coast, and six months after their move they took the children 'to see the high tide' at Cley. The next day the two boys, Raven and William, went back to see the results of the tide—in the form of wrecks.[1]

Wells too had its problems (illustrated overleaf) and could likewise suffer from severe flooding. In the storm of 14 January 1808 Wells Quay was under water, with boats washed against the buildings across the quay and some houses 'nearly washed away'.[2] At other times the *lack* of water affected commercial life. When William Hardy junior and a farming friend made a two-day trip to Wells to watch a ship being launched they were disappointed: 'William came home from Wells even[ing] past 9, the ship was not launched not being water enough.'[3]

High tides and surges damaged the cliffs found along the coast to the east. The location of the Hardys' tied house at Sheringham, the Crown, gave them constant anxiety. William Hardy senior and junior had to supervise repairs to the cliff and jetty from 1788 onwards in a vain attempt to shore up the public house perched dangerously on the edge. As described in volume 2, the Crown fell victim to erosion and collapsed into the sea on 22 October 1800.[4]

Jonathan Hooton devotes a series of chapters to the problems facing Blakeney and Cley with their silting harbours, and to the situation before and after the Act of 10 July 1817 which was designed to stem the decline; trade and shipping figures submitted to Parliament in 1806 chart the port's struggles.[5] It was to enable Blakeney to compete better for trade that improvements to the harbour were sought. Significantly, Cley harbour and the winding approach to Cley were not included in the scheme. The preamble to the Act sets out the hazards with precision: the existing channel was

[1] *wrecks* Diary MS: 20 Oct. 1781; *Diary 2*: 21 Oct. 1781. For the 'rages' see J. Hooton, *The Glaven Ports*, pp. 176–82

[2] *Wells* 11 vessels came to grief between Wells and Cromer (*Norw. Merc.* 30 Jan. 1808).
King's Lynn had its worst floods in 30 years, and the turnpike road to the south from Gt Yarmouth was under water (*Norw. Merc.* 23 Jan. 1808)

[3] *launch Diary 4*: 2 Oct. 1800

[4] *Crown* See vol. 2, chap. 9, under 'Lost to the sea'

[5] *problems* J. Hooton, *The Glaven Ports*, eg chaps 18, 19, 25, 28, 32, 33. Chap. 25 (pp. 166–75) offers an analysis of trade in the 18th century with useful tables and graphs. See esp. table 22 (p. 175), giving some comparative figures for 1792 and 1805.
The statistics confirm that London was the pre-eminent port of the kingdom. For a study of the profits to be made in London and the hazards faced, the records of Michael Hanley and Son 1770–1830 have been analysed by Simon P. Ville in *English Shipowning during the Industrial Revolution*

right A sight familiar to modern yachtsmen: Blakeney Quay at high water, looking west up the main channel; Agar Creek curves to the right in the distance. Here Mary Hardy and her family had tea on board *Nelly* in May 1801.

The quay is bounded by low-lying buildings, many of which get flooded in tidal surges. In the worst of conditions vessels would be washed up onto the quayside, both here and at Wells—as still happens today   [*MB · 2002*]

[1] *preamble* The Act , pp. 1–2; it runs to 44 pages and includes four schedules: harbour dues on vessels, duties on corn and manure, on other cargoes, and pilotage fees.

A Blakeney sloop, the 70-ton *Diana*, had been for sale in 1804—whether because she was too big for easy working is not stated (*Norw. Merc.* 1 Sept. 1804)

[2] *plan* NRO: MC 106/28/3; a 20th-century copy of Leak's plan of 1817.

As with the seaward end of the approach to Wells, the plan shows a refuge named 'Abraham's Bosom'. It is identified by a marker post with a triangular top, near the southern bank just before the Pit opens out to the east. Presumably this was the safest area for ships to ride out a storm, and may be the very spot where *Nelly* was destroyed in 1804.

The name derives from the biblical story of the beggar Lazarus, covered in sores and despised in life. The angels carry him from outside the rich man's gate safely into heaven and 'into Abraham's bosom' (Luke, chap. 16, vv. 19–26)

'very crooked in its course, whereby the navigation thereof is greatly impeded'. A new cut was needed to shorten a ship's passage and improve tidal scour; new buoys, beacons and mooring chains were required; and proper regulations were to be introduced to govern those using the port.[1]

The plan drawn up by Benjamin Leak of Holt to accompany the Bill depicted a treacherous waterway with numerous sandbanks in mid-channel, edged by mudflats and salt marshes. Much of the power of the tide would have been dissipated along creeks such as Morston and Agar Creeks running south from the large obstruction named Horn Sand, in the middle of the main channel east of the Pit; also the tidal force of the channel had to be shared between the havens of Cley and Blakeney. At Union Point, where the creeks to the quays at Blakeney and Cley merged, there was a jetty.[2] As a result of the improvements, ships as large as 150 tons (about 70 feet long or 21·5 metres) could again reach Blakeney Quay at average high water.

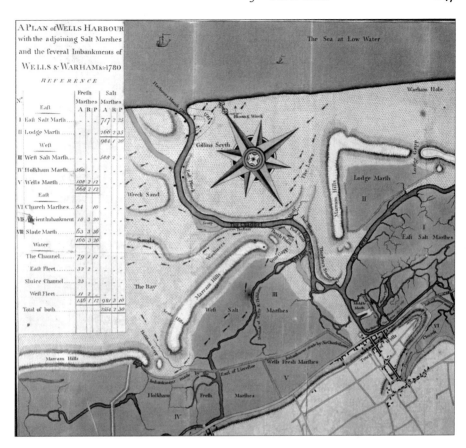

above Wells harbour in 1780, oriented north-northeast. The compass rose and beauty of the presentation will be familiar from the 1772 plan of the Aylsham navigation (chapter 2): this too is by H.A. Biedermann. At Wells he was under the direction of the Scottish civil engineer Robert Mylne.

Unlike the major ports of Gt Yarmouth and King's Lynn, the quays of this port had to be reached along narrow creeks winding through shifting sands and salt marshes. Cley, Blakeney, Burnham Overy and Brancaster Staithe offered similarly hazardous approaches. Dredging and deepening were resorted to, but provided only temporary relief: Mary Hardy noted in Oct. 1800 that a ship launch had to be postponed, there 'not being water enough'. Her diary also shows that Wells was used for passenger travel in preference to Blakeney.

The town itself was built on a grid plan (bottom right). The principal thoroughfare running south from the quayside is Staithe Street, on which the Hardys had their tied house, the Fighting Cocks; they also supplied two other outlets on the quay, the Jolly Sailor and the Fleece Inn.

What was found of *Nelly* in the way of shipwreck timber was sold here in Feb. 1804 [NRO: HMN 7/336, *detail*]

[1] *William* See vol. 2, chap. 11, table 2.11.5. The seven others were the lord of the manor Lord Calthorpe, who owned the marshes through which the new cut would be made; the merchant and shipowner Robert John Brereton, of the family which had founded the maltings and brewery owned by William; Thomas Drosier, trained as an attorney at Holt and also a miller, and married to a miller's daughter; John Temple and Thomas Johnson, both merchants; Pearson Walton, Esq.; and the Revd Benjamin Pullan (later Pulleyne), Master of the Free Grammar School, Holt 1809–57 and Curate of Blakeney; Pullan became the company clerk.

One of William's share certificates (no. 19, dated 16 Mar. 1818) is held in the Cozens-Hardy Collection.

Jonathan Hooton describes the provisions of the Act and the subsequent history of the company, which was wound up about 1914 (*The Glaven Ports*, pp. 228–34)

[2] *Bryce* TNA: PRO WO 30/100, pp. 147–63, report 12 Dec. 1803 to Lieut. Gen. Sir James Craig, KB, Colchester, Essex; lengthy extracts appear in *Diary 4*, app.

William Hardy junior took part in the promotion of the port as a very minor shareholder, although he relied heavily on Blakeney for supplies of coal and cinders and for shipping his farm and manufactured produce. He was one of the initial eight subscribers to the Blakeney Harbour Company, buying two £50 shares and thus securing access to the quay. The total issue was £2500, so his stake was minimal.[1]

One source departs from this depiction of a struggling port, although it should be emphasised that this independent observer was impressed not so much by the capabilities of the quays at Blakeney and Cley as by the anchorage of Blakeney Pit. His conclusions are to be found in the military papers of the Eastern District, responsible for home defence against the anticipated French invasion. An exceedingly detailed survey of the Norfolk coast was made in November–December 1803 by Major Alexander Bryce, the Commanding Engineer of the Eastern District, and is held in the National Archives. Extracts form an appendix to the fourth volume of Mary Hardy's diary.[2]

As well as inspecting the terrain and tramping across sands and undrained marshes in the cold and fog Major Bryce interviewed local seafarers and had a great deal to say on the relative merits of the anchorages, ports, havens and creeks of north Norfolk. He privately dismissed to General Craig the fears of villagers such as those at Mundesley—long used to unloading beached boats using cart gaps, and to resupplying Dutch fishermen at half-tide—that the Grande Armée would disembark in a similar manner: 'Although the inhabitants of this part seem to attach considerable importance to Mundesley, I can hardly bring myself to be of their opinion . . .' He did not think highly of Wells: 'Wells harbour is not so good or so easy as that of Blakeney. The vessels lie about a mile below the town.' However Holkham Bay west of Wells might provide the enemy with 'an extensive and good anchorage in six fathoms water'. Burnham Overy Staithe was 'an inconsiderable place at present, the mouth of the harbour being ruined by the sands'.

It was Blakeney and Cley which impressed Bryce: so much so that he recommended building a battery to protect the deep anchorage of Blakeney Pit, sheltered to the north by the long spit of Blakeney Point. It was never erected.

left Wells Quay, looking east past *Albatros*, a Dutch clipper built in 1899 at Middelharnis, near Rotterdam. With two masts and gaff-rigged, she used to trade between Holland and the Baltic. Her trading days ended in 1996, at which time she was the last sailing cargo ship in Europe. *Albatros* then turned to carrying passengers under sail and is here seen as a floating restaurant also offering bed and breakfast.

Public houses familiar to the Hardys line the quay: the Fleece Inn with shaped gables (right), and the Royal Standard of England (glimpsed beyond the distant gantry) [*Christopher Bird 2014*]

D4.C, pp. 467–71. Maj. Bryce's report is also covered in chap. 9 in this volume.

The report is very valuable in giving precise figures such as the depth of water on the bar at high water. He gained his information from local seafarers, fishermen and the commanding officer of the Sea Fencibles (a coastal Volunteer force: see chap. 9).

The problems experienced by Wells are narrated by John Barney, *The Trials of Wells Harbour* (Mintaka Books, Norwich, 2000)

Blakeney and Cley harbour is the best on this part of the coast. There is 20 feet water on the bar at high water. Since it has become well known it is much used by coasting vessels for shelter. The large vessels lie in what is called the Pit, and only those of small draught in general go to Cley or Blakeney Wharfs.

The Pit is not very extensive, and would not contain a large fleet. It might however be valuable to an enemy, in the event of wind becoming unfavourable, whilst attempting to disembark on the adjacent coast, when he might seek shelter here. On this account, and to protect the vessels in the harbour, a battery might be erected on the meals in front of Morston Marsh . . .[1]

It was not only the silting harbours of north Norfolk which suffered from neglect. Even the mighty River Tyne proved a hazard to shipping until the much-needed improvements of the mid-nineteenth century. The bar (the shoal which builds up across river mouths) caused ships to run aground, and the river was so shallow it was fordable at Newcastle at certain states of the tide. In short, it was 'a sluggish, wreck-strewn, shoal-studded waterway; difficult to get out of and dangerous to get into'.[2] This was the 'haven' awaiting a small sloop battling up the east coast.

[1] *Blakeney and Cley* TNA: PRO WO 30/100, pp. 159–60

[2] *Tyne* D. Keys and K. Smith, *Tall Ships on the Tyne* (Tyne Bridge Publishing, Newcastle upon Tyne, 2005), pp. 8, 6

¹ *Brown* House of Commons Parliamentary Papers 1826 (369), vol. IV, Minutes of evidence to the committee, p. 86, 26 Apr. 1826. The ship detained for 47 days waiting to get out was *Fancy*, under Capt. Cubitt, drawing 3–3·2 metres

² *London* Minutes of evidence to the committee, p. 86, 26 Apr. 1826. The second, smaller ship, *Hannah*, under Capt. Butcher, into which he next loaded his cargo, was detained 31 days. The final, successful ship, *Two Brothers*, under Capt. Tuck, drew 7½ feet (2·3 metres) and got the original transhipment of 27 Nov. out on 24 Dec. 1822 only 'with great difficulty' (p. 86).
  Crisp Brown cited other instances leading to financial loss and damage to the grain

³ *coals* Minutes of evidence to the committee, p. 88, 26 Apr. 1826.
  The engraving by Miller published just two years later (illustrated opposite) shows even a very small vessel in difficulty on the bar in a north-easterly gale

⁴ *ships* The entry for Gt Yarmouth in *The Norwich and Norfolk Complete Memorandum Book 1790* (unpag.)

Shipping, unloading and cargoes

The evidence given to the House of Commons Committee in 1826 by those pressing for a new exit to the sea presents Great Yarmouth as no longer a functioning port. The Norwich maltster and coal merchant Crisp Brown recited a litany of the 'very great' inconveniences he encountered when using wherries and then transhipping on the quays at Yarmouth. The 'very great interruptions' were attributable to Yarmouth Bar, which could hold up a ship for 47 days:

On that day [27 November 1822] I shipped malt and barley on board a vessel drawing about ten feet, or ten feet and a half of water, and there was not sufficient water on Yarmouth Bar to take her to sea till the 13th of January.[1]

The galling part of this experience, he explained, was that once the third ship which he eventually used had crossed this narrow shoal at the harbour entrance she got to London in just over 24 hours.[2]

It was not just merchants and manufacturers who suffered. The bulk of the population, dependent on coal for warmth and cooking fuel, was affected. Unless the coal merchants at Norwich and the inland ports held large stocks they had to pass on the rise in prices brought about by sudden shortages at Great Yarmouth. Again the bar was to blame. This question was posed to Crisp Brown:

Can you tell me whether the prices of coals at Norwich are liable to sudden and rapid rises in consequence of the state of Yarmouth Bar?

The merchant gave a characteristically precise response:

It is more frequently at Yarmouth than at Norwich: if the wind sets from the north-east the coals will rise 3s or 4s [per chaldron] in forty-eight hours, because they can get no more in.[3]

Such were the problems faced by those reliant on the sea for freight; and the captains and crews were even more directly affected. It would seem that many of these ships were not Yarmouth registered. In 1790 (a year of peace) the port had only fifteen ships and masters listed as trading to London, five to Hull, three to Newcastle, two to Sunderland and four to Rotterdam.[4] The colliers were largely northern-based.

above The mouth of the Yare, viewed from the sea and looking towards the cliffs at Gorleston; the River Yare curves away to the right on its long approach to the quays in the heart of Gt Yarmouth. In the stiff wind a single-masted coastal vessel is in difficulty on the bar; some Yarmouth beach-men, a volunteer rescue service in a small rowing boat, are seen in the foreground.

Bluff-bowed colliers, having negotiated the river at high water, lie alongside the south bank waiting for a favourable wind. Opposite, by the fort on the Denes, some wherries are being loaded with sea sand— one of the cargoes carried to Coltishall by keels and wherries, as noted by Mary Hardy [*painting by J. Stark; engraving by W. Miller 1828*]

If ships could not use the quays of a port there were other options, explored here: lightering, whereby goods were tran-shipped not in harbour but out at sea in the roads; alterna-tively, for those living close to the coast, unloading and load-ing on the beach and resorting to overland carriage. Both were troublesome and dangerous. A fourth option, and the way ahead, became a reality in the course of the eighteenth century: the wet dock. This manmade inland basin had water levels controlled by a lock at the dock entrance. While very expensive to build, it offered a safe, protected inland quayside and was not nearly so prone to silting.[1]

[1] *protected* From the force of the elements, both wind and tide, and from the pilfering which plagued Crisp Brown, as he told the committee (Minutes of evidence, pp. 86–9, 92, 94–5).

Wet docks had secure, controlled access by road and by water and are described later

[1] *Nelly* He was Robert Mathew: see the later inset 'The early years of *Nelly* 1792–1800'

[2] *draught* Lloyds Register of Ships 1802 also gives *Nelly* as 60 tons (<http://www.lr.org/en/research-and-innovation/historical-information/lloyds-register-of-ships-online>, 1802, p. 24, no. 104), acc. 1 Dec. 2014. Her captain is given as J. Coe; owner W. Hardy.
    Nelly appears in 1803 (p. 101, no. 5), again as 60 tons

[3] *accounts Diary 4*: app. D4.B, p. 454. With malt at 36s a coomb she was carrying a cargo worth £468. William had paid £590 for the ship in 1800, yet here he values the balance at £732, indicating perhaps a rebuild or some extra cargo not itemised.
    However in Sept. 1803, following the embargo and other difficulties after the resumption of hostilities with France, William valued ship and stores at only £350—despite the £590 purchase price (*Diary 4*: app. D4.B, p. 459 and note)

[4] *ship's tons* The knotty question of tonnage is summarised in chap. 4 under tonnages (pp. 165–6). No clear answer emerges

[5] *vital statistics* R. Kelham, 'Some gleanings

While the master of a coasting vessel would have been preoccupied with his ship's characteristics in such matters as stability, sailing rig and draught, the important feature for the owner was the tonnage burden. There was a delicate balance between carrying capacity on the one hand and speed and numbers on the pay-roll on the other if the ship were to pay her way. William Hardy junior's sloop *Nelly* was declared by her first master, from Dundee, to be of 56 tons.[1] Under William her capacity was adjusted upwards by four tons, although it is not known if this was as a result of some rebuilding work or as a reappraisal of her hold. Lloyds Register gives us more valuable pieces of information. *Nelly* was a single-deck ship, with a draught of nine feet (2·7 metres) when loaded,[2] draught being the distance from the ship's waterline to the bottom of the hull, plus a generous extra amount for safety needed for clearing the seabed.

However like many ships she would not always have sailed fully laden. As we have seen, the shallow Forth and Clyde Canal would have caused problems unless it was deepened within a very few years of its opening. In casting up his accounts on 22 September 1800 William Hardy junior listed his ship, then at sea, as carrying 13 last (130 quarters) of malt, the value of ship and cargo totalling £1200.[3] *Nelly* was then on her two-month voyage to Liverpool, but the malt was under half the full load a 56- or 60-ton ship could carry: 13 last weighs 26 tons (26·4 metric tonnes), or 29·1 ship's tons.[4] Taking the canal was thus a somewhat risky venture financially even before the delays encountered that autumn.

Registration details included tonnage (as tonnage burden), length and beam; also sometimes depth (not draught): the depth in the hold from the keelson or floor to the underside of the deck. The customs records in the National Archives and Richard Kelham's delvings among the surviving ship registers for Blakeney and Cley mean that we can try to compile the vital statistics of a sloop such as William Hardy junior's, even though *Nelly* herself has not been traced as the port books for those years have been lost. A 56-ton sloop is likely to have been approximately 50 feet long, with a beam of about 17½ feet (15·2 by 5·3 metres).[5]

For those vessels which could not reach a quay the most likely choice for loading and unloading was lightering. Reg-

left At Wells Quay
c.1900. The two-masted
coaster is moored in
the same spot as
Albatros (page 249)
[*Norfolk Heritage Centre,
Norwich, detail*]

from the ship registers',
The Glaven Historian,
no. 3 (2000); see esp.
the sloops *Blakeney
Packet, Faith* and *Hope-
well,* of 1826 and 1846
(pp. 53, 56, 62).
  As *Nelly* was built in
the north she is likely to
have been bluff-bowed
and thus squatter than
some sleeker southern
ships. Allowance has
accordingly been made
for a broader beam

istration of British ships was enforced under the Act of 1786, whereby the details of all such ships at sea had to be listed. Exemptions were allowed for lighters loading and unloading the large vessels in the roads,[1] and for new-built ships sailing in ballast; these had neither to be registered nor to obtain clearance from Customs.[2]

Interestingly for historians of inland shipping, any river vessel intending to sail by sea had to apply for registration. As a result we can trace those Norfolk keels and wherries venturing into unfamiliar waters—maritime and bureaucratic—as when in 1799 a Broadland keel owner applied to Customs at Great Yarmouth for his 25-year-old keel *Friendship* to carry timber to Southwold in Suffolk. The registration was forwarded to London, as the file copy of the letter shows. It is from the Collector of Customs and Comptroller of the port of Yarmouth to the Commissioners of Customs:

1 August 1799. Honourable Sirs—Mr Robert Riddelsdell applies to us to register his keel called the *Friendship* which we cannot do

[1] *roads* At Gt Yarmouth these were deep offshore waters in the channel between the east Norfolk beaches and Scroby Sands

[2] *lighters* TNA: PRO CUST 96/134, Customs Board to Collector of Wells, no. 78, p. 146, 21 Nov. 1802. However many historians of shipping have assumed lighters to be included in the numbers of registered ships at a port (eg Joyce Bellamy for Hull, as already stated in this chapter), and it is not clear for which years the exemptions were in place

above Cromer Beach in 1830, showing the
unloading and loading of three vessels.
Horses with their sturdy carts wait to pull
the cargo along the steep track to the cliff-
top, their hooves mired by the wet sand
[*painting by T. Creswick; engraving by E. Finden*]

[1] *raft* Timber: waves
would have broken over
the keel. Some timber
had to be towed, such
as ship's masts brought
over from the Baltic

[2] *keel* TNA: PRO CUST
97/31, p. 52, Collector
[John Bell] and
Comptroller [George
Thompson], Gt Yar-
mouth, to Board.
　For details of lighter-
ing by wherries and
keels see R. Clark,
Black-Sailed Traders, p.
111. The hazards would
have been great in the
days before steam

without your Honours' order, she being built before 1786, viz. in
or about the year 1774. The vessel is one of those in common use
upon our rivers for inland navigation and never used on the sea
but on particular occasions as to lighten or load ships in the roads
or to carry goods not subject to damage by water (as raft goods)
to a short distance on the coast.[1]

　This vessel is now wanted to carry deals to Southwold which is
the cause of this application. We registered a similar vessel under
similar circumstances the 13 April last pursuant to your order dated
11 of the said April, no. 63 . . . 　　　JOHN BELL, G. THOMPSON [2]

Unloading bulk goods not at a quay but on the beach where
the ship lay stranded was time-consuming and difficult. The
vessels were driven on shore either deliberately in fine
weather, as a way of supplying the needs of the local population, or helplessly by the force of a storm. The goods were
then hauled through cart gaps into the nearby town or
village and deeper into the countryside. The Cromer sur-

geon and artist Edmund Bartell jnr, a friend of William Hardy junior, considered that 70–80 tons was the maximum size of vessel that could perform this feat without mishap. Each beach cart, pulled by four horses, could carry only half a chaldron of coal up the sandy path to the cliff-top, the whole operation taking usually two tides. He adds:

> Perhaps there are few places, even at the distance of twenty miles from the sea, where coals are dearer than they are here; one principal reason of which is, the expense and hazard attending the unloading.[1]

The Cromer resident's viewpoint was somewhat different from that of the Norwich coal merchant. Crisp Brown considered it would not be economic to improve the dyke between Wayford Bridge and East Ruston, on the River Ant, in order to bring up coal by water from Great Yarmouth as people near the coast could buy their coal more cheaply by land carriage. Beached ships paid no dues or tolls, whereas Yarmouth Corporation took a cut on all coal passing through the seaport:

> The inhabitants of that part of Norfolk can buy their coals cheaper than from Yarmouth; at Barton [Bacton] and Mumsley [Mundesley] they can lay them out there, and there are no dues to be paid.[2]

This decidedly makeshift arrangement had been going on for centuries. Detailed coal-shipment records for 1508–11 held at Newcastle upon Tyne and discovered only in 1978 show that in the sixteenth century a vigorous trade existed, eleven north Norfolk settlements with no deepwater anchorages proving active in coaling.[3]

As would be expected, Yarmouth and Lynn in those three years made large numbers of return trips to the Tyne (at 305 and 104 respectively, against 207 from Dunwich in Suffolk and 148 from Boulogne in France). Nonetheless the harbourless towns and villages of Mundesley, Cromer, Beeston Regis, Sheringham, Holkham, Burnham, Brancaster, Titchwell, Thornham, Holme-next-the-Sea and Hunstanton taken together made 130 trips, eclipsing not only Wells (at 76) and Blakeney, Cley and Wiveton (at 58), but King's Lynn as well.[4] All the evidence points to ships being smaller then, but the number of beaching points is striking.

[1] *coals* E. Bartell jnr, *Cromer considered as a Watering Place*, p. 22. Given these difficulties 'the mercantile trade here is small', consisting of 'small exports of corn, and imports of coal, tiles, oil cake, London porter etc' (p. 21)

[2] *Brown* House of Commons Parliamentary Papers 1826 (369), vol. IV, Minutes of evidence to the committee, p. 95, 26 Apr. 1826

[3] *Newcastle* J. Wright, 'Coals from Newcastle', *The Glaven Historian*, no. 3 (2000), pp. 20–5. He calculates that an average of 16·9 chaldrons was carried per ship. This was the Newcastle chaldron, which he gives as approx. one ton (20 cwt) in the early 16th century; it was 18 cwt in the 1420s, but 53 cwt by 1698 (p. 25). For the coasting trade I owe a great deal to the researches of Jonathan Hooton, John Wright, Richard Kelham and others in *The Glaven Historian*, the journal of the Blakeney Area Historical Society

[4] *return trips* J. Wright, 'Coals from Newcastle', p. 22, table 1. Wiveton, lying in the estuary of the Glaven, still had access to the sea in the 16th century; embanking a century later ruined its trade

[1] *Gt Yarmouth* Instead the port has an outer harbour. Begun in 2007 and despite threats to its viability, it is, in 2019, in operation after further work including additional deepening

[2] *Ipswich* I am grateful to Colin Bridgland and Chris Marchbanks of the Brewery History Society for a wealth of notes accompanying the society's walking tour of 16 Sept. 2014

[3] *Liverpool* <http://www.liverpoolmuseums.org.uk/maritime/visit/old_dock_tours.aspx>, accessed 7 June 2019; the brick dock was re-discovered in 2001, having been buried in 1826

[4] *Hull Diary 4*: 13–30 May 1803

[5] *history* J. Tickell, *The History of the Town and County of Kingston upon Hull* (Hull, 1796)

Wet docks provided ships with what would have seemed a new world: a world with no mud, and no tidal rise and fall, but instead with extensive quays, secure purpose-built warehousing and firm access roads for carrying away the goods. Great Yarmouth never gained such a dock, but its Suffolk competitor Ipswich built a large wet dock in 1842.[1]

Wet docks however needed a deepwater approach, such as up the Humber and River Hull, or up the Thames estuary to the outskirts of the City of London. Ipswich's dock was created by widening and deepening the River Orwell, one of the riverbanks (on which the Customs House of 1844 still stands) being retained with its line of eighteenth-century warehouses and maltings.[2] The world's first enclosed commercial wet dock, controlled by means of a lock and with quays and warehouses, was Liverpool's Old Dock of 1715, holding up to 100 ships and built using part of the Mersey's natural 'pool'; *Nelly* may well have docked there.[3]

The first wet dock seen by Mary Hardy was at Hull, in 1803. When she had last visited the town after the family's gruelling voyage in 1775 (chapter 1) the dock scheme had been approved and the Hull Dock Company formed, but the basin was only opened three years later.[4] Raff or timber yards occupied the whole of the northern quay, demonstrating the importance of the Baltic timber trade to the town. It was also, like Dundee, a leading whaling port. The dock co-existed with the earlier wharves along the River Hull. A few of the old wharves are marked on the part of the plan of 1791 shown opposite, a pull-out insertion in the Revd John Tickell's massive 950-page history of the town.[5]

Immediately after breakfast on their first full day in Hull (14 May 1803) the Hardys made a point of seeing the dock and watching the vessels coming in and out. A lock taking shipping on this scale was a novelty to the diarist, although the construction would have reminded her of the one they had known at Coltishall years earlier (chapter 2).

left The steering wheel of the Thames sailing barge *Victor*, built in 1896 and moored in Ipswich wet dock by the Customs House.
   During the 18th century wheels replaced tillers on seagoing ships. The barge's gaff mainsail, such as *Nelly* also had, came into general use during the 16th to 18th centuries   [*MB · 2014*]

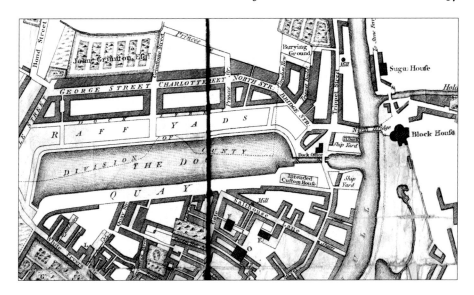

The success of Hull's remarkable civil engineering project would have brought it home to the Hardys how much their part of the world was being left behind.[1] The only port in Norfolk to be supplied with one or more wet docks, King's Lynn, did not acquire this facility until 1869, when the railway was about to reach the town.[2] Boston, up the coast in Lincolnshire, followed with a wet dock of its own in 1882–84, but it was smaller even than Hull's Humber Dock of 1809.

Before moving on to the coal trade which played such a prominent role we need to look at the other cargoes carried in and out of Norfolk.

[1] *Hull wet dock* No longer economic, it was filled in during 1930–34 to create public gardens.
  As seen elsewhere, the container port of Immingham down the Humber has taken over

[2] *King's Lynn* The Alexandra Dock 1869 and Bentinck Dock 1883 (P. Richards, *King's Lynn*, p. 140)

top Hull. In 1778 this was Britain's largest wet dock; William and Mary Hardy and Mary Ann toured it on their Hull visit of 1803. Ships approached up the Humber, turned north into the River Hull, and entered from the east, the lock being located beside the Dock Office. The basin covered nearly 10 acres. A second dock, of 7¼ acres, was opened in 1809. (The map has deep folds) [*plan of Kingston upon Hull, oriented north-northwest, by A. Bower 1791; engraving by I. Taylor 1792, detail*]

right The Hull Dock Company seal 1774. At the foot are the arms of Kingston upon Hull (the three crowns) and Trinity House (the anchor) [*engraving by I. Taylor 1790*]

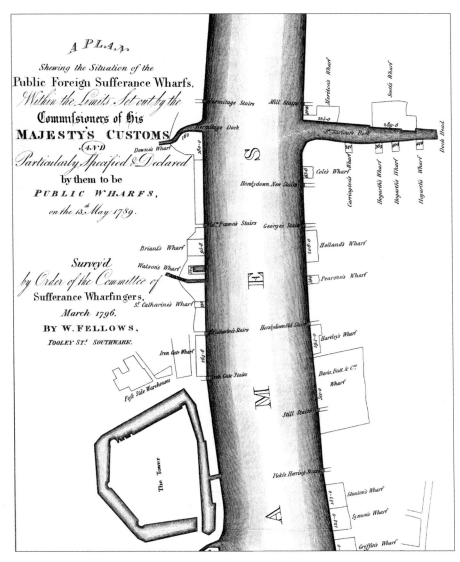

A PLAN

Shewing the Situation of the
Public Foreign Sufferance Wharfs,
Within the Limits Set out by the
Commissioners of His
MAJESTY'S CUSTOMS
(AND)
Particularly Specified & Declared
by them to be
PUBLIC WHARFS,
on the 13th May 1789.

Survey'd
by Order of the Committee of
Sufferance Wharfingers,
March 1796.
BY W. FELLOWS,
TOOLEY ST. SOUTHWARK.

above The Thames below the Tower of London 1796: part of the plan of the public foreign sufferance wharves. A table (seen in the full image in *Diary 4*, p. 129) lists each wharf, the length of its river frontage, the number of tons each warehouse and yard can contain, and the 'number of hogsheads of sugar each wharf can house'. Altogether 204,200 tons of merchandise could be held. London did not start to build its own long series of wet docks until 1800.

The Hardys were used to these wharves, Mary Hardy recording her Thameside visits during her London trips of 1777 and 1800. Her new Pembroke table was shipped from here to Blakeney in 1800 [*Author's collection*]

The Blakeney Harbour Act lists the duties payable on all the goods which could conceivably pass through the port in 1817. They total well over three hundred individual items: ale, beer and porter, shipped by the kilderkin, barrel, hogshead and butt; anchors by the ton; all manner of timber, deals, battens and bark; a full range of foodstuffs including salt and spices, oranges and olives; chairs, carpets and rugs; mats from Russia; linen, silk and wool and many other types of cloth; in the fish line anchovies, hake, cod, ling, haddock, cured herring, salmon and sprats; gunpowder (with a duty of sixpence per hundredweight); livestock; artists' paints; writing paper; a wide range of animal skins including bear, elk, moose, leopard, sable, panther, tiger, wolf and seal; individual wines and spirits; marble, grindstones and gravestones; tiles for roofing, flooring and malt-kilns; and wax, whale fins and woad.[1]

'Furniture' does not appear as such, but we know that household furniture passed through coastwise. While in London in 1800 Mary Hardy bought six painted chairs (which would have attracted a duty of threepence for the six after 1817) and a Pembroke table (with drop leaves) in Moorfields. Near the end of their long visit they 'packed up all the things we could spare to send home by Mr Temple's ship of Blakeney; I and Mr Hardy took a walk in the evening to Harrison's Wharf.'[2] Their son also used Thomas William Temple's ship until he bought his own. Early in 1800 William arranged to ship his malt to London by Mr Temple.[3]

There is a striking omission in the Blakeney list. Nowhere is what could pass as an anchor chain, unless included under the general heading, 'Anchors: the ton, 6d'. 'Anchor stocks' were of wood; items under 'Cables and cordage' could be tarred, showing they were not made of metal. Chains do not appear under the list of items made of iron. Did the Norfolk ships use hempen rope, and was *Nelly* lost as her anchor was held by hemp, which could rot in seawater unless regularly kept coated in pitch?

Some commodities were so essential as to require special provision: wheat, oats, barley and other grains; oilcake and manure. Ships belonging to Blakeney and Cley paid only half-rates (sixpence per last of grain or per ton of oilcake and manure); all other vessels paid one shilling.[4]

[1] *harbour duties* The Act, pp. 36–43.
Harbour dues were also payable by the ships themselves, irrespective of their cargo: $1\frac{1}{2}d$ per ton for each British vessel, and $3d$ for foreign vessels. Fishing and other boats loading or unloading along the coast on the open beaches were exempted (p. 36).
The duty on coal and coke was 6s per chaldron, but whether by London or Newcastle measure is not stated.
Gunpowder was needed not only for shooting game but for personal blunderbuses and public celebrations

[2] *furniture* Diary 4: 29 May, 11 June 1800.
William Hardy was back at Harrison's Wharf on 12 June, evidently the wharf favoured by Thomas William Temple, the Blakeney coal merchant

[3] *malt* Diary 4: 26 Feb., 11 Apr. 1800

[4] *grain* The Act, p. 36. Goods lightered from vessels in the Pit and destined for Cley Quay, Morston or Stiffkey did not pay these duties as they were not 'going through the intended new cut'—the straightened channel to Blakeney Quay (Act, p. 36).
Oilcake was animal feed as compressed cubes, and was derived

from crushed seeds.
Pilots also got special
mention (Act, p. 44)

---

[1] *customs* W. Marshall,
*The Review and Abstract
of the County Reports to
the Board of Agriculture,*
vol. 3, p. 312. He took
Kent to task over the
figures tabulated for the
four Norfolk customs
ports in Kent's *General
View of the Agriculture of
the County of Norfolk,*
pp. 147–9. Kent's tables
are reproduced in
Diary 2, p. 310 (for
Blakeney and Cley)
and p. 337 (Wells).
   For a considered
analysis of the data see
P. Mathias, *The Brewing
Industry in England
1700–1830,* pp. 428–37;
alas, he has to concen-
trate on the period
before 1780. He refers
to the Norfolk creeks
out of which many of
the goods were shipped
(p. 428). See also
J. Hooton, *The Glaven
Ports,* pp. 166–75, again
concentrating on the
period up to 1780

[2] *Rosebery* N. Kent,
*General View of the Agri-
culture of the County of
Norfolk,* p. 152

[3] *1770s* J. Hooton, *The
Glaven Ports,* p. 168,
tables 19, 18

[4] *1790s* N. Kent, *General View of the Agri-
culture of the County of
Norfolk,* p. 149. At Gt
Yarmouth, according

facing page Blakeney Quay at high water in the late 19th century.
Many of the granaries and warehouses present their gable ends
to the shipping, but lie so low as to be extremely vulnerable to
flooding—with the consequent loss of their perishable stores.
   Having the ships alongside at least eased the work of unloading and loading by hand, no signs of mechanisation, or even a
crane, being visible. This is a port in severe decline and lacking
investment over a long period   [*from an undated postcard*]

Grain shipments prove a contentious subject. Just how
much grain was shipped through the Norfolk ports in this
period? As so often, there is no precise answer. The customs
records have not survived for most of the diary years. Even
had they done so we could not rely on them, as pointed out
by William Marshall and Jonathan Hooton. Marshall, prone
to speak his mind and lacking Nathaniel Kent's urbanity,
dismissed the customs data relied on by Kent as 'not being
sufficiently accurate for the use of the Political Economist'.
He refrained from an analysis of the figures.[1]

Kent was well aware of the fallibility of his sources, and
reported Lord Rosebery's strictures on the trade figures:

The Custom-house books are not a rule to judge by, as every
exporter enters, at random, any quantity he pleases, and always
more than he is likely to export, to prevent the trouble and expense
of a second entry, there being no necessity or obligation for entering the exact quantity they are to export . . .[2]

Whatever the precise figures, all the sources and commentators point to the strength of the barley trade and the London market. In 1772, 31,133 quarters of barley were shipped
out of Blakeney and Cley, as opposed to 3035 quarters of
malt and only 135 quarters of flour and 10 of wheat. In 1771,
58 per cent of the ships were bound for London; in 1780 the
figure was 75 per cent.[3]

Kent produced annual average figures for the early 1790s.
At Blakeney and Cley the balance was still heavily in favour
of barley, at 59,176 quarters, with malt at 2525, flour 785 and
wheat 6378.[4] The ports covered all the creeks and beaches
within their area through which the goods were shipped, as
at Brancaster Staithe and Burnham Overy Staithe for the
port of Wells. Some of the largest maltings in Britain lay
beside those two staithes (volume 2, chapters 5 and 6).

Blakeney Quay.

This dip into the figures reveals the randomness of the picture, apart from the very evident pre-eminence of barley. Kent's informed approach of averaging should have evened out the effects of individual harvests, which fluctuated markedly owing to unpredictable weather in the diary years.[1] Even so, the figures seem unreconcilable: 135 quarters of flour in 1772, but 785 per annum in the 1790s; worse, 10 quarters of wheat in 1772, but 6378 per annum in the 1790s. Marshall, for all his testiness, was right to move on, rapidly.

Given the lack of consistent data, and for long periods any data at all, it might be hoped that Mary Hardy would help plug the gap. While at Coltishall her husband was reliant on Great Yarmouth for imports and exports; at Letheringsett her husband and son turned to Blakeney, Cley and Wells. Sadly she does not attempt to be methodical over recording shipments. As we have seen, the sea held little appeal (an attitude which the loss of *Nelly* would have entrenched), and she seems to have felt much less attachment to shipping than she had done to wherrying. Her nephew Henry Raven, also raised inland at Whissonsett, offers only snippets.

to Kent in those years, the annual average was barley 129,884 quarters, malt 66,579, flour 30,578 and wheat 22,466 (p. 147). Rye and peas were also listed.

The years were 1790–93 or 1792–95, Kent's explanation being unclear. Historians have gone with both

---

[1] *weather* See vol. 2, chap. 4 for graphs and tables depicting the fluctuations. Shipments would have reflected emergencies, such as a sudden shortage of flour in the capital: it was a time of intermittent famine

¹ *Norway* The Cley merchant John Ellis represented them there (*Diary 2*: 19 May 1792)

² *hops* The Hardys' purchase of Kentish hops by sample in London and Southwark and the shipping of the hops are described in vol. 2, chap. 5.

The diary volumes also index the factors and agents, where named. The wharfinger was another key figure, overseeing operations on the wharves and quays, such as James Church of Hull (*Diary 1*: 6 Oct., 16 Dec. 1775)

³ *beer* J. Hooton, *The Glaven Ports*, pp. 84–91

⁴ *strong beer* J. Hooton, *The Glaven Ports*, p. 173.

The Cawston and Reepham breweries could also have exported via Blakeney

⁵ *Liverpool* 'Received a letter from Mr Hardy informing us he had sold the cargo of corn and a 100 barrels of porter spoke for' (*Diary 2*: 20 Jan. 1788). 100 barrels equate to 3600 gallons (16,366 litres).

The ship had cleared Customs at Cley 3 Jan. and sailed from Blakeney 5 Jan. (Diary MS). She arrived about four weeks later, but 'had a bad passage and the flour and part of the barley and part of the malt is damaged' (*Diary 2*: 4 Feb. 1788)

The diaries of Mary Hardy and Henry Raven nevertheless show the Hardys' business conforming to the pattern of maritime trade in Norfolk: barley, malt, and sometimes wheat and flour, going out; coal, timber and hops coming in. The indexes in each volume of the published diaries list the shipments and their dates four ways: under the port of embarkation (also, if named, the port for which they were bound); under shipping; under the captain, shipowner or merchant (if named); and under the individual commodity. As neither diarist was keeping a full record no conclusions can be drawn on totals, but the hugely time-consuming, uncertain nature of this world comes across clearly.

Where possible William Hardy liked to oversee operations himself. We have already seen him checking on transhipping at Great Yarmouth from Coltishall (chapter 4), requiring a round trip by road of perhaps fifty miles. Surprising though it may seem, he and his son took the same care over checking on arrangements and negotiating sales in person in London, Liverpool, Yorkshire and Newcastle—not for every shipment, by any means, and not over sales in Norway, but when deemed necessary. They chose not to rely solely on intermediaries and agents.[1] Over one purchase vital to their needs as brewers they did not compromise. The London trip every September was a fixture in their calendar, to buy hops and arrange shipment: to Great Yarmouth while at Coltishall, and to Blakeney or Wells while at Letheringsett.[2]

Jonathan Hooton has traced sixteenth-century exports overseas of beer through the Glaven ports.[3] Shipment was a bold venture when the keeping qualities of beer were then not properly understood, the preserving power of the hop being introduced into brewing only gradually from the early or mid-sixteenth century onwards. The stronger the brew the better its keeping quality, and Jonathan Hooton notes strong beer in the export records for 1761[4]—probably the produce of the Binham and Letheringsett breweries.

The Hardys on the whole seem not to have shipped a great deal of beer. The first occasion at Letheringsett came in 1788 when 'corn' and strong beer were sent to Liverpool; sales of the corn and 100 barrels of porter had been secured well before the ship docked. William Hardy was waiting there for the ship, having travelled by road to arrange sales.[5]

Porter travelled best; yet even porter could pose problems, and losses could be heavy if the brew turned bad in the cask. While it would do well in a cool, steady temperature in the hold, there was no guarantee it would be properly cared for on the quayside, and casks must often have been exposed to sun, rain and frost while waiting to be loaded. Nonetheless William Hardy exported porter, apparently irregularly, between January 1788 and May 1795. He sent 30 barrels of porter to an unknown destination in June 1791, and 30 barrels of porter and ale to Norway in May 1792, these weighty consignments needing hired wagon teams to transport the barrels from the brewery to the port.[1] The port of Wells was also used, as when ten barrels were sent to Knaresborough in Yorkshire in June 1791, and nineteen barrels to Newcastle in May 1792.[2] Henry Raven twice refers to shipping beer to London via Blakeney, *after* war had broken out.[3]

The perils of transporting porter long distances by sea are illustrated in correspondence between the Treasury and the Excise. In 1786 Noah Squires, who predictably called his ship the *Ark*, petitioned the Treasury over 30 hogheads and 27 barrels of porter which his ship had carried for the London brewer Felix Calvert to Halifax, Nova Scotia in May 1784. But the recipient of the consignment in Halifax, Richard Seamark, declared the beer sour and unmerchantable and sent it back by Captain Squires. Calvert refused to have anything to do with the beer and would not even permit the casks to be unloaded. The unfortunate captain, caught in the middle and with a hold full of sour two-year-old beer which had twice crossed the Atlantic, thereupon turned to the authorities for redress. We do not learn how he fared.[4]

In this instance the bond between captain and shipper had broken down. Again speaking generally, the Hardys seem to have turned to trusted, known shipping merchants and went to some pains to become acquainted with the captains themselves, even in London, culminating in the purchase by William of a ship of his own.[5]

Other cargoes are mentioned. *Nelly* carried tallow to London for Mrs Jennis of Holt in 1801.[6] As seen already, the ship was carrying oilcake as well as coal when she was wrecked in 1804. In many ways trade was built around coal: it made sense to cultivate the Tyneside market for Norfolk

[1] *porter and ale* Diary 2: eg 9 June, 15–16 June 1791, 16 May 1792.
Another wagon team was needed to carry a shipload of porter bound for Liverpool 17 Aug. 1791. William Hardy jnr introduced porter brewing aged 17

[2] *Yorkshire, Newcastle* Diary 2: 7 June 1791, 11 May 1792

[3] *London* Diary 3: 'R. Bye to Blakeney with beer to put on board a ship to London' (15 Nov. 1794); the destination of the second shipment is not given (22 May 1795)

[4] *Ark* TNA: PRO CUST 48/22, p. 313. *Ark* had arrived back in London 21 Dec. 1785; Noah Squires' petition was dated 15 Feb. 1786 and forwarded 2 Mar. 1786

[5] *London* Capt. Bruce, of *Bruiser* (Diary 4: 16 June 1800; William Hardy saw him at Deptford).
Judging by the notices in the Norwich papers this was not always the case. Captains would advertise the date of their next voyage if they had space for more cargo and passengers: eg for Rotterdam, Hamburg and St Petersburg (*Norfolk Chronicle*, 21 July 1781; *Norw. Merc.*, 30 July 1774, 20 May 1775)

[6] *tallow* Diary 4: 13 Mar. 1801

right The start of the process of carrying coals to E. Anglia: the Causey Arch, in the former Co. Durham, the world's oldest surviving railway bridge. This huge single-span structure was built 1725–27 as part of the Tanfield Wagonway transporting coal in wooden trucks from the pits above Sunniside down to the south bank of the Tyne. There it was shipped into Tyne keels and then colliers plying the east coast. 930 horse-drawn trucks a day crossed this bridge in each direction

facing page A replica truck or 'chaldron'. Carrying 53 hundred-weight of coal, it gave its name to the Newcastle measure of coal and ran on wooden rails. The truck rolled down the slopes by gravity on the 'main way', being drawn on the flat by a horse which also pulled the empty truck on the way up along the 'bye way'. The wooden rails were replaced by iron in 1839 [*Christopher Bird 2014*]

[1] *mountains* D. Defoe, *A Tour through the Whole Island of Great Britain,* vol. 2, p. 250

[2] *Tanfield Wagonway* N. Neave and C. Douglas, '*Like Carrying Coals to Newcastle': The story of the Tanfield Way* (Summerhill Books, Newcastle upon Tyne, 2009), p. 8. The way, mostly without rails, survives as a set of pathways near Marley Hill, Sunniside, Whickham, Lobley Hill and Gateshead (p. 9)

barley, malt, wheat, flour and beer so that ships did not have to sail in ballast. (Finding a cargo to bring back from London, apart from seasonal hops, posed perhaps more of a problem for William.) The complexities—and heroism—of the coal trade form the subject of the next section.

The coal trade

The story of transporting coal to the Hardys' breweries in two Norfolk villages begins in the clusters of pits in Northumberland and in County Durham (now Tyne and Wear). Here Daniel Defoe had seen 'mountains of coal' in 1726,[1] and here the mined coal was taken by horse-drawn trucks or chaldrons from the hills above the Tyne's south bank. At its height the Tanfield Wagonway carried almost one-third of the total production of the Great Northern Coalfield.[2]

This triumph of civil engineering, with its early single-span bridge over the Causey Burn (opposite) and a gradient at times of 1 in 14, linked the pits in the coalfields to the staithes at Dunston, a short way upstream of Newcastle; until the way was constructed the coal had to be taken in panniers strapped to packhorses. First shipped into the keels working the Tyne and then transhipped into the brigs and schooners waiting at Newcastle, North Shields, Tyne-mouth and South Shields, only then was the coal ready to be taken along the coast.[1] This seacoal, as it was known, was a most precious commodity even in areas like East Anglia, London and the South generally considered to have been bypassed by the Industrial Revolution. It was differentiated from the higher-performance but much less prevalent Welsh coal, which had fewer impurities. While this Welsh or 'Welch' coal also came by sea it was not classed as seacoal.

The colliers of the North-East, including Blyth, the Tyne ports and Sunderland on the Wear, dominated the coasting trade. Quite apart from the shipping statistics and the evidence of the port books, the newspaper reports of ships driven ashore or wrecked on the Norfolk coast reveal the

[1] *Dunston* N. Neave and C. Douglas, '*Like Carrying Coals to Newcastle*', pp. 10–11, 18, 24. Owing to the Tyne Bridge and the river's shortcomings seagoing ships could not get so far upstream, so Tyne keels lay moored on the south-bank staithes from Dunston down to Redheugh to be loaded.

Given the huge volumes to be shifted winter and summer the loading was made as rapid as possible. At times, so a mid-18th century observer noted, one loaded chaldron (a truck, carrying more than 2½ tons) crossed the Causey Arch every 45 seconds (p. 25)

TABLE 4.5.1
Ships reported driven ashore on the coasts of north-east Norfolk and north Suffolk, 11–12 February 1804

source *Norwich Mercury*, 18 Feb. 1804   note A dash denotes lack of information

ship	home port	master	from	destination	cargo	crew's fate	ship's fate
Adeona	Blakeney	Jary	Sunderland	—	coal	saved	with cargo likely to be saved
Argo	Sunderland	Sibbald	Sunderland	—	coal	master and 7 men drowned; 5 saved	with cargo lost
——, collier	?Sunderland	—	Guernsey	Sunderland	in ballast	—	—
Dale, large barque	London	—	—	W. Indies	coal	all 20 men and 2 passengers saved by Sheringham fishermen	wrecked, part-salvaged; cargo lost
Enterprise, brig	Ipswich	Hill	Newcastle	—	coal	saved	with part of cargo likely to be lost
Friends Increase	?Blakeney	Burecroft	Blakeney	Dublin	corn [1]	saved	with cargo likely to be saved
Hannah, brig	Sunderland	—	—	—	—	Sheringham fishermen save 3 of 4 crew; mate's child dies	completely wrecked
Nancy	Hull	Dean	Gt Yarmouth	King's Lynn	furniture	? lost	likely to be lost
San Jozus, schooner	[Portugal]	Joze de Santos	Newcastle	Lisbon	coal	saved	lost
The Brothers	Whitby	Gobbit	Danzig	London	timber	saved	with cargo likely to be saved

[1] *corn* The Collector Customs, Gt Yarmouth, reported to London 13 Feb. 1804 that *Friends Increase* was carrying barley (TNA: PRO CUST 96/166, 17 Feb. 1804).

The wreck of *Nelly* was never reported in the press, and there will be other omissions

importance of these links. In the second half of the eighteenth century Sunderland was the pre-eminent coaling port serving Norfolk.[1] A glimpse of the nature of the traffic on the Norfolk coast is provided by table 4.5.1. Of the ten ships reported driven ashore on the night that *Nelly* was lost in 1804, six—possibly seven, if the brig *Hannah* is included—were colliers; of those seven, four were berthed at or bound for Sunderland, and two were sailing from Newcastle.

Mary Hardy and Henry Raven shed light on the reliance of local manufacturers on the services of Blakeney and Cley in supplying coal and cinders. Coal provided not only the principal domestic fuel, but also the means of firing the coppers in brewing. Slow-burning cinders gently and evenly heated the malt-kilns; tanners too relied on cinders for their processes.[2] By the period of the diaries of Mary Hardy and Henry Raven cinders seem generally not to have been shipped from the North-East, indicating that coking the coal was done at the Norfolk ports and inland staithes.[3]

Like some of the Broadland maltsters such as the Palgraves at Coltishall (as illustrated at the start of chapter 3) the Hardys acquired a cinder oven of their own soon after they arrived in north Norfolk. It was not at the Letheringsett maltings. Mary Hardy states that the Coltishall builder John Rolfe, brought over for the job, was building a cinder oven at the Hardys' malthouse at Cley in December 1781.[4]

[1] *Sunderland* J. Hooton, *The Glaven Ports*, p.189.
   Like Gt Yarmouth at the mouth of the Yare, Sunderland lies close by the coast at the mouth of the Wear, so many estuary hazards like those between Newcastle and Tynemouth were avoided. The bar still had be surmounted

[2] *malt-kilns* Brancaster malthouse, with its vast 360-coomb malting capacity, could store 500 chaldrons of coal in its coal house and its cinder ovens could coke 2½ chaldrons of cinders a day (*Norw. Merc.* 8 Apr. 1786)

[3] *cinders* The frequent press reports of shipwreck rarely refer to cinders as cargo. Also a table of goods imported in 1772 through Blakeney and Cley lists 3243 chaldrons of coal, but only 208 chaldrons of cinders (J. Hooton, *The Glaven Ports*, p. 186).
   Mary Hardy records coal and cinders on a ship wrecked at Cley 21 Oct. 1781; the boy was drowned (*Diary 2*)

[4] *Cley* Rolfe and his team built the oven 3–14 Dec. 1781 (*Diary 2*)

left **Mary Hardy records the start of work on their cinder oven at Cley, 3 Dec. 1781. Her husband was there too—keeping an eye on progress** [*Cozens-Hardy Collection*]

¹ *source* The brewery apprentice logs the collections made by cart from Letheringsett by the Hardys' workforce; coal was not carried in their wagons.

The quays at Blakeney and Cley lay four miles from Letheringsett.

Coal was used in brewing; cinders in malting

TABLE 4.5.2

Number of collections of coal and cinders by the Hardys from Blakeney and Cley 1793–97

source   Diary of Henry Raven ¹

fuel	Blakeney	Cley	total % of fuel
coal	15	35	42
cinders [coke]	15	55	58
% OF TOTAL COLLECTIONS	25	75	

² *Blakeney* J. Wright, 'The old "Guildhall" at Blakeney', *The Glaven Historian*, no. 5 (2002), p. 72.

Cinders were a little cheaper than coal. The Cromer merchant Mr Ditchell was selling Newcastle and Sunderland coal at 22s and cinders at 19s a chaldron (*Norw. Merc.* 3 June 1786). This was a summer price, in peacetime. Winter voyages, wartime rates and inland shipping raised coal prices to 29s 4d per chaldron at Norwich (*Norw. Merc.* 9 Nov. 1793)

³ *chaldron* As with 'childer' for children, she sometimes uses the older form 'chalder' for chaldron or chaldrons

⁴ *standardised* J. Wright, 'Coals from Newcastle', p. 25

⁵ *hypothesis* Richard Kelham's e-mail to me,

The Hardys' men had to journey from Letheringsett to collect both coal and cinders from the coal houses on the quayside at Blakeney and Cley. One particularly secure coal house was Blakeney's mediaeval building known as the Guildhall, its vaulted undercroft capable of storing 60 chaldrons of coal: as much perhaps as two or three shiploads.²

The vexed problem of the chaldron has already been set out in chapter 4, under tonnage. Mary Hardy uses the chaldron rather than the ton in relation to coal and cinders, thus quoting volume rather than weight.³ As we have seen, the chaldron was standardised in the late seventeenth century, stabilising as 53 hundredweight for the Newcastle measure and as half that for the London measure until the chaldron's abolition in 1963.⁴ Unfortunately the contemporary sources very rarely state which measure is being used.

Richard Kelham of Cley, who has written on measuring coal, ponders whether coal arrived at the north Norfolk ports as Newcastle chaldrons, which is how they left the ports of the North-East, but were then metered in by coal meters (men employed at the ports) to the local chaldron:

My hypothesis—that is all it can be at the present—is that the coal was shipped in the north-east as Newcastle chaldrons and received in, for example, Cley in the same measure; this would be necessary as the bills of lading and the duty payable would need to be consistent; and that once landed it would be sold to merchants and dealers using the local (London) measure; smaller quantities may well have been sold by the bushel?⁵

Henry Raven worked alongside the Hardys' workforce, and logged their tasks carefully day by day. One of their many errands, on top of their regular work on the farm, in the maltings and brewery and delivering beer, was to collect coal and cinders from the two nearest havens, Blakeney and Cley. They used the Hardys' carts, presumably as the axles of a fully loaded wagon could not cope with the rough roads and sloping terrain. It is from one of Henry's entries in 1797 that we can conclude with some certainty that the north Norfolk ports metered sales using the London measure:

AUGUST 1, TUESDAY W. Lamb and T. Baldwin to Blakeney 3 times each for 9 chaldron of coals from Mr Farthings, R. Bye unloaded them except 2 load . . . H. Raven in brewhouse.[1]

Each collection was thus 1½ chaldrons. There is no way a cart on such ground could withstand a load of 79½ hundredweight of coal (if sold as the Newcastle measure): just over four metric tonnes. Even at half that, 39¾ hundredweight (London measure), it would have been a struggle for man and horses.[2]

Over the four-year period October 1793–September 1797 Henry Raven records that the Hardys' workforce made fifty journeys by road to collect coal from Blakeney and Cley, and seventy journeys for cinders (table 4.5.2). Of these, thirty collections were made from Blakeney, and ninety from Cley. Since both havens were four miles from the brewery this might at first suggest that Cley was the busier place, were it not that the ground from Letheringsett to Cley (via Wiveton Bridge) is considerably more level than that to Blakeney, the 115-foot hill (35 metres) near Blakeney Church making it an unattractive prospect for coal carting. Individual totals and percentages for the collections are shown in the table.

We can calculate from the brewery apprentice's entries that of the fifty coal collections, 84 per cent were made at the height of summer (nine collections in June, six in July, seventeen in August). Of the cinder collections, only 5.7 per cent were made in late summer (two in July, one in August, one in September). This should not be taken to mean that coking was performed only in the winter, but that, as might be expected, the Hardys had little demand for cinders during the close season for malting. Brewing was by contrast a

---

27 Sept. 2013. We had a lengthy exchange of e-mails 2012–14.

A bill of lading was a docket on which the weight and marks of the goods coming into and leaving through the port were entered.

For further details see R. Kelham, 'The Blakeney and Cley port books', *The Glaven Historian*, no. 1 (1998), pp. 22–5, and R. Kelham, 'Taking the measure of the Blakeney coal trade in the 1780s', *Blakeney in the Eighteenth Century* (3rd edn Blakeney, 2010), pp. 21–2

---

[1] *Farthing* Robert, a Blakeney coal and cinder merchant (*Diary 3*).

Other coal and cinder merchants used by the Hardys at Blakeney at this time were Thomas Bond, Robert Brereton, Henry Chaplin, Thomas William Temple and Zebulon Rouse.

At Cley in the 1790s they were Corbett Cooke, John Ellis, Thomas Jackson, John Mann and Robert Farthing (again) (*Diary 3*)

[2] *39¾ cwt* Almost two tons (40 cwt). 79½ cwt equates to 4039 kg

[1] *seasonality* J. Hooton, *The Glaven Ports*, pp. 85, 132, 183. He shows the seasonal bias evident during the 16th and 17th centuries and for much of the 18th

[2] *costs of losses* In peacetime the Hardys insured their cargoes for at least one of the voyages using others' ships; this is not a subject either diarist covers. Henry Raven never mentions insurance; his aunt does so only twice.

In 1787, shortly before the first shipping of corn and porter to Liverpool, 17-year-old William travelled to Norwich to arrange the insurance (*Diary 2*: 30 Dec. 1787). It was a big moment for the family. William Hardy had taken his 14-year-old daughter to see the ship at Blakeney on 26 Dec. —an unusual business trip for Mary Ann.

The second mention comes with the loss of uninsured *Nelly* and her cargo, as seen at the chapter head (p. 231)

[3] *control* A thread running through the Hardys' story: see the reflections at the end of vol. 2, chap. 4. Even the development of Sunday schools nationally was in part for purposes of social control (vol. 3, chap. 2)

[4] *Camperdown* The reaction in the *Norwich*

constant, all-year process. The predominance of coal collection in summer suggests that the collier trade still favoured summer sailings where possible, even as late as the 1790s; the prices were lower too. Traditionally, in a past rather less hungry for coal, there had been a strong seasonality in collier sailings.[1] When times were hard colliers had to sail all year round, and *Nelly* was carrying Tyne coal when she was driven across Blakeney Bar to her end in the February storms.

Nelly under William Hardy jnr's ownership

Given all these difficulties and uncertainties it seems a strange move for William Hardy junior to go looking for a ship of his own. The French Revolutionary War still had more than eighteen months to run when father and son journeyed to Great Yarmouth in April 1800 to view a likely vessel. Until then they had not had to shoulder the extra responsibility of shipowning in their Letheringsett business, leaving it to others to bear the costs of losses and repairs.[2] Perhaps, as at Coltishall, they liked to bring as many aspects of their work as possible in-house. Having a vessel of their own, as with *William and Mary*, gave them the control they craved in their business, personal and spiritual lives.[3]

It was however an inauspicious time to diversify into shipowning. War brought additional problems for a merchant fleet already beset by natural hazards. The year 1795 had seen a highly unwelcome development for those on Britain's eastern seaboard: the annexation of the Netherlands by the French. Holland thereupon adopted the name the Batavian Republic. The two seafaring neighbours closely engaged in trade across the North Sea had perforce to become enemies.

For the people of England's east coast, having to regard the Dutch as hostile was a matter of some difficulty and even sorrow, as reflected in the tone of the press reports on the Battle of Camperdown in 1797.[4] Whereas rivalry and at times enmity had long characterised relations between Britain and the French and Spanish, the Dutch were seen as cultural, religious and trading cousins and were customarily treated with warm friendship. The children of Norfolk's merchant and manufacturing class would be sent over to Holland for the last part of their education and training to

```
NORWICH.  January  27.
This week a letter was received by the Mayor, from
the Right Hon. the Earl of Orford, Lord Lieutenant of the
county of Norfolk and the city of Norwich, setting forth
the expediency of the citizens being provided with arms
and ammunition, as the coast of Norfolk will be much
exposed to attacks, in consequence of the Dutch war.  On
which a full court of Mayoralty was summoned, and it
was unanimously resolved, to thank his Lordship for his
attention to the interest of this City, and that the Magis-
trates would recommend it to the citizens to concur with
the inhabitants of the county of Norfolk, in such measures
as may be thought necessary for the public safety.
```

left A shock to the customarily close trading relations between E. Anglia and Holland: the Dutch enter the American war early in 1781 on the side of the French and Spanish. As a result 'the coast of Norfolk will be much exposed to attacks.'

William's *Nelly* was in 1797 to become the victim of a later Anglo–Dutch war [*Norwich Mercury, 27 Jan. 1781: Norfolk Heritage Centre, Norwich*]

equip them for their future careers.[1] In peacetime the Norwich newspapers would marvel at the size of the Dutch fishing fleet putting in at Great Yarmouth for the traditional herring fair every September. Mary Hardy and her family had seen the Dutch fishermen at the port in 1775 as they waited for their ship to sail to Hull. After the warfare of 1781–83 the former close relations were quickly re-established, sixty Dutch ships and five hundred Dutchmen arriving in Great Yarmouth five years later.[2]

Once the war had escalated in 1795 the seas became even more threatening. Not even great setpiece naval battles could lessen the dangers besetting the British merchant fleet. Only two months after Admiral Duncan's victory off the Dutch coast in October 1797 the Scottish sloop *Nelly* was captured by a Dutch privateer as she sailed from Dundee to Hamburg with a cargo of oats.[3] All the belligerents would resort to privateering. A notice in the *Norfolk Chronicle* below the one advertising the Hardys' wherry in the summer of 1781 described a British 60-ton cutter transformed into a privateer and bristling with weaponry.[4]

The provincial newspapers alerted their readers to the dangers. One lucky ship bringing coal to the River Deben in Suffolk was rescued within hours of her capture by the enemy at night:

The *Œconomy* of Woodbridge, with coals, was captured off Cromer on the 4th instant, at 3 am, by a small cutter privateer with 30 men; she was retaken the same day by two pilot-cutters belonging to Lowestoft, and Sunday brought into Yarmouth Haven.[5]

Privateers interrupted trade routes, however strenuously the Royal Navy sought to protect these routes by patrol-

Mercury on 14 and 21 Oct. 1797, quoted in part in a note in *Diary 4*, pp. 13–14, reveals the sense of dislocation when these close trading nations were sundered by war

[1] *children* See vol. 1, chaps 5 and 6

[2] *Gt Yarmouth Diary 1*: 19 Sept. 1775; *Norw. Merc.* 20 Sept. 1788

[3] *Nelly* The capture is told later in this chapter under 'The early years of *Nelly*' (pp. 278–80)

[4] *British privateer Norfolk Chronicle*, 21 July 1781 (illustrated in *Diary 2*, p. 29). The Yarmouth-berthed cutter named *Argus*, 'a remarkable fast sailor', was for sale with 11 carriage guns, fourpounder guns and 'six swivels, with all her materials, ammunition and stores'

[5] *captured Norw. Merc.* 11 June 1803. This may be an early use of 'am' to denote morning

1 *trade routes* A.D. Harvey, *Collision of Empires*, p. 124. He gives statistics on the raiders operating off the British coast and describes the Royal Navy's efforts. 2218 enemy ships were taken by the British in those same years, many by privateers (pp. 123–7). On land the Militia, Volunteers and Sea Fencibles were mobilised to defend the coast (see chap. 9)

2 *Rosetta stone and outbreak of war* A. Petrides and J. Downs, eds, *Sea Soldier: An officer of Marines with Duncan, Nelson, Collingwood and Cockburn* (Parapress Ltd, Tunbridge Wells, 2000), pp. 49–50, 63, 66

3 *embargo* The Order in Council precipitated a temporary paralysis of trade. It was imposed on 15 May 1803, but was lifted 18 May for vessels employed in the coal and coasting trade; enemy ships were not allowed to leave port. See *Diary 4*: 17 May 1803, note; also *Norw. Merc.*, 21 May 1803

4 *skilled men* For these skills, and conditions at sea, see D. Davies, *A Brief History of Fighting Ships: Ships of the line and Napoleonic sea battles 1793–1815* (Constable & Robinson, London, 2002), pp. 20–56

ling the English coast and pinning down enemy shipping by blockading their harbours. Despite their efforts, 2861 British merchant ships were lost to enemy action, mostly to privateers, between 1793 and 1800.[1]

Not only the cargoes but the crews of the Merchant Navy fell prey to privateers. Seamen were inured to an exceptionally hard life at the best of times. They were particularly at risk from privateers and the press gang if they did not know war had broken out. Even the Regulars were perforce in a state of ignorance, as a young Royal Marine officer recounted to his sisters once he was safely back at Portsmouth in August 1803. Major T. Marmaduke Wybourn, RM had crossed the Mediterranean from Egypt to Malta bearing the object later known as the Rosetta Stone, which he describes. He left Malta in May, having transferred to a smaller ship:

. . . and might have made prize money had we known it was War for we passed several French and Dutch ships, who also knew nothing of the War; we were chased by an Englishman who made a variety of signals to us, but the Captain being desirous to make all haste home, would not stop to hear what he had to say; which he was most heartily sorry for since, as that ship knew of the War, so that the Capt. has lost prizes for his pains, when if he had stopped only 3 or 4 hours he might have taken those ships near us.[2]

One of the reasons behind the embargo imposed by the British Government on 15 May 1803—and referred to by Mary Hardy at Hull two days later on the resumption of hostilities between Great Britain and France—was to give an opportunity to press merchant seamen into the Royal Navy. The stoppage also alerted all shipping to the new danger.[3] As described in chapter 4, the Impress Service was ever on the lookout for men skilled in ship-handling, carpentry and ropework and with an ability to keep vessels in working order generally. Many of the men of the Royal Navy would have owed their service on board His Majesty's ships to the attentions of the press gang.[4]

To prevent attacks on the vital colliers and other British ships the Government reintroduced the convoy system instituted in the closing stages of the American war. In 1782 the Dutch had been busy seizing merchant shipping, making Royal Navy escort duties imperative; convoys also gave some reassurance that supplies would get through. Such

above Gt Yarmouth Roads, by the jetty. There was no harbour, but the larger merchant vessels and naval warships would anchor here to be unloaded and supplied by lighters. Rowing dinghies also linked them to the shore. The Herring Fair frequented by the Dutch in large numbers in peacetime was held on the beach.

The tall wooden lookout was used by the beachmen who manned rowing and sailing yawls to rescue crews in distress, these beach companies developing into the modern lifeboat service   [*drawing by J. Preston; engraving by J. Clark 1819*]

protection had again to be sought by all British ships within weeks of the outbreak of war in 1803; an Act imposed a swingeing fine of £1000 for any vessel leaving a convoy or sailing without one.[1] Reassurance of the populace, while desired, was not always achieved. Mary Hardy provided a rare frisson of excitement for her readers when her nephew Henry Goggs spotted what he took to be the might of the French fleet only a few miles from where she was writing:

[1803] AUGUST 8, MONDAY A very fine day. Mr Cook and Mr Goggs went to Sheringham morning 7, came back evening past 3, brought word there was a fleet of ships in sight off Sheringham supposed to be the French Fleet, proved to be coyers [colliers] or merchantmen under convoy . . .[2]

[1] *convoys Norw. Merc.* 15 June 1782, 9 July 1803. The Government responded quickly in both crises, all too aware that restraint of trade would damage the nation. The 1803 embargo was shortly further lifted for those trading with Russia, the Baltic and Norway; however other foreign ports remained out of bounds (*Norw. Merc.* 4 June 1803)

[2] *Diary 4.* For the difficulties presented by having to wait for a suitable convoy and then sail at the speed of the slowest vessel see S.P. Ville, *English Shipowning during the Industrial Revolution,* p. 126.

Ville also identifies a series of jumps in

right William Hardy jnr (1770–1842), who took over from his father as farmer, maltster and brewer in Oct. 1797 and greatly expanded all three branches of the business. By 1840 he could walk on his own land all the way to the sea at Cley (volume 1).

Of all the members of the immediate Letheringsett family William was the one most attracted to the sea. He alone did not fall seasick in the vexations of sailing to and from Hull in 1775, and he was also the only one in the circle of Hardys and Ravens (his mother's family) to own a sea-going ship—if only for four years. He also took up sea-bathing regularly in 1797, other members of the extended family later following his example.

He is seen aged about 56 in this unsigned, undated portrait [*Cozens-Hardy Collection*]

freight rates caused by war and by Napoleon's Continental Blockade in particular: 'The freight rate received by Henley vessels importing deals from Danzig rose to three times its prewar level.' And the bunching effect produced by convoys, with consequent pressure on wharves, may even have led to the rapid growth of the London docks (S.P. Ville, pp. 126, 39)

---

[1] *stamina* See House of Commons Papers, Accounts and papers (114), XII.367 (1806): 'An account of the totals of the imports

Given these hazards it might have been expected that the volume of imports and exports would go down. Yet, as stated at the opening of the chapter, the merchant fleet managed to stay resilient. Table 4.5.3, reproducing figures assembled by a watchful Commons from statistics provided by Customs, makes two telling points. In the last year of the French Revolutionary War there had indeed been a noticeable, but not too damaging, reduction in British ship movements compared with the last year of peace (January 1801 to January 1802, as against January 1792 to January 1793): a drop to nearly 10,500 voyages from just over 12,000. However the number of foreign vessels entering British ports had risen greatly: nearly 5500 voyages in 1801, as against nearly 2500 nine years earlier, with tonnages to match.

Taking years when William owned *Nelly* the parliamentary papers attest to the same stamina.[1] The key figures in a stream of data rest in the final column: 'Real value of British produce and manufactures exported'. Rounded, they show

TABLE 4.5.3

Number of voyages and tonnage of British and foreign ships entering British ports in a year of peace (1792) and of war (1801)

source   Returns presented by Customs to the House of Commons, 5 May 1806 [1]

| | BRITISH SHIPS | | FOREIGN SHIPS | |
	voyages	*tons*	*voyages*	*tons*
1792–93: peace	12,030	1,587,645	2477	304,074
1801–02: war	10,347	1,278,620	5497	780,155
REDUCTION in voyages	1683	200,025		
INCREASE in voyages			3020	476,081

[1] *source* House of Commons Parliamentary Papers, Accounts and papers (143), p. 721 (1806), 'A comparative account of the number and tonnage of British and Foreign Vessels that entered inwards at the several ports of Great Britain (including their repeated voyages) in different periods of peace and war', compiled by the Office of the Register General of Shipping, Custom House, London, 5 May 1806. The year is presumably the customs year, to 5 Jan., although this is not stated. The years were chosen as the last full year of peace before the outbreak of war in Feb. 1793, and 'the last whole year of war before the late peace' (the Peace of Amiens of Mar. 1802); however the truce had been agreed in Nov. 1801

British exports within the range £39–£42 million each year, apart from the full year 1801–02 (containing only a very few weeks of peace) when exports reached £48·5 million. Perhaps surprisingly, for those who expect more trade in years of peace, the one year of uninterrupted peace, ending 5 January 1803, recorded exports worth only £40·1 million.

It may have been an awareness of such buoyancy, gathered from converations with customs officials at Blakeney, Cley and Wells, that persuaded William to venture once again into the world of shipowning, this time on a larger scale, from which he had parted as a youngster of eleven. He had been present, with his companionable father, at the sale of the wherry he had known for five of his formative years.[2] In the end a natural disaster, not enemy action, led to the destruction of his hopes and the lives of all on board. The ship's boy, never named, would have been not much older than William at the close of his wherrying days.

and exports of Great Britain for the years ending 5 Jan. 1800, 1801, 1802, 1803, 1804, 1805 and 1806'. Hostilities had ceased between Nov. 1801 and May 1803

[2] *wherry William and Mary* was put up for auction at Horning 31 July 1781 (*Diary 2*), as illustrated in chap. 4 on p. 214

above The east coast of Scotland in 1780: Dundee, on the north bank of the Tay, and *Nelly*'s home port. The sloop was built in these busy shipyards in 1792, and it was from here that she sailed for Hamburg in 1797—only to be intercepted by a Dutch privateer and taken to Amsterdam.

Dundee and Hull were Britain's two principal whaling ports from the mid-18th century onwards, their timber yards and shipyards producing particularly tough, sturdy craft for this arduous trade. Dundee relied on its long foreshore; unlike Hull it had no wet dock at this time.

Nelly was only 56 tons burden, but this was not small when compared with the other ships built here at this time. William Hardy jnr had to buy a shallow-draughted vessel to suit the silted quays of north Norfolk. Inching up the creeks across the saltflats to Blakeney would have seemed ditch-crawling in comparison with the deep, spacious waters of the Tay, with its backdrop of green hills.

Adam Duncan, the future commander of the North Sea Fleet and victor over the Dutch, was born in 1731 in Seagate, one of the central streets near Dundee's foreshore [*engraving by Alex Robertson: courtesy Dundee City Council, Central Library*]

The story of *Nelly* begins in Dundee on the banks of the Tay in that last year of peace, 1792. It was a busy east coast port, with 116 ships counted in harbour in January 1792.[1] Hamish Robertson has chronicled the ships and their captains in detail from 1311 to 1980, and we find other ships named *Nelly* and *Charming Nelly* registered at the port in our period.[2] Trade was buoyant when William's *Nelly* was sailing the North Sea. Dundee's Trinity House was built in 1790, also hosting a School of Navigation and a hall for the Fraternity of Masters and Seamen.[3] By 1799, after six years of war, a contemporary source could rejoice:

> The shipping is wonderfully increased. Foreign tonnage is at least quadrupled. Vessels are well found and manned, and they voyage without interruption from Christmas to Christmas . . . Our home tonnage may be reckoned at from 8000 to 9000 tons.[4]

Robertson's long study yields a mass of information not only on the ships of this period but also on the citizens of Dundee who testified to the capture and recapture of *Nelly* in 1797 and 1799—the very people to whom William Hardy junior had to turn for the ship to be released for onward sale after her declaration as a prize by the Admiralty Court. They included *Nelly*'s original part-owner and master Robert Mathew and the shoremaster and magistrate Andrew Peddie; also James Sime, a Free Master of the Fraternity.[5] Theirs were good ships, able to withstand the rigours of the Arctic: the sloop *Peggy* was still in service at the age of 95.[6]

The dramatic story of *Nelly*'s early years from 1792 to 1800 is related on the following pages in the words of the time: in the deposition and petition of the sloop's first and last owners, and in the statements of others who examined the ship at Great Yarmouth. Their testimony begins with her registration in 1792 in Dundee and continues through her capture in December 1797, on her passage to Hamburg with a cargo of oats, by a Dutch privateer which brought her as a prize into the harbour of Amsterdam. They describe her recapture in April 1799 by a sloop-of-war of the Royal Navy, that ship's French name indicating she was herself a prize. They end the tale with *Nelly*'s identification at Great Yarmouth by James Sime in person—the very same seaman and shipowner who had known the sloop well in Dundee.

[1] *Dundee* A. Murray Scott, *Discovering Dundee: The story of a city* (Mercat Press, Edinburgh, 1999; 1st pub. 1989), p. 65.
As well as whaling and its thriving Baltic trade it was a linen town. In 1778 Dundee had 2000 linen handlooms at work; in 1791 it exported 8 million yards (p. 71). Sailcloth was another speciality

[2] *other ships* H. Robertson, *Mariners of Dundee: Their city, their river, their fraternity* (PDQ Print Services, Dundee, 2006), eg pp. 87, 273.
Nelly is a contraction of Helen, Ellen or Eleanor, as would be used in the family or for the maidservants

[3] *Trinity House* H. Robertson, *Mariners of Dundee*, p. 78

[4] *shipping* H. Robertson, *Mariners of Dundee*, p. 84. It had presumably quadrupled from 1792

[5] *citizens* H. Robertson, *Mariners of Dundee*, pp. 77, 82, 83, 87; for other relevant information see also pp. 76, 80–1, 84, 268, 271, 273

[6] *Peggy* Already built by 1767, she was sold for the last time in 1862 (H. Robertson, *Mariners of Dundee*, p. 71). Capt. R.F. Scott's Antarctic explorer *Discovery*, built in Dundee in 1901, is open to the public there

The early years of *Nelly* 1792–1800, including her capture by the Dutch and recapture by the British, as told to the Collector of Customs, Gt Yarmouth

source   TNA: PRO CUST 97/31, Customs outport book, Gt Yarmouth, 13 May 1800 [1]

[1] *source* The Collector of Yarmouth to the Board of Customs in London.

The clerk makes some errors: James Hardy for William Hardy jnr, and Hetheringsett for Lethereringsett. (James Hardy of Hethersett, south-west of Norwich, came from a well-known, non-brewing, Tory-voting family with which William's sister Mary Ann Hardy was also confused in the press announcement of her marriage: *Norw. Merc.* 16 Nov. 1805).

The spelling has here been modernised and punctuation inserted

[2] *L'Espiègle* Imp; Mischief. In her new life as a British warship the French ship had kept her old name following her capture by the Royal Navy on 30 Nov. 1793 off Ushant (M. Phillips and P. Marioné, Ships of the Old Navy: A history of the sailing ships of the Royal Navy <http://www.ageofnelson.org/Michael Phillips/info.php?ref=0848>, accessed 21 Nov. 2014)

[3] *Admiralty High Court* Gt Yarmouth had the privilege 1559–1835 of trying these maritime cases within the borough, at the Tolhouse (A.A.C.

ROBERT MATHEW OF DUNDEE in the county of Forfar, mariner, late master and part-owner of the sloop or vessel called the *Nelly*, of Dundee, of the measurement of fifty-six tons or thereabouts, MAKETH OATH AND SAITH that the said sloop or vessel was duly registered as a British-built ship at the port of Dundee on or about the twenty-first day of November one thousand seven hundred and ninety-two; AND that on the twenty-eighth day of December one thousand seven hundred and nine-seven the said sloop or vessel was captured upon the high seas by a DUTCH PRIVATEER and carried into Amsterdam; and at the time she was so captured the Certificate of Registry of the said sloop was demanded of and taken from this deponent as master of the said sloop by the commander of the said privateer; and this deponent further saith that in or about the month of April one thousand seven hundred and ninety-nine the said sloop or vessel was retaken by His Majesty's sloop-of-war *L'Espiègle*,[2] James Boarder, Esquire, commander, and sent into the port of Yarmouth, and that thereupon the said sloop or vessel was claimed in the High Court of Admiralty of England and have been since restored to the former owners and proprietors thereof upon payment of the SALVAGE;[3] AND this deponent further maketh oath that since the restoration of the said sloop or vessel the same hath been sold by this deponent and the other part-owners thereof and duly transferred by them according to law by BILL OF SALE dated the twenty-fifth day of April instant to WILLIAM HARDY the younger of HETHERINGSETT in the county of Norfolk in England, beer brewer ——

SWORN AT DUNDEE aforesaid the twenty-fifth day of April one thousand and eight hundred years   ROBERT MATHEW
Before me, ANDREW PEDDIE, magistrate, Dundee

JAMES SIME OF DUNDEE in the county of Forfar, shipmaster, MAKETH OATH AND SAITH that he was perfectly acquainted with and knew the sloop or vessel called the *Nelly*, of Dundee, whereof Robert Mathew was formerly master, and had frequently been on board thereof previous to her being captured by a Dutch privateer in or about the month of December one thousand seven hundred and ninety-seven and sent to Amsterdam; AND that he this deponent on or about the thirteenth day of June last past inspected and examined a certain sloop or vessel then laying in Yarmouth

Harbour which had been captured by His Majesty's sloop-of-war *L'Espiègle* and sent into the port of Yarmouth, and found the said sloop or vessel which he then examined to be the same vessel called the *Nelly*, of Dundee, of which the said Robert Mathew was formerly master; AND this deponent further saith that the said sloop or vessel called the *Nelly* was duly registered as a British-built ship at the port of Dundee on or about the twenty-first day of November one thousand seven hundred and ninety-two, and is the same vessel sold and transferred to JAMES HARDY the younger of HETHERINGSETT in the county of Norfolk in England, beer brewer, by a certain instrument of BILL OF SALE thereof bearing date the twenty-fifth day of April instant ——

SWORN AT DUNDEE aforesaid the twenty-fifth day of April one thousand eight hundred years JAMES SIME
Before me, ANDREW PEDDIE, magistrate, Dundee

JOHN MILLS of Great Yarmouth in the county of Norfolk, ship-wright,[1] and JAMES MANSER of the same town, tide surveyor,[2] SEVERALLY MAKE OATH that on the day of the date hereof they very minutely and accurately surveyed and examined a certain sloop or vessel lying in the port of Yarmouth late called the *Nelly*, of Dundee, and now belonging to William Hardy the younger of Hetheringsett in Norfolk, beer brewer, and that the said sloop or vessel has not had to the amount of fifteen shillings per ton laid out upon her in repairs in any foreign port ——

SWORN AT GREAT YARMOUTH abovesaid by the above-named John Mills and James Manser the ninth day of May 1800
JOHN MILLS, JAMES MANSER
Before me, WILLIAM STEWARD, a commissioner in His Majesty's Court of Exchequer

TO THE HONOURABLE THE COMMISSIONERS of His Majesty's Customs,[3] the petition of JAMES HARDY the younger of HETHERINGSETT in Norfolk, beer brewer, HUMBLY SHEWETH —— THAT the sloop or vessel called the *Nelly*, of Dundee in Scotland, which was duly registered at that port on the 21st day of November 1792, was captured on the 28th day of December 1797 by a DUTCH PRIVATEER and carried into Amsterdam;
THAT at the time of capture of the said vessel her Certificate of Registry was demanded by and delivered to the commander of the privateer by which she was captured,[4] as appears by the affidavit of ROBERT MATHEW, the then master of the said vessel hereunto annexed;

Hedges, *Yarmouth is an Antient Town*, p. 44)

[1] *John Mills* He was granted the Freedom of Gt Yarmouth in 1790 by apprenticeship to Nathaniel Palmer, ship-wright, who had himself been granted the Free-dom in 1761 through apprenticeship to William Danby Palmer; many of Nathaniel Palmer's other appren-tices also gained the privilege (*Calendar of the Freemen of Yarmouth 1429–1800*, pp. 236, 198)

[2] *tide surveyor* A customs officer in charge of a boarding or rummage crew; later known as a preventive officer

[3] *Commissioners* In London: the Lords Commissioners of the Board of Customs, to whom Collectors were directly responsible

[4] *certificate of registry* The Collectors of Customs and the Customs Board were much exercised by the loss or capture of certificates, which, if falling into enemy hands, enabled ships to sail under false colours and defraud the Revenue.
Mary Hardy was careful to note that the box containing *Nelly*'s papers was washed up on 13 Feb. 1804, the day after the shipwreck

The early years of *Nelly* 1792–1800, including her capture and recapture (*cont.*)

[1] *Boorder* Capt. James Boorder, RN emerges as a very effective officer in 1799 in the papers of Maj. T. Marmaduke Wybourn, RM. In an engagement in W. Friesland on 11 Oct. 1799 Boorder and his force of 157 men took on 670 and defeated them with no British losses: 'We had not a man hurt' (A. Petrides and J. Downs, eds, *Sea Soldier*, pp. 26–7)

[2] *George Thompson* Comptroller of the Port of Gt Yarmouth

[3] *Bell* Collector of Customs, Gt Yarmouth. He died in 1803 and was succeeded by William Palgrave jnr (*Norw. Merc.* 15 Oct. 1803), who is featured on the frontispiece to chap. 9

THAT in the month of April 1799 the said sloop or vessel was recaptured by His Majesty's sloop of war *L'Espiègle*, James Boorder, Esq. commander, and hath since been restored to the original proprietors thereof on payment of salvage and charges;[1]

THAT on the 18th of April last your petitioner purchased the said sloop or vessel by public auction at Great Yarmouth, and by bill of sale dated 25th ultimo the said sloop hath been duly transferred to your petitioner as the law directs;

THAT the said sloop or vessel has not had any foreign repairs, as appears by the affidavit of JOHN MILLS and JAMES MANSER hereunto annexed, and has been fully identified by a person who knew her before she was captured, as appears by the affidavit of JAMES SIME hereunto also annexed;

YOUR PETITIONER therefore most humbly request Your Honours will be pleased to give direction to the proper officers at the port of Yarmouth for registering the said vessel, and your petitioner will ever pray, etc   JAMES [WILLIAM] HARDY JUNIOR
Great Yarmouth, May 9/10th 1800

THE COLLECTOR AND COMPTROLLER of Yarmouth to report returning these papers,
By order of the Commissioners   H. MACLEAN

HONOURABLE SIRS, We see no objection to this petition being granted upon the petitioner's producing a bill of sale.
We are, etc   G. THOMPSON [2]
          JOHN BELL [3]

13 May 1800

facing page Early-19th-century Amsterdam: the Old Church and (left) the typical tall, narrow house of a merchant or craftsman.

  Nelly was brought into Amsterdam after being captured by a Dutch privateer at the end of December 1797. This was less than three months after the defeat of the Dutch Navy at Camperdown by the British naval squadron blockading the Texel under Duncan. Another east coast Scot, Admiral Keith, would shoulder that task 1803–07 [*drawing by W.J. Cooke; engraving by J. Poppel*]

Nelly was unlucky. From Hamish Robertson's researches it would seem that very few Dundee ships were captured in the French Revolutionary War 1793–1801. The fate of *Nelly* (rendered as *Nellie*), as sworn by Andrew Peddie in 1798, is reported merely in outline in Robertson's study.[1] However his summary of another ship's capture throws light on how *Nelly*'s master, and presumably her crew as well, managed to get back to Dundee while the war still raged. Merchant seamen, as non-combatants, were not held as prisoners of war. Even so the crew of the whaler *Tay* were particularly fortunate in the summer of 1799. *Tay*, returning from Greenland under Captain Webster as a 'full ship with nine whales', had almost reached her home port of Dundee when she was seized by a French privateer off Rattray Head, on the Aberdeenshire coast near Peterhead. The whaler's crew got back to Scotland from Norway just four weeks after their capture.[2]

The official record transcribed opposite and on the previous pages names *Nelly*'s saviour: the bold and energetic Royal Navy officer, Lieutenant James Boorder. His exploits are described in some detail in the chronicle of his sloop, HMS *L'Espiègle*, herself a former prize captured from the French off the coast of Brittany in November 1793 by HMS *Nymphe* and HMS *Circe*.[3]

Mary Hardy makes no mention at all of *Nelly*'s Scottish ancestry and adventurous past, and there is no hint in her diary of the ship's appearance in Admiralty Court proceedings. However the weekly Norwich newspaper was filled with snippets of 'Ship News' during the wars. So, on the assumption that William had not changed the ship's name, a search was made to locate a *Nelly* entering Great Yarmouth in the years leading to her sale there on 18 April 1800. Only one *Nelly* featured 1797–1800.[4] The *Norwich Mercury* on 20 April 1799 announced the triumphant return of *Nelly* to

[1] *capture* H. Robertson, *Mariners of Dundee*, p. 83. In 1801 the Dundee ship *Riga Merchant* on her passage to Norfolk, Virginia was captured off Ireland by a French 32-gun frigate. The merchant vessel was 'later recaptured by [a] British man-of-war and taken to Galway' (p. 87)

[2] *whaler* H. Robertson, *Mariners of Dundee*, p. 83. He adds, 'Ship and cargo valued at £6000. This was a heavy blow to Dundee. Crew landed at Aberdeen 28 July.' The privateer took the ship—and whales— over to Bergen

[3] *Boorder* See, on p. 278, the citation for the *Ships of the Old Navy* website. *L'Espiègle* was sold out of the Royal Navy in 1802, the year of peace

[4] *Nelly Diary 4.* I had no prior knowledge that *Nelly* was a Scottish ship which had been captured and recaptured. As diary editor I had to read each edition of the *Norwich Mercury* 1770–1810. It was the two-line newspaper item that alerted me to the ship's past

¹ *retaken* Recaptured. This also happened to James Sime's 101-ton brig *Aurora* just before he testified to *Nelly*'s provenance; presumably his journey from Dundee to Gt Yarmouth had been to identify his own vessel. *Aurora*, then under his command, was seized by a French privateer 22 Dec. 1798, only to be recaptured in 1799 by HMS *Iris* (TNA: PRO CUST 97/31, 8 Mar. 1800)

² *smallpox* For the introduction of the new vaccine, supplanting the earlier variolation, see vol. 3, chap. 8

³ *ship news Norw. Merc.* 20 Apr. 1799; names of ships [with my italics], masters and ports have been transcribed in their original spelling.

Shipping news had its own shorthand: '*Maria*, Turgens' denotes *Maria*, under Capt. Turgens. 'The *Courier* cutter' denotes a cutter named *Courier*, just as 'the *Scorpion* sloop' is a sloop named *Scorpion*.

Iris, like *L'Espiègle*, was a Royal Naval ship, both regularly bringing in prizes (TNA: PRO CUST 97/31, Collector of Yarmouth to Customs Board, 1799–1800).

A *dogger* and a *schuit* were types of Dutch vessels—a two-masted fishing boat and a flat-bottomed barge

British waters. She entered port on 14 April 1799 under a (merchant) captain named Patteson, with a cargo of oats, having been recaptured from enemy hands. The crucial words, apart from her name, were 'Scotland' and 'retaken'.¹

The item appeared in a miscellany of Yarmouth shipping news which included warship movements, the names of enemy merchant ships captured as prizes by HMS *L'Espiègle*; the arrival home of the body of the son of the Bishop of Lichfield and Coventry; and the birth of triplets on board HMS *Kent*—Admiral Lord Duncan's flagship anchored in Yarmouth Roads, and the ship where that same year the new Jenner smallpox vaccine was first used in Norfolk:²

On Wednesday died Mr Joseph Hallmarke, liquor merchant, of this place [Great Yarmouth].

April 14.   Arrived His Majesty's ship *Glatton*, from the Nore.

April 18.   Arrived His Majesty's ship *Monarch* with a frigate, from the Nore.

Sailed under the *Ganges*, Commodore McDouall, for the Texel, the *America*, *Monmouth*, and *Glatton*, with the *Scorpion* sloop.

On the 14th instant arrived the *Nelly*, Patteson, from Scotland, with oats, retaken; and *Young Elbert Wurster*, from Bordeaux, with brandy and wine, for Hamburgh, taken by the *Courier* cutter.

On the 15th, *De Hortidghand*, from Safia, with skins and gum, was sent in by the *Courier* cutter.

Same day *Juge*, Juff, Srauw [?], *Anna*, Jacobs, from Hamburgh to Amsterdam, with goods, was sent in by *L'Espiègle*. *Maria*, Turgens, from Ostend to Embden [Emden] in ballast, sent in by *Jalouse* cutter.

On the 16th, *Æolus*, Zubevie, from Stetin, with deals; *Sex Sosskende*, Barnkolds, from Norway, with ditto. *Anna*, Beer, from Norway, with bales, sent in by three of His Majesty's cruisers.

On the 17th, a dogger and a schoot were sent in by the *Iris*.

Thursday arrived a bye-boat, having on board the body of Mr Cornwallis, son of the Bishop of Lichfield and Coventry. His remains are to be interred at Broome, in Suffolk.

On the 4th instant a woman was delivered of three children on board the *Kent* man of war, all likely to live.³

William and his father arrived in Great Yarmouth only after *Nelly*'s tortuous year-long passage through the bureaucracy of the Admiralty High Court and Customs. His purchase of the ship for £590 (a sum not recorded other than in his mother's diary) marks the moment when Mary Hardy took up the tale of *Nelly* until the ship's end four years later.

As far as we know, William appointed only one captain in the four years he owned the sloop. This was John Coe, probably a local man as the name is common in north Norfolk. His bride, Hannah Lynes or Loynes, was almost certainly the nineteen-year-old daughter of the innkeepers at the King's Head at Cley, John and Edny/Edna Lynes. John Coe of Cley and his wife Hannah Lynes appear in the Cley registers at their marriage in 1784 and at the baptism of their children John, Robert and Hannah in 1784, 1788 and 1790; only Robert survived the early months of infancy.[1] Captain and Mrs Coe would occasionally call at the Hardys', and relations between owner and skipper seem to have been harmonious. Not once, in a family with a tendency to prickliness, is there any hint of discord with the Coes.

Mary Hardy's coverage of the sloop's movements is patchy, but we learn that on 16 October 1800 William Hardy junior received a written account from John Coe in Liverpool of the ten-week passage from Blakeney. As already discussed, this will have been a particularly troublesome passage, as an earlier shipment in January 1788, despite meeting rough weather, had taken only four weeks.[2] Sadly for her readers Mary Hardy mentions only in passing on 11 May 1802 that Captain Coe was about to sail to Norway for timber.[3] The advantage for William of having his own man at the helm, literally, was that he did not have to travel hundreds of miles overland around the country as much as his father and he himself had done in earlier years. He could trust his captain over arranging the sale of cargoes at the other end, and not once during his four years as a shipowner did William visit Newcastle, Hull or Liverpool or the surrounding areas.

At Coltishall the wherry had been a physical presence; at Letheringsett a distance of four miles separated the berth from the brewery. It is sometimes only by references to the Letheringsett workforce that *Nelly*'s movements can be tracked, as when the Hardys' men carried malt to the ship at Cley (not Blakeney) on 14 March 1801 for shipping to London. On that occasion *Nelly* sailed for the capital on 29 March and returned to Blakeney on 26 April 1801. Newcastle appears to have been the sloop's most regular port of call, as when Mary Hardy noted on 7 July 1800 and 17 October 1801 that *Nelly* had arrived home from Newcastle.

[1] *Cley* NRO: PD 270/5, 270/9, Cley parish registers of baptisms and burials 1779–1814, marriages 1754–1812. Hannah Lynes had been bapt. at Cley in 1765 (NRO: PD 270/4).
  The King's Head was tied to the Letheringsett brewery and kept by John Lynes 1793–1800. The Gazetteer of the Hardys' 101 public houses gives more details (vol. 2)

[2] *Liverpool Diary 4*. The captain in 1788, Francis Wells of Blakeney, went out of business in 1791 (*Norw. Merc.* 5 Feb. 1791).
  As part of the professionalisation of the merchant service skippers had to be able to write to owners, agents and customs officials. Masters of even small seagoing ships had to handle bills of lading, accounts, navigational aids and charts (S.P. Ville, *English Shipowning during the Industrial Revolution*, p. 68).
  The ADM 28 series in the National Archives reveals that many fishermen and seamen could sign their names: see the sections on shipwreck in this chapter and the Sea Fencibles in chap. 9

[3] *Norway Diary 4*. Likely outward-bound cargoes would have been porter and grain

¹ *Watson Diary 4*:
'William went to Blak-
eney afternoon (Mr
Watson valued the
sloop *Nelly* in order for
sale).' This was prob-
ably Capt. John Watson
of Wells.

Merchant ships were
being called up for
government service,
armed and ready: see
Diary 4, pp. 236–7, note
for 27 June 1803

² *North Pole* B. Cozens-
Hardy, 'Havens in North
Norfolk', *Norfolk Arch-
aeology*, vol. 35 (1972),
p. 356.

The author is William
Hardy jnr's great-great-
nephew

Despite the optimistic commercial picture given in much of this chapter the resumption of war with France may have affected the sloop's viability. Not only did William have a sale valuation made by Captain Watson at Blakeney on 27 June 1803, within six weeks of the breakdown of the Peace of Amiens, but no mention is made by Mary Hardy of *Nelly* and her sailings between that item of news and the entry for her last voyage.¹ On the other hand Mary Hardy, by then aged seventy, may just have become increasingly distanced from the world of the sea. It is probable therefore that no firm conclusion can be drawn from *Nelly*'s absence from the diary in those last few months.

Shipwreck

As a glance at an atlas will show, nothing except sea lies between the north Norfolk coastline and the North Pole. So declared Basil Cozens-Hardy. Consequently, 'These shores seem to catch and divert the tidal currents.'² Jonathan Hooton identifies the dangers posed by an accident of geography:

left The grave of Capt. Thomas Bond (d.1818 aged 55) and his wife Susanna (d. 1829 aged 61), near the west door of Blakeney Church.

William Hardy jnr and the Holt miller John Wade sailed on Capt. Bond's ship from Blakeney to Newcastle in June 1793. The Hardys sometimes bought coal and cinders direct from him, so he acted both as a sea-captain and a merchant.

This was a common pattern. Mary Hardy shows us that farmers and manufacturers would deal direct with the captains at Blakeney and Wells over arranging cargoes and voyages; at other times they used non-sailing intermediaries in the form of merchants at the ports.

Matters could be planned weeks in advance, as when William Hardy snr and jnr started buying barley at Holt market on successive Saturdays from 8 Dec. 1787 ready for the ill-fated voyage by Capt. Francis Wells to Liverpool four weeks later. Deliveries of grain to Blakeney by the Hardys' men also began weeks before the sailing date.

Having a ship of his own, with a trusted captain, eased the administrative burden for William [*MB · 2000*]

above Newcastle upon Tyne: the quay and Exchange. Unlike Blakeney it had a massive crane. *Nelly* called here on her round trips to collect coal, and it was from here that she made her final voyage [*drawing by W. Westall; engraving by E. Finden 1829, detail*]

The north Norfolk coast projects out at right angles from the trend of the rest of the east coast and acts like a vast breakwater waiting to trap ships sailing down the Yorkshire and Lincolnshire coasts, being driven southwards before an unrelenting northerly gale.[1]

Daniel Defoe and George Christopher Davies, 160 years apart, described in powerful language the fight for life of ships off the Norfolk coast.[2] Davies witnessed the awful situation of fishing vessels off Great Yarmouth, with ropes and anchor cables breaking as they tried to ride out a storm in what he calls 'the cruelty of the scene':

It was a pitiful sight to see at least a score of smacks riding at anchor in the Roads, waiting for the tide to turn, when there would be chance of gaining safety; the spindrift hid them every minute, and it appeared impossible that they could live for many hours in such a boil.[3]

[1] *breakwater* J. Hooton, *The Glaven Ports*, p. 265

[2] *Defoe* On his tour he listened to tales of the hazards of the coast. However strong the anchor and cable they still might not hold in a storm. The ships needed 'good ground tackle to ride it out, which is very hard to do there, the sea coming very high upon them' (D. Defoe, *A Tour through the Whole Island of Great Britain*, vol. 1, pp. 69, 70).

Anchor ropes have been touched on under 'cargoes' (p. 259)

[3] *cruelty* G.C. Davies, *Norfolk Broads and Rivers*, pp. 188–91

1 *Burgess* He had taken over from John and Edny/Edna Lynes at the King's Head, Cley on their deaths in 1800.

He may have been consulted as a parish officer involved in the administration of wreck (*The Whole Duty of Constables, by an acting magistrate* (2nd edn Norwich, 1815), pp. 70–2)

2 *Meakin* Revd John, Curate of Holt 1802–04

3 *Coke* Thomas William, of Holkham Hall, west of Wells. He could have been consulted in his capacity as a JP for his advice on wreck, or as lord of the manor with rights over the wreck.

Coroners' inquests were not then required for bodies washed ashore. An Act introducing special provisions for the burial of bodies cast ashore following shipwreck was not passed until 1808. It then became mandatory for church-wardens and overseers of the poor to recover the body 'and cause every such body to be decently interred in the churchyard . . . at the expense of the parish' (*The Whole Duty of Constables*, p. 71)

4 *Nelly Diary 4.* The double spread of Mary Hardy's entries for 5–17 Feb. 1804 is illustrated in *Diary 4*, p. 252

This was almost certainly *Nelly*'s situation, caught in a very severe storm as she approached her home port on her last passage from Newcastle. She was just outside the relative safety of Blakeney Pit, where she could have dropped anchor in the hope of riding out the storm. Instead she broke up. In the following days her owner and his farm steward George Phillippo, in an agonising search, found her mast and some of her wreckage and rigging along the shore where the turbulence and currents had carried them westwards. One crew member's body was found, swept ten miles along to Burnham Overy Staithe or Creek.

The loss of *Nelly* is best told by Mary Hardy herself:

[1804] FEBRUARY 11, SATURDAY . . . A very stormy night, wind very high.

FEBRUARY 12, SUNDAY Wind very high all day and stormy. Mr Hardy and I at home all day, the weather being very bad. Heard at evening that William's ship the *Nelly* was wrecked near Blakeney Pit and the whole crew consisting of the captain John Coe, 3 men and one boy perished. (She was coming from Newcastle loaden with coals and oil cake) no part of which was insured. William and Mary Ann went to Holt Church afternoon, Mr Joshua Smith, Rector of Holt, died this morning.

FEBRUARY 13, MONDAY A sharp frost. William and G. Phillippo went to Cley morning 7, called at Michael Burgess's [1] then went to Blakeney and from thence to Stiffkey by the seaside in search of the ship wreck, found a good deal of the rigging and mast and the cabin box where the Captain's papers were, came home evening 6. Mr Hardy went to Holt to meet the Commissioners of Income [Tax], came home evening 4.

FEBRUARY 14, TUESDAY A sharp frost. Mr Hardy at home all day. William and G. Phillippo went again to Blakeney and Stukey [Stiffkey] and Holkham in search of the ship wreck and had it removed to Wells. George came home evening 4, William went to Wells and slept there.

FEBRUARY 15, *Ash Wednesday* A frost in the morning, fine day. Mr Hardy at home all day. Mr Meakin dined, drank tea and supped here. [2] William went from Wells to Holkham, spoke to Mr Coke and went after the wreck all day, came home evening 10. One of the bodies of the *Nelly*'s crew was taken up at Burnham Overy, his name is Randall, he was carried to Wells Church . . . [3]

FEBRUARY 25, SATURDAY A sharp frost, wind high, a great [?deal] of snow fell in the night and continued great part of the day. William went to Wells morning 8 to sell the wreck of the ship *Nelly*, sold very little, came home evening 7. Mr Hardy at home all day . . . [4]

Nothing more is heard of *Nelly* and her crew; if further bodies were recovered the diarist does not mention them. The Wells register shows the dead man to have been Richard 'Randle', who was buried there on 16 February—the 28th anniversary of his public baptism at Cley.[1]

However Richard Randall has another memorial, as do his captain John Coe and a third man lost that night. This was John Lynes, almost certainly the captain's 41-year-old brother-in-law, who left a widow Ann and two surviving sons William and Thomas. While their ship is not named, we are told that all three men drowned; it would seem they did not die of exposure. Their service in the Blakeney and Sheringham Sea Fencibles sheds light on their movements and days of exercise, and gives the final entry against each of the three names: 'Drowned 12 February'. They were the only three men from that unit of Sea Fencibles who drowned in the month ending 24 February 1804. They did not exercise under their Royal Naval commanding officer Captain Peter Ribouleau on 29 January and 5, 12 and 19 February 1804, which would fit in with their voyage to Newcastle.[2]

The Sea Fencibles, as armed civilians, will be discussed more fully in chapter 9. Composed of fishermen, seamen, shipwrights and beachmen with useful skills, they were trained by petty officers and served under the command of full-time officers in the Royal Navy—a far cry from their more amateur counterparts, the land-based Volunteers. The records name large numbers of these men as service in the Sea Fencibles preserved them from the press gang, so there was quite a rush to sign up. The units were hurriedly formed in 1803 to meet the anticipated invasion threat, and the roll call of names for the 131 men in the Blakeney and Sheringham unit shows that *Nelly* would not have been at sea on certain days as Coe and Randall were exercising.[3]

Arguing from omission is an uncertain business, but Mary Hardy's terse record suggests that all her son's energies were directed to salvaging what he could and to administration. No mention is made in her diary of contact with the widows and families of captain and crew until William and his cousin Mary, daughter of the Whissonsett grocer Nathaniel Raven, called on Mrs Coe at Cley for tea on 21 June 1804.[4] Whether the widow was given any help and support

[1] *Randall* Son of Matthew and Alice, of Cley, he had been bapt. at Cley 16 Feb. 1776 (NRO: PD 679/7, for Wells; PD 270/4, for Cley, where the name Randall features regularly)

[2] *drowned* TNA: PRO ADM 28/14, Navy Board, Sea Fencibles pay lists, Cromer to Fosdyke Wash [Lincs] 1803–04.

John, son of John and Edna Lynes, was bapt. at Cley 14 Dec. 1762; Hannah Coe was thus his younger sister. He married Ann Mussett, and their children were bapt. at Cley in 1789, 1791, 1793 and 1795; William and Thomas were aged 14 and 11 at the time of their father's death.

The ship's boy was not old enough to serve in the Sea Fencibles and cannot be traced in these well-preserved and detailed records

[3] *roll call* John Coe and Richard Randall put their signatures to the days of exercise on 9, 16, 23 and 30 Oct. 1803 and collected their pay. Of the 131 men in the Blakeney and Sheringham unit, 38 could write their names (TNA: PRO ADM 28/14). The absences from days of exercise show that Coe and Randall did not always sail together

[4] *Mrs Coe Diary 4*

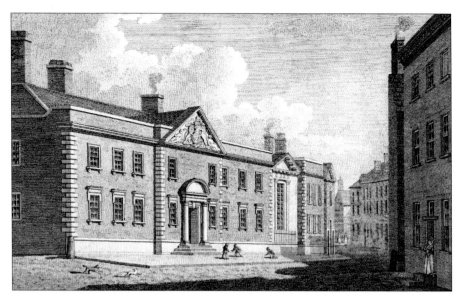

above Trinity House, in the centre of Hull. The buildings and chapel, dating from 1457, were remodelled in 1753 and 1772, with a hospital and training school attached.

Trinity House, the body responsible for safety at sea, was granted its royal charter in 1514; the placing of seamarks was added to its duties in 1566. Lowestoft was chosen in 1609 for the first lighthouse to be built in the British Isles, to improve the chances of colliers beating up and down the east coast at a very dangerous point along their route.

Mary and William Hardy and Mary Ann toured Trinity House on their visit to Hull in May 1803—having taken care to travel overland on their long round trip [*drawing by B. Gale; engraving by I. Taylor c.1790*]

---

[1] *nurse* Vol. 1, app. 1.c, pp. 712–13

[2] *curate* John Meakin, still in his twenties, was one of the Evangelicals admired by Mary Hardy and her children. This new breed chose to override parochial boundaries and also to focus on pastoral care (vol. 3, chap. 3). The curate came to the aid of a stricken friend who was not his parishioner

is not recorded. However the diarist hired the widowed Ann Lynes as a nurse in her last illness 1807–08, on a high wage, as noted in volume 1.[1]

The diary presents calamity as a private matter. The Holt curate, five years younger than William, made a long visit on 15 February in the hope of catching his friend. Ash Wednesday was a busy day in the Church's calendar and John Meakin's rector had just died, yet he stayed on for hours. No other friends of the Hardys are recorded as coming to offer sympathy.[2]

The emphasis of the diary is on the economic aspects— indeed, the commercial benefits—of shipwreck, as will be shown. The humanitarian side is rarely touched on, in marked contrast to the anguished accounts submitted to the press by individual correspondents: 'The morning's dawn exhibited such a scene of complicated distress, as excited horror in every breath . . . poor creatures lashed to the masts, and some on pieces of wreck . . .'[1]

We cannot conclude from the diarist's tight-lipped record that the Hardys and their circle were unfeeling. Leaders of local society, used to working together intermittently for twenty years to defend the coast from invasion and touched by the poignant scenes of seamen struggling for their lives in the surf, started to exert pressure to introduce the first lifeboat for Norfolk.[2] An early hint of this new humanitarian spirit appeared in November 1804, eight months after the storms in which *Nelly* and so many others were lost, in a report of a meeting at Cromer of 31 October. A committee had been appointed that night to provide a Cromer lifeboat at an estimated cost of £300, Edmund Bartell junior serving on the new body and his sister Charlotte immediately joining him in subscribing to the fund.[3] Within two weeks

[1] *distress Norw. Merc.* 7 Nov. 1789, referring to the morning of 31 Oct.

[2] *poignant* Edmund Bartell jnr depicted the horrors of shipwreck, and felt for the beach spectators suffering 'the most torturing anxiety for the safety of those who are so nearly allied to them . . .' (*Cromer considered as a Watering Place*, pp. 18–20)

[3] *fund* Charlotte Bartell and her father Edmund, the Holt surgeon, each gave a guinea; so did William Hardy jnr, as stated earlier (p. 232). Edmund jnr contributed 3 guineas.

Lord Suffield, of Gunton Hall, gave £21 (*Norw. Merc.* 3 Nov., 17 Nov. 1804)

left Sheringham fishermen in the early 20th century. Men and boys such as these were active in more than their prime trade. They were employed in unloading and loading beached ships, and long before lifeboats were introduced they risked their lives trying to save shipwrecked crews.

Table 4.5.1 (page 266) shows that on the night *Nelly* was lost Sheringham fishermen rescued all 20 crew and two passengers on the large barque *Dale*, bound for the W. Indies. They also saved three of the four crew of the Sunderland brig *Hannah*.

The Hardys were not given to trumpeting their charitable donations, but William Hardy jnr allowed his name to be published over his subscription of a guinea in support of the families of seven Sheringham fishermen drowned in the storms of 11 Nov. 1807 [*from a postcard dated 1907*]

1 *lifeboat fund Norw. Merc.* 15 Dec. 1804

2 *humanitarianism* This already existed over parish burials. Even before the mandatory requirement of the 1808 Act, Wells, like some other coastal parishes, customarily buried the remains of seamen with no means of identification. The Revd Samuel Horsfall, ignorant of the names of those brought in by the sea, noted the burials in the register: eg 'Anonymous: A stranger found dead upon the shore' (NRO: PD 679/6, 8 Oct. 1792, 14 Mar. 1793).

Such burials, like those of paupers, came at the expense of the ratepayers in a public display of humanity

3 *lifesaving* R. Malster, *Saved from the Sea* (Terence Dalton Ltd, Lavenham, 1974).

The impetus for the Cromer scheme came from the success of the Bawdsey lifeboat in Suffolk in rescuing eight people from the brig *Pallas* in the storms of Feb. 1804 (R. Malster, p. 72)

4 *Cromer boat* R. Malster, *Saved from the Sea*, pp. 72, 273, 274. Henry Greathead designed and built the first lifeboat, *Original,* for South Shields 1789–90 (D. Keys and K. Smith, *Tall Ships on the Tyne*,

the lifeboat fund had reached £295. Within six weeks it had reached £613, double the necessary figure, reflecting the diffusion of a public spirit beyond the inner circle of fishermen and beachmen who had traditionally shouldered the burden of rescue alone—and were still to risk their lives in the future as the backbone of the lifeboat crews.[1] It is stating the obvious that lifeboats did not save only local craft and crews, but rowed out to all ships plying the coast, whether from different parts of Britain or from abroad. The sea even in time of war fostered the spread of this humanitarianism.[2]

The story of the Cromer lifeboat and the wider context of lifesaving at sea is told by Robert Malster.[3] The town turned to Henry Greathead of South Shields, at the mouth of the Tyne, for the design of the 25-foot (7·6-metre) non-self-righting boat propelled by ten oars or sweeps. The Cromer boat, the first in a distinguished line, was transferred to Wells-next-the-Sea in 1830 where she continued her long and active service until 1851; Blakeney did not get a lifeboat until 1862.[4] Out of a series of maritime disasters came this symptom of a more general change in manners: a greater sensitivity; a determination to act; the suppression of prize-fighting, animal baiting and cockfighting. These threads are drawn together in chapter 7 in this volume.

For the Hardy family there was no public expression of sorrow. Possibly at William's request the loss of *Nelly* was not reported in the press alongside the accounts of the many other ships driven to their end that night. The Rector of Letheringsett, John Burrell, customarily provided detailed copy for the Norwich newspapers, but helping Holt's curate may have taken priority. He did not take up his pen for *Nelly*.

While a shipping disaster could bring personal and financial misery to those directly involved, it was to others a decided economic opportunity. As the local newspapers would frequently announce, coal, timber and other cargoes would wash up on the shore or, more usually, be sold from a beached or wrecked ship, the wreck herself then being sold in lots. Daniel Defoe, struck by the amount of shipwreck timber put to good use whether for barns or outside privies on the coast between Winterton and Cromer, described the phenomenon in his unsentimental way:

I was surprised to see . . . that the farmers, and country people had scarce a barn, or a shed, or a stable; nay, not the pales of their yards, and gardens, not a hogstye, not a necessary-house, but what was built of old planks, beams, wales and timbers, etc, the wrecks of ships, and ruins of mariners and merchants' fortunes . . . [1]

Echoing Defoe's observations, Hamish Robertson summarises a contemporary but unnamed source, writing in 1799 of a notorious North Sea hazard east of the Firth of Tay. Again the coastal farmers, and their livestock, benefited from the sea's bounty:

Regarding the need for a light on Bell Rock, it was estimated that in recent years 70 ships were wrecked on Bell Rock . . ., during which time vast quantities of wreckage was washed ashore in the Tay estuary. Farmers fenced yards with mahogany and teak, and pigsties were made of cedar. [2]

It was a fortunate merchant who could arrange for shipwreck sales to coincide with the local fair, thereby attracting more than the usual number of prospective customers. John Mann advertised on 17 July 1790 that he had wreck for sale on Cley Fair day, 30 July, in the form of 'Part of the wreck of the ship *Northumberland*', including planks, timber for posts, iron, rope, and masts; also her cargo of empty casks—100 wine pipes and 80 porter barrels. Following winter storms a few months later the shipwrecked *Diligence* was for sale at Trimingham and Mundesley, again in the form of planks, posts, beams, deck deals and iron; also the wreck of the three-year-old 70-ton brigantine *Keattie* on Trimingham beach. A year later *Leviathan*'s entire cargo of Norway timber was for sale at Cley. [3]

In the week that the recaptured *Nelly* was brought into Great Yarmouth the *Norwich Mercury* advertised the wreck of the sloop *Hopewell*, of Hull, stranded on Runton Beach; her anchors, cables, sails, yards and stores were for sale at Cromer, also six tons of alabaster forming part of the cargo. [4]

As well as William's ship two others named *Nelly* came to grief on the Norfolk coast early in 1804. 'Last week the *Nelly*, of Sunderland, struck on the Scroby Sand, was deserted by her crew, and on Sunday she drifted on the shore near the jetty' (at Great Yarmouth). The 244-ton *Nelly*, now given as of North Shields and lying by the ballast quay, was for auc-

pp. 27–8).

Edmund Bartell jnr in his 1806 Cromer work wrote of his great pleasure that 'one of Mr Greathead's lifeboats has been lately established here' (*Cromer considered as a Watering Place*, p. 20).

A boat very similar in age and design to Norfolk's first lifeboat is on display to the public at Redcar, N. Yorks. *Zetland*, also by Greathead, 29½ feet long (9 metres) and also with ten sweeps, saved over 500 lives at Redcar 1802–80 (D. Phillipson, 'The oldest lifeboat in the world', *The Lifeboat* (summer 2002), pp. 30–3)

---

[1] *wrecks* D. Defoe, *A Tour through the Whole Island of Great Britain*, vol. 1, p. 71. A wale, as in the gunwale of an open boat, is the ridge edging a vessel like the rim of a bowl

[2] *Bell Rock* H. Robertson, *Mariners of Dundee*, p. 84. Following the loss of HMS *York* in 1804 with all on board Robert Stevenson built a lighthouse there 1807–11, still in use today. Bell Rock is also known as the Inchcape Rock

[3] *sales Norw. Merc.* 11 Dec. 1790; 12, 26 Feb. 1791; 10 Mar. 1792

[4] *sloop Norw. Merc.* 6 Apr. 1799. Very

shortly afterwards the 400-ton British-built barque *Prudent* was for sale at Weybourne over the four days 20–23 May 1799, with her mast, bowsprit, 2½-inch-thick deck deals (6·4 cm), main and deck oak beams, floor timbers, and 'about 20,000 feet [6096 metres] of 2½, 3, 4, 5, and 6 inches oak plank' (*Norw. Merc.* 11 May 1799)

---

[1] *244-ton Nelly Norw. Merc.* 21, 28 Jan. 1804

[2] *300-ton Nelly Norw. Merc.* 10, 24 Mar. 1804

[3] *Dale Norw. Merc.* 24 Mar. 1804; the deals measured 4·6 to 12·2 metres

[4] *Customs* TNA: PRO CUST 96/165, 19 July 1798. Customs were keen to ensure that unloading shipwreck goods was nonetheless done in a controlled way, to prevent looting: 'We say that in all cases of shipwreck the labourers employed can only work when weather and light permit and that in the intervals they do not quit the spot but wait until opportunity offer to go on with their labour' (TNA: PRO CUST 97/31, p. 39, 13 July 1799). Wreck occupied five pages of guidance for the justices (J. Burn, *The Justice of the Peace,*

tion at Great Yarmouth, 'also her anchors, cables, etc', for the benefit of the underwriters.[1] A 300-ton *Nelly*, waiting by the south gate at Yarmouth to be repaired after gale damage, 'took fire by some accident in the cabin, which baffled all attempts to get it under—she is nearly destroyed'.[2]

The wreck of the large, 406-ton barque *Dale*, which was driven ashore the night that William's sloop foundered, and which features in table 4.5.1, was for sale at Lower Shering-ham where she lay broken on the beach; the hulk wreck, not her cargo, included 'new deck deals, from 15 to 40 feet in length, [and] a large quantity of English oak plank'.[3]

As the Customs confirmed, and unlike confiscated goods and prize goods, wreck was not subject to many controls. Sales to individuals could go ahead fairly promptly as long as centuries-old manorial rights on wreck were respected. Vessels lying at the mercy of the elements could quickly lose all value and leave little to be salvaged for the stricken owners and underwriters, and the speedy sale of hulk and cargo was recognised as essential. Stranded vessels were also vulnerable to pilfering, and those unloading the goods were required to stay by the wreck on guard night and day.[4]

We can chart the locals' reaction to the washing up of this bounty on their doorstep. Throughout her diary Mary Hardy records ships in distress and wrecked, both as press reports and, at Letheringsett, as news heard first-hand. At Coltishall she lived eleven miles from the sea at its closest point, and her husband is not recorded at any shipwreck sales in those years.

The situation changed once they moved to a village by the coast, and they quickly came to represent the type of house-holder remarked upon by Defoe and Robertson. From long before William pursued his cold and weary quest along the shore searching for the remains of *Nelly*, he and his father had been accustomed to profiting from shipwreck, assidu-ously attending shipwreck sales. At the time that the Hardys were pressing ahead with exports to Newcastle and Liver-pool they would have been conscious of the dangers of the sea. Nineteen-year-old William walked with the brewery clerk Robert Starling to Cley and Weybourne in November 1789 to view the wrecked shipping; two months later 'Lamb and William went to Weybourne for a ship mast.' William

Hardy senior and junior had a wasted journey to Weybourne in December 1792 expecting 'the sale of a shipwreck on that beach, it was not to be sold till tomorrow'.[1]

William Hardy, enticed by a cargo of grindstones, attended the auction of the Dutch sloop and former prize *Welden and Weldenken* at Cley in October 1781, and took his thirteen-year-old son William to the sale of the stranded 300-ton *Industry* at Blakeney two years later. The two were present at the sale of a stranded Portuguese ship, the 200-ton *Assumçao*, at Blakeney in 1789. William Hardy, the Revd John Burrell and Mr Cooper of Holt bought shipwreck at Weybourne in November 1789; in December 1792 William Hardy and others were back at Blakeney for the sale of the materials taken from the Danish ship *North Star* lying on Stiffkey Sands. Two weeks later the brewer went alone to a shipwreck sale at Weybourne.[2]

Unloading a vessel moored not at a quay but beached on land—whether deliberately, as part of the pattern of local trade, or helplessly stranded after being driven ashore by storms—was time-consuming and exacting. Mary Hardy describes the complexity of unloading a stranded collier at Salthouse in February 1791. Whereas the surgeon–artist at Cromer, in his customary highly-coloured language, had been captivated by the picturesque nature of the business with its grouping of horses and carts, men and boys, all 'connecting maritime with rural occupations',[3] the value of a more prosaic diary lies in its wealth of detail not generally available in customs records and press advertisements. Mary Hardy unselfconsciously depicts not only the laboriousness of unloading down the side of a ship in 1791 but the close working relationship of her husband and son:

[1791] FEBRUARY 3, THURSDAY Storms of hail and snow, wind high. Mr Hardy and William rid [rode] to Salthouse in little cart to see a ship that was driven on the beach loaden with coals, but could not git near her the marshes being all under water, came home evening 6…

FEBRUARY 9, WEDNESDAY A very fine day. Mr Hardy and William went to Salthouse about noon, bought a ship load of coals that was stranded on the beach last Wednesday night at 12s per chaldron, agreed with the fishermen to bring on shore for 5s per chalder [chaldron] and a quart of beer.

and Parish Officer (16th edn London, 1788), vol. 4, pp. 463–8)

---

[1] *wrecks* Diary MS: 8 Nov. 1789, 7 Jan. 1790, 31 Dec. 1792

[2] *sales* Diary 2: 12 Oct. 1781, 13 Nov. 1783, 12 Mar. 1789, 9 Nov. 1789, 17 Dec. 1792, 1 Jan. 1793. Mr Cooper, as a builder, benefited from local access to timber

[3] *picturesque* Edmund Bartell jnr, *Cromer considered as a Watering Place*, p. 22

above A narrow path beside the Customs House at Cley leads to the mill and quay from the former King's Head.

Customs officers and JPs shared the locals' desire to execute the speedy salvage of wrecks and sale of cargoes   *[MB·2003]*

facing page Wensleydale,
a schooner undergoing
the centuries-old and
laborious process of
unloading between
tides at Cromer in 1872.
  Cargoes were lifted
off ships wrecked on
the beach in the same
manner
[*photograph by D.W.
Savin, detail: Norfolk
Heritage Centre, Norwich*]

---

¹ *Salthouse Diary 2.*
The Hardys' tied house,
the Dun Cow, faced the
coast road at Salthouse,
and was well placed to
honour the promise of
beer for the men. One
of the beneficiaries of
the wreck, Elizabeth
Sheppard, ran the
Feathers at Holt

² *sales Diary 4*: 25 Feb.
1799, 21 Mar. 1799, 10
Apr. 1799, 21 May 1799,
11 Feb. 1800, 16 Jan.
1805, 25 Mar. 1807,
22 Mar. 1808

³ *barn floor Diary 4*:
25 Mar. 1807; this was
Michael Burgess, of the
King's Head at Cley.
  Revd Mr Burrell too
held a stock of ship-
wreck timber. During
their quarrel with the
rector the Hardys found
themselves barred at
their side door into the
churchyard by ship-
wreck planking put up
by the rector as fencing
(*Diary 2*: 25–26 Nov.
1790)

FEBRUARY 10, THURSDAY A dry day, wind very high. William went to Salthouse after breakfast to see to the coals, the men could git very few up to town the water being very rough, Lamb went for a wagonload. William came home evening 6. Mr Hardy walked up to Holt forenoon to sell some coals . . .

FEBRUARY 11, FRIDAY Wind very high forenoon . . . William brewed. Mr Hardy rid to Salthouse afternoon to see to the coals, Mrs Sheppard had 1½ chalders.

FEBRUARY 12, SATURDAY A fine day. William went to Salthouse morning 7 to see the coals measured out of the ship, came home evening 7 . . . Lamb went for 2 loads of coals to Salthouse . . . ¹

The unloading was still progressing at Salthouse on 14 and 18 February, and on 2 March 1791 father and son were at Trimingham by 6 am for the sale of the wrecked brigantine *Keattie*. Despite the constant risk of fire, the local malthouses and brewhouses required a large of amount of seasoned wood, and the Hardys' appetite for timber was rarely sated.

  In the later years of the diary William is recorded regularly attending sales of wreck, such as at Gimingham, Salthouse, Runton and Weybourne in 1799, Wells in 1800, Salthouse again in 1805, and Cley in 1807 and 1808.² Mary Hardy testifies to the truth of Defoe's observation on recycling: 'William went to Cley afternoon, bought some shipwreck off Burges for a barn floor, came home evening 8.'³

  The drama of the story of *Nelly*, a ship which in twelve years of service knew only two and a half years of peace, can obscure a hard economic reality. Only small vessels could reach north Norfolk's quays and Broadland's village staithes. Thus, whether relying on shallow-draughted seagoing ships like *Nelly* or on transhipping into keels and wherries from larger ships, the manufacturers in Norfolk's hinterland stood at some disadvantage over the supply of fuel to power their plant. The cinders and coal on which they depended could reach the maltings and breweries only in small loads: in the Hardys' case carried in keels and wherries of 12–16 chaldrons to Coltishall or in a 1½-chaldron cart to Letheringsett. A maltster and brewer at King's Lynn or Great Yarmouth was placed far more competitively. That small- and even medium-scale manufacturers away from major ports survived into the railway age is a testament to the dogged determination of the seamen, watermen and their vessels.

While the port of Blakeney and Cley supplied a vital need for the manufacturers and farmers deep in the hinterland beyond Fakenham and East Dereham by importing coal and exporting grain, it is doubtful whether small-scale maritime ventures were consistently profitable in the period of the diary. The transport ratios quoted earlier make sense only if applied to long sea passages on ships with good carrying capacity—and, probably, to passages made in time of peace. Mary Hardy reveals the many vicissitudes and uncertainties associated with the shipping trade, including day-to-day hurdles often overlooked, such as negotiations with shipmasters over dates of sailings and volumes of cargo.[1]

When preparing his annual accounts and seeing a marked fall in his *Nelly*'s value William might have echoed the words of an earlier Cley trader, William Jennis, that 'the ship is in debt to me.'[2] The London firm of Michael Henley and Son, which managed to succeed in making money from long-haul shipping, favoured ships of between 200 and 400 tons for, as their agent put it in 1788, 'Small vessels are in general but pickpockets.'[3]

[1] *hurdles* Negotiations could be protracted, especially when other manufacturers such as the Thornage miller William Cooke were using the same vessel to ship their produce: 'Mr Wells [the captain] and Mr Cook here forenoon, did not agree to the freight to Liverpool' (*Diary 2*: 12 Dec. 1787)

[2] *Jennis* R. Jefferson, 'The *William and Thomas*', *The Glaven Historian*, no. 5 (2002), p. 63. In 1726–33 William Jennis's ship would regularly voyage to Newcastle in ballast, returning with 32 chaldrons of coal; in 1729–31, of 15 round trips, 11 made a loss, with further losses 1731–33. After an expensive trip to Rotterdam in 1728, Jennis (d.1766) entered on the bottom line: 'The ship is in deate to me £9 5s 6d!' (p. 63). A table (pp. 60–1) shows that Jennis often imported cinders, suggesting that cinder ovens had not then been built at Cley Quay

[3] *pickpockets* S.P. Ville, *English Shipowning during the Industrial Revolution*, p. 44. See also his chap. 6 on profitability, rates of return and insurance in relation to transatlantic, Baltic and coastal trade (pp. 119–45)

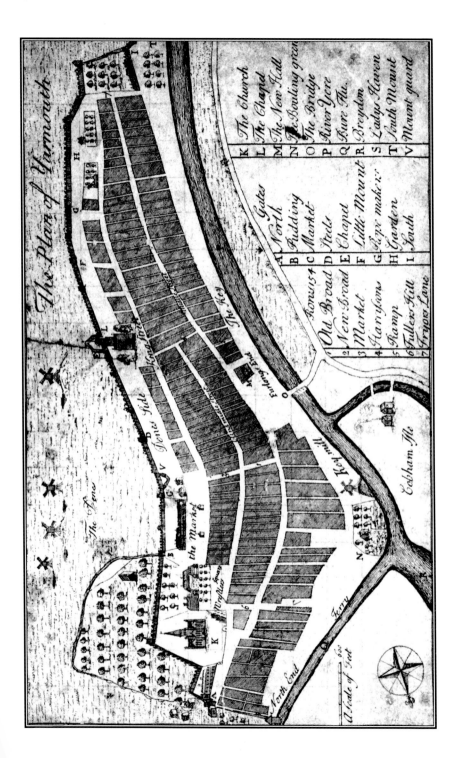

The Plan of Yarmouth

A	North		K	The Church
	Gates		L	The Chapel
B	Pudding		M	The New Hall
C	Market		N	The Bowling green
D	Steels		O	The Bridge
E	Chapel		P	River Yare
F	Little Mount		Q	Bure Flu.
G	Cap: maker:		R	Breydon
H	Garden		S	Ladys Haven
I	South		T	South Mount
			V	Mount guard

1	Old Broad	Row 154
2	New Broad	
3	Market	
4	Harrisons	
5	Ramp	
6	Fullers Hill	
7	Frijors Lane	

A Scale of feet

Strains placed on the Customs

Until now private enterprise, represented by merchants and manufacturers, traders and merchant seamen, has predominated in this chapter. This section and the next will feature an aspect mentioned only at intervals so far: the role of the State in the daily operation and support of seaborne trade. The customs service and, to a much lesser extent, the excise service regulated and oversaw maritime trade at the ports, backed up where necessary by the Royal Navy. Frequently run together as one in the modern mind, the Customs and the Excise were distinct services in Mary Hardy's time, with entirely different origins, histories and traditions. They did not unite as Customs and Excise until 1909.[1]

Customs houses, surviving today in forms recognisable to the diarist, graced the four Norfolk seaports of Great Yarmouth, Blakeney with Cley, Wells-next-the-Sea and King's Lynn (*plates 33–35*). Inside these handsome buildings the work was carried on at a frenetic pace, to judge from the letters and reports which have been preserved. Overloaded with tasks, required to work unsociable hours,[2] yet having to be painstaking in all their duties, the men of the customs service often went unsung at the time. In the extracts for *Nelly*'s early years we have already glimpsed the immense care taken by the officers at Great Yarmouth over just one insignificant Scottish sloop. This was during a conflict when between ten and eighteen prizes a week were being brought into that port, as the Collector's papers reveal.[3] And these prizes had to be handled on top of all the routine tasks of rummaging (searching ships), collection of import duties and clearing vessels coastwise and for foreign trade.

Nelly had required a very great deal of effort by the Collector of Customs and the Comptroller of the Port of Great

[1] *two services* Customs dated back to the reign of John in the early 13th century, and it still relied on 'farming' (the purchase of places, the leasing of collection of duties and pocketing of the fees) despite partial reforms in the 17th and 18th centuries. The Customs collected duties on imported goods.

The Excise dated only from the mid-17th century and was a tightly run, professional service which had as its prime focus the raising of indirect taxation through duties on malt, beer and other home-manufactured excise-able goods. For details see vol. 2, chap. 11.

Each service was run from the City of London by a Board of Commissioners

[2] *hours* The customs officers at Cley were still at work at about 9 pm when William Hardy jnr cleared his ship for Liverpool (*Diary 4*: 8 Aug. 1800)

[3] *prizes* TNA: PRO CUST 97/31, in summer 1799

---

facing page Gt Yarmouth: this plan of 1753, published 1779, is oriented east-southeast.

The long quay ['The Key'] runs from the Haven Bridge (centre) south towards the sea. The porticoed Town Hall [M] on Hall Quay stands on open ground downstream of the bridge. A ferry crosses the last stretch of the River Bure (left).

The town was built on this long spit in grid form, and is seen bisected by 154 very narrow rows leading away from the quays. The large parish church of St Nicholas [K] and chapel of St George [L] stand close to the Denes inside the seaward-facing wall [*plan by Henry Swinden: Norfolk Heritage Centre, Norwich*]

above Gt Yarmouth: South Quay *c*.1840.
A herring merchant's house of 1720 (left)
became the Customs House in 1802.
   In the French wars prizes were moored on
the River Yare from here down to the South
Gate. A huge public dinner was held here in
1814 for peace, as described in chapter 10.

The figures in the foreground appear to
be watching a flag-bedecked ship-launch
across the river at Southtown (on the far
right), where the hull runs down the slip
bearing a jubilant crowd
[*drawing by G. Fitt; lithograph by Day &
Haghe*]

---

[1] *Comptroller* In the
smaller ports the posts
of Collector and Comp-
troller were often vested
in one man

[2] *ship's papers* London
would regularly send
the Collectors lists of
ships whose registers
had been lost or been
captured by enemy
privateers. The Board
of Customs instructed
the Collector of Blak-
eney and Cley 9 Feb.
1802 to be vigilant over
detecting fraudulent
papers and 'to use
every means in your
power to detect any

Yarmouth and their staff.[1] They had to identify her original
passage and cargo; examine the authenticity of her alleged
capture by the Dutch and recapture by the Royal Navy; find
whether the ship's papers had been destroyed or been taken
by the enemy—a vital issue for the Navy and Customs;[2]
investigate the fate of the British and Dutch cargoes and
crews; arrange for interviews and obtain affidavits from
Scottish shipmasters in Dundee; and ensure smooth liaison
between the Admiralty High Court, which had the power to
declare (or 'condemn', as it was termed officially) the ship
as a prize, and the Board of Customs in London.
   All this took a year. Only then could William Hardy junior
make his purchase, with his father beside him at Yarmouth
to give advice; and only then could the purchase money be
put towards defraying all the expenses and recompensing
the owner Robert Mathew in Dundee. The balance was presumably forwarded to *Nelly*'s rescuers on HMS *L'Éspiègle*.

In 1798 the customs service at Blakeney and Cley had thirteen officers and boatmen including their head of station, the Collector. A small affair compared with the major ports it nevertheless offered a good range of services.[1] Recent research suggests that the 1790s marked the decade when the Customs became more professional; perhaps the strains of war made this imperative. Even so, whereas excise officers were kept distinct from the community they taxed, being posted at frequent intervals around England and Wales and always well outside their native area, customs officers were often local men remaining in post for years and even decades—with all the possibilities for influence and impropriety which long postings could encourage.[2]

What is striking about the customs records preserved in the National Archives is the contrast between the workloads of neighbouring ports. Great Yarmouth groaned under the weight of wartime business; but the small ports of Blakeney and Cley and Wells, with no Royal Navy presence owing to their silted harbours, handled mostly matters of personnel, petitions, trade and wreck; prizes lay well outside their normal routine. Even the considerable port of Newcastle had nothing to match Great Yarmouth's load. Newcastle lay too far north to be on the invasion coast, whereas the flagship of Admiral Duncan and later Admiral Keith would often be at anchor in Yarmouth Roads 1798–1805. Great Yarmouth's quaysides were kept busy with sloops of war bringing in their trophies, mostly with Dutch and Danish names.

Although not a royal dockyard Great Yarmouth worked closely with the Navy. It was one of few places outside the capital where the Admiralty High Court sat, and the proximity of Admiralty personnel and the warships' comings and goings added greatly to the workload of those administering the port. The excise cutter *Lively* also operated out of Great Yarmouth, the nearest other cutters north and south being based in Yorkshire (at Hull) and in Essex (at Harwich), as shown in table 4.5.4 on page 304.

One of the reasons for this pressure on Great Yarmouth lay in its geographical position on a seaboard confronting Britain's eastern enemies for many of the war years: the Batavian Republic (Holland) and Denmark. It was also that rare asset along the inhospitable east coast—a deepwater

imposition respecting the same, if attempted' (TNA: PRO CUST 96/166, 9 Feb. 1802; see also 96/166, 6 Sept. 1804)

---

[1] *Cley* TNA: PRO CUST 96/165, Board to the Collector 1798–1801, 20 July 1798

[2] *influence* William Palgrave jnr (frontispiece to chap. 9) served as Collector of Yarmouth from 1803 to 1826, working in the building only a few doors from one of his childhood homes. Charles Lamb, son of the Hardys' man William Lamb, was for many years a tidewaiter in the Customs at Cley, close to his childhood home.

Spike Sweeting has analysed the careers of 230 middle-ranking customs officers known as landwaiters (supervised by land surveyors, and dealing with imported cargoes). In the year 1784–85, before the reforms of the 1790s, one officer took £480 in fees (ie declared fees, from merchants); the average for such fees that year was £220 per officer (S. Sweeting, 'The Age of Corruption? Customs fraud in the Port of London, 1730–1785': a talk given at the Institute of Historical Research, London, 2 Oct. 2012)

facing page The Customs House for Blakeney and Cley, seen from Cley Quay. In July 1798 it had 12 officers and boatmen under the Collector; one Charles Lamb, was the son of the Hardys' farm servant William Lamb (chapter 1).

Three of this small complement were riding officers on patrol from Mundesley (the border of the jurisdiction with Gt Yarmouth) to Pit's Point (the border with Wells to the west)   [*MB · 2011*]

---

[1] *tonnages Norw. Merc.* 7 Sept. 1799

[2] *Board* See, for example, the orders to the Collector of Wells (TNA: PRO CUST 96/134, p. 78, 10 Oct. 1799)

[3] *quarantine* TNA: PRO CUST 96/134, pp. 100–2, 6 Dec. 1800

[4] *sinecurists* Customs officials, unlike the Exise, could hold down other jobs. The King's Lynn lawyer Philip Case was also a triple sinecurist customs comptroller (see 'Three attorneys', in vol. 3, chap. 8, drawn from John M. Barney's 'Building a fortune: Philip Case, attorney, 1712–92', *Norfolk Archaeology*, vol. 43, pt 3 (2000), pp. 441–56)

port. Although ships of the line had to ride at anchor, it is evident from the size of prizes for sale that the port routinely handled medium-sized ships. Just one press advertisement for Dutch prizes for sale in 1799 listed seven vessels with tonnages of 317, 232, 184, 164, 163, 87 and 70 tons respectively.[1] All had successfully cleared the bureaucratic hurdles of Admiralty and Customs.

In 1798–1800, three years (among many) when a French invasion was expected, hard-pressed customs officers were subjected to a mass of correspondence from the Board in London. As well as covering the handling of prize goods, selling prize cargo and coping with orders from the Admiralty High Court, the communications sent to the Collectors ranged from directions on naval allotments over seamen's pay to the sorting out of convoy duty and quarantine.[2]

These last two issues caused tensions with the Admiralty. Merchant ships were required in time of war to sail in convoy, as we have seen. However, waiting for a naval escort would frequently further delay merchant ships already subject to many vicissitudes in the form of adverse winds and tides, with consequent losses for the owners and crews. Matters became more heated when the Customs resisted the Admiralty by issuing strict injunctions over quarantine regulations, thus causing delays for the Royal Navy's vital despatches. While naval ships arriving in port from plague areas such as the Mediterranean were exempt from paying quarantine duty, they were still subject to quarantine restrictions. Customs officers were consequently accused of holding up the onward transmission of urgent despatches from the war zone. As a compromise the Customs decreed that despatches need only be dipped in vinegar before being cleared. The records do not divulge how the problem of protecting the ink from the vinegar could be overcome.[3]

The strains of office took their toll. Although popularly seen as a non-professional body filled with sinecurists, and portrayed somewhat unfavourably by historians when compared with hardworking, hard-driven excise officers, the Customs rose to wartime challenges.[4] Senior officers were overworked to the point of total exhaustion. Great Yarmouth's Collector John Bell, who had steered *Nelly* safely into the hands of William Hardy junior 1799–1800, died at

the height of the invasion crisis in October 1803. The press announcement does not mention the cause of death,[1] but the official port-books bear witness to his massive workload and his meticulous, conscientious approach to his task.

Even Newcastle upon Tyne, with its quieter demands than those of the more tumultuous Great Yarmouth, wore down its twin chiefs. In 1803–05, during repeated invasion fears, the Collector of Newcastle made no mention of prizes to the Commissioners of Customs in London. Only a very few naval ships, of the smallest type such as tenders and gun brigs, entered port. Nevertheless by 9 July 1804 the Comptroller of the port (at Newcastle a separate officeholder) was desperate for a holiday after two years without a break:

Honourable Sirs—The Comptroller humbly requests Your Honours' leave of absence for a month for the recovery of his health and to attend his private affairs—his last leave was by order 12 July 1802, no. 163, since which he hath not been absent from the post.[2]

[1] *Bell Norw. Merc.* 15 Oct. 1803

[2] *Newcastle* TNA: PRO CUST 84/36, Customs port book, Collector of Newcastle to Board 1803–05, p. 153.
There is no mention of William Hardy jnr's *Nelly* in the customs papers for Newcastle at the time of her demise, although Blakeney and Cley would presumably have informed the ship's port of embarkation that she had been wrecked and much of her cargo lost

¹ *Newcastle* TNA: PRO
CUST 84/36, p. 181

² *Gt Yarmouth* TNA:
PRO CUST 97/31, no. 96.
The accounts missed
the hoped-for coach
and were sent 23 May.
Bell's letters to the
Board in London are
full of the day-to-day
administration of prizes.
Another vessel was
brought into port as a
recaptured prize at the
same time as *Nelly*:
'. . . The *Love and Unity*
cutter was seized off
Dunwich on the coast
of Suffolk on the 10
March 1799 by the
Hunter cutter under his
[Mr Riches'] command:
. . . she was then under
Prussian colours and
there were on board
her 4 men, 3 of whom
appeared to be English
and the master appeared
to be a foreigner . . . and
he [Riches] put them
all on board one of His
Majesty's Ships in Yar-
mouth Roads and what
became of them after-
wards he does not know.'
The vessel had no
certificate of registry
on board at the time
that Riches re-seized
her. She was returned
into the Exchequer 9
Apr. 1799, was judged
to be a prize, and was
sold at Yarmouth 3 Mar.
1800 (TNA: PRO CUST
97/31, no. 126, 17 Apr.
1800)

³ *Diary 4*

⁴ Diary MS

London was not altogether impressed. The Comptroller received a prompt reply, as was customary with the correspondence of both Excise and Customs, and was granted a holiday from 19 July on the condition that he first clear his desk. Leave was 'to commence on or near the 19 instant when the Quarterly Accounts shall be finished'. He managed to get away. By 21 July papers were being signed by the Collector and the *Acting* Comptroller.[1]

The Collector of Yarmouth, John Bell, described what it was like to work in an office handling prizes and other wartime business. Writing on 15 May 1799, a month after *Nelly* had entered port at the start of her year-long voyage through Customs, he tried to convey to London what he was enduring. Again the quarterly accounts loomed large:

Honourable Sirs—In reply to Mr Secretary's letter of the 11th instant, no. 88, we humbly represent to Your Honours that it is not from neglect or inattention [but] from the increase of the common business of the office and the pressure of extraordinary business that Lady Day Quarter Accounts have not hitherto been sent. Not to mention the length of entries occasioned by the additional duties, the Navy allotments, the packets and the business consequent upon the prize ships take up so much of the clerks' time that these have been the occasion of the delay . . . No time shall be lost in finishing them [the accounts] and we hope to be able to send them by Monday's or Tuesday's coach . . . [2]

Given these preoccupations it was an impressive achievement that a year later, he and his staff detained the Hardys at the Customs House for only three to four days, Mary Hardy recording the absence of her husband and son in Great Yarmouth 15–19 April 1800.[3] Being more familar with the workload of Blakeney and Cley they may not have anticipated being away so long. The diarist, who was inclined to worry, noted on 18 April: 'Expected Mr Hardy and William home, [they] did not come'.[4]

The Excise at sea

It is widely held that customs officers and excise officers devoted their energies to catching smugglers at sea and on their patrols along the shore and cart gaps. The primary focus of the two services however lay not with combating smuggling but with gauging and levying duties on selected imported and home-produced commodities respectively. This was especially the case after the relaxation of some of the swingeing customs duties from 1784 onwards, with a move made in favour of taxation unrelated to the Customs. The new assessed taxes were levied from 1777 onwards on such items as riding horses, leisure carts, menservants and, briefly, maidservants. After 1799 came a new emphasis on direct taxation, largely through income tax. Smuggling as a result gradually became less lucrative. In 1784 the duty on tea had been reduced from 119 per cent to 12½ per cent; from then onwards much less was heard of smuggled tea.[1]

The number of reports of smuggling drops away during the war years; perhaps illegal operations were interrupted by the voracious privateers and other hostile ships waiting offshore. The official records confirm that it was the heavy demands of war rather than smugglers' wiles which overstretched the Customs. Unsurprisingly, to free them for their tasks, customs officers—like those in the Excise—were exempt from holding parish office and serving on juries, and could not be compelled by magistrates to do so.[2]

[1] *taxation* The position was different earlier. Before the American war the Excise Board had become alarmed at the rise in smuggling on the Norfolk coast. On 11 Apr. 1773 the tide surveyor Joseph Jackson, an excise officer based at Gt Yarmouth, was nearly run down by 19 armed smugglers in a large cutter. The Collector of Norwich told the Board 'that there are 6 or 8 smuggling vessels constantly employed between Holland and the coast of Norfolk' and feared 'much mischief will ensue'. One of these vessels carried 12 six-pounders, 18 swivel guns and 45 men, and, in the opinion of the Excise, needed one or two Royal Naval frigates rather than an excise cutter to intercept her (TNA: PRO CUST 48/18, pp. 413–14, 13 May 1773).

Such reports, being conveyed to the Treasury, may well have prompted the shift to direct taxation which over the years helped to undermine smuggling. Taxation is covered in vol. 2, chap. 11; income tax, introduced in 1799, proved a significant development

[2] *exempt* TNA: PRO CUST 96/134, pp. 83–6, 22 Feb. 1800

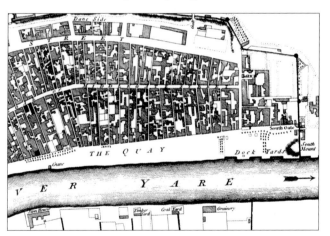

above Gt Yarmouth 1797: a detail from Faden's plan. Dockyards line the east bank of the Yare by the walled town's South Gate, where *Nelly* would have been held for a year awaiting a decision. Merchants' houses, the Palgraves' Yarmouth residence and the Customs House all faced west onto this quay with its trees and large crane (left)   [*Faden's Map of Norfolk 1797: Larks Press 1989*]

[1] *sundial* As in 'I count only the sunlit hours', a motto seen on sundials.
   For her qualities as a diarist see, in vol. 1, the Prologue and chap. 2

[2] *courted* The closest he came was early in the diary years, when he attended 'a great sale of gin and tea etc at the Custom House' at Gt Yarmouth (*Diary 1*: 13 Dec. 1774, and note); the goods were presumably ex-contraband

[3] *lawless* N. Holmes, *The Lawless Coast: Smuggling, anarchy and murder in North Norfolk in the 1780s* (Larks Press, Guist Bottom, 2009), author's preface, unpag.
   Unfortunately Neil Holmes does not cite his sources with the precision necessary to follow them up; he also makes errors such as calling the excise supervisors at Wells and Lynn superintendents.
   Kenneth Hipper had earlier written a wider-ranging, balanced study; but this too lacks detailed citation (apart from the dates of press reports), making it difficult to trace the sources: K. Hipper, *Smugglers All: Centuries of Norfolk smuggling* (Larks Press, Guist Bottom, 2001). He gives a useful survey of the difficulties facing the cutters in his chapter 'The conflict at sea' (pp. 72–88)

Mary Hardy tells us absolutely nothing about smuggling. It is hard to know what to make of this silence. As a diarist she engaged in self-censorship; her sundial tendencies can mask unpleasant realities.[1] On the other hand smuggling may well not have impinged on the Hardys' lives. As maltsters and brewers watched daily by the Excise they had to maintain high standards of probity. Reputation, once lost, was hard to recover. Having served twelve years as an excise officer William Hardy would have felt repugnance towards smugglers for their violent assaults on his former colleagues; he would certainly not have courted the men or their goods.[2]

His own products did not lend themselves to competition from smugglers. Malt and beer are bulky commodities, beer being a notoriously high-volume, low-value product. Yet two books chronicling Norfolk smuggling in the eighteenth century present this as 'the lawless coast', witnessing 'illegal running of contraband goods on an unprecedented scale'.[3] That may well be true; but we learn nothing of it, even by report, from Mary Hardy or Henry Raven.

TABLE 4.5.4

Cutters employed in the excise service in England and Wales, 30 September 1790

source   TNA: PRO CUST 48/25, p. 248, 1 June 1791

ship's name	tonnage	station
Resolution	103	Hull, Yorkshire
Lively	77	[Gt] Yarmouth, Norfolk
Fly	47½	Harwich, Essex
Wasp	45	Dover, Kent
Viper	45	Cowes, Isle of Wight
Lark	53½	Dartmouth, Devon
Eagle	45½	Plymouth, Devon
Fox	53	Falmouth, Cornwall
Ferret	45½	Milford, S. Wales
Dispatch	78	Pile Fowdrey, Lancashire
TOTAL TONNAGE	593	
MEAN TONNAGE	59⅓	

left Wells Quay: the Old Customs House, still with its Royal Arms (left). In 1853 the Customs House closed at Blakeney and Cley and its business was transferred here until 1881, when Wells too closed [*MB·2001*]

Like the Customs, the excise service was stretched by the demands of war. As well as customs cutters (such as the Yarmouth cutter *Hunter*, under Captain Thomas Riches in the 1790s),[1] there were ten armed excise cutters patrolling the coast in peacetime. The ships were very thinly spread, as seen in table 4.5.4, only four being stationed between Hull and Dover. On the outbreak of war constant adjustments were made by the Excise Board, and the vessels' numbers slightly increased. The cutters carried out a variety of tasks. As the table shows, there was a concentration on the smuggling coast with France in 1790, but even then, in peacetime, they were used in the Impress Service to add to naval strength: a directive of August 1790 informed the cutters that they could now be stood down from pressing.[2]

When war broke out in 1793 the workload once again increased. Within days of hostilities being declared the commanders of excise cutters were ordered by the Treasury to capture every French vessel they met with—a task requiring courage, given that the average size of an excise cutter was only 59 tons.[3] They also helped in the vital role of informing British and neutral masters and crews that a state of war existed. As seen earlier, crews could sometimes fall into enemy hands in the days before rapid communication as, being at sea, they were unaware of any declaration of war.[4]

[1] *Riches* The complement of customs personnel is listed in various printed sources, such as J. Crouse and W. Stevenson, *Crouse and Stevenson's Norwich and Norfolk Complete Memorandum Book 1790* (Norwich, 1790), unpag.

[2] *pressing* TNA: PRO CUST 48/25, p. 36, 17 Aug. 1790

[3] *courage* TNA: PRO CUST 48/26, p. 102, 9 Feb. 1793

[4] *informing crews* TNA: PRO CUST 48/26, p. 103, 11 Feb. 1793. The Treasury desired the Excise 'to give directions to your officers at every port and creek throughout the kingdom, and order all the vessels and boats belonging to each, to speak with every British and Dutch vessel they possibly can in order to give them notice of hostilities with France'; they were to inform the pilot boats as well.

The Dutch did not enter the war until 1795,

and it is a sign of the generally cordial relations between the two nations that the British were thinking of Dutch interests as well as their own in 1793

---

[1] *France* TNA: PRO CUST 48/26, p. 483, 4 Apr. 1794. As the subsequent volume shows (CUST 48/27), the cutters proved equal to the task.
   The Gt Yarmouth cutter *Lively* in the years 1794–95 arrested and detained not only smugglers but a Danish brig laden with provisions and a Swedish brig carrying corn

[2] *Emden* TNA: PRO CUST 48/27, p. 334, 9 Mar. 1795

[3] *Mercury* The *Norfolk Chronicle* and *Norwich Mercury* are mined by Kenneth Hipper and Neil Holmes for their studies on smuggling already cited on p. 304. They both give long accounts taken from the press

[4] *warehousing* TNA: PRO CUST 47/421, pp. 103–4, 20 Mar. 1801

[5] *world wars* A colonial conflict developed into a world war in 1778 with the intervention of France and then Spain on the side of the American colonists; the Dutch entered in 1781

The tasks multiplied alarmingly. On the personal orders of the King, commanders of excise cutters were expected to detain Danish and Norwegian ships bound for France with corn or naval and military stores.[1] Such were the desperate conditions facing the military in the Low Countries and Germany that excise cutters were ordered to cross the North Sea to help with the evacuation of sick and wounded British troops from Emden in the wake of the failed 1794–95 campaign. The commanders of excise cutters stationed from Hull to Weymouth in Dorset (which by then also had a cutter) were required by special request of the Treasury to leave their stations as speedily as possible to sail to Emden. There they would receive orders from 'the senior naval officer in the King's service at that station', or, if no Royal Navy officer could be found, from the officers commanding the land forces.[2] A feature of the minutes and orders of the time is the degree of improvisation expected from all those in official and service positions. It was not only Horatio Nelson's band of brothers in the Senior Service who displayed mental and operational agility when in action at sea.

The *Norwich Mercury* would give accounts of the exploits and seizures—both of ships and contraband—of 'the Lively Cutter' of Great Yarmouth.[3] The disruption caused by war to this part of *Lively*'s normal routine was immense, and any successes her crew enjoyed were particularly hard won in the context of the extra burdens imposed by hostilities.

The shore-based excise officers too were adapting to the demands of war. One of their tasks was to supervise the warehousing of prize goods, the increasing workload at Great Yarmouth requiring an additional excise officer to be posted there towards the end of the French Revolutionary War.[4] As argued at the start of this chapter, Great Yarmouth had a good war against the French in the sense of seeing its economy expand and certain aspects of its business booming, and the Revenue would have been satisfied with the increase in monies derived from the sale of prize goods.

Disparate elements of Government had to pull together during the trio of prolonged and intense world wars 1778–83, 1793–1801 and 1803–15 which form the backdrop to Mary Hardy's diary.[5] The multi-layered, co-operative approach to home defence which will emerge in chapter 9 was also discernible in maritime activity not directly connected with defence. Customs, Excise, the Admiralty High Court, merchant ships, captains and crews, shipowners and merchants all had to work at least fairly harmoniously with one another if their combined mission of keeping the nation provided with food and fuel were to be attained. As often shown in this four-volume study, efficient distribution proved the key to commercial success and national survival.

These five chapters forming the 'Wide horizons' of Mary Hardy's world have analysed the infrastructure necessary for efficient distribution: the roads, rivers and navigations, inland and coastal ports, and the busy highway of the North Sea. After a short leisure interlude three further chapters will chart the political and organisational thinking underpinning these structures. The American and French Revolutionary wars proved especially divisive politically, the country only coming together to meet the threat from Napoleon 1803–15. How they achieved this in Mary Hardy's Norfolk is told under the overall heading 'Human conflict'. The conflict was both external, against the foe, and internal, within the county, until the spectre of Boney frightened warring factions within the population into concerted action.

In her short life *Nelly* represented much that was typical of the way in which the nation was kept afloat. Despite a host of natural and manmade dangers she valiantly traded abroad. The Royal Navy demonstrated its command of the seas in bringing her home. And she carried coal and foodstuffs coastwise as a tiny cog in the mechanics of distribution. Yet her last owner never replaced her, and we do not learn why. The sloop may have been unprofitable; William's accounts certainly show a marked lessening in his estimate of her value as an asset.[1]

Only one member of William's workforce and that of his father was to die at work: the farm servant or labourer Stephen Moore, his skull crushed in a marlpit at Letheringsett.[2] Was William seared by the experience of sending five men to their deaths that same year? The emotional self-control displayed in his mother's written record means we can never know. But she tells us enough of *Nelly*'s story for its impact to remain imprinted on the mind of her readers.

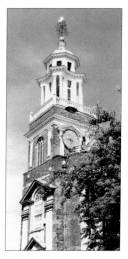

above Gt Yarmouth: the tall tower of St George's Chapel, built in 1716. Like the parish church it served as a landmark for those at sea and on the Broads [*MB · 2001*]

[1] *accounts* William's accounts, which have survived for the years 1798–1804 inclusive (apart from 1802), are transcribed in *Diary 4*, app. D4.B, with notes. He paid £590 for the ship in 1800, but valued her in Sept. 1803 at £360 *including* 'stores': 60% of her purchase price (*Diary 4*, p. 459 and note)

[2] *Moore Diary 4*: 1 Nov. 1804. See also vol. 2, chap. 1 on accidents befalling the Hardys' workforce

11 · Figures and tables

*Dramatic staging of
a popular novel, p. 350*

11 · Little time for play

Freemasons at Blakeney,
p. 333

DEVIL on two STICKS.

Stothard del.   Walker sculp.

above The Devil on Two Sticks, a farce based on the comic novel by Le Sage, author of *Gil Blas*. Mary Hardy and her 14-year-old son William saw this favourite of the touring players at Holt 4 Dec. 1784 in the town's makeshift theatre [*drawing by Stothard; engraving by Walker 1780*]

6

Leisure hours indoors

Rubbing off the rust

Mrs Hardcastle Is there a creature in the whole country but our-selves, that does not take a trip to town now and then, to rub off the rust a little?   OLIVER GOLDSMITH, 1773 [1]

A hot day. I poorly about noon with dimness in my eyes. We dined, drank tea and supped at Mr Raven's. We all went to the play, it was *She Stoops to Conquer, or The Mistakes of the Night* with *Robinson Crusoe, or Harlequin Friday.*   MARY HARDY, 1789 [2]

HOLIDAYS AND LEISURE ACTIVITIES do not make much of a showing in the diaries of Mary Hardy and Henry Raven. They were also a rare luxury for their workforce: the Hardys' maidservants and men were granted little free time. As seen in volume 3, even the children of the labouring poor were increasingly expected to spend their one day off a week in church and at Sunday school. While the gentry, mercantile and manufacturing classes enjoyed rather greater leisure opportunities, the ways in which they relaxed were still limited. Families often had to arrange trips separately to maintain cover at work, as related in Norwich at the chapter head (above). For the diarist this could mean walking home with two girls in the cold and dark, dressed in their best clothes.[3]

The sexes tended not to mix at certain outdoor events, such as wrestling and boxing matches (chapter 7). The indoor attraction of lingering in the public house was usually an all-male affair as well, apart from the work of the women who cooked the meals and served the drinks. These exceptions apart, the sexes and the generations could spend leisure hours together in Mary Hardy's class: attending pleasure gardens, fairs and plays; taking to the water and the road; visiting distant relatives; touring country houses

[1] *Mrs Hardcastle She Stoops to Conquer,* Act 1, scene 1. Oliver Goldsmith's social satire proved very popular. It was put on by William Scraggs's touring company for their second night at Holt in 1784 (see the inset on pp. 348–9)

[2] *the play Diary 2:* 11 May 1789; the second item, a two-act panto-mime by R.B. Sheridan, was first performed at Drury Lane in 1781.

Mary Hardy, her 15-year-old daughter Mary Ann and their Holt friend Sarah Bartell had travelled together to Norwich. They enjoyed an evening at the Theatre Royal after taking their meals at the King's Head; the innkeeper Henry Raven was not a relative

[3] *in the dark Diary 2:* 12 Nov. 1788. Mary Hardy, her daughter and her niece Mary Raven, aged 16, from the Whissonsett shop had gone to the Holt play then and on 8 Nov.

¹ *relaxing* For a study of the surge in leisure pursuits, for those who actually had some spare time, see J.H. Plumb, *The Commercialisation of Leisure in Eighteenth-century England: The Stenton Lecture 1972* (University of Reading, 1973)

² *holidays* See 'Tourism' on pp. 51–61, with the list of the 13 holidays (p. 52)

³ *retired life* F. de La Rochfoucauld, *A Frenchman's Year in Suffolk*, ed. N. Scarfe, p. 36. The 18-year-old French nobleman, writing in 1784, was inclined to arrive at sweeping generalisations, and the very *un*retiring lifestyle of the Hardys does not reflect the languor he saw in the class above theirs. It is however a telling remark that there was no equivalent in English for *je m'ennuie* (expressing boredom and lassitude).
See vol. 1, chap. 5, in 'The experience of childhood', for the inclusion of very young children in adults' social life

⁴ *players* T.L.G. Burley, *Playhouses and Players of East Anglia* (Jarrold & Sons Ltd, Norwich, 1928); E. Grice, *Rogues and Vagabonds; or The Actors' Road to Respectability* (Terence Dalton Ltd, Lavenham, 1977)

and cathedrals; and having carefree days at the seaside.¹ Tourism, defined as visits made other than to the family at Whissonsett and Sprowston, has been covered in chapter 1. Of the thirteen tourist holidays taken by Mary Hardy in the course of 36 years four were made without her husband, all four being before his retirement in October 1797. Six of the thirteen were a combination of business and pleasure. A few within Norfolk were very short, lasting only three or four days, including the long travel time. Apart from their Yorkshire visit of 1775 and until his retirement the diarist took only one other long holiday with her husband: to see his mother and brother Joseph in Wigan in 1787, seven months after Raven's death. William, aged seventeen, was resolutely capable of running the business in their absence: he was already taking it in a new direction by brewing porter.²

Having meals in each other's homes, especially tea and supper taken after the end of the working day, was the commonest form of relaxation enjoyed by those of the diarist's circle. It was usually a shared family experience, in which even the youngest children were included:

> They [English gentlemen] give the impression of being very happy in them [their homes]. In the country they live a very retired life . . . Their wives and children take up their leisure hours. They don't appear to know the meaning of boredom, although I'm persuaded, from certain examples, that they are concealing it. But what is remarkable . . . is that there is no word in English which expresses the reflexive verb *je m'ennuie*.³

Mary Hardy and Henry Raven record aspects of the use of spare time which appear not to have been preserved elsewhere. The nephew tells us of amusements available to apprentices (volume 2, chapter 5). His aunt reveals the heady reception accorded William Scraggs's touring Company of Comedians in the barn behind the White Lion at Holt. The actor–manager had an astonishing repertoire: 58 performances, of 53 productions, laid on in the space of twelve weeks, as listed later in the inset on his Holt season. Owing to the near-total absence of surviving records Scraggs's company has received very little attention from the historians of the East Anglian touring players, T.L.G. Burley and Elizabeth Grice.⁴ Mary Hardy's diary and the press notices advertising the performances fill a gap.

Not only the well-to-do attended the plays. The Hardys' farm servant, drayman and coachman William Lamb and the maidservants are each recorded as going once to Holt's 'theatre' to see a varied programme; they may have gone more often, the diarist not troubling to note their attendance. The repertoire was up to the moment, some of Scraggs's productions being works premièred within only the previous few months or very few years in London. The rural hinterland away from the provincial capital was no cultural desert, despite the inelegance of the theatrical stage when contrasted with Norwich's Theatre Royal.

The diarist also tells us of the vigour of Freemasonry in country areas at a time when the local press tended to report only the activities of Norwich Masons, and she hints at the interest women took in the masonic lodges.

above right Beccles [*MB · 2014*]

left Beccles, the Suffolk market town on the River Waveney bordering Norfolk. This view from the top of the parish church tower looks south-east to the market place below, with the creeper-clad King's Head.

In the centre is a large, long building with raised roof ventilation. This is the remains of the Fisher theatre, built by David Fisher jnr in 1819. It served as a playhouse until 1844, when it became the corn exchange; it is now fronted by Lloyds Bank in Sheepgate (with the steeply pitched hipped roof).

The former Independent chapel in Hungate, now the United Reformed and Methodist Church, its main front catching the western sun, lies a little beyond the old theatre.

Fisher's partner William Scraggs, once actor–manager of his own company, was buried in Beccles churchyard in 1808 aged sixty [*MB · 2000*]

¹ *fairs* Those referred to (and often attended) by Mary Hardy and Henry Raven are listed in chap. 7 in table 4.7.1.

The home fair was held in the area from which the farm servant or maidservant came.

The local fair took place in the area where they worked

² *sociability* For a survey of Norwich sociability in this period, with its 'vast array of clubs, a calendar of leisure and sociability all underpinned by the growing consumption of the city's grandees and "middling sort"', see A. Dain, 'An enlightened and polite society', in *Norwich since 1550*, ed. C. Rawcliffe and R. Wilson (Hambledon, London, 2004), pp. 193–218

³ *difference* Trevelyan's aphorism advances the cause of village cricket as promoting social cohesion, to the extent of preventing a revolution on the British side of the Channel: 'If the French *noblesse* had been capable of playing cricket with their peasants, their chateaux would never have been burnt' (G.M. Trevelyan, *Illustrated English Social History*, vol. 3 (Longmans, London, 1960), p. 112)

⁴ *purse clubs* See vol. 2, chap. 11

The poor, male and female, in contrast with the middle classes, largely spent out of doors what little leisure they had. The next chapter shows the immense value placed by the labouring poor on attendance at the home fair as a means of keeping in touch with family and friends, at a time when fashionable commentators tended to be dismissive of fairs and were becoming fearful of their latent riotousness.¹ Mary Hardy's lens swings across a world of outdoor pursuits in the century before sport, especially team sports, became a more general leisure activity. She ranges across boxing and wrestling, tenpins and bowls, cricket and horse racing. For the more leisured there were the field sports of hare coursing, shooting and fishing, in which the Hardys evinced almost no interest. These sporting activities, being comparatively rare in her circle, occupied little time. The bags she notes when shooting became more general from the 1780s, for those who could afford it, were exceptionally small by later standards: all the shooting engaged in by their friends on William Hardy junior's estate took the form of rough shoots. Two or three men and their dogs on a walk round the farm would bag only a handful of birds (table 4.7.2).

This chapter will cover indoor pursuits, such as reading, music, clubs and plays, before moving in the next chapter to outdoor activities. The sociability which underlay almost all leisure pursuits was a secure foundation on which to build a cohesive society among the upper and middling levels; but relatively few occasions arose when all the classes could join together in their free hours to engage in shared pastimes.² The playhouse and—to a more limited extent—cricket apart, there were cockfighting and badger-baiting, tenpins and bowls; but some of the clubs (Freemasonry proving an exception) seem to have perpetuated social difference, being designed to meet specific needs.³ Purse clubs were introduced for the working man as a means of support for his family in time of hardship, and did not form part of leisured clubbability.⁴

The study of leisure requires a clear exposition of chronology, for marked changes occurred during the diary years. The arguments in this chapter by no means hold good over the full 36-year span. Fairs were on the wane and sometimes actively suppressed. The theatre and Freemasonry (at least

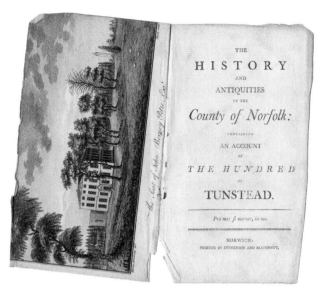

The start of John Burney Petre, Esq?

THE
HISTORY
AND
ANTIQUITIES
OF THE
County of Norfolk:
CONTAINING
AN ACCOUNT
OF
THE HUNDRED
OF
TUNSTEAD.

Pro me: si merear, in me.

NORWICH:
PRINTED BY STEVENSON AND MATCHETT.

left One of the books owned by the Hardys in 1797: Mostyn John Armstrong's multi-part history of Norfolk, published in 1781; this is the title page for Tunstead hundred.

Royce's frontispiece engraving is taken from Marcus Armstrong's depiction of Westwick House and grounds, between N. Walsham and Coltishall.

Jeremiah Cozens, who married Mary Ann Hardy, was raised at Westwick Old Hall nearby. Unlike his in-laws he was devoted to shooting, and spent as much time as possible in the field
[*Author's collection*]

in Norfolk) seem to have suffered a reverse during the war years from 1793 onwards. Long-established spectator sports involving a degree of violence, such as boxing, wrestling, cockfighting and badger-baiting, were on the decline, while shooting was becoming well-established. Frivolous pursuits as varied as cards and enjoying the companionship of friends in Norwich's pleasure gardens were becoming less popular in Mary Hardy's circle, while other light-hearted attractions, such as visits to the seaside, were on the increase.

The two leisure chapters will suggest some reasons for these developments. Improved roads encouraged travel within the county and further afield; a new moral earnestness accompanied the Evangelical Revival and Methodist onslaught; clubs became associated in the authorities' minds with seditious meetings. No study of leisure can be vague about dates. An appreciation of timescale is vital, and highlighting widespread enjoyment of a certain pursuit in one decade cannot be taken as indicating that it necessarily held sway in the next. Also any analysis has to be data-driven. Reliance on contemporary commentators can sow confusion, as Trevor Fawcett made clear in his presentation of some puzzling contradictions as to the vitality or otherwise of Norwich's artistic and cultural life 1780–1830.[1]

[1] *criteria* T. Fawcett, 'The culture of late-Georgian Norwich: a conflict of evidence', UEA Bulletin new series, vol. 5 (1972), pp. 1–10.
He emphasises the necessity of adhering to objective criteria: 'If we are to make sense of Norwich at this period we need better cultural indicators than the subjective testimony of contemporary spokesmen' (p. 4).
The picture is so confusing that he is unable to arrive at any overall conclusion

[1] *portraits* Reproduced on pp. 223 and 428. The diarist's love of fine lace remained constant however

[2] *tracts* Listed in vol. 3, chap. 4 under 'Heart religion'

[3] *newspapers* At Coltishall the auctioneer Robert Ansell may have acted as local agent for the Norwich papers: 'Mr Hardy . . . went to Boorne's afternoon to meet R. Ansell to send an advertisement to the printer' (*Diary 1*: 8 Feb. 1781), the notice duly appearing in the *Norwich Mercury* on 10 Feb.

A London paper taken at Letheringsett was the *Morning Herald* (*Diary 2*: 20 Feb. 1783). For the importance of newspapers see the section in chap. 8, pp. 427–36; also, in vol. 3, chap. 5, 'Looking beyond the county border'

[4] *books Diary 1*: 4 Dec. 1773; 7 Mar., 2 Apr. 1774. The second work was probably Combrune's *The Theory and Practice of Brewing* (1st pub. 1762)

[5] *large quantity Diary 2*, app. D2.C, pp. 411–12. Three stone is 42 lb (19 kg)

We have only to look at the two portraits of Mary Hardy to see what the passage of thirteen years could do. One was taken as she prepared to set off for the theatre at Holt in 1785; the other in the year when she was first recorded as a paid-up member of a Methodist congregation. The quite literal casting-off of frivolity in the rejection of frothy azure prettiness in favour of Quaker garb is immediately apparent. This chapter will show that she did not stand alone.[1]

From books to frolics

Taking first the solitary indoor activity of reading: it might be thought that the author of a manuscript which has spawned nine volumes in the present series, in addition to earlier studies, would be informative on the subject of books and reading. She is not. Apart from very occasional references to religious, contemplative works, such as the set of Wesleyan tracts, we learn little about the Hardys' reading preferences.[2] We know that they read a London newspaper, as well as the Norwich ones in which they sometimes placed advertisements and which they used for the many extracts interpolated in the diary text.[3] In Norwich William Hardy bought a spelling book for Raven in 1773 and a brewing manual by Michael Combrune in 1774.[4] For his long inventory of September 1797 he was painstaking in listing the books held at home in the counting house, transcribed in full as an appendix to *Diary 2*. None of those individually itemised among the titles was a work of fiction. In this motley collection, held alongside a 'razor, stone and strop [and] a bag of bottle corks', were included:

A large quantity of Acts of Parliament, old school books, newspapers, etc, etc, supposed three stone—3*s*; . . . about 40 small books and pamphlets etc—5*s*; . . . 27 small books of various kinds—7*s*; . . . [a] 10-volume History of England—£2 10*s* . . . [5]

The Hardys held a good selection of reference works, from manuals for parish officers, such as the four volumes by Burn, to a dictionary, a grammar, Armstrong's *The History and Antiquities of the County of Norfolk* (1781) in ten volumes, and Barlow's *Peerage*; also the family Bible. The only slightly unusual title was *The Bloody Tribunal*, presumably that by John Marchant (1770), its subtitle proclaiming it to

left Admiral the Hon. John Byng, notable in Mary Hardy's diary for being the subject of the only title she refers to as a work read for light relief: 'The Tryal of Admiral Bing'.

The admiral was executed in 1757 for showing cowardice in the face of the enemy off Minorca—according to Voltaire in *Candide* '*pour encourager les autres*'. The court martial of a man with a distinguished naval career was controversial at the time, some seeing it as political   [*from a contemporary engraving*]

below One of the many Acts of the type the Hardys stored for reference in their counting house at Letheringsett Hall, as William Hardy noted in his domestic inventory: 'a large quantity of Acts of Parliament'.

This Act of 17 Dec. 1798 sets out the duties on malt, mum (beer made from cereals other than barley), cider and perry (made from pears) for 1799   [*Author's collection*]

be a chronicle of 'the horrid cruelties of the Inquisition, as practised in Spain, Portugal, Italy, and the East and West Indies'. Only in connection with a borrowed work do we learn something of the Hardys' tastes in lighter reading:

[1778] JANUARY 19, MONDAY A very fine day. William Frary in malthouse, John Thompson and Zeb Rouse mending hedges and spreading muck. Mr Hardy went to Mr Ansell's forenoon, borrowed the Trial of Admiral Byng, went to club evening 6, came home evening 11.[1]

This was probably not a book but a pamphlet in the form of a letter, published anonymously 'by an old sea officer' in London in March 1757. This was the year Admiral Byng was shot on board HMS *Monarch* in Portsmouth harbour following a court martial held by many at the time to have been politically inspired and on charges which should not have been pressed.

Apart from recording his cousin William Hardy junior's attendance at the Holt book club in 1797 Henry Raven makes no mention of books.[2] Mary Ann Hardy married a

[1] *borrowed Diary 1*

[2] *book club Diary 3*: 10 Jan. 1797. For the few references to this club see the section 'Clubbability on the wane' (pp. 335–41)

right The original core of *c*.1700 of Coltishall Hall, home of Chapman and Sarah Ives. They treated their library of 500 books with rather more respect than did the Hardys with their far more meagre holdings: the Hall sale catalogue of 1796 after Chapman Ives's first bankruptcy included 'elegant bookcases'.

The Hardys still had no proper bookcase for their library 16 years after moving to Letheringsett, the volumes being heaped in the counting house or shoved into drawers alongside corks and a razor. Further, William Hardy valued some of their books by weight. As an indicator of priorities, the Hardys' only bookcases in 1797 held their account books. The total value of the counting-house bookcases and shelves, without their contents, was given in William Hardy's inventory as ten shillings   [*MB · 2011*]

¹ *Jeremiah Cozens* S. Cozens-Hardy, *Memorials of William Hardy Cozens-Hardy of Letheringsett*, p. 13; Sydney is quoting here from his father's reminiscences of 1895.

Mary Hardy's grandson relied on stimulae outside the limitations of his Sprowston home, many being provided by the intellectually curious William Hardy jnr, and on his own efforts at self-education, as his memoirs record. See also in vol. 1, chap. 5 all the central sections on nurturing children and developing a sense of wonder

² *Tompson Norw. Merc.* 13 Sept., 11 Oct. 1777

farmer with almost no interest in books, their son recording at the end of his life:

My father had a very meagre library, consisting of a few religious books, such as Bunyan's 'Pilgrim's Progress', Doddridge's 'Rise and Progress', Young's 'Night Thoughts', and the Methodist Magazine.¹

Although allowance has to be made for their impersonal approach to diary-keeping—one resembling a log, rather than an introspective journal—William and Mary Hardy can be seen as appearing unintellectual and limited in their pursuits within doors. Other brewers strike a contrast with the Hardys' uncultivated setting, Nockold Tompson of Norwich and Chapman Ives of Coltishall evidently priding themselves on their libraries and other treasures. The executors of Nockold Tompson, advertising the sale of household furniture at the brewer's former home fronting Tombland, referred to beautiful mahogany and walnut furniture and bookcases and 'very good paintings by Rubens and others'; also to his large collection of volumes covering law, history, agriculture, gardening and 'other arts and sciences'.²

Following his first bankruptcy Chapman Ives had to put on the market some precious household effects; these included 'elegant bookcases' containing his library of 500 books at Coltishall Hall.[1] On his death in 1794 James Moore senior, the former East Dereham innkeeper and governor of Gressenhall, left 'many volumes of books' which his sons had evidently decided not to keep.[2]

A love of books was commemorated in stone, as in the memorials to William Offley, MD at St Giles's, Norwich, to John Norris at Witton (volume 3, *plate 26*), and to John Langley Watts, the 37-year-old Mayor of Norwich who died of a fever while in office in 1774. William and Mary Hardy and their children were present at his funeral at Horstead, viewing the young woolcomber's dizzyingly asymmetrical memorial at Horstead on its installation a few months later.[3] They knew the Watts family of Horstead House, and the poignancy of a premature, sudden death, coupled with the Mayor's leaving a widow after just seven months of marriage, struck the diarist. The *Norwich Mercury* devoted six paragraphs to his passing, dwelling on the blending of his many private virtues and 'a most engaging complacency of manners' on the one hand with 'the assiduity, accuracy, and integrity of the merchant' and 'the address and affability of the gentleman' on the other.[4] His monument testifies to the love of learning and books to be found in the active man of business and not only in the retiring scholar.

Despite, or perhaps thanks to, his extremely patchy formal education William Hardy junior developed a lively, enquiring mind, his talents extending way beyond malting and brewing. Unlike his parents he treasured his wide-ranging books, his beautiful floor-to-ceiling mahogany fitted bookcases still lining his study at Letheringsett Hall.[5]

[1] *Ives Norw. Merc.* 1 Oct., 22 Oct. 1796

[2] *Moore Norw. Merc.* 12 July 1794

[3] *Watts Diary 1*: 10 Nov., 13 Nov., 14 Nov. 1774, 30 July 1775; the memorial is illustrated in *Diary 1*, p. 80. His widow gave birth to a daughter, Elizabeth, on 24 Feb. 1775

[4] *virtues Norw. Merc.* 12 Nov. 1774

[5] *William's books* Many, still held by the extended family, are illustrated in this study and the Diary volumes

above right St Giles's, Norwich: the Latin epitaph on the Rococo monument to Dr William Offley (d.1767), formerly Fellow of King's, Cambridge, opens with his love of classical learning from his youth: '*Literis humanioribus usq* [*usque*] *ab adolescentia instructus . . .*' A few of his beloved books are heaped under the eternal flame   [*MB · 2017*]

¹ *Coltishall* The 14 references to cards there span the years 1774–1780 (*Diary 1*). William Hardy played at cards until 3 am at the public-house club (*Diary 1*: 23 Jan. 1775)

² *Letheringsett Diary 2*: 27 Mar. 1786, 26 June 1787, 28 Apr. 1783. Quadrille was a game for four players.
   The Hardys also played cards at Mr Bartell's in 1783 (Diary MS: 29 Nov. 1783)

³ *silence* Self-censorship is not a likely explanation. The diarist gave up theatre-going before the rest of her family and friends, as this chapter will show, but she still recorded *their* attendance at the playhouse

⁴ *cards* The last reference came six months after Raven's death (Diary MS: 24 Aug. 1787).
   The 1797 inventory does not record the presence of a card table as such, but the Hardys had a range of tables which would have suited their purpose (*Diary 2*, app. D2.C)

⁵ *frolics Diary 4*: 18 Sept. 1799, 8 Dec. 1800. The shopkeeper John Davy's Twelfth-Night frolic, attended by William Hardy jnr, might have been classed as 'an entertainment' at Coltishall (15 Jan. 1805)

While living at Coltishall William and Mary Hardy regularly enjoyed card games. The two named by the diarist are brag (similar to poker) and commerce, and the friends they played with were principally the Bendys and the Neves. The curate Mr Farewell joined them once, and William Hardy was once recorded as playing cards on a club night at the Recruiting Sergeant, Horstead.[1] Card-playing was far less popular with the Hardys once they moved to Letheringsett. Here they played quadrille with the Burrells, very infrequently, and a friend lost a pound—borrowed from William Hardy—among card-sharpers at Holt Fair in 1783.[2]

Card-playing, whether by the Hardys or by others, may have ceased after August 1787, there being no reference to cards thereafter in either Mary Hardy's manuscript or (for the period 1793–97) in Henry Raven's. We cannot know if the diary's silence signals the end of this particular frivolity, or whether Mary Hardy's possible disapproval meant she chose not to mention that others were indulging in the pastime.[3] It seems unlikely that moral earnestness developed this early, some years before she was drawn to Nonconformity and long before she encountered the Evangelicals; nor is the dropping of cards likely to be related to the death of Raven in February 1787, when without doubt much of the joy was driven from the Hardys' lives. The diarist and her family still attended balls and the playhouse after Raven's passing, suggesting that bereavement did not occasion the apparent rejection of the card table.[4]

Frolics and 'entertainments' similarly underwent a downward trend from the 1780s, those mentioned in later years relating predominantly to specific feasts in the rural calendar such as harvest frolics and tithe frolics. This celebration over a meal and drinks could be hosted in the home or, more usually, at a public house; it was laid on free of charge by a grateful host such as a farmer when thanking his harvest team or a beneficed clergyman his tithe-payers. Even tithe frolics caught something of the changing mood, for after the move to Letheringsett Mary Hardy increasingly referred to them as tithe audits. Other types became very infrequent, with only three (the excise officers', the Holt bowling-green frolic and a Twelfth-Night frolic) being named in the later Letheringsett years 1797–1809.[5]

The picture in more carefree days at Coltishall had been very different. In the years 1773–80 no fewer than 48 frolics are mentioned, almost all attended by William Hardy and occasionally by his young sons as well; in none is a woman recorded as attending. This figure does not include numerous feasts and housewarmings at public houses; nor does it include the seven private 'entertainments' in the homes of leading members of village society, to some of which both men and women may have been invited, as two were hosted by women—Miss Sarah Palgrave and Mrs Rose Ives.[1]

Frolics were held in public houses in and around Coltishall. These included bowling-green frolics at the Recruiting Sergeant, the Hardys' harvest frolics at the same house, the wine-merchants' frolic at the White Horse, Great Hautbois, the innkeeper Thomas Neve's hunting frolic also at the White Horse, and unspecified frolics at Buxton, Horning, Horsham St Faith, Little Hautbois, Smallburgh and Tunstead. Four regattas or 'water frolics' at Hickling and Hoveton are mentioned 1776–80; also a Norwich frolic given in June 1780 by Captain Berney, a Freemason, attended by his fellow Masons William Hardy and Thomas Neve.[2]

Mary Hardy, perhaps uniquely in this period, records the load on women catering for these major events. For an intense two months in the autumn of 1776 there was an innkeeping interregnum at the Recruiting Sergeant, the Horstead house tied to her husband's brewery at Coltishall. The strains this imposed on her family and that of Zeb and Molly Rouse were severe. Having to help out there herself was extemely daunting given that she, like Molly, had a young family and a home of her own to run; Zeb's absence from the team also meant the Hardys were a man short on the farm and in the maltings and brewery.[3]

The hours at the Sergeant were very long when there were great meals to cook. The St Faith's Fair Supper was held on the opening day of the great livestock fair nearby:

Mr Hardy and I at the Sergeant all day. Roasted near 5 stone of pork, drew a barrel of nog, 2 gallons of rum, 2 bottles of gin and a small quantity of wine and brandy. Came home at 12 in the evening.[4]

She was back again all the next day, with her husband and her brother Robert Raven. A few days later she cooked a pig

[1] *Coltishall* Terminology poses problems, for the words frolic and entertainment may be interchangeable. Miss Palgrave held a 'frolic' on 27 Jan. 1774 and an 'entertainment' exactly a year later on 26 Jan. 1775 (*Diary 1*). Given the timing it is likely they were the same sort of event

[2] *frolics Diary 1*: entries spanning the dates 6 Dec. 1773–16 Oct. 1780.
The age of the frolic is not yet past. The annual frolic is a feature of the calendar of the Parson Woodforde Society: a weekend expedition to a part of the country, usually Somerset, Winchester, Oxford or Norfolk, associated with the clerical diarist

[3] *Rouses* Zeb (d.1804), the Hardys' hardworking farm servant, stepped in as temporary innkeeper, with his wife Molly helping as much as she could. See vol. 2, chap. 1 on the workforce, which reveals Zeb's contribution to the business.
He was the uncle of Zeb Rouse (d.1840), the Letheringsett miller and Methodist

[4] *Sergeant* Part of Mary Hardy's entry for 17 Oct. 1776 (*Diary 1*). She was on call Oct.–Dec. 1776. 5 stone is 70 lb (31·75 kg)

[1] *pig* Diary *1*: 29 Oct.
1776. The diarist and
Sally were also there all
afternoon and evening
on 2 Nov. 1776

[2] *tithe frolic* Diary *1*.
William and Hannah
Breese were about to
take over. They and the
diarist were back at the
Sergeant after breakfast
the next day, getting
home at 8 pm. Molly
was the diarist's second
maid Mary Riches;
Molly Rouse also
worked at the Sergeant

[3] *beef* NRO: PD 597/37,
18 Nov. 1788

[4] *Weston* J. Woodforde,
*The Diary of a Country
Parson*, ed. J. Beresford,
eg vol. 3, pp. 68–9, 2
Dec. 1788; pp. 315–16,
6 Dec. 1791. He had to
put up with a good deal
of disruption to his
domestic routines,
especially when the
tithe-payers got drunk
('rather full') and
became impudent

left Horstead, the Recruiting Sergeant: a landmark on the
Norwich–N. Walsham road at its junction with the route from
Aylsham to Gt Yarmouth.

William Hardy's brewery tap was a lively clubland scene 1773–
81, hosting a weekly club, music and bowls clubs, also specialist
lectures and a masonic lodge. Like most inns and the larger alehouses it hosted frolics: massive feasts which lasted from the
midday meal into the small hours. The diarist cooked for up to 70
people a night during an innkeeping vacancy in 1776 [*MB · 2015*]

for supper at the public house, with her maid Sally to help;
the evening 'broke up morning past 2' (past 2 am).[1] The
Revd Mr Hanmer's tithe frolic placed even greater demands
on the emergency team at the Sergeant. The diarist worked
consecutive shifts of eighteen and twelve hours to cope with
the load, and was probably on her feet most of the time:

[1776] DECEMBER 2, MONDAY …I and Molly went to Sergeant morning 8, Mr Hanmer's tithe frolic there, a very great company at dinner,
we stayed till morning 2 and left company there. William Breese
and his wife came and hired the house and came with us to lodge.[2]

These were big feasts. For his 1788 tithe frolic William Hanmer's successor Dr Grape ordered 39 lb of sirloin of beef.[3]
His fellow cleric James Woodforde chose not to turn to the
Hart at Weston for help. Instead he soldiered on with hosting tithe frolics at his parsonage year after year, his elaborate menus accompanied by punch, port and his much
admired—and powerful—home-brewed audit ale.[4]

For much of the Coltishall years Britain was at war. In the
latter stages the country was at full stretch in a conflict not
only with American colonists but with France, Spain and
Holland. Nevertheless these hostilities do not seem to have
impinged on the national consciousness as much as the
prolonged conflict with France—and additionally at times
Spain, the Batavian Republic and Denmark—in the last sixteen years of the diary. Higher levels of taxation and the
banking restriction of 1797 onwards may also be reasons for
the marked diminution in public-house junketings. There
was a change in behaviour too. At Letheringsett the tithe
frolics at the King's Head, often held in the second week of
January, were quieter affairs than at Horstead and Weston:
they started at the end of the working day and ended earlier.

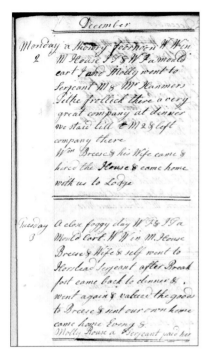

left An 18-hour stint at the Sergeant followed by one of 12 hours, by the woman who worked them: the diary for 2–3 Dec. 1776. At the end of the second entry she notes a payment: 'Molly Rouse at Sergeant, paid her'   [*Cozens-Hardy Collection*]

---

[1] *church choirs* Diary 1: 13 Apr. 1777, 30 Aug. 1778

[2] *singing* Diary 1: 29 Dec. 1778, 16 May 1779. Raven may have sung at Westwick with a newly formed choir from Coltishall or Horstead. The Hardys, when taking their children to Norwich's pleasure gardens from Coltishall, seem to have timed their arrival to fall *after* the concerts (vol. 1, chap. 5, 'Developing a sense of wonder')

[3] *funeral* Diary 2: 16 Feb. 1787

[4] *organ* Diary 1: 4 Oct., 5 Oct., 8 Oct. 1775

[5] *music club* Diary 1: 19 July, 2 Aug., 16 Oct., 15 Nov. 1780.
Trevor Fawcett, in his study of the county's musical life, gives due weight to the vitality of the market towns, but traces of public music-making in villages (to the existence of which Mary Hardy testifies) are harder to discern as such concerts were generally not advertised in the press. Fawcett does not cover home-based music-making: T. Fawcett, *Music in Eighteenth-Century Norwich and Norfolk* (Centre of E. Anglian Studies, Norwich, 1979), pp. 33–42, 1.
Exceptions can be found among the concerts associated with that firm believer in publicity, Chapman Ives: eg his notice for a grand concert and ball to be held at the King's Head, Coltishall in 1795 (*Norw. Merc.* 21 Mar. 1795)

Music

In this period of increasing seriousness other pursuits gained ground among the middling sort as represented by the Hardys. Music entered the family home. At Coltishall almost all mention of music had come in a context outside the home, such as the visits of church choirs to Coltishall from Wroxham and Norwich.[1] Mary Hardy records that her children 'began to learn to sing' at Christmas 1778, but the only subsequent reference came with Raven's participation at Westwick Church (where he might have been heard by the Cozens family into which his sister was to marry).[2] Raven evidently appreciated choral singing, for his family made arangements for Sharrington's choir to attend his funeral in 1787.[3] His mother seems to have had a particular fondness for the organ, hearing organ-playing at York Minster, Beverley Minster and King's Lynn.[4] A music club opened at the Recruiting Sergeant at Horstead in July 1780, with three concerts subsequently being performed there.[5]

[1] *organ* Recounted in vol. 3, chap. 7 under 'Sales and auctions'.
    Dancing, a pursuit primarily for children, is covered in vol. 1, chap. 6

[2] *Berry Diary 2*: entries beginning 21 Sept. 1789

[3] *organ Diary 2*: 26 Sept., 28 Sept. 1788; 15 May 1789; *Diary 4*: 8 July 1802.
    For William Love see T. Fawcett, *Music in Eighteenth-Century Norwich and Norfolk*, p. 26

[4] *piano Diary 2*: 18 Nov. 1789; *Diary 3*: 13 Apr., 3 May, 10 June 1797; for listings in the inventory see *Diary 2*, app. D2.C, pp. 414, 415.
    For the gradual introduction of the piano see T. Fawcett, *Music in Eighteenth-Century Norwich and Norfolk*, p. 48. This would have been the square pianoforte: like the grand piano developed early in the century its strings lie horizontally. The upright, with vertical strings, was invented in Philadelphia in 1800 (P.A. Scholes, *The Concise Oxford Dictionary of Music* (Oxford Univ. Press, London, 1952), p. 456)

[5] *Wells concerts Diary 2*: 30 Oct. 1789, 4 Oct. 1790. See also the index entries under 'music' in the Diary volumes

A marked change took place in the 1780s. A new emphasis was placed on private enjoyment of music and on instrumental rather than choral performance, apart from the singing tuition given to Letheringsett's Sunday school children recounted in volume 3, chapter 2. The gaity and delight which greeted the arrival of the Hardys' organ from Norwich in October 1785 strongly suggests that the very costly item was bought to provide pleasure for Mary Ann, rather than to give the family enhanced social consequence among their neighbours. Eleven young friends were invited to Letheringsett Hall for supper and a dance.[1]

From then onwards music is mentioned more frequently. The Wells organist Mr Berry, hired to teach the Sunday school, also started teaching William and Mary Ann in 1789, William deciding to take up the cello while his sister continued with the organ.[2] She had been taught the previous year by Mr Love of Norwich, who had helped to install the instrument and was probably the well-known musician William Love. Mary Ann played the organ, apparently spontaneously and for pure enjoyment, in the large churches she visited with her mother at Great Yarmouth and Cromer in 1789 and 1802.[3]

The first mention of a piano came in 1789—sixteen years after the earliest record of a piano in Norfolk. William and Mary Ann went to a supper and piano concert in the home of the Edgefield surgeon Thomas Theodorick, whose children were the Hardys' good friends. In May 1797 a piano, valued at £13 in the inventory that year and probably bought second-hand, arrived for Mary Ann from Southrepps, near Cromer, the instrument being housed in the keeping room. In the parlour stood the organ, valued at £20, with a ten-shilling music stool.[4]

References to choral concerts continued, such as those by the Sharrington choir, the Sunday school children at Letheringsett and the oratorio concerts under Mr Berry's direction at Wells Church, two of which the Hardys attended.[5] The years 1785–90 can be seen as a particularly rich period in the development of the Hardys' musical tastes. During the 1790s the diarist refers to church choral-singing far less frequently, and we hear no details of the introduction by the miller Zebulon Rouse of singing into Letheringsett

Church in 1798.[1] The existence of church choirs from the mid-1770s or earlier in the villages, an aspect not covered by Trevor Fawcett, would have meant that the labouring poor (assuming they attended services) would also have had the chance to participate in music-making. Many would already have learnt hymns and simple choruses at Sunday school, or have heard their children singing them.

Music had become a feature of theatrical performances through legal necessity. Under the licensing system of 1660, reinforced in 1737, only patent theatres (London's Covent Garden and Drury Lane being the only two to be granted perpetual patents) were permitted by law to perform plays.[2] In order to protect themselves from prosecution, for the justices who granted the temporary licences were watching them, travelling players had perforce to adopt the subterfuge of portraying themselves as musicians by injecting music into every performance. Operas, ballad operas, songs and musical interludes formed part of the repertoire of the troupes touring East Anglia, notably those belonging to Norwich's Theatre Royal and the companies under the management variously of William Scraggs and David Fisher. Assemblies and public balls gave further opportunities for the enjoyment of music. For the ball held in 'the assembly room' (the Shirehouse) at Holt in April 1790 it was announced that 'music will be provided from Norwich.'[3]

As in so many other aspects of the cultural and social life of the time public subscription concerts in market towns like Wells and Fakenham continued until 1790, after which time the press notices became far less frequent. The Hardys are not recorded as attending a public concert after 1790.[4] By the early 1790s Norwich's pleasure-garden concerts, such as those at the Pantheon, were tailing off, James Woodforde being most unimpressed on his last recorded visit in 1794. It was Assize Week, traditionally the busiest week by far in the city's social and cultural calendar. But there was 'not much company'. This was fortunate, for he endured 'a poor concert and worse singing, and coffee, tea and chocolate so indifferent that I did not so much as taste it'.[5] He had however the solace of the Weston choir in his own church. This received consistently favourable reviews, as in the singing of the Christmas anthem in 1792 and 1793.[6]

[1] *Rouse Diary 4*: 9 Sept. 1798

[2] *patent theatres* E. Grice, *Rogues and Vagabonds*, pp. 12, 14–16. Norwich's Theatre Royal claimed a patent for those performances given in the house, but Burley shows it was valid only for 11 years 1768–79 (T.L.G. Burley, *Playhouses and Players of E. Anglia*, pp. 7–10)

[3] *assembly* Norw. Merc. 24 Apr. 1790; none of the Hardys attended

[4] *town concerts* eg Mr Berry's at Wells (*Norw. Merc.* 24 Oct. 1789, 18 Sept. 1790). Although the Hardys attended the vocal and instrumental concerts in Wells Church, they did not stay for the evening balls at the Fleece Inn. A vocal and instrumental concert was given at Fakenham Town Hall for Mr Berry's benefit in 1790. It was not attended by the Hardys; nor did they go to the evening ball at the Red Lion that same day (*Norw. Merc.* 29 May 1790)

[5] *Pantheon* J. Woodforde, *The Diary of a Country Parson*, ed. J. Beresford, vol. 4, pp. 128–9, 15 Aug. 1794

[6] *Weston* J. Woodforde, *The Diary of a Country Parson*, ed. J. Beresford, vol. 3, p. 400; vol. 4, p.

87. His diary points to *c.*1793 as the onset of the decline in concert-going; however increasing infirmity may have meant he was just disinclined to attend. Tellingly, Trevor Fawcett's portrait of music-making in the city's pleasure gardens relates principally to the 1770s and 1780s (*Music in Eighteenth-Century Norwich and Norfolk*, pp. 29–32)

---

[1] *schools* Chronicled in vol. 3, chap. 2: see 'Dwindling of support' and 'A mixed picture'

[2] *Canada* Quoted by Peter Clark in *British Clubs and Societies 1580–1800: The origins of an associational world* (Oxford Univ. Press, 2001), p. 3

[3] *listings* Chase's Norwich directory 1783, p. 52, and Peck's of 1802, under addenda [!], p. 15

[4] *players* The performance of *Tamerlane the Great* at Holt in 1785 was followed by 'A Grand Ode on Masonry, . . . as performed at the Grand Lodge, Freemasons' Hall, Great Queen Street, London'; 'Brother Scraggs' was one of the singers (*Norw. Merc.* 8 Jan. 1785)

[5] *Aylsham Norw. Merc.* 26 Mar. 1791. Visiting Masons, 'the brethren',

As shown later, the country playhouse was also becoming less popular, attesting to a malaise even before the outbreak of war in February 1793—after which anxieties over the course of the war and sedition at home came to the fore. Clerical interest in Sunday schools, and public support for them, likewise died down after 1790; this sole musical avenue for the children of the labouring sort would in consequence have withered.[1]

The same pattern emerges in the life of the county's clubs. Among these was the high-profile society, 'The Most Ancient and Honourable Society of Free and Accepted Masons', otherwise known as the Freemasons.

Freemasonry—and a troubled lodge

It was 1759. Great Britain was at the high point of her *annus mirabilis*. Major General James Wolfe in Quebec had just died in his moment of victory over the French on the Heights of Abraham. As the drama unfolded, British troops strove urgently to establish a secure footing in their new conquest. Within days of their victory they had instituted the first Provincial Grand Lodge of Freemasons in Canada.[2]

In the same year the Provincial Grand Lodge of Norfolk was founded. There was little secrecy attaching to the society at this time, the members' meetings and processions which formed part of the social round occasionally being reported in the press. Their lodges too were named, with foundation dates and meeting places, in trade directories and annual memorandum books (as shown opposite).[3]

The theatrical profession had in its midst a high proportion of Masons and its own lodges: members were named in the playbills on masonic nights with the prefix 'Brother', William Scraggs being one such.[4] The playbills also identify local Masons. One was the Aylsham innkeeper William Strain, who hosted Scraggs's company in 1791 ahead of their procession and benefit performance in the town:

The brethren are desired to meet at 5 o'clock at Brother Strain's at the King's Head, Aylsham, in order to go in procession from thence to the theatre.[5]

William Hardy was a Mason, both at Coltishall and at Letheringsett. We learn something of rural Freemasonry from

A correct LIST of the REGULAR LODGES of the moſt ancient and honourable Society of Free and Accepted MASONS, in Norwich and Norfolk, according to their Seniority and Conſtitution.

PROVINCIAL GRAND MASTER,
Sir EDWARD ASTLEY, of MELTON, Bart.

R. Partridge, Eſq. P.D.G.M. Tho. Marks, Gent. P.S.G.W
J. Buttivant, ſen. P.J.G.W. Jas. Buttivant, jun. P.G.S.

No.
17 WHITE Swan, St. Peter's, Norwich, the firſt Wedneſday in the month, conſtituted May 11, 1724.
52 King's Head in Market-place, Norwich, laſt Thurſday 1736.
61 Chapter, Caſtle and Lion, third Thurſday, Royal George.
83 The Queen's Head, Acle, Norfolk, laſt Monday in the month, May 9, 1747.
85 Maid's-Head, Norwich, third Tueſday, January 5, 1784.
87 Red Cow, St. Giles's, Norwich, the firſt Tueſday, 1749.
94 Unicorn, St. Mary's, Norwich, the ſecond Monday, 1750.
96 Half Moon, Great Yarmouth, laſt Thurſday, June 6, 1751.
109 Three Jolly Dyers, St. George's Tombland, Norwich, firſt Wedneſday, Nov. 20, 1753.
115 Caſtle and Lion, Norwich, ſecond Thurſday every Month, conſtituted March 13, 1757.
132 The King's Head, Walſingham, Norfolk, called the Royal Edgar Lodge, the Monday before a full moon, June 17, 1755.
135 The Wounded Heart, St. Peters, Norwich, the fourth Tueſday, Sept. 16, 1755.
148 King's Arms, Blakeney, firſt Monday on or after the full moon.
153 King's Head, Coltiſhall, Norfolk, the Wedneſday on or neareſt the full moon, February 18, 1758.
185 Lodge of Friendſhip, Crown, Lynn-Regis, Norfolk, ſecond Friday, June 9, 1762.
213 Dormant, in Swaffham, Norfolk, called the Great Lodge, firſt Monday, December 17, 1756.
225 Black Horſe, Tombland, in Norwich, the laſt Friday, Feb. 11, 1766.
226 The White Hart, Thetford, called the Royal Edwin, (formerly held at Fakenham) the Monday before or on the full moon, 1766.

left Freemasonry: Norfolk's 18 lodges in 1790, listed under date of foundation.
William Hardy belonged to no. 148, meeting at the King's Arms, Blakeney on the 'first Monday on or after the full moon'.
He had previously belonged to no. 153, which in 1790 met at the King's Head, Coltishall on 'the Wednesday on or nearest the full moon'. In his time the lodge had met at his tied house, the Recruiting Sergeant, Horstead.
Unless the night were cloudy a full moon would help to light the Masons along their way to and from meetings.
Norwich hosted ten lodges. Acle, Gt Yarmouth, Walsingham, King's Lynn, Swaffham and Thetford hosted one each, although Swaffham's was dormant at the time [*Crouse and Stevenson's Norwich and Norfolk Complete Memorandum Book* (*Norwich, 1790*)]

Mary Hardy in 1779–81 (for Horstead's Lodge of Unanimity, when she fills in some of the missing years reported by the county's masonic historians), and then in 1787–89 (for Blakeney's Lodge of Friendship). But her references to their activities cease from December 1789.

were invited to attend *She Stoops to Conquer* on 5 Apr. 1791

Norfolk Freemasonry: Provincial Grand Masters and Grand Secretaries

source   F.R. Eaton, *An Outline of the History of the Provincial Grand Lodge of Norfolk 1759–1959* (Soman-Wherry Press, Norwich, 1960), pp. 11–25, 119–20 (dates and names only)

key   § denotes that the chosen candidate was not installed in office

dates	*Provincial Grand Masters 1759–1842*
1759–84	Edward Bacon, of Earlham, Recorder of Norwich, MP for Norwich (see page 449)
1785–98	Sir Edward Astley, Bt, of Melton, MP for Norfolk
1798–99	§ Hon. Henry Hobart, of Intwood, MP for Norwich, Colonel of 3rd Norfolk Militia
1800–07	Brig. Gen. William E. Bulwer of Heydon, Cdr of 2nd Norfolk Volunteer Cavalry
1810–13	§ Revd Samuel Summers Colman of Broome Place; Rector of Rushmere, Suff.
1813–16	§ William Palgrave jnr of Coltishall and Gt Yarmouth, Collector of Customs
1816–17	§ Sir Jacob Henry Astley, Bt, of Melton, MP for Norfolk, son of Sir Edward
1818–42	Thomas William Coke, of Holkham, MP for Norfolk, from 1837 Earl of Leicester

dates	*Provincial Grand Secretaries 1765–c.1809*
1765–74	Thomas Davey
1774–75	George Gilbert
1775–85	Joseph Stannard, ? Norwich barber, father of Revd Christopher Stannard
1785–92	James Buttivant, Norwich merchant
1792–96	James Buttivant jnr
1796–97	James Buttivant
1797–?1809	James Boyce, ? Norwich attorney (d.1809)

[1] *low ebb* F.R. Eaton, *An Outline of the History of the Provincial Grand Lodge of Norfolk 1759–1959* (Soman-Wherry Press Ltd, Norwich, 1960), p. 16

[2] *roots* H. le Strange, *History of Freemasonry in Norfolk 1724 to 1895* (Agas H. Goose, Norwich, 1896), pp. 1–9; F.R. Eaton, *Some Masonic Events relating to the Province of Norfolk 1724 to 1944* (Soman-Wherry Press Ltd, Norwich, 1945), pp. 5–11; F.R. Eaton,

Since the Masons' historian Frederic R. Eaton observes that by the early years of the nineteenth century 'Freemasonry was then at rather a low ebb in Norfolk' the diarist's silence is likely to point to a loss of vitality in the hinterland rather than to a change in her recording habits.[1]

Hamon le Strange and F.R. Eaton chart the events before and after the foundation of the county's Provincial Grand Lodge in 1759. By this time Freemasonry had formed strong roots in Norwich and Norfolk, there being twelve lodges in Norwich in 1758. The Maid's Head Lodge had been constituted in 1724, followed by King's Lynn's Duke's Head Lodge five years later and Great Yarmouth's Angel Lodge in 1751. Nevertheless Masonry remained at its strongest in Norwich. Since Norfolk was a masonic province from 1759, in this very real sense Norwich served as the provincial capital of Freemasonry.[2]

right The King's Arms at Ludham: one of the many homes found for William Hardy's extremely restless Lodge of Unanimity after its move from his tied house at Horstead [*MB·1993*]

An Outline of the History of the Provincial Grand Lodge of Norfolk, pp. 9–15

The biographical outlines of the early Provincial Grand Masters, added for the purposes of the inset opposite, might at first suggest that a conspiracy was afoot to infiltrate the political world's higher echelons with Masons and thereby exert influence. The pollbooks do not support this theory. The MPs listed, with the exception of the Pittite Hobart, were all Whigs of varying intensity. Yet, in spite of the Whiggish tendencies of city and county, masonic parliamentary candidates could not rely on electoral support from among their brethren, as the Coltishall entries in the county pollbooks demonstrate.[1] It is more likely that in their choice of Provincial Grand Masters the Masons were seeking the sanction and nominal leadership of elevated persons, some of whom went on to serve only in an honorific capacity and were inactive; only half were in fact installed in office.

Freemasonry is first mentioned by Mary Hardy in 1778, when she travelled to Norwich with her friend Mary Neve, wife of the Coltishall timber merchant and former innkeeper Thomas Neve. They dined at George Gilbert's (the former Provincial Grand Secretary, listed opposite) and watched the masonic procession to the Theatre Royal through the crowded streets of Norwich following the opening of the new lodge-room at the Angel Inn.[2] The diarist had already met George Gilbert: he had called at the Hardys' earlier in the month, apparently looking for a suitable lodge-room locally.[3] William Hardy and some of the Coltishall Masons went on to attend lodge meetings in Norwich at the Angel and the King's Head, both in the Market Place.[4]

[1] *Coltishall* In the 1802 Norfolk election, of the five voters identifiable from Mary Hardy's diary and H. le Strange's *History of Freemasonry in Norfolk 1724 to 1895* (p. 131) as Freemasons, only one (Charles William Bendy) voted for the Whig Sir Jacob Henry Astley. Even two former masters of the lodge (Robert Ansell and Chapman Ives) did not support him, although Sir Jacob was the son of the former Provincial Grand Master, Sir Edward.

In 1806, of the four voters identifiable as Coltishall Masons, only two voted for the Whig Freemason T.W. Coke

[2] *Norwich Diary 1*: 25 May 1778; *Norw. Merc.* 16 May, 30 May 1778.

The master of the Angel Lodge was the prominent banker Roger Kerrison

[3] *Gilbert Diary 1*: 5–6 May 1778; they looked over the White Horse, Gt Hautbois. Until 1776 this was Mrs Neve's home, Thomas Neve being the innkeeper.

Mrs Gilbert joined Mary Hardy and Mary Neve at Coltishall Fair 24 May 1779 (*Diary 1*)

[4] *Norwich Diary 1*: 22 Oct. 1779, 13 Oct. 1780

right The King's Head, Coltishall: the east front facing onto Lower Common. One of the large bay-windowed rooms may be the new masonic lodge-room built in 1793 by Chapman Ives, the brewer who owned this outlet.

The room was opened by the county MP Sir Edward Astley, Bt, Provincial Grand Master. The MP for Norwich, the Hon. Henry Hobart, was also present (*Norwich Mercury*, 19 Oct. 1793). But Ives used the Masons' funds to ease the debts fast building up in his brewing business   [MB · 1999]

[1] *Horstead Diary 1*: 20 Jan., 3 Feb. 1779; the female visitors appear to have looked round at the start of the February meeting

[2] *Stannard, Johnson Diary 1*: 31 Mar. 1779

[3] *Lodge of Unanimity Norw. Merc.* 13 July 1782, 1 Nov. 1788

[4] *Horstead Diary 1*: 4 Aug., 25 Aug. 1779

[5] *Ann Stannard Diary 1*: 2 June 1779.

Joseph and Ann Stannard's son Revd Christopher Stannard became a friend of the Hardys. He showed them round his Cambridge college, St John's, in May 1800 and called on them at Letheringsett 1800–03 (*Diary 4*).

He became Rector of St Peter Hungate, Norwich and of Gt Snoring with Thursford

In January 1779 a lodge was opened by William Hardy, Thomas Neve, Robert Ansell and others at the Recruiting Sergeant at Horstead, Mary Hardy and Mary Neve inspecting the lodge-room shortly afterwards.[1] The diarist records 28 monthly lodge meetings there, held first on Wednesdays and later on Mondays. All were attended by her husband from January 1779 until he moved to Letheringsett in 1781; he was present in addition at seven private lodge meetings 1779–80. The meetings frequently went on into the small hours. The opening night, 20–21 January 1779, lasted from 4 pm to 4 am; the second, on 3–4 February, lasted until 2 am, the timber merchant George Boorne and Coltishall schoolmaster John Smith apparently being initiated (*Diary 1*).

The new lodge received support from Norwich, Joseph Stannard, the Provincial Grand Secretary, and John Johnson arriving from the city for the meeting on 31 March 1779.[2] Mr Johnson was the proprietor of the coffee house in the Market Place where meetings of the Lodge of Unanimity had taken place before its move to Horstead; he was declared bankrupt in 1788.[3] Later in 1779 Captain Berney and Sir John Berney's steward Boorne Garrod attended from Norwich, and Joseph Stannard returned.[4] When Ann Stannard accompanied her husband to Horstead on a subsequent visit she stayed on for supper with Mary Neve and Mary Hardy while their husbands were at the lodge.[5] Flexible routines were swiftly established, the hours for the lodge meetings being from about 6, 7 or 8 pm until anything from 10 or 11 pm to 4 am. All the named Masons were working men with trades to run and young minds to teach: John Smith had to be back in command at Coltishall Free School a very few hours after some of the meetings had broken up.

Hamon le Strange, for over twenty years Provincial Grand Master for Norfolk and, like Frederic Eaton, a former Deputy Provincial Grand Master, enables the history of the Lodge of Unanimity to be resuscitated—apart from the missing years which include those at Horstead—from the patchy survivals in the archives. He confesses himself bewildered by this particular lodge. Tracing its moves around the city and county he lists its meeting places from its foundation in 1758 to the year he was compiling the record, 1896:

This Lodge has been more peripatetic than any other in the Province, having met at seven different towns or villages in Norfolk, to say nothing of a thirteen years' sojourn at Bungay in the neighbouring Province of Suffolk. Of the first thirty years of its existence no records have survived, the original warrant and the early minute books having alike disappeared; the places at which it met from 1758, when it was first warranted, down to 1787, when it moved to Coltishall, are given on the authority of the Warrant of Confirmation . . .

It had practically died out while at Johnson's Coffee-house in Norwich, and, according to a not infrequent practice of that day, it had sold its warrant, which had been bought by Brother Chapman Ives . . . [1]

The lodge had met at four public houses in Norwich 1758–1774 before moving to the Three Tuns at 'Aylsham' [? Bungay]. In 1778 it went back to the city, to Johnson's coffee house, at which point le Strange loses trace of it. We have seen that it met at Horstead from 1779 until, presumably, 1787, when the lodge was reconstituted at the King's Head, Coltishall—where it was reunited with its former Horstead hostess Ann Springthorp.[2] Le Strange recounts its history thereafter. It moved from Coltishall to the Maid's Head in Norwich, the Castle at Wroxham, the King's Head at Hoveton St John, the King's Arms at Ludham, and at Bungay the Three Tuns and then the King's Head. Finally it sought a safe haven in the King's Arms at North Walsham.[3] Le Strange enumerates other quirks associated with the lodge.

[1] *peripatetic lodge* H. le Strange, *History of Freemasonry in Norfolk 1724 to 1895*, pp. 118–20

[2] *Ann Springthorp* She and her husband William had come from Norwich in 1778 to take over the Sergeant; they prepared the new lodge-room and served as hosts from 1779. The Springthorps moved to the King's Head at Coltishall in 1784, William dying in 1785 and his widow continuing there until her death in 1794

[3] *removals* H. le Strange, *History of Freemasonry in Norfolk 1724 to 1895*, pp. 118–30. He also gives a list of masters of the lodge 1759–1895, with gaps for 1760–86 and 1798–1803 (pp. 131–2). William Boorne, son of George, became master in 1811 at Hoveton St John (p. 131).

There is even some doubt as to its identity. Chase's Norwich directory 1783 states that the lodge then meeting at the Recruiting Sergeant was not Unanimity but no. 131, the Lodge of Friendship, founded 17 June 1755 (W. Chase, *The Norwich Directory*, p. 52); it also shows a *separate* lodge, no. 152 (founded 18 Feb. 1758) at Johnson's coffee house in Norwich.

I have not traced a Three Tuns at Aylsham

¹ *quirks* Even in 1896 the lodge clung to its 'little local peculiarities' dating from the past (H. le Strange, *History of Freemasonry in Norfolk 1724 to 1895*, pp. 130, 120–1)

² *opening of lodge-room Norw. Merc.* 19 Oct. 1793. The following year Chapman Ives published a detailed rebuttal of the notion that the French Revolution was brought about by principles inculcated by Freemasonry (*Norw. Merc.* 26 July 1794)

³ *finances* H. le Strange, *History of Freemasonry in Norfolk 1724 to 1895*, pp. 122–3. Ives had form in taking money while a trustee of a Coltishall charity (vol. 1, chap. 6, 'An endowed village school', and vol. 2, chap. 8, 'The downfall of Chapman Ives')

⁴ *Blakeney* H. le Strange, *History of Freemasonry in Norfolk 1724 to 1895*, p. 105. Like the Lodge of Unanimity it was highly mobile, meeting in seven different Norwich public houses from its foundation in 1757 before settling in Gt Yarmouth from 1846 at a further four public houses in King Street and on Hall Quay

facing page The King's Arms, beside Blakeney harbour   [*MB · 2012*]

Whereas it was customary for Masons to celebrate the feast-day of St John Evangelist on 27 December, the Lodge of Unanimity insisted on observing the feast of St John Baptist on 24 June.[1] Coltishall's parish church was dedicated to the Baptist, but had in earlier centuries had a joint dedication to both Baptist and Evangelist, as displayed in the spandrels and flushwork at the west door; the victory of the Baptist may explain this preference for 'doing different'.

In Chapman Ives's time in office the lodge at first was flourishing. A new lodge-room at the King's Head was opened in 1793 by the Provincial Grand Master and Norfolk MP Sir Edward Astley in the presence of the Norwich MP Henry Hobart. The august assembly of 'respectable brethren', with their regalia and music, processed from the King's Head to Coltishall Church to hear a sermon before returning for 'an elegant dinner' and a collection for the poor.[2]

It ran into severe financial trouble at the time of the brewer's first bankruptcy in 1796, with arrears being due to the Grand Lodge. A leaf has been torn out of the minute book covering the years 1797–1803. However a surviving letter by Ives of 5 February 1801, transcribed in full by le Strange and oddly strained and defensive in tone, would seem to suggest that the brewer had used the funds to support his personal finances: he claimed that the lodge was his 'sole property'. The lodge was not back on a secure footing, having severed its Coltishall connection and moved to Hoveton St John, until 1804—the year of Ives's second bankruptcy. The minutes begin again in December 1804, at about the time of his death in Ireland.[3] The debts which bedevilled most forms of manufacturing, commercial and even social activity in this period had cast a long shadow over the lodge. Johnson and Ives were bankrupted within a few years of one another.

Masonic life was seemingly very much quieter at Blakeney, although mobility characterised that lodge as well. In 1787 the Lodge of Friendship had to move from its home at the Castle and Lion, in White Lion Street, Norwich. For no recorded reason it chose to uproot itself to a new world 25 miles away by the sea.[4] Here it remained at the King's Arms at Blakeney until 1792, when it returned to its urban setting,

this time more centrally at the White Lion in the Haymarket. Again the Provincial Grand Secretary, this time James Buttivant, who was also master of the lodge, took the lead.[1] And again female members of the Masons' families were anxious to capture something of the moment:

[1787] NOVEMBER 12, MONDAY A very fine day. Mr Dusgate drew Mr Hardy's tooth and dined here, Mr Hardy better. Mr and Miss Stannard and Mr Buttervant [Buttivant] came in afternoon, they were going to a Freemasons' Lodge at Blakeney.[2]

We learn far less about this lodge from the diarist, as her husband rarely attended. She records his presence at only two meetings in 1788, and one with his son in 1789. It is possible that the members, the great majority of whom lived in Norwich, made the journey only very infrequently to the port: le Strange notes that while sixteen Masons came from Blakeney and its neighbourhood, a further 32 hailed from Norwich.[3] No set pattern emerges from Mary Hardy's slender evidence, although on all three nights her husband did not get home until the small hours. It is likely that a fourth masonic meeting was held at the King's Arms, in August

[1] *James Buttivant* He is shown in the inset (p. 328) as instituted as Provincial Grand Secretary in 1785; but p. 52 of Chase's Norwich directory states he was in office by 1783

[2] *Blakeney Diary 2.* The lodge's move to the King's Arms had been announced in the press (*Norw. Merc.* 10 Nov. 1787). (Francis Dusgate was a Holt watchmaker, and presumably good with his hands)

[3] *Blakeney Diary 2:* 14 Nov., 15 Dec. 1788, 2 Dec. 1789 (a Friday, Monday and Wednesday); H. le Strange, *History of Freemasonry in Norfolk 1724 to 1895,* p. 110

¹ *Blakeney Diary 2*: 10
Aug. 1789 (a Monday);
William jnr went to the
port that night 'to meet
his father'

² *Norwich Diary 2*:
12 Dec. 1792. Hurrell,
briefly the Hardys'
maltster in 1782, could
have been ailing. He
died aged 44. His fine,
deeply incised head-
stone in Blakeney
churchyard (illustrated
in *Diary 2*, p. 237) may
have been funded in
part by grateful Masons

³ *the Ship* H. le Strange,
*History of Freemasonry
in Norfolk 1724 to 1895*,
pp. 169–70: it was an
'Ancients' or 'Atholl'
lodge. For the story of
the Lodge of Friend-
ship see his pp. 105–13

⁴ *listings* Chase's Nor-
wich directory 1783, p.
52; Peck's 1802, unpag.,
also addenda, p. 15

⁵ *leadership* As shown
in the list of Provincial
Grand Masters in the
inset, the next three
after Bulwer were not
installed in office

⁶ *Clark's conclusions* He
finds Norwich strong in
Masonry in 1778. He
does not comment on
the picture for the years
immediately following
(P. Clark, *British Clubs
and Societies 1580–1800*,
pp. 310, 309, 315, 316,
320–5; his chapter 'Free-
masons' is pp. 309–49)

⁷ *on the move* P. Clark,
British Clubs and Socie-

1789, attended by Robert Ansell and 'a Mr Bell' of Coltis-hall as well as her husband.¹

Lodges would have been dependent on the innkeepers who ran the premises, a factor which may explain the constant removals associated with some eighteenth-century lodges. The month before John Hurrell of the King's Arms died in December 1792 the lodge moved back to Norwich, even though his widow carried on the trade.² This was not the end of Freemasonry in Blakeney, for from 1801 there was a lodge at William Hardy junior's tied house, the Ship, but it did not prosper there.³

From the late 1790s there seems to have been a falling off of interest in Freemasonry, and the press reports diminish. The Norwich directory of 1802 does not point to decline, however. William Chase had listed nineteen lodges in 1783; dispersed around the city and county; nineteen years later Thomas Peck named 22 'Regular Lodges'.⁴ Henry Hobart was a dying man when he was chosen as Provincial Grand Master in 1798, and was never installed in office. His successor General William Earle Bulwer was often absent from Norfolk, on active service in home defence during the two French wars. Leadership may have been lacking at the top.⁵

Norfolk did not follow the national trend. Peter Clark concludes that the 1790s and early nineteenth century were witness to a strong era in masonic history following a period of 'dynamic growth' 1751–1800. In 1800, in an enumeration of just the 'Moderns' (among which the lodges Unanimity and Friendship were counted), there were 93 lodges in London, and 263 in the provinces in England and Wales; the lesser market towns were 'heavily represented', having 56 per cent of the total number of lodges. Clark's observations do however apply to Horstead and Coltishall in one significant aspect: men in trade and the professions were attracted and consolidated into the movement, but not the gentry, nor the poor. He considers that a mix of artisans, victuallers and tradesmen helped to form associational bonds and thus encourage social cohesion. The emphasis was on respectability, but not on social exclusivity.⁶

Freemasonry helped 'brethren' on the move.⁷ A newcomer to an area, and member of a distant lodge, could immediately feel a sense of belonging on being welcomed among his new neighbours in their lodge. All itinerants, unless they happen to be of an unusually sturdy and independent disposition, crave ready acceptance in their new setting; and, as this study emphasises time and again, itinerancy was a way of life in rural areas. Eaton supplies an illustration of this principle in action, at the time of the Seven Years War. A French prisoner at Great Yarmouth, 'Brother Mercier', applied in 1760 to Yarmouth's Angel Lodge for financial support during his sojourn in this country—and was unanimously granted seven pence a week by the Masons.[1] It was a pittance. Washerwomen and unskilled labourers would receive rather more for a *day*'s work. But the sympathy and brotherly solidarity shown towards a captured foe could have given solace.

Clubbability on the wane

Mary Hardy charts the decline of the club world generally. Just as frolics are mentioned less often as the years pass, so club meetings become fewer; exceptions are certain occasions such as annual school feasts and venison feasts for special commemorations. The Coltishall years 1773–81 had been brimful of clubbable spirit. She records the opening of the wine club at Coltishall King's Head, the music club at Horstead, her husband's attendance at the lottery club at Little Hautbois, and his visits to unnamed clubs at five public houses: at Horstead (where the club did not meet in the summer months, when bowls took over), Great and Little Hautbois, Neatishead and Tunstead.[2] William Hardy was especially faithful in his attendance at the Recruiting Sergeant's weekly club, going to 93 meetings in seven years; here he was in the company of farmers and maltsters, merchants and brewers, the curate and the schoolmaster.

After moving to Letheringsett, club life continued with a certain vitality at first. In the early years 1781–93 the diarist recorded her husband's participation in the lottery club at Holt King's Head and also in clubs at six public houses at Brinton, Cley, Holt and Letheringsett. However, even after acknowledging editorial abridgment in the Letheringsett years, there were far fewer visits to clubs. Only 29 recorded attendances are noted in the published text 1781–93; and during those twelve years only two visits came after 1789.[3]

ties 1580–1800, pp. 330–1; as a result, Masonry had broad appeal not only to strolling players but to the military, in bringing them, the 'outsiders', within 'the sociable community'

---

[1] *Frenchman F.R. Eaton, Some Masonic Events relating to the Province of Norfolk 1724 to 1944*, p. 9

[2] *bowls* As an outdoor pursuit they feature in the next chapter

[3] *abridgment* The Coltishall years are transcribed in full in *Diary 1*. Henry Raven's diary 1793–97 is transcribed in full in *Diary 3*. Both texts are fully indexed.
Mary Hardy's Letheringsett text 1781–1809 (in *Diary 2*, *Diary 3* and *Diary 4*) is abridged and indexed.
The Remaining Diary of Mary Hardy, also edited by Margaret Bird (2013), cited in this study as 'Diary MS', contains the missing entries 1781–1809; but it is not indexed. It completes the picture for those pursuing their own research: eg 'Mr Hardy went to Brinton club evening 6, came home past 10' (Diary MS: 2 Sept. 1782).
The editorial method is explained in detail at the start of each *Diary* volume

[1] *new clubs* Diary 3: 15 Nov. 1796, 10 Jan. 1797; 16 Dec. 1794

[2] *book club* Diary 3: 10 Jan. 1797. Mary Hardy last records William's attendance on 19 Jan. 1802 (*Diary 4*)

[3] *horse associations* Diary 4: 24 June 1801. These were commonly advertised in the local papers, together with lists of subscribers. In 1791 those belonging to the Holt Association included Cley merchants John Ellis and John Mann, the Glandford miller Richard Rouse, the owner of Swanton Novers' brickkiln John Dew and local farmers from a wide radius (*Norw. Merc.* 16 July 1791)

[4] *frothiness* P. Clark, *British Clubs and Societies 1580–1800*, p. 192. See also his presentation of the moral earnestness associated with Methodists and Revivalists (p. 96)

[5] *fervour* Mary Hardy's niece Rose and nephew-in-law Revd Thomas Skrimshire represent the new, earnest approach. Instead of talking about books into the small hours over numerous drinks at a public house the Fakenham schoolmaster instituted a public library in the town in 1801. As its first

During the middle Letheringsett years 1793–97 Mary Hardy's diary points to changing habits. A book club is first mentioned in 1796 at the Feathers at Holt, William Hardy junior and the Cley merchant John Ellis attending its dinners. Also William Hardy senior attended a club at Letheringsett King's Head 'for the first time' in 1794, indicating that it was not the one he used to go to in the 1780s: 'Mr Hardy went to a club at Dobson's for the first time, came home morning 1, William went a little while.'[1] Father and son thereafter attended it occasionally. Henry Raven was not a member of any club, and merely confirms his cousin William's attendance at Holt's book club.[2]

The same trend of decreasing clubbability emerges in the last of the Letheringsett diary years 1797–1809. William Hardy junior attended Holt book club dinners until 1802, and once went to the horse association dinner at Holt in 1801. Both men and women belonged to this, paying subscriptions towards the apprehension and prosecution of horse-stealers.[3] Father and son continued in a limited fashion to attend the club at Letheringsett, their five visits all falling in 1801–02. Thereafter the record falls silent.

We owe a great debt to the repetitive, rhythmic recordkeeping of a clubman's wife by which we can gauge changing habits. Mary Hardy's testimony tunes in to an extent with Peter Clark's tracking of various forms of sociability:

By the end of the eighteenth century several of the principal forms of Georgian sociability—pleasure gardens, promenades, assemblies, masquerades, the theatre—were in retreat as fashionable activities. This reflected wider economic and other changes in urban society, but it was also a result of the growing hostility, headed by the religious revival movement, to the perceived frothiness of much sociability, in contrast to the high seriousness of many voluntary societies.[4]

However these observations do not explain the conundrum that the men in Mary Hardy's immediate circle were neither Nonconformist nor Evangelical (at that time); in particular the once enthusiastic clubman William Hardy remained untouched by Revivalist fervour all his life.[5] Further, serious voluntary work was temporarily on the decline, as in the case of rural Sunday schools and even some urban ones (volume 3). Even the worthy philanthropy of Freemasonry was on the wane in Norfolk. In the authoritarian atmosphere of the 1790s clubs could be feared as potentially subversive. Developments which Clark goes on to identify, notably the differentiation of private social space between men and women, and family life's 'greater temporal and gender specialization', hold good only in part for Mary Hardy's experience of life among the middling sort: entertaining at home remained as central as ever during the 36 years of her record, with both sexes continuing to join in together. This hotly debated issue has a place of its own in the next chapter.[1] Clark also attributes an alleged lack of club life in country areas to dark nights and bad weather,[2] but Mary Hardy makes it clear that village clubs were especially active during the winter months. Outdoor pastimes such as bowls took over during the light summer evenings.

The evidence of her diary is that it would be inaccurate to characterise 'the associational world' portrayed by Clark as revolving mainly around clubs and Freemasonry, in which the camaraderie of political talk, drinking, office-holding and ritual helped to forge social bonds. He does not explore other gatherings in the multi-layered associational world of the rural middle class which had parish meetings as their focus. As described elsewhere, active participants might be parish officers, providers of public dinners for the poor or assistants in a Sunday school. In the last two roles, in contrast with the world of clubs, women played major parts.[3]

Networking in rural society was widespread, over dinners with the justices at quarter and petty sessions, and at town meetings.[4] The opportunities for office-holding presented by the old forms of parochial government demanded leadership ability and the exercise of far greater responsibility, and from an early age, than in running a club. Men in their twenties—like Mary Hardy's son and grandson—managed parish budgets, supervised the feeding of famished paupers, resettled labourers disabled by industrial accidents, organised emigration overseas and much more, all in their spare time. Public-spirited women also networked, as seen in volume 3 in the exchange of ideas over Sunday schools.

A highly significant vehicle for social bonding not considered by Peter Clark is represented by the Volunteers. As with parish meetings and Sunday schools these companies were

president he announced it would open on 10 Oct. (*Norw. Merc.* 25 Apr., 26 Sept. 1801)

[1] *'gender specialization'* P. Clark, *British Clubs and Societies 1580–1800*, p. 192; for 'the English pattern of collective sociability' and its predominantly urban setting, see eg his pp. 2, 19, 94, 131–2

[2] *dark nights* P. Clark, *British Clubs and Societies 1580–1800*, pp. 136–7, 142

[3] *serving the parish* See chap. 10 in this volume; and vol. 3, chaps 2 and 6

[4] *networking* P. Clark, *British Clubs and Societies 1580–1800*, pp. 98–100; here his observations on networking relate principally to political and philanthropic lobbying.

He concludes that 'The moderate achievements of British societies in their specialist or primary activity may also derive from the fact that . . . their secondary functions, whether promoting social alignments, facilitating social integration and social networking, or defining gender boundaries, were no less a priority', all of which 'were much easier to implement and accommodate within the distinctive structures of voluntary activity' (p. 444)

1 *comrades in arms* See chap. 9, under 'Mobilisation' and 'A militarised society'

2 *on Heads* Diary 1: 13 July, 17 July 1779. The topic may have been phrenology, then exciting some interest. The speaker may have been William Stevenson, publisher of the *Norfolk Chronicle* and the annual *Crouse and Stevenson's Memorandum Book.*
  Learned, artistic and scientific societies were being founded in Norwich: eg the United Friars (1785) and the Speculative Society (1790). Norwich's public (subscription) library dates from 1784: C.B. Jewson, *The Jacobin City*, pp. 143–56

3 *philosopher* Diary 2: 24 Sept. 1785. The Norwich Philosophical Society, with very wide-ranging interests, was not founded until 1812

4 *societies* The growth of scientific and philosophical (scientific) societies is examined in T. Kelly's *A History of Adult Education in Great Britain from the Middle Ages to the Twentieth Century* (3rd edn Liverpool Univ. Press, 1992; 1st pub. 1962), pp. 98–106

not clubs, but they were nonetheless intense forms of association forging bonds between disparate social elements. His study ends in 1800, before the great alarms of 1803–05, but even so the Volunteer units had been active in both rural and urban areas in 1781–83, once the American war had widened into more general conflict, and then with even greater urgency in 1795–1801. The Year of Peril, 1797, heralded a rush to arms by civilians. Serving part-time in arms became by far the most important activity for men away from the workplace in this militarised society 1798–1805.[1]

The advent of learned societies in cities and large towns fostered a new spirit which spilled over into the villages. There was a hunger for knowledge, for new ideas unconnected with workplace innovation of the type embraced by William Hardy and his son. Mary Hardy records lectures given at the Recruiting Sergeant in the 1770s, but with insufficient detail to enable the origins of this new interest to be traced; it is possible the societies springing up in Norwich had members prepared to tour public houses to give talks. On her way back home from Norwich with her sister Phillis Goggs, their brother Nathaniel and his wife the diarist's little group 'stopped at Sergeant to hear Stevenson's lectures on Heads'. It was evidently a success. Four days later the lecture was repeated, the diarist gathering a larger party: 'Mr and Mrs Neve and [Mr and Mrs] Boorne, I and Mr Hardy and Mr Slade went to Horstead Sergeant to hear Stevens's lecture on Heads.'[2] After the move to Letheringsett William and Mary Hardy and their seventeen-year-old son Raven joined the Davy family at the King's Head at Holt one evening 'to see a philosopher who is publishing a book'.[3]

The development of urban learned societies is well documented. One of the most famous, the Lunar Society of Birmingham, met between 1768 and 1799. Another, the Royal Institution, was founded in London in 1799 to teach science to the general public. Mary Hardy gives tantalising hints of this spirit of enquiry spreading into the countryside, but her slender entries do not enable us to form a clear picture; it may just be that such instances were extremely rare.[4]

The British Museum had opened in Bloomsbury in 1759. Although the diarist did not call there on her two London visits, in 1777 and 1800, the Hardys showed an eagerness to tour smaller museums and marvel at the 'curiosities' they contained. Mary Hardy described York Castle's gruesome relics in immense detail in 1775, probably for the benefit of her very young sons. Among the fourteen exhibits and murderous instruments which made a particular impression were 'the knife and fork used in quartering the rebels taken in the late Rebellion', 'the knife that one Knowles cut a woman's throat with at Knaresborough', and 'an iron rod a blacksmith run a man through the body with'.[1] She and her husband viewed Boulter's private museum in Great Yarmouth in 1783,[2] and Mary Ann noted in her mother's diary that she and her parents toured the Trinity House Museum in Hull in 1803: 'We all went to the Freemasons' Lodge, it is a large and very elegantly fitted up room, from thence we went to the Trinity House and saw the curiosities in it.'[3]

The Hardys had a museum right on their doorstep: at the rector's. The Revd John Burrell was a passionate and knowledgable naturalist, *The Universal British Directory* referring to his collection as early as 1794. He was evidently keen to show its contents to anyone who might be interested:

The Rev. John Burrell, rector, has a neat house in this village, and also a *nucleus musœi*, in which are a few articles believed to be unique, and deserving the attention of travellers.[4]

The notice following his death in 1825 reveals something of his intellectual pursuits within his Letheringsett home:

. . . In the Library there are about a thousand volumes on natural history, divinity, and miscellaneous subjects, in English, Latin, and French; amongst which are Shaw's Zoology, large paper, Shaw's Naturalists' Miscellany, Transactions of the Linnæan Society, Sowerby's English Botany, Martyn's English Entomologist, Curtis's Flora Londinensis, Curtis's Entomology, Zoological Journal, Donovan's British Insects, Zoological Miscellany, Pennant's Zoology, Gerarde's Herbal, Linnæus's System of Nature in Latin and English, and sundry other works of that author, Da Costa's British Conchology, Da Costa's Fossils, Lewin's Papilios, Harris's English Insects, Bolton's British Ferns, Sole's British Mints, Gyllenhal's Insecta Suecica, Hooker's Jungermanniae, Rees's Cyclopaedia, etc, etc.[5]

The Cabinet contains a portable Orrery by Jones, an ancient cornet, the tusks of the walrus, two Roman urns, a large quantity of shells, minerals, fossils, spars, etc, specimens of cloth manufactured by savage nations, and a variety of other curious articles . . .[5]

[1] *York Castle Museum Diary 1*: 26 Sept. 1775. The 'late Rebellion' was the Jacobite rising of 1745–46

[2] *Gt Yarmouth Diary 2*: 10 Nov. 1783. Daniel Boulter was a bookseller, silversmith, cutler, toyman and Quaker, his 'curiosities' featuring in the press (*Norw. Merc.* 15 Sept. 1787, 2 Aug. 1788, 4 Jan. 1794, 7 Feb. 1795, 18 Sept. 1802, 18 Aug. 1804). Members of the public were charged 1*s* admission

[3] *Hull Diary 4*: 28 May 1803. See also the illustrations and captions on pp. 230 and 231 of *Diary 4*

[4] *nucleus musœi The Universal British Directory*, vol. 3, pp. 280–1. The phrase means the nucleus of a museum (literally the kernel of a collection or seat of the Muses). The rector had a penchant for archaic forms of language

[5] *library, Cabinet Norfolk Chronicle*, 29 Apr. 1826. The full notice, still held as a newspaper snippet in the Cozens-Hardy Collection, is reproduced in *Diary 4*, p. 2.
A cabinet was not necessarily a free-standing cupboard or set of glass-fronted shelves for displaying objects: it could signify a small, private room

¹ *entomology* John
Burrell was elected a
Fellow of the Linnean
Society 17 June 1800.
The society's collection
was housed 1783–1809
at the Norwich home of
its founder Sir James
Edward Smith at 29
Surrey Street (A. Batty
Shaw, *Norfolk and
Norwich Medicine: A
retrospect* (The Norwich
Medico-Chirurgical
Society, Norwich, 1992),
pp. 101–2).
    For details of the
rector's life and publi-
cations see NRO: PD
547/42, Reprint of W.H.
Burrell's article 'Nor-
folk Natural History
Correspondence', *Trans-
actions of the Norfolk and
Norwich Naturalists'
Society*, vol. 11, pt 4
(1922–23), pp. 391–3;
it does however contain
errors relating to the
rector's antecedents
and relations with the
Hardys. The Gresham's
School Archive also
holds a set of notes
detailing some of his
intellectual pursuits

² *bowls* eg *Diary 2*:
30 Apr., 19 July 1781

³ *one extreme* The two
women make fascinat-
ing studies.
    Elizabeth Peach's
hedonistic way of life
damaged both her
family and her husband's
neglected parishioners
(C. Miller, *The Amiable
Mrs Peach* (The Lasse
Press, Norwich, 2016)).
    Mrs Bulwer-Lytton,

It may be a mark of how disengaged the diarist felt from such pursuits of the mind that not once does she mention the rector's collection, nor his interest in entomology.[1] The newspaper notice detailing the contents of the house, which also included 'many cases of stuffed birds', 'several lots of beautiful and fine old scarce china' and 'a collection of silver and copper coins, medals etc', was however preserved by her son and remains to this day in the family archives. Without doubt William Hardy junior appreciated John Burrell's intellectual strengths and shared some of his interests, while not being prepared to buy the collection so dear to the cleric: he wished only to purchase the house and its grounds.

Such pastimes were pursued in the home; museum visits however formed part of the surge in tourism recounted in chapter 1. It is doubtful whether Mr Burrell displayed his learning in talks at the various clubs infrequently mentioned by the diarist at Letheringsett and Holt. Unlike his sociable father, who would spend five hours playing bowls at a Holt inn with William Hardy, he was not a clubbable man.[2]

The frothiness identified by Peter Clark as 'in retreat', as quoted on page 336, was still the hallmark of some among the more leisured classes who were prepared to fritter away their days, nights and cash at the card table and in a vacuous way of life so repellant to serious-minded society—the very circles into which Mary Hardy and her daughter were moving. Two wealthier women can represent the throng at one end of the divide in a society fracturing along lines defined partly by religious observance, with the strict conduct some forms imposed, and partly by the way people spent their leisure hours. They are Betsy Peach, 'the amiable Mrs Peach' (1748–1815), whose first husband was Edward Leathes, the technically resident but often absent rector of Reedham, east of Norwich, and 'that odd rich old woman' Elizabeth Barbara Bulwer-Lytton (1773–1843), granddaughter of Elizabeth Jodrell of Bayfield and unhappily married to William Earle Bulwer of Heydon Hall. Only occasionally would devotion to earnest endeavour occupy these two women, who had so much to give. Aimless wandering, and a sense of having no secure foundation to their lives, were their fate.[3]

The idle rich or would-be rich pepper the pages of plays and novels, as in those by Sheridan, Jane Austen, Thackeray

above Norwich: Thomas Ivory's Theatre Royal in 1758, regularly attended by the Hardys on their Norwich visits in the early diary years. Mary Hardy last saw a performance here in 1792
[*drawing by 'TB' 1758, detail: Norfolk Heritage Centre, Norwich*]

Charlotte Bronte, George Eliot and Trollope. The gulf separating shallow Rosamond Vincy from worthy Dorothea Brooke in Eliot's *Middlemarch* (published in instalments 1871–72, but set 1829–32) is but one of a host of fictional divides. And the progression along the spectrum from 'perceived frothiness' to moral rectitude in Mary Hardy's time can be charted with precision by the fortunes of the playhouse and the reception accorded the strolling players of East Anglia.

The playhouse

The pattern of the Hardys' enjoyment of cultural pursuits was repeated in the theatrical world: a flowering during the 1770s and 1780s despite the backdrop of war 1775–83, succeeded by slow decline and near-extinction by 1809. The first indication of the Hardys' fondness for the theatre came in 1774. William Hardy attended a play at North Walsham after doing business at the inns in the town; his wife was left at Coltishall with the ironing and entertaining first the Bendys and then, until midnight, the curate.[1] At Great Yarmouth in 1775, once his business shipping malt for London was done, William Hardy went to the play; his wife, left in charge at home, received visits and cash from innkeepers.[2]

whom Mary Hardy would probably have seen as a young woman attending performances at Holt sponsored by her mother Elizabeth Warburton-Lytton and uncle Henry Jodrell, had an early life blighted by her parents' separation. Her father Richard, of Chesham, Bucks, later of Knebworth House and a member of the Lunar Society, broke her in early childhood by straining lovelessly to fill her brain with serious subjects which would leave no space for frivolity. Her development stalled by an appalling upbringing and equally ill-judged marriage, she was precipitated into an aimless life of endless rounds of visits to London, Bath and other spas and watering places (J. Preston, *That Odd Rich Old Woman: The life and troubled times of Elizabeth Barbara Bulwer-Lytton of Knebworth House 1773–1843* (Plush Publishing, Dorchester, 1998))

[1] *N. Walsham Diary 1*: 15 June 1774. Frances Boorne was there too, without her husband

[2] *Gt Yarmouth Diary 1*: 4 Dec. 1775. As was usual, the programme that night was advertised in advance (*Norw. Merc.* 2 Dec. 1775)

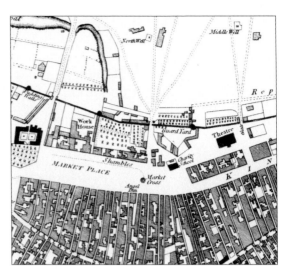

right Gt Yarmouth: its first play-house was built in 1778 beside the town walls; it is seen here well to the right of the market place.

In 1775 William Hardy saw the new comic opera *The Maid of the Oaks* and the farce *Cross Purposes*, performed by the company from Norwich's Theatre Royal. They were in makeshift premises in the Water Bailiff's Office on the quay, as described by John Preston in *The Picture of Yarmouth* (1819) [*Faden's Map of Norfolk 1797, detail: Larks Press 1989*]

below Players while on tour often had to make do with barns: the Leicester Company of Comedians tried to hire the Hardys' Horstead barn in 1779.

This is a small section of the magnificent 17th-century barn at Ludham Hall, near St Benet's Abbey on the Bure [*MB · 2001*]

[1] *theatre* For the dates of all references see the index entries under 'players' and 'plays' in the four published Diary volumes

Neither North Walsham nor Yarmouth had a purpose-built playhouse at this time, the visiting troupes having to shift for themselves.

Theatre-going in the Coltishall years 1773–81 could only rarely be a joint pastime for husbands and wives in the diarist's circle as the demands of running family businesses and caring for home and children intervened. It can be a mark of increasing prosperity if husbands and wives are re-corded going up to town together—a fair distance in the case of Norwich and North Walsham—for an event start-ing at 6 or 6.30 pm, for it indicates they had been able to leave behind a clerk in charge of the business, an assistant in the shop, a bartender in the public house or usher in the school. Of seven visits by the Hardys to the Theatre Royal in Norwich 1775–79, three were made by husband and wife together, nine-year-old Raven and his schoolmaster joining them on one occasion. On a further three William Hardy went alone or with friends; and once Mary Hardy went with the wife of the Norwich cabinetmaker Samuel Larrance.[1]

Women would frequently attend the theatre unaccompa-nied by their menfolk. A good deal of independence was required: working families with busy lives would have been very restricted in their leisure pursuits had they waited to find a time to suit both. Gender segregation could in this period be not so much a conscious social preference as an economic necessity when the playhouse, club or evening concert beckoned.

Mary Hardy records many of her friends who went to the Theatre Royal: the Coltishall schoolmaster John Smith and sometimes his family, his four visits all being in term-time and not confined to Saturdays as half-days; the innkeeper, later timber merchant, Thomas Neve and his wife Mary; the shopkeeping and mercantile family, the Boornes; and the diarist's first cousin Hannah, wife of the farmer Robert Raven. However on their 1777 visit to London William and Mary Hardy, in holiday mood, were able to attend together the Theatre Royal, Drury Lane.[1]

The diarist records a fascinating episode early in 1779 concerning licensing at the preliminary stage not entered in the quarter sessions records; nor was it the type of theatrical snippet announced in the press as it involved just the sort of magisterial rejection which actors wished to avoid. Circuit players on their journeys through East Anglia usually bypassed major centres such as Norwich, Great Yarmouth, King's Lynn, Bury St Edmunds and Ipswich favoured by the touring company from Norwich's Theatre Royal. They were evidently prepared to perform in very small villages, such as Horstead with its population twenty years later of only 370: it is testimony to the vitality of village culture at that time (or possibly to the comedians' desperation) that the company could contemplate putting on a series of shows there. The Hardys rented a large barn at Horstead along the Mill road from the Recruiting Sergeant:

[1779] JANUARY 23, SATURDAY... A Mr Fisher, Master of Leicester Company of Comedians, came to hire Horstead barn to act in, promised to come again on Monday next ...

FEBRUARY 1, MONDAY... Mr Fisher the player dined here, supped and slept here. Mr Hardy went with him after dinner to Horstead Sergeant [the Recruiting Sergeant], came back evening 4 ... Mr Baret refused to let the players come ...

FEBRUARY 2, TUESDAY... Mr Fisher and Mr Hardy walked to Horstead Sergeant after breakfast, came back at noon, Mr Fisher went away ...[2]

The *Norwich Mercury* records that 'Mr Fisher junior' was acting with the Leicester Company of Comedians that winter,

[1] *Drury Lane Diary 1*: 23 Sept. 1777; they saw Colman's comedy *The Jealous Wife* and Dauberval's opera *The Deserter*

[2] *Horstead Diary 1*. The system of licensing players at quarter sessions is explained under 'Puritanism re-emergent' later in this chapter. Actors, like cattle drovers, had to be licensed if they were to escape being classed as vagrants.

The justice Peter Baret (1705–81) lived at the property known later as Heggatt Hall, further along the lane from the Hardys' barn; he served as Sheriff of Norfolk in 1744.

His niece Lydia Baret (d.1823 aged 87) married Mary Hardy's first cousin Henry Raven, a Bramerton farmer who later moved to Gt Hautbois (vol. 1, chap. 4, fig. 1.4c). For the Barets see P. Millican, *A History of Horstead and Stanninghall*, pp. 97–102, 104–9.

It is not clear if 'Mr Fisher' is David Fisher (1729–82) or his young son David (1760–1832), pictured overleaf. It seems unlikely however that an 18-year-old would be running his own company: extreme youth would not have reassured the justices. The younger man was probably the 'Mr Fisher jnr' of the press notices

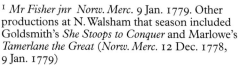

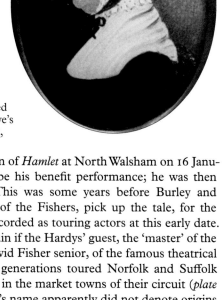

¹ *Mr Fisher jnr Norw. Merc.* 9 Jan. 1779. Other productions at N. Walsham that season included Goldsmith's *She Stoops to Conquer* and Marlowe's *Tamerlane the Great* (*Norw. Merc.* 12 Dec. 1778, 9 Jan. 1779)

² *Holkham* Mr and Mrs Thomas William Coke reinforced the Holkham connection by themselves announcing performances at Walsingham by the Leicester Company of Comedians: eg *Norw. Merc.* 26 Sept. 1778.

Both Burley and Grice chronicle the Fisher family, their theatres and circuit (T.L.G. Burley, *Playhouses and Players of East Anglia*, pp. 135–164; E. Grice, *Rogues and Vagabonds*, pp. 89–119).

The earliest date for David Fisher jnr's début quoted by Grice is 1786 (p. 90)

as their production of *Hamlet* at North Walsham on 16 January 1779 was to be his benefit performance; he was then aged eighteen.¹ This was some years before Burley and Grice, historians of the Fishers, pick up the tale, for the Fishers are not recorded as touring actors at this early date. It is thus not certain if the Hardys' guest, the 'master' of the company, was David Fisher senior, of the famous theatrical family which for generations toured Norfolk and Suffolk and built theatres in the market towns of their circuit (*plate 38*). The company's name apparently did not denote origins in Leicestershire, but derived from the earldom (of the first creation) of the Cokes of Holkham. Troupes of strolling players liked to cast themselves as associated with the nobility and gentry in order to protect themselves from being classed as vagrants, as they were always on the road.²

Respectability was consequently the quality they sought above all, as William Scraggs emphasised in the *Norwich Mercury*. That paper heralded the start of the winter season at Holt in 1784:

We are well assured that Mr Scraggs, (whose Company of Comedians, from its present respectability, has given such universal satisfaction at Eye [in Suffolk],) is preparing an elegant little theatre at Holt . . . which is now fitting up with entire new scenery and decorations, and will be opened early in the ensuing month; where, there is no doubt, but he will meet with that generous support the different performances have been constantly honoured with by the Nobility and Gentry of every place he has yet visited.[1]

There was also an attempt to ape Assize Week in Norwich, the few days a year when the King's representative came in pomp to sit in judgment and the county flocked to the city for summer balls, concerts, dinners, fireworks and the theatre. Holt hosted the county quarter sessions every October and January, and so 'Sessions Night' was devised (the sessions lasting one or at most two days). Scraggs arranged a Sessions Night programme for 27 September 1788, when an actress made her début at Holt: 'From the Theatre Royal, Richmond, being her first appearance on this stage, Mrs Stanley'.[2] The sense of occasion comes across strongly, a plea being made that ladies should no longer dress their heads with caps and hats as the gentlemen could see neither the ladies' faces nor the play. The injunction could have been directed at the female Hardys.[3]

[1] *Scraggs Norw. Merc.* 30 Oct. 1784

[2] *Sessions Night Norw. Merc.* 27 Sept. 1788. Theatre-goers at times had very little notice of the programme, the newspaper being published only weekly.
The Theatre Royal in Richmond, Yorks, had opened that year

[3] *hats Norw. Merc.* 16 Aug. 1788. The very large lace cap and ornate picture hat worn by Mary Hardy and Mary Ann for their portraits of 1785 show just what audiences had to contend with. One of the sittings took place on the day they went to *Romeo and Juliet* and *The Poor Soldier* at Holt with the artist Huquier and his wife (2 Feb.)

facing page Mary Fisher (1730–1819), née West, with her son David (1760–1832). It is not clear if it was he or, more probably, his father David (1729–82), who as actor–manager stayed with the Hardys early in 1779. The younger David, 'Mr Fisher jnr', was performing on tour with the Leicester Company of Comedians during the winter season 1778–79; the suffix could indicate his father was also active in the profession [*Norfolk Heritage Centre, Norwich*]

left David Fisher (1788–1858) in 1818, by then a theatre builder and actor–manager of his own company: son of the David Fisher seen opposite [*drawn and engraved by J. G. Walker 1818: Norfolk Heritage Centre, Norwich*]

¹ *'at the third act'* eg in Norwich (*Diary 2*: 22 Mar. 1783); and at Holt (*Diary 2*: 11 Dec. 1784, when the Hardys saw *The Power of Love, or Harlequin Animated*, described in the notice illustrated below: this London pantomime had as attractions 'the magic box, the living crocodile and the enchanted tailor')

Actors and audiences had to face long evenings in the converted premises. The curtain would rise at 6.30 pm and fall close to midnight; reduced prices were charged if only the farce were attended towards the end of the evening. Those with tasks to complete, as had both male and female members of the Hardy family, would sometimes come in only 'at the third act'—after the main performance and interlude.¹

All the Hardy family were enthusiastic theatre-goers in these early years. In the Holt seasons 1784–85 and 1788 one or more of the Hardys attended on a total of 26 nights. They also had round to their house some of the players from

right A typical notice placed regularly in the Norwich papers by William Scraggs during his winter season at Holt 1784–85; Holt's 'new theatre' was the White Lion's barn.

Scraggs announces that *The Merchant of Venice* has never before been performed at Holt (circuit companies tending to keep to a well-worn repertoire which they knew to be popular), and that the performance is at the request of Henry Jodrell— one of the leaders of local society and, even more importantly, a magistrate. Respectability was the watchword.

A neighbouring JP's son lends his name to the next performance. Captain Edward Astley, an officer in the Guards and thus clearly loyal to the Crown, was the son of the baronet Sir Edward—himself the commanding officer of the Melton Volunteers 1781–83.

The list of Scraggs's 58 performances at Holt that winter is given in the inset overleaf [*Norwich Mercury, 18 Dec. 1784: Norfolk Heritage Centre, Norwich*]

Never Performed Here.

By Defire of HENRY JODRELL, Efq; *of* BAYFIELD.

By Mr. Scraggs's Company of Comedians, *From the* THEATRES-ROYAL *London, York, & Edinburgh,* AT the new THEATRE in HOLT, on Saturday Evening, December 18, 1784, will be performed a Comedy, call'd,

The MERCHANT of VENICE.

To which will be added a Comedy in two Acts, call'd, The TOBACCONIST.

By Defire of Captain EDWARD ASTLEY, *of* MELTON.

On Tuefday Dec. 21, 1784, will be performed a Comedy, call'd,

The SCHOOL for SCANDAL.

From a correct Copy of the original Manufcript. (As written by RICHARD BRINSLEY SHERIDAN, Efq.) The above excellent Comedy (which is efteemed one of the very beft Productions of its ingenious Author) never having been publifhed, has feldom been performed in the Country but from fpurious and imperfect Copies. The Manager having with much Difficulty procured a true Copy of the Manufcript, hopes it will be found to deferve a Portion of that very liberal Approbation which attended its Reprefentation in London.

To which will be added a Pantomime Entertainment, call'd, The POWER of LOVE;

Or, HARLEQUIN ANIMATED.

In which will be introduced the Magic Box, the Living Crocodile, and the Enchanted Tailor, with many capital Scenes from the Pantomimes of Drury-Lane and Covent-Garden: The whole being calculated to excite Laughter, cure the Spleen, and difpel the Vapours.

And on Thurfday Dec. 23, 1784, (by Defire) a PLAY and FARCE, as will be exprefied in the Bills for the Day.

To begin at Half paft Six o'Clock. Tickets to be had at the Feathers Inn, Holt, the principal Inns in Cley and Blakeney, and Places to be taken of Mr. Gray, from Ten till Twelve, at the Theatre.

above The White Lion at Holt *c.*1912, at the north-east entrance to the market place; the Norwich coach, 'the Lobster', is heading for Cromer. Its route is shown as via Erpingham and Roughton, so it avoided the very steep hill above the Glaven headstream between Holt and Edgefield. Even five horses could not cope with a loaded coach on that gradient. The inn had been tied to the Hardys' brewery. The outbuilding behind it to the left may have been the barn which once served as the town's 'theatre' [NRO: MC 2043/2/132, 908 × 8, *Checkley Collection*]

Scraggs's company and from David Fisher's rival troupe.[1] The programmes advertised in the press and listed overleaf mimicked not only the productions of the provincial patent theatres but those of Drury Lane and Covent Garden in the capital; Mrs Siddons had, for instance, made the part of Euphrasia in *The Grecian Daughter* her own. Many of the plays and operas in the repertoire of Scraggs and Fisher were also up to date, such as those of 1773–77 by Goldsmith and Sheridan. New plays reached Norfolk quickly. G.E. Ayscough's tragedy *Semiramis* came to Norwich in 1777, when it had been first performed at Drury Lane only the previous year.[2] Nine-year-old Raven noted in the diary that he saw *Semiramis* and 'the entertainment called The Bankrupt' with his parents and schoolmaster. The curtain rose at 6.15 pm; the Coltishall party got home at midnight.[3]

[1] *Hardys* Scraggs and another player came to supper (Diary MS: 5 Jan. 1785); later he brought his new wife round (*Diary 2*: 18 Aug. 1788). David Fisher and his wife came to tea (*Diary 2*: 26 Mar. 1793). Other families, including the Burrells, hosted players

[2] *Semiramis* At the Theatre Royal (*Diary 1*: 19 Apr. 1777; *Norfolk Chronicle*, 19 Apr. 1777)

[3] *entertainment Diary 1*: 19 Apr. 1777

The 'theatre' at Holt: the repertoire of the actor–manager William Scraggs and his touring company in the winter season 1784–85

sources   *Norwich Mercury*, 13 Nov. 1784–29 Jan. 1785; Diary of Mary Hardy
note   The 'theatre' was the barn in the White Lion's backyard at Holt, cleared for action

date	production	author	type
1784			
Nov. 13	*Douglas*	Hume	tragedy
	and *The Poor Soldier*	O'Keefe/Shield	Irish ballad opera
16	*She Stoops to Conquer*	Goldsmith	comedy
	and a farce		[to be announced]
18	*King Richard the Third*	Shakespeare	history play
	and *The Citizen*		entertainment
20	*Love in a Village*	Bickerstaff/Arne	comic opera
	and *The Poor Soldier*	O'Keefe/Shield	Irish ballad opera
23	*The London 'Prentice* and	?Murphy	tragedy
	Catherine and Petruchio	Garrick	farce
25	*A Bold Stroke for a Wife*	Centlivre	comedy
	and a farce		[to be announced]
26	*The Beggar's Opera*	Gay	satirical ballad opera
	and *The Lying Valet*	Garrick	farce
27	*The School for Scandal*	Sheridan	comedy
30	*The Rivals*	Sheridan	comedy
Dec. 4	*The West Indian* and	Cumberland	comedy
	The Devil on Two Sticks	Le Sage	farce
7	*The Recruiting Officer*	Farquhar	comedy
	and *Bon Ton*	Garrick	farce
11	*The Busy Body* and	Centlivre	comedy
	The Power of Love		pantomime
14	*The Suspicious Husband*	Hoadley	comedy
	and a farce		[to be announced]
16	*The Beaux' Stratagem*	Farquhar	comedy
	and *Love à la Mode*	Macklin	farce
18	*The Merchant of Venice*	Shakespeare	comedy
	and *The Tobacconist*	Jonson/Gentleman	comedy
21	*The School for Scandal*	Sheridan	comedy
	and *The Power of Love*		pantomime
23	A play and a farce		[to be announced]

The 'theatre' at Holt: Scraggs's repertoire 1784–85 (*cont.*)

date		production	author	type
1785				
Jan.	1	*The Miser*	Fielding	comedy
		and *The Power of Love*		pantomime
	4	*The Constant Couple* and	Farquhar	comedy
		The Witches of the Rocks		pantomime
	8	*Tamerlane the Great* and	Marlowe	history play
		A Grand Ode on Masonry	Jackson	musical entertainment
		and *The Cobbler's Wife*		musical interlude
		and *The Invasion* [1]	Garrick/Boyce	speaking pantomime
	12	*King Henry IV* and	Shakespeare	history play
		The Soldier Laddy and		musical dialogue
		The Scotchman's Journey		
		to London and		interlude
		The Scheming Lieutenant	Sheridan	farce
	15	*The Wonder!* and	Centlivre	comedy
		The Lady of the Forest and		pantomime
		The Agreeable Surprise	O'Keefe/Arnold	comic opera
	19	*Love makes a Man*	Cibber	comic musical show
		and *The Poor Soldier*	O'Keefe/Shield	Irish ballad opera
	29	*The Grecian Daughter*	Murphy	tragedy
		and *The Oracle*		interlude
		and *The Maid of the Oaks*	Burgoyne	opera
Feb.	2	*Romeo and Juliet*	Shakespeare	tragedy
		and *The Generous Tar*	O'Keefe	interlude
		and *The Poor Soldier*	O'Keefe/Shield	Irish ballad opera
	6	*The Clandestine Marriage*	Garrick/Colman	comedy
		and *The Hypocrite*	?Bickerstaff	interlude
		and *The Mogul Tale*	Inchbald	new farce

---

[1] *The Invasion* Presumably *Harlequin's Invasion*, first performed at the end of Dec. 1759 at the Theatre Royal, Drury Lane, London. It has the song *Heart of Oak* written by David Garrick to the music of William Boyce in celebration of the year of victories—the *annus mirabilis* 1759: '*Come cheer up, my lads, 'tis to glory we steer, To add something more to this wonderful year…*'

right A dramatic scene from *The Devil on Two Sticks*, the French farce based on the novel *Le Diable Boiteux*.

The hero of the play, which takes place in 17th-century Spain, is Don Cleophas of Madrid; 'the devil' is a dwarf on two crutches, Asmodeus, released from his imprisonment in an evil magician's bottle. He shows Don Cleophas a series of events unfolding across the city as they fly above the rooftops [*drawing by Stothard; engraving by Heath 1780*]

[1] *Mrs Hardcastle* She warms to her theme in Act 2 of Goldsmith's *She Stoops to Conquer*: 'We country persons can have no manner at all. I'm in love with the town, and that serves to raise me above some of our neighbouring rustics . . . All I can do is to enjoy London at second-hand'

This was no rustic isolation, whatever Mrs Hardcastle might say about her strong but thwarted desire to 'rub off the rust', as quoted at the chapter frontispiece. She loved London, so she told Hastings—while never having actually gone there.[1] By the autumn of 1784 Scraggs's company was performing Macklin's farce *Love à la Mode* (1782) and Elizabeth Inchbald's *The Mogul Tale* (first produced in London that same year). The only piece performed in the 1784–85 Holt season four times, O'Keefe's popular ballad opera *The Poor Soldier*, had first opened in London in 1783.

Many of the plays themselves are full of social satire. These comedies of manners depict relations between the classes, the irrepressible servant often coming out on top, as in *The Rivals*. Others are commentaries on town-and-country debates, as in *She Stoops to Conquer*. Four of the productions in Holt's season 1784–85 were by the female playwrights Susannah Centlivre and Elizabeth Inchbald, who were not afraid of adopting the guise of comedy to confront topical issues such as women's rights and cultural conflict. Audiences reflected the social mix. Local gentry and servants were to be found in the audience; women attended the playhouse with other women or with their children. To get around the problem of being needed by their mistress, the Hardys' maidservants took it in turn on consecutive nights to attend at Holt, Molly Matsell going to *A Bold Stroke for a Wife* and Betty Mason to *The Beggar's Opera*.[1] The family's farm servant, maltster, drayman and coachman William Lamb drove his master and Mary Ann to Holt in the carriage in 1791 and stayed on for the play as well; he was then at plough the next day in a 'blustering' wind.[2]

By then some of the Hardys' interest had slackened. Mary Hardy's last visit to the theatre was in Norwich in 1792. The rest of the family attended fairly frequently at Holt in the season January–March 1793. But when the players came round in 1795 William senior and junior hardly went at all; Mary Ann chose to go once, as did Henry Raven. When 'Clarke's company of players' began performing at Holt in 1808 none of the Hardys was there, although the Revd Mr Burrell and his family attended during the tour.[3]

To enjoy the theatre as intensively as the Hardys did in the years 1784–91 required physical proximity. Although few thespians would have been very far from a temporary playhouse in north, east or central Norfolk it was certainly easier for the Hardys to attend from Letheringsett than from Coltishall. The Woodfordes at Weston Parsonage, who never seem to have attended Scraggs's performances at nearby Reepham, regarded the twelve-mile trip to Norwich as quite an undertaking and would spend a night or two there.[4]

[1] *maids Diary 2:* 25 Nov., 26 Nov. 1784

[2] *Lamb Diary 2:* 12 Jan., 13 Jan. 1791. More usually Lamb merely collected the Hardys late in the evening (eg Diary MS: 5 Feb. 1791)

[3] *Clarke Diary 4:* 24 Sept., 25 Oct. 1808. He did not advertise: the years of paying for considerable quantities of column inches in the press were for the moment over.

The marginal notes in the published Diary volumes give a great deal of additional detail about the theatre companies, the programmes and attendances by local people. Henry Raven went with his cousins William Hardy jnr and Nathaniel Raven jnr from the Whissonsett shop on 28 Apr. 1795 (*Diary 3*).

Mary Hardy's last visit, with her husband, was in Norwich on 23 May 1792 (*Diary 2*)

[4] *Reepham* A map of the Norwich circuit theatres, the 13 Fisher purpose-built theatres, and fit-up theatres like that at Holt illustrates the endpapers of Elizabeth Grice's *Rogues and Vagabonds*.

The Fishers built anew where there had been earlier theatres, as at Bungay; theirs opened in that town in 1828 (*plate 38*)

above A crowded Drury Lane on the night of 15 May 1800: James Hadfield, at the front of the stalls, tries to shoot the King in the Royal Box. The would-be assassin, aged 29, is the only man wearing a hat apart from the two Yeoman Warders clutching their pikestaffs and watching helplessly. Mary Hardy was in London at the time, but does not mention the King's brush with death: the shot narrowly missed.

The engraving shows the formal dress of women in the elegant boxes. Despite Holt's many charms as a Georgian market town, for the 18th-century theatre-goer its fitted-up barn could hardly have matched the social and aesthetic experience of an evening at formal playhouses like Ivory's spacious, classical Theatre Royal in Norwich. On 9 Feb. 1790 Parson Woodforde booked six seats in a box there, his niece having her hair specially dressed for the night out on the 10th.

Hadfield had served with courage under the Duke of York in the Low Countries in 1794, but a severe head wound had rendered him subject to delusions. At his trial he was declared insane and confined in Bedlam [*from a contemporary engraving*]

[1] *Mrs Patterson Diary* 2: 14 Feb. 1791; see also the chapter frontispiece to vol. 1, chap. 6. Her husband, a Freemason, was an actor in Scraggs's troupe (*Diary 2*: 19 Jan. 1791; *Norw. Merc.* 26 Mar. 1791)

The travelling troupes attracted people of talent who contributed to their success in a variety of ways. The costumes were elaborate, requiring inventive tailors and seamstresses; Mrs Patterson was almost certainly one such. She taught Mary Ann how to cut paper filigree and make flowers on Valentine's Day 1791.[1] Scenery and props were regarded as important parts of a production and had constantly to be updated. For Garrick's *A Christmas Tale*, seen by William

Hardy at the Theatre Royal in Norwich three years after its London opening, the scenery, machinery and dresses were 'entirely new'.[1] The year 1785 was one of balloon fever in Norwich. William Scraggs sought to capitalise on this and draw in a wider audience by a range of special effects and props: Harlequin and Columbine would make their escape from the stage in a hot-air balloon, and he would ride an ass in the finale. These enticing, if tricky, enhancements to the dramas were to take place at the Holt theatre.[2]

The artist Manuel Immanuel, who painted the Hardys' portraits in 1798, has for many years been the subject of intensive research by Mr S.H. Steel of Grantham. He has traced Immanuel as a specialist in backdrops and sets who worked on scenery design and painting at Covent Garden 1787–93 and in provincial theatres 1793–1831, notably in Berkshire, Norfolk, Lincolnshire and Northamptonshire. Immanuel was at the King's Lynn theatre 1804–05 and for a long period at Grantham, on the Lincoln Circuit.[3] The *Stamford Mercury*'s report in 1805 of a new theatre in Lincolnshire is typical of the coverage the artist attracted:

The new Theatre at Boston is nearly completed. The plan of the whole building is very judicious, and does great credit to the solid judgment of Mr Watson, the architect . . . The interior decorations, from the masterly pencil of Mr Immanuel, are in great forwardness, and evince a taste and genius which add to the reputation he has already acquired as an artist . . .[4]

Small towns and villages lost out as transport improved. With communication becoming easier the need for strolling players diminished; for the same reason itinerant salesmen were replaced by shops. And in some ways a small town could not fulfil the urban function of rubbing off the rust. The 'polishing every winter' after which Mrs Hardcastle hankered was best done in the metropolis, or at least the provincial capital. But the leap cannot then be made of portraying the market town deep in its rural setting as entirely different in character from the city. Urban distinctiveness lay in such superficial qualities as manners in a wide sense, civility and, by definition, urbanity: the yeasty froth at the top of the tankard. It was only 'manner' which set the city-dweller apart from the rustic—or so the satirists' characters would have it, as seen in the note earlier on Mrs Hardcastle.

[1] *scenery Norw. Merc.* 17 Feb. 1776; see also the note in *Diary 1* for 17 Feb. 1776

[2] *balloon Norw. Merc.* 8 Jan. 1785. Scraggs's long notice in the paper advertised the benefit performance for himself and his (first) wife in which she would deliver 'an Epilogue in the character of a Mason's wife'; also the 'speaking pantomime' *The Invasion; or Harlequin's Mouth Opened*, during which the new special effects would be unveiled. As a finale William Scraggs would perform *The Cries of London* while riding on an ass. Other productions were also listed

[3] *Immanuel* Local newspapers such as the *Stamford Mercury* and *Northampton Mercury* are a fruitful souce. I am very grateful to Mr Steel for his meticulous letters to me 2014–18 on Immanuel's travels, with full citation of sources

[4] *Boston Theatre Stamford Mercury*, 15 Nov. 1805 (copy sent to me by Mr Steel, 22 Oct. 2017).

More and more permanent structures were being built. N. Walsham got its first purpose-built playhouse in 1828; it was a Fisher theatre

[1] *puritanism* It is used here without an initial capital, signifying a style of living. When used with a capital it relates to the former broad political movement which developed following the Reformation and reached its zenith during the Commonwealth and Protectorate

[2] *licensing* NRO: C/S 1/14 (1785–91), 14 Jan., 7 Oct. 1789; NRO: C/S 1/15 (1791–1800), 22 Jan. 1795.
Scraggs was also granted permission at Holt on 20 Jan. 1791 to perform at Aylsham and Reepham. Fisher was granted a licence at Walsingham on 23 Apr. 1795 to perform at 'Lt Walsingham for 20 days and Fakenham 24 days', such orders exemplifying the restrictive terms of the licensing arrangements (C/S 1/14, 1/15)

[3] *Scraggs resigns Norw. Merc.* 14 Apr., 11 Aug. 1792. Ethel Mann states that Scraggs was the original manager of Nathaniel Godbold's theatre built in the Castle yard at Bungay in 1773, and that David Fisher [jnr] was his stage carpenter (E. Mann, *Old Bungay* (Heath Cranton Ltd, London, 1934), pp. 175–6).
Scraggs died at Beccles 5 Feb. 1808 aged 60 (*Norw. Merc.* 13 Feb. 1808)

New controls, and puritanism re-emergent

In the absence of firm data we have to rely partly on speculation as to why eighteenth-century pastimes and pleasures did not enter the next century intact. In the case of the decline in theatre-going from about the mid-1790s we have some hard evidence: growing hostility from the licensing authorities, and the re-emergence of seventeenth-century puritanism in its non-political form.[1]

As the Hardys' experience in 1779 with Mr Baret showed, Mr Fisher had to apply for permission from the magistrate on the spot to perform in William Hardy's barn at Horstead. The denial of permission by Mr Baret is the only such example cited in the diary or found in the local official records of the time. During the 1780s and 1790s William Scraggs and David Fisher would often petition the justices at Norfolk Quarter Sessions (in Norwich and by adjournment) to be licensed to perform for stated periods and in named towns. Authority was always granted, as these illustrations of the system at work show:

[NORWICH, 14 JANUARY 1789] Scraggs, Comedian, applied to this Court for a licence . . . to perform plays in the several towns of Walsingham, Swaffham, East Dereham, Downham, Diss and Fakenham in Norfolk. Granted by the Court . . .

[NORWICH, 7 OCTOBER 1789] No company of players to have a licence without having previously given notice to one or more justices of the division of an intention to apply for such licence at Sessions . . .

[HOLT, 22 JANUARY 1795] Ordered that David Fisher & Co. be licensed to perform plays within the parish of Holt for 24 days, *vide* petition.[2]

As a symptom of harder times, and perhaps indicating that the Hardys were representative of hardening public opinion in their rejection of the theatre, William Scraggs in April 1792 had to 'resign the management' of his company to David Fisher junior (b.1760). They carried on in harness together, and by August that year were reportedly playing to packed houses at the theatre in Sudbury, Suffolk.[3]

However an ominous note was struck in 1796. At Walsingham on 14 April only two magistrates were sitting, the Revd Charles Collyer of Gunthorpe and Henry Lee Warner of Walsingham. They decided to license David Fisher & Co.

to perform at Fakenham for twenty days between 1 July and 31 October 1796 only on condition that the company first obtain the approbation of the Revd Dixon Hoste (a local JP, of Godwick Hall, near Whissonsett) and the 'principal inhabitants' of Fakenham—a proviso not inserted hitherto.[1] From that moment the constant flow of requests from the players would seem to cease.

At the end of the fourth of her manuscript ledgers, covering the years 1790–1800, Mary Hardy committed her private thoughts to paper on the morality of attending the playhouse. Her long passage, headed 'Archbishop Tilotson['s] opinion on Plays', is a copy of the attack on theatre-going issued by the late-seventeenth-century Archbishop of Canterbury and stern Calvinist John Tillotson. This is his opening salvo:

As the stage now is, plays are intolerable, and not fit to be permitted in any civilised, much less Christian, nation. They do most notoriously minister both to infidelity [irreligion] and vice. By their profaneness they are apt to instil bad principles, and by their lewdness to dispose to lewd and dissolute practice . . . [2]

The diarist's entry is not dated, but may have been made about 1793, when she refused to attend the theatre at Holt even when the rest of the family was continuing to so do. It reveals her state of mind as being far removed from that of the theatre-lover of the previous twenty years, and her change of direction may have been inspired by the tone of the Methodist Conference's directions to its adherents.

Conference's accelerating puritanism following John Wesley's death in 1791 was characterised by a series of injunctions, classed as 'directions', against 'too great advances towards conformity to the world' such as dancing, showy dress and choral music other than plain communal singing. Theirs was a rigid, joyless mindset. In 1791 it was ruled that 'Those parents who employ dancing-masters for their children shall be no longer members of our Society.' In 1795 came the decision 'to exclude every person from the Society, who buys or sells on the Lord's Day' apart from essentials in the form of medicines and 'funeral necessaries', also a prohibition on adherents' encouraging their preachers to smoke.[3]

[1] *proviso* NRO: C/S 1/15, 14 Apr. 1796. By this date it is possible that the term 'comedian' no longer recommended itself to stern and sober Authority. Fisher was applying for 'a licence to perform *tragedies* etc' [my italics]

[2] *Tillotson Diary 2*, endnotes, p. 394, where the passage is transcribed in full. It ends with his sobering conclusion that those going to the playhouse, had it then existed in its present-day form, would have been 'shut out of the Communion of Christians . . . in the first ages of Christianity'. John Tillotson (1630–94), Archbishop of Canterbury 1691–94, had led the attacks on popery in Charles II's reign and taken a prominent role in the Exclusion Crisis. However the theatre a century later, under Garrick's guiding hand, was far removed from the bawdy excesses of Restoration drama

[3] *directions Minutes of the Methodist Conferences*, vol. 1 (London, 1812), p. 248 (1791); pp. 319, 320 (1795). Mary Hardy and other mothers in her circle had revelled in their children's dancing and strenuously given support to tuition in the 1770s and 1780s

[1] *bans* *Minutes of the Methodist Conferences*, vol. 1, p. 200 (1787); p. 350 (1796)

[2] *the King* His admiration for Wilberforce's reforming zeal was genuine, he and the Queen being examples of moral rectitude in their private lives. An ascetic, puritan element was in the King's nature (J. Black, *George III: America's last king* (Yale Univ. Press, London, 2006), pp. 189, 202–8)

[3] *balls* *Diary 2*: 29 Apr. 1789; her 10-year-old guest Phillis Symonds of Gt Yarmouth danced the night away. The family's gradual rejection of dancing is charted in vol. 1, chap. 6. William Hardy jnr, slower than his sister to embrace Methodism, attended a benefit ball at the King's Head, Holt in 1794 (*Diary 3*: 31 Dec. 1794)

[4] *dii majorum gentium* The superior deities (Cicero, *Tusculan Disputations*); senators in the Roman republic were divided into *majorum gentium* and *minorum gentium*

[5] *idolatry* D. Bogue and J. Bennett, *A History of Dissenters, from the Revolution in 1688 to the year 1808*, vol. 4 (London, 1812), pp. 40–1. Quintus Roscius Gallus (d.62 BC) was a Roman actor

There followed in 1796 a reassertion of a ban on anthems, and thus by extension choirs, it being essential to have all the congregation singing in 'joint worship' (an echo of an earlier injunction of 1787); there was also discouragement of 'lightness, expensiveness, or gaity of [wearing] apparel' (1796).[1] Advocating the adoption of a puritan style of life was thus contemporaneous with the formation of William Wilberforce's Campaign for the Suppression of Vice in 1787, a movement which attracted the solid support of the King.[2] But at this stage Mary Hardy was not prepared to give up her pleasures, nor to discourage her children from dancing. Only two years earlier she had dressed in all her finery for her portrait. As late as 1789 she still found balls 'very agreeable', attending a ball at Holt with her family and not getting home until 3 am.[3]

Two contemporary historians of Nonconformity epitomised puritan suspicion and hostility towards drama; it is illuminating that they also looked on conviviality generally with disdain. Writing of the state of the public mind earlier, c.1720–60, they attributed the prevailing lack of moral tone and seriousness to the baneful influence of the stage:

The worship of talent was the prevailing idolatry of this period, of which Shakespeare and Pope were *dii majorum gentium*.[4] Literary clubs were formed, where nightly sacrifices of conviviality were offered to the vanity of prostituted intellect . . .

Garrick, the Roscious of this age, infected it with a dramatic mania, which . . . rendered the sober realities of eternity gloomy or disgusting. While the playhouse was crowded to the neglect of the church, and Shakespeare . . . was studied more than the Bible, need it be asked what was the state of the public mind?[5]

What the faithful lost at the playhouse, however, they gained in the pew. Evangelical and Nonconformist preachers were masters of the theatrical sermon, as seen in volume 3's chapters on religion. These men worked on their hearers as subtly and as persuasively as the despised Garrick.

The stage was coming under attack on two fronts. It faced an unsympathetic and even repressive magistracy, and a populace increasingly uncomfortable over attending in the stern times of the 1790s. Control by the authorities, seemingly keen to restrict productions in barns and viewing a purpose-built theatre as more respectable, went hand in hand with self-denial by some at least of the prospective audience. Again the tone was set from the top. While happy to attend the leading patent theatres in his realm the moral monarch favoured the exertion of control:

> . . . George was not out of line with a dominant ethos that treated religion, conduct and morality not as private activities outside the ken of public supervision, but as matters of concern and control.[1]

It is a theme developed in the next chapter. Even greater efforts were made to restrict the pleasures of the poor. Sunday was for most of them—although not for the Hardys' workforce—their one day off a week, and customarily a time set aside for games, sports and merrymaking. The 'traditional' Sunday of sobriety and attendance in church or chapel is a nineteenth-century construct.[2] Mrs Trimmer, a respected nurturer of young minds, joined forces with the Wesleyans and Evangelicals to restrict the long-recognised liberty of the children of the poor to be idle, to roam and to play on the Lord's Day. Religion was seen not only as the best cement of society but as a restraint upon unruly conduct.[3] Robert Hole examines 'the concepts of restraint and sanctions, of social hierarchy and of the need for the poor to be content with their lot'.[4] Religion had long buttressed teaching on resignation to one's lot. Now, with the external and internal threats of the 1790s, political instability was added to the mix—just when, as Bogue and Bennett held, the French Revolution had taught the poor to think for themselves (related in volume 3, chapter 4).

With commonly voiced moral strictures came fears of riots, seditious gatherings and anything approaching excess. Such developments were all too distressingly visible across the Channel. Recognised companies of actors in elegant theatres patronised by the most distinguished in society were to be preferred to strolling players moving rapidly from one barn or outhouse to the next. Even Freemasons were not exempt from pressure. Were their private lodges and secret initiation ceremonies harbingers of sedition?[5] These misgivings may explain the decline in clubs patronised by the Hardys during the French wars, and the restrictions placed by JPs on travelling troupes. Life was serious, with political strife at home and the prolonged fight to survive as a nation.

[1] *control* J. Black, *George III*, p. 206

[2] *traditional Sunday* A. Tindal Hart, *The Curate's Lot: The story of the unbeneficed English clergy* (The Country Book Club, Newton Abbot, 1971), p. 24

[3] *best cement of society* See the section under that title, vol. 3, chap. 6

[4] *restraint, sanctions* R. Hole, *Pulpits, Politics and Public Order in England 1760–1832* (Cambridge Univ. Press, 1989), pp. 84–93

[5] *sedition* The Unlawful Societies Act of 1799 had implications for numerous bodies—even Parliament and the Inns of Court, as presented by Andrew Prescott at the conference of the Canonbury Masonic Research Centre, Univ. of Sheffield, 4–5 Nov. 2000.
He opened with the swirling atmosphere of suspicion in 1798 and 1799 which produced an Act 'to forestall the threat of revolution'; Habeas Corpus was already suspended. Debating clubs and Freemasons found themselves suspect (A. Prescott, 'The Unlawful Societies Act of 1799' <https://www.scribd.com/document/126937525/The-Unlawful-Societies-Act-of-1799> (unpag.), accessed 19 Mar. 2010)

above Hinsby's Gardens on the River Yare at Thorpe, beside the Yarmouth road downstream of Norwich. This part of the riverside gave people from the city an opportunity to relax and be reinvigorated after the labours of the day.

Here there is a good deal of messing about in small boats, and rather too much standing around helplessly on deck with hands in pockets. The Broads in Mary Hardy's time were not the pleasure grounds solely of the rich and leisured. They provided a setting for busy, industrious local people who enjoyed taking to the water.

Most could go boating only at the end of their day's work, paintings of the Norwich School showing numbers of small rowing boats and yachts on the river in Norwich in what appears to be soft evening light.

Belaugh, on the Bure just downstream of Coltishall, offered the same refuge at the end of a hard day. Thomas Engall's gardens were visited by Mary Hardy and her friends who twice had tea and fruit there in midsummer 1779: on foot and later by water, sailing in a keel
[*drawing by J. Stark; engraving by E. Goodall 1829, detail*]

7
Outdoor recreations

Openly licentious

A very fine warm day. William Frary in malthouse, Zeb Rouse at Corpusty. Isaac Pooley at plough forenoon, at Worstead Fair afternoon, T. Allen at plough . . .

A fine warm day. William Frary in malthouse, Zeb Rouse and T. Allen at muck cart, Isaac Pooley not come from the fair . . .

MARY HARDY, 1776 [1]

That Good Friday is little noticed in this country I think it my duty to inform your Lordship; and that the Lord's Day [Sunday] is most terribly profaned in this neighbourhood [West Somerton]; that people are buying and selling the whole day; shopkeepers, butchers, and alehousekeepers sell more of this, than of a common day . . . They [the people] are even so openly licentious, that they frequently appear in the face of the minister in large companies playing at ball and other diversions, and in church time I have frequently heard them in the marshes shooting of wild fowl.

REVD WILLIAM IVORY, 1784 [2]

NONE OF THE LEISURE ACTIVITIES described in the preceding chapter, apart from a very few exceptions such as harvest frolics and trips to the playhouse, was pursued by the labouring classes. The people, as the earnest Evangelical William Ivory called them, formed the bulk of his parishioners in their village between the River Thurne and the sea. Unlike members of the 'associational world' seen in chapter 6, the industrious poor—as also the idle poor—engaged in their leisure pastimes mostly out of doors. As a result they increasingly faced stern disapproval, as when confronted by their outraged minister during their ball games or their return from wildfowling. He had expected them to be listening attentively to his Sunday sermon.

In this same visitation return to his bishop the cleric lamented: 'The poor people complained, their masters will

[1] *fair Diary 1*: entries for 13–14 May 1776 (a Monday and Tuesday). Worstead Fair was held on the fixed date 12 May, but as this fell on a Sunday in 1776 it was moved to the Monday.

The Hardys expected their yearly-hired farm servant back at work on 14 May. But Pooley had taken two days off—the holiday period the men seem generally to have regarded as a right at fair time.

On 15 May Pooley was back delivering beer

[2] *shooting* William Ivory, Perpetual Curate of W. Somerton, reports to Dr Bagot, his new Bishop (NRO: DN/VIS 30/11, Flegg deanery visitation 1784, W. Somerton return). The parish population in 1801 was 162. Ivory features in vol. 3, chaps 1–4

top **Woodcock, a favourite delicacy for wildfowlers (table 4.7.2)** [*G.C. Davies, The Swan and her Crew (1876)*]

right **W. Somerton Church** from the north-west, with sweeping views from its ridge high above the reed-fringed waters of the northern Broads; the reed-thatched Norman nave dates from *c*.1200. Ivory's flock were down in those waters among the wildfowl [*MB · 2011*]

[1] *alehouse* For the arguments that working men could not handle leisure profitably and would spend it drinking, see K. Thomas, 'Work and leisure in pre-industrial society', *Past & Present* no. 29 (1964), pp. 50–66: 'With the awareness of the economic importance of labour comes a new insistence upon the duty of every man to work', a view traceable to the preaching of friars and Lollards in the Middle Ages (p. 59); 'With the coming of industrialism little was heard of the old incentives to labour which had existed in primitive society—joy, competition, craftsmanship, social responsibility' (p. 62).

See also B. Harrison, *Drink and the Victorians: The temperance question in England 1815–1872* (2nd edn Keele Univ. Press, 1994), pp. 21–62

[2] *profanation* NRO: DN/ VIS 34a/4, Ingworth

not pay them their wages 'till Sunday morning so that they are obliged to buy of a Sunday for want of money on a Saturday'. It is obvious what was in the masters' minds: the contents of a full pocket on a Saturday night would be spent not moderately at the local shop and butcher's but immoderately in the alehouse. Sunday pay was a sign of the growing fondness for controlling a potentially unruly workforce and for regulating lives outside the workplace.[1]

William Ivory's fellow Sabbatarian but non-Evangelical colleague, the Revd Lancaster Adkin, represents this strand of thought. He fulminated to a new Bishop ten years later over the commercial pursuits and merrymaking he witnessed on Sundays at Scottow, between Coltishall and North Walsham. Selected for special censure were farm servants like the Hardys' (together with their masters), and innkeepers such as the Hardys' former tenants at neighbouring Tunstead, Little Hautbois, Swanton Abbot and North Walsham:

Nothing but the profanation of the Sabbath by sports and pastimes sometimes at the time of divine service, sometimes immediately on coming out of church . . . Another mode of profanation is by collecting cattle together for driving them to the London markets . . . Farmers and their servants, butchers, and innkeepers are withheld from serving God . . .[2]

Views such as these helped to promote the suppression of wages to the lowest level possible and the maintenance of hours at the highest, on the argument that any surplus cash or time would be spent in the public house—despite the evidence of Mary Hardy and Henry Raven that low levels of workforce drunkenness do not appear to have presented much of a threat to good management and profitability.[1]

Many of the Norfolk clergy were more understanding of their parishioners' needs than the censorious Adkin and Ivory. The Revd John Smith, Vicar of Mattishall, reported in 1801 that 'several people' did not attend any place of public worship on a Sunday. They were 'chiefly weavers, who after having been confined during the rest of the week at their looms, are too apt to consider Sunday as their only time for relaxation and amusement'.[2]

Writing of developments in the first half of the nineteenth century, Brian Harrison observes:

Working men sensed that sabbatarians were trying to hold them down by restricting their activities on their one day of leisure . . . Sabbatarian restrictions weighed particularly heavily on the poor, because, in contrast to their superiors, they spent most of their lives in public. While in their clubs and homes the rich had independent facilities for recreation, food-preparation and travel, the poor had only the public facilities subject to legislative restriction. Radicals continually embarrassed the LDOS [Lord's Day Observance Society] by drawing attention to the bellringers, coachmen and servants whose Sunday labours enabled Respectability to attend church.

Furthermore, while the rich could store up their weekend food supplies on Saturday, the London poor were not paid till Saturday night and could not keep food fresh in their insanitary homes; hence the flourishing Sunday trade of small food shops and stalls.[3]

The amount of leisure time available to those in work had economic consequences; the type and timing of certain of the activities carried moral implications.[4] In a pincer movement against the poor, Sabbatarians and Evangelicals united with commercial employers and farmers actively to suppress old leisure pursuits and traditional holidays. This chapter will show that the fairs and sports such as boxing to which working people were attached did not die a slow, natural death. They were snuffed out rapidly, a high point in their suppression being that same decade c.1793–c.1803

deanery visitation 1794, Scottow return

[1] *drunkenness* These arguments are developed in vol. 2, chap. 1 on the workforce

[2] *weavers* NRO: DN/VIS 38/1, Hingham deanery visitation 1801, Mattishall return.
  He had made very similar observations in 1794. Nonetheless, in a large parish of 103 houses and with 100 Independents who were 'chiefly weavers' and one family of Quakers, he managed 30–40 communicants in his church—and this with no habitable parsonage. The ancient rectory was 'a very mean cottage, in a ruinous state' (DN/VIS 34a/2, 1794)

[3] *lives in public* B. Harrison, 'Religion and recreation in nineteenth-century England', *Past & Present*, no. 38 (1967), p. 109.
  The Anglican LDOS was not founded until 1831, but its Sabbatarian principles had been championed much earlier by the rather inappropriately-named Vice Society

[4] *economic consequences* '. . . The way man enjoys himself and the way his enjoyments are exploited—surely both are of considerable importance for eco-

nomic as well as social history' (J.H. Plumb, *The Commercialisation of Leisure in Eighteenth-century England*, p. 20)

---

[1] *bowling greens* S. Cozens-Hardy, *Memorials of William Hardy Cozens-Hardy of Letheringsett*, p. 21

[2] *skating Diary 2*: 10 Mar. 1786; *Diary 3*: 25 Jan. 1795, 5 Dec. 1796. The young people also 'spread a tent' on Salthouse Marshes—an unprepossessing location (*Diary 4*: 9 Aug. 1804). Tents had newly become associated with outdoor eating, as seen with the Turkish Tent, a permanent structure erected in the 1750s at Painshill, Surrey. Marquees were also coming into use at stock shows

[3] *lake* MS diary of W.H. Cozens-Hardy, p. 110 (Cozens-Hardy Collection). Similar hospitality had been extended in Dec. 1890 (p. 91). A slim, spry man, he skated into his eighties (p. 69, Dec. 1886–Jan. 1887)

[4] *conflict* See B. Harrison, 'Religion and recreation in nineteenth-century England', where he distinguishes strands of culture conflict in this field (pp. 121–2). Much of his analysis holds good for the late 18th century as well

which we have already seen as the decade of change in other recreational pursuits. Over a longer period certain areas of middle-class leisure became more sedate and more home-based under the influence of nineteenth-century respectability and a new yearning for domesticity. Whereas William Hardy, and to a lesser extent his son, had weekly played bowls on public-house greens over an evening's drinking, their Cozens-Hardy successors chose to play bowls in their secluded pleasure grounds at Letheringsett Hall and across the road at Glavenside. William H. Cozens-Hardy stated in his memoirs that he 'never played on public [bowling] greens'. Instead he was used to private greens such as those of his father Jeremiah and his uncle John Cozens at Sprowston.[1] The link between bowls and alcohol was severed.

Skating too had been enjoyed in public in Mary Hardy's time, she and her nephew Henry recording skating by William Hardy junior and other young members of the family. Chosen spots included Salthouse, Hempstead and Holt.[2] In 1853 her grandson constructed a large private lake in his grounds to provide a head of water to drive the turbine powering his circular saw at Hall Farm. It also provided ideal conditions for skating, as he noted in his diary. However, whereas playing bowls was confined to family and close friends, use of the frozen lake was granted to all. In January 1893 he had hundreds of local people on the ice:

We had very little appearance of winter till Xmas Day [Christmas 1892] when a rather sharp frost occurred and the ice on shallow waters would bear. This increased from day to day. When the ice on my lake was frozen to a great thickness—6 inches [15 cm] or thereabouts—and skating became very general several hundreds of men, women and children came from Holt and enjoyed the recreation for nearly 3 weeks.[3]

The tussles associated with working-class recreational pursuits have been characterised not so much as class conflict as culture conflict.[4] Robert Lee considers the ramifications of this conflict for the poor across a range of religious and social issues in the nineteenth century, although many had actually manifested themselves earlier. He explodes 'the myth of the passive, deferential nineteenth-century countryside', contrasting its widespread restiveness with the 'cyclical' and 'largely static' world familiar to James Woodforde:

left Letheringsett Hall, 21 July 1890: the Diamond Wedding of William Hardy Cozens-Hardy, right, and his wife Sarah, in the invalid carriage. Mary Hardy's husband had regularly played bowls on public-house greens. Here clubbability is renounced for the private, domestic space of these much-loved gardens.

Clement, the heir, stands far left beside Sydney; Herbert, the future peer, stands third from the left. Sailor-suited Basil Cozens-Hardy, aged five, sits on the grass. He became a life-long teetotaller, like his father Sydney. The image is shown in full at the start of the Epilogue [*photo A.E. Coe, of Norwich, 1890, detail: Cozens-Hardy Collection*]

Two *cultures* were clashing in the countryside of nineteenth-century Norfolk. One pre-dated living memory, was unwritten, popular . . .; the other was alien, legalistic, elite and authoritarian.[1]

Mary Hardy's diary is of great value in depicting some of the battle lines forming in rural areas and which appear time and again in the four volumes of this study. They include the pressure to use time profitably and not fritter it away, to raise children with a strong sense of this necessity, and to put aside the more boisterous, brutal pastimes of the past often involving cruelty to animals. Those who championed custom clung tenaciously to this vanishing world. Their ancestors who rose against authority and burned monastic records in 1381 and 1450 had similarly protested against the smothering of old values under the weight of two upstarts: the written and the printed word were beyond the reach of the unlettered.[2] In the diarist's world powerful forces were lining up for battle: custom versus capitalism, and custom versus Calvinism. Both conflicts feature in this chapter.

[1] *two cultures* R. Lee, *Rural Society and the Anglican Clergy, 1815–1914: Encountering and managing the poor* (The Boydell Press, Woodbridge, 2006), p. 2; see also his pp. 1–8

[2] *unlettered* Alienation from a set of values which prized the written word, as used in property deeds, above an oral, customary culture was nothing new. It had helped to spark medi-aeval peasant risings, as recounted by Roger Chartier in *Jack Cade, the skin of a dead lamb and hatred of the written word: The Hayes Robinson Lecture 2006* (Royal Holloway, University of London, 2006)

right Labour discipline: Mary Hardy's entries written at Coltishall 29–31 May 1775 recording Robert Manning's journeys with the beer cart. They show the precision with which she noted the times of day: this was clock time, not task time.

She annotates Monday as 'the Restoration of King Charles the 2^d' (to the throne, in 1660), but by this time 29 May was no longer kept as a public holiday.

William Frary [WF] and Robert Manning [RM] set off for Worstead on 31 May at 6 am ['M6'], but would have started work before 5 am as they had to load the cart and get the horses ready.

William Hardy did not get home until 11 pm ['E11'] after two days away, but his wife had carefully noted Frary and Manning's absence at Worstead until 4.30 pm. Zeb Rouse had gone a similar distance that day carting beer to Horning, five miles away, but had returned by lunchtime to complete an afternoon's ploughing.

Had they wished, Frary and Manning could also have spent the afternoon at work in the field or the malt-house ['M House']. Wasting time at Worstead on 31 May may well have contributed to Manning's summary dis-missal on 6 June.

The 18 days leading to the dismissal are summarised in table 2.1.5 in volume 2 [*Cozens-Hardy Collection*]

Restrictions on the poor's leisure

Capitalism is represented by the Hardys of this world: William Hardy, the thrusting, ambitious farmer, maltster and brewer, and his diarist wife who carefully logged the tasks and movements of the workforce day by day. The Calvinists are represented by the touring Anglican Evangelicals whom, as a voracious sermon taster, Mary Hardy followed around parishes within a twelve-mile radius of her home (volume 3, chapters 3 and 4). The twin pincer movement against custom exerted pressure on working men, women and children including even the Ben Leggatts, Briton Scurls and Sally Guntons of late-eighteenth century Norfolk—some of the annually-hired servants in their comfortable parsonage billet at Weston. Their sole protection was custom: the old ways of the prior culture, as honoured by more traditionally-minded employers like the Revd Mr Woodforde.[1]

It was the servant class especially who prized customary privileges such as attendance at fairs and frolics, although both types of event were attended by a much wider cross-section of the community. Time off was a valued commodity. Pressure for it proved a flashpoint in the Hardy household and at times even in the more relaxed regime at Weston. The restrictions imposed by capitalist employers who needed to extract all they could from their workforce were applauded by clergy of a more driven, authoritarian and less paternalistic tinge than Woodforde. One anonymous cleric, writing in a very popular work, expressed this chilling view to servants generally: 'When you hired yourselves, you sold your time and labour to your masters.'[2]

These forces of social change can be seen as occupying a spectrum. Towards one end the rector's establishment at Weston was largely governed by master–servant custom; towards the other end that at the Coltishall and Letheringsett breweries was dominated by capitalist–employee considerations. Close examination of the two diaries would suggest that Woodforde usually divided his day, and that of his team, 'our folk', by task time, whereas Mary Hardy most definitely noted even the most trivial events of the day by clock time. The notion that the predominance of clock time came in with factory-working during the industrial revolution is swept away.[3]

[1] *prior culture* For the implications for the young of its erosion see the last section in vol. 1, chap. 8 on the Hardys' maids and farm boys

[2] *chilling view* A Present for Servants, from their Ministers, Masters, or Other Friends (10th edn London, 1787), p. 35.

The unnamed author continues: 'And, besides the sin against God in idleness, you defraud your master, if you idle away an hour that should be employed in his business' (p. 35).

We have seen Mrs Sarah Trimmer take the same approach towards Sunday-school children: the idle young servant-girl was robbing her mistress (quoted in the inset in vol. 3, chap. 2, 'Sunday-school teaching at Coltishall 1813').

The three Hardy children were trained to respect clock time. As described in vol. 1, chap. 5, even six-year-olds would note the events of the day by the clock in their mother's diary. Marking the passing of the hours had come to stay

[3] *task time and clock time* These arguments are made in vol. 2, chap. 1 on the workforce. See esp. 'A rich and varied working life', 'The long working day', 'The long working year' and 'Watching the clock'

[1] *industrious* J. de Vries, 'The Industrial Revolution and the Industrious Revolution', *Journal of Economic History*, no. 54 (1994), pp. 249–70.

A voluminous literature exists on the decline of 'St Monday', the day supposedly taken off work in an era when Saturday working was the norm but saints' days were no longer granted as holidays. However any tradition of St Monday in existence in 18th-century E. Anglia (and none has been found) did not percolate to the Hardys' circle

[2] *turning point* E.P. Thompson, *Education and Experience* (Leeds Univ. Press, 1968), pp. 4, 9, 13

[3] *interfering* E.P. Thompson, *Education and Experience*, p. 10; see also p. 16.

Brian Harrison was to make a similar point, but without the political undercurrents, over the Lord's Day Observance Society: 'The LDOS was unpopular [with working men] for several reasons; it seemed to be depriving the people of their traditional recreations without providing any alternative beyond churchgoing . . .' (B. Harrison, 'Religion and recreation in nineteenth-century England', p. 108)

If there is an 'old culture', or prior culture, there must be a new one: strict labour discipline and social control. Yearly-hired servants, whether living in or living out, were increasingly finding themselves subject to the rule of the clock as part of the '*Industrious* Revolution'. This was Jan de Vries' phrase to describe the new long-hours culture, when work patterns changed between the seventeenth and early nineteenth centuries.[1] Taking time off during the working day, in the way that Frary and Manning lingered when delivering beer to Worstead in 1775 (pictured on the previous page), presented a direct threat to the profitability of a business.

When past traditions are no longer honoured and the old values are overturned, so chroniclers of the 'old culture' assert, attempts to mould a new tradition will set up social and labour tensions, as we shall see. Although E.P. Thompson's rapport with agricultural life seems to have lain more with the day labourer's toil than that of the yearly farm servant, whom he rarely mentions in his studies of labour history, he pinpoints precisely the nature and onset of the conflict which farm workers' leisure expectations produced. Unlike Brian Harrison, who opts for a later generation, Thompson identifies the crucial decade of the 1790s as the turning point from the old 'realistic paternalism' to the new 'fear of the revolutionary potential of the common people' and 'fear of an authentic popular culture beyond the contrivance and control of their betters'.[2]

Using a variety of literary and historical sources E.P. Thompson chooses not to highlight the moral reform and change in public manners which those pressing for spiritual renewal wrought in the more leisured class (as seen at the end of chapter 6 on puritanism's re-emergence). Instead he emphasises the social control of the poor increasingly achieved through Sabbatatarianism and authoritarianism:

In the counter-revolutionary mood engendered by the French Revolution—and the reform movements in England—paternalism changed its nature and emerged in a meaner, more interfering, and more authoritarian form.[3]

Struggling under the pressure of the pincer movement, and attempting to keep its identity intact, can be found what a long line of social commentators and historians, novelists and poets, have called the old culture—a respect for tradition and custom in social and labour relations. William Cobbett and George Borrow, with their rumbustious physicality, their acceptance of a ready resort to fisticuffs to settle an argument, and their honouring of former ways whether in diet or language, respected the old culture. So did George Bourne, who recorded the post-enclosure economic and social change visible in his Surrey homeland, this 'change in the village' being damaging to individual spirit, curiosity and enterprise.[1] Likewise Thomas Hardy in prose and verse lamented the replacement of church bands and their viols, cellos and merry, lilting tunes in favour of the organ—that instrument of sobriety beloved of two other Hardys, Mary and, especially, Mary Ann.[2]

Rudyard Kipling voiced his respect for hallowed traditions in his poem *The Land* (1917). Owners of the marshy, wealden Lower River-Field from the time of 'Julius Fabricius, Sub-Prefect of the Weald' to the poet himself, 'fortified with title-deeds, attested, signed and sealed', had over the centuries deferred to the wisdom of the local tiller and toiler, 'the aged Hobden', fount of knowledge on draining and liming and with a markedly independent train of thought and speech. Kipling, a newcomer to the farmland, conscious of his ignorance and firm opponent of the Game Laws, ends with this tribute to the Hobden of his time:

> *Not for any beast that burrows, not for any bird that flies,*
> *Would I lose his large sound counsel, miss his keen amending eyes.*
> *He is bailiff, woodman, wheelwright, field-surveyor, engineer,*
> *And if flagrantly a poacher—'tain't for me to interfere.*
>
> *'Hob, what about that River-bit?' I turn to him again,*
> *With Fabricius and Ogier and William of Warenne.*
> *'Hev it jest as you've a mind to, but'—and here he takes command.*
> *For whoever pays the taxes old Mus' Hobden owns the land.*[3]

The worker is treated not as a disposable item in the enterprise but valued as the mainstay of it. In return he has privileges which must be honoured. The most elegiac note was perhaps struck in the twentieth century by George Ewart Evans in his remarkable series of Suffolk interviews. He recorded on tape for posterity the lives of those whom he saw as shaped by a culture pre-dating universal schooling and mechanisation in the field.[4]

[1] *custom* G. Bourne's lament in *Change in the Village* (1912) over the effects on the human spirit of restricting the poor's freedom to roam is quoted in vol. I, chap. 10, in 'A general system of trespass'.

William Cobbett, in *Rural Rides*, inveighed in the 1820s against the loss of time-honoured traditions extended to the servant class which had eased their lives. But his ideal of Farmer Hodge, who dined at an oak kitchen table with his servants, was disappearing. William Hardy was no Hodge

[2] *church bands* Hardy's father had been a church musician. The bands' suppression was mourned in his verse and his novel *Under the Greenwood Tree* (1872)

[3] *Hobden* R. Kipling, *Kipling's English History*, ed. M. Laski (BBC, London, 1974), pp. 114–16.

E.P. Thompson, in his essay 'The Moral Economy Reviewed' in *Customs in Common* (Penguin, London, 1993), and John Rule, in *The Experience of Labour in Eighteenth-Century Industry* (Croom Helm, London, 1981) (esp. pp. 12–15, 56–7, 212–13), chart the decline of custom and the social effects on the poor

[4] *Evans* He articulates what he means by the

old culture most clearly in *Ask the Fellows who Cut the Hay* (Faber & Faber, London, 1965), esp. pp. 236–43; also in *Where Beards Wag All: The relevance of the oral tradition* (Faber & Faber, London, 1977), esp. pt 3, 'The village', pp. 159–232, where he recounts an anecdote told to him by an E. Anglian farmer: 'You don't order a farm-hand to do anything . . . In a case like George who's older than myself, more knowledgeable: give him an order about what you want him to do and if he doesn't agree he says: "That I aren't!"' (p. 187)

---

[1] *celebrations* For the first of these national, secular celebrations with their bellringing, bonfires and merry-making, see J.E. Neale, 'November 17th', in *Essays in Elizabethan History* (Jonathan Cape, London, 1963), pp. 95–106; the essay was first published in 1958, the 400th anniversary.

Such events were distinct from public fasts (days of 'national humiliation') and from general thanksgivings, both marked by religious services. Masters and mistresses were expected to grant paid time for their workforce to attend church.

Between 1689 and

above St Maurice, Briningham. Here, on a nine-mile round trip, the Hardys heard a succession of gospel preachers 1799–1809. These included the Revd William Atkinson, the Yorkshire-based brother of the influential Charles Simeon's Cambridge mentor Christopher Atkinson. The church served as the Evangelical hub of north Norfolk   [*J.B. Ladbrooke c.1823, detail*]

Recognition of paid annual leave had not yet entered labour agreements. With the possible exception of Christmas Day, the mediaeval Catholic tradition of granting days off had ended. After the Reformation the movable feasts (those not held to fixed calendar days but governed by the date on which Easter Day fell) were replaced by the commemoration of great national events on fixed dates, such as 17 November, the accession day of Queen Elizabeth I in 1558, or 29 May, Oak Apple Day, the day King Charles II was restored to his kingdom in 1660. But these lingered on only into the first part of the eighteenth century and did not survive the industrious revolution.[1]

An employer who hired a day labourer could look with greater equanimity on a hired hand who, in the manner of the self-employed, took a day off to attend his local fair or a boxing match, as he was simply not paid that day. However a time-aware master who took on a yearly servant was not so relaxed if that man pleaded to attend such an event:

calculating deductions for time off would have heralded the introduction of annual leave, then non-existent.

It is harder to offer precise definitions of the old culture than it is to recount the imposition of the new. In neither his voluminous history of the working class nor his survey of their culture and customs can E.P. Thompson formulate exact comparisons, willingly admitting to the elusiveness of the subject: 'Again and again the "passing of old England" evades analysis.'[1] That passing involved some loss of independence, both economic and social, linked to a loss of independence in thought, speech and manner such as Kipling's 'Briton of the Clay' enjoyed.[2] It was also associated with encroaching discipline and regulation, by employers and justices, over working practices and leisure activities. There was a lessening of a time to dance and a time to play and, generally, of many other forms of spontaneous recreation: 'As important in this passing as the simple physical loss of commons and "playgrounds", was the loss of leisure in which to play and the repression of playful impulses.'[3]

below A corbel grotesque at St Margaret, Lt Dunham—the Evangelical hub of central Norfolk in Mary Hardy's time. This smiling, horned creature, his features eroded by the passage of the centuries, resembles a green man; tendrils wind round his ears, and fleshy leaves are entangled with fronds of his hair.

Stern Calvinist preachers might scold the congregation, but such images from the days of Catholicism survived from a less constrained culture, firing the imagination of any of the flock whose eyes wandered during services   [*MB·2014*]

1870 there were 325 occasions of special worship for events of national significance. In this period, while observance was in some places willing and devout, 'it is evident that there was also indifference, dissent and defiance' (P. Williamson, 'Introduction: 1689–1870', in P. Williamson, A. Raffe, S. Taylor and N. Mears, eds, *National Prayers: Special worship since the Reformation, vol. 2, 1689–1870* (Church of England Record Soc., vol. 22, with the Boydell Press, Woodbridge, 2017), pp. liii, lxxxii). The massive volume examines each of the 325 occasions.

This topic is also considered in chap. 1 in vol. 3 under 'Themes and terminology', and in vol. 2, chap. 1, under 'The long working day'

[1] *elusiveness* E.P. Thompson, *The Making of the English Working Class* (Penguin, Harmondsworth, 1968), p. 456. The whole of that chapter, 'Community' (pp. 441–88), and his studies in *Customs in Common* (1993) nonetheless present a great deal of evidence

[2] *losses* For a consideration, from a position of hindsight, of the loss of a 'rustic tradition' with its accompanying self-reliance, and for evidence of longer working hours, lack of holidays and villagers' 'humiliation' see G. Bourne, *Change in the Village*, pp. 5–24, 67–8, 100–21

[3] *playfulness* E.P. Thompson, *The Making of the English Working Class*, p. 448

[1] *Wilberforce* E.P. Thompson, *The Making of the English Working Class*, pp. 441–2

[2] *pressures* E.P. Thompson, *The Making of the English Working Class*, p. 442

[3] *dumb creatures* Mrs [Sarah] Trimmer, *The Œconomy of Charity* (2nd edn London, 1801), vol. 1, p. 317

[4] *parents* Mrs [Sarah] Trimmer, *The Œconomy of Charity*, vol. 1, p. 317.

The poor could have been justified in thinking there was one rule for them and one for their masters. William Hardy and his capitalist circle were not in the least Sabbatarian by instinct in the 1770s: getting the most out of the workforce meant that Sunday working was endemic among professionals and tradesmen. The brewer even kept his men at work on Christmas Day (*Diary 1*: 25 Dec. 1778). Important business was often conducted on Sundays, including banking and ordering hops (eg *Diary 1*: 16 Nov., 30 Nov. 1777). Negotiations over the future of Browne's brewery at Coltishall opened on a Sunday evening (*Diary 1*: 22 Nov. 1778), while other pressing business might last all Sunday—in the public house (*Diary 1*:

In the chapter on community in his study of the working class Thompson sets out the moral and political thinking behind William Wilberforce's establishment of the Society for the Suppression of Vice, a body which 'clocked up 623 successful prosecutions for breaking the Sabbath laws in 1801 and 1802 alone'; Thompson goes on to connect the reformer's thinking with his anti-Jacobinism. It is significant that Wilberforce's efforts were at their zenith in the years from 1790 to 1810, the period which includes the decade of change, the 1790s, identifiable from Mary Hardy's evidence.[1] Thompson describes some of the pressures increasingly being exerted: control of the children of the poor, the creation of a disciplined workforce and enforcement of a sober, religious Sunday. At the same time the playhouse was in decline and old pastimes, sports and fairs under threat:

The pressures towards discipline and order extended from the factory, on one hand, the Sunday school, on the other, into every aspect of life: leisure, personal relationships, speech, manners.[2]

Attitudes shaping the Sunday-school movement have been set out in volume 3, chapter 2. In many ways they represented an assault on the 'old culture', as exemplified by the desire to remove 'rude and uncultivated' children from the streets. The emphasis on kindness to animals by the movement's early advocates presaged the banning decades later of such brutal pursuits as cockfighting and bear-, bull- and badger-baiting. As early as 1801 Sarah Trimmer was admonishing the schoolchildren's parents:

It is a very great cruelty to hurt dumb creatures; therefore parents should take care that their children do not make playthings of birds, kittens, etc or use cattle ill.[3]

Parents were expected to 'make a point of setting their children an example of sobriety and good behaviour', including regular attendance at church on Sundays. Mrs Trimmer's injunctions lend weight to the notion of a new authoritarian culture: one sympathetic to animals, but not necessarily to people clutching at the last vestiges of Sabbath freedom.[4]

Evangelicals, Nonconformists and abstainers from alcohol embraced the devout Sunday favoured by Messrs Ivory and Adkin and later the LDOS. Yet such a Sabbath, not seen

A

FORM

OF

PRAYER,

TO BE USED

In all Churches and Chapels throughout those Parts of the United Kingdom called *England* and *Ireland*, on *Wednesday* the Twenty-fourth Day of *March* 1847, being the Day appointed by Proclamation for a General FAST and Humiliation before Almighty God, in order to obtain Pardon of our Sins, and that we may in the most devout and solemn Manner send up our Prayers and Supplications to the Divine Majesty :

For the Removal of those heavy Judgments which our manifold Sins and Provocations have most justly deserved ; and with which Almighty God is pleased to visit the Iniquities of this Land by a grievous Scarcity and Dearth of divers Articles of Sustenance and Necessaries of Life.

By Her Majesty's Special Command.

LONDON:

Printed by GEORGE E. EYRE and WILLIAM SPOTTISWOODE, Printers to the Queen's most Excellent Majesty. 1847.

left The opening page of a service sheet for a general fast authorised by royal proclamation. This, of 24 Mar. 1847, praying for God's mercy during the Irish potato famine, was particularly well observed; different denominations even came together in worship, such was public distress at the plight of the starving in Ireland and parts of Scotland.

These days of special worship went against the instincts of time-aware employers: William Hardy snr and jnr usually did not allow their men time off to attend services.

Their rector's words in protest are quoted in full in the pen portrait of the Revd John Burrell in volume 3, chapter 1. In a revealing phrase he reported to Bishop Manners Sutton in 1806 that the 'good old *custom*' of the past of granting a fully paid day's holiday for the occasion was no longer being observed in 'this hitherto … exemplary parish'. And Letheringsett, he added, was not alone [*Author's collection*]

since the days of Lord Protector Cromwell and the Major-Generals in the mid-seventeenth century, was opposed to the interests of capitalists. William Hardy required his men not only to work on Sundays but on the two holiest days, Good Friday and Easter.[1] Good Friday was not observed as a day of fasting and religious observance when there was money to be made, as on 25 March 1796. The apprentice Henry Raven noted one man harrowing and then delivering beer; another drayman was helping the millwright to brew; the maltster and thresher were at work. Additionally four bricklayers and three carpenters were employed; the day labourer was working in the yard. None of the Hardy family attended a church service or meeting (*Diary 3*).

11 Feb. 1781). The Coltishall years are full of such examples, but these start to tail off during the 1780s

[1] *Easter* William Hardy posted Manning and Frary in his tied house five miles away for the whole of Easter Day; they had to keep possession of an absconding innkeeper's goods (*Diary 1*: 3 Apr. 1774)

facing page Part of
Cley's old fairstead on
Newgate Green. In
Mary Hardy's time the
fair was held here on
open ground facing the
Glaven estuary. Its tim-
ing in late July coincided
with the feast of St
Margaret of Antioch,
the church's patronal
saint   [*MB · 2010*]

---

[1] *matches, water frolics*
Both topics are covered
later in this chapter

[2] *Boyce and Girling*
Neither is recorded as
opposing his master
over leisure pursuits,
and neither is shown
as attending a fair.
    Although Girling's
mother and his sister
Ann went to Walsing-
ham Fair he did not
join them (*Diary 4*:
17 June 1805). As seen
in vol. 3, chap. 4, he
spent much of his
Sundays as boy and
then as brewery clerk
driving Mary Hardy to
Wesleyan meetings at
Cley and Briston 1800–
08. An uncharacteristic
element of light-heart-
edness was introduced
by Mary Hardy on
Easter Day 1801, when
he was 16. After hear-
ing Josiah Hill's Wesley-
an sermon on growing
in grace, Girling stayed
out 'all the evening for
the first time' (*Diary 4*:
5 Apr. 1801)

The weekly Norwich newspapers reflected the new mood. Before 1793 there had been regular reports of wrestling and boxing matches, attended by up to 20,000 spectators; some of the Hardys' men, including the luckless Manning, had enjoyed time off for these. Water frolics, as regattas were then known, similarly attracted huge numbers, William Hardy attending Hoveton Water Frolic in August 1776 and the Coltishall schoolmaster Hickling Water Frolic in July 1777.[1] Most of these large public gatherings appear to have ceased in the harsher times of the French wars; certainly many fewer bulletins about them were published.

The sober, industrious poor whom first Nonconformity and later Temperance resolved to fashion were just the sort of workers on whom capitalism could rely to do the job and who would turn their backs on traditional distractions such as fairs and wrestling matches. The contrast in the Hardys' workforce springs to mind between on the one hand such individuals as the independently minded and occasionally hard-drinking and mutinous William Frary, Robert Manning and Robert Bye, who clung as tenaciously as good sense permitted—or, with awful consequences, recklessly— to the old ways; and on the other Thomas Boyce and William Girling, adherents of orderly, blameless Methodism.[2]

It is against this confused backdrop of time-awareness, pressure to achieve productivity and profit, moral earnestness, Sabbatarianism and anti-Jacobinism that we should view the outdoor recreations of the poor.

Statistics on fairs, and their location

We learn of the central importance placed on fairs from the diaries of Mary Hardy and Henry Raven. They show more fairs in existence than those in the published county lists, and make it clear that the 'forgotten' fairs were not necessarily the haunt of just the lower orders. We watch as attempts to visit a fair would spark a crisis in relations between master and men, and see the varied strategems the men adopted to get to it. Public houses even miles distant would lay on vast fair suppers to feed the participants. The local fair would bring schools to a halt for up to a week, and other children at schools some distance away would be permitted time off to join their families and friends at the

[1] *1796 list* N. Kent, *General View of the Agriculture of the County of Norfolk*, pp. 166–7. He gives Binham as 25 July, Briston 26 May and Lyng 21 Nov. His text was evidently written some years earlier: Binham Fair had been suppressed in 1793, as this chapter will show.

Allowance has to be made for the skewing in table 4.7.1 (overleaf) produced by the Hardys' removal to Letheringsett in 1781. There are consequently more references to fairs in north-east and east Norfolk 1773–81, but more to north Norfolk 1781–1809.

The omission of Acle, Horning and Scottow after the diary's early years reflect this skew

[2] *Weybourne Fair* Its date was governed by the church calendar. The maid Sarah Jeckell and farm servant James Cornwell attended it on 1 June 1784, the year Easter fell on 11 Apr.

The farm servants William Lamb, Thomas Baldwin and Gunton Thompson went on 17 May 1796, the year Easter fell early, on 27 Mar. (*Diary 2, Diary 3*).

Cakerow was held on the first Monday in April unless it clashed with Easter Monday, when it moved to the Tuesday (*Diary 1*: 5 Apr. 1774)

grand reunion. Maidservants would be allowed time off for up to three days to get back home to be with family members and friends for whom this was their only chance of seeing one another from year to year. The fair was not solely a wholesale centre, nor a trading place, nor just a festival or junket. It was a much-prized gathering, a means of keeping in touch personally with loved ones when letter-writing was not a substitute available to the illiterate.

It is difficult to be precise about figures when none of the printed lists matches another. Crouse and Stevenson in 1790 named 74 Norfolk towns and villages hosting fairs (pictured overleaf), and city and county directories would also publish 'correct' lists of fairs. Yet Nathaniel Kent in his list published only six years later named three more: Binham, Briston and Lyng, all held on fixed dates.[1] And we know from Mary Hardy and Henry Raven that there were more fairs still. Cakerow Fair, held in the northern part of Horstead parish, was going strong in the 1770s. Weybourne Fair was still kept as late as 1796, yet neither Weybourne nor Cakerow (under this name) enters the published lists. Revealingly, whereas Cakerow was enjoyed by respectable and somewhat disreputable elements alike, as will be described, Weybourne Fair was attended by the Hardys' workforce and maidservants, but not their employers. It was these pleasure fairs, rather than worthy livestock and agricultural fairs, which as scenes of popular revelry invited suppression.[2]

34 Norfolk fairs, with years, recorded by Mary Hardy and Henry Raven

sources Diaries of Mary Hardy and Henry Raven

fair [1]	*years*	*fair* [1]	*years*
Acle	1774	Horstead: 'Hautbois'	
Aldborough	1774–75, 1799	['Cakerow Fair']	1774–79
Aylsham	1774, 1778–80, 1782,	King's Lynn [2]	1791, 1802
	1791	Kipton Ash	1801, 1803, 1807
Briston	1794, 1808	N. Elmham	1792
Cakerow, *see* Horstead		N. Walsham	1774, 1777–78, 1780,
Cawston Sheep Show	1802, 1804–06, 1808		1785–86, 1793,
Cley	1782, 1784, 1788,		1795
	1794–96, 1800,	Norwich: 'Tombland'	1778, 1780, 1794
	1802, 1806	St Faith's	1774–75, 1777–80,
Coltishall	1775–77, 1779–80		1788, 1798, 1801,
E. Dereham	1785, 1788, 1808		1805, 1807
Hempton Green	1781, 1783–84, 1792,	Scottow	1776–79
	1796–99, 1801–02,	Sprowston:	1776, 1778, 1780,
	1805, 1807–08	'Magdalen Fair'	1807
Holt	1781–88, 1790–99,	Swaffham	1806
	1801–02, 1805–08	Walsingham	1805
Horning	1774, 1776–77,	Weybourne	1784, 1796
	1779–80	Worstead	1774, 1776–79, 1807

[1] *34 fairs* 25 places are named here, but as some were held twice or even three times a year the number rises to 34. The 25 places are marked ✿ on the rear endpaper map

[2] *King's Lynn* The fair, still held in the town centre, is known as Lynn Mart

facing page The list of Norfolk fairs for the year 1790, showing 74 towns and villages if Norwich's two are treated as distinct. However, many towns such as Holt had two or even three fairs a year, making a total of 107 separate fairs. Some, like St Faith's (shown under 'F'), lasted up to three weeks.

Holt Fair was held on the fixed days April 25 and November 25 (not the 24th, as listed here; Mary Hardy confirms its November 25 date in 1789 and 1790). If a fair fell on market day or the Sabbath it was moved to a more convenient day. Dates of many were linked to religious movable feasts, such as Norwich's Tombland Fair on Maundy Thursday, or N. Walsham's Ascension Day fair. Dates would be changed if neighbouring fairs consequently fell too close together or clashed directly. Press notices would make these adjustments clear.

As other printed lists show, Norfolk had 22 fairs in 1792 governed by movable feasts, out of a total of 112—allowing for multiple counting of fairs held multiple times a year. Fairs not named by the two diarists are marked ✿ on the rear endpaper map [*Crouse and Stevenson's Norwich and Norfolk Complete Memorandum Book (Norwich, 1790)*]

A Correct List of the FAIRS in Norfolk.

Acle, Midsummer-Day
Alburgh, June 21
Attleborough, April 11, Holy Thursday, August 15
Aylesham, March 23, last Tuesday in September
Bacton, 1st Monday in August, November 30
Banham, January 22
Broomhill, July 7
Burnham, March 15, Aug. 1
Castleacre, April 18, July 25
Cawston, January 10, April 14, August 28
Cley, July 19
Coltishall, Whit-Monday
Cressingham Magna, Aug. 12
Cromer, Whit-Monday
Dereham, Th. before July 5 and Th. before Sept. 29
Diss, October 28
Downham, April 27, Nov. 2
Elmham, April 5
St. Faith's, October 17
Feltwell, November 20
Fincham, March 3
Forncet, 1st Th. in Sept. O.S.
Foulsham, 1st Tuesday in May
Frettenham, 1st Mon. in Apr.
Fring, May 10, November 30
Gaywood, June 11, October 6
Gissing, July 25
Gresllinghall, December 6
Harleston, July 5, Sept. 9
Harling East, May 4, Sept. 16 (Sheep Show), Oct. 24
Harpley, July 24
Hempnall, Whit - Monday, January 11
Hempton, Whit - Tuesday, November 22
Heacham, August 3
Hingham, March 7, Whit-Tuesday, October 2
Hockham, Easter Monday
Hockwold, July 25
Holt, April 25, November 24
Horning, Mon. after Aug. 2
Ingham, Mon. after Whit-Monday

Kenninghall, July 7, Sept. 30 (Sheep Show)
Kipton-ash (Sheep Show) Sept. 4
Litcham, November 1
Loddon, Easter Monday and Monday after Nov. 22
Ludham, Thurs. after Whits. week
Lynn, Feb. 14, October 16
Massingham, Tuesday before Easter, November 8
Mattishall, Tuesday before Holy Thursday.
Methwold, April 2
New Buckenham, May 29, November 22
Northwalsham, Holy Thurs.
Northwold, Nov. 30
Norwich, Day bef. GoodFri.
Do. (Bishop Bridge) Easter Monday and Tuesday
Do. (Do.) Whit-M. & Tu.
Oxburgh, March 25
Pulham St. Mary, Fortnight before Whit-Monday
Reepham, June 29
Rudham, May 17, October 13
Scole, Easter Tuesday
Scottow, Ditto
Shouldham, Sept. 19, Oct. 10
Southrepps, July 25
Sprowston (Magdalen), Aug. 2
Stoke, December 6
Stowbridge, Sat. after Whit-Sunday
Swaffham, May 12, July 21 November 3
Thetford, May 14, August 2, September 25
Walsingham, Monday Fortnight after Whit-Sunday
Watton, July 10, October 10, November 8
Weasenham, June 25
Worsted, May 12
Wymondham, Feb. 2, May 6
Yarmouth, Easter Friday and Saturday

facing page **Worstead Manor House, facing south onto the market square.** The annual fair was held in this large open space edged by manor house, church, grocer's store (probably that of the Hardys' friend William Bird) and, to the east, a row of weavers' houses.

This was the home fair of Jeremiah Cozens, who was raised in the neighbouring parish of Westwick   [*MB·2002*]

---

[1] *Cley Fair* eg *Diary 2*: 26 July 1782, 30 July 1784; *Diary 3*: 31 July 1795, 29 July 1796; *Diary 4*: 30 July 1802, 25 July 1806: all Fridays.

Cley Fair dated from 1253, and used to be held over three days 19–21 July (J. Hooton, *The Glaven Ports*, p. 61)

[2] *unreliable lists* Horning Fair's listing is also inaccurate. In theory it was held on the first Monday after 2 August, as seen on the previous page, but Mary Hardy twice records it in July (*Diary 1*: 19 July 1779, 20 July 1780—a Monday and a Thursday)

[3] *calendar change* It is explained in the Prologue in vol. I

[4] *vague* N. Kent, *General View of the Agriculture of the County of Norfolk*, p. 167

To act as a corrective to the lists, the 34 fairs mentioned by the diarists are tabulated, with dates (table 4.7.1). Adding to the confusion, the two diarists occasionally show that the dates quoted in print do not match the actual events held, the time difference being greater than the one or two days' shifting to allow for Sunday and market-day clashes. Cley Fair, in theory held on 19 July, the eve of the feast of the parish church's patron saint St Margaret of Antioch, was consistently held many days later, between 25 July and 31 July—and, according to the evidence of Mary Hardy and Henry Raven, always on a Friday.[1] It is they who tell us that Cley Fair had not only moved to its later date but was no longer on the fixed day 19 July shown in the 1790 Crouse and Stevenson list. Already by 1782 it had become a one-day affair held on the last Friday in July. The published lists thus cannot be treated as reliable.[2]

The persistent time shift is probably attributable to the loss of eleven days in 1752, when the Gregorian calendar was adopted in Britain.[3] Local people had to decide whether to keep their fair to the former, Julian fixed date, to become known as 'New Style', or to move it on, as Cley did, and as happened nationally in the quarter-days' adoption of 'Old Style'. Michaelmas, the feast of St Michael and All Angels, remained 29 September (New Style). From 1752 'Old Michaelmas Day', the adjusted rent day, was 10 October. The largest of Norfolk's fairs, held on open ground outside Horsham St Faith, used to start on St Faith's Day, 6 October. From 1752 it opened eleven days later, on 17 October.

There are further confusions. Kent says in 1796 in a somewhat vague fashion, as though wishing to impress on his readers that he was not much given to frequenting Norfolk fairs, that 'many of these are much upon the decline, but some of them rather increasing.'[4] His pronouncement contrasts with the assertion of the agriculturalist William Marshall in a work published only nine years earlier. Marshall caught the spirit and vitality of a Norfolk fair in 1782 when he visited Ingham, between Stalham and the coast, although he sounded a note of warning that their role as centres of exchange and trade was diminishing. Worstead, as their former home fair serving as a gathering place for the Cozens family, was seen to be on the decline:

Ingham Fair reaches four or five miles round on every side . . . This species of sociability and hospitality is not peculiar to Ingham: Walsham, Worstead, Southrepps, Aldborough, St Faith's etc etc have their fairs, more famed for their hospitality than the business transacted at them; except the last, which is one of the largest fairs in the kingdom.

Yorkshire has its *feasts*; other countries their *wakes*; and Norfolk its *fairs*.[1]

This marked change in tone between 1782 and 1796 reinforces the recurring theme: seriousness was increasingly extending its grip over rural revels.

Norfolk's fairs are located on the rear endpaper map, which distinguishes ones mentioned and sometimes attended by Mary Hardy and Henry Raven and those not appearing in their diaries. Reflecting its agricultural character the county had more fairs than the national average. In 1792 there were 1515 fairs in England and 176 in Wales. The highest number was found in Kent (130) and Sussex (119); Yorkshire came third (a total of 101 for the three ridings combined).[2] In 1801 the percentage of the population of England and Wales living in Norfolk was 3·1 per cent. Of the 1691 fairs in England and Wales in 1792 Norfolk had approximately 79 (including Binham). The county with just over 3 per cent of the population had 4·7 per cent of the fairs of England and Wales, and 5·2 per cent of England's.[3]

[1] *Ingham* W. Marshall, *The Rural Economy of Norfolk*, vol. 2, p. 261 [his italics]. His visit to Ingham Fair was on 28 May 1782; 'hospitality' is probably a synonym for heavy drinking.
Wakes as popular celebrations are covered later in this chapter

[2] *fairs* R. Perren, 'Markets and marketing', in *The Agrarian History of England and Wales, vol. VI, 1750–1850*, ed. G.E. Mingay (Cambridge Univ. Press, 1989) p. 223.
Statistics for fairs were compiled not on the actual number held, multiple fairs often being held in one place during the year (eg Cawston's three and Holt's two), but on the number of places or sites. The (approximate) figure of 79 is arrived at by counting those in the printed list of 1790; then adding a few extra from Kent's of 1796, from the Letheringsett diarists and from newspaper notices

[3] *population* Figures from the 1801 census data: population of England and Wales 8,872,980; England 8,331,434; Norfolk including Norwich 273,371. With calculations confined to England, Norfolk with just under 3.3% of the national population had 5·2% of its fairs

[1] *movable feasts* Of the 3203 fairs in 1753, 2684 were thus held on fixed dates (R. Poole, *Time's Alteration: Calendar reform in early modern England* (UCL Press, London, 1998), p. 146). See also his appendix on fair dates (pp. 213–16)

[2] *1753 data* R. Poole, *Time's Alteration*, pp. 145–6

[3] *decline of fairs* See D. Alexander, *Retailing in England during the Industrial Revolution* (Athlone Press, London, 1970), pp. 31–60; also C. Fowler, 'Changes in provincial retail practice during the eighteenth century, with particular reference to central–southern England', *Business History*, vol. 40, no. 4 (Oct. 1998), pp. 41–43. H-C. and L.H. Mui see fairs' near extinction by 1800: 'All that remained of the great fairs was the trade in livestock and some foodstuffs' (H-C. Mui and L.H. Mui, *Shops and Shopkeeping in Eighteenth-Century England* (McGill-Queen's Univ. Press, Canada, and Routledge, London, 1989) p. 27). The decline of itinerant selling and rise of fixed-place retailing is covered in vol. 3, chap. 7

[4] *role* D. Alexander, *Retailing in England during the Industrial Revolution*, p. 59

Taking England alone, Norfolk had a much higher number of fairs per capita than the English average. In England in 1792 there was one fair for every 5499 persons. In Norfolk and Norwich there was one fair for every 3460. These figures do not however allow for differences in size: Nottingham's eight-day Goose Fair was not a tiny affair like Scottow. In 1753, of the 3203 fairs held nationally, 519 (16·2 per cent) were held on movable feasts. This proportion is lower than Norfolk's 22 fairs out of 112 in 1792 (19·6 per cent).[1]

In his comprehensive study of fairs in the century of calendar change and of local variations in the adoption of New Style and Old Style dates (the latter adjusting for the 'lost' eleven days) Robert Poole shows that in 1753 there had been 3203 fairs in England and Wales.[2] As we have seen, nearly forty years later there were only 1691 fairs. A marked falling-off had thus occurred even before the arrival of the Anglican Evangelicals, the insurgent spread of Wesleyanism and fears over large public gatherings of the people which rose to new heights after the French Revolution. The story of the loss of fairs, or their suppression, is a complex, multi-faceted one.

Having grappled with the statistics, we can now turn to the type of business transacted at fairs. Historians of shopping generally agree that fairs' wholesale functions were fast disappearing by the end of the eighteenth century. Additionally retailing at fairs was being reduced to 'trifles' such as pedlars and hawkers would sell: lengths of fabric, ribbons, thread and other haberdashery; occasionally silverware. Their conclusions are the same, but they disagree as to the reasons. They cite the increase in fixed-place wholesale and retail shops as the distributive functions of fairs declined; improved road communications, and later the spread of railways; urban growth; and the building of indoor wholesale trading places such as cloth halls and corn exchanges.[3] Comparing the fair with the market, Alexander writes:

It was the fair which revealed the weakest powers of adaptation. As an exchange mechanism it operated usefully in predominantly rural societies, characterized by slow communications and transport, a low level of material demand and a high degree of local and personal self-sufficiency. It could not play a crucial distribution role in an urban, industrial society.[4]

The next section will demonstrate that it is premature to write off fairs simply as outmoded places of sale and exchange. They were valued, as Marshall recognised, for their sociability and as a vehicle for maintaining contact with family and old friends. And the map on the rear endpaper bears out David Alexander's thesis that they retained an economic role in non-industrial, non-urban areas poorly served by road comunications. Fairs were not evenly distributed across Norfolk. Comparatively few were found in the triangle bounded by Norwich, Great Yarmouth and Loddon in the populous area of the Southern Broads. The River Yare was a highway with a busy trade, and goods could be carried along its basin more cheaply than anywhere else within the county, coastwise carriage excepted.[1]

But the triangle bounded by King's Lynn, Burnham Market and Fakenham had a cluster of fairs (Lynn itself, Gaywood, Heacham, Fring, Rudham, Harpley, Kipton Ash, Massingham, Weasenham and Hempton Green). It was a fairly empty countryside with no fast roads other than the short stretch of 1770 turnpike from King's Lynn north to Snettisham; also the Nar navigation hardly penetrated this large area.[2] Fairs retained a role here in the north-west, as in other poorly served areas such as the Fens, with a cluster running from Downham Market to Thetford.[3] The Hardys' area of north Norfolk, densely populated and with good communications, had need of comparatively few fairs.

Trade in livestock and foodstuffs at fairs was holding up well in Norfolk. The fairs recorded by Mary Hardy at which such business was transacted were Holt (with its distinct beef, cattle and horse fairs), Hempton Green, just south of Fakenham (famous for bullocks), St Faith's (for cattle and horses), and Cawston and Kipton Ash (for sheep);[4] also horses were bought and sold at Cakerow and Tombland Fairs and many others. By far the greatest number of Mary Hardy's references to fairs relates to Holt Fair. Having a fair on the spot was still much valued.

Even fairs with a serious purpose had their lighter side, one summed up neatly by Mary Hardy in this anecdote during her Coltishall days. Cakerow Fair was held in Horstead near the deserted hamlet of Mayton, close to the crossing of the old course of the Bure at Little Hautbois:[5]

[1] *highway* Described in chaps 3 and 4 on river trade

[2] *roads* Depicted on the front endpaper map in this volume.
The navigable rivers are shown on that map and on the rear endpaper

[3] *the Fens* By contrast, this area had numerous short stretches of turnpike, as the front endpaper map shows; but the countryside with its numerous drains and rivers was not easy of access

[4] *stock fairs* Trade at all these fairs, and livestock fairs in neighbouring counties, received good coverage in the *Norwich Mercury*. It was the pleasure fairs, attracting little business other than in 'toys' for servants, which were ignored in the press

[5] *Cakerow* It seems to make an appearance as Frettenham Fair in the 1790 list illustrated on p. 375, but it was not held in Frettenham parish or in Lt Hautbois, another name by which it was known: 'Hobbis Fair' (*Diary 1*: 5 Apr. 1774).
The site today consists of arable fields close to the Mayton Wood landfill site and recycling centre

¹ *quite drunk Diary 1*; 'quite' means totally.
The Hardys were unimpressed with their Neatishead innkeeper, who had come over for a day at the fair. Three days later they required him to return the mare he had bought for them while his judgment was evidently impaired

² *drunk; Scarecrow Diary 1*: 'RM drunk at Hobbis Fair' (5 Apr. 1774); 7 Apr. 1777

³ *at Balls's Diary 1*; the Adam and Eve was tied to the Hardys. William Hardy, John Smith and the children went again to the fair together on 7 Apr. 1777, all getting home at 8 pm. Rather dangerously for those still incapable the next day, the press gang was in town (8 Apr. 1777)

⁴ *Cakerow Diary 1*: 5 Apr. 1779. Nearby Scottow Fair was held on Easter Tuesday; a clash was thus avoided that year

⁵ *Raven and William Diary 1*: 6 Apr. 1778

⁶ *sources* P. Millican, *A History of Horstead and Stanninghall*, pp. 14–17.
He quotes from a list of Norfolk fairs in 1595 which gives Cakerow as held not in April but on 6 November (p. 14).
Cakerow's ancient Friday market with its permanent stalls had died out by *c.*1620 (p. 16)

[1775] APRIL 3, MONDAY Thomas Scrape came morning 8, stayed till 12, got almost drunk, went to Cakerow Fair, bought us a horse, came back evening 8 quite drunk, stayed an hour and took our little colt home with him.¹

The impression created here is that drinking rather than trading predominated. Our first encounter with Cakerow is when the Hardys' farm servant Robert Manning got drunk at it in 1774. The diarist hints at its more disreputable side one year by calling it Scarecrow Fair.² It was certainly associated with drinking, the nearest public house, Henry Balls's Adam and Eve across the river at Little Hautbois doing a good trade into the small hours; he also probably supplied the drink at the fairstead itself. The Hardy boys evidently had the day or half-day off school, going with their father and their schoolmaster to the fair for about four hours:

[1776] APRIL 1, MONDAY . . . Mr Hardy went with the children and Mr Smith to Cacro Fair evening 2, sent the children home with Mr Smith evening 6, stayed himself at Henry Balls's till morning 1 . . .³

In 1779 the fair fell on Easter Monday, but it was not moved to the Tuesday. It appears that many of Coltishall's ratepayers attended Cakerow Fair, for when the annual town meeting ended early that year the customary midday dinner was not on offer. Instead William Hardy got home from the meeting by one o'clock and carried five-year-old Mary Ann to Cakerow, Raven and William going on foot.⁴ The presence of young children suggests that at least during the day the fair was respectable enough: Raven and William, aged ten and eight, had gone on their own the previous year.⁵

Cakerow has been given some prominence as in 1937 the historian of Horstead found that almost no archival sources survived.⁶ The fair stands as an illustration of the smaller type of gathering, combining business and pleasure, where local people and their children mingled for a half-day out— up to a point. After Manning's drunken behaviour there in 1774 the Hardys' men were kept to their tasks on fair day, although they could have gone to Cakerow in the evening. Also Mary Hardy makes no mention of women attending the event, apart from Mary Ann. Neither she nor her maidservants are recorded at Cakerow.

Fairs as reunions

There was a complex pattern of attendance by the Hardys' workforce and maidservants at other pleasure fairs, with priority evidently being given by their employer to the servants' home fair over the local fair (the one close to their place of work). The maidservants in the Hardys' household were consistently given greater latitude to stay away for up to three or four days, including journey time to and from their family home. By contrast master and mistress fretted if the male farm servants took more than one day off, as seen at the chapter head over Isaac Pooley's trip to Worstead. The link between servant and home fair is so strong as to act as an aid to modern genealogists. The struggle to get to a distant event and the longed-for reunion with 'friends', the eighteenth-century term for relatives, can often direct family historians to the servants' home area.

The annual gathering was a powerful urge felt across the country. William Marshall has already been quoted as linking Norfolk fairs to the type of gathering personified by the wakes of the Midlands and North; these were also known as rushbearings, when fresh rushes were carried to the church.[1]

above Hempton Green, its buttercup-strewn ground once trampled by the hooves of cattle at one of the county's leading livestock fairs.
 Less than five miles from Whissonsett, the twice-yearly event gave the diarists a chance to renew ties in the extended family   [*MB · 2011*]

[1] *wake* The word lives on as a funeral gathering. Like the fair it was a time of revelry with drinking, dancing, bell-ringing, pugilism, bull-baiting and other sports (R. Poole, *The Lancashire Wakes Holidays* (Lancashire County Books, Preston, 1994)

[1] *Wedgwood* E.P. Thompson, *The Making of the English Working Class*, p. 450. In this lengthy footnote, as well as quoting Josiah Wedgwood, Thompson cites evidence from 19th-century sources looking back in time. See also his p. 444, where he presents the fair's cultural importance in the life of the poor

[2] *Mattishall* J. Woodforde, *The Diary of a Country Parson*, ed J. Beresford, vol. 3, p. 22, 30 Apr. 1788; p. 94, 31 May 1791; p. 351, 15 May 1792.
    Mattishall Gaunt was held on the Tuesday before Ascension Day. Forby gives Gant or Gaunt as 'a village fair or wake', from the Anglo-Saxon *gan*, to go to; thus 'a place of resort' (R. Forby, *The Vocabulary of East Anglia* vol. 2 (London, 1830), p. 128)

[3] *Reepham* J. Woodforde, *The Diary of a Country Parson*, ed J. Beresford, vol. 3, p. 359, 30 June 1792; Reepham Fair was held on the fixed day 29 June.
    His maidservant Nanny Kaye walked seven miles to St Faith's Fair and back in one day (p. 222, 18 Oct. 1790). There was pressure to get back from St Faith's, as in 1800: 'I gave my maid Sally Gunton,

E.P. Thompson stresses the homing instinct associated with the wake. It was one which even the dour, hardworking Staffordshire potter Josiah Wedgwood could not suppress in a workforce customarily kept rigorously to their task:

> The Wakes were important kinship occasions, when the townsfolk visited their kin in the country . . . Even the disciplinary Wedgwood was defeated by the Wakes, 'which must be observ'd though the World was to end with them'.[1]

Both Mary Hardy and the Norfolk diarist resident a few miles away in Weston Parsonage represent a transitional point in attitudes to the fair. Woodforde was by no means a time-aware capitalist manufacturer like Josiah Wedgwood or William Hardy, yet even he regarded attendance at the fair not as a customary right but as something to be negotiated. The rector's maid Betty Dade was granted time off in 1788, 1791 and 1792 to see her family who lived more than six miles away at Mattishall, but she had to take her two days by agreement and by his leave. Her employer also decided to check where she was sleeping overnight:

> [1788] Mattishall Gaunt (alias Fair) today, my maid Betty, whose friends live at Mattishall, went thither and is to return home to-morrow . . .
> [1791] This being Mattishall-Gaunt Day, gave Betty leave to go and see her friends and stay out all night . . .
> [1792] Betty went with her Aunt Grey from Weston House this morning on foot to Mattishall Gant alias Fair. She has leave to sleep at her mother's tonight.[2]

Another of the rectory maids, Winfred, came from Witchingham. Her local fair was Reepham, nearly six miles north of Weston. For this she too was allowed up to two days off, her times away being noted most carefully: 'My maid Winfred went to Reepham Fair yesterday morn' and returned home about 4 this afternoon. Her mother lives at Witchingham.'[3]

But an ominous note was sounded about even so respectable a fair as St Faith's, one which the rector and his niece, and the county nobility, would sometimes attend. Woodforde's friend the Revd Thomas Jeans of Great Witchingham brought bad news on 12 October 1792, five days before the great fair was to begin:

Mr Jeans informed us that he had heard it rumoured about, that there would be a great mob collected at St Faith's Fair on Wednesday next, on account of the dearness of wheat and other provisions, but I believe rather from the late long propensity of the discontented to a general disturbance, so prevalent at present in France. The Norwich mob to meet the country mob on the above day at St Faith's.[1]

Although nothing in fact happened, the parson's fears of a rising at a fair reflect the attitudes which only encouraged further suppression. His association of popular discontent with the troubles in France in October 1792 (the King being beheaded three months later) and his nervousness at the rumoured co-ordination between 'the Norwich mob' and 'the country mob' may not have been widely shared by his fellow clergy. Woodforde and his niece were prone to fears about all manner of eventualities, including high winds. Nonetheless this outlook laid the seedbed for suppression.

With the exception of extremely few, including Aldborough and Weybourne, the 34 fairs listed in table 4.7.1 were attended by the Hardy family as well as their servants. The generally accommodating outlook of the kindly clerical employer was also that of Mary Hardy, who had control of the female staff on the Hardy establishment. Her approach seems to have been that it was only right to foster loyalty to the home, even if it meant quite a few days' disruption to routine. At Coltishall leave was extended to 'Nanny' (possibly Ann Rust) to travel twelve miles home to Upton to attend her mother, then seriously ill. A few months later, Nanny had time off for Acle's Midsummer Fair, the one nearest to Upton and about 13–14 miles from Coltishall; another two months later she was back again for a home visit following the death of her father.[2]

Scottow Fair proved an attraction for three of the Hardys' Coltishall maidservants, who then ran the risk of being berated by the Revd Mr Adkin; the Hardy children also attended one year.[3] Molly Greenacre attended Sprowston's Magdalen Fair on 2 August 1780,[4] and Betty Marlow went with Mary Hardy and the children to St Faith's on 19 October 1778. Each maid was granted time off for one fair a year, but during the Coltishall years none is recorded at the two most local fairs, Coltishall and Cakerow.

and my head servant-man Benjamin Leggatt, liberty to go . . . Sally and Ben returned from fair *in good time*' (vol. 5, p. 279, 17 Oct. 1800), [my italics]

---

[1] *mobs* J. Woodforde, *The Diary of a Country Parson*, ed J. Beresford, vol. 3, p. 377, 12 Oct. 1792.
 No mob materialised at St Faith's. Betty Dade, granted leave to attend two fairs that year, came back with the news: 'No mob at all' (p. 378, 17 Oct. 1792)

[2] *Upton, Acle Fair Diary 1*: 14 Mar., 24 June, 6 Aug., 14 Aug. 1774. Ann evidently liked the Coltishall area, taking a post with Mrs Baret at Horstead on leaving the Hardys (4 Sept., 10 Oct. 1774).
 Mary Hardy's treatment of her maids, including the grant of free time, is considered in much of vol. 1, chap. 8. See esp. the sections 'Maidservants' wages and time off' and 'Status, identity and fun'

[3] *Scottow Diary 1*: 9 Apr. 1776, 1 Apr. 1777, 6 Apr. 1779; also 21 Apr. 1778. It was held on Easter Tuesday

[4] *Magdalen Fair* It must have been moved by 11 days in 1752, the feast of St Mary Magdalene being 22 July

[1] *Molly Hales Diary 1:* 15 Mar. 1781. For the details of the 90 maids and their hiring see vol. I, app. I.C

[2] *Ann Chalders Diary 2:* 2–5 June, 16–19 Oct. 1781, 19–22 May 1782.
Molly Moys was given extra time to see her mother before the move (10 Mar. 1781).
As well as Molly Moys the farm boy Jonathan consented to be uprooted. The farm servant and maltster William Frary took his whole family with him to Letheringsett. He and his wife Rose died there five years later, both aged 50

The move to Letheringsett during the hiring year seems to have caused some heartache for the servants. One maid, Mary Hales, declined to venture the 22 miles, perhaps not being prepared to sever home and local links for the remaining six months of her contract; she may have taken a post in Norwich.[1] The other Mary, Molly Moys, accompanied the Hardys. She was joined by a new maidservant, recruited from Coltishall: Ann ('Nanny') Chalders, daughter of the parish clerk. Given Nanny's sacrifice her mistress extended new privileges as compensation. She was allowed as much as four days to go home for Coltishall Fair two months after the move, the farm boy and young William joining her on the trip; and she was granted a further four days to go home for St Faith's Fair in October 1781. The move proved a success for the adventurous pair, Molly and Nanny hiring themselves for a second year at Letheringsett. Again Nanny was given four days for Coltishall Fair in 1782.[2] Their mistress's sensitive handling of the move and the latitude she showed over the fairs which meant so much to them may have eased their pain at being plucked from their home area.

facing page St Nicholas, N. Walsham, as it looks after partial collapses of the tower in the 18th and 19th centuries. The Hardys granted their miller William Gunton Thompson an unusual amount of time off for fairs. In the one year, 1796, he attended not only his local fair (at Holt on 25 Apr.) and what may have been his home fair (at N. Walsham on 5 May), but also the much smaller fairs at Weybourne on 17 May and Cley on 29 July [*photograph dated 21 Sept. 1962: Norfolk Heritage Centre, Norwich*]

left One of a pair of massive stone gargoyles salvaged at N. Walsham Parish Church when the tower was being partially dismantled for safety's sake. Perched at the top the four mediaeval spouts had drained the roof. Bellringing was a feature of wakes and fairs. On 15 May 1724 the N. Walsham ringers had pulled for hours on their ropes so vigorously when ringing in the Ascension Day fair that the 170-foot (52-metre) structure was severely weakened. Two sides of the tower came crashing down at 9 am the following morning. No one was killed or injured [*MB · 2015*]

[1] *Smallburgh Diary 2*: 10
June 1781 (first Sunday
after Whitsun): see p. 31.
The village is near Ing-
ham, whose annual fair
was held on the Monday
after Whit Monday

[2] *Ann Chalders Diary
2*: 19 May 1782

[3] *Tunstead Diary 4*.
Mary Hardy too felt
the tug of the home fair.
Her childhood fair was
Hempton Green, held
on Whit Tuesday and
22 November, but at
Coltishall she never had
the chance to attend it.
  In her first two years
at Letheringsett she
made a point of getting
there, on the second
occasion with her young
children and meeting
her sister Phillis Goggs
(*Diary 2*: 5 June 1781;
Diary MS: 21–22 May
1782). She encouraged
her children to nurture
family ties, Mary Ann
and/or William often
going to the fair (eg
Diary 2: 5 June 1781,
22 Nov. 1781, 1 June
1784, 29 May 1792).
  Henry Raven also
heard the call of the
home fair (*Diary 3*: 17
May 1796, 6 June 1797;
Diary 4: 14 May 1799).
  Business brought the
adult William Hardy jnr
to Hempton Green. He
bought Scots bullocks
and cattle at the
autumn fair in the early
19th century (*Diary 4*:
18 Nov. 1801, 22 Nov.
1805, 23 Nov. 1807, 18
Nov. 1808)

These were long journeys for the young women. Just two
months after arriving in Letheringsett the diarist noted that
'Molly Moys set off for Smallburgh morning 5 upon our old
black mare'. The maid, the only one known to have been
able to ride, was probably bound for Ingham Fair.[1] At least
it was 'a fine dry day' for the 24-mile ride. A year later poor
Ann Chalders also set off at 5 am on a journey of at least
four hours, in the open, but on 'a very wet cold day'.[2]

The homecomings continued in the Letheringsett years,
despite the hardships of the journeys. Sarah Mortram's
family lived at Tunstead, about nineteen miles from Letheringsett. The long journey home, probably for the fair at Worstead, proved very difficult for her. She took the opportunity
three days early of a lift on the Hardys' beer wagon the eight
miles to Itteringham; she then walked eleven miles in tor-
rential rain which led the next day to flooding:

[1807] MAY 9, SATURDAY A very wet day, rain very heavy afternoon. Sarah Mortram went to Tunstead to see her friends, she rid
[rode] as far as Itteringham in our wagon and then walked . . .[3]

1 *Worstead Diary 4*: 12 May 1807. (After two bitter campaigns in 1802 and 1806 the county election went uncontested this time)

2 *St Faith's Diary 1*: 18 Oct. 1779

3 *N. Walsham* eg 'G. Thompson and wife had our cart and old mare to Walsham Fair' (*Diary 3*: 13 May 1795; they returned 15 May). Thompson also went to Weybourne and Cley fairs (*Diary 3*: 17 May 1796, 25 July 1794— and with his wife, 31 July 1795, 29 July 1796). The 1790 printed list of fairs, illustrated on p. 375, gives the date of N. Walsham Fair as 'Holy Thursday'. This can apply to both Maundy Thursday (the day before Good Friday) and Ascension Day (40 days after Easter Day—thus always a Thursday)

4 *Lamb* eg Holt and Weybourne (*Diary 3*: 25 Apr. 1796, 17 May 1796); he would have encountered Thompson at the latter

5 *Manning Diary 1*: 5–6 Apr. 1774; 5–6 June 1775. (He had just worked all Easter Day, 3 Apr. 1774)

6 *delivering beer* eg *Diary 1*: 19 May 1777. Trouble arose again in 1778 and 1779, so a compromise was reached in 1780 whereby the men

We do not learn when Sarah got back, as her mistress was staying at Mary Ann's home at Sprowston 11–14 May 1807 during the general election. Worstead Fair was still held on 12 May, and was attended by Jeremiah Cozens, revisiting the fair of his Westwick childhood, and the Revd Mark Wilks.[1]

Women and children often went to fairs on their own, with no apparent compromise of respectability, at least for those of the diarist's class; Anna Maria Woodforde's genteel seclusion at Weston may not have been typical. We have already seen the trio of masonic wives, Mary Hardy, Mary Neve and Mrs Gilbert of Norwich at Coltishall Fair in May 1779 (page 329). Mary Hardy and another masonic wife, Frances Boorne, also went to St Faith's Fair that year, where the diarist would have seen the family's farm servants Zeb Rouse and John Thompson.[2]

Management of the male establishment fell to William Hardy and, after 1797, to his son; the way the men were stringently controlled is covered in the chapter on the workforce (volume 2, chapter 1). Some were allowed time to attend the local fair, especially if it was also their home fair. The miller Gunton Thompson, perhaps as he enjoyed higher wages and status than the rest and as no hint of impropriety in the way of drunkenness attached to him, took three days off a year to go with his wife Ann to North Walsham's Ascension Day fair.[3] The reliable William Lamb, never recorded as drunk, hardly ever ill and thus always able to work, was sometimes given leave to attend two fairs a year.[4]

William Hardy's particular problems with his men over attendance at Coltishall's Whit Monday fair are chronicled in detail in the workforce chapter. Robert Manning was not only drunk at Cakerow Fair in 1774 and then at Coltishall's in 1775, but he also skipped work afterwards. He was drunk in the Recruiting Sergeant the morning after Cakerow Fair and did no work the rest of that day; and all the Hardys' men were drinking the whole day following Coltishall Fair even though they had been granted the fair day itself. Manning was dismissed that second evening; he may have been more insubordinate than the others.[5]

Given this experience the wily brewer contrived on some of the fair days to send his men delivering beer far afield during working hours.[6] However the men evaded tight control on other occasions. In 1778 all three of the Hardys' annually hired workforce arrived at Horning with beer on fair day—and then stayed on late instead of returning home promptly.[1] Time and again it is clear the men viewed two days as the customary annual holiday allowance, their drinking signalling their protest at being denied their rights.

Their master, probably incensed more by the loss of working time than the drinking, would react by often granting only one day or even a half-day. He held the cards. Some of the men, including Robert Manning, lived in cottages tied to the brewery; most, including Manning, had wives and young children: Susanna had been baptised at Coltishall on 31 December 1772.[2] The mutinous Manning lost his job and his home. Yet having time off for the fair, which he plainly regarded as his right, was so precious that he was prepared to jettison the security of his annual tenure.

Children were eager participants at fairs from an early age. It was general for schoolchildren in Norfolk and elsewhere to have only two months' holiday a year: from mid-December to mid-January, and mid-June to mid-July.[3] Thus being granted anything from a day to a week for the local fair during term was a much-prized privilege for day children. Pupils could be also be released from boarding school, by negotiation with the parents, for their home fair. Masters and mistresses understood the need to cement strong bonds with one's 'friends'—the extended family and circle of acquaintance; and teachers too wanted the chance to take time off for fairs. Coltishall Free School closed not only for the local fair but also for the first few days or even the opening week of St Faith's Fair. When off school in St Faith's Week six-year-old Raven accompanied his father on business to North Walsham on 20 October 1774. Mary Hardy took the children to Whissonsett for a St Faith's Week holiday 19–24 October 1776 after helping at the Recruiting Sergeant and cooking the celebration supper 16–18 October.[4]

While at North Walsham Free Grammar School Raven took three days off school to come home for Coltishall Fair, leave of absence probably having been agreed when his family had tea with the master a few days earlier.[5] The charge that fairs were 'openly licentious', to use Mr Ivory's phrase

were given a half-day for Coltishall Fair (15 May 1780)

[1] *Horning Diary 1*: 5 Aug. 1778

[2] *Susanna* Daughter of Robert and Ann Manning (NRO: PD 598/2)

[3] *holidays* Schooling is described in vol. 1, chap. 6

[4] *St Faith's Diary 1*. The large suppers at the Sergeant testify to the fair's prominence in the social calendar (17 Oct. 1776, 17 Oct. 1777, 17 Oct. 1778, 18 Oct. 1779, 17 Oct. 1780).
William and Mary Hardy would meet their friends: the Smiths, Shreeves, Neves, Boornes and even John Browne from Lt Ellingham, south-west of Norwich; the young brewery owner and his wife travelled 24 miles to reach the home fair

[5] *leave of absence Diary 1*: 4 May, 13–17 May 1780. Ten-year-old William accompanied his parents and the Neves to N. Walsham on 4 May for the town's fair and also called at the grammar school.
We have already seen the Hardy children and their schoolmaster John Smith taking time off for Cakerow Fair (1 Apr. 1776)

[1] *livestock* See vol. 2, chap. 1 on 'the working horse'; vol. 2 chap. 4 on cattle, pigs and sheep

[2] *beef* eg *Diary 2*: 25 Nov. 1784, 25 Nov. 1785, 27 Nov. 1786, 25 Nov. 1788; *Diary 3*: 25 Nov. 1793. Holt's horse fair took place in the morning. Provisioning a household is described in vol. 1, chap. 7

[3] *Binham Fair Norw. Merc.* 20 July 1793

[4] *Horning Fair Norw. Merc.* 11 July 1801, 10 July 1802, 9 July 1803. That paper showed the fair had been going strong in 1780 (*Norw. Merc.* 15 July 1780), a fact confirmed by Mary Hardy's record: her husband supplied the fair beer

above The entrance to the old Magdalen leper hospital which gave its name to Sprowston's fair   [*MB·2011*]

at the chapter head, cannot be sustained when middling-sort children were taken to them not only by their parents and other relatives but even occasionally by their teachers.

Suppression

This chapter considers the social aspects of fairs. The commercial and retail transactions which were the mainstay of the more prominent ones are described elsewhere: the sale and purchase of horses, sheep, bullocks, dairy cows and their calves;[1] also the purchase of beef by Mary Hardy, William Hardy junior and Mary Ann at Holt Fair.[2] On the whole stock fairs escaped censure, their value to the local economy being clearly evident. Also the system of driving cattle south from Scotland and fattening them on the marshes of East Anglia prior to their sale had long been established and regulated by the justices: drovers were licensed, and wore a badge to prove it. It was licentiousness, the throwing over of the constraints of the master–servant relationship for a day or two a year, which worried the authorities, the clergy and what Brian Harrison in the passage on the LDOS quoted earlier calls Respectability.

On 20 July 1793, five days before Binham Fair was to open, the Lord of the Manor of Binham let it be known in the press that there would be no more fairs at Binham.[3] That same year a new bishop came to the see of Norwich, a prelate with missionary zeal, who published the sermons he delivered in London to the Society for the Propagation of the Gospel. As Lord of the Manor of Horning, by virtue of his office of Abbot of St Benet's—and by which he took his seat in the House of Lords—the Rt Revd Dr Charles Manners Sutton could decree that his fair would be suppressed.

As an experiment he closed the fair in 1801 and 1802; in 1803 he announced that the ban would be permanent.[4] The Bishop chose not to state the reasons for the ban. However those hearing him preach at St Mary-le-Bow, Cheapside, in the City of London, would have drawn parallels between his attitude to the 'Mohawk Indian' in the United States and the approach he might take towards the equally uncultivated habitués of Horning and other fairs. In a long passage on 'the unconquerable love of savage life' of the native American he offered some uncompromising observations:

I fear there is but little reason to expect at his hands a voluntary exchange of his inveterate habits of pleasure and indolence for the advantages, however certain and obvious, of regular and daily labour. This radical change of manners and pursuits can result alone from early education or extreme necessity . . . [1]

The Bishop of Norwich's sermon on spreading the light of the Christian gospel to the Americans, whom the Society had at its inception in 1701 found 'in the lowest state of society, in the darkest stage of ignorance', may stand as the manifesto of the 'new culture' to be imposed on the ignorant, unrestrained English poor:

The Native Indian hath long been the object of our anxious commiseration. He is still however far withdrawn from the reach of our good offices. So long as the habits of erratic life prevail, it will be difficult, if not impossible, to make any lasting impressions upon his mind.[2]

The only effectual remedy, he repeated to his listeners in London, was 'early education'. And so we return to the arguments urged by the advocates of Sunday schools: change could only be brought about by starting at the fountain head—the very young.[3]

Coltishall bucked the trend of the time. It was announced in 1795 that the Whit Monday fair was being *extended* by 'the addition of a show of horses and neat stock', indicating that until then it had not been a horse and livestock fair. This must have proved a success, for the next Whit Monday the show of neat beasts and horses was continued, with 'the usual stalls and stall-stuff for petty chapmen'—the traditional retail aspect of a pleasure fair.[4]

Mary Ann's local fair after her marriage was Magdalen Fair, so named for the early-mediaeval leper hospital at Sprowston, north of Norwich's city walls. This came to an abrupt end a generation later. It was suppressed by the executors and trustees of the deceased lord of the manor in 1826 owing, so the estate bailiff declared, to the 'divers tumults and riotous proceedings' at previous fairs, to the 'terror and fear of the lives of the peaceable inhabitants' and with consequent damage to their property.[5]

Cakerow suffered the same fate at around the same time, although no date can be found for its demise; it had lasted

[1] *pleasure and indolence* C. Manners Sutton, *A Sermon Preached before the Incorporated Society for the Propagation of the Gospel in Foreign Parts* (London, 1797), p. 19. He had been admitted a member of that society in 1792.
  The pressure to be exerted on the 'Native Indian' was that of so squeezing the territory allowed him that he would have to turn from hunting and a nomadic life to cultivation of the land (pp. 18–19)

[2] *ignorance, erratic life* C. Manners Sutton, *A Sermon Preached before the Incorporated Society for the Propagation of the Gospel*, pp. 14, 17

[3] *education* C. Manners Sutton, *A Sermon Preached before the Incorporated Society for the Propagation of the Gospel*, p. 18

[4] *Coltishall Norw. Merc.* 23 May 1795, 7 May 1796

[5] *Magdalen Fair* Bailiff's notice, Sprowston, dated 15 July 1826 and published that day in the *Norfolk Chronicle*.
  Like the Oxford and Cambridge colleges the name was apparently pronounced 'Maudlin', Mary Hardy spelling it phonetically 'Maudling Fair' (*Diary 1*: 2 Aug. 1780)

[1] *Cakerow* P. Millican, *A History of Horstead and Stanninghall*, pp. 15, 16

[2] *Coltishall* R. Bond, *Coltishall: Heyday of a Broadland Village*, p. 18

[3] *Holt* For the later days of the fair see J. Hales, *Three Centuries at Holt* (Priest Publications, Hunstanton, 1967), pp. 20–1

[4] *drink-fuelled* Alcohol was widely available at fairs and sports; betting, often for high stakes, accompanied most endeavours from pugilism to cricket and racing.
    Most outdoor sports were held within reach of public houses; some took place in their yards. If no licensed outlet were close by, it seems a local innkeeper could set up a stall at the event, covered by his existing alehouse licence: no quarter sessions minutes and orders have been found recording the issue of special licences for outdoor events in this period.
    This may explain why Cakerow Fair was sometimes called Hautbois Fair. The landlord of the Adam and Eve (and thus William Hardy) supplied the drink

from before 1275.[1] St Faith's, which was an even older instituition of *c.*1100, lasted until 1872; the railways would have dealt it a severe blow. Coltishall outlasted its great stock-fair neighbour by a long way. There were those alive in the late twentieth century who could still recall the fair, but in a more disorderly form than even Robert Manning might have known it. For his work of 1986 Richard Bond interviewed Coltishall residents for whom recollections of the fair were still imprinted on their minds eighty years later:

The Whit Monday fair on the Upper Common invariably ended in a drunken brawl, with stalls overturned, benches scattered and fists flying. Villagers born around the the turn of the century have vivid childhood memories of gathering beside the common to watch the fracas with their friends.[2]

Like Coltishall, Holt Fair lingered on into the twentieth century.[3] Some took on new guises after a period in abeyance. Horning's regatta fair, held in late July or early August, was established in the 1930s; summer carnivals and festivals also draw great crowds to the towns and ports. But with universal literacy and the wide range of modern communications the irresistible pull of the home fair has lost its power.

The manorial bailiff at Sprowston had cited 'riotous proceedings' at the annual fair as the reason for its suppression, adding that these caused terror to the inhabitants and damage to property. Maintaining public order posed a very real problem for those responsible for fairs, sports and other outdoor events. Some of these affairs, such as boxing and cricket matches, attracted tens of thousands of onlookers. Many among the property-owning classes, like Woodforde with his fears of the mob in 1792, were in a fragile state of mind. With government legislation of the 1790s directed at combating treason, sedition and tumults it became more likely that anything liable to provoke disorder, such as drink-fuelled betting at boxing and wrestling matches and cock-fights, would stand in danger of suppression.[4] As ever the justices proved a safeguard. They were instructed to be precise and robust in interpreting the law. The poorer classes and not just property owners, so it was affirmed, had rights.

Magistrates perusing their fifteen pages of guidance on 'Riot, rout, and unlawful assembly' would find they had to tread carefully so as not to arrest those lawfully attending fairs, wakes, sports and other leisure events:

If a number of persons being met together at a fair or market . . . or on any other lawful and innocent occasion, happen on a sudden quarrel to fall together by the ears, they are not guilty of a riot, but of a sudden affray only, of which none are guilty but those who actually engage in it; because the design of their meeting was innocent and lawful, and the subsequent breach of the peace happened unexpectedly, without any previous intention concerning it.[1]

The directions indicated that unduly timorous individuals could be disregarded when alleging they had been terrorised by proceedings which the justices regarded as perfectly normal and lawful. Wakes and sports, while noisy and drawing huge crowds, were not inherently a threat to the Peace:

In every riot there must be some such circumstances, either of actual force or violence, or at least of an apparent tendency thereto, as are naturally apt to strike a terror into the people; as the show of armour, threatening speeches, or turbulent gestures; for every such offence must be laid to be done *to the terror of the people*: and from thence it clearly follows, that assemblies at wakes, or other festival times, or meetings for exercise of common sports or diversions, as bull-baiting, wrestling, and such like, are not riotous.[2]

The likes of William Ivory, James Woodforde and Sprowston's residents, it can be inferred, were being urged to show some backbone. Both custom and legal writ still exerted a force in favour of the labouring classes and their pursuits.

Sports and games

The familiar pattern repeats itself in the world of outdoor sports. The regulated and taxed activity of game-shooting, the preserve of the comfortably-off and the rich, took hold in the decade of the 1780s and expanded further in the early years of the next century. Cricket too had a growing following in this decade. It was regarded as respectable, judging by the tone of press reporting and absence of censure in the justices' minutes, despite the enormous bets placed on the outcome of matches.

However from the 1780s onwards the brutal pastimes associated principally, but not exclusively, with working men were on the decline. In her Coltishall diary Mary Hardy records four boxing matches, all but one attended

[1] *affray only* J. Burn, *The Justice of the Peace, and Parish Officer* (16th edn London, 1788), vol. 4, p. 97. The guidance on riots etc occupies pp. 96–110

[2] *not riotous* J. Burn, *The Justice of the Peace, and Parish Officer*, vol. 4, p. 98 [his italics]

above The Adam and Eve, close to the new navigation which had opened in 1775 to Lt Hautbois, is shown on a map of 1826. By then Cakerow Fair, held south-west of Mayton Hall ('Maton Hall' on the map) had ended.

In marked contrast with later attitudes the manor of Mayton in 1685 had prized having a fair nearby. It was 'to the advantage thereof, and to the benefit of the neighbour towns thereabouts' (quoted in chapter 2, page 67) [*Bryant's Map of Norfolk 1826: Cozens-Hardy Collection*]

[1] *matches Diary 1*: boxing at Coltishall, Horning, Blofield and Trowse (2 July, 26 Sept., 24 Oct. 1774, 17 July 1775); wrestling at Ingworth and Horstead and one unnamed location (4–5 July 1774, 18 Mar. 1775, 17 June 1774)

[2] *badger-baiting Diary 1*: 12 Mar. 1777; *Diary 4*: 29 May 1799. Bull- and bear-baiting are never noted in the diary

[3] *cockfighting* eg *Norw. Merc.* 11 Feb., 11 Mar. 1786, 3 Mar. 1787, 11 June 1791

[4] *threatened duel* See page 148

[5] *cruelty* For public attitudes to violence and animal cruelty, and the Vice Society's role in attempts to stamp out cruel sports as part of 'the efforts of nine-teenth-century Christians to remodel traditional patterns of recreation', see B. Harrison, 'Religion and recreation in nineteenth-century England', p. 99. See also pp. 116–19, where he highlights the selectivity of measures banning flogging of animals but not of human beings, and the many ways in which cruelty to animals was not confined to the lower orders. For the shift from prizefighting and cruel sports towards restraint, see P. Langford, *English-*

by her husband or the workforce and all in the very early years 1774–75; boxing is then never again mentioned. She recounts three wrestling matches watched by her husband, children or workforce, also all in 1774–75; wrestling is never again mentioned.[1]

William Hardy and the Coltishall schoolmaster John Smith watched a badger being baited at the Recruiting Sergeant in 1777. This was the last such occasion recorded until 1799, when there was badger-baiting at the King's Head, Letheringsett.[2] None of the Hardy family attended the second event, and baiting of animals departs from the record. Although cockfighting was advertised in the press no mention is made in the diary of the family or workforce going.[3]

We cannot ascribe this decline in reporting necessarily to self-censorship by a disapproving diarist. We do not know Mary Hardy's attitude to these sports, but we can guess that by the time she was a Methodist, if not earlier, she regarded them as unacceptable. Pugilism ceased to feature much in the local newspapers in the more serious age from 1790 onwards. Hitherto it had been written up in tones of awe—both over the dangerous, prolonged nature of the bouts, with the likelihood of one or other of the parties not surviving, and over the size of the purse at stake.

The last decade of the eighteenth century marked a change in manners and an embracing of more restrained conduct in public. The only threat of a duel in the diarist's circle came in 1775, in the early period at Coltishall, and was never repeated. Further, and significantly, the duel was not over a point of honour, but was sparked by Thomas Peirson's apparent rage at the violence inflicted on his school-age sons.[4] The moral reform of the 1790s onwards was characterised by increasing revulsion at cruelty to animals and a growing sensitivity about personal violence, but the seeds had been sown some years earlier.[5]

The question arises as to the mechanism by which these pursuits were suppressed before bans were enacted. Unlike shooting, with game-duty certificates, gamekeepers' licences and close seasons, pugilism was not yet governed by any code; baiting and cockfighting likewise went unregulated. But while the fights themselves were unfettered, the public houses in or near which they were usually held were not.

left Horning: the Swan Inn before its rebuilding in 1897. It was tied to the brewery William Hardy managed at Coltishall, five miles away. Deliveries of Hardy beer shot up at fair time. On 5 Aug. 1778 all three farm servants took beer carts to Horning—and did not return to the brewery until 10 pm.

The 20-year-old Henry Haylett, son of the Hardys' thresher, fought a fellow waterman in a 40-minute boxing match near this public house in 1774.

The Hardys' men Zeb Rouse and Robert Manning were there to watch [*photograph by J. Payne Jennings, detail: Norfolk Heritage Centre, Norwich*]

The justices were ever vigilant over disorderly houses. Heavy drinking by spectators, as also the loss of an employee's labour while he was watching an idle pursuit (even when leave had been obtained by a prudent servant or labourer), would have caused the justices some anxiety. And the withholding of a licence posed a real threat to the innkeeper.

Wrestling and boxing matches would often appear to have been arranged in natural amphitheatres to accommodate the crowds. When Manning was absent from work for one and a half days at the wrestling match at Ingworth in 1774—only two weeks after attending a bout elsewhere—it is likely the fixture was at the small alehouse built against a sheer escarpment in the village. The top of the cliff above the old yard at this former house provides an excellent viewing platform.[1] The Swan Inn at Horning is situated very close to another such escarpment on which a windmill used to stand, and it was at Horning that the Coltishall pugilist Henry Haylett fought Hindry the waterman in a boxing match in 1774.[2] A press report referred to a valley on Mousehold Heath outside Norwich as the setting for 'a sharp contest of near an hour', the spectators presumably being ranged along the slopes and looking down on the temporary stage.[3]

ness Identified: Manners and character 1650–1850 (Oxford Univ. Press, 2000), pp. 137–57

[1] *Ingworth Diary 1*: 4 July 1774. The house was probably the small cottage near the bridge.

Emma Griffin examines the varied public spaces in which sports took place (E. Griffin, *England's Revelry: A history of popular sports and pastimes 1660–1830* (The British Academy and Oxford Univ. Press, 2005)); but she does not mention amphitheatres

[2] *Horning Diary 1*: 26 Sept. 1774; *Norw. Merc.* 1 Oct. 1774

[3] *Mousehold Norw. Merc.* 11 Mar. 1775

[1] *Trowse Diary 1*: 17 July 1775. Haylett took an hour and 18 minutes to beat a Pockthorpe weaver; his prize was 20 guineas. 'After a strong contest . . ., during which great activity and skill in the boxing art was displayed by each party, victory declared itself in favour of the waterman. The odds in the middle of the controversy ran greatly against Haylett, by which the knowing ones were deeply taken in, and very considerable sums lost on this occasion' (*Norw. Merc.* 22 July 1775).

I am grateful to Michael Sparkes, Trowse born and bred, for showing me in 2000 the site of the old public house and the marlpits, now wooded, inland from Trowse Hythe. The marl slopes are now enjoyed as a dry ski run

[2] *Pockthorpe Norw. Merc.* 11 Mar. 1775

right These marlpits at Whitlingham, outside Norwich, adjoined the ones at Trowse and served local lime-kilns.

Such workings made a natural amphitheatre. Boxing and wrestling matches drew spectators in their thousands [*painting by J. Stark; engraving by W. Radclyffe 1828, detail*]

The boxing match at Trowse Newton, just south-east of Norwich, was attended by two of the Hardys' day labourers in 1775; they took the whole day off. It would have been laid on close to the public house at the foot of the marlpit slopes and thus right among the workings, affording a very good view for the spectators high on the rim. Even so, the Hardys' men may have had a restricted view in the crush, for they came away with a mistaken impression of the outcome. Their local man Henry Haylett was reported in the press as the victor; the men told Mary Hardy however that he had been beaten.[1]

Prizefighters were usually working men hoping to earn extra cash, despite the great risks involved. Haylett earned about a year's wage for a skilled man in less than two hours at Trowse. He and Hindry were both watermen: skippers or mates of keels and wherries. At Blofield a brick-striker and a mole-catcher, both from nearby Lingwood, fought a long bout during the working day, as the *Norwich Mercury* reported on 12 November 1774. The parish of Pockthorpe, one of the poorest in Norwich, provided three pugilists. On Mousehold in 1775 one of the contestants nearly lost his life, and almost a week later he was still 'very dangerously ill'.[2]

left The Recruiting Sergeant, Horstead: the venue not only for clubs and concerts but for the more boisterous pastimes of badger-baiting and tenpin matches. It was well known to the Hardy children, including toddler Mary Ann. The Hardys, conscientious parents, could feel confident over letting Raven and William attend harvest frolics here until very late without them   [*MB·1990*]

Other sports associated with public houses and drinking, but not attracting high stakes, were tenpins and bowls. Both were enjoyed by William Hardy. His son took up bowls but not tenpins—possibly as it may have ceased to be a popular pastime locally during William's childhood. Many of the larger public houses had good bowling greens, and drinks would be served on summer evenings from outdoor bars called drinking boxes, set up in the shade beside the greens. The 1841 sale notice of the Coltishall Brewery's White Lion, in North Walsham's market place, refers to its 'capital bowling green, enclosed by a quick-hedge [thorn hedge], with drinking box therein'. This was the green purchased for John Wells's brewery by William Hardy in 1773.[1]

Even the apparently harmless pastime of tenpins may not have survived the sterner world of the 1790s, for it lured devotees into staying away from work. Whereas William Hardy senior and junior mostly attended evening bowls clubs, tenpins required a greater time commitment.[2] Away matches meant that one or even two days' work would be lost. When William Hardy and the Letheringsett innkeeper Richard Mayes travelled to Horstead for a match they set off at 6 am and got back the next day at 10 pm. And when William Springthorp of the Recruiting Sergeant came for the return fixture he was 'at Mayes's tenpin-playing all day'.[3]

[1] *drinking box* NRO: MS 7351, 7D4, Sale of the Coltishall brewery and public houses, p. 19; *Diary 1*: 4 Dec. 1773.
The 1895 plan of the Crown at Southrepps shows hedged 'bowers' set in two corners of its large bowling green (Cozens-Hardy Collection). These could have been drinking boxes, where customers sat in comfort over a drink when watching the game. The plan is reproduced in *Diary 4*, p. 463

[2] *time commitment* 'Mr Hardy on tenpin ground all the afternoon' (Diary MS: 3 July 1782). It was a Wednesday

[3] *matches Diary 2*: 11 June 1782, 16 July 1782; Diary MS: 12 June, 14 July 1782. The Spring-

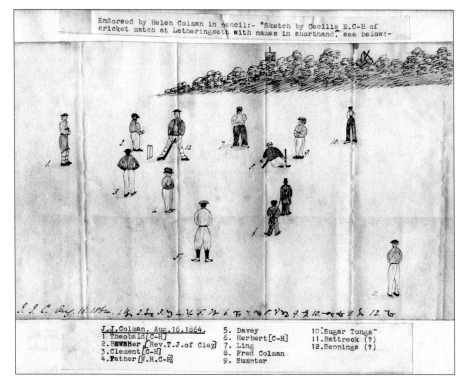

Endorsed by Helen Colman in pencil:- "Sketch by Cecilia E.C-H of cricket match at Letheringsett with names in shorthand." see below:-

J.J.Colman. Aug.16,1864.	5. Davey	10."Sugar Tongs"
1 Theobald[C-H]	6. Herbert[C-H]	11.Battreck (?)
2.Bawaher [Rev.T.J.of Cley]	7. Ling	12.Sennings (?)
3.Clement[C-H]	8. Fred Colman	
4.Father [W.H.C-H]	9. Sumpter	

above The mixing of the classes in village cricket on the Hall Farm meadow at Letheringsett on 16 Aug. 1864: detail of a sketch by Mary Hardy's great-granddaughter Cecilia showing her father William Hardy Cozens-Hardy and her brothers.

Clement [no. 3], by then of Cley Hall, is point. Herbert [no. 6], the future judge and the hunched figure in braces, is cover.

The cartoonist captions many of the other players only by their nicknames, indicating they formed part of the brewery workforce or were other working men; the long-legged mid-on [no. 10] has the nickname 'Sugar Tongs'. This is a very different representation of leisure from that of the private world of family bowls seen at the start of the chapter (page 363)   [*Cozens-Hardy Collection*]

---

thorps made a holiday of the event, spending three nights at Letheringsett; Mary Hardy entertained Ann Springthorp during the match

Worse, Edmund Beck, the carpenter and builder, lost half a day's work playing tenpins at the King's Head, Letheringsett in 1781—just when he was supposed to be busy about his work for the Hardys. The diarist compiled the charge sheet in endnotes at the back of her manuscript:

[1781] MONDAY 8 OCTOBER Memorandum, Edmund Beck at Richard Mayes drunk all day and I believe did no work.

WEDNESDAY 10 OCTOBER [Beck] lost half a day at tenpins at Mayes's.

FRIDAY 16 NOVEMBER [Beck] all day at Mayes's.[1]

It would not have escaped the notice of workmen such as Beck that William Hardy himself in this early period often spent all day in the public house. The difference was that the brewer was not being paid by others, and spent his time as he chose. It was the unprofitable wasting of time which employers and clients deplored; drunkenness and the undesirability of certain sports were less likely to be treated as a moral issue in that period. Beck was self-employed, and could not forfeit his livelihood as Manning had done.

Nevertheless he could lose a valuable client. Although he was still in the area and was hired for work inside the parish church the builder appears not to been engaged after 1781 in further projects at the Hardys' house and brewery. Tenpins at the King's Head could have been his undoing, as far as the Hardys were concerned. The pastime is not mentioned in the diary after 1782. It was not covered in the press, perhaps as it was not much patronised by the well-to-do.

Despite cricket's requirement of a similar commitment over away matches held during the working day, at grounds sited at or near public houses, the sport escaped censure.[2] Matches began early, while the grass was still wet, the one watched by Mary Ann Hardy on Monday 5 October 1789 beginning at 9 am.[3] It was engaged in not so much by the labouring class as the more affluent, and was based around club membership. Towns and villages came together to form teams. On Thursday 13 July 1797 the gentlemen of Aylsham, Blickling, Aldborough and Thurgarton in one team took on the gentlemen of Lyng and Elsing.[4] Gambling formed part of the attraction, with match purses becoming very large: two were for 500 guineas each.[5] Nonetheless working men were involved by the early nineteenth century, some playing as members of cricketing associations: 'There were "Trade" teams—teams of shoemakers, teams of innkeepers, of carpenters, of bricklayers, and even of stage-coachmen.'[6]

The Hardys lived in an area that was particularly strong in cricket,[7] but the sport largely passed them by. Father and son watched a match at Brinton in 1789, spending six hours at the ground. They took care to leave in time to get

[1] *Beck Diary 2*: endnotes, p. 393 (evidently written at the time of Beck's 1781 building work and indicating he was paid by the day)

[2] *cricket* See the regular press reports in the summer: eg *Norw. Merc.* 1 Sept. 1787; 21 June, 12 July, 9 Aug. 1788; 30 June, 21 July 1792; 2 July, 9 July 1796

[3] *9 am Norw. Merc.* 19 Sept. 1789; this was at Brinton. The innkeeper of the Thatched House at Brinton, John Barwick, was a keen promoter of the game

[4] *villages* The Lyng/ Elsing team won by seven wickets (*Norw. Merc.* 22 July 1797)

[5] *500 guineas* (£525) *Norw. Merc.* 24 June, 8 July 1797

[6] *trade teams* D. Armstrong, *A Short History of Norfolk County Cricket* (Larks Press, Guist Bottom, 1990), p. 6

[7] *Hardys' area* P. Yaxley, *Looking Back at Norfolk Cricket* (Nostalgia Publications, Toftwood, 1997), pp. 6–9

[1] *matches* Diary 2: 15 Aug., 5 Oct. 1789; Mary Ann Hardy and Elizabeth Burrell saw Brinton play Castle Acre for 50 guineas. The fixture ended in dispute (*Norw. Merc.* 31 Oct. 1789)

[2] *All England* Diary 3: 18 July 1797, where the match is depicted; *Norw. Merc.* 22 July, 29 July 1797. Two clergymen were also in the county team, which was heavily defeated: see P. Yaxley, *Looking Back at Norfolk Cricket*, pp. 6–7

[3] *Holt* The 1786 jubilee was to begin on 13 Mar. 1786, 'when much company is expected to be there'. These expectations were put on hold owing to bad weather (*Norw. Merc.* 4 Mar., 11 Mar. 1786)

[4] *grinning matches* Norw. Merc. 18 Jan. 1783; these involved pulling grotesque faces

[5] *hunting* Diary 2: 1 Feb. 1783

[6] *hunters' ball* Diary MS: 13 Apr. 1789

[7] *horse-racing* Diary 2: 13 Aug. 1781, 11 June 1788, 31 Mar. 1790, 22 Apr. 1793; Diary 3: 27 Sept. 1797. Stakes could be huge, two hunters being pitted against one another for 100 guineas (*Norw. Merc.* 6 Sept. 1788)

[8] *Holt races* Diary 4: 19 Oct. 1802

to Holt market, a far more pressing attraction. Mary Ann also watched a match there in the company of the rector's wife, Mrs Burrell coming from that village.[1] Henry Raven never mentions cricket. No more is heard of the game in Mary Hardy's diary until 1797, when her husband and some of her extended family attended the famous Norfolk *versus* All England contest on Swaffham racecourse. Two players named Raven were in the county team.[2]

The Hardys were not much attracted to horse-racing either. Holt's races were held on Holt Heath, looking over towards Edgefield on the high ground above the river valley, during the town's 'Jubilee' or festival. Little is recorded in the diary about the races, and the air of bustle and hints at patronage in the press notices may have borne little resemblance to reality.[3] In fact, among the featured deer-hunting, foxhunting and hare-hunting rather less select pursuits were laid on in festival week in 1783:

... On Thursday evening there will be a ball. On Friday morning, on the course, will be various amusements, such as ass-racing, sack races, grinning matches, etc, etc, etc ...[4]

Mary Hardy only twice mentions the Holt Jubilee, and when she does so it is merely in passing, as something of no direct concern; her husband and son would however have noticed the extra beer orders coming in. In 1783 the only reference to participation in the events came when her husband spent a little time watching the hunting while about his work that day: 'Mr Hardy went to Cley and hunting forenoon and went to market afternoon.'[5] They took no part in the other jubilee she mentions, in March 1787. There are no further references to the festival other than a possible note two years later: 'Hunters' ball at Holt, none of us went.'[6]

William Hardy occasionally went to Holt races with his wife's male relatives, and made a party with his wife and daughter in 1790—the only race-meeting either of the two women is recorded as attending.[7] As with so much else in this period, the dampening effect of the prolonged war years may have caused the town to lose its appetite for jollity and racing. In the later diary years William Hardy junior only once attended Holt races: in 1802, the solitary year of peace between the two French wars 1793–1801 and 1803–15.[8]

To judge from the evidence of the diaries of Mary Hardy and Henry Raven neither their family nor any in their circle took much part in deer-hunting or foxhunting. The terrain, especially in the marshes and fens and in Broadland, was ill suited to the chase. Foxes were scarce anyway in the county. Unlike rooks and rabbits they are not mentioned by the diarists as pests. The pastime was still something of a novelty:

> Fox hunting at its inception, at least in Norfolk, was far from being a rough sport enjoyed by farmers, as has been suggested elsewhere, but was an expensive innovation pioneered by the elite . . . Until the early 18th century catching foxes was still a woodland affair. They were caught by being dug out, or terriers were sent down to do battle underground . . . It is thought that fox hunting in the modern sense [as the chase] began in Yorkshire and the West Country. A possible reason for this is that in the 1720s there were relatively few foxes in Norfolk. Numerous entries in the Household Accounts show foxes being introduced to Holkham, where they were cared for and fed on rabbits and offal. Nor were they cheap: a large fox cub cost 10s, and it is no surprise therefore to find them making suitable gifts.[1]

A member of the diarists' close family attracted to hunting was Henry Raven's eldest brother Robert, his relatives watching him take part as the Holt meeting sped within sight of Letheringsett Hall Farm. Robert's aunt wrote:

> [1789] APRIL 14, TUESDAY Gentlemen came through the town [Letheringsett] a-hunting; Mrs Burrell, Mr Hardy, I and Mary Ann took a walk up of Mr Cobon's hills to see them. Robert Raven went with them [the huntsmen], came to dinner half past two . . .[2]

Hare-coursing seems to have held some appeal for William Hardy senior and junior, being proposed or engaged in during the early Letheringsett years: on four occasions by the father, and on two by the son. Their fellow sportsmen ranged from Whissonsett relatives to the Norwich coachmaker John Stoddart and the barrister Henry Jodrell.[3] Thereafter their interest waned. Almost as though rejecting any notion that he could be linked to the chase, William Hardy junior preferred in the later years not to course hares (as game) but to shoot them (as vermin).[4] Only once did his mother note that he coursed hares in this period, at Mr Wall's at Bayfield Brecks; his father had last coursed in 1790.[5]

[1] *elite* M.-A. Garry, 'Sport as a political meditator: Thomas Coke and the Layers of Booton', *Norfolk Archaeology*, vol. 43, pt 3 (2000), pp. 497, 498. The author draws on the archives at Holkham Hall to form her conclusions, and, in the early part of the extract, challenges observations by Linda Colley (L. Colley, *Britons: Forging the nation 1707–1837* (Yale Univ. Press, London, 1992), p. 170).
For a 400-page study of foxhunting in Norfolk and comparisons with other areas see J. Bevan, 'Foxhunting and the landscape between 1700 and 1900; with particular reference to Norfolk and Shropshire' (PhD thesis, UEA, 2011; in full online: <https://ueaeprints.uea.ac.uk/38809/1/2012BevanJPhD.pdf>, accessed 17 Apr. 2018)

[2] *a-hunting* Diary 2

[3] *coursing* Diary 2; the references 5 Dec. 1781–18 Oct. 1792 are indexed in the volumes under 'coursing'

[4] *shooting* William's companions were the enthusiastic shooters James Moore of Holt and Jeremiah Cozens of Sprowston (table 4.7.2)

[5] *coursing* Diary 4: 29 Dec. 1806; *Diary 2*: 17 Feb. 1790

¹ *bets* eg 'Young Harrold of Saxlingham trotted a little mare 50 miles. He was allowed five hours but performed it in four hours and 40 minutes, [he] set off from Holt and went seven miles beyond Dereham' (*Diary 2*: 7 May 1787, the phrase 'was allowed' indicating a wager); similarly: 'A shooting match at Dobson's for a hat, Mr Balls won it' (*Diary 4*: 18 Aug. 1803)

² *game-duty certificates* The theoretical qualification for sportsmen was that of holding a freehold landed estate worth £100 a year or more.
Yet not all those issued with licences appear to fall within this category, which was deliberately set high so as not to arm the population at large.
Norman Scarfe summarises the background and eligibility for certificates in his notes on the French nobleman's observations on shooting (F. de La Rochefoucauld, *A Frenchman's Year in Suffolk, 1784*, ed. N. Scarfe, pp. 40–1)

It is not known why field sports involving the chase finally fell out of favour with the Hardys. The work commitments of father and son, a distaste for betting, fear of injuring themselves in a fall or growing sensitivities about the treatment of animals may have been factors. When the diarist does recount bets being placed or matches engaged in for prizes, always outside the family, she writes dispassionately and without comment; we cannot therefore draw any conclusions.¹ A loss of appetite for the chase, for animal-baiting and many such 'time-wasting' activities, whether tenpins or cricket, is in tune with the puritanism increasingly pervading the leisure pursuits of the population at large from the early 1790s.

Shooting

Game-shooting bucked the trend; but it was the pursuit of those with daytime leisure to hand. It is a fairly straightforward matter to identify the moment when it established its hold: it began to be licensed and taxed in 1784. From then until 1807 both sportsmen and professionals (the gamekeepers) had to have a licence, on which duty was paid.²

Registration was at county level through the already overworked Clerk of the Peace, and historians of this recreation

are fortunate in having long lists published in the local press of shooters and gamekeepers who had taken out certificates. Not everybody registered for the year right at the start of the season in the early autumn, with the result that the names could appear in a series from September through to December. They reveal the holders of shooting licences, the names of estate owners who employed gamekeepers and the names of the keepers themselves.[1]

In the diary years the Hardys never had a gamekeeper. Their neighbour Henry Jodrell of Bayfield Hall employed Samuel Platten as keeper, Platten also serving the nearby estate of Sharrington and Saxlingham with the Members where the lord of the manor was Henry Jodrell's brother Richard Paul Jodrell of Lewknor in Oxfordshire.[2] William Hardy senior never took out a game licence and never shot. Any shooting by his son was on a small scale, as indicated in table 4.7.2 (overleaf). William junior did not buy a licence until after he had greatly expanded his landed estate by the purchase of 350 acres in 1800 and had obtained vacant possession in 1801, his Hall Farm land being dotted about with small woods affording cover for game birds. He bought his first licence in 1803, for which he paid the annual fee of three guineas.[3] He had shot on the coast at Salthouse on three occasions in earlier years, in the company of young friends including the younger Davys of Holt and London, his participation being covered by his hosts' certificates.[4]

The lists of licence holders, many of whom figure in the diary, show that shooting was enjoyed by farmers, tradesmen and members of the professions. Gentry, tenant farmers (some with only moderate holdings), millers, merchants, grocers, butchers, attorneys, naval and military officers and clergy all took to the sport. None was a woman. But the published lists also show that this was the preserve of the very few, about one hundred names at the most appearing in any one list.

The sportsmen who came walking over the turnips or across the barley stubble on William Hardy junior's land on a breezy autumn day were not necessarily local. His mother records that between 4 September 1788 (when shooting at Letheringsett is first recorded) and 23 November 1808 (her last entry on the subject) 25 people came to shoot on

[1] *lists* See, eg, *Norw. Merc.* 20 Sept., 4 Oct., 11 Oct. 1788; 26 Sept. 1789; 21 Oct. 1797; 4 Oct. 1800; 2 Oct. 1802; 24 Sept. 1803; 29 Sept., 6 Oct. 1804; 5 Oct. 1805.
Open and close seasons vary according to the bird. For partridge, then the most plentiful of the game birds, the start of the season on 1 September marked a major event in the sporting calendar. Partridge shooting ended on 1 February

[2] *Platten* He continued to serve throughout the period of registration and taxation, being listed for the same two estates in 1806 (*Norw. Merc.* 13 Dec. 1806)

[3] *William's licence Norw. Merc.* 24 Dec. 1803. He described himself not as beer brewer, the suffix he gave when voting in 1802, but as 'gent.'—perhaps to reassure the authorities

[4] *Salthouse Diary 2*: 16 Sept. 1788, 16 Aug., 19 Dec. 1791

facing page Common, or grey, partridge.
These plump birds, with their distinctive orange faces, have in recent years been on the Red List of endangered species [*G. C. Davies, The Swan and her Crew (1876)*]

[1] *William's 1808 shoots Diary 4*: 1 Sept., 2 Sept., 29 Sept. 1808

[2] *changes* For observations on quarry, habitat and changing technology see Lord Buxton's introduction to the diary of a north Norfolk gamekeeper of a later generation: N. Virgoe and S. Yaxley, eds, *The Banville Diaries: Journals of a Norfolk gamekeeper 1822–44* (Collins, London, 1986), pp. 9–14.

This unusual book, beautifully illustrated in full colour, gives a rare glimpse of the outlook of the keeper: the outspoken, Irish-born Larry Banville, often resentful of whose he served

[3] *bags Norw. Merc.* 8 Sept. 1804.

Other record bags were reported in the *Mercury*: 29 Sept. 1804, 28 Nov. 1807, 7 Jan. 1809. By later standards they were still small: 'Lord Paget has proved the most destructive pheasant shot this season in Norfolk. The two first days he killed 13 brace from his own single barrel' (*Norw. Merc.* 12 Oct. 1805). Pheasant shooting had only begun on 1 October; some young birds are seen at *plate 39*.

Bags increased markedly from 1807 onwards

the Hardys' land, of whom six were from London. Some of the others were strangers who arrived with friends of the Hardys.

William soon lost interest. He shot on eight occasions 1803–05. Thereafter he shot at Letheringsett on only three more days, with James Moore or Jeremiah Cozens; also on three other occasions in 1808: on Jonathan's Davey estate at Eaton Hall, Norwich, at his brother-in-law's farm at Sprowston and at Thornage Hall.[1] Jeremiah Cozens was an enthusiastic sportsman. He passed on his passion for shooting in full measure to his son William Hardy Cozens, whose 1840–41 season at Letheringsett is illustrated overleaf.

Their bags, where recorded, were small: just enough to supply the dinner tables of sportsmen taking part for a day or two. These rough shoots away from the huge estates were modest affairs, with no drives, no beaters, and no hand-reared birds. The gun technology of the time inhibited mass killing. This was still the age of the muzzle-loaded weapon, when powder was carried in a pouch and might get wet when being pushed down the barrel using a ramrod; there were no cartridges, and most guns were single-barrelled. Aiming had to be performed with precision, for once the gun had been fired there would be a great deal of smoke; the shooter would then have to wait for it to clear before taking aim once more. The advent of the breech-loader, the double barrel, the percussion cap, the smokeless cartridge and the involvement of a line of men forming the *battue* (the beating of woodland or cover to make the birds fly towards the guns) all contributed to a shift in the sport whereby the numbers bagged increased considerably.[2]

The tone of the press report would make it clear if the size of the bag were abnormally large. On 1 September 1804 Thomas William Coke hosted three shooting parties, mounting twelve guns, on his Holkham estate—the largest in Norfolk. With Coke using a double-barrelled gun they killed a total of 95 brace of partridge (190 birds), 18 brace of hares and 47 couple of rabbits. On the Townshend estate at Stiffkey that day Lord James Townshend and Major Loftus shot 43 brace of birds.[3] By contrast, in three seasons a total of just 17 brace of partridge and 17½ of pheasant was recorded at Letheringsett (opposite); some bags went unnoted.

TABLE 4.7.2

Shooting: three seasons on the Letheringsett Hall estate 1804, 1805, 1808

source Diary of Mary Hardy

notes Figures for bags relate to individual birds (partridge, pheasant and woodcock) and hares, and not to a brace or pair; a dash [—] denotes that no figure was recorded

season	guns	partridge	pheasant	woodcock	hare
1804–05					
Sept. 1	William Hardy jnr, James Moore of Holt, Edward Robinson of London	—	—	—	—
4	William Hardy jnr, Edward Robinson	—	—	—	—
13	Matthew Davy of London	—	—	—	—
Oct. 2	Myles Custance of London, Mr Humbert of London	—	—	—	—
3	Myles Custance, Mr Humbert, Henry Goggs of Whissonsett	—	—	—	—
22	William Hardy jnr, James Moore	1	11	1	0
Nov. 20	James Moore	—	—	—	—
Dec. 24	James Moore	0	8	0	0
Jan. 29	Benjamin Kittmer of Lt Walsingham, Thomas Balls of Saxlingham	1	3	0	0
31	James Moore	0	0	0	0
1805–06					
Sept. 19	James Moore, Thomas Gibbons of Wells	—	—	—	—
Oct. 5	William Hardy jnr, James Moore	4	6	0	0
Nov. 11	William Hardy jnr, James Moore	2	3	0	1
26	William Hardy jnr, Jeremiah Cozens of Sprowston	2	1	0	1
27	William Hardy jnr, Jeremiah Cozens	1	2	0	0
Jan. 30	Benjamin Kittmer, Thomas Balls	—	—	—	—
1808–09					
Sept. 20	William Hardy jnr, Jeremiah Cozens, James Moore	10	0	0	1
21	Jeremiah Cozens, James Moore	—	—	—	—
Oct. 20	Revd John Custance Leak of Holt	3	1	1	—
26	Jeremiah Cozens	5	0	0	0
27	Jeremiah Cozens	5	0	0	0
Nov. 22	Jeremiah Cozens	—	—	—	—
23	Jeremiah Cozens	—	—	—	—
	TOTALS	34	35	2	3

right Game shot in the 1840–41 season, noted by William Hardy Cozens shortly before he inherited the Letheringsett and Cley estates from his uncle William Hardy jnr.

He shot alone or with a companion; once he went out with his father on the Common Hills on his mother Mary Ann's birthday, 3 Nov. 1840; she was probably at the Hall that day seeing her brother.

Bags were still small. In the period 1 Sept. 1840 to 28 Jan. 1841 William H. Cozens and his companions shot these totals:

87 brace of partridge
6 brace of pheasant
23 woodcocks
1 snipe
180 hares
73 rabbits

[*Cozens-Hardy Collection*]

facing page From the period *c.*1910–14: the utterly different style of shooting from that of William Hardy jnr and his contemporaries and from the one recorded by William's nephew (above). They did not have beaters.

top Here the five sportsmen contemplate their bag. Sir Herbert Hardy Cozens-Hardy (1838–1920), second son of William Hardy Cozens and shortly to be ennobled, props himself up on his shooting stick (centre). On his left may stand the tall figure of one of his sons: William or, more probably, Edward, born in 1868 and 1873

below The men and boys who made the day's sport possible. The commanding figure of the head keeper on the Letheringsett estate now occupies the central position on the shooting stick: Stanley Frederick Wink (d.1963 aged 86), with his calm, steady gaze.

Around him are the beaters, many being taken off their normal duties on the estate. Allen Woodhouse, head gardener at the Hall, with the gun and crossover strap, stands middle right towards the rear. Jack Parling, another gardener, stands second left behind Jeary, who grasps a shooting stick.

The dog (far right), sniffing the kill, has not kept still and is blurred. The bag, while very much larger than in the time of Mary Hardy, is smaller than those seen on estates with extensive shoots in this period [*Cozens-Hardy Collection*]

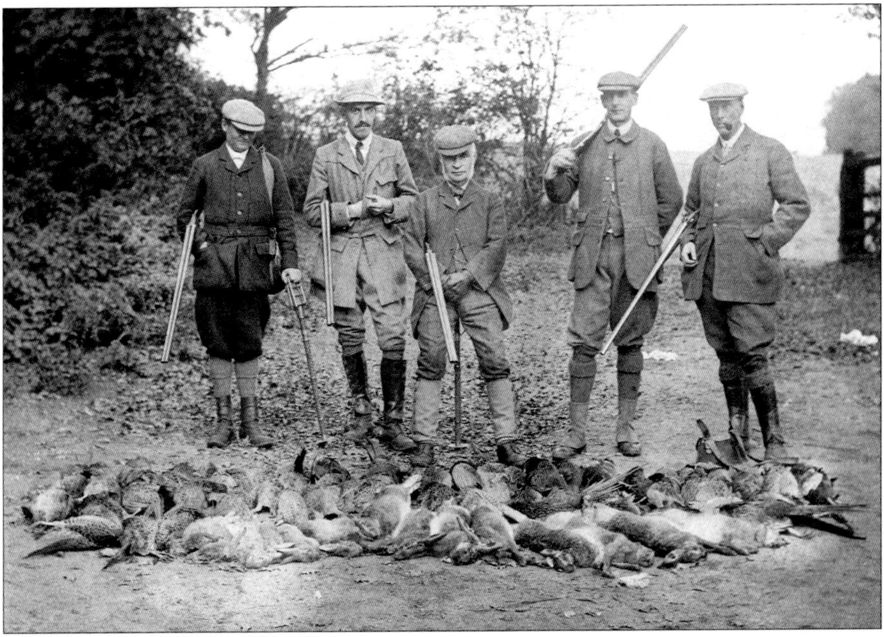

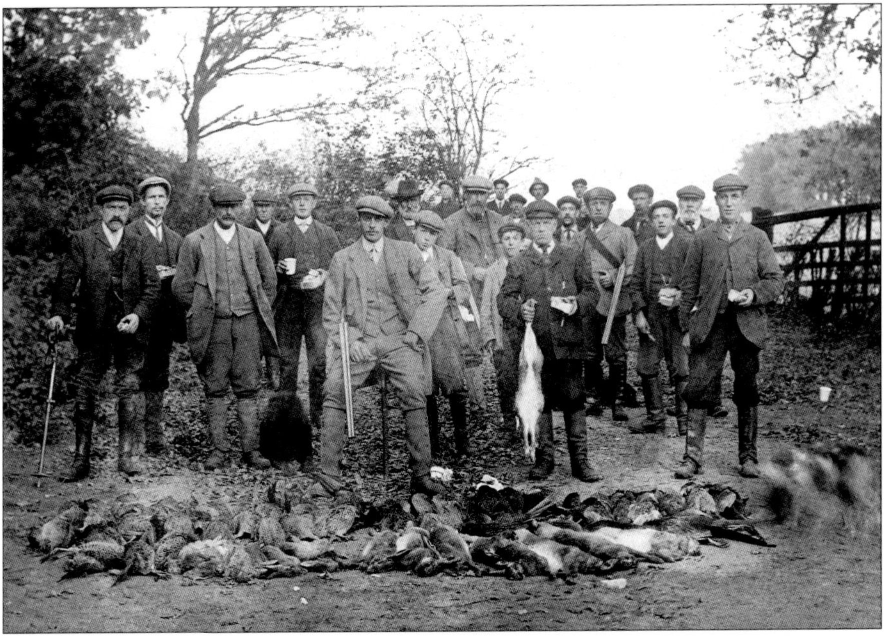

[1] *explosion, death* Norw. *Merc.* 22 Dec. 1787; *Diary 2*: 25 Feb. 1788

[2] *killed* S. Cozens-Hardy, *Memorials of William Hardy Cozens-Hardy of Letheringsett*, pp. 13, 20–1. Cozens was buried in Letheringsett churchyard by the church south wall.
His widow Ann, née Tooke, married his brother William in 1845. The ceremony was at Gretna, Dumfries, such unions being legal in Scotland (marriage certificate of William Cozens of St Pancras, Middx [London] and Ann Cozens of St Margaret's, King's Lynn, 8 Dec. 1845: Cozens-Hardy Collection)

[3] *shot by accident* MS diary of William Hardy [jnr] 1832–34, 23 Oct. 1832 (Cozens-Hardy Collection)

[4] *deaths* A.M.W. Stirling, *Coke of Norfolk and his Friends* (John Lane, The Bodley Head, London, 1912), pp. 278–9; C. Forder, *A History of the Paston School, North Walsham, Supplementary notes, pt 2* (N. Walsham, 1981), p. 42

[5] *suicide* Mary Hardy reported hearing on Saturday 30 Oct. that 'Mr John Barnwell of Bale shot himself last Thursday and was dead' (*Diary 2*: 30 Oct. 1790). His ledger stone gives 1 Nov. as the date of death

It was a dangerous sport. Gunpowder was a hazardous material, and the guns unreliable. In December 1787 the gamekeeper serving Henry Jodrell's mother Elizabeth on the Bayfield estate narrowly escaped death. Samuel Platten put some gunpowder in a pewter dish to dry over the fire in his kitchen. His cottage suffered a dreadful explosion; the windows were blown out and he and two of his children received extensive burns. Mary Hardy records that his daughter Amy died a little over two months later, and it is possible her death came as a result of the explosion.[1]

In 1832 Jeremiah Cozens' nephew of the same name, who lived in Bunhill Row, London and was the son of the London watchmaker William Cozens, was shot dead on the Letheringsett estate; he was aged 32. The gun handled by Joseph Wiley, husband of Mary Ann's stepdaughter Mary, went off unexpectedly. With them was the young man's first cousin William Hardy Cozens, who regarded Jeremiah Cozens as his 'best and sincerest friend':

I lent him a single-barrelled gun with which he was very pleased, but we had not been out an hour before Wiley's gun went off unexpectedly and killed him on the spot. It was a terrible shock to me and others, and I could not pluck up courage to shoot again that year. It is somewhat remarkable that this was the only time he [Jeremiah] ever went shooting.[2]

William Hardy junior, whose diary has much of the brevity of his mother's, recorded the incident: 'Tuesday 23 October: Poor Mr Jeremiah Cozens shot by accident and brought into the drawing room.'[3]

Despite the dangers, a fondness for shooting increasingly gripped the landholding class. Accidental death in the field struck Thomas William Coke's son-in-law Lord Andover in 1800, aged 24; also Captain Sir William Hoste's brother Charles in 1812, aged about thirteen, at the hand of their brother George while out shooting at Tittleshall.[4] Further, a gun could become a suicide weapon, as wielded by the 49-year-old farmer John Barnwell of Bale in 1790. He was interred in his parish church, beside his wife Anne who had predeceased him, and was commemorated by a fine ledger stone.[5]

While readers immersed in eighteenth- and nineteenth-century English history are accustomed to the idea that many men with leisure hours to spare chose to spend autumn and winter days roaming the countryside with a gun, their dogs and perhaps with a friend or two in tow, we do not generally hear exactly what was involved. However the Essex diarist Robert Marten, writing as an observer who had absolutely no desire to take part, gives more than a full page of detail on what actually happened on a shoot in 1825 while he was staying at Hockham Lodge, outside Attleborough. Here, apparently for the first time, Marten was introduced to shooting, with all its rituals: 'a novel sight'. He was much struck by the close working relationship between man and dog. But he was far less impressed by this manner of spending a day in 'hard labour', and soon lost interest:

I returned [to the house] after an hour or two, but the gentlemen continued between four and five hours and in this their *sport* (so called) they journeyed on foot somewhat encumbered with powder, shot and fowling piece more than twenty miles over ploughed land and through stubble and tall swedish turnips and potatoes— getting through hedges and over banks, and this almost daily for amusement—continued either in shooting or coursing from the first of September 'till the last of March.[1]

At least in the evening Marten found something to interest him. He closely examined the percussion mechanism of the fowling piece: 'I had never before seen a lock on that principle.'[2]

Pleasure boating

We now come to a slower, more tranquil leisure activity. It is sometimes argued that the Broads embarked on a new life as a holiday area only from the 1870s. Photography by men like George Christopher Davies and John Payne Jennings, together with the extended railway system, enabled the country at large to become aware of the watery paradise waiting to be explored.[3] While it is true that the hiring out of yachts and purpose-built pleasure wherries for commercial gain began in earnest in the late nineteenth century, taking to the water to engage with the beauties of the Broads had long been a feature of Norfolk life. Visitors from outside Broadland enjoyed sharing their hosts' waterborne activities.

When the younger members of the Crofts family from Gressenhall in central Norfolk came to stay with the Hardys,

[1] *in this their sport* E. Larby, ed., *Mr Marten's Travels in East Anglia: The 1825 journal of Robert Humphrey Marten* (Poppyland Publishing, Cromer, 2012), p. 108; see also pp. 106–7

[2] *mechanism* E. Larby, ed., *Mr Marten's Travels in East Anglia*, p. 108. Elizabeth Larby adds a note that the percussion cap was invented in 1807, enabling the new-style guns to be loaded with greater speed and safety than in the days of the flintlock.

I am grateful to Jeremy Cozens-Hardy and his son Raven, both with long experience of shooting in Norfolk, for their comments in Oct. 1998 on comparisons between 19th-century and modern shooting methods

[3] *discovering the Broads* 'Probably quite unwittingly, Davies' enthusiasm for the area is evident not only in his books but also through his photographs. He was quite simply the first and he became known as *The Man Who Found the Broads* . . . The sailing that Davies found when he first came to Norfolk [in 1871] was either the very, very rich at play or professional watermen plying their wherries for trade . . . He had come to a back-

right and *below* John Payne Jennings' *Sun Pictures of the Norfolk Broads*, a popular work which helped to promote tourism on the waterways following its publication in 1891. Its 100 pages of beautifully composed images, with captions by Ernest R. Suffling, contain scenes recognisable today.

Like other Broadland photographers of the late 19th century Jennings strove to capture only the dreamy idyll of the area's limpid 'lagoons', with vessels drifting in the lightest of breezes. Such images were thoroughly misleading. The working men and women of the waterways led pressured lives, struggling with the extremely heavy labour of loading and unloading and ever desperate to catch the tide.

Below on the left is Belaugh, where the Hardys worshipped and stopped for tea at Engall's Gardens. The new rectory is just visible, replacing the damp parsonage which gave Lancaster Adkin rheumatism (as related in volume 3, chapter 1) [*Payne Jennings, Sun Pictures of the Norfolk Broads (3rd edn Ashtead, Surrey, 1897), front cover and pp. 6, 7*]

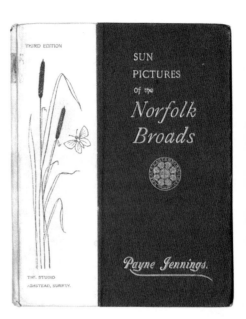

their old friends took them boating; the Coltishall school-master and his daughter joined the party and then had them back to tea at the Free School:

[1776] AUGUST 16, FRIDAY A showery day ... J. and B. and Miss Crofts, Mr and Miss Smith, Mr Hardy and self and Raven and Billy went in Mr Ansell's boat onto river, drank tea at Mr Smith's.[1]

This was on a Friday, in term-time. The schoolmaster John Smith appears to have enjoyed boating. He attended Hickling Water Frolic on a Tuesday ('a very wet day') in 1777, again taking time off from school to go on the water.[2] As with later regattas these frolics involved sailing and rowing matches.[3]

Mary Ann Hardy had not accompanied her parents and brothers in 1776 when she was two and a half, but at six she was judged old enough to be with her family and the family of their friend the timber merchant for a trip on a brilliant summer's day. They went out in the boat belonging to the Hardys' neighbour, William Palgrave of the Manor House:

[1780] JUNE 30, FRIDAY An excessive hot day ... Mr Hardy, I and children, Mr Boorne and children went down to Belaugh in Mr Palgrave's boat, drank tea at Mrs Prior's.[4]

The diarist does not mention what types of vessel these were. They could have been keels and wherries, their holds cleared for the trip, or purpose-built pleasure boats.

Riparian owners along the upper Bure were careful to secure parliamentary sanction for free passage on the Aylsham navigation. The nine miles of waterway newly dredged and embanked above Coltishall benefited not only trade but pleasure boating. One of the provisions of the Act of 1773 confirmed that owners and occupiers of lands adjoining the river could use 'pleasure boats' free of charges, so long as such boats were not carrying goods subject to tolls (quoted in full on page 77, in the inset on the navigation).

It was in the interests of Victorian promoters to extol the delights of the Broads to charm tourists into exploring a supposedly unknown and uncharted 'wilderness'. Their commercial instincts should not be allowed however to cloud the reality.[5] The Broads were appreciated for the delight they afforded the eye and the solace they offered the over-

water; an underused wilderness ...' (J. Campbell and C. Middleton, *The Man Who Found The Broads* (Hamilton Publications, Gorleston on Sea, 1999), p. 2

[1] *onto river Diary 1.* The Crofts had gone fishing with William Hardy the previous summer (*Diary 1:* 17 Aug. 1775), and William Hardy had attended Hoveton Water Frolic on 6 Aug. 1776. John and Ben Crofts, like their father, took Holy Orders

[2] *Hickling Diary 1:* 29 July 1777; the summer holidays customarily ended in mid-July

[3] *matches* As at Oulton Water Frolic (*Norfolk Chronicle,* 11 June 1814, advertising the event to be held near Lowestoft on 4 July, a Monday)

[4] *Belaugh Diary 1.* Mary Hardy's brisk style leaves no room for diary embellishment with descriptions of the picturesque

[5] *commercial instincts* Tom Williamson rightly points out that 'The Broadland rivers and lakes have been used by the local inhabitants for recreation and entertainment for centuries'. Also George Christopher Davies was 'to some extent, catering for a market which was

anyway expanding'. These publicity efforts spawned a vast array of tourist guides, an observer writing in 1897 that 'Surely no spot in the British Isles has been so "be-guided" as the Norfolk Broads' (T. Williamson, *The Norfolk Broads: A landscape history*, pp. 154, 155)

---

[1] *wealthy visitors* Lord Orford hosted a well-equipped pleasure-boating party on the Fenland waterways in 1774; Whittlesea Mere had not then been filled in. It was written up by three members of 'the Fleet' (J. W. Childers, ed., *Lord Orford's Voyage round the Fens in 1774* (Doncaster, 1868)).

I am grateful to Stephen Clarke for telling me of this published account at an Oxford conference in Jan. 2009

[2] *Yare valley* J. Stark and J. W. Robberds jnr, *Scenery of the Rivers of Norfolk*, pt 1 (London, 1828), unpag., a work full of literary, poetic and historical allusion.

As happened later in the century, commercial instincts underlay the guide: promotion of the Norwich–Lowestoft navigation (already described near the end of chaps 2 and 4)

worked body and overwrought mind before either the camera or the train was invented. Local people, and not just the wealthy ones, eagerly shared the waterways with visitors.[1]

The novelty lay not in a heightened awareness or 'discovery' of the Broads in the 1870s, but in changing patterns of leisure. Free time was severely curtailed until at least the mid-nineteenth century, so that trips on the water, such as those recorded by Mary Hardy, tended to be brief: a day at the most; often just an afternoon or evening. But many middle-class Victorians enjoyed holidays lasting a week or more. Pleasure boating then became more commercial and developed into a industry to serve an emerging market.

It is also true that, when drawing attention to the serenity and beauty of the area, authors of the early guides used a style unlikely to appeal to a mass market. This was the case with J. W. Robberds junior's ponderous prose in his *Scenery of the Rivers of Norfolk*, issued in four parts 1828–33. James Stark, his witty, observant illustrator, lightened the mood and depicted the people of the Broads at work and play, as seen at the chapter frontispiece. The Norwich artists would paint the glories of Norfolk on canvas; Robberds attempted the same in words. In 1828 he described 'the quiet loveliness' of the Yare valley near Norwich, which would 'enchaunt the sight'.[2] Yet the industrial, busy Yare was anything but quiet.

The long list of subscribers to Stark and Robberds' work, printed in the final part, is interesting. The authors drew support from much further afield than the confines of Norfolk. A very large number lived in London, with others in Canterbury, Birmingham, Manchester, Liverpool, Hull, Newcastle and Edinburgh, as well as in the towns of East Anglia. Some can be traced as having family connections with the county, such as the engineer to the Norwich–Lowestoft navigation William Cubitt, who had been born at Dilham in 1785. Even so, the list of subscribers shows that the picturesque scenery of the Broads had by 1833 been publicised in prose as well as in paint well beyond the county border.

The pleasure to be had from the natural beauties of Broadland was enhanced, as the painters of the Norwich School well knew, by the movement of boats going about their trade and by animated statheside scenes. Coltishall, not usually a place associated with the artists, was appreciated for these qualities, as the innkeeper of the King's Head near the river sensed as early as 1794. Jacob Watson sought to attract custom to his public house in terms recognisable to the nascent boat-hire industry of a century later:

The pleasant situation of the village of Coltishall is pretty generally known . . . The house [Watson's King's Head] is very near (and from some parts there is a view of) a pleasing navigable river, where vessels are almost constantly passing; and for parties fond of fishing or sailing, proper boats can always be had. It will also be his practice to keep cold provisions and bottled liquors in readiness to accommodate water parties, without any delay . . . [1]

This was no isolated example. The possibilities for outdoor recreation were highlighted at Wroxham six years later:

The beauties of the surrounding scenery, and the natural advantages of this charming expanse of water for sailing, render Wroxham Broad the most delightful rendezvous in the county of Norfolk for a water party.[2]

Some could afford to do it in style, anticipating the yachts which were to be fitted out with grand pianos and luxurious saloons a century later. A pleasure boat for sale, moored at Carrow Abbey, Norwich, had a dining cabin which would 'comfortably dine eight persons', while Mr Harmer of Wroxham Hall, whose grounds ran down to the Bure, had for sale 'a handsome pleasure boat with mast and sail'.[3] Merchants as well as gentry indulged their love of boating. Samuel Robinson, the maltster and coal merchant at Geldeston Staithe on the River Waveney, had for sale two pleasure boats, with sails and rigging.[4] When John Fiddy, the former playmate and dancing partner of the Hardy children, was selling his goods at Coltishall following his bankruptcy he offered a pleasure boat for sale in addition to two trading wherries; he was a farmer and liquor merchant.[5] None of these boat-owners could be classed as the very rich; nor were they professional wherrymen who had turned their boats into pleasure wherries for the day.

As so often in the eighteenth century, business was mixed with pleasure. In the summer months the Hardys occasionally walked two miles to Belaugh Church for the afternoon service. While Mary Hardy's father, her sister Phillis Goggs and her seven-year-old nephew Henry were on a visit to

[1] *Coltishall Norw. Merc.* 9 Aug. 1794

[2] *Wroxham Norw. Merc.* 12 July 1800, promoting the annual water frolic on Wroxham Broad. Breydon Regatta, held 30 July, was written up in the same paper three weeks later. And on 31 July the 'nymphs of the Yare and the dryads of Postwick Grove welcomed upon their deeps and under their shades the water parties of this city' for their annual regatta' (*Norw. Merc.* 2 Aug. 1800)

[3] *pleasure boats Norw. Merc.* 6 Sept. 1800, 23 Sept. 1775

[4] *Geldeston Norw. Merc.* 13 Jan. 1776. The notice is quoted in full as an inset in chap. 3, pp. 140–1

[5] *Coltishall Norw. Merc.* 16 May 1801.
   In the will dated 21 Jan. 1742 of Henry Smith (1676–1743), of Gt Hautbois, grandson of the regicide of the same name, he devised his boat 'with its appurtenances' to his son Henry [the Hardys' lawyer] *before* giving instructions as to his house, household goods, books, manuscripts, lands, tenements and monetary bequests (my warm thanks to Shirley Heriz Smith of Diss for her letter to me of 5 Feb. 2001, with her full transcript of the will)

[1] *Belaugh Diary* 1: 12 June 1774

[2] *Horning Diary* 1: it was a Thursday, during Raven's school holidays. This was a different John Clarke from their Strumpshaw innkeeper. Revd Anthony Barwick was Vicar of Horning, as already noted and illustrated on pp. 206–7. Mary Ann was not likely to have been included in the boating party, although the eight-month-old baby had come home three days earlier after being wet-nursed by Molly Rouse (vol. 1, chap. 5)

[3] *Farewell Diary* 1: 6 July 1774

[4] *Engall's garden Diary* 1

[5] *Merrie England* Referring to local gentry and clergy in Lancashire 1660–1800 Poole says: 'Their role at festival times changed from participant to patron, and from patron to figurehead, and it was not long before the condescending smile of the face of the figurehead became a disapproving scowl' (R. Poole, *The Lancashire Wakes Holidays*, p. 9). He dates 'the "merrie England" of myth and nursery rhyme' to the years after the Restoration (R. Poole, p. 5)

Coltishall in 1774 the Hardys took them to church by boat: 'Fine day . . . All went to Belaugh Church afternoon except Sister by water.'[1] The trip must have been a success. As we have seen, less than four weeks later the Hardys organised a more ambitious voyage, sailing nine or ten miles downriver to Horning in a keel belonging to John Clarke. They took the Coltishall curate with them on a visit to the wife (or possibly mother) of the Vicar of Horning, and had a five- or six-mile walk home in the gathering dusk:

[1774] JULY 7, THURSDAY Fine dry day . . . Mr Hardy, I and children and Mr Farewell went in Mr Clarke's keel to Horning to see Mrs Barwick, came home evening 10 walking.[2]

The curate had been boating with a parishioner the previous evening, and in the dark had ended up in the water; whether by accident or design is not stated. Both Richard Colby and Phillips Farewell were colourful characters.[3]

Despite the brevity of Mary Hardy's entries and the few opportunities she had for outings without the family—the only way of judging what she chose to do to please herself—it is evident that the diarist enjoyed boating on the Broads. She records a rare scene of relaxation away from the family circle one midsummer evening. A Friday, it had been a brewing day for the men; she and her son William had bathed in the large malthouse cistern; an innkeeper had called; and she and her great friend Mary Neve had come to the end of their working day. They took to the water at Coltishall skippered by Mr Starkey with his wife as mate, and in the last hours of daylight sailed down to Belaugh to Thomas Engall's garden:

[1779] JULY 2, FRIDAY A very warm day. Men brewed. I and Billy bathed. J. Clarke of Strumpshaw here. Mr Hardy at home all day. I and Mrs Neve drank tea with Mrs Starkey in their keel, went to Engall's garden after tea in Starkey's boat, home evening 9.[4]

The passing of old customs and 'merry ways'

Is it too fanciful to consider that the decades in which Mary Hardy wrote her diary saw a speeding up of the passing of Merrie England—an earthy, rumbustious, often violent England in which respectability and restraint had not yet become watchwords?[5] The powerful forces dominating this

left Norwich's great civic church of St Peter Mancroft from the north, hemmed in by narrow streets leading from the market.

Meandering past the tower's west face is Lady Lane, where St Peter's Wesleyan Chapel was built in 1824. It was largely financed by William Hardy jnr and Mary Ann Cozens (using her husband's name): see 'The religious dimension' in the Epilogue.

St Peter Mancroft was renowned for its bells, and in June 1775 Mary Hardy, her immediate family and her extended family from Whissonsett and Brisley heard the new peal of 12 bells rung in on Guild Day, when the new mayor was inaugurated.

Like the throngs massing in the market place at election time or around the Castle to witness public hangings this was a city and county event in which all could join. Bellringing was a feature of fairs and communal celebrations [*drawing by C. Wickes; lithograph by Day & Son 1858*]

volume ushered in a number of changes. Some were fleeting, lasting only until peace was resumed after 1815: a fondness for attending the theatre, for instance, found new strength in the second quarter of the century.[1] In other ways the old order had changed for good. Pleasure fairs never regained their popularity, leaving mainly the great stock fairs to continue their trade until the railways dealt them a final blow.

Life became more regulated under the weight of statute law, animals proving an early beneficiary of reforming legislation in the 1830s and 1840s—just when women and children too were starting to be protected at work. It would surely be unthinkable for any nineteenth-century Hardys and Cozens-Hardys to hang their dog because he had killed the pet rabbits: 'Dogs killed the tame rabbits, [we] hanged the dog Sancho.'[2] For the same reason, that of increasing sensitivity over expressions of violence, parents no longer took their young children to witness public hangings.[3]

[1] *theatre* The building of Fisher theatres in E. Anglia was revived after the end of the war, as recounted by T.L.G. Burley and Elizabeth Grice: see chap. 6

[2] *hanged Sancho Diary 1*: 31 July 1780. The cats did not suffer the same fate when they killed the Hardys' pigeons, however (*Diary 1*: 2 May 1774)

[3] *hangings* Crime is covered in vol. 3, chap. 6. Taking children to watch executions is discussed in vol. 1, chap. 5

[1] *loss of community*
J. Obelkevich, *Religion
and Rural Society: South
Lindsey 1825–1875*
(Clarendon Press,
Oxford, 1976), pp. 56–
61, 160–1, 217–19. He
concludes: 'When new-
style farmers recast
their relations with
them [farm labourers]
they had to make a
sweeping repudiation
of traditional pre-capi-
talist reciprocities that
formerly had bound the
two groups together',
reducing relations to
'the cash nexus' (p. 56).
    Special festivals such
as 'hopper feasts', mark-
ing the end of wheat-
sowing, 'were moribund
by the 1840s if not
quite extinct' (p. 57).
    And the harvest feast
or supper, 'the high
point of the festivities,
had died out—"under
the blighting influence
of Class Respectabil-
ity"' (p. 58, quoting the
diarist Henry Winn)

[2] *race Diary 1*: 14 Feb.
1774. There is a long,
level stretch of ground
behind the house

[3] *merry doings* There
was Whit Monday fun:
eg 'plowing for a pair of
breeches, running for a
shift, raffling for a gown
etc' (J. Woodforde, *The
Diary of a Country Par-
son*, ed. J. Beresford, vol.
3, p. 24, 12 May 1788;
see also vol. 2, pp. 137,
248, 31 May 1784, 5
June 1786; and at Mor-
ton, p. 188, 17 May 1785)

The process of shedding old customary ways took far longer than the 36 years of the diary; the various stages range across the mid-seventeenth to the mid-nineteenth centuries. In his classic 'Religion and society' study covering fifty years 1825–75 James Obelkevich identifies a loss of a sense of community, of old communal ways and village seasonal festivals, such as harvest celebrations. Work relationships shifted; at the same time Methodism and heart religion encouraged awareness of the individual self.[1] We have already seen in this volume the mission of the Evangelicals in recasting harvest frolics as religious services: temperance reigned; heavy drinking was deprecated. An elegiac tinge in the work of E.P. Thompson pervades his powerful analysis of loss as it hit the labouring classes. They found themselves no longer protected by custom, but exposed to the harsh realities of capitalism—the same tension seen in William Hardy's labour relations in this volume and in volume 2.

The poet and agricultural day labourer John Clare (1793–1864) attests to a sense of loss brought about in part by parliamentary enclosure and fen drainage. The greening of the shires in his Northamptonshire homeland to provide pasture for sheep, with the accompanying forefeiture of rights of common, impoverished his kind. In *The Shepherd's Calendar*, first published in 1827, he observes under June:

> *Thus ale, and song, and healths, and merry ways,*
> *Keep up a shadow still of former days.*

Clare also speaks in this poem of 'harmless fun', and it is the loss, indeed suppression, of fun to which Mary Hardy also testifies. The air of playfulness in the Coltishall years is much less apparent at Letheringsett; the Hardys' advance into middle age and the chronic pain which was its concomitant cannot provide the complete answer. In 1774 on Valentine's Day, not then a time purely for romance, a race was held at the White Lion, Coltishall.[2] This may have been a sack race, or a running race for a smock, such as the Rector of Weston sometimes recorded—perhaps wistfully—as he and Nancy heard of 'merry doings at the Heart'.[3]

Yet the countryside known to the Hardys did not groan under a punitive and oppressive regime. The sturdy independence fostered in the Middle Ages served as a counter-

left 'Merry doings at the Heart'.
 The former Heart, or Hart, where Whit-Monday events were laid on, lies over the road from Woodforde's church at Weston [*MB·2014*]

poise to attempts to exert control,[1] whether through Sunday schools, the work of puritanically-minded Evangelicals, or through the firm grip of the Wesleyan organisational machine. The flock refused to be cowed into submission.[2]

Norfolk JPs wielded a light touch. Public-house licences were not restricted, in marked contrast with other parts of the country.[3] A lavish provision of alehouses, the smaller type of establishment (like Weston's) particularly in the justices' sights as potentially unruly, was essential in lubricating most of the pleasures of the labouring class and the poor, as seen in this chapter over fairs and boxing matches, harvest frolics and Whit-Monday games. In the aftermath of the bread riots of 1795 justice dispensed at quarter sessions was relatively mild, particularly when judged against events at 'Peterloo' in 1819.[4] In many ways the magistrates had few powers. With no police force they had to rely on local tradesmen and farmers as back-up, or if necessary call in the military. It was this very powerlessness of the 'civil power' which led to the repression seen at Peterloo.[5] They feared loss of control. And exerting control defined the age: of the workforce, the labouring class on the Sabbath, of 'backsliders' failing to meet the standards expected by Methodist preachers, and of the poor in their outdoor leisure pursuits.

This was the backdrop to the febrile decade of the 1790s, when fear of sedition stalked government and courts. The divisive politics of the age dominate the next chapter.

[1] *Middle Ages* See the central part of chap. 5 in vol. 3, which analyses the nature of mediaeval property holding—and its consequences—in the parts of Norfolk where Mary Hardy wrote her diary

[2] *Sunday schools etc* Covered in the religious chapters (vol. 3, chaps 1–4)

[3] *licences* See vol. 2, chap. 9

[4] *bread riots* North Norfolk's are described in detail in vol. 3, chap. 6

[5] *Peterloo* The mocking name by which the encounter in St Peter's Field, Manchester came to be known after the brutal suppression by a charge of cavalry of a large but peaceful gathering there on 16 Aug. 1819, four years after the Battle of Waterloo. Tens of thousands of people had joined to call for the reform of parliamentary representation.
 About 18 were killed and hundreds injured

I · Impassable roads: Mary Hardy's entries in her diary for 27 Jan.–5 Feb. 1799. The severe winter prevented even determined individuals from getting about. On 3 Feb., in deep snow, the Curate of Whissonsett Thomas Skrimshire, based nearly six miles away, could not take the funeral of Nathaniel Raven: '. . . The roads all drifted up. My brother should have been buried, but it was impossible for Mr Skrimshire to come from Fakenham or scarce to get from house to house.' This was extremely unusual. As recounted in chapter 1, in roughly 12,850 diary entries Mary Hardy assessed the roads as impassable on only 32 days [*Cozens-Hardy Collection*]

2

2 · Gazebos on the River Lea at Ware, Hertford-
shire. William Hardy jnr would visit this great
malting centre, and malt-factors from the town
and surrounding area would call on him at
Letheringsett or during their annual 'summer
congress' at Cromer.

These late-17th-century and 18th-century
Dutch-style summerhouses were built at the
end of the gardens of inns and merchants'
houses away from the bustle and noise of
the High Street. The one second furthest
away has a date brick 1697   [MB · 2013]

3 · A creamware coffee jug, painted c.1800 by
William Absolon (1751–1815) and now in the
collection of the Norfolk Museums Service.

Absolon, of Gt Yarmouth, made a range of
souvenirs or 'trifles' for visitors. Many showed
a Yarmouth cart, a slim two-wheeler based on
the troll cart used for unloading at the quays and
negotiating the port's narrow rows. In 1783 the
Hardys built their own Yarmouth cart   [MB · 1989]

3

4

5

4, 5 · Swaffham Red Lion and New Buckenham King's Head. Public houses, especially coaching inns with large stables, were vital for road transport. Travellers 'bated' over meals, and their horses were swiftly changed. The Norwich turnpike opened in 1770 to Swaffham and in 1772 to New Buckenham   [MB · 2012, 2011]

6 · Strumpshaw grazing marshes beside the River Yare, now part of the nature reserve of the Royal Society for the Protection of Birds (RSPB). The entrance to the reserve is right by the former Strumpshaw Staithe, used by keels bringing bricks and tiles to Coltishall in the 1770s   [MB · 2012]

6

7 · Oxnead Bridge, looking upstream along the Aylsham navigation to Brampton. This canalised river had a series of humpback bridges shown on Biedermann's plan of 1772. They were destroyed in the 1912 flood which also ended the navigation's commercial life. The raised banks for controlling the flow and supplying a head of water for the locks are seen here. The rector Dr Charles Grape complained to King's College of the havoc they caused: drainage dykes from arable fields could no longer empty into the river [MB · 2011]

8, 9 · Sweet-smelling meadowsweet and catmint on the navigation [MB · 2011]

8

9

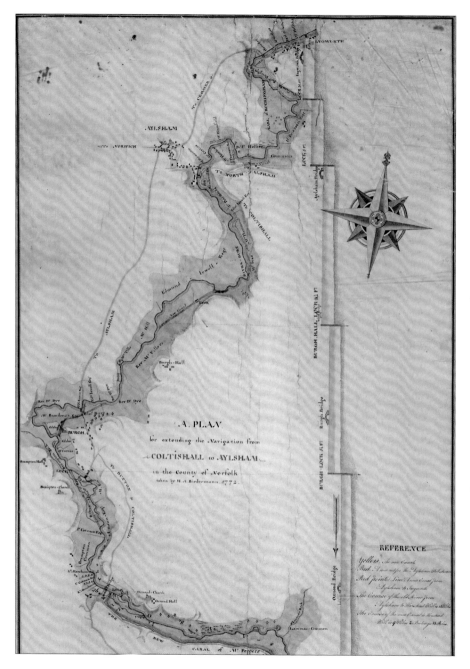

A PLAN

for extending the Navigation from

COLTISHALL to AYLSHAM

in the County of Norfolk

taken by M. A. Biedermann. 1772.

REFERENCE

10 · The upstream part of the plan of Oct. 1772 by the German-born surveyor Henry Augustus Biedermann for the proposed Aylsham navigation.

The whole course of the canalised and straightened River Bure was to be more than nine miles. Locks had to be built in new bypass channels near existing water-mills. The reaches above Aylsham and two locks were not built, on grounds of cost   [*Aylsham Town Council*]

11 · The lower part of the plan. The original is nearly 5 feet long (1·5 metres), and the Aylsham Town Archivist Lloyd Mills made this high-quality digital copy.

The precise draughtsmanship, picto-rial additions (such as the humpback bridges to accommodate wherries), blend of colours and muted tones form an attractive piece of data-rich graphic design by a surveyor still in his twenties [*Aylsham Town Council*]

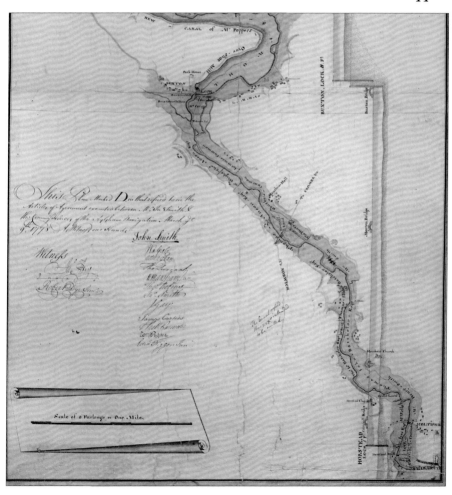

Stalham, Beccles and Aylsham— 13
three market towns formerly
reliant on navigable rivers:

12 · Wherries docked under the weather-
boarded granary of 1808 at Stalham
Staithe when loading and unloading
[*MB · 2001*]

13 · St Peter's House at Beccles, facing
the Old Market, has a long private
staithe at the rear where trading vessels
could moor [*MB · 2014*]

14 · 18th-century workforce cottages for
maltsters and tanners among a series
of imposing mercantile houses along
Northgate, Beccles [*MB · 2014*]

12

14

15 · These mercantile houses at Beccles have private staithes across Northgate— once an area of maltings, a tannery and coal and timber quays [*MB* · *2014*]

16 · Aylsham: the trading settlement of Millgate, beside the navigation, resembles the riverside area of Coltishall now called Anchor Street. Bure House (foreground), built 1768 for millers and maltsters, once had river frontage [*MB* · *2011*]

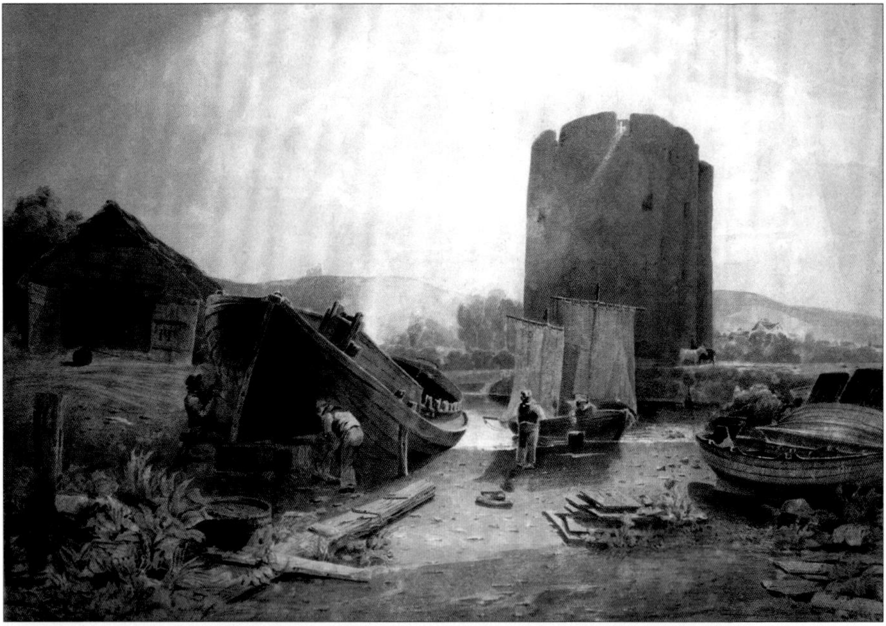

17

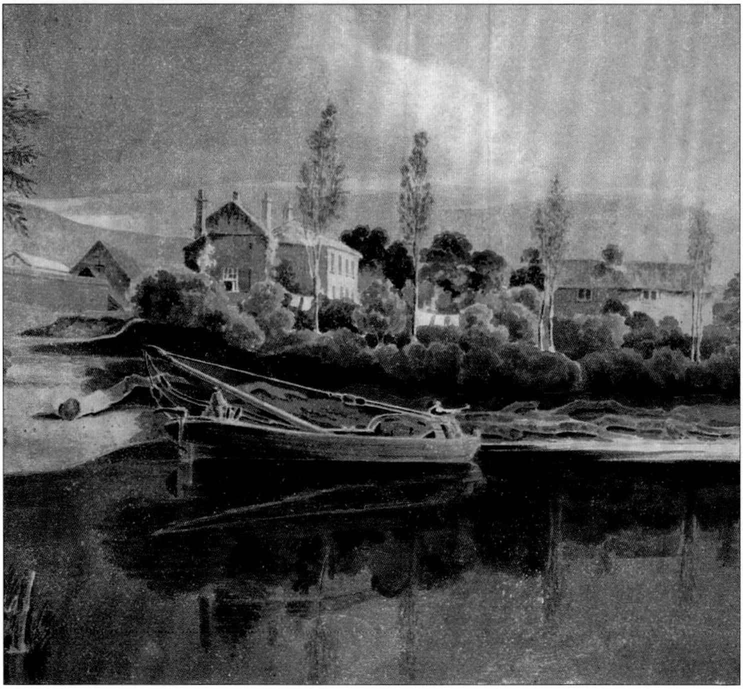

18

17 · *Boatbuilder's Yard, near the Cow's Tower, Norwich*, by John Thirtle *c*.1812. A wherry is under construction in the open, as *William and Mary* would have been at Wright's Yard, Coltishall. The artist's initials IT are on the shed door

18 · *View of the River near Cow's Tower, Norwich, c*.1810: detail of another view by Thirtle at this bend on the Wensum by Cow Tower. A keel is quanted along, the man by the cabin at the bow getting purchase for his pole against the bank. The centrally-stepped mast for the square sail is lowered for Bishop's Bridge [*both paintings Norfolk Museums & Archaeology Service (Norwich Castle Museum & Art Gallery)*]

19

19 · Midsummer sunrise at Reedham Ferry, the sole remaining vehicle ferry on the Norfolk Broads. William and Mary Hardy took Horning Ferry to reach Strumpshaw from Coltishall [*Julie Bird 2015*]

20 · The coming storm, with Norfolk reed bending in the strong wind. Hardley Cross stands at the confluence of the Chet and the Yare. The 16th-century shaft—no longer vertical—marks the boundary of the river jurisdiction between Norwich and Gt Yarmouth   [*Roger Bird 2015*]

20

21

22

21 · A transom-sterned clinker-built keel lies against the bank, laden with bundles of reed for thatching and fencing; further bundles are propped upright nearby. Her square tan sail is loosely furled; two pleasure yachts are under way [*Joseph Stannard, 'The River at Thorpe', ? early 1820s: Norfolk Museums & Archaeology Service (Norwich Castle Museum & Art Gallery)*]

22 · The transom stern of the Whitlingham keel *Dee-Dar*, in her steel cradle 26 Apr. 2012 shortly before her destruction. Like the keel in the painting she has a massive rudder   [*MB · 2012*]

23 · Looking towards *Dee-Dar*'s bow, showing a broad mossy plankway or catwalk   [*MB · 2012*]

24 · Blakeney: the main channel by the quay where William Hardy jnr's sloop used to moor and where Mary Hardy had tea on board.

In late 1803 Major Alexander Bryce explored the marrams, creeks and cliffs of the whole Norfolk coast. He reported on the strength of the Sea Fencibles and the likelihood of a French invasion at vulnerable points such as Blakeney Pit   [*MB · 2012*]

24

25, 26 · The trading wherry *Albion*, in
the care of the Norfolk Wherry Trust.
Built 1898, she is now used for charters
and members' cruises under volunteer
skippers and mates   [MB · 2001, 2012]

26

27

28

29

27 · The view from the helm: *Albion* sails up the Bure past St Benet's Abbey. The Hardys' much smaller wherry *William and Mary* would take this route on her passage home from Gt Yarmouth [*MB · 2001*]

28 · *Albion* sails down the Thurne. The sails of wherries and yachts appear to make their way across fields in the flat landscape of the Broads.

   In winter the towers of Thurne, Ludham, Horning, Ranworth and Upton churches can be seen from this vantage point close to Thurne Church   [*MB · 2018*]

29 · Strong bolts hold the keel *Dee-Dar*'s timbers together. A considerable amount of blacksmith's and plumber's work went into building keels and wherries, the heaviest item being the lead counter-poise at the foot of the mast [*Christopher Bird 2012*]

30 · King's Lynn: a view of quays, warehouses and cascades of pantiled roofs seen from the 16th-century lookout tower at Clifton House.

The view is north-west along the estuary of the Great Ouse to the North Sea   [*MB · 2012*]

31 · Clifton House: the tower. Merchants and shipowners built lookouts from which they would scan the horizon for their vessels. Many can be seen today in the Low Countries, as in Bruges and Middelburg   [*MB · 2012*]

32 · The front entrance to Clifton House in Queen Street has fine barley-sugar columns of 1708, described by N. Pevsner and B. Wilson (1999) as 'a Baroque motif rare in England' [*MB · 2012*]

32

33

33 · The Hanseatic port of King's Lynn, where William Hardy was stationed in the Excise in 1761 on the first of his Norfolk postings.

The Customs House of 1683 beside the Purfleet is by Henry Bell. The explorer George Vancouver, from a Lynn family, gazes out to sea [*MB · 2012*]

34 · Ceres, goddess of corn, and Bacchus, god of wine, adorn two of the Customs House windows [*MB · 2012*]

35 · The Customs' Royal Arms confer the sanction necessary in an intrusive tax-gathering service [*MB · 2012*]

34

35

36

36 · Letheringsett St Andrew, from the south-east. The headstone of 32-year-old Jeremiah Cozens, the nephew of Mary Ann's husband, killed during his only shoot, stands newly cleaned in the angle of the south porch and south-aisle wall.

From church pulpits could be heard the exhortations of Anglicans—Evangelical and, like Mr Burrell, otherwise—as they attempted to rein in what they saw as the unbridled pastimes of the poor. Sabbatarianism too was fast gaining ground at this time, decades before the Lord's Day Observance Society was founded in 1831   [*MB · 1989*]

37 · Bungay's butter cross of 1689, with Justice above   [*MB · 2012*]

38 · The Fisher Theatre of 1828 in central Bungay   [*MB · 2012*]

38

39 · Young hen and cock pheasants in barley stubble. These are at Westwick, where the diarist's son-in-law, the keen sportsman Jeremiah Cozens, was raised   [*MB · 2011*]

39

40

40 · 'Review of the Western Norfolk Battalion of Militia' (*plates 44, 45*). Lord Townshend (*plates 44, 45*), a man of immense energy and vision, was responsible for the Militia and Volunteers at county level as Lord Lieutenant at a time of great peril.

Here he is seen (centre) in riding boots and with his right arm outstretched in greeting [*painting commissioned in 1760 and ascribed to 'The Circle of David Morier'; reproduced courtesy the 8th Marquess Townshend*]

41 · Gt Yarmouth St Nicholas, a seamark even
without its former tall spire   [MB · 2001]

42 · The Fishermen's Hospital of 1702, a
herring lugger in the pediment   [MB · 2001]

43 · *Dutch Boats off Yarmouth*, by John Sell
Cotman ? 1823, with vessels beached in peace-
time. William Hardy jnr's sloop *Nelly* had been
in the Dutch fleet after her capture in 1798
[*Norfolk Museums & Archaeology Service
(Norwich Castle Museum & Art Gallery)*]

41

42

43

44

45

44 · Raynham Hall, just west of Whissonsett and seat of the Townshends. From here Field Marshal Marquis Townshend co-ordinated preparations to withstand a series of invasion threats during the French wars [*MB · 2012*]

45 · George, 1st Marquis and 4th Viscount Townshend (1724–1807), former Lord Lieutenant of Ireland and Master General of the Ordnance; Lord Lieutenant of Norfolk 1792–1807.

A career soldier of distinction and promoter of the Militia Act of 1757, he gave considered and effective leadership during recurrent crises
[*portrait by Mather Brown; reproduced courtesy the 8th Marquess Townshend*]

46 · Holt, decked out in
bunting on 25 May 2012
during the Diamond Jubi-
lee of the Queen's reign.
    Mary Hardy recorded
patriotic celebrations in
connection with the mon-
arch and with the end of
hostilities with foreign foes.
In November 1801 the Holt
innkeeper Samuel Love
could not keep the lamps
lit over this inn sign during
the peace festivities
[*Christopher Bird 2012*]

47 · 'Nelson, Berry, Victory':
the slogan on banners in
Norwich and Norfolk after
the victory over the French
at the Battle of the Nile in
1798. Captain Edward
Berry, RN, commander
of Nelson's flagship, had
strong Norfolk connections
[*painting by John Singleton
Copley; copyright National
Maritime Museum, London*]

48

49

48, 50 · The full-day joint expedition of the Norwich & Norwich Archaeological Society and Norfolk Industrial Archaeology Society to Letheringsett, 6 July 1996. Many members of the Cozens-Hardy family are in the front rows. They are seen in the brewery yard in front of the Hardys' tun room, and on the lawn at Glavenside, Basil Cozens-Hardy's former home   [*Christopher Bird 1996*]

51 · Eleven of the 15 descendants of Mary Hardy present at the launch of the Diary volumes on 26 Apr. 2013 are joined by the editor Margaret Bird; the setting is the refectory of Norwich Cathedral.

From the left: John Phelps, Sam Phelps, Margaret Bird, John Hirst, Sue Rosser (kneeling), Raven Cozens-Hardy, Graham Solberg, John Cozens-Hardy (seated), William Cozens-Hardy (at the back), Mina Holland, Caroline Holland (kneeling) and Jane Anderson   [*Christopher Bird 2013*]

49 · Glaven Cottage, built as 'Mill Cottage' beside his Letheringsett maltings by William Hardy in 1792. When his grandson William refronted it in 1870 he imposed the stamp of an estate property with the family crest and 'Fear One' motto [*Christopher Bird 2013*]

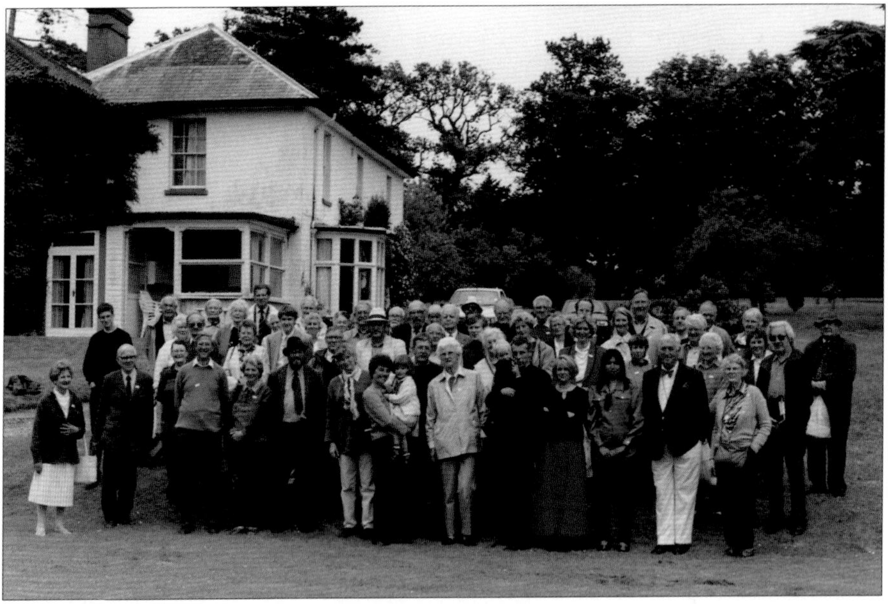

50

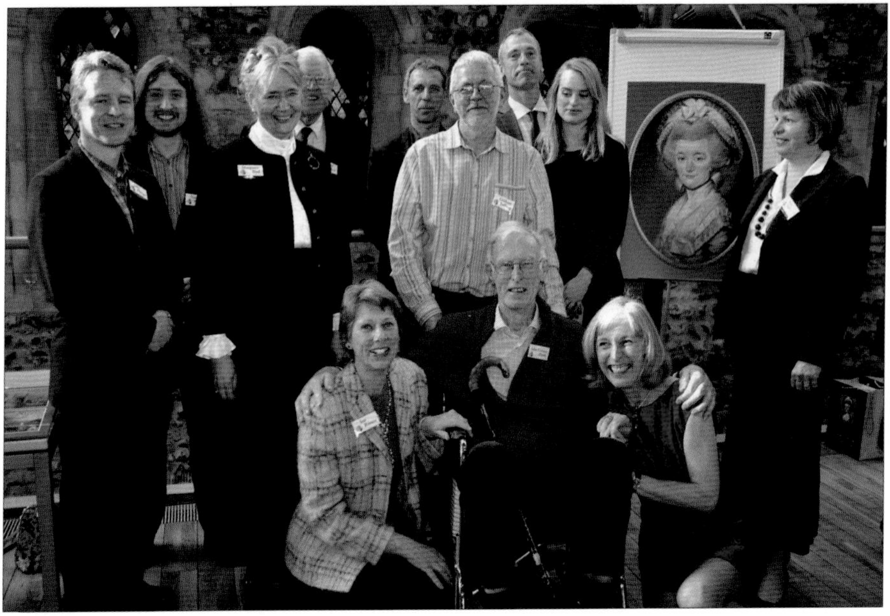

51

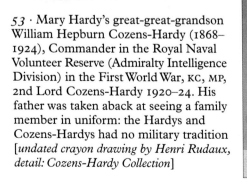

52 · First light: the pleasure wherry *Hathor* at anchor on Surlingham Broad, off the River Yare.

She was built at Reedham by Mary Hardy's descendants Ethel and Helen Colman in 1905 to replicate a trading wherry's lines, but was fitted out to a high standard for holiday use by the family.

She carries the Colman colours at her masthead, as the firm's trading wherries used to do.

For years *Hathor* has taken holiday parties with Norfolk Yacht Charter under skipper Peter Bower
[*Christopher Bird 2000*]

53

53 · Mary Hardy's great-great-grandson William Hepburn Cozens-Hardy (1868–1924), Commander in the Royal Naval Volunteer Reserve (Admiralty Intelligence Division) in the First World War, KC, MP, 2nd Lord Cozens-Hardy 1920–24. His father was taken aback at seeing a family member in uniform: the Hardys and Cozens-Hardys had no military tradition [*undated crayon drawing by Henri Rudaux, detail: Cozens-Hardy Collection*]

54 · Another group of descendants at the Diary launch. From the left: Graham Solberg, Raven Cozens-Hardy, John Cozens-Hardy (seated), the former Lord Lieutenant of Norfolk Sir Timothy Colman, (editor Margaret Bird) and Isabel Henniger, from Ontario [*Christopher Bird 2013*]

55 · The Hon. Beryl Cozens-Hardy (1911–2011) in 1984 (centre). In the Amalienborg Palace with HM Queen Ingrid (right) and HRH Princess Benedikte of Denmark, she is seen receiving the Olave Baden-Powell Award. For over half a century Beryl was custodian of Mary Hardy's manuscript [*photographer not known*]

54

55

56 · A popular mooring at Coltishall: the approach to the
former King's Head Staithe today, with Lower Common
on the right. The site of Joseph Browne's coaling business
known to the Hardys is glimpsed in the distance, where the
Rising Sun now does a busy riverside trade. The diarist's old
home and private staithe lie a short way up from this reach.

   These were the home waters of the Hardys' wherry
William and Mary, built in 1776 at Wright's yard just out of
sight round the bend   [*Christopher Bird 2015*]

57 · Candelabra primulas beside a dyke in S. Walsham's Fairhaven Gardens, looking towards the approach to Panxworth Staithe from the broad. Panxworth, a coaling wharf and home berth of keels in 1795—and home earlier that century to Jeremiah Cozens' grandfather—then occupied one arm of the broad. Pleasure boating, tourism and conservation now predominate.

This image, representing the contrast between the tranquillity of today and the lively trading world of the past, was chosen in 2019 to head the website home page of Burnham Press, publishers of Mary Hardy   [*MB · 2018*]

III · Figures and tables

T. W. Coke,
p. 451

III · Human conflict

Sᵗ ROBERT WALPOLE
EARL OF ORFORD
1744.

F. Zinke effig. p.1744

G. Vertue del. & sculp. 1748

8
Politics

A great riot... one man killed and several limbs broke

About three o'clock Mr Windham arrived in town, having returned from the Continent early on Wednesday, and was a stranger to his nomination till he came at Attleborough: from this hour the plot began to thicken ...   NORWICH MERCURY, 1780 [1]

Mr Hardy set off for Norwich in Mrs Sheppard's postchaise with Mr Bensley and Mr Bartell morning 8, William went upon our mare ...
Mr Hardy, William and Mr Burrell came home from Norwich evening 10. A great riot in Norwich yesterday, a great deal of mischief done: one man killed and several limbs broke. Hubbard [Hobart] got his election by a majority of 70. A scrutiny is talked of.   MARY HARDY, 1786 [2]

T HE PEOPLE OF NORFOLK AND NORWICH, whether or not they had a vote, revelled in elections. The county and city had a voracious appetite for what the press would call a hard contest. The Hardys were a highly politically aware family. In the diary's early years Mary Hardy and her young sons, while excluded from polling on the grounds of their sex and youth, would take their stand in the centre of Norwich to watch the proclamation of the results and the victorious candidates being chaired around the market

[1] *Norw. Merc.* 16 Sept. 1780. William Windham drove up unaware of his nomination to stand as MP for Norwich in the general election

[2] *riot Diary 1*: 15 Nov., 16 Nov. 1786. This by-election followed the raising of a Norwich MP to the Lords, but the Commons declared the by-election void.
The Letheringsett and Holt party had to journey more than 23 miles to Norwich to cast their votes, those of a like voting persuasion

top Norwich's Mercury brings the news, 1803 [*Norfolk Heritage Centre, Norwich*]

facing page The embodiment of Whiggery: Sir Robert Walpole (1676–1745), 1st Earl of Orford, celebrated in his Garter robes two years after he had left office following 21 years as Britain's first Prime Minister. He is festooned with symbols of authority and opulence. The plans of Houghton Hall, his splendid north Norfolk seat, lie heaped with other papers and coins in a jumble of regalia and instruments; a hand on a sceptre points to Houghton behind the Palladian screen.

While the pomp and display were not to the Hardys' taste, the powerful figure who governed Britain in the diarist's childhood stood for the values underpinning much of the family's Whig politics: stability, wealth creation, constitutional monarchy, religious toleration and solid, lasting achievement [*drawing by F. Zinke 1744; engraving by G. Vertue 1748: author's collection*]

below The Hon. Henry Hobart (1738–99), of Intwood; and *right* the Rt Hon. William Windham (1750–1810), of Felbrigg. Both feature in the extracts at the chapter head.

Hobart, son of the Earl of Buckinghamshire of Blickling Hall, was the only Tory for whom William Hardy polled in eight parliamentary elections spread over nearly 40 years (table 4.8.1). The anti-war Whig brewer chose on four occasions 1784–90, all in peacetime, to vote for Hobart, the loyal supporter of the administrations of William Pitt. He voted for Windham intermittently, usually when 'The Weathercock' was allied, at times uneasily, with the Foxite Whigs.

Of all the many MPs who represented Norfolk and its five parliamentary boroughs during the period of Mary Hardy's diary, Windham was the sole figure to hold high office. He was Secretary at War 1794–1801 during almost the whole of the French Revolutionary War, and Secretary for War and the Colonies 1806–07 during the Napoleonic War. Both were Cabinet posts [*posthumous painting of Hobart by John Opie 1802; painting of Windham by John Hoppner 1804: civic portraits Norfolk Museums & Archaeology Service (Norwich Castle Museum & Art Gallery)*]

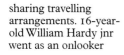

sharing travelling arrangements. 16-year-old William Hardy jnr went as an onlooker

place. And in 1806, at the age of 72, the diarist undertook the 47-mile round trip to be present for the end of polling.

Mary Hardy records the addiction of Norfolk men—and, if she is representative, women—to elections and electioneering. No time was allowed for mourning and reflection following the death in 1799 of the Hon. Henry Hobart, one of the Norwich Members of Parliament. In the same newspaper edition carrying the death announcement came news of the contest to succeed him, with Robert Fellowes and John Frere hastening to issue election statements.[1] The by-election was held only seventeen days after Hobart's passing and nine days after the press notice of his death, the published breakdown of the votes showing that while Fellowes had won among Norwich voters, the votes of others from the Cathedral Close, Great Yarmouth, the country areas of Norfolk and from London had swung the result to Frere.[2]

This chapter will chart the development of sophisticated psephology—the study of electoral patterns and statistics. The county newspaper the *Norwich Mercury* and its owner-editors Richard Bacon and his son Richard Mackenzie Bacon, publishers of valuable sets of pollbooks, played a major role locally in this new science.[3]

Terminology

Already some anachronistic terms have crept into this chapter. It may be useful at this early stage to introduce a few definitions and highlight certain differences between the political world then and now; the contrasts will be fleshed out later. The term by-election (a contest held outside the normal run of elections, as when a sitting MP retires, dies or is raised to the House of Lords) is for convenience adopted here although it was not an eighteenth-century one. It entered the political vocabulary as late as 1880.[4]

The pollbooks, Norfolk's first being illustrated overleaf, form the source of some of the tables in this chapter and will be analysed later in some depth; the earliest nationally, for Essex, dates from 1694.[5] This was the age of open polling, the sanctity of the secret ballot coming in very much later following the Ballot Act of 1872. Votes were publicly recorded at the polling booth giving the individual voter's name, place of residence and place of his property qualification. Shortly after the close of polling the votes cast were published in pollbooks containing often thousands of voting decisions. At a glance a landlord or patron could see whether his tenant, employee or protégé had bent to his

[1] *death Norw. Merc.* 18 May 1799

[2] *by-election Norw. Merc.* 1 June 1799. The Cathedral precincts, with their privileges and traditions, were often treated separately when compiling data ranging from the bishop's visitation returns to results of polls in parliamentary elections

[3] *Bacon* Mary Hardy knew the father as a valuer and auctioneer in 1781, and in 1789 had tea and supper at the *Norwich Mercury*'s Norwich offices in the tall, gabled building at the corner of Cockey Lane and Castle Street (*Diary 1*: 31 Jan.–13 Feb. 1781; *Diary 2*: 16 May 1789).
R.M. Bacon (1776–1844), editor 1804–44, also founded the Norwich Triennial Musical Festival

[4] *by-election* A contest held on a specific writ (E. Green, P. Corfield and C. Harvey, *Elections in Metropolitan London 1700–1850* (2 vols, Bristol Academic Press, Westbury-on-Trym, 2013), vol. 1, p. 15). The opening chapter, on terminology, gives an overview of contemporary usage (pp. 13–16)

[5] *Essex* E. Green, P. Corfield and C. Harvey, *Elections in Metropolitan London*, vol. 1, p. 131

right and *below* The earliest Norfolk poll-book: the general election of Feb. 1715 (1714 Old Style). The title page lists the four candidates. Sir Jacob Astley, Bt, of Melton, and Thomas de Grey of Merton were elected in a close contest. Astley was (newly) a Whig and de Grey (uneasily) also a Whig. All four candidates belonged to prominent Norfolk families who were politically active throughout much of the 18th century.

In uncontested elections, bargaining between supporters of opposing factions in two-member seats could at times secure an outcome satisfactory to both sides, with a Whig and a Tory being returned.

The entry for the diarist's home village of Whissonsett shows the layout of one type of pollbook, differing from that of 1806 (pictured later). Here the voters are arranged

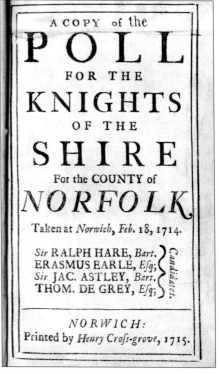

under the place of their property qualification, with place of residence (if different) given after their name. The dashes in the four final columns represent their votes.

Five with property in Whissonsett lived elsewhere, including the lord of the manor James Calthorpe, whose voting choices 11 of the 14 electors followed—among them Mary Hardy's grandfather Henry Raven. This suggests they were under Calthorpe's influence, for three who lived away from the village chose not to follow his example in the polling booth. There were no plumpers (those exercising only one vote). Each of the nine Whissonsett-based voters had to make a 46-mile round trip to Norwich, the sole polling centre for the county elections.

The 1715 general election resulted in a large Whig majority in the Commons of about 150 seats, although adherence to party was loose   [*Cozens-Hardy Collection*]

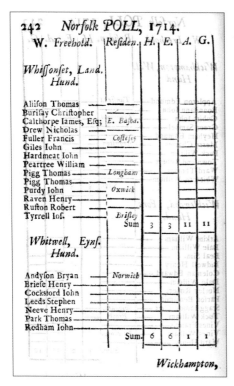

will and influence. Unless a by-election were being held the voter usually had two votes at his disposal; a minority would choose to exercise their right to withhold one of their votes and poll as plumpers—just for one candidate. The way plumping affected the voting will be considered later.

Party affiliations were not cited in the pollbooks; indeed many candidates would draw attention to their credentials as independently minded men devoted wholly to the interests of the electorate. A 'Party man' was a term of abuse. Political loyalties were fluid, and party adherence fluctuated: William Windham was lampooned as 'Weathercock Windham' for his changes of allegiance. A Tory might be characterised during the younger Pitt's years in power as a friend to the ministry, or a friend to government; or of the court party. The candidates and their labels will be discussed near the end of the chapter, but in portraying William Hardy as an anti-war, Foxite Whig we would probably be using terms he would not recognise. A staunch upholder of the Glorious Revolution settlement, the friend of Commerce, or friend of Peace, might more closely match his self-image. Labels are inserted nevertheless as guidance, as in table 4.8.1.

The suffrage, then all male, will occupy much of the central sections. It was perhaps surprisingly widely based in Mary Hardy's world in pre-Reform days, not only in the Freemen boroughs of Norwich and Great Yarmouth but even in the county. In some Norfolk parishes, including those known to the diarist, up to a quarter of the adult male population in a village might journey to Norwich to cast their votes. In her own home parish of Letheringsett 17·5 per cent of the adult males polled in 1806 (table 4.8.4).

Political participation

The passionate, even feverish preoccupation with contests extended beyond the political sphere, Mary Hardy following the protracted tussle between local attorneys to win the lucrative post of county coroner.[1] And when the Bishop of Norwich realised in 1791 that he could no longer serve both his new see and the Oxford college where for 22 years he had served as head, the *Norwich Mercury* breathlessly reported the struggle between two Fellows to succeed the Rt Revd Dr George Horne as President of Magdalen.[2]

[1] *coroner* 'The election for a coroner at Norwich: Sir John Leek, Mr Munhall, Mr Waller stood candidates. Munhall was chosen after a strong contest' (*Diary 2*: 26 Jan. 1791).

Each Norfolk freeholder had a vote in the two-day poll, the Baptist minister Revd Mark Wilks promoting himself as one of the nine contenders during the preliminaries. The Coltishall attorney Francis Munhall won (*Norw. Merc.* 11 Dec., 18 Dec. 1790, 22 Jan., 29 Jan. 1791).

Wilks's radical political views are described at the end of this chapter

[2] *Magdalen Norw. Merc.* 23 Apr. 1791.

The presidency was worth £1000 p.a., so the position was a coveted one. Martin Routh, aged 35, won by a single vote, staying in post until he died in his 100th year.

Elected when Louis XVI was still on the throne of the Capets, Routh died during the Crimean War, allegedly 'through chagrin at the fall of Russian securities' (J. Morris, *Oxford* (Faber and Faber, London, 1965), p. 197)

above **Weston Church: the arms of New College, Oxford, James Woodforde's patrons.**
Denied the chance to vote in Norfolk, the rector could have voted in the university seat—had not those elections gone uncontested as well   [*MB · 2014*]

---

[1] *other counties* In the 1784 general election only seven out of 40 counties and 63 out of 203 boroughs had a contested election (E. Green, P. Corfield and C. Harvey, *Elections in Metropolitan London*, vol. 1, p. 37). The Whigs were in disarray over the Fox–North Coalition

This chapter, like the portrait of local society in volume 3, chapter 5, illustrates one of the themes of this study: that in the eighteenth century Norfolk men and women looked outwards well beyond the county border and were deeply absorbed in discussion of national and international events. Large numbers participated in them, as we see in this volume. The sense of isolation so often spoken of by those who regard the Weston rector James Woodforde as typical can be misleading, for his diary is tinged with the depression of his middle and especially his last years. He never voted in a parliamentary election in Norfolk in the 27 years he lived in the county. As was common in other counties,[1] there was no contested poll for the county seat between the contested general elections of 1768 and 1802, giving him no opportunity to exercise his vote from his place of residence.

As a University man he could have voted in Oxford had he had the time to plan his journey, and the inclination to spend money on it. This was still the age of plural voting, lasting until the Act of 1948, when voters could take part in any contest for which they held the appropriate electoral qualification. (The Prime Minister, William Pitt, was one of the two MPs for Cambridge University 1784–1806.) However the Oxford University seat went uncontested in the general elections and one by-election held 1774–1802 inclusive. When at last Woodforde's chance came, for Norfolk in 1802, nervousness and ill-health precluded him from participating in that hard-fought county contest, as described later.

By contrast William Hardy voted eight times 1768–1806, in both Norwich and Norfolk parliamentary elections (table 4.8.1), his wife taking a keen interest in the campaigning and progress of the poll in a period when general elections were spread over a period of weeks. This chapter will examine the participation of the non-voters in the electoral process. Their presence as compliant observers when the successful candidates were chaired round the town centre, whether there had been a contest or not, provided three vital elements: consent, acclamation and thus validation. Unenfranchised women, children, apprentices and the poor could feel they had something to contribute to the stirring times they were living through. Those disappointed or angered by the result might resort to violence, as quoted at the chapter head.

Denial of a contest created a serious democratic deficit. These were the days of 'treating', as will be shown, when candidates wined and dined their prospective supporters and even paid for their return travel between Norwich and London. The capital outlays involved could be ruinous, so candidates would often conclude an electoral pact to run together despite marked political differences. A Foxite Whig (supporting C.J. Fox) and a ministerial Tory might stand together unopposed, or an anti-war Whig and an Independent Whig. This rarely happened in the Freemen boroughs with large electorates like Norwich and Great Yarmouth, but it was a feature of certain of the boroughs, the university seats and even politically active county seats like Norfolk.[1]

As a result of such pacts the power of an electorate already known to be unrepresentative was further diminished. (This was long before the Reform Acts of 1832 and 1867 widened the franchise.) The putative voters were conscious of the deliberate suppression of their chance to choose the very parliamentary decision-makers who would take the nation to war, sue for peace and impose the swingeing taxation required to pay for these adventures. Not only the parish officers but the chief constables and justices of the peace, all of whom had to implement the country's laws at local level in rural Norfolk, did not have the opportunity to vote for their political masters in the 32-year period 1769–1801.[2]

The Septennial Act, which in 1716 had swept away the Glorious Revolution's adoption of triennial parliaments, would have seemed irrelevant to large sections of the electorate.[3] Seven years may have been the theoretical maximum space between general elections, but often when those elections came along no contest took place. With meaningful participation in the democratic process sacrificed the foundations of the mandate from the people were seen as shaky. As a result a few landed grandees like Thomas William Coke, 'Coke of Norfolk', whom we meet later, faced the accusation that they were turning the proud county into a pocket borough, its electorate effectively powerless.

The divisiveness of the most contentious issue in English politics at this time, the reaction to the French Revolution and its aftermath, broke up the cosy arrangements between factional and party rivals. Whereas a certain level of unity

[1] *boroughs* Described, with analysis of the whole parliamentary electoral system, by Sir Lewis Namier in *The Structure of Politics at the Accession of George III* (2nd edn Macmillan, London, 1957; 1st pub. in 2 vols 1929); see esp. pp. 62–157, 299–401.

In pocket boroughs (like Castle Rising and Thetford in Norfolk), rotten boroughs and others in the grip of some interest (such as Treasury boroughs and corporation boroughs) it would be usual for both candidates to follow the political lead of the controlling person or institution, with again no contest

[2] *chief constables* Just as the parish constable of an individual parish was an elected officer, like the churchwardens, overseer of the poor and surveyor of the highways, so a chief constable served the group of parishes in the hundred. See vol. 3, chap. 6 on the Peace

[3] *Septennial Act* This remained in force until 1911. The prohibitive cost of electioneering every three years had been one of the reasons for its introduction, as also the 'more violent and lasting heats and animosities' in the populace at elections (W.C. Costin and J.S.

Watson, *The Law and Working of the Constitution: Documents 1660–1914* (2 vols, Adam & Charles Black, London, 2nd edn 1961; 1st pub. 1952), vol. 1, p. 127, where the Act is quoted at length)

---

[1] *divisions* Brian Lavery summarises the differing public reactions to the Seven Years War 1756–63 and the later wars: the American war 1775–83 ('almost a civil war') and the French Revolutionary War 1793–1801. Unity was more prevalent in the conflict with Napoleon 1803–15 (B. Lavery, *We shall fight on the Beaches*, pp. 32–4)

[2] *defining element* B.D. Hayes, 'Politics in Norfolk, 1750–1832' (unpub. 477-page PhD thesis, Univ. of Cambridge, 1957), p. 262; see also pp. 197, 204, 232, 262. It is a dazzlingly detailed and cogent analysis of the subject, by one who was supervised by J.H. Plumb and Lewis Namier

[3] *tensions* See chap. 9, where Townshend reassures the Home Secretary; also vol. 3, chap. 4 on the flock

[4] *sermons* Discussed in this chapter; see also vol. 3, chaps 1 and 4 on tensions between clergy and flock over politics

had prevailed in the middle years of the eightenth century, when the country was united against France in the Seven Years War, the American war fostered divisions which became a flood in the 1790s. The repercussions in Britain of the turmoil on the Continent find echoes in many parts of this study, as volume 3 explains. The last part of this chapter, as also much of the next, will focus on the response to the growing menace from France and the unsettled public mood in Norfolk. The Treason Trials and legislation against sedition came only a short while before the Year of Peril (1797).[1] Politics and the prosecution of the wars were intertwined: civilians were required to serve under arms and were to be mobilised when the invader struck. They had a direct role in the country's survival, yet large numbers were without the vote either directly through the limited franchise or indirectly since contests were shunned by the candidates.

With political consensus cast adrift, and so much at stake, contests at election time could no longer be ducked. B.D. Hayes in his thesis characterises the French Revolution as the defining element, a polarising force, in British political life. It broke the Whigs into factions, precipitating the prolonged split which was to give Pitt uninterrupted tenure.[2] It needed the Terror across the Channel to moderate the extremism of the Corresponding Societies at home, Mary Ann Hardy's future brother-in-law John Cozens, described later, cutting a leading figure in the Norwich Revolution Society. The wars, and the participation required in home defence, sharpened differences and gave the general population a heightened sense of political awareness. Pressing national issues supplanted local conflicts at election time.

Tensions were exposed, notably the Jacobinism of the 'Democratical' elements in Norfolk on which the Lord Lieutenant Lord Townshend reported to Government (*plate 45*). Set against this, the peaceable influence of the Wesleyans was relayed by parish clergy in their visitation returns to the Bishop of Norwich.[3] At Letheringsett Mary Hardy writhed as she listened to the 'political sermons' issuing from the rector, who voted Tory. She could not abide a political sermon, and would write 'in contradiction' to Mr Burrell.[4] Yet such sermons served as one of the weapons of control long relied on by the authorities to keep the population in check.

This heightened political awareness, and the public's zest for contested elections for a very wide variety of offices, has led the creators of the digital London Electoral Database and its companion London Electoral History website to characterise the eighteenth and early nineteenth centuries as witnessing the development of 'proto-democracy'. In the period 1733–1830 Middlesex had eleven recorded contests for the post of county coroner. More obscure posts such as bridgemaster of London Bridge attracted hotly-fought campaigns and wide participation in the voting process. Most of these elections spawned pollbooks from which patterns of voting can be charted for more than one million individual polling decisions in the London area 1700–1850.[1]

Theirs was 'a participatory world'. It was especially vivid and robust in the heated atmosphere of the capital, in the constituencies of London (the City), Westminster, Southwark and Middlesex; yet it extended to other parts of the country with large popular constituencies. Too often attention has concentrated on the oligarchic and rotten boroughs such as the one parodied by Dickens in *The Pickwick Papers* (1836). However Norwich, Great Yarmouth and even the county of Norfolk can be seen as having 'large popular constituencies' with cross-class participation:

There was extensive, though not universal, popular participation by the adult male population in the official electoral processes, undertaken to choose public representatives to serve in parliament and in a range of civic offices for a specified term . . .

Charles Dickens satirised the 'bad old' Eatanswill boroughs of England with such lethal comedy that their reputation for corrupt practices and meaningless, drink-driven partisanship is commonly taken to represent the pre-1832 electorate in its entirety. Yet there were also a number of large popular constituencies, where the state of play was quite different. Their alternative experiences are known in outline but have been insufficiently appreciated.[2]

Newspapers

It was the press which informed the electorate and wider population, shaping their political opinions and reinforcing their prejudices. One of the principal means by which the rural population kept in touch with events over the horizon was the weekly newspaper, Hannah Barker describing local papers as 'a vital link to the wider world'. Like the Sussex

[1] *proto-democracy* The pre-Reform age saw wide participation in the electoral process (E. Green, P. Corfield and C. Harvey, *Elections in Metropolitan London*, vol. 1, pp. 1, 21–2, 28–31, 55–8, 61–5; vol. 2, eg pp. 558–64).
Much is available online at London Electoral History, including full explanatory material and the database (<http://leh.ncl.ac.uk/>, accessed 6 July 2019)

[2] *popular constituencies* E. Green, P. Corfield and C. Harvey, *Elections in Metropolitan London*, vol. 1, p. 21

above The reassuringly traditional symbol of the *Norfolk Chronicle or Norwich Gazette* at its masthead, signalling stability and solidity.
In 1701 Norwich published Britain's first provincial newspaper, the *Norwich Post*. The *Norwich Gazette* followed in 1706 [*Norfolk Chronicle, 3 Apr. 1779: Norfolk Heritage Centre, Norwich*]

right Mary Hardy aged 64. Newspapers feature prominently in her diary, and it is evident that even without a vote she took a keen interest in politics.

As well as the Norwich newspapers (usually the *Mercury* rather than the *Chronicle*) she noted in Feb. 1783 that they had started taking a London paper, the *Morning Herald*; this was Foxite and radical.

Each newspaper was passed round three, four or five people in the Hardy household. They probably held onto them as they had a large stack of newspapers by 1797; many snippets from their hoard survive in the family archives today.

William Hardy had begun the practice in 1774 of committing to the diary short extracts from newsworthy items. The idea caught on and he, his wife and their son Raven embarked on a project which lasted until 1801 [*painting by Immanuel 1798: Cozens-Hardy Collection*]

---

¹ *newspapers* H. Barker, *Newspapers, Politics and English Society 1695– 1855* (Longman and Pearson Education Ltd, Harlow, 2000), p. 16. One copy of a paper had an average of five readers (pp. 47–8)

² *Herald Diary 2*: 20 Feb. 1783; *Norw. Merc.* 16 Nov. 1782.
   It is unlikely the Hardys took both the *Chronicle* and the *Mercury* at any one time

shopkeeper whom she quotes, the Hardys did not rely on one alone. As well as his Lewes paper Thomas Turner took the *London Gazette* on a regular basis.¹ It is evident from the long verbatim extracts copied by Mary Hardy and members of the family into her diary that the Hardys read both the *Norfolk Chronicle* and the *Norwich Mercury*, published weekly in Norwich. They decided in 1783, in the last weeks of the second Rockingham Administration, also to take the *Morning Herald*. This was one of many which could be supplied by agents in the capital to addresses in the country 'on very reasonable terms'.²

The Hardys read other papers and magazines as well. By 1797, when William Hardy made his inventory of the contents of their home, the counting house at Letheringsett

left William Hardy aged 66. The family relied on the Norwich newspapers for their commercial dealings, William Hardy snr and jnr occasionally placing notices over bankruptcies, public houses and other matters. The papers also provided the whole family with weekly intelligence, bringing the 'latest' despatches from the Americas, Europe, India and the empire.

In one early extract William Hardy neatly copied into his wife's diary the dramatic consequences of an earthquake in Guatemala. The topic was not as disconnected from Norfolk as it might appear, for hurricanes, earthquakes and other natural disasters affected sugar production across the Atlantic—and Mary Hardy came from a family of village shopkeepers [*painting by Immanuel 1798: Cozens-Hardy Collection*]

Hall held 37 numbers of *The Senator, or Clarendon's Parliamentary Chronicle*, also eight volumes of the *Spectator* and thirteen volumes of the *Westminster Magazine*. We know Mary Hardy read this last title as she made a separate note of a remedy for the relief of headache and asthma taken from a February 1780 issue of the *Westminster Magazine*, then presumably to hand.[1]

William Hardy's meticulous inventory reveals the family's desire to keep abreast of developments on the national stage. As manufacturers this was essential. Government regulations and changes in the various duties payable on malt, beer and licences, among many other items, spewed forth from Westminster and Whitehall. The Hardys held a large stock, measured by weight, of Acts of Parliament and newspapers.[2]

[1] *Letheringsett Diary 2*, app. D2.C, p. 411–12; *Diary 2*, endnotes, p. 393.
The Senator recorded the proceedings of the Lords and Commons, each issue costing 6d

[2] *stock* 'A large quantity of Acts of Parliament, old school books, newspapers etc etc, supposed 3 stone' (*Diary 2*, app. D2.C, p. 411, William Hardy's inventory, 12 and 13 Sept. 1797).
3 stone is 42 lb in weight (19 kg)

The *Norwich Mercury* is generally more useful than the *Norfolk Chronicle* for providing a commentary on the diary and picking up Mary Hardy's allusions. It was directed at the commercial classes, whereas the *Chronicle* gave greater coverage to clerical and gentry subjects likely to appeal to Church-and-King Tory readers. Most advertisements and public information notices, as would be expected, were duplicated, appearing in both papers on the same Saturday. The political tinge of the owners is not marked, and it is clear that in the Norwich press during the years of Mary Hardy's diary there was no single controlling elite.

In the early days their political stance had been more sharply defined. Henry Crossgrove, from 1706 owner and printer of the *Norwich Gazette* (later, under John Crouse and then William Stevenson, renamed the *Norfolk Chronicle or Norwich Gazette*), was a Jacobite Tory, while William Chase of the *Norwich Mercury* was a Whig.[1] By the 1770s, with Jacobitism long departed as an issue, the papers' political divide had become blurred. The *Mercury* was more informative in the French wars on the activities of the Volunteers (as seen opposite) than its rival, even though Volunteering was more likely to be close to the hearts of loyal, patriotic Tory readers than to Norfolk's often anti-war and Foxite Whigs. On the whole the Norwich press at this time was not as fiercely partisan as that of many other cities and towns; it seems to have wished to secure wide appeal.[2]

Both the Norwich newspapers gave very extensive coverage of the Court and Royal Family, governmental changes and parliamentary debates, diplomatic reports from embassies and wartime dispatches from the front, all customarily copied from the London press. It would be wrong however to characterise their readers as desiring only to broaden their minds. A myriad of tightly-set notices and advertisements would occupy the whole of at least two pages of the four-page broadsheet, the rules separating them forming an elaborate, synchopated chequerboard anchored by the strict discipline of the design. The dazzle worsened as advertising copy swelled during the diary years, resulting in more columns to the page and a very noticeably smaller type which would have proved ruinous to the eyes of the compositors and their readers. Very occasionally the

[1] *political stance* Where one town had two newspapers it was likely they represented differing views (H. Barker, *Newspapers, Politics and English Society*, p. 116; see also pp. 108–20). For the growth of provincial papers see pp. 30, 34–6; for the *Gazette*'s editorial lines see pp. 75, 134, 136.
    The provincial press blossomed after a slow start following the lapsing of the Printing Act in 1695. A useful list of titles and dates, with Norwich in the lead from Sept. 1701, is by G.A. Cranfield, *A Hand-list of English Provincial Newspapers and Periodicals 1700–1760* (Cambridge Bibliographical Society monograph no. 2, Bowes & Bowes, London, 1961).
    The paper that was to become the *Norwich Mercury* started possibly in 1714, although that title dates from 12 Feb. 1726 (G.A. Cranfield, *A Hand-list of English Provincial Newspapers and Periodicals*, pp. 16–17). The *Mercury* has since traced a continuous history to the *Eastern Daily Press* of the present day.
    William Chase snr, printer of the *Mercury* for 30 years, died in 1781 aged 53 (*Norw. Merc.* 3 Mar. 1781)

[2] *partisan* Hannah Barker gives an overview (*Newspapers,*

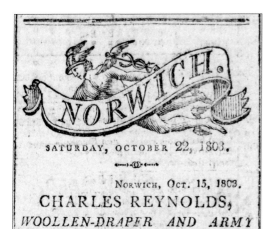

SATURDAY, OCTOBER 22, 1803.

✦━━━✦·⟨◉⟩·✦━━━✦

NORWICH, OCT. 15, 1803.

CHARLES REYNOLDS,
WOOLLEN-DRAPER AND ARMY CLOTHIER,

BEGS leave to inform his Friends and the Public in General, that he can supply every kind of Uniform, Arms, and Accoutrements, on the shortest notice, and most liberal terms—An Infantry Volunteer may be equipped with the following Articles ; viz. a Regulation Jacket, Cap, Feather, Stock and Clasps, Queue and Rosette, with Muskito Trowsers, for 2*l.* 7*s.*—Officers furnished with Regimental Hats and Accoutrements of every description, on the most liberal terms.

─────────────────

MILITARY PROMOTIONS,
From the London Gazette.

Swaffham Gentlemen and Yeomanry Cavalry.—Lawrence William Stephens, Gent. to be Lieutenant.

Brooke Volunteer Infantry.—John Dix, Esq. to be Captain ; John Whall, Gent. to be Lieutenant ; and Benjamin Johnson, Gent. to be Ensign.

Catton Volunteer Infantry.—Jeremiah Ives, Esq. to be Captain ; Sir Edward Berry, Knt. and the Hon. Frederick Paul Irby, to be Lieutenants ; James Agassis, Gent. to be Ensign.

Holt Volunteer Infantry.—Charles Hewitt, Esq. to be Captain ; William Withers and William Hardy, jun. Gents. to be Lieutenants.

Harleston Volunteers.—John Keirich, Esq. to be Captain ; Henry Fox and George Carthew, Gents. to be Lieutenants ; John Doughty, Gent. to be Ensign.

left The county noticeboard. Hermes (for the Greeks) or Mercurius (for the Romans), winged messenger of the gods, carries news bulletins across Norwich and Norfolk in Oct. 1803. This printer's ornament was a weekly feature of the *Norwich Mercury*, drawing the reader's eye to the start of local news.

The edition of 22 Oct. 1803 contains a military tailor's prices for equipping Volunteer forces with uniforms. Then follows a long series of appointments and promotions within the county's Volunteer units, of which this is just a part, copied from the *London Gazette*.

The Holt Volunteer Infantry has re-formed, and for the first time a Hardy is given as a member: William Hardy jnr is announced as a lieutenant in the unit. He served alongside and under two Holt attorneys, as the next chapter relates.

This paper and its rival, the *Norfolk Chronicle*, performed a vital service in keeping readers informed of local issues, political developments and the progress of the war; their vitality helped to form a highly politically aware electorate [*Norfolk Heritage Centre, Norwich*]

─────────────────

Politics and English Society, pp. 116–20)

─────────────────

[1] *broadsheet* For the first time since 1773, when the diary opened, the *Mercury* of 28 May 1803 carried a two-page (half-sheet) supplement to cover the outbreak of hostilities, the Navy at action stations and parliamentary debates

news reports were too long to squeeze into the four-page layout of the one large broadsheet, printed double-sided with a centre fold.[1]

[1] *text* For this reason the four volumes forming *The Diary of Mary Hardy 1773–1809* (2013) contain editorial sidenotes peppered on almost every page with extracts from the *Norwich Mercury*

[2] *innkeepers* Diary *1*: 26 Apr. 1774. Hickling's successor at the Black Lion, Robert Humphry, ended up in the debtors' gaol at the Castle. The brewer was about to meet Clarke's creditors, and may have decided to stay his hand until hearing from them (*Diary 1*: 28 Apr. 1774). An earlier Buxton notice composed by William Hardy is illustrated in *Diary 1*, p. 23

[3] *Boorne and Neve* Diary *1*: 8 Feb. 1781. The notice appeared in the *Norwich Mercury* only two days later (reproduced in *Diary 1*, p.409). The stock had been valued the previous week by Richard Bacon of Norwich (the future publisher of the *Mercury*)

[4] *agents Norw. Merc.* 6 Dec. 1788. Alsop was himself very soon to fall victim to the financial pressures of the time and see his house to let as part of his prolonged bankruptcy proceedings. William Hardy, as an assignee, submitted copy for the notices (eg *Diary 2*, p. 369)

The commercial advertisements provide valuable insights into eighteenth-century provincial life. No proper understanding can be gained of Mary Hardy's diary without reference to them, as they present the other side of the laconic one-sided conversation that is her text.[1] The public and private notices make sense of the world in which the Hardys traded. They proffer advice on how to comply with new taxes and duties and attest to the high turnover of breweries and public houses. More vividly than any table of rates of liquidation and bankruptcy the auction advertisements present a dismal catalogue of the ill-founded optimism, dashed hopes and financial ruin of farmers, merchants, shopkeepers, manufacturers, traders and innkeepers.

The diary enables us to follow how these notices came to appear. In March 1774 two of William Hardy's innkeepers at his tied houses were in difficulty. Matthew Hickling of Buxton soon had his goods seized in lieu of rent and John Clarke of Strumpshaw was about to be consigned to Norwich Castle for debt. William Hardy drafted notices for their houses but then changed his mind, recording in his wife's diary: 'Wrote two advertisements for the Black Lion [at Buxton] and Strumpshaw Shoulder of Mutton, did not send them to the printers'.[2] While still at Coltishall he drafted the long notice in the *Norwich Mercury* for the auction by Robert Ansell of the stock in trade of the timber merchants Boorne and Neve, who were far deeper in debt than the innkeepers. Mary Hardy noted that her husband 'went to Boorne's afternoon to meet Robert Ansell to send an advertisement to the printer, came home evening 10'.[3]

As Coltishall lay only seven miles from Norwich the auctioneer could get the notice quickly to the printers. Areas further from the offices were served by agents—often innkeepers—who would forward the copy to Norwich. In 1788 two innkeepers supplied by William Hardy, John Overton of Holt and Isaac Alsop of Cromer, were acting as agents for the *Norwich Mercury* and accepting notices from local people for publication.[4]

Although the two newspapers were published on Saturdays it would appear from the diary that the Hardys did not receive their copies until the Sunday, or at least they did not read them until then. Mary Hardy, her husband and son Raven tended to report items of news and write up the extracts on Sundays, presumably reflecting the time it took for carriers and agents to get the paper into the countryside. Holt, probably the central distribution point in Mary Hardy's part of north Norfolk, lay 23 miles from the city.[1]

The Norwich newspapers served as the public noticeboard for the whole county and even the region: Bury St Edmunds, Ipswich, Wisbech and Cambridge, as well as London, featured in the Norwich press. Local papers had a vital role as a public information service. In the days before railways and the penny post it was inconvenient and expensive for service providers and officialdom, whether civil or ecclesiastical, to send out individual letters to customers, clients, taxpayers, parish officers and the rest. Instead they expected the paper to be scanned for news of the next turnpike trust meeting, navigation commissioners' meeting, land-tax collection day, bishop's confirmation, archdeacon's visitation, or invitation to tender for supplying malt to a house of industry or bricks and timber for a navigation. Often the newspaper was the sole means by which committee members learned of the date and place of the next meeting; or parish officers were told of the date of the next quarter sessions; or farmers heard of the next stage in the complex process of enclosing the open fields and diverting roads.[2]

The private Act of Parliament of 1807, steered through the Commons by the Independent Whig county MP Sir Jacob Henry Astley, contained specific instructions on the method by which the enclosure commissioners for Holt and Letheringsett were to communicate with all those affected by the proposals:

. . . And be it further enacted, that the said Commissioners shall and they are hereby required to give or cause to be given public notice by advertisement to be inserted in the *Norwich Mercury*, or some other public newspaper to be circulated in the said county of Norfolk, of the time and place of their first and every other meeting for executing the powers hereby vested in them, eight days at the least before every such meeting . . .[3]

Largely unexplored is the press's function as a tool in the home education of children, and thus in the moulding of young minds who would, if holding an appropriate property

[1] *distribution* Hannah Barker emphasises that newspapers relied heavily on sales to country readers. The papers were by no means produced solely for the town or city where the presses were situated (H. Barker, *Newspapers, Politics and English Society*, pp. 41–2).
The role of newspapers is also covered at the end of vol. 3, chap. 5

[2] *meetings* See chap. 2 on the Aylsham navigation; also vol. 2, chap. 3 on enclosure, and vol. 3, chap. 6 on the Peace.
On 21 June 1794 the Norwich papers raised their prices from 3½d to 4d, reflecting the increased duty on paper; changes in stamp duty had earlier raised the price from 3d. They were however still available to all. Papers often passed through many hands, were read for free in the public house, and could be read aloud to the illiterate over a pint

[3] *Act* NRO: MS 18623/69, Holt and Letheringsett Enclosure Act 1807, p. 5. Despite the landed interest associated with enclosure it was not the Tory *Norfolk Chronicle* but the Whiggish trade-dominated paper which was singled out.
In the event both titles were used for the enclosure notices

[1] *petered out* Mary Hardy made her last, brief, reference to a newspaper item on 11 Nov. 1800. The last by her husband followed the press coverage of the celebration dinner the village gave its poor on the French truce of Nov. 1801 (*Diary 4*)

[2] *peace* See the section on the issues, where 62 peers and MPs voted for peace in an amendment to the King's Speech of Jan. 1794 (p. 485)

below right Nine-year-old Raven Hardy takes over in the diary: part of his long entry for 15 Mar. 1777, copied from the *Norfolk Chronicle* that day. His mother first notes the men's work, including beer deliveries to Horstead, Horning and Tuttington ('Tottontown').

Raven was fascinated by the trial and execution of James Hill for setting fire to a royal dockyard (a capital offence) and attempting to do so elsewhere. Hill was hanged at Portsmouth and gibbeted at Blockhouse Point.

News from home and overseas appealed to Raven from his early years, but he did not live to exercise his vote [*Cozens-Hardy Collection*]

qualification or Freedom of a borough, go to the polls from the age of 21. In an age when school textbooks and primers were dull and uninspiring, the newspaper, despite its tiny print and great unwieldiness for short arms, presented an absorbing, animated panorama. It gave vivid, often lurid coverage of criminal cases, the speech from the gallows, indelicate domestic disputes, accidents at home and on the road, attacks by rabid dogs, the last dying days of the consumptive, suicides, shipwrecks, heroic endeavours by the seamen and soldiers of His Majesty, and, for the women of the house, descriptions of the silk and silver-filigree gowns and ostrich feathers worn at court by the young princesses.

William Hardy had begun the practice in 1774 of committing to the diary short extracts from newsworthy items. The idea caught on, and he, his wife and Raven set off on a course which was to last until it petered out in the later Letheringsett years.[1] One of the brewer's own insertions into his wife's diary, on those voting for peace a year into the French war in 1794, is illustrated later in this chapter.[2]

The studious Raven, born in November 1767, evidently scanned the local paper with close attention from the time he could read fluently. He occasionally shouldered the burden—apparently willingly, since he kept to his task—of copying into his mother's diary long extracts from a strange assortment of news items. Some were exceptionally long, such as the marathon 5200-word transcription by the thirteen-year-old of a murder trial in Warwick at the time the family had just moved to their new home; he may have felt at a loose end in the disorder of the household.[1]

Raven favoured dramatic scenes as well as criminality: the execution at Portsmouth of James Hill, known as 'John the Painter', swinging from a specially-rigged gallows which had once served as the mizzenmast of HMS *Arethusa*; and, the following week, the execution of John Rye at Norwich for murder: Rye 'was but 25 years of age but had run a great length in wickedness'.[2] At Letheringsett Raven copied the detailed report of the capsizing of the first-rate ship of the line HMS *Royal George*—at the time of her launching the largest ship ever built for the Royal Navy—with the drowning of over 700 men, women and children including Rear-Admiral Richard Kempenfelt.[3]

The transcriptions were at their height when Raven was young and still at school. By contrast the less scholarly William, born in April 1770, made only one attempt at the task. He briefly relieved Raven during his elder brother's heroic transcription of the news of the storms of New Year's Day 1779 which wrought havoc around the kingdom. The children's report occupies sixteen pages and 3310 words in their mother's manuscript.[4]

William Hardy, who had led the way, evidently considered these extracts a useful exercise. They recorded for posterity the happenings of the time; perhaps he also wished to encourage his family to broaden their horizons and his sons to polish their handwriting. His younger son did not share this view. William decided against introducing newspaper extracts into the diary he started in 1793 for the apprentice Henry Raven to maintain (published in full in *Diary 3*), and into his own building diary for Letheringsett Hall 1832–34.

Mary Ann, born in November 1773 and for whom writing seems to have been something of an effort, never made

[1] *murder trial Diary 2*: 12 Apr. 1781; Diary MS: 12 Apr. 1781.
The transcription occupies 23 MS pages in the diary.
At the age of 15 Raven started studying for the Law with a N. Walsham attorney; he died in Feb. 1787 half-way through his articles.
For the training and schooling of the Hardy children see vol. 1, chaps 5 and 6

[2] *Hill and Rye Diary 1*: 15 Mar., 22 Mar. 1777. For the connections of John the Painter and his scheme to force the British Government to end its war in America, see N.L. York, 'Burning the dockyard: John the Painter and the American Revolution', *The Portsmouth Papers*, no. 71 (Portsmouth City Council, 2001)

[3] *Royal George Diary 2*: 27 Nov. 1782. The ship was in home waters off Southsea, but had been deliberately heeled over to clear an intake pipe while the lower gun-ports were kept open to load supplies for an expedition to Gibraltar

[4] *storms Diary 1*: 9 Jan. 1779. It was 'the most violent storm of wind ever remembered'.
From an early age William made entries in his mother's diary on day-to-day matters in the family business

[1] *diaries* Those of William Hardy jnr 1832–34 and his nephew W.H. Cozens-Hardy 1833–95, held in the private family collection, have not been published.
The surname Hardy in the diarist's branch of the family would have ended with the death of William Hardy jnr in 1842 had not the only child of his sister Mary Ann and her husband Jeremiah Cozens, named William Hardy Cozens, adopted the name Cozens-Hardy under the terms of his uncle's will.
The story of the family after Mary Hardy's death in 1809 is told in the Epilogue

[2] *town* The total population of Holt, one mile from Letheringsett, was 1004 in 1801.
Fakenham (11 miles from Letheringsett) had a population of 1236; Aylsham (13½ miles) 1667; N. Walsham (16 miles) 1959: see the front endpaper map

[3] *under-represented* L. Namier, *The Structure of Politics at the Accession of George III*, p. 62

[4] *pocket boroughs* Thetford fell under the influence of the Duke of Grafton and his family at Euston Hall, Suff., and Rising under that of the Earl of Orford and Earl of Suffolk

press extracts in her mother's diary. However she or her brother may have encouraged her son to adopt the practice. The 62-year-long diary of William Hardy Cozens-Hardy is crammed with news items relating to the weather, astronomical phenomena, politics and elections, and contains some pasted press clippings.[1]

Although the Hardys and (from 1842) Cozens-Hardys were firmly established in their beloved Norfolk soil in what might seem an isolated rural area, where a town of a thousand persons was the largest settlement in the neighbourhood, the newspapers helped them to feel connected to the regional capital of Norwich and to the seat of government in London.[2] Newspapers were instrumental in fostering a *county*wide spirit, a sense of a Norfolk community with a broad common experience, above the feeling of belonging to a village or market town with its set of elected parochial officers. It was largely by means of newspapers, and less by direct personal ways, that candidates in parliamentary elections communicated their (brief) political manifestoes to voters, and elections occupy the central part of this chapter.

The mechanics of elections

Eighteenth-century Norfolk, like many other areas, was severely under-represented in Parliament. It fell into the category of 'the northern counties'. This generous interpretation of the concept of the North embraces all the counties lying north of a line running from Bristol to the Thames estuary. More than 40 per cent of the House of Commons was elected by ten counties south of that line.[3] Norfolk returned twelve Members of Parliament from its six two-member seats: the county, the boroughs of Norwich, Great Yarmouth and King's Lynn, and the pocket boroughs of Thetford and Castle Rising, these last two being firmly under the influence of local grandees.[4]

The 245 English constituencies, of which 238 were two-member seats, returned 489 MPs at the time of Mary Hardy's diary. Norfolk, one of England's largest counties in geographical extent, had twelve MPs; but Cornwall had 44, Devon had 26 and Wiltshire 34. Cornwall's wealth of boroughs was responsible for its decided over-representation. Twenty-one Cornish boroughs, returning 42 Members, had a total electorate (those qualified to vote, but not necessarily turning up at the polls) between them of less than 1400. This figure was under half the number of those actually casting their votes for the seat of Norwich, in just *one* constituency.[1]

In 1801 the total population of Norfolk, including Norwich, was 273,371 persons.[2] Cornwall then had 192,281 persons. As a result Norfolk had one MP for every 22,781 persons; Cornwall had one Member for every 4370. Many other such calculations can be made to display the disparity across the country. The freedom from over-mighty 'interest' (influence) enjoyed by the great majority of the electors across Norfolk may explain the vitality and at times redbloodedness of its political life. Elections mattered, and the individual voter, other than in Thetford and Castle Rising, could see himself forming part of a large throng surging round town centre market places and engaging in a process far removed from the passivity of a tiny borough electorate.

As explained earlier, under the Septennial Act Britons in theory went to the polls only every seven years. We have seen that this could be circumvented for individual seats when candidates arranged to stand unopposed. However the system could work the other way in that the seven years might not run their full course. A general election had also to be held within six months of the death of the monarch, as for instance in February 1715 (after Queen Anne's death in 1714) and in March 1761 (after George II's death in 1760). Further, a by-election was required when the sitting Member accepted a government post, on the argument that he had thereby been 'bought'. By being transformed into a government lackey he had lost the independent judgment valued by his supporters, and must re-submit himself to the electorate for their approbation or rejection. And a lifespan of seven years could prove beyond the capabilities of individual administrations.

Mary Hardy covers, in varying degrees of detail, fourteen parliamentary elections between 1773 and 1809. These, consisting of eight general elections, four by-elections and two re-runs following Commons scrutinies disallowing the result, occurred in the years 1774, 1776, 1780, 1784, 1786, 1787, 1790, 1794, 1796, 1799, 1802, 1806, 1807, and again in 1807.[3] Thus in the 35½-year span of her diary she refers

[1] *Cornwall* L. Namier, *The Structure of Politics at the Accession of George III*, pp. 62, 299.
Pocket boroughs had their uses as bolt holes when candidates failed in their first-choice seat. When the 1806 Norfolk result was overturned after a scrutiny the unseated Windham secured the pocket borough of New Romney, Kent (R.W. Ketton-Cremer, *Felbrigg: The story of a house* (Futura Publications, London, 1982; 1st pub. 1962), p. 252). Other examples are given later

[2] *population* Discussed in vol. 1, chap. 1; see esp. table 1.1.1. These figures include women and children

[3] *14 elections* Individual campaigns are not described in detail here. Instead a brief account appears in the Diary volumes against the appropriate entry.
Coverage of Norfolk and Norwich politics in this period is also examined by B.D. Hayes, 'Politics in Norfolk, 1750–1832'; by C.B. Jewson, *The Jacobin City: A portrait of Norwich 1788–1802* (Blackie & Son, Glasgow and London, 1975); and M. Knights, 'Politics, 1660–1835', in *Norwich since 1550*, ed. C. Rawcliffe and R. Wilson (Hambledon & London, London, 2004), pp. 168–92

[1] *elections* The list of the dates, candidates and votes 1660–1790 inclusive is given by R. Beatniffe, *The Norfolk Tour*, pp. 298–9.

Two-member constituencies had also prevailed in 17th-century England. The situation was different in Wales and Scotland in the 17th and 18th centuries. All 24 Welsh MPs and 45 Scottish were in one-member seats. England elected almost 88% of the House of Commons (L. Namier, *The Structure of Politics at the Accession of George III*, p. 62; see also pp. 63–157 for an analysis of the system).

Namier lists the boroughs where the nomination lay with a controlling hand or hands or where influence was strong. As well as Thetford (both Members) the Duke of Grafton influenced the election of one for the corporation borough of Bury St Edmunds, Suff.; here its very small electorate of merchants and tradesmen consisted solely of those forming the corporation. The choice of the other candidate lay with the Earl of Bristol (L. Namier, pp. 145, 144). England had 27 corporation electorates

[2] *Norwich* R. Beatniffe, *The Norfolk Tour*, pp. 78–80

to fourteen elections in which she and her circle took an active interest, averaging one every two and a half years. All were for the borough of Norwich or the county of Norfolk. However not all were contested elections.

For these elections she actually records eighteen distinct campaigns out of 22, the breakdown being ten city campaigns (she omits two, for 1796 and 1802) and eight county (she omits those of 1790 and 1797). The eight general elections followed by the diarist were held in 1774, 1780, 1784, 1790, 1796, 1802, 1806 and 1807; the four by-elections in 1775, 1786, 1794 and 1799. As the list of dates shows, the administrations in power 1773–1809 were either unable to hold together for the full seven-year period or chose to dissolve themselves well before their seven years were up. The by-elections were occasioned variously by the demise of the sitting MPs Wenman Coke (Norfolk 1776) and the Hon. Henry Hobart (Norwich 1799), the raising of Sir Harbord Harbord to the peerage as Lord Suffield (Norwich 1786), and the acceptance by William Windham of a government post as Secretary at War (Norwich 1794). Parliamentary scrutinies followed the city by-election of 1786, resulting in a re-run the following year, and also the county poll of 1806, resulting in a re-run the following year—only two months before another general election in 1807.

The situation is rendered more complex by the fact that many of the eighteen election campaigns went uncontested; any image created by these bald statistics of an electorate constantly mounting the rickety stairs of the polling booth is deceptive. In the hundred-year period before William Hardy's death in 1811 there were only five contested elections at county level in Norfolk: in 1715, 1734, 1768, 1802 and 1806. This contrasts sharply with the experience of previous generations. In the 28 years 1668–96 there had been thirteen contested county elections, with two more in 1702 and 1710.[1] The dynamics of returning two men to represent Norfolk were very different in the eighteenth century from those of an earlier age. But the city of Norwich's 2500–3000 virile voters wanted a fight—and customarily were granted one, there being twelve contested city elections 1700–70.[2]

Norfolk was merely following the pattern of the time. In the decades before the diary opened in 1773 there were very few county polls. In 1747 only three of the forty counties went to the polls; in 1754 only five; and in 1761 four. None of these was Norfolk.[1]

The costs of a countywide campaign would often prove prohibitive. Norfolk had a large electorate. In the 1802 general election 7253 voters, casting 11,445 votes, clambered onto the polling booths. In the 1806 general election 6904 voters cast 11,205 votes.[2] Elections would be spread over days. The candidates' agents and stewards would bring in voters possessed of the requisite property qualification but who lived in London and other places beyond the county boundary. In his analysis of election expenses, B.D. Hayes records that in 1768 the victorious Sir Edward Astley and his defeated ally Wenman Coke spent £30,000, while Sir Armine Wodehouse (also defeated) and Thomas de Grey (elected) spent 'much more than £10,000'. In 1806 Colonel the Hon. John Wodehouse's outgoings amounted to £19,325, which proved insufficient to secure the seat. He had dropped out on the eve of the final day of polling, partly as he was behind on each day's results and partly as funds had run out. The expenses of the two who defeated him, T.W. Coke and William Windham, amounted to £33,000.[3] Such figures were not out of the ordinary in large, hotly-contested seats.[4]

The county poll stayed open for days, but only one vote-casting attendance was allowed per property qualification. The *Mercury*, fascinated by the electoral process, reported after the 1802 county contest that a 74-year-old watchmaker from Ashwellthorpe, William Huggins, had voted early and then died. His son and heir, so the newspaper announced, promptly came to the city and voted in the same election 'in right of the same freehold'.[5] However the pollbook records only one Huggins vote, presumably the father's, plumping for John Wodehouse; the son had made a futile journey.

Plumping, the casting of just one vote in multi-member constituencies, could have a pronounced effect on the result. It excited the psephologists of the time, as will be shown in the section on voters: John Wodehouse, the single Tory candidate, fell behind in 1806 in part as many of his supporters failed to heed his call for plumping. The creators of the London Electoral Database draw attention to the opportunities for sophisticated casting of votes in this period:

[1] *counties* L. Namier, *The Structure of Politics at the Accession of George III*, p. 65.
One of the five in 1754 was Oxfordshire, which had gone uncontested since 1710. The electors' hunger for a battle gave William Hogarth the opportunity to record the 'Guzzledown' campaign on canvas in his series *The Election*

[2] *Norfolk Norw. Merc.* 22 Nov. 1806; 'Comparative view of the Plumpers . . . 1802 and 1806', a table in R.M. Bacon's Norfolk pollbook of 1806 (unpag.); see also, in this chapter, table 4.8.3. A few votes had been disallowed in 1806, reducing the number from 6933

[3] *expenses* B.D. Hayes, 'Politics in Norfolk, 1750–1832', p. 431. This last figure for Coke and Windham included the cost of their defence against a petition to unseat them.
The greatest outlay for Edmond Wodehouse in 1817 was on entertainment at inns and on 'carriages, etc' to convey supporters who were being called out (Hayes, pp. 431–4)

[4] *expenses* L. Namier, *The Structure of Politics at the Accession of George III*, pp. 164–6

[5] *watchmaker Norw. Merc.* 24 July 1802

¹ *plumping* E. Green, P. Corfield and C. Harvey, *Elections in Metropolitan London*, vol. I, pp. 177–8.
'Splitters' divided their votes between parties, factions or allies, as did William Hardy in 1768 (table 4.8.1)

² *third man* James Mingay of Thetford was nominated without his knowledge to challenge Windham in the 1794 Norwich by-election. He wrote from London express-ing his astonishment (*Norw. Merc.* 19 July 1794)

³ *excise officer* He is shown under 'country voters' as an exciseman living at E. Dereham. For William Hardy's voting record 1768–1806 in city and county elections see table 4.8.1.
The Norwich property is never referred to in his wife's diary and has not been identified; the 1786 pollbook lists the place of his freehold as being in Timberhill, Norwich.
He probably sold it between 1790 and 1794, the last city poll in which he voted being the general election of 1790.
As he was not a Freeman of the city his voting rights were not acquired by that route

At the time of casting their votes, electors could distinguish between the candidate who stood at the head of the poll and one who was fighting for survival. This knowledge was reinforced because elec-tions frequently continued for some days, and the state of the poll was published on posters and in the newspapers . . .

Electors were under no obligation to use all, or indeed any, of their votes . . . It [plumping] meant not only casting one vote in favour of the preferred candidate, but, in effect, giving a negative to the others.

Election agents assiduously sought plumpers when their candi-date was standing without a running mate, since the tactical denial of votes to rival candidates could have a marked effect.¹

The city of Norwich presents a great contrast with Norfolk. Large boroughs with a diverse electorate did not like to be cheated of a contest. If it looked as though only two can-didates were venturing to come forward—understandably, given the possible financial commitment—there would be a frantic, last-minute search for the 'third man' even if, as in William Windham's case in 1780 quoted at the head of this chapter, the figure hit upon was wholly unaware of his nomination.²

Although she lived in the countryside Mary Hardy records the city elections. These were almost always excit-ing, hard-fought affairs both electorally and at street level; jibes, insults, fists and staves would fly during the poll and after the declaration, as she recorded in her entry for the city by-election of 1786 transcribed at the chapter head. The diarist also had a more direct interest. Her husband held property in Norwich which enabled him to vote in its elec-tions, his first appearance in a county or city pollbook being for Norwich in the general election of 1768 while he was still an excise officer in East Dereham and Raven was a baby.³

Many property-owning electors (as opposed to impov-erished Freemen, such as the Norwich handloom weavers) were able to cast their votes in more than one constituency. The polls thus had to be staggered to permit them to get to individual ballots. Nationwide, general elections would continue over a period of weeks. The poll for Norwich, usu-ally a one- or two-day affair, was held some days before that for Norfolk, which, while not so protracted as those in some other constituencies, was generally held over five days plus any intervening Sunday; that for 1802 lasted from 12 July

above Norwich market place and the church of St Peter Man-croft. Unstable-looking wooden polling booths were set up here for city and county elections, serving as the sole polling centre for both 　　*[drawing by J.P. Neale; engraving by J. Scott 1812]*

to 20 or 21 July. For colour and drama the 1806 Norfolk election has parallels with Oxfordshire in 1754 (Hogarth's 'Guzzledown'), and with Westminster in 1784—the latter famously open for forty days and the subject of a scrutiny and numerous prints and cartoons.[1]

Not only did the elector need to make arrangements to journey often long distances to cast his vote, with only one polling centre, but the candidate could judge whether to go to the expense of calling out his backwoodsmen. The results of the day's polling were published every evening, enabling the campaign to be dissected by the candidate's agents and pundits.[2] However the politically committed Hardy family did not wait to be called out. In 1802 father and son, on the first of the only two occasions during the long span of the diary on which they had an opportunity to cast their county

[1] *1806 Norfolk election* Its story is told with wit and gusto by R.W. Ketton-Cremer in 'The county election of 1806', *A Norfolk Gallery* (Faber and Faber, London, 1948), pp. 215–37

[2] *daily results* The breakdown day by day of the county poll was tabulated in the *Norwich Mercury*, 22 Nov. 1806.

In the 1784 city poll Windham defeated Hobart only through the weight of London voters brought up in his support (*Norw. Merc.* 3 Apr. 1784)

[1] *1802 election Diary 4.*
The diarist did not
attend, having three
visitors staying from
London. Coke is
pronounced 'Cook'; the
diarist also reveals the
pronunciation of the
Tory Wodehouse.
  Sir Jacob Henry
Astley had not yet
moved from his old
home at Burgh into
Melton Constable Hall.
Coke was well ahead of
his fellow Whig, with
the Tory close-tailing
Astley. The final result
was Coke 4317, Astley
3612, Wodehouse 3517.
  In 1806 neither
William Hardy nor his
son was able to get to
the polls early. William
was in London, and his
father minding the
business at home.
William voted the
moment he got to the
city on the third day,
and his father on the
fourth (*Diary 4*: 17
Nov., 18 Nov. 1806).
  They, and Jeremiah
Cozens from Sprows-
ton, voted for Coke and
Windham, the Lether-
ingsett pollbook entry
for 1806 being illus-
trated opposite.
  The 1806 Lethering-
sett voters made very
distinct choices. There
were five plumpers for
the Tory candidate,
including the rector
John Burrell and his
brother. Peter Rouse,
later of Letheringsett
Watermill, was a splitter

votes, arrived in Norwich near the start of polling, on the
second day:

[1802] JULY 13, TUESDAY A fine day. Mr Hardy and William set
off for Norwich to the county election morning 8. The contending
parties are Astley and Coke, Woodhouse [Wodehouse] and Windham, but Windham early declined. The contest began yesterday
and still continue very sharp . . .

JULY 15, THURSDAY A fine day. Mr Hardy and William came
home evening 8. The contest between Astley and Wodehouse still
continue very sharp . . .

JULY 21, WEDNESDAY A very wet day . . . The election closed for
the county of Norfolk this evening in favour of Mr Coke of
Holkham and Sir Jacob Astley of Borough [Burgh Parva].[1]

The diarist never mentions how her family voted, but the
pollbook shows that her husband and son and the miller
and millwright Thomas Youngman were the only three of
the eight Letheringsett residents in 1802 to vote for Astley and Coke; the rector plumped for Wodehouse. She is
inaccurate in saying that Windham was standing at first. He
had declined to do so at the outset after fighting Norwich
unsuccessfully a few days earlier, but it is interesting that
her family set off from Letheringsett expecting him to be
one of the candidates. From Whissonsett her nephew Nathaniel Raven voted as did the Hardys, but her other Whissonsett nephew Henry Goggs plumped for Coke.
  As recorded by the diarist in the quotation of 1786 at the
head of this chapter, the 'country' voters whom she knew
would sometimes club together to share the great expense of
travelling to Norwich. We never hear whether they claimed
their expenses from the candidates, but it is unlikely they
did so; the Hardys and many of their circle had a strong
appetite for politics and were hardly reluctant voters. However they might well have been dined for free, or 'treated', at
a city centre inn set aside for supporters.
  On those occasions when the diarist identifies the members of the local contingent taking to the road to attend an
election it can be concluded, using the pollbooks, that the
solidarity of the chaise or cart reflected shared political persuasions. This could be the case even for an uncontested
election or if the fellow traveller came only to cheer. When
William Hardy set off for Norwich with his wife for the 1806

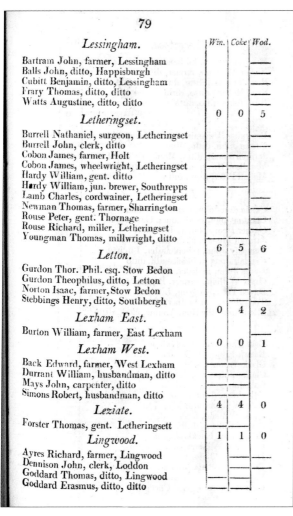

79	Win.	Coke	Wod.
Lessingham.			
Bartram John, farmer, Lessingham			—
Balls John, ditto, Happisburgh			—
Cubitt Benjamin, ditto, Lessingham			—
Frary Thomas, ditto, ditto			—
Watts Augustine, ditto, ditto			—
Letheringset.	0	0	5
Burrell Nathaniel, surgeon, Letheringset			—
Burrell John, clerk, ditto			—
Cobon James, farmer, Holt	—		
Cobon James, wheelwright, Letheringset	—		
Hardy William, gent. ditto	—		
Hardy William, jun. brewer, Southrepps			—
Lamb Charles, cordwainer, Letheringset			—
Newman Thomas, farmer, Sharrington			—
Rouse Peter, gent. Thornage	—		
Rouse Richard, miller, Letheringset	—		
Youngman Thomas, millwright, ditto	—		
Letton.	6	5	6
Gurdon Thor. Phil. esq. Stow Bedon	—		
Gurdon Theophilus, ditto, Letton	—		
Norton Isaac, farmer, Stow Bedon			—
Stebbings Henry, ditto, Southbergh			—
Lexham East.	0	4	2
Burton William, farmer, East Lexham			—
Lexham West.	0	0	1
Back Edward, farmer, West Lexham	—		
Durrant William, husbandman, ditto	—		
Mays John, carpenter, ditto	—		
Simons Robert, husbandman, ditto	—		
Leziate.	4	4	0
Forster Thomas, gent. Letheringsett			
Lingwood.	1	1	0
Ayres Richard, farmer, Lingwood			—
Dennison John, clerk, Loddon			—
Goddard Thomas, ditto, Lingwood			—
Goddard Erasmus, ditto, ditto			—

left A page from the Norfolk pollbook for the general election of 1806. Turnout was high, and the radical Whig T.W. Coke (with 4118 votes) and his uneasy ally, Pitt's former war minister William Windham (with 3722), defeated the Tory John Wodehouse (3365).

The divided opinion in Letheringsett (where the Revd John Burrell voted Tory) contrasts with Lessingham and W. Lexham, where local loyalties predominated.

This pollbook provides some of the raw material for the tables in this chapter. It is arranged by place of residence, the place name after the voter's occupation recording the whereabouts of his property qualification. For William Hardy jnr this was the Crown at Southrepps—one of his many tied houses which he could have quoted [*The Poll for Knights of the Shire for the County of Norfolk* (*R.M. Bacon, Norwich, 1806*): Cozens-Hardy Collection]

county election he went in a hired postchaise with his Cley attorney John Smith, who like his companion voted for Coke and Windham.[1] When the Revd John Burrell set off in 1796 for the county election he shared his whiskey on this day trip with the customs tidewaiter Charles Lamb (who, when a cordwainer, was—like the rector—to vote Tory in the county polls six and ten years later).[2] But William Hardy junior journeyed that same day with Charles Kendle of Holt,

[1] *1806 election Diary 4*: 18 Nov. 1806

[2] *1796 election Diary 3*: 2 June 1796; quoted in full in the next section on electioneering

[1] *1796 election Norw. Merc.* 4 June 1796; *Diary 3*: 31 May 1796: see also p. 446. The rector sometimes missed holding Sunday service at Letheringsett in order to vote (*Diary 4*: 16 Nov. 1806)

[2] *1802 election Norw. Merc.* 17 July 1802. The Norwich contest was bitter even by the city's standards, the *Mercury* calculating 24 July 1802 that the four candidates had spent a total of £35,000.

The defeated Windham, 'still smarting from the effects of a most severe and unusually expensive contest', declared that he could not possibly stand in the county contest to be held the next week (*Norw. Merc.* 10 July 1802). Hence the welcome bolt hole of a borough, with no costly electioneering to be endured

[3] *Jodrell Norw. Merc.* 10 July 1802; L. Namier, *The Structure of Politics at the Accession of George III*, p. 144. Jodrell had the support of the powerful Townshend family (B.D. Hayes, 'Politics in Norfolk 1750–1832', p. 378), who wielded influence over the Gt Yarmouth nominations (Namier, p. 104)

[4] *pocket boroughs* L. Namier, *The Structure*

and possibly Thomas Youngman (a fellow Whig in 1802 and 1806) and the blacksmith John Jex (who died a year later, but may be assumed to be a Whig).

It is not known how they all would have voted this time. At the last moment it transpired there would be no Norfolk contest and thus no 1796 county pollbook. The Tory magistrate Thomas Hare withdrew his candidature, leaving the field clear for the sitting members T.W. Coke (Whig) and Sir John Wodehouse, Bt (Tory). Hare's decision was announced only just in time to prevent the outlying troops having a wasted and expensive outing. The intelligence was not published in the *Mercury* until two days after the Letheringsett contingent's journeys, but these particular voters had heard two days before travelling that there would be no contest.[1]

One consequence of the staggered voting during general elections was that not only did the voter have an opportunity to vote in all those places where he was a forty-shilling freeholder, but a defeated candidate could, and did, put himself up in another seat in the same election. Thus when the sitting member William Windham was rejected at Norwich in 1802 by an electorate enraged at his pro-war stance he moved swiftly to secure, successfully, the pocket borough of St Mawes in Cornwall in that same general election.[2]

Similarly in 1802 the Hardys' neighbour, the Tory Henry Jodrell, was cast out by the Freemen and property-holders of Great Yarmouth whom he had represented for six years and over whom he was to preside as Recorder of Yarmouth for 21 years. But he was well regarded in London as a firm (if quiet) supporter of Government, and he found himself returned to Parliament for the pocket borough of Bramber in Sussex only days after the Great Yarmouth result.[3]

Staggered campaigns and pre-Reform 'reliable' boroughs had their uses for candidates rejected in the constituency of their first choice. The Government had a good reserve of such seats in the Treasury boroughs, Admiralty ports and especially in the pocket boroughs spread liberally around the southern counties, St Mawes and Bramber being two examples. Unlike turbulent Norwich, those pliable electors did not greatly trouble themselves if the candidate or Member (generally one and the same) rarely put in an appearance from one year to the next.[4]

Electioneering

Solidarity was fostered in advance of the election by supporters' dinners in inns and even in humble alehouses. The inns of the large towns have received most prominence, but Mary Hardy shows that such dinners were held in very small villages as well. In Norwich in this period the Angel Inn was the centre of the Coke camp on election days, the owner of the premises exercising control over the innkeeper. An aggrieved Henry Wake spoke out publicly at the Angel when, nine months after the 1806 county election, 14 per cent of his very substantial dinner expenses remained unpaid by the candidate's agents. He was summarily replaced, as recounted in the inset (overleaf); but he had been forced to bear the debt of £1300 for much of that time, and the sum of £214 still outstanding could have represented some years' net income even for a well-to-do innkeeper.

William Hardy junior dined with the Coke supporters at the Angel during the general election of May 1807, the county seat this time being uncontested. It was to be his mother's last election excitement, heard at second-hand from nearby at Sprowston. At the time that the innkeeper Henry Wake was footing the bill for this long-drawn-out dinner he was still unpaid from the 1806 election.[1]

The Duke's Head, King's Lynn's premier inn dominating the Tuesday Market Place (overleaf), had been the seat of Prime Minister Sir Robert Walpole's political headquarters and maintained this Whig tradition in the decades to follow:

The Duke's Head changed hands several times until 1773 when Samuel Browne, an immensely rich Lynn merchant whose mansion can still be seen in Nelson Street, owned the inn and let it for ten years to Samuel Horncastle of Fleet Street at £60 per annum rent, provided he '. . . will on any contested election for the Borough of King's Lynn or for the County of Norfolk . . . open the said house for such party as the said Samuel Browne, his heirs or assigns shall direct . . .'[2]

Mary Hardy gives valuable local colour to the 1796 county campaign. Even though Norfolk finally went uncontested, Letheringsett voters and supporters, Tory and Whig, were treated by local electors not to dinners (midday meals) but to suppers, taken towards the end of the day, when working men were more likely to be able to attend:

of Politics at the Accession of George III, pp. 81–3, 299–300, 303.
Henry Jodrell's father Paul had been Member (briefly, in 1751) for the famously rotten borough of Old Sarum, Wilts

---

[1] *1807 election* 'I and William set off for Sprowston [from Letheringsett] evening 2, stopped half an hour at Mr Hase's [an ironfounder], Saxthorpe, and got to Sprowston before 7 . . . William rid to Norwich forenoon to the election, dined at the Angel Inn with the gentlemen, came home evening 10. Mrs Cozens [the diarist's daughter Mary Ann] and I at home all day' (*Diary 4*: 11 May, 12 May 1807)

[2] *Browne* A. Gifford, 'History of the Duke's Head Hotel' (leaflet, King's Lynn, nd, circulated Sept. 2005).
In 1789 Samuel Browne's daughter Hester married Jacob Henry Astley, MP for Norfolk 1797–1806, 1807–17. In 1802 he succeeded to the baronetcy of his father Sir Edward, the former county MP. As a granddaughter of the Lynn attorney Philip Case Hester Browne came from a mercantile and professional background (J. Barney, 'Building a fortune', pp. 445–7)

[1] *Hare* See p. 444. The indefinite article 'a Mr Hare' shows him to live far from the diarist's area.

He was from Stow Bardolph in the Fens, to the south-west

[1796] MAY 30, MONDAY A very boisterous stormy day. Another candidate put up for the county election, a Mr Hare.[1] Mr Burrell gave a supper at Dobson's on behalf of him and Woodhouse . . .

MAY 31, TUESDAY . . . Mr Hardy walked up to Holt afternoon, drank tea at Mr Bartell's. The Feathers and King's Head [at Holt] opened for Mr Coke's friends. Mr Hardy came home evening 9, heard the contest was given up by Mr Hare . . .

'Gross deception': a Norwich innkeeper seeks to be reimbursed after treating T. W. Coke's supporters in the 1806 general election

source *Norwich Mercury*, 29 Aug. 1807

[2] *late election* The general election campaign of Nov. 1806 for the county seat, in which Thomas William Coke and William Windham were the successful candidates.

Wake had honoured the old tradition of keeping open house for Coke's supporters (of which William Hardy snr and jnr were two). The campaign managers forming 'Mr Coke's committee' had supervised him to check there was no undue extravagance. Yet nine months later they had still failed to reimburse him in full.

No public reply was made to the charge. But within six weeks Thomas Sadler had taken over the market place inn (*Norw. Merc.* 10 Oct. 1807)

TO ROBERT PLUMPTRE, ESQ., MR JOHN GRAND, MR JONATHAN DAVEY, and others, who composed Mr Coke's Committee at the late election in 1806 [2]

GENTLEMEN!

Did you or did you not intend to perform the promises which you made to the innkeepers who were in Mr Coke's interest at the late election? and do you or do you not hold yourselves responsible for the engagements you then entered into? If you answer these questions negatively, what gross deception you were guilty of towards many honest, industrious, and respectable tradesmen in this city, *by opening their houses*, as you must have intended they should understand by this that they might look to you for the payment of their bills.

If on the contrary you do consider yourselves bound by those engagements, (and this I consider you must, unless you have lost all sense of honour and honesty), why have you refused to pay bills contracted under such circumstances? I was told by several of the committee that they considered my bill a very just and reasonable one, and indeed I don't know how it could be otherwise, since it was made out precisely from the accounts of those men who were stationed in my house by you, for the express purpose of overlooking me and my servants and taking care that no improper items were placed to the account of the committee.

Now, Gentlemen, . . . how great was my surprise at having £1300 offered to me a few days since, as a full discharge for a bill amounting to £1514 . . . I have applied to several of you individually on the subject . . . Private applications having . . . been treated with contempt, I am driven to the necessity of publicly calling on you to explain your motives for withholding from me the sum of £214, which still remains unpaid . . .

I am, etc

HENRY WAKE

Angel Inn, Norwich, August 27, 1807

left King's Lynn: the upper windows of the elegant Duke's Head Hotel, attributed to Henry Bell and built 1683–89; it became the election headquarters of the Prime Minister Sir Robert Walpole. Its owner from 1773, the Lynn merchant Samuel Browne, controlled its political allegiance and the treating offered here at election time.

In 1796 Coke's Holt supporters laid on suppers at the Feathers and King's Head at Holt. The local Whig brewer William Hardy chose to exercise no control over his small Letheringsett tied house, the King's Head, and his innkeeper William Dobson: election suppers were held there in both the Tory and Whig interest in the 1796 campaign. In this village there was no pressure for a public house to declare for one side or the other if the owner were a tolerant man.

Such items tend not to be recorded other than in Mary Hardy's diary. She also reveals how like-minded voters clubbed together to share vehicles for the long round trip to Norwich [*MB·2012*]

JUNE 1, WEDNESDAY ... [by Henry Raven] Mr and William Hardy [snr and jnr] supped at the King's Head with a party of Cooke's friends. [by Mary Ann Hardy] Mr Hardy and William spent the evening at Dobson's, met Mr Cooke's friends ...

JUNE 2, THURSDAY [Mary Hardy resumes] A fine forenoon, showery afternoon. Mr Burrell and Charles Lamb went to Norwich in his whiskey to the election, came home evening 11. William went to Norwich with Charles Kendle morning past 6, Thomas Youngman and John Jex went. A wet night.

JUNE 3, FRIDAY Rained incessantly all day. Mr Hardy at home all day. William came home evening 10 very wet indeed. Mr Coke and Woodhouse brought in without opposition. Rained all night.[1]

Although Charles Lamb voted Tory this proved no bar to his working for the Hardys. He was busy on 5 June in the malthouse with his father, the Hardys' faithful yearly man William Lamb. They were probably trying to repair the damage caused by the heavy rain and flooding during which the drayhorse of a rival brewer, Mrs Booty of Binham, had drowned in the Letheringsett ford beside the malt-kilns.[2]

[1] *supped Diary 3.* None of these meals was reported in the press, which tended to be city-centric at election time. The last part of the entry for 1 June was made by Mary Ann, repairing the omission. Like her mother on 30 May and 3 June, and Henry Raven on 1 June, she was more used to hearing than reading the candidates' names

[2] *drowned Diary 3:* 4 June, 5 June 1796; for the accident see chap. 1. William put prodigious effort into polling: a 40-hour return trip with a 6 am start, in heavy rain

TABLE 4.8.1

William Hardy's voting record in Norwich and Norfolk parliamentary elections 1768–1806, with his self-styled occupation

source   Pollbooks for Norwich (for the city) and Norfolk (for the county)

notes   All were general elections, except for the city by-election of 1786 and its re-run in
1787 following a scrutiny. Party affiliations do not appear in the pollbooks, but are
added for this table: see also the section on parties. Winning candidates are marked ◆

year	poll	occupation	Hardy polls for	Hardy rejects
1768	city	*exciseman*	E. Bacon [*pro-Govt*]◆ T. Beevor [*Indep.*]	H. Harbord [*Indep.*]◆
1780	city	*beer brewer*	H. Harbord [*Indep. Whig*]◆ W. Windham [*anti-war Whig*]	E. Bacon [*pro-Govt*]◆ J. Thurlow [*Tory*]
1784	city	*beer brewer*	H. Harbord [*Coalition Whig*]◆ H. Hobart [*Indep. Tory*]	W. Windham [*Coalition Whig*]◆
1786	city	*beer brewer*	H. Hobart [*Pittite Tory*]◆	T. Beevor [*non-Foxite Whig*]
1787	city	*beer brewer*	H. Hobart [*Pittite Tory*]◆	T. Beevor [*non-Foxite Whig*]
1790	city	*gentleman*	H. Hobart [*Pittite Tory*]◆ W. Windham [*Whig*]◆	T. Beevor [*non-Foxite Whig*]
1802	county	*gentleman*	J.H. Astley [*Indep. Whig*]◆ T.W. Coke [*Foxite Whig*]◆	J. Wodehouse [*Tory*]
1806	county	*gentleman*	T.W. Coke [*Foxite Whig*]◆ W. Windham [*Govt Whig*]◆	J. Wodehouse [*Tory*]

[1] *canvassing Diary 2*:
30 Mar. 1784.
    R.W. Ketton-Cremer
gives a study of the
character and career
of his kinsman William
Windham, 'a national
celebrity of the first rank'
(p. 182) in *Felbrigg*, pp.
182–259. He also covers
the many parliamentary
elections fought by
Windham. Unlike Coke,
who fought very few

As well as the supporters' suppers in the countryside there
was the excitement of being canvassed. William Hardy had
never been canvassed while at Coltishall 1773–81, but he
was to receive three canvass calls in the succeeding 28 years
at Letheringsett, one of which came during a Norwich campaign. Even those standing in a city election might see to it
that the isolated 'country voter' received the compliment of
a courtesy call, although given the distances involved the
country-dweller was not always able to attend the poll.

    In 1784 William Windham's steward came canvassing
William Hardy during the general election campaign for the
Norwich seat,[1] but evidently did not persuade the brewer

of his cause. William Hardy voted against Windham, even though he had as a result to support the Tory Hobart (table 4.8.1); he never plumped. The table shows however that the brewer supported Windham in 1790 for the city seat, and even in the controversial 1806 county election, by which time the mercurial minister had become known as 'the Apostate' and 'Weathercock Windham' for the policy swings in which he engaged. Windham, who ironically was to serve in turn as Secretary at War and Secretary for War during the French wars, had embarked on his political career 1778–83 strongly opposed to the American war. Shaking off his old allies he turned vehemently pro-war 1792–1805 and did not return to the pacific fold until 1806. William Hardy could thereupon vote for him once more, probably as Windham had declared himself in harness—if uneasily—with Coke.[1] By contrast William Hardy's friend and trusted medical practitioner Edmund Bartell, with whom he sometimes journeyed to Norwich on polling days, voted for the winning team of Hobart and Windham in 1784.

For some reason not explained by his wife William Hardy no longer supported Sir Thomas Beevor, Bt of Hethel. In three successive elections the brewer chose to vote for the

contested elections in this period, Windham on his home ground rarely cruised to victory and equally rarely had his way eased by facing minimal opposition

---

[1] *Hardy* At first sight he emerges as a swing voter. Never a plumper, he was twice a splitter.

Table 4.8.1 shows he consistently supported Hobart and Coke—yet these men stood for very different principles. There was no farming 'interest', the farmers in Coltishall and Letheringsett polling for different candidates. The later section on party labels also examines voting choices

right Edward Bacon (1713–86), JP, of Earlham Hall, Recorder of Norwich, MP for Norwich 1756–84, occupying the seat held by his father 1705–10 and 1715–35. Like the Cokes, Astleys and Wodehouses he was a member of a prominent political dynasty in Norfolk.

Parties and factions being fluid, and political allegiance often depending on transient personal loyalties, William Hardy's voting record was not as inconsistent as the table opposite might imply.

In his first participation in a poll in his adopted county, in 1768, he voted for Bacon; but in 1780 he voted against him, presumably as the American war exercised polarising pressure. Bacon was by then a supporter of Lord North's policies
[aquatint by W. C. Edwards 1840, detail; from a painting from life by John van der Banck]

[1] *illness* In vol. 3, chap. 8.
For the electoral travails of Sir Thomas Beevor, 1st Bt (1725–1814) see A. Carter, *The Beevor Story* (Fundenhall, 1993), pp. 37–43. In the fracas that was the 1786 Norwich election Revd Mark Wilks, the firebrand radical, acted as his agent, spending huge sums on the baronet's behalf on the London supporters (pp. 40–1).
Thomas Beevor had deliberately distanced himself from C.J. Fox in the elections of 1786, 1787 and 1790; hence perhaps William Hardy's rejection of him

[2] *1784 election* Diary 2: 7 Apr. 1784. William Hardy attended the county declaration in Norwich nevertheless (14 Apr. 1784). Sir John was of Kimberley Hall, south of Norwich, far removed from Hardy country. He held the seat until his elevation to the Lords in 1797, precipitating the county by-election in which J.H. Astley was returned unopposed

[3] *farming* Vol. 2, chaps 2 and 4

[4] *Mrs Coke* Diary 3: 23 June 1796; Diary MS: 23 June 1796

[5] *pressure and Excise* L. Namier, *The Structure of Politics at the Accession of George III*, p. 93

Pittite Henry Hobart rather than the mild, consensual Beevor, brother of the Norwich physician John Beevor who for months, in his own home, had nursed William Hardy's brother-in-law Robert Raven through a mental complaint in 1777. Crucially, the baronet had turned against Fox.[1]

Given the absence of pollbooks in uncontested elections it is particularly helpful to have the diary as a source. While there is no pollbook to prove this, we know from a call by 'Mr Woodhouse' that William Hardy, by now a freeholder, possessed the county vote in 1784. He was canvassed on behalf of Sir John Wodehouse, who with his fellow baronet Sir Edward Astley was to be returned unopposed.[2] Twelve years later the local candidate himself, Thomas William Coke, whom we meet as an agricultural improver in the chapters on farming,[3] called at the Hardys' one evening after the 1796 general election, presumably to thank his host for his support even though Hare's last-minute withdrawal had rendered it unnecessary. The MP came to Letheringsett Hall accompanied by his wife Jane, as recorded by Henry Raven; Mary Hardy mentions only Mr Coke.[4]

In this series of brief references neither diarist records the content of any conversation, but it would have been impossible to pressurise either William Hardy or his son. Both were sturdy, independent voters beholden to no one for patronage. As a former excise officer William Hardy would have been particularly resistant to attempts at pressure, or what Namier presents as 'organized bullying which worked from the top downwards'. In 1753, during the canvass of Nottingham in support of the then Prime Minister, the Duke of Newcastle, 'the Excisemen were worked with due discretion (as the Commissioners were debarred by law from giving "directions to their officers about elections")', this restraint being further testament to the professionalism of the service.[5]

The candidates whom the Hardys knew best, as living in the hundred of Holt, were Sir Edward Astley and his son Jacob Henry. Perhaps feeling confident of their vote neither candidate paid a canvassing call on the Hardys. Only once did Sir Jacob and his wife Hester make a visit, perhaps as the MP wanted to discuss the new Holt and Letheringsett enclosure, over which he had exerted himself in Parliament,

left Coke the youthful countryman: an engraving of Gainsborough's 1778 portrait of Thomas William Coke (1754–1842, from 1837 1st Earl of Leicester of the 2nd creation).

It depicts the new county MP as the young man the diarist, her husband, her sons and brother had watched in Norwich two years earlier being publicly acclaimed in the uncontested by-election for his late father's seat. He liked to present himself as the artist shows him: a simple country dweller, as devoted to outdoor pursuits as to his electors' interests. The reality was more complex [*Author's collection*]

---

[1] *Astleys Diary 4:* 14 May 1808. See vol. 2, chap. 3 on enclosure, and vol. 1, chap. 10 for road diversions

[2] *dined at Holt Diary 4:* 21 Sept. 1803. The county MPs were evidently on tour: 'On Thursday se'nnight [8 Sept.] a numerous and respectable meeting of freeholders in the interest of Sir Jacob Astley and Mr Coke dined at the Castle Inn, Downham. Both members were present' (*Norw. Merc.* 17 Sept. 1803)

or in his capacity as a JP to check on the re-routing of the main road outside the Hardys' house earlier that year.[1] Members of Parliament worked at maintaining good relations with their 'friends', as their voters were described, even if there were no election in the offing. They would, it seems, meet them over supporters' dinners clear of any campaign: 'William dined at the [   ] at Holt, met Sir Jacob Astley and friends, came home evening 9.'[2]

above Holkham Hall from the south-west, the north Norfolk home of T.W. Coke, later Earl of Leicester. It was the regional fount of the radical brand of Whiggery espoused by Charles James Fox and the playwright and MP Richard Brinsley Sheridan.

The four Hardys attended the Glorious Revolution Ball here in 1788 to celebrate the centenary of the constitutional settlement which the Foxites vowed to uphold in the face of encroaching royal prerogative.

Responses to the ball invitations were used by Coke as a countywide canvass, entries in the register of replies still held at the Hall recording political sympathy—or lack of it. The Hardys were noted as 'civil' in their acceptance. Frances, wife of Captain Horatio Nelson, RN, as also the Revd James and Miss Woodforde, declined: they were pro-Government Tory families   [*MB · 2001*]

---

[1] *fury Norw. Merc.* 17 Apr. 1784. Coke was one of 160 of Fox's former supporters in the Commons, 'Fox's Martyrs', not to be returned in 1784 (J.S. Watson, *The Reign of George III 1760–1815* (Oxford Univ. Press, 1960), p. 272). For 'the most acrimonious and

No amount of canvassing could counter untoward developments at national level. The Whigs were thrown into disarray by the calling of a general election in 1784. After a rowdy campaign and on the eve of polling Coke found he had to withdraw from contesting the county seat he had held for eight years. Disillusionment and fury at Charles James Fox's shabby betrayal of principle, as it seemed, the previous year when lured by the prospect of office into forming the Fox–North Coalition vented itself on all Foxite Whigs including the Holkham squire.[1] This taint did not attach to the more independently-aligned Whiggery of Sir Edward Astley, who was returned for Norfolk in tandem with the Tory Sir John Wodehouse. Windham just scraped home in Norwich.[1]

Perhaps to repair his reputation in the county, as well as to obtain a sense of his standing among the county electors in readiness for the next general election, Thomas William Coke and his wife Jane gave a spectacular ball at Holkham Hall. It celebrated the centenary on 5 November 1788 of the landing at Torbay of William of Orange (shortly to become William III), an event which led to the Glorious Revolution of 1688–89. The spate of legislation which followed, including a Bill of Rights, freedom of worship, a royal prerogative bound by constitutional principles and three-yearly Parliaments, was precious to the Whigs of the persuasion of Coke and, indeed, the Hardys. In November 1788 George III fell dangerously ill. It was daily expected that a new Parliament would be called and the regency—or even kingship—of Fox's ally the Prince of Wales declared. The Prince himself was invited to the celebrations at Holkham, but on the way he learned of the King's illness and turned back to Windsor.

Guided by lists of the principal residents and beneficed clergy across the county, the Cokes invited a huge number of guests: 900 to the ball (the electors and their families), and 5000 to the festivities and fireworks outdoors in the park (largely the tenantry);[2] among the indoor guests were William Hardy and his family. No attention was paid to previously declared political views, even where feared hostile. Unlike the Revd James Woodforde, who did not receive his 'gilt card' until 29 October as it had been waiting some time at the post office in Norwich,[3] the Hardys' arrived gratifyingly early. Mary Hardy noted on 17 October: 'Received a card of invitation from Mr Coke of Holkham'.[4] The Cokes then carefully logged the replies, drawing voting inferences from the degree of condescension in the choice of wording.

Mrs Christine Hiskey, the Holkham Hall Archivist, wrote on 17 April 1996 in response to my enquiry as to whether the Hardys' reply were still lodged in the family papers:

. . . I have now discovered the register of replies, and some of the replies themselves, with other papers evidently put to one side by Mrs Stirling when she was writing her book—and apparently not seen since then!

bitterly contested election of the century' see L.G. Mitchell, *Charles James Fox* (Penguin, London, 1997), pp. 66–71

[1] *Windham* He was nearly beaten by Hobart, the Norwich results for 1784 being Harbord 2305, Windham 1297, Hobart 1233

[2] *ball* Described by A.M.W. Stirling, *Coke of Norfolk and his Friends* (John Lane, The Bodley Head, London, 1912; 1st pub. 1908), pp. 214–33; and by S. Wade Martins, *Coke of Norfolk 1754–1842: A biography* (The Boydell Press, Woodbridge, 2009), pp. 77–80.
The ball was fully written up in the Norwich newspapers of 8 Nov. 1788. The local press had also reported 1 Nov. on the Glorious Revolution dinners held in Norwich inns

[3] *Woodforde* J. Woodforde, *The Diary of a Country Parson*, ed. J. Beresford, vol. 3, p. 59.
His poor niece might have appreciated a bit of excitement away from their solitary parsonage; but the rector declined on behalf of them both

[4] *invitation* Diary 2

[1] *register of replies* I am very grateful to Mrs Hiskey for her letter of 17 Apr. 1996 and for searching the hundreds of replies among the papers used in the biography by Mrs Stirling, Coke's great-granddaughter, first published in 1908

[2] *Nelson* A.M.W. Stirling, *Coke of Norfolk and his Friends*, illustration facing p. 216 of the 1912 edition

[3] *Windham* In 1792 he changed from a vehemently anti-war Whig 1778–91 into a pro-war, anti-Jacobin zealot as the French Revolution also changed its character and the menace of France increased.

Coke's sympathies still lay with what had begun as the French insurgency in favour of liberty and equality for all

[4] *angry* A.M.W. Stirling, *Coke of Norfolk and his Friends*, p. 216

[5] *large and brilliant* Diary 2

[6] *letter* J. Woodforde, *The Diary of a Country Parson*, ed. J. Beresford, vol. 3, pp. 90–1, 14 Mar. 1789

The register of replies merely records, 'Mr and Mrs Hardy & fam^y [family], Letheringsett, y[es], civil.' The last word is in the column headed '*Nature of Answers*'.

The actual reply, which is in a tightly bound bundle, reads: 'Mr and Mrs Hardy, and son and daughter, present their compliments to Mr and Mrs Coke. Intend doing themselves the honor of waiting on them, on the 5th Nov. next agreeable to their kind invitation.

Letheringsett, 20th October 1788.'[1]

There was a distinct coolness about some. In her biography Mrs Stirling reproduced Mrs Nelson's reply from Burnham Thorpe dated 31 October 1788 on behalf of her husband Horatio, then chafing at his enforced peacetime rest from the Royal Navy in his six years 'on the beach': ' . . . It is not in his power to accept their invitation for Nov. 5th.'[2] Other replies were regarded as warmer: 'Friendly' appears in the final column, and, under Windham, 'An amicable and decisive friend'. The friendship was to be strained to the limits by Windham's about-turn four years later.[3] Another reply was 'Insolent', while Archdeacon Warburton and family were 'Very angry at the lateness of the card'.[4]

The 'civil' Hardys, part of the inner circle of electors who attended the ball and supper, set off from home at 5 pm and got back to Letheringsett at ten the next morning. In honour of the Holkham Jubilee the diarist permitted herself some adjectives:

[1788] NOVEMBER 5, WEDNESDAY A very fine day . . . Spent the evening at Thomas William Coke's Esquire at a grand entertainment of a ball and supper given in commemoration of the Glorious Revolution of 1688. The entertainment was elegant and the company large and brilliant, the company stayed all night . . . [5]

Having marshalled his returns the hopeful Coke followed up the canvass with individual letters. Woodforde must have drafted his invitation response the previous autumn with his customary urbanity, for he received an equally polite communication a few months later: '. . . a letter this evening from Mr Coke of Holkham, desiring my vote and interest at the next election for the county of Norfolk'.[6]

The Weston rector did not have the opportunity of showing his political hand. Like other county Members nationwide Coke made every effort to spare himself a contest.

The election was not held for another fifteen months, the incumbent MP Sir Edward Astley dropping out at the last moment and Coke and Sir John Wodehouse being returned unopposed. As we have seen, by the time the rector's sole opportunity in Norfolk arrived in 1802 he was too indifferent in health to contemplate braving the tumult of the booths, even though he was summoned to the polls by one of Colonel Wodehouse's agents arriving post-haste at the parsonage when the opposing factions' race for the second seat was running neck and neck.[1] One man did vote from Woodforde's household, however. His loyal farm servant Ben Leggatt, with property in the Kimberley heartland at Crownthorpe, plumped for Wodehouse. His master would almost certainly have done the same.[2]

Uncontested polls meant that the voters, those very freeholders whose approbation Coke and the county Members sought, were in effect disenfranchised. The 'happy union and good agreement of King and People' referred to in the Triennial Act of 1694 was no longer to be achieved by frequent journeys to the polls.[3] The misgivings about Coke and the way he wielded his wealth and influence to circumvent the spirit of the very Revolution settlement he honoured so flamboyantly will be described later in this chapter.

Meanwhile, how accurate was his general election canvass during and after the centenary ball, and what can be deduced from Humphry Repton's elegant hand-coloured electoral map accompanying it?[4]

Exerting and mapping influence

Before examining Coke's canvass of 1788–89 and charting the geographical spread of votes actually cast during the 1806 general election we need to look in further detail at the principal source, the pollbooks, and then define what was meant by 'interest'—or, put more crudely, influence.

County pollbooks have already been illustrated. These printed and bound volumes record the votes cast for individual candidates by named voters, variously arranged by place of residence or place of property qualification according to the publishers' preferences. The voter often did not live in the property or even the town or village from which he derived his electoral entitlement. A few are indexed by

[1] *summoned* J. Woodforde, *The Diary of a Country Parson*, ed. J. Beresford, vol. 5 (Oxford Univ. Press, 1931), pp. 398–402, 30 June–17 July 1802. 'A Dr Ogilvie from Norwich came post-haste in a postchaise after me to go back with him to Norwich to vote for Colonel Wodehouse. Sir Jacob Astley is running him hard—but I was too ill to go anywhere at present, therefore was obliged to decline going. He stayed about half an hour' (p. 402, 16 July 1802)

[2] *Leggatt* Stevenson and Matchett's *Poll for the Knights of the Shire of the County of Norfolk* (Norwich, 1802), p. 49.
The 10 Weston voters spread their votes: eight for Wodehouse, three for Coke and one for Sir Jacob Henry Astley

[3] *happy union* Preamble to the Triennial Act (W. C. Costin and J. S. Watson, *The Law and Working of the Constitution*, vol. 1, p. 79)

[4] *map* Reproduced in colour in S. Wade Martins, *Coke of Norfolk*, plate 5, and reproduced as a chart, with her explanation, in 'Voting in the late 18th century', *An Historical Atlas of Norfolk*, ed. P. Wade-Martins (Norfolk Museums Service, Norwich, 1993), pp. 120–1

[1] *indexed* eg the county election of 1768, in *The Poll for Knights of the Shire for the County of Norfolk* (W. Chase, Norwich, 1768), pp. i–xxxv, with names set across a total of 105 columns

[2] *occupations* The *Norwich Mercury* publishers R. and R.M. Bacon recorded them in their editions of the 1802 and 1806 polling; the *Norfolk Chronicle* publishers did not.

Pollbooks are a rich source for family and business historians. From Bacon's 1802 Norfolk pollbook we learn that William Oakes (a plumper for Coke) had moved to a Horstead farm (thus freeing the Old House at Coltishall for Siday Hawes to move into and expand the maltings and brewery: vol. 2, chap. 8). Since the Horstead ratebook does not survive for this time the pollbook is likely to be the sole source for Billy Oakes's move

[3] *haste The Poll for the Knights of the Shire for the County of Norfolk* (R. Bacon, Norwich, 1802), p. iv

[4] *Bylaugh* Table 4.8.4 should thus record *six* voters under Belaugh, not five, especially as Ingham, Archer's place of qualification, is very much closer to Belaugh than to Bylaugh

voter's surname and forename.[1] They provide an invaluable series of data on voting patterns from the early eighteenth century (the first in Norfolk being for the Norwich election of 1710) until open voting ended in 1872.

Some pollbooks give the voter's occupation, as stated by him to the returning officer's clerk in the polling booth. These are necessarily brief statements in an age when people had multiple trades. Robert Ansell of Coltishall called himself a plumber when plumping for Wodehouse in 1806; but he was also a glazier, valuer, auctioneer and boat owner. William Hardy junior called himself a brewer in 1802 and 1806; he was also a farmer and maltster.[2] Other pollbooks merely give the social status of the voter as 'Esq.', or 'Gent.'; a clergyman appears as 'Clerk'. William Hardy rose in social standing over the years, by his own description, from exciseman via beer brewer to gentleman (table 4.8.1).

From the point of view of compiling voting data matched against census returns, the choice of a pollbook arranged by place of residence is essential to avoid a trawl through all 200 pages and 7000 names in a search for other mentions of the home village. In a pollbook arranged by qualification, William Hardy junior is listed not under Letheringsett but under Southrepps, in North Erpingham hundred, since in the polling booth he quoted the Crown at Southrepps as his freehold. R.M. Bacon's 1806 book has thus been used as one of the sources for table 4.8.4 when calculating the percentage of adult males with the vote, the population figure being estimated as the mid-point between the 1801 and 1811 census results. (Unlike industrial Britain, Norfolk villages had relatively stable populations during that decade.)

There are errors. As Richard Bacon readily admitted in 1802, 'Accuracy and haste are seldom united'—and rival publishers wanted to get their books out right after the poll.[3] Pronunciation of place names was notoriously hard to catch in Norfolk, especially in the hubbub that was Norwich at election time. Possibly the Robert Archer who plumped for Wodehouse in 1806 was not from Bylaugh, on the Wensum near East Dereham, but from Belaugh, on the Bure near Coltishall; both are pronounced locally 'Beeler'. Mary Hardy refers to the Archer family, and Robert, at Belaugh (*Diary 1*), and the Archers appear in local parish registers.[4]

Pollbooks do not necessarily record the voter's real intentions, nor his true political allegiance. J.R. Vincent goes so far as to assert that before 1872 'Votes often represented the wishes of anyone but the voter.'[1] Candidates and their electoral team would try to identify individuals and chart areas of influence so as to be able to call out supporters, as when Colonel Wodehouse's agent tried for half an hour to get just one voter, James Woodforde, to the poll. If a local landowner could be persuaded to vote in that 'interest' he would be expected to carry his tenants with him: their votes formed one part of his property portfolio.[2]

While it is possible that those who could vote freely were all of one mind in a village, the estate villages under the control of one dominant landowner stand out in the pollbooks. Whissonsett in 1715 was one such (illustrated near the start of this chapter on page 422). Although the lord of the manor, James Calthorpe, did not live in his manorial seat of Whissonsett Hall he appears to have carried most of the village with him, including Mary Hardy's grandfather. It was not this time a matter of political allegiance. Calthorpe and the great majority of the Whissonsett voters polled for a Whig (Astley) and a Tory (de Grey). Lessingham in 1806, illustrated in the section on the mechanics of elections (page 443), was another. The coastal outpost where the Hardys' draymen had faithfully delivered to the Star lay within a few miles of Witton, the home in 1806 of Colonel Wodehouse.[3] All five Lessingham voters plumped for Wodehouse.

Coltishall and Letheringsett were open villages socially and electorally, as analysed in volume 3, chapter 5. With no single dominant landlord and a good number of tradesmen as voters there was a better chance the elector could decide for himself. A client was generally unlikely to remove his custom from a skilled blacksmith or conscientious carpenter just because he had voted on the other side from his own, and neither Mary Hardy (with one notable exception) nor Henry Raven ever records instances of falling out politically with neighbours, shopkeepers and tradesmen, nor any political pressure whatsoever. The exception was the Rector of Letheringsett, Mary Hardy's antipathy to John Burrell's political sermons being confided to her diary. By contrast, B.D. Hayes finds very many examples of pressure.[4]

[1] *intentions* J.R. Vincent, *Pollbooks: How Victorians voted* (Cambridge University Press, London, 1967), p. 8

[2] *portfolio* This was particularly true of estate villages, with one major landowner, though any landlord might be expected to carry his tenants with him (B.D. Hayes, 'Politics in Norfolk 1750–1832', p. 43).
The contrast between open and estate villages, and how these are to be defined, is discussed in vol. 3, chap 5 on the social backdrop

[3] *Lessingham* The isolated position of the Star is illustrated in vol. 2, pp. 603, 606 and 607

[4] *pressure* Hayes quotes numerous illustrations of pressure and even coercion by male and female landowners (B.D. Hayes, 'Politics in Norfolk 1750–1832', pp. 41–8). The Hills, brewers and tradesmen of Wells, exerted themselves in 1784 to procure votes against T.W. Coke out of personal spite (p. 44).
In the 1768 county poll 51 clergy voted whose patrons were still living and had known views; of these, 44 voted as their patron would have wished (p. 47).
Hayes has also found instances of tenants refraining from voting if their landlord took no part in the poll (p. 43)

[1] *Colkirk* TNA: PRO IR 23/61, p. 763, Land tax assessment 1798 for Colkirk. Robert Goggs, who paid £38 10s 8d, an exceptionally large sum, is listed as occupier of one of the two large and valuable properties in the village belonging to Marquis Townshend.

Townshend in the last decades of his life was not a party man; as Lord Lieutenant of Norfolk he did not wish to be divisive (chap. 9). His natural inclination seems to have been to support the government of the day, given the foreign threats to the country; 'ministerial' or 'Court' might thus be his political label

[2] *de Grey* B.D. Hayes, 'Politics in Norfolk 1750–1832', p. 41

[3] *Coke* 'I give each man credit for his opinions, and I wish him to vote according to his conscience. I have on my estate some who have been very active partisans against me, but I have never removed them from their farms on that account' (quoted in A.M.W. Stirling, *Coke of Norfolk and his Friends*, p. 170)

[4] *sheep* Quoted in vol. 2, chap. 4, in 'Championing the Norfolk Horn'

[5] *Coke* W. Cobbett, *Rural Rides*, ed. P. Cobbett (London, 1893), p. 64

The picture is contradictory over the extent to which influence was exerted, and examples can be quoted either way. Colkirk, a parish north of Whissonsett, was an estate village, Marquis Townshend of nearby Raynham Hall owning much of the land (*plates 40, 44, 45*). However the pollbooks suggest it was free from electoral control. Mary Hardy's nephew Robert Goggs rented a very substantial farm at Colkirk from Lord Townshend (who, through being pro-Government rather than as a Tory, favoured Pitt),[1] but he was able to choose for himself. He voted in 1802 for Coke and Astley (both Whigs), by right of a Horningtoft property. In 1806 the Colkirk voting did not reflect the Townshend 'interest', the pollbook showing six votes for Coke, four for Windham and two for Wodehouse. Robert Goggs voted for Coke and Windham, both Whigs. (His brother Henry at Whissonsett chose the unusual combination of Coke and Wodehouse, the only one of the village's twelve electors to do so; his vote was the sole one polled there for the Tory.)

The county Members claimed they did not exert pressure: their object was to serve sturdy, independently minded Norfolkmen. In 1768 Thomas de Grey, a Tory, observed on his victory that he had 'obtained what I most ardently wished— the voices of a free and disinterested people'.[2] It was a boast of T.W. Coke's that he never turned out tenants who voted against him.[3] Were such claims valid? Coke was not, by his own account, so tolerant over farming. At one of his Holkham sheepshearings he announced that he was determined to extirpate the Norfolk Horn breed, and would feel himself justified in raising the rent of any unenlightened tenant who clung to the native breed of sheep.[4]

William Cobbett, surprisingly, given their marked political differences, comes to Coke's support. He was prepared to think highly of the MP following the panegyric he had heard on 15 December 1821 from the farmers at Holt market— one of whom was likely to have been William Hardy junior:

Here, as everywhere else, I hear every creature speak loudly in praise of Mr Coke. It is well known to my readers that I think nothing of him as a public man; . . . but it would be base in me not to say that I hear, from men of all parties, and sensible men too, expressions made use of towards him that affectionate children use towards the best of parents. I have not met with a single exception.[5]

below Commemorating Thomas William Coke: the plinth of the Leicester Monument built 1845–50 in Holkham Park, near the coast at Wells.

Three bas-relief friezes designed by Donthorn pay tribute to Coke the countryman and agricultural improver; a plough, a seed drill and a Devon Longhorn bull can be seen on top of the corner projections

above Coke in his full maturity: a close-up of the bas-relief seen on the left. The overhang casts perpetual shade over the upper parts of the figures.

The MP's complex character revealed a number of contradictions. While declaring himself a passionate adherent of the 1689 settlement, he exerted himself to bypass its spirit: the elections in which he stood were neither frequent nor contested. Vast outlays lent weight to the accusation that he was turning Norfolk into a pocket borough, with an emasculated electorate. Lukewarm over home defence in the American war and early part of the French Revolutionary War, the French menace led him to form a local Volunteer force. By 1803 the inspecting officer could judge the unit to have horses 'superior to any in England' (table 4.9.2)

Coke was much admired locally, William Hardy snr and jnr voting for him when they had the chance in 1802 and 1806 [*MB · 2003*]

Influence could take many forms and was not necessarily only by landlord over tenant: the city journeymen complained in 1786 of pressure from their masters.[1] One way in which influence could have been exerted was through the candidates' work as justices of the peace, for most parliamentary hopefuls were also JPs. Did they perhaps withhold licences from brewers for tied houses where justice and manufacturer held differing opinions? While William Hardy did encounter trouble at licensing sessions, as recorded by his wife, not once is there a hint of political pressure behind the hitches. The techicalities of licensing, and the need to get innkeeper, brewer and those standing surety all turning up for the right day and place were usually to blame.[2]

Freemasonry offered a possible avenue for exerting influence, or at least for calling upon ties of loyalty. The Norwich and Norfolk MPs Edward Bacon, Sir Edward Astley and the Hon. Henry Hobart were very prominent Masons, all three serving in turn as Provincial Grand Masters. We cannot be sure whether they could rely on support from their brethren, but William Hardy's consistent voting record for the Tory Hobart may be a significant pointer (table 4.8.1).[3]

Hard evidence, rather than anecdote, is needed to try to determine what forces, if any, were at work. How independent *were* the county electors? Hayes doubted they were, compiling 'maps of the county showing voting in contested elections by hundreds . . . disfigured by blocs of solid party strength'.[4] Coke's novel method of canvassing by interpreting replies to his ball invitations provides a starting point.

It was in 1788–89, during his six-year retirement from Westminster, that Coke undertook his rigorous canvass of Norfolk assisted, among others, by the farmer John Repton. Repton, a fellow agricultural improver, lived at Oxnead on the Aylsham navigation upriver from Coltishall (chapter 2). The wording of the farmer's letter of 12 November 1788 would suggest that a group of like-minded Whigs was urging on Coke the desirability of a canvass:

We all agree that the present position of affairs with regard to the King's health does not ought [*sic*] to relax our attention to the business we have undertaken . . . We therefore suppose you will join us in thinking that no time should be lost in preparing for a canvass which may suddenly be called for.[5]

[1] *journeymen Norw. Merc.* 29 July 1786; this was in the Norwich by-election

[2] *licensing* See also party labels (p. 481); and vol. 2, chap. 9.
No brewing lobby has been traced locally. Chapman Ives, John Patteson and Edmund Lacon, three leading brewers, voted Tory; the Bootys of Binham, Birchams of Reepham (Hackford) and Dawson Turner of Gt Yarmouth voted Whig

[3] *Freemasons* Discussed in chap. 6. William Hardy, Robert Ansell, George Boorne, Chapman Ives and others in their circle were active Masons. However Hardy voted once against Bacon, in 1780.
The King's Head at Coltishall, owned by Chapman Ives, hosted a major masonic event in 1793, with the two MPs Astley and Hobart present at the opening of the new lodge room: see the caption in chap. 6 on p. 330

[4] *maps* B.D. Hayes, 'Politics in Norfolk 1750–1832', p. 42; the maps are in his thesis (maps II and III). The hundreds to which he refers are the administrative divisions of the county

[5] *John Repton* A.M.W. Stirling, *Coke of Norfolk and his Friends*, p. 233

Repton's artistic brother Humphry, friend of Windham and Coke, was then living near Cromer. His work as a landscape gardener was not so demanding as to preclude him from politics, and he mapped the areas of influence on which he thought Coke could rely for the coming general election.[1]

The map is colour-coded to represent the political tinge of wealthy landowners: blue for T.W. Coke's supporters, yellow for Sir Edward Astley's and red for Sir John Wodehouse's; Norwich is depicted as red and blue in equal measure.[2] Interestingly Lord Townshend is shown as blue: the family, formerly close allies of Sir Robert Walpole, had traditionally been Whig. The French Revolution and war with France were to cause great shifts in allegiance. Launditch hundred is mixed. Sir Edward Astley was then lord of the manor of Whissonsett, though resident at Melton; as we have seen, the village seems to have followed the manorial lead. In this hundred containing the old Coke heartland of Godwick, between Whissonsett and Tittleshall, blue is the predominant colour; only the Barnwells nearby at Mileham are red.

William Hardy does not feature on the map, his 56 acres being far too insignificant. His neighbour at Bayfield, Elizabeth Jodrell, is blue; but her son Henry, who inherited it from her, was a Pittite Tory and not a Whig. Not only a Tory MP himself, he seconded the nomination of Colonel Wodehouse in 1806;[3] his political stance is seen later. Chapman Ives, the farmer, maltster and brewer at Coltishall, is shown as red, the reports he placed in the *Norwich Mercury* confirming him as a loyal supporter of the Tory Government in the 1790s when treason and sedition were perceived as rife.[4]

The question arises of how far the tenantry, if any, followed the lead of the landowner. Henry Jodrell had very few tenants at Bayfield, a small estate which his mother had bought for herself in her widowhood. Chapman Ives had virtually none, unless his large tied estate is counted, the Ives public houses being dotted around a wide radius. Broadland, as Susanna Wade Martins confirms in her analysis, was largely free from influence and pressure.[5] It is doubtful if Repton's map proved crucial for Coke, as the notion that landowners could command swathes of votes would not have held good across the board. It is thus something of a relief to look at the actual votes cast, and not at a canvass of opinon.

[1] *Repton's map* It is analysed in B.D. Hayes, 'Politics in Norfolk 1750–1832', pp. 38–9

[2] *colours* The map, as already cited, is seen as plate 5 in Susanna Wade Martins' *Coke of Norfolk*. Blue was then a Whig colour

[3] *Jodrell Norw. Merc.* 8 Nov. 1806; see also the section on party labels

[4] *Ives* As Grand Master of the Most Ancient and Honorable Order of Gregorians he issued a statement in 1792 avowing allegiance to King and Constitution. This was at the time of Tom Paine's trial *in absentia* in London over the *Rights of Man* (*Norw. Merc.* 22 Dec. 1792).

As this chapter and the next chapter will show, T.W. Coke was vehemently pro-peace at this time and for a few years more to come, having nothing to do with the Militia, the Volunteers and other expressions of patriotic fervour. In this he was out of step with a large body of voters

[5] *Broadland* S. Wade Martins, 'Voting in the late 18th century', p. 120.

The Broads, an area of Danish settlement and sokemen, had a distinct social structure and few estate villages (see vol. 3, chap. 5, on the mediaeval period)

right An example of the statistics published in pollbooks. This, from R.M. Bacon's pollbook for the county election of 1806, breaks down the areas of influence of each candidate. The columns show the total votes polled in each hundred (or borough) for Windham, Coke and Wodehouse.

These figures include the votes of property-holding residents with a county qualification in four boroughs: Gt Yarmouth, King's Lynn, Thetford and Norwich.

Norwich and Thetford were evenly balanced between the candidates. In Lynn Windham may not have been pulled home, as elsewhere, 'on Coke's coat-tails', since he was strong in the adjoining Freebridge Marshland.

However Windham overtook Coke in only three areas, one being his home ground of N. Erpingham hundred.

Wodehouse laid claim to Tunstead and Happing, around his wife's Witton base, and to Forehoe, in which his own ancestral seat of Kimberley stood. Depwade, Wayland and Mitford bordered Forehoe

[*Cozens-Hardy Collection*]

ALPHABETICAL LIST
OF
THE HUNDREDS AND BOROUGHS,
WITH
The Number of Votes for each Candidate.

				Win.	C.	Wod.
Blofield				70	73	31
Brothercross				71	71	4
Clackclose				218	230	86
Clavering				42	46	95
Depwade				61	91	117
Diss				104	123	86
Earsham				64	87	91
Erpingham North				129	112	62
Erpingham South				98	119	120
Eynsford	Win.	Co.	Wo.	114	122	86
Flegg East	51	56	36	474	492	337
YARMOUTH	423	436	301			
Flegg West				27	33	81
Forehoe				68	93	187
Freebridge Lynn	115	127	91	379	413	157
LYNN	264	286	66			
Freebridge Marshland				126	125	75
Gallow				70	77	26
Greenhoe North				158	180	34
Greenhoe South				37	59	93
Grimshoe				36	45	119
Guiltcross				52	72	96
Happing				49	55	113
Henstead				56	59	21
Holt				124	126	57
Humbleyard				22	32	45
Launditch				135	162	99
Loddon				53	60	69
Mitford				84	116	137
Shropham	107	89	101	152	143	156
THETFORD	45	54	55			
Smithdon				75	83	15
Taverham				52	61	32
Tunstead				50	57	139
Walsham				57	62	73
Wayland				40	31	91
NORWICH				129	132	105
SUFFOLK				89	99	135
LONDON, WESTMINSTER, &c.				68	71	24
DISTANT VOTERS				89	101	71
				3722	4118	3365

The table produced by R.M. Bacon of the breakdown of votes in the 1806 county election by hundred, illustrated opposite, displays with precision and by area the type of data Repton's map had sketched in 1788–89. Some parts of the county were more susceptible to influence than others, as seen in the caption comments. One area familiar to Mary Hardy did not return a solid block of votes in support of an 'interest'. Like much of the rest of Broadland, South Erpingham hundred, where Coltishall lay, shows a good balance between the three candidates; the edge given to Wodehouse probably reflects the presence of his estate at Witton, near North Walsham. Launditch hundred, the home area of Mary Hardy and Henry Raven in their childhood and youth, demonstrates a certain balance compared with many, this time Coke taking the lead in his ancestral hundred.

North Norfolk, by contrast, was solid Whig territory, on Coke's home ground in North Greenhoe, Brothercross and Gallow hundreds, on Windham's in North Erpingham in the north-east, and on Sir Jacob Henry Astley's in Holt hundred. There is no suggestion in the diaries or in Hayes's many examples that this show of Whig strength was achieved through coercion.[1] There was a strong undercurrent of personal regard for Coke, to which Cobbett readily testified at the time. This was extended to Windham in 1806 as the two men were presenting themselves in alliance to the voters.

[1] *Hayes's examples*
Already cited in this section: B.D. Hayes, 'Politics in Norfolk 1750–1832', pp. 41–8. He marshals a formidable body of evidence that pressure and even coercion were to be found elsewhere

---

below left **Part of the great monument by Nicholas Stone 1641 in Tittleshall Church to Sir Edward Coke (1552–1634), Lord Chief Justice in James I's reign and champion of the common law. The Coke family memorials fill the chancel of the parish church, yet none is to be found to Edward Coke's descendant Thomas William Coke, who is also buried here.**

The Chief Justice knew the area of the two diarists' family homes very well. His stepfather lived close by at Whissonett Hall, the home of the Ravens in the diary years and seat of the manor courts.

T.W. Coke had a strong personal following in this hundred of Launditch, but the map of the 1806 results (overleaf) shows that he commanded loyalty in much of eastern Norfolk as well [*MB · 2011*]

464

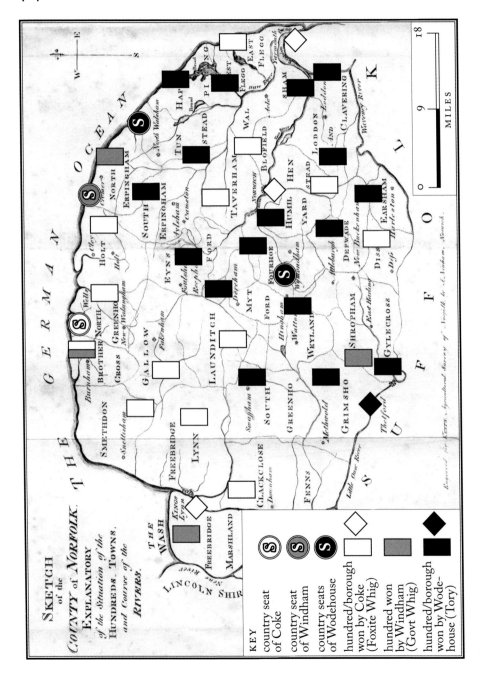

SKETCH
of the
COUNTY of NORFOLK.
EXPLANATORY
of the Situation of the
HUNDREDS. TOWNS.
and Course of the
RIVERS.

KEY

country seat
of Coke

country seat
of Windham

country seats
of Wodehouse

hundred/borough
won by Coke
(Foxite Whig)

hundred won
by Windham
(Govt Whig)

hundred/borough
won by Wode-
house (Tory)

MILES
18   9   0

FIGURE 4.8A (*facing page*)
The 1806 county election: voting patterns in the 33 hundreds and four boroughs of Norfolk

source   Figures tabulated by Richard Mackenzie Bacon in his Norfolk pollbook of 1806 (illustrated on page 462)

A display of the clusters of influence around the country seats where the candidates lived at the time of the general election of Nov. 1806. The fold-out map accompanying Nathaniel Kent's *General View of the Agriculture of the County of Norfolk* (1796) serves as the background.

Although it would appear from the map that Thomas William Coke [*white*] and the Hon. John Wodehouse [*black*] defeated the Rt Hon. William Windham [*grey*], in fact Coke and Windham won owing to the dynamics of dual voting. Windham was then Secretary for War and the Colonies in the short-lived Ministry of All the Talents.

Coke, with his strong following among farmers of all political persuasions, aug-

mented his unpopular's ally's polling. The great majority of those who voted for Coke also voted for his fellow Whig. The two tied in Brothercross hundred, in the north-west, even though it lay next to Coke's seat.

663 (20%) of the total of 3365 who voted for Wodehouse did not plump for him but cast a second vote—usually for Coke (seen in 12 hundreds in table 4.8.2). Windham's failure to attract the second votes of Tories helped to put him behind Coke.

The boroughs had their own candidates and polls (Norwich, Gt Yarmouth, King's Lynn and Thetford). They are represented here only through the *county* votes of their residents, as listed in Bacon's table [*background engraving by J. Ninham 1796*]

The map opposite represents pictorially the evidence from Bacon's table in the 1806 pollbook. It displays the outright winner in every hundred and borough,[1] even though he might have won by just a single vote or handful of votes; it therefore gives a rather stark portrait of the situation on the ground. Humphry Repton charted two or three colours in many of the hundreds on his map, or none at all if no influence could be detected. Thus Bacon's table is needed as a refinement to this map to give the votes cast and reflect the strength of support for each candidate in each hundred.

As shown by Bacon, the final results for the county were Coke 4118, Windham 3722 and Wodehouse 3365. It was Coke's declaration of his joint candidature with Windham, despite historic and continuing differences, which boosted the weaker Whig's tally. Without that stand Wodehouse would have beaten Windham and won a seat in Parliament. However the actions of the plumpers in this poll were not decisive in swinging the vote away from Wodehouse.

[1] *borough* Bacon's table omits the county polling by residents of Castle Rising, the fifth and last of the county's boroughs. The numbers were so tiny as not to merit separate recording, and they are probably included in Bacon's totals for the hundred of Freebridge Lynn.

The actual votes cast at Castle Rising by the three voters who polled from there were Windham 1, Coke 2 and Wodehouse 2. On fig. 4.8A this would appear as a Coke/Wodehouse borough tie were they not negligible

above **Witton Church:** detail of the memorial to Elizabeth Norris (d.1769), first wife of John Norris, and to Norris himself (d.1777). His only child Charlotte Laura married Col. John Wodehouse [*MB · 2011*]

[1] *N. Greenhoe* One of the six was Coke! By plumping for himself he broke his agreement with Windham in 1806. Windham voted for himself *and* for Coke

[2] *Tories* Wodehouse tried to maintain good relations in public with Coke, conscious of the strength of the agricultural interest: 'No opposition was ever intended to Mr Coke, of whose popularity, derived however from causes totally distinct from his political opinions, I was fully sensible' (J. Wodehouse,

'Keep plumpers in sight!'

Table 4.8.2 (opposite) relates to the same 1806 county election, but is based on another table by R.M. Bacon in his county pollbook, entitled 'Comparative view of the plumpers given at the elections of 1802 and 1806'. It analyses the votes of 1767 of the voters who cast two votes—or one, if they decided to plump in favour of one candidate—to elect the two county members. Chosen from areas of Norfolk well known to Mary Hardy, these 1767 persons represent one-quarter of the total number of voters who came up to Norwich from all parts of the county and beyond. In all, 6904 voters took part in the 1806 election: roughly the same number as the 7253 who polled in another hotly-contested county election in 1802. Of these 6904 persons, 470 (6·8 per cent) were resident outside the county in Suffolk, London and elsewhere, yet they rode or drove up to Norwich for the poll. The occupations and places of residence and qualification of the 'Distant voters' are recorded in Bacon's pollbook.

Table 4.8.2 shows clearly that much of Broadland was not directly influenced by any of the three candidates. There was a moderately even distribution of votes in South Erpingham, Taverham and Walsham hundreds and, to a lesser extent, in Blofield. Those who voted for Wodehouse often did not plump for him but cast a second vote, usually for Coke. However in those parts of the Broads under Wodehouse influence in Tunstead and Happing hundreds there was very marked polling, and plumping, for the local man, presumably out of loyalty or obligation to the inheritor by marriage of the Norris estate at Witton. Wodehouse's own ancestral area of Forehoe hundred is not shown here.

Coke did not always succeed in persuading his voters to cast their second votes for Windham; hence the mismatch between their tallies. The thought of voting for the former pro-war minister evidently proved too much for six Coke supporters in and around Holkham in North Greenhoe.[1] The only hundred in which Windham attracted any sort of plumper following and overtook his ally in the poll was his own, that of North Erpingham. Table 4.8.3 (opposite) gives an overview of the 1802 and 1806 plumpers. Tories seem to have respected Coke for his farming and his consistency and were prepared to countenance his re-election.[2] But they

TABLE 4.8.2

The 1806 county electorate: voting figures in 12 north Norfolk hundreds, by total number of votes cast in each hundred and for each candidate

source R.M. Bacon's Norfolk pollbook of Nov. 1806: 'Comparative view of the plumpers'

note The figures in square brackets in the candidate columns are the numbers of plumpers (voters choosing to exercise only one of their two votes), as a subset of the total votes cast for that candidate

HUNDREDS			CANDIDATES [1]					
hundred	no. of voters	total of votes cast	Coke Foxite Whig		Windham Govt Whig		Wodehouse Tory	
Blofield	107	174	73	[2]	70	[1]	31	[28]
Brothercross	74	146	71	[0]	71	[0]	4	[2]
Gallow	97	173	77	[5]	70	[2]	26	[15]
Happing	156	217	49	[2]	55	[0]	113	[94]
Holt	177	307	126	[1]	124	[1]	57	[40]
Launditch	225	396	162	[1]	135	[1]	99	[57]
N. Erpingham	170	303	112	[0]	129	[8]	62	[46]
N. Greenhoe	196	372	180	[6]	158	[2]	34	[12]
S. Erpingham	197	337	119	[2]	98	[1]	120	[78]
Taverham	84	145	61	[1]	52	[1]	32	[23]
Tunstead	182	246	57	[1]	50	[0]	139	[117]
Walsham	102	192	62	[0]	57	[3]	73	[36]
TOTAL [2]	1767	3008	1149	[17]	1069	[20]	790	[538]

[1] *candidates* Coke's seat of Holkham lay near Wells in N. Greenhoe hundred; his huge estate stretched into Brothercross and Gallow. The much smaller estate of his ally Windham was at Felbrigg, near Cromer in N. Erpingham.

Wodehouse's hereditary seat at Kimberley, near Wymondham, lay in Forehoe hundred (an area which does not feature to any great extent in Mary Hardy's diary), but by marrying Char-lotte Norris he acquired the wealthy estate at Witton, near N. Walsham in Tunstead hundred

[2] *total* The final countywide poll mirrored the results shown in this part of north, north-east and north central Norfolk:

Thomas William Coke, Esq.	4118
Rt Hon. William Windham	3722
Col. the Hon. John Wodehouse	3365

deplored what was seen as Windham's apostasy and sudden shifts in political allegiance. For the Whigs his long service as minister in the War Department caused resentment in a county decidedly ambivalent over going to war with France.

election address, 23 Oct. 1806, from the Budget in R.M. Bacon's pollbook 1806, p. 7)

right John (1771–1846), later 2nd Baron
Wodehouse of Kimberley, who as Colonel
the Hon. John Wodehouse of the East
Norfolk Militia fought the county elections
of 1802 and 1806. In 1796 he married Charlotte Laura Norris, heiress of the Witton
squire whose funeral procession from London was recorded by Mary Hardy in 1777.

He was from the foremost family of
Norfolk Tory MPS, and gave a lifetime of
public service. His grandfather Sir Armine
Wodehouse, 5th Bt, was Member for Norfolk 1737–68; his father Sir John (1741–1834)
was Member 1784–97, having moved swiftly
to secure Norfolk with Sir Edward Astley
after a defeat in 1784 at Gt Yarmouth.

The 2nd Lord Wodehouse was Lord
Lieutenant of Norfolk from 1821 until his
death. He served in the Commons 1820–26
as MP for Marlborough, Wilts
[*miniature by W.C. Ross; engraving by
S. Cousins: Cozens-Hardy Collection*]

[1] *Wodehouse* His
admiration for Coke is
quoted on p. 466. But a
few days later his agent,
posing anonymously as
'An Elector', published
an address to the
Norfolk freeholders,
urging anti-Windham
electors 'not to lend
your aid to this foul
conspiracy [by
Windham] against the
Colonel, but *to give
your single votes only for
him*' (R.M. Bacon's
pollbook 1806, Budget,
p. 11, my italics).

For editorial
comment and illustra-
tions relating to the
1806 city and county
elections see *Diary 4*,
Oct.–Nov. 1806

The candidates needed to calculate in advance how
far plumping would give them an advantage. What they
declared in public on the matter and what their electoral
agents urged proved very different. Colonel Wodehouse,
the sole Tory, openly professed his admiration for Coke
and stated he had no desire to oppose him. But his agent
called for plumpers.[1] Coke and Windham could not call for
plumpers as they were standing together, the harness working to the controversial Windham's advantage—but not to
Coke's. Windham had a low personal following. In 1806
only 54 voters plumped for him in the whole of Norfolk, and
he seems to have pulled down Coke. When Coke stood in
tandem with the moderate Whig Sir Jacob Henry Astley in
1802, Astley received the support of 70 plumpers and Coke
160. In 1806 Coke had only 76, including himself: a drop of
52 per cent (table 4.8.3).

As the campaign became more vicious and the opening
day of the election approached, Wodehouse's self-imposed
restraint evaporated. He steered a course as near as he
dared to asking the freeholders to exercise only one of their
precious two votes. On 5 November 1806 he wrote from

Norwich, a wealth of meaning contained in his italics. This is a coded call for plumping:

... It only remains for me to inform you that the day of election is fixed for Thursday, the 13th instant; and to remind you, that as I shall have two opponents directed against *me singly*, that it is on your *decided* support our final success must depend . . .[1]

Hours later, with the canvas returns coming in, the pretence dropped and he went all out for plumpers, both in his own direct appeal to the voters and in a series of rhythmic drumbeat marching songs composed by his supporters. One, called 'Plumpers! Plumpers! Plumpers!', opens:

Ye Norfolk Freeholders! keep Plumpers in sight,
'Twas by Plumpers that Patteson beat Blue and White;
By your Plumpers a Wodehouse resolve to elect;
C——'s [Coke's] presumption the cause, let him feel the effect . . .[2]

Wodehouse's support stayed constant with the plumpers when the difference between the two election results is viewed in context. 2692 voters plumped for him in 1802, and 2702 in 1806 (table 4.8.3). While a very slight percentage increase, it is made more considerable when set against the backdrop of a five-per-cent decrease in the electorate.

[1] *me singly* R.M. Bacon's pollbook 1806, Budget, p. 14 [Wodehouse's italics]

[2] *keep plumpers in sight* R.M. Bacon's pollbook 1806, Budget, p. 39. Wodehouse's simple, one-sentence appeal, made from Norwich 5 Nov. 1806, is on p. 38. The Whigs' local colours were blue and white, or, sometimes, blue and buff. The ditty refers to the wresting of Norwich from the Whigs in Nov. 1806 by the new MP John Patteson; also to Coke's highhandedness. Patteson, the sole Tory, received 1783 votes of which 1287 were plumpers (the highest number ever for Norwich), thereby denying his

TABLE 4.8.3
The 1802 and 1806 county elections: the candidates' plumpers

source R.M. Bacon's Norfolk pollbook of Nov. 1806: 'Comparative view of the plumpers'
notes Table 4.8.1 shows the party affiliations of the candidates in the polls during the general elections of 1802 and 1806. Table 4.8.2 provides further data on the plumpers of 1806

	1802			1806		
	Coke	Astley	Wodehouse	Coke	Windham	Wodehouse
total votes cast	4317	3612	3516	4118	3722	3365
plumpers [3]	160	70	2692	76	54	2702
plumpers as % of total votes	3·7	1·9	76·6	1·8	1·5	80·3

[3] *plumpers* Voters who exercise only one of their two votes at the polling booth. They are here shown as a subset of the total number of votes cast for the individual candidate

Whig opponents a vote
(*Norw. Merc.* 8 Nov.
1806)

---

[1] *voting* For analysis of
the voting in 1802 and
1806 by the upper
gentry, see B.D. Hayes,
'Politics in Norfolk
1750–1832', pp. 38–40

[2] *property* L. Namier,
*The Structure of Politics
at the Accession of
Geroge III*, p. 64.
    In Norfolk copyhold
tenure was extremely
common and was
treated as freehold
for electoral purposes

[3] *every class* B.D. Hayes,
'Politics in Norfolk
1750–1832', p. 41.
He goes on to give this
percentage breakdown
from a sample of 2161
voters in 1802 from 12
hundreds to the south
and west of the county
(his p. 42, note):
	%
baronets, esquires	3·5
gentlemen	8·7
clergymen	5·4
Dissenting ministers	0·1
professional men	2·4
entrepreneurs	2·1
shopkeepers	5·3
craftsmen	14·6
farmers, graziers	41·7
yeomen, husbandmen	3·1
labourers	3·1
miscellaneous	10·1

[4] *Freemen boroughs* The
electorate is examined
in vol. 3, chap. 8 in
connection with trades

The number of voters declined from 7253 to 6904 over four years, but there was little fall in the Whig turnout caused by disenchantment with Coke's alliance with Weathercock Windham. The Tory vote fell rather more, for the Whigs' total dropped by 89 votes and the Tories' by 151 votes.[1]

The voters

Who were the voters? From the evidence of occupations in the pollbooks it is very clear that electors were no longer drawn only from the leading families of the shire. The minimum qualification of a forty-shilling (£2) freehold had been fixed in 1430 in the reign of Henry VI and never adjusted for inflation over the centuries. Also there was a good measure of fluidity over 'freehold': leasehold tenure and mortgaged property were for instance acceptable.[2] As a result, the electors were a more varied group, even at county level, than the traditional image of squirearchy, gentry and clergy. Hayes goes so far as to state that those entering the polling booths were 'representatives of every class except the paupers'.[3]

The declared intention behind the pre-twentieth-century maintenance of a property-owning electorate, in contrast with the modern system of universal adult suffrage, was that the voters should have a vested interest in political stability. Handing over the selection of the legislature to those without a stake in society was seen as precipitating rule by the mob. Whereas the franchise was getting seriously out of line with the new wealth of the industrialising regions before the Great Reform Act of 1832, Norfolk and many other agricultural and pastoral shires did not suffer from that imbalance. It could fairly be said that in Mary Hardy's Norfolk the electors did form the great bulk of the wealth-owning and wealth-creating classes—if wealth creation by labour, by women and by the very young are to be ignored.

Most propertyless labourers, all females, and all those aged twenty and under did not have the vote at county level, although the first of these three categories did vote in the Freemen-dominated boroughs of Norwich and Great Yarmouth. There, poor weavers and tailors, dyers and finishers, ropemakers and caulkers had the vote, holding their Freedom by means of apprenticeship or by birth as the son of a Freeman.[4] C.B. Jewson calculates that in the Norwich election of 1790 only 295 of the 2480 voters were freeholders (of whom William Hardy was one): the rest (88 per cent) were Freemen.[1] Richard Bacon stated in 1802 in his county pollbook that three-quarters of Norfolk freeholders resided in parishes where their property lay, justifying his layout of voters under place of qualification, not residence.[2]

Something under 11 per cent of adult males took part in the Norfolk general election of 1802,[3] and just under 10 per cent in a sample in 1806 (table 4.8.4, overleaf). The twenty parishes in the table for 1806 have been chosen to cover areas directly associated with Mary Hardy. Its range extends from market towns and the harbours of Blakeney and Cley down to the two small villages of Belaugh (downstream of Coltishall) and Horningtoft (next to Whissonsett, and home to some of her extended family). She had become familiar with a wide area around Coltishall through supplying the public houses, such as nearby Horstead and Tunstead; also the riverside part of Hoveton and the villages of Upton and Strumpshaw on the Broads. Field Dalling she had come to know well from its Church of England gospel preacher, and it is one of seven towns and villages near Letheringsett to appear in the table. By 1806 she had been journeying weekly to Cley and Briston for Methodist meetings.[4] Mileages are calculated using White's 1845 Norfolk directory, with occasional adjustments for inconsistencies or to reflect the route likely to have been taken to Norwich.

The small size of some of the villages in the sample can obviously affect the percentages. It needed only one resident to fail to get to Norwich for the position of his home parish in the ranking in the final column to be altered.

Nevertheless the pollbook yields valuable data. All votes had to be cast in person in the sole centre for the county poll. The booths were set up in the heart of Norwich, with the voters ascending the steps to enter covered stalls serving small groups of hundreds.[5] Although just under 10 per cent of the adult male population voted in these rural parishes in an election held 26 years before the Great Reform Act, probably a great many more would have made the long journey to Norwich had they been able to leave their place of work. It was hard for the shopkeepers, innkeepers and craftsmen of the market towns to abandon their counter,

[1] *Norwich* C.B. Jewson, *The Jacobin City*, p. 21

[2] *place of qualification* R. Bacon, Norfolk pollbook 1802, 'Address', p. vi. His son altered the ordering for the 1806 Norfolk poll. Stevenson and Matchett, printers of the *Chronicle*, adopted the opposite system in 1802 and 1806 from that of the *Mercury*'s printers. Taken together the four pollbooks are very helpful

[3] *adult males* The census shows the total male population in Norfolk and Norwich in 1801 to be 129,842; approx. 48% of these (62,324) will be adult males, as explained in the table notes. The number of voters in the 1802 county election living within the county boundary, and discounting the distant voters, was 6858 (11 per cent of the adult males); adjustment must then be made for population increase 1801–02

[4] *religion* Covered in vol. 3, chaps 1–4

[5] *booths* Chase's 1768 county pollbook sets out the arrangement of the 15 booths that year. Coltishall's voters were ranged under N. and S. Erpingham hundreds in Booth 11; Letheringsett was next door in Booth 12, shared by Holt and

Eynsford hundreds. Whissonsett in Launditch hundred was alongside Clackclose in Booth 14. Pollbooks arranged by hundred and not by place name reflected the order of the booths. Treating at inns too was run openly according to the hundred (*Norw. Merc.* 8 Nov. 1806)

[1] *turnout* Holt's shows few tradespeople and surprisingly few shopkeepers. No one of the Davy and Baker shopkeeping families came to Norwich, and no innkeeper. The draper Charles Sales voted— like most of Holt—for Coke and Windham, as did a bevy of seven small manufacturers in the shape of a cooper, shoemaker, hatmaker, wheelwright, basketmaker and two bakers. A patten-maker and bricklayer (builder) plumped for Wodehouse. One blacksmith voted for Coke and Wodehouse; a second voted for Coke and Windham.
The total votes from Holt in Nov. 1806 were: Coke 19, Windham 18, Wodehouse 5

[2] *11 hours Diary 4*: 18 Nov., 22 Nov. 1806

[3] *Lynn and Downham* Shown in the pollbook, but not displayed in table 4.8.4

parlour or workshop for the day or two days which attendance at polling required. The towns make a poor showing. All five market towns in the sample shown in table 4.6.4 appear in the bottom half of the ranking. Aylsham is the lowest, although only twelve miles from Norwich. Only 5·8 per cent of its total adult males made the effort.[1]

A marked feature is the inconsistency between the places listed in the table, even when allowance is made for the small numbers involved. Upton and Strumpshaw were very comparable villages, both with good communications. Yet three times as many turned out from Upton as from Strumpshaw, which made a poor showing. Whissonsett and Horningtoft are similarly comparable in character and location, if not in size; yet again there is great variation. More than twice as many voters, in percentage size, turned out from Whissonsett as from neighbouring Horningtoft.

One of the real surprises in the table is that mileage did not determine turnout. Some of the most eager pollers faced very long return journeys. Living in Letheringsett, second in the table, imposed a round trip of 47 miles and thus great commitment to the cause and to civic duty. Yet 17·5 per cent of its adult males voted in Norwich and were prepared to spend the eleven hours on the road which it took Mary and William Hardy for the round trip.[2] Letheringsett, while a politically active village, was surpassed by Upton, on the River Bure near Acle, and the same distance from the city as low-ranking Aylsham. A little under one quarter of Upton's adult males polled.

The average distance from Norwich of the twenty parishes in the table is just over sixteen miles. Those in the hundreds not shown here would have had endured far longer journeys, but all her life Mary Hardy lived within 23½ miles of Norwich and thus the table is somewhat city-centric. The 334 voters from King's Lynn each had a round trip of 84 miles; Downham Market's 54 voters also each journeyed 84 miles.[3] With great distances such as these it was probably not so much the loss of time and income as expenditure on horses and chaises which would have affected turnout, unless help were at hand from the candidates over expenses.

Given this level of commitment many voters chose to treat election week the way they did Assize Week, as a great coun-

TABLE 4.8.4

The 1806 county electorate: number of those voting, and voters as a percentage of the population in 20 rural Norfolk parishes

sources National censuses 1801, 1811; R.M. Bacon's Norfolk pollbook of Nov. 1806

notes Market towns are shown in small caps. The parishes, chosen as a geographical spread of a sample featuring in Mary Hardy's diary, are arranged by the percentage of resident adult males casting their vote, as shown in the final column

parish	miles [1]	total males [2]	no. of voters [3]	% of total males voting	% of adult males voting [4]
Upton	12	181	21	11·6	24·2
Letheringsett	23·5	131	11	8·4	17·5
Belaugh	8·5	65	5	7·7	16·0
Hoveton St John	7·5	108	7	6·5	13·5
Whissonsett	22	196	12	6·1	12·8
Briston	19	356	21	5·9	12·3
Field Dalling	24	139	8	5·8	12·0
Sprowston	2	139	8	5·8	12·0
Tunstead	10	230	12	5·2	10·9
Coltishall	7	290	14	4·8	10·1
HOLT	23	470	22	4·7	9·8
N. WALSHAM	15	951	44	4·6	9·6
Thornage	22	111	5	4·5	9·4
Horstead	6·5	182	8	4·4	9·2
Blakeney	27	246	10	4·1	8·5
Strumpshaw	8·5	151	6	4·0	8·3
FAKENHAM	25	573	20	3·5	7·3
Horningtoft	21	104	3	2·9	6·0
CLEY	27	247	7	2·8	5·9
AYLSHAM	12	784	22	2·8	5·8
TOTAL	322·5	5654	266		
AVERAGE	16·1			4·7	9·8

[1] *miles* From Norwich, the sole polling centre

[2] *total males* Figure calculated as the mid-point between the 1801 and 1811 census figures for the total male population (children included)

[3] *voters* The number of parish residents actually travelling to Norwich and registering their votes, the pollbook giving their place of residence

[4] *adult males* Percentage estimated from the (incomplete) census returns of 1821, from which it can be calculated that approx. 48% of the male population of England and Wales was aged 21 and over and thus of voting age (B.R. Mitchell and P. Deane, *Abstract of British Historical Statistics* (Cambridge Univ. Press, 1971), p. 11)

[5] *Fakenham* The number of total males in 1806 is estimated from the *total* population in 1801 of 1236; a figure for males was not printed in 1801

[1] *validity* E. Green, P. Corfield and C. Harvey, *Elections in Metropolitan London*, vol. 1, pp. 61–2. The crowds were present 'as public witnesses, marking these events as ones of communal note' (p. 61)

[2] *Hogarth* The other three, all of 1754, are 'An Election Entertainment' at an inn; 'Canvassing for Votes' in the street; and the riotous 'Chairing the Member'. The bystanders, as non-voters, are very much to the fore. See E. Baudey, 'The liberty of voting restored: William Hogarth's *Election* series as a vision of electoral (dis)order', in *Hogarth's Election Entertainment: Artists at the hustings* (Sir John Soane's Museum and Apollo Magazine, London, 2001), pp. 12–14. See also J. Brewer, *The Common People and Politics 1750–1790s* (Chadwyck-Healey, Cambridge, 1986), esp. pp. 27–9

[3] *elections* See, eg, *Diary 2*: 5 Apr. 1784, 15 Mar. 1787; *Diary 4*: 27 May 1799, 15 Nov., 20 Nov. 1806

[4] *women* See chap. 10; also vol. 1, chaps 2–4; vol. 2, chaps 8–10; vol. 3, chaps 2, 4 and 8

[5] *safeguarded* E. Green, P. Corfield and C. Harvey, *Elections in*

ty event. Whereas the assizes came to Norwich every July, a contested Norfolk election might come only once in a generation or perhaps once in a lifetime. Even when there was no contest, wives, children and other non-voters swelled the throng as spectators, and it was their participation in giving the Members not their votes but public acclamation which gave additional validity to the electoral outcome in the days before universal suffrage.[1] The cheers ringing through the Norwich streets as the new Members were chaired around the market place meant a great deal: ceremony as much as suffrage distinguished elections. Only one of Hogarth's four large *Election* canvases depicts the actual polling process.[2]

The non-voters

The impression can be given by coverage at the time and by paintings and engravings that a disenfranchised rabble roamed the hustings during polling and the declaration. Mary Hardy's own account, based on her husband's experience as a voter at one city by-election, reinforces the image of disorder and riot, as quoted at the chapter head. It is natural that the actions of the mob, being newsworthy, should jostle to the fore. But they crowd out the steady presence of what the newspapers liked to call a respectable concourse, of which the diarist's circle formed a part: herself, her children (including Mary Ann), the brewery apprentice and diarist Henry Raven, and William Hardy junior's farm steward George Phillippo. All were present in Norwich at various elections, contested and uncontested, as participants in the exuberence and vitality of the occasion, while themselves being debarred from taking any part in the actual polling.[3]

For one who never had the vote Mary Hardy was exceedingly interested in elections. The active role of women in the family, in business and trade and in organised religion is discussed in many parts of this work, their participation being often under-reported.[4] It may be that in the political sphere women considered their interests to be safeguarded by their menfolk.[5] This was an age when family solidarity was essential for survival. With no state services, nursing was performed in the home, as were often education and training for work: many occupations in Mary Hardy's circle were carried on in the home and counting house. The family thought of itself as a unit, riding out in gritty solidarity the storms of pain, sickness, debt, premature death of bread-winners and mothers and all the uncertainties that life might bring. Individualism, as in striking out for oneself, could conflict with this unitary imperative. Mary Hardy gives every sign of sharing her husband's political persuasions, but since she does not speak out other than in opposition to the rector (a feeling William Hardy shared) we cannot be certain where her sympathies lay, nor whether she felt aggrieved at not possessing the vote. However custom and upbringing make it unlikely she harboured such resentment.

She would have been reared from early childhood to be politically aware, as were her children. She was too young to remember the county general election of 1734, when her father Robert Raven, a shopkeeper and maltster, travelled to Norwich and polled for the successful candidates Sir Edmund Bacon, Bt and William Wodehouse. At the time of her twelfth birthday she would have been vividly aware of the peril in which the country stood from the Scots under Prince Charles Edward Stuart as they marched on London. They did not reach further south than Derby, but the Jaco-bite rising created a profound shock across the country which at its height lasted for months and dominated press reports. She would have heard political sermons ringing out from the pulpit in 1745 and 1746 on the royal proclamation days of public fast and thanksgiving.[1]

The first three elections recorded by Mary Hardy in her diary went uncontested. On the second, following the city election earlier in the month, she accompanied her hus-band to Norwich for the county general election of October 1774, when Sir Edward Astley, Bt and Wenman Coke were returned for Norfolk.[2] The Hardys had no qualms about taking their young children off school at election time—and for public hangings, fairs, mayor-making and other note-worthy events. Norwich lay only seven miles from Coltis-hall. As responsible parents, eager to develop a sense of civic awareness in their offspring, they took them to the city.

The first election witnessed by Raven and William was the county by-election of May 1776. T.W. Coke succeeded not only to the Coke estates following his father's death but to his parliamentary seat, unopposed.[3] This was six-year-old

---

Metropolitan London, vol. I, p. 25

---

[1] *Jacobites* Such ser-mons were preached on the public fast 18 Dec. 1745 at the time of greatest danger, and on the thanksgiving of 9 Oct. 1746, six months after Culloden, called in honour of 'the suppression of the late unnatural rebellion'.

Two published sermons by Revd Dr Philip Williams, a Norfolk rector, are what the diarist would have called political. His second did not mince words: 'By the rebellion at home our lives, property, and religion were in the utmost danger: superstition stood ready to enter our churches; arbitrary rule our courts of justice ...' (P. Williams, *A Sermon preached in the Parish Church of Starston in Norfolk, upon the day of thanks-giving* ... (Cambridge, 1746), p. 9); see also P. Williams, *A Sermon preached in the Parish Church of Starston in Norfolk, upon the fast day* ... (Cambridge, 1745)

[2] *1774 election Diary 1:* 11 Oct., 26 Oct. 1774

[3] *by-election Diary 1:* 8 May 1776. The rearing of the Hardy children is described in vol. I, chaps 5 and 6

above Mary Hardy's daughter Mary Ann (1773–1864) and her husband Jeremiah Cozens (1766–1849), in unsigned and undated portraits. They formed part of a Nonconformist, radical circle close to their Sprowston farm, although Jeremiah's brother John Cozens and brother-in-law Jonathan Davey were far more active.

Mary Ann's granddaughter Caroline married Jeremiah Colman, later MP for Norwich; Caroline's brother Herbert became MP for N. Norfolk, Master of the Rolls and was raised to the peerage. His son, the MP for S. Norfolk, was the 2nd Lord Cozens-Hardy (*plate 53*). All were Liberals, with politics in the blood   [*Cozens-Hardy Colleection*]

[1] *Holkham* Narrated in vol. 2, chap. 4 and vol. 1, chap. 10

[2] *affection Norw. Merc.* 29 Oct. 1774. The wording emphasises the unity fostered by an uncontested election, with no divisiveness and no hostile antagonists; the electors were willing to play their part even when no polling had taken place. Both MPs were moderate Whigs. What Tory supporters thought is not stated

William's first sight of the new MP, aged only 22, who in later life was to invite him to the sheepshearings at Holkham Hall and whom William was to support as a friend, voter and adviser on tree-planting.[1] The tone of the press at the 1774 general election shows that public acclamation, not passive witness, was a vital part of the process:

On Wednesday last Sir Edward Astley, Bart. and Wenman Coke, Esq. were unanimously elected representatives in Parliament for the county of Norfolk. The numerous appearance of the freeholders (though no contest was expected), and the joy visible in every countenance, strongly proved their affection to and entire confidence in the integrity of their worthy Members.[2]

There was a studied choreography about an uncontested election, when even those qualified found themselves without a vote. This was particularly true in March 1807. The victors of November 1806, Coke and Windham, had been unseated. Following that controversial campaign the House of Commons had conducted their 'Great Constitutional Enquiry' into the county poll. On 20 February 1807 Norwich heard the news that the Commons had declared the poll invalid: the wining and dining ('treating') by Coke and Windham had far exceeded what was allowed by law.

Two new candidates had to be found, both Whigs, as Wodehouse declined to stand again and risk financial ruin. Sir Jacob Henry Astley had the relief of a safe return without undue expenditure; controversially the second candidate was the unseated Member's younger brother Edward Coke of Longford, Derbyshire, the northern family seat of the Cokes. He had immediately resigned as MP for Derby on hearing of his brother's disqualification, and stood for Norfolk. Equally promptly T. W. Coke was returned unopposed for Derby in his place. William Windham, as we have seen, was swiftly returned for New Romney, a convenient Kentish pocket borough.[1] The Coke brothers swapped seats again very shortly afterwards at the general election of May 1807, both being returned unopposed. Tory charges that the high-handed Cokes were turning Norfolk into the worst sort of borough were, perhaps understandably, renewed.[2]

The crisis of February and March brought onto the Norwich streets a show of strength in support of the new county MPs to give sanction to what could otherwise be seen as peremptory treatment of the freeholders. In the presence of the two unseated county Members, the new candidates rode into the city on election day, 4 March, at the head of a thousand-strong procession wending on horseback and on foot from Mile Cross beyond the city gates.[3] William and Mary Hardy had already struggled in deep snow to Sprowston, their daughter's new marital home; William Hardy junior arrived in readiness on 3 March. Mary Ann's brother-in-law William Cozens, born and raised near North Walsham, came up from London, and Henry Goggs and his wife came from Whissonsett for the uncontested election.

A large family party, including the diarist, dined at John Cozens' shop in the market place, from where those not in the procession could watch the chairing.[4] Mary Hardy's

[1] *scrutiny and new poll* For the House of Commons findings and the Norwich reaction see the *Norwich Mercury* of 21 Feb. and 7 Mar. 1807

[2] *Tory charges Norw. Merc.* 7 Mar. 1807

[3] *procession Norw. Merc.* 7 Mar. 1807

[4] *party Diary 4*: 18 Feb.–7 Mar. 1807. From the leaded roofs of the shop's bow windows John Thelwall (1764–1834), acquitted in the 1794 London Treason Trials, had addressed a huge crowd during the 1796 general election.

The Hardys were probably not alone among Norfolk families in treating the county election as the occasion for a huge family reunion: 'Mr Hardy and I, Mr and Mrs James [Cozens] and Mr William Cozens, Mr and Mrs Davey [Jonathan and Emma, née Cozens], Mr [Thomas Druery] Hawkins, Mrs Case [née Elizabeth Cozens], . . . sixteen in number, dined at Sprowston, our William went home after dinner' (5 Mar. 1807). This circle is described later in the chapter.

Mary Ann, the ever-valiant hostess, was then a new mother, her only child William being born 1 Dec. 1806

¹ *proclamation* R.M.
Bacon's pollbook 1806,
Budget, pp. 20–1. The
small caps and italics of
the original, designed
as guidance when read
aloud, are retained here.
The Budget has the
vigour of spoken English.
It contains 90 pages of
election addresses, pleas
and scurrilous attacks
of varying degrees of
savagery

² *influence Norw. Merc.*
15 Nov. 1806.
Charges of bribery
and corruption had
also been lodged (*Norw.
Merc.* 21 Feb. 1807)

above Bayfield Hall,
down the Glaven from
the Hardys' home. The
Tory MP Henry Jodrell
could rise above party
politics, as befitted a
part-time judge, but he
and the Hardys did not
socialise other than
through his work as a
local JP   [*MB · 2012*]

circle, many of whom had the county vote but were twice prevented from exercising it in 1807, played their part in the public acceptance of what otherwise could have seemed manipulation of proud, independently-minded freeholders.

These had been a searing few months, with party strife, factionalism and private ambition rampant just when the nation was engaged in a prolonged struggle on many fronts against France, Spain and the Dutch, at a great cost in lives, lasting personal injuries and to public finances. This attack on Coke, in a handbill published for the 1806 election contest, conveys something of the prevailing rancour:

PROCLAMATION —We, THOMAS WILLIAM, by our own presumption, PERPETUAL DICTATOR of *Norfolk* . . .

The inefficiency of our former Nominee [Astley] to represent our *Borough of Norfolk* is acknowledged: his retirement being necessary, the appointment of his successor [Windham] belongs, as everyone knows, *to us alone*. Our power to make this appointment is as honourable to our loving subjects, and as agreeable to the laws and constitution, as the means by which our power was acquired . . .

The Independent Cause was hourly increasing in popularity and real strength, and was known to have the good wishes of many of our *Dependents* [Coke's tenants]. Wodehouse and the supporters of this cause must however *be crushed*—WE ORDAIN IT . . .

It is the duty of subjects to obey . . .

Done at Holkham, in the fifth year of our reign.

THOMAS WILLIAM, *Perpetual Dictator* ¹

Bacon, editor of the *Norwich Mercury* and an avid election-watcher, deplored the 'influence' (pressure) which had been brought to bear on voters in November 1806, the majority of the complaints being directed against Windham.² The defeated candidate, Wodehouse, had been vindicated by the Commons, yet could not stand again as the expense was too great. To spare his purse earlier, Wodehouse had withdrawn from the poll on the penultimate evening, which would help to explain the drop in the Tory vote already noted.

Candidates and party labels

The pollbook budgets, or appendices of addresses, squibs and anonymous letters, highlight the issues debated during individual campaigns. These often centred round local preoccupations and prejudices as much as on national policies.

As pollbooks and their associated budgets were published only for contested elections, newspapers form the principal, regular source by which we can gain some sense of the candidate's political or party stance. The issues will be discussed in the next section; here some attempt is made to bracket the candidates and their affiliations, however elusive and contradictory they might appear at times.

Public positions were constantly shifting: it was not only Windham who swung in the wind. Of Edward Bacon, the MP for Norwich whom William Hardy in turn supported and rejected (table 4.8.1), it could fairly be said that he kept to his principles while others shifted around him. Paradoxically both men, the Member and the voter, showed consistency. Bacon adopted the stance of the 'Ministerialist'. Whatever the colour of the party in power, such men stood calmly and steadfastly behind the administration of the day in order to uphold the work of the King's ministers. Party came second or, more often, was not a consideration at all.[1]

Such a stand, they held, was particularly required when the country was at war. Support for the government, and by extension the Crown and the Armed Forces, was essential to present a united front. However, judged by the issues, the Bacon of 1768 (in peace) was a different man from the Bacon of 1780 (in war, and keeping an increasingly unpopular North administration in power). William Hardy, whose expression of his personal antipathy to war in his wife's diary is illustrated in the next section, was likewise consistent in his votes for and against Bacon. As excise officer and then brewer he championed trade and manufacturing; war affected them adversely and led to higher taxation.[2]

Henry Jodrell of Bayfield Hall, MP for Great Yarmouth and then for Bramber, has already been labelled a Tory. He was one of three prominent Tories and justices in the county who each subscribed £50 to the petition for the Great Constitutional Enquiry which swiftly unseated T.W. Coke and Windham in February 1807.[3] Yet for him party came second only a few weeks later. Following the near civil war of those months in Norfolk's political circles, Jodrell pledged to support Sir Jacob Henry Astley, a Whig, in the May general election. His long eulogy of Astley as he proposed his old friend's nomination was published in the *Norwich Mercury*.[4]

[1] *Bacon* See his biography in B.D. Hayes, 'Politics in Norfolk 1750–1832', pp. 348–50.
Bacon the ministerialist is depicted: 'He was less a politician than a man of business . . . Bute [the Prime Minister] found Bacon a sure government man and he [Bacon] supported each administration in turn until the Rockinghams came into office . . .' (pp. 348–9). The period covered is from May 1762, when the Earl of Bute was appointed First Lord of the Treasury, to Mar. 1782, with the formation of the Second Rockingham Administration

[2] *taxation* As a manufacturer William Hardy paid huge amounts of excise duty. A list of tax totals over time from Sir John Sinclair's *The History of the Public Revenue of the British Empire* (London, 1785) was copied in 1791 into the diary (*Diary 2*: p. 394, endnote)

[3] *petition* Norw. Merc. 14 Feb., 21 Feb. 1807. The other two named subscribers were Sir George Chad, Bt of Thursford Hall and John Custance—Revd James Woodforde's Squire Custance of Weston and Bath

[4] *Jodrell* Norw. Merc. 16 May 1807

[1] *neighbours* A point rammed home by B.D. Hayes, 'Politics in Norfolk 1750–1832', pp. 30–40

[2] *gentlemen; friends* Diary 4: 12 May 1807, 21 Sept. 1803.
Party labels rarely described a position adequately. William Windham would not have regarded himself as a Tory, but he sat in Pitt's Cabinet. The Duke of Portland, Pitt's Home Secretary and a Whig, took a group of Portland Whigs into Pitt's administration in July 1794

[3] *Tory, Whig* S. Johnson, *A Dictionary of the English Language* (London, 1755), vol. 2, unpag.
'Wigs' appear in Mary Ann Hardy's MS recipe book. Hers are far more elaborate than pure whey, being a light baked pudding made from flour, butter, eggs, yeast, new milk, sugar and carraway seeds.
The book, held in the Cozens-Hardy Collection, is featured in vol. I, app. I.B, with some examples of her recipes.
Dr Johnson would have delighted in giving his culinary definition first, followed by the disparaging meaning; the two were unrelated etymologically

Healing deep wounds came before party. Personal sympathies and loyalties would often trump political or party allegiance. Neighbours in the countryside, who would work and socialise companionably at quarter and petty sessions and afterwards at the inns, as stewards at assembly balls, at school feasts and shooting parties, recognised they needed to rub along together.[1]

Mary Hardy rarely refers to political debate other than in the newspaper extracts committed to her diary; Henry Raven never does. The loyalties of her husband and son William lay with the Whigs (with the exception of William Hardy senior's unswerving support for Henry Hobart), but they were not ostensibly party men. Neither diarist employs the epithets Whig, Tory, radical, Foxite, Jacobin, ministerialist or any of the other terms used at the time to describe an individual's leanings. For Mary Hardy, the freeholders gathering in Norwich to support T.W. Coke on election day were simply 'the gentlemen'; Sir Jacob Henry Astley merely hosted his 'friends' at a supper at Holt.[2]

In general terms a Whig supported the constitutional settlement of 1688–94 more wholeheartedly than a Tory. In Norwich the Whigs were drawn particularly from Nonconformist circles rather than the Established Church. That connection can however be over-emphasised, William Hardy cleaving faithfully to the Church of England to the end of his days. A Whig was more likely to be in trade, and thus to favour fiscal prudence and be fearful of waging war with all the consequent commercial disruption. A Tory was likely to have fewer qualms than a Whig about George III's use of the royal prerogative to circumvent Parliament, and was often classed as a 'Church and King' man.

The great lexicographer was airily dismissive. In the first edition of his work, in 1755, he balked at defining a Whig. By presenting a Tory as principled and a Whig as unprincipled Dr Johnson mischievously betrayed his own party affiliation:

TORY.   One who adheres to the ancient constitution of the state, and the apostolical hierarchy of the Church of England, opposed to a Whig.

WHIG.   1. Whey.
          2. The name of a faction.[3]

In his election address each candidate would present himself as upholding the Constitution and good government against the assaults of the others. Candidates proclaimed they were championing probity and stability in public life so routinely that even in the highly contentious general election campaign of 1806 the Norfolk freeholders would have been hard put to determine from election addresses just where the divide lay other than at a purely personal level.[1]

Occasionally a candidate would resort to practical politics, as Coke did in 1796 when he realised he might be facing a contested election. He declared that he had been against the American war, and would continue to press for peace with France in a conflict he had always abhorred:

. . . A speedy peace and the most rigid economy in every department of government can alone, I am persuaded, restore this country to its former flourishing state, and preserve to us and our descendants the blessing of the British Constitution as established at the glorious revolution of 1688 . . .[2]

Ten years later Coke's manifesto speech to the electors in Norwich a week before the opening of the poll was the only one by any of the three county candidates to refer in set terms to issues and to rise above personal vendatta; Windham and Wodehouse confined themselves to personal assaults on the unprincipled tactics adopted by the other. In one attack, by Windham on Wodehouse, the Felbrigg squire alleged that the Witton squire had imposed the ultimate sanction on innkeepers. Unless they voted for Wodehouse their licences would not be renewed at the next sessions— the very pressure point already identified, without finding evidence either way, in the section on influence (page 460). As justices of the peace the candidates held latent power.[3]

Coke's platform in 1806 remained as of old, according to the press report:

. . . He had endeavoured to promote the interests of the county in its agricultural concerns, and by an independency of parliamentary conduct, in supporting the principles of the constitution as established in 1688, to merit their [the freeholders'] good opinion . . .[4]

Political differences could be identified other than by party labels. Rather than dividing along personal or ideological

[1] *1806 election* The Norwich papers would give the candidates a good amount of space at election time to spell out what they hoped to achieve by representing their 'native county' at Westminster.
They chose to talk in vague terms of service, independence, activity and perseverance, with very little attention paid to the ends to which these exertions would be put

[2] *Coke Norw. Merc.* 21 May 1796. He could with justice claim that throughout his long career he had remained unusually consistent

[3] *Windham* 'In a speech of considerable length' he made the very specific allegation that 'even magisterial authority had been exerted among various publicans, who had been told that their licences should not be renewed, unless they voted for Col. Wodehouse' (*Norw. Merc.* 8 Nov. 1806).
As stated earlier, no such hint can be picked up from Mary Hardy's diary for the Hardys' parts of the county. By then they had few tied houses in areas under Wodehouse 'interest', compared with their Coltishall years

[4] *Coke Norw. Merc.* 8 Nov. 1806

[1] *court* One such gulf opened in the 1786 Norwich campaign: the 'Court interest' (Hobart) and the 'Independent interest' (Beevor) (*Norw. Merc.* 5 Aug. 1786).
That prolonged city by-election campaign proved so violent that the defeated Beevor called for a Commons scrutiny and had Henry Hobart deposed; a re-run took place a few months later (*Norw. Merc.* 29 July, 5 Aug., 16 Sept., 23 Sept., 30 Sept. 1786; 3 Feb., 24 Feb., 17 Mar. 1787). Hobart scraped in again

[2] *Windham* R.M. Bacon's Norfolk poll-book 1806, Budget, p. 11, by an anonymous Wode-house supporter. The italics are his

[3] *Roberts* T.W. Coke's difficulties over the Holkham inheritance and the rejection of the Roberts line by the Dowager Countess of Leicester are vividly described by A.M.W. Stirling, *Coke of Norfolk and his Friends*, pp. 50–62. Norfolk and Holkham were utterly unfamiliar to Wenman and T.W. Coke

[4] *own country* L. Namier, *The Structure of Politics at the Accession of George III*, p. 5. In 1761, 49 out of 80 knights of the shire 'can be said to have inherited their seats' (Namier, p. 73)

lines the age-old fracture of 'Court' and 'Country' was one with which electors could identify. Those forming the loose grouping of the country party regarded themselves as a fiercely independent body of freeholders, their chosen man uncontaminated by office and by place-seeking.[1] That Windham, although back in the Whig fold, was also by 1806 once more in receipt of monies from the public purse as Secretary for War and the Colonies proved ground for abuse from the very side which had supported him wholeheartedly as Secretary at War under Pitt, as this (Tory) address to the freeholders of Norfolk illustrates:

> . . . *Mr Windham* lends himself to Mr Coke as *his tool*, to enable him to verify his assertion, that he can at any time secure the election of any candidate of his own nomination: and Mr Windham having got his hand once more in the *public purse*, no longer pleads his poverty as an excuse for not engaging in the contest . . . Such among you, therefore, as deem the independence of the county worth struggling for, and that it may not be represented in parliament like a *venal borough*, by any person whom a gentleman sitting in his parlour may choose to name, I would admonish you not to lend your aid to this foul conspiracy against the Colonel . . .[2]

The County Member, as a knight of the shire with antecedents in the reign of Edward III, had to demonstrate not only his independence from pressure but also his solid bonds with his county. The young Thomas William Coke had to work hard at representing himself as worthy of the high regard of the Norfolk freeholders, for his father Wenman Roberts (1717–76) had not been born a Coke, nor had he known anything, other than by report, of Norfolk until he, the father, was elected MP for Norfolk in 1774 in the same general election that saw him returned as MP for Derbyshire; he resigned from the latter seat. Only in 1750 had Wenman Roberts assumed his mother's surname of Coke. The family estate lay at Longford, in Derbyshire.[3]

Father and son faced the real danger that as strangers to the county they might not be acceptable to the freeholders. A county MP could not be 'parachuted', to use the modern idiom, into the constituency. The country dwellers who sat as knights of the shire in the House of Commons desired above all 'primacy in their own "country" ';[4] hence the significance of the Hardys, with their very young sons, turning out in Norwich to cheer the 22-year-old Coke in May 1776, as described earlier. It was only venal boroughs, to use the term adopted by Coke and by Windham's opponents, which were compliant over accepting candidates foisted on them by Government or by those wielding local influence.

Coke, while a man of immense charm and generosity in other spheres, was vehemently partisan in politics. When he displayed a tendency to treat Norfolk in imperious fashion there was a good deal of restiveness and, at times, outright opposition—and not just from diehard Tories. The Lord Lieutenant, George Walpole, third Earl of Orford, grandson of the great Whig Prime Minister and an admirer of the young Coke, distanced himself later from his actions, addressing him with these reproachful words: 'Sir, I respect you as an agriculturalist, but you must not turn the county of Norfolk into a borough.'[1] Jane Coke, who, as we have seen, would accompany her husband on the canvass and when making political calls and who did so much to promote his interests, had an arresting phrase to describe a contested election. It has the ring of the autocracy that Coke deplored in his sovereign. Putting up a candidate to oppose her husband was 'to disturb the peace of the county'.[2]

The peace, used here in the senses both of good order and of absence of strife, was certainly disturbed at election time. But that was what the Glorious Revolution, by which Coke set so much store, had brought in its wake. Even in an uncontested election his unconcealed hatred of the Tories emerged. In his declared opinion, both Norfolk MPs had to be Whigs. If possible they had also to be Foxite Whigs and not, as was traditionally the case in an uncontested election, one Whig and one Tory in order to represent an electorate which the county polling figures consistently show in this period to be fairly equally balanced between the two parties. Looking back on his long life in politics 1776–1831 as the ferment over the Great Reform Bill reached its height, Coke observed that his only object in standing for election had been this: 'To see Norfolk represented by two Members who followed the principles of Mr Fox; . . . I could not bear to see Norfolk represented by one Whig and one Tory . . .'[3]

He had perforce to bear it. The county was indeed represented by one Whig and one Tory between 1784 and 1797,

[1] *Orford* Quoted in A.M.W. Stirling, *Coke of Norfolk and his Friends*, p. 96.
  She does not cite the date of his letter, but it was written on the third occasion on which Coke sought Orford's support for his candidature, and was thus either 1784 or, more probably, 1790; the Lord Lieutenant died in 1791.
  By his reference to 'a borough' he means a pocket borough

[2] *Jane Coke* Quoted in A.M.W. Stirling, *Coke of Norfolk and his Friends*, p. 136. The letter is dated 4 Apr. 1784

[3] *Coke* Quoted in A.M.W. Stirling, *Coke of Norfolk and his Friends*, p. 326, from a report in the *Norwich Mercury* from May 1831. There is much material on the subject in her study (pp. 320–37).
  Coke retired from the strife of elections in 1833, and in 1837 was raised to the peerage as 1st Earl of Leicester of the 2nd creation (the earlier Holkham line having died out, but then passing via the female line to the Roberts branch of the family)

[1] *Wilkes's Head* The outlet, its licensing and innkeeper Ben Ginby feature in *Diary 1* and in vol. 2, chaps 9 and 10.
For its name changes see the entry in the Gazetteer of the Hardys' 101 public houses in that volume: it was the Windmill in 1751

[2] *Wilkes* J.D. Alsop, 'Contemporary remarks on the 1768 election in Norfolk and Suffolk', *Norfolk Archaeology*, vol. 38, pt 1 (1981), p. 79; H. Barker, *Newspapers, Politics and English Society*, pp. 152–6

[3] *events* Mary Hardy's entry for 23 May 1794 gives a flavour of the non-committal way she reported them: 'From the newspapers: The British troops defeated with great loss in France [the actions near Courtrai on 15 May and Lille 16 May]. Many people taken up in England for sedition and treason, the Habeas Corpus Act suspended' (*Diary 3*).
She does not develop such entries to reveal the family's reactions, although issues like these would have been discussed around the table and on visits to friends and family; nor does she link them to the political platforms on which parliamentary candidates stood

and the only Foxite Whigs who were returned for Norfolk in the 36-year span of Mary Hardy's diary were himself, for 27 years, and, for two months in 1807, his brother.

The issues

When they lived at Coltishall 1772–81 the Hardys had a tied house at nearby Tunstead named the Wilkes's Head. It had been the Windmill in the mid-century. In 1795 it became the Horse and Groom, the name it retained into the twenty-first century.[1] The adoption and then dropping of the name of the divisive Middlesex MP John Wilkes reflected changing political opinions. He was popularly feted 1763–1770 under such slogans as 'Wilkes for ever' for his resistance to arbitrary power in the form of general warrants and attacks on a free press. The turbulent 1768 general election was fought partly on this issue; in 1770, on his release from prison, 45 textile workers marched through Norwich to the sound of a band.[2] But his name, and what he stood for, were considered dangerous in the 1790s in the government clampdown on sedition. To be sure of keeping its licence it was thought politic to change the name of Tunstead's small thatched outlet again. The dominant issues of the day shaped not only political divides but even justices' attitudes to licensing.

We know from the newspapers and the actions of the circle into which Mary Hardy's daughter married that there were some fundamental differences over issues and over reactions to events by which political parties defined themselves. These included the American war 1775–83, the French Revolution 1789–93, the use of the royal prerogative, agitation in the 1790s for parliamentary reform, the French wars 1793–1815 and the high taxation demanded by war. With the exception of reform Mary Hardy refers to all these, but she does not link them specifically to political debate.[3]

Since a desire for parliamentary reform was treated as incipient sedition by a government alarmed by developments across the Channel, that topic will be examined shortly in relation to the Corresponding Societies 1792–93 and the Treason Trials of 1794 in which the Norwich figures John Cozens, Jonathan Davey and Mark Wilks were involved.

William Hardy's views are expressed forcibly in his wife's diary in January 1794 (opposite). In his entry on the anti-

On Tuesday if 21st Instant the Parliament met and the Kings Speech being Read a Voat of Thanks was proposed. but an Amendment was wished for in order to put an end to the French War the following Members being the Minority Voates for Amendment

Peers

Albemarl. Bedford. Chedworth. Cholmondely. Derby
Guilford. Lansdown. Lauderdale. Egmont. Norfolk
St John. Stanhope.

Commons

Wm Adams	R S Milnes	P J Townshend
N L Antonie	Cunliffe Shaw	Sir E Vane
Sir J Aubrey	Jos Jeckyll	B M Vaughan
— Bouverie	Sir Wm Lemon	R Viner
J R Burch	N Machleod	J Walwyn
G Bing	Hon T Maitland	C C Western
J B Church	Sir Wm Milner	J Wharton
T W Coke	Dudl North	J Whitbread Jun
E Coke	Wm Plumer	T Whitmore
Wm Colhoun	— Powlett	R Wilbeham
J Courtenay	Sir M W Ridley	Sir E Wennington
J C Crespigny	L Wm Russell	R Milbank
T Erskine	W C Shawe	J Crew
Sir H Featherstone	A B Sheridan	Lord Wycombe
Rt Hon R Fitzpatrick	W Smith	
Sir H Fletcher	H Speed	
Hon T Foley	C Sturt	
Rt Hon C J Fox	And St John	Tellers
Ph Francis	Ld R Spencer	W. Adams
Chas Grey	B Tarlton	Chas Grey
Jas Hare	M A Taylor	These are the 62
J Hercourt	J Thomson	Vertuous Members
Film Honeywood		who Voted in this
H Howard		
S Howell		
W Hussey		
great Contest for PEACE against 277		

¹ taxation 'New taxes to be raised this year to pay the interest of eleven millions [pounds sterling]' (Diary 3, where the full extract is transcribed). Again it is a newspaper extract, cataloguing additional duties on bricks and other building materials, paper, spirits and attorneys' clerks

² Coke From a speech in honour of the new Mayor of Lynn given at King's Lynn 29 Sept. 1830, by which time William IV was on the throne; a long extract appeared in the Norfolk Chronicle, 23 Oct. 1830

³ births, deaths eg the birth of the King's son Prince Adolphus Frederick, and death of the King's sister the Queen of Denmark (Diary 1: 24 Feb. 1774, 20 May 1775)

⁴ birthday Diary 1: 4 June 1775, 4 June 1779. After the early years she ceased to treat her diary as additionally a type of almanac, and the marginal glosses changed their form.

Years later the Hardys viewed the King's birthday illuminations in the capital (Diary 4: 4 June 1800)

⁵ joy of all Diary 2, p. 394, endnotes, Feb. 1789.

George III's prolonged illness proved a turning point in his

war amendment to the King's Speech which he copied from the newspaper it is not merely his words which betray his outlook: it is his orthography. His highlighting of the words 'RT HON. C.J. FOX', 'R.B. SHERIDAN', and 'PEACE' leave no doubt in the reader's mind, as he will have intended, over where his sympathies lay. He was at that time without question a Foxite Whig incensed by a war which he abhorred and by the consequent high taxation, this last being demonstrated at that time in the wording of his wife's press extract of 7 February 1794.¹

The extracts, and to a lesser extent his voting record, identify William Hardy as a Foxite Whig. However in his loyalty to George III—the person as well as the ruler—he was a mainstream Whig, in the style of Thomas Beevor and the Astleys. The Foxite faction by contrast distanced themselves from the King over his use of the royal prerogative. Coke and other Foxites were appalled by what they saw as unconstitutional meddling by the sovereign in matters which ought properly to belong to Parliament. Coke was outspoken in his condemnation of the King: 'the worst man that ever sat on a throne—George III, that bloody King'.²

Mary Hardy's references to the Royal Family are those of a traditionally loyal supporter of the monarchy. She notes births and deaths,³ twice records the King's birthday as a marginal gloss,⁴ and appears truly relieved and thankful on the King's recovery of his health in February 1789 despite the fact that it delayed by 22 years the regency so devoutly desired by Fox and his faction. The enthusiastic celebration of the news by the Hardy family and the rest of the village is touched on in chapter 10 and described in volume 3, chapter 6. Her own words, not taken from a newspaper, reveal her joy. Under the general heading 'Remarkable events' at the back of ledger 3 of her manuscript diary she notes the name of the new excise officer and the death of her uncle Thomas Raven. She then makes a series of observations about the progress of the King's affliction, ending:

. . . when to the joy of all he perfectly recovered the use of his reason. The Prince of Wales had been chosen Regent under certain restrictions but had not begun to act in that capacity when his Father was pronounced perfectly well and took on himself the reins of Government.⁵

The question of peace or war proved the major defining issue of the day. Norwich was not very badly hit by the start of the American war as the county did not export its cloth across the Atlantic. But when the conflict escalated in 1778 into war with the French and Spanish, and then the Dutch, the trade of Norfolk's seaboard suffered. War with France in early 1793 dealt another great blow, to be exacerbated in 1795 when the French gained control of Holland. For centuries the Low Countries had been the place of trade for East Anglia, serving as its gateway to the Continent. Now the North Sea was further infested with privateers, and exports were very badly affected. On 27 January 1795 the Mayor, Sheriffs and Common Council of Norwich, on behalf of the citizens, drew up petitions to the King and Commons, suing for the end of:

The present most calamitous and destructive war; a war which has nearly annihilated the manufactories and trade of this once-flourishing city, and consequently reduced the majority of its inhabitants—the industrious poor—to a state of extreme distress.[1]

There was however no unity, even in Norwich, as indicated by the hard evidence of an election result rather than the more subjective assessment of the state of public opinion based on petitions and newspaper coverage. The Norwich by-election of July 1794, occasioned by the acceptance by William Windham of the government post of Secretary at War, was fought on the peace issue. James Mingay, a Thetford lawyer, was nominated (without his knowledge) to stand against Windham as the peace candidate.[2] The voters were not persuaded by the peace lobby, resoundingly supporting the man who was one of the principal figures leading the prosecution of the armed struggle against France. The result at Norwich was Windham 1236, Mingay 770. Anti-war sentiment in Norfolk and Norwich politics should not be over-emphasised. The minister had won more than three-fifths (62 per cent) of the vote.[3]

The pro-war Whigs as well as the Tories threw their weight behind the Government at this time of national emergency. One element of the multi-faceted crisis was the threat of sedition. This threat grew out of another defining political issue: Britain's reaction to the French Revolution. Turmoil

public acceptance. A grass-roots wave of genuine affection and loyalty swept the country. For a careful analysis of the changing public profile of the King and its effect on national unity see L. Colley, 'The apotheosis of George III: Loyalty, royalty and the British nation 1760–1820', *Past & Present*, no. 102 (Feb. 1984), esp. pp. 97, 104–6, 110–13, 120

[1] *petitions Norw. Merc.* 7 Feb. 1795

[2] *Mingay* His message from London of 14 July to the Norwich voters presages the Mayor's petitions six months later: '...The present distressed state of your trade and manufactures must give pain to every feeling mind; and I shall look forward with anxious hope for the arrival of that day in which we may all again enjoy the inestimable blessings of PEACE' (*Norw. Merc.* 19 July 1794).

Mingay was however astonished that his name had been put forward without his knowledge. He was ineligible to stand, as he held a place from the Crown (*Norw. Merc.* 19 July 1794)

[3] *result Norw. Merc.* 19 July 1794

[1] *revolution Norw. Merc.* 1 Dec. 1787. Following the storming of the Bastille, reports were feverish with excitement that the French people were about to emulate the British and discover true freedom: 'Thus has this great Revolution been effected', read the bulletin from Paris of 17 July 1789 (*Norw. Merc.* 25 July 1789)

[2] *radicals* The Paris Jacobins were members of the radical club led by Robespierre which overthrew the Girondists in 1793; the rule of the Committee of Public Safety followed

[3] *division* B.D. Hayes, 'Politics in Norfolk 1750–1832', p. 262

[4] *legislation* It followed the issuing in France in 1792 of the Edict of Fraternity (which called on the lower orders to rise), and included the Suspension of Habeas Corpus 1794, the Aliens' Act 1794, the Seditious Meetings Act 1795 and the Seditious Practices Act 1795.
Enforcement lay with magistrates, but Norwich's took a relaxed attitude to meetings in public houses, to the fury of the city MP William Windham. See vol. 2, chap. 9 on regulation; also C.B. Jewson, *The Jacobin City*, p. 33–49 on the legislation

in France had early been anticipated. The *Norwich Mercury* closely followed the worsening situation over the Channel and the French King's difficulties: 'What will be the upshot of this business no one can foresee, but the people talk of a revolution in the Government . . .'[1]

But once the initial joy had subsided, and especially once the Terror had started to take a hold, the Whigs in England split into factions. These ranged from the reticent, who feared what the harvest would be, to the extreme radicals, classed as Jacobins, who still held to the nobility of the cause despite the aberrations of some of its proponents.[2] Hayes sees the Revolution as a polarising force in the city of Norwich, but less so in the county at large; it was the division between 'an inclination towards authority and an instinct for conservation on the one hand, and a love of liberty and a readiness for change on the other'.[3]

William Hardy appears to have straddled these two strands in contemporary local politics, personifying the phenomenon identified by Hayes of the diminution of polarity in the country areas. He was anti-war, but pro-monarchy; in favour of the promotion of trade and fiscal prudence, but wholly untouched by Jacobinism. As he had no opportunity to vote between 1790 and 1802 we are left ignorant of how he would have polled during that important decade.

The future brother-in-law of his only daughter took a very different line. Three of the close circle into which Mary Ann married—but not her husband Jeremiah Cozens—were active members of extreme radical groups in Norwich. John Cozens, Jonathan Davey and the Revd Mark Wilks all maintained links with the London Corresponding Society (LCS) as members of the Norwich Revolutionary Society. This was later renamed the Norwich Patriotic Society in an attempt to reassure the authorities after Pitt's legislation was passed 1792–95 stemming what was seen as a tide of sedition.[4]

Jewson has described the febrile state of Norwich politics in the early 1790s. The wholesale and retail grocer John Cozens, who was to become known as the Sprowston Fox as his politics closely matched those of the famous Westminster politician, was only 23 years of age when he instituted a correspondence with the LCS. Less than two years later these letters (transcribed in part overleaf) were seized

above Emma, née Cozens (1764–1841), and her husband Jonathan Davey (1760–1814), painted in 1824 and 1811. Among Emma Davey's brothers were Mary Ann Hardy's husband Jeremiah and the 'Sprowston Fox' John Cozens.

John and his brother-law were partners 1791–93 as the wholesale and retail grocers Cozens & Davey in Norwich market place. Both stood on the extreme radical wing of Whig politics in Norwich, Davey attending the Treason Trials in London in 1794 and bringing news of the acquittals to Norwich.

As late as 1812 Davey, who had stood unsuccessfully for Mayor in 1807, declared he 'would make a hole in the King's head'. He carried out his threat, demolishing his inn of that name beside his old shop and creating the walk to the Castle still known as Davey Place (volume 3, chapter 7) [*portraits by Sir William Beechey, RA: Cozens-Hardy Collection*]

by the Government as part of its prosecution of Thomas Hardy, John Thelwall and others in what became known as the Treason Trials of 1794.[1]

The platform of the LCS was reform, not revolution. It pressed for universal manhood suffrage and annual parliaments, and adopted the principles not so much of the Jacobins as of John Locke. However supporting part of the intellectual and political programme of those who from late January 1793 were the enemy could strike the authorities

[1] *John Cozens* For his career as a Norwich grocer see vol. 3, chap. 7. His shop, from which Mary Hardy was to see the 1806 election, was in the market place, but he also had a villa and garden at Sprowston; hence his soubriquet

left Mary Ann Hardy's brother-in-law John Cozens (1769–1841), whose facial features strongly resemble those of his sister Emma Davey and brother Jeremiah. Mary Ann appears to have adjusted harmoniously to the extreme views of this circle based in Norwich and nearby Sprowston, to which her parents and brother also became accustomed. John Cozens and his wife Mary remained very close to the Letheringsett family for the rest of their lives.

Mary Cozens came from a family of Nonconformist Norwich shopkeepers. She was the sister of Thomas Druery Hawkins, the sugar-factor in the City of London from whom her husband bought supplies for his Norwich business and who married Mary Hardy's niece Mary Raven in 1806 [*photograph of an unlocated portrait: Cozens-Hardy Collection*]

[1] *riots* Discussed in vol. 3, chap. 6 on upholding the Peace. Mary Hardy and Henry Raven, living at the centre of some of these bread riots, described them in their diaries in a series of entries for Dec. 1795 and Jan. 1796 (*Diary 3*)

[2] *Saint* C.B. Jewson, *The Jacobin City*, pp. 47–8, 73. Saint was innkeeper of the Pelican, in the Nonconformist area by Wilks's chapel and close to the Old Meeting in which John Cozens was active.

The first was Calvinistic Baptist; the second Independent

as treachery. And when these papers fell into government hands the emphasis on secrecy and concealment so marked in the letters to John Cozens from London would have aroused further suspicions of treasonable activity.

In 1792–93 Cozens was secretary of the Norwich Revolution Society; Jonathan Davey was to become treasurer of the successor organisation. Both men stood in great danger. The penalties for treason were severe, as shown in the sidenotes opposite. The Government was not to know that the revolution in France would fail to be exported to Britain, and had no means of foreseeing that the war against Napoleon would put agitation for reform on hold for a generation. Adding to the sense of alarm, the disastrous harvest of 1795 precipitated riots and local unrest.[1] John Cozens' successor as secretary, Isaac Saint, was arrested and held for months under the suspension of Habeas Corpus in May 1794, the same month that the Treason Trial defendants were arrested. Saint was taken to London and questioned by the Privy Council; the Lord Chancellor led the interrogation.[2]

Despite, or because of, the dangers, the combative Baptist minister Mark Wilks did not hesitate to preach fearless

Working to restore the Constitution to its ancient purity: the London Corresponding Society's letters to John Cozens of Norwich 1792

source TNA: PRO TS 24/10, Treasury Solicitor's papers, Nov. and Dec. 1792 [1]

FROM MAURICE MARGAROT: LETTER 16, 26 Nov. 1792 [2]

Fellow Citizens,—Your letter of the 11th instant was by the Secretary [Thomas Hardy] laid before the Committee of Delegates of the London Corresponding Society. Having never before heard of your Society [in Norwich] they wish to have some farther information concerning it as to its origins, its principles and the number of its members ... They do not thoroughly comprehend how it would be possible to incorporate with our Society three of your members residing in Norwich inasmuch as it would be impossible to communicate to them at that distance all our correspondence and they could not attend our committees where the business is transacted ...

As to the object they have in view they refer you to their addresses. You will therein see they mean to disseminate political knowledge and thereby engage the judicious part of the nation to demand a restoration of their rights in annual parliaments, the members of those parliaments owing their election to the unbought and even unbiased suffrage of every citizen in possession of his reason and not incapacitated by crimes ...

[Giving advice on how to run the society in Norwich:] Above all, be careful to preserve peace and good order among you, let no dispute be carried to excess—leave monarchy, democracy and even religion entirely aside; never dispute on those topics ...

They [the LCS] likewise recommend the appointment of one of the least conspicuous of your members to receive such letters as may be sent to the Society lest if he be well known about your town to be a member some interruption might take place in the delivery ...

FROM THOMAS HARDY: LETTER 19, 14 Dec. 1792 [3]

[to] Norwich, Mr John Cozens:

Dear Sir,—In answer to your letter of the 12th instant I am authorised to answer you in the name of our Society that not one of our members will affix his signature to any declaration or profession of being fully satisfied with the existing abuses engrafted on our Constitution nor to any paper expressing a wish that those abuses may be continued. We look back to our original Constitution and we associate for the purpose of restoring it to its ancient purity; the pressure of business is such that we have not time at present to give you a full account of what paper but if you can point out to us any method of conveyance safer than the post we will send you some copies of different letters and addresses which may inform and encourage your Society in that laudable pursuit.

I am with sincerity, Your humble servant [   ]

[1] *source* These papers of the London Corresponding Society (LCS) were held by the Government when preparing the prosecution case for the Old Bailey trial of Thomas Hardy (1752–1832), the LCS's secretary, and 12 other defendants on a charge of High Treason following their arrest in May 1794. (Hardy was no relation to William Hardy of Letheringsett)

[2] *Margarot* Maurice (1745–1815), founder member and chairman of the London Corresponding Society, represented Norwich's and other revolution societies at a convention in Edinburgh in 1793 pressing for parliamentary reform. He was arrested there and tried in Scotland.

He and others were found guilty of sedition and sentenced to 14 years' transportation to Botany Bay, the group becoming known as the Scottish martyrs.

This letter is the draft of an address he proposed to send to John Cozens's Norwich Revolutionary Society

[3] *From Hardy* Unsigned. It is in the shoemaker Thomas Hardy's hand, to judge from other letters in the collection

'*Treason! Treason!*': Revd Mark Wilks's sermon 1795 in support of Thomas Hardy and his fellow defendants in the London Treason Trials of 1794

source   S. Wilks, *Memoirs of Rev. Mark Wilks* (London, 1821); extracts pp. xxxvii–lxiii

[1] '*Athaliah*' The first of the two sermons Wilks delivered at St Paul's Baptist Church, Norwich, 19 Apr. 1795 and then published himself; his daughter Sarah later included them as appendices to her memoir.

Wilks gave two collection sermons on the one day to help pay for the defence expenses of the trial in Dec. 1794 of Thomas Hardy, John Horne Tooke, John Thelwall and the other defendants; his afternoon sermon (S. Wilks, *Memoirs*, pp. lxiv–lxxxiv) was even more overtly political.

The Hardys often heard Mark Wilks preach at St Paul's 1804–08, where he served as minister, and at chapels at Briston and Cley Methodists, 1802–05

[2] *Hardy etc* The defendants. See the introduction to the eight-volume facsimile edition of the trial papers: J. Barrell and J. Mee, eds, *Trials for Treason and Sedition, 1792–1794* (Pickering & Chatto, London, 2006, 2007)

'ATHALIAH; OR THE TOCSIN SOUNDED BY MODERN ALARMISTS'

2 Kings, Chap. xi. 14. *Treason! Treason!* Never since the world began was a charity sermon preached from a text like this; nor was ever charity sermon preached on a like occasion. The text contains neither law nor gospel, neither exhortation nor dehortation; neither precept nor promise is to be found in it: it alludes to an historical narration of facts, and contains the hideous yell of a crafty alarmist [Athaliah], who in order to rouse the fears of her partisans, and excite to war, raises the cry of *treason! treason!* . . .

Tell me, citizens, have not we among us, no infamous calumniators, has not the ghost of Athaliah lately haunted the pulpit, the bar, the senate, the court, and has not the cry of treason! treason! been vociferated through the island? . . .

But the word that has inspired the most dread in a British senate, and the adoption of which appears most criminal is that of 'citizen—citizen'! How terrific! how inauspicious! how inimical to the interest of all nations, and subversive of good government! . . . Notwithstanding the word citizen has so much to recommend it to general use, as it is an epithet expressive of the doctrine of equality; of the annihilation of slavery and vassalage; of the abolition of privileged orders, and feudal customs; it is not strange it should excite disgust: but as its genuine meaning is only a freeman, the adoption of it cannot be treason . . .

In opposition to every thing insinuated in the king's message, and to every thing advanced in both Houses of Parliament, I ask, what says an English jury? I hear the clerk of the Arraigns call out, Thomas Hardy, hold up your hand; turning to the jury, I hear him enquire, Gentlemen of the jury, is the prisoner guilty of the treason whereof he is charged, or not guilty? Hear Englishmen— hear with transport! hear with grateful thankfulness to God! hear the foreman of the jury, as the mouth of all, give the lie to the lip of slander, and rescue innocence from the jaws of death, by the just and inevitable reply of NOT GUILTY!! . . .

But for the jurisprudence of this country, the just decision of an incorruptible jury, and the superintending care of God, I might have called, Hardy, Tooke, Thelwall, Holcroft, Richter, Joyce, Bonney, Kid, where are you?[2] and have received no answer! yes, I might have interrogated myself with, where am I? and have found myself on a Newgate drop.

and inflammatory sermons in his Norwich chapel built by the Evangelical Church of England priest Revd Thomas Bowman of Martham.[1] Like Cozens and Davey, Wilks was not prosecuted. But a West Country Baptist minister from Plymouth was charged with sedition, tried at Exeter Assizes, and imprisoned in Newgate for four years. On his release he travelled up to Norwich in 1798 to preach from Wilks's pulpit at St Paul's Baptist Church.[2] As the extracts from 'Athaliah' show, Wilks might have been found guilty too had he been brought before a Tory jury at Norwich Assizes.

Just as the Norwich magistrates kept their heads, so did those in the countryside. No witch-hunt was reported in the press, and Mary Hardy makes no mention either of seditious meetings or of prosecutions of innkeepers.[3] The commanding presence of T. W. Coke in north Norfolk, himself a justice of the peace, may have afforded some protection, for he was as outspoken as any. The diarist's record is however often found wanting on subjects not intimately connected with the family and the family business. While not recording the existence of any revolution societies in her area she likewise fails to record the patriotic meetings. One such was the anti-Paine village feast given near Letheringsett by the Rector of Edgefield, where the author of *The Rights of Man* was burnt in effigy.[4] Tom Paine, the Thetford-born former excise officer, was seen by loyal sections of the Norfolk population as a traitor. It is hard to judge from the newspaper reports how deep-seated this hostility to him was in reality among the labourering poor, who may have been willing to take part in any displays offering free beer and feasting.

Apart from the Norwich correspondence seized and held in London, the sermons of Wilks and the memoir by his daughter Sarah illustrate the type of talk that would have been heard in the Norfolk revolution societies. Given his extraordinary volubility, the statement by his daughter that 'By those who best knew my father, it is said, his politics were active not talkative' suggests that a whirlwind of activity must have surrounded him and his crusade for reform. Sarah Wilks emphasises the danger to his liberty and even his life faced by her father in his endeavours, on which she takes care not to elaborate even after the lapse of nearly thirty years. When he ended 'Athaliah' with the words, 'I

[1] *Bowman* J. Browne, *History of Congregationalism and Memorials of the Churches in Norfolk and Suffolk* (London, 1877), pp. 196–7.
For the important figure of Bowman (d.1792), see vol. 3, chap. 3. His influence stretched from Martham not only across central and eastern Norfolk but into Norwich. It was in Bowman's former city pulpit that Wilks gave 'Athaliah' and other sermons which risked being interpreted as seditious

[2] *Newgate* C.B. Jewson, *The Jacobin City*, p. 87. The minister, William Winterbotham, feted by various Nonconformist congregations in Norwich

[3] *sedition* Fanny Burney, while staying at Aylsham in 1792, asserted that there was a network of 'little revolution societies' in the villages which transmitted their ideas to Norwich and thence to London (quoted by C.B. Jewson, *The Jacobin City*, p. 39, where other evidence is also cited)

[4] *Paine Norw. Merc.* 12 Jan. 1793. Other similar patriotic displays took place at Corpusty and Swaffham.
Revd Bransby Francis, Rector of Edgefield 1764 –1829, changed his

right The firebrand Mark Wilks (1748–1819).
The Gibraltar-born field preacher began his
religious career in W. Bromwich, near Birmingham, as a Baptist. He later joined Lady
Huntingdon's Connexion to be trained in her
college at Trevecca, S. Wales, and first served
as a Calvinistic Methodist in Norwich.

William Hardy would, most unusually,
accompany his wife to a meeting if Wilks
took the pulpit. They often saw him at his
Sprowston farm and at their daughter's
nearby, and had him to stay at Letheringsett
[*painting by Branwhite; engraving by Ridley
1810, from the frontispiece to Sarah Wilks's 1821
memoir: Norfolk Heritage Centre, Norwich*]

political stance over the
years, voting Whig (for
Sir Edward Astley and
Wenman Coke) in 1768,
but plumping for the
Tory John Wodehouse
in 1802 and 1806. The
searing 1790s may have
played their part in
shaping his opinions

[1] *Wilks* S. Wilks,
*Memoirs of Rev. Mark
Wilks, Late of Norwich*
(London, 1821), pp. 71,
76–81. He campaigned
against Windham's re-
election in Norwich in
1794 and against the
Seditious Meetings Bill

[2] *sermons* S. Wilks,
*Memoirs of Rev. Mark
Wilks*, pp. iii–xxxiv

[3] *seaside Diary 4*: 2 Aug.
1802, 25 July 1803, 20
May 1805, 21–23 July,
28 July 1807.

His significance as a
preacher is covered in
vol. 3, chap. 3

might . . . have found myself on a Newgate drop,' he was
making a serious point as well as relishing the use of language sufficiently arresting to keep his congregation alert
during the long watches of his sermons.[1]

Wilks's sermons on the French Revolution, preached on
14 July 1791, the second anniversary of the storming of the
Bastille, were similarly incendiary. The first opened with the
strident declamation, 'Jesus Christ was a Revolutionist'. In
his second he launched a savage assault on the British system of civil government. Its upholders, he asserted, viewed
the revolutionaries in France as an 'irrational, unprincipled,
proscribing, confiscating, plundering, ferocious, bloody,
and tyrannical democracy'. He then devoted the rest of his
sermon to demonstrating that true liberty rested with the
French under their new regime. It was the English who were
enchained in 'political darkness'.[2]

It is typical of Mary Hardy that although we meet this
preacher, bath owner (at Heigham), farmer and election
agent fairly frequently in her diary not a hint of his conversation is set down. Instead we learn at what hour he arrived,
and whether he stayed for tea. She does shed light on the
variety of the meeting houses in which he preached and the
range of listeners he attracted, including even her staunchly
Anglican husband. Also we learn something of his domestic
habits not recorded elsewhere. Wilks, like John Cozens,
enjoyed the unrevolutionary activity of going to Cromer,
Sheringham and Salthouse for short breaks by the seaside.[3]

Politics and war were intertwined. The next chapter will show that the struggle against Napoleon was, generally, not so divisive as the French Revolution and the ensuing conflict had been for England. Given the alarms of the 1790s the authorities in the shape of the Lord Lieutenant and the Bishop of Norwich took care to be watchful. Through their correspondence with Deputy Lieutenants, justices of the peace and commanders of Volunteer companies on the one hand, and with the Anglican clergy on the other, they were in close communication with the leaders of local society.[1]

These they alerted to be on the look-out for what Lord Townshend would, with relative equanimity, characterise as the 'Democratical' tendencies of Norfolk's labouring sort. Nevertheless the calming effects of Wesleyan Methodism—a very different strand of Nonconformity from that of Wilks, who was never a Wesleyan—and the unity of purpose required in defending the island against 'Boney' helped to suppress for well over a decade the political restiveness which had surfaced in the 1790s.

The paradox is that just when a marked degree of unity was emerging over the pressing need to counter the invasion threat, and when even Coke was organising Holkham's armed Volunteer cavalry unit from 1798, electoral strife was rampant in Norfolk and Norwich. No county election had been fought right through to a poll from before the American war to the eve of the Napoleonic War, during which time there was talk of revolution at home and a spate of legislation to suppress it. But then, as though tensions had been pent up too long in the 1790s, near civil war broke out in three county campaigns in 1802, 1806 and early 1807: Hayes depicts the 1802 and 1806 polls as distinctly political elections.[2] Only in a fourth in that series, the May 1807 general election, were party divisions thrown aside and wounds allowed to heal, as we have seen in Henry Jodrell's actions.[3]

In politics at this time participation was a key element; Norfolk and Norwich, like the constituencies in and around London, had large, boisterous electorates. Participation was to be the key in repelling the invader. Voters and non-voters, peaceable and riotous, the landed gentry and propertyless poor, were handed arms by central government and transformed into trusted forces protecting their home areas.

[1] *intertwined* The country's institutions and key players are drawn in the next chapter as interlocking circles representing the forces working closely together at local level to defend Norfolk from invasion (fig. 4.9B)

[2] *political elections* 'In a sense the contests of 1802 and 1806 [for the county] were the belated expression of the antagonisms of the nineties. The parties engaged in those contests had real political content . . .' (B.D. Hayes, 'Politics in Norfolk 1750–1832', p. 274)

[3] *Jodrell* See pp. 478–80

above **Salthouse:** according to his daughter, Mark Wilks took seaside breaks here, where he would have drunk Hardy beer at their outlet the Dun Cow. He had once run a bathing place on the Wensum at Heigham [*MB·2001*]

above The spectacular uniform of the young lieutenant commanding the Yarmouth Volunteer Cavalry in 1798. It is no mere vain display. The Yarmouth troop received consistently favourable reports as one of the best in Norfolk.

William Palgrave jnr (1771–1838), son of the Hardys' neighbour at Coltishall Manor House, is depicted by his sister Mary Turner. He took over from John Bell as Collector of Customs at Gt Yarmouth in 1803, and was posted as Collector of Dublin in 1826 *[engraving by J. Brown 1798]*

9

Civilians at war

An invasion apprehended from the French

If an enemy should land upon our shores, every possible exertion should be made immediately to deprive him of the means of subsistence. The Navy will soon cut off his communication with the sea; the Army will confine him on shore in such a way as to make it impossible for him to draw any supplies from the adjacent country. In this situation he will be forced to lay down his arms, or to give battle on such disadvantageous terms as can leave no doubt of his being defeated . . . GOVERNMENT DIRECTIVE TO EVERY PARISH, 1798 [1]

Mr Hardy, Mary Ann and William went to our church afternoon, no sermon, Mr Burrell harangued the people on taking up arms in defence of the country, an invasion being apprehended from the French. MARY HARDY, 1798 [2]

FOR TWO-THIRDS OF THE SPAN of Mary Hardy's diary, during 23½ of its 35½ years, the nation was at war. Additionally, eight childhood years of the diarist and her future husband were spent during the War of the Austrian Succession, which ended in 1748 when they were aged fourteen and sixteen. They married in 1765, two years after the close of the Seven Years War. That conflict and the American and French wars of the diary were effectively world wars.[3] During these, over varying periods, Britain was engaged in campaigns on land and sea against France, Spain, Holland,[4] Denmark and Russia stretching from the Americas across to the Indian sub-continent and the East Indies.

Mary Hardy died in 1809, and William Hardy in 1811. Neither lived to see the resolution of the struggle against Napoleon, nor the tumultuous celebrations sparked by his abdication and banishment in 1814 and described in the next chapter. Both would have been conditioned from childhood to be politically aware, Norwich and York having a

[1] *exertion* TNA: PRO WO 30/141, p. 3; it is a 30-page printed directive of Apr. 1798

[2] *harangued Diary 4*: 29 Apr. 1798. The verb illustrates the anti-war family's reaction to the rector's address in place of a sermon. He was however speaking not as their priest but as their parish superintendent, an administrative post in charge of civilians in the event of invasion (fig. 4.9B)

[3] *wars of the diary* The American War of Independence (or American Revolutionary War) 1775–83, the French Revolutionary War 1793–1801 and the Napoleonic War 1803–15

[4] *Holland* The name adopted for brevity. The country was known as the United Provinces to 1795 and then as the Batavian Republic to 1806, when it became the Kingdom of Holland under Louis Napoleon. Mary Hardy solved the problem by

referring simply to 'the Dutch'.

Across the southern border until 1794 lay the Austrian Netherlands (present-day Belgium), thereafter annexed to France.

All changed once more in 1810 and 1814

---

[1] *politically aware* See chaps 8 and 10 for the Norfolk newspapers, fasts and thanksgivings.

The *York Mercury: or, A General View of the Affairs of Europe* was founded in 1719 and became the *York Journal* in 1724. From 1725 there was also the rival *York Courant* (G.A. Cranefield, *A Hand-List of English Provincial Newspapers and Periodicals*, pp. 24–5)

[2] *taxation* See vol. 2, chap. 11

[3] *Volunteers* For clarity the terms Regulars, Militia and Volunteers are given an initial capital, even when used as adjectives. This is to distinguish them from militias in general, which can be confused with the old trained bands, *levées en masse* and private armies; also from the volunteers, sometimes lured by bounties, who came forward willingly to serve in the various branches of the Armed Forces

range of weekly newspapers from the early years of the eighteenth century. From before the Jacobite rising of 1745–46 they would have been accustomed to following great national events in the newspapers and attending church for the solemn services of public fast and national thanksgiving which by turn marked moments of crisis and the respite of individual victories.[1]

These were not only world wars but nascent total wars in the narrow sense of widescale civilian participation; unrestricted total war, with all resources directed at the war effort, did not arrive until the First World War. Not merely did taxation have to rise markedly, under the variety of new measures already chronicled,[2] but severe shortages of manpower in the Royal Navy, Army and Militia meant that strategems of coercion had to be adopted ranging from the press gang to quotas and the ballot which were a form of compulsion imposed on the poor. Various exemptions and the buying of substitutes removed the element of compulsion for the wealthier classes, so this was not conscription.

Further, towards the end of the American war and during most of the French wars, military service was expected from patriotic civilians who had until then been spared such participation. This took the form of the Volunteers.[3] As will be shown, one-fifth of the male population of Norfolk in the age group seventeen to 55 was armed and engaged in home defence in the early nineteenth century, *not including* those serving as Regulars in the Royal Navy and British Army. Yet these years immediately followed the wheat famines of 1795 and 1800, with their accompanying social unrest, riots and rick-burning (volume 3, chapter 6). Fear of Bonaparte impelled the Government into issuing arms to the very section of the people associated with that unrest.

The repeated invasion scares during the wars meant that families near the invasion coast, such as the Hardys, were directly exposed to the billeting of soldiers, to army camps, manoeuvres and exercises, and to having to plan for evacuation in the event of an enemy landing. These experiences were logged by Mary Hardy and Henry Raven. Apart from mentions in the Norwich newspapers, the diarists may be the only source of information on the extraordinary welcome accorded the Royal Horse Artillery in 1795 and 1796

as they wheeled their gun-carriages to the coast and laid on field days and displays for the admiring crowds who flocked to the rough windswept ground that was Weybourne Military Camp. The Hardys' workforce got to know the camp too, as William Hardy senior and junior secured the contract for supplying beer to the military in both years.

War also threatened interruptions to trade. The Hardys were heavily dependent on the merchant fleet which brought them their coal and cinders for the brewery and maltings and exported their agricultural and manufacturing produce. The ravages of privateers and paralysis of trade by embargo, blockade and enemy attack directly affected a shipowning family, as chapter 5 has shown. The fear of French invasion damaged the local economy in 1803, and was blamed for forcing down the price of lambs at the great sheep fairs.[1]

Mass mobilisation: families touched by war

A later section on the militarised society of the Hardys' time will explore the Norfolk numbers involved. In summary they were so large as to mean that most families were affected at a personal level. The American war, a local colonial dispute at the start, escalated and set a trend for the later conflicts:

above Salthouse from Bard Hill, west of the site of Weybourne Military Camp.
The hills near the shore on this stretch of coast gave commanding views for troops daily expecting an invasion by the French.
The shingle bank seen here by the sea forms part of modern coastal defences against flooding. Much of the low ground was marsh in the Hardys' day (page 293)
[*Christopher Bird 2009*]

[1] *lambs Norw. Merc.* 3 Sept. 1803 (at Ipswich, Suff.); 10 Sept. 1803 (at Kipton Ash)

[1] *American war* S. Conway, 'The politics of British military and naval mobilization, 1775–83', *English Historical Review*, vol. 112, no. 449 (Nov. 1997), p. 1180

[2] *French wars* J.E. Cookson, *The British Armed Nation, 1793–1815* (Oxford Univ. Press, 1997), p. 5

[3] *Militia* An overview of the structures is given in later sections and figs 4.9A and 4.9B

above Holt Church. The Volunteers would turn out in uniform for special church services. The Holt unit, disbanded in 1783, still provided a guard of honour at the funeral of their old commander, the JP and attorney Edmund Jewell, in Nov. 1784. Mary Hardy went to watch   [*MB·2001*]

By the close of the War of American Independence, about 300,000 of George III's British and Irish subjects were serving in the army, navy, militia, fencibles, and various volunteer corps. In the course of the struggle, around half a million were at one time or another members of the official or unofficial armed forces. In other words, between one in seven and one in eight males of the appropriate age served in some kind of military or naval capacity during the war. This was less impressive than British mobilization in the war against revolutionary and Napoleonic France.[1]

The demands of the two French wars were such that by the early nineteenth century the British had been transformed into an armed nation—and this well over a century before conscription came to be introduced during the First World War. The manpower contribution of 1793–1815 had trebled from that of the American war:

> Counting militia and volunteers, the size of the armed forces reached about three times the highest total achieved during the American War, and the debt also was trebled: government expenditure per annum averaged £16 million in 1786–90 and £97 million in 1811–15.[2]

As a result the country had to grapple with the administrative and psychological consequences of mass mobilisation. Never before had so much been asked of the general population. The hunger of the Army and Royal Navy for recruits, who generally served overseas, was rarely sated. As will be explained, the Militia, roughly the equivalent of the Territorials (reservists) of a later age, depended on forcible recruitment by means of a ballot. Despite its strong county affiliation a Militia unit never served on local soil for fear of going native, its task being not only to resist the invader but to suppress civil riot and commotion at home. The Militia was deployed elsewhere around the country and in Ireland, thereby also releasing the Regular Army for service abroad.[3]

The third arm, the equivalent of the Home Guard of 1940, was provided by the Volunteers. These were infantry companies and troops of cavalry led and manned by civilians with little or no professional military training. Their coastal counterparts, the Sea Fencibles, were likewise composed wholly of civilians, but were trained by full-time serving Royal Naval officers and petty officers—a distinction which never ceased to irk the inshore Volunteer defenders of home and hearth. Their voluble protests will be heard later, and the workings of this carefully layered structure of home defence described.[1]

Again the numbers were impressive. In 1798 the Volunteer establishment in 1798 in Britain amounted to 116,000 men; by 1801 it was 146,000. On 16 December 1803 it reached 380,000. As John Cookson observes, these numbers were 'never less than half the total home force, and sometimes as high as two-thirds':

This huge mobilization, simply the greatest popular movement of the Hanoverian age, has always been regarded as the leading feature of the British armed nation, even its definition.[2]

Comparisons with other countries indicate that the British populace made a far greater contribution as armed personnel than their counterparts. In 1805 the British Government calculated there were 385,151 members of Volunteer units, the same number as those in the Royal Navy and Regular Army combined. Additionally 30,000 Sea Fencibles guarded Britain's shores. Once the Militia was included, and with the findings of the first national census (of 1801) to hand, it became clear that nationwide above one in five of the active British male population was under arms.

By contrast France, Russia and Austria were each ranked as having almost one in fourteen under arms, and Prussia almost one in ten. However a large percentage of the Prussian army, it was remarked at the time, were foreigners. It thus could hardly be regarded as a national force.[3] It was the presence of the Volunteers—a phenomenon unknown on the Continent—which heightened the British contribution, and it is they who play the chief part in this chapter on the civilians' role. Even the unmilitary Hardys supplied one man, William Hardy junior, in the moment of his motherland's greatest need. However William lasted a mere three and a half months towards the close of 1803; and for four weeks of that time he was in London meeting the needs not of internal defence but of his own commercial business.[4]

Later sections will cover the administration of this extraordinarily large home defence force. It was never melded into one cohesive whole, but relied on local county and

[1] *home defence* Internal defence was the term used most frequently at the time to denote the protection of the home territory and population from foreign invasion. Home defence and internal defence are here used interchangeably.
Civilians played a major role, but this was not civil defence. The 20th-century term relates to fire-watching, air-raid precautions and other specialist protective measures on the home front

[2] *mobilisation* J.E. Cookson, *The British Armed Nation, 1793–1815*, p. 66

[3] *comparisons* J.E. Cookson, *The British Armed Nation, 1793–1815*, p. 95

[4] *commercial needs* In this William was probably serving his country more effectively than by wielding a weapon: 'The British armed nation, then, did not arise out of a society that was highly militarized either in terms of the social esteem given to military men or actual military participation by the élite; George III set this tone by firmly presenting himself as a civilian king . . . There was equally a cult of commerce, which upheld commerce as

the basis of British power' (J.E. Cookson, *The British Armed Nation, 1793–1815*, p. 22)

---

[1] *its defence* J.E. Cookson, *The British Armed Nation, 1793–1815*, p. 91

[2] *Townshend* Told to me at Raynham Hall 28 Aug. 2012 by Charles, 8th Marquess Townshend, with whose kind permission the paintings at Raynham are reproduced (*plates 40, 45*). He added, with a mischievous grin, that Wolfe had strongly disapproved of his subordinate's choice of dress!
Lord Townshend's title is now Marquess. His ancestor the Lord Lieutenant had adopted the usage Marquis

[3] *stake* In the mobilisation of civilians 'the ruling classes of 1803 were assuming a high level of morale and a huge degree of commitment to the war among those who had little formal stake in the country' (B. Lavery, *We shall fight on the Beaches*, p. 76).
The issue of suffrage is discussed in chap. 8; the Militia ballot in this chapter. See also the inset 'Ours is a maritime county' in this chapter (pp. 564–5)

urban leaders to liaise with central government. The psychological demands of this massive effort will also run through the story.

Paradoxically, although 'Britain was the only European power that based its defence on a volunteer force,' the British did not see themselves as a military society.[1] They became militarised largely through civilian, part-time service in the Militia and the Volunteers, the routes by which war directly touched people's lives in the circle known to Mary Hardy. Militia officers served full-time, in war and peace. The men served full-time only once the Commander-in-Chief of the Army had called them out as danger threatened. They were then embodied, to use the contemporary term. George III's predecessor, his grandfather George II, proved to be the last British sovereign to appear (if somewhat ceremonially) at the head of his army in battle at Dettingen on the Main in 1743. George III set the course of the monarchy thereafter by no longer providing military leadership in person.

A career officer still in his teens present at Dettingen was George Townshend of Raynham Hall (*plates 40, 44*), close to Mary Hardy's childhood home at Whissonett. By the time he became Lord Lieutenant of Norfolk in 1792 he was Marquis Townshend (*plate 45*), and it was he who gave energetic home defence leadership at county level until his death in 1807. The present Lord Townshend, a descendant, recounts that even this devoted Army officer who rose to the rank of Field Marshal chose to be painted in the scarlet of the Norfolk Militia—the very uniform he had worn in 1759 when leading the capture of Quebec for the British following the death of General Wolfe.[2] Like his sovereign he seems to have eschewed some of the trappings that could have been his by right. Both men, in the topmost positions of influence, reflected the mindset of British society at that time.

Much of the brunt of the war effort had to be borne by those with no stake in society and little opportunity to vote; hence perhaps some of the nationwide restiveness over the Militia ballot.[3] The Raven, Hardy and Cozens families were decidedly unmilitary, but so were many others in their immediate circle. Not one member of the two diarists' families is known to have joined the Armed Forces or Militia in

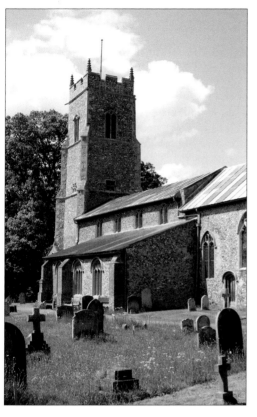

left St Mary, Wroxham, high above the Bure. Families of all walks of life were touched by war, the Hardys being lucky in escaping bereavement brought about by the conflicts.

The son of the Revd Daniel Collyer, Vicar of Wroxham with Salhouse, was killed during the Peninsular War. In the chancel a mural tablet records that Capt. George Collyer of the Royal Engineers fell during the siege of San Sebastian 31 Aug. 1813. He was 24.

On the same day, at the same siege, the eldest son of the Rector of Stanfield, by Whissonsett, was killed. The Stanfield ledger stone records that Lieut. George Norris was 22 years old.

The dead were interred close to where they fell; usually only the officer class received any sort of memorial.

They were not carried back to the churchyards they had known from childhood. Their families did not have the solace of tending their graves on home soil, as Capt. Collyer's mural tablet makes clear:

> *... Mourn not! he lies where Soldiers lie,*
> *And Valour envies such a Grave ...*

[*MB · 2011*]

the long span of Mary Hardy's diary. One possible exception is Henry Raven's brother William, whom his aunt recorded in 1804 as newly arrived home 'from a voyage to the West Indies'.[1] Since he has not been traced in naval and army lists he could have been a planter rather than a sailor or soldier. Mary Hardy does not tell us in 36 years of a single person known to her who was killed or injured in any of the fighting, or who even participated in any of the action.

The Hardys did have two close brushes with the Militia. The first, when their innkeeper William Breese was drawn in the ballot during the invasion fears of 1779, has already been described. William Hardy had to appear before the justices at Wroxham Bridge to extricate this most troublesome of tenants from his latest misfortune.[2]

[1] *W. Indies Diary 4*: 24 Sept. 1804. William Raven is not in the Royal Naval or Army lists; the merchant service's records for this period have not survived

[2] *justices Diary 1*: 22 Mar. 1779. See also the references to Breese's innkeeping career in vol. 2, chaps 9 and 10. He spent some time as a debtor in Norwich Castle

[1] *wages* See vol. 3, chap 1 on the clergy; also vol. 2, chap. 1 on the Hardys' workforce. In 1797 their farm servants each received £20 16s p.a. —calculated, and presumably paid, weekly

[2] *Girling Diary 4*: 11 Oct.–29 Oct. 1803. It was an anxious time for the Girling family, William Girling's mother coming to breakfast and dinner at the Hardys' on 20 Oct. and taking her son home for the next few days. The diarist was pleased to have her driver back, Girling as clerk resuming his old role when farm boy of taking her to and from Methodist meetings. See vol. 2, chap. 5 for the brewery clerks

above Letheringsett King's Head, scene of a shooting match won by a neighbouring farmer in Aug. 1803 [*MB·2010*]

The second occasion, even closer to home, was when the Hardys' trusted farm boy was drawn in the Militia ballot immediately after he had left them for a new post. William Girling was drawn on 15 October 1803, just two days after he had embarked on a new life in the service of the Revd John Longe nearly twenty miles away at Spixworth, near Coltishall. His name would still have been on the Holt hundred lists, and it was at Holt that he was drawn. Mary Hardy does not record who paid for the purchase of a substitute, which could rise to as much as £30 (the equivalent of a curate's annual salary for two parishes, or eighteen months' wages for a farm servant),[1] but it was almost certainly the Hardys. Girling would, in his new master's eyes, have been a fresh and untried figure at his rectory.

William Hardy junior was at Holt when the ballot was under way, and he moved fast. It was he who arranged with two magistrates, from Bayfield and Sheringham, the swift swearing-in of the substitute whom Girling had found, and it was he who secured Girling his promotion to clerk at the Letheringsett brewery.[2]

While Mary Hardy and Henry Raven remain largely silent over service by local men in the Regular forces and Militia the rumble of war can still be heard in the village thanks to the conscientious rector. The clergy were mindful of the need to keep an eye on the mobile population represented by an army on the move when it came to baptisms and burials; noting places of birth and baptism also helped to establish clarity in settlement cases. A few of the flock had their lives disrupted by military service, or by marrying into the Army. The Letheringsett parish register yields information which Mary Hardy frequently denies us, her distancing from matters military seemingly being habitual.

In 1802 and 1804 the register records the private baptisms of Susanna and Louisa, daughters of George Duffield and Mary Ann, née Suckling. Mr Burrell added against Louisa: 'NB: Duffield is enlisted into Artillery; family followed him to Woolwich July 26th 1804.' Mrs Duffield had to organise and undergo the journey from Letheringsett to London with Susanna aged under two years and Louisa aged only four weeks. In 1805 the rector recorded the cordwainer William Mayes serving with the Army in Ireland at the time that Mayes's son William died aged three months; the baby had been born and baptised privately in May 1805. Mayes's wife, the former Susanna Westby, was left behind in Letheringsett for the birth and burial: 'NB: Mayes was a cordwainer in this village, but is now serving in the Army in Ireland, having enlisted at Norwich.'[1]

The Royal Artillery features in the Letheringsett register in 1806 and 1807, and again reveals the pressures of family life on the move. Isaac Ward was employed briefly by Mary Hardy's daughter and son-in-law as a builder at their home in Sprowston, yet there is no mention in the diary that he was a sergeant in the Artillery. When Mary Ann, their first child, was born in December 1805 to Ward and his wife Lydia, née Edridge, Mr Burrell observed: 'NB: Ward is a Serjeant in His Majesty's Artillery.' A son followed soon afterwards, but he came into the world at Colchester in Essex, where Ward was presumably stationed at the barracks. The parents held over the new arrival's public baptism until they were back at Letheringsett.[2]

Nearby at Cley in October 1795 two local women married serving members of the Royal Horse Artillery, presumably at the time the men were being transferred to new quarters after a summer spent at Weybourne Camp. The first groom stood witness at his comrade's wedding three days later. The brides, like Mrs Duffield and Mrs Ward, were embarking on a married life dominated by the needs of the military.[3] Sometimes, as with Mrs Mayes, the wife would be left behind, as Mary Hardy noted with the daughter of their farm servant John Ramm: 'George [   ], a Serjeant in the Army, married Susan Ramm, he soon went away and left her.'[4] This Army wife died seven years later and was buried in her home village.

Mary Hardy notes a lighter side to the contemporary preoccupation with all things military. On 18 August 1803, at one of the most critical invasion periods, a shooting match was organised at their outlet, the King's Head, Letheringsett; the prize was not money but a hat. The winner was the Hardys' farming friend from nearby Saxlingham, Thomas Balls (page 400). Behind the fun perhaps lay the realisation that a Frenchman could provide the next target as he leapt ashore at Weybourne Hope.

[1] *register* NRO: PD 547/2, 18 Sept. 1802, 28 June 1804 (the Duffield girls being christened within hours of their birth); 17 May 1805, 31 Aug. 1805 (for Mayes, the cordwainer or leather-worker)

[2] *Ward* NRO: PD 547/2, 26 Jan. 1806 (the date of Mary Ann's public baptism; she had been born 26 Dec. 1805 and privately baptised two days later, the rector adding that the parents had been married at Marsham, near Aylsham). Ward helped to lay the hall floor at Sprowston 15 Dec. 1806 (*Diary 4*).

Their second child Thomas Youngman Ward was born at Colchester, baptised privately there, and received into the church at Letheringsett 11 Oct. 1807, Mary Hardy however noting that event as held on 4 Oct. (*Diary 4*)

[3] *Cley* PD 270/9, 17 Oct. 1795 (Robert Crick of Weybourne to Rebecca Juler of Cley, both making marks); 20 Oct. 1795 (Matthew Magness of Weybourne to Anne Bell of Cley, both signing). Both marriages were by licence

[4] *Ramm Diary 2*: 16 Oct. 1790 and note. The parish register supplies the groom's surname: Deighton

[1] *Herbert* His career is summarised in the Epilogue in this volume.
See also the Cozens-Hardy family tree (fig. 4B)

[2] *horrors* Written at Letheringsett 6 Aug. 1915. The MS autobiography and the typed and bound transcript are held in the Cozens-Hardy Collection; this extract is from pp. 27–8 of the typescript.
The peer was baffled at his elder son's enthusiastic engagement in the armed struggle, William H. Cozens-Hardy serving in Intelligence while in the RNVR (*plate 53*).
Herbert's brother Sydney gave up his Letheringsett home, Glavenside, as an Army recruiting base and then Red Cross hospital for wounded service personnel, as illustrated in *Diary 4*, p. 73

[3] *coast* See P. Kent, *Fortifications of East Anglia* (Terence Dalton, Lavenham, 1988), p. 173. Apart from a fort at the estuary at Gt Yarmouth and modest batteries at Mundesley, Cromer and Holkham (Kent, pp. 183–5) the Norfolk coast was left unprotected and, as explained in chap. 10, was not included in the line of martello towers 1808–10

The Hardys' lack of contact with the Navy and Army was perpetuated through the generations until the First World War. Only then did the younger men join up, including Raven Cozens-Hardy (heir to the Letheringsett and Cley estates built up by Mary Hardy's son) and his cousin Basil Cozens-Hardy (as referred to in the Prologue in volume 1). That conflict claimed Raven's life at Polderhoek in 1917. A marked distancing from naval and military matters, amounting to a distaste, emerges from the unpublished autobiography of Mary Hardy's great-grandson Herbert (1838–1920), Master of the Rolls and from 1914 the first Lord Cozens-Hardy.[1] Writing in his retirement at Letheringsett a year into the Great War, he reveals a sense of dislocation:

The horrors of war are not to be transcribed here. Suffice it to say that soldiers are to be seen in almost every village, that Letheringsett Hall was occupied for several months by Staff Officers and that soldiers were quartered in almost every cottage. As a family we have hitherto had no intimacy with military men and little desire for a closer acquaintance, but now almost all the younger men are in Khaki . . . Money is being spent like water and a huge debt is being contracted.[2]

Decentralised structures and flexible response

Great Yarmouth lies far nearer to the coast of Holland than to London: 95 miles across the North Sea, as against 123 miles to the capital. Norfolk has approximately one hundred miles of unprotected coastline, only the tortuous shallow creeks of its northern shores and the treacherous sands off the north-east and eastern beaches giving pause to those contemplating invasion. There are no rocks to act as off-shore fixed defences for its open beaches.[3]

Traditionally close bonds of friendship existed with Holland, whose seamen were often to be seen in Norfolk's ports in peacetime (*plate 43*). When the Dutch joined Britain's foes during the American and French wars the East Anglian coast instantly became vulnerable to those expert navigators. The Dutchmen were familiar with negotiating their way through the creeks and sands, and knew which beaches were the most open of access, as the Eastern District's Commanding Engineer Major Alexander Bryce observed at Mundesley in 1803:

The beach . . . is good, and well known to the Dutch fishermen, who have been in the habit of grounding their boats here at half tide, for the purpose of watering. And the anchorage off is reputed safe, being protected by the Happisburgh and other sands.[1]

France had secured the Austrian Netherlands in 1794 and Holland in 1795, thereby acquiring additional bases from which to launch an assault on the East Anglian coast. While it was anticipated that the principal invasion expedition would set off from a point much closer to the British shore than the Dutch seaboard facing Norfolk, the British planners feared that a diversionary force might attack from the estuary of the Scheldt or even the Texel.[2] At the opening of the Napoleonic War the Scottish general in command of the Eastern District (figure 4.9A) downplayed the likelihood of Norfolk's being chosen by the French as an invasion point. Lieutenant-General Sir James Craig wrote to his Commander-in-Chief, HRH the Duke of York, in June 1803:

The coast of Norfolk, both from its distance from the opposite coast and from its own nature is certainly, next to that of Lincolnshire, the least exposed of any part of the [military] District.[3]

Pressure was brought to bear on the Duke that Craig was being too sanguine. As Norfolk's Lord Lieutenant Marquis Townshend was careful to point out, via his own channels to the new Home Secretary in London three months later, the county was indeed in danger, 'situated as it is opposite the enemy's ports, with an accessible line of coast'; further, it was 'unprotected by any Regular troops stationed in it for its security'. A few days later Townshend launched the sally that General Craig, whose base was at Colchester, had not himself seen the Norfolk coast.[4]

It was fast brought home to Craig by the Commander-in-Chief (C-in-C) that a proper survey must be made of the whole Norfolk coast from Great Yarmouth to King's Lynn. Only six months after his June assessment, and having received Bryce's masterly report, Craig had considerably revised his opinion. He was now convinced that provision should be made for limited fixed defences on the Norfolk coast in the form of batteries at Mundesley and Cromer, in case the French were blown off course or, 'from having

[1] *Mundesley* TNA: PRO WO 30/100, p. 154, 12 Dec. 1803, part of Bryce's long report to Gen. Sir James Craig, Commander of the Eastern District, pp. 152–63 (referred to in chap. 5 and quoted extensively in *Diary 4*, app. D4.C).
The bound volume contains much on the threat assessment and preparations to defend the Eastern District 1797–1805. This area included Cambridgeshire and Huntingdonshire, and was one of nine military districts in the kingdom in 1803

[2] *attack* Napoleon later told his captors on St Helena that he had decided to land in July/ Aug. 1805 on the south-eastern corner of England between Deal and Margate, with no plan in mind to attack the E. Anglian shore (R. Glover, *Britain at Bay: Defence against Bonaparte, 1803–14* (George Allen & Unwin Ltd, London, 1973), pp. 82–3)

[3] *least exposed* TNA: PRO WO 30/100, p. 83, letter from Colchester 23 June 1803. Craig later allowed that Yarmouth 'is a point that requires attention' (p. 84)

[4] *Townshend* TNA: PRO HO 50/80, 27 Sept., 7 Oct. 1803, writing from Raynham to the Home Secretary Charles Yorke

FIGURE 4.9A

Norfolk home defence: command and communication within the governmental, naval and military structures and county leadership 1798–1805

sources TNA: PRO HO 42/37, HO 42/49; HO 50/80; WO 30/76, WO 30/100, WO 30/141
notes Three Cabinet posts occupy the top line. Armed civilians are below the dotted line

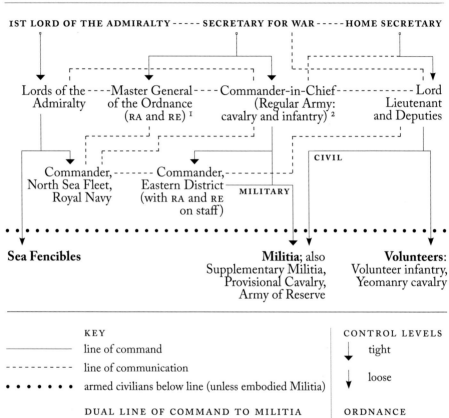

KEY

———————— line of command

- - - - - - - - - - line of communication

• • • • • • • armed civilians below line (unless embodied Militia)

DUAL LINE OF COMMAND TO MILITIA

MILITARY defence against enemy attack on home soil

CIVIL suppression of civil commotion at home

(Militia officers served full-time. The men trained
as civilians in peacetime, but served full-time under
military discipline once the Militia was embodied)

CONTROL LEVELS

↓ tight

↓ loose

ORDNANCE

RA Royal Artillery

RE Royal Engineers

LOSS OF CABINET POSITIONS

[1] *Master General of the Ordnance* Ceased to be a Cabinet post in June 1798
[2] *Commander-in-Chief* (C-in-C) Ceased to be a Cabinet post in Jan. 1795

$\mathcal{M}^{B\,20}_{20}$

been fallen in with by our cruisers', were dispersed up the coast by the Royal Navy.

The rest of the vulnerable shore could be protected by mobile field guns at Cley and Wells, with Holt playing a central part in the deployment of further artillery. Holt, as 'the most centrical place' in north Norfolk, was to host a brigade of heavy guns consisting of twelve-pounders and howitzers.[1] They had been there before, from the moment the Dutch coast fell under French control, as described in the section on Weybourne Camp at the end of this chapter. In 1795–98 and from December 1803 Norfolk was accepted officially as standing on the front line of attack.

A country so frequently placed on a war footing 1740–1815 developed a way of coping by devising an effective command structure. This could be implemented at very short notice not through Parliament but by royal prerogative exercised through the prime minister. That structure is charted in figures 4.9A and 4.9B. The chain of command (figure 4.9A) begins at the top with Cabinet-level control in the persons of the First Lord of the Admiralty (for the Navy and Sea Fencibles), Secretary for War (Ordnance, Army and Militia) and Home Secretary (Militia and Volunteers).

Once embodied the Militia came under the political control of the Secretary for War unless it were being deployed to suppress civil disturbances, when it remained with the Home Secretary. The Volunteers were to fall under military control and thus under the Secretary for War only once the invader had stepped ashore. This never came to pass, to everyone's ill-concealed relief: to that of the C-in-C and the Army high command, ever suspicious of the amateurs' effectiveness; and to that of the Volunteers, terrified of finding themselves subject to military discipline.[2] The political post of Secretary for War was senior to that of Secretary at War, the latter being the civilian head of the Army. The junior appointment was tasked with such matters as personnel, pay, welfare and administration. In the period covered by the chart opposite it too was a Cabinet post.[3]

The structure's success depended on rapid, willing co-operation and communication between the departments and forces, thereby counteracting the lack of effectiveness

above **Strategically placed Holt, its large inns able to billet hundreds of soldiers and horses, became an area military hub in the French wars** [*MB·2011*]

[1] *Craig* TNA: PRO WO 30/100, pp. 147–52, 20 Dec. 1803. Craig was extremely concerned however that the Royal Navy was not patrolling the coast from Mundesley to Gt Yarmouth in sufficient numbers (TNA: PRO WO 30/100, p. 148, 20 Dec. 1803)

[2] *relief* As described later in this chapter

[3] *Cabinet posts* When William Windham, the Norwich MP, was Secretary at War in the French Revolutionary War and Secretary for War and the Colonies in the Napoleonic War he occupied key Cabinet positions

1 *Keith* George Keith Elphinstone (1746–1823), Adm. Lord Keith; his steady blockade and patrols played a crucial anti-invasion role, as seen later

2 *co-operation* TNA: PRO WO 30/75, 21 Oct., 18 Oct. 1803, WO 30/78, pp. 5–16, 11 July 1804; WO 30/76, pp. 225–6, 12 Nov. 1803, p. 240, 8 Dec. 1803; HO 50/80, HO 50/341.
    For Townshend see also NRO: MS 5363, 5 B6, eg over the unimportance of the party stance of Capt. Samuel Barker of the Yarmouth Volunteer Infantry, 1 July, 3 July 1798

3 *Craig* K. Navickas, 'Lieut. General Sir James Henry Craig's orders to commanders in the Eastern Military District, 1803–04', in A. Franklin and M. Philp, *Napoleon and the Invasion of Britain* (Bodleian Library, Oxford, 2003), p. 66; see also pp. 64–5. This superb catalogue accompanied the invasion bicentenary exhibition of 2003.
    Craig had a brilliant career. He secured S. Africa for Britain and later became Governor General of Canada

4 *despatches* eg TNA: PRO ADM 2/1360, 8 June, 22 June 1803; ADM 2/1361, 2 July, 4 July 1803; ADM 2/1363, 22 July 1805

caused by shortfalls in ships, arms, equipment and personnel. The official papers in the Public Record Office's Admiralty, War Office and Home Office classes in the National Archives reveal on the whole a pattern of inter-service and inter-departmental co-operation. Admiral Keith,[1] the Commander of the North Sea Fleet, would send despatches while at sea to the Commander-in-Chief of land forces with intelligence about the French and with recommendations for the blockade, in reply to the Duke of York's questions posed three days earlier. General Craig displayed expert knowledge of the types of French transports and their problems with winds and east-coast surf. The Duke of York pressed the Home Secretary for professional training of the Volunteers, who fell outside his area of supervision. Lord Townshend kept up the pressure by daily relaying to Whitehall the reports he received from correspondents in Norfolk and his recommendations for commissions and promotions in the Militia and Volunteers, without permitting any party-political bias.[2] General Craig took care to brief the Lord Lieutenants of the counties which made up the Eastern Military District, as in his attendance at the meeting of the Essex Lieutenancy on 24 June 1803.[3]

Lengthy secret letters and despatches, often with multiple enclosures, would be sent and absorbed, and replies issued, all within 24 to 36 hours. These winged their way between the Lords of the Admiralty in Whitehall and the flagship of the North Sea Fleet at anchor off Sheerness or the Downs.[4] Lord Townshend moved frequently between his ancestral seat at Raynham, south of Fakenham, where he was in regular communication countywide with the Deputy Lieutenants and magistrates, and his London house in Weymouth Street. Built in 1775 on Marylebone Fields, north of Oxford Street, it lay within easy walking distance through the great squares to St James's and Whitehall.

The archives exhibit an impressive degree of departmental co-operation, conscientious attendance by those at the top, efficient paperwork in Whitehall and beyond, confidence over swift decision-taking, and flexibility of thought. However the command structure often broke down in the field, notably in the very difficult area of 'conjunct operations': amphibious assaults during which the wretched troops were let down by poor planning and lack of support, as in the failure of the expeditions to the Helder in 1799 and Walcheren in 1809.[1] Walcheren fever became a catch-all term for malaria, dysentery, typhoid and typhus. It incapacitated more than half the expeditionary force and killed forty times more men than did the enemy.[2]

The persistent British difficulties over combined operations and opposed landings did however carry with them the reassurance that the French would encounter similar problems—if not worse, given the huge scale—were their invasion barges to make it to the shores of England. In the sphere of home defence to withstand invasion, one directly affecting Mary Hardy and her circle on the North Sea coast, repeated threats during the Seven Years War, American war and French Revolutionary War had produced a well-honed response. By 1803, when Napoleon was preparing his Grande Armée in Boulogne and further north for the assault on England, effective measures based on a system of layered defence were in place to defeat him.[3]

Figures 4.9A and 4.9B present the framework of layered defence, showing to whom the various individual forces were responsible politically and militarily and the flow of communication between them. To combat the feared invasion a supreme effort was made by the civilian local authorities as well as by the Regular forces, as both charts illustrate: nascent total war.

The study of taxation (volume 2, chapter 11) showed the strength and power of the centralised British State in the area of tax collection. It was the efficiency, and the relative social justice, with which money was raised for government coffers which enabled the country to wage war for so long, the Excise being the chief player. A completely different system operated over waging war and resisting invasion. Here was a fragmented, decentralised State, with power vested in numerous bodies under devolved procedures dating from mediaeval and Tudor times. Of especial significance was the Lord Lieutenant, an office dating from Henry VIII's reign, whereby one prominent local figure represented the monarch in each county. Whereas the role is now primarily ceremonial it was in Mary Hardy's period vital to defence against insurrection and against a foreign foe.[4]

[1] *expeditions* For a vivid depiction of the hardships and dangers of combined operations in the words of the Royal Marine officer Maj. T.M. Wybourn 1797–1813, see A. Petrides and J. Downs, eds, *Sea Soldier*, esp. pp. 1–27, 139–48.

Writing to his sister 3 Dec. 1799 while on board HMS *Isis* at Gt Yarmouth on his return he recalls 'the common slaughter' of his 'brave troops' during the opposed landing in Den Helder: 'We shall ever remember the wretchedness we experienced in Holland: so wet, so full of canals and dykes that the whole country is full of swamps enough to kill anyone' (p. 25)

[2] *Walcheren fever* P. Mathias, 'Swords and ploughshares: the armed forces, medicine and public health in the late eighteenth century', in P. Mathias, *The Transformation of England* (Methuen, London, 1979), p. 268

[3] *layered defence* Richard Glover in *Britain at Bay* analyses the many anti-invasion measures and the principles underpinning them

[4] *fiscal–military State* For a study of the paradox of a centralised fiscal State yet devolved military authority, and for con-

trasts with the systems of France and other powers, see J. Brewer, *The Sinews of Power: War, money and the English state, 1688–1783* (Unwin Hyman, London, 1989), esp. pp. xvi–xx, 22.

Two of Mary Hardy's descendants served as Lord Lieutenant of Norfolk: Russell James Colman, eldest son of Jeremiah James Colman and Caroline, née Cozens-Hardy (fig. 4B, the Epilogue), during 1929–44; and his grandson Sir Timothy Colman, KG, during 1978–2004 (*plate 54*)

---

[1] *voluntary-minded* P. Langford, *A Polite and Commercial People: England 1727–1783* (Oxford Univ. Press, 1992), p. 692; 'No other country proved so successful at shifting from the demands of peacetime commercial expansion to wartime concentration on military objectives and then back again' (also p. 692)

[2] *flexible response* P. Langford, *A Polite and Commercial People*, p. 693; the post-1783 wars were not so limited

[3] *chart* It also appears in vol. 3, chap. 6 (as fig. 3.6A) in connection with civil unrest

[4] *confused* B. Lavery, *We shall fight on the Beaches*, p. 93

An earlier chapter showed that local government at parish level could be almost republican in character (volume 3, chapter 6). Similarly there could appear to be a voluntaristic, unauthoritarian feel to local resistance in time of danger, for Britain in the eighteenth century was not a military State, but 'above all the product of a decentralized, pluralistic, voluntary-minded society':[1]

When it made war the British State seemed remarkably efficient, even centralized, in its capacity to find funds, and raise forces. It was precisely when fighting wars, especially the relatively limited wars of the period, none of which produced an actual invasion by a foreign army, that the State showed its capacity for flexible response. In peacetime, and for many purposes in wartime, it remained a highly decentralized system.[2]

Yet, as later sections on the full-timers and a militarised society will show, those in the ranks had little sense they were living in a voluntary-minded State. The quotas for the Royal Navy and the Militia, together with frequent ballots when insufficient volunteers came forward, roused vocal opposition which at times became violent.

The chart opposite (figure 4.9B) depicts the decentralised, complex structure of internal defence remarked upon by so many commentators.[3] Brian Lavery points to the feudal origins of some of these elements, and to 'the many contradictions, with areas of overlapping responsibility and confused boundaries'.[4] However what can be overlooked in the study of home defence is the vital role played by civilians in positions not of power but of influence: the ability to exhort and to encourage was almost as important as the power to coerce. This chapter will include the exerters of influence, such as the Bishop and clergy; it will also highlight the role of those wielding civil power, such as the justices of the peace, parish superintendents and parish officers. Too often they can be overlooked in the focus on the Militia and Volunteers. Often they merged: there was no bar to a clergyman or parish officer becoming a Volunteer commander.

Administering the devolved power illustrated in the overlapping circles imposed enormous strain on magistrates, in and out of quarter sessions, and on parish officers. Militiamen's families had to be supported at parish level, and con-

FIGURE 4.9B   513

'Decentralized and complex': the holding of military and civil power over and within Norfolk during invasion threats 1798–1805

sources TNA: PRO HO and WO classes; announcements in the *Norwich Mercury*

note The quotation in the title is by B. Lavery, *We shall fight on the Beaches*, p. 93, on power in relation to home defence

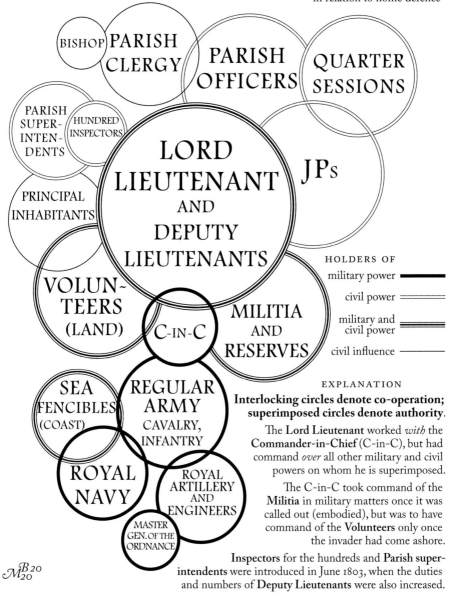

BISHOP PARISH CLERGY

PARISH OFFICERS

QUARTER SESSIONS

PARISH SUPER-INTEN-DENTS

HUNDRED INSPECTORS

LORD LIEUTENANT AND DEPUTY LIEUTENANTS

JPs

PRINCIPAL INHABITANTS

VOLUN-TEERS (LAND)

C-IN-C

MILITIA AND RESERVES

SEA FENCIBLES (COAST)

REGULAR ARMY CAVALRY, INFANTRY

ROYAL NAVY

ROYAL ARTILLERY AND ENGINEERS

MASTER GEN. OF THE ORDNANCE

HOLDERS OF

military power

civil power

military and civil power

civil influence

EXPLANATION

Interlocking circles denote co-operation; superimposed circles denote authority.

The **Lord Lieutenant** worked *with* the **Commander-in-Chief** (C-in-C), but had command *over* all other military and civil powers on whom he is superimposed.

The C-in-C took command of the **Militia** in military matters once it was called out (embodied), but was to have command of the **Volunteers** only once the invader had come ashore.

Inspectors for the hundreds and **Parish super-intendents** were introduced in June 1803, when the duties and numbers of **Deputy Lieutenants** were also increased.

$\mathcal{M}^{B}_{20}$ 20

¹ *Militia families* See the quarter sessions orders in contested cases, eg NRO: C/Sce 1/8, 16 Jan. 1782

² *Gay* The 12th child of the Hardys' innkeepers at Ingworth, James Gay (b.1756) left his wife and children chargeable to the parish when he became a substitute in the embodied Militia 1780–83 (NRO: PD 521/26, Ingworth town book 1768–98).

I am grateful to Valerie Belton of Ingworth for giving me details of James Gay and his family in her letter of 1 Dec. 1991

tested cases were regularly brought before the magistrates.¹ In the case of James Gay, the son of two of the Hardys' innkeepers and hired as a Militia substitute in 1780, the overseer of the poor of Gay's parish of Ingworth, near Aylsham, had regularly to journey 42 miles on a return trip to Thurton (the parish of the balloted man who had hired Gay) to claim back these expenses.²

Huge increases in the county levy, paid by Norfolk's ratepayers, had to be granted to enable the County Treasurer to meet his responsibilities. By the start of 1799 the levy had for the first time reached £1800 for the coming quarter, £1200 of which had within the month to be paid 'to the

below The Whole Duty of Constables, written by 'An acting magistrate of the county of Norfolk' (2nd edn Norwich, 1815).

It shows the great range and volume of administration relating to war-preparedness which fell on unpaid civilian officials, from Deputy Lieutenants to parish constables. These are two of the eight pages devoted to the Militia   [*Cozens-Hardy Collection*]

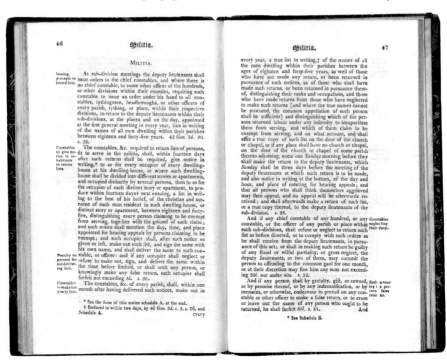

left Ranworth Church:
the chancel, south wall.
Matthias Kerrison
(d.1844) voted as a
splitter in 1806: Tory
(for Wodehouse) and
Whig (for the war
minister Windham).

Here he portrays his
father John (d.1804) as
uncompromisingly a
loyalist: strenuously
supporting the King
and Constitution and
sporting martial ele-
ments in his funerary
sculpture. Militaria
increasingly adorned
commemorative tablets.

'Principal inhabit-
ants' appear in the chart
(figure 4.9B) as playing
a key role in leading the
civilian effort on the
home front [*MB · 2011*]

Court of Guardians in Norwich . . . on account of their expenditure for the maintenance of Militia families'.[1] Six months later the levy was £2400 for the coming quarter.[2]

As a gesture towards easing the strain on local finances and to show patriotic fervour at times of crisis the better-off local inhabitants would voluntarily pay into funds set up ad hoc at county level for the defence of the country.[3] The lists of subscribers published in the press convey a sense of national solidarity and strong leadership by the prominent citizens (male and female). They may also have offered reassurance to the hard-pressed county lieutenancy who, as shown on pages 564–5 under 'Ours is a maritime county', found more solid support frequently lacking even from sheriffs and magistrates. The published lists form one of the few sources on the engagement of women in the war effort.

[1] *county rate* NRO: C/S 1/15, 16 Jan. 1799. In the American war it had been a mere £450 to £1200 a quarter (eg C/Sce 1/8, 25 Apr. 1781, 7 Oct. 1778)

[2] *levy* NRO: C/S 1/15, 24 July 1799

[3] *funds Diary 1*: 28 Jan. 1778. For details of a Holt meeting to fund the Volunteers, see the lengthy annotation to Mary Hardy's entry for 3 May 1794 (*Diary 3*), with lists of subscribers

[1] *subscribers Norw. Merc.* 5 May 1798

[2] *Holt Norw. Merc.* 26 May 1798. The Rector of Holt Joshua Smith and the Lord of the Manor of Letheringsett Laviles James Hewitt each paid £10; the great majority paid £1 1s or 10s 6d

[3] *loyalism* J. Cookson, *The British Armed Nation, 1793–1815,* pp. 24–37

[4] *Holt* It likewise harboured almost no gentlemen and gentlewomen: it was not a resort for the leisured. The *Universal British Directory* of 1794 (vol. 3, p. 279) named only four individuals under 'gentry'

[5] *sums Norw. Merc.* 17 Mar. 1798. 'Jacobinical' and 'democratical' Norfolk's civilian response will be further examined under 'A militarised society'.

On a cautionary note, conurbations should be measured not only by population size but by wealth and as 'a resort for the conspicuously rich'. In this Norwich could hardly compete with Bath. See P.J. Corfield, 'From second city to regional capital', in *Norwich since 1550,* ed. C. Rawcliffe and R. Wilson (Hambledon and London, 2004), p. 155, and her table 6.3 (p.158)

Some of the Hardys' circle paid in, such as Mary Hardy's cousin Ben Raven of Horningtoft, and her cousin Judith's husband John Moy.[1] In May 1798 the Norwich paper published the names of thirty subscribers living in the parish of Holt, seven of whom were female heads of households such as the Cley merchant John Mann's widow Priscilla Mann, the widow of the former Vicar of Hempstead and Binham Mrs Tilson, the schoolmistress Miss Mary Alpe and the milliner Miss Ann Leak. The servants at the Feathers, the leading inn, also clubbed together and sent in eleven shillings between them to the fund.[2]

Patriotism and loyalty to King and Country are often held to have been the preserve of Tories, but John Cookson offers a useful distinction between loyalism, with its Tory overtones, and national defence patriotism, an attribute of many in the Hardys' Whiggish circle. It was this second and far more widespread characteristic which produced the desire to participate in national defence, whether through subscriptions or actual service in the Volunteers. It was not loyalism which led to the surge of mass mobilisation.[3]

Analysis of the Holt subscription list of May 1798 when set against the pollbooks bears out Cookson's thesis. The town's polling record shows it harboured very few Tories.[4] Only one of the 23 men in the Holt list of 1798 who also voted in the 1802 or 1806 county elections under Holt was a Tory. This was the surgeon Nathaniel Burrell, younger brother of the Rector of Letheringsett (also a Tory).

True to form, the Hardys' names never appeared in these published lists. Norfolk generally did not shine when it came to financial contributions. Despite valiant efforts by the Norwich papers to drum up support for the voluntary funds in 1798, the *Norwich Mercury* had to report a disappointing total of only £4139 13s 9d at Norwich by 17 March, much below that of some comparable cities. Bristol by that date had contributed £25,000; Bath £15,000; and York £5000. Industrialising Manchester had gathered £19,000, while Cambridge, at £9000, had found well over twice the provincial capital's paltry sum.[5]

The decentralised military structure supporting internal defence offered flexibility and swiftness of execution. But it could also prove authoritarian and arbitrary, and it placed huge burdens on the unpaid justices of the peace, high constables, petty constables, tithingmen and overseers of the poor on whose shoulders fell its day-to-day administration. Collecting the county rate; recruiting; balloting; trying to meet the very challenging manpower quotas; billeting; providing carriages, horses and drivers for officers and baggage trains accompanying troops on the march; calling up the Militiamen when war threatened and for annual exercises in time of peace; rounding up deserters: these, and more, fell to the hard-pressed local officials.[1] The guineas and half-guineas subscribed to defence by some of the more prominent figures in Holt society and elsewhere were tokens of goodwill, but much more than that would be required.

Full-timers: the Royal Navy and Regular Army

Mary Hardy felt absolutely no rapport with the sea and shipping which, apart from voyages to and from Hull in 1775, she avoided as a means of long-distance travel (chapters 1 and 5). The Royal Navy receives scant coverage in her diary entries. Exceptions are three set battles: Les Saintes (1782),[2] Camperdown (1797) and Trafalgar (1805)—each noted so soon after the action that no name had yet been accorded them for posterity. Also we learn of the occasional capture: 'A French sloop brought into Yarmouth by the *Fly* and *Ariadne*, sloops of war'.[3]

She refers to Horatio Nelson only twice: on the day of his death, and on the day of national thanksgiving for his victory and the country's deliverance.[4] She omits to name Adam Duncan as the victor of Camperdown.[5] John Jervis's achievements are left out entirely. More understandably, given the restricted subject matter of his farm and brewery diary written during the French Revolutionary War, her nephew and fellow diarist Henry Raven does not mention the names and actions of naval and military commanders.

Their manuscripts thus do not reflect the public mood as reported in the press on such occasions. An event which captured the public imagination and filled the news pages in Norfolk was the victory over the French in the Battle of the Nile, off the coast of Egypt at Aboukir Bay, on 1 August 1798. Norwich feted two heroes with local attachments: Nelson, the fleet commander, born and raised in the rectory

[1] *burdens* These duties, and more, are set out in *The Whole Duty of Constables* (1815)

[2] *Les Saintes* Also known as the Battle of the Saints and (to the French) the Battle of Dominica. Mary Hardy refers by name to Adm. Rodney on this victory of 12 Apr. 1782 over the French fleet at Les Iles des Saintes in the W. Indies (*Diary 2*: 20 May 1782).
Raven Hardy reports Adm. Kempenfelt's drowning that same year on board HMS *Royal George* in his long account of the disaster (page 435; also *Diary 2*: 27 Nov. 1782)

[3] *Yarmouth Diary 1*: 16 June 1780. The *Norwich Mercury* did not report the capture until 24 June. The diarist seems to have heard the news from her husband, who was there on the day that the warships and their prize, a 20-gun Dunkirk privateer, entered port

[4] *Nelson Diary 4*: 21 Oct. 1805 (her entry being squeezed in a few weeks later on learning of the victory); 5 Dec. 1805

[5] *Camperdown Diary 4*: 19 Dec. 1797, when Mary Hardy notes the day of national thanksgiving 'for the victory gained over the Dutch fleet October 11 1797'

[1] *Berry's portrait* High moral and physical courage were essential for service in the Army and Navy. These were still the days of hand-to-hand fighting, as the press was fond of emphasising. Many naval men such as Horatio Nelson and his Norfolk protégé Capt. William Hoste (victor of Lissa in 1811) bore the marks of their wounds and suffered chronic pain for the rest of their often short lives

[2] *Berry Norw. Merc.* 29 Sept. 1798. The visit to Norfolk nearly a year later by Edward Berry was reported 15 June, 3 Aug., 17 Aug 1799, his father-in-law giving a ball in Norwich on the first anniversary of the battle. The new knight was granted the Freedom of Norwich (*Norw. Merc.* 28 Sept. 1799)

[3] *whiskey Diary 4*: 13 Aug. 1799

[4] *new command Norw. Merc.* 17 Aug., 14 Sept 1799

at Burnham Thorpe and educated at the Free Grammar School, North Walsham; and the commander of his flagship, Edward Berry, London-born cousin and husband of Louisa Forster, daughter of the Master of Norwich School. The captain and his lady were shortly to reinforce the local link by renting a house outside Norwich at Catton.

Captain, later Rear-Admiral, Sir Edward Berry, Bt (1768–1831) is pictured in John Singleton Copley's huge canvas at *plate 47*. The sword at his side is by no means ornamental, for naval officers even of the rank of captain were required to fight their way to victory hand to hand.[1] County pride was heightened by the realisation that Norfolk learned the news of the destruction of the French fleet a day ahead of London, the despatches from overseas arriving at Great Yarmouth on 25 September.[2] The diarist however names Berry not for his naval exploits, but only in connection with her son's purchase of his whiskey (a light gig) in August 1799.[3]

During the French wars individual members of the Navy, and to a noticeably much lesser extent the Army, were lionised as saviours of the country. The people of Norfolk could feel close to their heroes. Through the pages of the press they followed their conflicts and their movements, as when Captain, now Sir Edward, Berry, posted to his new command (and no longer in need of his whiskey in Norwich), took leave of His Majesty in August 1799. He had recovered his health after 'his severe service in the Mediterranean and the cruel treatment of [by] the French after he was taken in the *Leander*'.[4]

The Mediterranean command, which also extended across the Atlantic to the West Indies and American seaboard, received the great majority of the press coverage. Its senior

---

facing page The key to the 360-degree panorama of the Battle of the Nile exhibited in London. It may have been the 'pomerany' seen by Mary Hardy and Mary Ann 13 June 1800 in 'Leicester Fields' [Leicester Square] during their long London visit. The French flagship *L'Orient* (top left), 110 guns, had blown up after a fire spread to the magazine. The 74-gun HMS *Orion* is top right.

The battle of 1 Aug. 1798, with Nelson as fleet commander on Captain Berry's HMS *Vanguard*, 74 guns (bottom right), caught the imagination of the people of Norfolk when the news arrived in late September.

Mary Hardy shows us that women from a family with no Forces connections would go unaccompanied to view a wholly naval commemoration   [NRO: BUL. 4/298, 614×4]

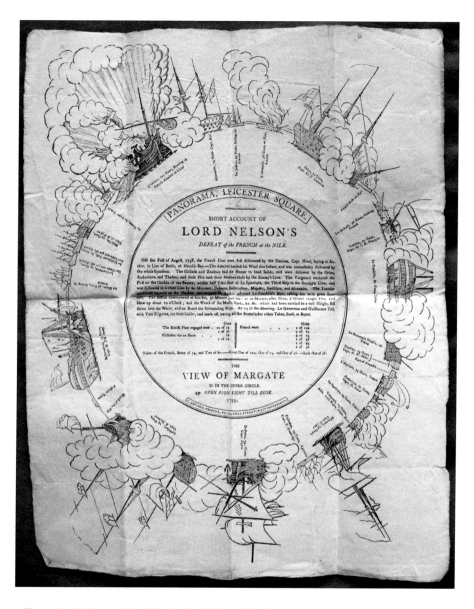

officers similarly received the bulk of the adulation.[1] It was however the North Sea Command which carried out the grind, day by day, winter and summer, of blockading the eastern Channel and Flemish and Dutch ports. The tautness of that blockade proved crucial in the salvation of Britain.

[1] *officers* The names of officers would be given in news bulletins on losses. Senior rates and men were not named. There were too many

D— n your boots and your shoes too
_ where I sit is my own little land in
the ocean _ and if you attempt to stir
a foot _ there's a few of my wooden walls
in the offing shall give you a Pretty
Peppering

Hollo you Jean Bull _ take notice
I have got on my seven League
Corsican Boots, that never fails me
depend upon it Ill step across the
Water one of these days and Pay you
a visit Master Bull.

CONVERSATION acrofs the WATER

above 'Conversation across the Water': a cartoon from the last days of peace, 16 Apr. 1803; hostilities resumed against France on 18 May.

Bonaparte jeers, 'I'll step across the water ... and pay you a visit, Master Bull.' A stolid, unruffled John Bull, still in civilian clothes, has every confidence the Royal Navy massed on the horizon will protect him from the insolent Corsican: '... If you attempt to stir a foot there's a few of my wooden walls in the offing shall give you a pretty peppering.' Four months later John Bull would be in uniform as a Volunteer.

The Royal Navy's blockade did indeed save Britain, as a result of which the anti-invasion military leadership was never put to the test

[*photo Bodleian Libraries*: Curzon b.12(7)]

---

[1] *Keith* See C. Lloyd, ed., *The Keith Papers: vol. 3, 1803–1815* (Navy Records Soc., 1955).

The stern Scot's 'disapproval of "frivolous enterprises" brought him into conflict with his adventurous subordinate, Sir Sidney Smith', but earned him the respect of the Admiralty Board (C.

The admiral with by far the most significant anti-invasion role, Lord Keith, goes unrecorded by Mary Hardy. As Commander of the North Sea Fleet in the early years of the Napoleonic War, Admiral Keith was responsible for preventing the Grande Armée's barges from setting out from northern France and the Low Countries. Thanks to Duncan in 1797 and then Keith the military preparations for internal defence featured in this chapter were never put to the test. But Keith, whose nature it was to shun popular acclaim, received very little attention in the Norwich press, and no full acknowledgment of the debt owed to him.[1] It is possible that readers of the two local newspapers had only a hazy notion of his vital role and his calm, steady leadership.

Nelson's mercurial personality was such that he did not excel at blockading, with all its drudgery and monotony, and he was posted as second-in-command of the Channel and North Sea Fleets in turn for only the two years 1800–01. Blockading rarely brought the public adulation he craved.[1] Apart from Duncan's engagement at Camperdown in 1797 and Sir Hyde Parker's and Nelson's at Copenhagen in 1801 the preservation of Britain from invasion generally involved preventing a battle rather than seeking one.

Army and Navy heroes sometimes chose to enter politics. Admiral Sir John Jervis served as MP for Great Yarmouth until being raised to the peerage with the title of his great victory at Cape St Vincent. Jervis, who appreciated Keith's sterling qualities, was briefly Nelson's superior officer in the Channel Command before taking a key post in Henry Addington's Cabinet 1801–04 as First Lord of the Admiralty (figure 4.9A).[2]

As seen in chapters 2 and 4, Mary Hardy does make references to the darker side of the Royal Navy—impressment. These come only during her Coltishall years, 'pressing' posing a real danger for keelmen and wherrymen; the activities of the press gang do not feature in the Letheringsett diary 1781–1809. All Marines, whether officers or men, the seaborne infantry, were volunteers. They were never impressed, conscripted, or drawn by ballot.[3]

Under the six Quota Acts of 1795 and 1796 watermen— the skippers and mates of river craft—received some protection from impressment during the French Revolutionary War. The first Quota Act had some success in raising 15,000 seamen for the Royal Navy by imposing a compulsory quota on all parishes nationwide, but it was yet another in a long line of unpopular measures for long-suffering parish officers to implement. Requiring individual men to serve, by State decree, was seen as much a deprivation of the liberty of the subject as the recent suspension of Habeas Corpus.[4]

During the process of raising seamen from the hundred of Holt William Hardy, a parish officer for Letheringsett, missed his dinner. His wife, her mind on compulsory recruiting for the Army, was confused over what was going on:

Lloyd, p. 3).

The North Sea Fleet patrolled from Selsey Bill in Sussex to the Shetlands; the Channel Fleet patrolled westwards from Sussex. As well as blockading the enemy shore, notably at Boulogne and Flushing, the North Sea Fleet guarded home waters and escorted convoys. The work became even more onerous after Spain declared war on Britain on 12 Dec. 1804

[1] *Nelson* Tom Pocock, like many other Nelsonian biographers, traces the vanity that was part of this complex personality, and the exasperation it caused other very able commanders such as Lord Keith (T. Pocock, *Horatio Nelson*, eg pp. 210–11, 213)

[2] *Cabinet* The post of First Lord of the Admiralty had been held earlier by Viscount Howe and then Earl Spencer; St Vincent was succeeded in 1804 in the second Pitt administration by Viscount Melville

[3] *Marines* Known as the Royal Marines from Apr. 1802

[4] *compulsory* J. Ehrman, *The Younger Pitt: The consuming struggle*, p. 126. The shortness of

time allotted to debating the controversial proposal for the suspension of Quota Act exemptions and protections in May 1798 occasioned the Prime Minister's famous duel with the Foxite George Tierney on Putney Heath's gibbet hill (J. Ehrman, pp. 126–9)

¹ *justice sitting* Diary 3

² *Quotamen* Clive Emsley sets out the intentions behind the six Acts, and their effects at local level: C. Emsley, ed., *North Riding Naval Recruits: the Quota Acts and the Quota Men 1795–1797* (N. Yorks County Council, Northallerton, 1978); see esp. pp. 7–9, 10–12, 16–18. He portrays the careers of individuals and dismisses allegations as to the Quotamen's quality generally

³ *Wells Norw. Merc.* 27 Aug. 1803. See also TNA: PRO HO 42/71, f. 18, Lord Lowther in Cumberland to Lord Pelham in London, 31 July 1803, on arming all merchant ships

⁴ *13 districts* Mapped as at 1805 by B. Lavery, *We shall fight on the Beaches*, p. 102. He also includes the Royal Naval Commands around the coast

[1795] APRIL 4, SATURDAY A close foggy cold day. Mr Hardy rid [rode] up forenoon to the justice sitting to fix on a plan for raising soldiers [sailors] for Government according to an Act of Parliament lately made [for] that purpose, dined nowhere, drank tea at Mr Bartell's . . .¹

The Quota Acts also posed problems for the Merchant Navy, which lost some very capable sailors. Those entering His Majesty's service by this route were by no means all felons and riff-raff, as the Quotamen were sometimes portrayed.² Further disruption was caused to the merchant fleet by the centuries-old requirement to supply civilian vessels, armed and ready, for the Government in time of war. In 1803 the shipowners of Wells offered 22 vessels, totalling 1992 tons.³

The element of compulsion which met so much opposition on the ground is a thread running through this chapter in relation to the Navy, Army and Militia. Service in the Volunteers, the very name suggesting freedom from coercion, offered a way of escaping the uncongenial, compulsory service far from home endured by full-timers in those three services. Anyone recruited into the Volunteers and Sea Fencibles was spared the anxiety and uncertainty of the quota and the ballot. It is no wonder their numbers soared.

The Army was for Mary Hardy much closer to home. Her choice of the generic term 'soldier' often makes it impossible to determine whether she is referring to Regular cavalry and infantry (under the Commander-in-Chief), the Royal Horse Artillery, Royal Artillery and Royal Engineers (under the Master General of the Ordnance), or the Militia and, from 1796, Supplementary Militia (under the dual command of the Lord Lieutenant and C-in-C). All passed through Holt, and some were stationed there. Soldiers, however imprecisely defined, became a constant presence in her diary.

The British mainland was divided for purposes of internal defence into thirteen military districts. In August 1803 General Sir James Craig had 17,500 men under his command, all Regulars, in the Eastern District. General Sir David Dundas in the Southern District had 24,000, this being considered the most likely area chosen by Napoleon for his assault. The other eleven districts were tiny in manpower terms in comparison with these two.⁴

The disposition of troops could vary a great deal, again making accurate identification difficult. Whereas three regiments of Regulars were quartered in Norwich in May 1795, a table ten years later showed that the only Regular troops in Norfolk were the 1st Shropshires, with 725 officers and men in Norwich under Major General Milner.[1] As already quoted, Lord Townshend stated in September 1803 that no Regulars at all were stationed in the county at that time.

References to the military in the *Norwich Mercury* can create the misleading impression of a well-defended county, when the paper was in fact reporting the passage of troops on the march. Huge numbers would arrive at Great Yarmouth when returning from expeditions to the Low Countries during the French Revolutionary War. In 1799, in just one week, 3746 British troops were landed from Den Helder before marching through Norwich on their way south. The Whig paper was happy to do honour to the war-weary but magnificent soldiers, their hats perforated by musket balls: 'The Guards are without doubt the finest body of men in the English service.' Most stood, it said, between six feet and six feet four inches in height (1·83–1·93 metres). They towered over the populace who cheered them, with women and children rushing to relieve them of the burden of their muskets and baggage and showing them to their quarters.[2]

Not all may have moved on. Mary Hardy may be referring to the returning Helder troops when she records ninety soldiers taking up winter quarters that same month at Holt, presumably at the inns and in private houses. With Holt 'full of them' six had to be billeted at the King's Head, Letheringsett, the arrangements requiring the presence of the local excise supervisor and excise officer 'all day and almost all night'.[3] If these troops were some of the survivors from the Helder we hear nothing of the miseries they had endured. They could instead however have formed part of the East Norfolk and West Norfolk Militia, who were also billeted at that time in the towns of Aylsham and Reepham.[4]

Individual, unnamed soldiers feature in Mary Hardy's record. One was given a military funeral at Holt in 1781; another committed suicide there three weeks later.[5] Two Army officers were at the Hardys' towards the end of the American war,[6] and both Mary Hardy and Henry Raven

[1] *Regulars Norw. Merc.* 16 May 1795; TNA: PRO WO 30/78, pp. 261–2, table dated 1 June 1805

[2] *Den Helder Norw. Merc.* 2 Nov. 1799.
Another 3500 arrived in Norwich from Holland the following week (9 Nov.), and over a short period 20,000 English troops and several hundred Russians landed at Gt Yarmouth (the Helder being an Anglo-Russian amphibious operation during the War of the Second Coalition) and moved on to Norwich. The Duke of York himself landed on 4 Nov. (*Norw. Merc.* 9 Nov. 1799).
The Gt Yarmouth innkeepers 'sustained great inconvenience and loss' over billeting these huge numbers (*Norw. Merc.* 23 Nov. 1799)

[3] *winter quarters Diary 4*: 18 Nov., 22 Nov. 1799. Holt must indeed have been full. The 90 soldiers represented nearly one-tenth of the town's 1801 population of 1004

[4] *billeted Norw. Merc.* 23 Nov. 1799

[5] *Holt Diary 2*: 22 July, 11 Aug. 1781. The second man 'shot himself intentionally' at 8 in the evening

[6] *officers Diary 2*: 15 Oct. 1782

[1] *gardening Diary 3*: 15 Mar., 18 Mar., 19 Mar. 1794

[2] *guns Diary 4*: 4 June 1804. It was presumably the King's birthday salute

[3] *Mousehold* William Hardy and William Ansell witnessed the review (*Diary 1*: 24 Apr. 1776); another was held there a year later (*Diary 1*: 23 Apr. 1777). Nearly 20,000 people watched the first (*Norw. Merc.* 27 Apr. 1776), William Hardy meeting many friends and acquaintances that day

[4] *Holt* 'William went up to Holt forenoon to see the cavalry exercise' (*Diary 4*: 13 Aug. 1804)

[5] *Dereham road Diary 3*: 9 June 1795. See also *Diary 4*: 14 May 1804 and note. The Royal Artillery and their anti-invasion role will be covered towards the end of the chapter

[6] *by-election* In chap. 8

[7] *flourished* Described in chap. 5. The Excise noted complacently that 'The business of the town and port of Yarmouth is greatly increased' (TNA: PRO CUST 47/454, p. 117, 1 Oct. 1807)

[8] *training* S. Conway, 'The politics of British military and naval mobilization, 1775–83', p. 1191

record soldiers at work in the Hardys' garden a year into the French Revolutionary War.[1] One year after the start of the Napoleonic War William Hardy junior watched the Artillery and Volunteers firing their guns on Spout Hills, the roar and smoke of the cannon on Holt's common land being less than a mile from the Hardys' home.[2]

The Hardys personify the ambivalence of the relationship between much of the anti-war sections of the population and the military whose individual members they wished to honour. We have seen William Hardy's bitterness over the defeat of the peace vote in Parliament in 1794 (chapter 8); yet only the following year he was happy to secure the beer contract for Weybourne Military Camp, as described later.

The peace-loving Hardys showed themselves keen followers of the military. They took their place alongside the many thousands of spectators flocking to cavalry exercises, field days and regimental reviews. These were held on Mousehold Heath near Norwich in 1776,[3] at Weybourne Camp in 1795 and 1796 and at Holt in 1804.[4] Henry Raven noted his cousins William and Mary Ann Hardy driving miles down the Dereham road from Holt to meet and escort the Royal Artillery as they brought their guns and howitzers north to Holt and Weybourne.[5] As the Norwich voters showed in 1794, when they returned William Windham in the city by-election on his appointment as Secretary at War,[6] it would be wrong to characterise the county and city generally as anti-war. Some areas were more than usually enthusiastic in their support for the Forces. Great Yarmouth, one of the hosts of the North Sea Fleet, flourished on the back of war.[7]

Full-timers: the embodied Militia

The embodied Militia was the term given to reservists once they were called out for full-time active service. In peace-time the Militia remained in being, but with only its officers, adjutants and non-commissioned officers serving full-time. They were needed for training the men, ever rotating, who were recruited in three ways: voluntarily; as drawn men in the ballot, called 'principals'; or hired as substitutes by balloted men. The men trained alongside the Regulars often in camps, as at Weybourne or Hopton.[8] The crucial feature of the Militia was that it remained a body drawn from civilians

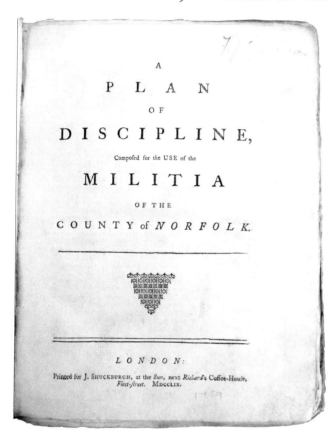

A

P L A N

O F

D I S C I P L I N E,

Compoſed for the USE of the

M I L I T I A

O F T H E

C O U N T Y of *N O R F O L K.*

L O N D O N:

Printed for J. SHUCKBURGH, at the *Sun,* next *Richard's* Coffee-Houſe,
Fleet-ſtreet. MDCCLIX.

left This book, of 1759, was the fruit of a close collaboration between two active proponents of the reconstituted Militia: George Townshend (as he was then), MP for Norfolk 1747–64, and from 1792 the Lord Lieutenant, and William Windham (1717–61), of Felbrigg, father of the Norwich MP who features in chapter 8.

The Militia was of ancient foundation, its origins lying with the Saxon requirement for all able-bodied men aged 16–60 to serve within their counties. Under the Tudors and early Stuarts it had been revived under statute, only to fall into abeyance from 1640. The new body sprang from the Militia Act of 1757, driven through the Commons and Lords by Townshend, whose brainchild it was [*Norfolk Heritage Centre, Norwich*]

who served only a fixed term, usually five years, with a few weeks set aside for training each year. The men's military age boundaries post-1762 were set at eighteen to 45 years.

Rotation had its advantages, as claimed in an anonymous tract of 1781 referred to by Stephen Conway:

A true militia, it was claimed, must draw by rotation on all men able to bear arms, for without rotation militiamen 'gradually lose their *civil capacity,* and from *free citizens,* are apt to become mere *Soldiers'.*[1]

Significantly, the tract then went on to argue that, such was the Militiaman's vital contribution to the State, he should be granted the right of suffrage.[2] However this was not to

[1] *rotation* S. Conway, 'The politics of British military and naval mobilization, 1775–83', p. 1196

[2] *suffrage* S. Conway, 'The politics of British military and naval mobilization, 1775–83', p. 1197

right One of 49 plates by William Windham in his book on the Norfolk Militia
designed to give directions over dress and
drill. Here the Militiaman is seen in the
correct pose for the '3rd motion' when
carrying his firelock on his right arm.

Much of the inspiration derived from
manuals for the Prussian Army. George
Townshend wrote the preface. R.W. Ketton-
Cremer gives its genesis in *Felbrigg: The story
of a house*, Windham composing the work
while at Hilsea Barracks, Portsmouth.

In the early years Townshend command-
ed the Western Battalion of the Norfolk
Militia and his fellow Norfolk MP Sir
Armine Wodehouse the Eastern Battalion.
These later developed into the Western and
Eastern Regiments of the Norfolk Militia.

The larger or more populous counties
each had two or more regiments. In Eng-
land and Wales these were Devon, Essex,
Gloucester, Hampshire, Kent, Lancashire,
Lincolnshire, Middlesex, Norfolk, Somerset,
Suffolk, Surrey, Tower Hamlets and York.
Scotland had no Militia until 1797
[*W. Windham, A Plan of Discipline . . . for the
use of the Militia of the County of Norfolk
(1759): Norfolk Heritage Centre, Norwich*]

---

[1] *censure* Conway
points up the paradox
already identified that
rural Norfolk, known
for its democratic and
anti-war instincts,
should have witnessed
prominent opponents
of the American war
coming forward to lead
Volunteer (not Militia)
units. He instances Sir
Edward Astley of
Melton as one such (S.
Conway, 'The politics
of British military and
naval mobilization,
1775–83', p. 1197)

be, and the Militia came to share all that was disliked, even
detested, in the popular imagination in connection with
standing armies. The Volunteers escaped this censure.[1]

The reconstituted Militia, as it became known, owed its
existence to the drive and energy of the 33-year-old Norfolk
MP George Townshend, a Regular Army officer with a very
long political and professional military career. His Bill was
passed in 1757 at a time of some danger, a French inva-

sion being feared in the Seven Years War.[1] In 1778 it was again embodied in reaction to the French intervention in the American war; Spain joined France the following year.

The principal role of the Militia was to free the Regulars to serve overseas, thus enabling the Army to protect the British Empire worldwide and to wage wars against the foe on the European mainland and further afield. The Militia also formed one of the many layers of home defence against invasion during other conflicts. Townshend's vision of a citizen force who in time of peace could remain in their homes and pursue their usual employment was accentuated by the strong county affiliation of the Militia. The new body had a sense of local identification long before the Regulars' regiments were to forge county links.[2]

As well as being recruited from the county, Militia units were led by prominent, propertied county families: it was considered essential that officers in charge of an armed peasantry should have a personal stake in social stability. The social composition of those in the ranks of the Militia (and Volunteers) will be covered later under 'A militarised society'. Unlike their men's, the officers' swagger, bright scarlet uniforms were beautifully tailored and adorned with blue facings, braided button holes, sashes and gold lace. At senior officer level the Militia had certain weaknesses owing to the small pool of talent from which the leaders could be drawn. A Militia colonel had to possess land worth £1000 a year or be heir to land worth £2000, while a major was required to meet £400 and £800 respectively.

Thus the force was led by scions of the county's nobility and greater gentry with scant regard for their competence, as John Barney and Sir Angus Fraser illustrate by numerous instances.[3] Landed inheritance distinguished the senior officer class, given the tremendous hurdle set by Parliament, as when 27-year-old Captain John Wodehouse, later the Tory candidate for Norfolk and a peer, became colonel of the East Norfolks on the resignation of his father Sir John in 1798 (chapter 8). He was the third generation of Wodehouses to hold the colonelcy of the East Norfolks since 1759.

Militiamen in the ranks were excused service if they had already had a five-year spell in the Militia. They had little opportunity to acquire a high level of expertise unless they

[1] *Townshend* His conviction that the nation needed a citizen military force may have grown out of his impatience with the attitudes of the Regulars. His descendant Charles, 8th Marquess Townshend told me at Raynham 28 Aug. 2012 that as a young officer in 1746 Townshend had been sickened by the butchery of the Hanoverian troops under HRH the Duke of Cumberland at Culloden and spoke out against it; he promptly resigned his Commission. He thereafter drew and circulated many caricatures of the Duke. Townshend showed humanity and tolerance to the Highlanders, whom he called Scottish *sans-culottes*. He was not hostile to public protest and could sympathise with the views of civilians (conversation with Lord Townshend 2012)

[2] *county affiliation* Points made by Matthew McCormack, of the University of Northampton, in 'The material life of the Militiaman: uniforms 1757–1815', a talk given at the Institute of Historical Research, 27 June 2012

[3] *leadership* J. Barney, *The Defence of Norfolk 1793–1815: Norfolk in the Napoleonic Wars* (Mintaka Books, Nor-

wich, 2000), p. 29; A. Fraser, 'Lord Orford's droll-dressed Militia men', *Parson Wood-forde Society Quarterly Journal*, vol. 29, no. 1 (spring 1996), pp. 5–32.

See also L. Colley, *Britons: Forging the Nation 1707–1837* (Pimlico, London, 2003; 1st pub. 1992), pp. 285–93, 312–19.

Richard Glover is more positive over the Militia and its leadership: *Britain at Bay*, pp. 43–4, 127–8

[1] *terms of service* For a study of the post-1757 Militia and changes over time, see J. Gibson and M. Medlycott, *Militia Lists and Musters 1757–1876* (Federation of Family History Societies, 2nd edn Birmingham, 1990), pp. 5–10.

For the Militia in Norfolk, see R.W. Ketton-Cremer, 'Norfolk and the threat of invasion', *Norfolk Portraits* (Faber and Faber, London, 1944), pp. 143–55

[2] *civil power* Militia units were constantly on the move, and almost never served in the counties from which they were drawn (L. Colley, *Britons: Forging the nation 1707–1837*, pp. 313–16; J. Barney, *The Defence of Norfolk*, pp. 28, 31–2).

It was thought safer and more effective for

above 'Present, as center rank, a side view'. Militia officers, like the Regulars, wore scarlet tunics dyed with cochineal which kept their brightness. The men's tunics, as seen here, were of a duller, ruddier red made from madder. The manual's emphasis is on rapid rate of fire, good discipline and obedience to orders [*W. Windham, A Plan of Discipline . . . for the use of the Militia of the County of Norfolk (1759): Norfolk Heritage Centre, Norwich*]

elected to be there for the long-term as recurrently-serving substitutes.[1]

The dual chain of command has been described earlier, and depicted in figures 4.9A and 4.9B. In peace the Militia regiments remained under the direction of the Lord Lieutenant on the authority of the Privy Council, and under the Deputy Lieutenants and JPs of the counties to which they were posted, for the purpose of suppressing civil insurrection and riot—an armed policing role in support of the civil power.[2] In time of war they also came under the control of the Commander-in-Chief, via the military district into which they were posted, for the purpose of resisting enemy attack and manning forts and guard-posts—a soldiering role. The Militia was thus under military command and subject to military discipline only once it was embodied.

Regarded as a very useful adjunct to the Regulars, their numbers kept increasing. In 1758 the quota set for Norfolk's two battalions of Militia was 960 men. By 1803 there were 1814 men in the ranks, the numbers being swelled by the Supplementary Militia introduced in 1796—an extension to and 'augmentation' of the Militia, also recruited by ballot.[1] Those volunteering for the Supplementary Militia were paid a bounty of not more than four guineas by the parish overseers of the poor. In 1796 Pitt's administration intended to raise by ballot an extra 60,000 infantry (through the Supplementary Militia) and 20,000 cavalry (the Provisional Cavalry): 'easily the largest requisition of military manpower the British state had ever made'.[2] By June 1804 numbers in the Militia nationwide equalled those in the Regular Army stationed at home: 90,000 in each.[3] One of the reasons for first national census in 1801 was to ascertain for the first time the number of men available for service in the Militia.[4]

The augmentation of the Militia proved insufficient.[5] Pitt's government thereupon sought to create new ways of forming Militia-like supplements to the Regular Army: notably the Provisional Cavalry (in being 1797–98) and the Army of Reserve of 50,000 men (1803–04)—names deceptively hinting that no actual service would be demanded. In a vain attempt to reassure, or at least to placate, a suspicious populace the authorities made assertions which even the most patriotic spirit would be likely to question. Those in the Supplementary Militia were to be prepared 'on the shortest notice, properly armed and clothed, and in readiness to join the Militia of their counties', this being effected, so it was alleged, 'with little inconvenience to individuals'.[6]

Under the Act for the Provisional Cavalry a quota system was again devised 'for enabling His Majesty to raise a provisional force of cavalry to be embodied in case of necessity for the defence of these kingdoms'. One horseman, clothed, furnished and mounted, had to be ready to serve for every ten horses in the hundred (the local area) kept for the purposes of riding or of drawing carriages.[7] While the Hardys kept well under ten such horses William junior was in danger of being drawn in the ballot as one of the hundred's horsemen; his father was above the service age. Within days of this announcement William had been required to enter

members of the Pembrokeshire Militia, from the far western shores of mainland Britain, to advance with fixed bayonets on Norfolk bread-rioters at Wells-next-the-Sea than for a Norfolk Militiaman to do so (vol. 3, chap. 6).

Also the likelihood of desertion lessened away from the home area

---

[1] *numbers* TNA: PRO HO 50/80, Lord Townshend to Lord Hobart, 10 June 1803. The Supplementary Militia was discontinued in 1816; the Local Militia had been introduced in 1808

[2] *manpower* J. Cookson, *The British Armed Nation, 1793–1815*, p. 36

[3] *numbers* B. Lavery, *We shall fight on the Beaches*, p. 243

[4] *census* B. Lavery, *We shall fight on the Beaches*, p. 37

[5] *numbers Norw. Merc.* 21 May 1803; also *Norw. Merc.* 8 Aug. 1801, 6 Nov. 1802. For the new body's institution see *Norw. Merc.* 29 Oct., 12 Nov., 19 Nov., 3 Dec. 1796. Norfolk including Norwich had to find an extra 1992 men, Suffolk 1470, Essex 1756 and Cambridgeshire 646

[6] *in readiness Norw. Merc.* 12 Nov. 1796

[7] *horses Norw. Merc.* 4 Feb. 1797

into what his mother described as a 'society' or band of local horse-owners who together could muster a group of ten riding horses: 'William went to Holt forenoon, entered into [a] society relating to the Cavalry to be raised, . . . went to market afternoon'.[1] William proved lucky in the ballot at Holt that month,[2] and the unpopular scheme was very shortly dropped by the Government.

As seen in the section on mass mobilisation, and later under 'A militarised society', the ballot loomed large in people's lives. While it should not be overlooked that those imbued with patriotic fervour or enduring economic hardship were willing to come forward as volunteers, enticed by the bounties on offer, Militia ranks were largely formed of those whom the balloted men had bought; very few principals served. Scotland experienced particular difficulty. In Edinburgh in 1804 only 41 principals were taken in a batch of 944 recruits.[3] Being hired as a substitute was overwhelmingly the customary entry route, and when the life was found to hold little appeal desertion would sometimes follow. The newspapers often carried items seeking information on the whereabouts of absconders, as seen below.

It is difficult to generalise over the sums paid for a substitute. Cookson states that the average cost per substitute in the 1807–8 ballots was more than £27.[4] As seen in the inset 'Ours is a maritime county', Pembrokeshire offered to pay the Government 25 guineas (£26 5s) for each man not found for the Supplementary Militia in 1796. There was no set sum, local employers and parish funds all helping out.

right A 'principal', or drawn man, deserts from the Militia during the American war. The parish officers advertise for news of him.

Robert Gibson came originally from Smallburgh, near Stalham, a village supplied by the Hardys from Coltishall. He moved to the north of the county to find work at Bodham, and was employed on the land at Bayfield and Glandford, next to Letheringsett, when he was drawn in the Holt ballot. Like many, 22-year-old Gibson was mobile [*Norwich Mercury, 15 Apr. 1780: Norfolk Heritage Centre, Norwich*]

April 12. 1780.
RAN away from Bayfield, near Holt, where he was employed by the Week, ROBERT GIBSON, Husbandman, who was drawn to serve in the Militia for Bayfield and Glandford, in Holt Hundred. He is about 22 Years of Age, of a florid Complexion, is very much Pock mark'd, and that Disorder still looks fresh in his Face, is stout limb'd, about 5 Feet 8 or 9 Inches high, walks drooping, wears his Hair short, and sometimes a small Curl over the same, of a lightish Colour; wears an old light coloured Cloth Cloak, bound at the Neck, without a Collar, and a Slop under it, and a Pair of Leather Breeches; his Friends live at Smallburgh, near Northwalsham; he was lately at work at Bodham, and is now supposed to be in the Neighbourhood of Aylsham; he is a dangerous Person for any Farmer to have in his House, his Honesty not being Proof. Any Person giving Information of him so as he can be secured, before the 24th of this Month, shall receive HALF a GUINEA for their Trouble, of us
THOMAS FOSTER,
THEOPHILUS IVES.

Holt hundred, and thus Letheringsett, lay within the recruiting area of the Western Regiment of the Norfolk Militia; South Erpingham hundred, and thus Coltishall, in the Eastern Regiment's. Under the tight control of the County Lieutenancy and down through the magistrates and the petty constables of each parish the command structure operated swiftly when required. By the time war was resumed on 18 May 1803 both regiments of the Norfolk Militia had already been embodied for some weeks, and in its first issue after the renewal of hostilities the *Norwich Mercury* announced that the Supplementary Militia was now also called out.[1]

Similarly the Militia was stood down or disembodied as soon as was thought expedient. At the close of the American war the preliminary articles of peace were signed between Britain, France and Spain at Versailles on 20 January 1783, the Dutch entering into a separate agreement. The Peace of Paris was concluded in the February. On 15 March the *Norwich Mercury* announced that the Militia was standing down.

The Militia and Supplementary Militia of Great Britain fulfilled almost all the essential requirements for a militia laid down by Carl von Clausewitz. They were directed at home defence and not at attack; and they were not organised on the lines of the Prussian model, of which Clausewitz was critical, to form part of the Regular Army and thus be deployed to invade enemy territory:

. . . The concept of a militia embodies the idea of an extraordinary and largely voluntary participation in the war by the whole population, with its physical strength, its wealth, and its loyalty. The less the institution resembles this model, the more a militia will become a regular army under another name. It will then have the advantages of a regular army, but it will also be lacking in the advantages of a genuine militia: a reservoir of strength that is much more extensive, much more flexible, and whose spirit and loyalty are much easier to arouse . . . Its organisation must leave scope for the participation of the populace . . .[2]

The Prussian officer was writing after the defeat of Napoleon Bonaparte in a struggle in which he had served from its beginnings in 1793. He was not thinking necessarily of the British model, and he does not allude to Britain in this passage. But his characterisation of the best, home-based type

above 'Prime and load, 7th motion, ended' [*W. Windham, A Plan of Discipline . . . (1759): Norfolk Heritage Centre, Norwich*]

[1] *called out Norw. Merc.* 21 May 1803

[2] *militia* C. von Clausewitz, *On War*, ed. M. Howard and P. Paret (Princeton Univ. Press, New Jersey, 1984), book 6, chap. 6, p. 372.

Put together from essays made during the final years of the Napoleonic War and in its aftermath, the work was revised by the author in 1827

[1] *invasion* The press voiced fears of a Dutch invasion in the area of Gt Yarmouth (*Norfolk Chronicle*, 13 Jan. 1781)

[2] *corps* This term, like that of 'company', was then employed more loosely. It did not have the later, more precise meaning relating to numbers of military personnel

[3] *Holt and Letheringsett* Although this early unit 1781–82 contained the name Letheringsett no record of the villagers' participation has been found.

Holt and its surrounding area did not have a Volunteer unit in the French Revolutionary War, perhaps reflecting anti-war and Jacobin sympathies locally, despite the country being put on an anti-invasion footing: the Supplementary Militia was embodied in Mar. 1798 (*Norw. Merc.* 17 Mar. 1798).

The Holt Volunteer Infantry, described later, was formed in the summer of 1803

[4] *exercises Diary 2*: 15 Apr. 1781 (Easter Day), quoted later in this chapter

[5] *volleys Norw. Merc.* 9 June 1781. Mary Hardy noted the Volunteers' loyal salute the following year (Diary MS, 4 June 1782)

of Militia can fairly be attributed to Britain's, with the major reservation that British participation was by no means voluntary. In most rural areas, and certainly in Norfolk, the names of the chosen were not lifted from the pool of the willing but dragged from the slough of despond of the balloted or from despairing individuals prepared to be bought for military service through a lump sum rather than endure further deprivation. Lifelines were extended in the form of part-time service with the Volunteers and Sea Fencibles, guaranteeing exemption from the ballot.

Clausewitz's voluntary principle thus attached far more to the Volunteers than to the Militia. The explosion of loyalty and the desire to participate, identified as strengths by the Prussian, proved characteristics of the new body formed during the last years of the American War of Independence. This force later became enshrined in law under William Pitt's enabling Defence Act of 1794.

Part-timers: the Volunteers

The Volunteers were composed of and led by part-timers: civilians anxious not to be severed from their home, family and place of work, yet who felt they wished to contribute something more to the war effort than loyalty and taxes. As earlier with the Militia, strong leadership was given by Lord Townshend. In 1781, an invasion being feared,[1] he formed the first Volunteer corps in the county, the Norfolk Rangers.[2] This was a troop of cavalry, or yeomanry, drawn from the area around his estate at Raynham (*plate 44*).

Other units quickly followed. The Holt and Letheringsett Volunteers, as they were known in the American war,[3] seem to have been one of the earliest companies formed in Norfolk, Mary Hardy referring to their exercises at Holt as early as mid-April 1781.[4] On 4 June 1781, the King's birthday, the unit fired 'three excellent volleys' in the market place and adjourned to the Feathers for dinner and loyal toasts.[5] Her husband was playing bowls at Holt that day and the diarist had tea at the surgeon's, but no mention was made of the parade; William Hardy was never to play any part in the Volunteer movement.

In 1782, as the war with France, Spain and Holland continued to rage, the press started to give more coverage to the movement. Sir Edward Astley formed the fifty-strong Melton Company 'for the defence of the coast of Norfolk'; the Earl of Orford, Lord Lieutenant of Norfolk and Colonel of the Western Regiment of Militia, had one hundred in his Volunteer force. By then the Norfolk Rangers had risen to a strength of 150.[1] Henry Jodrell of Bayfield and William Brereton of Holt, both lawyers, became officers in the Melton Volunteers; even the fervently anti-war Thomas William Coke was planning to form a corps of Volunteers.[2] Edmund Jewell, Chairman of Holt Quarter Sessions, commanded the Holt and Letheringsett company.[3] His lieutenants, John Thomlinson and John Johnson, were both prosperous men from Cley, while various local landowners, gentry and clergy subscribed sums of money to the corps.[4]

Norwich also took an early interest. Just two weeks after the rumours of an imminent Dutch invasion companies of Volunteers were being formed in the city.[5] More followed in May 1782, the *Norwich Mercury* informing its readers that 'some young gentlemen of spirit and prosperity in this city' intended 'to raise Volunteer companies of independent men who are interested in the protection and security of the kingdom, and the preservation of our most excellent constitution'.[6] The words 'prosperity' and 'independent' are significant in linking the leaders of the Volunteers with the propertied class. As with the Militia, the property hurdle for officers was designed to ensure that the interests of the commanders of armed labourers, servants and artisans were vested firmly in the stability of the State.

The lower property qualification for Volunteer commissioned officers enabled the lesser gentry, farmers, merchants and the professional class to command a Volunteer corps. They had to have an annual income from land of not less than £50, or to pay rent of not less than £100. Exemptions were permitted, for half-pay Regular officers, anyone with sufficient military experience, and the sons of the propertied class.[7] Despite these lower hurdles very few of the Hardys' immediate circle served as officers in the Volunteers.

The full name of the new force, the Local Defence Volunteers, remained intermittently in use until July 1940, when the Prime Minister Winston Churchill resolved to rename the LDVs the Home Guard. Even allowing for the improvi-

[1] *Astley etc Norw. Merc.* 31 Aug., 14 Sept. 1782

[2] *Melton, Coke Norw. Merc.* 21 Sept. 1782.
Susanna Wade Martins refers to Coke's force as a militia (S. Wade Martins, *Coke of Norfolk*, pp. 74, 75), but at no time did he take a Militia role. His patriotic efforts were channelled into the Volunteers in the form of his Holkham troop of cavalry

[3] *Jewell Norw. Merc.* 21 Sept. 1782.
The description of his funeral at Holt in 1784, watched by William and Mary Hardy in the pouring rain (Diary MS: 15 Nov. 1784), attributes the creation of the Holt unit to him as 'captain of an independent company raised by himself during the late war, when this country was threatened with a foreign invasion' (*Norw. Merc.* 20 Nov. 1784)

[4] *Holt corps Norw. Merc.* 2 Nov. 1782, stating that His Majesty had ordered 'a supply of new arms and accoutrements' (illustrated in *Diary 2*, p. 66)

[5] *Norwich Norfolk Chronicle*, 27 Jan. 1781

[6] *Norwich Norw. Merc.* 18 May 1782

[7] *income* J. Barney, *The Defence of Norfolk*, p. 33, giving further details

[1] *terms of service* Held in TNA: PRO HO 50/80 (eg 4 Sept. 1803), and NRO: MS 5363, 5 B6 (eg Dec. 1800)

[2] *hedge-fighting* J. Money, *Major General Money's Letter to the Officers of Volunteer Corps* (Norwich, [? 1803]), p. 7. General Edward Braddock died leading a failed expedition in Pennsylvania in 1755, during the Seven Years War, during which the native Americans had fought alongside the French.

Money wished that men in Britain's maritime counties 'should be irregulars, such as riflemen, mounted riflemen or sharp shooters' (p. 8).

Although his *Letter* is not dated he refers to the Army of Reserve, introduced in 1803, and to government directives of 1803

[3] *camouflage* 'In Canada, during the American War, we had two companies of Woodmen in dark brown, nearly the colour of the bark of trees, which in that country [countryside] was decidedly the most eligible.' 'Well armed and well trained marksmen' were the key (J. Money, *Major General Money's Letter to the Officers of Volunteer Corps*, pp. 12, 22)

sation which famously characterised those later units the Volunteers possessed little of the relative homogeneity of the Second World War force. The Volunteers of Mary Hardy's time were granted a huge measure of freedom. As will be described, they even set their own terms, unit by unit, on which they wished to serve. Some saw themselves as military back-up for the Regulars and Militia on their home patch, or across the hundred or county, or within the country as a whole; while others regarded themselves as on stand-by to help put down incipient Jacobinical elements and secure the countryside against insurrection. A very few viewed themselves as irregulars, anticipating the Spanish guerrillas of the Peninsular War who acted independently of each other, and with little overall control, against the invader. In the French wars Lord Townshend would patiently and conscientiously forward to London the individual terms of service of each Norfolk unit, periodically collating the information into tables in case his individual letters were mislaid in London.[1]

What was the inspiration for this entirely new force? As we have seen, there was nothing like it on the Continent. It came into being in the closing years of the American war, when the campaign was going badly for the British, and it may well be that a military bruised by the colonists' successes wished to emulate some of their tactics. One such in Norfolk was Major, later Major General, John Money (1752–1817), of Crown Point, near Norwich. In his *Letter to the Officers of Volunteer Corps*, written long after his American service and when Napoleon's invasion threat was at its height, the veteran wrote of the 'hedge-fighting' in which he had participated alongside 'the Indians' (native Americans and Canadians):

> . . . Not but I had rather see the Volunteers with common fowling-pieces in their hands, to act as irregulars, than with soldiers' musquets [muskets] . . . One who knows his piece [gun] will act more deliberately; he will, by strategem, like an Indian, get near enough his enemy before he fires, and will become the braver by it. The Indians never use rifles or soldiers' firelocks, and yet they defeated and killed General Brad[d]ock, near Fort Stanix [Stanwix]. I have served with Indians, yet I never saw a musquet or a rifle amongst them.[2]

Eighty years before the British Army adopted khaki, Money proceeded to make a powerful case for camouflage dress.[3]

Townshend, who shared some of Money's disillusionment[1] with Regulars (especially the officer class), as well as his outspokenness, chose green for his Rangers. Green and black, designed to blend into the landscape, were to be worn by very many Volunteer companies. The scarlet tunic and white breeches of the 'thin red line' endangered their wearer.[1]

The thrust of Money's address is that a lightly armed sharpshooter, blending into the landscape, who believes his cause to be just and that he is protecting his home territory, will harass the foe and fight with more passion, more local knowledge and far more effectiveness than the demoralised, over-disciplined infantryman weighed down by his arms and his kit. In such notions lay the probable origins of the Volunteers. Experience of the American theatre of war had given the British commanders pause for thought, as Hew Strachan points out. Skirmishes, not set battles, had characterised contests against the colonists, who played to their strength of knowing their home ground. In this 'petty war' with its 'revolution in tactics'[2] the colonists had been lightly armed and had avoided the British fondness for marching in columns. The Americans were 'a population brought up to the use of arms', in the manner of the citizen force which Townshend had long been advocating.[2]

William Windham, the son of Townshend's old Militia comrade, became persuaded of this view in 1803, and drew up careful plans for the training of his own Volunteer force at Felbrigg. They were kitted out in green, with black or tan leather buttons and gaiters of dark grey or brown:

Firing at a mark, . . . firing from behind trees, retiring upon call, and resuming a new station; these are all the heads upon which I should propose them [the Felbrigg corps] to be exercised.[3]

It is hard not to conclude that despite the seriousness of the threat this novel method of warfare held great appeal, and the Norfolk Volunteers underwent their training with gusto. A new Commandment was added to the ten of the Old Testament: 'Six days shalt thou labour, and the seventh shalt thou train.'[4] 'Sham fights' would be organised, invariably resulting in the surrender of the 'French', such as took place on the Denes at Great Yarmouth and at Bramerton Heights on the lightly-wooded slopes running down to the Yare.[5]

[1] *disillusionment* 'Good God! how are men . . . to be pitied, who are so situated: bridled, curbed, martingaled, half disciplined as regular soldiers, and under the command of men who know not how to conduct them into the presence of an enemy, or how to dispose of them [dispose them] when he has got them there?' (J. Money, *Major General Money's Letter to the Officers of Volunteer Corps*, p. 23). By contrast, the man fighting on his own soil for everything he held dear, 'if he is a good marksman, and cautious as well as brave, . . . may kill a Frenchman a day, perhaps his brace [a pair]' (J. Money, p. 23). Volunteers' uniforms are discussed in this chapter on pp. 550–1

[2] *revolution in tactics* H. Strachan, *European Armies and the Conduct of War* (Routledge, London, 1983), pp. 28–9

[3] *Windham* R.W. Ketton-Cremer, *Felbrigg: The story of a house*, pp. 246, 247

[4] *new Commandment* B. Lavery, *We shall fight on the Beaches*, pp. 335–6

[5] *sham fights* eg *Norw. Merc.* 19 Nov. 1803; Bramerton Heights were near the Woods' End public house

¹ *Patteson* See vol. 2, chap. 8 for his career as a brewer

² *Bramerton Norfolk Chronicle*, 16 June 1804.
The spectators had been drawn by the prediction that the sham fight would be 'the grandest military spectacle ever witnessed in this county' (*Norfolk Chronicle*, 9 June 1804).
It was probably one of the most entertaining

John Patteson, the prominent Norwich brewer and Tory MP, certainly knew how to give his men a good time.¹ On Monday 11 June 1804 his Volunteers arranged two pontoons of wherries alongside one another straddling the wide river, and planked them over. John Harvey's troop of Light Horse Volunteers then attacked from the far bank as 'the invading enemy', riding across the boats and managing to seize an English howitzer in front of 'an immense concourse' of onlookers. Even the newspaper had to admit there was more fun than military merit in the spectacle: 'Some of the operations might have appeared rather incongruous in the eyes of military men.'²

The Aylsham lawyer William Repton, son of Humphry, took a rather more serious approach to training his men.

facing page Bramerton Common by the River Yare, a popular spot for relaxation over the centuries. In the early 19th century the Norwich brewer John Patteson would organise military exercises here for his Volunteers. In June 1804 he pitted his men against a troop of Volunteer cavalry. The horsemen took the role of the enemy and attacked by crossing from the far bank on pontoons formed of wherries.

As was to be expected, the 'French' lost the Battle of Bramerton Common. The victors were regaled with barrels of Norwich porter; the 'French' had to make do with brown stout [*MB·2011*]

right Bramerton Common also hosted military reviews and inspections.

John Patteson's company and both of John Harvey's were prepared to stand guard duty at Gt Yarmouth for long periods in the 1803 invasion crisis.

It was such commitments away from home which probably persuaded William Hardy jnr to resign his commission in the Holt Volunteers [*Norwich Mercury, 22 Oct. 1803: Norfolk Heritage Centre, Norwich*]

confirmed the declaration by three hearty cheers for their King and Country.

We are authorised to state, that Lieut.-Colonel Patteson having received a letter from Marquis Townshend, Lord Lieutenant of this county, in which his Lordship requested to be informed whether the battalion of Norwich Volunteers, under the Colonel's command, would voluntarily undertake permanent duty at Yarmouth, under certain circumstances of imminent danger threatened to that place, from the forwardness of the enemy's preparations,—it was unanimously agreed by the battalion, to undertake such permanent duty, on Invasion, or imminent danger thereof.

On Tuesday last, the day of review and inspection on Bramerton Common, the two Troops of Norwich Light Horse Volunteers, under the command of Major John Harvey, previous to their entering on the ground, were formed into a hollow square, and addressed by the Major, as to the expectation of their being called out by Government

The Major read a letter from Marquis Townshend, the Lord Lieutenant, requiring whether the Corps would volunteer their service on permanent duty at Yarmouth : In putting this question, he said that he felt it his duty, as their commanding Officer, to declare his own sentiments; and pledged himself upon his Honour to march with his comrades whenever Government should demand their services. The Officers and Gentlemen of the Corps laid their hands on their breasts, as an appeal to their Honour, to undertake that Duty whenever it should be required.

Aged only twenty, and commanding officer of one of the two companies of the Loyal Aylsham Light Infantry, he found himself responsible in 1803 for teaching drill and military manoeuvres and seems to have had to rely on his crib card to keep one step ahead of his men.[1]

All this was thoroughly unnerving for the Regulars, whose very name stood for order and regularity, and yet who would be called upon to direct the vain-glorious amateur captains of the Volunteers once an invasion force had landed. Anxious memoranda would fly between the full-time military commanders as the menace of Bonaparte grew larger.[2] Near the end of the French Revolutionary War, General Henry Calvert, writing from Horse Guards, off Whitehall, summarised to Lieutenant General Balfour the part the Volunteers were to play in the Eastern District, as envisaged by the Commander-in-Chief:

. . . With respect to the Yeomanry and Volunteer corps, the whole of the former, and as many of the latter as are contiguous, will on the first appearance of the enemy be employed in driving the country to the extent that may be deemed necessary . . . That important

[1] *Repton* W. and M. Vaughan-Lewis, *Aylsham: A Nest of Norfolk lawyers*, p. 183. The crib survives

[2] *memoranda* Preserved in the archives of the Eastern District (TNA: PRO WO 30/100). This file contains a mass of proposals over supplying wagons and carts, requisitioning foodstuffs and fuel, liaising with millers and bakers, driving livestock, and hoisting red flags on church towers and lighting beacons as warnings 1797–1805 (eg pp. 1–31, relating to 1797; pp. 135–45 for 1803). Volunteers did not shine at logistics

[1] *internal tranquillity* TNA: PRO WO 30/100, p. 77, 20 Apr. 1801. Yeomanry were mounted Volunteer cavalry.
The memorandum shows that one of the Volunteers' principal roles as envisaged by the authorities was a policing one: to maintain public order and put down civil unrest

[2] *roads* Henry Motz, civilian Commissary General of the Eastern District, was as outspoken as the C-in-C in his report to the Duke: '. . . If the mode of doing this [driving the country and evacuating civilians] is not properly regulated, they [the locals] will choke up the roads and throw fatal impediments into the way of the operations of the Army' (TNA: PRO WO 30/100, p. 31, 27 Dec. 1797)

[3] *inspections* The Duke to Charles Yorke, Home Secretary (TNA: PRO WO 30/76, p. 248, 30 Dec. 1803). It was accepted at the time that when campaigning in Flanders and the Netherlands in 1793–95 and 1799 the Duke's already lacklustre performance as a battlefield commander had been further undermined by ill-trained troops weakened by disease and

service completed . . . a third, or perhaps the half of these corps, will be most advantageously employed in preserving the internal tranquillity of the country, in forming continual patrols on all the roads in the vicinity of the great towns, in enforcing the orders and requisitions of the committees of magistrates (which would be constantly sitting), in protecting the market people, and in securing the regular and accustomed supplies of the markets.[1]

Despite the protestations of the more combative Volunteers, they were not to interfere with the operations of the military. As the observations by the Duke of York illustrate (opposite) on 'Clogging the movements of the Army', the Regulars had a horror of having to clear the roads of indisciplined, physically frail Volunteers and independently-minded citizenry just when rapid deployment was most necessary.[2]

The correspondence between the military and civil powers entrusted with the country's preservation during the last years of the French Revolutionary War and opening years of the Napoleonic War reveal certain tensions and incompatibility of aims between them, with the unfortunate Lord Lieutenant caught in the middle. Lord Townshend and other county lieutenants were being pressed by central government and the Commander-in-Chief of the Army either to mould the Volunteers into an effective force or to make the geriatric leaders of individual corps recognise their limitations and serve only in a minor capacity as a policing body guarding against 'Jacobinical insurrection'.

In the autumn of 1803 the Duke, a firm believer in 'regularity' and 'uniformity' as the way to impose discipline, had instituted a system of inspection of the Volunteers by senior serving officers known as inspecting field-officers. Their task was 'to connect the experience of the Regular Army with this new description of force, so as to obtain the certainty of discipline and uniformity of system and exercise'.[3] The Duke emerges in the Horse Guards papers (catalogued very much later as War Office papers) as knowledgeable and competent, a man of some charm and great good sense, but the bluntness of his speech betrays his anxiety over the effectiveness of the Volunteers.

He regarded the Volunteer officers as untrained amateurs 'wholly unaccustomed to service'; while the whole force had 'a want of uniform system and previous habit of moving in

'Clogging the movements of the Army': some of the Commander-in-Chief's reservations about the Volunteers, November–December 1801

sources TNA: PRO WO 30/76, pp. 107, 246–7, 12 Nov., 30 Dec. 1803

DOUBTS OVER THE VOLUNTEERS' EFFECTIVENESS, 12 NOV. 1803 [1]

In considering the means of producing the Volunteer force in the field with the greatest promptitude and effect, it has appeared to me, from the constitution of these corps, a certain deficiency must be expected in each (upon their being called on actual service), arising from the state of health of many whose zeal and loyalty (and the sake of example) may have led to engage in this service, without due attention either to their period of life or physical strength.

And as it is probable that you will agree with me in the propriety under any circumstance of invasion, of a portion of the Volunteer force being intrusted with the police of the country, I submit to the consideration of His Majesty's Government that the senior, and most inefficient part of every corps, should be formed into separate companies expressly for this duty.

The greater part of those who would compose these companies, being either householders or married men, they would feel a greater interest in the preservation of property and checking any attempt at Jacobinical insurrection, whilst the military operations, deriving every aid from efficient numbers, will not be embarrassed by the care, or charge of provisioning, men whose want of activity would clog the movements of the Army . . .

CONTINUING DOUBTS OVER THEIR EFFICIENCY, 30 DEC. 1803 [2]

I have since received a copy of the book presented to the House of Commons,[3] containing the establishment of the corps which have been accepted in the different counties, and which offers better means than any hitherto obtained for laying the groundwork of such arrangements. I am however to observe that the *numbers* therein stated are those which have been accepted by His Majesty —but that the *efficiency* of those numbers is still unknown to me . . .

The state of equipment and discipline also is far from being generally ascertained, and where known is reported in many instances to be defective.

These remarks have appeared to me indispensably necessary, that we may not be supposed to possess means which do not exist, and that His Majesty's Government may not as yet place too great a reliance upon the operations of those bodies of support intended to be formed from the Volunteers of the inland counties.

I again however offer the fullest assurance that no exertion shall be wanting on my part to animate this great engine of our national defence to every exertion of which it is capable . . .

[1] *doubts* From the Duke of York, as C-in-C of the British Army, at Horse Guards, London, to Lord Hobart, Secretary for War (TNA: PRO WO 30/76, p. 107).

HRH Prince Frederick Augustus (1763–1827), Duke of York and Albany, was the second son of George III and Queen Charlotte. As a career officer he had been sent when young to study Austrian and Prussian military manoeuvres.

He served as C-in-C of the Army from 1795 (effective 1798) to 1809 and 1811–27, and was responsible for the disposition and direction of British troops during the invasion scares 1798–99 and 1803–05. He was seen then, and has been since, as an able and effective C-in-C: a hard-working leader, with imagination and drive

[2] *continuing doubts* From the Duke to Charles Yorke, Home Secretary (TNA: PRO WO 30/76, pp. 246–7). The Duke's underlinings are shown in italics

[3] *since received* Since the Duke's letter to Yorke of 8 Dec. 1803, pressing for returns on the numbers and standard of the Volunteers

exposure, poor supply lines and lack of clear strategic objectives: hence the Duke's desire to improve effectiveness at all levels.

Mark Urban highlights poor leadership by senior officers—the consequence of promotion through political patronage—as another source of the Army's failings, and one the Duke managed partially to remedy as C-in-C (M. Urban, *Generals: Ten British commanders who shaped the world* (Faber and Faber, London, 2005), pp. 100–1, 103–4)

---

[1] *the Duke's anxiety* TNA: PRO WO 30/76, p. 240, 8 Dec. 1803

[2] *regularity* TNA: PRO WO 30/76, p. 240, 8 Dec. 1803

[3] *Volunteers' anxieties* These poured almost daily into Townshend's in-tray (TNA: PRO HO 50/341 and HO 50/80).

For a man held to have had a short fuse he bore up well—at least in his emollient written replies and his comments accompanying the forwarded correspondence

[4] *Cromer established Norw. Merc.* 26 May 1798. Names changed frequently among the Volunteer corps

collected bodies', and was likely to be thoroughly in the way in an emergency.[1] The Duke feared that without rigorous training the Volunteers would disintegrate at the first shock of engagement with the enemy, should that come to pass, or even while supporting the civil power. The object of instilling 'regularity' into the Volunteers was to enable them to conduct themselves correctly, with 'punctual observance of orders', when facing 'new and trying situations'. For all his flattering words about this 'great engine of our national defence', quoted in the inset on the previous page, it is obvious that the King's son considered the Volunteers as likely to prove little more than a disorderly rabble when it came to 'real action', as he termed it.[2]

Such a thorough-going regime was not at all to the taste of civilians. Some of the commanding officers of the Volunteers were emphatic on many contentious points in their letters to Lord Townshend. They were not prepared to serve outside their own immediate home area; shortages of manpower in the Regulars notwithstanding, they urgently needed more professional soldiers to train them in the use of arms which also were in very short supply; on absolutely no account were they to be treated as part of the Regular Army until the very last moment when the invader actually stepped ashore; and they were not to be subject on any occasion whatever to military discipline and punishments.[3]

The Duke's rigorous approach would have been alarming to most of Norfolk's Volunteer officers, as vividly exemplified by the commanding officer of the Cromer Loyal Association. In 1803 this was renamed the Cromer Battery Volunteers, and by 1806 it had become the Cromer Loyal Volunteer Artillery. It was commanded by 'Captain' Thomas Mickelburgh, a local merchant, whose second-in-command was William Hardy junior's great friend Edmund Bartell junior. It had been formally established by May 1798.[4]

Mickelburgh possessed the mentality abhorred by the Duke, and the letters reveal a peevish, inflexible, querulous side to the Cromer man's nature. Following a local exploratory meeting on 3 April 1797 Mickelburgh sent a list of nine resolutions to Townshend, many of which related more to what the Government was to do for his prospective corps than what the corps proposed to do for the country. The purpose of the new body was threefold: 'To protect our coast as well as to support internal tranquillity' and 'aid the civil magistrate'; so the Cromer force did not want to be channelled solely into a policing role. The captain and his fellow signatories (one of whom was Edmund Bartell junior) required that the corps be subject only 'to such regulations as shall be made by the committee hereafter named'— the nine members comprising local surgeons, shopkeepers, merchants and a surveyor. The Cromer committee was particularly firm on two other points:

*Resolved . . .*That they shall not be subject to military punishment nor be liable to be marched out of the said hundred [of North Erpingham] without their consent, on any occasion whatsoever.[1]

The peremptory tone of one of his later letters, addressed to the Under Secretary of State at the War Department in August 1803 and forwarded to London by Townshend, was not one calculated to impress a capital hourly expecting a French landing and a march on London:

Sir—. . . I have to inform you that our first drill commenced this day, and shall be glad to have arms and accoutrements sent down as soon as possible as we are quite [ie totally] in a defenceless state in this part of the county; we are drilling the men with a few old rusty muskets. I beg leave to be informed when we are to have an order from Government to be clothed [issued with uniform] and what the allowance is per man if made here, and whether our pay commence from the first drill. With an anxious expectation of an immediate reply,
    I have the honour to be, Sir, Your most obedient servant,
THOMAS MICKELBURGH [2]

Unlike William Hardy junior, Edmund Bartell junior stuck with the Volunteers. At the opening of the Napoleonic War he was once more lieutenant to Mickelburgh, being promoted less than two years later in the newly reorganised Volunteers as adjutant in the 4th Battalion of Cromer Volunteer Infantry. John Parslee, the Holt printer, stationer and bookseller, served that unit as quartermaster.[3]

Mickelburgh and his committee in 1797 had defined the hundred as the area in which they were prepared to serve. Very precise restrictions would be set by other commanding officers. In 1800 Captain Samuel Barker's 1st Company of

[1] *resolutions* TNA: PRO HO 50/341, enclosure to letter by Townshend 1 May 1797, forwarding the Cromer resolutions to the Duke of Portland, Home Secretary.
    The resolutions had been drawn up at a meeting at the Cromer Hotel, one of the Hardys' tied houses, and could well have been lubricated by Letheringsett beer.
    One of the signatories was John Smith, like Bartell a local surgeon. His leg was to be shot off in a misfire by the Cromer Battery Volunteers (P. Kent, *Fortifications of East Anglia*, p. 184).
    By 14 May 1798 the resolutions had been reduced to seven, an oddly querulous tone still pervading them (*Norw. Merc.* 26 May 1798)

[2] *letter* TNA: PRO HO 50/80, 8 Aug. 1803, forwarded to London by Townshend 12 Sept. 1803 and one of a series issuing from Mickelburgh. He wanted field artillery to be sent to Cromer; he noted that the local Sea Fencibles had serving naval officers training them, unlike his neglected men . . .

[3] *Bartell, Parslee* TNA: PRO HO 50/80, 26 Aug. 1803; *Norw. Merc.* 8 Oct. 1803, 6 Apr. 1805

[1] *Gt Yarmouth* NRO: MS 5363, 5 B6, 3 Dec. 1800

[2] *N. Walsham* NRO: MS 5363, 5 B6, 2 Dec. 1800. Coltishall, seven miles distant, fell outside its recruiting area

[3] *Fleggs* NRO: MS 5363, 5 B6, 26 Apr. 1798

[4] *Bulwer's troop* NRO: MS 5363, 5 B6, 2 Apr. 1798; also a table by Lord Townshend, Dec. 1800.
In the Napoleonic War those so minded

above Heydon Hall, seat of the Bulwer family. The Yeomanry troop led from here by Gen. Bulwer (d.1807) was one of the 20% of corps prepared to serve not just in Norfolk but anywhere in Gt Britain [*drawing by H. Repton; engraving by W. Ellis 1780, detail*]

Yarmouth Loyal Volunteer Infantry was 'not to be called out to serve beyond the liberties of the town and borough of Great Yarmouth except with their own consent'. By contrast Barker's son-in-law William Palgrave junior, commander of the Yarmouth Volunteer Troop of Cavalry, would 'assist the civil power whenever called upon' and would 'serve in case of need anywhere within twelve miles of Yarmouth'.[1] The North Walsham Volunteer Infantry resolved to extend its service 'at the requisition of the civil magistrate to a circuit of five miles round North Walsham'.[2]

In 1798 the Flegg Associated Cavalry, drawn from the sparsely populated pastoral area of north-east Broadland and the coast north of Great Yarmouth, set very precise terms. The force offered to assist the civil power in quelling riots only in the hundreds of East and West Flegg; also to give aid in escorting prisoners, provisions and military stores, as required by the local magistrates, within twenty miles of the boundary between Caister-on-Sea and Great Yarmouth but only within the county of Norfolk. The commanding officer thought it necessary to emphasise it was under the supervision of the justices and not the military.[3]

The townsfolk of Coltishall are not recorded as playing any active part in the Volunteers in the three wars. The brewer Chapman Ives, who gave strong leadership in many aspects of local life, was preoccupied with his financial problems and bankruptcies at the height of the invasion threats 1797–98 and 1803–04. The very low profile of this mercantile and manufacturing centre may have been occasioned by the fact that the South Erpingham and Eynsford Troop of Yeomanry Cavalry, into which recruits would have been drawn from Coltishall, was led by the extremely active and committed professional soldier William Earle Bulwer of Heydon. His troop was one of only six out of a total of thirty Volunteer troops and corps of infantry existing in Norfolk in 1800 prepared to serve outside the county in any part of Great Britain 'in case of actual invasion or for the suppression of riots and tumults'. Such a proposition was unlikely to appeal to Coltishall entrepreneurs with small firms to run requiring their constant presence, and with specialist workforces on whom they were heavily reliant and who could not be spared.[4]

A further six units out of the thirty were prepared to serve within the Eastern Military District; but ten, including five of the Norwich corps, would serve only their own town or city and the immediate neighbourhood. The remaining eight were prepared to serve within the hundred or within some specified radius ranging from three to twenty miles. The Holt Volunteers are not named in Lord Townshend's correspondence and tables on the subject 1798–1800, providing further evidence that the town played no part in Volunteering during the French Revolutionary War.

William's service in the Volunteers 1803

Readers of the *Norwich Mercury* learned in October 1803 that Holt and the surrounding area had reconstituted the Volunteer infantry corps of the American war: 'Holt Volunteer Infantry—Charles Hewitt, Esq. to be Captain; William Withers and William Hardy junior, Gents, to be Lieutenants'.[1] The reason for a change of heart at Holt in 1803 is not recorded in the official papers.

Both national and local press announcements of military promotions, as they were classed, lagged behind officialdom. William would have come forward in late August 1803, for the Lord Lieutenant, writing from Raynham, confirmed to the Home Secretary on 2 October 1803 that the commissions of the three Holt officers had been granted by the King on 16 September, and the Holt Volunteer Infantry already had 120 men by 14 September.[2] The *Mercury* would wait to see the appointments published in the *London Gazette* before going into print. The paper does not appear to have gathered information direct from Raynham, Lord Townshend being very correct in waiting for His Majesty's approbation of his recommendations.

Most of Mary Hardy's references to her son's activities in the Volunteers appear in the later section 'A militarised society'. They show him to have been active during the one extremely brief spell 7–11 September 1803 in training men drawn from the ranks of Letheringsett's poor (*Diary 4*). No reliable conclusion can be drawn from her near total absence of references thereafter. Either William had disengaged from participation, or his mother was oblivious to or disapproving of his Volunteering and chose not to record it.

at Coltishall could have joined the Loyal Aylsham Light Infantry, more than 200 strong in Nov. 1803—except that they too, like Bulwer's troop, were ready to serve 'in any part of Gt Britain' (TNA: PRO HO 50/80, 22 July 1803).

The other five corps prepared to serve nationwide were the Norfolk Rangers (under Townshend), Cackclose (Thomas Hare), E. Dereham (Thomas Wodehouse), Tunstead and Happing (Charles Laton) and Norwich Light Horse (John Harvey).

Tunstead and Happing bordered the Fleggs, which had taken a totally contrary view. The marked differences reflected the outlook of individual COs.

Norfolk's 30 corps of Dec. 1800 had risen to 59 by Dec. 1803 (table 4.9.2)

---

[1] *Holt Norw. Merc.* 22 Oct. 1803 (illustrated on p. 431 in the section on newspapers).

Hewitt, from whom William Hardy jnr had bought the manorial estate of Letheringsett Laviles in 1800, was, like Withers, a Holt attorney

[2] *Lord Lieutenant* TNA: PRO HO 50/80, 2 Oct. 1803

[1] *59 units* Lt Col. Metzner inspected 18 troops of cavalry and 41 corps of infantry across Norfolk in a few weeks. Extracts from 12 of these inspections are given in table 4.9.1

[2] *resignation* TNA: PRO HO 50/80

[3] *coach Diary 4*: 8 Nov., 7–8 Dec. 1803; Diary MS: 10 Nov. 1803. William had stayed the night of 7–8 Dec. at Whissonsett, very close to Raynham Hall.
For Mindham's professional work see vol. 1, chaps 7 and 10

[4] *killed Diary 4*: 18 Jan. 1804. Queen Charlotte celebrated her 59th birthday on 18 Jan. The Holt corps was probably firing a loyal salute and the unlucky Volunteer could have been the victim of a misfire

[5] *promotions Norw. Merc.* 31 Mar. 1804

[6] *terms of service* J. Cookson, *The Armed British Nation, 1793–1815*, p. 77

[7] *long hours* Described and tabulated in vol. 2, chap. 1

[8] *rush to join* R. Glover, *Britain at Bay*, pp. 14, 77; J. Terraine, *Trafalgar* (Wordsworth Editions Ltd, Ware, 1998), pp. 12–29

William set off on his long visit to London on 10 November 1803, two days after the Duke of York's inspecting officer had reviewed the Holt corps—one of 59 units he examined.[1]

On the day that William returned home on 8 December his resignation was forwarded tersely by Lord Townshend to the Home Secretary: 'Holt Volunteers: Mindham, Gent. to be Ensign, vice Hardy, resigned'.[2] William had evidently persuaded his architect and builder William Mindham to take over in a more junior capacity, and may have called at Raynham Hall in the snow on his way back to Letheringsett after travelling on the London–Fakenham coach.[3]

The *Norwich Mercury* announced the Holt changes on 17 December, and thereafter the Holt corps received very little attention in the press. Unlike many other Volunteer units it seems to have had no officers anxious to furnish the public with details of its activities. As though confirming her opinion of the organisation, Mary Hardy recorded the following month that a Volunteer had been killed by a gun at Holt; the news did not reach the *Mercury*.[4] Mindham stayed on for at least some months, being promoted lieutenant in March 1804, with the new innkeeper of the Feathers, Benjamin Ellis, as ensign.[5] Ellis was bankrupted that same year, as noted in the Gazetteer of the Hardys' public houses (at the end of volume 2).

Up to 1804 no Volunteer, whether in the ranks or an officer, engaged as a soldier for a fixed term.[6] Most were trying to hold down often demanding jobs: labourers faced pressures through their exceptionally long hours.[7] Turnover was high even among officers, as Townshend's letters and the press notices confirm, and William Hardy junior was free to leave at any time. The officers were not drawn from the leisured class, but were professional men, manufacturers, merchants and tradesmen. It was their input, as labour and as wealth creators, which formed Britain's economic base and enabled the country to prosecute a war.

We can only speculate over the reasons behind William Hardy junior's decisions; his mother offers no explanations. He joined at a moment of great national peril and when there was a rush to respond to the emergency.[8] Also on 6 August 1803 Townshend had proclaimed that unless more Norfolkmen came forward as volunteers they would face the compulsory provisions of the General Defence Act passed on 27 July for the military training of men aged 17–55.[1]

William's resignation after what appears to have been a lacklustre two months under arms, not counting his four-week stay in London, may have been influenced by the growing trend for the Volunteers to serve outside their home area. In what the press characterised as 'the march of our Volunteers to the coast' (an item of probably unwelcome news on Mary Hardy's seventieth birthday) even inland units would serve on two-weekly rotas of garrison duty to free the Regulars and Militia.[2] Mary Hardy noted ominously on the day of the Holt inspection that 'Raynham Rangers and Fakenham Volunteers were sent to Yarmouth to guard the coast.'[3] As many as 280 Volunteers marched from Norwich to Great Yarmouth. Even the North Walsham Light Infantry, from a town conspicuously restrictive over its terms of service in the previous war, was scheduled to undertake a fortnight's duty at Yarmouth at that perilous time.[4]

We have seen in many other parts of this study that being in control of their lives mattered to the Hardys and those of their mindset. This ranged from control of the workforce and maidservants to control of an individual's spiritual destiny; even the Sunday school movement took root partly as an instrument of social control. By joining the Volunteers William had compromised his ability to control his hours and his movements. It could not last.[5]

On the day that the Volunteers were inspected at Holt William characteristically had other matters demanding his attention. He had to journey eight miles to Binham to be admitted as copyholder of his new tied house—presumably after the inspection that afternoon, as he arrived home from Binham at 8 pm. Had he too been 'sent to guard the coast' forty miles away at Great Yarmouth the profitability of his farm, maltings and brewery would have been damaged. Whereas in the previous war the Volunteers had set their own terms, pressure from Parliament to regularise the force was about to remove some of this freedom. A Bill was soon in progress to make attendance compulsory. Those currently serving in the Volunteers were to be permitted to resign, but those remaining had to engage to serve and attend regularly for five years or the continuation of the war.[6]

[1] *Act* See J. Barney, *The Defence of Norfolk*, pp. 41–7. Under the Act able-bodied men were to be formed into local armed units, with selection by ballot—a perilously 'near approach to compulsory conscription' (p. 41)

[2] *march to the coast Norw. Merc.* 12 Nov. 1803. The pledges of some of the Norwich units have been illustrated in the press extract of 22 Oct. 1803 describing sham fights at Bramerton (on p. 536)

[3] *Yarmouth Diary 4:* 8 Nov. 1803

[4] *Yarmouth Norw. Merc.* 12 Nov. 1803. The paper was full of announcements that autumn and winter of the movements of the Volunteers as though they were an embodied Militia—presumably heightening the Hardys' fears.

The 74-strong Wells Volunteers passed through Norwich on their way to garrison duty at Gt Yarmouth (*Norw. Merc.* 24 Dec. 1803). The commitments continued for years. As late as 1807 the Bungay Volunteers were doing duty at Lowestoft (*Norw. Merc.* 19 Sept. 1807)

[5] *control* Analysed at the end of vol. 2, chap. 4

[6] *terms of service Norw. Merc.* 4 Feb. 1804

BONEY ATTACKING THE ENGLISH HIVES
or the CORSICAN caught at last in the Island

above A cartoon from Aug. 1803, when William Hardy jnr was joining the newly formed Holt Volunteers. George III is defended by loyal swarms of bees from the hives protecting his realm: the mobilised coastal counties of Kent, Sussex, Suffolk, Wales and Scotland and—the large hive in the foreground—London's commercial sector and the Bank of England producing 'Threadneedle Street Honey'.

Britain is dependent on the commercial class as well as the military and naval—the 'Salt Water Bees'. Further, the English Constitution sturdily supports the protectors.

The 'plundering little Corsican villain', as the King calls him, exclaims ruefully: 'I did not think this nation of shopkeepers could have stung so sharp.' Napoleon's 'shop-keeper' jibe had riled the British
[*photo Bodleian Libraries*: Curzon b.11(11)]

---

[1] *Lacon* NRO: MS 67, p. 7, Lt Col. Metzner's inspection, 21 Dec. 1803. Just one of the 48 horses of the Yarmouth troop did not come up to standard (see p. 548, table 4.9.1)

It could be argued that other brewers managed to combine the demands of work with the command of Volunteer companies. On taking up the busy post of Collector of Customs William Palgrave junior had been succeeded by the very successful Yarmouth brewer Edmund Knowles Lacon, who was judged by the inspecting field officer in December 1803 to have 'an excellent troop'.[1] John Patteson of Norwich, then owner of the largest brewery in the county, managed to be active as Lieutenant Colonel of the Norwich Battalion of Volunteer Infantry. However his exceptionally large corps with 222 men present in the ranks did not receive the same glowing report as Lacon's when it was seen at Bramerton at the start of the Norfolk inspection process in October 1803.[1]

Unlike most of the county's brewers, Lacon and Patteson had large teams in their extensive concerns. William Hardy junior was head brewer of his, and could not be spared. Others may have shared William's predicament. John Heath, the Fakenham doctor, resigned his lieutenancy in the Fakenham Volunteers as early as 30 August 1803.[2] Britain was not only a nation of shopkeepers, in Adam Smith's phrase (and later Napoleon's), but of conscientious professionals, craftsmen and labourers who knew their employment contribution to be vital to the nation's survival.

Those who, like William Hardy junior, elected to resign as quickly as possible were not necessarily casting their backs on their country just when it needed them most. The malt and beer taxes paid by William and other manufacturers who managed to keep their businesses running at peak production were undoubtedly far more valuable to the Armed Forces reliant on these taxes than his half-hearted attempts at soldiering. To arrange his affairs in London and order the year's supply of Kentish hops for his brewery was for William rather more pressing than exercising village labourers in the Six Acres,[3] and so it was that on his return from his business trip he tendered his resignation. The payments to the State coffers from an expanding Letheringsett maltings and brewery probably outweighed anything else he could have done for the war effort. 'The English hives' of the 1803 cartoon (opposite), representing financial and economic muscle, helped preserve the country from Boney. They arguably achieved as much as the Navy—the massed hives of the 'Salt Water Bees' blocking the approach from Calais.

As part of the process of improving and regularising the Volunteers the Duke of York's inspecting field-officers toured the country in the opening years of the Napoleonic War. As quoted earlier in the extracts from the Duke of York's letters of 1803, the Commander-in-Chief wanted to gauge not

[1] *Patteson* NRO: MS 66, p. 12, 18 Oct. 1803. Seven men were sick. One captain, one sergeant and 62 privates were absent (perhaps at the brewery, or delivering beer). It was nonetheless a 'steady, remarkable clean good corps'

[2] *Heath* TNA: PRO HO 50/80, letter from Townshend to the Home Secretary, 30 Aug. 1803

[3] *Six Acres Diary 4*: 8 Sept. 1803

above Fakenham, the sanctuary: Dr Heath's wife Frances, née Money, was buried in 1808 with their stillborn child.

John Heath held the shortest commission of any Volunteer officer in Norfolk in the invasion crisis 1803–05. A busy medical practitioner could not leave his patients and march to the coast with his men [*MB · 2011*]

TABLE 4.9.1

State of readiness: the inspecting officer's report on the Norfolk Volunteers, October–December 1803

source NRO: MS 66, 67, vols 1 and 2, Inspection of Yeomanry Cavalry and Volunteer Infantry of Norfolk by Lt Col. Metzner, Inspecting Field Officer, 18 Oct.–21 Dec. 1803 [extracts]

company: CO	present	observations and state of discipline
CAVALRY		
Dereham Corps J. Crisp	53	Officers and NCOS 'attentive and willing to improve'; trumpeters 'indifferent'; men under arms 'lately formed'; horses 'middling'. Arms and horse furniture 'good'. 'Improving; promise to make a good troop'
E. Dereham Troop J. Hyde	61	Officers and NCOS 'very steady'; trumpeters 'improving'; men 'attentive'; horses 'good in general'. Arms 'new, purchased by the captain'; horse furniture 'good of every specie'. 'Very willing and attentive'
Holkham T.W. Coke	40	39 horses, 'superior to any in England'. Arms 'very good'; horse furniture 'all new'. 'Bold horsemen, charge sturdily and well'
Yarmouth E.K. Lacon	53	1 captain, 1 cornet, 1 chapain, 1 surgeon, 7 NCOS, 1 trumpeter, 42 privates, 48 horses. Officers and NCOS 'remarkably steady', trumpeters 'good'; men 'very steady and very willing to improve'. Arms 'good'; one horse rejected. 'An excellent troop, complete and well appointed; steady in evolutions, charge bold and well'
INFANTRY		
Aylsham Hon. G. Walpole	210	7 officers and 9 sergeants 'very attentive'; men 'steady'. Arms 'good'. 'Very steady, a stout body of men, attentive and silent'
Cromer Battery T. Mickelburgh	83	Officers and NCOS 'alert and steady'; drummers and fifers 'good'; men under arms 'steady, upright and quick'. 'Carabines remarkably clean'. 'Much praise' is due the captain
Felbrigg W. Windham	92	'Arms of different kinds'. 'This corps just raised is over the establishment [by] 25; application for augmentation is made'
Gunton & Blickling Rifle Corps W.A. Harbord	388	20 officers, 18 sergeants, 18 corporals all 'very attentive'; the 326 privates 'steady and alert'. Arms 'capital new rifles and swords'. 'This corps shows superior attention to military tactics, are active and silent (mostly daily labourers)'
Holt C. Hewitt	115	Officers 'attentive and desirous to improve'; drummers and fifers 'very good'; men under arms 'steady'. Prussian arms. 'A drill sergant is ordered; march well'
Little Walsingham C. Adcock	54	Officers and NCOS 'just appointed'; men under arms 'not steady'. Prussian arms. Corps 'not at all disciplined, [as] . . . just embodied'
Twyford S.H. Savory	57	Officers and men 'attentive'. 'The whole corps has been completed and furnished with every necessary without the aid of Government . . . This company improving'
1st Wells J.G. Bloom	70	Officers and NCOS 'very attentive and steady'; drummers and fifers 'very good'; men under arms 'steady'. Prussian arms 'very good and clean'; 'knapsacks very neat'. Company 'throughout steady and well disciplined'

just the numbers but the effectiveness and efficiency of the force, and the state of their equipment and discipline. The half-pay officer despatched to Norfolk, Lieutenant Colonel Metzner, carried out his two-month tour of inspection with remarkable tact and tried hard to be encouraging. But his relief is palpable when he finds 'an old soldier' in charge, as in the case of the Swaffham Volunteer Infantry: 'The commanding officer (as an old soldier) has been indefatigable in bringing this corps to great perfection and cleanliness.'[1]

Those new to the task could nevertheless earn his praise. 'Major' Richard Mackenzie Bacon, publisher of the *Norwich Mercury* which did so much to promote the Volunteer movement, received a good report for his Norwich Rifle Corps.[2] The Lord Lieutenant—or possibly even those in London smarting from Thomas Mickelburgh's barbs—may have briefed Metzner to be diplomatic about the Cromer Battery Volunteers: 'Much praise is due the captain for the soldier-like appearance of this corps.'[3] As might be expected, the Norfolk Rangers, raised by a field marshal who had served since Dettingen, received a very good report.[4]

As table 4.9.1 shows, Metzner could be critical where he judged it necessary. On occasion he had to speak out when he found a corps 'undisciplined' or even 'totally undisciplined', or the officers 'not yet perfect in their duty'.[5] The Holt Volunteers did not shine, the most favourable remarks being reserved for the drummers and fifers. Under the leadership of the two lawyers and a brewer whose mind was on keeping his appointment at the King's Arms at Binham that day the unit was probably not prospering. It did however, unlike many, have some Prussian arms, and the men were adjudged steady, and good at marching.[6] Metzner too, like William, must have been at full stretch on 8 November, as in that one day he inspected six companies: Felbrigg, Barningham, Holt, Little Walsingham, Cromer and Wells.[7]

An interesting test of commitment was whether the company had done garrison duty at Yarmouth. Only 26 of the 59 units inspected had served there by the time Metzner was compiling his statistics, presumably at the end of December 1803. Holt, like Aylsham and Holkham, had not; the South Erpingham and Eynsford troop, likewise Tunstead and Happing's and Patteson's Norwich Battalion, had.[8]

---

[1] *Swaffham* NRO: MS 67, p. 15. Similarly the Yarmouth Volunteer Infantry under Lt Col. W. Gould, despite suffering many sick and other absentees, received the accolade: 'This is one of the steadiest and best corps in the county, the lieutenant colonel an old officer of the line' (MS 67, p. 30).
The Tunstead and Happing Yeomanry Cavalry, inspected at Wroxham the day before Holt, excelled under Capt. Laton: 'The commanding officer has great merit (was in the Army)' (MS 66, p. 8)

[2] *Norwich* NRO: MS 67, p. 28

[3] *Cromer* NRO: MS 66, p. 24

[4] *Norfolk Rangers* NRO: MS 66, p. 7

[5] *critical* At Wymondham (NRO: MS 66, p. 11); at Southrepps (MS 66, p. 13); and at Norwich in Robert Harvey's corps (MS 66, p. 13)

[6] *Holt* NRO: MS 66, p. 22

[7] *Metzner* That order is suggested by the page-numbering of the MS. It would have made sense on the day to arrange the itinerary so as to achieve greater economy of effort

[8] *Gt Yarmouth* NRO: MS 67, p. 32

¹ *1804 inspections* The classes and results are explained by John Barney in *The Defence of Norfolk*, pp. 55–6 and app. I, pp. 74–6

² *foppery* R.W. Ketton-Cremer, 'Norfolk and the threat of invasion', p. 162

³ *Holt* NRO: MS 66, p. 22.
The Loyal Aylsham Corps of Volunteer Infantry chose an unusual uniform of 'grey fustian jacket and round hats' (MS 66, p. 28)

⁴ *Melton Norw. Merc.* 14 Sept. 1782

⁵ *Norwich, Gunton* NRO: MS 67, p. 28; MS 66, p. 29.
The 2nd Wells Company of Volunteer Infantry chose green, black and gold (MS 66, p. 26)

Metzner's inspections the following year, by which time William Hardy junior had severed his connection, were more rigorous, enabling the Commander-in-Chief to judge the capabilities of the individual corps more accurately. The results were poor. Eight (including Yarmouth under Gould) were in the top class; sixteen (including Holt, Holkham, and Cromer) in the middle; and seventeen (including Felbrigg, under Windham) in the lowest—these last being backward and unpromising. Lack of training explained the failures.[1]

Thanks to Metzner's reports we know something of the 'clothing' worn by the Norfolk Volunteers; he could not bring himself to call it uniform, there being nothing uniform about the units' choices. He was greeted by all the colours of the rainbow except purple, plus others: grey and black, gold and silver. A criticism sometimes levelled at the Volunteers was their 'foppery of dress', as Windham put it in 1803:[2] a desire for lavish display, with a myriad of colours in their uniforms. As shown by the engraving of Lieutenant Palgrave (page 496), there was a passion for feathers: not small alpine-style feathers, but great arching creations taller than the shakos and bearskins on which they were sported.

The colours red and blue, with black accoutrements (knapsack, belt etc), as worn by William Hardy junior at Holt,[3] were fairly popular in the county, but the striking feature of the reports is the number of companies that chose green. As already observed, green may have been adopted in honour of Townshend's Norfolk Rangers, who chose that colour from the start of the Volunteer movement. The Melton Volunteers, another very early unit, wore green and orange.[4] Riflemen and sharpshooters often wore green, such as Bacon's Norwich corps with 'clothing all green'. The Gunton & Blickling Rifle Corps wore green and black, with round hats, green feathers and black accoutrements.[5]

Green was at that time an unmilitary colour, signalling the Volunteers' distance from the red-coated Regulars and Militia. It might have been associated with the Lincoln green of Robin Hood and, as John Money was urging, there are hints it was indeed deliberately adopted to offer camouflage for a force intended not so much to hold the line as deploy as irregulars—as had the Merry Men in the greenwood. William Windham was a strong advocate of such a role for the Volunteers, and Metzner noted that green was the chosen colour of Windham's corps.[1]

This was no wild scheme. The orders in General Craig's copybook 1803–04 show that he too envisaged that the Volunteers would be most effective when putting their local knowledge to best use by harassing the enemy and shooting at the French from 'behind every tree and stone':[2]

The Military High Command realized that an approach was necessary which mirrored the elements of rapidity, the use of almost guerrilla-like sharp shooters and light artillery and the mobilization of the mass population in defence.[3]

Mary Hardy only very infrequently lets slip her own view of the mass of legislation putting the country on a military footing. However the actions, or inaction, of her family speak volumes. Her husband, aged fifty in January 1782, was young enough to have served as a Volunteer at the end of the American war; their son was of an age to be a Volunteer during the whole of the French wars, still being only 45 in June 1815. But, apart from William's very brief encounter with the Volunteers in 1803, father and son remained aloof from military service. For all that they lived in a militarised society 1778–82, 1794–1801 and 1803–c.1810, neither father nor son was minded to bear arms.

The Hardys represent the very type over whom the Lord Lieutenant and his advisers agonised. They had a farm to run, a maltings and brewery to maintain in constant production, a large number of retail outlets to supply and a very hardworking team to supervise. With the exception of George Phillippo, living in the manor farmhouse at Letheringsett from 1801, they had no foreman or steward to whom they could delegate any of these burdens: brewery clerks like William Girling had no supervisory role.

As Colonel Money, as he then was, expressed it in his trenchant style to Lord Townshend in 1794, the retention of the key phrase 'an *appearance* of invasion' in the Defence Act establishing the terms of service of the Volunteers was 'a scarecrow to the honest farmer and the man of business'.[4] While there remained the danger that they could be called out well before the actual moment of invasion, or be posted elsewhere on garrison duty, the Hardys would not serve.

[1] *Windham* R.W. Ketton-Cremer, 'Norfolk and the threat of invasion', pp. 162–3 (referring to Windham's celebrated speech to the House of Commons 20 June 1803); NRO: MS 66, p. 20 (for Metzner).

On the appreciation of the need for camouflage, particularly for snipers, and the adoption of guerrilla tactics see also B. Lavery, *We shall fight on the Beaches*, pp. 333, 337

[2] *harassing* K. Navickas, 'Lieut. General Sir James Henry Craig's orders to commanders in the Eastern Military District', p. 64

[3] *sharp shooters* K. Navickas, 'Lieut. General Sir James Henry Craig's orders', p. 65

[4] *scarecrow* TNA: PRO HO 50/341, 6 Apr. 1794.

While Money wrote with great good sense, the vehemence of his expressions would probably have alienated readers in positions of authority who were already harried by their mounds of correspondence.

The C-in-C at his Horse Guards HQ had to respond to 300 letters a day, but had only 35 people on his staff at most with which to run the Army (M. Urban, *Generals*, pp. 113, 104)

[1] *Metzner* Information from Mark Wishon of University College London, in his talk 'Brother-soldiers or "other" soldiers? Perception and social interaction in the British and German Armies 1689–1815', given at the Institute of Historical Research, 24 Feb. 2010.

German soldiers were integral to the British and Allied coalitions in Europe, and 20,000 German soldiers fought on the British side in the American war and in home defence 1776–1810

[2] *Fencible* An archaic term for a defender or guard. One of the definitions of 'to fence' given by Dr Johnson in his 1755 dictionary is 'to guard against', fencible being the adjective. The Volunteer infantry were sometimes called Fencibles.

The Sea Fencibles do not feature in the studies already cited by Linda Colley, John Cookson and Richard Glover, among others

[3] *Hoste* TNA: PRO ADM 28/14; in the same file Capt. Bentinck commanded the King's Lynn unit in Feb. 1804

[4] *pay* The Navy Board's pay lists 1798–1810 for the Sea Fencibles survive at Kew under the

The tactful Lieutenant Colonel Metzner moved on, leaving for posterity his sets of immaculately presented reports. By 1805 he was at Bexhill-on-Sea in Sussex, serving as General Metzner with the King's German Legion at its infantry headquarters. He may well have been in the Legion from the autumn of 1803, when it was formed as a unit of expatriate Germans within the British Army.[1]

Despite so much ink expended in the reports, reviews and correspondence of the time we have no way of gauging how these part-time Volunteers would have performed under conditions of 'real action', in the Duke of York's telling phrase. He was ever pressing for more rigorous, professional standards to be applied to them. These were to be found in their coastal counterparts, the Sea Fencibles.

Part-timers: the Sea Fencibles

The Sea Fencibles have been ignored in many studies of home defence.[2] The reason for their shadowy presence lies in the professionalism of their training. Since they were led and trained by serving officers and senior NCOs in the Royal Navy their papers, which are voluminous, are housed in the Admiralty files. Some of the officers were of high rank and had distinguished careers, the Wisbech and Spalding Sea Fencibles being under the command of Nelson's protégé Captain William Hoste in July 1804. Captain William Bentinck, soon Rear-Admiral, commanded the King's Lynn Sea Fencibles that same year; he was from the area.[3]

The units fell under the direct command not of the North Sea and Channel Fleets but of the Lords of the Admiralty, and their members were paid by the Navy Board (figure 4.9A).[4] These civilians under arms were fishermen, ferrymen, shipwrights, ropemakers and merchant seamen with good local knowledge of creeks, tides and landing places. The fact that they were outside the control of the County Lieutenancy gives them their elusive quality, and they sit on the periphery of the tight system of home defence illustrated in figure 4.9B. They are rarely mentioned in the War Office and Home Office papers in the National Archives, filled to bursting with preparations to withstand invasion. The mists of the fog-bound marram-edged creeks and salt flats in which they operated seem to surround them still.

left Salt marshes at Stiffkey, west of Wells. Major Alexander Bryce recommended flooding the marshes to make the terrain uninviting to an invader.

The coast was the haunt of the Sea Fencibles. At Wells, with an 1801 population of 1023 males (including children and the elderly), 66 Sea Fencibles took part in weekly exercises in Feb. 1805
[*Christopher Bird 2014*]

They were first established in March 1798, were stood down in October 1801, reactivated on a much larger scale in July 1803 and stood down once more in October 1810. As the Home Secretary was informed in July 1803, their great strength lay in their expert knowledge:

Sea Fencibles should attack the enemy by sea. The Sea Fencibles, being composed of merchant seamen, fishermen, shipwrights, sailmakers, ropemakers and others who are either constantly or occasionally employed on the *water,* would have great advantages over the best disciplined troops in the world *in their own element . . .*[1]

They were not called up by ballot, nor were their numbers set by quotas. They were volunteers who thereby secured exemption from the Militia and—a key consideration—from impressment into the Royal Navy. While, like the land-based part-timers, they were not put to the test, the manner of their training made it likely they would have been more effective than the Volunteers. They were seen as a desirable and effective body by the Ordnance and Army at the highest levels: from Bryce, the Commanding Engineer of the Eastern District, to the C-in-C himself.[2] It was envisaged by the military that the Sea Fencibles would be deployed on land

ADM department, with orders appointing Royal Naval officers to them 1803–07 (eg ADM 6/55, ADM 11/14)

[1] *great advantages* TNA: PRO HO 42/71, f. 18, written by Lord Lowther at Lowther, Cumb. to Lord Pelham, Home Secretary, 31 July 1803. (Lowther's underlinings have been italicised)

[2] *C-in-C* 'The Sea Fencibles should be again enrolled upon the same or a similar plan to what was adopted in the late war, under the superintendance of active and intelligent naval officers' (TNA: PRO WO 30/76, pp. 4–5,

C-in-C's letter to Lord Hobart, Secretary for War, 21 June 1803)

---

[1] *Mundesley* TNA: PRO WO 30/100, pp. 148–9, 12 Dec. 1803. Bryce appears to have been persuaded by the locals against his better judgment that Mundesley, with its deepwater access to the cart gap in the cliffs, needed a good measure of protection. He had reported to Craig on 12 Dec. 1803: 'Although the inhabitants of this part seem to attach considerable importance to Mundesley, I can hardly bring myself to be of their opinion . . .' (quoted more fully in *Diary 4*, app. D4.c)

Just being on coast watch was a useful task (B. Lavery, *We shall fight on the Beaches*, p. 337)

[2] *Cley* TNA: PRO WO 30/100, p. 159, 12 Dec. 1803

[3] *numbers* TNA: PRO WO 30/100, 20 Dec. 1803: pp. 149, 151.

In late 1803, 149 were enrolled between Emsworth and Beachy Head in Sussex, with 59 boats. Bigbury, in Devon, had 146 Sea Fencibles (B. Lavery, *We shall fight on the Beaches*, pp. 337–8)

to man mobile artillery and small batteries as required as part of a rapid-response team harassing and 'annoying' landing parties. On the strength of Bryce's findings General Craig considered that the guns of the proposed battery at the small fishing station of Mundesley on the Norfolk coast 'might considerably annoy an Enemy'; the active and committed local Sea Fencibles would man the battery.[1]

Both Major Bryce and General Craig reveal that the Sea Fencibles were present in large numbers on the north Norfolk coast. As Bryce observed at Cley, they were 'numerous on this part of the coast and well acquainted with the beach and roads through the marshes'.[2] In the autumn of 1803 Mundesley had between forty and fifty men in the corps, when the total male population in 1801 was 88. There were 48 at Cley and Blakeney (with male populations in the census of 235 and 258) in the latest returns Sir James Craig had been given by the naval officer in charge, while Wells had eighty (in a total male population of 1023).[3] These were sizeable additions to the civilian fighting force. The numbers would have been drawn not just from those named parishes but from neighbouring coastal villages such as Morston for Blakeney and Stiffkey for Wells. The reports from the Eastern District suggest that its senior (military) officers worked closely with the Royal Navy personnel posted to the coast, who would have supplied them with the data.

Originally, in 1798, the Sea Fencibles were divided into five districts, stretching from Emsworth on the Hampshire/ Sussex border to Great Yarmouth; shortly afterwards the coverage was extended. In 1803 the whole of Norfolk was supplied with Sea Fencible units as the number of districts was greatly increased. The muster lists were meticulously kept since the men's pay depended on their attendance, as seen already when tracing the members of *Nelly*'s crew (chapter 5, page 287). Names, dates and payments are recorded for the units on the north Norfolk coast at King's Lynn, Thornham, Burnham, Wells, Blakeney (including Cley), Sheringham and Cromer.

Of the 131 at Blakeney and Sheringham in October 1803 38 men (29 per cent) could write their names. *Nelly*'s captain heads a group of fencibles who each signed for their pay on 30 October 1803: John Coe, William Harvey, John

Starling, Richard Randall (lost with Coe a few months later on *Nelly*), Christopher Jackson, Thomas Leake, Edward Silence and William Farthings. Most men manged to attend on at least two days a month. A few of the 131 could not be present on occasion, being 'at sea', or 'fishing'. One, who had enrolled early, was absent all that month. The reason was later noted against his name: 'drowned'.[1]

In February 1804, the month that *Nelly* was wrecked at Blakeney, the King's Lynn unit under Captain Bentinck numbered 257.[2] By the end of 1805 this former Governor of St Vincent and the Grenadines in the West Indies, now Rear-Admiral Bentinck, had a supervisory role for a long stretch of coastline: 'Superintendent of the Enrolment of Sea Fencibles between Cromer and Foss Dyke Wash'. In that capacity he disbursed £3427 6s 9d to the units.[3]

There was no maximum age limit. At Lowestoft, which also embraced Pakefield, Corton and other nearby coastal villages, the great majority in 1803 were in their twenties

[1] *musters* TNA: PRO ADM 28/14. The records are not in paginated ledgers, but form a jumble of loose papers

[2] *Lynn* TNA: PRO ADM 28/14

[3] *Bentinck* TNA: PRO ADM 28/15; the total is for the period 12 Oct. 1803 to 13 Dec. 1805.
Details of numbers, attendances and payments are also noted east round the coast at Overstrand (Beckhithe), Trimingham, Mundesley, Bacton, Happisburgh, Winterton, Gt Yarmouth, Gorleston and Lowestoft

left A sturdy clinker-built fishing boat rots on Blakeney marshes. Those familiar with the creeks and marshes for their work were recruited for defence against invasion. Capt. Peter Ribouleau (d.1847), already with a very distinguished record, commanded Sea Fencible units at Sheringham, Blakeney and Wells in 1803. He died a Vice-Admiral.

Exercises were taken seriously. In October that year the newly formed Wells unit took part in exercise routines every week, all but one of the 84 on the books appearing in person. An additional four were petty officers, possibly drawn from the unit, so there was a ratio of 5:84 during training.

The Navy Board ran a tight ship over pay. Capt. Ribouleau's pay that month was £42. Once the men's pay (1s for each attendance) and the petty officers' was included the expenses of the Wells unit for the month totalled nearly £96 (TNA: PRO ADM 28/14). This was a far cry from the pleadings of Volunteer company commanders for their men to be paid   [*Christopher Bird 2013*]

[1] *ages* TNA:PRO ADM 28/17, July and Aug. 1803. At Gt Yarmouth the majority of the 160 members were in their thirties and forties

[2] *Allen* TNA:PRO ADM 28/18, 10 Nov. 1805

[3] *literacy* TNA:PRO ADM 28/18, Nov. 1805

[4] *Hunter* TNA:PRO ADM 28/18, Mar. 1805.

Tremblett, aged 29, had travelled 232 miles from Bath to take up his post at Gt Yarmouth in July 1803, for which he claimed 1*s* 3*d* per mile (ADM 28/17).

Thomas Thurst, aged 36, the Hardys' inn-keeper at the White Horse, Overstrand, was allowed to sign his name when he was appointed 'an officer' (confusingly given later as 'petty officer') in the Overstrand unit, his daily rate being 2*s* 6*d* (ADM 28/17, July 1803; ADM 28/18, Mar. 1805)

[5] *gunnery* NRO: MC 216/1, 668 x 3, The farming journal of Randall Burroughes, (unpag. MS), week of 16 July 1798. Burroughes was one of a large party of visitors. HMS *Contest* was a 75-foot (23-metre) 14-gun gun-boat launched at Deptford in 1797 (Britain's Navy, Fighting Ships (<http://britainsnavy.co.uk/Ships/HMS%20Contest/HMS%20Contest%20(1797)%201.htm>,

and thirties; one was 63.[1] One member of the Cromer unit failed to appear on 10 November 1805 (just after news of the victory at Trafalgar had reached Norfolk). Robert Allen had died on 30 October 'of old age'.[2]

Literacy rates appear markedly lower at first sight than on Mary Hardy's part of the coast. Of the 71 men at Gorleston in December 1805 only eight signed their names. Of the 21 at Cromer the previous month just one signed. At Beckhithe, Trimingham and Mundesley all made marks. All four exercising one day at Bacton and seven at Happisburgh made marks.[3] Appearances can however be misleading. It is likely that an impatient Royal Navy captain, wanting to press on with training, did not give his men the chance to line up in turn to sign. With Captain William Henry Tremblett in charge David Hunter has a mark against his name at Cromer. But under other commanding officers he signs.[4]

Although she lived only four miles from two coastal havens, one of which, Cley, she visited regularly once a week for a Methodist meeting, Mary Hardy may well have been only vaguely aware of the activities of the Sea Fencibles. True to form, she never mentions them. However the Wymondham farmer Randall Burroughes gives a rare and useful picture of the training of the Sea Fencibles in gunnery. In July 1798 he watched these exercises himself at Great Yarmouth on board HMS *Contest*:

> On Wednesday [18 July] I saw the Sea Fencibles exercised at the great guns by Capt. Killock in the morning, went on board the *Contest* Gun Boat, [commanded by] Lieutenant Short, armed with 20 carronades, 18-pounders and 28-pounders. The guns were fired while our party was on board and I saw the ball soon after it had left the gun and ultimately fall into the sea.[5]

The inspecting field officers' reports on numbers in the Volunteers, with the meticulous Royal Navy records for the Sea Fencibles (a boon for family historians), provide substance for the claim that this was a militarised society. The members of these forces became acquainted with military and naval life either willingly or as a means of avoiding the ballot and the press gang. Many thousands of Norfolk civilians were training weekly or more often in a huge wave of mass mobilisation.

A militarised society

In 1803 William Windham, squire of Felbrigg, former Secretary at War and soon to be appointed Secretary for War, saw Norfolk as an unmilitary county and one lacking proper leadership. The restless Windham found the local gentry, in his words, to be stupid and spiritless, supine and apathetic. He even had harsh things to say about Colonel the Hon. John Wodehouse—commanding officer of the Eastern Regiment of the Norfolk Militia.[1]

The lower orders were not allowed to be supine. Political debates on arming the people accompanied the American War: just as the previous conflict had witnessed the reconstitution of the Militia, so a colonial revolt ushered in the Volunteers.[2] Service in the ranks would make a restive people more biddable: 'I apprehend the people accustomed to military subordination and discipline would be much more orderly and manageable than they are at present.'[3]

Experience of military service became common for working men during the French wars, an aspect of the labourer's lot which, apart from brief references to the Regulars, E.P. Thompson largely omits in his influential work *The Making of the English Working Class* (1968). Taking only those drawn temporarily into military service, rather than Regulars in the Royal Navy and Army, and confining the figures to men in the ranks of the Militia, in various branches of the Volunteers and in the Sea Fencibles in Norfolk, it is likely that 20 per cent of the county's 'industrious sort' of serving age were under arms soon after the start of the Napoleonic War; the percentage may have been even higher.

Linda Colley counters Thompson's thesis: 'the pressures of war, rather than the experience of work or the example of political revolution' may have transformed lives, ideas and expectations.[4] In the Volunteers alone, nationwide in December 1803, there were 3976 infantry companies, 604 cavalry units and 102 artillery companies; their members formed the total of 380,000 given at the start of the chapter.[5] Metzner's totals (table 4.9.2, overleaf) show approximately 6300 privates in the land-based Norfolk Volunteers, not including the sick and those absent without leave on the day of inspection. They constituted a large body of artisans and labouring poor with some acquaintance of military life.

accessed 7 Aug. 2019).
It is very unlikely that a gun-vessel could have carried 20 carronades (powerful short-range naval guns) in addition to the other guns. The website gives her armament as four 24-pounder guns and ten 18-pounder carronades

---

[1] *Windham* Strictures reported by R.W. Ketton-Cremer in 'Norfolk and the threat of invasion', pp. 164–6

[2] *American war* S. Conway, 'The politics of British military and naval mobilization, 1775–83', pp. 1194–7

[3] *biddable* S. Conway, 'The politics of British military and naval mobilization, 1775–83', pp. 1194–5. The quote of 1782 by James Wodrow echoed a similar observation by Lord Barrington, a former Secretary at War

[4] *transforming* Linda Colley identifies 'training in arms under the auspices of the state' as 'the most common collective working-class experience' at this time, rather than labour in a factory, or political or (then illegal) union activity (L. Colley, *Britons: Forging the nation 1707–1837*, p. 312)

[5] *numbers* B. Lavery, *We shall fight on the Beaches*, p. 333

[1] *exemptions* Licensed teachers, former Militiamen, Regular soldiers and seamen and those upholding the Peace such as judges, JPS and constables were also exempt.

The height restriction was reduced to 5 feet 2 inches (1·57 metres) in the summer of 1803

[2] *estimate* Derived from percentage calculations using the partial returns of 1821 (B.R. Mitchell and P. Deane, *Abstract of British Historical Statistics*, p. 11)

[3] *Townshend* TNA: PRO HO 50/80, Lord Townshend to Lord Hobart, 10 June 1803.

The breakdown in Lord Townshend's report is two regiments each of 907 men. Of these 1814 men, 605 were in the Supplementary Militia. Officers and NCOs are excluded from these figures

[4] *wider age group* L. Colley, *Britons: Forging the nation 1707–1837*, app. 2, pp. 378–9 (a nationwide table).

These figures were gathered partly to determine how many might be expected to serve in the Volunteers

[5] *Holt inspection Diary 4*: 8 Nov. 1803, where Mary Hardy promotes Lt Col. Metzner to the rank of general

A large number of exemptions applied to service in the Militia. Henry Raven, for instance, being an indentured apprentice, was exempt from the ballot, as were the Revd John Burrell (as a clergyman) and Edmund Bartell junior (as a medical practitioner). All those under five feet four inches in height (1·63 metres) were also excluded.[1]

The total male population of Norfolk, including Norwich, of all ages, was given in the 1801 census as 129,842. The Militia Ballot lists, containing the names of all men of serving age between eighteen and 45, have not survived for Norfolk. Using the partial returns on age distribution in the 1821 census, and making a rough allowance for exemptions, it can be estimated that the number of those liable to be balloted was no more than 38,000.[2] As already seen, in June 1803 Lord Townshend relayed to Lord Hobart, Secretary for War, that 1814 men made up the ranks of the Norfolk Militia and Supplementary Militia[3]—nearly five per cent of those estimated as eligible to be drawn. By that stage Militia service was for five years, having risen from three, so the continuous programme of drafting affected considerably more than five per cent of men over the years. This estimated figure of 38,000 is compatible with the total of 49,345 as the number of all men aged seventeen to 55 in Norfolk in the 1804 defence returns, with no provision for exemptions as this represented the age range of the Volunteers.[4]

At the end of 1803 in Norfolk 910 troopers from the Yeomanry and 5398 privates in the Volunteer infantry reported for inspection (table 4.9.2). These totals show part-time service in the Volunteers, while not so intense as full-time military service in the embodied Militia, to have been far commoner as a working-class experience: approximately 6300 men as against 1800. Briefly among the additional 818 Volunteer officers and NCOs could be found William Hardy junior, Mary Hardy referring to the inspection in her diary.[5]

Metzner sometimes reported on the background of the 6300 men filling the ranks. In the impressive Gunton and Blickling Rifle Corps, under the command of William Assheton Harbord (later second Baron Suffield and Lord Lieutenant of Norfolk 1808–21), the majority of the 326 privates were of the labouring sort: 'daily labourers', who were 'steady and alert', 'active and silent' (table 4.9.1).

TABLE 4.9.2

Numbers: the inspecting officer's returns for the Norfolk Volunteers 1803

source   NRO: MS 67, Inspection of Yeomanry Cavalry and Volunteer Infantry of Norfolk
by Lt Col. Metzner, Inspecting Field Officer: effective returns, p. 31, 21 Dec. 1803 [1]

rank	*cavalry* [18 troops]	*infantry* [41 corps]
COMMISSIONED OFFICERS		
lieutenant colonel	—	7
major	3	10
captain	21	81
lieutenant	21	80
cornet /	21	—
ensign	—	71
STAFF OFFICERS		
chaplain	2	2
adjutant	1	5
quartermaster	18	4
surgeon	4	6
mate	—	1
NON-COMMISSIONED OFFICERS		
sergeant	52	302
corporal	31	256
trumpeter /	17	—
drummer/fifer	—	160
OTHER RANKS		
trooper /	910	—
private	—	5398
TOTAL PERSONNEL [2]		7126
HORSES	1010	

[1] *source* These returns include only personnel actually inspected by Metzner during Oct., Nov. and Dec. 1803.
  He excluded from the returns any who were sick or otherwise absent

[2] *total* Metzner records that the total fell only slightly short of the total county establishment. The cavalry were at full officer strength, but were short of 2 trumpeters, 64 troopers (privates) and 66 horses.
  The infantry were short of 3 officers, 3 NCOs, 4 drummers and fifers and 212 privates.
  The *Norwich Mercury* gave the county establishment on 10 Sept. 1803 as 7524. Allowing for the sick and absent, Norfolk had exceeded that figure by Dec. 1803

When Mary Hardy first mentions the Volunteers in 1781 they would appear to have been of a more gentlemanly complexion than in the French wars, when the general population rushed to join. The diarist's use of language is interesting. On Easter Day 1781, only ten days after the Hardys' move to Letheringsett, she notes that 'Children and maids went to Holt after tea to see the Gentlemen exercise.'[3] Since tea was taken at about six o'clock in that household they

[3] *gentlemen Diary 2*: 15 Apr. 1781, where her entry is illustrated

[1] *church services* When William Hardy walked up to Holt with his children and brother Joseph in 1782 'to see the Volunteers exercise' it was following afternoon service at Letheringsett Church (*Diary 2*: 22 Sept. 1782)

[2] *tradesmen* They predominated in the N. Walsham Volunteer Infantry in 1803. Writing from his London house Townshend forwarded to Lord Hobart (Secretary for War) the names and occupations of the 66 officers and men. They included a hairdresser, servant, ostler, shoemaker and cordwainer (TNA: PRO HO 50/80, 11 June 1803)

[3] *poor men Diary 4*: 7 Sept., 8 Sept. 1803

[4] *Holt Diary 4*: 9 Sept., 11 Sept. 1803

[5] *numbers* TNA: PRO HO 50/80, Lord Townshend to the Home Secretary, 14 Sept. 1803

[6] *official returns* Tabulated by Linda Colley in *Britons: Forging the nation 1707–1837*, app. 2, pp. 378–81. Many counties far exceeded Norfolk's percentage: Derbyshire at 55 %, Devonshire 51 %, Northumberland 76 %. Neighbouring Suffolk had 36 %, Lincolnshire 31 %, Essex 20 %. Argyll had 91 %; Ross 71 %

must have been watching at well after seven in the evening. By 'the Gentlemen' she means the Holt and Letheringsett Volunteers. Even Easter Day was a working day, the builder, carpenter and gardener all having been at work at the Hardys' that Sunday (as they had been on Good Friday). The choice of the evening for drill means that the Gentlemen were not only taking care to be clear of morning and afternoon church services but were also enabling working men to take part.[1] Even then, at the start of the movement, the Volunteers must have made provision for participation by people in full-time employment as tradesmen and manufacturers, servants and labourers.[2]

By contrast, in the French wars the diarist no longer describes the Volunteers as 'the Gentlemen'. In September 1803 she observes: 'The poor men of this parish began to learn their exercise;' the following day they were drilling in the evening in the Six Acres, one of the Hardys' arable fields at Letheringsett. Both entries were on weekdays.[3] On the third day, a Friday, 'William went up to Holt in the evening with the men to exercise,' neither the lieutenant nor his men being free until after work. However on the following Sunday William went with the men to Holt in the morning to exercise, presumably with the rest of the corps and possibly for a church parade.[4] The Holt Volunteer Infantry at that time numbered 120 men plus three officers.[5]

The total of approximately nine thousand officers and men in the two regiments of Norfolk Militia and the Volunteers in 1803 does not include all civilians under arms as it does not cover the Sea Fencibles. Ever-shifting numbers in the Royal Navy pay lists make compilations tricky, but at a conservative estimate Norfolk had more than one thousand men in the Sea Fencibles. These calculations produce the percentage total quoted earlier: male civilians under arms in Norfolk in 1803–04 formed more than 20 per cent of the total of 49,345 men in the age group seventeen to 55. Under the official returns submitted via each Lord Lieutenant to Government, Norfolk already had 3019 men in uniform in the Regular Army. The official calculation in May 1804 was that 37 per cent of Norfolkmen aged seventeen to 55 were under arms: well over one-third. It was actually far more. These returns do not include the Navy and Sea Fencibles.[6]

The Militia, Volunteers and Sea Fencibles were essential defenders on the home front, especially at times of heightened danger from invasion. The Regular Army on service overseas was spared reluctantly and spread relatively thinly for duties at home. John Barney shows that while there were 87,000 Regular soldiers stationed in Great Britain in 1804 there were 80,000 in the Militia and 380,000 Volunteers, including the mounted Yeomanry.[1] The additional land forces thus outnumbered the Regular Army at home by more than five to one.

Arming thousands of craftsmen, artisans and labourers as civilian volunteer privates who were not subject to military discipline, and having amongst these more than nine hundred armed cavalrymen in the county, could well have made Norfolk's authorities tremble (table 4.9.2). The Year of Peril in 1797, during which two of the Royal Navy fleets mutinied in home waters, and some of the more extreme measures taken for home defence under the Defence of the Realm Act in 1798 came in the troubled decade of the 1790s. Jacobinism, the revolution societies and corresponding societies, civil unrest, rick-burning and the bread riots of 1795 and 1800 inflamed the minds of working people and fanned their sense of grievance; repressive legislation was passed to curb incipient insurrection (chapter 8).

Yet even in allegedly Jacobin Norfolk came no reports that the Volunteers abused their power.[2] On the contrary, almost all accounts in the newspapers and from official sources as relayed to the Lord Lieutenant show those in the ranks to have been alert and attentive, willing and biddable—if not always well drilled. Metzner's neatly-minuted observations during his Norfolk tour were for the eyes of the General Commanding the Eastern District, Sir James Craig, in addition to the Commander-in-Chief of the British Army; the C-in-C was the man to whom inspecting field officers were ultimately responsible. The arming of the masses represented a vote of confidence in the working class by central government, Regular officers and the local law-enforcers of the day: 'For the first time, the generals trusted the masses to be armed and to fight as auxiliaries to the Army.'[3] The spectre of Bonaparte did much to unite all classes and to calm some of the recent social tensions, if only temporarily.

[1] *numbers* J. Barney, *The Defence of Norfolk,* p. 60.
The Duke of York broke down the troop strength across the (then) nine military districts of the country three months after the outbreak of hostilities. The Militia appears to be included with the Regulars (TNA: PRO WO 30/76, p. 112, 25 Aug. 1803):

Southern	55,000
Eastern	30,000
Western	12,000
London, Home and Inland	10,000
North West	10,000
South West	8,000
Yorkshire	6,000
Severn	2,000
TOTAL	139,000

[2] *abuse* Vigilance was required. Rule 9 of the rules of the Wells Loyal Volunteers dated 11 May 1798 was intended to prevent irregular use of ammunition: 'Rule 9. Any man who on field-days shall secrete cartridges instead of using them shall be liable to a fine of sixpence' (NRO: MS 5363, 5 B6, Printed version of the rules 1800)

[3] *auxiliaries* K. Navickas, 'Lieut. General Sir James Henry Craig's orders to commanders in the Eastern Military District, 1803–04', p. 66

[1] *Money* Quoted near the end of the section on William's Volunteer service (p. 551)

[2] *democratical* TNA: PRO HO 50/341, Townshend's letter of 7 Apr. 1794 to Dundas enclosing that by Money of 6 Apr. urging this course

[3] *magistrates* Mr Adair, a new JP, irritated Townshend in his letter of 17 Nov. 1796 from Trowse Newton, outside Norwich (where he would have been a neighbour of Money's), at the height of opposition to the Supplementary Militia Act.

Mr Adair thought implementing the new measures would be attended with great difficulty, the opposition being inflamed on two counts: 'One of these is the idea of compulsion; the other, that of being torn (as they express it) from their wives and families' (TNA: PRO HO 50/26, letter forwarded by Townshend to the Duke of Portland, Home Secretary).

Large numbers of Norfolk JPs identified closely with those on 'their patch' and kept their heads even during riots (a theme explored in vol. 3, chap. 6 on the Peace)

A very active Lord Lieutenant, George Townshend was determined to take Norfolk with him and not to exacerbate the 'democratical' sentiments of some of the population, as he described them to Government ministers. From the start of his lieutenancy he was tireless in coaxing rather than harrying the people of Norfolk into military service, and he remained respectful of local feeling. He was all too aware of local sensitivities in 1794, the year of the Treason Trials and a time when the Norwich Revolution Society was still operating. Writing from his London house to the Home Secretary Henry Dundas, Lord Townshend offered his views on the chances of raising corps of Volunteers even in 'that part of the county where the most opposition may be expected'.

He pushed Dundas for an alteration to the terms under which the Volunteers were to serve. He believed that Norfolk people would be prepared to join the force only if given the reassurance that they would not be called out to leave their homes, farms and businesses and enter into armed combat until the *actual* moment of invasion rather than under a *threat* of invasion—the highly problematic Article 14 of the 1794 Defence Act seized on as a 'scarecrow to the honest farmer and man of business' by John Money in his letter to Townshend of the previous day.[1] Townshend shared the military lobbyist's apprehensions. If a more sensible approach were to be adopted by Government, 'it would seem that we shall succeed in raising Corps in spite of the most democratical parts of the county.'[2]

The Marquis occasionally shed his customary urbanity in his reports. At times of tension he did not always receive support from the magistrates, the very body on whom he could have hoped to rely, for some JPs went native and aligned themselves with local resistance to compulsion.[3] Some of the extracts from the protests of maritime counties in 1796 (overleaf) show that he met a certain hesitancy even from Robert John Buxton, a Deputy Lieutenant and Tory MP for Thetford. Buxton, like Mr Lowther for the Penrith area of Cumberland (also overleaf), was of the opinion that the ballot for the Supplementary Militia could not be conducted in his area of south Norfolk without the presence of the Regular Army—a course which, as he hinted directly to the Home Secretary, he thought inadvisable.

In the French Revolutionary War there was a coolness over military service and a disinclination to participate at various levels of Norfolk society. This stance was taken by many of the justices and other prominent leaders, to Townshend's regret in 1796 (overleaf); also by farmers and commercial men, as recognised by Townshend and the JPs lobbying him;[1] and by the poor who, if drawn in the ballot, could not afford to buy themselves out of military service. Some in this last category were prepared to disrupt the ballot by physical violence (also as seen in the extracts overleaf).

As observed in volume 2, chapter 2, this was an age with an appetite for systematic data collection. But many feared the data provided a springboard for launching new taxes. Those who were illiterate had a particular fear of texts which undermined their freedoms. Words on paper, such as property deeds, or ballot lists, which they could not decipher, were used as shackles to limit their independence and determine the course of their lives. Centuries earlier the revolts under Jack Straw, Wat Tyler and Jack Cade in 1381 and 1450, characterised in part by violent hatred of the written word, had seen the destruction of legal records; Norfolkmen had risen in some numbers in 1381.[2] This deep-seated suspicion of data collection, and of ballot and quota lists, may help to explain the disinclination of the people of Holt and parts of Holt hundred 1793–1801 to reconstitute the Volunteer infantry of the American war. Townshend considered that the French Revolution too had an influence (note, overleaf). In Cumberland the rioters went further and burned the Militia Ballot lists, the instruments of their oppression.

Lord Townshend and the justices in correspondence with him made little or no play with Norfolk's seafaring tradition, yet this may have been a factor. The Chairman of Pembrokeshire Quarter Sessions could have spoken for many such chairmen at Norwich, Holt, Walsingham, Lynn or Swaffham: 'Ours is a maritime county, and the inhabitants have an utter aversion to the army.'[3] Norfolk is bordered on two sides by the sea; the county of Cumberland had a very long expanse of coastline. Pembrokeshire however had an even greater seaboard in proportion to its area, and the authorities there proved unable 'to procure a single man' for the Supplementary Militia (overleaf).

[1] *lobbying* eg by Revd Daniel Collyer, JP, Vicar of Wroxham with Salhouse, on the non-combatant, policing roles which he thought some of his leading parishioners might be persuaded to adopt in preference to more active defence roles (TNA: PRO HO 50/341, forwarded by Lord Townshend 27 Apr. 1798, and quoted later under local leadership)

[2] *written word* 'Burn all the records of the realm' (*Henry VI*, Part Two, act IV, scene 7). Roger Chartier examines the suspicion of written testimony in his lecture 'Jack Cade, the skin of a dead lamb, and hatred of the written word' (Royal Holloway, University of London, 2006).

Many Norfolk manorial rolls, such as those for Neatishead, Tunstead and Westwick, survive only post-1381; earlier ones had gone up in flames. See B.M.S. Campbell, 'Population pressure, inheritance and the land market in a fourteenth-century peasant community', in *Land, Kinship and Life-Cycle*, ed. R.M. Smith (Cambridge Univ. Press, 1984), pp. 92–3

[3] *Pembrokeshire* TNA: PRO HO 50/26, 21 Dec. 1796, quoted in full overleaf

'Ours is a maritime county': opposition to the Supplementary Militia Act in the coastal counties of Pembrokeshire, Cumberland and Norfolk 1796

source   TNA: PRO HO 50/26, Internal defence, Militia correspondence 1796 [1]

[1] *source* The letters, not filed under page numbers, are either addressed directly to the Home Secretary, the Duke of Portland, or were forwarded by the county's Lord Lieutenant

[2] *I hope* Mr Philipps got a sharp reply from 'WB' in London that no payment of a fee could be accepted and that Militia service must be *in person* or the parish overseers would be fined

[3] *My Lord* The Lord Lieutenant of Cumberland: James Lowther (d.1802), 1st Earl of Lonsdale 1784.

His distant cousin Sir William Lowther, Bt (d.1844), who appears to have been a JP but not a Deputy Lieutenant, later states that he has not made representations direct to the Secretary of State as he is 'leaving it to Your Lordship to do what is proper'

[4] *papers* Sir William Lowther explains later that he cannot organise another ballot 'without a military force', and even that would prove difficult 'as the books which contained the amended lists [of names for the ballot] was burnt'

FROM HAVERFORDWEST, PEMBROKESHIRE, SOUTH WALES

May it please your Grace [the Duke of Portland],

The magistrates, constables and overseers of the county of Pembrokeshire have done all in their power to raise requisition men for the army, but have not been able to procure a single man. Ours is a maritime county, and the inhabitants have an utter aversion to the army. If Government will accept of twenty-five guineas instead of a man the money will be immediately paid. I should think the Government would be gainers thereby, as men might certainly be raised in the inland counties for much less money. I hope your Grace will accept of the money which shall be forthwith paid; otherwise I know not what can be done, for we cannot raise the men.[2]

I am with great respect

Your Grace's most obedient servant

JOHN PHILIPPS
Chairman of the Pembrokeshire Quarter Sessions
Williamston, near Haverford West

December 21 1796

FROM PENRITH, CUMBERLAND, NORTH-WEST ENGLAND

My Lord,[3]

This day the men were to have been ballotted at Penrith for Leath Ward under the Supplementary Militia Act. Two gentlemen and myself attended on that occasion, and after we had ballotted about thirty men a set of desperate fellows with sticks or bludgeons in their hands ... broke into the room and burnt and destroyed all the papers,[4] except the book in which we enter the orders and which I got from a man at the door who had taken it by violence.

We summoned above one hundred of the principal inhabitants of Penrith to keep the Peace, and very few of them appeared. About three o'clock the mob threatened to pull down the George Inn where we were assembled if we would not disperse the constables who came out of the country, and, as they began to press much upon us and as night was coming on and we could have but little dependence upon many of the constables who seemed unwilling to discover the names of the rioters, we discharged them ...

I am, my Lord etc

W. LOWTHER

December 22nd 1796

'Ours is a maritime county' (*cont.*)

[1] *My Lord* The Duke of Portland: Robert John Buxton goes straight to the top and not via the Lord Lieutenant.

He begins by forwarding a letter from the local Rector of Garboldisham enclosing a handbill, taken down from a signpost, opposing the new Militia Act. Buxton adds, 'I am very sorry to add, it [the poster] speaks the sentiments of too many of the lower class of the people in this part of the country'

[2] *Shirehouse* Marquis Townshend's letter to Portland concerns the 'mob' at Norwich 15 Nov. 1796 which interrupted the meeting he and his deputies were to hold over ways of achieving the quotas for the Supplementary Militia and Provisional Cavalry.

Like the other correspondents in this long catalogue of woes sent from round the country to central government, Townshend (the Lord Lieutenant) observes that some of the prominent people who should have been present did not attend, so he was without the necessary support.

He adds that 'the resistance to these laws in other parts of England' and the 'Revolution' in France further stimulated the mob

FROM LARLINGFORD, NEAR THETFORD, NORFOLK

My Lord,[1]

... Mr Hare and myself, the two acting Deputy Lieutenants for these hundreds, held our meeting this day at Larlingford for the purpose of receiving the Militia lists and of hearing appeals. We were there assailed by a violent mob who forced into the house and so interrupted our proceedings that we were obliged to leave the business undone. Their object seemed to be to prevent the execution of the new Militia Act, which I am of opinion cannot be executed without the aid of a strong military force, the propriety of which His Majesty's ministers will judge of.

I have the honour to be ...

ROBERT JOHN BUXTON
Shadwell Lodge, near Thetford

November 23rd 1796

FROM NORWICH, NORFOLK

My Lord,

... I am very sorry to say that our proceedings at the Shirehouse were obstructed by a very numerous and outrageous mob,[2] which had taken possession of all the approaches to the Grand Jury Room using the most violent expressions and menaces. The High Sheriff was not there, nor had we more than one constable. As the minds of these people had been poisoned by seditious handbills, they called out to know what was the purpose of the Acts of Parliament. I told them that if they would [? come] quietly into the court house they should be acquainted therewith.

We then went into the court house, where I informed them that the Acts were no more than a provision for the defence of this country against our enemies, and by measures the most mild and the least burdensome to individuals, and that provisions were made for the pay of those who were to be called forth, and for their families in their absence ... The ringleaders of the party still continued their uproar ... The noise continuing so great it was then thought proper to adjourn to the Angel Inn, where we proceeded upon the business of the day ...

I remain ...

TOWNSHEND
Raynham [near Fakenham]

November 17th 1796

right 'An officer marching at the head of his company';
facing page 'Ensign carrying the colours'.
  The Militia held little appeal in the popular imagination, and very few flocked willingly to march in the
ranks behind the colours. Norfolk was always having
difficulty in meeting its Government-set quotas
[*W. Windham, A Plan of Discipline . . . for the use of the
Militia of the County of Norfolk* (*1759*): *Norfolk Heritage
Centre, Norwich*]

[1] *insulated* L. Colley,
*Britons: Forging the
nation 1707–1837*, p.
292; see also the county
comparisons in her app.
2, pp. 378–81, which
reinforce her thesis

[2] *Nonconformists* See
vol. 3, chaps 3 and 4

[3] *naval service* Linda
Colley does not make
allowance for the very
strong role played in a
maritime county by the
Royal Navy, Merchant
Navy and Sea Fencibles
in siphoning off young
and middle-aged men
to serve their country.
In the 1804 (military)
defence returns Cum-
berland is shown as the
county with the lowest
score (9%) in England,
and the second lowest
in Britain; the figures
for Pembrokeshire are
incomplete (L. Colley,
*Britons: Forging the
nation 1707–1837*,
pp. 378–81)

[4] *quotas* Holt and Letheringsett were among

Linda Colley ponders whether it was the East of England's geographical isolation and strong Nonconformist
leanings which hindered military recruitment and engendered the disloyalty suggested by the region's poor showing
in the defence returns of 1804, as already quoted: 'The rural
hinterland of East Anglia was simply too sparsely populated,
too insulated, too complacent within itself to care much
about the nation beyond its borders.' [1] But the region was
not isolated in the eighteenth century, and there is little hint
in the official records that the Baptists, Independents and
Methodists exerted any influence in the matter in Norfolk
1784–1813. On the contrary (and Wilks apart), the clergy's
visitation returns to the Bishop emphasised time and again
that the Nonconformists generally gave no trouble and were
quiet and peaceable, with no evidence that either itinerant
or local preachers were stirring up disloyalty. [2]
  Linda Colley comes to her conclusion on the basis of the
County Lieutenancy records alone, which, in by-passing the
Admiralty chain of command, omit all types of naval service
and the Sea Fencibles. [3] However, even when allowance is
made for this additional element in the Volunteer movement
it is evident that Norfolk was struggling to meet its quotas. [4]

Owing to the shortage of manpower during the French wars new legislation and directives poured into the provinces from London over recruiting for the Royal Navy, Militia, Supplementary Militia, Provisional Cavalry and Army of Reserve. At times of crisis the *Norwich Mercury* would contain weekly bulletins on the Militia and Volunteers, on the difficulties of recruitment, and how Norfolk was faring over reaching its quotas.[1]

Given Norfolk's reputed aversion to military service it is significant that Mary Hardy makes no mention of rioting or other visible opposition associated with the ballots. The diarist notes six ballots at Holt between 1796 and 1803;[2] yet, mirroring the absence of unrest at Coltishall and Horstead over the opening of the Bure navigation to Aylsham (chapter 2), she does not record any trouble at them. We know that she does not suppress references to rioting, in that she alludes to protests against the Methodists at Holt and gives a full account of the serious bread riots of 1795 (volume 3, chapters 3 and 6).

many parishes fined £20 each at quarter sessions for not supplying their quota for the Army of Reserve (NRO: C/S 1/17, 23 Feb. 1805), these fines having to be met by local ratepayers

---

[1] *bulletins* See, eg, the spate of items week by week in the *Norwich Mercury* 5 Apr.–17 May 1794, 29 Oct.–19 Nov. 1796, 17 Mar.–26 May 1798, 13 Aug.–31 Dec. 1803, and continuing into 1804 and 1805

[2] *ballots Diary 3*: 12 Dec. 1796, 14 Jan. 1797 (for the Supplementary Militia); 25 Feb. 1797 (for the Provisional Cavalry).

Three Militia ballots are noted in *Diary 4*: 30 June 1798 (when Theophilus Pye Hastings, future father-in-law of the rector's son Shambrook Burrell, was drawn); 25 June 1803 (when Thomas Reynolds let himself as a substitute for 16 guineas); and 15 Oct. 1803 (when William Girling was drawn).

It is possible there was trouble at the first, in Dec. 1796, since a further ballot was held the following month

1 *Astley Crouse and Stevenson's Norwich and Norfolk Complete Memorandum Book* (1790), unpag., giving the names of the peacetime complement of officers in the two regiments of Norfolk Militia

2 *friend* Thomas Henry Mountain Neve, son by his first marriage of the Hardys' former close friend, the Coltishall timber merchant and innkeeper Thomas Neve, served in the East Norfolks as ensign and then lieutenant (TNA: PRO HO 50/80, 5 Oct. 1803; *Norw. Merc.* 2 June 1804). He never appears in the diary.
    Parson Woodforde however moved on the edge of Militia circles, being well acquainted with Squire Custance's eldest son Hambleton, who was promoted to major in the West Norfolk Militia (TNA: PRO HO 50/80 50/80, 29 Mar. 1803)

3 *Hurn Norw. Merc.* 11 June 1803

4 *Jennis Norw. Merc.* 11 June 1803

5 *Ireland Norw. Merc.* 13 Aug. 1803. In 1798, a desperately troubled year for Ireland, an Act had been passed permitting the English Militia to serve there (J. Ehrman, *Pitt the Younger: The consuming struggle*, p. 125)

Very few indeed of their acquaintance are noted by Mary Hardy as coming forward to serve. With the exception of the future Norfolk MP Jacob Henry Astley, none at all was a Militia officer. Astley had joined the Eastern Regiment of Norfolk Militia during the years of peace, being a captain in 1790,[1] but he could hardly be counted a close friend.[2]

To Letheringsett falls the doubtful distinction of having the sole Militia deserter in the whole of Holt hundred in 1803, at the time when the Western Regiment of the Norfolk Militia was being embodied shortly before the outbreak of war. Robert Hurn of Letheringsett had been drawn in the ballot, but he had managed to find a substitute in Norwich, a 29-year-old weaver named William Allen. Although it was Allen who had absconded, both Hurn (the 'principal' or drawn man) and Allen (his substitute) were classed as deserters.[3] Over at Horningtoft Robert Jennis had just been drawn, and his substitute 28-year-old Samuel Daniels of Norwich also failed to join the regiment.[4] The city's poor and unemployed provided a rich seam for the moneyed or insured to mine, ballot insurance schemes being instituted as protection for those who could afford the premiums. To cap it all a further blow hit recruitment. There was talk of both regiments of Norfolk Militia being sent to Ireland.[5]

facing page Protection from being forced to serve in the Militia on being drawn in the ballot was provided by Militia societies.

These insurance clubs, run from inns and taverns and providing funds for buying a substitute, were occasionally advertised in the local press. This printer's ornament, specially designed to highlight items of news over Militia recruitment and service, heads a notice about the Dove Tavern's society in Norwich [*Norwich Mercury, 17 Oct. 1807: Norfolk Heritage Centre, Norwich*]

Invasion preparedness and local leadership

With the benefit of centuries of hindsight it is all too easy to feel confident that Britain would have been well placed to defend herself. At the time, however, Napoleon's chilling pronouncements and his colossal army encamped on the shores facing the south-east corner of England were perceived as posing real threats. Such prognostications as 'It is necessary for us to be masters of the sea for six hours only and England will have ceased to exist' may have proved baseless puff, but to contemporaries the danger was real.[1]

Brian Lavery presents the defensive measures taken to withstand the coming assault, and the careful use of intelligence: 'The British built up a very detailed picture of their enemy and his means of attack.'[2] When intelligence was passed on to the defending forces' staff headquarters, at Colchester, existing plans had often to be modified. General Craig was at first sceptical about the likelihood of an invasion in East Anglia. But on the strength of Alexander Bryce's report at the end of 1803 he became persuaded that precautions were essential after all. He decided that a proper use of resources would be to station troops at Great Yarmouth, to defend a likely invasion point, and also at Norwich, as a good central location from where they could quickly march to positions along the coast as necessary: the principle of flexible response in action.[3] Holt fulfilled this role as a north Norfolk hub, and like Norwich became a garrison town.

It has been emphasised many times in this chapter that the Hardys did not mix in circles conspicuous in coming forward to support the war effort. There were two exceptions. The first was the parish or local superintendent in their neighbourhood: civilians (always male) charged with organising fellow parishioners in a civil emergency such as

[1] '*six hours only*' Napoleon's boast of 1805, made while his Grande Armée was encamped facing the English shore, was used as the strapline on the poster for the Bodleian's commemorative exhibition at Oxford in 2003. Napoleon actually would have needed at least six *tides* (and thus three days) and a south or south-easterly wind for his vast armada to reach Margate or Deal

[2] *picture* B. Lavery, *We shall fight on the Beaches*, p. 135. The tactics of the invader, as let slip by a French official and then transmitted to the British authorities, would have been to gain a foothold at 'some tenable point or post'; *schuits* or *schuyts* (shallow-bottomed Dutch craft, as seen in *plate 43*) were to be run upon the bluff shore and not steer for harbour (Lavery, pp. 128–9; see also his p. 152 on intelligence-gathering and surveys). Maj. Bryce had warned in Dec. 1803 of the dangers of *schuits* approaching Norfolk's beaches by running across the offshore sands (*Diary 4*, app. D4.C, p. 471)

[3] *Gt Yarmouth and Norwich* TNA: PRO WO 30/100, p. 84, Letter by Gen. Sir James Craig from

Colchester. For a case-study of invasion preparations, plans for the rapid movement of troops and flexible response see P.A.L. Vine, *The Royal Military Canal*, pp. 11–12, 23–7, 71–2

---

[1] *superintendents* TNA: PRO HO 42/71, f. 87, 'Plan for establishing a system of communication throughout each county', June 1803 [printed].

The new or revised posts of Deputy Lieutenant, inspector and superintendent were established under the Defence Act of June 1803, Lord Hobart issuing explanatory information 24 June (TNA: PRO HO 42/71, ff. 84–6). Letheringsett was probably too small to merit the appointment of agents to assist the superintendent

[2] *parishes* See vol. I, chap. I, table 1.1.1

[3] *solid citizens* The type best suited to this post was identified in 1798 by Revd Daniel Collyer, JP, Vicar of Wroxham with Salhouse. He was the brother of Revd Charles Collyer, also a JP, who lived near the Hardys and who was nominated in 1803 to be superintendent of his Gunthorpe parish. Daniel Collyer wrote

a mass evacuation. The Hardys knew many who held that post in their area of the county. The second exception was in following the Royal Artillery with marked enthusiasm when units were in the Holt area, the Hardys (male and female) walking or driving in procession as the mobile field guns were brought up from the south and attending field days and reviews at Weybourne Camp. We do not learn whether the family would have displayed such commitment had they not secured the contract to supply the forces at the camp with beer.

As figure 4.9B shows (page 513), on decentralised structures, the parish superintendent came under the direction of the Lord Lieutenant. The post was established in 1803; at the same time the duties of the county Deputy Lieutenants were extended. Another innovation was the post of inspector of the district, or of the hundred, in overall charge of a group of superintendents.

The tasks to be carried out by superintendents were couched in vague terms:

Each parish to be placed under the charge of such gentleman, clergyman or principal farmer, resident therein, as will engage to superintend the execution of the measures which may be directed to be taken within the same, who may be denominated *Superintendents of Parishes* . . . The *Superintendents of Parishes* will select such a number of Agents in their respective parishes, to assist them in the detail of business, as the extent or population of the parish may require.[1]

In observance of the new regulations Lord Townshend would receive nominations of resident parishioners for the post from the inspectors and would pass the names to the Home Secretary for confirmation of the appointment—a colossal load for Whitehall, since England and Wales had more than 11,000 parishes.[2] The County Lieutenancy and the parochial unit thus came into play once more over invasion preparedness, as they so often did in other aspects of local administration and government.

Superintendents could not be in military service. In Norfolk they tended to be solid citizens such as lesser landowners, farmers, beneficed and unbeneficed clergy; professionals such as attorneys; and tradesmen such as grocers.[3]

above and *right* A reminder of local military activity: an artillery-piece probably from the Napoleonic era, discarded when it suffered some damage. Other such guns are occasionally set upright in towns and give long service as traffic bollards.

This one has been planted on the village green at Wiveton, near Cley and Blakeney and within sight of the estuary of the Glaven. A cannon ball has been wedged in the muzzle of the gun, which can no longer fire; following a mishap the barrel casing has a gaping hole   [*MB · 2012*]

to Townshend recommending ways in which his non-combatant acquaintance might be persuaded to adopt a policing role. The Lord Lieutenant forwarded the letter to London with the observation that Collyer, who lived 'in a large and populous division of the county' [on the northern Broads], had 'conferred with many respectable inhabitants who do not seem willing to engage in a military capacity, but are well disposed to associate for preserving internal tranquillity and maintaining a proper police' in such matters as moving cattle from the coast in the event of an imminent invasion (TNA: PRO HO 50/341, 27 Apr. 1798)

They were required to explain to villagers the measures the Government was enforcing, to keep them orderly and free from panic, and prevent the blocking of roads. The resident rector was appointed for Letheringsett. Some of those known to the Hardys were nominated for this task in August 1803:

NOMINATIONS FOR PARISH SUPERINTENDENT 1803

CLERGY John Burrell (*Letheringsett*), Joseph Church (*Coltishall*), John Crofts (*Fakenham*), Charles Collyer (*Gunthorpe*), William W. Wilcocks (*Bale*), Richard T. Gough (*Blakeney*), Bransby Francis (*Edgefield*), William Girdlestone (*Salthouse and Kelling*)

LANDOWNER Horatio Batcheler (*Little Hautbois*)

FARMERS Robert Worts (*Belaugh*), John Savory (*Glandford cum Bayfield*), Stephen Frost (*Langham*), Thomas Balls (*Saxlingham*), Henry Paul (*Stody*), Thomas Curties (*Hunworth*), John King (*Holt*), Robert Waller (*Briningham*)

FARMER AND BRICK-KILN OWNER John Dew (*Swanton Novers*)

ATTORNEY William Williams (*Thornage*)

MERCHANTS Thomas Jackson (*Cley*), John Temple (*Weybourne*)

SHOPKEEPERS John Brereton (*Brinton*), Thomas Woodcock (*Briston*)[1]

[1] *nominations* TNA: PRO HO 50/341, Letter from Townshend at Raynham to Lord Hobart, 2 Aug. 1803, giving a list of the nominations for superintendent in all the parishes of the hundreds of N. and S. Erpingham, Tunstead, Holt, Gallow and Brothercross. The occupations are not stated in the original document, where the names are ordered by hundred and parish, and not by occupation.
    Lord Townshend

submitted many more nominations than are transcribed in this extract

---

[1] *Burrell* Extracts are given in vol. 3, chap. 1

[2] *meetings* J. Barney, *The Defence of Norfolk*, pp. 41–2

[3] *small corps* Parochial armed associations such as these were to be established under the General Defence Act of July 1803 to act as auxiliaries. The rush to Volunteer and form larger units rendered these projected parish units superfluous

[4] *charge* C. Manners Sutton, *An Address to the Clergy of the Diocese of Norwich* (Norwich, 1803), p. 11.
The Bishop seems to have modified his views. In the previous war some at least of his clergy understood that he had no objection to the 'brethren' serving in fully armed Volunteer companies. Revd John Longe jnr (1765–1834), son of the Spixworth rector, was resident vicar of Coddenham, Suff., in the Norwich see. He took an active part in the Ipswich Volunteer Troop of Light Horse in 1798 and paid for his uniform and horse (Suffolk Record Office (Ipswich): Bacon Longe Collection,

Using clergymen to act in this capacity would have brought problems, for the American war and recent French war had been politically divisive. A superintendent had to work on behalf of *all* those in his care and ensure their safety. A difficulty at Letheringsett was that John Burrell tended to be immoderate in his language and his attitudes, as exemplified by Mary Hardy's choice of the verb 'harangued' to describe his call to arms to the parishioners in April 1798, quoted at the head of this chapter. The rector's published address of February 1801, 'The vortex of Gallic fury', reproduced in volume 3, shows the heights of vituperation he could reach.[1]

By contrast, the Bishop of Norwich was more measured in tone (opposite), as befitting a future Archbishop. He took part in weekly planning meetings with the senior Deputy Lieutenants and senior Army officers and was thus well briefed.[2] He saw it as his task to offer guidance to the clergy over appropriate ways in which they might come forward at the time of great crisis in August 1803. He emphasised that his 'brethren' must give leadership. A clergyman should take his place 'at the head of his parishioners' even in a military sense as commanding officer of a small defence corps or parochial association. No lower position was acceptable, for fear of the ribaldry he might suffer if consigned to the ranks.[3]

The Bishop saw it as the clergyman's task 'to rouse the indignant spirit of the people'—presumably against the foe, rather than against the priest, as Mr Burrell was wont to do. Thus it was that the post of superintendent, which had no attendant military functions, was seen as one proper to an ordained minister, and at the very end of his address or 'charge' the Bishop explicitly applauded 'the readiness with which you have accepted the offices of inspectors of hundreds and superintendents of parishes'.[4]

Mary Hardy took no part in emergency-planning meetings which were treated at local level as extraordinary parish meetings. She makes only brief references to the subject in 1798, 1801 and 1803, her husband and son likewise not being actively engaged. Although parish superintendents had not been appointed as early as 1798 Mr Burrell was to the fore even then:

'The only resident gentleman' in a parish: the Bishop of Norwich on clerical leadership, August 1803

source C. Manners Sutton, *An Address to the Clergy of the Diocese of Norwich* (Norwich, 1803) [1]

REV. BRETHREN, I have called you together at a moment the most anxious perhaps this country ever experienced ... The duties of our profession incapacitate us in great degree for those personal services in the field to which every other class in society is invited. We cannot enlist in military associations, without neglecting in part, duties of a higher order, and of an antecedent claim. Whatever be our zeal for the defence of our country (and in this respect I trust we are second to none), we cannot forget that our labours are already engaged ...

The legislature, in contemplation of these facts, have exempted the clergy from military array.

What then, are we the only order of men precluded from forming part of that impenetrable phalanx, which shall assuredly line our coasts whenever the enemy shall be desperate enough to approach them? Are we the only description of Britons from whom the proud invader shall experience no inconvenience, no check, no resistance? God forbid! We have families to protect; we have laws to maintain, we have a king to uphold, we have a country to defend, we have a religion which, under the blessing of God, no power on earth shall wrest from us ...

We must not lose sight of the geographical character of the two counties over which, as Bishop, I unworthily preside. The broad front they oppose to the enemy, is sufficiently obvious to every one who passes his eye over the map. It follows, that government cannot undertake the protection of every mile of their extensive coasts ... Part must be left to the defence of its own inhabitants; and this defence is best provided for, by parochial associations.

In a parish then, situated upon the sea coast, or in the neighbourhood of the sea coast, I know not how the clergyman, who is perhaps the only resident gentleman, or the only person in whom the parishioners are disposed to confide,[2] can refuse to accept the command of a corps established for this purpose. The existence of the corps may depend on his acceptance of the command, and the security of the parish on the existence of the corps.

In truth this is the only description of military service, so far as the clergy are concerned, to which I am at present disposed to acquiesce.[3] ... It leaves the clergyman, in respect of his parish, in the same situation in which it found him—namely, at the head of his parishioners ... It removes him from the licence and ribaldry, to which I fear he would be occasionally exposed, were he placed in the ranks ... Whatever has a tendency to rouse the indignant spirit of the people, and to point it to its proper object, falls within the just limits of our exertions ...

[1] *source* These extracts are from a charge delivered to the Norfolk clergy (for the northern half of his see) at Norwich and the Suffolk clergy (for the southern) at Stowmarket, pp. 3–4, 6–7, 8–9. The printed version is dated 29 Aug. 1803 from Lowestoft.

Mary Hardy heard the Bishop preach at Holt during his primary visitation (*Diary 3*: 4 July 1794)

[2] *to confide* To have confidence. (Nelson first drafted his 1805 signal as 'England confides ...')

[3] *command* It was rare for a clergyman to command a Volunteer company. Revd Thomas Lloyd of N. Walsham may have done so. Vicar of Happisburgh 1781–1814 and Rector of Westwick 1797–1814, he had been usher at the Free Grammar School from 1778 (in Raven Hardy's time) and may have served as assistant until 1805 (C. Forder, *A History of the Paston School, North Walsham*, Norfolk (2nd edn N. Walsham, 1975), pp. 84, 92).

Capt. Thomas Lloyd led the N. Walsham Volunteer Infantry in 1800 (NRO: MS 5363, 5 B6, his letter to Townshend, 2 Dec. 1800). Metzner found Capt. H. Cooper in command in Dec. 1803 (NRO: MS 66, p. 18)

HA 24/50/19/4.3 (2), Diary of Revd John Longe jnr, series of entries Apr.–Oct. 1798; see esp. 23 Apr. 1798 and his expenses on the flyleaf). His sermons on home defence are so constructed as to command wider appeal than Mr Burrell's (eg HA 24/50/19/4.4 (6), 28 July 1803)

<hr />

[1] *invasion Diary 4.* Town (parish) meetings were customarily held at the King's Head. Hosting this one in his own home perhaps enhanced the rector's authority and made it easier for him to run proceedings as he wished

[2] *safety Diary 4.* Mary Ann was in Whissonsett, otherwise she would have accompanied her mother and aunt to Communion.

The last sentence is not intended as irony. It refers to the rector's series of talks on theological and ecclesiastical topics.

Some of the paperwork handled by Mr Burrell had been sent to the clergy by the Bishop on 3 Aug., then at Norwich during his summer visitation. These schedules were to be 'carefully filled up and expeditiously returned' (*Norw. Merc.* 15 Aug. 1801)

right Juno, of Morston, in Blakeney Creek.

Mary Hardy records alarms over rumours of the French being sighted along this coast during a 22-year period. Whatever the final outcome of the conflict, the region's residents felt themselves at the time to be at the centre of a danger zone   [*MB · 2012*]

[1798] MAY 7, MONDAY A very fine day. Mr Hardy and William at home all day . . . A town meeting at Mr Burrell's to contrive for the safety of the inhabitants in case of an invasion from the French which is much expected. I bathed.[1]

Three years later the diarist's marked sense of detachment from events still prevailed, with no hint of any involvement by her menfolk; Mr Burrell was still in charge. William was in London, and his father distanced himself from Communion and apparently from emergency planning:

[1801] AUGUST 9, SUNDAY A hot day. I and Sister Goggs went to our church forenoon, a Sacrament; we went to Briston [Methodist] meeting afternoon. Mr Burrell met the parishioners to sign a paper for their safety in case of an invasion, had a lecture.[2]

The pattern appears to have been broken in 1803, mirroring William's sudden participation in the Volunteers that summer and autumn. On the evenings of 14 and 15 November, a few days after William had left for London, there were first a vestry meeting and then a town meeting at the King's Head, which, although his wife's language is ambiguous, William Hardy seems to have attended. These were held 'to consider of the best plan to remove the inhabitants to a place of safety in case of an invasion on our coast'.[1]

Despite the diarist's restrained tone, these preparations would have had a sense of urgency hanging over them. A recurrent apprehension was felt by those near the coast, as reflected in Mary Hardy's references to enemy fleets sighted offshore over a 22-year period. In the American war she 'heard the Dutch fleet were seen off Yarmouth'.[2] In the summer of 1803 her nephew Henry Goggs and his London friend thought they had seen the French navy off the north Norfolk coast at Sheringham, only to learn subsequently that the ships were merchant vessels under Royal Navy convoy.[3] The following August there were more alarms: 'A report prevailed this evening that the French fleet were seen on the Suffolk coast.'[4]

For two summers during the French Revolutionary War the anxious residents of north Norfolk had the reassurance that the professionals stationed there would protect them and repulse the invader. The Royal Artillery had arrived, resplendent in the blue coats, red facings and white breeches worn by all ranks.[5] Weybourne Camp was to become a feature of daily life not only for these Regulars but also for the Militia who trained there and for the local populace, riveted in their thousands by the spectacle. The review of the Norfolk Militia's Western Battalion conveys something of the colour and drama of massed military might (*plate 40*).

[1] *remove to a place of safety Diary 4*

[2] *Dutch Diary 2:* 13 May 1782

[3] *convoy Diary 4:* 8 Aug. 1803; quoted in full on p. 273. At the end of July the Dutch had reportedly been seen cruising off the Dogger Bank (*Norw. Merc.* 27 July 1782)

[4] *Suffolk Diary 4:* 6 Aug. 1804. The *Norwich Mercury* fuelled the sense of imminent danger with reports and rumours during all three wars (eg 15 June 1782; throughout Feb. and Mar. 1798; 11 Aug. 1804)

[5] *Artillery* The Royal Horse Artillery, formed only in 1793, was also present as a mobile troop of light guns (P.R.F. Bonnet, *A Short History of the Royal Regiment of Artillery* (The Royal Artillery Historical Trust, 1994), pp. 5–9; see also the notes and captions in *Diary 4*, pp. 264–7)

left The site of Weybourne Camp. Muckleburgh Hill (centre) overlooked the camp from a height of 223 feet; Telegraph Hill, just to the south, is 246 feet high (68 and 75 metres). The wholesale brewery ['Brewhouse'] was not there in Mary Hardy's time.

Trade at the Hardys' nearby outlets soared when the Army came to town [*Bryant's Map of Norfolk 1826: Cozens-Hardy Collection*]

[1] *archives* I am very grateful to Brig. K.A. Timbers, RA, Historical Secretary to the Royal Artillery Historical Trust, for examining the records at the Old Royal Military Academy, Woolwich, in response to my enquiries (his letter of 19 Apr. 1995); also to Col. M.B. Cooper, later Regimental Colonel, Royal Artillery, Woolwich, for putting me in touch with Brig. Timbers

[2] *Hopton* Two RA companies mustered at Hopton in the summer of 1795 (letter of Brig. Timbers, 19 Apr. 1995). Clausewitz dates the rejection of pitched camps as *c.*1801: 'Since the wars of the French Revolution, armies have given up tents because of the mass of baggage they involve.' Rapid deployment was more important, despite the 'wear and tear on the troops' exposed to the elements (C. von Clausewitz, *On War*, ed. M. Howard and P. Paret, book 5, chap. 9, p. 312)

[3] *camp* Norw. Merc. 29 Aug. 1795. More than 2000 watched the troops in Norwich (*Norw. Merc.* 7 Nov. 1795)

[4] *heights* TNA: PRO HO 50/80, 7 Oct. 1803; see also *Diary 3*, note and caption for 26 June 1795. In Apr. 1941 the War

Supplying Weybourne Military Camp

For reasons not given by the diarists Mary Hardy and Henry Raven, nor recorded in the archives of the Royal Artillery at Woolwich, Weybourne Camp was established in the three wars covered in this study only for the two summer seasons of 1795 and 1796.[1] Hopton Military Camp, further down the coast between Great Yarmouth and Lowestoft, was likewise established only for summer 1795.[2] Significantly, this was the year the French annexed Holland. The two camps and the movement of the troops deploying to them were described with patriotic fervour by the *Norwich Mercury*:

The camp at Weybourn, in this county, forms a most pleasing spectacle, and on field-days attracts a numerous concourse of people; not less than between 3 and 4000 persons appeared on the ground on Monday last [24 Aug. 1795] and were reviewed by Marquis Townshend . . . The above camp is composed of a part of the Royal Artillery and Queen's Bays, with the Norfolk Rangers etc . . .[3]

The comparatively safe anchorage of Weybourne Hope, while not a recognised harbour, is deep enough to allow disembarkation at all states of the tide. The cliffs to the east drop down to a cart gap beside a rivulet once powering a watermill, and an invasion party could rapidly establish themselves and start to deploy inland if not immediately repulsed. For centuries in time of war Weybourne has been defended against a possible landing, whether by the Spanish in 1588, the French in 1795–96 or the Germans in 1940–41.

This weak point was referred by the Lord Lieutenant in October 1803 when pressing the Secretary for War for a military force once more to be despatched to defend Weybourne Hope, which he regarded as open to the enemy:

The heights which command the most accessible part of the beach are semicircular on which they [the Regulars, Artillery and Militia in 1795] were stationed, and [such troops] might check the enemy before the force from our interior could reach them.[4]

The authorities reacted by sending a more mobile force to the area. It appears to have been housed partly under canvas, in public houses and with local residents. The growing dislike of pitched camps ascribed by Clausewitz to this period (note 2, left) seems to have been shared by the British.

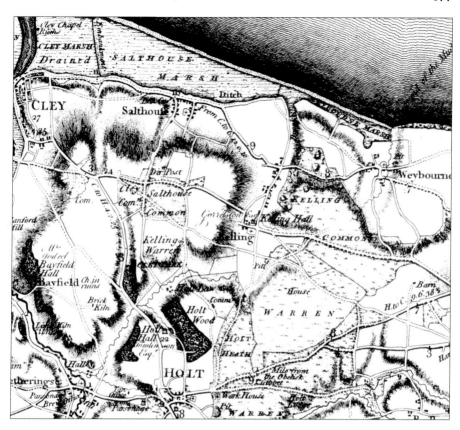

above The site of Weybourne Camp, on the open ground by the sea at Weybourne (top right); Muckleburgh Hill is shown as the hatched slopes north of Kelling Common. The camp overlooked a possible landing place for the French by the rivulet north of the church [+].

Provisioning was comparatively easy, with Cley to the west and Holt to the south. The beer had to come only from the Hardys' Letheringsett brewery ['Brew Office'], (bottom left), less than five miles away   [*Faden's Map of Norfolk 1797: Larks Press 1989*]

The county seen as cool towards personal military service nevertheless had a marked weakness for parades. The new camp proved a magnet for the Hardys, and father and son secured the beer contract even before the Artillery had brought up their guns. Henry Raven recorded William

Office considered Weybourne a likely enough invasion point to launch an exercise; war diaries record the 'attack' from the defenders' point of view at Weybourne, Kelling Hard and the surrounding hills—the same points defended in 1795–96 (TNA: PRO WO 166/4432, War diaries of the 8th Bn Lincolnshire Regiment, Norfolk Division)

AYLSHAM *Celebration of a FESTIVAL for the PE*

above and *facing page* The doodled frieze at the foot of Humphry Repton's watercolour of the peace celebrations at Aylsham (seen on the frontispiece to chapter 10). The towns-folk's procession of 15 July 1814 around the market place matches the joyousness of the civilians' parades from Holt to Weybourne Camp in 1795.

The Hardys were caught up in the excitement. Mary Hardy and her daughter followed the Artillery in the chaise and her husband rode on horseback. Their home became a centre of hospitality for a string of visitors wanting to see the camp [*Private collection. Photograph: Photographic Survey, Courtauld Institute of Art; details*]

[1] *serving the camp Diary 3*: 1 June 1795.

The information on provisioning the camp is unique to the two diarists and does not appear in either the newspapers or in the Royal Artillery records.

Since the military fell outside the licensing system the magistrates were not involved, as discussed on p. 581

[2] *Sheringham* The contents of Samuel Sanderson's canteen were sold early in 1797, when it was presumably clear it was presumably not returning to the camp (*Diary 3*: 12 Jan., 13 Jan. 1797)

[3] *first delivery Diary 3*: 6 June 1795

[4] *moving north Diary 3*: 8 June, 9 June 1795

[5] *followed the regiment Diary 3*

Hardy senior and junior at Weybourne and Sheringham on 1 June 1795, his aunt giving the reason: 'Mr Hardy and William went to Weybourne and Sheringham to get the serving the Camp with beer, came home evening past 11.'[1] Their innkeeper from the Crown at Sheringham took up a new role running the camp canteen.[2]

The Hardys moved fast. The first beer was delivered during a thunderstorm a few days later, Henry Raven's entry that two men were deputed for the task suggesting it was a large order.[3] Despite the rain William and Mary Ann rode up to Holt to watch the advance party come into town on their way to the camp, while the next day brother and sister rode over to Briningham, nearly five miles away on the East Dereham–Holt road, to watch the Artillery moving north. Meanwhile their parents 'walked up to Holt forenoon to see another regiment of Artillery expected at Holt, they did not come'.[4] On 10 June William and Mary Hardy and Mary Ann rode up in their chaise to Holt on a wet, foggy day to watch the Artillery arrive and be 'lodged at Holt that night'. Maintaining their eager interest, the family went in procession and in some style to Weybourne:

[1795] JUNE 11, THURSDAY A fine pleasant morning, foggy after-day. Mr Hardy on horseback, I and Mary Ann in chaise morning 8 followed the regiment from Holt to the Camp at Weybourne, came home evening 2. William brewed.[5]

PEACE. July 15. 1814. 1200 Persons Dined.

The excitement continued throughout that summer and autumn, both diarists making numerous references to the camp. It was Henry Raven's task to log the beer supply, and he took care to differentiate between supplying Edward Hall at the Crown (the Hardys' licensed public house at Weybourne) and the military camp. He records eighteen deliveries between 6 June and 29 October 1795, and nine between 28 April and 3 September 1796:[1] there may have been fewer troops stationed there in 1796, or the contract may have been awarded to other brewers as well. Henry was able to sample the atmosphere at the camp for himself, visiting it three times in 1795 and once in 1796.[2]

As had been the case with the increased business for the little Swan at Sharrington at the time of the bread riots, so tumults and rumours of war created a thirst. Beer was much in demand, and business was brisk. Deliveries to Edward and Mrs Hall at the Crown at Weybourne shot up in the summer and early autumn of 1795 and 1796. Whereas fourteen deliveries to the Crown were made during the whole of 1794, and six in 1797 up to mid-August (Henry's diary ending shortly afterwards), there were 26 deliveries to the Crown in 1795 and 21 in 1796.[3] Deliveries tripled to Sanderson's old public house, the Crown, another Hardy tied house at Sheringham.[4]

The Hardys took many of their acquaintance on a series of visits to the camp in both summers, including not only many of the Goggs, Raven and Fox families from the Whissonsett area but the farmers Messrs Everitt and Keeler and Miss Billing from Guestwick, who as their barley suppliers were thus indirectly involved in provisioning the camp. Henry Goggs took his farm steward, and the Rector of Whissonsett went with his wife. Mary Cozens, the wife of the 'Sprowston Fox', accompanied them, but there is no

[1] *deliveries Diary 3.* One of these is recorded not as a delivery to the camp but to Sanderson. Their former innkeeper had dined at the Hardys' on 16 Mar. and 9 Apr. 1796, presumably when arrangements were being drawn up for the new season

[2] *Henry's visits Diary 3*: 14 June, 14 July, 10 Aug. 1795, 8 July 1796

[3] *in demand Diary 3.* For the riots and the Sharrington Swan see vol. 3, chap. 6.

The Crown was one of two public houses at Weybourne, the other being the Ship. Both were sited prominently on the main east–west coast road and thus close to the camp

[4] *Sheringham* The full sets of deliveries to Weybourne and Sheringham are indexed for Henry Raven's diary in *Diary 3* under the names of the villages and the innkeepers.

Robert Johnson and then John Edwards, in quick succession, took over at the Sheringham Crown

above The standard field artillery-piece of the time: a bronze six-pounder British field gun cast in London in 1796 and on display at Firepower, the Museum of the Royal Artillery at the Royal Arsenal, Woolwich. It is of the type used against the French in the Peninsular War.

The *Mercury* reported 19 May 1804 that four such guns, with two howitzers, had come to Holt on 14 May   [*MB · 2002*]

[1] *visits* Henry Raven records 11 visits to the camp made by those calling at the Hardys' between 17 June and 18 Sept. 1795 and 29 June and 29 July 1796 (*Diary 3*).
   Mary Hardy records far more, by guests of all ages, including many visits paid by her son on his own (*Diary 3* and Diary MS)

[2] *Askew Diary 3*: 29 July 1795.
   On the field day of 24 Aug. 1795 three Hardys took a party of friends and extended family to Weybourne. All were given dinner, tea and supper at the Hardys' and stayed overnight (Diary MS).
   On 18 Sept. 1795 William Hardy drove his sister-in-law Phillis Goggs to the camp, while on 8 July 1796 five of the young Raven cousins and Julia Rowden went there from the Hardys' house (Diary MS)

[3] *novelty* M.J. Armstrong describes Weybourne as 'defenceless' in the American war (*The History and Antiquities of the County of Norfolk*, Holt hundred, p. 117).
   The review of the Norfolk Militia (*plate 40*) took place at King's Lynn: the town's Red Mount Chapel can be seen in the background

mention that her husband John could bring himself to contemplate a military spectacle which presumably represented much of what he abhorred.[1] There is similarly no reference at the time or by his biographers that Thomas William Coke, normally at the forefront of local affairs, showed any enthusiasm for the camp.

The Letheringsett diarists' numerous references leave the reader in no doubt that very many men and women, young and old, from farming, clerical and shopkeeping backgrounds and with no direct military connection, were fascinated by the camp and its firepower. In addition to five field days recorded by Mary Hardy, when 'the cannon were fired', there was the excitement of a Holt ball on 3 August 1795 for the officers, which the Hardys did not attend; Mr Askew, from the Royal Artillery, had however dined at the Hardys' a few days earlier.[2] There is every indication that the camp was a novelty for the locals. There had been no military presence at Weybourne in the American war.[3]

It all ceased in 1796 when William Hardy junior went to Weybourne as the camp broke up and the troops moved to Woodbridge, William buying some of the goods from the canteen that winter.[1] The frequency of visits by William to Weybourne suggests that the diversification of the brewery's business was at his instigation rather than his father's. However William Hardy senior's apparent distancing from the beer contract cannot be interpreted as coolness towards the military: he was as enthusiastic as any in his family over supporting the Artillery.[2]

Camp canteens proved a source of anxiety for the side-lined local magistrates as they had no control over these unregulated, unlicensed outlets. In 1780 some justices (in an unnamed county) raised the matter with the Secretary at War, complaining that traders dealing in spiritous liquors were serving military camps without a spirits licence. In time-honoured fashion the Secretary at War passed it to the Treasury, who thereupon sought the opinion of the Excise Board; the Board promptly declared it was a matter for the Stamp Office. No record was made of the eventual outcome, and the matter was probably quietly dropped.[3]

The Artillery returned to Holt 1804–05, as already noted in the section on the Army, and the townsfolk had troops billeted on them for seventeen months.[4] But the intense interest shown during the summer of 1795 and, to a lesser extent, in 1796 was not reawakened. Weybourne Camp was not revived during Mary Hardy's lifetime.[5]

Puzzling contradictions surround Norfolk's contribution to the military and the war effort over the 23 years 1776–83 and 1793–1809 chronicled by Mary Hardy. The county's strong naval traditions aside—and setting aside the achievements of its most famous hero Horatio Nelson markedly imbalances any attempt at an audit—much of this chapter and chapter 8 will have suggested ways in which it was not a particularly military or even patriotic county. Mass mobilisation was at the behest of the State, and the rush to join the Volunteers and Sea Fencibles was probably, in the main, a means of escaping the ballot, the quota and the press gang.

There was violent opposition in some parts to the ballots. Parishes failing to meet their quotas were fined. The ambiva-

[1] *broke up Diary 3:* 9 Sept. 1796; 12 Jan., 13 Jan. 1797

[2] *William Hardy* As when he walked up to Holt in the rain to watch the Artillery come into Holt during their second season; William was also at Holt that day (Diary MS: 15 June 1796)

[3] *unregulated* TNA: PRO CUST 48/20, p. 88, 22 Apr. 1780; p. 98, 24 May 1780

[4] *return to Holt* See also, for details of the troop movements, the annotation to *Diary 4:* 14 May 1804.

There had been a camp at Sheringham in peacetime, visited by William Hardy (*Diary 2:* 24 July 1792)

[5] *Weybourne Camp* For its earlier and subsequent history see P. Kent, *Fortifications of East Anglia,* pp. 176–9, 182–3, 185–7, 189, 194.

The army camp has lived on since 1988 in a new form as the popular military museum the Muckleburgh Collection. The public are given live tank and armoured-car displays, and can take windswept rides in an open Gama Goat personnel carrier, bumping and circling over the same ground on which the Artillery had exercised in 1795 and 1796

[1] *Regulars* L. Colley, *Britons: Forging the nation 1707–1837*, p. 312; the figure relates to the later stages of the Napoleonic War

[2] *a first* R.W. Ketton-Cremer, 'Norfolk and the threat of invasion', pp. 152–4; A. Fraser, 'Lord Orford's droll-dressed Militia men', p. 5.
Ketton-Cremer depicts Lord Orford at the head of his men: 'This first march across England of a body of county militia, commanded by their Lord Lieutenant in person, was a notable event; and they were reviewed by George II in Hyde Park amid the acclamations of the populace' (R.W. Ketton-Cremer, 'George Walpole, third Earl of Orford', *A Norfolk Gallery* (Faber and Faber, London, 1948), pp. 170–1).
Horace Walpole lost no opportunity of indulging in a dig at his nephew's expense: 'How knights of shires, who have never shot anything but woodcocks, like this warfare, I don't know; but the towns through which they pass adore them' (Ketton-Cremer, 'George Walpole', p. 171)

lence of its 'Jacobinical' and 'democratical' citizens towards the French in the war of 1793–1801 unsettled the authorities. The pacifist tendencies of some Norwich manufacturers and other figures, as exemplified by the MP T.W. Coke, the grocer John Cozens and the brewer William Hardy, were widespread. Many prosperous residents were parsimonious or worse over subscriptions towards national defence. And there was little in the way of willing military participation, even part-time, in the Hardys' wide circle of acquaintance. Beyond that circle, as we have seen, and in their villages, very many families were touched by war. The Hardys, spared the anxiety of having loved ones exposed to danger, cannot be seen as typical. Nationwide half a million men were serving in the Royal Navy and Regular Army at home and overseas at this time, not including the Militia and Volunteers.[1]

These elements, while by no means peculiar to Norfolk, combine to paint a picture of an area uneasy over waging war until the fear of Bonaparte dispelled many of these misgivings. As a result the explosion of interest in Weybourne Camp in the tumultuous years of the mid-1790s could be seen as out of tune with the mood of the times. Yet the prevalence of national patriotism, as in Windham's retention of his Norwich seat in 1794, indicates that generalisations within a county or even within the limits of a city are unwise.

Reinforcing the patriotic paradox, Norfolk occasionally scored 'firsts' in military terms. At moments of crisis it made notable contributions. Against strong opposition in 1757 its county MP George Townshend steered the Militia Bill, which he had originated and drafted, through Parliament. A Norfolk squire devised and illustrated the Militia's first drillbook. On 30 May 1759, contrary to what had been proposed only two years previously, Parliament agreed that Militia battalions could be posted beyond their home county. In July 1759 Norfolk's two battalions had the honour of becoming the first so to be deployed, marching impressively from Norwich to Portsmouth behind the Lord Lieutenant, their Colonel-in-Chief George Walpole, Earl of Orford; the crowds of admiring Londoners who cheered them included William Pitt the Elder. Lord Orford's waspish uncle Horace Walpole could not resist a tart remark, however noble the Earl looked in his scarlet regimentals faced with black.[2]

The fervent support for the camp could in part have been motivated by simple gratitude on the part of Norfolk's beleaguered inhabitants who considered themselves in grave danger of attack from the Low Countries. The camp apart, the evidence is strong that here, as in other parts of England, the public mood was entirely different in the French Revolutionary War from that of the Napoleonic: the conflicts cannot be run together as one. The Vicar of Wroxham's telling words to Townshend, quoted in the section on local leadership, that many of his 'respectable' parishioners would be prepared to come forward only in a policing role is highly significant: they 'do not seem willing to engage in a military capacity, but are well disposed to associate for preserving internal tranquillity'. It was made in April 1798. It would probably have had less validity after May 1803.[1]

A great deal rested on the leadership and drive of the Earl of Orford's successor. This chapter has put the Lord Lieutenant firmly at the centre of anti-invasion preparations and overseeing the arming of civilians. Despite many calls on his time George Townshend never lost his interest in the Militia and Volunteers. In daily communications during emergencies he informed, liaised, soothed, encouraged and cajoled. Through him and his deputies, down to the JPs, superintendents and parish officers, the creaking structure of Norfolk's internal defence retained its cohesion and operated effectively—while not being put to the ultimate test.

Without the remarkable energy and attention to duty of a man who was aged 68 when he was appointed Lord Lieutenant in 1792 and had reached 79 when war resumed in 1803 the county for which he was responsible would have had an even less glorious record on the home front.[2] The assessment in the *Oxford Dictionary of National Biography* that the positions to which Townshend was appointed in his latter years 'could not disguise a rather lacklustre end to a tumultuous political and military life' is surely wide of the mark, as is the lack of full recognition of the achievement of the Militia Act of 1757 and its lasting significance.[3]

Given the county's unmilitary tendencies, it espoused peace with especial fervour. Norfolk's citizenry, male and female, excelled at laying on the parish celebrations which form the subject of the final chapter.

[1] *policing role* See note 3 on pp. 570–1 for the citation

[2] *less glorious record* As expressed in the defence returns of 1804, when out of the nearly 50,000 Norfolkmen aged 17–55 it was thought only 37% were under arms as civilians and in the Regulars—a low percentage nationally (discussed in the section 'A militarised society', where it is emphasised that these figures relate only to land-based service)

[3] *Townshend Oxford Dictionary of National Biography*, ed. H.C.G. Matthew and B. Harrison (Oxford Univ. Press, 2004), vol. 55, p. 159, entry by Martyn J. Powell. Reference to the peer's zealous championing of the Volunteers is altogether omitted.

Given the immense contribution made in the last 15 years of Townshend's life and the mass of documents in the National Archives and Norfolk Record Office relating to this topic it is odd that crucial aspects of his career are overlooked in this long entry (*Oxford DNB*, vol. 55, pp. 155–60)

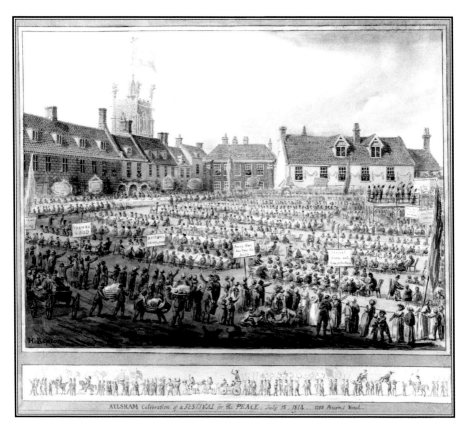

AYLSHAM *Celebration of a FESTIVAL for the* PEACE *. July 15. 1814 . 1200 Persons Dined .*

above The country's deliverance, 15 July 1814: Humphry Repton's watercolour of the dinner of roast beef for 1200 poor people (the non-ratepayers) in Aylsham market place following the end of hostilities.

Two placards in the foreground attribute the townsfolk's salvation to God and to 'BRITONS ARMY & NAVY'; a third asserts that 'Every Man has done his Duty.' A military band entertains the throng. The subscribers (the ratepaying class) watch the proceedings and help serve the food and drink.

In Oct. 1801 a triumphal arch had been erected in Aylsham's Red Lion Street, and 600 poor dined in the market place. Both interludes in the fighting proved shortlived.

Mary Hardy helped to organise and cater for the Letheringsett public dinners celebrating the restoration of the King's health in 1789 and the peace of 1801. With manageable numbers of 150 and 182 poor on those occasions all the men, women and children could be served under cover in a barn [*Private collection. Photograph: Photographic Survey, Courtauld Institute of Art*]

facing page, top A favourite emblem used for painted back-lit transparencies created at home when celebrating great national events and victories. This crown adorns the inn board of the Crown at Colkirk, near Whissonsett   [*MB · 2011*]

10
Deliverance

A large transparent painting of War vanquished

The principal walk in the garden terminated with a large transparent painting of War vanquished and disarmed at the approach and powerful influence of Peace near her temple . . . A Gothic portico and some other ornamental structures were erected for the displaying of a great number of lamps to unite the different divisions of the garden.   WILLIAM HARDY, FROM THE NEWSPAPER, 1801 [1]

England by her example, perseverance, and her heroes has preserved the world. May Europe appreciate her merits. God save the King.   PLACARD, GREAT YARMOUTH BONFIRE, 1814 [2]

HINDSIGHT MAKES IT DIFFICULT at first to understand the great outpouring of relief and joy at the overthrow of Napoleon Bonaparte in Paris in April 1814. Rich and poor in towns and villages across Great Britain throughout that spring and summer feasted and revelled into the night, secure in the certainty that the French war machine had ground to a halt, the fearsome enemy was in exile on the island of Elba, the Volunteers and the Militia could be stood down and all combat would cease. Families could once more be reunited and prisoners return. The war, waged with only an eighteen-month break since early in 1793 was now—so it seemed to all—at last thankfully over. The name of Waterloo, a small village outside Brussels, conveyed nothing.

   Yet to come were the Hundred Days: the escape from Elba, the Emperor's triumphal entry into Paris on 20 March 1815, and the resolution and the desolation of Waterloo on 18 June. Following Napoleon's final overthrow there was little appetite for celebration in Great Britain, apart from services of thanksgiving in churches across the land. All energy was spent. It was during April to August 1814 that the defeat

[1] *garden Diary 4*: endnotes, p. 421. William Hardy copies into his wife's diary the report in the *Norfolk Chronicle* 5 Dec. 1801 on the celebrations at Letheringsett for the truce which ended the French Revolutionary War and led to the Peace of Amiens of Mar. 1802.
   Here the newspaper describes the Hardys' garden. Further extracts are given on p. 595

[2] *England* Part of the inscription on the 'funeral pile of the Buonapartean dynasty' at Gt Yarmouth 19 Apr. 1814 (illustrated p. 602) during festivities for the overthrow of Napoleon on 6 Apr. and the decision five days later to banish the deposed Emperor to Elba.
   A 30,000-strong crowd watched the spectacular bonfire, which contained casks of tar among the faggots and effigies. Towns and villages nationwide staged public celebrations in 1814

[1] *celebrations* While there were other times of general thanksgiving, such as for the victory over the Dutch at Camperdown in 1797, these four occasions marked the principal moments of public rejoicing in this period.
    The death of Nelson at Trafalgar in 1805 cast a long shadow over the nation's deliverance. Joy was accompanied by grief.
    Public rejoicing at national events had a long history. The accession of a Protestant queen in 1558, the foiling of the Gunpowder Plot in 1605 and the monarchy's restoration in 1660 sparked fervent jubilation: see J.E. Neale, 'November 17th', in his *Essays in Elizabethan History* (Jonathan Cape, London, 1963), pp. 95–106

[2] *open villages* See vol. 3, chap. 5. Estate villages were subject to a greater degree of social control by the local landowner

[3] *enterprises Diary 2* (for 1789); *Diary 4* (for 1801); also *A Narrative of the Grand Festival at Yarmouth on Tuesday the 19th of April 1814*, attributed to Robert Cory and illustrated by John Sell Cotman (Gt Yarmouth, 1814).
    Dawson Turner may have helped to oversee its publication

of France and her allies was commemorated, even in small villages, with the ringing of church bells, feasts of roast beef and beer, races, matches and martial music. The night sky shone bright with colourful illuminations, fireworks and bonfires.

Neither Mary Hardy nor her husband lived to join in the general thanksgiving. But they had helped to organise earlier celebrations at Letheringsett, the diarist's account giving us certain insights into these affairs which do not usually enter the public record. The tone of the celebrations differed markedly from place to place across Norfolk. The county was however as fervent as any in its relief at a happy outcome—whether the King's recovery in March 1789 after the Regency Crisis (and the country's consequent salvation from the rule of the Prince of Wales under the boisterous guidance of Charles James Fox), the naval defeat of the French at the Battle of the Nile in August 1798, the truce in the autumn of 1801 which preceded the Peace of Amiens, or the developments in France of April 1814.[1]

The differences lay principally in two areas: in the lack of bombast discernible in those towns and villages which chose to be mindful of local sensibilities over the prosecution of the war; and in the level of social condescension in the reporting. The open villages, like Coltishall, were much less deferential than the closed, where the influence of the squire and the 'big house' prevailed.[2]

Public celebrations

These communal efforts were tremendous feats of organisation and teamwork. By their focus on the face presented to the public, however, the press reports failed to give due credit to those who meticulously planned the events. The diary of Mary Hardy (covering March 1789 and October–November 1801) and the careful minuting of the festivities at Great Yarmouth in April 1814 shed light on how these ambitious celebrations were staged. The diary in particular reveals the contribution, otherwise overlooked, made by local women to the success of the various enterprises.[3]

Such events required forethought, leadership, generosity with time and money and a spirit of co-operation. Party and factional politics tended not to intrude, for these were days

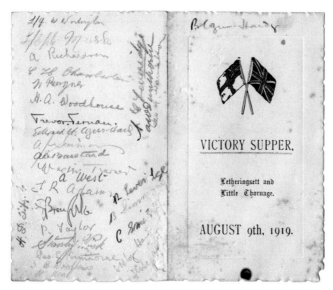

VICTORY SUPPER,

𝕷𝔢𝔱𝔥𝔢𝔯𝔦𝔫𝔤𝔰𝔢𝔱𝔱 𝔞𝔫𝔡
𝕷𝔦𝔱𝔱𝔩𝔢 𝕮𝔥𝔬𝔯𝔫𝔞𝔤𝔢.

AUGUST 9th, 1919.

left Letheringsett 1919:
the front and back
covers of Basil
Cozens-Hardy's copy
of the Victory Supper
menu for 9 Aug. 1919
after the peace treaty of
Versailles which ended
the First World War.
The signatures of
Edward H. Cozens-
Hardy (later 3rd Lord
Cozens-Hardy) and
Basil's father Sydney
appear in the bottom
half; that of the Hall
gardener H.A. Wood-
house is near the top.
  Mary Hardy records
similar celebrations at
times of national deliverance, the 20th-century
events being modelled
on the 18th century's—
except that women and
children took part in
her period
[*Cozens-Hardy Collection*]

[1] *1200* The figure
recorded by Repton
in his watercolour

[2] *8000 A Narrative of
the Grand Festival at
Yarmouth*, pp. 13–14.
  The *Norfolk Chronicle*
devoted a column and
a half to an account of
the Yarmouth celebra-
tions (23 Apr. 1814),
this lengthy coverage
being eclipsed when it
came to the turn of the
paper's home city. On
18 June 1814 it pub-
lished a spread of 3¾
columns, with further

when all, or nearly all, came together in unity. There was no overall direction at county or hundred level by the Lord Lieutenant, his Deputies or the justices. Individual boroughs, towns and villages would organise their celebrations to suit themselves, drawing on a mix of church bells, parades, flags, floats, military bands, guns, fireworks, back-lit transparencies, and home-drawn mottoes borne aloft on placards. As depicted by Humphry Repton, at the chapter frontispiece, the mottoes could be roughly written and uncertainly spelt.

  Dinners for the multitude were held either in the open or, if numbers were fairly small, in a shirehall or barn. Numbers were such as to make open-air dining a necessity in market towns, even in the wind and rain. In July 1814 Aylsham's market place seated twelve hundred poor,[1] while three months earlier eight thousand of Great Yarmouth's citizenry from the Mayor downwards had seated themselves on the quay in flurries of rain which mercifully soon cleared up.[2]

  These communal occasions set the pattern for the future, through the public celebrations for Queen Victoria's jubilees of 1887 and 1897 and into the twentieth century: public dinners, processions, street parties and garden fetes would mark a succession of royal events and victory parades.

items relating to Norwich a week later. Lesser places received less attention: eg E. Harling, Bungay and Beccles (4 June); Wroxham (18 June); and a mass of towns and villages in Norfolk and Suffolk on 25 June and 2 July

[1] *Whissonsett Norw. Merc.* 1 Dec. 1798. Many other Nile celebrations were reported: eg 13 Oct. 1798.

Local brewers such as the Hardys would generally give freely of their beer. But the balance sheet for Letheringsett's fund for the Diamond Jubilee of 1897 (reproduced in *Diary 2*, p. 271) shows that in that sterner age not beer but mineral waters and tea were provided for the villagers. Also Morgans, very briefly brewing ginger beer in the village, claimed in expenses more than they donated in cash.

There appears to have been a village revolt. Only five years later beer and stout were once more laid on, but in extremely limited quantities: a little over £2-worth for 180 people, including children (illustrated, right)

The protracted struggle against France, Spain and their allies was no remote contest, despite the far-flung theatres in which the wars were fought. The repeated threats of invasion 1779–1808 meant that for the British it was a fight for survival, as described in the previous chapter. Through their taxes, the embargoes and the military and naval service of their loved ones, most families had felt some privation at the hand of the enemy and saluted those who ventured out, if unwillingly at times, to champion Britannia. Even the less intense celebrations of 1798 extended into the villages of the hinterland. As well as the processions through Norwich on the day of the general thanksgiving, 29 November, when the city's parishes were illuminated, Whissonsett laid on its own festivities. The farmers provided a dinner for the labourers and poor widows, to the ringing of the church bells in the tower which Mary Hardy's father had helped to restore.[1]

Letheringsett Coronation Festivities, June 26th, 1902.
BALANCE SHEET.

RECEIPTS.		£	s.	d.	EXPENDITURE.		£	s.	d.
Lord Justice Cozens-Hardy	...	5	0	0	Mr. A. J. Cunningham, Dinner for 180	...	18	0	0
Clement Cozens-Hardy, Esq.	...	5	0	0	„ „ Beer and Stout		2	3	0
Rev. A. A. Eady	...	3	3	0	„ „ Mineral Waters		1	10	0
Sidney Cozens-Hardy, Esq.	...	2	0	0	„ „ Buns	...	0	12	6
W. H. C. Chevalier, Esq.	...	1	0	0	Mr. A. Preston, Printing		0	7	0
Morgan's Brewery Company, Ltd.	...	1	0	0	Sundry Expenses	...	0	6	6
Mrs. Clement Cozens-Hardy	...	1	0	0					
Mrs. A. Webb	...	0	10	0					
Mr. Jas. Simmons	...	0	10	0					
Mr. G. Hewitt	...	0	10	0					
Mr. P. Fisher	...	0	10	0					
Mr. E. Hewitt	...	0	5	0					
Mr. R. Scott	...	0	5	0					
Mr. R. Turner	...	0	5	0					
Mr. J. Chastney	...	0	5	0					
Mr. A. J. Cunningham	...	0	5	0					
Subscriptions under 5/-	...	1	11	0					
					SPORTS FUND.				
SPORTS FUND ONLY.					Prizes for Sports	...	4	12	6
Sir A. Jodrell, Bart.	...	3	3	0	Mr. A. Preston, Printing	...	0	9	0
Mrs. Waldy	...	2	0	0	Sundry Expenses and postage	...	0	1	6
		£28	2	0			£28	2	0

GEORGE HEWITT,
Acting Treasurer.

ARTHUR PRESTON, PRINTER. HOLT.

above Letheringsett celebrated Edward VII's coronation in 1902. The arrangements were more formal than in the past, and drink and catering were in the hands of the King's Head innkeeper Alfred John Cunningham. The villagers had had a merrier time of it in 1789. The beer had flowed more freely, and the beef for 150 poor had been organised and cooked by two women: Mary Hardy and the rector's wife Elizabeth Burrell. Gunpowder (for fireworks) had featured in the 1789 expenses   [*Cozens-Hardy Collection*]

Great joy greeted the truce of 1801. Although the Peace of Amiens was not signed until 27 March 1802, the cessation of hostilities had been agreed in London and ratified by the King on 1 October 1801—just too late for the Norwich papers of Saturday 3 October, the news being brought to the city by the Expedition coach at 9 am that day. Instead of proceeding to his inn, the White Swan, the coachman drove round the market 'to the astonishment and joy of those present, the inhabitants running from all quarters towards the market to ascertain the truth' on hearing the bells ring out and the volleys fired by the Volunteers.[1]

War had damaged the city's economy, especially textile manufacture; at the same time taxes had risen. When Norwich announced the date of its 1814 celebration the choice of words was significant. The festivities were to be held on 16 June, so the newspaper declared, for 'the happy and glorious termination of *a long and most expensive war*'.[2]

The Quakers, known formally as the Society of Friends, were highly respected in Norfolk and Norwich. In the same edition of the *Norfolk Chronicle* a long letter to the editor was published from an anonymous Norwich member of the Society of Friends in which he vehemently disassociated the Society from the celebrations. Referring to the proposed general illumination, when householders would vie with one another in producing colourful back-lit transparencies for public view in their windows, he announced that he and his fellow Quakers 'decline to unite with their fellow-citizens in such a measure' as they could heartily share 'in their feelings of *joy*! but not in those of *triumph*'. The Friends, he wrote, were not only opposed to all war, but to the intemperance and riot which, so he asserted, often attended peace festivities. Further, they were appalled that under the peace treaty (of 30 May 1814) France was permitted to carry on the slave trade in her West Indian possessions.[3]

It was perhaps with these sentiments in mind, and a desire by the city fathers not to cause unnecessary offence to such members of local society as the prominent Quaker bankers the Gurneys, that Norwich's celebrations set a rather more lofty and restrained tone than did the red-blooded affair at Great Yarmouth, described later. Although Yarmouth's seamen were particularly exposed to the hazards of war, the

[1] *truce Norw. Merc.* 10 Oct. 1801. It was ratified in Paris on 5 Oct.
   The Ipswich Mail, trying to emulate its rival, arrived bedecked with flags in Norwich's market place on Sunday morning 4 Oct., but came to grief. Its coachman tried to direct the horses to drive round the market, but the hard-driven animals were tired and turned sharply towards their accustomed rest in the King's Head yard, overturning the vehicle in their haste (*Norw. Merc.* 17 Oct. 1801)

[2] *expensive war Norfolk Chronicle*, 11 June 1814 [my italics]

[3] *Quakers Norfolk Chronicle*, 11 June 1814 [his italics]. There had been rejoicings in Norwich when the London coaches brought news of the signing of the definitive treaty of peace in Paris on 30 May (*Norfolk Chronicle*, 4 June 1814).
   Not all Quakers maintained this firm stance, and pacifist views were not permitted always to stand in the way of business. One of the principal contractors building martello towers was a Quaker, William Hobson (N. Longmate, *Island Fortress: The defence of Great Britain 1603–1945* (Hutchinson, London, 1991), p. 278)

right Holt: the King's Head's ornate inn sign. The lamps lighting up a crown fixed to the iron-work kept blowing out in the 1801 celebrations [*MB · 2011*]

1 *French ports* See the opening part of chap. 5. Gt Yarmouth's wartime buoyancy occupies the last part of that chapter

2 *Spout Hills The Festival at Holt given on August 12th 1814 in commemoration of the Happy Return of Peace* (Holt, 1814). This anonymous 32-page booklet printed by the Holt bookseller James Shalders was seen by L.B. Radford when composing his *History of Holt: A brief study of parish, church, and school* (Holt, 1908), pp. 80–1. No copy of the booklet survives in the British Library, Norfolk Record Office or Norfolk Heritage Centre

3 *1789 celebrations* See vol. 3, chap. 6, on 'Mixing with the poor'

4 *Letheringsett Norw. Merc.* 28 Mar. 1789. The barn was demolished in the 1830s to make way for a large rectory on the site—now the Old Rectory.

Huge quantities of beef were required, but how these were sourced is not recorded

port had on the whole done well out of the conflict. By contrast the French ports had languished during the blockade.[1]

In August 1814 Holt laid on a large celebration for peace, evidently far more ambitious than those the Hardys had seen in the town in 1789 and 1801. This time it was given for seven hundred townsfolk not in the market place but on Spouts Common. As at Great Yarmouth, a booklet was published to commemorate every detail of the event which lasted more than ten hours, from the firing of a signal gun in the market place at noon to the afternoon sports and evening dances on the common; it ended with the last flash of the fireworks at night.[2]

Mary Hardy's record of the Letheringsett celebrations for the King's recovery in 1789 is described in volume 3.[3] On 24 March, in very good weather, she and the rector's young wife 'cooked all the victuals' for 150 poor people, the men, women and children all dining together in the large barn just west of the church; William Hardy provided a barrel of beer. The press report, in concentrating on the good conduct of the poor and the transparencies in the windows, did not go into the planning and into the mechanics underpinning the operation.[4] It was Mary Hardy who recorded the provisioning required, and itemised the cash donations by the farmers, brewer, miller and village innkeeper to fund expenditure on food, drink, carpentry and gunpowder.[1]

The day after Letheringsett's celebrations William Hardy junior attended the festivities at Fakenham:

[1789] MARCH 25, WEDNESDAY A dry sharp day . . . Fakenham gave the poor a dinner in the market place and illuminated the town in the evening and had a ball, William came home evening 12 . . .[2]

Transparent paintings became a feature of public celebrations, placed in prominent positions such as public buildings and any houses visible from the road; being back-lit they showed up at night. A transparency was a screen of paper or thin fabric such as gauze or starched muslin on which the picture would be painted, illuminated by candles and lamps. A more robust solution, and one which produced something of the effect of stained glass, was to gum the paper onto glass and seal it with varnish or isinglass. The Hardys might have adopted this device since isinglass, used in finings for beer, was readily to hand in a brewery.[3]

It would often be reported that rain and wind extinguished the lights, impairing the effect intended. The weather was against many of the 1801 celebrations, as Samuel Love, of the King's Head at Holt, was to discover. The inn's swirling wrought-iron sign still jutting over the main street through Holt (*plate 46* and opposite) is almost certainly the same sign on which the innkeeper had done his patriotic best:

Mr Love had prepared a crown, formed of variegated lamps, in order to place it over his sign, but the wind would not suffer the lights to keep in.[4]

Professional artists and drawing masters may have produced many of these lighting devices and transparencies for communal areas and public buildings, although the names are rarely reported. Individual households would also produce their own illuminations and transparencies, the men and women of the family being engaged in their preparation. Ideas were borrowed from others. While busy planning Letheringsett's 1801 event William Hardy junior and Mary Ann went up to have a look at the more restrained of Holt's two celebrations for the truce:

[1] *expenditure Diary 2*: 23–24 Mar. 1789. Mary Hardy's MS entry in her diary is illustrated in *Diary 2*, p. 269. Her record of Holt's 1789 celebrations is also in vol. 3, chap. 6

[2] *Fakenham Diary 2*. The towns of Aylsham, Bungay, E. Dereham and Hingham also laid on public festivities, and Cromer gave a dinner for 400 poor people (*Norw. Merc.* 28 Mar. 1789). Norwich's Sunday school children were given special treats of cakes and ale (vol. 3, chap. 2)

[3] *illuminations* See Trevor Fawcett, 'Patriotic transparencies in Norwich, 1798–1814', *Norfolk Archaeology*, vol. 34 (1968), pp. 245–52.
His list of artists responsible for transparencies, gathered from the press, includes famous local names such as Crome, Sillett and Ladbrooke (pp. 251–2)

[4] *Love Norw. Merc.* 14 Nov. 1801.
For the story of these public celebrations and the religious thanksgivings at their heart see N. Mears, A. Raffe, S. Taylor and P. Williamson (with L. Bates, eds, *National Prayers: Special worship since the Reformation, vol. 1, 1533–1688* (Church of England Record Soc., vol.

right Part of the report in the *Norwich Mercury* of the Letheringsett celebrations on 24 Nov. 1801 for the coming of peace. It was probably written by the rector, John Burrell, whose gardens are described at the top of this column. He frankly acknowledges the disappointments caused by the weather. He had hung several hundred lamps, but the weather was too bad for him to light them.

The Hardys too were unable to show off their festoons of lamps to full effect. However the Chinese-style lighting of William Hardy jnr's garden bridge was a success, and the family's allegorical transparency of War and Peace was positioned to be admired from the road.

The report shows how the celebrations united the classes in the village: 'The illumination extended to every cottage. One tradesman had a transparent painting— a Crown, under it the word "Peace".'

The Tory paper, the *Norfolk Chronicle*, carried an even longer and rather differently worded account, with which the Hardys were evidently much pleased. William Hardy copied the whole of the *Chronicle*'s version into the end of his wife's diary [*Norwich Mercury, 5 Dec. 1801: Norfolk Heritage Centre, Norwich*]

flowers and evergreens, with various emblems of Peace; admidst which the candles were placed with pleasing effect. Mr. Burrell's garden, adjoining pastures, and the skirting shrubbery, were prepared with several hundred lamps in festoons, &c. the whole terminated by a spiral display of near an hundred more around the mount, on the top of which they were arranged in a lofty pyramid; but the evening being unfavourable at its commencement, prevented the whole being lighted up. The same cause very much damaged the illumination in Mr. Hardy's garden, where a gothic portico which terminated one walk, and the ornamental festoons of lamps which should have united the various divisions of the garden into one beautiful whole, was broken in upon. The bridge, notwithstanding, was prettily lighted up with coloured lamps *à la Chinoise*, and the walk seen from the public road was terminated by a transparent painting—" War asleep upon his shield, his instruments scattered about broken & useless near the Temple of Peace; the Goddess of which appeared in vestal neatness and elegance." Colours were flying in the Inn yard and on the Steeple. The Workhouse formed a pleasing distant object; and the Church was well lighted. The illumination extended to every cottage.—One tradesman had a transparent painting—a Crown, under it the word " Peace;" and the others had various transparencies, mottoes, &c. in short, to do justice to the whole requires a more powerful pen; and the conviviality of the day and evening appeared to be equalled only by the gratitude of the poor, and the joy of the beholders.

Pot ash, pearl ash, and rock salt, are

20, with the Boydell Press, Woodbridge, 2013). This exhaustive study, more than 860 pages long, reveals the events' mediaeval origins (in AD 1009!) and continuity of thinking (p. lxxii). A successor volume came out in 2017, bringing the story to 1870

[1] *Holt Diary 4*

[2] *householders Norw. Merc. 14 Nov. 1801*

[1801] OCTOBER 28, WEDNESDAY A close cold day . . . William and Mary Ann . . . walked up to Holt after tea to see Miss Burcham's illuminations, only three or four houses besides was illuminated . . . [1]

The diarist's record is important, for Miss Burcham's artistry was not acknowledged in the press. It was her father or brother, the surveyor, auctioneer and valuer John Burcham, who as head of the illuminated household was named at the time of the second celebration and poor's dinner on 5 November. The private householders with illuminations at their windows were reported as the attorney and captain of the Volunteers Charles Hewitt; the printer and bookseller John Parslee; and 'Mr Bircham' (John Burcham).[2] There were many, male and female, who went unrecorded as artists since the press tended to name only the head of the household. Even professional artists such as Immanuel, who had painted the Hardys' portraits in 1798 (reproduced on pages 428 and 429), were not named. We know from Mary Hardy's diary that the artist made prolonged visits to them in the weeks leading up to the day of celebration in 1801. It was probably Immanuel as much as his pupil Mary Ann, or her brother, who was responsible for the graceful effects produced by the transparencies and other artwork in the Hardys' garden, as described in the *Norfolk Chronicle*.[1]

The Letheringsett report of 1801 was probably submitted to both the Norwich papers by the rector. Although John Burrell was a pronounced pro-war Tory it is evident that the politics of peace had been delicately handled in his parish, given its complement of anti-war Whigs. Emphasis was placed not on belligerent defiance and triumphalism (the

[1] *Hardys' garden Diary 4*; extracts from the report in the *Norfolk Chronicle* of 5 Dec. 1801, as transcribed by William Hardy, are given overleaf. In addition to his earlier visits Immanuel stayed with the Hardys over the period of the festivities 20–26 Nov.

Mary Hardy never gives his full name. He was Manuel Immanuel (d.1834), with a long professional career in London, Lincolnshire, Norfolk and other parts of England; he customarily did not sign his work: see vol. 1, chaps 2 and 6. I am very grateful to Mr S.H. Steel of Grantham for the identification

left Allegorical artwork by Rudolph Ackermann, a professional artist who often designed for commemorative and patriotic occasions. The Royal Arms, the Lion of England, Neptune and other gods, goddesses and Britannia would also feature in amateurs' artwork, as described in the Norwich press. Here swatches of his wallpapers and fabrics are pasted onto his printed advertisement.

On their long London visit in the summer of 1800 Mary Hardy and her daughter visited Ackermann's shop in the Strand to view his transparencies. Mary Ann and her drawing master Immanuel, a portrait painter, were almost certainly responsible for some of Letheringsett's illuminations [*Author's collection*]

above Norwich: the city's arms above the entrance to the Free Grammar School.

In June 1814 the artist John Crome, who taught at the school, painted a transparency above this arch showing Victory crowning Britannia seated on a rock, with Discord in chains   [*MB · 2011*]

<hr>

[1] *allegorical creations* T. Fawcett, 'Patriotic transparencies in Norwich', pp. 247, 250; *Norfolk Chronicle*, 5 Dec. 1801 (opposite)

[2] *Holt* Diary MS: 4 Nov. 1801; *Diary 4*: 5 Nov. 1801. Immanuel's name does not appear in any of the press reports

[3] *meeting Diary 4*: 30 Oct. 1801

[4] *barn Diary 4*

tone set at Great Yarmouth), but on thankfulness; not on the valour of the troops and sailors who had sustained the long struggle (as at Aylsham), but on the nation's deliverance and the hoped-for reconciliation with France. This measured tone would have been acceptable even to the Hardys.

As the next section will show, the placards for the 1814 festivities at Great Yarmouth, appreciated by those could read, were far more down to earth than the elegant classical allegories in Norwich and Letheringsett. The city and village, probably under the influence of the master of the grammar school and the rector respectively, had a penchant for Latin tags and for allegorical creations such as Britannia and Gallia, Neptune, Fame and Honour, Euphrosyne (one of the Graces), and the 'Genius of the Fine Arts'.[1]

Immanuel is likely also to have helped the people of Holt with their second celebration, held on 5 November. He was there the day before, and stayed at the Hardys' on the night of 5 November following the dinner given to Holt's poor (after a stormy morning) and the illuminations that evening. All the Hardys went up to watch except the diarist, who was ill all day with stomach pains; the Hardys' maidservants later walked up in the dark to see the illuminations.[2]

The workload for these events was such that it had to be shared. First came the planning, which for Letheringsett was probably instigated at the special town meeting called more than three weeks before the dinner.[3] As the village's turn approached the weather worsened. Four of the Whissonsett relations arrived to help their aunt and her family as they prepared the hot meal to be provided for 182 from the labouring class (the non-ratepayers) assembled in the barn behind the rector's house. Mary Hardy, her mind on the work in hand, is characteristically terse and her tone far removed from the fulsome praise in the newspapers:

[1801] NOVEMBER 23, MONDAY Very cold windy day. All very busy making preparations for illuminations of our house and gardens and providing a dinner for the poor. Nathaniel, Ann and Phillis Raven came to tea, slept here.

NOVEMBER 24, TUESDAY A close foggy morning, very wet afternoon, held up evening 6 but the wind being rather high could not keep many of the lamps light [lit]. Mr Goggs came evening 2, several people dined here, the poor people dined in Mr Burrell's little barn.[4]

The *Norfolk Chronicle*'s account of the peace celebrations at Letheringsett, 24 November 1801

source   Diary 4, endnotes, p. 421: part of William Hardy's transcription from the *Norfolk Chronicle* of 5 Dec. 1801, reporting events at Letheringsett 24 Nov. 1801

...THE NORTH FRONT OF THE REVD MR BURRELL'S house 24 windows presented a profusion of lights displayed with taste and variety,[1] and in the eastern aspect was a transparency representing two beautiful figures of Gallia and Britannia in the act of uniting hands under the influence of Peace.[2] His garden mount and adjoining pastures were prepared for the reception of several hundred lamps, but the weather and unfavourableness of the evening prevented the display of them.

Mr Hardy displayed very great taste and variety in decorating his house and garden.[3] The windows with illuminated pyramids, amidst some wreaths of flowers and emblematic devices of peace, had a very pleasing effect. The principal walk in the garden terminated with a large transparent painting of War vanquished and disarmed at the approach and powerful influence of Peace near her temple; the beautiful bridge that led to it was superbly illuminated with variegated globe lamps in great taste, and its beauties were much increased by its vivid reflection in the stream below it. A Gothic portico and some other ornamental structures were erected for the displaying of a great number of lamps to unite the different divisions of the garden.

The church, workhouse and every cottage was [were] illuminated; a bonfire and colours flying etc enlivened the scene, the decorum and regularity of the poor was worthy the highest commendation; the visitors from the neighbouring towns as well as distant parts were genteely treated, and the day passed with much pleasure.

[1] *north front* Facing the main Cromer–King's Lynn road. The '24 windows' at the house later known as The Lodge were either 12 transomed casements, with twin openings, or the upper and lower parts of 12 sash windows. By 1880 The Lodge's north front had 14 sash windows (seen below)

[2] *eastern aspect* Facing the lane to Lt Thornage, then called Friday Street

[3] *Mr Hardy* William Hardy snr. Parts of the garden described here, such as the ornamental bridge over the Glaven, were his son's recent creation (vol. 1, chaps 9 and 10)

left The mid-18th-century north front of The Lodge, Letheringsett, over the road from the church. This was the rector's privately owned house, there being no parsonage in Mary Hardy's time.

During the 1801 celebrations all the indoor lamps stayed lit in these windows. Plans for the gardens had to be scrapped [*photograph A.E.Coe, of Norwich, 1880: Cozens-Hardy Collection*]

[1] *portions* William Hardy's list for a dinner in 1800 for labourers, minor tradesmen and their wives and children (illustrated in vol. 3, chap. 6 and in *Diary 4*, pp. 184, 185) shows 72 children among the 136 persons he allowed for. Children comprised 53% of that section of the parish population.

Two single men, Ed Sheppard and David Sidney, were allotted 2 lb beef each (0·9 kg).

For the 1801 peace event there were 182 diners from a total parish population of 236. In 1902 there 180 diners, from a population of 234 which in 1901, unlike 1801, included the inhabitants of neighbouring Bayfield and Glandford

[2] *Holkham* Its celebrations were written up in effusive detail in the *Norfolk Chronicle*, 20 Aug. 1814

[3] *Weston* J. Woodforde, *The Diary of a Country Parson*, ed. J. Beresford, vol. 3, p. 89, 8 Mar. 1789 (when the Custances did not even come to church for the day set aside for general thanksgiving, although they were in residence at Weston House); and p. 91, 18 Mar. 1789 (when Woodforde gave 'our people in the kitchen' a bottle of gin—but did not drink with them)

Among the precious survivals in the Cozens-Hardy archives is a scrap of paper on which the diarist noted the amount of food for the 1801 dinner. Unfortunately the large quantity of beef weighing ten stone (63·5 kilograms) noted by Mary Hardy and illustrated opposite proved insufficient for 182 persons, but there was no obvious failing by the commissariat. Taking as her guide the 1789 consumption of beef there should have been ample, especially given the large number of children in the village—presumably with smaller appetites than their parents'. Also it is clear that William Hardy did not stint on the beef in his long lists for other huge dinners prepared by his wife.[1]

Towns were able to lay on patriotic displays to celebrate the King's recovery and the nation's great victories. But there were many villages where little if anything was done, to judge from the relatively small number of villages sending in reports to the Norwich papers in 1789, 1798 and 1801. Doubtless some celebrations would have gone unrecorded when crowded out by the extensive coverage devoted to the national news and to Norwich, Holkham and other large towns and estate villages.[2] Holt's big event, for instance, in August 1814 was not reported by the *Norfolk Chronicle*.

At Weston there was persistent lack of leadership, both by the local squire and magistrate John Custance and his family and by the resident incumbent James Woodforde. This is surprising as both were loyal Tories with none of the anti-war tendencies of some of Letheringsett's inhabitants. In his latter years Woodforde was weakened by ill-health and bouts of depression, but even when fit he seems to have concluded that he could do nothing unless given the lead by Squire Custance—although other clergy did not consider themselves so constrained.

Woodforde would compose short, spontaneous thanksgivings on hearing good news in wartime, would draw his little band of servants together for drinks and toasts, and gave permission for some of them to attend festivities such as the ambitious affairs arranged in Norwich.[3] However the parson did not gather the parish together as a whole. It was no wonder his niece railed against her surroundings at great moments of public celebration such as the King's recovery.

left Letheringsett's public dinner for the poor in 1801. Mary Hardy's jottings record the main ingredients for the meal of roast beef, plum pudding and beer: the traditional fare of Old England. The diarist was pre-occupied with provisioning the 182 diners: '10 stone beef, not enough'. There was, however, bread to spare.

It was natural for her to be perplexed. The diarist was used to these undertakings, having catered for 136 the year before. On the basis of the 7½ stone of beef consumed by 150 diners in 1789 she should have had sufficient for 200 this time. Instead the beef ran out. With individual portions averaging three-quarters of a pound of beef (0.35 kg) there should have been plenty, washed down by a barrel and a half of beer (432 pints).

Following the recent series of wheat famines the grateful recipients may have tucked into their platefuls with unanticipated gusto [*Cozens-Hardy Collection*]

Nancy had become 'very discontented of late, and runs out against living in such a dull place'.[1]

The same pattern emerged after the Battle of the Nile in 1798. Woodforde confided in his diary on the day of general thanksgiving: 'No rejoicings at all at Weston. I should have been very glad to have contributed towards some, if Mr Custance had come forward.' Instead the rector merely gave his servants some strong beer and punch to drink the health of the admiral and of 'all the other officers with him and all the brave sailors with them . . .' Several people journeyed from Weston to watch the illuminations at Norwich, but neither the rector nor Nancy saw anything of them.[2]

His farm servant Ben Leggatt attended Norwich's event in 1801, and his manservant Bretingham Scurl the 'great rejoicings' in the village of East Tuddenham. Mrs Custance and her daughters attended the peace ball held at East Dereham.[3] But for the residents of Weston as a whole and the unhappy pair confined to the rectory there was nothing to mark the coming of peace.

[1] *dull place* J. Woodforde, *The Diary of a Country Parson*, ed. J. Beresford, vol. 3, p. 91, 17 Mar. 1789

[2] *1798 events* J. Woodforde, *The Diary of a Country Parson*, ed. J. Beresford, vol. 5, p. 149, 29 Nov.; p. 150, 30 Nov. 1798. The Custances are not noted at church

[3] *1801 events* J. Woodforde, *The Diary of a Country Parson*, ed. J. Beresford, vol. 5, p. 346, 21–22 Oct.; p. 347, 26 Oct.; pp. 346–7, 22 Oct. 1801. 'None from Weston House at church today, nor Miss Woodforde' (p. 347, 25 Oct. 1801)

Grinning matches and diving into flour: Coltishall celebrates peace with 'lots of fun', 24 June 1814

source   Norfolk Chronicle, 2 July 1814, reporting events at Coltishall 24 June 1814

[1] *festivals* The *Norwich Mercury* and *Norfolk Chronicle* carried numerous such reports during the spring and summer of 1814. The newspaper's italics are retained here

[2] *se'nnight* Week; ie 24 June (patronal festival of St John Baptist, to whom Coltishall Church is dedicated)

[3] *marched* This type of informal, joyous procession is illustrated by Humphry Repton's Aylsham frieze (frontispiece to this chapter, and, as a larger detail, on pp. 578, 579)

[4] *St Peter's* The parish of St Peter Mancroft, Norwich. The only resident named Woodward listed in Peck's 1802 Norwich directory is John Woodward, of the Eating House, 36 St Stephen's Street

PEACE FESTIVALS [1] ... Amongst the numerous village *Fêtes*, we are informed that at Coltishall, yesterday se'nnight,[2] was pre-eminent in respect both to the gaiety of the scene and the regularity with which it was conducted.

At one o'clock, nearly 400 persons were assembled around a most excellent martial band, and preceded by two natives of this place, bearing insignia of their having fought in various battles by the side of our immortal Nelson, marched through the village, and afterwards took their respective stations in the field devoted to the occasion, over which proudly waved a profusion of banners.[3]

At three, appeared the Roast Beef and Plum Puddings—in one of the latter was placed a small union jack, inscribed '*Peace to the World—Plenty to the Poor*', executed in the most beautiful style. During dinner, the ladies and gentlemen of the parish seemed to vie with each other in attendance on their neighbours, and the partakers of the feast in their turn as gratefully acknowledged it. After the repast, many loyal toasts were pledged in true amber, each accompanied by a discharge of artillery, ringing of bells, and well-selected tunes.

The whole concluded with '*Lots of Fun*'—foot-racing, sack-jumping, diving in bowls of flour (which afforded great merriment), and grinning matches; in the last, however, one performer was so adept a performer in the art, that the contending parties speedily resigned the prizes.

The fireworks displayed at night were furnished by Mr Woodward, of St Peter's, in this city, and gave general satisfaction to the spectators.[4]

facing page Litcham: in 1814 there was dancing on the green facing the Bull after the dinner for 350 of the village poor.

The Hardys had lived at Litcham before their move to Coltishall. William was born there in 1770, and the Bull had been his father's excise office [*MB·2011*]

For the parishioners this was one of the disadvantages of living in a village evidently totally dependent on the drive of the squire or parson. Other places felt able to come together and plan the whole affair on a co-operative basis, the parish ratepayers contributing their time and labour, their skills, some food and drink and their cash. The tone of the press reports gives a clue. At Cley in 1814 the contribution of the Thomlinsons of Cley Hall was all important. Nearly four hundred of the poor were given roast beef and plum pudding and 'several barrels of ale' on tables arranged on the fairstead 'beside the trees of the park of J.W. Thomlinson,

Esq. who was the principal contributor to this festive scene'. Near the newly constructed triumphal arch 'Mrs Thomlinson, Miss Chad, and several ladies honoured the tables with their assistance.'[1] At Crostwick, near Horstead, the report singled out the prominent local landowner. The inhabitants 'through the liberality of Henry Palmer Watts, Esq. celebrated the downfall of Napoleon, the Desolator of Europe, in the most magnificent manner'.[2] By contrast at Litcham there was no hint of deference. 'A little band of village musicians played during dinner' for 350 of the poorer inhabitants, who then took to dancing on the green by the public house familiar to William Hardy from his excise days.[3]

The report of Coltishall's celebrations (opposite) stands out from other press items in its emphasis on 'lots of fun' and in that not one benefactor is named. It was a genuinely communal gathering, and not a feast bestowed on a deferential populace by social superiors. The publicity-minded Chapman Ives was dead; the former leaders of village society, the Perkins family, were in decline. Many prominent merchants like the Fiddys were bankrupt. The sole brewer still trading was Siday Hawes, the probable donor of the beer— the 'true amber'. He or his wife may have written the account sent to the Norfolk Chronicle, for Elizabeth Hawes ran the Sunday school and knew the village children.[4] The rector, Dr Charles Grape, wrote a memorandum of the event identical in wording to the press report. Whether he was the author of both or was merely copying the published item into the parish record is not clear.[5]

Coltishall's light-hearted festivities betrayed no hint of social control, yet benefited from meticulous planning. The military component may have been supplied by part of the East Norfolk Yeomanry Cavalry, for the Tunstead and Happing Troop of Volunteers had been summoned by the cavalry's commanding officer to a parade at Coltishall ten days before the actual celebration.[6]

The author claims that Coltishall was pre-eminent in the gaiety of the scene; certainly there was rather more emphasis on revelry there than elsewhere. Also the claim that 'two natives' of the place had 'fought in various battles by the side of our immortal Nelson' was an unusual addition. Neither the newspaper nor parish register discloses their names.

[1] Cley Norfolk Chronicle, 2 July 1814. Frances Thomlinson was the former Miss Chad of Thursford, her assistant thus being her relative

[2] Crostwick Norfolk Chronicle, 16 Apr. 1814. Watts's sister Maria (b.1781) became Edmund Bartell jnr's second wife in 1837

[3] Litcham Norfolk Chronicle, 2 July 1814

[4] Sunday school See vol. 3, chap. 2

[5] Coltishall P. Millican, A History of Horstead and Stanninghall, p. 63; O. Sinclair, When Wherries Sailed By: Recollections of a Broadland village (Poppyland Publishing, N. Walsham, 1987), pp. 36–7

[6] cavalry Norfolk Chronicle, 11 June 1814, Lt-Col. C. Laton of the 'ENYC' ordering the parade 'in Review Order' for 14 June from his home at Drayton Lodge. The actual festivities were held on 24 June

facing page The Norfolk Pillar (1819): the county's monument to Nelson on the Denes where the 1814 bonfire was held   [*MB·2001*]

¹ *unclassical* One of the mottoes on the 1814 procession through Gt Yarmouth proclaimed, 'England, the sheet anchor of Europe'.

The sole classical allusion came in the person of Neptune drawn on a float. This was more John Bull than Neptune, the particularly belligerent sea-god pointing his trident at an effigy of Napoleon on a sledge while his attendants held a drawn sabre over the defeated Emperor's head and a pistol to his ear (*A Narrative of the Grand Festival at Yarmouth*, pp. 11–13).

The wording of the placard on the bonfire (overleaf) has echoes of the dying Pitt's last public speech on 9 Nov. 1805, as news of victory at Trafalgar came to London: ' . . . England has saved herself by her exertions, and will, as I trust, save Europe by her example' (J. Ehrman, *The Younger Pitt: The consuming struggle*, p. 808)

² *Norfolkman* T. Pocock, *Horatio Nelson* (The Bodley Head, London, 1987), p. 217

'England has preserved the world'

The unnamed Quaker who wrote to the *Norfolk Chronicle* in 1814 (page 589) had declared that he and like-minded citizens could not support public celebrations as they frequently descended into intemperance and riot. This claim runs counter to the accounts submitted to the Norfolk press recording such events from 1789 to 1814. Unless the papers deliberately suppressed reports of riotousness, as is possible, it would appear to be an unfounded slur on the revellers.

The reports transcribed in this chapter for Letheringsett and Coltishall are typical of the praise accorded the poor for their consistent good conduct, 'regularity' and decorum. Revelry is not equated with drunkenness; diving into bowls of flour is classed as merriment, not riot. The great mass of the population, 'the poor', had borne the weight of national resistance as sturdily as the ratepaying classes, and the fleeting moment of social bonding represented by the celebrations honoured everyone's contribution, rich and poor.

There is no mistaking the distinctly unclassical sentiments of the Great Yarmouth citizenry. Shunning allegory, they opted for recognisable representations of real-life heroes and the foes they had fought.¹ Very many local men had served at sea and on the Continent. Those who stayed behind had cheered the naval and army commanders sailing in and out of their port: it was at Great Yarmouth that Nelson had declared to a delighted crowd in November 1800 that he gloried in being a Norfolk man.² In 1814 effigies and depictions of the 'tyrants' would be consigned to the flames. Yet even when patriotic fervour had been ignited literally and metaphorically there were no reports of civil disorder, nor of drink-fuelled rampages through the streets.

The fears about civilians held at the time and aired by even such a clear-headed and well-informed figure as HRH the Duke of York have been identified in chapter 9. Civilians, so the argument ran, could not be relied on to organise themselves effectively to resist the invader. Military discipline and drill—second nature to line regiments—was necessary if raw Volunteers were to serve alongside seasoned Regulars and if mass evacuations were to be achieved quickly and in good order. Some of the senior professionals (but not Field Marshal Marquis Townshend) had reservations about the 'democratical' tendencies of the free-spirited masses and the fierce local pride which might have impeded effective action.

Thanks to the Royal Navy it was never discovered if these suspicions were well grounded. But the organisation of the public dinners suggests they were not. On these very large occasions hot meals had to be provided swiftly to a mass of people—including young children—totally unaccustomed to synchronised movement in response to given signals. The scenarios are admittedly different. A populace gathering together to receive a free hot meal and beer has a strong incentive to behave in an orderly fashion and is not in the same frame of mind as one responding to an enemy landing.

The documenting of Great Yarmouth's peace celebrations of 19 April 1814 reveals how one town, under the direction of the mayor Jacob Preston and a General Committee, performed prodigious feats of organisation. It took only seven days to devise and execute an event involving 8023 ticket-holders. On the day these were seated at tables 'without the least bustle or confusion', and food and drink were brought to the tables in only a few minutes: 'Extraordinary as it may appear, the whole fifty-eight tables were completely covered in less than seven minutes.' The dinner was conducted 'with as much order and decorum, and with as much comfort, as could have been enjoyed in any private family'.[1]

The various stages of the meal were controlled by the firing of guns to signal the moment to move to the seats, to say grace at each table, to remove the dishes, 'which was done in a very few minutes' (while leaving the beer mugs behind), to say grace after the meal, and to drink the health of the King; a fifth gun triggered a royal salute from the warships moored alongside. A sixth gun thereupon announced the delivery of a pipe and tobacco to every man. A further four-teen toasts were drunk, each preceded by a signal gun and followed by 'three hearty cheers, given in rapid succession along the line, which produced an irristibly exciting effect on the feelings of the spectators'.[2] These spectators were not the participants, but the 20,000 visitors (many probably from the surrounding area) who were parading around the tables during the dinner and soliciting spare food and ale 'which the presidents at the different tables politely grati-fied'.[3]

[1] order A Narrative of the Grand Festival at Yarmouth, pp. 2, 13, 14. The carving was by stewards at each table

[2] toasts A Narrative of the Grand Festival at Yarmouth, pp. 15, 16, 17. An emotional toast was to 'The speedy return of our townsmen imprisoned in France' (p. 17, note)

[3] visitors A Narrative of the Grand Festival at Yarmouth, pp. 17–18

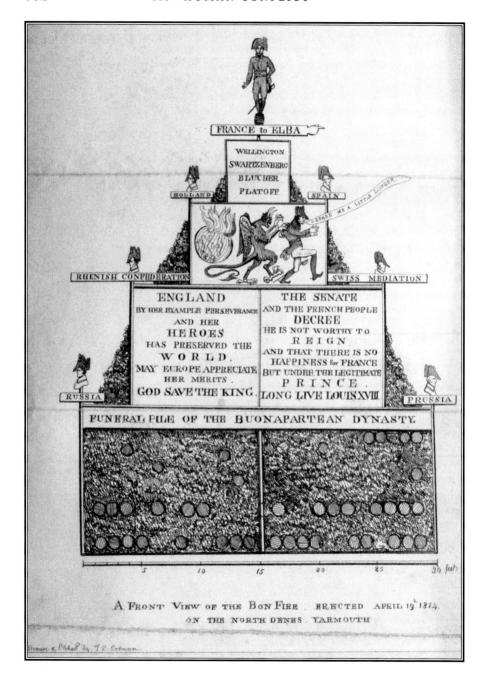

FRANCE to ELBA

WELLINGTON
SWARTZENBERG
BLUCHER
PLATOFF

HOLLAND

SPAIN

SPARE ME A LITTLE LONGER

RHENISH CONFEDERATION

SWISS MEDIATION

ENGLAND
BY HER EXAMPLE PERSEVERANCE
AND HER
HEROES
HAS PRESERVED THE
WORLD.
MAY EUROPE APPRECIATE
HER MERITS.
GOD SAVE THE KING.

THE SENATE
AND THE FRENCH PEOPLE
DECREE
HE IS NOT WORTHY TO
REIGN
AND THAT THERE IS NO
HAPPINESS for FRANCE
BUT UNDER THE LEGITIMATE
PRINCE.
LONG LIVE LOUIS XVIII

RUSSIA

PRUSSIA

FUNERAL PILE OF THE BUONAPARTEAN DYNASTY

A FRONT VIEW OF THE BON FIRE. ERECTED APRIL 19th 1814.
ON THE NORTH DENES. YARMOUTH

The refrain constantly voiced in the press on these occasions was heard again at Yarmouth over 'the multitude of the poorer class of the inhabitants, with happiness beaming in their faces, . . . seated with the most perfect regularity'.[1] These were the masses from whose ranks the Volunteers had been drawn, who had been trusted to take up arms while remaining civilians, and who had not betrayed that trust by turning on the propertied classes. The immense crowd, once more marshalled by means of gunfire, again paraded through the town and onto the Denes to march around the bonfire and receive more beer.[2] There were no accidents, even with the guns and combustibles, and no disorder even after the seventy barrels of strong ale provided that day had been exhausted.[3]

The organisers paid for 6844 pounds of beef, which like the rest of the meal was cooked in large numbers of private homes and some specialist bakeries; much of the provisioning, as at Letheringsett, rested with the female inhabitants. The food supplied not only those at the quayside tables but the residents of the Fishermen's Hospital, gaol and other institutions, bringing the total fed to about nine thousand. Each average beef portion was thus approximately three-quarters of a pound (0.35 kilogram), matching Letheringsett's average in 1801; but Letheringsett's had fallen short while at Great Yarmouth there was food to spare.[4]

[1] *regularity A Narrative of the Grand Festival at Yarmouth*, p. 18

[2] *parade A Narrative of the Grand Festival at Yarmouth*, pp. 18–20. The whole affair was financed by private subscriptions, as at Letheringsett, the total donations—by women as well as men—reaching £1106 (p. 69). The committee recommended that the nicely judged surplus of £35 go to Yarmouth's prisoners of war returning from France (p. 72)

[3] *beer A Narrative of the Grand Festival at Yarmouth*, p. 70. The Yarmouth brewers were not expected to donate that number of barrels, and the beer appears on the expense account

[4] *food A Narrative of the Grand Festival at Yarmouth*, pp. 70, 21–2

---

facing page 'ENGLAND . . . HAS PRESERVED THE WORLD. MAY EUROPE APPRECIATE HER MERITS.' The bonfire on the North Denes at Gt Yarmouth to celebrate the (temporary) cessation of hostilities in Apr. 1814, nine days before Napoleon sailed for Elba.

The Norwich artist John Sell Cotman was drawing master to Dawson and Mary Turner's daughters in their home above the Hall Quay banking firm. He helped with the festivities, including the illustrated seating plan and this elaborate pyre over 30 feet wide and 44 feet high (9 x 13.5 metres), with its array of casks of tar and gunpowder and 'a vast collection of other combustibles' wedged among the furze faggots. It was surmounted by the effigy of the fallen Emperor, his head filled with gunpowder.

The whole town came together for a public dinner for over 8000 people ranged on 58 huge tables along the quayside from Sir Edmund Lacon's brewery at one end to the house of the brewer Samuel Paget at the other, a distance of 856 yards (783 metres).

Donkey races and a pig hunt on the Denes, facing the sea on the sandy spit, preceded the lighting of the bonfire in the presence (it was claimed) of 30,000 spectators [NRO: *Frontispiece by J. S. Cotman to A Narrative of the Grand Festival at Yarmouth on Tuesday the 19th of April 1814 (1814)*]

[1] *heroes* All four were acknowledged, with varying degrees of public awareness, as having the greatest competence and showing resolve when it was most needed. Just one of the quartet appears to have captured the local imagination. Only Dundee-born Adam Duncan was awarded the accolade of having Norfolk public houses named after him, as at Caister-on-Sea, north of Gt Yarmouth, where the King's Head was renamed the Lord Duncan between Sept. 1798 and Sept. 1799 (NRO: C/Sch 1/16)

[2] *French* Napoleon's agreement with the Tsar at Tilsit in July 1807 altered the balance of power in favour of France, for the Russians were deploying in the Mediterranean and off Portugal.

By 1808 France had large numbers of ships in different theatres including the invasion launch-pads of the French harbours and Antwerp. For France's powerful Navy after 1805 see R. Glover, *Britain at Bay*, p. 19

[3] *warships* R. Glover, *Britain at Bay*, pp. 28–9

[4] *martellos* P. Kent, *Fortifications of East Anglia*, pp. 20–2, 59–63, 91–98, 131–4, 145–6

Cotman's view of the bonfire is dominated by a huge placard attributing the victory to England through 'her example, perseverance and her heroes'. Actually it was Scottish heroes who should have been honoured. If any one country in the Union had to be singled out it should have been Scotland. During the height of the invasion scares the crucial blockades were by Admirals Duncan and Keith, both east-coast Scots, while the command of the Eastern and Southern Military Districts, containing the two most vulnerable coasts, were by Generals Craig and Dundas, both from Scottish families. All four were men of proven ability whose achievements spanned decades. The eastern coastal regions were very fortunate that these commanders' postings came at crucial moments for home defence.[1]

Nelson's victory at Trafalgar, while often regarded as decisive and complete, brought only temporary respite. The French Navy regrouped and posed further danger to Great Britain. Villeneuve's Mediterranean fleet, with the Spanish, which Napoleon had intended to deploy to secure safe passage for his Grande Armée on its precarious crossing of the Dover Straits or southern North Sea, was smashed at Trafalgar in October 1805 only *after* the Emperor had drawn his troops away from the coast at Boulogne to attack Austria in late August 1805. Trafalgar did not spark the withdrawal.[2]

Only three years later the warships of France and her allies, including Russia, outnumbered British ships by the large margin of 155 to 113.[3] Invasion thus remained a possibility. Had the threat been removed after 1805 there would have no need to build the hugely expensive line of 29 martello towers up the coast of Essex and Suffolk in 1808–10.[4]

There were no major joyous celebrations between those of 1801 and 1814: not even following another Norfolk captain's victory over the French Navy in the Mediterranean, by William Hoste at Lissa in 1811. While the threat lasted and while British prisoners of war remained in the custody of the French the prevailing mood was one of determined resilience. The sense of thanksgiving occasioned by Napoleon's enforced abdication on 6 April 1814 and the decision to banish him on 11 April was thus all the more intensely felt—until he escaped from Elba in February 1815 and set off on the road to Waterloo.

left and *below* Two martello towers on the Suffolk coast at East Lane, Bawdsey and built at about the time of Mary Hardy's death. Both have been converted from defunct garrisons to houses.

Each armed with three 24-pounders on the roof, the east-coast towers were considerably more formidable than earlier martellos along the south coast.

Years after Trafalgar a French invasion still remained a very real threat   [*MB · 1996*]

By 1814 Mary and William Hardy were lying by their son Raven in the quiet of Letheringsett churchyard. More than half their lives had been spent against the backdrop of war, and their deaths coincided with times of danger for the country. The diarist died 23 March 1809, shortly after the opening of the investigation into the Duke of York which was to unseat this capable prince as Commander-in-Chief, and just after the country had learned of the death at Corunna of General Sir John Moore—another Scot. This was a time when the Peninsular campaign was going badly; and a few months later 235 ships and transports were to set sail across the North Sea on the ill-fated and ineptly-led Walcheren Expedition.[1] The general fast only the month before the diarist's death had been held to implore God's 'blessing on our arms, for the restoration of peace and prosperity'.[2]

Her husband was buried with her in August 1811, when Wellington was enduring reverses in the Peninsula after being forced to raise the second seige of Badajoz and to see his army unable to move through sickness and dysentery.[3]

[1] *Walcheren* E. Longford, *Wellington: The Years of the Sword* (Granada Publishing Ltd, 1971), pp. 214–18

[2] *general fast Norw. Merc.* 4 Feb. 1809

[3] *Peninsula* E. Longford, *Wellington: The Years of the Sword*, pp. 320–3

[1] *King* Linda Colley's depiction of the great celebrations of the King's reign closely mirrors the Hardys' experiences: the public dinners; the key role of women; the preparation of illuminations; and, after the defeat of the Fox–North Coalition, the way the King acted as the focus of national unity (L. Colley, 'The apotheosis of George III', esp. pp. 97, 104–6, 110–14, 120)

[2] *Beryl Cozens-Hardy* Her parents were first cousins once removed: see the family tree in the Epilogue (fig. 4B)

above **From a design by Humphry Repton for a transparency celebrating the introduction of the Norwich Mail service in 1785, with a cameo of George III** [*Norfolk Heritage Centre, Norwich, detail*]

The King was permanently incapacitated and his eldest son newly declared Prince Regent.[1]

It was the Hardys' son and daughter who in their middle and later years prospered in the decades of relative peace (on the international stage, if not in Britain), and it was under William Hardy junior that the Letheringsett estate and the family business reached its apogee. To bid farewell to Mary and William Hardy amid the perils and uncertainties of 1809 and 1811 is untimely, and the Epilogue will carry the tale of their descendants into the twenty-first century.

'They were part of the political nation'

This 39th chapter in the four-volume study can be seen as a microcosm of the diarist's larger world. The barrels of beer given at the great communal celebrations were the end-result of the labour of the Hardys and their workforce from first ploughing the land and sowing the barley seed: malting, brewing, distribution and the careful running of their vertically integrated business have been described in volume 2.

In organising their village festivities the Hardys planned and toiled as a team, just as in their married lives they had joined hands through 44 years of endeavour. They had endured the pressures of the excise service at East Dereham and then at Litcham; they had ventured into tenant farming and managing a maltings and brewery at Coltishall; finally they laid down roots which lasted into modern times at Letheringsett. Their double descendant Beryl Cozens-Hardy died at their old home in 2011 just short of her hundredth birthday and was buried with them in the family vault.[2]

This chapter has portrayed not only harmony over family relationships but the teamwork underpinning the running of a home; the extended family from the diarist's beloved Whissonett helped at moments of greatest striving. This entire volume has highlighted the Hardys' outward-looking approach to life. While active farmers and brewers in the small village they had made their base from 1781 they were not constrained by its boundaries. The wide horizons of the opening chapters of this volume, the family's sociability, and the Hardys' engagement with the political issues of the day and the crises of war and threats of invasion: all formed part of their shared experience and that of their circle.

above Letheringsett churchyard, by the back of the Hall: the last resting place of Mary and William Hardy, their sons Raven and William and many of their Hardy and Cozens-Hardy descendants. They would daily have been able to see the place of their burial from the windows of their home.

The railings above the large brick vault date from 1997. This was taken on the day of the thanksgiving, 23 Apr. 2010, for Jeremy Raven Cozens-Hardy, son of the lawyer and historian Basil. Both had been custodians of a large part of the private family archive, the Cozens-Hardy Collection   [*MB·2010*]

We are left with this most remarkable diary. As a reviewer of the published *Diary of Mary Hardy* put it when reflecting on the significance of the lives of Mary and William Hardy:

> While neither belonging to nor aspiring to join the polite elite of their county, [they] nonetheless exerted influence in the commercial world and were part of the political nation.[1]

Part of the political nation. For a woman with no vote and unable to take up arms it is a considerable tribute. Yet as she looked back on her life Mary Hardy might well have considered her most enduring legacies to be her long marriage and the bringing of her three much-loved children to maturity. Above all she died, as she had lived, fast in the faith.[2] Meeting her Maker, and being reunited with her son Raven, would surely have been among her last thoughts in this world.

[1] *book review* Prof. G.M. Ditchfield, reviewing the four-volume set *The Diary of Mary Hardy* (2013) and the companion volume *The Remaining Diary of Mary Hardy* (also 2013) in the *English Historical Review*, vol. 130, no. 542 (Feb. 2015), p. 219

[2] *fast in the faith Watch ye, stand fast in the faith, quit you like men, be strong*: St Paul's words to the people of Corinth (I Cor. 16, v. 13)

above Letheringsett Hall, 21 July 1890: the
Diamond Wedding of Jeremiah and Mary Ann
Cozens' only child William Hardy Cozens-Hardy
(1806–95), centre, and his wife Sarah (1808–91),
née Theobald, in the invalid carriage. With them
are the surviving seven of their nine children and
other close family, named in the caption opposite.
Laura had died in 1838, Cecilia Willans in 1879.

On inheriting the Letheringsett estate from
William Hardy jnr in 1842 William had taken the
name Cozens-Hardy by royal licence. After his
death his eldest son Clement (far left), his partner
in the maltings and brewery, sold the business and
tied houses to Morgans, the Norwich brewers
[*photograph A.E. Coe, of Norwich, 1890:
Cozens-Hardy Collection*]

right Basil Cozens-Hardy (1885–1976), son of
Sydney, seen here *c.*1933 and in the group photograph (*top*) beside Gladys, the future Lady Cozens-
Hardy and mother of Beryl. He carefully preserved
the family records and published extracts from the
diary in 1957 and 1968 which introduced Mary
Hardy to the public   [*Cozens-Hardy Collection*]

Epilogue

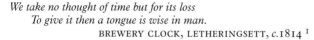

The enduring record

Giving time a tongue

We take no thought of time but for its loss
To give it then a tongue is wise in man.
BREWERY CLOCK, LETHERINGSETT, *c.*1814 [1]

. . . a spontaneous tribute of respect to his memory
And an enduring record of the zeal
With which he supported the cause of
Wesleyan Methodism . . .
EPITAPH TO WILLIAM HARDY JNR, HOLT, 1842 [2]

T HIS IS A DIFFICULT PART of the story to relate. It should in theory be a straightforward matter to tie up the loose ends at the close of this long undertaking and chart the outlines of the family's history in the century or so after Mary Hardy's death. That it is not a simple task is due to her grandson and one of her great-grandsons, Herbert Hardy Cozens-Hardy, the future peer. By 1900 they had destroyed quantities of family papers, obliterated parts of the story and created what might be termed the Letheringsett legend.

Apart from the weeks early in 1820 which marked the brief struggle for life of that grandson's cousin William, the only child of William Hardy junior, there was just one heir

[1] *time* One of three inscriptions on the clock tower built by William Hardy jnr but destroyed in the 1936 fire. The words are from *Night Thoughts*, Edward Young's devotional poem of 1742

[2] *zeal* From the epitaph in Holt Methodist Church believed to have been composed by William's nephew. It was Mary Hardy who introduced her family to Methodism and who first supported the Sunday schools later alluded to in this epitaph. Her legacy too endures

top The brewery clock [? *by Cecilia Willans (1840–79), detail: Cozens-Hardy Collection*]

facing page BACK ROW, standing, from left: Clement (*son*), Sydney (*son*), Herbert (*son; 1st Lord Cozens-Hardy*), ? William (*2nd Lord*) or ? Harry (*sons of Herbert and Theobald*), Edith (*Clement's daughter*), Theobald (*son*), Helen (*Clement's wife*), Sarah Anna (*Theobald's wife*), **William Hardy Cozens-Hardy**, Jeremiah James Colman (*Norwich MP, mustard manufacturer, husband of Caroline*), Ethel Colman (*Caroline's daughter*), James Willans (*husband*

of William's deceased daughter Cecilia and of Cecilia's younger sister Kathleen)
FRONT ROW, seated, from left: Gladys (*Clement's granddaughter*), Agnes Cozens-Hardy (*daughter*), Basil (*Sydney's son*), Jessie (*Sydney's wife*), Winifred Willans (*granddaughter*), SARAH Cozens-Hardy (*in bath chair*), Caroline Colman (*daughter*), Hilda Willans (*granddaughter*), Kathleen Willans (*daughter*). A family tree is overleaf (fig. 4B)

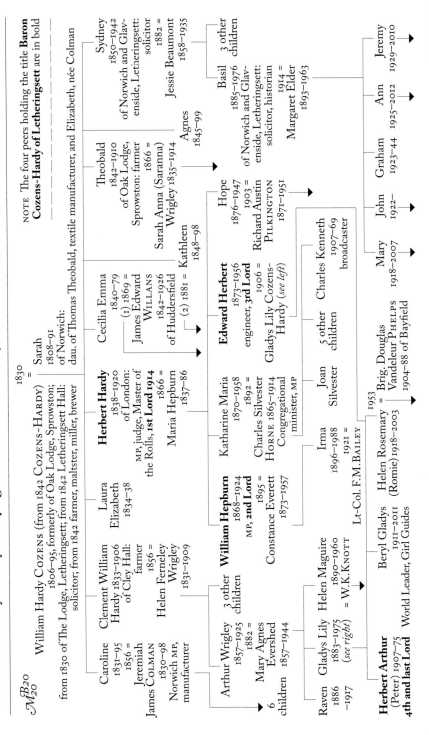

FIGURE 4B
The Cozens-Hardys: Mary Hardy's grandson William Hardy Cozens-Hardy and his descendants (*selective*)

NOTE The four peers holding the title **Baron Cozens-Hardy of Letheringsett** are in bold

to the Letheringsett estate and the family business: Mary Ann's son. William Hardy Cozens-Hardy owed everything to his uncle. His reverence for William shines through in his writings, published and unpublished, as does the lasting love for Letheringsett and its surroundings which he passed on in full measure to all his children.

That love did not extend to the maltings and brewery which had brought the family to the village in 1781. The running down of William Hardy junior's cherished manufacturing concern in the half-century after his death sheds light on the mindset of Mary Hardy's great-grandchildren. With the exception of the eldest great-grandson, Clement (and his son), they showed little taste for the commercial life which the diarist, her husband and son had embraced wholeheartedly. They were moving in new directions.[1]

William Hardy Cozens-Hardy eliminated from the family lore much that concerned central aspects of their moulding or tended to diminish the role in the creation of the village's physical appearance played by his uncle. When in the mid-twentieth century Basil Cozens-Hardy came to publish his history of Letheringsett and edit his great-great-grandmother's diary he showed a flimsy grasp of the family's antecedents. He was only a boy of ten when his grandfather died in April 1895, his faculties intact; but Basil's father Sydney, the youngest of the nine children of William and Sarah Cozens-Hardy, lived to 1942—again with his mind and memory clear to the last (figure 4B, opposite).

Had the older members of the family chosen to pass on to succeeding generations the story of their Letheringsett progenitor's coming to Norfolk there would surely have been many opportunities to do so: they were most united, and on close terms with one another. Instead Basil had perforce to speculate, writing of the diarist's Yorkshire-born husband that he was 'a young farmer' and that 'For some reason now unknown he came south to East Dereham in Norfolk.'[2] When, near the start of my work on this project, I discovered in the National Archives that William Hardy had been *posted* to Norfolk as an excise officer during his twelve years in the service on various postings around the country (as told in volume 1, chapter 2) this came as a complete surprise to the various branches of the family.

[1] *maltings and brewery* These later came back into the family, as we shall see.

The brewery fire of 1936 proved a catalyst. It left a partially demolished set of buildings, defunct for decades, across the road from Letheringsett Hall and over the river from Glavenside. Lord Cozens-Hardy and Basil Cozens-Hardy, as owners of these properties, negotiated with Morgans for the purchase of the maltings and brewery site. In 1943 Lord Cozens-Hardy's son Peter (later the 4th lord), with Basil, became co-owners.

There was no suggestion the buildings could be used for their original purpose

[2] *'now unknown'* B. Cozens-Hardy, *The History of Letheringsett*, p. 64; B. Cozens-Hardy, ed., *Mary Hardy's Diary*, p. 1. He states in both that William Hardy's father was a farmer at Scotton, then in the W. Riding, but I have found no evidence of his occupation.

Basil, in referring to the small farm and maltings at Coltishall, omits to mention in the Diary introduction that William Hardy was the brewery manager there (p. 1). Yet it was the *brewery* which had attracted him

[1] *enquiries at Coltishall* Conversations with Mr Stibbons and Mrs Morse at The Limes, Oct. 1988.
    In Aug. 1990, thanks to a chance encounter on the river with Ivan Spinks, I managed to identify the Hardys' home as Holly Lodge, south of the church (as described in vol. 1 on pp. 465–6)

[2] *tributes* For Sarah Cozens-Hardy (1891), Caroline Colman (1896), her son Alan (1898), Raven Cozens-Hardy (1918), William Hardy Cozens-Hardy (1936), Sydney Cozens-Hardy (1944), and more.
    There is also a very full and scholarly biography of Jeremiah James Colman by his daughter Helen (1905), and Sydney wrote of his Letheringsett home, Glaveside (1935)

[3] *visitors* These included the radical William Cobbett, the Ware malt-factor Joseph Taylor and the Methodist preacher William Stones (see vol. 1, chaps 1, 9 and 10)

[4] *obituaries* The broadsheet *Eastern Daily Press* of 30 Apr. 1895 devoted more than 2½ full-page columns of very small type to the father's life, politics, Methodism and public service. Brewing does not feature at all

Slowly over the years I have tried to crack the outer shell of family tradition to get at the kernel. Basil Cozens-Hardy, genuinely in the dark, had endeavoured to do the same. William Stibbons and his sister Mabel Morse, of Coltishall, told me in 1988 that they had heard of his enquiries many years earlier as to where the Hardys had lived in the village. Nothing then survived in the Cozens-Hardy family memory of where this home had been, and Basil had to drop all mention of its whereabouts in his published works.[1]

What had happened? This was a family passionate about the record. They kept diaries and wrote voluminous letters. When a loved one died they privately circulated long printed tributes, beautifully composed, illustrated and bound.[2] However the Letheringsett photographs show only family groups and the Hall with its gardens and grounds: the idyll. When in July 1880 and 1890 William and Sarah Cozens-Hardy celebrated their Golden and Diamond Weddings the Norwich photographers A.E. Coe were commissioned to capture various scenes treasured by the family. The maltings and brewery, the source of the family's wealth, were ignored.

The days of William Hardy junior were long gone. He had eagerly and proudly shown his visitors the wonders of his brewing concern and reduced even the voluble William Cobbett to speechlessness.[3] The lengthy obituaries in the press to the later partners in the concern, William Hardy Cozens-Hardy and his son Clement, bore almost no mention of their work as maltsters and brewers. Instead the focus was on their public service on the bench and in other fields, and on their religion and their happy family lives.[4]

We have already seen this tendency to sweep aside any part of the tale which did not fit the image they wished to present to the world in William Hardy Cozens-Hardy's suppression of William Mindham's role as architect of the 1818 road bridge at Letheringsett. Although he would have known the true picture he asserted that it was all his uncle's work (volume 1, chapter 10). Thus Basil failed to give credit where it was due. He had absorbed the family lore, and knew nothing of Mindham's many architectural projects for the Hardy and Cozens families at Letheringsett, Holt and Sprowston.

In writing of his wife William Hardy Cozens-Hardy does not reveal that her father was a Norwich textile manufacturer.[1] Yet their daughter Caroline Colman's husband was an eminent and highly respected mustard manufacturer living beside the works in Norwich, Colman's already being a name known nationally and internationally. Such contradictions make it hard to arrive at the truth.

London-based Herbert Hardy Cozens-Hardy, the judge and future first Baron Cozens-Hardy, adopted the stance of his father. Like his brother Sydney and sister Caroline he had a somewhat blinkered vision of Letheringsett. He determinedly destroyed an extremely large cache of family papers in the weeks following his father's death. As a result not one of Mary Hardy's letters survives, and only one each by her husband and son, presumably as they cast light on Herbert's father as a toddler in 1808 and at his marriage in 1830.[2] We are lucky that the five great ledgers in which Mary Hardy's diary were written escaped the purge. These went off to Cley Hall, Clement's home, returning to Letheringsett Hall in the third lord's time.[3] Possibly the malting and brewery ledgers from the Hardys' time were destroyed then. In his letter to Caroline of 9 June 1895 Herbert recounted that he had spent 'many hours' tearing up the family archives and had very much more still to do.[4] Twelve years later he was made Master of the Rolls—keeper of the public record and custodian of the nation's memory.

Later sections in this Epilogue will try to analyse the various reasons for that generation's actions. Factors at work included aversion to alcohol, which for some developed into total abstinence; creeping gentrification coupled with a wish to enter or remain in the professions and not in trade; and a new puritanism fostered by a Dissenting schooling at Amersham Hall for Herbert and his two younger brothers.

Familiarity with Whissonsett, the Ravens' old seat, now ceased. Mary Hardy's maiden name was retained: for Clement's grandson Raven Cozens-Hardy and great-granddaughter Sylvia Mary Raven Lyne, née Knott; also for Basil's son Jeremy Raven Cozens-Hardy, and Jeremy's son Raven and his great-granddaughter Vida Raven. But the Raven homes and occupations were forgotten. Sydney tried to remedy this, and kept in touch for years with James Nathaniel Flaxman, a Somerset schoolmaster who was the grandson of Mary Hawkins, daughter of the diarist's brother Nathaniel.[5]

[1] *father* Thomas Theobald (S. Cozens-Hardy, *Memorials of William Hardy Cozens-Hardy of Letheringsett*, pp. 14–15). See also vol. 2, chap. 11 and *plate 42* in that volume

[2] *two letters* One is the frontispiece to vol. 1, chap. 5 (p. 294); the other is also illustrated in vol. 1 (on p. 630)

[3] *diary* Information from Beryl Cozens-Hardy, 29 Dec. 1994

[4] *letter* Pasted into one of the red albums in the Cozens-Hardy Collection. The family papers were then kept in the gun room at Letheringsett Hall. Herbert does not mention the manuscript diaries of Mary Hardy and Henry Raven, although they also would have been at the Hall in his father's time

[5] *Flaxman* They corresponded 1905–14, Sydney going over to Whissonett to try to locate the Raven graves and learn more. His father had evidently not told him anything of the Raven and Goggs background which had featured so prominently in the Hardys' lives (vol. 1, chaps 3 and 4).

J.N. Flaxman (b.1844) loved Whissonsett from his West Country exile as deeply as the Cozens-Hardys loved Letheringsett

right Whissonsett Church: four of Mary Hardy's descendants at the week-long festival celebrating the two diarists in Aug. 2013.

This was the church of Mary Hardy and Henry Raven. They were christened here and worshipped here, and here she married the 33-year-old excise officer in 1765.

Some of the hundreds of visitors tried their hand at writing diaries of their experience of the exhibition, church, talk, organ recital and Raven trail around the village which formed part of the festivities.

Here Basil Cozens-Hardy's granddaughters Sue Rosser (second from left) and Angela Calvo (right) write diary entries with Angela's daughter Chloe (second from right) and Angela's niece Joanna Ripoll.

Sue came over from Lt Thornage, near Letheringsett; the others had travelled from Spain [*Jean Hart 2013*]

---

[1] *Robert Raven* B. Cozens-Hardy, ed., *Mary Hardy's Diary*, p. 1

[2] *Whissonsett* I am very grateful to Lesley Pegg

Despite this new connection Basil made little headway over the Whissonsett background. He concludes: 'Robert Raven appears to have been a prominent farmer and townsman.'[1] He gives no hint that Robert Raven earned his living as a maltster for much of his life and had earlier followed the family calling of village grocer. Robert's father Henry, mother, brother and son (two Nathaniels) were shopkeepers and manufacturers; his daughter Mary Hardy often refers to her old home as 'the Malthouse' (volume 1, chapter 3).

Mary Hardy's commercial origins explain her easy dealings with shopkeepers and her ability to support her husband and son in their business lives. William Hardy Cozens-Hardy knew these origins intimately. He and his uncle had kept in touch with many members of the Whissonsett family despite the Raven and Goggs diaspora, as we know from his diary and that of his wife and from his annotations to some press cuttings in the family albums. Yet it is only from 1988 and the start of the Mary Hardy project that Whissonsett has fully re-entered Cozens-Hardy consciousness. And the way the home village has adopted its diarists Mary Hardy and Henry Raven is one of the joys of this work.[2]

The picture is not clear-cut. While, as this Epilogue will show, there were key moments when the family chose to shed the traditions which had moulded them, theirs was not a constant progression in the late nineteenth century into landowning and the professions. The Cley Hall branch of the Cozens-Hardys provides a reminder we should be wary of generalisations. David Cannadine, in his penetrating portrait of the Hardys and Cozens-Hardys in the two centuries after Mary Hardy's death, depicts Clement's son Arthur W. Cozens-Hardy, raised at Cley Hall, as enjoying country pursuits at Cley and serving as a JP and on the Board of Guardians. Likewise Arthur's son Raven, killed in October 1917, was 'devoted to country life and country pursuits'.[1]

As a corrective Arthur's great-grandson Richard Lyne points out that Arthur, head of the family after his father's death in 1906, had earned his living through *brewing*:

He actually spent his working life, before he inherited the Letheringsett and Cley estates in 1906, as a brewer based in Burton upon Trent and Kendal working for Evershed's brewery (which later merged with Marstons). He married the daughter of the boss, Sydney Evershed MP.[2]

The ambivalence is striking. That boss's daughter, Mary, compiled a moving tribute to their only son Raven, cut down at Polderhoek leading his platoon in a dawn attack. He was born in 1886 at Kendal in the Lake District, educated at the grammar school there and at Exeter College, Oxford, and worked as a stockbroker in London with Foster & Braithwaite until obtaining his commission early in the First World War. Apart from holidays his life had been spent away from Norfolk. Yet on the title page of his mother's tribute Raven is described as of the 4th Norfolks and Cley Hall. Ancestral associations exerted a strong pull.[3]

The Cozens-Hardys proved a diverse and talented family, the third Lord Cozens-Hardy busy as an electrical engineer in Lancashire for most of his adult life until retiring to Letheringsett Hall in 1938. Many had a strong public-service ethos and devoted their lives to others. Beryl Cozens-Hardy, custodian of the manuscript diary of Mary Hardy, summed up the diarist's descendants in one of our discussions in 1992: 'The Cozens-Hardys have always been workers.'

for her enthusiastic engagement with Mary Hardy over the years and in the exhibitions of 2000 and 2013 which she and others spearheaded.

The Raven and Goggs diaspora is touched on briefly in vol. 1, chaps 3 and 4. In the mid-19th century certain branches of the families emigrated to Canada, the United States, Australia and Tasmania; others moved within England

---

[1] *Cley Hall family* D. Cannadine, *Aspects of Aristocracy: Grandeur and decline in modern Britain* (Yale Univ. Press, London, 1994), p. 189; his study of the Cozens-Hardys is on pp. 184–209

[2] *Richard Lyne* His e-mail to me of 9 Apr. 2015; his mother Sylvia, née Knott, bore Raven as one of her names.

Sporting prowess characterised the family through the generations, Arthur playing county cricket for Westmorland

[3] *Raven* [M. Cozens-Hardy], *A Beloved Memory: Raven Cozens-Hardy* (Cley, 1918), in which Raven emerges as a kind and delightful personality. 'Lovable' is the attribute used repeatedly in others' memories of him

[1] *maltings, brewery and watermill* See vol. 2, chaps 5–8. The mill also receives detailed study in D.W. Durst, *Letheringsett: The industrial history of a Norfolk village* (Norfolk Industrial Archaeology Soc., 2013), a compilation of earlier NIAS articles

[2] *trees* William jnr's plantations in fact

Estate expansion

We parted from Mary and William Hardy in chapter 10. The foundations they had laid were built on to great effect by their surviving son. The dynamic, imaginative William brought the Hall and the enlarged estate, maltings and brewery to the point of their greatest brilliance; he also added the watermill to his diversified portfolio of assets and proceeded to improve and expand its machinery.[1] In the words of his epitaph in Letheringsett Church 'he clothed the once barren hills with foliage.'[2] His life, work and achievements are covered in all four volumes of this study.

left and *facing page* Letheringsett Hall and Church: a magnificent panorama of the east front (far left) rebuilt by William Hardy jnr 1832–34. Bathed in winter sun across the meadow used for village cricket, they were captured in 1892 by Cecilia's son, the talented 20-year-old photographer Gerald Cozens-Hardy Willans.

His grandfather William Hardy Cozens-Hardy, Mary Ann's son, stands to the left of the porch in the shadows by the drawing room wall. The arched window containing brilliantly coloured stained and painted glass has a prominent place over the porch. William Hardy jnr's study to the right of the porch overlooks the brewery across the road, here hidden by the trees on the left.

The long stable block to the north was built by W. H. Cozens-Hardy in 1848 on roughly the site of the Hardys' old chaise house and stables. The River Glaven runs northwards through the meadow this side of the railings. The decaying elm (extreme left), planted about 1814, was felled by him in 1894, seventeen man-days being needed for the task; he observed in his diary that the elms his uncle had planted did not stand for many years.

William Hardy jnr died alone in his study in June 1842, as did Beryl Cozens-Hardy in that same room in September 2011 [*Cozens-Hardy Collection*]

Their ancestral home served as the stimulus for many of the family's undertakings into the late nineteenth century. In the year that his mother died, 1809, William changed the look of the south front completely by superimposing on the existing fenestration the heavy Greek Doric portico which that summer transformed an unremarkable house into one of the county's minor country seats, a position it retains to this day. Further signalling his new status, he carved a park out of part of the manorial estate he had bought in 1800 and out of land released by diverting the main road running past his windows to form a sweeping bend eight years later.

adorned some hills that were not 'barren': this may be more hyperbole by his successor (vol. 1, chaps 9 and 10).

William H. Cozens-Hardy continued the work of afforestation. His coffin was made of estate oak, from a tree he had chosen 30 years earlier (*Eastern Daily Press*, 11 May 1895)

¹ *house* See vol. 1, chaps 7, 9 and 10

² *country seat* David Watkin, then at the start of his long career, analysed the house and gardens: 'Letheringsett Hall, Norfolk', *Country Life*, 5 Jan. 1967, pp. 18–21, with superb 1966 photographs; also J. Musson, 'Restoration and retirement: Peterhouse, Cambridge', *Country Life*, 22 Apr. 2009, pp. 95–6, where Letheringsett Hall is referred to as Watkin's first assignment for *Country Life*. David Watkin died in 2018

facing page **Letheringsett Hall's south front of 1809, with its Greek Doric: a very early example of that order in the Greek Revival** [*photograph A. E. Coe, of Norwich, 1880: Cozens-Hardy Collection*]

right **'Elegant neo-Greek decoration' in 'the surprising but graceful curves of the staircase and landing': David Watkin's praise in 1967 on the work of 1832–33 is quoted more fully in volume 1.**
    William Hardy jnr's MS diary names the architect, Mindham, and the workmen [*Country Life Picture Library 1966*]

The east front of 1832–34, by contrast, followed the L-shaped plan of his parents' time and appears more understated in style. Both phases of rebuilding owed much to William Mindham.¹ By 1834 William had rebuilt his home and malt-kilns and improved and reclad his brewery and tun room. His nephew and heir had only to expand the stables and dig out the lake (for water power to drive the estate sawmill and a greenhouse ram, rather than for ornament) to complete the look of a fine country seat. The Hall was then left largely untouched until in 1936 the third Lord Cozens-Hardy added a small extension to the north.²

Clear evidence of William Hardy junior's progression up the social scale through property acquisition is given in his own jottings of 1838 in which he made a tally from the time of his father's handover in 1797. Under farms, land and houses the biggest item was the purchase in 1800 of the manorial estate of Letheringsett Laviles, with its ancient farmhouse, the Old Hall (£10,500). He bought other Letheringsett properties including the rector's house (£1500), known later as The Lodge, in which he installed his nephew William Hardy Cozens just prior to the younger William's marriage to Sarah Theobald in 1830. He spent £5000 on buying and improving the watermill.

Other major land purchases included Pereers Wood (on the Holt/Letheringsett border), Kelling Wood and Holt Wood, and Wiveton and Cley Marshes. William calculated that he had spent £63,209 in total, although his tally seems very far from complete. There is no mention of *Nelly*, nor of how much the extensive improvements and remodelling of Letheringsett Hall and the maltings and brewery had cost.[1]

[1] *tally* William Hardy jnr's scribbled list is set as a table in vol. 2, chap. 11 (table 2.11.5). He never lived at the Old Hall (Hall Farm).

The list names nine public houses acquired by purchase (others would have been secured by lease), large sums invested in new chapels including £1700 for St Peter's Methodist Chapel in Norwich (as described later), personal gifts to family members including his father's £300 annuity, and a gift of £3500 to his nephew, and large sums in stocks and shares

above The top lawn, 21 July 1880. These Hall gardens, created by William jnr from manor farmland, were embellished by his nephew; the conservatory is also W. H. Cozens-Hardy's.
Here, in seclusion and in contrast with William Hardy's practice, the family played bowls (page 363) [*photograph A.E. Coe, of Norwich, 1880: Cozens-Hardy Collection*]

[1] *acres* Vol. 2, table 2.2.2

The purchase of Cley Marshes was the precursor to a far more significant purchase: the 1294-acre Cley Hall estate, in 1839. William Hardy junior's huge expansion after 1797 of the modest 56 acres of his father's home farm, plus 12 acres bought by his father at Holt, proved beneficial to succeeding generations.[1] William's baby son had died in 1820, but his nephew's marriage brought children a-plenty, and William's acquisitions were put to good use as family homes. William H. Cozens-Hardy's eldest son Clement moved in 1855 into Cley Hall; Theobald got the Sprowston house and farm formerly their father's childhood home. Sydney, on the death of his unmarried sister Agnes in 1899, got The Lodge at Letheringsett, which she had inherited from their father. Clement also got the Mill House (later Glavenside) bought by William Hardy junior in 1827, with the watermill, for £3500. Such a portfolio of the family's land and houses would have been unrecognisable to Mary Hardy.

The story of this expansion has been related in these volumes, and by others. William knew how to seize opportunities as they arose, the death of John Winn Thomlinson of Cley Hall in 1836 putting in train a series of moves which culminated in the 1839 purchase. As a result he could now walk on his own land all the way from his home to the sea.[1]

The tale is not one of hard-headed farm and business development alone. A deep, lasting love infused the writings of the nineteenth-century family in relation to Letheringsett in particular. These accounts reached their apogee in the tribute of Sydney Cozens-Hardy to Glavenside, the name he gave in 1902 to his sunny Mill House country home with the river flowing through its carefully tended gardens. He and his wife Jessie decided they would prefer to live there rather than at The Lodge, which gave them less scope for one of her passions, landscape gardening. In 1900 Clement and Sydney swapped properties, Clement taking The Lodge while continuing to live at Cley Hall, and Sydney gaining vacant possession of the Mill House in 1901. 'A source of joy and happiness', in his words, it became a much-loved retreat from working life in Norwich.[2]

above Creating a country seat—and rick-burning: William Hardy jnr's building diary for 19 Jan. 1833, when Letheringsett Hall's east window was put in. This contained the quirky heraldic glass, depicting flowers, trees and acorns and probably designed by Edmund Bartell jnr; it is seen in colour in volume 1 (*plate 50*).

Here the village carpenter James Tinker is taken off work on the architraves around the first-floor doors to help put out an arson attack on a farmer's stacks [*Cozens-Hardy Collection*]

[1] *expansion* See vol. 1, chaps 4 and 7 for Sprowston; vol. 1, chap. 10; and vol. 3, chap. 5 for the creation of an estate village. William in 1840 owned 2026 acres in total.

For Letheringsett properties in the 19th and 20th centuries see B. Cozens-Hardy, *The History of Letheringsett*, pp. 104–64.

John Ebdon tells the Cley Hall story, with many maps and illustrations: 'History of the Cley Hall Estate: The emergence of the Hardys 1839–1855', *The Glaven Historian*, no. 12 (2010), pp. 83–94; 'History of the Cley Hall Estate, pt 2', *The Glaven Historian*, no. 14 (2014), pp. 61–84

[2] *Glavenside* S. Cozens-Hardy, *Glavenside* (Norwich, 1935), pp. 1–5, 11. It was also his son Basil's home where, overlooking the grounds gently sloping to the river, he wrote his many books and articles.

The house is seen in *plate 50*, in the group photograph for the Norfolk and Norwich Archaeological Society's 150th-birthday trip to Letheringsett in 1996 in celebration of earlier visits organised by Basil when excursion secretary of the society. The Norfolk Industrial Archaeological Society shared the trip

below Detail of a large portrait of the farmer Joseph Wiley (d.1855 aged 52), of Buxton Lodge, beside Buxton Watermill. He married Mary Cozens (1802–37), the half-sister of W.H. Cozens-Hardy. Like her mother she died young of tuberculosis, having borne Joseph six children 1826–36.

In 1832 Joseph Wiley accidentally killed his brother-in-law's first cousin and best friend Jeremiah Cozens, of London, while out shooting (page 406 and *plate 36*) [*courtesy Reginald and Felicity Wiley*]

above Lt Plumstead Manor House, seat of the descendants of Mary Hardy's son-in-law Jeremiah Cozens by his first wife Mary Petchell (1774–1805); aged 39, he married Mary Ann Hardy in the year of his wife's death. Under Mary Ann's marriage settlement the Sprowston property that became her marital home could not be devised by Jeremiah to his elder children Mary and Jeremiah jnr (1804–29). The Hardys, who settled £7000 on her as a marriage portion, also ensured that the valuable Sprowston farmland just outside Norwich remained with the Letheringsett estate.

W.H. Cozens-Hardy installed his son Theobald in 1865 in his old home known later as Oak Lodge, Sprowston. Joseph and Mary Wiley's son Jeremiah Cozens Wiley (b.1833) and his Danish wife Camilla Fugl moved to Lt Plumstead and raised a family. In 1896 W.H. Cozens-Hardy's executors sold the Sprowston land for housing, the house staying with Theobald and his family   [*MB·2003*]

---

[1] *male ultimogeniture* Inheritance by the youngest son, common under manorial law in central Norfolk in the 18th and early 19th centuries: see vol. 1, chaps 3 and 4

When William Hardy Cozens-Hardy died in 1895 he was careful to keep the various properties all within the ownership of his eldest son. Unlike his grandmother Mary Hardy he evidently did not favour the system of male ultimogeniture.[1] The maltings, brewery and tied houses similarly were devised to Clement alone. Having the diverse estates intact kept the family within the category of lesser gentry, as Pam

Barnes describes in her study of Norfolk landowners from the late nineteenth century. Her map shows the Letheringsett estate, including Cley and Sprowston, at its height to have been at the top end of the county's smaller estates in 1883, totalling 2929 acres.[1]

When times became hard, having land suited to housing proved a great asset. This proved true at Sprowston, where the land which Jeremiah Cozens had farmed was sold:

The Cozens-Hardy family of Letheringsett owned particularly valuable land only two miles from the centre of Norwich in Sprowston and Old Catton, having frontages on to three main roads and situated in 'one of the most populous suburbs'. This land was sold in 1896, following the death of William H. Cozens-Hardy the previous year, and much of it was bought for comparatively high-density housing in terraces. 483 acres realised £16,745, double the value of agricultural land.[2]

The needs of a huge family meant that assets had to go. At the time of their 1890 Diamond Wedding William and Sarah Cozens-Hardy had seven surviving children, 26 grandchildren and five great-grandchildren (with many more to come). This concluding part of the Hardy story sketches the disintegration of the unified estate: first the sale in 1896 of the maltings, brewery and public houses and, concurrently, the Sprowston farmland—but not the farmhouse, Mary Ann's marital home, known in her time as Sprowston Villa and later as Oak Lodge; also the Holt farm and wood (the original purchase in 1796 by William Hardy senior becoming part of the grounds of Gresham's School in the early twentieth century); and, piecemeal over a century, the Cley Hall estate. Part of William Hardy junior's Cley Marshes, sold after the death of Arthur W. Cozens-Hardy in 1925, became the first nature reserve to be owned by the Norfolk Naturalists' Trust.[3] In 1992 the nephew of the fourth Lord Cozens-Hardy, John Phelps, sold Letheringsett Hall, Hall Farm and the estate to Robert Carter. He also sold the Letheringsett maltings and brewery which, as we shall see, had come back into Cozens-Hardy ownership in 1943.

Apart from the obvious need to help support a very large family in difficult times for country houses and agriculture from the 1870s there were other pressures, not least the mindset of individual family members. They just did not

[1] *lesser gentry* Pam Barnes, *Norfolk Landowners since 1880* (CEAS, Norwich, 1993), pp. 9, 87. Others in this lesser category included the Gurneys of Sprowston Hall and the Jodrells of Bayfield Hall; also the Custances of Weston, Durrants of Scottow, Macks of Tunstead and Marshams of Stratton Strawless (p. 87)

[2] *Sprowston* P. Barnes, *Norfolk Landowners since 1880*, p. 63. She reproduces the 1896 sale catalogue's opening page facing p. 51

[3] *Cley Marshes* Letter to me from Beryl Cozens-Hardy, 1 May 1989.
Letheringsett Hall and estate were bought by Edward H. Cozens-Hardy, later the third lord, in 1918 from his father-in-law Arthur. Thus from 1918 to 1920 the first lord was his *son's* tenant, not his nephew's. Riverside Farm in Letheringsett was sold to Basil, also Drewery's Farm in Lt Thornage: all had been W.H. Cozens-Hardy's.
There is a very large archive of Cley papers and maps in Basil Cozens-Hardy's uncatalogued deposits in the Norfolk Record Office.
Some Cley papers remain with the family, including a map of the estate of William Woodbine, Esq. at Cley, by J.

Burcham 1792; also the MS inventory and valuation of three of Clement's farms by Salter, Simpson & Sons 1906

[1] *aversion to inherited wealth* eg by John Wells (d.1736), the Coltishall brewer (vol. 2, chap. 8)

[2] *letters* Pasted into the family albums.
Even to a visiting former and future Prime Minister the close bonds of family love were very evident at Letheringsett. Catherine and William E. Gladstone wrote a two-page letter 20 July 1890 from 27 Grosvenor Square to congratulate William and Sarah on their Diamond Wedding, 'earnestly hoping that all may be blessed unto you and yours and continue to give the comfort of seeing happy and loved faces around to cheer and help. We often think of our delightful visit and of all the kindness we received' (Cozens-Hardy Collection).
Published tributes to family members refer to the sustaining power of Letheringsett's beauty: eg C. Colman, *In Memoriam: Sarah Cozens-Hardy* (Norwich, 1891), pp. 5, 6

[3] *schools* See vol. 1, chap. 6

view themselves as brewers, and, as seen with a few other figures in this study, some expressed a desire to carve out a living by their brains and not rely on inherited wealth.[1] These issues will be explored in the following sections.

Gentrification and ennoblement

The Cozens-Hardys expressed their love for each other as openly and naturally as they expressed their love of Letheringsett. The Hall and grounds formed the backdrop to a united, affectionate family, many of their letters to one another having survived the purge of papers after the 'patriarch's' death in 1895. Caroline, writing from the Colmans' Carrow works and their seaside retreat at Corton; Herbert, from London, where he practised as a barrister and later judge; and Sydney, from his solicitor's practice in Norwich: these three seem to have been particularly close. In the mid-century the parents too had written lovingly to their children away at school, and continued to do so as the young people grew into adulthood.[2]

That they were sent far away to boarding school marks a significant departure. William and Mary Hardy had, it is true, sent their elder son and their daughter to boarding school, but only for limited periods and to market towns nearby: Raven for less than two years and as a weekly boarder at the Free Grammar School, North Walsham, when he was aged eleven to thirteen; and Mary Ann to an establishment at Fakenham when she was aged ten to nearly thirteen.[3]

William Hardy junior however had displayed a marked reluctance to attend school. With Raven by his side he accepted Coltishall Free School, two minutes' walk from home, until he was nine. Attendance at his next two schools was irregular in the extreme, and he gave up entirely at thirteen. The Free Grammar School at Holt, the forerunner of Gresham's, was probably as glad as he was over the parting of the ways: his whole focus was on malting and brewing. Almost certainly the diarist's children spoke with Norfolk accents. We can see it in their writing, and in Henry Raven's diary. Much later Clement was sent to Greyfriars Priory in Norwich, but the Baptist establishment in Buckinghamshire, Amersham Hall, attended by his three younger brothers may well have diluted or even eradicated any Norfolk intonation.

At the same time boarding schools encouraged a different outlook on life, as Herbert's letters make very clear. He particularly valued his companions at the Dissenting academy as 'gentlemanly boys', comparing them unfavourably with the rougher types he had known when at the Priory School, Norwich, who had to be restrained by corporal punishment—which, he said, was rarely resorted to at Amersham Hall.[1] This was presumably the Greyfriars Priory to which his father had been sent as a day boy from Sprowston and where, under the Unitarian Mr Drummond, William Hardy Cozens had 'learnt little or nothing from his teaching'.[2]

Amersham Hall under Mr West had high academic standards, Herbert in his letters referring to the pressure on the boys to score highly in the London Matriculation Examination; this for some would lead to university entrance. Such considerations were a world away from the attitudes of Mary and William Hardy, who cared not a jot for such matters. The age of the competitive examination had arrived.[3]

As a further consequence of this physical distancing from the home territory Letheringsett became not a place of work and wealth creation, as known for three generations, but a retreat from the world, a sanctuary. Herbert expressed his sentimental attachment in a letter from Letheringsett Hall to his sister Caroline a few days after their father's death. He had just agreed with Clement to take the Hall as his tenant:

Every inch of ground is to me consecrated by the memories of those who are gone, and I believe both Mother and Father would have liked to feel that the garden they so loved would fall to my care. Agnes [their sister] seems much brighter since I told her this morning, and the old retainers and the villagers will, I think, be glad . . . And it will be a good thing for me and for my descendants to have a place to which we can at all times resort for quiet and rest and holiday. Assuredly there is no spot to which my feet will turn more eagerly than to Letheringsett.[4]

The pressures of the world were indeed great. In addition to their exceptionally demanding jobs, Caroline's husband Jeremiah James Colman and her brother Herbert were Liberal MPs for Norwich 1871–95 and north Norfolk 1885–99 respectively. The feelings of the Cozens-Hardy brothers towards Letheringsett were to shape their attitude to the brewery when they came to decide on its fate.

[1] *Herbert* His letter to his mother from school, 6 Oct. 1855, when he was 16. He had a very high opinion of Amersham Hall and the headmaster Ebenezer West (d.1895), and he twice refers in this letter to the 'gentlemanly boys'.
The school moved in 1861 from Buckinghamshire to Caversham, Berks. It educated sons of notable E. Anglian families including some of the Colmans, E.T. Boardman and Sir Samuel Morton Peto's elder sons (C. Binfield, 'Architectural cousinhood', *Religious Dissent in East Anglia*, ed. N. Virgoe and T. Williamson (CEAS, Norwich, 1993), p. 109)

[2] *Priory* S. Cozens-Hardy, *Memorials of William Hardy Cozens-Hardy of Letheringsett*, p. 8. His half-brother Jeremiah went to Mr Pigg's 'academy' in Magdalen Street, Norwich (p. 8; his quotes)

[3] *standards* Expressed by the pupil and also by Ebenezer West himself in his letter to W.H. Cozens-Hardy from the school, 14 Dec. 1854 (Cozens-Hardy Collection)

[4] *consecrated ground* Letter from Herbert H. Cozens-Hardy, 5 May 1895 (Cozens-Hardy Collection). Caroline died two months later

'Fear One': the evolution of the family arms

top Letheringsett Hall: the upper panels of the east window, noted by William as installed 19 Jan. 1833. This is an early display of 'Fear One' as the family motto, also of the chevron coat of arms with two fireballs or grenades   [*MB · 1998*]

above The bookplate of Herbert H. Cozens-Hardy, first Baron Cozens-Hardy of Letheringsett. The crest is a dexter arm embowed (a right arm, bent at the elbow) grasping an eagle's head (Hardy), with a lion rampant (Cozens)   [*Cozens–Hardy Collection*]

top The arms and crest developed from this first representation by William Hardy jnr, seen in the hand-drawn bookplates which may have been his own artwork or that of his friend Edmund Bartell jnr. The motto, a suitably reverent one for a devout family, also appears in this bookplate design   [*Cozens–Hardy Collection*]

above Detail from the railings put up in 1997 by Beryl Cozens-Hardy around the family graves in Letheringsett churchyard, showing the lion rampant fretty (latticed); the dexter arm is also used   [*MB · 2011*]

As recounted in the chapter on Politics, the diarist's husband William styled himself at the polling booth first as an exciseman, then as a beer brewer and lastly, after his retirement in 1797, a gentleman. He was not an esquire. His son William first appears in the 1802 pollbook as a beer brewer, but he very soon became an esquire; as lord of the manor he was entitled to the suffix. William thereupon devised some arms for himself and by 1833 he had become armigerous, as seen opposite.

In his diary for 15 August 1842 William Hardy Cozens recorded that he took the name of Hardy in addition to his present surname 'by virtue of the Queen's License dated this day'.[1] Confirmation, with special instructions over the quartering of the arms, followed in the *London Gazette* on 26 August 1842. The Cozens-Hardy crest combines the right arm holding an eagle's head, for Hardy, and the red lion rampant with its textured, latticed surface (immensely satisfying to photographers in a slanting light), for Cozens.[2] Landowner, with nearly 3000 acres, and resident all the year round on the country seat he loved: the gentrification of Mary Hardy's manufacturer grandson was complete.

His descendant Richard Lyne, reflecting on the family's rise, considered that William Hardy junior had striven to establish their new social status on lasting foundations:

I am sure that you are absolutely right about the 'gentrification' of the family after William Hardy Cozens-Hardy inherited the estate in 1842. I have an inscribed silver plate given to Clement William Cozens-Hardy from his parents on his twenty-first birthday in 1854, which has the family coat of arms heraldically differenced for the son and heir . . .

Looking at William Hardy junior's will (written in 1840), I wonder if this 'gentrification' process might have perhaps begun in part before William Hardy Cozens-Hardy actually took over? In his will, William styles himself as an Esquire and stipulates that William Hardy Cozens should not only take the name of Hardy but the arms as well. So do you think that he might have come to see the future in dynastic terms as well as in business terms?[3]

The family crest can be seen today on many buildings in the Letheringsett area and on bookplates in second-hand bookshops. By the 1870s Mary Hardy's grandson had stamped his mark architecturally, creating the feel of an estate village.

[1] *diary* MS vol. 1, for 1833–55 (Cozens-Hardy Collection)

[2] *royal licence* I am very grateful to Joy Lodey of Etling Green for sending me the printout from the 1842 *Gazette* on 8 Aug. 2013.

In the announcement from Whitehall 15 Aug. 1842 the Queen refers to William Hardy Cozens and his father as gentlemen, as also William Hardy [snr]; but his maternal uncle William Hardy, under the terms of whose will the change of surname was required, is an esquire (*London Gazette*, 26 Aug. 1842, p. 2302).

The announcement also contains the authorisation for the recipient of the licence to bear the arms of Hardy and Cozens quartered, 'such arms being first duly exemplified according to the laws of arms, and recorded in the Heralds' Office' and in the College of Arms.

For the latticed effect see *plate 49*, showing the crest on the clerk's riverside cottage of 1792 at the brewery, remodelled by W.H. Cozens-Hardy

[3] *gentrification* Richard Lyne's e-mail to me of 9 Apr. 2015. I had sent him and other family members an early draft of this Epilogue

¹ *Mindham* Wide eaves, gault brick, blind arcading and associated flint panels (vol. 1, chap. 7)

² *Raven Hardy* For his illness see vol. 1, chap. 5. For the legal profession in the diarist's time and for Raven's articles see vol. 3, chap. 8 and *Diary 2*, app. D2.B.
    The Norwich firm which her great-grandson Sydney founded is now (in 2019) Cozens-Hardy LLP. In his time and his son Basil's it was known as Cozens-Hardy & Jewson

Much of the property, both land and the built environment, was his. He adopted a distinctive architectural style, just as his uncle had done through William Mindham's trademark style, and branded the buildings with his crest.¹ The nephew eschewed Mindham's heavy, imposing classicism, and his form is more vernacular; but both styles rely on texture and plasticity, shown to good effect in the clear Norfolk light.

One further stage in the family's rise to fame followed on 1 July 1914: ennoblement. Herbert H. Cozens-Hardy's schooling had been the springboard, but the pursuit of the Law, by which the peerage was attained, was indeed a throwback to the diarist's time. Her beloved son, her lost Raven, had been halfway through his articles with a North Walsham attorney when he was cut down in 1787. Thereafter a legal career was the choice of many members of the family, including her grandson and two great-grandsons.²

left 'Fair if not beautiful': a Spy cartoon from *Vanity Fair*, 24 Jan. 1901. 'Spy' (Sir Leslie Ward) painted two other cartoons of Herbert Hardy Cozens-Hardy, who made his name as an equity court judge. One of those cartoons is in volume 1, at the end of chapter 2   [*Cozens-Hardy Collection*]

above Sir Herbert Hardy Cozens-Hardy, the Master of the Rolls, a post he held 1907–18. Ennobled in 1914, he retired in 1918 [*miniature by Walter Everitt: Cozens-Hardy Collection*]

above William Hardy Cozens-Hardy's crest is set high up on many of the properties he built or refronted in Letheringsett, Holt and

Lt Thornage (*plate 49*). The rows of knapped-flint houses in Letheringsett, of 1870–71, are known as 'Fear One' Cottages   [*MB·2008*]

The peerage proved relatively short-lived, the title dying out with the passing of the fourth lord, Peter, in 1975 (figure 4B). Interestingly the first lord seems from his own testimony to have been embarrassed by his elevation. A notably unassuming man, he was 'not in favour of hereditary titles' and wished to be known still as the Master of the Rolls and not as Lord Cozens-Hardy; he regarded the House of Lords as 'a relic of the past'.[1] In expressing himself in his direct way he gave renewed life to the Letheringsett legend. To his elder son Willie he wrote:

I trust you will always be a united family. Remember that you have no blue blood in your veins. We come from a middle class puritan stock. I hope you will never forget your origins or forsake the traditions of your family.[2]

'From puritan stock'. Mary Hardy's husband might have spluttered into his tankard on reading this. It offers another

[1] *hereditary titles* His repugnance is stated at length in his unpublished autobiography (p. 27 in the typescript by Basil Cozens-Hardy in the family collection)

[2] *no blue blood* Letter to William Hepburn Cozens-Hardy from Letheringsett Hall 21 Nov. 1918, on the eve of his 80th birthday (Cozens-Hardy Collection). Willie held the peerage 1920–24, having to resign his seat in Parliament on succeeding to the title (*plate 53*)

[1] *William Hardy* His drinking sessions are recorded in *Diary 1* and *Diary 2*; see also vol. 1, chap. 2

[2] *denominations* See vol. 1, chaps 2 and 4; vol. 3, chaps 1–4

[3] *Dissenters* D. Cannadine, *Aspects of Aristocracy*, pp. 185, 208. His study of the family is perceptive and often openly admiring, but a few misconceptions need to be corrected as this influential work is much quoted.

William Hardy jnr never lived at Hall Farm, the old manorial seat which he bought in 1800 (his p. 186); and the improvements he made to his house were all at Letheringsett Hall, his home from the age of eleven. Also William jnr amassed an estate not of 1000 acres (his p. 186) but of over 2000 acres: at Letheringsett, Holt, Saxlingham, Wiveton, Kelling and Cley.

When the Sprowston estate reverted to Jeremiah Cozens' younger son—hardly a 'distant relative' of William jnr (p. 186), but a most beloved nephew whom William had watched over from birth—this was not because Jeremiah Cozens' children by his first wife had predeceased him (his p. 187), but as a result of the terms of Mary Ann's marriage settle-

illustration of the tendency to recast the past which is such a feature of the Cozens-Hardy writings in the two generations after William Hardy junior. William Hardy was never a Nonconformist, and his lifestyle in the Excise, at Coltishall and in the early years at Letheringsett was the reverse of puritanical. His tolerant wife might have observed tartly 'If only', as she recalled how often she had seen him 'not well' or 'ill all day' after a heavy session at the Recruiting Sergeant, or the White Horse, or the King's Head.[1]

Their son William adopted a more sober lifestyle, but was likewise hardly in the puritan mould. While a promoter of the Methodist cause he did not turn his back on the Established Church to which he was committed, on the evidence of his mother's diary. Like her, during much of her later life, he was probably double-minded: both an Anglican and a Wesleyan. And on the Cozens side nothing has been found to show that Jeremiah Cozens senior of Westwick was a Nonconformist, although his wife Emma Hubbard may well have been a Calvinistic Baptist, like their eldest son Jeremiah. The other Cozens children, it is true, were also drawn to various Nonconformist denominations, as were the Theobalds of Norwich, on the maternal side of the 'puritan stock'.[2]

By overstating their puritan, Dissenting antecedents the late-nineteenth-century family constructed a version of their past which evidently appealed to them, but was not solidly grounded in fact. This has implications for those of us who study the family and try to set them in their broad historical context. So all-pervasive is the legend that David Cannadine, guided by the later memoirs and statements, portrays William Hardy senior and junior as Dissenters. Methodists are not Dissenters; and both men were Anglicans.[3]

The Epilogue does not attempt to relate the history of the Cozens-Hardys. The broad sweep of their achievements is compellingly delineated by David Cannadine. The alliterative title he chose for his chapter in *Aspects of Aristocracy*, 'Landowners, Lawyers and Litterateurs: The Cozens-Hardys of Letheringsett', marks them out from the others under his microscope—among them Curzon, Churchill, the Devonshires and Harold Nicolson and Vita Sackville-West. He rightly draws attention to the multi-faceted nature of the family's contribution as magistrates and lawyers, in Parliament and on local councils, in education and journalism, and as poor-law guardians; two of Mary Hardy's descendants, Russell James Colman and Sir Timothy Colman (*plate 54*), have served as Lord Lieutenant of Norfolk.

Referring to William Hardy's original fifty-acre purchase of 1780, Cannadine observes:

> Yet it was from this inauspicious beginning that a dynasty developed which played a major role in the affairs of the county of Norfolk and the city of Norwich for the best part of the next two hundred years.[1]

The legacy of this dynasty has had a direct impact on the writing of this long study of Mary Hardy. Quite apart from the family's massive archive of manuscripts, printed books, maps and photographs (the Cozens-Hardy Collection), a formerly privately-owned library has been invaluable. The Colman Collection, consisting of printed books, pamphlets and engravings and strong on religious tracts, is publicly available in the local studies department of Norwich Library, the Norfolk Heritage Centre. The near-complete run of copies of the *Norwich Mercury* held at the *Eastern Daily Press* offices in the city is again a Colman legacy.[2]

The dustjackets and colour plates chosen for this Burnham Press edition of first the diary and now the world of Mary Hardy have drawn on the bequests to Norwich Castle Museum and Art Gallery of the Norwich School paintings formerly owned by Jeremiah James and Russell James Colman, the husband and son of Mary Hardy's great-granddaughter Caroline. The Stannard painting on the front cover of this volume (also as *plate 21*)—a canvas so large that it envelops the viewer, and so striking in its impact as to take one's breath away—once graced the Colman family homes, as did John Sell Cotman's *Dutch Boats off Yarmouth* (*plate 43*, and seen as the front cover of *Diary 4*).

'The gardens rang with laughter'

This concentration on the hardworking, worthy and God-fearing approach to life of the Letheringsett family should not mask another reality about which we hear little in their writings. Life was also fun, as Sarah Cozens-Hardy tells us.

ment of 1805. It was Hardy money which had secured and expanded the Cozens property, and to Letheringsett it returned

---

[1] *dynasty* D. Cannadine, *Aspects of Aristocracy*, p. 185. The 56 acres were in Letheringsett and Saxlingham (vol. 2)

[2] *Eastern Daily Press* Another of Mary Hardy's descendants, Archibald Cozens-Hardy, son of Theobald, was editor of this regional daily paper for 40 years 1897–1937. He spent all his long life at the Sprowston farmhouse, Oak Lodge

above **Sarah Cozens-Hardy at 78. Her unpublished diary shows her as a spirited, fun-loving young woman who was never idle**
[*photograph A.E. Coe, of Norwich, 1887, detail: Cozens–Hardy Collection*]

Joan Silvester Horne's reply to John Betjeman's poem *Lord Cozens-Hardy*

source   Reproduced by kind permission of David Horne; a printed version is held in the
Cozens-Hardy Collection

note   Joan S. Horne, granddaughter of the 1st Lord Cozens-Hardy, makes play with
Lord Cozens-Hardy, published in the fuller editions of Betjeman's *Collected Poems*

Oh my dear John Betjeman
    Your poem is quite wrong,
You do not know my Letheringsett
    That home where we belong.
How could you glimpse our feelings,
    The love in children's hearts
For every yew and oak tree,
    The farm, the pony carts,
And, most of all, John Betjeman,
    The chestnut on the lawn,
When from the 'Chestnut' bedroom
    We watched that Norfolk dawn.

You never walked with Grandfather
    Once Master of the Rolls,
You never watched him playing
    The village team at bowls.
Nor learnt from him each bird call,
    Nor saw a long-tailed tit—
(On eggs in downy lichened nest
    A pair of birds would sit).
He'd lead us to the stables,
    Or row us on the lake,
At Christmas time we'd take round gifts
    Of tea and fruit and cake.

It may well be, John Betjeman,
    A mausoleum to you—
To us and to our family
    Its mem'ry will renew
Those carefree happy days of old
    When nine of us would go
To spend the weeks at Letheringsett
    And watch the Glaven flow.
The gardens rang with laughter,
    Far happier than most—
I know my darling Grandfather
    Could never be a ghost.

left 'The chestnut on the lawn' recalled by Joan Horne: Letheringsett Hall's entrance porch and east front.

    Betjeman referred in his 1955 poem to the 'Doric portico' (on the south front) round which the grandchildren of the Master of the Rolls played. One of those children disperses the chill of his mood in the warmth of her spirited riposte [*MB·2000*]

Although an exceptionally busy wife and mother, with three children aged under four while she was yet in her mid-twenties, Sarah Cozens-Hardy kept a diary which has survived for 1835 in the family archive. She and William were still at The Lodge, and a great deal fell to her in the way of nursing the sick and offering hospitality to a wide circle of family and friends; at the same time she took a lively interest in politics, religion, legal cases and gardening. When her brother-in-law Edward Blakely arrived on a visit the family trooped off to nearby Bayfield Hall, the home of Henry Jodrell's widow and her second husband George Nathaniel Best. Sarah's diary conjures up the unforgettable image of these serious-minded people, whose thoughts on sermons and election addresses fill their writings, laughing uproariously as they pushed one another over on the wet grass:

[1835] 22 JULY Mr Blakely came. In the morning we took luncheon at Mr Best's summer house and had a great deal of fun. The grass so slippery that a slight push laid us prostrate.

That same sense of fun and laughter is seen in the poem opposite, a riposte by the granddaughter of the first Lord Cozens-Hardy, Joan Silvester Horne, to a strange poem by John Betjeman entitled *Lord Cozens-Hardy*. He never knew the Master of the Rolls: the peer, who stalks the verses as a ghost, died in 1920 when Betjeman was fourteen. His poem is a work of impish imagination drawn from the genius of the place following a visit in 1955, but it reads as oddly savage. From the Doric portico 'Waiting eyes are drawn'—

> To the half-seen mausoleum
> In the oak trees on the hill.

Betjeman fancies the villagers will not go near the root house on the top lawn on starlit November nights—

> For fear of seeing walking
> In the season of All Souls
> That first Lord Cozens-Hardy
> The Master of the Rolls.[1]

Joan's younger brother Kenneth Horne, who spent his life making others laugh, is one of the children she describes as revelling in the Letheringsett gardens and countryside.[2]

[1] *Betjeman's poem* David Cannadine reproduces it in *Aspects of Aristocracy*, p. 209.
It is on the Literary Norfolk website <http://www.literarynorfolk.co.uk/Poems/lord_cozens_hardy.htm>, accessed 9 Aug. 2019.
The poem refers to parts of the Letheringsett Hall gardens: see vol. 1, p. 621. There is no mausoleum, nor has there ever been one.
Various members of the Cozens-Hardy family loved Joan Horne's version and printed it with the original as a greetings card. Her nephew Duncan Gordon wrote to me from Isleworth, Middx on 16 May 2007: 'It ended up OK, because Betjeman had Joan to lunch and they seem to have got on pretty well'

[2] *Kenneth Horne* His father was Charles Silvester Horne, the preacher and MP. Kenneth (1907–69) was the youngest of the seven Horne children (fig. 4B, p. 610). His childish hand is seen in the Letheringsett Hall visitors' book on their many stays.
His own biography *Solo for Horne* (Angus & Robertson, London, 1976) is by Norman Hackforth, the 'mystery voice' of the radio show *Twenty Questions*

1 *Cley Hall* Conversations with Beryl Cozens-Hardy at Letheringsett 1989–98, and with Richard Lyne in Kingston upon Thames 24 Apr. 2015. Both sprang from the Cley Hall branch and told me of its 20th-century Anglican tradition

2 *strong views* Theobald 'never read a novel, never entered a theatre, never played cards' on any day of the week (*Eastern Daily Press* obituary, 18 Feb. 1910). Jeremy Cozens-Hardy would reminisce, in appalled recollection, about the gloom of his grandfather Sydney's Sundays, with no books allowed other than the Bible or a prayer book; newspapers were forbidden; walking was about the only leisure pursuit permitted. Helen Colman, Sydney's niece, observes that 'Music made only a limited appeal to him' and gives instances of his Sabbatarianism: no trains, cars or bicycles were used on Sundays (H.C. Colman, *Sydney Cozens-Hardy: A memoir* (Jarrold & Sons, Norwich, 1944), pp. 75, 63)

3 *newspapers* See chap. 6, the section on newspapers. News items were copied into the diary on Sundays by various members of the 18th-century family

The religious dimension

The question arises of how a family which for its livelihood relied on brewing and supplying beer, and on the supporting activities of farming and malting, could square their manufacturing of demon drink with their social consciences. How far did their religious scruples affect their decisions over the future of the maltings and brewery? The answers are not straightforward. In their letters individual members might express a decided opinion (in this family all opinions were firmly held, and stated forcefully), but was there some underlying consideration not expressed in writing? How far can we take what they said at face value?

First we need to explore the nature of their religion and the extent to which it impinged on the direction of their lives. We have already seen the way Mary Hardy's great-grandsons, unlike her own children and grandson, were sent away to boarding school far from home; three were at a Baptist academy. We have also seen wide variations over religious adherence in the Hardy and Cozens-Hardy family. Some embraced the Church of England, as did the Cley Hall branch after Clement's death in 1906.[1] Others were double-minded: Anglican and Nonconformist. But the family members who influenced the decisions on the fate of the family concern were uncompromisingly Nonconformist in outlook: Caroline, Clement, Herbert, Theobald (while kept at a distance) and Sydney. These last two were also strict Sabbatarians, with strong views on leisure pursuits.[2]

Their strands of Nonconformity varied: Baptist, Congregational and Free Methodist for Caroline; Free Methodist for Clement; a relaxed approach by Herbert, who nonetheless attended his son-in-law C.S. Horne's Congregational meetings in Kensington (Allen Street) and Tottenham Court Road (Whitefield's Tabernacle); Free Methodist for Theobald; and Congregational for Sydney in Norwich (Princes Street) and at Briston, and Free Methodist at Holt. This was one of the legacies of Mary Hardy, the first to adopt Nonconformity. But hers was of a markedly tolerant strain. She was double-minded almost to the last; and Sabbatarianism was far from the Hardys' style then. The family worked on Sundays and expected their men and maidservants to do the same; newspaper extracts too were written up on Sundays.[3]

above Dorothy and Oliver Horne, two of the 1st Lord Cozens-Hardy's grandchildren, photographed by Basil Cozens-Hardy on the footbridge at the Glaven ford in Riverside Road in the early 20th century (seen also on page 47). Joan, author of the skit on John Betjeman, and Kenneth Horne, in later life from *Beyond our Ken* and *Round the Horne*, were their younger sister and brother.

In this period they lived near Tottenham Court Road, where their father served as a Congregational minister. The Letheringsett holidays provided a carefree change from London life   [*Cozens-Hardy Collection*]

More to the point, William Hardy was happy to be seen drinking in public houses on Sundays and conducting a good deal of business there and at home on the Sabbath. To at least the mid-nineteenth century there was no obvious dichotomy between brewing and devout religious observance.[1] Even in Methodist Wales, where temperance was to be taken up far more fervently than in England, beer and Bibles went happily hand in hand until the 1830s.[2]

Mary Hardy's daughter and son carried her standard for Methodism long after her passing. Mary Ann started to accompany her mother to Wesleyan Methodist meetings at Briston in 1797, aged 23; she married Jeremiah Cozens, a Calvinistic Baptist, in 1805. Husband and wife were content each to go their own ways denominationally and to attend one another's meeting houses in Norwich. For Jeremiah this was St Paul's, under Mark Wilks, and for Mary Ann first Cherry Lane and then Calvert Street Wesleyan Methodist.[3]

[1] *dichotomy* Its hardening 1828–72 is charted by Brian Harrison in *Drink and the Victorians: The temperance question in England 1815–1872* (2nd edn Keele Univ. Press, 1994), pp. 167–81

[2] *Wales* B. Glover, *Prince of Ales: The history of brewing in Wales* (Alan Sutton Publishing, Stroud, 1993), pp. 23–7. As in England, parish meetings were customarily held in public houses (p. 24)

[3] *meetings* Described in vol. 3, chaps 3 and 4

¹ *five chapels* Listed by
William in 1838 (vol. 2,
chap. 11, table 2.11.5).
They were all Wesleyan:
Holt (1813 and 1838),
Briston, Aylsham and
St Peter's in Norwich.
   The notes to the table
give details, as also vol.
3, chaps 3 and 4

² *opulent friends* W.
Lorkin, *A Concise His-
tory of the First Estab-
lishment of Wesleyan
Methodism in the City of
Norwich in the year 1754*
(Norwich, 1825), p. 45

³ *donations* The
financial records of St
Peter's Chapel list the
capital sums received
1824–25 from these
two benefactors who
largely paid for the
whole building work
(NRO: FC 27/7)

William Hardy junior, who was to devote some of his
wealth to funding five chapels, came later to Wesleyanism.¹
He took it up regularly only in 1804 when he was aged 34,
and unlike his sister he still continued to attend Church of
England services. The chronicler of Norwich Wesleyanism,
William Lorkin, writes that 'Some of our more opulent
friends subscribed in a most liberal manner,' and the Letheringsett brewer was certainly one of these.² His donation
of £1700 to St Peter's was technically a loan, as also was
Jeremiah Cozens' of £1000 (probably on behalf of his wife),
and both men received interest at four per cent for a few
years; but the 'loans' seem not to have been repaid. By 1849
Jeremiah Cozens' had become part of a consolidated fund.³
However when William's nephew fell out spectacularly with
the Wesleyans in 1850 the Holt sums were seen to be loans.

The significance of William Hardy junior's generosity
towards the Wesleyans lies in the fact that he was both an
'opulent' brewer and an active Nonconformist as late as
1838–39: he evidently felt no unease that his Methodism
might be regarded as undermined by his lifelong trade. Similarly there is no evidence anywhere that his Methodist
nephew experienced qualms over making a living from beer.

The struggle waged in the mid-century by that nephew against the high-handed expulsion by the 1849 Methodist Conference of those pushing for more lay leadership has been outlined in volume 3, chapter 4.[1] The Cozens-Hardy standpoint is contained in the diary of W.H.Cozens-Hardy and in the autobiography of his son Herbert, both unpublished. Given his uncle's history of chapel-building the elder writer objected strongly to what he portrayed as the new Conference attitude towards lay benefactors: 'The chapels are ours, the debts are yours.' In his diary account of his successful Chancery case in resistance to the Wesleyans, heard as the Wesleyan Conference v. Cozens-Hardy and others, he wrote of 'a most iniquitous suit . . . a signal defeat'.[2]

Out of this struggle was born the Wesleyan Reform Movement, or Free Methodists. They represented a fourth strand of Methodism in addition to the Wesleyans, Primitives, and the Calvinistic Methodists of Lady Huntingdon's Connexion—many of whom became Independents (Congregationalists).

[1] *struggle* See also E.J. Bellamy, *Methodism in Holt: A short history* (Holt, 1988), pp. 4–10

[2] *diary* Entry for 7 May 1851 (Cozens-Hardy Collection).

In the Lincoln, Louth and Market Rasen Circuits in Lincolnshire there were 'disastrous secessions' from the Wesleyans: 'over half the rural membership in these circuits was lost, never to be regained' (J. Obelkevich, *Religion and Rural Society: South Lindsey 1825–1875* (Clarendon Press, Oxford, 1976), p. 184)

facing page St Peter's Chapel, Norwich, also known as Lady Lane Chapel, facing St Peter Mancroft. This Wesleyan Methodist chapel was demolished to make way for the Norwich Central Library of 1963. William Hardy jnr and his brother-in-law Jeremiah Cozens (for Mary Ann) were major contributors to its building in 1824 [*J. Sillett 1828*]

left Holt Methodist Church of 1862–63, on Obelisk Plain; William Hardy jnr's large mural tablet was moved here from the 1838 Holt chapel when his nephew broke away from the Wesleyans. W.H. Cozens-Hardy fought a Chancery case in 1851 which led to the formation of the Wesleyan Reformers, also known as the Free Methodists and the United Methodists, in reaction to what he saw as Methodist Conference tyranny.

He built this very large, prominently-sited church at his own expense, using as his architect Thomas Jekyll. It is a most unusual Nonconformist chapel, its lancet windows Early English in inspiration, and has striking polychromatic brickwork [*MB·2011*]

[1] *abstainers* B. Harrison, *Drink and the Victorians*, pp. 167–8. The figures relate just to ministers. The Primitive Methodists in 1848 represented 19%, the Calvinistic Methodists 12%. John Wesley had not seen anything strange in recommending 'soft warm ale' to ease the parched throats of his preachers (*Minutes of the Methodist Conferences*, vol. 1 (London, 1812), p. 21). This injunction came in Wesley's closing words to his first Conference

[2] *toddler* See, eg, his grandmother's account of his stay in 1808 (*Diary 4*: 16 May–21 June 1808, and notes)

[3] *diary* The sharp frost meant the temperature was 20 degrees below freezing (12°F, or −11°C) *inside* the brewery: '*Icicles of 6 inches in length* were even seen *inside* the Brewhouse and *the Cocks were also frozen*' (Cozens-Hardy Collection; his italics)

[4] *steep* Vol. 2, chap. 6

[5] *letter book* These are his rough copies, probably drafted first in the book and then copied in best as the outgoing letter. Most are in shorthand, presumably using Holdsworth & Aldridge's system known to many in the family and taught by John Cozens

The embracing of a stricter type of Nonconformity by the younger generation of Cozens-Hardys was to have a profound effect on the fate of the maltings and brewery. The religious dimension mattered; and the particular denomination mattered. Some Nonconformists were overwhelmingly more likely by the mid-century to be more temperance-minded than Anglicans or Wesleyans, with the congregations following the lead of their ministers.

Of 566 clerical total abstainers in 1848, just four per cent were Anglican. The Congregationalists (Herbert and Sydney Cozens-Hardy's future spiritual home) by contrast represented one-quarter; the Baptists fifteen per cent. The Wesleyans contributed only five per cent, and as late as 1841 the Wesleyan Conference *condemned* teetotalism. The future however lay with the non-drinkers: 'The pioneering teetotal ministers were relatively energetic, and became influential in the [temperance] movement.'[1]

A family dilemma: to brew or not to brew

When William Hardy Cozens succeeded his uncle as owner of the maltings, brewery and tied houses and added the name Hardy to his surname he had had a very long time to prepare for this moment. His fond grandparents had loved having him as a toddler to stay with them, and relations between Sprowston and Letheringsett remained very close throughout his childhood and youth.[2] Installed by his uncle at The Lodge, Letheringsett from 1830 he had twelve years to learn the trade while also practising as a rural solicitor. He was being prepared for the handover when death should claim the master craftsman and entrepreneur.

However there is little to show he ever had the feel for business that had marked his uncle and grandfather's time in charge. The first reference in his diary to malting, brewing or wholesaling comes on 18 April 1849, *sixteen years* after the opening of the volume—and then when marvelling at the severe weather rather than at any development across the road.[3] As recounted in volume 2, the capacity of the steep, the gauge of a maltings' production levels, was halved from 80 coombs to 40 coombs on his watch.[4]

His letter book 1850–57 has survived, and shows he kept the innkeepers on a shorter rein than had his predecessors.[5]

The past and the future: the sill to the barley steep of 1814

above and *right* In 1814 William Hardy jnr rebuilt the brick steep or cistern for the barley in the lean-to at the south end of his Letheringsett maltings (volume 2, chapter 6) [*MB · 2004, 2014*]

below William placed a date stone (left) on the east-facing outer wall of the steep.

In 2014 the builders converting the maltings and brewery to housing moved the date stone to a prominent position (right) at the west end of the steep, which had become a wide alley leading from the brewery yard to the riverside cottage [*MB · 2001, 2014*]

above Lt Walsingham: the Bull, centrally placed facing Shirehall Plain. The outlet is never mentioned by Mary Hardy or Henry Raven and is not included by William Hardy jnr in his acquisitions 1797–1838 (volume 2, table 2.11.5). It came late to the Letheringsett property portfolio [*MB · 2011*]

right From William Hardy Cozens-Hardy's letter book, containing copies of his outgoing corrrespondence: a brusque missive 26 Apr. 1852 to the Bull's innkeeper Gilbert Hunt. 'I must request peremptorily that you will deliver me or any agent the key of the house . . .; and unless you do so I shall be compelled to take legal means to eject you.'

Hunt had only recently arrived. Like so many he did not last, White's 1854 Norfolk directory showing Thomas Stribling in charge. The house was sold with 28 other Cozens-Hardy tied houses to Morgans on 12 Mar. 1896   [*Cozens-Hardy Collection*]

He writes with verve and brusqueness when dealing with innkeepers, as seen opposite. To Robert Harper, of the Buck, Syderstone, an outlet secured by William Hardy junior for the brewery in 1792, he wrote on 18 November 1852:

Sir, Notwithstanding the business you are doing your debt is yearly increasing till it now amounts to more than £200. I must therefore request that you will send £2 extra every time the cart goes, to reduce this heavy balance.

I shall be glad if you will come over once a year to settle the account.[1]

His uncle and grandfather had occasionally allowed debts for beer and rent to mount to a rather greater extent. In 1804 the innkeeper at the Crown, Southrepps had owed nearly £300, William Hardy junior's accounts logging the details of many other large debts which had built up over the years.[2] His successor as brewer had a firm way of ejecting unsatisfactory retailers like one Mr Bullock. To Jonas Raven at the Red Lion at Hindolveston he wrote:

Sir, If Bullock wishes to quit immediately you may take possession, but if he refuses to leave I can get him out at a month's notice. I will thank you to let me know what he intends to do and whether you can come to any understanding as to his quitting.[3]

As well as installing a modern wedge-wire floor in the malt-kilns (volume 2, chapter 6) he made an addition to the complex: the open-fronted cart house erected against the west wall of the malthouse near the malt-mill and waterwheel (illustrated overleaf). The new building does not feature on Manning's detailed map of Letheringsett of 1834.[4]

The maltings and brewery were gradually being run down; so too the outlets. The Norwich auctioneer and valuer C.C. Rix Spelman, who surveyed all thirty tied houses in June 1895, a few weeks after W.H. Cozens-Hardy's death on 29 April, observed in his report that he found them 'generally in good substantial repair, but they are old-fashioned houses and require some external painting and renovating'.[5] The family knew by then that they were going to part with the business; it was not to have a large injection of capital. Arriving at that decision had taken many years and had involved intense family debate. Sydney's temperament had been pivotal to the outcome.

[1] *every time the cart goes* On every beer delivery (Letter book, Cozens-Hardy Collection).
See the Gazetteer at the end of vol. 2 for details of the outlets

[2] *accounts* Transcribed in *Diary 4*, app. D4.B; see also the tables of debts in vol. 2, chap. 11

[3] *Hindolveston* Letter book of W.H. Cozens-Hardy, 19 June 1852 (Cozens-Hardy Collection).
The later years of his diary similarly have almost nothing on the maltings, brewery and public houses. Instead they contain a great deal on politics, the weather and gardening: he was quite obsessive about his dahlias.
He was keenly interested in the water-mill upstream, which he also owned, as water power fascinated him. The last decades of his diary reveal him as absorbed in constructing the lake and repairing the brewery reservoir, the pipes, cascade, mill dam and sluices

[4] *map* Seen in colour in vols 1 and 2 and on the rear dustjacket of vol. 2

[5] *old-fashioned* Quoted and discussed in vol. 2, chap. 10, in the section 'Into the nineteenth century'. Spelman's report, held in the Cozens-Hardy archive, is dated 22 June 1895

right The fate of the Letheringsett brewery hangs on the outcome of these discussions in 1867 between the owner William Hardy Cozens-Hardy and his elder sons Clement (aged 34) and Herbert (28) over the future of the business. The part played by Sydney (aged 17), the youngest son, will determine the issue.

This opening letter in the debate is from the father, from Manchester on 29 July 1867, addressed to Clement, long settled at Cley Hall. The father had told Sydney 'some time ago that it would be very desirable for him to turn his attention to the Brewing and Malting business. There is you know a pretty good and steady trade already established which is capable of considerable improvement . . .'

He then admits that he himself has 'not had any practical experience in the business' [*Cozens-Hardy Collection*]

---

[1] *Burton* The very course Clement's elder son Arthur was to adopt, as seen earlier, and suggesting perhaps that as late as *c.*1875 Clement was holding out for a continuation of the business with an eye to the succession.

Clement went into partnership with his father in 1877 as Cozens-Hardy & Son, signalling continuity

[2] *private customers* The private trade became important for brewers after the deregulation of 1830 (T.R. Gourvish and R.G. Wilson, *The British Brewing Industry 1830–1980* (Cambridge Univ. Press, 1994), pp. 65–6). After the Beer Act, and the loss of tax

The opening salvo had been launched on 29 July 1867 by William Hardy Cozens-Hardy (above); Sydney had just left Amersham Hall. The father was canvassing the views of his two elder sons as to whether Sydney should be trained in the family business. Clement replied speedily on 3 August, agreeing that 'if Sydney would like it' (in the event the condition by which the plan failed) it would be good for him to emulate 'Young Bullard' (of the Norwich brewing family) who had been sent to Burton upon Trent in Staffordshire to learn the trade.[1] Clement showed some grasp of the matter, pointing his father in the direction not of increasing production and a continued reliance on the tied trade but (and perhaps as a more genteel way of earning a living) of expanding the existing very meagre private-customer base.[2]

The initial response of the barrister son Herbert in London on 17 October 1867 followed a conversation over his father's redrafting of his will and took a very different line:

left The Letheringsett brewery yard, 23 June 2001; the tun room casts its shadow across the yard. This addition to the complex, against the malthouse's west wall, was built almost certainly by W.H. Cozens-Hardy after 1842: it has none of the architectural distinction of his uncle's style. The three arched bays of the ground floor (later boarded with doors) proclaim its original function as an open-fronted cart house.

It later became a piggery, the name by which Jeremy Cozens-Hardy, a former owner, habitually called it. A petrol pump, still in place in 1993 and a memento of the brewery's days as a base for a motor haulage company, stood where the broken pallets rest against the wall. The central opening at first-floor level was probably for pitching hay into the hayloft from a cart or wagon.

Work is seen progressing on repairs to the kiln roofs following restoration of the cowls by Gainsborough Construction Ltd of Thaxted, Essex, the firm which had bought the maltings and brewery from Robert Carter in May 2000; the new cowls had gone up on 22 June 2001. The malt-kilns were set aside as a bat sanctuary   [*MB · 2001*]

right Precision-made mid-grey bricks lining the floor of the malthouse steep, revealed during restoration and conversion in 2014 by the new owners D. and M. Hickling Properties Ltd of Roughton, near Cromer.

Henry Raven called such bricks 'clinkers', a local dialect word for bricks fired at very high temperatures in the kiln. They would then become non-porous, and thus suited to wet areas such as breweries and wash houses.

The steep's capacity was altered as production rose and fell. An 80-coomb steep under William Hardy jnr, it had shrunk to 40 coombs—its size when William Hardy had bought the business in 1780—by the time of the sale to Morgans in 1896   [*MB · 2014*]

I understood you to say that you intend to leave Sydney the brewery and public houses and to bring him up as a brewer. But is it desirable to split up the Letheringsett property? Ought not the Hall and the premises immediately opposite to go together . . .?

advantages, much private brewing ceased, the gentry turning to wholesale brewers' ales

¹ *no magisterial duties*
It is not at all clear
why Herbert should
consider that anyone
not living at the Hall
was thereby precluded
from serving on the
bench. He had already
made it clear that it
would not be pressure
of work which would
prevent the brewer
from becoming a JP.
An element of social
snobbery seems to lie
behind his case

² *quartered* As stated
earlier, Clement and
Theobald had been
established on the Cley
and Sprowston estates.
If Sydney were to get
the manufacturing and
retail side (and perhaps
also the Letheringsett
estate) only Herbert
would be out in the
world earning an
independent living

³ *at Letheringsett* As
shown earlier, Herbert
regarded his childhood
home as a retreat, an
escape from working
life for just a while. For
some reason he could
not see it as a place
humming with activity:
malting, brewing, mill-
ing, water engineering
and estate management.
He was also very
outspoken about the
'narrow cliqueishness'
of Norwich solicitors,
seen as 'very dreadful',
and pressed for Sydney
to try his luck in Lon-
don (as quoted more
fully in vol. 3, chap. 8)

Herbert then showed his true hand. He wished to see Sydney enter the professions and not rely on the family business.
Whereas Clement in his letter of 3 August 1867 was expressing the view that 'it would be well for him [Sydney] to see
how some of the best Brewers make their good Ales' the
London-based brother held a contrary view. In the same letter of 17 October, by which time Sydney was trying his hand
at being trained as head brewer, the future peer urged their
father to think again. His mindset, in favouring brainpower
and the professions, implies a rejection of much of what
their Hardy predecessors had built up across more than seventy years, from William Hardy's leaving the Excise in 1769
to the death of his son in 1842, for they had defined themselves, and been seen, as farmers, maltsters and brewers:

Again, is not the brewery business in itself much more suitable as
an addition and appendage to the Hall property than as a separate
affair? There is a large amount of invested capital, which no doubt
yields a good steady income, but even Gales [the head brewer]
does not seem to have enough work to employ him fully. How then
can the business occupy the time of a clerk [? James Simmons] *and*
of a brewer who will have nothing else to do—no farm to manage
or other property to look after, and no magisterial duties? ¹
  Again is it desirable that three out of your four sons should be
quartered upon the estate? ² Ought not two of us at least to try to
get a living by means of our brains?

The barrister son abhorred what he evidently regarded as
'an idle life' at Letheringsett:

All this is irrespective of Sydney's wishes. It may be that he likes
the notion of an idle life at Letheringsett with a competent income
. . . But for my part I have great faith in hard work, especially for a
young man, and I am pretty confident that he would be a better
and a happier man if put into a profession or into some business
which would keep him awake and call forth all his energies . . . I
believe he feels the same.³

He spent the rest of his letter, using his considerable powers
as an advocate, in pressing for Sydney to become a solicitor.
  It is a highly significant expression of his views. In other
letters he states that Caroline and their mother concurred.
Nothing has been retained in the archive of the views of
others in the family—perhaps more letters expunged in the
1895 clearances? He was wrong about there being 'but little

right Sydney Cozens-Hardy (1850–1942), an unsigned, undated caricature probably by his talented sister Cecilia (1840–79). He is seen not long after he had declined, aged 17, to be trained as head brewer after a short spell at the job.

Soon a committed Congregationalist, strict teetotaller and Sabbatarian, giving impassioned addresses in his twenties to the Band of Hope, he was not an obvious type to be head brewer. His father and brothers had agonised over his future and supported him in his chosen career.

Instead of brewing he was articled to J.O. Taylor & Son of Norwich in 1868 just before his 18th birthday and qualified as a solicitor. He founded the Norwich firm later known as Cozens-Hardy & Jewson and then Cozens-Hardy LLP.

By the age of 26 he had built their chambers near Norwich Castle, and went on to serve on the board of numerous charities. David Cannadine characterises Sydney as in his time 'one of the most important men in Norwich' (*Aspects of Aristocracy*, p. 188)   [*Cozens-Hardy Collection*]

society in Norwich which will be congenial to Sydney'. His brother, twelve years his junior, carved out a most distinguished career on the back of his brains, certainly, and of his extraordinary capacity for hard work and public service leading to high office, as described by Professor Cannadine.

As it happens the family confabulations were to be overtaken by Sydney himself. A young man who addressed Band of Hope gatherings on the evils of drink was hardly promising material for a head brewer and putative owner of a brewery.[1] Very soon his course was set not as a brewer but as a solicitor and, in his words to Herbert on 15 November 1867, 'for something more intellectual and requiring more brain work'.[2]

Had Sydney showed the requisite interest and aptitude, and had he been conditioned from childhood as William Hardy junior had been, the brewery might have had the chance to go from strength to strength, modernise its production methods and extend its network of public-house outlets. Instead Clement's advice was overridden. Sydney was not sent away to Burton. Amersham Hall and then

[1] *Band of Hope* The temperance (abstinence) movement: H.C. Colman, *Sydney Cozens-Hardy*, pp. 69, 78

[2] *course set* H.C. Colman, *Sydney Cozens-Hardy*, pp. 19–20. Her memoir contains a great deal on Sydney's upbringing and personality and on the choices available to him.

Cecilia, the sister and caricaturist after whom Sydney named his own daughter (who also died young, at 13), married James E. Willans, uncle of the future Prime Minister Herbert Henry Asquith. The widowed Willans married his sister-in-law Kathleen

¹ *sale* There is a small archive in the Cozens-Hardy Collection on the sale, being papers retained by the vendor.

They are publicly available in the Norfolk Record Office (NRO), catalogued in the BR 10 and BR 160 series and representing the copies of the agreements for the buyers, Morgans. Key documents include BR 160/6, Sale of Tompsons brewery, Norwich to Morgans 1845; and BR 160/38, Clement Cozens-Hardy's sale to Morgans 12 Mar. 1896, with coloured plans of the public houses.

Further records of the 12 individual public houses held copyhold can be found in the manor court book of the appropriate place, eg Fakenham, Stody; Syderstone's court book is in the archives at Houghton Hall. The manor court stewards wrote up the transfers of 1896 in minute detail

² *Spelman* This valuation came into the Cozens-Hardy Collection only in Mar. 1993 through the kindness of Mr L. Price of Cromer, who had bought the Spelman ledger, with its valuation of the tied houses, at an auction.

The 30 outlets were valued at £25,020 (see vol. 2, chap. 10, table 2.10.1)

chapel life, in which he was very actively engaged, would have played their part too. Like his two Norfolk-based brothers and his father he was an active poor-law guardian, and the increasing perception that drink, drunkenness and impoverishment were linked may have helped to shape the younger generation's attitude to brewing.

The fate of the maltings and brewery

Clement may not have given up on the idea of training a younger member of the family to steer the business into the twentieth century. He went into partnership with his father as Cozens-Hardy & Son in 1877 when his son Arthur was already at Burton upon Trent. However by then Arthur's brewing course was set north, for Kendal and Eversheds. When the photographers came to Letheringsett, as noted on page 612, to commemorate the Golden and Diamond Weddings through a series of local scenes—including even the lake and parish church—they had no instructions to capture the maltings, brewery and brewery tap for posterity.

The partnership agreement (opposite), put in writing in 1894 after the Partnership Act, would have eased matters when parting with the business on the older brewer's death. Although Clement, Herbert and Sydney were their father's executors, managing the sale fell to the surviving partner.[1]

Unusually, and in complete contrast with the Coltishall breweries like Wells's (1744) and Hawes's (1841), in volume 2, there was no detailed valuation of the maltings and brewery prior to the sale; nor were any particulars printed. Almost certainly this was envisaged as a private sale, negotiated out of sight, and the lack of a full inventory may suggest that it was obvious from the start that the new owners would not want to malt and brew using the antiquated plant. C.C. Rix Spelman's Letheringsett valuation of 22 June 1895 refers to the freehold brewery with beer stores, stabling, yards and outbuildings including the fixed plant and machinery; and the malthouse for 20 quarters [thus a 40-coomb steep] and malt store; also the cottage and garden adjoining occupied by the coachman. He valued them at a very modest £1450.[2]

The 1895 valuation gives no clue as to production levels. As the business was not advertised the newspapers are no help. In fact, the maltings and brewery were not publicly on

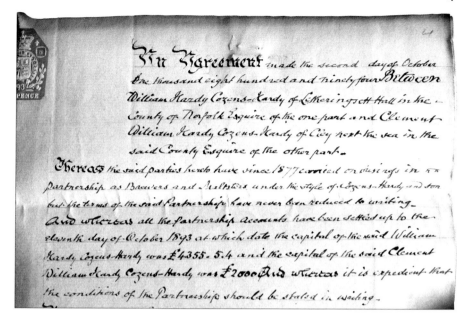

above The preamble to the partnership agreement between William Hardy Cozens-Hardy and his eldest son Clement, 2 Oct. 1894. The partnership had been formed in 1877, but following legislation in 1890 they had now to commit the terms to paper.

The maltings and brewery appear under-capitalised. The father had £4355 tied up in the business and Clement £2000. Clement was taking a minimum of £350 p.a. from the profits, and his father the residue—which may have been less, a later clause referring to £250 as his share of the profits. A century earlier, in 1797, William Hardy's annual profit had been £2170 (volume 2, table 2.11.4).

All repairs to the 30 public houses were to be at the charge of the father, whose private property they were to remain; he alone also received their rents, totalling £485 p.a.

On his father's death Clement was to have the option of buying all 30 tied houses for £8000 (an option he took on 3 June 1895). This was just under one-third of their market value. The thirty were professionally valued in June 1895 at £25,020.

The agreement was witnessed by the brewery clerk, James Simmons. Nearly seven months later the senior partner died [NRO: BR 10/1, *Copyhold papers of the Bell, Fakenham 1763–1896*]

the market between 1780 and 1998—an extraordinary testament to the resilience of the family connection over four generations and then to the desire for privacy by various parties over negotiations during the twentieth century.[1]

Economics did not favour manufacturing at Lethering-sett. The railway station, which had come to Holt in 1884, stood much too far distant to offer any possibility of a goods

[1] *annual production levels* The only firm figures date from William Hardy's time: 2000 barrels of strong beer in 1795–96, and 2100 in 1796–97 (vol. 2, chap. 11, table 2.11.4)

¹ *ceased* Letheringsett WI Village Notes, vol. 1, typed, unpag. (Cozens-Hardy Collection).

Margaret Cozens-Hardy was very active in the organisation and helped with the notes' preparation. She would have known the true situation from her husband Basil, whom she had married in 1914, and from her father-in-law Sydney. (Basil was also teetotal, like Sydney.)

Some of the other WI members would have been the sisters, wives, widows and daughters of the old workforce, so it is very likely to be an authoritative statement

yard close to the brewery. The nearby ports, as seen in chapter 5, had silted badly and offered no prospect of bulk shipment unless by lightering and transhipment on leaving the quays. The rural hinterland had no rapidly increasing population thirsty for beer. The men, about whom we hear hardly a word in the surviving records in the family archive after William Hardy junior's death, would have faced a very uncertain future indeed. Strangely, we are not told whether malting and brewing did in fact cease immediately. However a terse entry in the two-volume Letheringsett Women's Institute Village Notes, prepared in 1937, states categorically that 'Beer ceased to be brewed in the Brewery in 1895.' ¹

Three long conveyances, on large legal paper, document the details of the sale; all are dated 12 March 1896. The three are not consistently between the same named parties, as copyhold properties could not be transferred to a firm or company but only to a named individual. Clement William

right The Cozens-Hardys did not take photographs of their maltings, brewery, brewery tap or watermill; nor did they photograph members of the workforce.

This undated image survives in the archive. He is Richard Cooper, one of the brewery carpenters. Seen here extensively retouched as it was in poor condition, it was not taken by the professionals such as Sawyer & Bird or A.E. Coe whom his employers used.

Another blurred image, and a mid-20th-century addition to the archive, shows the workforce at the end of the brewery's working days (opposite page). Cooper stands in the front row, second from the right.

In his *History of Letheringsett* (p. 153) Basil Cozens-Hardy states that Richard Cooper was one of the first trustees of the Primitive Methodist Chapel built in 1898 on land in Riverside Road given by Clement Cozens-Hardy. We can surmise that the carpenter was also teetotal   [*Cozens-Hardy Collection*]

The Letheringsett brewery team in 1895 or 1896: the last brew?

above A tiny, faded image, a mid-20th-century gift to the family archive, is seen here greatly enlarged and enhanced. The employees of the Letheringsett brewery line up in the yard at the close of its working days; Morgans would have made the purchase to acquire the tied estate, an out-of-date brewery not being an economic proposition.

This moment was probably organised by the men, who are seen by the south wall of the brewhouse and malt-mill. Their tools denote their trade: the drayman's apron, the malt shovel, the carpenter's tool, the paint tin.

Basil Cozens-Hardy has named almost all the men. William High (left of centre, front) was killed when delivering at Wighton on 16 Dec. 1908. His son Walter, who had kept the undated photograph, served as Sydney and Basil's gardener at their Letheringsett home for 60 years; he was also a special constable for 38 years and retired in 1962.

There is no clerk in the group. The central figure, Jeremiah Mortram, seems to be holding a tankard. Does it contain the last brew? [*gift of Walter High 1953: Cozens-Hardy Collection*]

BACK ROW, from left: Herbert Chapman (*bricklayer*), John Loynes (*bricklayer*), [unidentified figure], Alfred Boyce (*driver*), Herbert 'Fiddler' Lines (*bricklayer*)
CENTRE ROW, from left: Billy Eastaugh (*carpenter, wheelwright*), Alfred Moore, Walter Pratt (*gardener*), 'Young' Tom Lines

FRONT ROW, from left: Esrom Boyce (1840–1926) (*carpenter*), Buck Loades (*painter*), Charles 'Podger' Moore (maltster), William High (*1st drayman*), Jeremiah Mortram (*3rd drayman*), 'Big' Jack Lines (*2nd drayman*), George High (*maltster*), Richard Cooper (*carpenter*), Ernest Loades (*painter*)

[1] *sale* The three conveyances are in the Cozens-Hardy Collection. Clement's side of the transaction was handled by Cozens-Hardy & Jewson, Sydney's firm; Clement's son Ferneley (1862–1918), a Norwich lawyer, handled the copyholds. William H. Cozens-Hardy's will dated 19 Oct. 1891 (proved in the Norwich District Registry 29 June 1895) named three of his sons, Clement, Herbert and Sydney, as his executors. Clement had scrupulously sought their permission and authority to pursue the sale. Theobald, as so often in the family discussions, seems to have been sidelined

[2] *water* See vol. 1, chaps 7 and 10 and vol. 2, chap. 7. The scope of the 15 covenants was wide, giving the family the right to inspect the waterwheel and culvert. The new owners could not put up a chimney, and had to keep the river and sluices clear of mud

[3] *manor courts* See vol. 2, chap. 9

[4] *Morgans* A.P. Davison, *Justly Celebrated Ales: A directory of Norfolk brewers 1850–1990* (Brewery History Soc., 1991), pp. 28–9. (The Letheringsett entry (p. 20) is very inaccurate)

Hardy Cozens-Hardy sold the maltings, brewery and 29 outlets to Morgans Brewery Co. Ltd, of the King Street Old Brewery, Norwich (the Conisford home of the Tompsons' brewery in the Hardys' time) for £29,000. The King's Head, Letheringsett was not named in the sale. The twelve copyhold tied houses comprised £11,700 of the total.[1]

The principal conveyance, with a plan of the brewery and water systems, detailed the freehold maltings and brewery and the restrictive covenants. The parties were 'the vendor' Clement, of Cley Hall; his brother Herbert, of 50 Ladbroke Grove, Notting Hill, 'Middlesex' (now London), 'the mortgagee'; and Morgans Brewery. Herbert was involved as in 1890 he had made a loan of £12,000 to his father on the security of rights of way and water rights now passing from Clement, as heir and vendor, to Morgans. Additionally Herbert, as Clement's tenant, faced a loss of amenity at the hands of the brewery's new owners if care was not taken to protect him and his successors at the Hall over the use of the brewery reservoir (built in 1787 in the Brewhouse Pightle) which also supplied the Hall with drinking water.[2] More restrictive covenants followed when Sydney acquired the Mill House in 1901, as he wished to protect himself from unsightly developments over the river from his grounds.

The second conveyance was between Clement and one named director of Morgans, William John Morgan, of Alexandra Mansions, Prince of Wales Road, Norwich. It related to the twelve named copyhold tied houses; like the others, many of these had parcels of land attached. The unfortunate director had then to embark on a Norfolk tour to be admitted to each outlet in their respective manor courts.[3] He was a busy man: Morgans had bought four breweries since 1889.[4] The third conveyance named as parties the executors Clement, Herbert and Sydney, and Morgans Brewery, and related to the seventeen freehold public houses.

Spelman's valuation of 1895 had amounted to a total of £26,470. This figure included the King's Head, Letheringsett, beside the brewery (valued at £850). It is not stated why the outlet was withdrawn from the negotiations, but given its location opposite the Hall the family may have wished to retain control over its future. The sale went through at £29,000, stamp duty being calculated at £3000. The Brew-

left Letheringsett
as a branch store for
Morgans ginger beer:
four stoneware, two-
tone bottles, one (right)
still with its internal
screw stopper.

Letheringsett, listed
between Newcastle-on-
Tyne and Yarmouth, is
one of twelve stores;
other places include
Holt and King's Lynn.
The bottles date from
the early 20th century.
By 1925 Morgans had
let the brewery site to
the motor haulage
contractors Warne &
Bicknell, who stored
lorries and fuel there.

Basil Cozens-Hardy
states that in the early
years of their owner-
ship Morgans brewed
ginger beer at Lether-
ingsett. It was a very
short-lived enterprise.
They did not brew beer
[*Author's collection*]

house Pightle, the field which, as explained in volumes 1
and 2, had been sold with the maltings and brewery from
the mid-eighteenth century onwards and which contained
the vital reservoir on its slopes, went to Morgans.

'For a short while', in Basil Cozens-Hardy's words, Morgans brewed not beer but ginger beer at Letheringsett.[1]
They fast realised that even this limited operation had to
cease, and by 1906 Letheringsett was merely a branch store
for their ginger beer, as the lettering on the many surviving
stoneware bottles attests. As a result the company no longer
needed liquor from the reservoir.[2] Malting, if it had continued at all, also ended. A bombshell followed. Sydney
Cozens-Hardy wrote to Herbert on 2 May 1906 with news
that Morgans were prepared to sell back the brewery and
maltings to the family. Clement's son Ferneley reported
that his father had called on him just before his death:

[1] *ginger beer* B. Cozens-
Hardy, *The History of
Letheringsett*, p. 154. He
has almost nothing on
the sale of the brewery

[2] *water* A later confirmation is held in a public
archive. Morgans'
surveyor told the firm
they could 'give up the
right to take water from
the reservoir' (NRO: BR
10/1, Letter from Fred-
erick Lacey, 4 June
1907)

[1] *Sydney* Letter in the Cozens-Hardy Collection. Ferneley bore a family name from his mother Helen's side

[2] *fire* Reported in the *Eastern Daily Press* the next day and transcribed in full as an inset in vol. 2, chap. 7. The carpenter's shop, closed in 1896 on the sale to Morgans, became a fire-engine house, later Fire Station Cottage

[3] *fire engine* Letheringsett WI Village Notes, vol. 1, unpag.

above 'The clock gave its dying chime at 4.30 am and directly afterwards crashed with the roof' (*Eastern Daily Press*, 25 Apr. 1936). The brewery clock's west face, from an archive photograph [*Cozens-Hardy Collection*]

Ferneley said it was about Morgans closing the malthouse and ginger beer factory. He said that Morgans had written to him [Ferneley], informing him of this, and suggested that I [Sydney] might like to purchase! They said the building would make good stables!! [1]

Sydney told his brother that he considered the malthouse and other buildings would be 'a white elephant' as far as he was concerned, although he would be interested in acquiring the fire station and the riverside cottage, which could be useful for a gardener or coachman. (William Hardy had built the cottage against the malthouse east wall in 1792 for his clerk, although its first occupant was his millwright. In 1896 the Hall coachman Robert Moore lived there.) In 1906 the Cozens-Hardys declined to buy any of the buildings.

In the end the maltings and brewery were let by Morgans to Warne & Bicknell, motor haulage contractors. When the disastrous fire struck on Friday 24 April 1936 it was a mercy the underground petrol tank in the yard did not explode. Two lorries and a steam wagon were destroyed. The malt-mill and brewery complex, except for the tun room, were gutted. The waterwheel in its tunnel did not escape and was left a charred ruin; Mindham's imposing brewery clock crashed to the ground after sounding its dying chime. The malthouse, steep, kilns, cart house, stables, cottage and Cooper's former carpenter's shop survived.[2] Ironically a fire engine given to the parish by Herbert Cozens-Hardy in 1901, a manual Merryweather housed right by the brewery, had been handed over to Holt four years before the fire.[3]

In 1937 the brewery site was let to a local farmer until shortly before John Phelps's sale in 1992 of the Letheringsett Hall estate, maltings, brewery and Brewhouse Pightle to Robert Carter, John Phelps retaining ownership of the King's Head and Letheringsett Watermill. For nearly 55 years the brewery hosted agricultural machinery, pigs and straw bales. Gaping holes were gashed in the sides of the malthouse and tun room to house vehicles; floor pamments were ripped out. Their upper floors removed, the cool, dim, ivy-clad malthouse and tun room faced one another quietly across the dishevelled yard: two cathedral-like spaces.

This unwanted, broken, crippled site, its original building line created by William Hardy junior savagely shaved after

left Converting the south end of the malt-house, 29 Mar. 2013.

This view from the steep shows an internal wall being built to separate two of five homes newly being created out of the huge structure [*Christopher Bird 2013*]

---

[1] *new building line* Illustrated in vol. 1, chap. 10; vol. 2, chap. 7; and *Diary 3*, pp. 3, 77

[2] *sale* Further restrictive covenants were imposed, and old ones dropped where no longer needed (Cozens-Hardy Collection).
Basil's son Jeremy sold that side of the family's share in the maltings and brewery in exchange for land.
On his death in 1975 Peter, the 4th Lord Cozens-Hardy, left the whole site, with the Hall estate and other properties, in trust to John, the son of his sister Rosemary (Romie) Phelps

the fire to improve road safety, found itself, at Basil Cozens-Hardy's instigation, back in the family fold in the dark days of the Second World War.[1] The third Lord Cozens-Hardy, Herbert's younger son, had retired from Pilkingtons in Lancashire and he too wanted the site back in the control of the family. With his wife Gladys, daughter of the Kendal brewer Arthur Cozens-Hardy, he came to live permanently at Letheringsett Hall in 1938. In April 1943 Morgans sold Glaven Cottage (the clerk's cottage of 1792) to Basil Cozens-Hardy; they also sold the maltings and brewery to Basil and to Lord Cozens-Hardy's only son the Hon. Herbert Arthur Cozens-Hardy (known as Peter) as co-owners.[2]

From 1992 successive owners engaged in a twenty-year attempt to obtain planning permission for converting the buildings to housing. Early in 2013 Derek and Melanie Hickling, the husband-and-wife team trading as D. and M. Hickling Properties Ltd, began the long task of conversion in as sympathetic and sensitive a manner as possible.[3] The first of nine homes came onto the market in the spring of 2015. The malthouse, cart house, tun room, stables and riverside cottage, handsomely refashioned, had come into their own.

[3] *successive owners* I am extremely grateful to John Phelps, Mr and Mrs Carter, Ian Irvine-Fynn of Gainsborough Construction, and Mr and Mrs Hickling and their foreman Martin Bridges and the building team for allowing my family and me to wander at will around the site and take photographs 1989–2014

1 *the mould* For the national scene see L. Richmond and A. Turton, eds, *The Brewing Industry: A guide to historical records* (Manchester Univ. Press, 1990), with an overview by Richard Wilson (pp. 1–20). He characterises the mid- to late-1890s as 'years of exceptional prosperity for brewers' (p. 8)—chosen by the Cozens-Hardys as the very moment at which to shed their concern

2 *short-lived* See the detailed analysis of ownership structure and outcomes in T.R. Gourvish and R.G. Wilson, *The British Brewing Industry 1830–1980*, pp. 226–66

3 *predecessors* John Brereton, John Priest and Henry Hagon; Priest was bankrupted (vol. 2, chap. 8)

4 *partnership* C. Clark, *The British Malting Industry since 1830* (The Hambledon Press, London, 1998), p 92. She analyses partnerships in malting and brewing and also training the young, and gives a wealth of examples (pp. 92–103). She too stresses the short-lived ownership of most businesses (p. 92), and confirms that 'not all partnerships, especially those between fathers and sons, involved formal

The third-generation syndrome

The tale of the Letheringsett concern constitutes a pleasant change for business historians. The voices of the articulate Hardy and Cozens-Hardy family animate what is usually, up to about 1870, a silent commercial scene. Even thereafter, lists of assets, debts and wages and the appointment and shedding of partners and directors tend to form the standard bill of fare. The Coltishall and Letheringsett breweries are unusually well documented for their time; additionally the diaries of Mary Hardy and Henry Raven provide a feast in a very early period in business history terms. The experience of the Hardys and Cozens-Hardys in many aspects fitted the mould; in other ways they broke free of it.[1]

Firstly they can be judged as quite exceptionally successful just by owning and directly running their concern through four generations. In the eighteenth and nineteenth centuries most traders' time proved short-lived.[2] None of William Hardy's three Letheringsett predecessors had been able to pass on the torch to the next generation.[3]

At Coltishall too there had been remarkable continuity. In the early eighteenth century the Browne, Wells and Ives families founded manufacturing dynasties lasting three generations; Hawes later lasted two. Two indomitable widows, Sarah Ives and her daughter-in-law Rose, were instrumental in keeping the threatened business afloat until their sons John and Chapman could take over (volume 2).

Choosing to appoint a manager—not a course considered at Letheringsett, on the evidence of the surviving papers—enabled the owners to extend their years in the industry. John Wells's preference for a series of managers enabled first William Hardy and then Siday Hawes to establish themselves firmly as practitioners. External forces were ranged on the manufacturer's side for upriver Broadland maltings and breweries set deep in the hinterland: Geldeston and Beccles too enjoyed good river communication with the sea. Bringing coal direct to the business and being able to despatch the produce by water proved a notable advantage.

When William Hardy Cozens-Hardy made his 44-year-old son a partner in 1877 he was following the trend in the industry; incorporation as a limited company, the choice of Morgans in 1887, was not the norm.[4] The most effective way of achieving continuity was to train up the next generation, as William Hardy had done and as his son had tried to do.

Family capitalism, and the well-worn path from manufacturing and trade into the professions, land and gentility, has been debated for centuries. The business stereotype is presented as spanning three generations. The founder is a man (it is almost always a man) with energy and imagination. His successor (often a talented son, or perhaps a keen nephew) is even more adept at expanding the business and takes it to its apogee. The original focus becomes diffused in the third generation. Fresh interests are pursued (as recorded by William Hardy Cozens-Hardy in his diary), and the young ones find they have no heart for the daily grind.[1]

The grind had without doubt become harder by W.H. Cozens-Hardy's time, for he took over in 1842 just as the first railways were about to transform familiar patterns of distribution. Goods trains steamed over rivers and estuaries, crossed valleys, and made bulk carriage an entirely different proposition. As touched on earlier, by the 1880s malting and brewing would have become a struggle at Letheringsett. Morgans' near-immediate cessation of manufacturing in this inhospitable territory is telling. The future lay elsewhere, with investment in multi-floored, mechanised maltings and breweries beside goods yards, as at East Dereham and Beccles stations or by the quays of Great Yarmouth.

Again as illustrated by Morgans in the late nineteeth century, concentration was becoming the way ahead. There was a steep rise in larger brewing concerns; smaller ones were obliterated.[2] The third and fourth generations at Letheringsett could not be expected to withstand this juggernaut. Cozens-Hardy & Son was squeezed out, just as other long-established breweries not especially well placed, as at Reepham, Fakenham and Wymondham, were being absorbed or shut down, preyed on for their tied estate. Coltishall's last wholesale brewery, despite all its advantages, closed in 1841; some of the larger maltings lasted far longer, into the 1930s.

Even making allowance for all these adverse developments we are left with a nagging doubt. *Could* Letheringsett have turned itself around? Why were the minds and hearts of the Cozens-Hardys no longer in their malting and brewing,[3] many years before new forces gave them little room for

arrangements (p. 94): here the Cozens-Hardys fit the mould.

Like Clyde Binfield in 'Architectural cousinhood', Christine Clark identifies malting families bound by networks of kinship and shared religious belief. Very many manufacturers were Dissenters (pp. 96–103)

[1] *third generation* The problem of ensuring a smooth succession is examined in a 'family business' edition of the journal *Business History* (vol. 35, no. 4 (Oct. 1993)). See esp. the studies by G. Jones and M.B. Rose, 'Family capitalism', pp. 1–16; R. Church, 'The family firm in industrial capitalism: International perspectives on hypotheses and history' (pp. 17–31); and S. Nenadić, 'The small family firm in Victorian Britain' (pp. 86–96)

[2] *concentration* T.R. Gourvish and R.G. Wilson, *The British Brewing Industry 1830–1980*, p. 126; L. Pearson, *British Breweries: An architectural history* (The Hambledon Press, London, 1999), p. 4

[3] *minds and hearts* Nowhere in his 30-page autobiography, with its anguished reflections and self-analysis, does Herbert H. Cozens-

Hardy mention even a word about the maltings and brewery. As Sydney thought, they were a white elephant

---

[1] *debate* F.M.L. Thompson guides us through the issues, as raised by Weber, Wiener, Rubinstein and others, eg as to whether gentlemanly values caused a loss of the industrial spirit: *Gentrification and the Enterprise Culture: Britain 1780–1980* (Oxford Univ. Press, 2001); see esp. pp. 1–13, 122–61

[2] *Smith, Defoe* Discussed by F.M.L. Thompson, *Gentrification and the Enterprise Culture*, p. 9

[3] *farming projects* See vol. 2, chaps 2 and 4

manoeuvre? With the notable exception of Clement, who stuck out for a brewing future the longest, his generation had suppressed their manufacturing gene. In the end there was no brewery for Clement's son Arthur to come home to.

Many commentators have identified a visible pivot point around 1850–70. But eighteenth-century observers had much to say on gentrification long before then, and well before it had become a disputed area of academic debate.[1] F.M.L. Thompson quotes Adam Smith's adage: 'Merchants are commonly ambitious of becoming country gentlemen;' Daniel Defoe, an acute observer, too had watched the merchant turn into the gentleman and landowner.[2] In many ways the Letheringsett maltings and brewery were fortunate in having as their hands-on owner for 45 years an inventive man who, while expanding his house and country estate and venturing into shipping, chapel-building and assorted new farming projects, still devoted himself to the craft and business model he had revelled in since childhood.[3] Despite his rise in social status William Hardy junior never cast aside that early love.

right A living text: descendants of 'Podger' Moore, the Letheringsett maltster seen in the group photograph of 1895/96 (page 649). When the faded image went up on the website for Mary Hardy's diary in summer 2013 it caught the attention of the great-great-grand-daughter of Charles 'Podger' Moore.

Teri Warsop, née Moore, and her son Arnie, of Sparham, then came to the Whissonsett festival in Aug. 2013. They are seen here in the same pose as Podger's, holding a malt shovel from the exhibition. This image too was uploaded to the website, in Aug. 2013: now [in 2019] <https://www.burnham-press.co.uk/6-june-2013-norwich-a-talk-on-malting-and-brewing>.

Teri and Arnie are descended not only from three generations of Letheringsett maltsters but from the river engineer employed by the Hardys for dredging the Glaven and maintaining the waterwheel culvert, Jeremiah Moore (d.1818 aged 68)   [*Jean Hart 2013*]

A living text

The Diary volumes came out in 2013, some years before these volumes of commentary and analysis could follow. It soon became clear that readers were responding enthusiastically. The feedback was exciting; the tone of the reviews unexpectedly positive, given the diarists' terse written style.[1] The introduction common to each volume of *Mary Hardy and her World* contains my own reflections (pages xii–xvii), but as the 32-year project draws to a close I should like to give two instances of readers' interaction with the material by drawing on threads from this final volume. They relate to the brewery workforce photograph (on page 649) and to the long-disused staithes (chronicled in chapters 2, 3 and 4).

The indexes to the four Diary volumes name many hundreds of people in Mary Hardy's circle. Family historians, reading about the lives of their forebears, can flesh out the bones of parish register entries of baptism, marriage and burial. The eighteenth century, predating the photographic era, is in some ways still the Dark Ages. It is also well outside the reach of oral-history evidence, even allowing for the way the human lifespan leaps the centuries. As a child I spent months a year on the Broads with my parents and wandered the lanes and creeks of riverside villages such as Coltishall, then the home berth of our boat. Just 17½ years separate the life of my father from the life of Mary Hardy's daughter, with whose birth at Coltishall the diary opens in 1773. The diary was to become for me a living, breathing text.

So it has proved for some of the family and local historians, writers and researchers who have contacted me at the talks and seminars I have given since 2006,[2] or on receiving the compliments slip packaged with the books; others use the contact form on the publishers' website.[3] On chancing on a news item on the website Teresa (Teri) Warsop and her son Arnie came to the Whissonsett festival of 2013, as described opposite. She had been researching the Letheringsett maltster Podger Moore, who lived at Little Thornage across the Glaven from Letheringsett. The internet search engine had drawn her to the Burnham Press website—and to the photograph of her ancestor with his brother and other workmates. The Diary volumes even chronicle the working lives of a few of her family from Mary Hardy's time.[4]

[1] *book reviews* Extracts from the five principal Diary reviews 2013–15 are given at the start of this volume, before the half-title page

[2] *talks* As the Letheringsett maltings and brewery came on the market in 2015 in their new guise as homes I gave a talk on their history, at the invitation of the parish clerk Louise Stevens.
It was held on 4 June 2015 in a packed Letheringsett Village Hall, built in 1910 by Herbert Hardy Cozens-Hardy as a gift to the village.
Some of the talks feature as posts on the News pages of the Burnham Press website

[3] *contact form* On the Burnham Press website, as of 2019: <https://www.burnham-press.co.uk/burnham-press/contact-us>

[4] *Podger Moore* Teri Warsop brought her family tree on her Whissonsett visit. Podger was born Charles Moore at Thornage in 1852; his younger brother Alfred Moore stands behind him in the photograph.
Jeremiah Moore, the river specialist, was a member of Mary Hardy's Wesleyan cottage meeting at Letheringsett in 1808 (vol. 3, chap. 4)

¹ *Panxworth* Following a talk I gave to the Norfolk Wherry Trust in Ludham Village Hall in Oct. 2014 I was invited by Richard Bond and Mundy Ellis to write 'When working boats sailed from Panxworth Staithe' (published in the *Marshland Mardler*, the magazine for Upton, S. Walsham, Ranworth and Panxworth (Dec. 2014), pp. 9, 11)

² *channel* Des O'Brien's e-mail to me of 15 Jan. 2015. (LiDAR imaging is used for shoreline mapping and hydrographic surveying.) The images he sent to me clearly show the outlines of a very wide waterway—which it once needed to be to accommodate the 40-ton keel *Trial* (see the illustrations in chap. 2, under 'Navigating the waterway', and chap. 4, 'Firm data from the Gt Yarmouth register').

I am very grateful to David Pooley, owner of 60 acres at Panxworth Carrs, for allowing me to walk round the area upstream from the old staithe, and to Richard Bond for leading me on the exploration in Apr. 2015

³ *micro-brewery* This possibility was explored by Basil Cozens-Hardy's son John in the 1980s. In July 1990 Ray Ashworth, co-founder

Articles written for various local history and specialist journals and published from 2010 onwards have sparked interest from readers who find they trigger new lines of thinking. Desmond O'Brien, a landscape history student at the University of East Anglia (UEA), is one such. Living near the Broads at Panxworth, ancestral home of the Cozens family, he was struck by a short piece I wrote in 2014 for a magazine circulated in his area.¹

As a research tool he uses LiDAR imaging (Light Detection and Ranging), a remote sensing method for examining the surface of the Earth three-dimensionally from the air using light in the form of a pulsed laser. He called up the LiDAR imaging for Panxworth at the point where the parish borders South Walsham Inner Broad (seen opposite, and as described in chapter 4). The LiDAR results show how much wider the stream had once been where the Panxworth keels berthed at the staithe in 1795:

> The Google Earth image of this area is interesting in itself, although it now shows no watercourse of note. Being a landscape history student it occurred to me that field drainage locally, as part of general improvements in agricultural methods, may have had some bearing on the apparent disappearance of the waterway . . .
>
> The LiDAR images are attached. I was rather surprised by the apparent breadth and extent of the channel they appear to reveal, in comparison with other satellite imagery and Environment Agency mapping of the area.²

The rivers and broads are fast clogging up and narrowing; carr woodland is spreading across once open waterways (*plate 57*). The old, laborious ways of dredging and of mowing the banks for marsh litter, thus preventing the growth of invasive vegetation, are not cost-effective in an age which no longer turns to these once great highways for trade. Tourism, pleasure boating, other leisure activities and ecological projects have replaced a centuries-old economy. Malting at Letheringsett would similarly prove hopelessly uneconomic now, although a craft micro-brewery could have established itself there.³

left The likely area of old Panxworth Staithe, on the northern Broads. Home berth of two keels in the 1795 register, it is viewed looking towards the Inner Broad from the lane between Ranworth and S. Walsham.

As with many former staithes this start of a shipping highway to Gt Yarmouth and the North Sea is now silted and narrowed. But vital coal from the North-East was once landed here, and goods could go out to the Baltic and the Low Countries.

LiDAR imaging shows this channel to have been a very much wider waterway in the past   [*MB·2015*]

For the maltster Podger Moore's descendants, for a landscape historian intrigued by a long-forgotten staithe, and for the host of others who have told me of their reactions and investigations, Mary Hardy and Henry Raven do indeed 'give time a tongue', as the brewery clock proclaimed. The diarists capture the passing moment, seeing it as having a significance which would otherwise be lost. The richness lies partly in their structured, repetitive daily entries from which we can gradually build up a picture of the reality of their lives and the lives of those around them.

By maintaining 'an enduring record', the phrase chosen for William Hardy junior's epitaph in one of the Methodist chapels he built, his mother and cousin have opened our eyes. Through their testimony we are not only exposed to past truths but can more clearly understand the present. As a result we have a greater chance to become informed custodians, for the generations to come, of what survives.

in 1981 of Woodforde's Norfolk Ales, told me at Woodbastwick that he had visited the Letheringsett site soon after the start of his business at Drayton, near Norwich, but had decided that the buildings were 'too far gone' to enable him to carry out any such plan.

Mains water came to Letheringsett in 1955 (vol. 2, chap. 7). But the precious springs, the source of pure brewing liquor, still bubble up from the ground, as they do at Coltishall

Appendix 4.A

A chronology of the Hardys' lives 1732–1811

The diarist's family	*The family business*	*Background events*

——— F O U N D A T I O N Y E A R S 1 7 3 2 – 1 7 7 1 ———

1732
William Hardy born 26 Jan.
to William and Ann Hardy
at Scotton, W. Riding, Yorks,
the eldest of five children

1732
Breweries of John Wells at
Coltishall and John Brereton
at Letheringsett already well
established in rural Norfolk

1733
Mary Raven, the diarist, born
12 Nov. to Robert Raven, of
Whissonsett, Norfolk, grocer
and farmer, and Mary, née Fox

1733
Rebuilding work at Wells's
maltings, Coltishall

1733
English replaces Latin as
language of record; Kay invents
flying shuttle; Excise Crisis

1740
John Wesley and George White-
field part to promote Arminian
Methodism and Calvinistic
Methodism respectively;
Arne's *Rule Britannia*

1742
Sir Robert Walpole resigns
as Prime Minister; Handel's
Messiah

1744
Robert Wells of Coltishall dies
with 22 public houses tied to
his brewery across a wide area;
a further 27 are tied or supplied

1744
War with France begins;
first Wesleyan Methodist
Conference held in London

1745
Diarist's father Robert buys
Whissonsett maltings and
attached grocer's shop at house
named Gurneys

1745
Jacobite rising; Arne's *God Save
the King*

1748
Robert Raven as churchwarden
repairs/rebuilds church tower

1748
Royal Navy promotions
granted on merit; War of
Austrian Succession ends

1751
Diarist's mother Mary dies 26
July leaving four children

1751
Brewer William Wells of
Coltishall dies

1756
John Priest bankrupt as
maltster, brewer and miller
at Letheringsett

1756
Seven Years War with France
begins

The diarist's family	*The family business*	*Background events*
1757 Diarist's sister Phillis marries Burnham Thorpe farmer Henry Goggs and settles at Whissonsett	**1757** William Hardy joins excise service in Yorkshire and is posted to Evesham, Worcs; Henry Hagon buys Letheringsett farm, maltings and brewery **1758** Owing to increased manufacturing Coltishall is promoted from division to excise district	**1757** Thomas Mendham registers property at Holt, Norfolk as a Nonconformist meeting house; Militia Act; British Museum opens to public in London **1758** Theatre Royal opens in Norwich
1759 Diarist's sister Phillis has first of two surviving children	**1759** William Hardy dismissed from the Excise at Stroud, Gloucs **1760** William Hardy is reinstated and posted to Garstang, Lancs **1761** William Hardy dismissed, is reinstated and posted to King's Lynn, Norfolk **1762** William Hardy is posted to E. Dereham, Norfolk	**1759** *Annus mirabilis* of victories, including Quebec **1760** Accession of George III **1761** William Pitt the Elder resigns; Lady Huntingdon, patroness of Whitefield, opens her first chapel at Brighton **1763** Seven Years War ends; trial of John Wilkes in London
1765 Mary Raven and William Hardy marry 22 Dec. at Whissonsett and settle at E. Dereham **1767** Raven Hardy born 9 Nov. at E. Dereham **1768** William Hardy first votes in Norwich city election	**1765** Holt and Cley excise divisions move from Lynn Collection to Norwich Collection **1768** William Hardy is posted to Litcham, Norfolk; his £50 annual salary has also to provide for his horse **1769** William Hardy resigns from Excise; Coltishall brewer John Browne dies	**1765** Hargreaves invents Spinning Jenny **1768** General election, first county poll in Norfolk since 1734; Lady Huntingdon opens training college at Trevecca, S. Wales **1769** Watt patents condenser; Arkwright patents waterframe
1770 William Hardy jnr born 1 Apr. at Litcham; diarist's brother Robert marries Ann Smith **1771** Diarist's brother Nathaniel marries their cousin Ann Fox	**1771** Davy Postle becomes manager of Browne's brewery, Coltishall	**1770** Boston 'massacre'; Lord North becomes Prime Minister **1771** First water-powered spinning mill, Cromford, Derbys

The diarist's family	*The family business*	*Background events*

BREWING AT COLTISHALL 1772–1781

1772 Hardys move to Coltishall to riverside house south of church (later named Holly Lodge); Mary Hardy provides finance for husband's post at Wells's	**1772** William Hardy becomes tenant farmer of 60 acres at Coltishall and Horstead and manager of John Wells's 34-coomb maltings and brewery at Coltishall	**1772** Thomas Paine one of signatories to excise officers' petition to Parliament; Norfolk and Norwich (free) Hospital opens
1773 Robert Raven snr builds barn at Whissonsett Hall; Mary Ann Hardy born 3 Nov. at Coltishall; with husband's help MARY HARDY BEGINS DIARY on 28 Nov.	**1773** His wife's diary to 1781 shows that over those years 31 public houses are supplied by Wells's, of which 22 are tied to the brewery	**1773** Turnpike Act; Aylsham navigation authorised by Act of Parliament; Boston Tea Party; Goldsmith's *She Stoops to Conquer*
1774 William joins brother Raven at Coltishall Free School	**1774** William Hardy seeks to expand by acquiring more outlets	**1774** General election; John Wilkes Lord Mayor of London
1775 Family visits Yorkshire; Mary Ann starts school	**1775** Coltishall Lock opens for lower part of Aylsham navigation; Hardys' malt shipments to London begin	**1775** Briston chapel opens in Norfolk in Lady Huntingdon's Connexion; Gurneys bank opens in Norwich; American war begins; Sheridan's *The Rivals*
1776 Ansells lodge with Hardys; William and Mary Ann inoculated against smallpox; diarist helps at Recruiting Sergeant, Horstead	**1776** Hardys' wherry *William and Mary* built and launched; all farming concentrated at Horstead; interregnum at Recruiting Sergeant	**1776** Tom Paine's *Common Sense*; American Declaration of Independence; Bridgewater Canal links Manchester to sea
1777 Brother Robert Raven develops mental illness; his son Henry born 31 Aug.; visit to London	**1777** Norwich brewer Nockold Tompson dies; Hardys' beer shipments to London begin	**1777** Elland Society formed in Yorkshire for training Evangelical clergy
1778 Father Robert Raven dies 14 Feb.; mother-in-law Ann Hardy arrives on one-year visit; diarist begins bathing in steep	**1778** William Hardy fails to buy Tompson's and 13 tied houses; merger talks begin with Browne's brewery, Coltishall	**1778** Contour lines first used on a British map by Charles Hutton; war with America widens to include France
1779 William Hardy joins new Horstead masonic lodge; Raven starts at Free Grammar School, N. Walsham; William is withdrawn from Free School	**1779** Coltishall brewer Chapman Ives succeeds mother Rose; William Hardy underwrites Boorne and Neve for £1000; excise case against him fails	**1779** Crompton's spinning mule combines the jenny and the waterframe; navigation opens fully to Aylsham
1780 Diarist visits Suffolk with her friend Mary Neve	**1780** Hardys buy Letheringsett house, 56-acre farm, 40-coomb maltings and brewery for £1610 with £1000-mortgage	**1780** Malt duty increased; Gordon Riots in London; general election; Robert Raikes promotes Sunday schools

The diarist's family   *The family business*   *Background events*

—— B R E W I N G   A T   L E T H E R I N G S E T T   1 7 8 1 – 1 7 9 7 ——————

1781
Hardys buy their first chaise; they move 5 Apr. from Coltishall to Letheringsett to house named Rawlings (later Letheringsett Hall); sons day boys at Free Grammar School at Holt, Mary Ann day girl at Holt
1782
Raven leaves school 18 Dec. aged 15

1783
Diarist's brother Robert dies 30 Sept. at Whissonsett Hall leaving eight children; William leaves school aged 13; Raven articled at 15 to N. Walsham attorney Charles Buck
1784
Diarist's brother Nathaniel inherits larger Whissonsett shop from uncle; Mary Ann starts boarding at Fakenham private school

1785
Huquier paints family portraits; William watches balloon flight in Norwich; diarist's garden bath built; organ bought

1786
Revd John Burrell succeeds father as rector, founds Letheringsett Sunday School and is assisted by diarist; Raven falls ill; Mary Ann leaves school at 13
1787
Raven dies from tuberculosis 12 Feb. at Letheringsett; major rebuilding work in house; diarist and husband visit London and Lancashire

1781
William Hardy runs both breweries from Letheringsett; building work in house, malt-mill and brewhouse

1782
Brewing copper from Wells's installed at Letheringsett; mash vat finished; Siday Hawes takes over from William Hardy as manager of Wells's maltings and brewery, Coltishall
1783
William works full-time in his father's business; brewery mortgage transferred from John Davy of Mileham to Thomas Howard of Rudham

1784
New malt-mill built; waterwheel installed to power malt-mill and brewery from River Glaven; cornmilling starts in brewery

1786
Legal dispute with upstream miller Richard Rouse over water rights; Hardys' malt shipments to London resume

1787
Hardys' malt and flour shipments to Liverpool begin; William starts brewing porter and is tutored by Mr Scott; iron kiln floors installed

1781
Britain at war with America, France, Spain and Holland; Gen. Cornwallis surrenders; Volunteers active during invasion threat; Gurneys bank expands from Norwich into country branches in Norfolk
1782
Lady Huntingdon first registers a chapel under the Toleration Act; fall of Lord North; loss of HMS *Royal George*; hostilities cease

1783
Preachers first ordained in Lady Huntingdon's Connexion; William Pitt the Younger forms first administration; Montgolfier brothers' first balloon flight

1784
General election; assessed taxes and excise duties increased; Samuel Whitbread places order for steam engine to replace horse power in his Chiswell Street brewery; John Wesley ordains preachers; balloon fever
1785
Norwich–London mail coach service begins; Cartwright invents powerloom; Meikle invents horsepowered threshing machine

1787
208 water-powered cotton-spinning mills at work in England and Scotland; John Wesley registers chapels under Toleration Act

The diarist's family

1788
William Hardy joins new Blakeney masonic lodge; Hardys attend Glorious Revolution Ball at Holkham
1789
Diarist sees Norwich doctor over eye trouble; she and Mary Ann visit Gt Yarmouth; three-year breach with her brother Nathaniel Raven begins
1790
Diarist ceases teaching at Sunday school and three-year dispute with rector begins; William Hardy last votes in Norwich city election
1791
William begins tree-planting schemes

1792
Diarist's friend Elizabeth Smith registers Cley property as a Wesleyan Methodist meeting house; diarist's nephew Henry Raven comes to live with family aged 15; she ceases to attend playhouse
1793
Diarist's life-threatening illness lasts two months from 16 Aug.

1794
Both diarists lead quiet lives socially at Letheringsett Hall, then called Rawlings; William Hardy supports peers and MPs pressing for peace with France
1795
Mary Hardy starts regular attendance at Methodist meetings; Mary Ann gives up dancing; farm in poor state at Whissonsett Hall, Henry Raven's childhood home

The family business

1788
First brewery clerk Robert Starling starts; 208-barrel cask installed; brewery counting house rebuilt
1789
Loss of posts in massive excise service reorganisation; Holt and Cley return to Lynn Collection from Norwich; Coltishall remains as district
1790
Excise bring Exchequer case against William Hardy on charge of mixing beer; new brewing copper, boiling back and three casks installed
1791
Diarist's nephew William Raven briefly becomes Hardys' brewing pupil; porter shipments to Yorkshire, Newcastle and Liverpool begin
1792
Hardys' porter and other beer shipments to Norway begin; tun room chamber converted to wheat and flour store; Henry Raven arrives on trial as brewery apprentice
1793
With William's help HENRY RAVEN BEGINS FARM AND BREWERY DIARY on 10 Oct.
1794
Henry Raven with his mother Ann signs articles as William Hardy's brewery apprentice 19 July; he will live with his aunt's family another six years
1795
Hardys secure Weybourne Camp beer contract with Regular Army; new pump and hop back installed in brewery; wheat harvest fails

Background events

1788
Whig celebration of Glorious Revolution centenary; Regency crisis begins
1789
Celebration dinners for poor on George III's recovery; Declaration of Rights of Man, Paris; fall of Bastille

1790
General election; Burke's *Reflections on the Revolution in France*

1791
Tom Paine's *Rights of Man*; Thomas Mendham's *Rights of Man*; preparations begin for Ordnance survey of Britain

1792
September Massacres in Paris; England in ferment over fears of sedition; Lady Huntingdon's theological training college moves from Trevecca to Cheshunt, Herts

1793
Execution of Louis XVI; war with France begins; Jacobins seize power in France
1794
Increased taxes and duties to fund war; suspension of Habeas Corpus; treason trials

1795
Ordnance Survey begin map-making; Seditious Meetings Act; bread riots

The diarist's family

1796
Domestic counting house rebuilt; Mary Ann has suite of rooms converted for her use; she starts to join her mother at Methodist meetings; Letheringsett House of Industry opens after parish townhouses rebuilt

1797
Piano installed in the Hardys' keeping parlour; William Hardy's itemised inventory values house and garden at £600 and furniture at £526

The family business

1796
Chapman Ives's steam brewery at Coltishall with maltings and tied houses for sale; William Hardy pays off £1000-mortgage on his own brewery; he buys 12-acre farm at Holt Heath when enclosure first proposed

1797
Henry Raven brews unsupervised 19 Jan.; William Hardy semi-retires in Sept.; he values total property at £16,274 including outlets; he hands control and ownership to William with annual strong-beer production at 2100 barrels for 42 public houses including 25 tied outlets; HENRY RAVEN'S DIARY ENDS on 25 Oct.

Background events

1796
General election; Jenner develops smallpox vaccine; Supplementary Militia and Provisional Cavalry established to engage more civilians in anti-invasion measures; Catherine the Great of Russia dies

1797
Year of Peril; banks stop conversion of banknotes into cash; naval mutinies; naval battles of Cape St Vincent and Camperdown; first large-scale county map of Norfolk published by William Faden of London

WILLIAM HARDY JUNIOR TAKES OVER 1797

—— EXPANSION AT LETHERINGSETT 1798–1811——

1798
Portraits of Mary and William Hardy by Immanuel; she ceases outdoor bathing at 64; her first recorded Wesleyan Methodist Communion and Wesleyan membership; Zebulon Rouse holds Wesleyan meetings at Letheringsett Watermill

1799
Diarist's brother Nathaniel Raven dies 28 Jan.; William buys his first whiskey (gig); Elizabeth Smith builds first Methodist chapel at Cley; Hardys begin to hear Anglican Evangelical preachers

1798
William fails to buy 112-acre estate [Riverside Farm], Letheringsett; Zebulon Rouse rebuilds and enlarges watermill and Hardys cease cornmilling

1799
Dundee sloop *Nelly* recaptured from Dutch by Royal Navy and taken to Gt Yarmouth; Hardys have latest recorded harvest; very poor barley harvest, beer price rises

1798
New assessed taxes introduced; heightened fears of French invasion; plans drawn up for civilian evacuation from coastal areas; Battle of the Nile

1799
Income tax introduced; Napoleon Bonaparte becomes First Consul; Jenner's vaccine first used in Norfolk, on HMS *Kent* off Gt Yarmouth; Joseph Boyce patents horse-drawn reaping machine

The diarist's family

1800
Visit by diarist, husband and daughter to Cambridge and London; they hear Charles Simeon and John Newton; diarist attends seven Anglican and 26 Nonconformist services in London in five weeks and goes to Synagogue

1801
As part of national celebrations for truce Hardys arrange Letheringsett dinner for poor and village illuminations

1802
William Hardy snr and jnr first vote in Norfolk county election; William jnr extends major tree-planting schemes and begins closure of road to Hall Farm past Hardys' home

1803
On visit to Hull with husband and daughter, diarist attends 17 Methodist and five other Nonconformist meetings in two weeks; William briefly joins Holt Volunteers as lieutenant; he acquires his first game licence

1804
Mary Ann starts to attend Anglican services only rarely; William starts regularly accompanying mother and sister to Methodist meetings

1805
William Mindham bankrupt; Mary Ann marries Sprowston farmer Jeremiah Cozens 12 Nov. with £7000 dowry; Raven family leaves Whissonsett Hall

1806
William Hardy makes last will; Mindham rebuilds Sprowston farmhouse; diarist's sister Phillis Goggs dies 14 Sept.; Mary Ann's only child William Hardy Cozens born 1 Dec.

The family business

1800
William christens new 100-barrel cask; he buys sloop *Nelly* for £590; he buys [Old] Letheringsett Hall, 351-acre manor farm and lordship for £10,500; Hardys' wheat harvest fails; Henry Raven leaves

1801
Excise finds manufacturing in north Norfolk in decline; new copper; George Phillippo becomes William's farm steward; they buy Norfolk Horn flock

1802
William attends his first Holkham sheepshearing; *Nelly* sails to Norway for timber; William Mindham first works as builder for Hardys; Chapman Ives's 20,000-barrel steam Coltishall brewery for sale

1803
William has 20 friends to tea in new mash vat; William Girling becomes ninth brewery clerk; William values farm livestock and crops at £2305 and brewery stock (malt, beer, coal etc and ship, not plant and public houses) at £3669

1804
William Hardy becomes a local income tax commissioner; *Nelly* wrecked off Blakeney on voyage from Newcastle, captain and all hands lost

1805
William rebuilds open-air basin to soften brewing liquor; Siday Hawes expands malting at Coltishall and unites three village breweries on defunct Wells site

Background events

1800
Fulton's successful trials of submarine *Nautilus* on River Seine

1801
First national census; Battle of Copenhagen; Trevithick's steam locomotive trials

1802
First Norfolk county poll since 1768; experimental mechanical threshing introduced to Norfolk

1803
War recommences, embargo imposed; measures to defend home front, Supplementary Militia embodied; first steam-powered watermills in Norwich

1805
Jenner's vaccine is given systematically in Norfolk; Nelson dies at Trafalgar

1806
Pitt and Fox die; Norfolk county poll in general election; Napoleon imposes Continental System against British trade

The diarist's family

1807
Diarist falls seriously ill; on recovery she no longer attends Anglican services

1808
William diverts main road for reconstruction of Letheringsett Hall and grounds; diarist founds Wesleyan Methodist meeting house at her washer-woman's cottage

1809
MARY HARDY'S DIARY ENDS 21 Mar., just before her sudden death at Letheringsett Hall on 23 Mar.; William builds Greek Doric portico in summer when remodelling south front of Hall

1810
Diarist's sister-in-law Ann, widow of Robert Raven, and her daughter Mary keep house for Hardys at Letheringsett Hall

1811
William Hardy dies 18 Aug. at Mary Ann's farmhouse outside Norwich named Sprowston Villa (later Oak Lodge); he is buried Letheringsett 22 Aug. in churchyard vault with wife and son Raven

The family business

1807
First Holt and Letheringsett Enclosure Act

1808
Coltishall reduced by Excise from division to two rides; King's Head rebuilt on new site at Letheringsett; enclosure claims published

1809
Second Holt and Letheringsett Enclosure Act

1810
William's architect William Mindham designs and builds first Foundry Bridge, Norwich

1811
William owns 350 acres in Letheringsett, of which 268 are arable; on his father's death he succeeds to their home Letheringsett Hall, with 20 acres, and his father's farmland at Saxlingham and Holt

Background events

1807
General election; British Orders in Council for blockade of France; first street gaslight-ing in Pall Mall, London

1808
Construction of east coast martello towers begins; alehousekeeper's licence doubles to two guineas

1809
Death of Gen. Moore at Corunna; Wellesley returns to the Peninsula; Walcheren expedition; British (Noncon-formist) schools established

1811
Prince of Wales becomes Regent; second national census; National (Church of England) schools established; Primitive Methodist Connexion founded

Glossary

Technical terms, area, weights and measures

This glossary relies in part on the published works cited below, and in part on inferences drawn from the diarists' texts as to the Hardys' practice.

Terms and measures varied according to region and even within a county, the imperial standard not being made compulsory until 1826. In some parts of England the statute acre was used; in others the customary acre. Beer barrelage varied, also coal measure. Most produce was measured by volume and not by weight. There were thus wide variations according to the crop and its moisture content. A bushel of barley might weigh from 49 lb to 56 lb; a bushel of wheat from 56 lb to 62 lb.

These terms may have other definitions not given here, the glossary being tailored to the diarists' usage. United States measures, while bearing the same names, often differ markedly from the British, and conversion tables need to be used.

Words in italics have their own listed entry.

sources These sometimes conflict, but guidance has been sought from C. McCoy, *McCoy's Dictionary of Customs & Excise* (H.H. Greaves, London, 1938); P. Mathias, *The Brewing Industry in England 1700–1830* (Cambridge Univ. Press, 1959); G.E. Mingay, ed., *The Agrarian History of England and Wales: Volume VI 1750–1850* (Cambridge Univ. Press, 1989), pp. 1117–55 (the statistical appendix); and public notices in the *Norwich Mercury*

acre   4840 square *yards* (0·405 hectares): 6 acres = 2.43 hectares, 640 acres = one square mile. Norfolk used the statute acre (4 *roods* to the acre), not the customary acre (3 roods). There were 40 *perches* to the rood, land measure being quoted as 'a　r　p'

ale   Technically, *unhopped* malted liquor; however by the Hardys' time it was used indiscriminately to mean also hopped liquor (ie *beer*), as a strong brew, made with pale or amber *malt*

alehouse   Another name for a public house: on-licensed premises for the sale of *beer* and often for wine and spirits as well, for which additional licences were required. Technically only a tavern had these additional licences, but this distinction had largely faded

assignee   A person to whom property is legally transferred so that it can be used for the benefit of the creditors. It differs from a receiver, where the management, but not the ownership, of the debtor's property is vested in a person appointed by a court

back   Any coopered vessel used in brewing
bag   A sack of *hops*: 2½ *cwt* (127 kg), measuring 7½ *feet* long and 8 feet in circumference (2·3 and 2·4 metres), the canvas weighing 4 *lb*; together with the *pocket* the standard size for selling hops

baiting, bating   Pausing (as in bated breath), eg when breaking a journey for refreshment; also (as baiting) setting dogs against other animals for sport, usually in a confined space such as an inn yard

barrel   A coopered vessel in which beer is transported. Also a liquid measure:
ale: in theory, from 1531 to 1803, 34 *gallons* in country districts (154·6 litres), 32 gallons in London (145·5 litres); after 1803, 36 gallons nationally (163·7 litres), the figure it remains today;
beer: in theory, from 1531 to 1803, 34 gallons in country districts (154·6 litres), 36 gallons in London (163.7 litres); after 1803, 36 gallons nationally, the figure it remains today.

However, many sources show that in 18th-century Norfolk, and earlier, both ale and beer barrels contained 36 gallons (eg *Norw. Merc.* 2 Apr. 1785, 24 Mar. 1787; see also *Diary 3*, app. D3.B, note; *World*, vol. 2, chap. 7)

basin An open reservoir, set high, in which brewing *liquor* can soften (ameliorate) for brews such as *porter* requiring soft water

beer A generic term for such brews as bitter, *fourpenny*, mild, nog, porter, sixpenny and *small beer*, all of which were produced commercially using only *liquor, malt, hops*, yeast and finings. Sugar was not permitted in brewing until 1847

bottle Wine: 5 bottles = one *gallon* after 1803

bran The fourth grade of flour; coarse flour

British spirits Distilled in the British Isles, eg whisky, and not imported, eg brandy; thus subject to excise and not customs duty

bundle See *load*

bushel Until the imperial bushel became the standard in 1824 the Winchester bushel of 1695 was widely used in England and Wales, the measure (the shovel) being round, with an even bottom, 18½ inches wide throughout and 8 inches deep (47 cm and 20·3 cm)

apples: 4 heaped *pecks* or 33 dry quarts

barley: cubic capacity, one bushel = 1¼ cubic *feet* (0·042 cubic metres), with a weight variation range of 49 to 56 *lb* (22·2–25·4 kg)

malt: approx. 42 lb (19·1 kg), malt weighing less than the same volume of barley as its moisture is lost in processing

oats: approx. 38 lb (17·2 kg)

wheat and *meal*: variation range 56 lb to 62 lb (25·4–28·1 kg)

cask A very large closed vessel for storing *beer* undergoing secondary fermentation while it matures. William Hardy's largest cask in 1788 could hold 208 *barrels* (7488 *gallons*, or 59,904 *pints*), but city brewers such as those in Norwich could have much larger casks

chaldron The usual measure for coal; also for the tonnage ('burthen') of 18th-century vessels including those on inland waterways:

nationally: one chaldron = 36 heaped bushels or 12 sacks

north Norfolk: the port of Blakeney and Cley in the Hardys' time used the London measure of 26½ *cwt* (1346·2 kg, or 1·35 metric tonnes) to the chaldron (*Diary 3*: 1 Aug. 1777), not the Newcastle measure of 53 cwt (2·69 metric tonnes)

Yarmouth, mid-18th century: one chaldron = 20 sacks, each *sack* weighing 137 *lb*; a Broadland chaldron was thus 24½ *cwt*

(1242·8 kg). As the Hardys' *wherry William and Mary* was of 12 chaldrons' burthen the vessel can be estimated at 16 *tons* or 14½ tons, depending on the method of calculating tonnage (R. Clark, *Black-Sailed Traders* (David & Charles, Newton Abbot, 1961), p. 100)

chamber A bedroom, or storage room

cinders Coke; pit coal specially fired in cinder ovens to render it smokeless for roasting barley by slow, even heat and without tainting; (charcoal, with similar properties, is made from wood). Culm, or anthracite, can also be used in *malt*-kilns. Coal can be used for heating the brewing copper, but not in malting as it gives a sulphurous taste to the malt

cistern A very large open-topped tank within the malthouse in which barley is soaked (steeped) at the start of malting: see *steep*

cleansing Removing the yeast head and running the beer from the fermentation vessel into casks, thus ending primary fermentation

coal meter Coal measurer: a person appointed to measure and weigh coal, *culm* and *cinders* and certify them. If for purposes of levying customs duty the appointment (established 1695) was made by the Commissioners of Customs; it was also a post in an incorporated borough such as Gt Yarmouth. See also *chaldron* and *sack*

colt A young male horse not put to full work

comb, coomb 4 *bushels* or half a *quarter*, and the customary grain measure used by the Hardys: one coomb of barley = approx. 2 cwt or 16 *stone* (101·6 kg); one coomb of wheat = approx. 18 stone (114·3 kg)

combs, culms Unwanted shoots from *malted* barley, removed by *screening*; estimated to represent 4% of the weight of the barley on which malt duty had been paid; for culm, see *cinders*

common brewer A licensed wholesale commercial brewer supplying retail outlets (public houses) and who could, with the appropriate licence, also sell retail direct; the later term 'brewer for sale' included the functions of the common brewer

cooler A wide, shallow vessel into which the *wort* passes after boiling in the *copper* and before being run into the fermenting tun; see also *hop back*

copper   A closed vessel for boiling the *liquor*, the *grist malt* after *mashing*, and the *hops*, these forming the brew to which yeast is added; in private brewhouses the copper was often an open vessel. When installing the copper the bricklayer had to take care to 'hang' or offset it correctly

couch   A separate area within a wooden frame on the malthouse floor near the *steep* where the wetted barley was spread after steeping and was allowed to germinate; here the excise officer gauged the piece of *malt*

counting house   Literally accompting house, the room where the books, ledgers and petty cash were stored and business with clients transacted. Both the dwelling house and the brewery complex had counting houses

crone   An old ewe

culm, culms   See *cinders*; *combs*

cwt   See *hundredweight*

drawer   A publican (innkeeper or alehouse-keeper), a term particularly applied to those supplied by or tied to a *common brewer*. *Beer* was not pumped up to the parlour but 'drawn' out of the *barrel*

drawing house   A public house supplied by a *common brewer* (not therefore one where the innkeeper did his own brewing as a publican brewer), where the house was tied in some way to the brewery: either by direct ownership freehold, copyhold or leasehold and then being let or sublet to the *drawer* by the brewer, or by the drawer being tied to the brewer by a mortgage or bond

dressing   Cleaning and removing impurities in grain and *malt*; also recutting grooves in millstones by a trained millwright

engine   A pump

faggot   Strictly, a piece of wood 3 *feet* long by 24 *inches* in circumference (0·91 by 0·61 metres); loosely, a small length of hewn timber

firkin   A butter measure: 56 *lb* (25.4 kg)

foot   12 *inches* or one-third of a *yard* (30·48 cm)

fourpenny   (4^d) Strong *beer* stronger than *twopenny* but weaker than *sixpenny* and probably classed as *X* by the Hardys; so called from its retail price per quart: see also *nog*; *porter*

gallon   Liquid measure: 8 *pints* (4·55 litres)

geneva   Gin, a spirit flavoured with juniper

gig   A light, two-wheeled vehicle drawn usually by one horse; similar to a *whiskey*

goaf, goaft, goft   A rick of corn, usually one being transported by cart or wagon

grist   *Malt* crushed in a malt-mill either by metal rollers or by millstones

gyle, gile, guile   A brew. It was broken down into two or three parti-gyles (then spelt 'party guile'). The strongest *beer* came from the first *mash* creating the first parti-gyle (`/`), the next strongest from the second (`//`), and the weakest from the third (`///`). See also *gyle vat*; *mash tun*

gyle vat   Another name for a fermenting tun

hop back   A vessel containing *hops* and perforated at the bottom to form a coarse sieve through which the *wort* passes from the *copper* to the *cooler*, thus removing the solids

hops   *Humulus lupulus*, a native wild hardy perennial climbing plant cultivated for its fruits and first licensed for brewing in England and Wales by Edward VI; when dried and added in brewing the cones give *beer* its distinctive bitter aroma. See *bag* and *pocket*

hundredweight   (cwt)   112 *lb* (8 *stone*, or 50·8 kg); 20 cwt = one ton. The rough measure was half a hundredweight = one *bushel* (56 pounds, or 25·4 kg). It was often called 'hundred' at the time, this being the Hardys' usage

inch   One-twelfth of a *foot* (2·54 cm)

keel   An open commercial Broadland sailing vessel, then often larger than the *wherry*, developed from mediaeval times with a single square sail, centrally positioned mast, winch at the stern, and skipper's cabin at the bow; later ones, from the late 18th century onwards, were sometimes hatched

keeping room   The family sitting room, less formal than the parlour

lading   Cargo, the bill of lading being the customs certificate of cargo carried whether coastwise (around Britain) or abroad

last   10 *quarters* or 20 *coombs* (approx. 2032 kg or 2 metric tonnes): the largest unit of grain measure

lb   See *pound*

liquor   Water used in brewing, usually from a spring or well and sometimes left to soften in a *basin* set high at the start of the gravity feed

load   A dry measure:
gravel: one cubic *yard* (0.76 cubic metre);
hewn timber: one *ton*
new hay: 19¼ *cwt* (36 trusses of 60 *lb* each: 977.9 kg);
old hay: 18 cwt (36 trusses of 56 lb each: 914.4 kg), new hay weighing more owing to its greater moisture content
rushes: 63 bundles

malt   Barley roasted to create fermentable maltose, and crushed or milled for brewing. Different types of malt produce individual *beers*; see also *bushel*; *grist*; *porter malt*

marl   A chalky-clay mixture occurring naturally in layers in chalky areas and lying beneath the top layer of clay; quarried in deep open-cast pits and spread as fertiliser for crops

mash tun   A vessel in which the *grist malt* is mixed with hot *liquor*. The strongest brew comes from the first mash; weaker brews from the second, or occasionally third, mashes, the same malt being used for the mashes but with additional hot liquor. See also *gyle*

meal   The second grade of flour, less fine than the top grade

meeting   A religious service conducted by Methodists and other Protestant Nonconformists on dedicated premises (the meeting house); these might be officially licensed or unlicensed. The premises could range from a purpose-built chapel to a labourer's kitchen or smallholder's outhouse

mild   A more lightly hopped *beer* than bitter, allowing a sweeter flavour

mile   1760 *yards* (1.61 km)

muck   Farm manure; animal dung

nog   A strong, long-maturing *beer* particularly associated with Norfolk and one of the Hardys' staple brews; also called by them *fourpenny* and *X*

ounce (oz)   One-sixteenth of a *pound* (weight)

peck   One-quarter of a *bushel*, or 2 *gallons* dry measure

perch   A small area of land:
40 perches = one *rood*; 4 roods = 1 *acre*

pint   Half a *quart* (0.57 litres), or one-eighth of a *gallon*

pipe   A wine cask; also a liquid measure:
port: 138 *gallons* (627.4 litres)
sherry: 130 gallons (591 litres)
wine: 126 gallons (572.8 litres)

pocket   A sack of *hops*: 1¼ cwt (63.5 kg), measuring 7½ *feet* long by 5¾ feet in circumference (2.3 and 1.75 metres), the canvas weighing 4 *lb*; together with the *bag* the standard size for selling hops

pollard   Very coarse, fourth-grade flour suited only to animal feed

porter   Strong, long-maturing *beer* of varying strengths (*XX* or, for the Hardys, more usually *X*) with good lasting properties, made from special dark *porter malt*. It first became popular in London in the early 18th century. Owing to the capital costs associated with its large *casks* and slow maturity most village *common brewers* did not attempt to brew it

porter malt   Barley further roasted after the process of *malting* has been completed, to darken the colour of the *beer* and enhance its bitter flavour; the chocolate-coloured grain becomes shrunken and very hard

pound (lb: weight)   16 *ounces* (0.45 kg)

puncheon   Liquid measure: *beer*: 72 *gallons* (327.3 litres); wine: 84 gallons (381.9 litres)

quart   2 *pints* (1.14 litres), or one-quarter of a *gallon*

quarter   8 *bushels*, or 2 *coombs*, or one-tenth of a *last*

quicking   The process of weeding and destroying, usually by burning, field couch grass or 'quicks' (*Triticum repens*)

quire   A paper measure: 24 sheets; 20 quires = one ream (480 sheets)

rider   Travelling salesman; the sales representative of a merchant or manufacturer

rood   One-quarter of a statute *acre*:
40 *perches* = one rood; 4 roods = 1 acre

sack   Coal: usually 3 *bushels*, each sack measuring 50 *inches* by 26 inches (127 by 66 cm); Gt Yarmouth measure 137 *lb* (62.1 kg); flour or meal: 5 bushels or 280 lb (127 kg)

screening   Removing shoots and foreign bodies from grain and *malt*, usually by sieving; all commercially produced malt had to be screened

se'nnight   A week (literally seven nights)

shearling   A young sheep which has had one shearing. A two-year shearling has been shorn twice

sixpenny   (6^d), the strongest of the Hardys' brews, apparently classed by them *XX* and comparatively rarely brewed; so called from its high retail price per quart. The Treasury in 1779 regarded it as the product only of 'brewers of fine and particular strong beers and ales' (TNA: PRO CUST 48/20, p. 27)

small beer   The weakest *beer*: more commonly brewed by private brewers and brewing victuallers (publican brewers) in country houses, parsonages and public houses, whereas *common brewers* concentrated on varieties of *strong beer*. See also *gyle*

society   The local congregation of paid-up members of a Methodist *meeting house*

staithe   A quay or landing place often to be found up cuts ('dykes') and purpose-built canals linking the hinterland to rivers and navigations; sometimes just a grassy bank on the riverside, usually with access to roads, where boats can be loaded and unloaded

steep   A *cistern* for soaking barley at the start of *malting*, the process being called steeping. The majority of rural maltings in Norfolk in the 1770s had steeps for 25 or 30 *coombs* of barley (50 or 60 *cwt*/2½ or 3 *tons*/2·54 or 3·05 metric tonnes); Letheringsett's in 1780 was 40 coombs. In Norwich at this time brewers often had one or more 50- to 60-coomb steeps (5·08 to 6·1 metric tonnes)

stone (st.)   14 *pounds* avoirdupois (6·35 kg). Butcher's meat was often regarded as dead weight and measured at 8 lb to the stone, but Mary Hardy used the avoirdupois reckoning, calculating meat as live weight; otherwise she could not have referred, eg, to '2 St. 12 lb' of beef (*Diary 1*: 19 Aug. 1774)

strong beer   *Beer* such as *sixpenny*, best, *nog* and *porter* made from the first *mash* and subject to the highest levels of excise duty, its strength determining the level of duty according to a scale

tandem   The harnessing of horses one behind the other and not abreast

tasking   Threshing; a tasker is a thresher

tea   Black: defined 1767 as Bohea, Congou, Souchong and Pekoe; green: all other varieties

tent   Sweet red Spanish wine, technically from the Alicante region

tied house   See *drawing house*. A secondary meaning applies to a tenant or subtenant, such as a farm servant, occupying the property only while employed by its owner or tenant, thus guaranteeing him local accommodation. Both parsonages and farm cottages can be tied houses

ton   2240 *lb* or 20 *hundredweight* (1016 kg, 1·016 metric tonnes); in a ship's measure 40 cubic feet or 2000 lb = one ton

trashing   Threshing

truss   See *load*

tun room   A large, lofty store room, also called a vat house, where beer is left in *casks* to condition or mature; see also '*white hall*'

twopenny   (2^d), a weak brew, so called from its retail price per *quart*; the Hardys do not use the term

underback   The vessel under the *mash tun* to receive the *wort* before it runs into the *copper*

vat   Usually a synonym for a *cask*: a very large closed vessel for storing *beer*; however see also *gyle vat*

waterman   The skipper or mate of a *keel* or *wherry*

wether   A castrated male sheep

wharfinger   The occupier of a wharf, usually in a sea port or large inland port, such as Norwich, rather than at a village *staithe*

wherry   A commercial single-sailed Broadland vessel developed in the 18th century, and then often smaller than the *keel*, with a winch at the bow and skipper's cabin in the stern; by 1800 it was usually hatched to protect the cargo. By the mid-19th century it had superseded the keel owing to its superior design, its mast, placed for'ard, allowing a unique, simple fore-and-aft rig and an uncluttered hold

whiskey   A light, two-wheeled vehicle usually pulled by one horse; see *gig*. (Whisky the drink was often called *usquebaugh* or *aqua vitae* at this time: Gaelic and Latin for water of life)

'white hall'   A term specific to the Letheringsett brewery for the chamber holding the *casks* and presumably whitewashed; it is not clear if this was separate from the *tun room*.

above The Wensum in Norwich in 1828: a busy riverside scene in this large inland port, looking upstream to Bishop Bridge. This area near the Cathedral, its spire glimpsed on the left, was by a ferry; the next crossing downstream, Foundry Bridge, had only been built in 1810.

As is the case today on the Broads, some of the staithes are piled to protect the bank as vessels come in; others are left unboarded. Coltishall, also an inland port at the head of navigation, would have had something of this appearance in the Hardys' day, with keels and wherries drawing alongside.

A sturdy rowing boat collects barrels by the ferryman's cottage on the left; a small pleasure yacht sails towards it. A wherry is moored at a warehouse near the black-faced sheep; on the opposite bank a much larger, high-sided wherry is loaded or unloaded while a crew member does a bit of angling from beside the skipper's cabin or cuddy.

The size of a vessel was measured by its carrying capacity in chaldrons. The contemporary and specialist terms in this Glossary were in regular use by the Hardys' circle [*painting by J. Stark; engraving by J.C. Vorrall 1828*]

In an adjoining chamber the fermented *beer* was run off into *barrels*, as a young beer; or into a subterranean tank, from where it was pumped into *casks* if a long-maturing brew

wort   Liquid run off from the *mash tun*, *copper* and *cooler*; fermentation has to take place before it can be called *beer* or *ale*

X, XX   Strong *beer*—the greater the number of Xs, the stronger the beer. The notation was derived from the chalk marks scribbled on the vessels, *barrels* and *casks*. Brewers would draw a horizontal bar through the letter X to denote XX, and two bars for XXX (X̶, X̶̶)

yard   Linear measure: 3 *feet* (0·914 metres)

ʼI, ʼII, ʼIII   Parti-gyles: up to three brewings from the one batch of *malt*. See *gyle*

Bibliography

Volume 4

Manuscript sources

The National Archives of the UK (TNA): Public Record Office (PRO)

Sea Fencibles

ADM 2/1360–1363, Admiralty out-letters: Secret letters 8 June 1803–22 July 1805

ADM 6/55, Admiralty service records: Officers commissioned for hired cutters, signal stations and Sea Fencibles 1803–07

ADM 11/14, Admiralty service records: Entry book of orders appointing officers to hired cutters, signal stations and Sea Fencibles 1804–05

ADM 28/14–15, Navy Board: Sea Fencibles pay lists, Cromer to Fosdyke Wash [Lincs] 1803–05

ADM 28/17–18, Navy Board: Sea Fencibles pay lists, Southwold to Cromer 1803–05

CUST 47/198–463, Excise Board and Secretariat: Minute books 1751–1809

CUST 48/18–37, Excise Board and Secretariat: Correspondence with Treasury 1767–1805

Customs Board and Collectors of Customs

CUST 84/36, Collector to Board: Outport books, Newcastle upon Tyne 1803–05

CUST 96/134, Board to Collector: Outport books, King's Lynn, Wells, Blakeney and Cley, Wisbech 1793–1806

CUST 96/165–166, Collector to Board: Outport books, King's Lynn, Wells, Blakeney and Cley, Wisbech 1798–1805

CUST 97/31, Collector to Board: Customs outport books, [Gt] Yarmouth, Lowestoft, Southwold 1799–1800

Internal defence: Militia and Volunteers

HO 42/37, Home Office: Domestic correspondence, George III, letters and papers 1795

HO 42/49, Home Office: Domestic correspondence, George III, letters and papers 1800

HO 42/71, Home Office: Domestic correspondence, George III, letters and papers 1803

HO 50/26, Home Office: Military correspondence, Militia 1796

HO 50/80, Home Office: Military correspondence, Supplementary, Norfolk (Volunteers) 1803

HO 50/341, Home Office: Military correspondence, Supplementary, Norfolk (Volunteers) 1794–1813

IR 23/61, Land tax assessments 1798: Norfolk

IR 30/23/146, Tithe Commission: Coltishall tithe map [surveyed 1841]

TS 24/10, Treasury Solicitor's papers on sedition, London Corresponding Society and Norwich Revolution Society, Nov.–Dec. 1792

Internal defence: Military measures

WO 30/75, General defence of the country: Defence reports 1803–04

WO 30/76, General defence of the country: Commander-in-Chief's letters 1803–04

WO 30/78, General defence of the country: Defence reports 1804–05

WO 30/100, Eastern District: Reports and proposals for measures of defence 1797–1805

WO 30/141, General defence of the country in the event of invasion: Printed directive Apr. 1798

WO 166/4432, War diaries of the 8th Bn Lincolnshire Regiment, Norfolk Division, 1940–41

British parliamentary papers: House of Commons parliamentary papers

Accounts and papers (114), xii.367 (1806): An account of the totals of the imports and exports of Great Britain for the years ending 5 Jan. 1800–5 Jan. 1806

Accounts and papers (143), p. 721 (1806): 'A comparative account of the number and tonnage of British and Foreign Vessels that entered inwards at the several ports of Great Britain . . . in different periods of peace and war', 5 May 1806

1826 (369), Norwich and Lowestoft Navigation Bill, Minutes of evidence before the committee

Norfolk Record Office (NRO)

ANF (1805), f. 50, no. 34, Archdeaconry of Norfolk, will of James Amies, of Barton Turf, 'boatman', proved 1 Apr. 1805

Business and brewery records

BR 10/1, Fakenham: abstract of title to copyhold property, the Bell, 1763–1896, including admission of W.J.Morgan [of Morgans Brewery, Norwich] to the Bell, 24 Apr. 1896, and letter to Morgans Brewery Co. Ltd from F. Lacey, 4 June 1907

BR 160/6, Sale of Tompsons Brewery, Norwich to Morgans Brewery 1845

BR 160/38, Clement W.H. Cozens-Hardy's sale of the Letheringsett maltings and brewery and 29 tied houses to Morgans, 12 Mar. 1896

Wells family and brewery papers

BRA 926/xii 56/4, 110 x 4, Agreement over a watercourse in Horstead permitted by Henry Palmer Watts to John and Anne Darby and Charles Grape, 9 Jan. 1790

BRA 926/xiii/28, 110 x 1, Tripartite indenture 21 Feb. 1775, with one-year lease of meadow land owned by Henry Palmer Watts and Mrs Margaret Smith, 20 Feb. 1775

BRA 1164/16/18, 760 x 7, Assignment by Robert Wells's executor Mr [John] Simpson of leases and ownership of estates to Mr [William] Wells, 23 June 1744

Clerk of the Peace, Norfolk

C/S 1/15, Norfolk Quarter Sessions, minute book 1791–1800

C/S 1/16, Norfolk Quarter Sessions, minute book 1801–04

C/S 1/17, Norfolk Quarter Sessions, minute book 1805–11

C/Sce 1/8, Norfolk Quarter Sessions, order book 1773–84

C/Sch 1/16, Register of Norfolk public houses 1789–99

DN/TA 438, Coltishall tithe apportionment 1841, with tithe map

DN/TER 48/3, Coltishall glebe terrier, 20 June 1770

FC 27/7, Records of St Peter's [Wesleyan Methodist] Chapel, Norwich

Mary Hardy and Henry Raven, facsimiles

FX 376, Photocopies of the MS diaries of Mary Hardy and Henry Raven (deposited 10 Apr. 2013):

MS diary of Mary Hardy 1773–1809:
FX 376/1, 28 Nov. 1773–6 Jan. 1778
FX 376/2, 7 Jan. 1778–21 Feb. 1784
FX 376/3, 22 Feb. 1784–20 July 1790
FX 376/4, 21 July 1790–7 May 1800
FX 376/5, 8 May 1800–21 Mar. 1809
MS diary of Henry Raven 1793–97:
FX 376/6, 10 Oct. 1793–25 Oct. 1797

HMN 7/336, Plan of Wells harbour 1780 by H.A. Biedermann

MC 106/13, 560 x 7, Act 'For Improving the Harbour of Blakeney, within the Port of Blakeney and Clay' 1817

MC 106/28/3, Plan of Blakeney harbour 1817 by Benjamin Leak [20th-century copy]

MC 216/1, 668 x 3, MS farming journal of Randall Burroughes 1794–99

MC 662/15/1, Map of Scottow and area c.1742 by Samuel Bellard

MC 1858/17, 860 x 5, Holt hundred: Thornage surveyor's [account] book 1776–1816

MS 66, Lt Col. Metzner's inspection of Norfolk Yeomanry Cavalry and Volunteer Infantry, vol. 1, 18 Oct.–19 Nov. 1803

MS 67, Lt Col. Metzner's inspection of Norfolk Yeomanry Cavalry and Volunteer Infantry, vol. 2, 30 Nov.–21 Dec. 1803

MS 3332, 4 B3 (Clayton MSS 123), A particular of the manor of Meyton [Mayton] in the county of Norfolk (nd, c.1673)

MS 5363, 5 B6, Rules of the Wells Loyal Volunteer Infantry 1798, 1800; correspondence of Lord Townshend 1800

MS 7351, 7 D4, W.W. Simpson's sale particulars of the Coltishall Brewery and estate, for auction at Norwich 14–17 Sept. 1841

MS 18623/69, Holt and Letheringsett Enclosure Act 1807

NRS 18386, 33 B7, Horstead churchwardens' account book 1724–1803

Parish deposits

PD 270/4, Cley parish register of baptisms 1744–79, marriages 1744–53 and burials 1744–78

PD 270/5, Cley parish register of baptisms 1779–1812 and burials 1779–1812

PD 270/9, Cley parish register of marriages 1754–1812

PD 521/26, Ingworth town book 1768–98

PD 547/1–5, /44, Letheringsett parish registers of baptisms, marriages and burials 1653–1996

PD 547/42, Reprint of W.H. Burrell's article 'Norfolk Natural History Correspondence', *Transactions of the Norfolk and Norwich Naturalists' Society*, vol. 11, pt 4 (1922–23)

PD 597/78, Revd Dr C. Grape, 'A sketch or outline of the parish of Horstead, taken 29th April 1788'

PD 598/2, Coltishall parish register of baptisms, marriages and burials 1714–1812

PD 598/14, Coltishall parish register of burials 1813–58

PD 598/37, Coltishall churchwardens' account book 1776–1830

PD 692/2, Horning parish register of baptisms, marriages and burials 1686–1812

PD 692/4, Horning parish register of marriages 1754–1812

PD 679/6, Wells-next-the-Sea parish register of baptisms and burials 1754–1801

PD 679/7, Wells-next-the-Sea parish register of baptisms and burials 1802–1812

Great Yarmouth Corporation

Y/C 38/3, Gt Yarmouth register of keels and wherries 1795–98

Suffolk Record Office (Ipswich)

Bacon Longe Collection

HA 24/50/19/4.3 (2), Diary of Revd John Longe jnr of Coddenham, Suff. 1797–99

HA 24/50/19/4.4 (6), Revd John Longe jnr's Address to the inhabitants [of Coddenham] on the defence of the country, 28 July 1803

Aylsham Town Council, Norfolk: Aylsham town archives

Aylsham navigation: Plan by H.A. Biedermann of the proposed 11 miles from Ingworth to Coltishall 1772

Box 34, Aylsham navigation: Accounts of treasurer Thomas Durrant 1773–81

Box 36, Aylsham navigation: Commissioners' minute book 1772–1811

King's College, Cambridge

Manorial records of Horstead and Coltishall:

KCAR/5/1/26 76, Survey and valuation of Horstead manorial estate by John Josslyn jnr of Belstead, Suff. to William Johnson at King's College, 2 June 1802

KCAR/6/2/38, COL/505, Report on the Coltishall manorial estate by John Josselyn jnr from Belstead, Suff., 24 Jan. 1805

KCAR/6/2/38/8, COL/407, Sales particulars for Coltishall Manor House estate, 7 Sept. 1822

KCAR/6/2/38/9, COL/517, Letter from Henry Smith of Coltishall to the Bursar of King's, 27 Dec. 1773 [typed copy], with attached sketch map [original] of Coltishall Lock and new canal, 27 Dec. 1773

KCAR/6/2/38/9, COL/ 517, Notes by F.L. Clarke, dated May 1911, on the contents of a letter from Henry Smith dated 21 July 1725

KCAR/6/2/087/4, HOR/24, Report on the Horstead and Coltishall estates, Oct. 1725

KCAR/6/2/087/6, HOR/90, Coltishall: Sketch map of staithe area by River Bure at lower confluence with lock stream, nd [19th century]

KCAR/6/2/087/6, HOR/136, Manors of Horstead and Coltishall, estate map by Robert Corby, Jan. 1811

KCAR/6/2/087/14, HOR/18, Letter from Revd Dr C. Grape to Provost of King's, 27 June 1791

Norfolk Heritage Centre, Norwich

Best, D., 'The Aylsham Navigation' (unpub. thesis, Keswick Hall, 1976)

Douglas-Sherwood, T., 'The Norfolk keel' (unpub. thesis, St Andrews, 1987)

Hayes, B.D., 'Politics in Norfolk, 1750–1832' (unpub. PhD thesis, Univ. of Cambridge, 1957)

Websites

Britain's Navy, Fighting Ships <http://britainsnavy.co.uk/Ships/HMS%20Contest/HMS%20Contest%20(1797)%201.htm>, accessed 7 Aug. 2019

Literary Norfolk <http://www.literarynorfolk.co.uk/Poems/lord_cozens_hardy.htm>, accessed 9 Aug. 2019

Lloyds Register of Ships 1802 <http://www.lr.org/en/research-and-innovation/historical-information/lloyds-register-of-ships-online>, 1802, p. 24, no. 104, accessed 1 Dec. 2014

London Electoral Database, with commentary at London Electoral History <http://leh.ncl.ac.uk/>, accessed 6 July 2019

The Marlpit, community magazine for Coltishall, Horstead and area <www.themarlpit.co.uk>, accessed 25 May 2019

National Museums Liverpool, Merseyside Maritime Museum <http://www.liverpoolmuseums.org.uk/maritime/visit/old_dock_tours.aspx>, accessed 7 June 2019

Norfolk Wills: Amis/Amies of Barton Turf
<www.norfolkwills.co.uk/1805-001.pdf>,
<www.norfolkwills.co.uk/1846-001.pdf>,
accessed 4 Nov. 2014

Phillips, M. and Marioné, P., **Ships of the Old Navy: A history of the sailing ships of the Royal Navy** <http://www.ageofnelson.org/MichaelPhillips/info.php?ref=0848>,
accessed 21 Nov. 2014

Royal Naval Museum, Portsmouth <http://www.royalnavalmuseum.org/info_sheet_impressment.htm>, accessed 4 June 2019

SCRIBD: A. Prescott, 'The Unlawful Societies Act of 1799' <https://www.scribd.com/document/126937525/The-Unlawful-Societies-Act-of-1799> (unpag.), accessed 19 Mar. 2010

University of East Anglia, PhD theses:
J. Bevan, 'Foxhunting and the landscape between 1700 and 1900; with particular reference to Norfolk and Shropshire' (PhD thesis, UEA, 2011 <https://ueaeprints.uea.ac.uk/38809/1/2012BevanJPhD.pdf>, accessed 17 Apr. 2018)

Printed works

Pre-1900 works

Armstrong, M.J., *The History and Antiquities of the County of Norfolk* (Norwich, 1781)

Bartell jnr, E., *Cromer considered as a Watering Place* (enlarged 2nd edn London, 1806)

Beatniffe, R., *The Norfolk Tour, or Traveller's Pocket Companion* (5th edn Norwich, 1795)

Bogue, D. and Bennett, J., *History of Dissenters from the Revolution in 1688 to the year 1808* (4 vols, London, 1812)

Browne, J., *History of Congregationalism and Memorials of the Churches in Norfolk and Suffolk* (London, 1877)

Bryant, A., *Map of the County of Norfolk* (London, 1826)

Burn, J., *The Justice of the Peace, and Parish Officer* (4 vols, 16th edn London, 1788)

Childers, J.W., ed., *Lord Orford's Voyage round the Fens in 1774* (Doncaster, 1868)

Cobbett, W., *Rural Rides*, ed. P. Cobbett (London, 1893)

Colman, C., *In Memoriam: Sarah Cozens-Hardy* (Norwich, 1891)

Crouse, J. and Stevenson, W., *Crouse and Stevenson's Norwich and Norfolk Complete Memorandum Book 1790* (Norwich, 1790)

Cubitt, W., *A Report and Estimate on the River Waveney between Beccles Bridge and Oulton Dyke towards making Beccles a Port* (London, 1829)

Davies, G.C., *Norfolk Broads and Rivers* (London, 1883)

The Festival at Holt given on August 12th 1814 in commemoration of the Happy Return of Peace (Holt, 1814)

Forby, R., *The Vocabulary of East Anglia* (2 vols, London, 1830)

Johnson, S., *A Dictionary of the English Language* (2 vols, London, 1755)

Kent, N., *General View of the Agriculture of the County of Norfolk* (London, 1796)

Lorkin, W., *A Concise History of the First Establishment of Wesleyan Methodism in the City of Norwich in the year 1754* (Norwich, 1825)

Macpherson, D., *Annals of Commerce, Manufactures, Fisheries and Navigation* (London, 1805)

Manners Sutton, C., *An Address to the Clergy of the Diocese of Norwich* (Norwich, 1803)

Marshall, W., *The Rural Economy of Norfolk* (2 vols, London, 1787)

Marshall, W., *The Review and Abstract of the County Reports to the Board of Agriculture*, vol. 3 (York, 1818; 1st pub. 1811)

Minutes of the Methodist Conferences, vol. 1 (London, 1812)

Money, J., *Major General Money's Letter to the Officers of Volunteer Corps* (Norwich, [?1803])

A Narrative of the Grand Festival at Yarmouth on Tuesday the 19th of April 1814 (Gt Yarmouth, 1814)

The Norfolk Chronicle 1770–1814

The Norwich Mercury 1770–1829

Palmer, C.J., and Tucker, S., eds, *Palgrave Family Memorials* (Norwich, 1878)

Paterson, D., *A Description of all the Direct and Principal Cross Roads in England and Wales* (10th edn London, 1794)

The Poll for the Knights of the Shire for the County of Norfolk (Norwich, 1768)

The Poll for the Knights of the Shire for the County of Norfolk (Norwich, 1802)

The Poll for the Knights of the Shire for the County of Norfolk: A Budget, containing all the addresses and papers published during the late contested election for the county of Norfolk (Norwich, 1806)

A Present for Servants, from their Ministers, Masters, or Other Friends (10th edn London, 1787)

Priestley, J., *Historical Account of the Navigable Rivers, Canals, and Railways, throughout*

Great Britain (David & Charles Reprints, Newton Abbot, 1969; 1st pub. 1831)

Sinclair, J., *The History of the Public Revenue of the British Empire* (London, 1785)

Southey, R., *The Life of Wesley and Rise and Progress of Methodism* (new edn London, 1864; 1st pub. 1820)

Stark, J. and Robberds jnr, J.W., *Scenery of the Rivers Yare and Waveney, Norfolk, pt 2* (London, 1830)

Stone, F. & Son, *Picturesque Views of the Norfolk Bridges, pts 1–4* (Norwich, 1830, 1831)

Stones, W., *The Garden of Norfolk, or The rural residence* (Norwich, [c.1823])

Storer, J., *The Antiquarian and Topographical Cabinet* (London, 1807)

Strange, H. le, *History of Freemasonry in Norfolk 1724 to 1895* (Norwich, 1896)

Sutton, C. Manners, *A Sermon Preached before the Incorporated Society for the Propagation of the Gospel in Foreign Parts* (London, 1797)

Trimmer, Mrs [Sarah], *The Œconomy of Charity; or, An Address to Ladies, . . . with a particular view to the cultivation of religious principles, among the lower orders of people* (2 vols, 2nd edn London, 1801)

The Universal British Directory, 5 vols (London, 1793–98)

White, F., *History, Gazetteer and Directory of Norfolk* (Sheffield, 1854)

White, W., *History, Gazetteer and Directory of Norfolk* (Sheffield, 1845)

The Whole Duty of Constables, by an acting magistrate (2nd edn Norwich, 1815)

Wilks, S., *Memoirs of Rev. Mark Wilks, Late of Norwich* (London, 1821)

Williams, P., *A Sermon preached in the Parish Church of Starston in Norfolk, upon the fast day . . .* (Cambridge, 1745)

Williams, P., *A Sermon preached in the Parish Church of Starston in Norfolk, upon the day of thanksgiving . . .* (Cambridge, 1746)

Windham, W., *A Plan of Discipline composed for the use of the Militia of the County of Norfolk* (London, 1759)

Young, A. *General View of the Agriculture of the County of Norfolk* (London, 1804)

Post-1900 printed works

Agnew, J., ed., *The Whirlpool of Misadventures: Letters of Robert Paston, First Earl of Yarmouth, 1663–1679* (Norfolk Record Soc., vol. 76 (2012))

Alexander, D., *Retailing in England during the Industrial Revolution* (Athlone Press, London, 1970)

Allthorpe-Guyton, M., *John Thirtle 1771–1839: Drawings in Norwich Castle Museum* (Norfolk Museums Service, Norwich, 1977)

Alsop, J.D., 'Contemporary remarks on the 1768 election in Norfolk and Suffolk', *Norfolk Archaeology*, vol. 38, pt 1 (1981)

Armstrong, D., *A Short History of Norfolk County Cricket* (Larks Press, Dereham, 1990)

Aslet, C. and Musson, J., 'Restoration and retirement: Peterhouse, Cambridge', *Country Life*, 22 Apr. 2009

Barber, S., 'The Coltishall Commons Management Trust', *The Marlpit: The community paper for the villages of Horstead, Coltishall and Great Hautbois* (Horstead, Sept. 1991)

Barker, H., *Newspapers, Politics and English Society 1695–1855* (Longman and Pearson Education Ltd, Harlow, 2000)

Barnes, P., *Norfolk Landowners since 1880* (CEAS, Norwich, 1993)

Barney, J., *The Defence of Norfolk 1793–1815: Norfolk in the Napoleonic Wars* (Mintaka Books, Norwich, 2000)

Barney, J., *The Trials of Wells Harbour* (Mintaka Books, Norwich, 2000)

Barney, J.M., 'Building a fortune: Philip Case, attorney, 1712–92', *Norfolk Archaelogy*, vol. 43, pt 3 (2000)

Barrell, J. and Mee, J., eds, *Trials for Treason and Sedition, 1792–1794* (8 vols, Pickering & Chatto, London, 2006, 2007)

Barringer, C., *Exploring the Norfolk Market Town* (Poppyland Publishing, Cromer, 2011)

Batty Shaw, A., *Norfolk and Norwich Medicine: A retrospect* (The Norwich Medico-Chirurgical Society, Norwich, 1992)

Baudey, E., 'The liberty of voting restored: William Hogarth's Election series as a vision of electoral (dis)order', in *Hogarth's Election Entertainment: Artists at the hustings* (Sir John Soane's Museum and Apollo Magazine, London, 2001)

Bellamy, E.J., *Methodism in Holt: A short history* (Holt, 1988)

Bellamy, J.M., *The Trade and Shipping of Nineteenth-Century Hull* (E. Yorkshire Local History Soc., 1971)

Belton, V., *The Norwich to Cromer Turnpike* (Ingworth, 1998)

Binfield, C., 'Architectural cousinhood', *Religious Dissent in East Anglia*, ed. N. Virgoe and T. Williamson (CEAS, Norwich, 1993)

Bircham, N., 'My Opinion', *Bulletin of the Broads Society* (Sept. 1970)

Bird, M., ed., *The Diary of Mary Hardy 1773–1809* (4 vols, Burnham Press, Kingston upon Thames, 2013)

Bird, M., ed., *The Remaining Diary of Mary Hardy 1773–1809* (Burnham Press, Kingston upon Thames, 2013)

Bird, M., 'When working boats sailed from Panxworth Staithe', *Marshland Mardler: the magazine for Upton, South Walsham, Ranworth and Panxworth* (Dec. 2014)

Black, J., *George III: America's last king* (Yale Univ. Press, London, 2006)

Blayney Brown, D., Hemingway, A. and Lyles, A., *Romantic Landscape: The Norwich School of Painters* (Tate Gallery Publishing, London, 2000)

Bond, R., *Coltishall: Heyday of a Norfolk Village* (Poppyland Publishing, N. Walsham, 1986)

Bonnet, P.R.F., *A Short History of the Royal Regiment of Artillery* (The Royal Artillery Historical Trust, 1994)

Bourne, G., *Change in the Village* (Gerald Duckworth & Co., London, 1955; 1st pub. 1912)

Bower, P., *Hathor: The story of a Norfolk pleasure wherry* (Broads Authority, Norwich, 1989)

Boyes, J. and Russell, R., *The Canals of Eastern England* (David and Charles, Newton Abbot, 1977)

Bray, D., *The Story of the Norfolk Wherries* (Jarrold Colour Publications, Norwich, [1978])

Brewer, J., *The Common People and Politics 1750–1790s* (Chadwyck-Healey, Cambridge, 1986)

Brewer, J., *The Sinews of Power: War, money and the English state, 1688–1783* (Unwin Hyman, London, 1989)

Brown, J., *The English Market Town: A social and economic history 1750–1914* (The Crowood Press, Marlborough, 1986)

Burley, T.L.G., *Playhouses and Players of East Anglia* (Jarrold & Sons Ltd, Norwich, 1928)

Burton, A., *The Canal Builders* (2nd edn David & Charles, Newton Abbot, 1981)

Butler, A. and A., *Somerleyton Brickfields* (Somerleyton, 1980)

Campbell, B.M.S., 'Population pressure, inheritance and the land market in a fourteenth-century peasant community', *Land, Kinship and Life-Cycle*, ed. R.M. Smith (Cambridge Univ. Press, 1984)

Campbell, J. and Middleton, C., *The Man Who Found The Broads* (Hamilton Publications Ltd, Gorleston on Sea, 1999)

Cannadine, D., *Aspects of Aristocracy: Grandeur and decline in modern Britain* (Yale Univ. Press, London, 1994)

Carrodus, C., ed., *Life in a Norfolk Village: The Horning story* (Soman-Wherry Press, Norwich, 1949)

Carter, A., *The Beevor Story* (Fundenhall, 1993)

Chartier, R., *Jack Cade, the skin of a dead lamb, and hatred of the written word* (Royal Holloway, University of London, 2006)

Chartres, J., 'The eighteenth-century English inn: a transient "Golden Age"?', in *The World of the Tavern: Public houses in early modern Europe*, ed. B. Kümin and B.A. Tlusty (Ashgate, Aldershot, 2002)

Church, R., 'The family firm in industrial capitalism: International perspectives on hypotheses and history', *Business History*, vol. 35, no. 4 (Oct. 1993)

Clark, C., *The British Malting Industry since 1830* (The Hambledon Press, London, 1998)

Clark, P., *British Clubs and Societies 1580–1800: The origins of an associational world* (Oxford Univ. Press, 2001)

Clausewitz, C. von, *On War*, ed. M. Howard and P. Paret (Princeton Univ. Press, New Jersey, 1984)

Cocke, S., and Hall, L., *Norwich Bridges Past & Present* (Norwich Soc., Norwich, 1994)

Cole, V.G., 'Birthplace of the wherries', *The Norfolk Magazine*, vol. 6, no. 6 (Nov.–Dec. 1953)

Colley, L., 'The apotheosis of George III: Loyalty, royalty and the British nation 1760–1820', *Past & Present*, no. 102 (Feb. 1984)

Colley, L., *Britons: Forging the nation 1707–1837* (Yale Univ. Press, London, 1992)

Colley, L., *Britons: Forging the Nation 1707–1837* (Pimlico, London, 2003; 1st pub. 1992)

Colman, H.C., *Sydney Cozens-Hardy: A memoir* (Jarrold & Sons, Norwich, 1944)

Conway, S., 'The politics of British military and naval mobilization, 1775–83', *English Historical Review*, vol. 112, no. 449 (Nov. 1997)

Cookson, J.E., *The British Armed Nation, 1793–1815* (Oxford Univ. Press, 1997)

Copeman, W.O., *Copemans of Norwich 1789–1946* (Jarrold and Sons, Norwich 1946)

Corfield, P.J., *The Impact of English Towns 1700–1800* (Oxford Univ. Press, 1982)

Corfield, P. J., 'From second city to regional capital', *Norwich since 1550*, ed. C. Rawcliffe and R. Wilson (Hambledon and London, 2004)

Cossons, A., 'The turnpike roads of Norfolk', *Norfolk Archaeology*, vol. 30 (1952)

Costin, W. C. and Watson, J. S., *The Law and Working of the Constitution: Documents 1660–1914* (2 vols, Adam & Charles Black, London, 2nd edn 1961; 1st pub. 1952)

Cozens-Hardy, B., 'The Glaven valley', *Norfolk Archaeology*, vol. 33 (1965)

Cozens-Hardy, B., 'Havens in North Norfolk', *Norfolk Archaeology*, vol. 35 (1972)

Cozens-Hardy, B., *The History of Letheringsett in the County of Norfolk with extracts from the diary of Mary Hardy (1773 to 1809)* (Jarrold & Sons, Norwich, 1957)

Cozens-Hardy, B., 'The Holt road', *Norfolk Archaeology*, vol. 31 (1957)

Cozens-Hardy, B., ed., *Mary Hardy's Diary* (Norfolk Record Society, vol. 37 (1968))

[**Cozens-Hardy**, M.], *A Beloved Memory: Raven Cozens-Hardy* (Cley, 1918)

Cozens-Hardy, S., *Glavenside* (Norwich, 1935)

Cozens-Hardy, S., *Memorials of William Hardy Cozens-Hardy of Letheringsett, Norfolk* (Norwich, 1936)

Cranfield, G. A., *A Hand-list of English Provincial Newspapers and Periodicals 1700–1760* (Cambridge Bibliographical Society monograph no. 2, Bowes & Bowes, London, 1961)

Dain, A., 'An enlightened and polite society', in *Norwich since 1550*, ed. C. Rawcliffe and R. Wilson (Hambledon, London, 2004)

Davies, D., *A Brief History of Fighting Ships: Ships of the line and Napoleonic sea battles 1793–1815* (Constable & Robinson, London, 2002)

Davison, A. P., *Justly Celebrated Ales: A directory of Norfolk brewers 1850–1990* (Brewery History Soc., 1991)

Defoe, D., *A Tour through the Whole Island of Great Britain* (2 vols, J.M. Dent & Sons, London, 1962; 1st pub. 1724–6)

Digby, A., *Pauper Palaces* (Routledge & Keegan Paul, London, 1978)

Ditchfield, G. M., 'The Diary of Mary Hardy 1773–1809 (4 vols) and The Remaining Diary of Mary Hardy 1773–1809' (book reviews), *English Historical Review*, vol. 130, no. 542 (Feb. 2015)

Duncan-Jones, R., *The Economy of the Roman Empire* (2nd edn Cambridge Univ. Press, 1982)

Durst, D. W., *Letheringsett: The industrial history of a Norfolk village* (Norfolk Industrial Archaeology Soc., 2013)

Dutt, W. A., *The Norfolk Broads* (Methuen, London, 1903)

Earl, D. C., *On the Absence of the Railway Engine* (University of Hull, 1980)

Eaton, F. R., *An Outline of the History of the Provincial Grand Lodge of Norfolk 1759–1959* (Soman-Wherry Press Ltd, Norwich, 1960)

Eaton, F. R., *Some Masonic Events relating to the Province of Norfolk 1724 to 1944* (Soman-Wherry Press Ltd, Norwich, 1945)

Ebdon, J., 'History of the Cley Hall Estate: The emergence of the Hardys 1839–1855', *The Glaven Historian*, no. 12 (2010)

Ebdon, J., 'History of the Cley Hall Estate, pt 2', *The Glaven Historian*, no. 14 (2014)

Ecclestone, A. W., *The Old White Lion, Great Yarmouth, and the Symonds Family* (E. Lacon & Co. Ltd, Gt Yarmouth, nd [*c*.1946])

Eden, P., 'Land surveyors in Norfolk 1550–1850, pt 2', *Norfolk Archaeology*, vol. 36, pt 2 (1975)

Ehrman, J., *The Younger Pitt: The consuming struggle* (Constable, London, 1996)

Emsley, C., ed., *North Riding Naval Recruits: the Quota Acts and the Quota Men 1795–1797* (N. Yorks County Council, Northallerton, 1978)

Evans, G. E., *Ask the Fellows who Cut the Hay* (Faber & Faber, London, 1965)

Evans, G. E., *Where Beards Wag All: The relevance of the oral tradition* (Faber & Faber, London, 1977)

Faden, W., *Faden's Map of Norfolk* (Larks Press, Dereham, 1989; 1st pub. 1797)

Fawcett, T., 'The culture of late-Georgian Norwich: a conflict of evidence', *UEA Bulletin* new series, vol. 5 (1972)

Fawcett, T., *Music in Eighteenth-Century Norwich and Norfolk* (Centre of E. Anglian Studies, Norwich, 1979)

Fawcett, T., 'Patriotic transparencies in Norwich, 1798–1814', *Norfolk Archaeology*, vol. 34 (1968)

Forder, C., *A History of the Paston School, North Walsham, Norfolk* (2nd edn N. Walsham, 1975), with *Supplementary notes to the second edition of 1975, pt 2* (N. Walsham, 1981)

Fordham, M., *Halesworth Quay and the Blyth Navigation* (Halesworth and District Museum, 2012)

Fowler, C., 'Changes in provincial retail practice during the eighteenth century, with particular reference to central–southern England', *Business History*, vol. 40, no. 4 (Oct. 1998)

Fraser, A., 'Lord Orford's droll-dressed Militia men', *Parson Woodforde Society Quarterly Journal*, vol. 29, no. 1 (spring 1996)

French, V., 'Ice, wind and snow', *The Lifeboat*, issue 596 (summer 2011)

Garry, M.-A., 'Sport as a political meditator: Thomas Coke and the Layers of Booton', *Norfolk Archaeology*, vol. 43, pt 3 (2000)

George, M., *The Land Use, Ecology and Conservation of Broadland* (Packard Publishing, Chichester, 1992)

Gibson, J. and Medlycott, M., *Militia Lists and Musters 1757–1876* (Federation of Family History Societies, 2nd edn Birmingham, 1990)

Gifford, A., 'History of the Duke's Head Hotel' (leaflet, King's Lynn, nd, pre-2005)

Glover, B., *Prince of Ales: The history of brewing in Wales* (Alan Sutton Publishing Ltd, Stroud, 1993)

Glover, R., *Britain at Bay: Defence against Bonaparte, 1803–14* (George Allen & Unwin Ltd, London, 1973)

Green, E., Corfield, P. and Harvey, C., *Elections in Metropolitan London 1700–1850* (2 vols, Bristol Academic Press, Westbury-on-Trym, 2013)

Grice, E., *Rogues and Vagabonds; or The Actors' Road to Respectability* (Terence Dalton Ltd, Lavenham, 1977)

Griffin, E., *England's Revelry: A history of popular sports and pastimes 1660–1830* (The British Academy and Oxford Univ. Press, 2005)

Hackforth, N., *Solo for Horne: the biography of Kenneth Horne* (Angus & Robertson, London, 1976)

Haines, C.W., 'Norfolk milestones, Part 2', *Journal of the Norfolk Industrial Archaeology Society*, vol. 4, no. 2 (1987)

Haines, C.W., 'Norfolk milestones, Part 7', *Journal of the Norfolk Industrial Archaeology Society*, vol. 6, no. 2 (1997)

Hales, J., *Three Centuries at Holt* (Priest Publications, Hunstanton, 1967)

Harrison, B., *Drink and the Victorians: The temperance question in England 1815–1872* (2nd edn Keele Univ. Press, 1994; 1st pub. 1970)

Harrison, B., 'Religion and recreation in nineteenth-century England', *Past & Present*, no. 38 (1967)

Harvey, A.D., *Collision of Empires: Britain in three World Wars 1793–1945* (Phoenix, London, 1994)

Hewitt, R., *Map of a Nation: A biography of the Ordnance Survey* (Granta Publications, London, 2010)

Hipper, K., *Smugglers All: Centuries of Norfolk smuggling* (Larks Press, Guist Bottom, 2001)

Hodskinson, J., *Hodskinson's Map of Suffolk in 1783* (Larks Press, Guist Bottom, 2003; 1st pub. 1783)

Hole, R., *Pulpits, Politics and Public Order in England 1760–1832* (Cambridge Univ. Press, 1989)

Holman, P., 'The Bure Navigation 1779–1912', *A Backwards Glance: Events in Aylsham's Past*, ed. G. Gale *et al.* (Aylsham Local History Soc., 1995)

Holmes, N., *The Lawless Coast: Smuggling, anarchy and murder in North Norfolk in the 1780s* (Larks Press, Guist Bottom, 2009)

Hooton, J., *The Glaven Ports: A maritime history of Blakeney, Cley and Wiveton in north Norfolk* (Blakeney History Group, Blakeney, 1996)

Hoskins, W.G., *The Making of the English Landscape* (Penguin Books Ltd, Harmondsworth, 1970)

Jefferson, R., 'The William and Thomas', *The Glaven Historian*, no. 5 (2002)

Jewson, C.B., *The Jacobin City: A portrait of Norwich 1788–1802* (Blackie & Son, Glasgow and London, 1975)

Jones, G. and Rose, M.B., 'Family capitalism', *Business History*, vol. 35, no. 4 (Oct. 1993)

Kelham, R., 'Some gleanings from the ship registers', *The Glaven Historian*, no. 3 (2000)

Kelly, T., *A History of Adult Education in Great Britain from the Middle Ages to the Twentieth Century* (3rd edn Liverpool Univ. Press, 1992; 1st pub. 1962)

Kemp, R.A.F., *Staithes: A survey and register* (The Broads Authority, Norwich, 1986)

Ketton-Cremer, R.W., 'The county election of 1806', *A Norfolk Gallery* (Faber and Faber, London, 1948)

Ketton-Cremer, R.W., *Felbrigg: The story of a house* (Futura Publications, London, 1982; 1st pub. 1962)

Ketton-Cremer, R.W., 'George Walpole, third Earl of Orford', *A Norfolk Gallery* (Faber and Faber, London, 1948)

Ketton-Cremer, R.W., 'Norfolk and the threat of invasion', *Norfolk Portraits* (Faber and Faber, London, 1944)

Ketton-Cremer, R.W., 'The Tour of Norfolk', *Norfolk Assembly* (Faber and Faber Ltd, London, 1957)

Keys, D. and Smith, K., *Tall Ships on the Tyne* (Tyne Bridge Publishing, Newcastle upon Tyne, 2005)

Kipling, R., *Kipling's English History*, ed. M. Laski (BBC, London, 1974)

Kirby, M., *Albion: The story of the Norfolk trading wherry* (Norfolk Wherry Trust and Jarrold Publishing, Norwich, 1998)

Knights, M., 'Politics, 1660–1835', *Norwich since 1550*, ed. C. Rawcliffe and R. Wilson (Hambledon & London, London, 2004)

Langford, P., *Englishness Identified: Manners and character 1650–1850* (Oxford Univ. Press, 2000)

Langford, P., *A Polite and Commercial People: England 1727–1783* (Oxford Univ. Press, 1992)

Larby, E., ed., *Mr Marten's Travels in East Anglia: The 1825 journal of Robert Humphrey Marten* (Poppyland Publishing, Cromer, 2012)

Lavery, B., *We shall fight on the Beaches: Defying Napoleon and Hitler, 1805 and 1940* (Conway, London, 2009)

Lee, R., *Rural Society and the Anglican Clergy, 1815–1914: Encountering and managing the poor* (The Boydell Press, Woodbridge, 2006)

Levine, G.J., *A Concise History of Brundall and Braydeston* (Brundall, 1977)

Lloyd, C., ed., *The Keith Papers: vol. 3, 1803–1815* (Navy Records Soc., 1955)

Longford, E., *Wellington: The Years of the Sword* (Granada Publishing Ltd, 1971)

Longmate, N., *Island Fortress: The defence of Great Britain 1603–1945* (Hutchinson, London, 1991),

Macnair, A. and Williamson, T., *William Faden and Norfolk's 18th-century Landscape* (Windgather Press, Oxbow Books, Oxford, 2010)

Malster, R., *The Mardler's Companion: A dictionary of East Anglian dialect* (The Malthouse Press, Holbrook, 1999)

Malster, R., *The Norfolk and Suffolk Broads* (Phillimore, Chichester, 2003)

Malster, R., *Saved from the Sea* (Terence Dalton Ltd, Lavenham, 1974)

Malster, R., *Wherries and Waterways* (Terence Dalton Ltd, Lavenham, 1971)

Mann, E., *Old Bungay* (Heath Cranton Ltd, London, 1934)

Mathias, P., *The Brewing Industry in England 1700–1830* (Cambridge Univ. Press, 1959)

Mathias, P., 'Swords and ploughshares: the armed forces, medicine and public health in the late eighteenth century', in P. Mathias, *The Transformation of England* (Methuen, London, 1979)

Mears, N., Raffe, A., Taylor, S. and Williamson, P. (with L. Bates), eds, *National Prayers: Special worship since the Reformation*, vol. 1, 1533–1688 (Church of England Record Soc., vol. 20, with the Boydell Press, Woodbridge, 2013)

Middleton, C.S., ed., *The Broadland Photographers* (Wensum Books, Norwich, 1978)

Miller, C., *The Amiable Mrs Peach* (The Lasse Press, Norwich, 2016)

Millican, P., *A History of Horstead and Stanninghall, Norfolk* (Norwich, 1937)

Millican, P., 'The rebuilding of Wroxham Bridge in 1576', *Norfolk Archaeology*, vol. 26 (1938)

Mitchell, B.R. and Deane, P., *Abstract of British Historical Statistics* (Cambridge Univ. Press, 1971)

Mitchell, L.G., *Charles James Fox* (Penguin, London, 1997)

Mollard, T. and Gale, G., eds, *Millgate, Aylsham* (2nd edn Aylsham Local History Soc., 2006; 1st pub. 1993)

Morris, J., *Oxford* (Faber and Faber, London, 1965)

Mui, H-C. and Mui, L.H., *Shops and Shopkeeping in Eighteenth-Century England* (McGill-Queen's Univ. Press, Canada, and Routledge, London, 1989)

Namier, L., *The Structure of Politics at the Accession of George III* (2nd edn Macmillan, London, 1957; 1st pub. in 2 vols 1929)

Navickas, K., 'Lieut. General Sir James Henry Craig's orders to commanders in the Eastern Military District, 1803–04', in Franklin, A. and Philp, M., *Napoleon and the Invasion of Britain* (Bodleian Library, Oxford, 2003)

Neale, J.E., 'November 17th', *Essays in Elizabethan History* (Jonathan Cape, London, 1963)

Neave, N. and Douglas, C., '*Like Carrying Coals to Newcastle': The story of the Tanfield Way* (Summerhill Books, Newcastle upon Tyne, 2009)

Nenadić, S., 'The small family firm in Victorian Britain', *Business History*, vol. 35, no. 4 (Oct. 1993)

Obelkevich, J., *Religion and Rural Society: South Lindsey 1825–1875* (Clarendon Press, Oxford, 1976)

Oxford Dictionary of National Biography, ed. H.C.G. Matthew and B. Harrison (Oxford Univ. Press, 2004)

Pargeter, V. and L., *Maud: A Norfolk wherry* (Ingatestone, 1990)

Pearson, L., *British Breweries: An architectural history* (The Hambledon Press, London, 1999)

Perren, R., 'Markets and marketing', *The Agrarian History of England and Wales: Volume VI 1750–1850*, ed. G.E. Mingay (Cambridge Univ. Press, 1989)

[**Perryman**, J.] alias 'Boy John', 'The Norfolk keel', *Journal of the Norfolk Wherry Trust* (spring 1989)

Petrides, A. and Downs, J., eds, *Sea Soldier: An officer of Marines with Duncan, Nelson, Collingwood and Cockburn* (Parapress Ltd, Tunbridge Wells, 2000)

Phillipson, D., 'The oldest lifeboat in the world', *The Lifeboat* (summer 2002)

Plumb, J.H., *The Commercialisation of Leisure in Eighteenth-century England: The Stenton Lecture 1972* (University of Reading, 1973)

Poole, R., *The Lancashire Wakes Holidays* (Lancashire County Books, Preston, 1994)

Poole, R., *Time's Alteration: Calendar reform in early modern England* (UCL Press, London, 1998)

Preston, J., *That Odd Rich Old Woman: The life and troubled times of Elizabeth Barbara Bulwer-Lytton of Knebworth House 1773–1843* (Plush Publishing, Dorchester, 1998)

Radford, L.B., *History of Holt: A brief study of parish, church, and school* (Holt, 1908)

Ransom, P.J.G., *The Archaeology of the Transport Revolution 1750–1850* (The Windmill Press, Kingswood, 1984)

Richards, P., *King's Lynn* (Phillimore, Chichester, 1990)

Richmond, L. and Turton, A., eds, *The Brewing Industry: A guide to historical records* (Manchester Univ. Press, 1990)

Robertson, H., *Mariners of Dundee: Their city, their river, their fraternity* (PDQ Print Services, Dundee, 2006)

Rochefoucauld, F. de la, *A Frenchman's Year in Suffolk, 1784*, ed. N. Scarfe (The Boydell Press and Suffolk Records Soc., vol. 30 (1988))

Rolt, L.T.C., *Victorian Engineering* (Penguin, Harmondsworth, 1974)

Rule, J., *The Experience of Labour in Eighteenth-Century Industry* (Croom Helm, London, 1981)

Scholes, P.A., *The Concise Oxford Dictionary of Music* (Oxford Univ. Press, London, 1952)

Scott, A.M., *Discovering Dundee: The story of a city* (Mercat Press, Edinburgh, 1999; 1st pub. 1989)

Sinclair, O., *When Wherries Sailed By: Recollections of a Broadland village* (Poppyland Publishing, N. Walsham, 1987)

Smith, W., *The Drovers' Roads of the Middle Marches: Their history and how to find them today* (Logaston Press, Woonton Almesley, 2013)

Sparkes, M., 'A passage in time, industry and sport on the Norwich River', *Harnser: The magazine of the Broads Society* (Apr. 2014)

Sparkes, M.J., 'The *William and Mary* and the *Nelly*', *Journal of the Norfolk Wherry Trust* (spring 1988)

Spooner, S., ed., *Sail and Storm: The Aylsham navigation* (Aylsham Local History Society, 2012)

Stirling, A.M.W., *Coke of Norfolk and his Friends* (John Lane, The Bodley Head, London, 1912; 1st pub. 1908)

Strachan, H., *European Armies and the Conduct of War* (Routledge, London, 1983)

Taylor, P., *The Tollhouses of Norfolk* (Polystar Press, Ipswich, 2009)

Terraine, J., *Trafalgar* (Wordsworth Editions Ltd, Ware, 1998)

Thomas, K., 'Work and leisure in pre-industrial society', *Past & Present*, no. 29 (1964)

Thompson, E.P., *Education and Experience* (Leeds Univ. Press, 1968)

Thompson, E.P., *The Making of the English Working Class* (Penguin, Harmondsworth, 1968)

Thompson, E.P., 'The Moral Economy Reviewed', in E.P. Thompson, *Customs in Common* (Penguin, London, 1993)

Thompson, F.M.L., *Gentrification and the Enterprise Culture: Britain 1780–1980* (Oxford Univ. Press, 2001)

Tindal Hart, A., *The Curate's Lot: The story of the unbeneficed English clergy* (The Country Book Club, Newton Abbot, 1971)

Tinniswood, A., *A History of Country House Visiting: Five centuries of tourism and taste* (Basil Blackwell and the National Trust, Oxford and London, 1989)

Trevelyan, G.M., *Illustrated English Social History*, vol. 3 (Longmans, London, 1960)

Urban, M., *Generals: Ten British commanders who shaped the world* (Faber and Faber, London, 2005)

Vaughan-Lewis, W. and M., *Aylsham: A Nest of Norfolk lawyers* (Itteringham History, 2014)

Venn, J.A., *Alumni Cantabrigienses 1752–1900*, (6 vols, Cambridge Univ. Press, 1940–54)

Ville, S.P., *English Shipowning during the Industrial Revolution: Michael Henley and Son, London Shipowners, 1770–1830* (Manchester Univ. Press, 1987)

Vince, J., *Discovering Carts and Wagons* (3rd edn Shire Publications Ltd, Princes Risborough, 1987)

Vincent, J.R., *Pollbooks: How Victorians voted* (Cambridge University Press, London, 1967)

Vine, P.A.L., *The Royal Military Canal: An historical account of the waterway and military road from Shorncliffe in Kent to Cliff End in Sussex* (Amberley Publishing, Stroud, 2010)

Virgoe, N. and Yaxley, S., eds, *The Banville Diaries: Journals of a Norfolk gamekeeper 1822–44* (Collins, London, 1986)

Vries, J. de, 'The Industrial Revolution and the Industrious Revolution', *Journal of Economic History*, no. 54 (1994)

Wade Martins, S., *Coke of Norfolk 1754–1842: A biography* (The Boydell Press, Woodbridge, 2009)

Wade Martins, S., 'Voting in the late 18th century', *An Historical Atlas of Norfolk*, ed. P. Wade-Martins (Norfolk Museums Service, Norwich, 1993)

Watkin, D., 'Letheringsett Hall, Norfolk: The home of the Lady Cozens-Hardy', *Country Life*, 5 Jan. 1967

Watson, J.S., *The Reign of George III 1760–1815* (Oxford Univ. Press, 1960)

Whyman, S.E., *The Pen and the People: English letter writers 1660–1800* (Oxford Univ. Press, 2009)

Willan, T.S., 'River navigation and trade from the Witham to the Yare, 1600–1750', *Norfolk Archaeology*, vol. 26 (1938)

Williamson, P., 'Introduction: 1689–1870', in P. Williamson, A. Raffe, S. Taylor and N. Mears, eds, *National Prayers: Special worship since the Reformation*, vol. 2, 1689–1870 (Church of England Record Soc., vol. 22, with the Boydell Press, Woodbridge, 2017)

Williamson, T., *The Norfolk Broads: A landscape history* (Manchester Univ. Press, 1997)

Wilson, A., *Wherries and Windmills* (Barton Turf, 1982)

Woodforde, D.H., ed., 'Nancy Woodforde: A diary for the year 1792', *Woodforde Papers and Diaries* (Parson Woodforde Soc. and Morrow & Co., Bungay, 1990)

Woodforde, J., *The Diary of a Country Parson*, ed. J. Beresford (5 vols Oxford Univ. Press, 1924–31)

Wright, J., 'Coals from Newcastle', *The Glaven Historian*, no. 3 (2000)

Wright, J., 'The old "Guildhall" at Blakeney', *The Glaven Historian*, no. 5 (2002)

Yaxley, J., *A Jam round Barton Turf* (Barton Turf, 2006)

Yaxley, P., *Looking Back at Norfolk Cricket* (Nostalgia Publications, Toftwood, 1997)

Yaxley, S., ed., *Sherringhamia: The journal of Abbot Upcher 1813–16* (Larks Press, Guist Bottom, 1986)

York, N.L., 'Burning the dockyard: John the Painter and the American Revolution', *The Portsmouth Papers*, no. 71 (Portsmouth City Council, 2001)

Index

Volume 4

These contractions are used to denote
Mary Hardy's family:

Hs	the Hardys
MH	Mary Hardy [*diarist*]
WH	William Hardy [*husband*]
RH	Raven Hardy [*son*]
WHj	William Hardy jnr [*son*]
MA	Mary Ann (Cozens) [*daughter*]
JC	Jeremiah Cozens [*son-in-law*]
HR	Henry Raven [*nephew/diarist*]

A

'**Abraham's Bosom**', refuges for ships, 246

Absolon, William, of Gt Yarmouth, potter and artist, *pl. 3*, **32**

accidents, collapse of N. Walsham church tower, **384**; danger from block running along iron horse on wherries, 215; destructive fire at Letheringsett, 652; steam vessels' wash capsizes other boats, 226; Stephen Moore crushed to death in marlpit, 307; wherry capsizes at Lamas, 63, **81**, 210; wherry skipper Thomas Pooley killed on boat by winch handle, 193, **210**; wherry sinks on Yare after collision, 213
drownings:
  in rivers: five boys in Humber, 50; John Oliver drowns in Bure, 208; keelmen and wherrymen, **161**, **183**; men die in flight from press gang, 188; Norwich waterman at Coldham Hall, **210**, 211; two on wherry on Breydon, **210**, 211
  at sea, 48, 266, 555; more than 700 on HMS *Royal George*, 435; seven Sheringham fishermen, 232; ship's boy, 267: *see also Nelly*, shipwreck; shipwreck
  military: Cromer surgeon's leg shot off in Volunteers' exercise, 541; deaths caused by guns and gunpowder, 406, **622**; Holt Volunteer killed by gun in loyal salute, 544
  road: caused by rutted roads, 46; deaths of William III and Sir Robert Peel in falls from horse, 44; drayman William High killed while delivering, **649**; death of William Salter, stage-coach driver, 45, **45**; drink a factor in falls, 44; excise super-

accidents, road (*cont.*)
  visor breaks thigh in fall from horse, 45; fatal incidents at fords, 30, **46**, 47, **47**, 447; fewer horseback falls as vehicle use rises, 5, 44, 48; hazards, 19–20, 25; horse poses greatest danger to workforce, 44; MH injured in fall from runaway donkey cart driven by MA, **40**, 48; postchaise's good safety record, 48; Robert and Hannah Raven fall from horse, 31; series of deaths and injuries with vehicles, 44–6, 48; stage coach and postchaise relatively safe, 44; three deaths in falls from horses in early diary years, 44–5
see also deaths and funerals; shooting, deaths

Ackermann, Rudolph (1764–1834), London artist and printseller; **593**

acknowledgments, by author, xviii–xxi

Acle, Norf., county bridge and turnpike, 26, **53**, **69**, 167; Freemasons' lodge, **327**; ? Hs' wherry moves to after sale, 226; named as home berth in register of vessels, 194; new road to, **161**, 195: *see also* fairs

actors, *see* players

Acts of Parliament, 316, **317**; Blakeney Harbour, 232–3, 243, **244**, 245–6; burial of bodies cast ashore, 286; county bridges, 27, 30; enclosure, 122–3, 433; large stock held by Hs, 429; Militia service in Ireland, 568; protection of animals, and of women and children at work, 413; provisions enforced by justices, 20–1; register of commercial vessels on inland waterways, **92**, 93, 186–7, 190; roads, 17, 18, 19, 22:

B

D

Dunston, Co. Durham, staithes at end of Tanfield Way, 265

Dunwich, Suff., captured cutter retaken off, 302; coal trade with Tyne, 255

Durrant, Davy (1704–59), of Scottow Hall, barrister; **87**

Durrant, Thomas (d.1790 aged 56), Bt 1784, of Scottow Hall, son of Davy; careful recording, 82–3; Commissioner and Treasurer of Aylsham navigation, 81–2; at loggerheads with Horstead rector, 99–100

Durrant family, of Scottow; 623

Dusgate, Francis (d.1801 aged 77), Holt watchmaker; draws WH's tooth, 333

Dutch, the, *pl. 43*, 189; British excise cutters to Low Countries to evacuate troops, 306; Camperdown, 517, 521, 586; clipper *Albatros*, **249**; close relations with east-coast Britain in peace, 270–1, **271**, 305–6, 506; commercial decline, 234, 235; engagement in W. Friesland, 280; failure of British expeditions to Den Helder and Walcheren, 511, 523; fishermen resupplied on beaches, 248, 507; fishing fleet, 271, **273**; Norfolk's trade with Rotterdam, 250, 295; passengers to Rotterdam, 263; privateer brings *Nelly* to Amsterdam, 231, 277, 278–80, **281**; proximity to Gt Yarmouth, 506; seamen at Gt Yarmouth and Mundesley, 50, 506; smuggling operations run from Holland, 303; threat to east-coast Britain, 299–300, 533, 583; tonnages of prizes, 300; United Provinces annexed by French, 270, 305, 487, 497, 506, 576; use of shallow-draughted craft for invasion, 569; WH to sale of Dutch prize at Cley, 293: *see also* war

duties, *see* taxes

Dye, Isaac, keel skipper; 168

E

Earlham, Norf., county bridge, 26; Hall, **449**

earthquake, in Guatemala, **429**

Earsham, Norf., five county bridges, 26

Eastaugh, William (Billy), Letheringsett carpenter and wheelwright; **649**

East Dereham, Norf., 24, 640, 655; celebrations for King's recovery, 591; in dense network of lesser roads, 18; peace ball, 397; turnpike, 23

East Harling, Norf., 588

Easto, Nathaniel, Coltishall butcher; at wherry launch, 157, 219;

Eaton, Christopher, Gt Yarmouth merchant; 141

Eaton, Norwich, shooting, 402

East Ruston, Norf., 255

East Tuddenham, Norf., 597

Ebbage, William, of Ranworth; skipper of Panxworth-berthed keel, 196

Edgefield, Norf., 13, 324; avoided by coaches, **347**; Hs buy trees, 24; Hs' innkeeper dies in fall from horse, 44; treacherous roads, 19–20, 21; Tom Paine burnt in effigy, 493

Edinburgh, 410

Edmund, 90-ton keel berthed at Gt Yarmouth, **186**; needs crew of four, **186**, 187–8

Edwards, Henry (d.1817 aged 77), of Coltishall, Hs' maltster and farm servant; builds road across common to lock for WH, 149: *see also* workforce

Edwards, John, Sheringham innkeeper; 579

Egypt, Battle of the Nile, 517, 586, 588, 597

elections, 437–9, **441**; by-elections, 438; by-election when MP accepts government post, 437, 487; called more often than every seven years, 437; independence prized in candidates, 482–3; Norfolk's six two-member seats in Commons, 436; Oxfordshire, 439, 441; party labels, 448; pocket boroughs, 436, 437, 444–5, 477; public appetite for hot contests, 419, 427, 437, 440; rotten boroughs, 445; scrutinies, 438, 441, 448, 477, 482; venal boroughs, 483; Westminster, 441; WH votes in eight elections for Norwich and Norfolk, 424, 440, 442–3, 448

canvassing: candidates' committees, 446; charting influence, **462**, 463, **465**, 465; Coke's Glorious Revolution Ball as canvass, **452**, 453–4; of Hs, 448–9, 450

contested elections, **422**, 424, 427, 438–40, 448–9; dynamics of dual voting, **465**, 466, 467, 468, 469; electoral pacts to avoid contest create democratic deficit, **422**, 425–6, 454, 455, 483–4; near civil war in 1802, 1806 and early 1807, 495; none for Norfolk county between 1768 and 1802, 424, 474; turnout, 471–3; university seats uncontested, **424**

individual polls:
  by-election, 1776: 475–6;
  by-election, 1786: 448, 482; WH and WHj to, riot at Norwich, Hobart elected, declared void, 419, 474;
  by-election, 1787: 448, 482
  by-election, 1794: fought on peace issue, Windham still wins, 487, 494, 524, 582
  by-election, 1797: 450
  by-election, 1799: voting for Fellowes and Frere, 421

J

Jewell, Edmund (d.1784 aged 65), Holt attorney, Chairman of Quarter Sessions; **500**, 533

Jex, John (d.1797 aged 52), Letheringsett blacksmith; voting, 444, 447,

Jodrell, Mrs Elizabeth (d.1794 aged 79), née Warner, of Bayfield Hall, wife of Paul; 340, 406, 461

Jodrell, Henry (1752–1814), MP, of Bayfield Hall, barrister, Recorder of Gt Yarmouth, son of Paul; 399, 401, 461, **478**; helps unseat T.W. Coke and Windham, unites parties after election strife, 479–80, 495; and Holt theatre, 341, **346**; joins Volunteers, 533; loses Gt Yarmouth seat, returned for Bramber, Suss., 444; widow Johanna Elizabeth, Mrs Best, 633

Jodrell, Paul (d.1751), MP, 445

Jodrell, Richard Paul (1745–1831), MP, of Lewknor, Oxon, scholar and playwright, son of Paul; 401

Jodrell family, of Bayfield; 623

John and Elizabeth, 40-ton keel for sale at Gt Yarmouth, John Clarke skipper, 168; ? used by Hs for trip to Horning, 206

John and Joseph, keel for sale at Coltishall, 168; owned by John Fiddy and Joseph Browne, 169

John and Mary, wherry berthed at Coltishall, 190

Johnson, John, of Cley; 533

Johnson, John (d.1789 aged 47), Norwich coffee-house owner; bankrupt, 330; hosts Freemasons' lodge, sells warrant to Chapman Ives, 331

Johnson, Robert, Sheringham innkeeper; 579

Johnson, Samuel (1709–84), lexicographer and writer; 480, 552

Johnson, Thomas, Blakeney merchant; 248

Jonathan, Hs' farm boy; 384

Josselyn, John jnr, of Belstead Hall, Suff., surveyor; reports to King's College on Horstead and Coltishall manors, 63, 65, 102–5, **102**

Juler, Rebecca, of Cley; marries soldier from Weybourne Camp, 505

July Flower, 80-ton keel plying Coltishall–Gt Yarmouth, 191

juries, excise and customs officers exempt from service on, 303

justices of the peace, **478**, 644; and bridges, 30; Clerk of the Peace, 26; consulted over shipwrecks, 286, 292; contradictory evidence for pressure over polling, 460, 481; and county budget, 26, 28; Cumberland's not

justices of the peace (*cont.*)
supported by local leaders of society, 564; denied chance to vote in general elections, 425; effective oversight, 21; enforce Acts of Parliament, monitor parish officers' performance, 20–1; identify with those in local area, 562; light touch over political meetings, 488, 493; networking at sessions and dinners, 337; order Faden's map for Grand Jury chamber, 22; and roads, 451

home defence: do not always support lord lieutenant, 515, 562–3, 565; exempt from Militia service, 558; Militia ballot and substitutes, 503, 504; raising Militia and maintenance of Militia families, 512, 514, **514**, 516–17; role in home defence command structure, 513, 528, 531; Volunteers choose to be under supervision of justices, not Army, 542

and labouring class: light touch over riots, 415; lord lieutenant and others on watch for popular risings, 495; middle path between removing sources of disorder and preserving celebrations and rights of poor, 390–1, 415; prosecutions for breaking Sabbath laws, 370; and Sunday working, 204; urge habits of work on, 51, 393

licensing: drovers, 388; met by WH at brewers' sessions, 82; not involved in military camp canteens, 578, 581; regulation of public houses, 393, 415, 460, 481, 488 travelling players': granting of temporary licences, 325, 343; increasing restrictiveness, 354–5; Peter Baret rejects David Fisher's application at Horstead, 343, 354:

see also sessions

K

Kaye, Ann (Nanny), Revd James Woodforde's maidservant; 382

Keeler, Thomas, Guestwick farmer; 579

keelmen, **176**, **177**; daily hardships, 208–9; *Dee-Dar*'s skippers 'Dilly' Smith and 'Tiger' Smith, 177; flout bar on Sunday working, 204; Freemen of Norwich, 208; names of skipper and boy on register of vessels, 190; protected by Quota Acts, 521–2; socialise with local residents, 207; Stephen Cox skippers Symonds' keel, 205; strike of Tyne men over pressing, 188; wealth of data from register, 186–200

crews: do not load and unload, 203; *Edmund*, 90 tons, needs three men helping skipper,

M

navigations, problems (*cont.*)
age of water, 110; some not deep enough
for seagoing ships, 65; tolls, 95, 140; trade
bypassed by coastal cart gaps, 110:
see also Acts, authorising navigations;
Aylsham navigation; Blyth navigation;
Bungay navigation; canal; inland ports;
locks; New Cut; North Walsham and
Dilham Canal; rivers; Royal Military
Canal; staithes

Neatishead, Norf., beer deliveries, 5; loading
bay under warehouse for vessels, 139;
manorial records, 563
White Horse: club, 335; Thomas Scrape at
Cakerow Fair, 380

Nelly, William Hardy jnr's 60-ton sloop, *pls 24,
43*, 241; 12-year history, with only 2½ years
of peace 270–95, 307; home ports Dundee,
later Blakeney, 48, **232**, 238, **246**, **276**; measurements and tonnages, 252–3; other local
ships named *Nelly*, 291–2; owned by Robert
Mathew, captured by Dutch, retaken by
Royal Navy as prize, 231, 277; shallow
draught, **276**
cargoes: 130 quarters of malt to Liverpool,
252; coal and oilcake, 231, 286; malt from
Cley to London, 283; ship and cargo not
insured when lost, 286; ship unable to sail
fully laden, 252, 294; tallow to London,
263; timber from Norway, 283;
shipwreck: crew die of drowning, 287; death
of Richard Randall, **231**, 286; lost near
Blakeney Pit with captain and all crew on
way home from Newcastle, 231, 246, 286;
not reported in press, 290; records of Sea
Fencibles identify crew, 287; ship's boy,
275, 287; ship's papers washed ashore,
279, 286; timber sold at Wells, **247**; WHj
and George Phillippo recover parts of
wreck, 286; WHj and Mary Raven call
on Mrs Coe, 287
valuations: bought by WHj at Gt Yarmouth
for £590, 231, 275, 277, 302; calculations
by WHj, 252; decline in value, 295, 307;
sale valuation in war, 284
voyages: Blakeney to Liverpool via Forth
and Clyde Canal, 241, **242**, 283; cleared
by Customs, 297–8, 302; London and
Newcastle, 283, 286; Norway for timber,
283:
see also Coe, Capt. John

Nelson, Mrs Frances (1761–1831), formerly
Mrs Nisbet, née Woolward, later Viscount-
ess Nelson, wife of Horatio; declines Holkham invitation, **452**, 454

Nelson, Horatio (1758–1805), Vice-Admiral
Viscount, RN, *pl. 47*, 306, 552, 573, 581, 586,
598, 599; Norfolk Pillar, **600**; not suited to
blockading, 521; victories and thanksgiving,
517–18, 521, 600, 604; wife declines invitation to Holkham ball, **452**, 454

Nene navigation, 111; John Smith's work for,
90; 44 locks, 110

Neve, John (d.1780 aged 89), Coltishall
carpenter; 88

Neve, John jnr (d.1814 aged 84), Coltishall
carpenter; 88

Neve, L., Hs' wherry skipper; 214; abandons
wherry, 222, 225; lodges at Recruiting
Sergeant, 220, 225; reckons with WH, 225

Neve, Mrs Mary, née Flamwell, 2nd wife of
Thomas; enjoys cards, 320; to fair, 386;
friend of H.A. Biedermann, 86; holiday
in Nacton, 52, 53, **54**; to lecture, 338; to
playhouse, 343; on Starkey's keel to Belaugh
with MH, 206, 412; views new masonic
lodge-room at Horstead, 330; watches
masonic procession with MH, 329

Neve, Thomas, innkeeper of White Horse, Gt
Hautbois –1776, Coltishall timber merchant
in partnership with George Boorne 1776–81,
innkeeper of King's Head, Coltishall 1802–
06; 148; attends Freemasons' frolic, 321;
collects MH from Suffolk, **54**; contractor to
navigation, closing-down timber sale, 83, 109;
enjoys cards, 320; Freemason, 330; friend of
H.A. Biedermann, 83, 86; holds frolics, 321;
to lecture, 338; partnership fails, 109, 432;
partnership underwritten by WH for £1000,
89; to playhouse, 343; requires lock-builders
to drink outside at White Horse, 83

Neve, Thomas Henry Mountain, son of
Thomas by 1st wife; in Militia, 568

Nevison, John, alias William Nevinson (*c*.1639–
85), highwayman; 61

New Buckenham, Norf., *pl. 4*

Newbury, Berks, violent opposition from
Reading as old head of navigation, 107

Newcastle, Thomas Pelham-Holles (1693–
1768), 1st Duke of; Prime Minister, 450

Newcastle-under-Lyme, Staffs, **4**

Newcastle upon Tyne, 49, **285**, 410;
chaldron as measure, 165, **264**; customs
comptroller overworked, 301; Hs' beer
shipped to, 12–13, 263; maritime trade and
shipping, 237–8, 241, 249, 250, 255, 263,
266, 267, 295; miller John Wade sails to with
WHj, 50–1, **284**; *Nelly*'s most regular port of
call, 283; *Nelly* wrecked on way home from
with coal and oilcake, 231; quiet by compari-

O

P

T

U

V

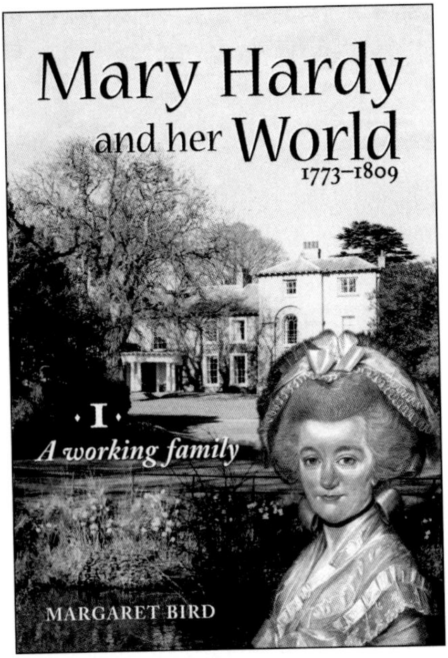
Mary Hardy
and her World
1773–1809
· 1 ·
A working family
MARGARET BIRD

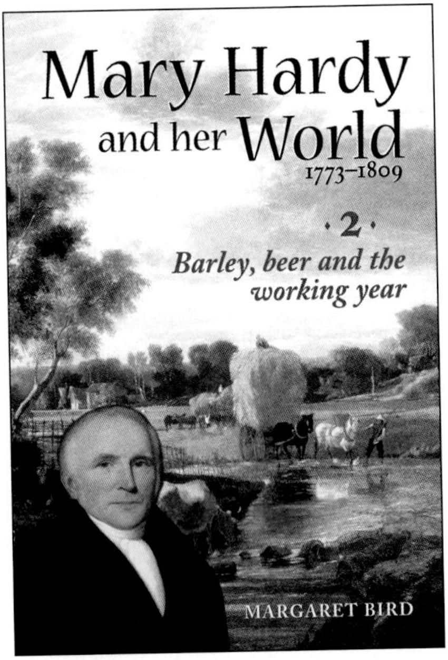
Mary Hardy
and her World
1773–1809
· 2 ·
Barley, beer and the
working year
MARGARET BIRD

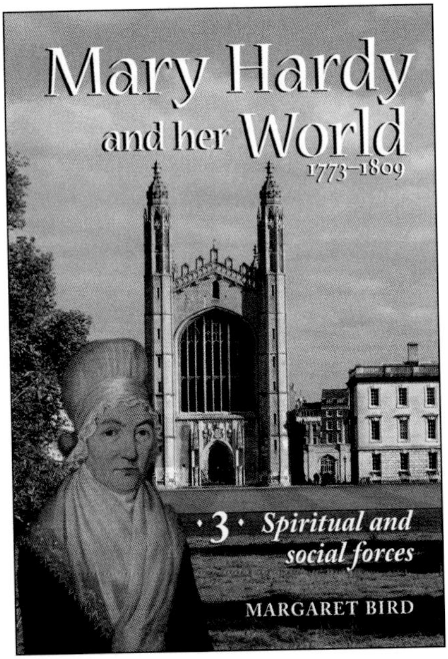
Mary Hardy
and her World
1773–1809
· 3 · Spiritual and
social forces
MARGARET BIRD

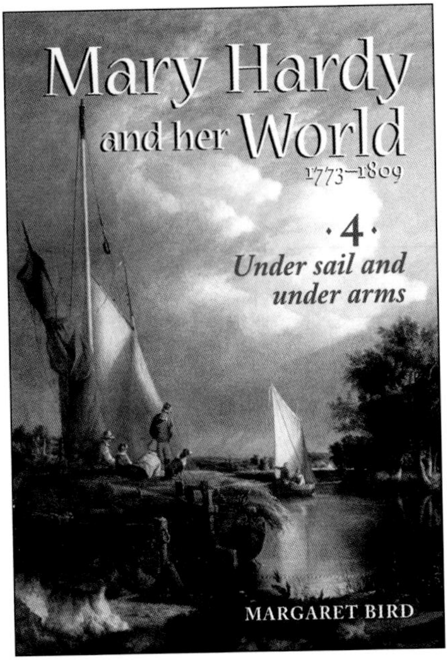
Mary Hardy
and her World
1773–1809
· 4 ·
Under sail and
under arms
MARGARET BIRD

Mary Hardy and her World 1773–1809 by Margaret Bird
The eleven books, with 39 chapters, in the four-volume commentary

The list of figures, tables and chapter contents in each of the eleven books appears at the beginning of every book. Each volume has its own bibliography and index.

rear endpaper Itinerants relied on market towns to provide support services. Bishops on their visitations; Collectors of Excise and Receivers General of the Land Tax; Wesleyan Methodist itinerant preachers stationed on their circuits: all needed a market town base during their tours.

Fairs held a very important place in working people's lives as a time of reunion with family and friends.

Attendance at the home fair or at the local fair near the workplace was prized by farm servants and maidservants as a customary right to be granted by employers as annual holiday.

Fairs retained a retail function in remote areas. The map displays density of distribution in locations not well served by towns [*map © Margaret Bird 2020*]